Territorial Growth of the United States

1820 Date of state's admission to the Union
● Geographic center of population by decade

CANADA

MAINE 1820

VT. 1791

N.H.

MASS.

CONN.

R.I.

NEW YORK

PENNSYLVANIA

NEW JERSEY 1790

DELAWARE

MARYLAND

MASON-DIXON LINE

THIRTEEN COLONIES

THE ORIGINAL

VIRGINIA

WEST VIRGINIA 1863

NORTH CAROLINA

SOUTH CAROLINA

GEORGIA

OHIO 1803

INDIANA 1816

ILLINOIS 1818

KENTUCKY 1792

TENNESSEE 1796

MICHIGAN 1837

WISCONSIN 1848

MINNESOTA 1858

IOWA 1846

MISSOURI 1821

MISSOURI COMPROMISE LINE 36°30'N — 2000

ARKANSAS 1836

MISSISSIPPI 1817

ALABAMA 1819

LOUISIANA 1812

THE ORIGINAL UNITED STATES
(By Treaty with Britain, 1783)

(Seized from Spain, 1810, 1813)

FLORIDA
(By Treaty with Spain, 1819)

FLORIDA 1845

Lake Superior

Lake Michigan

Lake Huron

Lake Erie

Lake Ontario

St. Lawrence R.

Mississippi R.

Gulf of Mexico

ATLANTIC OCEAN

BAHAMAS

CUBA

HAITI

DOMINICAN REPUBLIC

| 0 | 150 | 300 Km. |
| 0 | 150 | 300 Mi. |

90°W 80°W 70°W 60°W

N

PUERTO RICO
(Acquired from Spain, 1898)

VIRGIN IS.
(Acquired from Denmark, 1916–1917)

PUERTO RICO

VIRGIN ISLANDS

19°N

18°N

68°W 67°W 66°W 65°W

| 0 | 25 | 50 Km. |
| 0 | 25 | 50 Mi. |

LIBERTY, EQUALITY, POWER

LIBERTY, EQUALITY, POWER

A HISTORY OF THE AMERICAN PEOPLE

VOLUME 2: SINCE 1863

Sixth Edition

—◆—

John M. Murrin
Princeton University, Emeritus

Paul E. Johnson
University of South Carolina, Emeritus

James M. McPherson
Princeton University, Emeritus

Alice Fahs
University of California, Irvine

Gary Gerstle
Vanderbilt University

Emily S. Rosenberg
University of California, Irvine

Norman L. Rosenberg
Macalester College

WADSWORTH
CENGAGE Learning™

Australia • Brazil • Canada • Mexico • Singapore • Spain • United Kingdom • United States

WADSWORTH
CENGAGE Learning™

Liberty, Equality, Power: A History of the American People, Sixth Edition, Volume 2: Since 1863
John M. Murrin, Paul E. Johnson, James M. McPherson, Alice Fahs, Gary Gerstle, Emily S. Rosenberg, and Norman L. Rosenberg

Senior Publisher: Suzanne Jeans
Senior Sponsoring Editor: Ann West
Senior Development Editor: Margaret McAndrew Beasley
Assistant Editor: Megan Chrisman
Media Editor: Robert St. Laurent
Senior Marketing Manager: Katherine Bates
Marketing Coordinator: Lorreen Pelletier
Marketing Communications Manager: Caitlin Green
Associate Content Project Manager: Anne Finley
Senior Art Director: Cate Rickard Barr
Production Technology Analyst: Jeff Joubert
Senior Print Buyer: Judy Inouye
Senior Rights Acquisition Specialist, Text: Katie Huha
Senior Image Rights Acquisition Specialist: Jennifer Meyer Dare
Text Designer: Shawn Girsberger
Cover Designer: Hecht Design
Cover Image: *Untitled*, 1985 by Romare Bearden (1911–1988)/ Christie's Images/CORBIS © Romare Bearden Foundation/Licensed by VAGA, New York, NY
Production Service and Compositor: Integra Software Services, Inc.

For product information and technology assistance, contact us at **Cengage Learning Customer & Sales Support, 1-800-354-9706**

For permission to use material from this text or product, submit all requests online at **www.cengage.com/premissions**. Further permissions questions can be e-mailed to **permissionrequest@cengage.com**.

Library of Congress Control Number: 2010936690

ISBN-13: 978-0-495-91588-1
ISBN-10: 0-495-91588-2

Wadsworth
20 Channel Center Street
Boston, MA 02210
USA

Cengage Learning is a leading provider of customized learning solutions with office locations around the globe, including Singapore, the United Kingdom, Australia, Mexico, Brazil and Japan. Locate your local office at **international.cengage.com/region**

Cengage Learning products are represented in Canada by Nelson Education, Ltd.

For your course and learning solutions, visit **www.cengage.com**.
Purchase any of our product at your local college store or at our preferred online store **www.cengagebrain.com**.

Printed in the United States of America
1 2 3 4 5 6 7 14 13 12 11 10

JOHN M. MURRIN

Princeton University, Emeritus

John M. Murrin studies American colonial and revolutionary history and the early republic. He has edited one multivolume series and five books, including two essay collections, *Colonial America: Essays in Politics and Social Development*, Sixth Edition (2010), and *Saints and Revolutionaries: Essays in Early American History* (1984). His own essays range from ethnic tensions, the early history of trial by jury, the emergence of the legal profession, and the political culture of the colonies and the new nation, to the rise of professional baseball and college football in the 19th century. He served as president of the Society for Historians of the Early American Republic in 1998–99.

PAUL E. JOHNSON

University of South Carolina, Distinguished Professor Emeritus

A specialist in early national social and cultural history, Paul E. Johnson is also the author of *The Early American Republic, 1789–1829* (2006); *Sam Patch, the Famous Jumper* (2003); *A Shopkeeper's Millennium: Society and Revivals in Rochester, New York*, 1815–1837, 25th Anniversary Edition (2004). He is coauthor (with Sean Wilentz) of *The Kingdom of Matthias: Sex and Salvation in 19th-Century America* (1994), and editor of *African-American Christianity: Essays in History* (1994). He has been awarded the Merle Curti Prize of the Organization of American Historians (1980), the Richard P. McCormack Prize of the New Jersey Historical Association (1989), and fellowships from the National Endowment for the Humanities (1985–86), the John Simon Guggenheim Foundation (1995), the Gilder Lehrman Institute (2001), and the National Endowment for the Humanities We the People Fellowship (2006–07).

JAMES M. McPHERSON

Princeton University, Emeritus

James M. McPherson is a distinguished Civil War historian and was president of the American Historical Association in 2003. He won the 1989 Pulitzer Prize for his book *Battle Cry of Freedom: The Civil War*

Era. His other publications include *Marching Toward Freedom: Blacks in the Civil War*, Second Edition (1991); *Ordeal by Fire: The Civil War and Reconstruction*, Third Edition (2001); *Abraham Lincoln and the Second American Revolution* (1991); *For Cause and Comrades: Why Men Fought in the Civil War* (1997), which won the Lincoln Prize in 1998; *Crossroads of Freedom: Antietam* (2002); and *Tried by War: Abraham Lincoln as Commander in Chief* (2008), which won the Lincoln Prize for 2009.

ALICE FAHS

University of California, Irvine

Alice Fahs is a specialist in American cultural history of the 19th and 20th centuries. Her 2001 *The Imagined Civil War: Popular Literature of the North* and *South, 1861–1865* was a finalist in 2002 for the Lincoln Prize. Together with Joan Waugh, she published the edited collection *The Memory of the Civil War in American Culture* in 2004; she has also edited Louisa May Alcott's *Hospital Sketches* (2004), an account of Alcott's nursing experiences during the Civil War first published in 1863. Fahs has been published on the cultural history of the Civil War and gender in such journals as the *Journal of American History* and *Civil War History*. Her honors include an American Council of Learned Societies Fellowship and a Gilder Lehrman Fellowship, as well as fellowships from the American Antiquarian Society, the Newberry Library, and the Huntington Library. She is currently at work on a study of popular literary culture in the late 19th and early 20th centuries, focused on the emergence of mass-market newspapers during an age of imperialism.

GARY GERSTLE

Vanderbilt University

Gary Gerstle is the James G. Stahlman Professor of American History at Vanderbilt. A historian of the twentieth-century United States, he is the author, co-author, and co-editor of six books and the author of more than thirty articles. His books include *Working-Class Americanism: The Politics of Labor in a Textile City, 1914–1960* (1989); *American Crucible: Race and Nation in the Twentieth Century* (2001), winner of the Saloutos Prize for the best work in immigration and ethnic history; *The Rise and Fall of the New Deal Order, 1930–1980* (1989); and *Ruling America: Wealth and Power in a Democracy* (2005). He has served on the board of editors of both the *Journal of American History* and the *American Historical Review*. His honors include a National Endowment for the Humanities Fellowship, a John Simon Guggenheim Memorial Fellowship, and membership in the Society of American Historians.

EMILY S. ROSENBERG
University of California, Irvine

Emily S. Rosenberg specializes in U.S. foreign relations in the 20th century and is the author of *Spreading the American Dream: American Economic and Cultural Expansion, 1890–1945* (1982); *Financial Missionaries to the World: The Politics and Culture of Dollar Diplomacy* (1999), which won the Ferrell Book Award; and *A Date Which Will Live: Pearl Harbor in American Memory* (2004). Her other publications include (with Norman L. Rosenberg) *In Our Times: America Since 1945*, Seventh Edition (2003), and numerous articles dealing with foreign relations in the context of international finance, American culture, and gender ideology. She has served on the board of the Organization of American Historians, on the board of editors of the *Journal of American History*, and as president of the Society for Historians of American Foreign Relations.

NORMAN L. ROSENBERG
Macalester College

Norman L. Rosenberg specializes in legal history with a particular interest in legal culture and First Amendment issues. His books include *Protecting the "Best Men": An Interpretive History of the Law of Libel* (1990) and (with Emily S. Rosenberg) *In Our Times: America Since 1945*, Seventh Edition (2003). He has published articles in the *Rutgers Law Review, UCLA Law Review, Constitutional Commentary, Law & History Review*, and many other journals and law-related anthologies.

BRIEF CONTENTS

17 RECONSTRUCTION, 1863–1877 462

18 A TRANSFORMED NATION: THE WEST AND NEW SOUTH, 1865–1900 486

19 THE RISE OF CORPORATE AMERICA, 1865–1914 512

20 CITIES, PEOPLES, CULTURES, 1890–1920 538

21 PROGRESSIVISM 562

22 BECOMING A WORLD POWER, 1898–1917 594

23 WAR AND SOCIETY, 1914–1920 620

24 THE 1920s 648

25 THE GREAT DEPRESSION AND THE NEW DEAL, 1929–1939 680

26 AMERICA DURING THE SECOND WORLD WAR 714

27 THE AGE OF CONTAINMENT, 1946–1953 742

28 AFFLUENCE AND ITS DISCONTENTS, 1953–1963 768

29 AMERICA DURING ITS LONGEST WAR, 1963–1974 800

30 UNCERTAIN TIMES, 1974–1992 832

31 ECONOMIC, SOCIAL, AND CULTURAL CHANGE IN THE LATE 20TH CENTURY 860

32 A TIME OF HOPE AND FEAR, 1993–2011 884

CONTENTS IN DETAIL

MAPS   xvii

HISTORY THROUGH FILM   xviii

LINK TO THE PAST   xviii

MUSICAL LINK TO THE PAST   xviii

VISUAL LINK TO THE PAST   xviii

TO THE STUDENT   xix

PREFACE   xxv

SUPPLEMENTS AND ACKNOWLEDGMENTS   xxix

17   RECONSTRUCTION, 1863–1877   462

Wartime Reconstruction   464
Radical Republicans and Reconstruction   464

★ CHRONOLOGY   464

Andrew Johnson and Reconstruction   465
Johnson's Policy   465
Southern Defiance   466
The Black Codes   467
Land and Labor in the Postwar South   467
The Freedmen's Bureau   467
Land for the Landless   467
Education   468

The Advent of Congressional Reconstruction   469
Schism between President and Congress   469
The 14th Amendment   469
The 1866 Elections   470
The Reconstruction Acts of 1867   471

The Impeachment of Andrew Johnson   472
The Completion of Formal Reconstruction   472
The 15th Amendment   472
The Election of 1868   473

The Grant Administration   474
Civil Service Reform   474
Foreign Policy Issues   475
Reconstruction in the South   475
Blacks in Office   475
"Carpetbaggers"   477
"Scalawags"   477

The Ku Klux Klan   477
The Election of 1872   478

★ HISTORY THROUGH FILM   479
The Birth Of A Nation (1915)
The Panic of 1873   480

The Retreat from Reconstruction   480
The Mississippi Election of 1875   480
The Supreme Court and Reconstruction   481

★ LINK TO THE PAST   482
Frederick Douglass on the Supreme Court and Civil Rights
The Election of 1876   482
Disputed Results   482
The Compromise of 1877   483
The End of Reconstruction   484

Conclusion   484

Chapter Review   484

18   A TRANSFORMED NATION: THE WEST AND NEW SOUTH, 1865–1900   486

An Industrializing West   488

★ CHRONOLOGY   488
The Homestead Act   489
Railroads   489
Chinese Laborers and the Railroads   490
The Golden Spike   491
Railroads and Borderlands Communities   491
Mining   491
Ranching   492
Cattle Drives and the Open Range   492
The Industrialization of Ranching   494
Industrial Cowboys   494
Mexican Americans   494

★ HISTORY THROUGH FILM   495
Oklahoma! (1955)
Itinerant Laborers   496
Homesteading and Farming   497
The Experience of Homesteading   497
Gender and Western Settlement   497

Conquest and Resistance: American Indians in the Trans-Mississippi West   498

Conflict with the Sioux   499

Suppression of Other Plains Indians   500

The "Peace Policy"   500

The Dawes Severalty Act and Indian Boarding Schools   500

The Ghost Dance   501

Sitting Bull and Buffalo Bill: Popular Myths of the West   501

★ VISUAL LINK TO THE PAST   502

Indian Children at the Hampton Institute

Industrialization and the New South   503

Race and Industrialization   504

Southern Agriculture   504

Exodusters and Emigrationists   504

Race Relations in the New South   505

The Emergence of an African-American Middle Class   506

The Rise of Jim Crow   506

The Politics of Stalemate   507

Knife-Edge Electoral Balance   507

★ LINK TO THE PAST   508

Waving the Bloody Shirt

Civil Service Reform   508

The Tariff Issue   509

Conclusion   509

Chapter Review   510

---

19   THE RISE OF CORPORATE AMERICA, 1865–1914   512

A Dynamic Corporate Economy   514

Engines of Economic Growth   514

★ CHRONOLOGY   514

Technological Innovation   515

The Rise of Big Business   515

Corporate Consolidation   516

Mass Production and Distribution   518

Revolution in Management   518

Corporations and American Culture   520

Standardized Time   520

A National Consumer Culture   520

Ideas of Wealth and Society   520

Sharpened Class Distinctions   521

Obsession with Physical and Racial Fitness   522

Changes in Middle-class Women's Lives   522

Middle-class Women and Work   522

The Women's Club Movement   523

The "New Woman"   523

Higher Education and Professional Organizations   523

Workers' Resistance to Corporations   523

★ VISUAL LINK TO THE PAST   524

The New Woman

Industrial Conditions   525

The Great Railroad Strike of 1877   525

★ HISTORY THROUGH FILM   526

The Molly Maguires (1970)

The Knights of Labor   527

Haymarket   527

The American Federation of Labor (AFL)   528

The Homestead Strike   529

The Depression of 1893–1897   529

The Pullman Strike   529

Farmers' Movements   530

Resistance to Railroads   531

The Greenback and Silver Movements   531

Grangers and the Farmers' Alliance   532

The Rise and Fall of the People's Party   533

The Silver Issue   533

The Election of 1896   533

"Robber Barons" No More   534

Conclusion   536

Chapter Review   536

---

20   CITIES, PEOPLES, CULTURES, 1890–1920   538

The Rise of the City   540

★ CHRONOLOGY   540

Immigration   544

European Immigration   545

Chinese and Japanese Immigration   546

Immigrant Labor   547

Living Conditions   548

Building Ethnic Communities   549

A Network of Institutions   549

The Emergence of an Ethnic Middle Class   549

Political Machines and Organized Crime   550

African American Labor and Community   551

★ MUSICAL LINK TO THE PAST   553

Ragtime

Working-class and Commercial Culture   554

Popular Literature   554

The New Sexuality and the Rise of Feminism   555

★ HISTORY THROUGH FILM   556

Coney Island (1917)

Re-Imagining American Nationality   558

Conclusion 560

Chapter Review 561

21 PROGRESSIVISM 562

Progressivism and the Protestant Spirit 564

Muckrakers and the Turn toward "Realism" 564

★ CHRONOLOGY 565

Settlement Houses and Women's Activism 566
Hull House 566
The Cultural Conservatism of Progressive
   Reformers 567
A Nation of Clubwomen 569

Socialism 570
The Several Faces of Socialism 570
Socialists and Progressives 571

Municipal Reform 572
The City Commission Plan 572
The City Manager Plan 572
The Costs of Reform 572

Reform in the States 573
Restoring Sovereignty to "the People" 573
Creating a Virtuous Electorate 573
The Australian Ballot 573
Personal Registration Laws 574
Disfranchisement 574
Disillusionment with the Electorate 575
Woman Suffrage 575

★ LINK TO THE PAST 577
Humor and the Woman Suffrage Movement
Robert La Follette and Wisconsin
   Progressivism 578
Progressive Reform in New York 579
Scientific Management on the Factory Floor 579

A Campaign for Civil Rights 580
The Failure of Accommodationism 580

★ HISTORY THROUGH FILM 581
The Great White Hope (1970)
From the Niagara Movement to the NAACP 582

★ MUSICAL LINK TO THE PAST 583
Before Jazz: An Early African American
   Orchestra

The Roosevelt Presidency 583
Regulating the Trusts 584
Toward a "Square Deal" 584
Expanding Government Power: The Economy 585
Expanding Government Power:
   The Environment 585

Progressivism: A Movement for the People? 585
The Republicans: A Divided Party 586

**The Taft Presidency: Progressive Disappointment
   and Resurgence 586**
Battling Congress 587
The Ballinger-Pinchot Controversy 587
Roosevelt's Return 587
The Bull Moose Campaign 587
The Rise of Woodrow Wilson 588
The Election of 1912 588

The Wilson Presidency 589
Tariff Reform and a Progressive Income Tax 589
The Federal Reserve Act 589
From the New Freedom to the New
   Nationalism 589

Conclusion 591

Chapter Review 592

22 BECOMING A WORLD POWER, 1898–1917 594

The United States Looks Abroad 596

★ CHRONOLOGY 596
Protestant Missionaries 596
Businessmen 597
Imperialists 598

The Spanish-American War 599
"A Splendid Little War" 600

The United States Becomes a World Power 603

★ VISUAL LINK TO THE PAST 604
Spanish-American War Rifles
The Debate over the Treaty of Paris 604

★ MUSICAL LINK TO THE PAST 605
Music for Patriots
The American-Filipino War 605
Controlling Cuba and Puerto Rico 607
China and the "Open Door" 608

Theodore Roosevelt, Geopolitician 609
The Roosevelt Corollary 609

★ HISTORY THROUGH FILM 610
Tarzan, The Ape Man (1932)
The Panama Canal 610
Keeping the Peace in East Asia 612

William Howard Taft, Dollar Diplomat 614

Woodrow Wilson, Struggling Idealist 615

Conclusion 617

Chapter Review 618

23   WAR AND SOCIETY, 1914–1920   621

Europe's Descent into War   622

★ CHRONOLOGY   622

American Neutrality   624

Submarine Warfare   624

The Peace Movement   625

Wilson's Vision: "Peace without Victory"   626

German Escalation   626

American Intervention   626

Mobilizing for "Total" War   628

Organizing Industry   629

★ LINK TO THE PAST   630

"A Storm of Our People Toward the North"

Securing Workers, Keeping Labor Peace   630

Raising an Army   631

Paying the Bills   632

Arousing Patriotic Ardor   633

Wartime Repression   635

★ MUSICAL LINK TO THE PAST   636

A Light-Hearted Poke at Army Life

The Failure of the International Peace   637

The Paris Peace Conference and the Treaty of
    Versailles   638

The League of Nations   639

Wilson versus Lodge: The Fight over Ratification   639

The Treaty's Final Defeat   641

The Postwar Period: A Society in Convulsion   641

Labor-Capital Conflict   642

Radicals and the Red Scare   642

Racial Conflict and the Rise of Black
    Nationalism   643

★ HISTORY THROUGH FILM   644

Reds (1981)

Conclusion   646

Chapter Review   647

24   THE 1920s   648

Prosperity   650

★ CHRONOLOGY   650

A Consumer Society   650

A People's Capitalism   651

The Rise of Advertising and Mass Marketing   651

Changing Attitudes toward
    Marriage and Sexuality   653

An Age of Celebrity   653

Celebrating Business Civilization   654

Industrial Workers   655

Women and Work   655

The Women's Movement Adrift   657

The Politics of Business   658

Harding and the Politics of Personal Gain   658

Coolidge and Laissez-Faire Politics   659

Hoover and the Politics of Associationalism   659

The Politics of Business Abroad   660

**Farmers, Small-Town Protestants, and Moral
Traditionalists   661**

Agricultural Depression   661

Cultural Dislocation   662

★ MUSICAL LINK TO THE PAST   663

Women Singers and the Birth of Modern Country Music

Prohibition   664

★ VISUAL LINK TO THE PAST   665

The Banjo

The Ku Klux Klan   665

Immigration Restriction   666

Fundamentalism versus Liberal Protestantism   667

The Scopes Trial   669

Ethnic and Racial Communities   669

European American Ethnics   669

African Americans   670

★ HISTORY THROUGH FILM   672

The Jazz Singer (1927)

The Harlem Renaissance   674

Mexican Americans   675

**The "Lost Generation" and Disillusioned
Intellectuals   675**

Democracy on the Defensive   677

Conclusion   678

Chapter Review   678

25   THE GREAT DEPRESSION AND
THE NEW DEAL, 1929–1939   680

Causes of the Great Depression   682

Stock Market Speculation   682

Mistakes by the Federal Reserve Board   682

An Ill-Advised Tariff   682

★ CHRONOLOGY   683

A Maldistribution of Wealth   684

Hoover: The Fall of a Self-Made Man   684

Hoover's Program   684

The Bonus Army   685

A Culture in Crisis   686

The Democratic Roosevelt   687

An Early Life of Privilege   687

Roosevelt Liberalism   687

The First New Deal, 1933–1935 688

Saving the Banks 689
Economic Relief 689
Agricultural Reform 690
Industrial Reform 691
Rebuilding the Nation's Infrastructure 692
The TVA Alternative 693
The New Deal and Western Development 694

**Political Mobilization, Political
Unrest, 1934–1935 694**

Populist Critics of the New Deal 694
Labor Protests 696
Anger at the Polls 696
Radical Third Parties 697

★ VISUAL LINK TO THE PAST 698
Monopoly

The Second New Deal, 1935–1937 698

Philosophical Underpinnings 698
Legislation 699

★ HISTORY THROUGH FILM 700
Mr. Deeds Goes To Town (1936)
Victory in 1936: The New Democratic Coalition 700
Rhetoric versus Reality 701
Men, Women, and Reform 702
Labor in Politics and Culture 704

America's Minorities and the New Deal 706

Eastern and Southern European Ethnics 706
African Americans 706

★ MUSICAL LINK TO THE PAST 707
An African American Rhapsody
Mexican Americans 707
American Indians 708

The New Deal Abroad 709

Stalemate, 1937–1940 711

The Court-Packing Fiasco 711
The Recession of 1937–1938 711

Conclusion 711

Chapter Review 712

26 AMERICA DURING THE SECOND
WORLD WAR 714

The Road to War: Aggression and Response 716

The Rise of Aggressor States 716
U.S. Neutrality 716

★ CHRONOLOGY 716
The Mounting Crisis 717
The Outbreak of War in Europe 717
The U.S. Response to War in Europe 717
An "Arsenal of Democracy" 719
Pearl Harbor 719

**Fighting the War in Europe and
the Pacific 720**

Campaigns in North Africa and Italy 721
Operation OVERLORD 721
Seizing the Offensive in the Pacific 722

★ HISTORY THROUGH FILM 723
Saving Private Ryan (1998)
China Policy 724
U.S. Strategy in the Pacific 725
A New President, the Atomic Bomb, and Japan's
Surrender 726

The War at Home: The Economy 728

Government's Role in the Economy 728
Business and Finance 728
The Workforce 730
The Labor Front 731
Assessing Economic Change 732
A New Role for Government? 732

The War at Home: Social Issues 732

Selling the War 732
Gender Issues 733
Racial Issues 734

★ MUSICAL LINK TO THE PAST 735
Songs of the Second World War
Internment of Japanese Americans 736
Challenging Racial Inequality 736

★ LINK TO THE PAST 738
Civil Liberties in Wartime: Korematsu v. United States

Shaping the Peace 738

International Organizations 739
Spheres of Interest and Postwar Settlements 739

Conclusion 740

Chapter Review 740

27 THE AGE OF CONTAINMENT,
1946–1953 742

**Creating a National Security State,
1945–1949 744**

Onset of the Cold War 744

★ CHRONOLOGY 744
The Truman Doctrine and Containment Abroad 745
Truman's Loyalty Program and Containment at
Home 745
The National Security Act, the Marshall Plan, and the
Berlin Crisis 746
The Election of 1948 747

The Era of the Korean War, 1949–1952 748

NATO, China, and the Bomb 748
NSC-68 and the Korean War 748
Korea and Containment 752

Pursuing National Security at Home 753
Anticommunism and the U.S. Labor Movement 753
Containing Communism at Home 754
Targeting Difference 754

★ VISUAL LINK TO THE PAST 755
It's Okay—We're Hunting Communists
The "Great Fear" 756
Joseph McCarthy 756
The National Security Constitution and the Structure of Governance 757

Postwar Social-Economic Policymaking 757
The Employment Act of 1946 and Economic Growth 758
Truman's Fair Deal 758
Civil Rights 759

Signs of a Changing Culture 761
The Baseball "Color Line" 761
The New Suburbia 761
Postwar Hollywood 763

★ HISTORY THROUGH FILM 764
High Noon (1952)

The Election of 1952 765
Continuing Containment 765
A Soldier-Politician 765

Conclusion 766

Chapter Review 766

28 AFFLUENCE AND ITS DISCONTENTS, 1953–1963 768

Reorienting Containment, 1953–1960 770
Eisenhower Takes Command 770

★ CHRONOLOGY 770
The New Look, Global Alliances, and Summitry 770
Covert Action and Economic Leverage 772
The Third World 772

★ LINK TO THE PAST 774
A Warning About the Future:
President Dwight Eisenhower's Farewell Address, 1961

Affluence—A "People of Plenty" 774
Economic Growth 774
Highways and Waterways 776
Labor–Management Accord 777
Political Pluralism 777
A Religious People 778

Discontents of Affluence 778
Conformity in an Affluent Society 778
Restive Youth 779
The Critique of Mass Culture 780

Debating the Role of Government 781

The New Conservatism 781
The Case for a More Active Government 782

New Frontiers, 1960–1963 783
The Election of 1960 783
Foreign Policy 784
Cuba and Berlin 785
Southeast Asia and Flexible Response 785
Domestic Policymaking 786

The Politics of Gender 786
The New Suburbs and Gender Politics 786
Signs of Women's Changing Roles 787
A New Women's Movement 787

The Expanding Civil Rights Movements, 1953–1963 788
The Brown Cases, 1954–1955 788
The Montgomery Bus Boycott 789
The Politics of Civil Rights: From the Local to the Global 791
The Politics of American Indian Policy 791
Spanish-Speaking Communities and Civil Rights 792
Urban-Suburban Issues 793
New Forms of Direct Action, 1960–1963 793

November, 1963 795
Policy Choices 795

★ HISTORY THROUGH FILM 796
JFK (1991)
The Assassination of John F. Kennedy 797

Conclusion 797

Chapter Review 798

29 AMERICA DURING ITS LONGEST WAR, 1963–1974 800

The Great Society 802
Closing the New Frontier 802

★ CHRONOLOGY 802
The Election of 1964 803
Lyndon Johnson's Great Society 805
Evaluating the Great Society 805

Escalation in Vietnam 806
The Gulf of Tonkin Resolution 806
The War Continues to Widen 808

★ VISUAL LINK TO THE PAST 809
Shocking Images
The Media and the War 809

The War at Home 810
The Movement of Movements 810

★ MUSICAL LINK TO THE PAST 811
The Folk-Rock Movement and the Sixties
A New Left 811

The Counterculture   812
Civil Rights and Black Power   813

★ HISTORY THROUGH FILM   815
Malcolm X (1992)
The Antiwar Movement   816

1968   817
Turmoil in Vietnam, 1968   817
Turmoil at Home   818
The Election of 1968   819

Continued Polarization, 1969–1974   821
Lawbreaking, Violence, and a New President   821
Social Policy   821
Environmentalism   822
Controversies over Rights   823
The Economy   824

Foreign Policy in a Time of Turmoil, 1969–1974   825
Détente   825
Vietnamization and the Nixon Doctrine   825
The United States Leaves Vietnam   826
Expanding the Nixon Doctrine   827

A Crisis of Governance, 1972–1974   827
The Election of 1972   828
The Watergate Investigations   828
Nixon's Resignation   829

Conclusion   829

Chapter Review   830

30   UNCERTAIN TIMES, 1974–1992   832

Searching for Direction, 1974–1980   834
★ CHRONOLOGY   834
A Faltering Economy   834
Welfare and Energy Initiatives   836
Negotiation and Confrontation in Foreign Policy   836
The New Right   838

The Reagan Revolution, 1981–1992   839
The Election of 1980   839
Supply-Side Economics   840
Curtailing Unions, Regulations, and Welfare   840
Reagan to Bush   842

★ HISTORY THROUGH FILM   843
The First Movie-Star President

Renewing and Ending the Cold War   844
The Defense Buildup   844
Deploying Military Power   844
The Iran-Contra Controversy   845
The Cold War Eases   845
Post-Cold War Policy and the Persian Gulf War   845
The Election of 1992   848

The Politics of Social Movements   848
Women's Issues   849

★ LINK TO THE PAST   850
Cultural Disagreements: Equality for Women?
Sexual Politics   850
Activism Among African Americans   851
Activism Among American Indians   852
Activism in Spanish-Speaking Communities   853
Activism Among Asian Americans   855
Anti-Government Activism   856

Conclusion   858

Chapter Review   858

31   ECONOMIC, SOCIAL, AND CULTURAL CHANGE IN THE LATE 20TH CENTURY   860

A Changing People   862
An Aging, Shifting Population   862
★ CHRONOLOGY   862
The New Immigration   864
The Metropolitan Nation   865

Economic Transformations   868
New Technologies   869
Changes in the Structure and Operations of Business   869
The Financial Sector   872
The Sports-Entertainment Industry   873

Culture and Media   875
The Video Revolution   875
Hollywood   875
The Changing Media Environment for Pop Music   876

★ HISTORY THROUGH FILM   877
Star Wars (1977)
The New Mass Culture Debate   878

★ MUSICAL LINK TO THE PAST   879
Hip-Hop Leaps in
The Religious Landscape   879

Conclusion   882

Chapter Review   882

32   A TIME OF HOPE AND FEAR, 1993–2011   884

The Politics of Polarization, 1993–2008   886
★ CHRONOLOGY   886
A New Democrat   886
A Decade of Legal Investigations and Trials   888
The Investigation and Trial of a President   888

★ HISTORY THROUGH FILM   889
The Big Lebowski (1998)

The Long Election and Trials of 2000   890

A Conservative Washington, 2001–2008   892

Politics and Social-Cultural Issues   893

Foreign Policies of Hope and Terror: 1993–2008   894

Clinton's Internationalist Agenda   894

Globalization   895

Protecting the Planet   895

September 11, 2001 and the Bush Doctrine   896

Unilateralism and the Iraq War   896

National Security and Presidential Power   898

Divisions over Foreign Policy Direction   898

An Economy of Bubble and Bust, 1993–2008   900

Deregulation of the Financial Sector During the
1990s   900

Economics for a New Century, 2000–2006   901

The Bubble Bursts, 2006–2008   902

The Election of 2008   902

Changing Times, 2009–   903

Political Polarization   904

The Culture of Social Networking and Liberty, Equality,
Power   904

★ VISUAL LINK TO THE PAST   905
The Future of Print Media?

Conclusion   906

Chapter Review   907

APPENDIX   **A-1**

GLOSSARY   **G-1**

MAPS and FEATURES

Maps

Map 17.1 Black and White Participation in Constitutional Conventions, 1867–1868 473

Map 17.2 Reconstruction in the South 475

Map 17.3 Hayes-Tilden Disputed Election of 1876 483

Map 18.1 Railroad Expansion, 1870–1890 490

Map 18.2 Mining and Cattle Frontiers, 1870s 493

Map 18.3 Indian Reservations, 1875 and 1900 499

Map 19.1 Industrial America, 1900–1920 519

Map 19.2 Presidential Election of 1896 535

Map 20.1 African American Population, 1910 552

Map 21.1 Cities and Towns Electing Socialist Mayors or Other Major Municipal Officers, 1911–1920 571

Map 21.2 Woman Suffrage Before 1920 578

Map 21.3 Presidential Election, 1912 589

Map 21.4 Federal Reserve Districts 590

Map 22.1 Spanish-American War in Cuba, 1898 603

Map 22.2 American South Pacific Empire, 1900 606

Map 22.3 Colonial Possessions, 1900 611

Map 22.4 United States Presence in Latin America, 1895–1934 611

Map 22.5 Panama Canal Zone, 1914 613

Map 22.6 Route of the Great White Fleet, 1907–1909 615

Map 23.1 Europe Goes to War 623

Map 23.2 America in the First World War: Western Front, 1918 628

Map 23.3 African American Migration, 1910–1920 632

Map 23.4 Europe and the Near East After the First World War 640

Map 24.1 Automobile Civilization: Cars, Roads, and the Expansion of Travel Horizons in Oregon, Illinois 652

Map 24.2 Urbanization, 1920 664

Map 24.3 Presidential Election, 1928 673

Map 24.4 Mexican Population in the United States, 1930 676

Map 25.1 Presidential Election, 1932 685

Map 25.2 Dust Bowl, 1935–1940 692

Map 25.3 Tennessee Valley Authority 693

Map 25.4 Federal Water Projects in California Built or Funded by the New Deal 695

Map 25.5 Presidential Election, 1936 701

Map 26.1 German Expansion at Its Height 718

Map 26.2 Allied Military Strategy in North Africa, Italy, and France 722

Map 26.3 Allied Advances and Collapse of German Power 724

Map 26.4 Japanese Expansion and Early Battles in the Pacific 725

Map 26.5 Pacific Theater Offensive Strategy and Final Assault Against Japan 727

Map 27.1 Presidential Election, 1948 748

Map 27.2 Divided Germany and the NATO Alliance 749

Map 27.3 Korean War 751

Map 27.4 Presidential Election, 1952 766

Map 28.1 Israel, the Middle East, and the Suez Crisis, 1956 773

Map 28.2 Presidential Election, 1960 784

Map 28.3 Shifts in African American Population Patterns, 1940–1960 790

Map 29.1 Vietnam War 807

Map 29.2 Presidential Election, 1968 821

Map 29.3 Presidential Election, 1972 828

Map 30.1 Presidential Election, 1976 835

Map 30.2 Presidential Election, 1980 839

Map 30.3 Collapse of the Soviet Bloc 847

Map 30.4 Presidential Election, 1992 848

Map 31.1 Population Shifts Toward the Sunbelt 863

Map 31.2 Regional Shifts in Congress 864

Map 31.3 New Americans: Percentage of Persons Who Are Foreign Born and Foreign Born Population by Region of Birth, 2000 866

Map 31.4 Urbanization: Percentage of Persons Who Live in Urban Areas in 2000 867

Map 32.1 Presidential Election, 2000 891

Map 32.2 Presidential Election, 2008 903

History through Film

The Birth Of A Nation (1915)   479
Oklahoma! (1955)   495
The Molly Maguires (1970)   526
Coney Island (1917)   556
The Great White Hope (1970)   581
Tarzan, The Ape Man (1932)   610
Reds (1981)   644
The Jazz Singer (1927)   672
Mr. Deeds Goes To Town (1936)   700
Saving Private Ryan (1998)   723
High Noon (1952)   764
JFK (1991)   796
Malcolm X (1992)   815
The First Movie-Star President   843
Star Wars (1977)   877
The Big Lebowski (1998)   889

Link to the Past

Frederick Douglass on the Supreme Court and Civil
  Rights   482
Waving the Bloody Shirt   508
Humor and the Woman Suffrage Movement   577
"A Storm of Our People Toward the North"   630
Civil Liberties in Wartime: *Korematsu* v. *United States*   738

A Warning About the Future: President Dwight
  Eisenhower's Farewell Address, 1961   774
Cultural Disagreements: Equality for Women?   850

Musical Link to the Past

Ragtime   553
Before Jazz: An Early African American Orchestra   583
Music for Patriots   605
A Light-Hearted Poke at Army Life   636
Women Singers and the Birth of Modern Country Music   663
An African American Rhapsody   707
Songs of the Second World War   735
The Folk-Rock Movement and the Sixties   811
Hip-Hop Leaps In   879

Visual Link to the Past

Indian Children at the Hampton Institute   502
The New Woman   524
Spanish-American War Rifles   604
The Banjo   665
Monopoly   698
It's Okay—We're Hunting Communists   755
Shocking Images   809
The Future of Print Media?   905

Why Study History?

Why take a course in American history? This is a question that many college and university students ask. In many respects, students today are like the generations of Americans who have gone before them: optimistic and forward looking, far more eager to imagine where we as a nation might be going than to reflect on where we have been. If anything, this tendency has become more pronounced in recent years, as the Internet revolution has accelerated the pace and excitement of change and made even the recent past seem at best quaint, at worst uninteresting and irrelevant.

But it is precisely in these moments of change that a sense of the past can be indispensable in terms of guiding our actions in the present and future. We can find in other periods of American history moments, like our own, of dizzying technological change, rapid alterations in the concentration of wealth and power, and basic changes in patterns of work, residence, and play. How did Americans at those times create, embrace, and resist these changes? In earlier periods of American history, the United States was home, as it is today, to a broad array of ethnic and racial groups. How did earlier generations of Americans respond to the cultural conflicts and misunderstandings that often arise from conditions of diversity? How did immigrants of the early 1900s perceive their new land? How and when did they integrate themselves into American society? To study how ordinary Americans of the past struggled with these issues is to gain perspective on the opportunities and problems that we face today.

History also provides an important guide to affairs of state. What role should America assume in world affairs? Should we participate in international bodies such as the United Nations, or insist on our ability to act autonomously and without the consent of other nations? What is the proper role of government in economic and social life? Should the government regulate the economy? To what extent should the government promote morality regarding religion, sexual practices, drinking and drugs, movies, TV, and other forms of mass culture? And what are our responsibilities as citizens to each other and to the nation? Americans of past generations have debated these issues with verve and conviction. Learning about these debates and how they were resolved will enrich our understanding of the policy possibilities for today and tomorrow.

History, finally, is about stories—stories that we all tell about ourselves; our families; our communities; our ethnicity, race, region, and religion; and our nation. They are stories of triumph and tragedy, of engagement and flight, and of high ideals and high comedy. When we tell these stories, "American history" is often

the furthest thing from our minds. But, often, an implicit sense of the past informs what we say about grandparents who immigrated many years ago; the suburb in which we live; the church, synagogue, or mosque at which we worship; or the ethnic or racial group to which we belong. How well, we might ask, do we really understand these individuals, institutions, and groups? Do our stories about them capture their history and complexity? Or do our stories wittingly or unwittingly simplify or alter what these individuals and groups experienced? A study of American history helps us first to ask these questions and then to answer them. In the process, we can embark on a journey of intellectual and personal discovery and situate ourselves more firmly than we had thought possible in relation to those who came before us. We can gain a firmer self-knowledge and a greater appreciation for the richness of our nation and, indeed, of all humanity.

Analyzing Historical Sources[1]

Astronomers investigate the universe through telescopes. Biologists study the natural world by collecting plants and animals in the field and then examining them with microscopes. Sociologists and psychologists study human behavior through observation and controlled laboratory experiments.

Historians study the past by examining historical "evidence" or "source" materials: government documents; the records of private institutions ranging from religious and charitable organizations to labor unions, corporations, and lobbying groups; letters, advertisements, paintings, music, literature, movies, and cartoons; buildings, clothing, farm implements, industrial machinery, and landscapes: anything and everything written or created by our ancestors that give clues about their lives and the times in which they lived.

Historians refer to written material as "documents." Excerpts of dozens of documents, some in *Link to the Past* boxes and others in the text narrative itself, appear throughout the textbook. Each chapter also includes many visual representations of the American past in the form of photographs of buildings, paintings, murals, individuals, cartoons, sculptures, and other kinds of historical evidence, some featured in *Visual Link to the Past* boxes. The more you examine all this "evidence," the more you will understand the main ideas of this book and of the U.S. history course you are taking. This introduction to studying historical evidence will help you learn how to look at evidence the way your instructor does. Improving your skills in this area will enhance your ability to interpret the past.

---

[1] Some material in this section refers to content and page numbers from the comprehensive volume of *Liberty, Equality, Power*, sixth edition.

Source Material Comes in Two Main Types: Primary and Secondary

"Primary" evidence is material that comes to us exactly as it was spoken, written, or drawn by the person who created it. The easiest way to locate examples of primary evidence in this textbook is to sample several *Link to the Past* features, each of which focuses on one primary document. See, for example, a passage from the speech that John Winthrop, the leader of the Massachusetts Bay colony, gave to his fellow Puritans on the ship that was taking them from England to New England in 1630 (p. 58); an excerpt from a speech by Frederick Douglass, the black civil rights leader, in which he criticizes an 1875 Supreme Court decision (p. 482); and a humorous poem written in 1915 by an early 20th-century female suffragist (someone who believed that the right to vote ought to be extended to women) (p. 577).

"Secondary" evidence is an account constructed by an individual, usually a historian, about an event, organization, idea, or personality of historical significance. Stories about Abraham Lincoln by his Secretary of War would give us primary source information about Lincoln by someone who knew him. But imagine an account about Lincoln's performance as president written by someone who did not know Lincoln and was born 50 or 100 years after Lincoln had lived. This individual would have to consult all the available primary sources he or she could find: Lincoln's own writings, letters, memos, and speeches; the accounts of Lincoln's presidency appearing in newspapers and magazines of the time; the writings and speeches of Lincoln's allies and enemies in civilian and military life; letters to Lincoln written by his supporters and opponents; documents pertaining to the performance of various government departments during Lincoln's presidency; and so on. Typically, someone studying Lincoln in such detail would do so with the ambition of writing a book about the man and his presidency. That book would be considered a secondary source of information about Lincoln.

In this textbook, we include lists of secondary sources at the end of each chapter under the heading, "Suggested Readings." These are books by historians pertinent to important issues discussed in that chapter. If you turn to the suggested readings for Chapter 17, for example, you will notice that two books listed there examine Lincoln's role in Reconstruction, the project begun during Lincoln's presidency to emancipate the slaves and establish racial equality in the South. These books evaluate Lincoln's intentions and performance in regards to Reconstruction. Like the other titles listed in the suggested readings, these books are secondary sources.

"Reading" and Studying Photographs, Artwork, and Movies

Your experience of this textbook will be enriched, we believe, if you take the time to study the artwork, photography, movies, and other forms of visual representation that are integral to it. For an example of what the textbook offers in its art program, and how you might study the art, consult the

1877 painting by Winslow Homer that appears below and in Chapter 17, Reconstruction, 1863–1877. At the center of the painting are four young African Americans who are reading the Bible or listening to it being read. On the right is their watchful grandmother.

Certain features of the painting immediately stand out. First, Homer treats his African American subjects with respect: each of them is represented as thoroughly absorbed in either reading or listening to the Bible. Second, each (with the possible exception of the boy at the left) has taken care to arrange his or her clothes well and modestly. This communicates an air of dignity. Third, the Bible reading is being done by the children and not, as was often the case in Sunday school, by adults. Fourth, the two black children who are reading are lighter skinned than the two who flank them and are listening.

Winslow Homer, *Sunday Morning in Virginia,* 1877. Cincinnati Art Museum John J. Emery Fund. Acc.#1924.247

A historian might ask questions about the painting such as those that follow to try to learn more about African American life during Reconstruction. The more you study Reconstruction and, more generally, black life in the South before, during, and after the Civil War, the more information this painting will reveal. Good study begins with good questions. Consider these:

1. After taking a close look at what the four children and the grandmother are wearing, what do you judge to be their social and economic status? Do they seem wealthy, poor, or somewhere in between?

2. What does the centrality of the Bible to this image suggest about the religiosity of African Americans during the 1860s and 1870s?

3. One way of interpreting the children taking the lead in reading the Bible is to suggest that the grandmother was herself unable to read. How many African Americans born in slavery, as this grandmother likely was, learned to read either while they were slaves or after they were emancipated in the 1860s? After emancipation, how and when did African American children learn to read? Were

their opportunities for education greater than they had been during slavery? For those receiving an education, who taught them? Did they learn at school, in church, or at home? Did girls have as much access to education as boys?

4. What kind of room or building are these African Americans in? Why are there only a bench and chairs and no table? Why are there no decorations on the walls?

5. What significance, if any, are we to attribute to Homer's decision to paint two of the African American children as light skinned and two as dark skinned? And what significance, if any, are we to attribute to Homer's decision to depict the two light-skinned children as the principal Bible readers?

6. That this painting is organized around four children and a grandmother suggests that this is a family scene. What, if anything, are we to make about the presence of a grandparent and the absence of the parents themselves? More broadly, how did African Americans organize their family life in the South during slavery and then during freedom?

7. Keep in mind that most pieces of art such as these do not simply communicate "facts" about the time in which the subjects of the painting lived. The artist imparts to the painting a point of view. On the basis of this painting, how would you characterize Homer's attitudes toward African Americans? Winslow Homer was a white northerner. How might a white southern artist have rendered an image of African American life in 1877?

8. To learn how one white southerner portrayed black life during Reconstruction, please find an opportunity to watch the movie *The Birth of a Nation*, which is the *History through Film* entry for Chapter 17 (see p. 479). This movie was made by D.W. Griffith, a white southerner by birth and upbringing. How would you compare Griffith's depiction of black life during Reconstruction with that of Winslow's?

Reading and Studying Maps

Historical events do not just "happen." They happen in a specific place. It is important to learn all you can about that place, and a good map can help you do this.

Your textbook includes many different kinds of maps, including those that show political boundaries, election results, population, topography, military battles, and irrigation and transportation networks. To study maps effectively, you should first take the time to identify and study map labels. Take a look at the foldout map inside the front cover, a geographic-political map of the United States. This map provides four kinds of basic labels. They do the following:

1. Identify the states and the countries bordering the U.S.
2. Identify the state capitals and major cities
3. Identify the rivers, large lakes, major bays, gulfs, and oceans
4. Identify the mountain ranges, important individual mountains, plateaus, plains, and deserts

In addition, this map contains a distance scale in miles and kilometers. It appears in the lower right-hand corner of the map. This scale permits a reader to determine the actual size of different parts of U.S. territory and the distances between them. This map also contains insets to show parts of the United States that are either too far from the mainland to be drawn to scale (Alaska and Hawaii) or are too small to show up clearly on the map (Puerto Rico and the Virgin Islands).

Many of the maps in this book contain legends that use colors and other forms of coding to convey important information without cluttering up the map with words. Most maps in this book also have captions written by the textbook authors. Each caption is meant to describe the basic purpose of the map and to draw readers' attention to particular details.

Using Maps to Study Geographic-Political Change

Across the 235-plus years of U.S. history, the political boundaries of the country and the number of states belonging to the United States have changed a great deal. Maps can help us to see and study those changes.

Example #1: The Territorial Growth of the United States and the Emergence of New States Compare the following maps: 3.1 (this notation refers to the first map in the third chapter), which shows how small the area of English settlement was in 1700; 6.5, which shows the original thirteen states at the time of Independence as well as their claims to western land; 13.1, which shows the free and slave states in 1848, as well as the huge western territories that the United States had added to its land mass but had yet to divide into states; and 19.2, which charts the distribution of electoral votes in the 1896 election by states and, in the process, reveals that America, by that time, had acquired its modern continental

Map 3.1

Map 6.5

States, and Map 18.3, which shows the small reservations in the West in which Indian tribes had been concentrated by 1875 and 1900.

Example #3: Changes in the Internal Political Boundaries of Europe, 1919–1989 Map 23.4 shows the vast changes in the internal political boundaries of Europe and the Middle East that resulted from the defeat and disintegration of the Austro-Hungarian and Ottoman empires during the First World War. The legend for Map 23.4 identifies the 14 different visual devices required to show all the territorial shifts and boundary changes. Map 30.3 is really two maps: the first shows how far the Soviet Union extended its political control into eastern and southern Europe during the Cold War (1945–1989). The second shows the territories that achieved national independence after the Soviet Union collapsed in 1989.

A comparison of Maps 23.4 and 30.3 reveals that most of the new nations created in Europe after the First World War were the ones that the Soviet Union deprived of their independence after the Second World War. Many of these countries had actually lost their independence earlier than 1946, as the Nazis began, as early as 1938, to extend their control through central, eastern, and southern Europe (see Map 26.1). These countries, in other words, enjoyed barely 20 years of freedom before being plunged into 50 years of servitude. The Soviet Union's collapse in 1989 gave the peoples inhabiting these lands their second twentieth-century chance for freedom and self-government, and most embraced the opportunity.

These maps demonstrate the instability of Europe's internal borders through much of the twentieth century. That instability, in turn, helps to explain why the United States fought four wars in Europe across the last 100 years: the First World War, the Second World War, the Cold War, and the 1990s War in the Balkans.

boundaries. By 1896, the United States possessed 45 of its 50 states, missing only Oklahoma, Arizona, New Mexico, and Alaska (all of which were, by 1896, territories of the United States) and Hawaii, which would be acquired in 1898.

Once you study these four maps, focus on the second one, 6.5, and answer this question: which new states were added to the United States out of the western lands that the original thirteen states ceded to the national government between 1784 and 1802?

Example #2: The Shift and Shrinkage of Indian Lands in the Continental United States Compare Map 1.8, which shows how mound-building Indian societies once extended throughout the eastern half of the modern United

Map 13.1

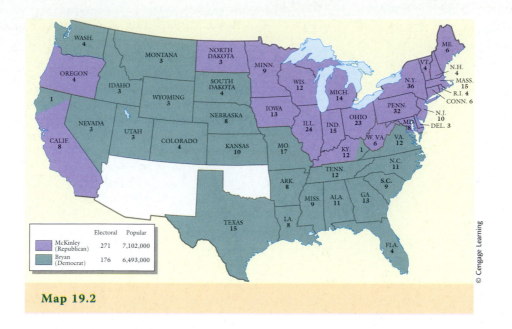

	Electoral	Popular
McKinley (Republican)	271	7,102,000
Bryan (Democrat)	176	6,493,000

Map 19.2

© Cengage Learning

Using Maps to Study Battles

Maps can convey a wealth of knowledge about military battles in a compressed and efficient way. See, for example, Map 16.2, which charts the progress of the Battle of Chancellorsville (and Fredericksburg) during the Civil War. The boxed legend defines the ten different kinds of bars and arrows that are used on the map to show the position of the Union and Confederate forces on the five different days of the battle and to demonstrate how the two armies conducted their advances and retreats. From studying the map itself, can you determine which side won the Battle of Chancellorsville? What information in the map led you to that conclusion?

Using Maps to Study the American Economy

The most detailed legend in the book is attached to Map 19.1, which shows the distribution of industries across America in the years 1900–1920. Twenty-two industries are identified by icons in the legend, and those icons, in turn, demonstrate where those industries were concentrated in the 48 states. A second legend to the right of the first uses color coding to identify the scale of manufacturing (measured in the dollars of factory production generated in each state in 1919). After examining this map, try to answer these questions:

1. In what states were the meatpacking, textile, and petroleum-refining industries concentrated?
2. Which state had no significant industrial output of any sort?
3. Which seven states had the highest factory output, as measured in dollars? Which six states had the lowest factory output? Were the highest and lowest factory output states clustered in particular regions? If so, which ones?
4. In how many cities did factory production in 1919 exceed $1 billion? Which cities earned this distinction?
5. Do you think that the uneven distribution of industry in the United States shaped American politics and culture in the 20th century?

We invite you to explore the maps mentioned in this guide as well as the many others offered in the textbook.

We are pleased to present the sixth edition of *Liberty, Equality, Power*. Like the first five editions, this one captures the drama and excitement of America's past, from the pre-Columbian era through our own time. It integrates social and cultural history into a political story that is organized around the themes of liberty, equality, and power, and synthesizes the finest historical scholarship to create a narrative that is balanced, lively, and accessible to a broad range of students.

The *Liberty, Equality, Power* Approach

In this book, we tell many small stories, and one large one: how America transformed itself, in a relatively brief period of world history, from a land inhabited by hunter–gatherer and agricultural Native American societies into the most powerful industrial nation on earth. This story has been told many times before, and those who have told it in the past have usually emphasized the political experiment in liberty and equality that took root here in the 18th century.

We, too, stress the extraordinary and transformative impact that the ideals of liberty and equality exerted on American politics, society, and economics during the American Revolution and after. We show how the creation of a free economic environment—one in which entrepreneurial spirit, technological innovation, and industrial production have flourished—underpinned American industrial might. We have also emphasized the successful struggles for freedom that, over the course of the last 230 years, have brought—first to all white men, then to men of color, and finally to women— rights and opportunities that they had not previously known.

But we have also identified a third factor in this pantheon of American ideals—that of power. We examine power in many forms: the accumulation of vast economic fortunes and their influence on the economy and on politics; the dispossession of American Indians from land that they regarded as theirs; the enslavement of millions of Africans and their African American descendants for a period of almost 250 years; the relegation of women and of racial, ethnic, and religious minorities to subordinate places in American society; and the extension of American control over foreign peoples, such as Latin Americans and Filipinos, who would have preferred to have been free and self-governing. We do not mean to suggest that American power has always been turned to these negative purposes. Subordinate groups have also marshaled power to combat oppression, as in the abolitionist and civil rights crusades, the campaign for woman suffrage, and the labor movement. The government has at times used its power to moderate poverty and to manage the economy in the interests of general prosperity. And it has used its military power to defeat Nazi Germany, World War II Japan, the Cold War Soviet Union, and other enemies of freedom.

The invocation of power as a variable in American history impels us to widen the lens through which we look at the past and to enrich the stories we tell. Ours has been a history of freedom and domination; of progress toward realizing a broadly democratic polity and of delays and reverses; of abundance and poverty; of wars for freedom and justice and for control of foreign markets. In complicating our master narrative in this way, we think we have rendered American history more exciting and intriguing. Progress has not been automatic, but the product of ongoing struggles.

In this book, we have tried to capture the diversity of the American past, both in terms of outcomes and in terms of the variety of groups who have participated in America's making. American Indians are not presented simply as the victims of European aggression but as peoples diverse in their own ranks, with a variety of systems of social organization and cultural expression. We give equal treatment to the industrial titans of American history—the likes of Andrew Carnegie and John D. Rockefeller—and to those, such as small farmers and poor workers, who resisted the corporate reorganization of economic life. We celebrate the great moments of 1863, when African Americans were freed from slavery, and of 1868, when they were made full citizens of the United States. But we also note how a majority of African Americans had to wait another 100 years, until the civil rights movement of the 1960s, to gain full access to American freedoms. We tell similarly complex stories about women, Latinos, and other groups of ethnic Americans.

Political issues are only part of America's story. Americans have always loved their leisure and have created the world's most vibrant popular culture. They have embraced technological innovations, especially those promising to make their lives easier and more fun. We have, therefore, devoted considerable space to a discussion of American popular culture, from the founding of the first newspapers in the 18th century and the rise of movies, jazz, and the comics in the early 20th century to the cable television and Internet revolutions in recent years. We have also analyzed how American industry has periodically altered home and personal life by making new products—such as clothing, cars, refrigerators, and computers—available to consumers. In such ways, we hope to give our readers a rich portrait of how Americans lived at various points in our history.

New to the Sixth Edition[1]

The fifth edition won praise for its successful integration of political, cultural, and social history; its thematic unity; its narrative clarity and eloquence; its extraordinary coverage of pre-Columbian America; its extended treatment of the Civil War; its history of economic growth and change; and its excellent map and illustration programs. It also received high marks both for its *History through Film* series, which now discusses 32 different films (one per chapter) that treat important aspects of American history, and for its *Musical Link to the Past* feature, which discusses 15 different songs from the middle of the 18th century to the present, each set in its historical and cultural context. *History through Film* features encourage students to think critically about what they see on screen and allow instructors to stimulate students' historical interest through a medium they enjoy. For the sixth edition, we are pleased to introduce 4 new films to our series: *Gangs of New York, Coney Island, Saving Private Ryan,* and *The Big Lebowski.* In addition, we have moved two films—*The Great White Hope* and *The Jazz Singer*—from Chapters 20 and 21 to Chapters 21 and 24 respectively.

Musical Link to the Past covers a great range of songs and artists: from revolutionary era odes to liberty to 20th-century country music laments about women's domestic burdens; from Stephen Foster and John Philip Sousa to Duke Ellington and Grandmaster Flash. We are pleased to announce that this edition expands the number of *Musical Links* from 15 to 18 through the addition of three new entries: Stephen Foster, "Oh Susannah" (Chapter 10); Scott Joplin, "Maple Leaf Rag" (Chapter 20); and Irving Berlin, "Oh, How I Hate to Get Up in the Morning" (Chapter 23). Dr. Harvey Cohen, a specialist in American cultural history who teaches at King's College London, has once again drafted the texts of these musical features, as he did for the original 15. We wish to thank Dr. Cohen for his important contributions to this textbook.

To make the *Musical Links* come alive in classrooms, we have assembled a CD containing many of the musical selections that we discuss. All instructors who adopt our textbook will, upon request, receive a free copy of this CD to play in their classrooms.

The success of *Musical Link to the Past* has inspired us to expand our primary source program in yet another direction for this edition: we have added an entirely new feature, *Visual Link to the Past.* Each of the new 15 *Visual Links* focuses on a single piece of art, material culture, or photography that reveals something important about the historical era in which it was produced. In an extended caption we explore the historical significance of the object in question, and then pose a question for students to answer. The objects that we explore range from a statue of George III erected in 1766 (Chapter 5) to the banjo (Chapter 24), and from an abolitionist woodcut protesting the lynching of slaves (Chapter 12) to *Monopoly*, the 1930s board game that made mimicking the ruthless competitive behavior of "plutocrats" a popular diversion (Chapter 25).

The *Visual Links* supplement not only our strong program of *Musical Links* but also our traditional program of **Link to the Past** that, for several editions now, has explored important written documents from the American past. These three series of *Links*, in combination, endow our sixth edition with one of the most comprehensive, diverse, and intriguing programs of primary sources available in a U.S. history textbook. In addition to sources featured in the text, we have added a few *Primary Source Icons* to the margins of each chapter indicating documents which are available on the ⊡ CourseMate website.

As in past editions, we have continued to make sure that the textbook's last chapter (32) is up to date and gives adequate attention to the important developments in politics, economics, and culture of the 21st century. George W. Bush's victories in 2000 and 2004; the destruction of the World Trade Center towers on September 11, 2001; the resulting wars on terrorism and on Saddam Hussein in Iraq and the Taliban in Afghanistan; Obama's victory in 2008; the financial crash of 2008–2009; and the BP oil spill in the Gulf of Mexico: all receive substantial treatment.

In preparing for this revision, we solicited feedback from professors and scholars throughout the country, many of whom have used the fifth edition of *Liberty, Equality, Power* in their classrooms. Their comments proved most helpful, and many of their suggestions have been incorporated into the sixth edition. Thus, for example, at the prompting of reviewers, we have shortened the overall word length of the textbook by five percent. We have also undertaken for this edition a major reorganization and overhaul of Chapters 19 and 20. The new Chapter 19 now brings together and reworks material on late 19th-century economics, technology, and labor that in earlier editions had appeared in multiple chapters. The new Chapter 20, in turn, focuses on cities, peoples, and cultures during that same period of time. Much of the material in Chapter 20 is new and deepens our textbook's engagement with cultural and intellectual history.

We have carried over and, in some cases, enhanced pedagogical changes that we made to earlier editions and that have proved popular with professors and students. **Chapter outlines** and **chronology boxes** continue to appear at the beginning of each chapter. We have added new *Focus Questions* for many chapters; these questions both frame major sections of chapters and are gathered at each chapter's end along with *Questions for Critical Thinking*. We have updated our *Identifications* (boldfaced terms that appear throughout the text) and supply the definitions for these terms in a comprehensive *Glossary* appearing at the end of the book. Each map in our outstanding map program comes equipped with a brief caption instructing students about how to interpret the geographical and topographical data it contains. Many of the maps are also animated on the CourseMate website. We have updated our *Suggested Readings* for each chapter while keeping the lists brief. Extensive bibliographic essays for each chapter are still available on the website.

We believe that both instructors and students will find these aids to be useful and well-placed tools for reviewing

---

[1] Some material in this section refers to content and page numbers from the comprehensive volume of *Liberty, Equality, Power*, sixth edition.

what they have learned and for pushing outward the frontiers of their knowledge.

Finally, we have scrutinized each page of this textbook, making sure our prose is clear, the historical issues well presented, and the scholarship up to date and accurate.

Specific Revisions to Content and Coverage

Chapter 17   Condensed material on the Treaty of Washington.

Chapter 18   New material on mining; new Visual Link to the Past feature, "Indian Children at the Hampton Institute."

Chapter 19   (MAJOR REVISION) Completely revised and reorganized. Now titled "The Rise of Corporate America, 1865–1914," it incorporates material from Fifth Edition Chapters 19 and 20 so that the story of the growth of American corporations is told in one place. New Visual Link to the Past feature, "The New Woman."

Chapter 20   (MAJOR REVISION) New title, Introduction, and Conclusion; added two substantial sections, "The Rise of the City" and "Re-Imagining American Nationality"; substantially revised section, "Working-Class and Commercial Culture" (formerly, "The Joys of the City"); new Musical Link to the Past feature, "Ragtime"; new History through Film feature, *Coney Island;* added Focus Questions and glossary terms and reworked Chronology.

Chapter 21   Added sections on the IWW and Frederick W. Taylor and scientific management; added Focus Questions; reduced number of major headings.

Chapter 22   New Visual Link to the Past feature, "Spanish-American War Rifles."

Chapter 23   New Musical Link to the Past feature, "A Light-Hearted Poke at Army Life"; revised Chronology.

Chapter 24   New Visual Link to the Past feature, "The Banjo"; moved History through Film feature on *The Jazz Singer* here from Chapter 20.

Chapter 25   New Visual Link to the Past feature, "Monopoly"; added Focus Questions.

Chapter 26   Streamlined and revised prose to provide stronger narrative; condensed sections on European and Pacific Theaters into one; increased attention to role of West in "Business and Finance" and "Assessing Economic Change" sections; expanded coverage of Japanese internment and added mention of Italian and German internees; revised Focus Questions; added History through Film feature, *Saving Private Ryan;* added Link to the Past feature, "Civil Liberties in Wartime: *Korematsu* v. *United States.*"

Chapter 27   Revised Korean War section, giving greater emphasis to war's impact; substantially revised discussion of containment; updated material on McCarthy; added material on farm issues; revised Fair Deal section; added discussion of integration of armed forces; revised end of chapter in light of recent scholarship on significance of Election of 1952; new Visual Link to the Past feature, "It's Okay—We're Hunting Communists"; revised Focus Questions.

Chapter 28   Combined coverage of civil rights movement into one section; revised coverage of conservatism in sections "Debating the Role of Government" and "The Case for a More Active Government"; refocused final section of chapter; added material on rural America and farm policy; added Link to the Past feature, "A Warning about the Future: President Dwight Eisenhower's Farewell Address, 1961."

Chapter 29   (MAJOR REVISION) Streamlined and reorganized to clarify and focus narrative; reframed section, "A Crisis of Governance"; reworked civil rights material; added discussion of Environmentalism; revised accounts of 1964 election and Gulf of Tonkin; revised Focus Questions; new Visual Link to the Past feature, "Shocking Images"; added Musical Link to the Past feature, "The Folk-Rock Movement and The Sixties."

Chapter 30   (MAJOR REVISION) Completely reorganized chapter along thematic lines; new section, "The Reagan Revolution," includes a more focused discussion of the central themes of the administration of Ronald Reagan; added Link to the Past feature, "Cultural Disagreements: Equality for Women?"

Chapter 31   Revised section on the financial sector; included work of George Herring in Suggested Readings.

Chapter 32   (MAJOR REVISION) Revised and updated entire chapter; reworked economic discussion; new Visual Link to the Past feature, "Does Print Media Have a Future?"; new History through Film feature, *The Big Lebowski;* revised Focus Questions.

Supplements

For the Instructor

PowerLecture CD-ROM with ExamView® and JoinIn®
This dual platform, all-in-one multimedia resource includes the Instructor's Resource Manual; a test bank written by Andria Crosson of the University of Texas at San Antonio; Microsoft® PowerPoint® slides of both lecture outlines and images and maps from the text that can be used as offered, or customized by importing personal lecture slides or other material; and *JoinIn®* PowerPoint® slides with clicker content. Also included is ExamView, an easy-to-use assessment and tutorial system that allows instructors to create, deliver, and customize tests in minutes. Instructors can build tests with as many as 250 questions using up to 12 question types, and using ExamView's complete word-processing capabilities, they can enter an unlimited number of new questions or edit existing ones.

Musical Links to the Past CD Available free to adopters, this CD contains audio recordings of many of the musical selections from the text's new *Musical Link to the Past* feature.

HistoryFinder This searchable online database allows instructors to quickly and easily download thousands of assets, including art, photographs, maps, primary sources, and audio/video clips. Each asset downloads directly into a Microsoft® PowerPoint® slide, allowing instructors to easily create exciting PowerPoint presentations for their classrooms.

eInstructor's Resource Manual Prepared by Roger Hall of Allan Hancock College, this manual has many features, including instructional objectives, chapter outlines and chronologies, lecture outlines, suggested essay topics, and other readings and resources. Available on the instructor's companion website.

WebTutor™ on Blackboard® or WebCT® With WebTutor's text-specific, pre-formatted content and total flexibility, instructors can easily create and manage their own custom course website. WebTutor's course management tool gives instructors the ability to provide virtual office hours, post syllabi, set up threaded discussions, track student progress with the quizzing material, and much more. For students, WebTutor offers real-time access to a full array of study tools, including animations and videos that bring the book's topics to life, plus chapter outlines, summaries, learning objectives, glossary flashcards (with audio), practice quizzes, and weblinks.

History CourseMate Cengage Learning's History CourseMate brings course concepts to life with interactive learning, study, and exam preparation tools that support the printed textbook. Watch student comprehension soar as your class works with the printed textbook and the CourseMate content developed for *Liberty, Equality, Power*. History CourseMate goes beyond the book to deliver what you need! History CourseMate includes an integrated eBook, interactive teaching and learning tools including quizzes, flashcards, videos, and more, and EngagementTracker, a first-of-its-kind tool that monitors student engagement in the course. Go to login.cengage.com to access these resources, and look for this icon which denotes a resource available within CourseMate.

Online Instructor's Resources include detailed plans and instructions for three Group Projects for classroom use: 1) Re-creating the '60s: Teaching History through Teach-ins; 2) Commemorating the Boston Massacre: Teaching History through Public Memory; and 3) Reconstruction and the Meaning of Freedom: Teaching History through Public Debate. In each of the projects, students examine the choices facing people in a particular era from the various perspectives of the different groups involved in the historical event.

Supplements are available to qualified adopters. Please consult your local sales representative for details.

For the Student

History CourseMate For students, CourseMate provides an additional source of interactive learning, study, and exam preparation outside the classroom. Students will find outlines, focus questions, flashcards, quizzes, primary source links, and video clips. In addition, CourseMate includes an integrated *Liberty, Equality, Power,* sixth edition eBook. Students taking quizzes will be linked directly to relevant sections in the ebook for additional information. The ebook is fully searchable and students can even take notes and save them for later review. The ebook links out to rich media assets such as video and MP3 chapter summaries, primary source documents with critical thinking questions, and interactive (zoomable) maps. Students can use the ebook as their primary text or as a companion multimedia support. Go to login.cengagebrain.com to access these resources, and look for this icon to find resources related to your text in CourseMate.

CL eBook This interactive multimedia ebook links out to rich media assets such as video and MP3 chapter summaries. Through this ebook, students can also access self-test quizzes, chapter outlines, focus questions, essay questions (for which the answers can be emailed to their instructors), primary source documents with critical thinking questions, and interactive (zoomable) maps. Available at www.cengagebrain.com.

Cengagebrain.com Save your students time and money. Direct them to www.cengagebrain.com for choice in formats and savings and a better chance to succeed in your class. *Cengagebrain.com*, Cengage Learning's online store, is a single destination for more than 10,000 new textbooks, eTextbooks, eChapters, study tools, and audio supplements. Students have the freedom to purchase a-la-carte exactly what they need when they need it. Students can save 50% on the electronic textbook, and can pay as little as $1.99 for an individual eChapter.

Wadsworth American History Resource Center Wadsworth's American History Resource Center gives your students access to a "virtual reader" with hundreds of primary sources including speeches, letters, legal documents and transcripts, poems, maps, simulations, timelines, and additional images that bring history to life, along with interactive assignable exercises. A map feature including Google Earth™ coordinates and exercises will aid in student comprehension of geography and use of maps. Students can compare the traditional textbook map with an aerial view of the location today. It's an ideal resource for study, review, and research. In addition to this map feature, the resource center also provides blank maps for student review and testing.

Reader Program Cengage Learning publishes a number of readers, some containing exclusively primary sources, others a combination of primary and secondary sources, and some designed to guide students through the process of historical inquiry. Visit Cengage.com/history for a complete list of readers.

Rand McNally Atlas of American History, 2e This comprehensive atlas features more than 80 maps, with new content covering global perspectives, including events in the Middle East from 1945 to 2005, as well as population trends in the U.S. and around the world. Additional maps document voyages of discovery; the settling of the colonies; major U.S. military engagements, including the American Revolution and World Wars I and II; and sources of immigrations, ethnic populations and patterns of economic change.

Major Problems in American History Series Volumes in this series contain primary source documents (6-10 per chapter), secondary sources (2-3 per chapter), chapter introductions, separate introductions to documents and essays in every chapter, bibliographies, and full documentation of sources.

Documenting America's Past: Primary Sources in US History Provides access to over 900 readings to create the ideal supplement or text for any U.S. History course. With its unique combination of primary source documents, students can gain deeper insight to the events, people, and movements that helped shape U.S. History.

Custom Options Nobody knows your students like you, so why not give them a text that is tailor-fit to their needs? Cengage Learning offers custom solutions for your course— whether it's making a small modification to *Liberty, Equality, Power* to match your syllabus or combining multiple sources to create something truly unique. You can pick and choose chapters, include your own material, and add additional map exercises along with the Rand McNally Atlas to create a text that fits the way you teach. Ensure that your students get the most out of their textbook dollar by giving them exactly what they need. Contact your Cengage Learning representative to explore custom solutions for your course.

Acknowledgments

We recognize the contributions of reviewers who read portions of the manuscript in various stages:

Sam Abrams, The Beacon School
William Allison, Weber State University
Angie Anderson, Southeastern Louisiana University
Kenneth G. Anthony, University of North Carolina, Greensboro
Paul R. Beezley, Texas Tech University
David Bernstein, California State University at Long Beach
Sue Blanchette, Hillcrest High School
Jeff Bloodworth, Ohio University
Michael R. Bradley, Motlow College
Betty Brandon, University of South Alabama
Daniel Patrick Brown, Moorpark College
Ronald G. Brown, College of Southern Maryland
Susan Burch, Gallaudet University
Thomas M. Cangiano, The Lawrenceville School
Jeffrey W. Coker, Belmont University
Phil Crow, North Harris College
Lorenzo M. Crowell, Mississippi State University
Amy E. N. Darty, University of Central Florida
Thomas M. Deaton, Dalton State College
Norman C. Delaney, Del Mar College
Ted Delaney, Washington and Lee University
Andrew J. DeRoche, Front Range Community College
Rebecca de Schweinitz, Brigham Young University
Bruce Dierenfield, Canisius College
Brian R. Dirck, Anderson University
Maura Doherty, Illinois State University
R. Blake Dunnavent, Lubbock Christian University
Eileen Eagan, University of Southern Maine
Derek Elliott, Tennessee State University
B. Jane England, North Central Texas College
William B. Feis, Buena Vista University
David J. Fitzpatrick, Washtenaw Community College
Van Forsyth, Clark College
Michael P. Gabriel, Kutztown University of Pennsylvania
Gary Gallagher, Pennsylvania State University
Kevin M. Gannon, Grand View University
Gerald Ghelfi, Santa Ana College
Michael Goldberg, University of Washington, Bothell
Kathleen Gorman, Minnesota State University, Mankato
David E. Hamilton, University of Kentucky
Michael J. Haridopolos, Brevard Community College
Mark Harvey, North Dakota State University
Brenda Hasterok, Spain Park High School
Kurt Hohenstein, Hampden Sydney College
Mark Huddle, University of Georgia
Samuel C. Hyde, Jr., Southeastern Louisiana University
Thomas N. Ingersoll, Ohio State University
J. Michael Jeffries, Northeastern Technical College

Frank Karpiel, Ramapo College of New Jersey

Anthony E. Kaye, Pennsylvania State University

Michael Kazin, Georgetown University

Michael King, Moraine Valley Community College

Michael Krenn, Appalachian State

Frank Lambert, Purdue University

Pat Ledbetter, North Central Texas College

Jan Leone, Middle Tennessee State University

Michelle LeMaster, Eastern Illinois University

Craig Livingston, Montgomery College

Robert F. Marcom, San Antonio College

Suzanne Marshall, Jacksonville State University

Brenda Taylor Matthews, Texas Wesleyan University

Joanne Maypole, Front Range Community College

Jimmie McGee, South Plains College

Nora E. McMillan, San Antonio College

Jerry Mills, Midland College

Charlene Mires, Villanova University

Brock Mislan, Watchung Hills Regional High School

Rick Moniz, Chabot College

Michael R. Nichols, Tarrant County College, Northwest

Linda Noel, Morgan State University

Christy Olsen, Skyline High School

Richard B. Partain, Bakersfield College

William Pencak, Pennsylvania State University

Teresa Thomas Perrin, Austin Community College

David Poteet, New River Community College

Howard Reed, University of Bridgeport

Jonathan Rees, Colorado State University–Pueblo

Thomas S. Reid, Valencia Community College

Anne Richardson, Texas Christian University

Lelia M. Roeckell, Molloy College

Thomas J. Rowland, University of Wisconsin, Oshkosh

Roy Scott, Mississippi State University

Reynolds J. Scott-Childress, State University of New York at New Paltz

Katherine A. S. Sibley, St. Joseph's University

Herb Sloan, Barnard College

M. Todd Smallwood, Manatee Community College

John Smolenski, University of California, Davis

Steve Stein, University of Memphis

Michael J. Steiner, Northwest Missouri State University

Jennifer Stollman, University of Mississippi

Siegfried H. Sutterlin, Indian Hills Community College

Richard O. Swanson, Duxbury High School

John Wood Sweet, The University of North Carolina at Chapel Hill

Teresa Fava Thomas, Fitchburg State College

Xiansheng Tian, Metro State College of Denver

Jamie Underwood, Montana State University Northern

Vincent Vinikas, University of Arkansas, Little Rock

Vernon Volpe, University of Nebraska

Harry L. Watson, The University of North Carolina at Chapel Hill

William Benton Whisenhunt, College of DuPage

David K.White, McHenry County College

Laura Matysek Wood, Tarrant County College, Northwest

We wish to thank the members of the Wadsworth/Cengage staff, many of them new to the company, for embracing our textbook wholeheartedly and for expertly guiding the production of this sixth edition. We are indebted to Ann West, our new Senior Sponsoring Editor, for her savvy, inspiration, and commitment. She is one of the best editors we have worked with, and, in her brief time with our book, has already contributed mightily to it. Project Manager Anne Finley has done a superb job supervising work on the sixth edition while Project Editor Lauren Traut, Elm Street Publishing Services, has expeditiously coordinated the numerous tasks required to bring this book to press. We thank photo editor Sarah Everston for collecting many of the beautiful photographs and illustrations that grace these pages. We owe a great debt, yet again, to our long-time developmental editor, Margaret McAndrew Beasley who has worked with us on five editions and, by now, knows the book as well as we do. Margaret's editing skills, organizational expertise, wisdom, good cheer, and belief in this book and its authors keep us going.

A big thanks, too, to Wadsworth/Cengage's marketing department and to the sales representatives who have worked hard and creatively to generate interest in our book among university, college, and high school teachers across America.

No project of this scope is completely error free. A special thanks, for that reason, to Kaylee Dorman, an undergraduate user of the textbook, for taking the time to write us about an error that she discovered. We hope that others will follow Ms. Dorman's lead and take the time to send us queries, suggestions, and corrections. The book will be enriched by such feedback. Please send comments to senior sponsoring editor, Ann West at **ann.west@cengage.com**.

Finally, each of us would like to offer particular thanks to those historians, friends, and family members who helped to bring this project to a successful conclusion.

Personal Acknowledgments

JOHN M. MURRIN Mary R. Murrin has provided the kind of moral and personal support that made completion of this project possible. James Axtell and Gregory Evans Dowd saved me from many mistakes, mostly about Indians. John E. Selby and Eugene R. Sheridan were particularly helpful on the Revolution. Fred Anderson and Virginia DeJohns Anderson offered acute suggestions. Several former colleagues and graduate students have also contributed in various ways, especially Stephen Aron, Andrew Isenberg, Ignacio Gallup-Diaz, Evan P. Haefeli, Beth Lewis-Pardoe, Geoffrey Plank, Nathaniel J. Sheidley, and Jeremy Stern.

PAUL E. JOHNSON My greatest debt is to the community of scholars who write about the United States between the Revolution and the Civil War. Closer to home, I owe thanks to the other writers of this book, particularly to John Murrin. The Department of History at the University of South Carolina provided time to work, while my wife, Kasey Grier, and stray dogs named Lucy, Bill, Buddy, and Patty provided the right kinds of interruptions.

JAMES M. McPHERSON My family provided an environment of affection and stability that contributed immeasurably to the writing of my chapters, while undergraduate students at Princeton University who have taken my courses over the years provided feedback, questions, and insights that helped me to understand what students know and don't know, and what they need to know.

ALICE FAHS Thanks are due to Gary Gerstle, whose keen editorial eye and judgment helped greatly with revisions of Chapter 19. Our "team leader" among the authors, Gary has given generously of his time to the rest of us, providing constant support. Margaret Beasley continues to be a crucial resource of intelligence and good cheer as our development editor; we all know we are very lucky. I am grateful as well to Ann West, our editor at Cengage, for her exceptional leadership and commitment to excellence; and to James M. McPherson for the initial invitation to become part of *Liberty, Equality, Power*. At the University of California, Irvine, David Igler was an important resource for past revisions of Chapter 18. My students, both undergraduate and graduate, have continued to be a source of inspiration to me in conceptualizing this textbook. Finally, my family continues to listen patiently to history anecdotes over breakfasts, lunches, and dinners—whether in California or Texas. To Charlie and to Mimi, many thanks.

GARY GERSTLE A long time ago, Jerald Podair, Thomas Knock, and the late Roy Rosenzweig gave me exceptionally thorough, thoughtful, and insightful critiques on early drafts of my chapters. This textbook still benefits from their good and generous work. Former graduate students Kathleen Trainor, Reynolds Scott-Childress, Linda Noel, Kelly Ryan, Robert Chase, Marcy Wilson, Thomas Castillo, and Katarina Keane offered skillful research assistance on earlier editions. Monte Holman made many indispensable and timely contributions to this edition. Alice Fahs helped me a great deal with the redesign of Chapter 20. Thanks to Alice and the rest of my fellow authors for their intelligence, wit, and deep commitment to this project, and to Ann West and Margaret Beasley for their leadership and support.

EMILY AND NORMAN ROSENBERG We would like to thank our children—Sarah, Molly, Ruth, and Joe—for all of their help and good cheer over the years. Successive generations of students at Macalester College, who helped us refine our ideas about the past and about specific features in this book, also deserve thanks. Graduate students at the University of California, Irvine, have helped sharpen and clarify themes. We also want to acknowledge all of the people who offered both supportive and helpfully critical comments on earlier versions of *Liberty, Equality, Power*. Finally, our deepest thanks go to our development editor, Margaret Beasley, who has offered personal friendship and expert guidance through the many editions of this text, and to Ann West, our editor at Cengage, whose care and talent is unsurpassed.

John M. Murrin, Paul E. Johnson, James M. McPherson, Alice Fahs, Gary Gerstle, Emily S. Rosenberg, Norman L. Rosenberg

LIBERTY, EQUALITY, POWER

Winslow Homer, *Sunday Morning in Virginia*, 1877. Cincinnati Art Museum John J. Emery Fund. Acc.#1924.247

Sunday Morning in Virginia

This painting by Winslow Homer (1877) of four young black people and the grandmother of two of them is full of symbolism that illustrates important themes in both slavery and Reconstruction. The two lighter-skinned children, probably siblings, are reading the Bible while the dark-skinned children on either side—probably brother and sister—follow along as they too learn to read. The grandmother listens with a wistful look into the distance, perhaps wishing that she was young enough to acquire the powerful tool of literacy denied to slaves. The religiosity of freedpeople, their humble homes, the partly white ancestry of some, and their thirst for education all are portrayed in this splendid painting.

Reconstruction, 1863–1877

F ROM THE BEGINNING of the Civil War, the North fought to "reconstruct" the Union. Lincoln at first attempted to restore the Union as it had existed before 1861, but once the abolition of slavery became a Northern war aim, the Union could never be reconstructed on its old foundations. Instead, it must experience a "new birth of freedom," as Lincoln had said at the dedication of the military cemetery at Gettysburg.

But precisely what did "a new birth of freedom" mean? At the very least, it meant the end of slavery. The slave states would be reconstructed on a free-labor basis. But what would liberty look like for the 4 million freed slaves? Would they become citizens equal to their former masters in the eyes of the law? Would they have the right to vote? Should Confederate leaders and soldiers be punished for treason? On what terms should the Confederate states return to the Union? What would be the powers of the states and of the national government in a reconstructed Union?

Wartime Reconstruction
  Radical Republicans
    and Reconstruction

**Andrew Johnson
and Reconstruction**
  Johnson's Policy
  Southern Defiance
  The Black Codes
  Land and Labor in the Postwar
    South
  The Freedmen's Bureau
  Land for the Landless
  Education

**The Advent of Congressional
Reconstruction**
  Schism between President and
    Congress
  The 14th Amendment
  The 1866 Elections
  The Reconstruction Acts of 1867

**The Impeachment of
Andrew Johnson**
  The Completion of Formal
    Reconstruction
  The 15th Amendment
  The Election of 1868

The Grant Administration
  Civil Service Reform
  Foreign Policy Issues
  Reconstruction in the South
  Blacks in Office
  "Carpetbaggers"
  "Scalawags"
  The Ku Klux Klan
  The Election of 1872
  The Panic of 1873

The Retreat from Reconstruction
  The Mississippi Election of 1875
  The Supreme Court and
    Reconstruction
  The Election of 1876
  Disputed Results
  The Compromise of 1877
  The End of Reconstruction

Wartime Reconstruction

Lincoln pondered these problems long and hard. At first he feared that whites in the South would never extend equal rights to the freed slaves. After all, even most Northern states were denying full civil equality to the few black people within their borders. In 1862, Lincoln encouraged freedpeople to emigrate to all-black countries such as Haiti, where they would have a chance to get ahead without having to face the racism of whites. Black leaders, abolitionists, and many Republicans objected to that policy. Black people were Americans. Why should they not have the rights of American citizens instead of being urged to leave the country?

Lincoln eventually embraced the logic and justice of that view. But in beginning the process of reconstruction, he first reached out to Southern *whites* whose allegiance to the Confederacy was lukewarm. On December 8, 1863, Lincoln issued his Proclamation of Amnesty and Reconstruction, which offered presidential pardon to Southern whites who took an oath of allegiance to the United States and accepted the abolition of slavery. In any state where the number of white males aged 21 or older who took this oath equaled 10 percent of the number of voters in 1860, that nucleus could reestablish a state government to which Lincoln promised presidential recognition.

Because the war was still raging, this policy could be carried out only where Union troops controlled substantial portions of a Confederate state: Louisiana, Arkansas, and Tennessee in early 1864. Nevertheless, Lincoln hoped that once the process had begun in those areas, it might snowball as Union military victories convinced more and more Confederates that their cause was hopeless. But those military victories were long delayed, and in most parts of the South, reconstruction did not begin until 1865.

Another problem that slowed the process was growing opposition within Lincoln's own party. Many Republicans believed that white men who had fought *against* the Union should not be rewarded with restoration of their political rights while black men who had fought *for* the Union were denied those rights. The Proclamation of Reconstruction stated:

> . . . any provision which may be adopted by [a reconstructed] State government in relation to the freed people of such State, which shall recognize and declare their permanent freedom, provide for their education, and which may yet be consistent, as a temporary arrangement, with their present condition as a laboring, landless, and homeless class, will not be objected to by the national Executive.

This seemed to mean that white landowners and former slaveholders could adopt labor regulations and other measures to control former slaves, so long as they recognized their freedom and made minimal provision for their education.

Radical Republicans and Reconstruction

These changes were radical advances over slavery, but for many Republicans they were not radical enough. Led by Thaddeus Stevens in the House and Charles Sumner in the Senate, the radical Republicans wanted to go much further. If the freedpeople were landless, they said, provide them with land by confiscating the plantations of leading Confederates as punishment for treason. Radical Republicans also distrusted oaths of allegiance sworn by

CHRONOLOGY

1863	Lincoln issues Proclamation of Amnesty and Reconstruction
1864	Congress passes Wade-Davis bill; Lincoln kills it by pocket veto
1865	Congress establishes Freedmen's Bureau ◆ Andrew Johnson becomes president, announces his reconstruction plan ◆ Southern states enact Black Codes ◆ Congress refuses to seat Southern congressmen elected under Johnson's plan
1866	Congress passes civil rights bill and expands Freedmen's Bureau over Johnson's vetoes ◆ Race riots in Memphis and New Orleans ◆ Congress approves 14th Amendment ◆ Republicans increase congressional majority in fall elections
1867	Congress passes Reconstruction acts over Johnson's vetoes ◆ Congress passes Tenure of Office Act over Johnson's veto
1868	Most Southern senators and representatives readmitted to Congress under congressional plan of Reconstruction ◆ Andrew Johnson impeached but not convicted ◆ Ulysses S. Grant elected president ◆ 14th Amendment is ratified
1870	15th Amendment is ratified
1871	Congress passes Ku Klux Klan Act
1872	Liberal Republicans defect from party ◆ Grant wins reelection
1873	Economic depression begins with the Panic
1874	Democrats win control of House of Representatives
1875	Democrats implement Mississippi Plan ◆ Congress passes civil rights act
1876	Centennial celebration in Philadelphia ◆ Disputed presidential election causes constitutional crisis
1877	Compromise of 1877 installs Rutherford B. Hayes as president ◆ Hayes withdraws troops from South
1883	Supreme Court declares civil rights act of 1875 unconstitutional

ex-Confederates. Rather than simply restoring the old ruling class to power, asked Charles Sumner, why not give freed slaves the vote, to provide a genuinely loyal nucleus of supporters in the South?

These radical positions did not command a majority of Congress in 1864. Yet the experience of Louisiana, the first state to reorganize under Lincoln's more moderate policy, convinced even nonradical Republicans to block Lincoln's program. In the occupied portion of Louisiana (New Orleans and several parishes in the southern half of the state), enough white men took the oath of allegiance to satisfy Lincoln's conditions. They adopted a new state constitution and formed a government that abolished slavery and provided a school system for blacks. But despite Lincoln's private appeal to the new government to grant literate blacks and black Union soldiers the right to vote, the reconstructed Louisiana legislature chose not to do so. It also authorized planters to enforce restrictive labor policies on black plantation workers. Louisiana's actions alienated a majority of congressional Republicans, who refused to admit representatives and senators from the "reconstructed" state.

At the same time, though, Congress failed to enact a reconstruction policy of its own. This was not for lack of trying. In fact, both houses passed the Wade-Davis reconstruction bill (named for Senator Benjamin Wade of Ohio and Representative Henry Winter Davis of Maryland) in July 1864. That bill did not **enfranchise** blacks, but it did impose such stringent loyalty requirements on Southern whites that few of them could take the required oath. Lincoln therefore vetoed it.

Lincoln's action infuriated many Republicans. Wade and Davis published a blistering "manifesto" denouncing the president. This bitter squabble threatened for a time to destroy Lincoln's chances of being reelected. Union military success in fall 1864, however, combined with sober second thoughts about the consequences of a Democratic electoral victory, reunited the Republicans behind Lincoln. The collapse of Confederate military resistance the following spring set the stage for compromise between the president and Congress on a policy for the postwar South. Two days after Appomattox, Lincoln promised that he would soon announce such a policy, which probably would have included voting rights for some blacks and stronger measures to protect their civil rights. But three days later, Lincoln was assassinated.

Abraham Lincoln, Proclamation on the Wade-Davis Bill (1864)]

Andrew Johnson and Reconstruction

Q **FOCUS QUESTION** What were the positions of Presidents Abraham Lincoln and Andrew Johnson and of the moderate and radical Republicans in Congress on the issues of restoring the South to the Union and protecting the rights of freed slaves?

In 1864, Republicans had adopted the name Union Party to attract the votes of War Democrats and border-state Unionists who could not bring themselves to vote Republican. For the same reason, they also nominated Andrew Johnson of Tennessee as Lincoln's running mate.

Of "poor white" heritage, Johnson had clawed his way up in the rough-and-tumble politics of east Tennessee. This region of small farms and few slaves held little love for the planters who controlled the state. Andrew Johnson denounced the planters as "stuck-up aristocrats" who had no empathy with the Southern yeomen for whom Johnson became a self-appointed spokesman. Johnson, although a Democrat, was the only senator from a seceding state who refused to support the Confederacy. For this stance, the Republicans rewarded him with the vice presidential nomination, hoping to attract the votes of pro-war Democrats and upper-South Unionists.

Booth's bullet therefore elevated to the presidency a man who still thought of himself as primarily a Democrat and a Southerner. The trouble this might cause in a party that was mostly Republican and Northern was not immediately apparent, however. In fact, Johnson's enmity toward the "stuck-up aristocrats" whom he blamed for leading the South into secession prompted him to utter dire threats against "traitors." "Treason is a crime and must be made odious," he said, soon after becoming president. "Traitors must be impoverished. . . . They must not only be punished, but their social power must be destroyed."

Radical Republicans liked the sound of this pronouncement. It seemed to promise the type of reconstruction they favored—one that would deny political power to ex-Confederates and would enfranchise blacks. They envisioned a coalition between these new black voters and the small minority of Southern whites who had never supported the Confederacy. These men could be expected to vote Republican. Republican governments in Southern states would guarantee freedom and would pass laws to provide civil rights and economic opportunity for freed slaves. They would also strengthen the Republican Party nationally.

Johnson's Policy

From a combination of pragmatic, partisan, and idealistic motives, therefore, Radical Republicans prepared to implement a progressive reconstruction policy. But Johnson unexpectedly refused to cooperate. Instead of calling Congress into special session, he moved ahead on his own. On May 29, 1865, Johnson issued two proclamations. The first provided a blanket **amnesty** for all but the highest-ranking Confederate officials and military officers, and those ex-Confederates with taxable property worth $20,000 or more—the "stuck-up aristocrats." The second named a provisional governor for North Carolina and directed him to call an election of delegates to frame a new state constitution. Only white men who had received amnesty and taken an oath of allegiance could vote. Similar proclamations soon followed for other former Confederate states. Johnson's policy was clear: He would exclude both blacks and upper-class whites from the reconstruction process.

Although at first many Republicans supported Johnson's policy, the radicals were dismayed. They feared that restricting the vote to whites would lead to oppression of the newly freed slaves and restoration of the old power structure in the South. They began to sense that Johnson (who had owned slaves) was as

Andrew Johnson and Frederick Douglass. By 1866, the president and the leading black advocate for equal rights represented opposite poles in the debate about Reconstruction. Johnson wanted to bring the South back into the Union on the basis of white suffrage; Douglass wanted black men to be granted the right to vote. Johnson's resistance to this policy as Republicans tried to enact it was a factor in his impeachment two years later.

dedicated to white supremacy as any Confederate. "White men alone must govern the South," he told a Democratic senator. After a tense confrontation with a group of black men led by Frederick Douglass, who had visited the White House to urge black suffrage, Johnson told his private secretary: "I know that damned Douglass; he's just like any nigger, and he would sooner cut a white man's throat than not."

Moderate Republicans believed that black men should participate to some degree in the reconstruction process, but in 1865 they were not yet prepared to break with the president. They regarded his policy as an "experiment" that would be modified as time went on. "Loyal negroes must not be put down, while disloyal white men are put up," wrote a moderate Republican. "But I am quite willing to see what will come of Mr. Johnson's experiment."

Southern Defiance

As it happened, none of the state conventions enfranchised a single black. Some of them even balked at ratifying the 13th Amendment (which abolished slavery). The rhetoric of some white Southerners began to take on a renewed anti-Yankee tone of defiance that sounded like 1861 all over again. Reports from Unionists and army officers in the South told of neo-Confederate violence against blacks and their white sympathizers. Johnson seemed to encourage such activities by allowing the organization of white militia units in the South. "What can be hatched from such an egg," asked a Republican newspaper, "but another rebellion?"

Then there was the matter of presidential pardons. After talking fiercely about punishing traitors, and after excluding several classes of them from his amnesty proclamation, Johnson began to issue special pardons to many ex-Confederates, restoring to them all property and political rights. Moreover, under the new state constitutions, Southern voters were electing hundreds of ex-Confederates to state offices. Even more alarming to Northerners, who thought they had won the war, was the election to Congress of no fewer than nine ex-Confederate congressmen, seven ex-Confederate state officials, four generals, four colonels, and even the former Confederate vice president, Alexander H. Stephens. To apprehensive Republicans, it appeared that the rebels, unable to capture Washington in war, were about to do so in peace.

Somehow the aristocrats and traitors Johnson had denounced in April had taken over the reconstruction process. Instead of weapons, they had resorted to flattering the presidential ego. Thousands of prominent ex-Confederates or their tearful female relatives applied for pardons, confessing the error of their ways and appealing for presidential mercy. Reveling in his power over these once-haughty aristocrats who had disdained him as a humble tailor, Johnson waxed eloquent on his "love, respect, and confidence" toward Southern whites, for whom he now felt "forbearing and forgiving." More effective, perhaps, was the praise and support Johnson received from leading Northern Democrats. Although the Republicans had placed him on their presidential ticket in 1864, Johnson was after all a Democrat. That party's leaders enticed Johnson with visions of reelection as a Democrat in 1868 if he could manage to reconstruct the South in a manner that would preserve a Democratic majority there.

The Black Codes

That was just what the Republicans feared. In the fall of 1865, their concern that state governments devoted to white supremacy would reduce the freedpeople to a condition close to slavery was confirmed when some of those governments enacted **"Black Codes."**

One of the first tasks of the legislatures of the reconstructed states was to define the rights of 4 million former slaves. The option of treating them exactly like white citizens was scarcely considered. Instead, the states excluded black people from juries and the ballot box, did not permit them to testify against whites in court, banned interracial marriage, and punished blacks more severely than whites for certain crimes. Some states defined any unemployed black person as a vagrant and hired him out to a planter, forbade blacks to lease land, and provided for the apprenticing to whites of black youths who did not have adequate parental support.

These Black Codes aroused anger among Northern Republicans, who saw them as a brazen attempt to reinstate a **quasi-slavery**. "We tell the white men of Mississippi," declared the *Chicago Tribune*, "that the men of the North will convert the State of Mississippi into a frog pond before they will allow such laws to disgrace one foot of the soil in which the bones of our soldiers sleep and over which the flag of freedom waves." And in fact, the Union army's occupation forces did suspend the implementation of Black Codes that discriminated on racial grounds.

Land and Labor in the Postwar South

The Black Codes, although discriminatory, were designed to address a genuine problem. The end of the war had left black–white relations in the South in a state of limbo. The South's economy was in a shambles. Burned-out plantations, fields growing up in weeds, and railroads without tracks, bridges, or rolling stock marked the trail of war. Nearly half of the livestock in the former Confederacy and most other tangible assets except the land had been destroyed. Law and order broke down in many areas. The war had ended early enough in the spring to allow the planting of at least some food crops. But who would plant and cultivate them? One-quarter of the South's white farmers had been killed in the war; the slaves were slaves no more. "We have nothing left to begin anew with," lamented a South Carolina planter. "I never did a day's work in my life, and I don't know how to begin."

Despite all of this trouble, life went on. Soldiers' widows and their children plowed and planted. Slaveless planters and their wives calloused their hands for the first time. Confederate veterans drifted home and went to work. Former slave owners asked their former slaves to work the land for wages or shares of the crop, and many did so. Others refused, because for them to leave the old place was an essential part of freedom. In slavery times, the only way to become free was to run

away, and the impulse to leave the scene of bondage persisted. "You ain't, none o' you, gwinter feel rale free," said a black preacher to his congregation, "till you shakes de dus' ob de Ole Plantashun offen yore feet" (dialect in original source).

Thus the roads were alive with freedpeople who were on the move in summer 1865. Many of them signed on to work at farms just a few miles from their old homes. Others moved into town. Some looked for relatives who had been sold away during slavery or from whom they had been separated during the war. Some wandered aimlessly. Crime increased as people, both blacks and whites, stole food to survive, and as whites organized vigilante groups to discipline blacks and force them to work.

The Freedmen's Bureau

Into this vacuum stepped the U.S. Army and the **Freedmen's Bureau**. Tens of thousands of troops remained in the South as an occupation force until civil government could be restored. The Freedmen's Bureau (its official title was Bureau of Refugees, Freedmen, and Abandoned Lands), created by Congress in March 1865, became the principal agency for overseeing relations between former slaves and owners. Headed by antislavery General Oliver O. Howard and staffed by army officers, the bureau established posts throughout the South to supervise free-labor wage contracts between landowners and freedpeople. The Freedmen's Bureau also issued food rations to 150,000 people daily during 1865, one-third of them to whites. Southern whites viewed the Freedmen's Bureau with hostility. Without it, however, the postwar chaos and devastation in the South would have been much greater—as some whites privately admitted. Bureau agents used their influence with black people to encourage them to sign free-labor contracts and return to work.

In negotiating labor contracts, the bureau tried to establish minimum wages. Lack of money in the South, however, caused many contracts to call for **share wages**—that is, paying workers with shares of the crop. At first, landowners worked their laborers in large groups (called gangs). But many black workers resented this arrangement as reminiscent of slavery. Thus, a new system evolved, called **sharecropping**, whereby a black family worked a specific piece of land in return for a share of the crop produced on it.

Land for the Landless

Freedpeople, of course, would have preferred to own the land they farmed. "What's de use of being free if you don't own land enough to be buried in?" asked one black sharecropper (dialect in original). Some black farmers did manage to save up enough money to buy small plots of land. Demobilized black soldiers purchased land with their bounty payments, sometimes pooling their money to buy an entire plantation on which several black families settled. Northern philanthropists helped some freedmen buy land. But most ex-slaves found the purchase of land impossible. Few of them had money, and even if they did, whites often refused to sell their land because it would mean losing a source of cheap labor and encouraging notions of black independence.

The Freedmen's Bureau. Created in 1865, the Freedmen's Bureau stood between freed slaves and their former masters in the postwar South, charged with the task of protecting freedpeople from injustice and repression. Staffed by officers of the Union army, the bureau symbolized the military power of the government in its efforts to keep peace in the South.

Sharecroppers Working in the Fields. This photograph shows two families of sharecroppers picking cotton. Freed slaves resisted landowners' efforts to work them in gangs as they had in slavery, so the owners rented land to black families in return for a share of the crop. These croppers do not appear to be overjoyed with the new system.

Several Northern radicals proposed legislation to confiscate ex-Confederate land and redistribute it to freedpeople, but those proposals went nowhere. The most promising effort to put thousands of slaves on land of their own also failed. In January 1865, after his march through Georgia, General William T. Sherman had issued a military order setting aside thousands of acres of abandoned plantation land in the Georgia and South Carolina low country for settlement by freed slaves. The army even turned over some of its surplus mules to black farmers. The expectation of **"40 acres and a mule"** excited freedpeople in 1865, but President Johnson's Amnesty Proclamation and his wholesale issuance of pardons restored most of this property to pardoned ex-Confederates. The same thing happened to white-owned land elsewhere in the South. Placed under the temporary care of the Freedmen's Bureau for subsequent possible distribution to freedpeople, by 1866 nearly all of this land had been restored to its former owners by order of President Johnson.

Education

Abolitionists were more successful in helping freedpeople obtain an education. During the war, freedmen's aid societies and missionary societies founded by abolitionists had sent teachers to Union-occupied areas of the South to set up schools for freed slaves. After the war, this effort was expanded with the aid of the Freedmen's Bureau. Two thousand Northern teachers, three-quarters of them women, fanned out into every part of the South. There they trained black teachers to staff first the mission schools and later the public schools established by Reconstruction state governments. After 1870, the missionary societies concentrated more heavily on making higher education available to African Americans. Many of the traditionally black colleges in the South today were founded and supported by their efforts. This education crusade, which the black leader W. E. B. Du Bois described as "the most wonderful peace-battle of the nineteenth century," reduced the Southern black illiteracy rate to 70 percent by 1880 and to 48 percent by 1900.

A Black School During Reconstruction. In the antebellum South, teaching slaves to read and write was forbidden. Thus about 90 percent of the freedpeople were illiterate in 1865. One of their top priorities was education. At first, most of the teachers in the freedmen's schools established by Northern missionary societies were Northern white women, but as black teachers were trained, they took over the elementary schools, such as this one photographed in the 1870s.

The Advent of Congressional Reconstruction

Political reconstruction shaped the civil and political rights of freedpeople. By the time Congress met in December 1865, the Republican majority was determined to control the process by which former Confederate states would regain full representation. Congress refused to admit the representatives and senators elected by the former Confederate states under Johnson's reconstruction policy and set up a special committee to formulate new terms. The committee held hearings at which Southern Unionists, freedpeople, and U.S. Army officers testified to abuse and terrorism in the South. Their testimony convinced Republicans of the need for stronger federal intervention to define and protect the civil rights of freedpeople. Many radicals wanted to go further and grant the ballot to black men.

Most Republicans realized that Northern voters would not support such a radical policy, however. Racism was still strong in the North, where most states denied the right to vote to the few blacks living within their borders. Moderate Republicans feared that Democrats would exploit Northern racism in the congressional elections of 1866 if Congress made black suffrage a cornerstone of Reconstruction. Instead, the special committee decided to draft a constitutional amendment that would encourage Southern states to enfranchise blacks but would not require them to do so.

Schism between President and Congress

Meanwhile, Congress passed two laws to protect the economic and civil rights of freedpeople. The first extended the life of the Freedmen's Bureau and expanded its powers. The second defined freedpeople as citizens with equal legal rights and gave federal courts appellate jurisdiction to enforce those rights. To the dismay of moderates who were trying to heal the widening breach between the president and Congress, Johnson vetoed both measures. He followed this action with a speech to Democratic supporters in which he denounced Republican leaders as traitors who did not want to restore the Union except on terms that would degrade white Southerners. Democratic newspapers applauded the president for vetoing bills that would "compound our race with niggers, gypsies, and baboons."

The 14th Amendment

Johnson had thrown down the gauntlet to congressional Republicans, and they did not hesitate to take it up. With

"PARDON, Columbia—'Shall I Trust These Men'?"   "FRANCHISE—'And Not This Man'?"

Cartoons for Freedom. One of the best political cartoonists in American history, Thomas Nast drew scores of cartoons for *Harper's Weekly* in the 1860s and 1870s advocating the use of federal power to guarantee the liberty and enforce the equal rights of freed slaves. This illustration (1865) is an eloquent graphic expression of a powerful argument for giving freedmen the right to vote: Black men who fought for the Union were more deserving of this privilege than white men who fought against it. Several of the kneeling figures are recognizable Confederate leaders: Alexander Stephens and Robert E. Lee in the foreground, Jefferson Davis to Lee's left, and John C. Breckinridge, Joseph E. Johnston, and Robert Toombs behind and to Davis's left.

more than a two-thirds majority in both houses, they passed the Freedmen's Bureau and Civil Rights bills over the president's vetoes. Then on April 30, 1866, the special committee submitted to Congress its proposed 14th Amendment to the Constitution. After lengthy debate, the amendment received the required two-thirds majority in Congress on June 13 and went to the states for ratification. Section 1 defined all native-born or naturalized persons, including blacks, as American citizens and prohibited the states from abridging the "privileges and immunities" of citizens, from depriving "any person of life, liberty, or property without due process of law," and from denying to any person "the equal protection of the laws." Section 2 gave states the option of either enfranchising black males or losing a proportionate number of congressional seats and electoral votes. Section 3 disqualified a significant number of ex-Confederates from holding federal or state office. Section 4 guaranteed the national debt and repudiated the Confederate debt. Section 5 empowered Congress to enforce the 14th Amendment by "appropriate legislation." The 14th Amendment had far-reaching consequences. Section 1 has become the most important provision in the Constitution for defining and enforcing civil rights.

The 1866 Elections

Republicans entered the 1866 congressional elections campaign with the 14th Amendment as their platform. They made clear that any ex-Confederate state that ratified the amendment would be declared "reconstructed" and that its representatives and senators would be seated in Congress. Tennessee ratified the amendment, but Johnson counseled other Southern legislatures to reject the amendment, which they did. Johnson then prepared for an all-out campaign to gain a friendly Northern majority in the congressional elections.

Johnson began his campaign by creating a National Union Party made up of a few conservative Republicans who disagreed with their party, some border-state Unionists who supported the president, and Democrats. The inclusion of Democrats doomed the effort from the start. Many Northern Democrats still carried the taint of having opposed the war effort, and most Northern voters did not trust them. The National Union Party was further damaged by race riots in Memphis and New Orleans, where white mobs, including former Confederate soldiers, killed 80 blacks, among them several former Union soldiers. The riots bolstered Republican arguments that national power was necessary to protect "the fruits of victory" in the South. Perhaps the biggest liability of the National Union Party was Johnson. In a whistle-stop tour through the North, he traded insults with hecklers and embarrassed his supporters by comparing himself to Christ and his Republican adversaries to Judas.

Republicans swept the election: They gained a three-to-one majority in the next Congress. Having rejected the Reconstruction terms embodied in the 14th Amendment, Southern Democrats now faced far more stringent terms. "They would not cooperate in rebuilding what they destroyed," wrote an exasperated moderate Republican, so "we must remove the rubbish and rebuild from the bottom. Whether they are willing or not, we must compel obedience to the Union and demand protection for its humblest citizen."

The Reconstruction Acts of 1867

In March 1867, the new Congress enacted over Johnson's vetoes two laws prescribing new procedures for the full restoration of the former Confederate states to the Union. These laws represented a complex compromise between radicals and moderates that had been hammered out in a confusing sequence of committee drafts, caucus decisions, all-night debates on the floor, and frayed tempers. The Reconstruction acts of 1867 divided the 10 Southern states into five military districts, directed army officers to register voters for the election of delegates to new constitutional conventions, and enfranchised males aged 21 and older (including blacks) to vote in those elections. The acts also disenfranchised (for these elections only) those ex-Confederates who were disqualified from holding office under the not-yet-ratified 14th Amendment—fewer than 10 percent of all white voters. When a state had adopted a new constitution that granted equal civil and political rights regardless of race and had ratified the 14th Amendment, it would be declared reconstructed, and its newly elected congressmen would be seated.

These measures embodied a true revolution. Just a few years earlier, Southern whites had been masters of 4 million slaves and part of an independent Confederate nation. Now they were shorn of political power, with their former slaves not only free but also politically empowered. In 1867 the emancipation and enfranchisement of black Americans seemed, as a sympathetic French journalist described it, "one of the most radical revolutions known in history."

Like most revolutions, the reconstruction process did not go smoothly. Many Southern Democrats breathed defiance and refused to cooperate. The presence of the army minimized anti-black violence, but thousands of white Southerners who were eligible to vote refused to do so, hoping that their nonparticipation would delay the process long enough for Northern voters to come to their senses and elect Democrats to Congress.

Blacks and their white allies organized **Union leagues** to inform and mobilize the new black voters into the Republican Party. Democrats branded Southern white Republicans as **"scalawags"** and Northern settlers as **"carpetbaggers."** By September 1867, the 10 states had 735,000 black voters and only 635,000 white voters registered. At least one-third of the registered white voters were Republicans.

President Johnson did everything he could to block Reconstruction. He replaced several Republican generals in

NEW YORK, SATURDAY, MAY 26, 1866.

according to Act of Congress, in the Year 1866, by Harper & Brothers in the Clerk's Office of the District Court for the Southern District of New

The Burning of a Freedmen's School. Because freedpeople's education symbolized black progress, whites who resented and resisted this progress sometimes attacked and burned freedmen's schools. This dramatic illustration shows a white mob burning a school during anti-black riots in Memphis in May 1866.

command of Southern military districts with Democrats. He had his attorney general issue a ruling that interpreted the Reconstruction acts narrowly, thereby forcing a special session of Congress to pass a supplementary act in July 1867. He encouraged Southern whites to obstruct the registration of voters and the election of convention delegates.

Johnson's purpose was to slow the process until 1868 in the hope that Northern voters would repudiate Reconstruction in the presidential election of that year, when Johnson planned to run as the Democratic candidate. Off-year state elections in fall 1867 encouraged that hope. Republicans suffered setbacks in several Northern states, especially where they endorsed referendum measures to enfranchise black men. "I almost pity the radicals," chortled one of President Johnson's aides after the 1867 elections. "After giving ten states to the negroes, to keep the Democrats from getting them, they will have lost the rest."

The Impeachment of Andrew Johnson

FOCUS QUESTION Why was Andrew Johnson impeached? Why was he acquitted?

Johnson struck even more boldly against Reconstruction after the 1867 elections. "What does Johnson mean to do?" an exasperated Republican asked another. "I am afraid his doings will make us all favor impeachment." In February 1868, Johnson removed from office Secretary of War Edwin M. Stanton, who had administered the War Department in support of the congressional Reconstruction policy. This appeared to violate the Tenure of Office Act, passed the year before over Johnson's veto, which required Senate consent for such removals. By a vote of 126 to 47 along party lines, the House impeached Johnson on February 24. The official reason for **impeachment** was that he had violated the Tenure of Office Act (which Johnson considered unconstitutional). The real reason was Johnson's stubborn defiance of Congress on Reconstruction.

Under the U.S. Constitution, impeachment by the House does not remove an official from office. It is more like a grand jury indictment that must be tried by a petit jury—in this case, the Senate, which sat as a court to try Johnson on the impeachment charges brought by the House. If convicted by a two-thirds majority of the Senate, he would be removed from office.

The impeachment trial proved long and complicated, which worked in Johnson's favor by allowing passions to cool. The Constitution specifies the grounds on which a president can be impeached and removed: "Treason, Bribery, or other high Crimes and Misdemeanors." The issue was whether Johnson was guilty of any of these acts. His able defense counsel exposed technical ambiguities in the Tenure of Office Act that raised doubts about whether Johnson had actually violated it. Several moderate Republicans feared that the

precedent of impeachment might upset the delicate balance of powers between the executive branch, Congress, and the judiciary that was an essential element of the Constitution. Behind the scenes, Johnson strengthened his case by promising to appoint the respected General John M. Schofield as secretary of war and to stop obstructing the Reconstruction acts. In the end, seven Republican senators plus all Democrats voted for acquittal on May 16, and the final tally fell one vote short of the necessary two-thirds majority.

The Completion of Formal Reconstruction

The impeachment trial's end cleared the poisonous air in Washington, and Johnson quietly served out his term. Constitutional conventions met in the South during winter and spring 1867–68. Hostile whites described them as "Bones and Banjoes Conventions" and the Republican delegates as "ragamuffins and jailbirds." In sober fact, however, the delegates were earnest advocates of a new order, and the constitutions they wrote were among the most progressive in the nation. Three-quarters of the delegates to the 10 conventions were Republicans. About 25 percent of those Republicans were Northern whites who had relocated to the South after the war; 45 percent were native Southern whites who braved the social ostracism of the white majority to cast their lot with the despised Republicans; and 30 percent were blacks. Only in the South Carolina convention were blacks in the majority.

The new state constitutions enacted **universal male suffrage**, putting them ahead of most Northern states on that score. Some of the constitutions disenfranchised certain classes of ex-Confederates for several years, but by 1872, all such disqualifications had been removed. The constitutions mandated statewide public schools for both races for the first time in the South. Most states permitted segregated schools, but schools of any kind for blacks represented a great step forward. Most of the constitutions increased the state's responsibility for social welfare beyond anything previously known in the South.

Violence in some parts of the South marred the voting on ratification of these state constitutions. The **Ku Klux Klan**, a night-riding white terrorist organization, made its first appearance during the elections. Nevertheless, voters in seven states ratified their constitutions and elected new legislatures that ratified the 14th Amendment in spring 1868. That amendment became part of the U.S. Constitution the following summer, and the newly elected representatives and senators from those seven states, nearly all Republicans, took their seats in the House and Senate.

The 15th Amendment

The remaining three Southern states completed the reconstruction process in 1869 and 1870. Congress required them to ratify the 15th as well as the 14th Amendments. The 15th Amendment prohibited states from denying the right to vote on grounds of race, color, or previous condition of servitude. Its

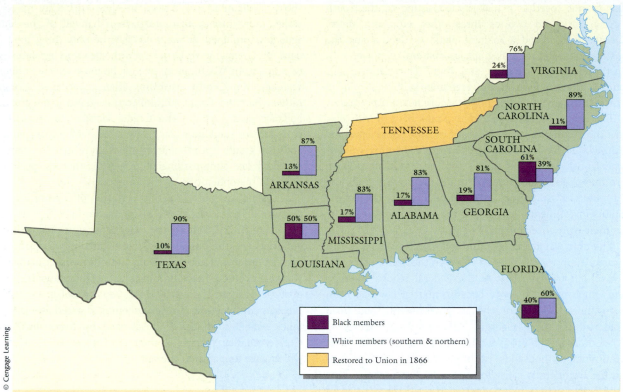

Map 17.1 Black and White Participation in Constitutional Conventions, 1867–1868. Although black participation in these state constitutional conventions matched the African American percentage of the population only in South Carolina and Louisiana, the very presence of any black delegates in states where slavery had prevailed three years earlier was revolutionary.

purpose was not only to prevent the reconstructed states from any future revocation of black suffrage, but also to extend equal suffrage to the border states and to the North. With final ratification of the 15th Amendment in 1870, the Constitution became truly color blind for the first time in U.S. history.

But the 15th Amendment still left half of the population disfranchised. Many supporters of woman suffrage were embittered by its failure to ban discrimination on the grounds of gender as well as race. The radical wing of the suffragists, led by Elizabeth Cady Stanton and Susan B. Anthony, therefore opposed the 15th Amendment, causing a split in the woman suffrage movement.

This movement had shared the ideological egalitarianism of abolitionism since the Seneca Falls Convention of 1848. In 1866, male and female abolitionists formed the American Equal Rights Association (AERA) to work for both black and woman suffrage. Although some Republicans sympathized with the suffragists, they knew that no strong constituency among male voters favored granting the vote to women. Most members of the AERA recognized that although Reconstruction politics made black enfranchisement possible, woman suffrage would have to wait until public opinion could be educated up to the standard of gender equality.

Stanton and Anthony refused to accept this reasoning. Why should illiterate Southern blacks have the right to vote, they asked, when educated Northern women remained shut out from the polls? The 15th Amendment would establish "the

most odious form of aristocracy the world has ever seen: an aristocracy of sex." When a majority of delegates at the 1869 convention of the AERA voted to endorse the 15th Amendment, several women led by Stanton and Anthony walked out and founded the National Woman Suffrage Association. The remaining delegates reorganized as the American Woman Suffrage Association. For the next two decades, these rival organizations, working for the same cause, remained at odds with each other.

The Election of 1868

Just as the presidential election of 1864 was a referendum on Lincoln's war policies, so the election of 1868 was a referendum on the Reconstruction policy of the Republicans. The Republican nominee was General **Ulysses S. Grant**. Although he had no political experience, Grant commanded greater authority and prestige than anyone else in the country. As general-in-chief of the army, he had opposed Johnson's Reconstruction policy in 1866 and had broken openly with the president in January 1868. That spring, Grant agreed to run for the presidency in order to preserve in peace the victory he had won for Union, and liberty he had won in war.

The Democrats turned away from Andrew Johnson, who carried too many political liabilities. They nominated Horatio Seymour, the wartime governor of New York, bestowing on him the dubious privilege of running against Grant.

Hoping to put together a majority consisting of the South plus New York and two or three other Northern states, the Democrats adopted a militant platform denouncing the Reconstruction acts as "a flagrant usurpation of power . . . unconstitutional, revolutionary, and void." The platform also demanded "the abolition of the Freedmen's Bureau, and all political instrumentalities designed to secure negro supremacy."

The vice presidential candidate, Frank Blair of Missouri, became the point man for the Democrats. In a public letter, he proclaimed: "There is but one way to restore the Government and the Constitution, and that is for the President-elect to declare these [Reconstruction] acts null and void, compel the army to undo its usurpations at the South, disperse the carpet-bag State Governments, [and] allow the white people to reorganize their own governments."

The only way to achieve this bold counterrevolutionary goal was to suppress Republican voters in the South. This, the Ku Klux Klan tried its best to do. Federal troops failed to prevent much of the violence because martial law had been lifted in the states where civilian governments had been restored. In Louisiana, Georgia, Arkansas, and Tennessee, the Klan or Klan-like groups committed dozens of murders and intimidated thousands of black voters. The violence helped the Democratic cause in the South, but probably hurt it in the North, where many voters perceived the Klan as an organization of neo-Confederate paramilitary guerrillas. In fact, many Klansmen were former soldiers, and such famous Confederate generals as Nathan Bedford Forrest and John B. Gordon held high positions in the Klan.

Seymour did well in the South, carrying five former slave states and coming close in others, despite the solid Republican vote of the newly enfranchised blacks. Grant, however, swept the electoral vote 214 to 80. Seymour actually won a slight majority of the white voters nationally; without black enfranchisement, Grant would have had a minority of the popular vote.

The Grant Administration

Grant is usually considered a failure as president. That indictment is only partly correct. Grant's inexperience and poor judgment betrayed him into several unwise appointments of officials, who were later convicted of corruption, and scandals that plagued his back-to-back administrations (1869–77). His secretary of war was impeached for selling appointments to army posts and Indian reservations, and his attorney general and secretary

AMERICANS ABROAD
Dan Sickles

of the interior resigned under suspicion of malfeasance in 1875. (For a story about one of Grant's infamous ministerial appointments, see the Americans Abroad feature "Dan Sickles Tries to Provoke War with Spain.")

Although he was an honest man, Grant was too trusting of subordinates. He appointed many former members of his military family, as well as several of his wife's relatives, to offices for which they were scarcely qualified. In an era notorious for corruption at all levels of government, many of the scandals were not Grant's fault. The Tammany Hall "Ring" of

"Boss" William Marcy Tweed in New York City may have stolen more money from taxpayers than all of the federal agencies combined. It was said that the only thing the Standard Oil Company could not do with the Ohio legislature was to refine it. In Washington, one of the most widely publicized scandals, the **Credit Mobilier** affair, concerned Congress rather than the Grant administration. Several congressmen had accepted stock in the Credit Mobilier, a construction company for the Union Pacific Railroad, which received loans and land grants from the government. In return, the company expected lax congressional supervision, thereby permitting financial manipulations by the company.

What accounted for this explosion of corruption in the postwar decade, which one historian has called "The Era of Good Stealings"? During the war, expansion of government contracts and the bureaucracy had created new opportunities for the unscrupulous. Following the intense sacrifices of the war years came a relaxation of tensions and standards. Rapid postwar economic growth, led by an extraordinary rush of railroad construction, further encouraged greed and get-rich-quick schemes of the kind satirized by Mark Twain and Charles Dudley Warner in their 1873 novel *The Gilded Age*, which gave its name to the era.

Civil Service Reform

Some of the apparent increase in corruption during the Gilded Age was more a matter of perception. Reformers focused a harsh light into the dark corners of corruption, hitherto unilluminated because of the nation's preoccupation with war and reconstruction. Thus reformers' publicity may have exaggerated the actual extent of corruption. In reality, during the Grant administration, several government agencies made real progress in eliminating abuses that had flourished in earlier administrations.

The chief target of civil service reform was the **"spoils system."** With the slogan "To the victor belongs the spoils," the victorious party in an election rewarded party workers with appointments as postmasters, customs collectors, and the like. The hope of getting appointed to a government post was the glue that kept the faithful together when a party was out of power. An assessment of 2 or 3 percent on the beneficiaries' government salaries kept party coffers filled when the party was in power. The spoils system politicized the bureaucracy and staffed it with unqualified personnel who spent more time working for their party than for the government. It also plagued every incoming president (and other elected officials) with the "swarm of office seekers" that loom so large in contemporary accounts (including those of the humorist Orpheus C. Kerr, whose nom de plume was pronounced "Office Seeker").

Civil service reformers wanted to separate the bureaucracy from politics by requiring competitive examinations for the appointment of civil servants. This movement gathered steam during the 1870s and finally achieved success in 1883 with the passage of the Pendleton Act, which established the modern structure of the civil service. When Grant took office, he seemed to share the sentiments of civil service reformers;

several of his cabinet officers inaugurated examinations for certain appointments and promotions in their departments. Grant also named a civil service commission headed by George William Curtis, a leading reformer and editor of *Harper's Weekly*. But many congressmen, senators, and other politicians resisted civil service reform because **patronage** greased the political machines that kept them in office. They managed to subvert reform, sometimes using Grant as an unwitting ally and thus turning many reformers against the president.

Foreign Policy Issues

A foreign policy controversy added to Grant's woes. The irregular procedures by which his private secretary had negotiated a treaty to annex Santo Domingo (now the Dominican Republic) alienated leading Republican senators, who defeated ratification of the treaty. Politically inexperienced, Grant acted like a general who needed only to give orders, rather than as a president who must cultivate supporters. The fallout from the Santo Domingo affair widened the fissure in the Republican Party between "spoilsmen" and "reformers."

But the Grant administration had some solid foreign policy achievements to its credit. Hamilton Fish, the able secretary of state, negotiated the Treaty of Washington in 1871 to settle the vexing Alabama Claims. These were damage claims against Britain for the destruction of American shipping by the C.S.S. *Alabama* and other Confederate commerce raiders built in British shipyards. The treaty established an international tribunal to arbitrate the U.S. claims, resulting in the award of $15.5 million in damages to U.S. ship owners and a British expression of regret.

The events leading to the Treaty of Washington also resolved another long-festering issue between Britain and the United States: the status of Canada. The seven separate British North American colonies were especially vulnerable to U.S. desires for annexation. In fact, many bitter Northerners demanded British cession of Canadian colonies to the United States as fair payment for the wartime depredations of the *Alabama* and other commerce raiders. Such demands tended to strengthen the loyalty of many Canadians to Britain as a counterweight to the aggressive Americans. In 1867, Parliament passed the British North America Act, which united most of the Canadian colonies into a new and largely self-governing Dominion of Canada. The Treaty of Washington reduced Canadian-American as well as Anglo-American tensions. It resolved disputes over American commercial fishing in Canadian waters. American demands for annexation of Canada faded away. These events gave birth to the modern nation of Canada.

Reconstruction in the South

During Grant's two administrations, the "Southern Question" was the most intractable issue. A phrase in Grant's acceptance of the presidential nomination in 1868 had struck a responsive chord in the North: "Let us have peace." With the ratification of the 15th Amendment, many people breathed a sigh of relief

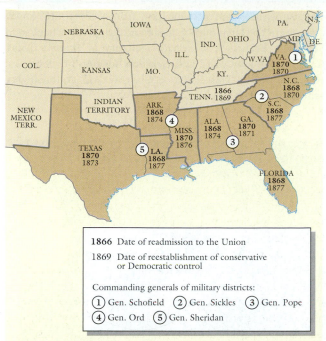

1866 Date of readmission to the Union

1869 Date of reestablishment of conservative or Democratic control

Commanding generals of military districts:
1 Gen. Schofield 2 Gen. Sickles 3 Gen. Pope
4 Gen. Ord 5 Gen. Sheridan

© Cengage Learning

Map 17.2 Reconstruction in the South. The dates for each state listed on this map show how short-lived "Radical Reconstruction" was in most Southern states.

at this apparent resolution of "the last great point that remained to be settled of the issues of the war." It was time to deal with other matters that had been long neglected. Ever since the annexation of Texas a quarter-century earlier, the nation had known scarcely a moment's respite from sectional strife. "Let us have done with Reconstruction," pleaded the New York *Tribune* in 1870. "LET US HAVE PEACE." But there was no peace. Reconstruction was not over; it had hardly begun. State governments elected by black and white voters were in place in the South, but Democratic violence against Reconstruction and the instability of the Republican coalition that sustained it portended trouble.

Blacks in Office

Because the Republican Party had no antebellum roots in the South, most Southern whites perceived it as a symbol of conquest and humiliation. In the North, the Republican Party represented the most prosperous, educated, and influential elements of the population, but in the South, most of its adherents were poor, illiterate, and landless.

About 80 percent of Southern Republican voters were black. Although most black leaders were educated and many had been free before the war, most black voters were illiterate ex-slaves. Neither the leaders nor their constituents, however, were as ignorant or as venal as stereotypes have portrayed them. Of 14 black representatives and two black senators elected in the South between 1868 and 1876, all but three had attended secondary school and four had attended college. Several of the blacks elected to state offices were among the best-educated men of their day. Jonathan Gibbs, secretary of state in Florida from 1868 to 1872 and state superintendent of education from 1872 to 1874, was a graduate of Dartmouth College and Princeton Theological Seminary. Francis L. Cardozo, secretary of state in South Carolina for four years and treasurer for another four, was educated at the University of Glasgow and at theological schools in Edinburgh and London.

It is true that some lower-level black officeholders, as well as their constituents, could not read or write, but the fault for that situation lay not with them but with the slave regime that had denied them an education. Illiteracy did not preclude an understanding of political issues for them any more than it did for Irish American voters in the North, some of whom

Library of Congress, Prints and Photographs Division

Library of Congress, Prints and Photographs Division

Robert B. Elliott, c.1875 (litho), American Photographer, (19th century) / Schlesinger Library, Radcliffe Institute, Harvard University / The Bridgeman Art Library International

Three African American Members of Congress During Reconstruction. Pictured clockwise from upper left are Blance K. Bruce, Robert Smalls, and Robert B. Elliott. Born into slavery, Bruce and Smalls became the two most prominent blacks in Congress during the 1870s. Bruce was elected to the United States Senate from Mississippi in 1875 and served his full six-year term despite the takeover of Mississippi by white-supremacist Democrats later in 1875. Smalls gained fame when he delivered the Confederate dispatch steamer *Planter* to the Union blockade fleet outside Charleston in 1862. After working as a pilot for the navy, Smalls emerged as a leader of the South Carolina Republican party during Reconstruction and served several terms in the House. Of West Indian descent, Elliott was born in England and immigrated to South Carolina in 1867. He was elected to the House for two terms and became an eloquent spokesman for civil rights.

were also illiterate. Southern blacks thirsted for education. Participation in the Union League and the experience of voting were forms of education. Black churches and fraternal organizations proliferated during Reconstruction and tutored African Americans in their rights and responsibilities.

Linked to the myth of black incompetence was the legend of the "Africanization" of Southern governments during Reconstruction. The theme of "Negro rule" was a staple of Democratic propaganda. It was enshrined in folk memory and in generations of textbooks. In fact, blacks held only 15 to 20 percent of public offices, even at the height of Reconstruction in the early 1870s. No states had black governors (although the black lieutenant governor of Louisiana acted as governor for a month), and only one black man became a state supreme court justice. Nowhere except in South Carolina did blacks hold office in numbers anywhere near their proportion of the population; in that state, they constituted 52 percent of all state and federal elected officials from 1868 to 1876.

"Carpetbaggers"

Next to "Negro rule," carpetbagger corruption and scalawag rascality have been the prevailing myths of Reconstruction. Carpetbaggers did hold a disproportionate number of high political offices in Southern state governments during Reconstruction. More than half of the Republican governors and nearly half of the congressmen and senators were Northerners. A few did resemble the proverbial adventurer who came south with nothing but a carpetbag in which to stow the loot plundered from a helpless people. Most of the Northerners were Union army officers who stayed on after the war as Freedmen's Bureau agents, teachers in black schools, business investors, pioneers of a new political order—or simply because they liked the climate.

Like others who migrated to the West as a frontier of opportunity, those who settled in the postwar South hoped to rebuild its society in the image of the free-labor North. Many were college graduates at a time when fewer than 2 percent of Americans had attended college. Most brought not empty carpetbags but considerable capital, which they invested in what they hoped would become a new South. They also invested human capital—themselves—in a drive to modernize the region's social structure and democratize its politics. But they underestimated the hostility of Southern whites, most of whom regarded them as agents of an alien culture and leaders of an enemy army—as indeed they had been—in a war that for many Southerners was not yet over.

"Scalawags"

Most of the native-born whites who joined the Southern Republican Party came from the upcountry Unionist areas of western North Carolina and Virginia, eastern Tennessee, and elsewhere. Others were former Whigs who saw an opportunity to rebuild the South's economy in partnership with equally Whiggish Northern Republicans. Republicans, said a North Carolina scalawag, were the "party of progress, of education, of development. . . . Yankees and Yankee notions are just what

we want in this country. We want their capital to build factories and work shops, and railroads."

But Yankees and Yankee notions were just what most Southern whites did not want. Democrats saw that the Southern Republican Party they abhorred was a fragile coalition of blacks and whites, Yankees and Southerners, hill-country yeomen and low-country entrepreneurs, illiterates and college graduates. The party was weakest along the seams where these disparate elements joined, especially the racial seam. Democrats attacked that weakness with every weapon at their command, from social ostracism of white Republicans to economic intimidation of black employees and sharecroppers. The most potent Democratic weapon was violence.

The Ku Klux Klan

The generic name for the secret groups that terrorized the Southern countryside was the Ku Klux Klan, but some went by other names (the Knights of the White Camelia in Louisiana, for example). Part of the Klan's purpose was social control of the black population. Sharecroppers who tried to extract better

Two Members of the Ku Klux Klan. Founded in Pulaski, Tennessee, in 1866 as a social organization similar to a college fraternity, the Klan evolved into a terrorist group whose purpose was intimidation of Southern Republicans. The Klan, in which former Confederate soldiers played a prominent part, was responsible for the beating and murder of hundreds of blacks and whites alike from 1868 to 1871.

terms from landowners, or black people who were considered too "uppity," were likely to receive a midnight whipping—or worse—from white-sheeted Klansmen. Scores of black schools, perceived as a particular threat to white supremacy, went up in flames.

The Klan's main purpose was political: to destroy the Republican Party by terrorizing its voters and, if necessary, by murdering its leaders. No one knows how many politically motivated killings took place—certainly hundreds, probably thousands. Nearly all of the victims were Republicans; most of them were black. In one notorious incident, the Colfax Massacre in Louisiana (April 18, 1873), a clash between black militia and armed whites left three whites and nearly 100 blacks dead. Half of the blacks were killed in cold blood after they had surrendered. In some places, notably Tennessee and Arkansas, Republican militias formed to suppress and disarm the Klan, but in most areas the militias were outgunned and outmaneuvered by ex-Confederate veteran Klansmen. Some Republican governors were reluctant to use black militia against white guerrillas for fear of sparking a racial bloodbath—as happened at Colfax.

The answer seemed to be federal troops. In 1870 and 1871, Congress enacted three laws intended to enforce the 14th and 15th Amendments. Interference with voting rights became a federal offense, and any attempt to deprive another person of civil or political rights became a felony. The third law, passed on April 20, 1871, and popularly called the Ku Klux Klan Act, gave the president power to suspend the writ of **habeas corpus** and send in federal troops to suppress armed resistance to federal law.

Armed with these laws, the Grant administration moved against the Klan. Because Grant was sensitive to charges of "military despotism," he used his powers with restraint. He suspended the writ of habeas corpus in only nine South Carolina counties. Nevertheless, there and elsewhere federal marshals backed by troops arrested thousands of suspected Klansmen.

Federal grand juries indicted more than 3,000, and several hundred defendants pleaded guilty in return for suspended sentences. To clear clogged court dockets so that the worst offenders could be tried quickly, the Justice Department dropped charges against nearly 2,000 others. About 600 Klansmen were convicted; most of them received fines or light jail sentences, but 65 went to a federal penitentiary for terms of up to five years.

The Election of 1872

These measures broke the back of the Klan in time for the 1872 presidential election. A group of dissident Republicans had emerged to challenge Grant's reelection. They believed that conciliation of Southern whites rather than continued military intervention was the only way to achieve peace in the South. Calling themselves Liberal Republicans, these dissidents nominated Horace Greeley, the famous editor of the New York *Tribune*. Under the slogan "Anything to beat Grant," the Democratic Party also endorsed Greeley's nomination, although he had long been their antagonist. On a platform denouncing "bayonet rule" in the South, Greeley urged his fellow Northerners to put the issues of the Civil War behind them and to "clasp hands across the bloody chasm which has too long divided" North and South.

This phrase would come back to haunt Greeley. Most voters in the North were still not prepared to trust Democrats or Southern whites. Powerful anti-Greeley cartoons by political cartoonist Thomas Nast showed Greeley shaking the hand of a Klansman dripping with the blood of a murdered black Republican. Nast's most famous cartoon portrayed Greeley as a pirate captain bringing his craft alongside the ship of state, while Confederate leaders, armed to the teeth, hid below waiting to board it.

Grant swamped Greeley on election day. Republicans carried every Northern state and 10 of the 16 Southern and

IT IS ONLY A TRUCE TO REGAIN POWER ("PLAYING POSSUM").
H. G. "Clasp hands over the bloody chasm."
C. S. "Freely accept the hand that is offered, and reach forth thine own in friendly grasp."

One of Thomas Nast's Anti-Greeley Cartoons. This cartoon appeared in *Harper's Weekly* during the 1872 election campaign. It shows Greeley and Charles Sumner (whose bitterness toward President Grant caused him to support Greeley) trying to get a black man to "clasp hands across the bloody chasm" with a member of the Ku Klux Klan whose hand is dripping with the blood of the man's wife, whom he has murdered. On the Klansman's left stands a Nast caricature of an Irishman, while in the background are scenes from the New York draft riot in 1863, when Irish-Americans lynched blacks. Nast portrays this unholy alliance as the essence of the Liberal Republican/Democratic coalition in 1872.

HISTORY THROUGH FILM

The Birth Of A Nation (1915)

Directed by D. W. Griffith.
Starring Lillian Gish (Elsie Stoneman), Henry B. Walthall (Ben Cameron), Ralph Lewis
(Austin Stoneman), George Siegmann (Silas Lynch).

Few if any films have had such a pernicious impact on historical understanding and race relations as *Birth of a Nation.* This movie popularized a version of Reconstruction that portrayed predatory carpetbaggers and stupid, brutish blacks plundering a prostrate South and lusting after white women. It perpetuated vicious stereotypes of rapacious black males. It glorified the Ku Klux Klan of the Reconstruction era, inspiring the founding of the "second Klan" in 1915, which became a powerful force in the 1920s (see Chapter 24).

The first half of the film offers a conventional Victorian romance of the Civil War. The two sons and daughter of Austin Stoneman (a malevolent radical Republican who is a thinly disguised Thaddeus Stevens) become friends with the three sons and two daughters of the Cameron family of "Piedmont," South Carolina, through the friendship of Ben Cameron and Phil Stoneman at college. The Civil War tragically separates the families. The Stoneman and Cameron boys enlist in the Union and Confederate armies and—predictably—face each other on the battlefield. Two Camerons and one Stoneman are killed in the war, and Ben Cameron is badly wounded and captured, to be nursed back to health by—you guessed it—Elsie Stoneman. After the war, the younger Camerons and Stonemans renew their friendship. During the Stonemans' visit to South Carolina, Ben Cameron and Elsie Stoneman, and Phil Stoneman and Flora Cameron fall in love. If the story had stopped there, *Birth of a Nation* would have been just another Hollywood romance. But Austin Stoneman brings south with him Silas Lynch, an ambitious, leering mulatto demagogue who stirs up the animal passions of the ignorant black majority to demand "Equal Rights, Equal Politics, Equal Marriage." A "renegade Negro," Gus, stalks the youngest Cameron

daughter, who saves herself from rape by jumping from a cliff to her death. Silas Lynch tries to force Elsie to marry him. "I will build a Black Empire," he tells the beautiful, virginal Elsie (Lillian Gish was the Hollywood beauty queen of silent films), "and you as my queen shall rule by my side."

Finally, provoked beyond endurance, white South Carolinians led by Ben Cameron organize the Ku Klux Klan to save "the Aryan race." Riding to the rescue of embattled whites in stirring scenes that anticipated the heroic actions of the cavalry against Indians in later Hollywood Westerns, the Klan executes Gus, saves Elsie, disperses black soldiers and mobs, and carries the next election for white rule by intimidating black voters. The film ends with a double marriage that unites the Camerons and Stonemans in a symbolic rebirth of a nation that joins whites of the North and South in a new union rightfully based on the supremacy of "the Aryan race."

The son of a Confederate lieutenant colonel, David Wark (D. W.) Griffith was the foremost director of the silent movie era. He pioneered many precedent-setting cinematic techniques and profoundly influenced film-making throughout the world. *Birth of a Nation* was the first real full-length feature film, technically and artistically superior to anything before it. Apart from its place in the history of cinema, though, why should anyone today watch a movie that perpetuates such wrongheaded history and noxious racist stereotypes? Precisely because it reflects and amplifies an interpretation of Reconstruction that prevailed from the 1890s to the 1950s, and thereby shaped not only historical understanding but also contemporary behavior (as in its inspiration for the Klan of the 1920s). Although *Birth of a Nation* aroused controversy in parts of the North and was picketed by the NAACP, some 200 million people saw the film in the United States and abroad from 1915 to 1946. The story, and director Griffith, demonstrated in dramatic fashion how the South, having lost the Civil War, won the battle for how the war and especially Reconstruction would be remembered for more than half a century. ▟

© Bettmann/CORBIS

Ben Cameron (Henry B. Walthall) kissing the hand of Elsie Stoneman (Lillian Gish) in *Birth of a Nation.*

border states. Blacks in the South enjoyed more freedom in voting than they would again for a century. But this apparent triumph of Republicanism and Reconstruction would soon unravel.

The Panic of 1873

The U.S. economy had grown at an unprecedented pace since recovering from a mild postwar recession. In eight years, 35,000 miles of new railroad track had been laid down—equal to all the track laid in the preceding 35 years. The first transcontinental railroad had been completed on May 10, 1869, when a golden spike was driven at Promontory Summit, Utah Territory, linking the Union Pacific and the Central Pacific. But the building of a second transcontinental line, the Northern Pacific, precipitated a Wall Street panic in 1873 and plunged the economy into a five-year depression.

Jay Cooke's banking firm, fresh from its triumphant marketing of Union war bonds, took over the Northern Pacific in 1869. Cooke pyramided every conceivable kind of equity and loan financing to raise the money to begin laying rails west from Duluth, Minnesota. Other investment firms did the same as a fever of speculative financing gripped the country. In September 1873, the pyramid of paper collapsed. Cooke's firm was the first to go bankrupt. Like dominoes, thousands of banks and businesses also collapsed. Unemployment rose to 14 percent, and hard times set in.

The Retreat from Reconstruction

Q **FOCUS QUESTION** Why did a majority of the Northern people and their political leaders turn against continued federal involvement in Southern Reconstruction in the 1870s?

It is an axiom of American politics that the voters will punish the party in power in times of economic depression. That axiom held true in the 1870s. Democrats made large gains in the congressional elections of 1874, winning a majority in the House for the first time in 18 years.

Public opinion also began to turn against Republican policies in the South. The campaign by Liberal Republicans and Democrats against "bayonet rule" and "carpetbag corruption" that left most Northern voters unmoved in 1872 found a growing audience in subsequent years. Intraparty battles among Republicans in Southern states enabled Democrats to regain control of several state governments. Well-publicized corruption scandals also discredited Republican leaders. Although corruption was probably no worse in Southern states than in many parts of the North, Southern postwar poverty made waste and extravagance seem worse. White Democrats scored propaganda points by claiming that corruption proved the incompetence of "Negro-carpetbag" regimes.

Northerners grew increasingly weary of what seemed to be the endless turmoil of Southern politics. Most of them had never had a strong commitment to racial equality, and they were growing more and more willing to let white supremacy regain sway in the South. "The truth is," confessed a Northern Republican, "our people are tired out with this worn out cry of 'Southern outrages'!!! Hard times & heavy taxes make them wish the 'nigger,' 'everlasting nigger,' were in hell or Africa."

By 1875, only four Southern states remained under Republican control: South Carolina, Florida, Mississippi, and Louisiana. In those states, white Democrats had revived paramilitary organizations under various names: White Leagues (Louisiana), Rifle Clubs (Mississippi), and Red Shirts (South Carolina). Unlike the Klan, these groups operated openly. In Louisiana, they fought pitched battles with Republican militias in which scores were killed. When the Grant administration sent large numbers of federal troops to Louisiana, people in both North and South cried out against military rule. The protests grew even louder when soldiers marched onto the floor of the Louisiana legislature in January 1875 and expelled several Democratic legislators after a contested election. Was this America? Republican Senator Carl Schurz asked in a widely publicized speech: "If this can be done in Louisiana, how long will it be before it can be done in Massachusetts and Ohio? How long before a soldier may stalk into the national House of Representatives, and, pointing to the Speaker's mace, say 'Take away that bauble!'"

The Mississippi Election of 1875

The backlash against the Grant administration affected the Mississippi state election of 1875. Democrats there devised a strategy called the Mississippi Plan. The first step was to "persuade" the 10 to 15 percent of white voters still calling themselves Republicans to switch to the Democrats. Only a handful of carpetbaggers could resist the economic pressures, social ostracism, and threats that made it "too damned hot for [us] to stay out," wrote one white Republican who changed parties.

The second step in the Mississippi Plan was to intimidate black voters because, even with all whites voting Democratic, the party could still be defeated by the 55 percent black majority. Economic coercion against black sharecroppers and workers kept some of them away from the polls, but violence was the most effective method. Democratic "rifle clubs" showed up at Republican rallies, provoked riots, and shot down dozens of blacks in the ensuing melees. Governor Adelbert Ames—a native of Maine, a Union general who had won a medal of honor in the war, and one of the ablest of Southern Republicans—called for federal troops to control the violence. Grant intended to comply, but Ohio Republicans warned him that if he sent troops to Mississippi, the Democrats would exploit the issue of "bayonet rule" to carry Ohio in that year's state elections. Grant yielded—in effect giving up Mississippi for Ohio. The U.S. attorney general replied to Ames's request for troops:

> The whole public are tired out with these annual autumnal outbreaks in the South, and the great majority are now ready to condemn any interference on the part of the government. . . . Preserve the peace by the forces in your own state, and let the country see that the citizens of Mississippi who are . . . largely Republican, have the courage to fight for their rights.

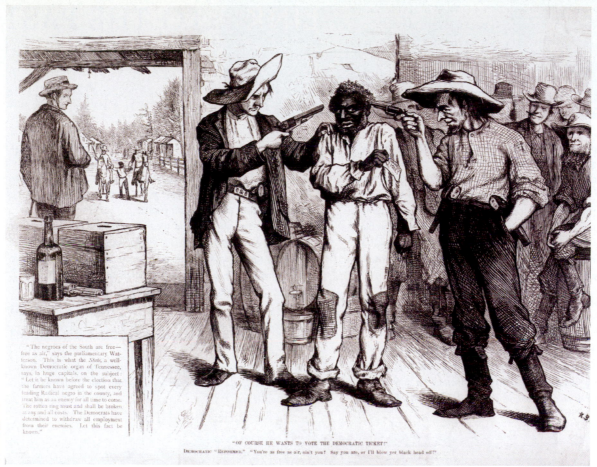

"The negroes of the South are free—free as air," says the parliamentary Watterson. This is what the *State*, a well-known Democratic organ of Tennessee, says, in huge capitals, on the subject: "Let it be known before the election that the farmers have agreed to spot every leading Radical negro in the county, and treat him as an enemy for all time to come. The rotten ring must and shall be broken at any and all costs. The Democrats have determined to withdraw all employment from their enemies. Let this fact be known."

"OF COURSE HE WANTS TO VOTE THE DEMOCRATIC TICKET!"

DEMOCRATIC "REFORMER." "You're as free as air, ain't you? Say you are, or I'll blow yer black head off!"

How the Mississippi Plan Worked. This cartoon shows how black counties could report large Democratic majorities in the Mississippi state election of 1875. The black voter holds a Democratic ticket while one of the men, described in the caption as a "Democratic reformer," holds a revolver to his head and says: "You're as free as air, ain't you? Say you are, or I'll blow your black head off!"

Governor Ames did try to organize a loyal state militia, but that proved difficult—and in any case, he was reluctant to use a black militia for fear of provoking a race war. "No matter if they are going to carry the State," said Ames with weary resignation, "let them carry it, and let us be at peace and have no more killing." The Mississippi Plan worked like a charm. In five of the state's counties with large black majorities, the Republicans polled 12, 7, 4, 2, and 0 votes, respectively. What had been a Republican majority of 30,000 in 1874 became a Democratic majority of 30,000 in 1875.

The Supreme Court and Reconstruction

Even if Grant had been willing to continue intervening in Southern state elections, Congress and the courts would have constricted such efforts. The new Democratic majority in the House threatened to cut any appropriations for the Justice Department and the army intended for use in the South. In 1876, the Supreme Court handed down two decisions that declared parts of the 1870 and 1871 laws for enforcement of the 14th and 15th Amendments unconstitutional. In *U.S.* v. *Cruikshank* and *U.S.* v. *Reese*, the Court ruled on cases from Louisiana and Kentucky. Both cases grew

out of provisions in these laws authorizing federal officials to prosecute *individuals* (not states) for violations of the civil and voting rights of blacks. But, the Court pointed out, the 14th and 15th Amendments apply to actions by *states:* "No State shall . . . deprive any person of life, liberty, or property . . . nor deny to any person . . . equal protection of the laws" and the right to vote "shall not be denied . . . by any State." Therefore, the portions of these laws that empowered the federal government to prosecute individuals were declared unconstitutional.

The Court did not say what could be done when states were controlled by white-supremacy Democrats who had no intention of enforcing equal rights. Meanwhile, in another ruling, *Civil Rights Cases* (1883), the Court declared unconstitutional a civil rights law passed by Congress in 1875. That law banned racial discrimination in all forms of public transportation and public accommodations. If enforced, it would have effected a sweeping transformation of race relations—in the North as well as in the South. Even some of the congressmen who voted for the bill doubted its constitutionality, however, and the Justice Department had made little effort to enforce it. Several cases made their way to the Supreme Court, which in 1883 ruled the law unconstitutional—again on grounds that the

Frederick Douglass on the Supreme Court and Civil Rights

The Civil Rights Act of 1875 anticipated many of the provisions of the Civil Rights Act of 1964, which is the law of the land and has been upheld by the U.S. Supreme Court. But the law of 1875 was ahead of its time, or at least ahead of the Supreme Court of its time, which declared it unconstitutional on the grounds that the 14th Amendment prohibited discrimination by states but not by individuals. The black civil rights leader Frederick Douglass denounced the Court's decision in language that anticipated the Supreme Court's reasoning in the last third of the 20th century.

This decision of the Supreme Court admits that the Fourteenth Amendment is a prohibition of the States. It admits that a State shall not abridge the privileges or immunities of citizens of the United States, but commits the seeming absurdity of allowing the people of a State to do what it prohibits the State itself from doing. . . . It is said that this decision will make no difference in the treatment of colored people; that the Civil Rights Bill was a dead letter, and could not be enforced. There is some truth in all this, but it is not the whole truth.

That bill, like all advance legislation, was a banner on the outer wall of American liberty, a noble moral standard, uplifted for the education of the American people. . . .

This law, though dead, did speak. It expressed the sentiment of justice and fair play. . . . If it is a bill for social equality, so is the Declaration of Independence, which declares that all men have equal rights; so is the Sermon on the Mount, so is the Golden Rule . . . so is the Constitution of the United States.

FREDERICK DOUGLASS

From a speech in Washington, D.C., October 22, 1883

Q What is Douglass's response to the argument that the Civil Rights Act was a dead letter even before the Supreme Court declared it so?

14th Amendment applied only to states, not to individuals. Several states—all in the North—passed their own civil rights laws in the 1870s and 1880s, but less than 10 percent of the black population resided in those states. The mass of African Americans lived a segregated existence.

The Election of 1876

In 1876, the remaining Southern Republican state governments fell victim to the passion for "reform." The mounting revelations of corruption at all levels of government ensured that reform would be the leading issue in the presidential election. In this centennial year of the birth of the United States, marked by a great exposition in Philadelphia, Americans wanted to put their best foot forward. Both major parties gave their presidential nominations to governors who had earned reform reputations in their states: Democrat Samuel J. Tilden of New York and Republican Rutherford B. Hayes of Ohio.

Democrats entered the campaign as favorites for the first time in two decades. It seemed likely that they would be able to put together an electoral majority from a "solid South" plus New York and two or three other Northern states. To ensure a solid South, they looked to the lessons of the Mississippi Plan. In 1876, a new word came into use to describe Democratic techniques of intimidation: *bulldozing*. To bulldoze black voters meant to trample them down or keep them away from the polls. In South Carolina and Louisiana, the Red Shirts and the White Leagues mobilized for an all-out bulldozing effort.

The most notorious incident, the Hamburg Massacre, occurred in the village of Hamburg, South Carolina, where a battle between a black militia unit and 200 Red Shirts resulted in the capture of several militiamen, five of whom were shot "while attempting to escape." This time Grant did send in federal troops. He pronounced the Hamburg Massacre "cruel, blood-thirsty, wanton, unprovoked . . . a repetition of the course that has been pursued in other Southern States."

The federal government also put several thousand deputy marshals and election supervisors on duty in the South. Although they kept an uneasy peace at the polls, they could do little to prevent assaults, threats, and economic coercion in backcountry districts, which reduced the potential Republican tally in the former Confederate states by at least 250,000 votes.

Disputed Results

When the results were in, Tilden had carried four Northern states, including New York with its 35 electoral votes. Tilden also carried all of the former slave states except—apparently—Louisiana, South Carolina, and Florida, which produced disputed returns. Because Tilden needed only one of them to win the presidency, while Hayes needed all three, and because Tilden seemed to have carried Louisiana and Florida, it appeared initially that he had won the presidency. But frauds and irregularities reported from several bulldozed districts in the three states clouded the issue. For example, a Louisiana parish that had recorded 1,688 Republican votes in 1874

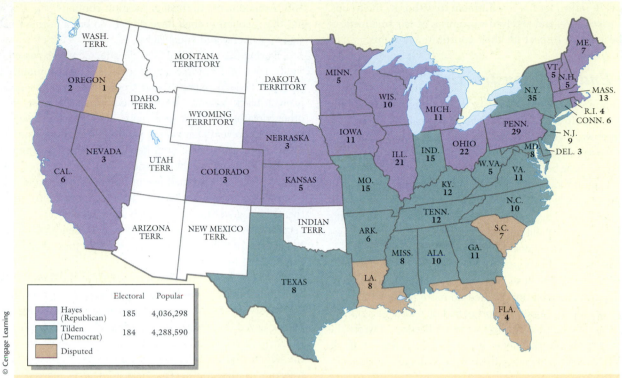

	Electoral	Popular
Hayes (Republican)	185	4,036,298
Tilden (Democrat)	184	4,288,590
Disputed		

© Cengage Learning

Map 17.3 Hayes-Tilden Disputed Election of 1876. A comparison of this map with those on pp. 473 and 475 shows the persistence of geographical voting patterns once Southern Democrats had overthrown most Republican state governments and effectively disfranchised many black voters.

reported only 1 in 1876. Many other similar discrepancies appeared. The official returns ultimately sent to Washington gave all three states—and therefore the presidency—to Hayes, but the Democrats refused to recognize the results, and they controlled the House.

The country now faced a serious constitutional crisis. Armed Democrats threatened to march on Washington. Many people feared another civil war. The Constitution offered no clear guidance on how to deal with the matter. A count of the state electoral votes required the concurrence of both houses of Congress, but with a Democratic House and a Republican Senate, such concurrence was not forthcoming. To break the deadlock, Congress created a special electoral commission consisting of five representatives, five senators, and five Supreme Court justices split evenly between the two parties, with one member, a Supreme Court justice, supposedly an independent—but in fact a Republican.

Tilden had won a national majority of 252,000 popular votes, and the raw returns gave him a majority in the three disputed states. But an estimated 250,000 Southern Republicans had been bulldozed away from the polls. In a genuinely fair and free election, the Republicans might have carried Mississippi and North Carolina as well as the three disputed states. While the commission agonized, Democrats and Republicans in Louisiana and South Carolina each inaugurated their own separate governors and legislatures (Republicans in Florida gave up the fight at the state level). Only federal troops in the capitals at New Orleans and Columbia protected the Republican governments in those states.

The Compromise of 1877

In February 1877, three months after voters had gone to the polls, the electoral commission issued its ruling. By a partisan vote of 8 to 7—with the "independent" justice voting with the Republicans—the commission awarded all of the disputed states to Hayes. The Democrats cried foul and began a **filibuster** in the House to delay the final electoral count beyond the inauguration date of March 4, to throw the election to the House of Representatives, an eventuality that threatened to bring total anarchy. But, behind the scenes, a compromise began to take shape. Both Northern Republicans and Southern Democrats of Whig heritage had similar interests in liquidating the sectional rancor and in getting on with the business of economic recovery and development. To wean Southern Whiggish Democrats away from a House filibuster, Hayes promised his support as president for federal appropriations to rebuild war-destroyed **levees** on the lower Mississippi and federal aid for a southern transcontinental railroad. Hayes's lieutenants also hinted at the appointment of a Southerner as postmaster general, who would have a considerable amount of patronage at his disposal—the appointment of thousands of local postmasters.

Most important, Southerners wanted to know what Hayes would do about Louisiana and South Carolina. Hayes signaled his intention to end "bayonet rule," which he had for some time considered a bankrupt policy. He believed that the goodwill and influence of Southern moderates would offer better protection for black rights than federal troops could provide. In return for his commitment to withdraw the troops, Hayes asked for—and received—promises of fair treatment of freedpeople and respect for their constitutional rights.

The End of Reconstruction

Such promises were easier to make than to keep, as future years would reveal. In any case, the Democratic filibuster collapsed, and Hayes was inaugurated on March 4. He soon fulfilled his part of the Compromise of 1877: ex-Confederate Democrat David Key of Tennessee became postmaster general; in 1878, the South received more federal money for internal improvements than ever before; and federal troops left the capitals of Louisiana and South Carolina. The last two Republican state governments collapsed. The old abolitionist and radical Republican warhorses denounced Hayes's actions as a sellout of Southern blacks.

But voices of protest could scarcely be heard above the sighs of relief that the crisis was over. Most Americans, including even most Republicans, wanted no more military intervention in state affairs. "I have no sort of faith in a local government which can only be propped up by foreign bayonets," wrote the editor of the New York *Tribune* in April 1877. "If negro suffrage means that as a permanency then negro suffrage is a failure."

Conclusion

Before the Civil War, most Americans had viewed a powerful government as a threat to individual liberties. That is why the first 10 amendments to the Constitution (the Bill of Rights) imposed strict limits on the powers of the federal government. During the Civil War and especially during Reconstruction, however, the national government had to exert an unprecedented amount of power to free the slaves and guarantee their equal rights as free citizens. That is why the 13th, 14th, and 15th Amendments to the Constitution contained clauses stating that "Congress shall have power" to enforce these provisions for liberty and equal rights.

During the post–Civil War decade, Congress passed civil rights laws and enforcement legislation to accomplish this purpose. Federal marshals and troops patrolled the polls to protect black voters, arrested thousands of Klansmen and other violators of black civil rights, and even occupied state capitals to prevent Democratic paramilitary groups from overthrowing legitimately elected Republican state governments.

By 1875, many Northerners had grown tired of or alarmed by this continued use of military power to intervene in the internal affairs of states. The Supreme Court stripped the federal government of much of its authority to enforce certain provisions of the 14th and 15th Amendments. Traditional fears of military power as a threat to individual liberties came to the fore again.

The withdrawal of federal troops from the South in 1877 constituted both a symbolic and a substantive end of the 12-year postwar era known as Reconstruction. Reconstruction had achieved the two great objectives inherited from the Civil War: (1) to reincorporate the former Confederate states into the Union, and (2) to accomplish a transition from slavery to freedom in the South. That transition was marred by the economic inequity of sharecropping and the social injustice of white supremacy. A third goal of Reconstruction, enforcement of the equal civil and political rights promised in the 14th and 15th Amendments, was betrayed by the Compromise of 1877. In subsequent decades, the freed slaves and their descendants suffered repression into segregated, second-class citizenship. Not until another war hero-turned-president sent troops into Little Rock (Chapter 28), 80 years after they had been withdrawn from New Orleans and Columbia, did the federal government launch a second Reconstruction to fulfill the promises of the first.

CHAPTER REVIEW

REVIEW QUESTIONS

1. What were the positions of Presidents Abraham Lincoln and Andrew Johnson and of moderate and radical Republicans in Congress on the issues of restoring the South to the Union and protecting the rights of freed slaves?
2. Why was Andrew Johnson impeached? Why was he acquitted?
3. Why did a majority of the Northern people and their political leaders turn against continued federal involvement in Southern Reconstruction in the 1870s?

CRITICAL THINKING QUESTIONS

1. The two main goals of Reconstruction were to bring the former Confederate states back into the Union and to ensure the equal citizenship and rights of the former slaves. Why was the first goal more successfully achieved than the second?

2. Why have "carpetbaggers" and "scalawags" had such a bad historical image? Did they deserve it?

IDENTIFICATIONS

Review your understanding of the following key terms, people, and events for this chapter (terms in bold in text are included in the Glossary).

amnesty, p. 465
Black Codes, p. 467
quasi-slavery, p. 467
Freedmen's Bureau, p. 467
share wages, p. 467
sharecropping, p. 467
40 acres and a mule, p. 468
enfranchise, p. 465
Union leagues, p. 471
scalawags, p. 471
carpetbaggers, p. 471
impeachment, p. 472
universal male suffrage, p. 472
Ku Klux Klan, p. 472
Ulysses S. Grant, p. 473
Credit Mobilier, p. 474
spoils system, p. 474
patronage, p. 475
habeas corpus, p. 478
filibuster, p. 483
levees, p. 483

SUGGESTED READINGS

The most comprehensive and incisive history of Reconstruction is **Eric Foner, *Reconstruction: America's Unfinished Revolution 1863–1872* (1988). For a skillful abridgement of this book, see Foner, *A Short History of Reconstruction*** (1990). Also valuable is **Kenneth M. Stampp, *The Era of Reconstruction, 1865–1877*** (1965). Incisive interpretations can be found in **Thomas J. Brown, *Reconstruction: New Perspectives on the Postbellum United States*** (2006). A superb study of the South Carolina Sea Islands as a laboratory of Reconstruction is **Willie Lee Rose, *Rehearsal for Reconstruction: The Port Royal Experiment*** (1964).

Two important studies of Andrew Johnson and his conflict with Congress over Reconstruction are **Hans L. Trefousse, *The Radical Republicans: Lincoln's Vanguard for Racial Justice*** (1969); and **Michael Les Benedict, *The Impeachment and Trial of Andrew Johnson*** (1973). Two books by **Michael Perman** connect events in the South and in Washington during Reconstruction: *Reunion without Compromise: The South and Reconstruction, 1865–1868* (1973) and *The Road to Redemption: Southern Politics 1868–1879* (1984). The emotional undertones of Reconstruction politics are analyzed in **Mark Wahlgren Summers, *A Dangerous Stir: Fear, Paranoia, and the Making of Reconstruction*** (2009). For counter-Reconstruction violence in the South, see **George C. Rable, *But There Was No Peace: The Role of Violence in the Politics of Reconstruction*** (1984) and **Nicholas Lemann, *Redemption: The Last Battle of the Civil War*** (2006). The evolution of sharecropping and other aspects of the transition from slavery to freedom are treated in **Roger L. Ransom and Richard Sutch, *One Kind of Freedom: The Economic Consequences of Emancipation*** (1977).

Of the many books on African Americans in Reconstruction, the following are perhaps the most valuable: **Thomas Holt, *Black over White: Negro Political Leadership in South Carolina during Reconstruction*** (1977) and **Laura F. Edwards, *Gendered Strife and Confusion: The Political Culture of Reconstruction*** (1997). Both black and white churches are the subject of **Daniel Stowell, *Rebuilding Zion: The Religious Reconstruction of the South, 1863–1877*** (1998).

CourseMate

Visit the CourseMate website at www.cengagebrain.com for additional study tools and review materials for this chapter.

CHAPTER 18

© Bettmann/CORBIS

The Golden Spike

This carefully posed scene records the merging of the Central Pacific and Union Pacific Railroads at Promontory Point, Utah, on May 10, 1869, to create the nation's first transcontinental railroad. A celebration of the industrialization of the American West, the photograph includes hundreds of white laborers, but reflects the racial prejudice of the time in excluding Chinese railroad workers who also played a central role in building the railroad.

A Transformed Nation: The West and the New South, 1865–1900

"**H**OW I DO WISH YOU** could all come out here," the new Kansas homesteader Mary Abell wrote to her family back east in 1871. "It is such a beautiful country—I did not know there was any thing so beautiful in the whole world as the country we passed over in coming here." Just arrived from New York with her husband, Abell was clearly excited about the prospect of a new life in the West: "Robert has got a piece of land that suits him," she told her sister. "It seems so fortunate." She knew there was much to do in the days ahead—"There is a house to be built fences to make—a well to be dug and a cow to be got." But Abell didn't seem to mind: "I should never be content to live East now," she said. "Things there would look very little."

Abell was part of a great wave of settlement in the post–Civil War era that would transform the West. From 1865 to 1890, the white population in the trans-Mississippi west increased some 400 percent to 8,628,000—a figure that includes both native-born and white immigrants. The dream of western lands also inspired many African Americans, whose cherished hopes for liberty led hundreds of thousands to leave the South for points west from 1880 to 1910. At the same time, immigrants from China, Mexico, and other countries were drawn to the economic opportunities of the West as part of a global movement of peoples in this period.

All of these men and women were driven by desires for a better life, but this motivation often conflicted with the rights and desires of the diverse peoples who already inhabited the West, including, among others, a variety of Indian cultures and societies; borderlands villages of Spanish-speaking peoples;

An Industrializing West
 The Homestead Act
 Railroads
 Chinese Laborers and the
  Railroads
 The Golden Spike
 Railroads and Borderlands
  Communities
 Mining
 Ranching
 Cattle Drives and the Open Range
 The Industrialization of Ranching
 Industrial Cowboys
 Mexican Americans
 Itinerant Laborers
 Homesteading and Farming
 The Experience of Homesteading
 Gender and Western Settlement

**Conquest and Resistance:
American Indians in the
Trans-Mississippi West**
 Conflict with the Sioux
 Suppression of Other Plains
  Indians
 The "Peace Policy"
 The Dawes Severalty Act and
  Indian Boarding Schools
 The Ghost Dance
 Sitting Bull and Buffalo Bill:
  Popular Myths of the West

**Industrialization and the New
South**
 Race and Industrialization
 Southern Agriculture
 Exodusters and Emigrationists
 Race Relations in the New South
 The Emergence of an African-
  American Middle Class
 The Rise of Jim Crow

The Politics of Stalemate
 Knife-Edge Electoral Balance
 Civil Service Reform
 The Tariff Issue

settlements of Chinese miners and laborers; and Mexicans in California. Settlement set in motion conflict and resistance in numerous locations. Who would gain power over Western lands? Whose liberty would be respected? What efforts would be made to achieve equality—or deny equality—to all of these peoples? This chapter explores the transformation of the West and the South during the late 19th century, part of a larger process of industrialization in this period.

An Industrializing West

Q How did the industrialization of the West change American lives?

FOCUS QUESTION

Traditionally, historians have associated industrialization with the East in the post–Civil War era, but in fact the West also industrialized in this period. That industrialization had many linked components: the settlement of the West, including the creation of farms, communities, and western cities; the production of commodities such as cattle and timber that could be shipped east; the creation of western consumers and thus the demand for manufactured goods; the extraction of resources through mining and logging; and the shipment of commodities using a national transportation network. These western processes of resource extraction may have looked different from the factory-centered industrialization that developed in the East and Midwest at this time (see Chapter 19), but they still involved the transformation of an agrarian economy to

CHRONOLOGY

1862	Sioux uprising in Minnesota; 38 Sioux executed
1864	Colorado militia massacres Cheyenne in village at Sand Creek, Colorado
1866	Cowboys conduct first cattle drive north from Texas
1869	President Grant announces his "peace policy" toward Indians
1876	Sioux and Cheyenne defeat Custer at Little Big Horn
1880	James A. Garfield elected president
1881	Garfield assassinated; Chester A. Arthur becomes president
1883	Pendleton Act begins reform of civil service
1884	Grover Cleveland elected president
1887	Dawes Severalty Act dissolves Indian tribal units and implements individual ownership of tribal lands

1888	Benjamin Harrison elected president
1889	Government opens Indian Territory (Oklahoma) to white settlement
1890	Wounded Knee massacre ◆ New Mississippi constitution pioneers black disenfranchisement in South ◆ Republicans try but fail to enact federal elections bill to protect black voting rights ◆ Congress enacts McKinley Tariff
1892	Grover Cleveland again elected president
1895	Booker T. Washington makes his Atlanta Compromise address
1896	*Plessy* v. *Ferguson* legalizes "separate but equal" state racial segregation laws
1898	*Williams* v. *Mississippi* condones use of literacy tests and similar measures to restrict voting rights

an industrial society. Like eastern industrialization, western industrialization also had global reach, pulling immigrants from China, Peru, Chile, Hawaii, European, and Mexico to the already diverse West.

The Homestead Act

Settlement of the West was part of the larger process of industrialization. Mary Abell and her husband, for instance, were able to become homesteaders because of legislation that took effect on January 1, 1863—the same day that the Emancipation Proclamation became law. Meant to provide free land for western settlers, the **Homestead Act** was the result of a dream that stretched back decades. "Go West, young man!" had been a famous saying during the 1850s, associated with an extended campaign for a homestead law by newspaper editor Horace Greeley. The saying embodied a cherished American ideal: the belief that individual ownership of land by farmers was at the heart of a virtuous citizenry and a sound democratic republic. That ideal had fueled Jeffersonian agrarianism, too.

In the 1850s, many people believed that a western "safety valve" was necessary to ward off the potential evils of industrialization, urbanization, and capitalist expansion. Free land in the West would help prevent a system of perpetual wage labor, or "wage slavery," by allowing individual farmers to support themselves. Thus free land would ultimately help preserve American values of democratic individualism. Yet settlement of the West was not so much an escape from industrialization as an important factor in the ongoing industrialization of the West.

The provisions of the Homestead Act were remarkably egalitarian for their day—at least up to a point. Both men and unmarried women were eligible to file for up to 160 acres of surveyed land in the public domain, as long as they were over the age of 21. (Married women were assumed to be dependents of their homesteading husbands.) Immigrants who affirmed their intention to become citizens were also eligible. As long as homesteaders lived on the land for five years, not only cultivating it but also "improving" it by building a house or barn, they could receive full title for a fee of only $10. Utilizing these provisions, white homesteaders ultimately claimed some 285 million acres of land, a remarkable redistribution of public acreage by the government.

However, despite a surface egalitarianism, the Homestead Act privileged white farmers over African Americans and Hispanics, who rarely had the resources necessary to homestead. Even free land required tools, seed, plus often-costly transportation to a far-away place. Experts in the Agriculture Department estimated such needs at $1,000, a huge sum for most Americans at the time. The act also denied access to Chinese laborers, who could not become U.S. citizens and had few property rights. It made no provisions for the truly poor.

Furthermore, the Act severely affected such groups as New Mexico sheepherders and Native Americans for whom such settlement did not open up land but instead took it away. The Homestead Act was in fact part of a larger process of conquest, driven by the twin pressures of industrialization and white settlement, through which Indians were irrevocably stripped of their lands.

A final problem with the Act was corruption in its implementation. Those who agitated for a Homestead Act in the antebellum period had been fueled by a sense of idealism. Ironically, however, through chicanery, outright fraud, and government giveaways, more public land actually fell into the hands of railroads, other corporations, and speculators, than into the hands of individual farmers during this period.

Was the Homestead Act a success or failure in American life? To younger sons in Norwegian or German farm families who could expect to inherit no land at home, the opportunity to obtain 160 acres in Minnesota or Nebraska seemed miraculous. But clearly, that perspective was not shared by Native Americans.

Railroads

Nothing was more important to the industrialization of the West than the railroad. Just as free land for homesteaders was a long-held dream for many Americans, so, too, was the creation of a transcontinental railroad that would link East and West. The two dreams were connected: the settlement of the West would be greatly facilitated by the extension of the railroad into far-flung territory. Thus it was no accident that in 1862, the year the government passed the Homestead Act, it also passed the Pacific Railroad Bill, which provided large loans and extremely generous subsidies of land to two railroad companies, the Union Pacific (working west) and the Central Pacific (working east), in order to enable them to build a transcontinental line stretching from Omaha, Nebraska, to Sacramento, California. (Railroad lines already existed from Omaha to the East.) Two years later, the government also provided a substantial monetary subsidy for each mile of track laid in the West. Ultimately, the government would give away 131 million acres of land to support transcontinental railroads, including huge land subsidies to three additional railroads: the Atchison, Topeka, and Santa Fe (following the Santa Fe Trail between Missouri and the Southwest); the Southern Pacific (from Southern California to New Orleans); and the Northern Pacific (from the Great Lakes to the Columbia River).

These lavish subsidies set off a frenzy of railroad building; they also made a few individuals very rich, including the "Big Four" of the Central Pacific: Leland Stanford, Collis P. Huntington, Mark Hopkins, and Charles Crocker. Big in every way (they collectively weighed 860 pounds), the four men had come to California during the Gold Rush and had shrewdly sized up its entrepreneurial opportunities. They now avidly seized the historic opportunity at hand and formed a partnership that effectively split up the work necessary in such a giant task, including the work of influencing lawmakers. Like so many others involved in the notoriously corrupt postwar railway boom, they were not shy about using bribery or graft to achieve their aims. The leader of the Union Pacific, Thomas C. Durant, was not shy either, having been the chief architect of the scandalous Credit Mobilier scheme (see Chapter 17).

Having provided generous subsidies, the government expected the railroads to obtain their own financing, and so various railroads sold millions of dollars of stocks or bonds, many selling as much stock as the market would bear without

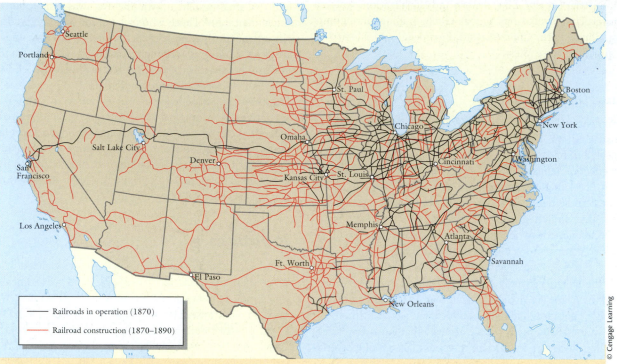

Map 18.1 Railroad Expansion, 1870–1890. This map provides a vivid illustration of the spanning of the western half of the United States by steel rails in two short decades.

much relationship to the actual value of the railroads. This "watered" stock was part of the runaway corruption that surrounded financing railroads. The Big Four participated wholeheartedly in this corruption, creating construction contracts, for instance, that paid them $90 million for work that only cost them $32.2 million.

Once financing had been arranged for this complex venture, the Union Pacific and Central Pacific embarked on a daunting task that would engage some 20,000 workers at a time. From 1865 on, the two railroads raced against one another, as whoever laid the most track stood to gain in government subsidies as well as later commerce. The Union Pacific employed primarily Irish laborers, while the Central Pacific employed a workforce that was by 1867 almost 90 percent Chinese. All worked almost constantly.

Chinese Laborers and the Railroads

A global economy had drawn thousands of Chinese laborers to California during the Gold Rush, beginning in 1849. Mostly peasants emigrating from the Pearl River delta of Guangdong Province in southeast China, they were pushed from home by poverty and unstable political conditions related to China's defeat in the British Opium Wars; they were pulled to America by their hope to make a better living in "Gold Mountain." While only a few hundred men emigrated in 1849 and 1850, by the mid-1850s, thousands of Chinese immigrants arrived annually. By 1870, there were some 63,000 Chinese in the United States, with over three-quarters settled in California.

Almost entirely men, Chinese immigrants intended to be sojourners, not permanent settlers: they planned to take their hard-earned savings home to the wives and families they had left behind. At first they worked as independent prospectors panning for gold, but as gold profits dwindled, they moved into other areas of work. In the 1860s, labor contractors in China actively recruited young men to come to America to build the transcontinental railroad, as well as to work as agricultural laborers, to develop fisheries and vineyards, and to help reclaim California swamplands. Some 12,000 Chinese laborers ultimately built the Central Pacific Railroad, often under exceptionally harsh conditions, and with substantially less pay than white laborers.

Even before they began working on the railroads, Chinese miners and laborers faced extremes of prejudice from white nativists. In 1850, the California State legislature responded to anti-foreigner agitation with a Foreign Miners' Tax aimed at all foreigners; two years later, the legislature specifically targeted Chinese immigrants. Western labor leaders, particularly Dennis Kearney of the Workingman's Party of California, inflamed nativist crowds of white workers with anti-Chinese rhetoric: in 1877, during the national Great Railway Strike (see Chapter 19), mobs of white workers rioted against Chinese workers in San Francisco's Chinatown. Violence against Chinese workers occurred in numerous places in the West during the 1870s and 1880s, including a massacre in Rock Springs, Colorado, after the Union Pacific Railroad decided to hire Chinese workers. Twenty-eight Chinese died in an attack that included burning down Chinese homes; similar attacks soon occurred throughout the West.

At the local level, Chinese immigrants faced a host of discriminatory ordinances specifically targeting them, from queue ordinances regulating the length of men's hair (forbidding the distinctive braid worn by Chinese men); to sidewalk ordinances preventing the carrying of baskets on shoulders. At the state level, California laws denied Chinese the right to own land, to testify in court, to intermarry with whites, and to immigrate. Under these conditions, Chinese workers created communities of their own against stiff odds. Yet by 1850, a thriving Chinatown had emerged in San Francisco, and Chinese sections emerged in numerous communities throughout the West.

In 1882 the federal government weighed in with its first discriminatory law targeting a specific immigrant group. The **Chinese Exclusion Act** suspended Chinese immigration for 10 years with the exception of a few job categories. Wealthy Chinese businessmen and merchants were allowed entry because of the U.S. government's interest in trade with China. But the law forbade Chinese laborers, who were said to endanger "the good order of certain localities." Renewed in 1892, the Chinese Exclusion Act achieved its aim: The population of Chinese declined from 105,465 in 1880 to 89,863 in 1900, during a period in which immigration swelled for other groups (for more on Chinese immigrants, see chapter 20).

The Golden Spike

By the early spring of 1869, what one commentator called the "irrepressible railroad" was almost an accomplished fact. The only question was where East and West would meet. In the final stages of track-laying, the two railroads—which would receive money, after all, based on miles of track built—actually built some track parallel to one another before finally being instructed by no less than President Grant to determine a meeting point.

The result, on May 10, 1869, was the historic driving of a "golden spike" in Promontory, Utah, to mark the merging of the two lines. Present that day, we know from the historical record, were "men of every color, creed, and nationality," including the Chinese laborers who had built the railroad and laid the very last track. But official photographs of the event leave them out—a silence that speaks volumes about racial prejudice at the time.

Soon, others followed this first trans-continental railroad, although there were numerous difficulties and abortive attempts. The Northern Pacific ran out of capital in 1873 and went into receivership; the Santa Fe fell short of its goal. Still, by 1893, a total of five trans-continental railroads would be in service, and track mileage west of the Mississippi would increase from 3,272 miles at the end of the Civil War to 72,473 miles. No single factor was as important to the industrialization of the West as the building of railroads, which provided an infrastructure for the western economy as well as connection to eastern markets.

Railroads and Borderlands Communities

Railroads changed ordinary people's lives across the West. The arrival of the railroads, as well as the Anglo settlers who followed swiftly in their wake, dramatically changed established patterns of life in the borderlands communities of northern New Mexico and southern Colorado. In the 1870s Hispanic villagers lived communally in this area, grazing sheep and cattle on the open range. That way of life had not changed much even after the conquest of New Mexico in 1848.

But the coming of the railroads in the 1880s put new pressure on Hispanic village life. In places like Rio Arriba County, New Mexico, Hispanic villagers who had done a thriving trade freighting—hauling goods by wagons—found themselves replaced by the railroads. As a result, communities that had combined trade with grazing and farming were now forced to go back only to farming and grazing, even though this combination had never produced quite enough for their needs. Even worse, in a pattern repeated throughout the West, Hispanic villagers found that Anglo settlement and fencing of once-open lands reduced the available range for grazing.

As Anglo-owned livestock companies moved in, bringing in better breeds and buying up grazing land, they began to squeeze out the Hispanic farmers. By the 1890s villagers began to depend on credit for the first time; in the turbulent economy of that decade, many of them were unable to pay their debts. The end result was the loss of their sheep—and livelihood—to Anglo businessmen who had extended credit to them. Many ended up working for livestock companies, sometimes caring for herds they had once owned themselves. Eventually others ended up as miners, forced to become wage laborers.

Resentment became active resistance in the 1880s, when a secret organization, *las Gorras Blancas* (White caps), rode mostly at night to cut fences, tear up railroad track, and burn bridges. "Our purpose is to protect the rights of the people in general and especially those of the helpless classes," the group declared in its platform. But the group had only limited success in achieving these goals.

Mining

A similar process held true in mining. The California Gold Rush of 1849 and the early 1850s had drawn miners from across the United States—and from Mexico, Europe, China, Chile, and other countries, as well—to pan for gold. After the Civil War, mining continued but the image of the individual prospector striking it rich on his own claim became increasingly quaint. By the 1870s the majority of miners were wage laborers who worked for corporations, not for themselves. Mining was big business, with groups of investors consolidating holdings in some of the richest mines. George Hearst, for instance, began by investing in 1859 in the legendary Comstock Lode in Nevada—the richest vein of silver in America. "If you're ever inclined to think that there's no such thing as luck," Hearst remarked, "just think of me." In 1877, Hearst and business partners bought the Homestake Mine in the Black Hills, and then enriched their holdings still further by buying up the claims of surrounding miners. Other financiers invested in the industries related to mining, including railroads, lumber companies, and smelters.

Gold Rush prospectors had worked the surface of the earth with picks, shovels, and tin pans. But soon miners and mining companies developed new technologies to extract ore, whether on the surface of the earth or underground. Hydraulic mining, used as early as the 1850s, employed high-pressure jets of water to wash away banks of earth and even mountains in order to extract gold. By the 1880s, hydraulic mining produced 90 percent of California's gold, but it also ravaged the environment, tearing away indiscriminately at earth, boulders, and trees, and leaving desolate landscapes in its wake. The debris (tailings) from hydraulic mining clogged rivers and caused floods, ruining farms with muddy waste. Other types of mining destroyed landscapes as well: copper mining in particular created strip-mining moonscapes.

Railroads played a central role in the development of industrial mining, not only providing access to mines but also enabling a new kind of mining late in the century. Gold discoveries had propelled the first waves of western settlement, but by the 1870s, silver eclipsed gold in volume and some years even in value. Copper mining became profitable after the arrival of the railroads, which allowed transportation of huge quantities of ore. In Butte, Montana, mining had centered around on diminishing supplies of silver until 1881. But the arrival of railroads that year made it possible to extract Butte's rich lode of copper, known as the "richest hill on earth." The same held true for large-scale copper mining in southern Arizona, which was also catalyzed by the arrival of the railroads in the 1880s. Such large-scale resource extraction was at the heart of western industrialization.

Miners' working conditions in heavily mechanized hard-rock mines grew steadily worse. Mining on the Comstock Lode involved work in mines with temperatures of well over 100 degrees—sometimes as much as 150 degrees deep underground. Miners died of the heat, of poor ventilation, of the release of toxic gases, and of accidents with mining equipment. Accidents disabled one out of every 30 miners in the 1870s. By the end of the 19th century, mining was the most dangerous industry in the country.

Unions gained a limited foothold in the 1870s and 1880s, but wage cuts in the early 1890s initiated a new burst of labor radicalism and resistance. After a violent confrontation between miners and the National Guard at Coeur d'Alene, Idaho, in 1892, mining unions met at Butte, Montana, in 1893 to form the **Western Federation of Miners (WFM)**, whose radical politics included a call radically to transform the American economic system. That year, a violent strike at Cripple Creek, Colorado, broke out over mine owners' attempts to move from an eight-hour to a ten-hour day. These strikes were part of nationwide labor activism and resistance in the 1890s (see Chapter 19). Ultimately the WFM would help to found the 20th-century Industrial Workers of the World (IWW) (see Chapter 20). The IWW's leader, William "Big Bill" Haywood, later remembered being approached by a WFM organizer as a young man in Idaho. "I had never heard of the need of workingmen organizing for mutual protection," Haywood

said, but he soon became a leader of the WFM himself. The industrialization of the West became a radicalizing political experience for many.

Ranching

It wasn't just miners who went on strike: by the 1880s, even cowboys attempted strikes for better pay and better working conditions. The idea of a striking cowboy might seem incongruous, but cowboys were employees, too, and increasingly in the late 19th century they were employees of large industrial corporations. Contrary to most Hollywood images, they were also a diverse group: approximately one-third of the trail cowboys were African American, Mexican, or Indian.

Cattle Drives and the Open Range

A postwar boom in the range cattle industry had its beginnings in southern Texas. The Spaniards had introduced longhorn cattle there in the 18th century. This hardy breed multiplied rapidly: by the 1850s, millions of them roamed freely on the Texas plains. The market for them was limited in this sparsely settled region—the nearest railhead was usually too far distant to make shipping them north and east economically feasible.

The Civil War changed all that. Beef supplies in the older states dropped drastically, and prices rose to the unheard-of sum of $40 per head. The postwar explosion of population and railroads westward brought markets and railheads ever closer to western cattle that were free to anyone who rounded them up and branded them.

Astute Texans quickly saw that the longhorns represented a fortune on the hoof—if they could be driven northward the 800 miles to the railhead at Sedalia, Missouri. In spring 1866, cowboys hit the trail with 260,000 cattle in the first of the great drives. Disease, stampedes, bad weather, Indians, and irate farmers in Missouri (who were afraid that the Texas fever carried by some of the longhorns would infect their own stock) killed or ran off most of the cattle.

Only a few thousand head made it to Sedalia, but the prices they fetched convinced ranchers that the system would work, if only they could find a better route. By 1867, the rails of the Kansas Pacific had reached Abilene, Kansas, 150 miles closer to Texas, making it possible to drive the herds through a sparsely occupied portion of Indian Territory. About 35,000 longhorns reached Abilene that summer, where they were loaded onto cattle cars for the trip to Kansas City or Chicago. This success resulted in the interlocking institutions of the cattle drive and the Chicago stockyards. The development of refrigerated rail cars in the 1870s enabled Chicago to ship dressed beef all over the country. Abilene mushroomed overnight from a sleepy village where one bartender spent his spare time catching prairie dogs, into a boomtown where 25 saloons stayed open all night. The railroad made almost as much money shipping liquor into town as it did shipping cattle out.

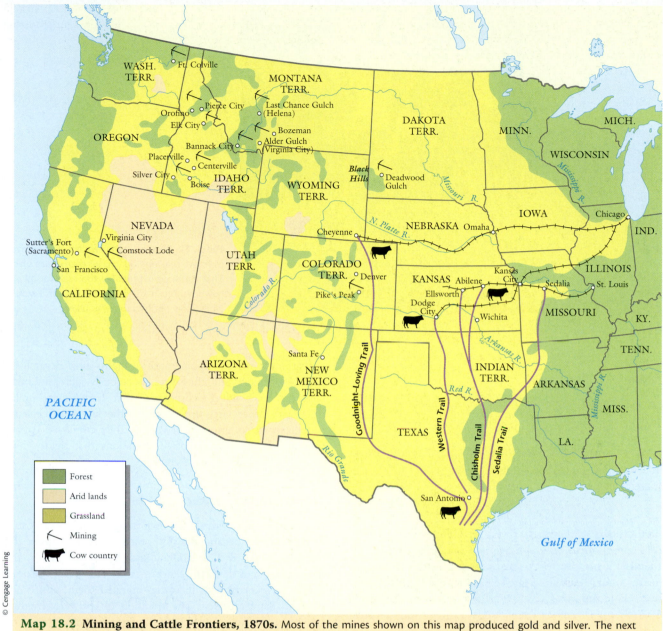

Map 18.2 Mining and Cattle Frontiers, 1870s. Most of the mines shown on this map produced gold and silver. The next generation would begin to exploit copper in Montana and Arizona, and later generations would extract oil from Texas and Oklahoma and coal and oil from Wyoming.

More than a million longhorns bellowed their way north on the **Chisholm Trail** to Abilene over the next four years, while the railhead crept westward to other Kansas towns, chiefly Dodge City, which became the most wide-open and famous of the cow towns. As buffalo and Indians disappeared from the grasslands north of Texas, ranches moved northward to take their place. Cattle drives grew shorter as railroads inched forward. Ranchers grazed their cattle for free on millions of acres of open, unfenced government land. But clashes with "grangers" (the ranchers' contemptuous term for farmers), on the one hand, and with a growing army of sheep ranchers on the other—not to mention rustlers—led to several "range wars." Most notable was the Johnson County War in Wyoming in 1892. Grangers and small ranchers there (who had sometimes gotten their start by rustling) defeated the hired guns of the Stock Growers' Association, which represented larger ranchers.

By that time, open-range grazing was already in decline. The boom years of the early 1880s had overstocked the range and driven down prices. Then came record cold and blizzards on the southern range in the winter of 1884–85, followed by even worse weather on the northern plains two years later. Hundreds of thousands of cattle froze or starved to death. These catastrophes spurred reforms that ended open-range grazing. The ranchers who survived turned to growing hay and supplemental feed for the winter. They reduced the size of their herds, started buying or leasing land and fencing in their cattle, and invested in scientific breeding that crossed longhorns with higher-quality stock to produce a better grade of beef.

Black Cowboys. Some studies of cowboys estimate that one-quarter of them were black. That estimate is probably too high for all cowboys, but it might be correct for Texas, where this photograph was taken.

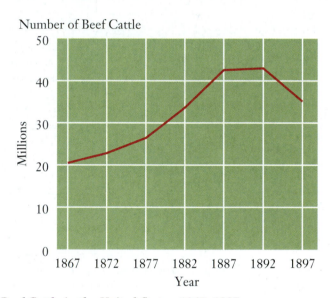

Number of Beef Cattle

Beef Cattle in the United States, 1867–1897.

backgrounds—or perhaps because of them—they never liked each other much. Still, they were enormously successful business partners, building a corporation that shared many similarities with other large companies in the late 19th century. Mobilizing large amounts of capital, they employed over a thousand laborers in extensive operations that tightly connected ranchlands with the city.

Industrial Cowboys

Cowboys did not just ride the open range in the Texan cattle drives that have became the stuff of legend; they also rode the extensive Miller & Lux landholdings. Before the 1870s, the most valuable of the firm's cowboys were *vaqueros*, Mexican cowboys who rounded up cattle, branded them, and drove them to San Francisco. The tradition of the *vaqueros* had arrived in the New World with the Spanish, who introduced herding by men on horseback. By the late 19th century, the raising of cattle herds by *vaqueros* had been practiced for centuries in California.

Not surprisingly, the head *vaquero* at Miller & Lux was a Mexican American, Rafael Cuen. His was a position of skill and respect, but his salary was not as high as that of his white coworkers, which reflected prevalent discrimination against Mexicans. It's possible this carried an especially sharp sting since his father had once owned (and lost) a piece of the Miller & Lux land. The arrival of railroads took a toll on the positions of *vaqueros* like Cuen: after the 1870s cattle were shipped to market by rail.

Mexican Americans

Throughout the late 19th century, Mexican Americans, many of whom had owned their land for generations, lost both property and political influence to incoming Anglo-American settlers. Many elite *Californios*, who were ranchers in southern

The Industrialization of Ranching

As open-range grazing declined, industrialized ranching expanded. We don't usually think of ranching as an industrial process—industrialization tends to conjure up images of eastern factories belching smoke—but in fact major ranching companies operated as big businesses by the end of the century. As historian David Igler has shown, by 1900 the California corporation Miller & Lux was one of the largest industrial enterprises in the country, having integrated raising cattle on vast landholdings together with meatpacking in San Francisco. Its two founding partners were German immigrants who had started out working as butchers in San Francisco but soon owned their own shops. Despite their remarkably similar

HISTORY THROUGH FILM

Oklahoma! (1955)

Directed by Fred Zinnemann.
Starring Gordon MacRae (Curly); Shirley Jones (Laurey); and Rod Steiger (Jud).

Only a history textbook would ask you to connect the great Rodgers & Hammerstein musical *Oklahoma!* to the range wars of the late-19th-century West. But think about it: when the cast sings "The Farmer and the Cowman" during a square dance, right before launching into a colorful fistfight, they express the different viewpoints of farmers and cattle ranchers. "Whyn't those dirtscratchers stay in Missouri where they belong?" asks a cowman, and another protests, the farmer "He come out west and built a lot of fences. /And built 'em right acrost our cattle ranges!" It's up to the song's refrain to tell us how to resolve this dispute:

The farmer and the cowman should be friends,
Oh, the farmer and the cowman should be friends.
One man likes to push a plough,
The other likes to chase a cow,
But that's no reason why they cain't be friends.

Oklahoma! isn't really about Oklahoma, even if it is set in 1907 right before the territory became a state. It's really about a mythic Western space in Americans' imagination, where Americans come together in harmony at square dances and box suppers and where a cowboy like the masculine hero Curly is not a wage laborer for life, but instead is about to become a prosperous farmer. *Oklahoma!* may be set in Indian Territory, but there are no Native Americans here. It is an entirely white, native-born world except for the peddler Ali Hakim, and he is clearly just passing through. There's certainly

no indication of Oklahoma's arid climate and the devastating drought of the Great Depression, which would have been in recent memory when the musical was written in 1943. In fact, some of the people associated with the musical were uneasy about the title "Oklahoma," precisely because they were afraid it would remind audiences of the "Okies," the poverty-stricken farmers forced to flee the arid plains during the Depression. Instead, this is a world of green abundance where "the corn is as high as an elephant's eye." The only shadow in this sunlit world with its "bright golden haze on the meadow," is Jud, the hired hand.

And perhaps that's why Jud is the most interesting character in this movie musical. Played with a heavy, menacing scowl by none other than Rod Steiger, Jud is the dark side of the Western dream, a man with a deep violent streak (unlike the boys-will-be-boys scuffling of the cowboys) and an unhealthy liking for "girly pictures." All of these negative qualities are loaded onto his status as the "hired hand"; he provides an uneasy reminder that class lines did exist in the West and that not everyone was on the brink of becoming prosperous. Jud is the only real problem in the mythic world of *Oklahoma!*, and the musical blithely dispatches him by having him fall on his own knife in a fight with Curly.

A huge hit right in the midst of World War II, the show's determined exuberance and confidence struck deep chords. The show's brilliant choreographer, Agnes DeMille, remembered that soldiers and sailors would stand weeping at the back of the theater, so deeply did *Oklahoma!* evoke what they considered the essence of America. "Oh, what a beautiful mornin'" sings Curly at the beginning, and it reassured Americans that having grown up on that mythic frontier, they were at the dawn of a new era. ◪

Vibrant movie posters for the 1955 movie musical *Oklahoma!* emphasized the fresh-faced, homespun appeal of romantic leads Gordon MacRae (Curly) and Shirley Jones (Laurey), who began her movie career with this role.

California, for instance, had to sell their lands to pay outstanding debts after devastating droughts in the 1860s virtually destroyed the ranching industry. But even as early as 1849 in the northern California goldfields, resentment of "foreigners" provoked violence against Mexican American miners—and the Foreign Miners' Tax of 1850 effectively forced Mexican

Destruction of the Buffalo. Historians estimate that as many as 30 million bison (popularly called buffalo) once roamed the grasslands of North America. By the mid-19th century, however, expansion of the European American settlement, the demand for buffalo robes in the European and eastern U.S. markets, and competition from Indian horses for grazing lands had reduced the herds by many millions. Such pressures intensified after the Civil War—as railroads penetrated the West and new technology enabled tanners to process buffalo hides for leather. Professional hunters flocked to the range and systematically killed the bison. By the 1880s, the buffalo were almost extinct, leaving behind millions of bones, which were gathered in piles, as in this photograph of buffalo skulls, and shipped to plants that ground them into fertilizer.

Kansas State Historical Society, Topeka, Kansas

Americans out of the goldfields (even though they were not "foreigners"). As the 19th century progressed, hordes of Anglo-American "squatters" invaded the expansive holdings of *Californios*, who were forced to seek relief in the courts. Although their claims were generally upheld, legal proceedings often stretched on for years. After exorbitant legal fees and other expenses were taken into account, a legal triumph was often a Pyrrhic victory. In the end, most Mexican American landholders in northern California, like those in southern California, had to sell the very lands they had fought to keep in order to pay their mounting debts.

The migration of Anglos into eastern Texas had played a role in fomenting the war for Texas independence and in bringing about the war with Mexico (see Chapter 13). By the latter half of the 19th century, eastern Texas was overwhelmingly Anglo; most *Tejanos* (people of Mexican origin or descent) were concentrated in the Rio Grande Valley of southern Texas. As in California, Anglos in Texas used force and intimidation, coupled with exploitative legal maneuvering, to disenfranchise the *Tejanos*. The Texas Rangers often acted as an Anglo vigilante force that exacted retribution for the real or imagined crimes of Mexican Americans. Eventually, Mexican Americans in Texas were reduced to a virtual state of peonage, dependent on Anglo protectors for political and economic security.

Similar patterns prevailed in New Mexico, but the effects were mitigated somewhat because New Mexicans continued to outnumber Anglo-American settlers. Earlier in the 19th century, international trade along the Santa Fe Trail had strengthened the political and economic status of the New Mexican elites. Now these same elites consolidated their position by acting as power brokers between poorer New Mexicans and wealthy Anglos. Throughout the Southwest, Spanish-speaking peoples maintained their cultural traditions in the face of Anglo settlement, with the Roman Catholic Church serving as an important center of community life. An influx of immigrants from Mexico toward the end of the century created a new basis for community as well.

Itinerant Laborers

The *vaquero* Rafael Cuen was a highly skilled worker of great value to his employer; he was one of the lucky employees who had long-term employment. But for many workers in the West, itinerancy was the norm; a virtual army of workers and wanderers traveled the western countryside. Most low-level jobs in ranching were seasonal, meaning that workers were forced to move from place to place periodically in search of work. And as western industrialization uprooted many workers from their traditional lives, more and more people took to the road. As Henry George said in his bestselling 1879 book, *Progress and Poverty*, a scathing indictment of the current economic system, "the 'tramp' comes with the locomotive." For George, who had been a prospector before becoming a newspaper editor in California, the fault lay in a system of "land monopoly" that allowed control of land and resources by the few at the expense of the many.

At Miller & Lux, itinerant laborers were Chinese, Portuguese, Italian, Mexican, and Mexican American, in addition to white, native-born Americans. One itinerant laborer on an irrigation crew, Joseph Warren Matthews, was a farmer who had heavy debts. To pay his debts he had taken on a series of grueling temporary jobs, including wage labor for a lumber company in the Pacific Northwest, work in the Alaskan goldfields, pipe laying for a water company, ore smelting, and digging ditches. His situation underlined the precariousness of many lives in the industrializing West.

Homesteading and Farming

Homesteaders and farmers shared that precariousness: not only were 49 percent of all homesteaders unable to "prove up" their claims, but many were ultimately forced off their homesteads by the unforgiving climate of the Great Plains.

For much of the antebellum period, the Great Plains region was known as the Great American Desert and assumed to be uninhabitable. By the 1850s, however, many boosters of western expansion promoted the idea that the Great Plains was a potentially lush American garden perfect for settlement. In this view, aridity was not a problem; the folk belief that "rainfall follows the plow"—that settlement would somehow prevent droughts—even gained credence among some geologists and other experts.

A great wave of settlement of the Great Plains occurred during the late 1870s to the mid-1880s, when rainfall was in fact relatively abundant. But the truth was that the average normal rainfall on the Great Plains was scarcely enough to support farming except in certain river valleys. Years of drought inevitably followed, beginning in 1886 and lasting through the mid-1890s—and fueling farmers' discontent and protests (see Chapter 19). Homesteaders and farmers in Minnesota, Iowa, and parts of Kansas and Nebraska were relatively lucky—those areas had rich soil and adequate rainfall. In Iowa, for instance, farmers had great success with a "corn and hog" farm economy. But other land was arid and unproductive, producing heartbreak for homesteaders and farmers. Between 1888 and 1892, half the population of Kansas and Nebraska was forced to give up and move back east to Illinois or Iowa.

The Experience of Homesteading

Homesteading families on the Great Plains literally built their houses from the ground up: in an environment without trees, they cut the dense prairie sod into blocks and stacked them up to form walls, providing a small window and a door in a "soddy" of around 18 by 24 feet. **Soddies** were a practical solution to a difficult problem on the plains, but they were also dark, dank, and claustrophobic.

As Kansas homesteader Mary Abell explained to her sister: "Imagine living in a place dug out of the side of a hill (one side to the weather with door and window—top covered with dirt and you have our place of abode). No one east would think of putting pigs in such a place." Abell's letters from 1871 to 1875 make clear the hard labor involved in homesteading: in addition to caring for five children, in the fall of 1873, she had been her husband's "sole help in getting up and stacking at least 25 tons of hay and oats." Less than a week later, "one of those dreadful prairie fires" swept through the Abells' land, and they lost not only their hay and oats but also chickens and farm equipment. In 1874, she faced both drought and grasshoppers, and wrote to her family that "none of you have the least conception" of "actual want, destitution." In 1875, Abell died at the age of 29.

Not all homesteaders faced dire straits. Of the 4 million immigrants who came from Germany, the Czech region of the Austro-Hungarian Empire, and the Scandinavian countries from 1865 to 1890, many settled in the upper Midwest and northern plains and became successful farmers. The northern plains region had the highest proportion of foreign-born residents in the nation during the last quarter of the century. These European immigrants formed homogenous ethnic enclaves that maintained the distinctive culture and traditions of their homelands. Swedish immigrants in Minnesota, for instance, spoke Swedish with one another and centered their lives around the Swedish Lutheran church; their children attended Swedish schools and learned to read the Swedish bible, sing Swedish songs, and recite Swedish history; and both men and women wore traditional Swedish dress on holidays. By the end of the century, there were also homogenous ethnic communities of Germans, Czechs, Poles, Hungarians, and Norwegians dotting the northern landscape.

Gender and Western Settlement

The Homestead Act was unusual in allowing unmarried women to make claims; between 5 and 15 percent of homestead entries in different locales went to women in the late 19th century. Many of these women probably "proved up" only to immediately sell their land, rather than farm it themselves: but still, the existence of women homesteaders reminds us that in some ways, gender arrangements were different in the West than in other regions of the country.

The most pronounced difference was in mining camps and towns, which were overwhelmingly masculine. During the Gold Rush, California was up to 93 percent male, and many ranches, including Miller & Lux holdings, were exclusively male as well. Mining towns were known as violent places, and many observers were anxious to establish a more respectable family life there.

Prostitutes from all over the world were drawn to mining towns throughout the late 19th century, but nowhere except in San Francisco were women systematically forced into sexual slavery. There, the situation of Chinese laborers encouraged an exploitative world trade in women. Although by the last decades of the century Chinese merchants were allowed to bring their wives and daughters to America, laborers had no such rights. Furthermore, respectable single women were expected to stay home. The number of Chinese women in America never rose above 5,000 during the 19th century.

The absence of Chinese women encouraged a brutal international trade in prostitution. Chinese women who were kidnapped or purchased from poor parents were sold into indentured servitude or slavery and unknowingly shipped to America to become prostitutes. In San Francisco, an estimated 85 to 97 percent of Chinese women were prostitutes in 1860; around 72 percent in 1870; and between 21 and 50 percent in 1880. They faced a harsh existence. However, some women managed to escape prostitution. Some women married men who had saved up enough money to purchase the contracts that bound them; Protestant missionaries worked to rescue prostitutes, as well.

As these few examples show, settlement patterns of the West produced—at least for a short period of time—societies with unequal numbers of men and women, with different

A Nebraska Soddy. This young family stands proudly in front of their Nebraska soddy in 1884 or 1885, during a time when rainfall was abundant on the Great Plains. A long-term drought began in 1886, however, making us wonder whether this family was able to hang on to its homestead through the coming difficult times.

results in different places. The impact of these disparities continues to intrigue historians, who still puzzle, for instance, over the reasons why several western states were the first to grant woman suffrage (see Chapter 21).

Conquest and Resistance: American Indians in the Trans-Mississippi West

 How did the Indian peoples of the trans-Mississippi West respond to white settlement and U.S. government policies?

The westward expansion of ranching and farming after 1865 doomed the free range of the Plains Indians and the buffalo. In the 1830s, eastern tribes had been forcibly moved to preserves west of the Mississippi so as permanently to separate whites and Indians. Yet in scarcely a decade, white settlers had penetrated these lands via the overland trails to the Pacific Coast. In the 1850s, when the Kansas and Nebraska territories opened to white settlement, the government forced a dozen tribes living there to cede 15 million acres, leaving them on reservations totaling less than 1.5 million acres. Thus began what historian Philip Weeks has called the "policy of concentration": No longer were Indians to be pushed ever westward. Instead, they were to be concentrated onto reservations a fraction of the size of where they had formerly hunted freely.

Even before the Civil War, the nomadic Plains Indians, whose culture and economy were based on the buffalo, faced pressure not only from the advancing tide of white settlement but also from the forced migration of eastern tribes into their domain. In the aftermath of the Civil War, the process of concentrating Indian tribes on reservations accelerated. Chiefs of the five "civilized tribes"—Cherokees, Creeks, Choctaws, Chickasaws, and Seminoles—had signed treaties of alliance with the Confederacy. At that time, they were living in Indian Territory (most of present-day Oklahoma), where their economy was linked to the South. Many of them, especially members of the mixed-blood upper class, were slaveholders. Bitter toward the United States, the tribal leaders cast their lot with the Confederacy on the principle that "the enemy of my enemy is my friend." The Cherokee leader Stand Watie rose to brigadier general in the Confederate army and was the last Confederate commander to surrender, on June 23, 1865.

But siding with the Confederacy proved to be a costly mistake for these tribes. The U.S. government "reconstructed" Indian Territory more quickly and with less contention than it reconstructed the former Confederate states. Treaties with the five tribes in 1866 required them to grant tribal citizenship to their freed slaves and reduced tribal lands by half. The

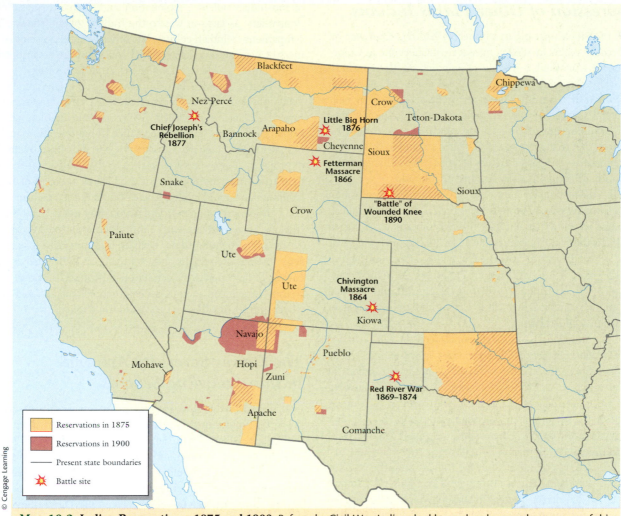

Map 18.3 Indian Reservations, 1875 and 1900. Before the Civil War, Indians had hunted and trapped over most of this vast region. The shrinking areas on which they were confined by the reservation policy vividly illustrate that for the first Americans, the story was not "the expansion of America" but "the contraction of America."

government then settled Indians who had been dispossessed from other areas on the land it had taken from these tribes.

Conflict with the Sioux

The Civil War set in motion a generation of Indian warfare that was more violent and widespread than anything since the 17th century. Herded onto reservations along the Minnesota River by the Treaty of Traverse des Sioux in 1851, the Santee Sioux were angry in the summer of 1862 that annuity payments did not arrive, threatening starvation. Warriors began to speak openly of reclaiming ancestral hunting grounds. Then on August 17, a robbery in which five white settlers were murdered seemed to open the floodgates. The warriors persuaded Chief Little Crow to take them on the warpath, and over the next few weeks, at least 500 white Minnesotans were massacred.

Hastily mobilized militia and army units finally suppressed the uprising. A military court convicted 319 Indians of murder and atrocities and sentenced 303 of them to death. Appalled by this ferocious retaliation, Lincoln personally reviewed the trial transcripts and reduced the number of executions to 38—the largest act of executive clemency in American history. Even so, the hanging of 38 Sioux on December 26, 1862, was the largest mass execution the country has ever witnessed. The government evicted the remaining Sioux from Minnesota to Dakota Territory.

In the meantime, the army's pursuit of fleeing Santee Sioux provoked other Sioux tribes farther west. By 1864, and for a decade afterward, fighting flared between the army and the Sioux across the northern plains. It reached a climax in 1874 and 1875 after gold-seekers poured into the Black Hills of western Dakota, a sacred place to the Sioux. At the **Battle of Little Bighorn** in Montana Territory on June 25, 1876, Sioux warriors led by **Sitting Bull** and Crazy Horse, along with their Cheyenne allies, wiped out George A. Custer and the 225 men with him in the Seventh Cavalry. In retaliation, General Philip Sheridan carried out a winter campaign in which the Sioux and Cheyenne were crushed.

The largest and most warlike of the Plains tribes, the Sioux were confined to a reservation in Dakota Territory where poverty, disease, apathy, and alcoholism reduced them to a desperate condition.

Suppression of Other Plains Indians

Just as the Sioux uprising in Minnesota had triggered war on the northern plains in 1862, a massacre of Cheyenne in Colorado in 1864 sparked a decade of conflict on the southern plains. The discovery of gold near Pike's Peak set off a rush to Colorado in 1858–59. The government responded by calling several Cheyenne and Arapaho chiefs to a council, and with a combination of threats and promises, persuaded the chiefs to sign a treaty giving up all claims to land in this region (guaranteed by an earlier treaty of 1851) in exchange for a reservation at Sand Creek in southeast Colorado.

In 1864, hunger and resentment on the reservation prompted many warriors to return to their old hunting grounds and to raid white settlements. Skirmishes soon erupted into open warfare. In the fall, Cheyenne Chief Black Kettle, believing that he had concluded peace with the Colorado settlers, returned to the reservation. There, at dawn on November 29, militia commanded by Colonel John Chivington surrounded and attacked Black Kettle's unsuspecting camp, killing 200 Indians, half of them women and children.

The notorious **Sand Creek massacre** set a pattern for several similar attacks on Indian villages in subsequent years. Ever since the earliest battles between colonists and Indians in the 17th century, whites had followed the strategy of burning Indian crops and villages as a means of destroying or driving off the Indians. Sherman and Sheridan had adopted a similar strategy against the Confederates and followed it again as military commanders responsible for subduing the Plains Indians. Their purpose was to corral all of the Indians onto the reservations that were being created throughout the West. In addition to trying to defeat the Indians in battle, which proved to be difficult against the mounted Plains Indians, the army encouraged the extermination of the buffalo herds. Professional hunters slaughtered the large, clumsy animals by the millions for their hides, thus depriving Plains Indians of both physical and spiritual sustenance. When the buffalo became nearly extinct in 1883, the Plains Indians understood that their old way of life was gone forever. "Nothing happened after that," recalled one Crow warrior. "We just lived. There were no more war parties, no capturing horses from the Piegan and the Sioux, no buffalo to hunt. There is nothing more to tell."

The Indians were left with no alternative but to come into the reservations, and by the 1880s, nearly all of them had done so. Chief Joseph of the Nez Percé pronounced the epitaph for their way of life when federal troops blocked the escape of his band from Montana to Canada in 1877:

> I am tired of fighting. Our chiefs are killed. The old men are all dead. It is cold and we have no blankets . . . no food. . . . The little children are freezing to death. . . . Hear me, my chiefs; I am tired; my heart is sick and sad. From where the sun now stands, I will fight no more forever.

The "Peace Policy"

Many Eastern reformers condemned America's suppression of the Indians. The most prominent was Helen Hunt Jackson, whose *A Century of Dishonor* (1881) was an outraged indictment of anti-Indian violence, exploitation, and broken treaties. Yet as sympathetic as Jackson was to the Indians' plight, she was not sympathetic to Indian culture; like other white Protestant reformers of her day, she believed that Indians must be stripped of their culture in order to assimilate to American society.

In this she was in alignment with the government. In 1869 President Grant had announced a new "peace policy" toward Indians, urging "their civilization and ultimate citizenship." "Civilization" meant acceptance of white culture, including the English language, Christianity, and individual ownership of property. It also meant allegiance to the United States rather than to a tribe. In 1869, Grant established a Board of Indian Commissioners and staffed it with humanitarian reformers. In 1871, the century-long policy of negotiating treaties with Indian "nations" came to an end. From then on, Indians became "wards of the nation," to be "civilized" and prepared for citizenship, first on reservations and eventually on individually owned parcels of land that were carved out of the reservations. Most Indians acquiesced in the "reconstruction" that offered them citizenship by the 1880s—they had little choice.

The Dawes Severalty Act and Indian Boarding Schools

In order to further the goal of Indian ownership of private property, Protestant reformers in the 1880s found themselves in a strange alliance with land-hungry westerners, who greedily eyed the 155 million acres of land tied up in reservations. If part of that land could be allotted directly for individual ownership by Indian families, the remainder would become available for purchase by whites. The 1887 **Dawes Severalty Act** combined these impulses toward greed and reform. This landmark legislation called for the dissolution of Indian tribes

The Dawes Severalty Act of 1887

as legal entities, offered Indians the opportunity to become citizens, and allotted each head of family 160 acres of farmland or 320 acres of grazing land, as long as they were "severed" from their tribe.

For whites who were eager to seize reservation land, the Dawes Act brought a bonanza. At noon on April 22, 1889, the government threw open specified parts of the Indian Territory to "Boomers," who descended on the region like locusts and by nightfall had staked claim to nearly 2 million acres. Indians did not just lose the lands legally opened for white settlement: many Indians who received individual land titles through the Dawes Act also lost these lands to unscrupulous whites through fraud and misrepresentation. Eventually, whites gained title to 108 million acres of former reservation land.

For Indians, the Dawes Severalty Act was a disaster. Private ownership of land was an alien concept to most tribes, yet Indians received little training for a transition to farming, much less the appropriate tools and supplies. Moreover, the poor quality of their land allotments made farming difficult, if not impossible. In an attempt to strip Indians of their culture, the Dawes Act forbade Indian religions and the telling of Indian myths and legends, as well as the practices of medicine men.

Indian boarding schools, established beginning in the late 1870s, were another attempt to strip Indians of their culture. Children were taken from their families to the Hampton Institute in Virginia and the Carlisle Institute in Pennsylvania, among other schools. There they were forbidden to speak Indian languages or wear Indian clothing. As one 1890 set of instructions from the U.S. Bureau of Indian Affairs put it: "Pupils must be compelled to converse with each other in English, and should be properly rebuked or punished for persistent violation of this rule." The writer Zitkala-Sa, a Yankton Sioux, later remembered her life in an Indian school: "the melancholy of those black days has left so long a shadow that it darkens the path of years that have since gone by."

Indian schools may have had assimilation to white culture as a goal, but they also had a very narrow vision of the place Indians would hold in a white world. Girls were educated for menial jobs as servants; many spent long hours working in school laundries as virtual servants of the schools that were supposed to teach them. Students resisted as best they could by running away, often only to be caught and returned to school again; many adults later resisted the training they had received by returning to Indian traditions. This was the case with Zitkala-Sa. After graduation from an Indian boarding school, Zitkala-Sa taught at the Carlisle School and became a much-praised writer in New York. But later she would undergo a spiritual crisis: she compared herself to a "slender tree" that had been "uprooted from my mother, nature, and God," and lamented that she had "forgotten the healing in trees and brooks." Eventually she left New York, married a Sioux, and became an activist for Native American rights.

The Ghost Dance

At a time of despair for many Indians, a new visionary religious movement swept through Indian peoples in 1890, offering a different kind of resistance to white domination. The **Ghost Dance** began with the visions of the Paiute shaman Wovoka, who counseled Indians that if they gave up alcohol, lived a simple life, and devoted themselves to prayer, white men would disappear from the earth, Indian lands would be restored, and dead Indians would rejoin the living. This message of hope was embodied in the Ghost Dance ritual, involving days of worship expressed in part through dance.

When the Ghost Dance religion spread to those Sioux led by Sitting Bull, and they began days of ecstatic dancing, Indian agents grew alarmed: As one agent telegraphed authorities, "Indians are dancing in the snow and are wild and crazy. *We need protection and we need it now.*" The results of the ensuing confrontations between Indians and authorities were tragic: first Sitting Bull and his grandson were killed in a skirmish with reservation authorities; then a few days later, a trigger-happy military—members of the Seventh Cavalry, Custer's old regiment—opened fire on Sioux men, women, and children at **Wounded Knee** in the Pine Ridge Reservation, killing 146 Indians, including 44 women and 18 children, as well as 25 soldiers. For many, the massacre at Wounded Knee symbolized the death of 19th-century Plains Indian culture. While Indians throughout the West would adapt to a new world with great resilience, working to preserve their cultural practices, there was no question that their old world had been demolished.

Sitting Bull and Buffalo Bill: Popular Myths of the West

Only a few years before he was killed, Sitting Bull had been one of the prime attractions in the entertainment extravaganza known as Buffalo Bill Cody's Wild West Show. Sitting Bull had been a canny negotiator of fees for his appearances in 1885; he required an interpreter, several attendants, and a salary that came to half the annual salary of the typical Indian agent. He also used press interviews while on the Wild West tour to ask the U.S. government to live up to its promises to Indians. If Cody was using Sitting Bull, Sitting Bull was certainly using Cody right back.

Smithsonian Institution, Bureau of American Ethnology

The Ghost Dance. This photograph shows a Sioux performing the Ghost Dance with a sacred whistle in 1890. This religious dance became part of a movement of resistance to white domination that ended tragically in the Wounded Knee Massacre of 1890.

Indian Children at the Hampton Institute

At the Hampton Institute, Indian girls taken from reservations led a regimented life and learned domestic skills such as cooking and sewing. Yet the second photograph here shows girls apparently at leisure: playing checkers and reading, and a doll prominently displayed in the small chair. "Before-and-after" shots like these were used by a number of educational and charitable institutions in the late nineteenth century in fundraising efforts aimed at potential donors.

Q What messages do you think such "before-and-after" photographs were supposed to convey?

Courtesy of the Peabody Museum of Archaeology and Ethnology, Harvard University. 2004.29.5634

Courtesy of the Peabody Museum of Archaeology and Ethnology, Harvard University. 2004.29.5635

these shows revealed just how tightly linked industrialization and conquest were in Americans' thinking—and even in their entertainment.

Industrialization and the New South

FOCUS QUESTION

How did industrialization shape African-American experience in the post-Reconstruction South?

Like the West, the South underwent a surge of industrialization in the last decades of the 19th century. Boosters like the energetic and influential Henry Grady, editor of the Atlanta *Constitution*, proclaimed that a New South had emerged, one hospitable to industry and to Northern investment.

Some people scoffed at such promotional talk in a world that was still decidedly rural, but in fact the pace of industrialization quickened in the last decades of the century, with textiles leading the way. In 1880, the South had only 5 percent of the country's textile-producing capacity; by 1900, it had 23 percent and was well on its way to surpassing New England a generation later. Tobacco also industrialized, with James B. Duke of North Carolina transforming the industry (see Chapter 19).

Railroads and iron also saw a surge in growth. Between 1877 and 1900 the South built railroads faster than any other region in the country. In 1880 the former slave states produced only 9 percent of the nation's pig iron; by 1890, after a decade of extraordinary expansion for the industry nationwide, that proportion had doubled. Most of the growth was concentrated in northern Alabama, where the proximity of coal, limestone, and ore made the new city of Birmingham the "Pittsburgh of the South."

But there were limits to Southern industrialization. It was difficult to catch up with well-established Northern industries. Thus Southerners competed in the few areas in which they could find markets for local crops and resources: textiles produced from their own cotton; cigarettes manufactured from Southern tobacco; as well as lumber, sugar, and iron.

Not all of the wealth from the new industries went into the pockets of Southerners, though. Over the late 19th century, Southern industry attracted more and more Northern capital in a pattern that held true across industries. At first, for instance, Southerners supplied most of the capital in the expansion of the textile industry. But after 1893, an increasing amount came from the North, as New England mill owners began to recognize the benefits of relocating to the low-wage, nonunion South. In the tobacco industry, too, initial Southern capital gave way to Northern financing, especially after James Duke moved to New York in the 1880s. But most dependent on Northern capital were the railroads and iron industries. When in 1886 Southern railroads switched their tracks from the regional gauge to the national standard, the symbolic domination of the North seemed complete.

Sitting Bull and Buffalo Bill. Before he was killed in 1890 during the Ghost Dance movement, the renowned Sioux leader Sitting Bull became an important part of Buffalo Bill's Wild West Show, negotiating shrewdly for his salary. In this remarkable 1885 staged image, the elaborately costumed Buffalo Bill and Sitting Bull appear as virtual equals, both resting a hand on the same rifle.

Having "real" Indians in his show was of vital importance to Cody, who capitalized on the public's hunger for "authentic" spectacular entertainments in his popular Wild West shows. Cody was an extraordinary mix of the new industrializing West, the frontier West, and an emerging culture of mass entertainment. Having begun his career as a soldier in the Civil War, Cody then worked for one of the transcontinental railroad lines (where he gained the nickname "Buffalo Bill" for slaughtering buffalo) before becoming a scout for the Fifth Cavalry. When Cody became the subject of a popular dime Western novel, the most improbable turn in Cody's career occurred: he decided to dramatize his own life in a series of theatrical entertainments. By the year Sitting Bull joined Buffalo Bill's Wild West Show with its band of trick riders and sharpshooters, it required 18 railroad cars to transport performers (including a number of Indians), work crews, animals, and equipment.

The Wild West Show celebrated the white conquest of the West in a series of acts called "The Drama of Civilization," which showed scenes of an emigrant train crossing the prairie, Buffalo Bill rescuing a pioneer family from Indians, and a mining camp. Billed as "America's National Entertainment,"

Heavy Northern investment in Southern industry meant that the South had less control over economic decisions that affected its welfare. Some historians have referred to the South's "colonial" relationship to the North in the late 19th century. One result was that the low wages prevailing in the South made for inequitable distribution of the economic benefits of industrial growth. Average Southern per capita income remained only two-fifths of the average in the rest of the country well into the 20th century.

Race and Industrialization

Even those low wages were unequally distributed, as the politics of race influenced the structuring of industrial jobs. Along the piedmont from Virginia to Alabama, new cotton mills sprang up for a white labor force drawn from farm families on the worn-out red clay soil of this region. About 40 percent of the workers were women, and 25 percent were children aged 16 and younger. Living in company towns, workers labored long hours for wages about half the level prevailing in New England's mills, with their cheap labor giving mill owners a competitive advantage.

At first, African Americans assumed that there would be jobs for them in this new textile industry. And why not? Blacks had worked in mills before the Civil War, and they continued to work in tobacco factories in the postwar era, albeit in the lowest-paid jobs and performing the dirtiest work. There seemed no reason why such a large and inexpensive workforce might not become a mainstay of the mills.

But industrialization did not mean progress for blacks. Instead, it went hand in hand with segregation in the increasingly white supremacist world of the 1880s and 1890s. To attract white workers, mill owners promised them segregated environments. The bargain offered was this: mill workers might not earn very much, but they would gain what one historian has called the "wages of whiteness," a sense of racial superiority that could serve as compensation for their low economic status. Thus the emerging industrial economy of the New South was built around the politics of race. For most African Americans agricultural work was thus the only option.

Southern Agriculture

A major success story, however, was increasing black ownership of land in the post-Reconstruction period, with almost 200,000 farmers achieving that cherished goal. Most black landowners in the South were in the Upper South or coastal areas; others were in the trans-Mississippi West.

Still, most blacks were tenants rather than landowners, and many blacks and whites faced lives of grinding rural poverty. Those who owned land risked sliding into tenantry; those who did not own land found it impossible to make the leap to land ownership. One-crop specialization, overproduction, declining prices, and an exploitative credit system all contributed to the problem. The basic institution of the Southern rural economy was the crop lien system, which came into being because of the shortage of money and credit in the war-ravaged South. Few banks had survived the war, and land values had plummeted, which left farmers unable to secure a bank loan with their land as collateral. Instead, merchants in the crossroads country stores that sprang up across the South provided farmers with supplies and groceries in return for a lien on their next crop.

This system might have worked well if the merchants had charged reasonable interest rates and if cotton and tobacco prices had remained high enough for the farmer to pay off his debts after harvest with a little left over. But the country storekeeper charged a credit price 50 or 60 percent above the cash price, and crop prices, especially for cotton, were dropping steadily. Cotton prices declined from an average of 12 cents per pound in the 1870s to 6 cents in the 1890s. As prices fell, many farmers went deeper and deeper into debt to the merchants. **Sharecroppers** and tenants incurred a double indebtedness: (1) to the landowner whose land they sharecropped or rented, and (2) to the merchant who furnished them supplies on credit. Because many landowners became merchants, and vice versa, that indebtedness was often to the same man.

One reason cotton prices fell was overproduction. Britain had encouraged the expansion of cotton growing in Egypt and India during the Civil War to make up for the loss of American cotton. After the war, Southern growers had to face international competition. By 1878, the Southern crop had reached the output of the best antebellum year, and during the next 20 years, output doubled. This overproduction drove prices ever lower. To obtain credit, farmers had to plant every acre with the most marketable cash crop—cotton. This practice exhausted the soil and required ever-increasing amounts of expensive fertilizer, which fed the cycle of overproduction and declining prices.

It also reduced the amount of land that could be used to grow food crops. Farmers who might otherwise have produced their own cornmeal and raised their own hogs for bacon became dependent on merchants for these supplies. Before the Civil War, the cotton states had been nearly self-sufficient in food; by the 1890s, they had to import nearly half their food at a price 50 percent higher than it would have cost to grow their own. Many Southerners recognized that only diversification could break this dependency, but the crop lien system locked them into dependency.

Exodusters and Emigrationists

Given the difficulties rural African Americans faced—from persistent poverty to dependence on white owners to racial discrimination and violence—it is not surprising that many dreamed of leaving the South entirely. In the late 1870s, a movement called Exodus gained momentum among African Americans who believed that they might have to "repeat the history of the Israelites" and "seek new homes beyond the reign and rule of Pharaoh." Most pinned their hopes on internal emigration to the West, although some explored the possibility of emigration to Liberia as well. In 1875, Benjamin Singleton, a former Tennessee slave, helped a group of African Americans establish new lives in an agrarian colony in western Kansas; three years later, he circulated an advertisement picturing prairie abundance in the hopes of enticing a few hundred more settlers. Instead, in the spring of 1879, some 20,000 African Americans began an exodus to Kansas from all over the Southwest—drawn not just by the advertisement but also by rumors that there was free land available for settlers as well as free supplies from the government. The rumors were false, but many of these **Exodusters** stayed on in Kansas anyway, although not as homesteaders amidst the prairie abundance but as domestics and laborers in Kansan towns, including some they founded, such as Nicodemus.

Race Relations in the New South

The desire to emigrate for better jobs, autonomy, and a place where African Americans could be truly free did not end with the Exodusters. "The disposition among the colored people to migrate now is strong, and is increasing," commented a white Southerner in 1889. There was a net loss of 537,000 African Americans in the South between 1880 and 1910. Economic reasons were important, but so too was the worsening world of white supremacy that arose in that period.

Adherence to the industrial ideology behind the New South, with its emphasis on racial cooperation, was shallow at best among broad classes of whites. Many refused to let go of the legacy of the defeated plantation South. They celebrated the Lost Cause by organizing fraternal and sororal organizations such as the United Daughters of the Confederacy (UDC). The UDC, like the Daughters of the American Revolution (DAR) on which it was modeled, was open only to white women who could prove their relation to the "first families" of the South. Its members decorated the graves of Confederate soldiers, funded public statues of Confederate heroes, and sought to preserve a romanticized history of the slavery era. Several white Southern authors became famous writing stories about this fabled South. Thomas Nelson Page's racist sentimental story "Marse Chan" created a national craze for Southern literature in the 1880s. Published in a Northern magazine, the story was written in what Page claimed to be authentic black dialect, with an aging freedman telling of the glorious days before the war when slaves supposedly had little work to do. Such stories romanticized the Southern plantation, cleansing it of the horrors of slavery.

The national appeal of such stories made it clear that anti-black racism was not just a Southern phenomenon. Certainly, there was shockingly little Northern reaction to the wave of lynchings of black men in the South in the 1890s. Lynchings rose to an all-time high, averaging 188 per year, while the viciousness of racist propaganda reached an all-time low. At a time when many middle-class blacks were steadily gaining economically even as a downward spiral in the rural economy frustrated whites, lynchings of black men were not just extraordinarily violent acts. They were also clear symbolic messages to entire black communities to keep their "place" in a white-dominated society. Ritualized expressions of white power, lynchings were not secret or furtive events, but often well-orchestrated community affairs advertised in advance and sometimes even including men, women, and children as spectators.

In 1892, three respected African American businessmen who owned a grocery store in Memphis, Tennessee, were

Ida B. Wells. A passionate crusader for justice, the renowned journalist Ida B. Wells received death threats after she began a campaign against lynching in her Memphis, Tennessee newspaper, *Free Speech*, in 1892. Forced to leave Memphis, Wells moved to Chicago and continued her anti-lynching crusade in pamphlets, newspaper columns, and public lectures delivered both in the U. S. and in England. Together with Booker T. Washington, Wells was one of the most prominent African American leaders of the 1890s.

taken from the jail where they awaited trial and lynched by a white mob. Their ostensible crime was attempted murder—firing on three white intruders who had burst into their store—but their real offense was successfully challenging the dominance of a white grocery store in their area.

In response to the lynching, the African American journalist **Ida B. Wells** embarked on an extensive anti-lynching campaign involving an economic boycott as well as a series of fiery editorials in her newspaper, *Free Speech*, that called into question the usual white rationale for lynching: the supposed rape or molestation of a white woman. Exposing this common trumped-up charge as "the old racket," Wells ignited the wrath of white Memphis residents and was forced to flee for her life to the North. But there her anti-lynching campaign met with indifference from Northerners until Wells traveled to England on a speaking tour. She received widespread publicity as she called into question how civilized America could be if it tolerated a barbaric practice like lynching; she also touched a nerve back home. Upperclass white Northerners indifferent to the murder of blacks but sensitive to English opinion finally sat up and began to notice her campaign. Her English travels were a brilliant strategy to shake up Northern complacency and challenge Northern complicity in lynching.

The Emergence of an African-American Middle Class

Wells was part of an extensive African-American middle class that came of age in the 1880s and 1890s. These men and women, educated in the emerging black colleges, became teachers, doctors, lawyers, ministers, and business owners. They formed numerous civic organizations, such as the 1896 National Association of Colored Women, which was part of the women's club movement of the late 19th century (see Chapter 19). Echoing the moral reform activities of white middle-class women, its president, Mary Church Terrell, called on middle-class black women to work with "the masses of our women" and to "uplift and claim them."

Such institution building, combined with increasing prosperity, gave middle-class blacks great optimism that "racial uplift" might reduce or even eliminate racism in American society. "We as a race are enjoying the brightest rays of Christian civilization," wrote one bishop in the African Methodist Episcopal (AME) Church. Middle-class blacks believed that through education and self-improvement, they could become "best men" and "best women," seen as equals by middle-class whites. These were not naïve hopes as black entry into the middle class surged in the 1880s and early 1890s.

The Rise of Jim Crow

But these visible successes of middle-class African Americans enraged white supremacists, who denied any possibility of class solidarity across racial lines. Serious anti-black riots broke out in Wilmington, North Carolina, in 1898 and in Atlanta in 1906. Several states adopted new constitutions that disenfranchised most black voters by means of literacy or property qualifications (or both), poll taxes, and other clauses implicitly aimed at black voters. The new constitutions contained "understanding clauses" or "grandfather clauses" that enabled registrars to register white voters who were unable to meet the new requirements. In *Williams* v. *Mississippi* (1898), the U.S. Supreme Court upheld these disenfranchisement clauses on the grounds that they did not discriminate "on their face" against blacks. State Democratic parties then established primary elections in which only whites could vote.

During these same years, most southern states passed **Jim Crow laws** (the name came from black-face minstrelsy; see Chapter 10) mandating racial segregation in public facilities of all kinds. Many African Americans resisted: in 1884, Ida B. Wells, at the time a young schoolteacher, refused to give up her seat in a railway "ladies' car." The conductor "tried to drag me out of the seat," she remembered, "but the moment he caught hold of my arm I fastened my teeth in the back of his hand. I had braced my feet against the seat in front and was holding to the back, and as he had already been badly bitten he didn't try it again by himself. He went forward and got the baggageman and another man to help him and of course they succeeded in dragging me out." Wells sued the railroad, winning her case in a lower court before losing it on appeal.

In 1896 came a tremendous setback for American equality. In the landmark case of ***Plessy v. Ferguson*** (1896),

Booker T. Washington. The most powerful African American leader of his time, Washington built an excellent secondary school and industrial training institute at Tuskegee, Alabama, and gained great influence with philanthropists and political leaders. But several prominent African American writers and activists, including W. E. B. Du Bois, accused Washington of acquiescing in segregation and second-class citizenship for African Americans in exchange for the crumbs of philanthropy.

the Supreme Court sanctioned Jim Crow laws so long as the separate facilities for blacks were equal to those for whites—which, in practice, they never were. At this "nadir" of the black experience in freedom, as one historian has called the 1890s, a new black leader emerged as successor of the abolitionists and Reconstruction politicians who were fading from the scene. **Booker T. Washington**, a 39-year-old educator who had founded Tuskegee Institute in Alabama, gave a speech at the 1895 Atlanta Exposition that made him famous—and has been controversial ever since.

Speaking to a white audience at this celebration of Southern industry and progress, Washington was introduced as "a representative of Negro enterprise and civilization." Assuring his audience that he wanted to "cement the friendship of the races," Washington talked of the "new era of industrial progress" and told the industrialists before him that they should hire African Americans rather than immigrants. "Cast down your bucket where you are," he told them, "among the eight million of Negroes whose habits you know." If they did so, Washington said, they would not only find people to "run your factories," but could also be assured that they would be surrounded by a "faithful, law-abiding, and unresentful" people. In the most famous sentence of the speech, Washington then promised that "in all things that are purely social we can be as separate as the fingers, yet one as the hand in all things essential to mutual progress." In effect, Washington accepted segregation as a temporary accommodation between the races in return for white support of black efforts for education, social uplift, and economic progress.

It was a complex, canny speech, much like the man himself, and Washington's listeners came away with very different impressions. Many African Americans applauded his appeal for black inclusion in the new industrial order; many white audience members simply took away the idea that Washington approved of segregation, vocational training for blacks, and a permanent, second-class status. An eloquent response to Washington came from the emerging African-American leader **W. E. B. Du Bois** in his 1903 masterpiece *The Souls of Black Folk*, a set of essays written between 1897 and 1903. Criticizing Washington for a policy of conciliation and submission, Du Bois reminded his audience that "only a firm adherence to their higher ideals and aspirations will ever keep those ideals within the realm of possibility."

The Politics of Stalemate

Q **FOCUS QUESTION** Why did politicians fail to address many of the most serious economic and social issues facing the nation in the post-Reconstruction world?

During the 20 years between the Panic of 1873 and the Panic of 1893, serious economic and social issues beset the American polity. The strains of rapid industrialization, an inadequate monetary system, agricultural distress, and labor protest built up to a potentially explosive force. The two mainstream political parties, however, seemed indifferent to these problems. Partisan memories of the Civil War mired Americans in the politics of the past. Paralysis gripped the national government.

The Republican Party did not disappear from the South after 1877. Nor was the black vote immediately and totally suppressed. Republican presidential candidates won about 40 percent of the votes in former slave states throughout the 1880s, and some blacks continued to win elections to state legislatures until the 1890s. Until 1901, every U.S. Congress but one had at least one black representative from the South. Independent parties occasionally formed coalitions with Republicans to win local or state elections, especially in Virginia.

Even so, "bulldozing" of black voters (Chapter 17) continued to keep the southern states solid for the Democrats. In 1880, the Democratic Party hoped to build on this foundation to win the presidency for the first time in a generation. Taking their cue from the Republicans, the Democrats nominated a Civil War hero, General Winfield Scott Hancock for president. His opponent was another Civil War general, James A. Garfield. The popular vote was extremely close: Hancock carried every southern state, while Garfield won all but three northern states—and the election.

Knife-Edge Electoral Balance

The five presidential elections from 1876 through 1892, taken together, were the most closely contested elections in American history. No more than 1 percent separated the popular vote of the two major candidates in any of these contests except 1892, when the margin was 3 percent. The Democratic candidate won twice (Grover Cleveland in 1884 and 1892), and in two other elections carried a tiny plurality of popular votes (Tilden in 1876 and Cleveland in 1888) but lost narrowly in the Electoral College. During the 20 years covered by these five administrations, the Democrats controlled the House of Representatives in seven Congresses to the Republicans' three, while the Republicans controlled the Senate in eight Congresses to the Democrats' two. During only six of those 20 years did the same party control the presidency and both houses, and then by only razor-thin margins.

The few pieces of major legislation during these years—the Pendleton Civil Service Act of 1883, the Interstate Commerce Act of 1887, and the Sherman Antitrust Act of 1890—were enacted by bipartisan majorities only after they had been watered down by numerous compromises. Politicians often debated the tariff, but the tariff laws they passed had little real impact.

Divided government and the even balance between the two major parties made for political stalemate. Neither party had the power to enact a bold legislative program; both parties avoided taking firm stands on controversial issues. At election time, Republican candidates "waved the bloody shirt" to keep alive the memory of the Civil War. They castigated Democrats as former rebels or Copperheads who could not be trusted with the nation's destiny. Democrats, in turn, especially in the South, denounced racial equality and branded Republicans as the party of "Negro rule"—a charge that took on added intensity in 1890 when Republicans tried (and failed by one vote in the Senate) to enact a federal elections law to protect the voting rights of African Americans. From 1876 almost into the 20th century, scarcely anyone but a Confederate veteran could be elected governor or senator in the South.

Availability rather than ability or a strong stand on issues became the prime requisite for presidential and vice presidential nominees. Geographical availability was particularly important. The solid Democratic South and the rather less solid Republican North gave each party a firm bloc of electoral votes in every election. But in three large northern states—New York, Ohio, and Indiana—the two parties were so closely balanced that the shift of a few thousand votes would determine the margin of victory for one or the other party in the state's electoral votes. These three states alone represented 74 electoral votes, fully one-third of the total necessary for victory. The party that carried New York (36 electoral votes) and either of the other two won the presidency.

Of 20 nominees for president and vice president by the two parties in five elections, 16 were from these three states. Only once did each party nominate a presidential candidate

Waving the Bloody Shirt

The Civil War cast a long shadow over the politics of the generation that had fought it. For decades after the war, political speakers in both North and South called on voters to "vote as you shot." In the North, this was called "waving the bloody shirt." Colonel Robert Ingersoll, who had commanded an Illinois cavalry regiment during the war, was a master of this genre; a speech he gave to Union veterans in 1876, urging them to vote Republican in the presidential election, is a classic example.

Every state that seceded from the United States was a Democratic State ..., Every man that tried to destroy this nation was a Democrat. Every man that loved slavery better than liberty was a Democrat.

The man that assassinated Abraham Lincoln was a Democrat.... Every man that raised blood-hounds to pursue human beings was a Democrat.... Soldiers, every scar you have got on your heroic bodies was given to you by a Democrat.

Q A. Why did Ingersoll invoke the issues of the Civil War during an election that took place more than a decade after that war had ended?

(Wit, Wisdom, Eloquence, and Great Speeches of Col. R. G. Ingersoll, ed. J. B. McClure, Chicago (Rhodes & McClure Publishers, 1881), pp. 27 and 29)

---

from outside these three states: Democrat Winfield Scott Hancock of Pennsylvania in 1880 and Republican James G. Blaine of Maine in 1884—both lost.

Civil Service Reform

The most salient issue of national politics in the early 1880s was civil service reform. Old-guard factions in both parties opposed it. Republicans split into three factions known in the colorful parlance of the time as Mugwumps (the reformers), Stalwarts (who opposed reform), and Half-Breeds (who supported halfway reforms). Mugwumps and Half-Breeds combined to nominate James A. Garfield for president in 1880. Stalwarts received a consolation prize with the nomination of Chester A. Arthur for vice president. Four months after Garfield took office, a man named Charles Guiteau approached the president at the railroad station in Washington and shot him. Garfield lingered for two months before dying on September 19, 1881.

Described by psychiatrists as a paranoid schizophrenic, Guiteau was viewed by the public as a symbol of the spoils system at its worst. He had been a government clerk and a supporter of the Stalwart faction of the Republican Party but had lost his job under the new administration. As he shot Garfield, he shouted, "I am a Stalwart and Arthur is president now!" This tragedy gave a final impetus to civil service reform. If the spoils system could cause the assassination of a president, it was time to get rid of it.

In 1883, Congress passed the Pendleton Act, which established a category of civil service jobs that were to be filled by competitive examinations. At first, only one-tenth of government positions fell within that category, but a succession of presidential orders gradually expanded the list to about half by 1897. State and local governments began to emulate federal civil service reform in the 1880s and 1890s.

Like the other vice presidents who had succeeded presidents who had died in office (John Tyler, Millard Fillmore, and Andrew Johnson), Arthur failed to achieve nomination for president in his own right. The Republicans turned in 1884 instead to their most charismatic figure, James G. Blaine of Maine. His 18 years in the House and Senate had included six years (1869–75) as Speaker of the House. He had made enemies over the years, however, especially among Mugwumps, who believed that his cozy relationship with railroad lobbyists while Speaker and rumors of other shady dealings disqualified him for the presidency.

The Mugwumps, heirs of the old Conscience Whig element of the Republican Party, had a tendency toward self-righteousness in their self-appointed role as spokesmen for political probity. They were small in number but large in influence. Many were editors, authors, lawyers, college professors, or clergymen. Concentrated in the Northeast, particularly in New York, they admired the Democratic governor of that state, Grover Cleveland, who had gained a reputation as an advocate of reform and "good government." When Blaine won the Republican nomination, the Mugwumps defected to Cleveland.

In such a closely balanced state as New York, that shift could make a decisive difference, but Blaine hoped to neutralize it by shaving a few percentage points from the normal Democratic majority of the Irish vote. He made the most of his Irish ancestry on the maternal side, but that effort was rendered futile late in the campaign when a Protestant clergyman characterized the Democrats as the party of "Rum, Romanism, and Rebellion." Although Blaine was present when the Reverend Samuel Burchard made this remark, he failed to repudiate it. When the incident hit the newspapers, Blaine's hope for Irish support faded. Cleveland carried New York State by 1,149 votes (a margin of one-tenth of 1 percent) and thus became the first Democrat to be elected president in 28 years.

The Tariff Issue

Ignoring a rising tide of farmer and labor discontent, Cleveland decided to make or break his presidency on the tariff issue. He devoted his annual State of the Union message in December 1887 entirely to the tariff, maintaining that lower duties would help all Americans by reducing the cost of consumer goods and by expanding American exports through reciprocal agreements with other nations. Republicans responded that low tariffs would flood the country with products from low-wage industries abroad, forcing American factories to close and throwing American workers out on the streets. The following year, the Republican nominee for president, Benjamin Harrison, pledged to retain the protective tariff. To reduce the budget surplus that had built up during the 1880s, the Republicans also promised more generous pensions for Union veterans.

The voters' response was ambiguous. Cleveland's popular-vote plurality actually increased from 29,000 in 1884 to 90,000 in 1888 (out of more than 10 million votes cast). Even so, a shift of six-tenths of 1 percent put New York in the Republican column and Harrison in the White House. Republicans also gained control of both houses of Congress. They promptly made good on their campaign pledges by passing legislation that almost doubled Union pensions and by enacting the McKinley Tariff of 1890. Named for Congressman William McKinley of Ohio, this law raised duties on a large range of products to an average of almost 50 percent.

The voters reacted convincingly—and negatively. They handed the Republicans a decisive defeat in midterm congressional elections, converting a House Republican majority of 6 to a Democratic majority of 147, and a Senate Republican majority of eight to a Democratic majority of six. Nominated for a third time in 1892, Cleveland built on this momentum to win the presidency by the largest margin in 20 years, but this outcome was deceptive. On March 4, 1893, when Cleveland took the oath of office for the second time, he stood atop a social and economic volcano that would soon erupt. When the ashes settled and the lava cooled, the political landscape would be forever altered.

Conclusion

In 1890, the superintendent of the U.S. Census made a sober announcement of dramatic import: "Up to and including 1880 the country had a frontier of settlement, but at present the unsettled area has been so broken into by isolated bodies of settlement that there can hardly be said to be a frontier line. . . . any longer."

This statement prompted a young historian at the University of Wisconsin, Frederick Jackson Turner, to deliver a paper in 1893 that became the single most influential essay ever published by an American historian. For nearly 300 years, said Turner, the existence of a frontier of European-American settlement advancing relentlessly westward had shaped American character. To the frontier Americans owed their upward mobility, their high standard of living, and the rough equality of opportunity that made liberty and democracy possible. "American social development has been continually beginning over again on the frontier," declared Turner. He continued:

> This perennial rebirth, this fluidity of American life, this expansion westward with its new opportunities . . . furnish the forces dominating American character. . . . Frontier individualism has from the beginning promoted democracy [and] that restless, nervous energy, that dominant individualism . . . and withal that buoyancy and exuberance which comes with freedom—these are traits of the frontier, or traits called out elsewhere because of the existence of the frontier.

For many decades, Turner's insight dominated Americans' perceptions of themselves and their history. Today, however, the Turner thesis is largely discredited as failing to explain the experiences of the great majority of people throughout most of American history who lived and worked in older cities and towns or on farms or plantations hundreds of miles from any frontier, and whose culture and institutions were molded more by their place of origin than by a frontier. The whole concept of a frontier as a line of beyond which lay empty, uninhabited land has also been discredited.

Frederick Jackson Turner, *The Significance of the Frontier in American History* (c. 1890)

The Turner thesis also ignored the environmental consequences of the westward movement. The virtual destruction of the bison, the hunting almost to extinction of other forms of wildlife, the ravaging of virgin forests by indiscriminate logging, and the plowing of semi-arid grasslands on the plains drastically changed the ecological balance in the West. These ecological changes stored up trouble for the future in the form of soil erosion, dust bowls, and diminished biodiversity. Thoughtful Americans began to express concern about these problems in the 1890s, foreshadowing the launching of a conservation movement in the following decade.

For most Americans, however, the exploitation of the West was a matter of pride, not concern. The positive claims of the Turner thesis reflected beliefs shared widely among whites. They *believed* that liberty and equality were both at least partly the product of the frontier, of the chance to go west and start a new life. And now that opportunity seemed to be ending. In fact, to many Americans it seemed that a new and worrisome power had overtaken American life, threatening American liberty: the power of the corporation. ✒

CHAPTER REVIEW

REVIEW QUESTIONS

1. How did the industrialization of the West change American lives?
2. How did the Indian peoples of the trans-Mississippi West respond to white settlement and U.S. government policies?
3. How did industrialization shape African-American experience in the post-Reconstruction South?
4. Why did politicians fail to address many of the most serious economic and social issues facing the nation in the post-Reconstruction world?

CRITICAL THINKING QUESTIONS

1. Both the South and the West industrialized in the late 19th century. What were the major differences in the industries that developed in each section, and why?
2. How were ordinary people's experiences of industrialization different in the two regions? Why? Assess the opportunities that were provided by industrialization as well as its drawbacks in the West and South.

IDENTIFICATIONS

Review your understanding of the following key terms, people, and events for this chapter (terms in bold in text are included in the Glossary).

Homestead Act, p. 489
Chinese Exclusion Act, p. 491
Western Federation of Miners (WFM), p. 492
Chisholm Trail, p. 493
vaqueros, p. 494
soddies, p. 497
Battle of Little Bighorn, p. 499
Sitting Bull, p. 499
Sand Creek massacre, p. 500
Dawes Severalty Act, p. 500
Ghost Dance, p. 501
Wounded Knee, p. 501
sharecroppers, p. 504
Exodusters, p. 505
Ida B. Wells, p. 505
Jim Crow laws, p. 506
Plessy v. Ferguson, p. 506
Booker T. Washington, p. 506
W. E. B. Du Bois, p. 507

SUGGESTED READINGS

For general histories of the West, see **Robert V. Hine and John Mack Faragher**, *The American West: A New Interpretive History* (2000); **Richard White**, *"It's Your Misfortune and None of My Own": A New History of the American West* (1991); **William Deverell, ed.**, *A Companion to the American West* (2004); and **Patricia Nelson Limerick**, *The Legacy of Conquest: The Unbroken Past of the American West* (1987).

On industrial ranching, see especially **David Igler**, *Industrial Cowboys: Miller & Lux and the Transformation of the Far West, 1850–1920* (2001). Influential and useful treatments of the industrial transformation of the West are **William Cronon**, *Nature's Metropolis: Chicago and the Great West* (1991), and **William G. Robbins**, *Colony and Empire: The Capitalist Transformation of the American West* (1994).

Histories that explore the Chinese in America include **Ronald Takaki**, *Strangers from a Different Shore: A History of Asian Americans* (1989, rev. 1998); **Yong Chen**, *Chinese San Francisco, 1850–1943: A Trans-Pacific Community* (2000); **Judy Yung**, *Unbound Feet: A Social History of Chinese Women in San Francisco* (1995); **Erika Lee**, *At America's Gates: Chinese Immigration during the Exclusion Era, 1882–1943* (2003); and **Sucheng Chan**, *This Bittersweet Soil: The Chinese in California Agriculture, 1860–1910* (1986). For a discussion of Southwest borderlands, see **Sarah Deutsch**, *No Separate Refuge: Culture, Class, and Gender on an Anglo-Hispanic Frontier in the American Southwest, 1880–1940* (1987). On mining, see **Elizabeth Jameson**, *All That Glitters: Class, Conflict, and Community in Cripple Creek* (1998). On women, see **Rebecca J. Mead**, *How the Vote Was Won: Woman Suffrage in the Western United States, 1868–1914* (2004); and **Peggy Pascoe**, *Relations of Rescue: The Search for Female Moral Authority in the American West, 1974–1939* (1990).

On the 19th- and 20th-century myths of the frontier, see **Richard White and Patricia Nelson Limerick**, *The Frontier in American Culture* (1994). The Indians' response to the reservation system after the 1860s is discussed in **Frederick Hoxie, Peter C. Mancall, and James H. Merrill, eds.**, *American Nations: Encounters in Indian Country, 1850 to the Present* (2001) and **Robert M. Utley**, *The Indian Frontier of the American West, 1846–1890* (1984).

On the New South, see especially **Edward I. Ayers**, *The Promise of the New South: Life after Reconstruction* (1992). The Lost Cause ideology is examined in **Gaines M. Foster**, *Ghosts of the Confederacy: Defeat, the Lost Cause, and the Emergence of the New South* (1987). The rising tide of white racism is chronicled by **Joel Williamson**, *A Rage for Order: Black-White Relations in the American South Since Emancipation* (1986).

On African-American political action after the war, the best book is **Steven Hahn, *A Nation under Our Feet: Black Political Struggles in the Rural South from Slavery to the Great Migration*** (2003). On black experience after Reconstruction, see **Glenda Elizabeth Gilmore,** *Gender and Jim Crow: Women and the Politics of White Supremacy in North Carolina, 1896–1920* (1996); and **Michele Mitchell,** *Righteous Propagation: African Americans and the Politics of Racial Destiny after Reconstruction* (2004).

 Visit the CourseMate website at www.cengagebrain.com for additional study tools and review materials for this chapter.

The Ironworkers' Noontime

This 1880 painting by Thomas Anshutz depicts workers on their noon break in a nail factory in Wheeling, West Virginia. Providing a striking contrast between the muscular, well-lit bodies of workers at leisure and the dense, dark smoke and grime of the factory in the background, this painting offers visual commentary on the new corporate order of post-Civil War America.

The Rise of Corporate America, 1865–1914

I N THE SUMMER OF **1877**, the same year that President Ruther-ford B. Hayes withdrew federal troops from the South and effectively ended Reconstruction, he called out the military to suppress the most serious labor uprising in the nation's history. The Great Railroad Strike was no local, isolated disturbance: it was a national event that ultimately involved hundreds of thousands of people across America; claimed at least 100 lives; resulted in injuries to hundreds more; and caused the destruction of millions of dollars of property. It also caught many onlookers by surprise: "Sudden as a thunderburst from a clear sky," one journalist wrote, "the crisis came upon the country. It seemed as if the whole social and political structure was on the very brink of ruin."

But the strike was not so sudden as it seemed to shocked middle-class observers: tensions between capital and labor had been building for years. The end of the Civil War had inaugurated an era of rapid economic expansion, but industrialization left many work-ers as permanent wage earners, with little hope of the independence that had been a cherished part of antebellum free-labor ideology. As a roller-coaster economy also subjected employers to boom-and-bust cycles, many resorted to periodic price-cutting and wage-cutting, even while demanding longer hours. The result was that capital and labor had never been more at odds with one another.

America's preoccupation with sectional issues before the Civil War and the gnawing problems of Reconstruction after the war had diverted attention from the economic and social problems asso-ciated with industrialization. But in 1877, those problems burst spectacularly into view. The Great Railroad Strike raised troubling questions that would continue to haunt Americans over the next few decades: Who held power in the emerging corporate order? How was liberty now defined, and whose liberty would the govern-ment uphold? Had America become a permanently unequal society?

A Dynamic Corporate Economy
Engines of Economic Growth
Technological Innovation
The Rise of Big Business
Corporate Consolidation
Mass Production and Distribution
Revolution in Management

Corporations and American Culture
Standardized Time
A National Consumer Culture
Ideas of Wealth and Society
Sharpened Class Distinctions
Obsession with Physical
    and Racial Fitness

Changes in Middle-class Women's Lives
Middle-class Women and Work
The Women's Club Movement
The "New Woman"
Higher Education and
    Professional Organizations

Workers' Resistance to Corporations
Industrial Conditions
The Great Railroad Strike of 1877
The Knights of Labor
Haymarket
The American Federation
    of Labor (AFL)
The Homestead Strike
The Depression of 1893–1897
The Pullman Strike

Farmers' Movements
Resistance to Railroads
The Greenback and Silver
    Movements
Grangers and the Farmers' Alliance

The Rise and Fall of the People's Party
The Silver Issue
The Election of 1896

"Robber Barons" No More

A Dynamic Corporate Economy

 FOCUS QUESTION What were the main engines of American economic growth in the late 19th and early 20th centuries?

The decades following the Civil War saw an unprecedented surge of growth in the economy. The gross national product was $9 billion for the five-year period from 1869 to 1873; it was $37 billion for the period from 1897 to 1901. In the 1880s, manufacturing began to outstrip agriculture as a source of new value added to the economy, underlining America's ongoing transformation to an industrial society. America moved from fourth in the world in production in 1865 to first in 1900; its industrial production now outstripped the combined output of France, Germany, and Great Britain.

But this tremendous economic growth was also accompanied by spectacular volatility. Cycles of overexpansion and overproduction were followed by inevitable cycles of contraction. The boom years right after the Civil War were followed by a crash in 1873 and a depression lasting through 1878, and there were additional depressions from 1882 to 1885 and from 1893 to 1897. Around 10 percent of businesses failed each year, many of these small enterprises. During the depression years of the 1870s, bankruptcies rose from 5,000 in 1873 to more than 10,000 in 1878. The rate of collapse was even greater during the depression years of the 1890s.

Significant labor uprisings correlated with economic downturns, as employers and businesses sought to cut their losses by cutting wages or laying workers off. The **Great Railroad Strike of 1877** occurred during an extended depression; 1886, another depression year, saw 1,400 strikes involving half a million workers. The great Homestead Strike of 1892 followed the announcement of a wage cut of 18 percent.

Still, the enormous growth of the economy in this period meant great opportunity and increased prosperity for many Americans. Titans of industry piled up previously unimaginable fortunes. A flourishing middle class achieved new power. But the working class shared unequally in this rising prosperity.

Engines of Economic Growth

What fueled the dynamic economy of the post–Civil War era? We can start with railroads, the largest single employer of labor in this period. An important spur to economic growth, railroads increased in miles of track from 30,000 in 1860 to some 200,000 in 1900. Railroad expansion meant a greater need for coal and iron, and later steel, to build railroad cars and lay track: steel production soared from 732,000 tons in 1878 to 10,188,000 tons by 1900. The steel industry in turn was a catalyst for a host of other industries, in a pattern repeated across the American industrial landscape.

As a result, manufacturing expanded dramatically in this period. In 1859, the value of American manufactured goods was $1.9 billion, but by 1899 it had risen to $13 billion.

Just before the Civil War, there were 140,000 factories and manufacturing shops across the country; by 1899 this figure had risen to 512,000 and included the rise of industrial giants such as Carnegie Steel.

Growth after 1900 was also dramatic. Employment in Chicago's International Harvester factory, where agricultural implements were built, nearly quadrupled from 4,000 in 1900 to 15,000 in 1916. Delaware's DuPont Corporation, a munitions and chemical manufacturer, employed 1,500 workers in 1902 and 31,000 workers in 1920.

CHRONOLOGY

1869	Knights of Labor founded
1873	Financial panic begins economic depression
1877	Railroad strikes cost 100 lives and millions of dollars in damage
1883	Railroads establish four standard time zones
1886	Knights of Labor membership crests at 700,000 ◆ Haymarket triggers antilabor backlash ◆ American Federation of Labor founded
1888	Edward Bellamy publishes *Looking Backward*
1890	Congress passes Sherman Antitrust Act
1892	Homestead Strike fails ◆ Populists organize the People's Party
1893	Financial panic begins economic depression
1894	"Coxey's army" of the unemployed marches on Washington ◆ Pullman Strike paralyzes the railroads and provokes federal intervention
1896	William McKinley defeats William Jennings Bryan for the presidency
1897	Depression ends; prosperity returns
1899	Theodore Roosevelt urges Americans to live the "strenuous life"
1901	U.S. Steel is formed from 200 separate companies ◆ Andrew Carnegie devotes himself to philanthropic pursuits ◆ 1 of every 400 railroad workers dies on the job
1909	Henry Ford unveils his Model T

The Great Railway Strike. On August 11, 1877, the national magazine *Harper's Weekly* printed this illustration with the caption, "The Great Strike—the Sixth Maryland Regiment Fighting Its Way Through Baltimore." At first glance the illustration seems sympathetic to the strikers being fired upon in the foreground. The article accompanying this illustration, however, talked of the "reign of terror inaugurated by the railroad strikers" and "scenes of riot and bloodshed," such as "we have never before witnessed in the uprising of labor against capital."

Technological Innovation

Growth in manufacturing spurred technological innovation, while invention in turn spurred increased and more efficient manufacturing. Railroads, for instance, ran on a promise of reliability and efficiency, but poorly constructed tracks and rails were a significant hindrance to delivering on that promise. Technological advances like automatic signals and air brakes not only improved railroad efficiency, but aided railroad growth; similarly, the switch from iron to steel tracks not only aided efficient production of railroad tracks but also promoted the tremendous growth of the new steel industry.

No one understood the link between technological innovation and manufacturing growth better than **Thomas Alva Edison**, who invented an astonishing array of devices in this period, from a patented vote-recording machine before he was 21, to the phonograph, the incandescent light bulb, and the kinetoscope (or movie camera). "The Wizard of Menlo Park" was a savvy businessman and self-promoter who kept a sharp eye on the market. "I have always kept," he once told a reporter, "strictly within the lines of commercially useful inventions." In 1876, Edison moved a group of workers to Menlo Park, New

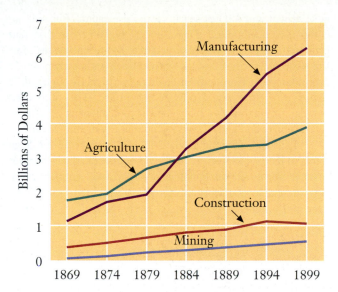

Value Added by Economic Sector, 1869–1899 (in 1879 Prices).

Jersey, to set up an "invention factory" that deliberately mimicked the world of manufacturing. An inventor-entrepreneur, Edison incorporated the Edison Electric Light Company in 1878.

Scientists had long been fascinated by electricity, but only in the late 19th century did they find ways to make it practically useful. The work of Edison, George Westinghouse, and Nikola Tesla not only produced the incandescent bulb that brought electric lighting into homes and offices but also the alternating current (AC) that made electric transmission possible over long distances. From 1890 to 1920, the proportion of American industry powered by electricity rose from virtually nil to almost one-third. Older industries switched from expensive and cumbersome steam power to more efficient and cleaner electrical power. New sectors of the metalworking and machine-tool industries arose in response to the demand for electric generators and related equipment. Electric power, in short, stimulated capital investment and accelerated economic growth.

In addition to the harnessing of electric power, the gasoline-powered internal combustion engine was one of the most important new technological innovations of this period. The first gasoline engine was patented in the United States in 1878, and the first "horseless carriages" began appearing on European and American roads in the 1890s. A host of other inventions in this period spurred economic growth as well, from Kodak cameras to the Otis elevator to Alexander Graham Bell's telephone.

The Rise of Big Business

But technological breakthroughs alone do not fully explain the nation's spectacular economic boom. New corporate structures and new management techniques—in combination with new technology—created the conditions that powered economic growth. Before the Civil War, most American businesses were local, family-run affairs that received little or no aid from the government and did not sell stock to raise capital. But railroad companies inaugurated a new era of big business that had profound effects on business practice. Many businesses after the Civil War organized as corporations rather than single proprietorships: Corporations could raise capital through selling shares in a company directly to the public. They also used boards of directors as a management tool, allowing for shared responsibility and a new scale and complexity of enterprise.

Railroads were big business in every way, requiring huge tracts of land as well as enormous amounts of capital. In order to encourage railroad building, between 1862 and 1871 the government stepped in with extremely generous land subsidies—over 100 million acres of federal lands—as well as monetary subsidies based on miles of track built. This largesse signaled the beginning of a close relationship between government and business in the postwar period—so much so that throughout the late 19th century and into the 20th century, government supported the rights of corporations rather than the rights of workers in a series of legal cases as well as major strikes.

Railroad companies stood to gain greatly if they built enough miles of track. But in order to build, they first needed often-staggering sums of money. The answer to this dilemma came in the form of financiers, bankers, and a wealthy elite—many of whom seized a golden opportunity to obtain power in the new industrial order. The savvy young banker **J. P. Morgan**, for instance, not only helped finance the Albany & Susquehanna Railroad in upstate New York but joined its board in 1870. Morgan would become the most celebrated and powerful banker of the late 19th century, in large part through his shrewd investing in a variety of industries, including Edison's first electric power plant in 1882. By the turn of the century, Morgan's banking firm had built a financial empire. Numerous other bankers would also gain new power through providing the finance capital needed by industry.

But there were financial losers as well as winners in the railroad-building frenzy of the post–Civil War era. More than 300 companies, most of them railroads, were listed on a greatly expanded New York Stock Exchange right after the war. But shaky financing characterized much of the railway boom, which was accompanied by a speculative fever reminiscent of the Gold Rush. The most notorious speculator was the secretive Jay Gould, who built a railroad empire using bribery, trickery, and manipulation. Ordinary investors who hoped to make their fortunes by investing in the railroads often lost their shirts instead when rickety financial scaffoldings collapsed.

The most spectacular and far-reaching downfall of the postwar years was that of Jay Cooke, the legendary financial genius behind the sale of Union bonds during the Civil War. Cooke was undone by his attempts to finance the Northern Pacific Railroad: He ran out of capital in 1873 after selling risky bonds and mortgaging government property. When the Northern Pacific went into receivership, Cooke was forced to close his powerful Philadelphia banking house. Within hours, his closure triggered the crash of the New York Stock Exchange, which in turn began the Panic of 1873. In the severe depression that followed, 18,000 businesses went under.

But it wasn't only Jay Cooke or Jay Gould who participated in the late 19th-century culture of speculation. A wider culture of speculation prevailed in the new corporate society. During periods when the economy was hot, many ordinary people also engaged in speculation—only to lose everything when the economy suddenly cooled off again.

Corporate Consolidation

Corporations began looking for ways to insulate themselves from harrowing downturns in the business cycle. The railroads led the way in tackling this problem. Rather than engaging in ruinous rate wars, railroads began cooperating. They shared information on costs and profits, established standardized rates, and allocated discrete portions of the freight business among themselves. These cooperative arrangements were variously called "pools," "cartels," or "trusts." Still, the railroads' efforts rarely succeeded for long because they depended heavily on voluntary compliance. During difficult economic times, the temptation to lower freight rates and exceed one's market share could become too strong to resist.

Corporate efforts to restrain competition and inject order into the economic environment continued unabated, however. A number of corporate titans innovated with corporate organization, including **Andrew Carnegie**, the industrial leader who built giant Carnegie Steel after the Civil War. An immigrant from Scotland in 1848 at age 12, Carnegie began his career as an errand boy with the railroads, then spent 12 years in positions of increasing authority before striking out on his own, determined to make a fortune. First forming a rail-making concern and then a locomotive factory in 1866, Carnegie turned to steel in 1872, employing the new Bessemer process that allowed efficient production of steel from pig iron. Carnegie kept close track of expenses, paying punitively low wages to workers and forcing them to work long hours.

Carnegie contributed an important innovation to 19th-century business organization: vertical integration. Carnegie steadily took control of all parts of the steel-making process, starting with the mining of the raw material of iron ore and ending with the transportation and marketing of the final product. Vertical integration was a powerful new form of business organization that allowed for unprecedented consolidation and the building of business on a previously unimagined scale.

Another titan, **John D. Rockefeller** of Standard Oil, also innovated with business structure. A legendarily ruthless competitor who led a private life of quiet, prim rectitude, Rockefeller either bought out or ruined his rivals through practices such as "predatory pricing" (selling below cost until he bankrupted a competitor) and demanding secret rebates from railroads that wanted his business. Having invested in oil during the Civil War, Rockefeller incorporated in 1870, and then in the 1880s pioneered a new form of corporate structure, the trust, as a way of making a determined assault on competitors in the oil refinery business. A vehicle for the creation of a monopoly (a term Rockefeller avoided later in life, preferring to talk of "cooperation" among businesses), a trust was initially used by Rockefeller to gain control over the oil refining industry and to create the horizontal integration of one aspect of his business. Soon, like Carnegie, he engaged in vertical integration as well in order to gain control over every aspect of the oil industry, from extraction of crude oil to marketing. By the

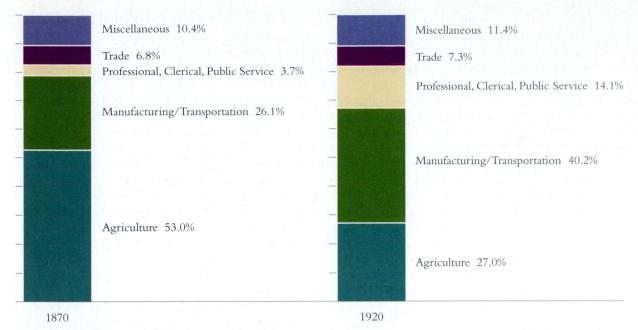

Change in Distribution of the American Workforce, 1870–1920.
Source: Data from Alba Edwards, *Comparative Occupational Statistics for the United States 1870–1940*, U.S. Bureau of the Census, Sixteenth Census of the United States, 1940, Population (Washington, D.C., 1943).

1890s, Rockefeller controlled an astonishing 90 percent of the oil business, with Standard Oil a major force on the world stage.

Andrew Carnegie. Industrialist and business magnate, Carnegie (1835–1919) was an immigrant from Scotland who created a vast fortune in steel, often using ruthless methods to achieve his goals. A classic rags-to-riches story, Carnegie later disavowed the pursuit of money for its own sake, arguing in his famous 1889 "Gospel of Wealth" that the rich should act as "trustees" of their wealth for the public good. One of several "robber barons" who later became philanthropists, Carnegie was famous in his own day for providing free public library buildings around the nation.

Mergers also emerged as an important instrument of corporate expansion and consolidation. By the 1890s, investment bankers such as J. P. Morgan possessed both the capital and the financial skills to engineer the complicated stock transfers and ownership renegotiations that mergers required. Smoking tobacco manufacturer James Buchanan Duke led the way in 1890 when he and four competitors merged to form the American Tobacco Company. Over the next eight years, the quantity of cigarettes produced by Duke-controlled companies quadrupled, from 1 billion to almost 4 billion per year. American Tobacco used its powerful position in cigarette manufacture to achieve dominance in pipe tobacco, chewing tobacco, and snuff manufacture as well.

The **merger movement** intensified as the depression of the 1890s lifted. In the years from 1898 to 1904, many of the corporations that would dominate American business throughout most of the 20th century acquired their modern form: Armour and Swift in meatpacking, Standard Oil in petroleum, General Electric and Westinghouse in electrical manufacture, American Telephone and Telegraph (AT&T) in communications, International Harvester in the manufacture of agricultural implements, and DuPont in munitions and chemical processing. The largest merger occurred in steel in 1901, when Andrew Carnegie and J. P. Morgan together fashioned the U.S. Steel Corporation from 200 separate iron and steel companies. U.S. Steel, with its 112 blast furnaces and 170,000 steelworkers, controlled 60 percent of the country's steelmaking capacity. Moreover, its 78 iron-ore boats and 1,000 miles of railroad gave it substantial control over procuring raw materials and distributing finished steel products.

A weak federal government and a conservative Supreme Court set few limits on corporations in this period, despite significant antitrust agitation in the 1880s and 1890s. By then, many Americans feared the power wielded by tycoons who had established monopolies or monopoly market shares not only in oil and steel, but also in sugar, tobacco, and transportation, among other industries. The **Sherman Antitrust Act of 1890** was an attempt to declare any form of "restraint of trade" illegal, but it was so vague as to be almost useless in the actual prosecution of corporations. Several states passed antitrust legislation, but other states virtually negated this legislation by passing laws favorable to trusts. In 1895, the Supreme Court dealt a crippling blow to the already weak Sherman Antitrust Act when it ruled in *U.S.* v. *E.C. Knight Company* that the federal government did not have authority over manufacturing because it was not commerce—a form of semantic hair-splitting that revealed the conservative Court's unwillingness to curtail the power of big business. Only in the 20th century would the Supreme Court begin seriously to tackle the questions raised by the consolidation of giant businesses and the concentration of power in the hands of a wealthy few.

Mass Production and Distribution

In 1900, Henry Ford was an eccentric 37-year-old mechanic who built race cars in Michigan. In 1909, Ford unveiled his Model T: an unadorned, even homely car, but reliable enough to travel hundreds of miles without servicing and cheap enough to be affordable to most working Americans.

Ford had dreamed of creating an automobile civilization with his Model T, and by the 1920s Americans were buying his car by the millions. The stimulus this insatiable demand gave to the economy can scarcely be exaggerated. Millions of cars required millions of pounds of steel alloys, glass, rubber, petroleum, and other material. Millions of jobs in coal and iron-ore mining, oil refining and rubber manufacturing, steelmaking and machine tooling, road construction, and service stations came to depend on automobile manufacturing.

Ford innovated with **mass-production** techniques that increased production speed and lowered unit costs. Mass production often meant replacing skilled workers with machines that were coordinated to permit high-speed, uninterrupted production at every stage of the manufacturing process. Mass-production techniques had become widespread in basic steel manufacturing and sugar refining by the 1890s, and they spread to the machine-tool industry and automobile manufacturing in the first two decades of the 20th century.

Such production techniques were profitable only if large quantities of output could be sold. Although a burgeoning domestic market offered a vast potential for sales, manufacturers often found distribution systems inadequate. This was the case with North Carolina smoking tobacco manufacturer James Buchanan Duke, who almost single-handedly transformed the cigarette into one of the best-selling commodities in American history. In 1885, at a time when relatively few Americans smoked, Duke invested in several Bonsack cigarette machines, each of which manufactured 120,000 cigarettes per day. To create a market for the millions of cigarettes he was producing, Duke advertised his product aggressively throughout the country. He also established regional sales offices so that his sales representatives could keep in touch with local jobbers and retailers. As cigarette sales skyrocketed, more corporations sought to emulate Duke's techniques. Over the course of the next 20 years, those corporations that integrated mass production and mass distribution, as Duke did in the 1880s and 1890s, came to define American "big business."

Revolution in Management

The growth in the number and size of corporations revolutionized corporate management. The ranks of managers mushroomed, as elaborate corporate hierarchies defined both the

Cigarette-making Machine. James Albert Bonsack's 1880 invention of a cigarette-making machine revolutionized the production of cigarettes. Skilled individual workers were able to produce around 200 cigarettes an hour. With the Bonsack machine, that rate soared to some 12,000 an hour.

From the General Negative Collection, North Carolina State Archives, Raleigh, NC.

status and the duties of individual managers. Increasingly, senior managers took over from owners the responsibility for long-term planning. Day-to-day operations fell to middle managers who oversaw particular departments (e.g., purchasing, research, production, labor) in corporate headquarters or who supervised regional sales offices or directed particular factories. Middle managers also managed the people—accountants, clerks, foremen, engineers, salesmen—in these departments, offices, or factories. The rapid expansion within corporate managerial ranks created a new middle class, whose members were intensely loyal to their employers but at odds both with blue-collar workers and with the older middle class of shopkeepers, small businessmen, and independent craftsmen.

As management techniques grew in importance, companies tried to make them more scientific. Firms introduced cost-accounting methods into purchasing and other departments charged with controlling the inflow of materials and the outflow of goods. Many corporations began requiring college or university training in science, engineering, or accounting for entry into middle management. Corporations that had built their success on a profitable invention or discovery sought to maintain their competitive edge by creating research

Map 19.1 Industrial America, 1900–1920. This map shows that the Northeast, Midwest, and California dominated factory production in the United States from 1900 to 1920. It also reveals the state-by-state distribution of various industries—clothing in New York, automobiles in Michigan, petroleum refining in Texas and Oklahoma, and lumber in Oregon, Washington, and Idaho.

View an animated version of this map or related maps on the CourseMate website.

departments and hiring professional scientists—those with doctorates from American or European universities—to come up with new technological and scientific breakthroughs. Such departments were modeled on Thomas Edison's industrial research laboratory.

Corporations and American Culture

FOCUS QUESTION

How did the rise of corporations reshape the everyday experiences of Americans?

New technological innovations reshaped almost all Americans' lives. Electricity, streetcars, and elevators were just a few of the industrial innovations that changed urban dwellers' everyday relationship to physical space. Even people's relationship to time changed. The world of mass-produced consumer goods also provided a new standardization of experience, and created a new national consumer culture.

Standardized Time

Before the post–Civil War boom in railroads, there was no such thing as "standard" time: instead, many localities and cities kept their own time, derived from the sun's meridian in each locality. If the clock read noon in Chicago, for instance, it read 11:50 in St. Louis, 11:38 in St. Paul, and 11:27 in Omaha, with many other local times in between. This situation played havoc with railroad timetables.

In a sign of corporations' power over American life, in 1883 a consortium of railroad companies agreed to standardize North American time with the creation of four different time zones—much as they exist today—in which all clocks would be set to exactly the same time. This was a corporate act, not an official government act, and some grumbling followed about the arrogance of railroad presidents changing "God's time." But people everywhere quickly adopted "railroad time," although Congress did not officially sanction standard time zones until 1918.

A National Consumer Culture

Consumer goods also standardized American experience as manufacturers produced national brands such as Ivory soap, Quaker oats, and Jell-O. Advertising firms such as J. Walter Thompson and N. W. Ayer & Son began working hand in hand with manufacturers to create national marketing campaigns. Expenditures on advertising increased enormously: from some $50 million in 1867 to $500 million by 1900.

Technological improvements in lithography and the half-tone process in the 1880s and 1890s allowed advertisers to create bright, colorful images that were distributed nationally. Advertising had featured little visual imagery before the 1880s, but multicolor advertising trade cards (including baseball cards from cigarette companies) became a national fad in the 1880s, followed by increased visual imagery in ads in the 1890s and early 1900s. Advertisements became part of a shared national visual culture.

A series of technological breakthroughs in printing allowed new popular magazines and mass-circulation newspapers to reach hundreds of thousands of readers nationally, as well. The conservative *Ladies' Home Journal*, for instance, founded in 1893, achieved enormous success with its profusion of illustrations and photographs, soon reaching over 500,000 readers. Newspapers expanded greatly as well, responding to the demands of a growing population with the first color comics, women's pages, Sunday sections, society pages, and sports pages—where readers could follow the standings of the first national teams in baseball.

Advertising revenues from department stores fueled the growth of newspapers in large cities around the country. These new department stores were glittering "palaces of consumption" that dramatically changed the urban experience of buying consumer goods. In a major retailing innovation, stores such as Marshall Field & Co. in Chicago (1865) and R. H. Macy's in New York (1866) sold a wide variety of items—from perfume to shoes to hats to clothing to household goods—all under one roof in different departments, instead of in different stores. Customers strolled down carpeted aisles—arranged to mimic city streets—and gazed at a dazzling array of goods arrayed in glass cases. Ornate interiors with mirrors and lights added to a sensory experience of profusion, color, and excitement.

Outside of cities, men and women could participate in the new national culture of consumption through mail order. Mail-order catalogues were the brilliant idea of A. Montgomery Ward, who had worked at Marshall Field's firm in Chicago. Starting with a single price sheet of items in 1872, Ward expanded to an 8-page-booklet within two years, then a 72-page catalogue, and by 1884 was producing a thick, 240-page catalogue that listed close to 1,000 items for sale—everything from women's underclothing to entire houses.

Ideas of Wealth and Society

A profusion of consumer goods reached a wide national audience in this period. But among the wealthy, some also practiced what the economist Thorstein Veblen described in *The Theory of the Leisure Class* (1899) as "conspicuous consumption." They sent agents to Europe to buy paintings and tapestries from impoverished aristocrats. In their mansions on Fifth Avenue and their summer homes at Newport, Rhode Island, they entertained lavishly. At one famous costume ball in New York in 1897, guests in satin gowns sewn with jewels impersonated aristocrats. Such aristocratic pretensions extended to marriage: between 1874 and 1911, 72 American heiresses married British peers. The extravagant habits of a wealthy elite gave substance to Mark Twain's labeling of this era as the Gilded Age. The estimated number of *millionaires* (a word that came into use during this era) in 1860 was 300; by 1892, the number was 4,000. While this was not a large proportion of the population, it was nevertheless a highly visible group.

Many among the wealthy, and eventually among a broader middle class as well, justified their right to wealth with an emerging post–Civil War vocabulary of **Social Darwinism**. "The growth of a large business," wrote John D. Rockefeller, "is merely a survival of the fittest, the working out of a law of nature and a law of God." In assuming that market forces were in fact laws of nature, Rockefeller and other industrial titans such as Andrew Carnegie drew upon the influential work of the English author Herbert Spencer, who had coined the phrase "survival of the fittest" in applying the evolutionary theories of Charles Darwin to human society. Social Darwinism was popular among both white intellectuals and a wider middle-class reading public to explain existing racial and class hierarchies in society: according to its tenets, human history could be understood in terms of an ongoing struggle among races, with the strongest and the fittest invariably triumphing. The wealth and power of the Anglo-Saxon race were ample testimony, in this view, to its superior fitness.

Social Darwinism reflected a widely shared belief that human society operated according to principles that were every bit as scientific as those governing the natural world. The ability of 19th-century biologists, chemists, and physicists to penetrate the mysteries of the natural world generated confidence in science, in people's ability to know and control their physical environment. That confidence, in turn, prompted intellectuals to apply the scientific method to the human world. The social sciences—economics, political science, anthropology, sociology, psychology—took shape in the late 19th century, each trying to discover the scientific laws governing individual and group behavior. Awed by the accomplishments of natural scientists, social scientists were prone to exaggerate the degree to which social life mimicked natural life; hence the appeal of Social Darwinism, a philosophy that allegedly showed how closely the history of human beings resembled the history of animal evolution.

At first popular mostly among intellectuals, Social Darwinism was quickly adopted as a way of explaining social and racial hierarchy by a broader public, with "survival of the fittest" becoming a popular catchphrase. Social Darwinism provided a comfortable way of understanding the glaring social inequality of the post–Civil War era: workers were doomed to be permanent wage laborers not because of some fault in the emerging corporate system, but because they were not "fit." The rich, meanwhile, were entitled to every dollar that came their way.

Sharpened Class Distinctions

The well-publicized activities of the wealthy sharpened a growing sense of class distinction in this era. "No observing person can help being aware of an increasing tendency toward a strong *demarcation of classes* in this country," the antebellum abolitionist Lydia Maria Child wrote to a friend in 1877. Different classes "are as much strangers to each other, as if they live in different countries." Throughout the late 19th century, many Americans worried over the class distinctions they saw emerging around them as part of the corporate reordering of American life. Was this sharpened sense of class distinctions acceptable in a republican society that promised equality for all? A source of uneasiness at first, class distinctions became a source of alarm among numerous observers in the 1880s and especially the 1890s, when widespread labor activism challenged the existing social order.

The rise of corporations helped to produce a new, "white-collar" middle class. Corporations needed salaried managers, engineers, office workers, and retail clerks. The expansion of this "white-collar" work—a term that entered common usage during the late 19th century and referred to detachable, starched white collars for shirts—marked a significant change from the antebellum period. Agricultural labor dropped from 53 percent of the gainfully employed in 1870, to 35 percent in 1900, and to 21 percent in 1930; clerical work in the same period rose from less than 1 percent to over 8 percent. The profession of engineer, directly related to the expansion of manufacturing, leapt by an astonishing 586 percent, between 1870 and 1900.

Many members of this new corporate middle class sought to distinguish themselves from the "lower classes." The post–Civil War suburbanization movement was one important spatial realization of this drive for distinction. As early as 1873, *Scribner's* magazine noted that "the middle class, who cannot live among the rich, and will not live among the poor . . . go out of the city to find their houses." By the end of the 19th century, suburban communities of detached houses, surrounded by lawns, were markers of the middle-class status of businessmen and professionals who worked by day in cities and traveled back and forth by train or streetcar to their homes.

Theater, literature, and art were also arenas of class distinction. Before the Civil War, performances of Shakespeare had often been rowdy, participatory, cross-class events. By the end of the century, however, the middle class not only claimed Shakespeare as an icon of "high" culture, but also succeeded in imposing a new set of standards for audience behavior at the theater. Noisy and enthusiastic audience participation gave way to an expectation of total silence during performances as a marker of gentility.

Within literary magazines and books, middle-class critics sought to create permanent "genteel" standards and decried the vulgarity of an extensive popular "low" literature of dime novels and westerns. *Century* and *Harper's New Monthly* published serial novels by great authors and a variety of articles and "tasteful" fiction, including an emerging literature of nostalgia for slavery with virulently racist portrayals of blacks. This white nostalgia for black subordination paralleled growing middle-class alarm over the "insubordination" of the working class in late 19th-century labor strife.

A new art movement, American Impressionism, also expressed a middle-class desire for gentility. Influenced by French Impressionism, artists such as William Merrit Chase and Childe Hassam painted light-flecked landscapes or flower-filled urban parks, recording middle-class pleasures in cities strikingly devoid of workers.

Yet increasingly over the late 19th century, mere gentility began to seem arid to some middle-class artists and writers. Painters such as Thomas Eakins and Thomas Anshutz pioneered a style that would develop into the "realism" of the early 20th century, with its grittier view of city life and less idealized vision of the human form. The dean of American letters, William Dean Howells, called for a new "realism" based on close observation of and engagement with life. His novels explored issues that had rarely been touched by American authors, including divorce, the moral bankruptcy of capitalism, and interracial marriage. Discouraged by the widening gulf between the classes, in 1886 Howells even broke with most of his class in his plea for clemency for the defendants in the **Haymarket** affair (see later section).

The gulf between the classes also alarmed Edward Bellamy, whose 1888 utopian novel, *Looking Backward*, imagined a world in the year 2000 in which "labor troubles" and social inequities had been eradicated through a form of socialism called Nationalism. Bellamy's powerful fictional indictment of Gilded Age society resonated with half a million readers, making his novel one of the most popular of the 19th century. More than 160 Nationalist clubs sprang up in which members of the middle class mulled over the possibilities of government ownership of industry. For some authors and artists in the 1880s and 1890s, the desire to pull away from genteel standards was inspired by a sense of the considerable social costs of the new corporate order.

Obsession with Physical and Racial Fitness

The fractious events of the 1890s induced many middle-class and wealthy Americans to engage in what Theodore Roosevelt dubbed **"the strenuous life."** In an 1899 essay with that title, Roosevelt exhorted Americans to live vigorously, to test their physical strength and endurance in competitive athletics, and to experience nature through hiking, hunting, and mountain climbing. Other writers, too, argued that through sport and vigorous activity, men could find and express their virility.

The 1890s were a time of heightened enthusiasm for competitive sports, physical fitness, and outdoor recreation.

Theodore Roosevelt, The Strenuous Life (1899)

Millions of Americans, both women and men, began riding bicycles and eating healthier foods. Young women began to engage in organized sports and other athletic activities. A passion for athletic competition also gripped American universities. The power and violence of football helped make it the sport of choice at the nation's elite campuses, and, for 20 years, Ivy League schools were the nation's football powerhouses.

In the country at large, the new enthusiasm for athletics and the outdoor life reflected a widespread dissatisfaction with the growing regimentation of industrial society. Among middle-class and wealthy Americans, the quest for physical superiority reflected a deeper and more ambiguous anxiety: their *racial* fitness. Most of them were native-born Americans whose families had lived in the United States for several generations and whose ancestors had come from the British Isles, the Netherlands, or some other region of northwestern Europe. Having embraced the principles of Social Darwinism, they liked to attribute their success and good fortune to their "racial superiority." They saw themselves as "natural" leaders, members of a noble Anglo-Saxon race endowed with uncommon intelligence, imagination, and discipline. But events of the 1890s challenged the legitimacy of the elite's wealth and authority, and the ensuing depression mocked their ability to exert economic

leadership. The immigrant masses laboring in factories, despite their poverty and alleged racial inferiority, seemed to possess a vitality that the "superior" Anglo-Saxons lacked.

Changes in Middle-class Women's Lives

FOCUS QUESTION What were the major changes in middle-class women's lives in the late 19th and early 20th centuries?

After the Civil War, many middle-class women continued to adhere to the ideology of domesticity, assuming that their place was in the home. Yet an increasing number of women began to explore the world of work—whether out of necessity in the turbulent economy of the late 19th century, or because they chose to enter a wider sphere of life. Significant changes in middle-class women's lives included access to higher education and an embrace of a new, energetic athleticism.

Middle-class Women and Work

Historians are not sure how many middle-class women went to work: Statistics of the period do not separate out working-class and middle-class women. By 1900, however, 21 percent of all women were in the workforce, as opposed to 9.7 percent of women in 1860. After the Civil War, women moved into nursing and office work, while continuing to be a mainstay in teaching. By the end of the 19th century, middle-class women were also becoming editors, literary agents, and journalists in larger numbers, while also entering the professions of medicine and law in small numbers. Many college women moved to cities to take up work, living in apartments on their own as "bachelor girls."

The increased interest in work was reflected in literature of the period. Louisa May Alcott's 1873 novel *Work*, for instance, imagined an ideal cross-class, cross-race world of supportive female workers, while Elizabeth Stuart Phelps spoke for many discontented middle-class women in her 1877 novel *The Story of Avis*, in which the despairing heroine ultimately gave up being an artist for her marriage. But it was writer and economist Charlotte Perkins Gilman's 1892 biting novella *The Yellow Wallpaper* that spoke most powerfully of a new domestic claustrophobia. In that brief work, the unnamed heroine desires to write after the birth of a child but is told by her husband and doctor that she must rest instead. As a result she becomes virtually imprisoned in her home. Drawing upon Gilman's own experiences, the novel is a bitter indictment of an unequal society.

Few middle-class observers—men or women—were able to imagine women combining work with family. And yet many women had to do so: the nationally known journalist Jane Croly, for instance, who wrote columns under the name "Jenny June," supported her sick husband and four children as an editor and author during the 1880s before becoming the first female professor of journalism at Rutgers University.

The Women's Club Movement

Jane Croly began one of the most important movements among middle-class women in the late 19th century: the women's club movement. In 1868, the New York Press Club decided to bar women journalists from a celebratory dinner for the great novelist Charles Dickens, who was touring the United States. Croly was insulted and furious, but turned that fury toward a positive purpose: forming the women's club Sorosis (the name was chosen to suggest sisterhood). Composed primarily of professional women writers, Sorosis met regularly to discuss topics of the day and to exchange professional advice.

Sorosis inaugurated a movement of women's clubs among working and nonworking middle-class women in communities across the nation. Distinct from antebellum moral reform societies, the new women's clubs were secular and had a variety of different purposes, from intellectual discussion to civic reform. Providing sociability for women without male involvement or supervision, women's clubs also offered leadership opportunities and provided a bridge to middle-class women's activism during the Progressive era. While many clubs in the 1860s and 1870s did not support woman suffrage, by the turn of the 20th century, the women's club movement was an important source of support for the revived suffrage movement (see Chapter 21). What's more, by 1900, women had used the women's club movement to move into and even take over a variety of civic organizations—a way of practicing politics by other means in an era before women had the vote.

This was especially important in the Jim Crow South, where black men were disfranchised in the 1890s (see Chapter 21). Middle-class black women drew on their extensive experiences in church organizations and Republican aid societies to create effective new networks of public civic organizations. African American women also joined the largest women's social organization of the late 19th century, the Woman's Christian Temperance Union (WCTU). Under the leadership of Frances Willard beginning in 1879, the WCTU engaged in a variety of social reform activities nationally and endorsed woman suffrage in 1884.

The "New Woman"

A clear indication that white middle-class women's positions in society were changing by the turn of the 20th century was the ubiquitous discussion of the **"New Woman"** in the 1890s. A cultural icon of cartoons, illustrations, paintings, short stories, and essays, the New Woman was depicted as a public figure who was athletic, self-confident, young, and independent: she wore the new, less confining fashion of shirtwaists and skirts; rode a bicycle; and even smoked in some images. The painter John Singer Sargent captured this dawning moment of confidence for women in several compelling portraits of strong women.

But to some observers, the New Woman was a fearsome thing, threatening the sanctity of the home and traditional gender roles. A backlash against middle-class women's new roles took different shapes but was often rooted in new "scientific" expertise. Arguing against women's higher education, for instance, the Harvard Medical School professor Edward H. Clarke asserted in 1873 that intellectual work damaged women's reproductive organs. "A girl could study and learn," he warned, "but she could not do all this and retain uninjured health, and a future secure from neuralgia, uterine disease, hysteria, and other derangements of the nervous system."

The Comstock Law (1872) made it illegal to send reproductive literature or devices through the mails on the grounds that they were "obscene," eroding women's already-limited control of reproduction. As women took to bicycles during the bicycle craze of the 1890s, experts warned that it would be unhealthy for women to expend so much strength in physical activity. Women actively resisted these attacks in articles, lectures, and through their own actions, both large and small. Frances Willard of the WCTU, for instance, took up bicycling at age 53 in part, she said, because she knew her example would "help women to a wider world."

Higher Education and Professional Organizations

Women moved into higher education in large numbers in the late 19th century. In the Midwest and the West, public universities as well as land-grant universities (a result of the 1862 Morrill Act) expanded and began to admit women in the 1860s. In the East there were fewer coeducational institutions, but the founding of women's colleges—with Vassar leading the way in 1865—meant that by 1890, women were approximately 40 percent of all college graduates nationally.

Oddly enough, this move into higher education did not translate into greater ease of access to professional education. Women had broken into medical training in 1849 with the admission of Elizabeth Blackwell to Geneva Medical College in upstate New York. But as separate medical colleges gave way to medical schools within universities in the late 19th century, women began to lose ground in medical education. Professional organizations often excluded women as well; at the turn of the 20th century, the American Medical Association, a gatekeeper to the profession, was an all-white, all-male organization. As other national professional organizations were founded in the 1870s and 1880s—including the American Bar Association, the American Historical Association, and the American Economic Association—they too erected barriers to the entry of women and blacks. Professionalization was thus a double-edged sword: while new professional organizations established much-needed uniform standards and training in a variety of professions and disciplines, they also closed ranks against women and minorities.

Workers' Resistance to Corporations

FOCUS QUESTION

How effective was workers' resistance to the new corporations? Why?

A national culture of consumption had grown up in the last decades of the 19th century, but not everyone had equal access to it. Wages that did not keep pace with the booming

The New Woman

John Singer Sargent's 1897 portrait of Mr. and Mrs. I. N. Phelps Stokes captures the vibrant, athletic independence of the emerging New Woman. Dressed in a shirtwaist and carrying a straw boater, Edith Minturn Stokes radiates an air of vitality and energy; her husband by contrast is very much in the background.

The New Woman was a much-discussed phenomenon of the late nineteenth century—the term variously described women who were entering the work force in greater numbers; attending colleges or universities; playing such sports as golf and tennis; and sometimes living independently from parents and family.

Although most New Women were middle-class whites, historians now recognize that there were also New Women among both working-class and African American women.

Many women writers celebrated the New Woman as a sign of women's progress in American life. But a number of conservative critics mounted a fierce counterattack on the New Woman, arguing that women were biologically unsuited both for work and higher education.

Q Why were some critics alarmed by the emergence of the New Woman? Why do you think the New Woman was controversial?

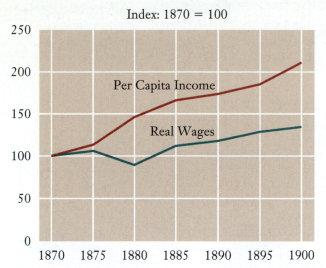

Index: 1870 = 100

Real Wages of Workers and Per Capita Income of All Americans, 1870–1900.

economy meant less money to spend, not to mention a struggle to put food on the table.

Although the average per capita income of all Americans increased by 35 percent from 1878 to 1893, real wages advanced only 20 percent. That advance masked sharp inequalities of wages by skill, region, race, and gender. Many unskilled and semiskilled workers made barely enough to support themselves, much less a family; many families, especially recent immigrants (who formed a large part of the blue-collar workforce), needed two or three wage earners to survive.

"Eight hours for work, eight hours for rest, eight hours for what we will" was a famous slogan of the labor movement in the post–Civil War era. In the demand for "eight hours for what we will," workers voiced their belief that they had a right to leisure time under their own control. As one worker told a Senate committee in 1883, "a workingman wants something besides food and clothes in this country. . . . He wants recreation. Why should not a workingman have it as well as other people?"

Why not indeed? While some alarmed middle-class observers believed that all workers were revolutionaries who wanted to overturn the American government, only a small percentage were political radicals, much less revolutionaries. The truth was more prosaic: workers wanted fair wages and fair conditions in the workplace. They wanted equality in a system in which power had been systematically stripped from them, and liberty seemed to accrue more to corporations than to individuals. Broad-based workers' movements throughout the late 19th century attempted to rectify a situation in which equal opportunities no longer seemed to be available to all.

Industrial Conditions

Conditions in the industrial workplace were often dangerous. The drive for even greater speed and productivity on railroads and in factories gave the United States the unhappy distinction

of having the world's highest rate of industrial accidents. The railroads were particularly hazardous, with over 72,000 deaths of employees on the tracks between 1890 and 1917. What one historian has called "mechanized violence" characterized other industries as well: coal mines threatened underground collapses, explosions, and the release of toxic gases; iron mills and steel mills required work with molten metals at open hearths; textile mills threatened mutilation and dismemberment.

Yet there was little government regulation of industrial safety, and workmen's compensation did not appear until the 1930s. As a result, many families were impoverished by workplace accidents that killed or maimed their chief breadwinner. This was one source of a rising tide of labor discontent. Another was the erosion of worker autonomy in factories, where new machinery took over tasks once performed by skilled workers and where managers made decisions about the procedures and pace of operations once made by workers. Many crafts that had once been a source of pride to those who practiced them became just a job that could be performed by anyone. Labor increasingly became a commodity bartered for wages rather than a craft whereby the worker sold the product of his labor rather than the labor itself. For the first time in American history, the census of 1870 reported that a majority of employed persons worked for wages paid by others rather than working for themselves.

Skilled artisans considered this an alarming trend. Their efforts to preserve or recapture independence from bosses and robber barons fueled much of the labor unrest in the 1870s and 1880s. In 1866, the leaders of several craft unions had formed the National Labor Union, which advocated for an eight-hour day at a time when many industries required workers to work for 10 or even 12 hours daily. Labor parties sprang up in several states; the Labor Reform candidate for governor of Massachusetts in 1870 won 13 percent of the vote. While the advocacy of an eight-hour day would remain a central demand of the postwar labor movement, the National Labor Union would fade in the 1870s. During the depression that followed the Panic of 1873, workers were virtually powerless to push their agenda.

The National Labor Union withered away in the depression of the 1870s, but industrial violence escalated. In the anthracite-coal fields of eastern Pennsylvania, the Molly Maguires (an amalgam of a labor union and a secret order of Irish Americans) carried out guerrilla warfare against mine owners. In the later 1870s, the Greenbackers (a group that urged currency expansion to end deflation) and labor reformers formed a coalition that elected several local and state officials plus 14 congressmen in 1878. In 1880, the Greenback-Labor candidate for president won 3 percent of the popular vote.

The Great Railroad Strike of 1877

The worst labor violence in U.S. history up to that time, the Great Railroad Strike of 1877 underscored the deep discontent of workers nationwide. In July, the Baltimore and Ohio Railroad cut wages by 10 percent—its third recent wage reduction. B & O workers had seen their wages drop steadily ever since 1873, a depression year. When workers in Martinsburg, West Virginia walked out in protest, workers up and down the B & O line joined them.

HISTORY THROUGH FILM

The Molly Maguires (1970)

Directed by Martin Ritt.
Starring Richard Harris (James McParlan), Sean Connery (Jack Kehoe),
Samantha Eggar (Mary Raines).

The gritty realism of *The Molly Maguires* offers a compelling portrait of labor conditions in 19th-century coal mines. Filmed on location in the anthracite region of eastern Pennsylvania, the film takes the viewer deep into the earth where Irish American miners labored long hours for a pittance at the dangerous, back-breaking, health-destroying job of bringing out the coal that heated American homes and fueled American industry.

These mining communities constituted a microcosm of ethnic and class tensions in American society. Most of the mine owners were Scots-Irish Presbyterians; many foremen, skilled workers, and police were English or Welsh Protestants; most of the unskilled workers were Irish Catholics. This was a volatile mixture, as vividly depicted in the movie. The skilled miners had formed the Workingmen's Benevolent Association, which had won modest gains for its members by 1873. Many Irish belonged to the Ancient Order of Hibernians, which aided sick miners and supported the widows and orphans of those who died—and there were many such. The inner circle of this order called itself the Molly Maguires, after an anti-landlord organization in Ireland that resisted the eviction of tenants. In Pennsylvania, the Mollies retaliated against exploitative owners, unpopular foremen, and the police with acts of sabotage, violence, intimidation, and murder.

The economic depression following the Panic of 1873 exacerbated tensions and violence. The owners hired the Pinkerton detective agency to infiltrate and gather criminal evidence against the Mollies. Detective James McParlan went to work in the mines, gained the confidence of his fellow Irish Americans, and was eventually admitted to the Molly Maguires. For more than two years, he lived a dangerous double existence (foreshortened in the movie) that would have meant instant death if the Mollies had discovered his mole role. In a series of widely publicized trials from 1875 to 1877 in which McParlan was the main witness, dozens of Molly Maguires were convicted and 20 were hanged.

Sean Connery (Jack Kehoe, right) and Art Lund (a fellow Molly Maguire) prepare to dynamite a coal train in *The Molly Maguires.*

© Bettmann/CORBIS

Richard Harris and Sean Connery are superb as McParlan and Jack Kehoe, the Mollies' leader. The real Jamie McParlan courted the sister-in-law of one of the Mollies; the film expands this into a poignant romance between McParlan and a retired miner's beautiful daughter. The love interest fits with the film's effective presentation of McParlan's conflicted conscience and the moral ambiguity of his role as the agent of justice (as defined by the ruling class), which requires him to betray the men with whom he had lived, sung, plotted, swapped stories, and carried out raids. What were McParlan's real motives? The film does not successfully answer that question, but neither does history. Most viewers, however, will take from this movie a feeling of empathy with the Mollies, whose protest against terrible conditions drove them to desperate acts of violence. ◢

The strike touched a nerve nationally and spread rapidly; within a few days, what had begun as a local protest had traveled to Baltimore, Philadelphia, Pittsburgh, New York, Louisville, Chicago, St. Louis, Kansas City, and San Francisco. Women as well as men joined angry crowds in the streets; workers from a variety of industries walked out in sympathy; and in some places the strike crossed both gender and racial lines. Strikers and militia in a number of cities fired on each other, and workers set fire to railroad cars and depots. Alarmed at the possibility of a "national insurrection," President Hayes called in the army. The strike finally ended in early August—"The strikers have been put down by *force*," Hayes noted in his diary.

Urban Fortresses. In the 1880s and 1890s, numerous armories were built in cities across the country to protect against a perceived threat from the "dangerous classes"—workers and the poor. This immense, castle-like 1894 armory in Brooklyn, New York, was meant to inspire awe.

But this spontaneous, unorganized labor upheaval did not produce solutions to workers' dilemmas. On the contrary, fears of a workers' "insurrection" led to a new cohesion in the middle class, which began to talk of a "war" between capital and labor. Not only did the middle class strongly support military intervention in the wake of 1877, but it also supported the construction of armories in the nation's largest cities.

The Knights of Labor

Many workers in the wake of 1877 looked to a new labor organization for inspiration. The **Knights of Labor** had been founded in 1869 in Philadelphia as a secret fraternal organization, one of many such artisan societies in eastern cities. Under the leadership of Terence Powderly, a machinist by trade, it became public in 1879 and then expanded rapidly in the wake of the Great Railroad Strike, finally achieving hundreds of thousands of members nationally in the 1880s.

The Knights of Labor offered workers an inspiring vision of an alternative to competitive corporate society. Rooted in the artisan republicanism of the antebellum era

(see Chapter 7), with even its name suggesting a nostalgic look backward, the Knights opposed the wage labor system, declaring "an inevitable and irresistible conflict between the wage-system of labor and republican system of government." Instead it offered an inclusive vision of a "cooperative commonwealth" that would include both men and women and would not discriminate by race. In its platform it called for an eight-hour day, equal pay for women, public ownership of railroads, abolition of child labor, and a graduated income tax.

By the late 1870s, the Knights were a potent national federation of unions—or "assemblies," as they were officially known—and departed in several respects from the norm of labor organization at that time. Most of its assemblies were organized by industry rather than by craft, giving many unskilled and semiskilled workers union representation for the first time. It was also a more inclusive labor organization than most, although in local practice the Knights did not live up to its lofty ideals. Only some assemblies admitted women or blacks. Tendencies toward exclusivity of craft, gender, and race divided and weakened many assemblies.

A paradox of purpose also plagued the Knights. Most members wanted to improve their lot within the existing system through higher wages, shorter hours, better working conditions—the bread-and-butter goals of working people. This meant collective bargaining with employers; it also meant strikes. The assemblies won some strikes and lost some. Powderly and the Knights' national leadership discouraged strikes, however, partly out of practicality: a losing strike often destroyed an assembly, as employers replaced strikes with strikebreakers, or "scabs."

Another reason for Powderly's antistrike stance was philosophical. Strikes constituted a tacit recognition of the legitimacy of the wage system. In Powderly's view, wages siphoned off to capital a part of the wealth created by labor. The Knights, he said, intended "to secure to the workers the full enjoyment of the wealth they create." This was a goal grounded both in the past independence of skilled workers and in a radical vision of the future, in which workers' cooperatives would own the means of production. "There is no reason," said Powderly, "why labor cannot, through cooperation, own and operate mines, factories, and railroads."

Terence Powderly, *Thirty Years of Labor* (1890)

The Knights did sponsor several modest workers' cooperatives. Their success was limited, though, partly from lack of capital and of management experience and partly because even the most skilled craftsmen found it difficult to compete with machines in a mass-production economy. Ironically, the Knights gained their greatest triumphs through strikes. In 1884 and 1885, successful strikes against the Union Pacific and Missouri Pacific railroads won prestige and a rush of new members, which by 1886 totaled 700,000. Expectations ran high, but defeat in a second strike against the Missouri Pacific in spring 1886 was a serious blow. Then came the Haymarket bombing in Chicago.

Haymarket

Chicago was a center of labor activism and radicalism. In 1878, the newly formed Socialist Labor Party won 14 percent of the vote in the city, electing five aldermen and four members of the Illinois legislature. With recovery from the depression after 1878, the Socialist Labor Party fell onto lean times. Four-fifths of its members were foreign-born, mostly Germans. Internal squabbles generated several offshoots of the party in the 1880s. One of these embraced anarchism and called for the violent destruction of the capitalist system so that a new socialist order could be built on its ashes. Anarchists infiltrated some trade unions in Chicago and leaped aboard the bandwagon of a national movement centered in that city for a general strike on May 1, 1886, to achieve the eight-hour workday. Chicago police were notoriously hostile to labor organizers and strikers, so the scene was set for a violent confrontation.

The May 1 showdown coincided with a strike at the McCormick farm machinery plant in Chicago. A fight outside the gates on May 3 brought a police attack on the strikers in which four people were killed. Anarchists then organized a protest meeting at Haymarket Square on May 4. Toward the end of the meeting, when the rain-soaked crowd was already dispersing, the police suddenly arrived in force. When someone threw a bomb into their midst, the police opened fire. When the wild melee was over, 50 people lay wounded and 10 dead, 6 of them policemen.

Haymarket set off a wave of hysteria against labor radicals. Police in Chicago rounded up hundreds of labor leaders. Eight anarchists (seven of them German-born) went on trial for conspiracy to commit murder, although no evidence turned up to prove that any of them had thrown the bomb. All eight were convicted; seven were sentenced to hang. One of the men committed suicide; the governor commuted the sentences of two others to life imprisonment; the remaining four were hanged on November 11, 1887. The case became a cause célèbre that bitterly divided the country. Many workers, civil libertarians, and middle-class citizens who were troubled by the events branded the verdicts judicial murder, but most Americans applauded the summary repression of radicalism they regarded as un-American.

The Knights of Labor were caught in this anti-labor backlash. Although the Knights had nothing to do with the Haymarket affair and Powderly had repeatedly denounced anarchism, his opposition to the wage system sounded to many Americans suspiciously like socialism, perhaps even anarchism. Membership in the Knights plummeted from 700,000 in spring 1886 to fewer than 100,000 by 1890.

The American Federation of Labor (AFL)

As the Knights of Labor waned, a new national labor organization waxed. Founded in 1886, the American Federation of Labor (AFL) was a loosely affiliated association of unions organized by trade or craft: cigar-makers, machinists, carpenters, typographers, plumbers, painters, and so on. Most AFL members were skilled workers. The leader of the AFL, **Samuel F. Gompers**, was a onetime Marxist and cigar maker who was reelected to the AFL presidency every year from 1896 until his death in 1924.

Many workers understood that the only hope for economic improvement lay in organizing unions powerful enough to wrest wage concessions from reluctant employers. But this was no easy task. Federal and state governments had shown themselves ready to use military force to break strikes. The courts, following the lead of the U.S. Supreme Court, repeatedly found unions in violation of the Sherman Antitrust Act, even though that act had been intended to control corporations, not unions. Judges in most states usually granted employer requests for injunctions—court orders that barred striking workers from picketing their place of employment (and thus from obstructing employer efforts to hire replacement workers). Before 1916, no federal laws protected workers' right to organize or required employers to bargain with the unions to which their workers belonged.

This hostile legal environment retarded the growth of unions from the 1890s through the 1920s. It also made the AFL, the major labor organization of those years, more timid and conservative than it had been before the depression of the 1890s. Few AFL members were women and blacks. The AFL accepted capitalism and the wage system. Instead of agitating for governmental regulation of the economy and the workplace, it concentrated on the bread-and-butter issues of better conditions, higher wages, shorter hours, and occupational safety within the system—"pure and simple unionism," as Gompers called it.

The AFL had concluded that labor's powerful opponents in the legislatures and the courts would find ways to undermine whatever governmental gains organized labor managed to achieve. That conclusion was reinforced by a 1905 ruling, *Lochner v. New York*, in which the U.S. Supreme Court declared unconstitutional a seemingly innocent New York state law that limited bakery employees to a 10-hour day.

Yet in its early years the AFL showed considerable vitality under the leadership of Gompers, with its membership quadrupling from less than a half million in 1897 to more than 2 million in 1904. Craft unions negotiated contracts, or trade agreements, with employers that stipulated the wages workers were to be paid, the hours they were to work, and the rules under which new workers would be accepted into the trade. These agreements were accorded the same legal protection that American law bestowed on other commercial contracts.

Still, the AFL had limited success. Its 2 million members represented only a small portion of the industrial workforce. Its concentration among craft workers, moreover, distanced it from most workers, who were not skilled. Unskilled and semiskilled workers could only be organized into an industrial union that offered membership to all workers in a particular industry. Gompers understood the importance of such unions and allowed several of them, including the United Mine Workers (UMW) and the International Ladies Garment Workers Union (ILGWU), to participate in the AFL. But AFL ranks remained dominated by skilled workers who looked down upon the unskilled, especially immigrants. AFL members demonstrated even worse prejudice toward black workers, with more than 10 AFL unions excluding African Americans from membership in the early 20th century.

The Homestead Strike

During the 1890s, strikes occurred with a frequency and a fierceness that made 1877 and 1886 look like mere preludes to the main event. The most dramatic confrontation took place in 1892 at the **Homestead** plant (near Pittsburgh) of the Carnegie Steel Company. Carnegie and his plant manager, Henry Clay Frick, were determined to break the power of the country's strongest union, the Amalgamated Association of Iron, Steel, and Tin Workers. Frick used a dispute over wages and work rules as an opportunity to close the plant (a "lockout"), preparatory to reopening it with non-union workers. When the union called a strike and refused to leave the plant, Frick called in 300 Pinkerton guards to oust them. (The Pinkerton detective agency had evolved since the Civil War era into a private security force that specialized in antiunion activities.) A full-scale gun battle between strikers and Pinkertons erupted on July 6, leaving nine strikers and seven Pinkertons dead and scores wounded. Frick persuaded the governor to send in 8,000 militia to protect the strikebreakers, and the plant reopened. Public sympathy, much of it pro-union at first, shifted when an anarchist tried to murder Frick on July 23. The failed Homestead strike crippled the Amalgamated Association; another strike against U.S. Steel (successor of Carnegie Steel) in 1901 destroyed it.

The Depression of 1893–1897

By the 1890s, the use of state militias to protect strikebreakers had become common. Events after 1893 brought an escalation of conflict. The most serious economic crisis since the 1873–78 depression was triggered by the Panic of 1893, a collapse of the stock market that plunged the economy into a severe four-year depression. The bankruptcy of the Reading Railroad and the National Cordage Company in early 1893 set off a process that by the end of the year had caused 491 banks and 15,000 other businesses to fail. By mid-1894, the unemployment rate had risen to more than 15 percent.

An Ohio reformer named Jacob Coxey conceived the idea of sending Congress a "living petition" of unemployed workers to press for appropriations to put them to work on road building and other public works. "Coxey's army," as the press dubbed it, inspired other groups to hit the road and ride the rails to Washington during 1894. This descent of the unemployed on the capital provoked arrests by federal marshals and troops, and ended in anticlimax when Coxey and others were arrested for trespassing on the Capitol grounds. Coxey's idea for using public works to relieve unemployment turned out to be 40 years ahead of its time.

The Pullman Strike

The explosive tensions between capital and labor fueled the **Pullman strike** of 1894. George M. Pullman had made a fortune in the manufacture of sleeping cars and other rolling stock for railroads. Workers in his large factory complex lived in the company town of Pullman just south of Chicago, with paved streets, clean parks, and decent houses rented from the company. But Pullman controlled many aspects of their lives, including banning liquor from the town and punishing workers whose behavior did not suit his ideas of decorum. When

Pennsylvania Militia at Carnegie's Homestead Steel Mill, 1892. After the shootout between striking workers and Pinkerton guards, the Pennsylvania militia reopened the mills and protected strikebreakers from striking workers. This photograph shows the militia using steel beams manufactured by the mill as a makeshift barricade.

the Panic of 1893 caused a sharp drop in orders for Pullman cars, the company laid off one-third of its workforce and cut wages for the rest by 30 percent, but did not reduce company house rents or company store prices. Pullman refused to negotiate with a workers' committee, which called a strike and appealed to the American Railway Union (ARU) for help.

The ARU had been founded the year before by Eugene V. Debs. A native of Indiana, Debs had been elected secretary of the Brotherhood of Locomotive Firemen in 1875 at the age of 20. By 1893, he had become convinced that the conservative stance of the various craft unions in railroading (firemen, engineers, brakemen, and so forth) was divisive and contrary to the best interests of labor. He formed the ARU to include all railroad workers in one union. With 150,000 members, the union won a strike against the Great Northern Railroad in spring 1894. When George Pullman refused the ARU's offer to arbitrate the strike of Pullman workers, Debs launched a boycott by which ARU members would refuse to run any trains that included Pullman cars. When the railroads attempted to fire the ARU sympathizers, whole train crews went on strike and quickly paralyzed rail traffic.

Over the protests of Illinois Governor John P. Altgeld, who sympathized with the strikers, President Grover Cleveland sent in federal troops. That action inflamed violence instead of containing it. The U.S. attorney general (a former railroad lawyer) obtained a federal injunction against Debs under the Sherman Antitrust Act on grounds that the boycott and the strike were a conspiracy in restraint of trade. This creative use of the Sherman Act was upheld by the Supreme Court in 1895 and became a powerful weapon against labor unions in the hands of conservative judges.

For a week in July 1894, the Chicago railroad yards resembled a war zone. Millions of dollars of equipment went up in smoke. Thirty-four people, mostly workers, were killed. Finally, 14,000 state militia and federal troops restored order and broke the strike. Debs went to jail (for violation of the federal injunction) for six months. He emerged from prison a socialist.

To many Americans, 1894 was the worst year of crisis since the Civil War. The Pullman strike was only the most dramatic event of a year in which 750,000 workers went on strike and another 3 million were unemployed. But it was a surge of discontent from farmers that wrenched American politics off its foundations in the 1890s.

Farmers' Movements

Q FOCUS QUESTION What provoked the farmer protest movements in the last third of the 19th century?

Between 1870 and 1890, America's soaring grain production increased three times as fast as the American population. Only rising exports could sustain such expansion in farm production. But by the 1880s, the improved efficiency of large farms in Eastern Europe brought intensifying competition and consequent price declines, especially for wheat, just as competition from Egypt and India had eroded prices for American cotton. Prices on the world market for these two staples of American agriculture—wheat and cotton—fell about 60 percent from 1870 to 1895, while the

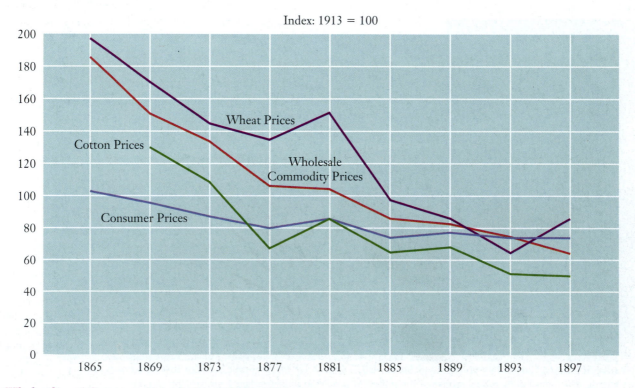

Index: 1913 = 100

Wholesale and Consumer Price Indexes, 1865–1897.

wholesale price index for all commodities (including other farm products) declined by 45 percent during the same period. Not surprisingly, distress was greatest and protest loudest in the wheat-producing West and the cotton-producing South.

Victims of a world market largely beyond their control, farmers lashed out at targets nearer home: railroads, banks, commission merchants, and the monetary system. In truth, these institutions did victimize farmers, although not always intentionally.

Resistance to Railroads

The power wielded by the railroad companies inevitably aroused hostility. Companies often charged less for long hauls than for short hauls in areas with little or no competition. The rapid proliferation of tracks produced overcapacity in some areas, which led to rate-cutting wars that benefited some shippers at the expense of others—usually large shippers at the expense of small ones. To avoid "ruinous competition" (as the railroads viewed it), companies formed "pools" by which they divided traffic and fixed their rates. Some of these practices made sound economic sense, but others appeared discriminatory and exploitative. Railroads gave credence to farmers' charges of monopoly exploitation by keeping rates higher in areas with no competition (most farmers lived in areas served by only one line) than in regions with competition. Grain elevators, many of which were owned by railroad companies, came under attack for cheating farmers by rigging the classification of their grain.

Farmers responded by organizing cooperatives to sell crops and buy supplies. The umbrella organization for many of these cooperatives was the Patrons of Husbandry, known as the Grange, founded in 1867. But because farmers could not build their own railroads, they organized "antimonopoly" parties and elected state legislators who enacted "Granger laws" in several states. These laws established railroad commissions that fixed maximum freight rates and warehouse charges. Railroads challenged the laws in court. Eight challenges made their way to the U.S. Supreme Court, which in *Munn* v. *Illinois* (1877) ruled that states could regulate businesses clothed with a "public interest"—railroads and other common carriers, millers, innkeepers, and the like. It was a landmark decision.

The welter of different and sometimes conflicting state laws, plus rulings by the U.S. Supreme Court in the 1880s that states could not regulate interstate railroad traffic, brought a drive for federal regulation. After years of discussion, Congress passed the Interstate Commerce Act in 1887. This law, like most such laws, reflected compromise between the varying viewpoints of shippers, railroads, and other pressure groups. It outlawed pools, discriminatory rates, long-haul versus short-haul differentials, and rebates to favored shippers. It required that freight and passenger rates must be "reasonable and just." What that meant was not entirely clear, but the law created the Interstate Commerce Commission (ICC) to define the requirement on a case-by-case basis. Because the ICC had minimal enforcement powers, however, federal courts frequently refused to issue the orders the ICC requested. Staffed by men who were knowledgeable about railroading, the ICC often sympathized with the viewpoint of the industry it was supposed to regulate. Nevertheless, its powers of publicity had some effect on railroad practices, and freight rates continued to decline during this period as railroad operating efficiency improved.

The Greenback and Silver Movements

The long period of price deflation from 1865 to 1897, unique in American history, made credit even more costly for farmers. When the price of wheat or cotton declined, farmers earned even less money with which to pay back loans from country

The Kansas State Historical Society Topeka, Kansas

Returning to Illinois, 1894. This photograph shows one of the thousands of farm families who had moved into Kansas, Nebraska, and other plains states in the wet years of the 1870s and 1880s, only to give up during the dry years of the 1890s. Their plight added fuel to the fire of rural unrest and protest during those years.

store merchants. Thus it was not surprising that angry farmers who denounced banks or country store merchants for gouging them also attacked a monetary system that brought deflation.

The federal government's monetary policies worsened deflation problems. The 1862 emergency wartime issuance of treasury "greenback" notes (see Chapter 15) had created a dual currency—gold and greenbacks—with the greenback dollar's value relative to gold rising and falling according to Union military fortunes. After the war, the Treasury moved to bring the greenback dollar to par with gold by reducing the amount of greenbacks in circulation. This limitation of the money supply produced deflationary pressures, with the South and West suffering from downward pressures on prices they received for their crops. Western farmers were particularly vociferous in their protests against this situation, which introduced a new sectional conflict into politics—not North against South, but East against West.

Many farmers in 1876 and 1880 supported the Greenback Party, whose platform called for the issuance of more U.S. Treasury notes (greenbacks). Even more popular was the movement for **"free silver."** Until 1873, government mints had coined both silver and gold dollars at a ratio of 16 to 1—that is, 16 ounces of silver were equal in value to one ounce of gold. However, when new discoveries of gold in the West after 1848 placed more gold in circulation relative to silver, that ratio undervalued silver, so that little was being sold for coinage.

Silver miners joined with farmers to demand a return to silver dollars. In 1878, Congress responded by passing, over President Hayes's veto, the Bland-Allison Act requiring the Treasury to purchase and coin no less than $2 million and no more than $4 million of silver monthly. Once again, silver dollars flowed from the mint. But with increased production of new silver mines, the market price of silver actually dropped to a ratio of 20 to 1.

Pressure for "free silver"—that is, for government purchase of all silver offered for sale at a price of 16 to 1 and its coinage into silver dollars—continued during the 1880s. The admission of five new western states in 1889 and 1890 contributed to the passage of the Sherman Silver Purchase Act in 1890. That act increased the amount of silver coinage, but not at the 16-to-1 ratio. Even so, it went too far to suit "gold bugs," who wanted to keep the United States on the international gold standard.

President Cleveland blamed the Panic of 1893 on the Sherman Silver Purchase Act, which caused a run on the Treasury's gold reserves triggered by uncertainty over the future of the gold standard. Cleveland called a special session of Congress in 1893 and persuaded it to repeal the Sherman Silver Purchase Act, setting the stage for the most bitter political contest in a generation.

Grangers and the Farmers' Alliance

Agrarian reformers supported the free silver movement, but many had additional grievances concerning problems of credit, railroad rates, and the exploitation of workers and farmers by the "money power." Both the Grange and the Farmers' Alliance, a new farmers' organization that expanded rapidly in the 1880s, addressed these political concerns. Both also addressed farm families' social and cultural needs, providing them with a sense of community that helped reduce rural isolation. The Grange sponsored picnics and cultural events, actively encouraging the participation of women. Local chapters were required to have female members, and women took up positions of leadership at the local level and also attended national meetings. The Grangers were not anti-consumption, but they desired to avoid middlemen: this made them a good audience for the new mail-order catalogues. Indeed, the innovative retailer Montgomery Ward first gained a foothold in the mail-order business by styling himself the official supply house for the Grange.

Like the Grange, the Farmers' Alliance also provided a sense of community for farmers. Starting in Texas as the Southern Farmers' Alliance, it expanded into other southern states and the North. By 1890, the movement had evolved into the National Farmers' Alliance and Industrial Union, which was affiliated with the Knights of Labor. It was also affiliated with a separate Colored Farmers' Alliance, formed by African Americans who recognized the utility of the Farmers' Alliance but were not welcome in the larger whites-only organization. Reaching out to 2 million farm families, the Farmers' Alliance set up marketing cooperatives to eliminate the middlemen who profited as "parasites" on the backs of farmers. Like the Grange, the Alliance served the social needs of farm families as well as their economic needs, organizing picnics and educational institutes in addition to camp meetings. Appealing to women as well as men, the Alliance helped farmers to overcome their isolation, especially in the sparsely settled regions of the West. The Alliance also gave farmers a sense of pride and solidarity to counter the image of "hick" and "hayseed" being purveyed by an increasingly urban American culture.

The Farmers' Alliance developed a comprehensive political agenda. At a national convention in Ocala, Florida, in December 1890, it set forth these objectives: (1) a graduated income tax; (2) direct election of U.S. senators (instead of election by state legislatures); (3) free and unlimited coinage of silver at a ratio of 16 to 1; (4) effective government control and, if necessary, ownership of railroad, telegraph, and telephone companies; and (5) the establishment of "subtreasuries" (federal warehouses) for the storage of crops, with government loans at 2 percent interest on those crops. The most important of these goals, especially for southern farmers, was the subtreasuries. Government storage would allow farmers to hold their crops until market prices were more favorable. Low-interest government loans on the value of these crops would enable farmers to pay their annual debts and thus escape the ruinous interest rates of the crop lien system in the South and bank mortgages in the West.

These were radical demands for the time. Nevertheless, most of them eventually became law: the income tax and the direct election of senators by constitutional amendments in 1913; government control of transportation and communications by various laws in the 20th century; and the subtreasuries in the form of the Commodity Credit Corporation in the 1930s.

Anticipating that the Republicans and the Democrats would resist these demands, many Alliancemen were eager to form a third party. In Kansas they had already done so, launching the People's Party, whose members were known as

Populists, in summer 1890. White Southerners, mostly Democrats, opposed the idea of a third party for fear that it might open the way for the return of the Republican Party, and African Americans, to power.

In 1890, farmers helped elect numerous state legislators and congressmen who pledged to support their cause, but the legislative results were thin. By 1892, many Alliance members were ready to take the third-party plunge. The two-party system seemed fossilized and unable to respond to the explosive problems of the 1890s.

The Rise and Fall of the People's Party

Q **FOCUS QUESTION** | Why did many Americans find Populism appealing in the 1890s?

Enthusiasm for a third party was particularly strong in the plains and mountain states, five of which had been admitted since the last presidential election: North and South Dakota, Montana, Wyoming, and Idaho. The most prominent leader of the Farmers' Alliance was Leonidas L. Polk of North Carolina. A Confederate veteran, Polk commanded support in the West as well as in the South. He undoubtedly would have been nominated for president by the newly organized People's Party had not death cut short his career at the age of 55 in June 1892.

The first nominating convention of the People's Party met at Omaha a month later. The preamble of their platform expressed the grim mood of delegates. "We meet in the midst of a nation brought to the verge of moral, political, and material ruin," it declared. "The fruits of the toil of millions are boldly stolen to build up colossal fortunes for a few. . . . From the same prolific womb of governmental injustice we breed the two great classes—tramps and millionaires." The platform called for unlimited coinage of silver at 16 to 1; creation of the subtreasury program for crop storage and farm loans; government ownership of railroad, telegraph, and telephone companies; a graduated income tax; direct election of senators; and laws to protect labor unions against prosecution for strikes and boycotts. To ease the lingering tension between southern and western farmers, the party nominated Union veteran James B. Weaver of Iowa for president and Confederate veteran James G. Field of Virginia for vice president.

Despite winning 9 percent of the popular vote and 22 electoral votes, Populist leaders were shaken by the outcome. In the South, most of the black farmers who were allowed to vote stayed with the Republicans. Democratic bosses in several southern states dusted off the racial demagoguery and intimidation machinery of Reconstruction days to keep white farmers in line for the party of white supremacy. Only in Alabama and Texas, among southern states, did the Populists get more than 20 percent of the vote. They did even worse in the older agricultural states of the Midwest, where their share of the vote ranged from 11 percent in Minnesota down to 2 percent in Ohio. Only in distressed wheat states such as Kansas, Nebraska, and the Dakotas and in the silver states of the West did the Populists do well, carrying Kansas, Colorado, Idaho, and Nevada.

The party remained alive, however, and the anguish caused by the Panic of 1893 seemed to boost its prospects. In several western states, Populists or a Populist-Democratic coalition controlled state governments for a time, and a Populist-Republican coalition won the state elections of 1894 in North Carolina. Women as well as men campaigned for the Populists: Mary Lease, one of the few women practicing law in Kansas, became famous for her impassioned speeches against corporate power.

In 1893, President Cleveland's success in getting the Sherman Silver Purchase Act repealed drove a wedge into the Democratic Party. Southern and western Democrats turned against Cleveland. In what was surely the most abusive attack on a president ever delivered by a member of his own party, Senator Benjamin Tillman of South Carolina told his constituents in 1894: "When Judas betrayed Christ, his heart was not blacker than this scoundrel, Cleveland, in deceiving the Democracy. He is an old bag of beef and I am going to Washington with a pitchfork and prod him in his fat ribs."

The Silver Issue

Clearly the silver issue stirred deep emotions. For many people silver meant far more than a mere change in monetary policy: it also represented a widespread yearning for a more equitable society in which corporations and banks held less power. Thus when Democratic dissidents stood poised to take over the party in 1896, they adopted free silver as the centerpiece of their program. This stand raised possibilities for a fusion with the Populists, who hoped the Democrats would adopt other features of their platform as well. Meanwhile, out of the West came a new and charismatic figure, a silver-tongued orator named **William Jennings Bryan**, whose shadow would loom large across the political landscape for the next generation. A one-term congressman from Nebraska, Bryan had taken up the cause of free silver. He came to the Democratic convention in 1896 as a young delegate—only 36 years old. Given the opportunity to make the closing speech in the debate on the silver plank in the party's platform, Bryan brought the house to its feet in a frenzy of cheering with his peroration: "You shall not press down upon the brow of labor this crown of thorns, you shall not crucify mankind upon a cross of gold."

This speech catapulted Bryan into the presidential nomination. He ran on a platform that not only endorsed free silver but also embraced the idea of an income tax, condemned trusts, and opposed the use of injunctions against labor. Bryan's nomination created turmoil in the People's Party. Although some Populists wanted to continue as a third party, most of them saw fusion with silver Democrats as the road to victory. At the Populist convention, the fusionists got their way and endorsed Bryan's nomination. In effect, the Democratic whale swallowed the Populist fish in 1896.

The Election of 1896

The Republicans nominated William McKinley, who would have preferred to campaign on his specialty, the tariff. Bryan

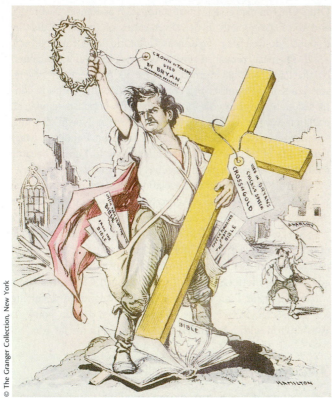

An Anti-Bryan Cartoon, 1896. This cartoon in *Judge* magazine, entitled "The Sacrilegious Candidate," charged William Jennings Bryan with blasphemy in his "Cross of Gold" speech at the Democratic national convention. Bryan grinds his Bible into the dust with his boot while waving a crown of thorns and holding a cross of gold. In the background, a bearded caricature of an anarchist dances amid the ruins of a church and other buildings.

made that impossible. Crisscrossing the country in an unprecedented whistle-stop campaign covering 18,000 miles, Bryan gave as many as 30 speeches a day, focusing almost exclusively on the free silver issue. Republicans responded by denouncing the Democrats as irresponsible inflationists. Free silver, they said, would mean a 57-cent dollar and would demolish the workingman's gains in real wages achieved over the preceding 30 years.

Under the skillful leadership of Ohio businessman Mark Hanna, chairman of the Republican National Committee, McKinley waged a "front-porch campaign" in which various delegations visited his home in Canton, Ohio, to hear carefully crafted speeches that were widely publicized in the mostly Republican press. Hanna sent out an army of speakers and printed pamphlets in more than a dozen languages to reach immigrant voters. His propaganda portrayed Bryan as a wild man from the prairie whose monetary schemes would further wreck an economy that had been plunged into depression during a Democratic administration. McKinley's election, by contrast, would maintain the gold standard, revive business confidence, and end the depression.

The 1896 election was the most impassioned and exciting in a generation. Many Americans believed that the fate of the nation hinged on the outcome. The number of voters jumped by 15 percent over the 1892 election. The sectional

pattern of South and West versus Northeast and North Central was almost as pronounced as the North–South split of 1860. Republicans won a substantial share of the urban, immigrant, and labor vote by arousing fear about the Democratic 57-cent dollar and by inspiring hope with the slogan of McKinley as "the advance agent of prosperity." McKinley rode to a convincing victory by carrying every state in the northeast quadrant of the country. Bryan carried most of the rest. Republicans won decisive control of Congress as well as the presidency. They would maintain control for the next 14 years. The election of 1896 marked a crucial turning point in American political history away from the stalemate of the preceding two decades.

Whether by luck or by design, McKinley did prove to be the advance agent of prosperity. The economy pulled out of the depression during his first year in office and entered into a long period of growth—not because of anything the new administration did (except perhaps to encourage a revival of confidence) but because of the mysterious workings of the business cycle. With the discovery of rich new goldfields in the Yukon, in Alaska, and in South Africa, the silver issue lost potency, and a cascade of gold poured into the world economy. The long deflationary trend since 1865 reversed itself in 1897. Farmers entered a new—and unfamiliar—era of prosperity. Bryan ran against McKinley again in 1900 but lost even more emphatically. The nation seemed embarked on a placid sea of plenty. But below the surface, the currents of protest and reform that had boiled up in the 1890s still ran strong.

"Robber Barons" No More

 FOCUS QUESTION How and why did American elites seek to alter their "robber baron" image in the late 19th and early 20th centuries?

The depression of the 1890s—along with the Populist movement and labor protests such as the Homestead and Pullman strikes—shook the confidence of members of the industrial elite. Industrialists were terrified when in 1892 anarchist Alexander Berkman marched into the office of Henry Clay Frick, Andrew Carnegie's right-hand man, and shot him at point-blank range (Frick survived). Although such physical assaults were rare, anger over ill-gotten and ill-spent wealth was widespread. In the 1890s, popular rage forced Mrs. Bradley Martin and her husband to flee to England after she spent $370,000 (roughly $3.5 million in 2007 dollars) on one evening of entertainment for her friends in New York's high society.

Industrial titans were often called **"robber barons."** Seeking a more favorable image, some industrialists began to restrain their displays of wealth and use their private fortunes to advance the public welfare. As early as 1889, Andrew Carnegie had advocated a "gospel of wealth." The wealthy, he believed, should consider all income in excess of their needs as a "trust fund" for their communities. In 1901, the year in which he formed U.S.

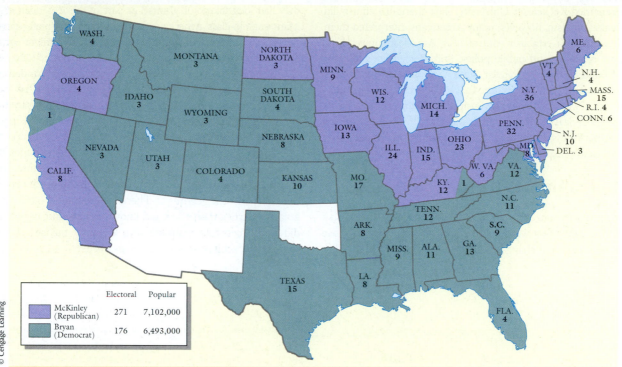

Map 19.2 Presidential Election of 1896. Once again, note the continuity of voting patterns over the two generations from the 1850s to the 1890s by comparing this map with those on pages 383, 406, and 483.

Steel, Carnegie withdrew from industry and devoted himself to philanthropic pursuits, especially in art and education. By the time he died in 1919, he had given away or entrusted to several Carnegie foundations 90 percent of his fortune. Among the projects he funded were New York's Carnegie Hall, Pittsburgh's Carnegie Institute (now Carnegie-Mellon University), and 2,500 public libraries throughout the country.

Other industrialists, including John D. Rockefeller, soon followed Carnegie's lead. A devout Baptist with an ascetic bent, Rockefeller had never flaunted his wealth, but his ruthless business methods in assembling the Standard Oil Company and in crushing his competition made him one of the most reviled of the robber barons. In the wake of journalist Ida Tarbell's stinging 1904 exposé of Standard Oil's business practices, and of the federal government's subsequent prosecution of Standard Oil for monopolistic practices in 1906, Rockefeller transformed himself into a public-spirited philanthropist. Between 1913 and 1919, his Rockefeller Foundation dispersed an estimated $500 million. His most significant gifts included money to establish the University of Chicago and the Rockefeller Institute for Medical Research

LEADING INDUSTRIALIST PHILANTHROPIC FOUNDATIONS, 1905–1925

Foundation	Date of Origin	Original Endowment
Carnegie Corporation of New York	1911	125,000,000
Carnegie Endowment for International Peace	1910	10,000,000
Carnegie Foundation for the Advancement of Teaching	1905	10,000,000
Carnegie Institution of Washington	1902	10,000,000
Duke Endowment	1924	40,000,000
John Simon Guggenheim Memorial Foundation	1925	3,000,000
Rockefeller Foundation	1913	100,000,000
Rosenwald Fund	1917	20,000,000
Russell Sage Foundation	1907	10,000,000

Source: from Joseph C. Kiger, *Operating Principles of the Larger Foundations* (New York: Russell Sage Foundation, 1957), p. 122.

(later renamed Rockefeller University). His charitable efforts did not escape criticism, however; many Americans interpreted them as an attempt to establish control over American universities, scientific research, and public policy. Still, Rockefeller's largesse helped build for the Rockefeller family a reputation for public-spiritedness and good works, one that grew even stronger in the 1920s and 1930s. Many other business leaders, such as Julius Rosenwald of Sears Roebuck and Daniel and Simon Guggenheim of the American Smelting and Refining Company, also dedicated themselves to philanthropy during this time.

Conclusion

For many Americans, the strikes and violence and third-party protests of the 1890s were a wake-up call. They realized that wrenching economic change threatened the liberty and equality they had long taken for granted as part of the American dream. Many middle-class Americans began to support greater government power to carry out progressive reforms that might cure the ills of an industrializing society.

The rise of corporate America created a fundamental paradox: on the one hand, the new industrial landscape denied workers independence and subjected them to harsh conditions, which they resisted as best they could in a series of strikes in the late 19th and early 20th centuries. Yet that same corporate world provided significant opportunities for a better life—opportunities that were especially embraced by the millions of immigrants who settled in American cities at the turn of the century. There, immigrants often found greater liberties than they had known before. But opportunity did not necessarily translate into equality: the search for a more equal society was far from finished.

CHAPTER REVIEW

REVIEW QUESTIONS

1. What were the main engines of American economic growth in the late 19th and early 20th centuries?
2. How did the rise of corporations reshape the everyday experiences of Americans?
3. What were the major changes in middle-class women's lives in the late 19th and early 20th centuries?
4. How effective was workers' resistance to the new corporations? Why?
5. What provoked the farmer protest movements in the last third of the 19th century?
6. Why did many Americans find Populism appealing in the 1890s?
7. How and why did American elites seek to alter their "robber baron" image in the late 19th and early 20th centuries?

CRITICAL THINKING QUESTIONS

1. Some historians have argued that corporate power went virtually unchecked in the 19th century. Is this true? Why or why not?
2. How did the ongoing struggle between capital and labor reshape American society in the late 19th century?

IDENTIFICATIONS

Review your understanding of the following key terms, people, and events for this chapter (terms in bold in text are included in the Glossary).

Great Railroad Strike of 1877, p. 514
Thomas Alva Edison, p. 515

J. P. Morgan, p. 516
Andrew Carnegie, p. 516
John D. Rockefeller, p. 516
merger movement, p. 517
Sherman Antitrust Act of 1890, p. 518
mass production, p. 518
Social Darwinism, p. 521
"the strenuous life", p. 522
Haymarket, p. 522
"New Woman", p. 523
Knights of Labor, p. 527
Samuel F. Gompers, p. 528
Homestead (Strike), p. 529
Pullman Strike, p. 529
free silver, p. 532
William Jennings Bryan, p. 533
"robber barons", p. 534

SUGGESTED READINGS

For a general overview of the period, see **Alan Dawley,** *Struggles for Justice: Social Responsibility and the Liberal State* (1991) and **Nell Irvin Painter,** *Standing at Armageddon: The United States, 1877–1919* (1987). On economic growth and corporate development, see **Harold G. Vatter,** *The Drive to Industrial Maturity: The United States Economy, 1860–1914* (1975); and **Glenn Porter,** *The Rise of Big Business, 1860–1910* (1973). For culture in the Gilded Age, see **Rebecca Edwards** , *New Spirits: Americans in the Gilded Age, 1865–1905* (2006); and **Alan Trachtenberg,** *The Incorporation of America: Culture and Society in the Gilded Age* (1982). On changing ideas of masculinity and civilization, see **Gail Bederman**, *Manliness and Civilization: A Cultural History of Gender and Race in the United States, 1880–1917* (1995). On the middle class see especially **Sven Beckert**, *The Monied Metropolis: New York City and the Consolidation of the American Bourgeoisie, 1850–1896* (2001); and **Stuart Blumin**, *The Emergence of the Middle Class: Social Experience in the American City, 1760-1900* (1989).

The rise of the department store is examined in **William Leach**, *Land of Desire: Merchants, Power, and the Rise of a New American Culture* (1993). The labor movement is treated in **David Montgomery**, *The Fall of the House of Labor: The Workplace, the State, and American Labor Activism* (1987). For the Knights of Labor, see **Leon Fink**, *Workingman's Democracy: The Knights of Labor and American Politics* (1983). On Haymarket and Pullman, see **Carl Smith**, *Urban Disorder and the Shape of Belief: The Great Chicago Fire, the Haymarket Bomb, and the Model Town of Pullman* (1995).

For a fresh interpretation of Populism see **Charles Postel**, *The Populist Vision* (2007); and the classic **Lawrence Goodwyn**, *Democratic Promise: The Populist Moment in America* (1976).

 Visit the CourseMate website at www.cengagebrain.com for additional study tools and review materials for this chapter.

Hester Street

This 1905 painting by George Luks recreates a busy corner of the Lower East Side, then home to New York City's immigrant Jewish community. Peddlers and consumers, men and women, adults and children crowd this painting, which stresses the energy, diversity, and commerce of this bustling urban district.

Cities, Peoples, Cultures, 1890–1920

The Rise of the City

Immigration
European Immigration
Chinese and Japanese Immigration
Immigrant Labor
Living Conditions

Building Ethnic Communities
A Network of Institutions
The Emergence of an Ethnic
  Middle Class
Political Machines
  and Organized Crime

**African American Labor
and Community**

**Working-class and
Commercial Culture**
Popular Literature

**The New Sexuality and the Rise
of Feminism**

Re-Imagining American Nationality

AMERICA'S CITIES grew rapidly in the late 19th and early 20th centuries, both to accommodate expanded production and trade and to house the toiling masses that worked on the wharves, streets, and factories. Growth called forth technological advance: running water, electric lighting and trolley lines, steel suspension bridges, skyscrapers, and elevators. Immigration soared to remedy severe labor shortfalls in manufacturing and construction; foreign languages and cultures, as a result, became an ever more noticeable feature of American urban life.

The new economic elites wanted to impress their importance and aspirations upon the cities in which they resided. They built mansions in posh residential districts either in the cities themselves or in tony suburbs that were sprouting on urban rims. They also sought to impart to their cities an architectural elegance and cultural *gravitas* that, in their minds, rivaled those of the greatest cities in history—London, Paris, Rome, Athens, Berlin. The elites' determination to uplift their cities through physical transformation and promotion of the arts was in part an effort to counteract urban distress and unruliness. It expressed the elites' anxiety about the masses that seemed to have other, and less lofty, ideas about city living. Labor-capital conflict was one area in which the ideas of rich and poor clashed in late-19th century America; struggles over culture were another. A vigorous commercial culture took root in working-class and ethnic districts of the city, appearing in dance halls, **nickelodeons**, and amusement parks. Exuberance rather than refinement, adventure rather than education defined these leisure pursuits. Young, working-class women pioneered a sexual revolution in the districts of this commercial culture, and immigrants began to emphasize both hybridity and diversity as signature features of American life. A new—and modern—America was taking shape in the country's cities, a development that aroused both great hopes and great fears.

The Rise of the City

Q **FOCUS QUESTION** In what ways did urban elites seek to shape the physical and cultural character of their cities in the years between 1890 and 1910?

By the late 19th century, cities were changing the face of America. Their populations, their physical size, and their capacity to transform the landscapes they inhabited dwarfed those of cities a mere 50 years earlier. The rate of urban growth was staggering. Chicago, for example, grew from 30,000 residents in 1850 to 500,000 in 1880 to 1,700,000 by 1900. Chicago joined two other cities, New York and Philadelphia, in surpassing the million-inhabitants mark. The number of cities with more than 100,000 residents soared from 18 in 1870 to 38 in 1900.

A new kind of building, the skyscraper, came to symbolize the aspirations taking shape in these expanding urban milieux. These modern towers were made possible by the use of steel rather than stone in the framework and by the invention of electric-powered elevators. Impelled upward by rising real estate values, they were intended to evoke the same sense of grandeur as Europe's Gothic cathedrals. But these monuments celebrated man, not God; material wealth, not spiritual riches; science, not faith. Reaching into the sky, dwarfing Europe's cathedrals, they were convincing embodiments of America's urban might.

If advances in construction made possible America's urban areas' vertical reach, technological advances encouraged horizontal expansion. Most important in this regard was the application of electricity to urban transportation systems. Between 1890 and 1920, virtually every major city built electric-powered transit systems to replace horse-drawn trolleys and carriages. By 1912, some 40,000 miles of electrical railway and trolley track had been laid. In Boston, electricity made possible the construction of the first subways in 1897, and New York and Philadelphia soon followed suit.

As a result of these transportation improvements, it now became possible for urban dwellers to live miles away from where they worked. As recently as the 1870s, many of America's urban centers had been **walking cities**. They were compact entities, with residential areas abutting work districts, and different income and ethnic groups living in close proximity to each other. By the 1890s, these walking cities had given way to metropolitan entities, with core areas of work and commerce— "downtowns"—now surrounded by expanding rings of residential areas offering inhabitants their own homes and gardens, and the promise of tree-lined streets. The intensifying congestion, dirt, poor air, and poverty of urban cores made these new residential areas into refuges of peace and quiet, and they drew those with ample economic resources. In some cases, these areas were jurisdictionally separate from cities, becoming prototypes of the independent 20th-century suburb: Brookline, Massachusetts, a town southwest of Boston, and Evanston, Illinois, a town north of Chicago, were two early examples of this phenomenon. In other urban centers, the new residential

CHRONOLOGY

1893	Columbia Exposition opens
1900	Chicago joins New York City and Philadelphia as the only U.S. cities with populations exceeding 1 million
1900–1914	Immigration averages more than 1 million per year
1907	Congress establishes Dillingham Commission to study immigration problems
1907–1911	An average of 73 of every 100 Italian immigrants return to Italy
1908	Israel Zangwill's play, *The Melting-Pot*, debuts
1909	Immigrants and their children constitute more than 96 percent of labor force building and maintaining railroads
1910	Black skilled tradesmen in northern cities reduced to 10 percent of total skilled trades workforce ◆ 20,000 nickelodeons dot northern cities
1911	Triangle Shirtwaist Company fire kills 146 workers
1914	Theda Bara, movies' first sex symbol, debuts ◆ *The Masses*, a radical journal, begins publication
1915	Horace Kallen publishes "Democracy versus the Melting Pot"
1916	Randolph Bourne publishes "Trans-National America"
1919	Japanese farmers in California sell $67 million in agricultural goods, 10 percent of state's total
1920	Nation's urban population outstrips rural population for first time

districts arose as part of the cities themselves. The old cores, meanwhile, increasingly became home to the poor, to immigrants, and to racial minorities.

These changes in the appearance of cities above ground were matched by important changes below. None were more important than water and sewage systems. By 1900, Chicago was pumping 500 million gallons per day to its inhabitants through 1,900 miles of water pipes. Another 1,500 miles of sewage pipe carried used water and other waste products away from Chicagoan households. The 139 gallons that Chicago and other American cities were pumping a day for each of its inhabitants dwarfed the 20–40 gallons per capita that British and German cities were distributing to their residents. The scale and power of these water systems made flush toilets and bathtubs standard equipment in every American middle-class urban home in America by 1900. Such improvements came more slowly to the urban poor. In cities such as Pittsburgh, for example, water supplies and water pressure were much steadier in the prosperous neighborhoods than they were in those of the poor. As late as the First World War, a significant percentage of working-class families still lacked running water in their homes. Still, America's urban poor had better access to running water than did their counterparts in Europe.

These water systems were impressive engineering feats. In New York City, a network of aqueducts that one historian has described as "the greatest project in water engineering since the Roman Empire," carried water in tunnels that were more than thirteen feet in diameter a distance of thirty miles from upstate reservoirs. If measured by their ability to procure, pump, and carry away huge volumes of water, these American systems were unrivalled in the world.

If measured by efforts to control costs, to ensure the safety of workers building tunnels and aqueducts, and to enhance public health, these waterworks were less impressive. The construction and administration of these projects occurred within political systems that were often notorious for their corruption. City and state officials expected to receive kickbacks for awarding contracts. Some regarded the size of the kickback as a more important consideration in choosing a contractor than the firm's competence or the prudent use of taxpayer monies. Expenditures on urban construction projects were therefore high. Those in charge of designing and building this infrastructure often did not do enough to protect laborers from the hazards of working underground, to ensure that consumers used the water efficiently, or to protect local lakes, rivers, and oceans against contamination from sewage. Typhoid and other water-born epidemics periodically struck the inhabitants of America's cities. In Chicago in 1882, the city's polluted water gave rise to a typhoid fever outbreak that killed more than 20,000 people. In some cities, nonbacterial contaminants compromised water quality, limiting its use for drinking. A Philadelphia newspaper reported in 1895 that the local water tasted "like a solution of gum boots and coal tar."

By 1900, the problems caused by contaminated water had begun to yield to the insistence of urban reformers that cities improve water treatment. Urban governments were installing water filtration systems and developing safer processes for sewage disposal and treatment. Newly paved roads reduced the amount of dirt, mud, and stagnant pools of water on city streets and thus further curtailed the spread of disease. As a result, urban mortality rates began to fall.

Advances in water systems, in transportation, and in housing reflected the breadth of the commitment in America's urban centers to improving the lives of urban dwellers. This commitment extended well beyond questions of physical well-being to those of education and morals. In the late 19th century, urban elites undertook one of the most intensive cultural improvement campaigns in all of American history. Symphonies, opera companies, museums, and libraries sprouted in countless cities, often housed in imposing buildings that transformed the urban landscape. In cities such as New York, Cleveland, and Philadelphia these institutions, interwoven with newly designed urban parks, anchored ambitiously conceived urban districts meant to be places where city dwellers might escape the struggles of daily life and cultivate their higher sensibilities. Thus in New York City, the Metropolitan Museum of Art and the American Museum of Natural History each took shape in the 1870s alongside Central Park, the first landscaped public park in the United States. The park's principal designer, **Frederick Law Olmsted**, imagined his 50-block-long masterpiece, with its 5 million plantings, as a refuge from the city, a place where people "may stroll for an hour, seeing, hearing, and feeling nothing of the bustle and jar of the streets." If these same people took another hour to contemplate the artistic masterpieces of the Metropolitan Museum or marvel at the holdings of the American Museum of Natural History, so much the better. Museums and parks were part of the same civic, civilizing, and regenerating enterprise. Olmsted's success with parks in New York gave him an opportunity to replicate it in numerous other cities, including Atlanta, Boston, Brooklyn, Hartford, Detroit, Chicago, Louisville, and Washington, D.C. No other single individual exercised as large an influence on American urban landscapes.

Urban elites of the late 19th century were drawn to Beaux-Arts architecture, a Paris-based style that merged neoclassical size and scale with Italian Renaissance and Baroque decorative influences. By 1902, the Metropolitan Museum had acquired its signature Beaux-Arts façade, which defines the exterior look of the museum to this day. A few years earlier, the Boston Public Library, then the finest public library in the world, moved into magnificent new quarters, whose features included a massive reading room resembling a Roman basilica and a central courtyard modeled on a 16th-century Italian Renaissance cloister. Free and open to the public, the library was celebrated by local newspapers as a "palace of the people" and as "feeding the most careless or unconscious eye with the food of high artistic loveliness."

The scale and ornateness of these buildings revealed the ambitions of the urban elites who founded them. These elites were constructing palatial institutions for posterity, imagining that the buildings would stand as permanent monuments to their civic vision and influence. They were, at the same time, making a deep investment in their cities, proclaiming their concern not simply with their private lives but with the public life and well being of others who lived in the cities they loved. Founders of the Metropolitan expressed this sentiment in 1880, when they talked about diffusing "knowledge of art in its higher forms of beauty" so as to "educate and refine a practical and laborious people."

The energy that they poured into these institutions, however, also revealed anxieties about their own social status. For the newly wealthy in their ranks, museums, symphonies, operas, and the like offered a form of alchemy that converted their riches into cultural prestige and authority: as one museum leader said, these institutions would "convert pork into porcelain, grain and produce into priceless pottery, the rude ores of commerce into sculptured marble, and railroad shares and mining stocks . . . into the glorified canvas of the world's masters."

Elites worried, too, about plebeian resistance to their civilizing projects. What if the masses ignored these institutions? Or misused them? Both the New York museums and Central Park were sites of conflict in the late 19th century between administrators and the people: the former laying down fastidious sets of rules about dress and comportment when using these institutions, the latter repeatedly declaring their intention to be left alone or demanding a role in the shaping of park and museum rules. In the 1880s, 100 labor organizations, representing 50,000 workers, presented petitions to the Metropolitan and Natural History museums asking that these institutions open their doors to the public on Sunday, the only day that was free of work for most of New York City's inhabitants. Religious groups and religious members of the Boards of Trustees brought intense pressure on these museums to keep their doors closed on the Sabbath. By 1892, however, both institutions decided to open on Sundays, handing a victory to the city's labor movement. Privately, at least, the more visionary museum leaders had to be pleased that the demand among the city's poor for access had become so strong.

The conflicts of urban life were acutely felt in Chicago. As the fastest growing American city, it was also one of the hardest to control. Rapid growth spurred innovation but also generated a great gulf between the rich and the poor, violent labor-capital conflict (see Chapter 19), and widespread corruption. The city had also suffered from disasters such as the typhoid epidemic of 1882 and the Chicago Fire of 1871, which destroyed the homes of 100,000 residents across a stretch of land four miles long. The massive destruction caused by the fire actually accelerated urban creativity and innovation. One of the most interesting groups of American architects, the so-called Chicago School, arose in the city a decade after the fire. It included men such as Louis Sullivan and John Wellborn Root and a young draftsman by the name of Frank Lloyd Wright. America's most daring skyscraper designs came out of this group, as did buildings (mostly Sullivan's creations) that merged crisp modern lines, functionality, and wondrous ornamentation. At a later time, Wright would take what he learned as Root's and Sullivan's assistant and develop a distinctive American form of modernist architecture that made his buildings in Chicago and elsewhere among the most original and admired in 20th-century America.

Chicago's remarkable ascent as a center for manufacturing, trade, and architectural innovation made it the choice for hosting the Columbia Exposition of 1893, a world's fair to celebrate the 400th anniversary of Columbus's discovery of America. The fair's two square miles of area made it three times as large as the fair in Paris four years before, and the giant Ferris wheel unveiled by Exposition planners was meant to rival the Eiffel Tower as an iron and steel architectural marvel.

At the heart of this enterprise was a monumental set of gleaming buildings called the **"White City,"** meant to evoke the classical grandeur of Greece and Rome and to trumpet the maturation of American civilization. One set of buildings—Agriculture, Transportation, Manufacturing, among them—devoted itself to inventorying America's achievements in various economic sectors. Other buildings celebrated American women, the histories, cultures, and peoples of the individual states, and the contributions of

The White City. This photograph captures the scale, grandeur, and classical lines of the Columbia Exposition's White City. The massive Agriculture building sits to the right of the Basin.

foreign nations to the story of human progress. The Transportation Building, designed by Sullivan, was the most innovative of the fair's structures, while the Manufactures Building was the largest, covering more than twice as much area as the Great Pyramid of Egypt and being lit by 120,000 incandescent lamps. Steel skeletons held the buildings up; they were sheathed in perishable stucco, unlikely to survive even one Chicago winter. The stucco was easy to work with, however, and thus allowed architects to unleash their decorative instincts in their building designs.

The individual buildings were carefully laid out around a manmade lagoon created by landscape master Olmsted himself, who imparted a neoclassical unity to the entire enterprise. Broad, open courts studded with statuary and interspersed with fountains and parks connected the buildings to each other. It is remarkable that exposition planners invested so much effort in a "city" meant to exist only for a few months.

The planners nevertheless hoped that their work would endure as a design and influence, if not as an actual urban space. Indeed, the White City, an exemplar of Beaux-Art principles, gave rise to a movement of urban architectural renovation that would become known as the **City Beautiful movement**. Its carefully composed vision of urban order, it was hoped, would offer city planners an inspiration for imposing a similar kind of order on the actual urban environments in which they lived. Metaphorically, the rise of this White City out of the swamps of Jackson Park south of Chicago symbolized the city's and the nation's capacity for rebirth. A utopian dream of an ordered city and a triumphant industrial civilization, the White City embodied America's quest for and belief in perfection.

With paid admissions at $21,480,141 in a nation with a population of 63 million, the Columbia Exposition was by far the most successful fair in American history. Americans from all over the country came to marvel at this reincarnation of ancient Rome and to record their impressions in special printed books that thoughtfully guided them through the fair, beginning with the category "My first day in the 'White City.'" The White City did fill many fairgoers with pride and inspiration, much as the planners

of the fair hoped it would. Visitors, however, also found their attention drawn to another part of the fair, one that focused on amusement rather than education, and on the dissonances of modern life rather than its classical symmetry. The **Midway Plaisance** was a long strip located at some distance from the White City, full of concessions where one could buy food and drink, engage in games, line up for rides, including the Ferris Wheel, and gaze upon the curiosities that countless small entrepreneurs had gathered into their traveling dime museums and freak shows. This, Daniel Burnham, the fair's head designer understood, was "the lighter and more fantastic side of the Fair." The chaotic variety of its sights and smells proved irresistible to tourists.

Part of Midway's variety was deliberately ethnographic, as numerous pavilions displaying life in areas of Africa and Asia were housed here. The accent was on the primitive and exotic: the pavilions did not display the modernizing elites of these faraway places, or their achievements in manufacture or transportation, but rather native peoples supposedly barely touched by civilization. It was hard to miss the implication that civilization occurred in America and Europe, as represented in the White City, while primitivism belonged to people of color from Africa, the Middle East, and Asia.

The very structure of the fair thus embodied and reinforced a racial hierarchy that posited the superiority of white, middle-class civilization. African Americans understood how much this hierarchy organized not only America's relationship with much of the world but also life within the United States itself. The anti-lynching crusader Ida B. Wells (see Chapter 18) published a pamphlet, with contributions from several black leaders, titled "The Reason Why the Colored American Is Not in the World's Columbian Exposition." Exploring the intertwined histories of American slavery and racism, this pamphlet offered a detailed accounting of the refusal of fair organizers to include African Americans. "Theoretically open to all Americans, the Exposition practically is, literally and figuratively, a 'White City,'" the pamphlet asserted. Wells boycotted the fair on "Colored American Day," but former abolitionist Frederick

Union Station, Washington, D.C. The capital city's train station, which opened in 1908 and is still being used today, is an exemplary piece of City Beautiful architecture. Its lines and landscaping reveal how much it was influenced by Chicago's White City. Indeed, the two projects shared an architect, Daniel Burnham. This color lithograph dates from 1928.

Midway Plaisance. Columbian Exposition fairgoers were drawn to this lively entertainment strip. They rode the giant Ferris wheel, poked their heads in shops, mounted camels, and explored the exotic cultures on display in Asian and African pavilions.

Douglass attended in order to give a stirring speech. "Men talk of the Negro problem," he said. "There is no Negro problem. The problem is whether the American people have honesty enough, loyalty enough, honor enough, patriotism enough to live up to their own Constitution." Try as it might, the Columbia Exposition could not erase the question of race; nor could all the striving for unity and placidity in the White City erase the presence in Chicago and every other major American city of polyglot populations of diverse ethnic origins. These international populations constituted the peoples of the American city, and they would stake a claim to define it as much as the elites who built the palatial museums, opera houses, and White Cities.

Immigration

FOCUS QUESTION From which parts of the world did immigrants come in the years between 1880 and 1920? What caused them to migrate? What were their patterns of work and residence in the United States?

The United States had always been a nation of immigrants, but never had so many come in so short a time. Between 1880 and 1920, some 23 million immigrants came to a country that numbered only 76 million in 1900. From 1900 to 1914, an average of 1 million immigrants arrived each year. In many cities of the Northeast and Midwest, immigrants and their children constituted a majority of the population. In 1920s Boston, New York City, Chicago, and Milwaukee, immigrants accounted for more than 70 percent of the total population; in Buffalo, Detroit, and Minneapolis, more than 60 percent; and in Philadelphia, Pittsburgh, and Seattle, more than 50 percent. Everywhere in the country, except in the South, the working class was overwhelmingly ethnic.

European immigration accounted for approximately three-fourths of the total. Some states received significant numbers of non-European immigrants—Chinese, Japanese,

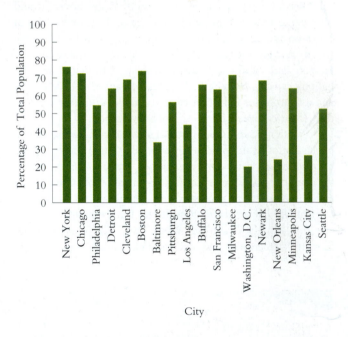

Immigrants and Their Children as a Percentage of the Population of Selected Cities, 1920.
Source: Data from U.S. Department of Commerce, Bureau of the Census, *Fourteenth Census of the United States, 1920, Population* (Washington, D.C.).

and Filipinos in California; Mexicans in California and the Southwest; and French Canadians in New England. Although their presence profoundly affected regional economies, politics, and culture, their numbers, relative to the number of European immigrants, were small. Immigrants from Latin America were free to enter the United States throughout this period, but few did until 1910, when the social disorder caused by the Mexican Revolution propelled a stream of refugees to southwestern parts of the United States. Half a million French Canadians had migrated to New England and the upper

Midwest between 1867 and 1901. After that, the rate slowed as the pace of industrialization in Quebec quickened.

European Immigration

Most of the European immigrants who arrived between 1880 and 1914 came from Eastern and Southern Europe. Among them were 3 to 4 million Italians, 2 million Russian and Polish Jews, 2 million Hungarians, and an estimated 5 million Slavs and other peoples from eastern and southeastern Europe (Poles, Bohemians, Slovaks, Russians, Ukrainians, Lithuanians, Serbians, Croatians, Slovenians, Montenegrins, Bulgarians, Macedonians, and Greeks). Hundreds of thousands came as well from Turkey, Armenia, Lebanon, Syria, and other Near Eastern lands abutting the European continent.

These post-1880 arrivals were called "new immigrants" to underscore the cultural gap separating them from the "old immigrants," who had come from northwestern Europe—Great Britain, Scandinavia, and Germany. Old immigrants were regarded by many native-born Americans as racially fit, culturally sophisticated, and politically mature. The new immigrants, by contrast, were often regarded as racially inferior, culturally impoverished, and incapable of assimilating American values and traditions. This negative view of the new immigrants reflected in part a fear of their alien languages, religions, and economic backgrounds. Few spoke English, and most adhered to Catholicism, Orthodoxy, or Judaism rather than Protestantism. Most, with the exception of Jewish immigrants, were peasants, unaccustomed to urban industrial life, but they were not as different from the old immigrants as the label implied. For example, many of the earlier-arriving Catholic peasants from Ireland and Germany had had no more familiarity with American values and traditions than did the Italians and Slavs who arrived later.

In fact, the old and new European immigrants were more similar than different. Both came to America for the same reasons: either to flee religious or political persecution or to escape economic hardship. The United States attracted a small but steady stream of political refugees throughout the 19th century: labor militants from England; nationalists from Ireland; socialists and anarchists from Germany, Russia, Finland, and Italy. Many of these people possessed talents as skilled workers, labor organizers, political agitators, and newspaper editors and thus exercised influence in their ethnic communities. However, only the anti-Semitic policies of Russia in the late 19th and early 20th centuries triggered a mass emigration (in this case Jewish) of political refugees.

Most mass immigration was propelled instead by economic hardship. Europe's rural population was growing faster than the land could support. European factories absorbed some, but not all, of the rural surplus. Industrialization and urbanization were affecting the European countryside in ways that disrupted rural ways of life. As railroads penetrated rural areas, village artisans found themselves unable to compete with the cheap manufactured goods that arrived from city factories. These handicraftsmen were among the first to emigrate. Meanwhile, rising demand for food in the cities accelerated the growth of commercial agriculture in the hinterland. Some peasant families lost their land. Others turned to producing crops for the market, only to discover that they could not compete with larger, more efficient producers. In addition, by the last third of the 19th century, peasants faced competition from North American farmers. Prices for agricultural commodities plummeted everywhere. The economic squeeze that spread distress among American farmers in the 1880s and 1890s caused even more hardship among Europe's peasantry, and many of them decided to try their luck in the New World.

An individual's or family's decision to emigrate often depended on having a contact—a family member, relative, or fellow villager—already established in an American city. These people provided immigrants with a destination, inspiration (they were examples of success in America), advice about jobs, and financial aid. Sometimes whole villages in southern Italy or

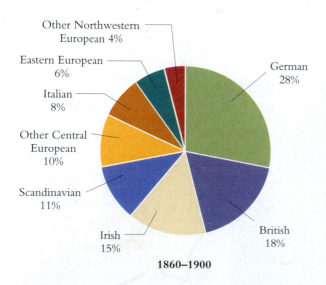

1860–1900

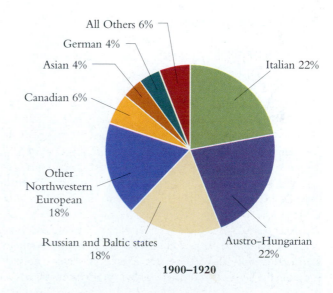

1900–1920

Sources of Immigration.
Source: Data from *Historical Statistics of the United States, Colonial Times to 1970* (White Plains, NY: Kraus International, 1989), pp. 105–9.

western Russia—or at least all of the young men there—seemed to disappear, only to reappear in a certain section of Chicago, Pittsburgh, or New York. Villages without contacts in the United States were relatively unaffected by the emigration mania.

Most immigrants viewed their trip to the United States as a temporary sojourn. They came not in search of permanent settlement but in search of high wages that would enable them to improve their economic standing in their homeland. For them, America was a land of economic opportunity, not a land to call home. This attitude explains why men vastly outnumbered women and children in the migration stream. From 1899 to 1910, three-fourths of the immigrants from Southern and Eastern Europe were adult men. Some had left wives and children behind; more were single. Most wanted merely to make enough money to buy a farm in their native land. True to their dream, many did return home. For every 100 Italian immigrants who arrived in the United States between 1907 and 1911, for example, 73 returned to Italy. Before the First World War, an estimated 60 to 80 percent of all Slavic immigrants eventually returned to the land of their birth.

The rate of return was negligible among certain groups, however. Jews had little desire to return to the religious persecution they had fled, and only 5 percent returned to Europe. The rate of return was also low among the Irish, who saw few opportunities in their long-suffering (although much-loved) Emerald Isle. In the early 20th century, however, such groups were exceptional. Most immigrants looked forward to returning to Europe. Not until the First World War shut down transatlantic travel did most immigrants begin to regard their presence in the United States as permanent.

Immigration tended to move in rhythm with the U.S. business cycle. It rose in boom years and fell off during depressions. It remained high during the first 14 years of the new century when the U.S. economy experienced sustained growth, broken only briefly by the Panic of 1907–08.

Chinese and Japanese Immigration

The relatively small numbers of Chinese and Japanese immigrants who came to the United States in the late 19th and early 20th centuries reflected the efforts of native-born Americans and their allies to keep them out. As many as 300,000 Chinese immigrants arrived in the United States between 1851 and 1882, and more than 200,000 Japanese immigrants journeyed to Hawaii and the western continental United States between 1891 and 1907. They contributed in major ways to the development of two of the West's major industries: railroad building and commercial agriculture. These two immigrant groups might have formed two of America's largest, each numbering in the millions, but the U.S. government began to exclude Chinese immigrant laborers in 1882 (The Chinese Exclusion Act) and Japanese immigrant laborers in 1907 (see Chapter 22). The government also interpreted a 1790 law to mean that Chinese, Japanese, and other East Asian immigrants were ineligible for citizenship. These exclusions remained in force until the 1940s and 1950s. They expressed the racial prejudice felt by most native-born white Americans toward nonwhite Asian immigrants, and they also revealed how determined America was to remain a nation of European immigrants and their descendants.

The factors propelling Chinese and Japanese immigrants were similar to those motivating their European counterparts. The rural population in those countries was increasing at a rate faster than the rural economies could support. Chinese and Japanese rural peasants were being integrated into an international market for agriculture, contributing to the global

© Bettmann/CORBIS

Immigrant Japanese Children Arrive at Angel Island, San Francisco Harbor, 1905. Beginning in 1907, as a result of the "gentlemen's agreement" between the United States and Japanese governments, it would no longer be possible for Japanese immigrants such as these children to come to the United States.

oversupply of agricultural goods and depressing prices. Many Chinese and Japanese immigrants, like their European counterparts, intended to move abroad just long enough to make enough money to establish themselves economically in their homelands. Thus the early streams of Chinese and Japanese migration to the United States were overwhelmingly composed of men looking for work. Similar to the European immigrants, the Chinese and Japanese sojourners tended to follow precise migratory paths—from one region or village in China or Japan to one city or region in the United States.

Conditions in China were more desperate than those in Japan, where industrialization had begun to generate new wealth and absorb some of the rural population. Chinese immigrants, as a result, often suffered greater hardship than did their Japanese counterparts. In the 19th century, many were forced to sign contracts with suppliers of overseas laborers that subjected them to slave-like conditions: They were herded onto boats for the transpacific voyage, bound to particular employers for years on end, thrust into dangerous working conditions, and paid paltry wages. The conditions of their labor in the western states where they tended to settle inflamed the sentiments of white working men, who saw the Asian migration as a threat to their own wages and livelihoods. These white workers might have made common cause with Asian immigrant workers, but the racial prejudice they harbored toward the "yellow hordes" was simply too great. White workers became leaders of the movements in the western states to keep these immigrants out.

Significant numbers of Chinese and Japanese immigrants continued to try to enter the United States during the period of Asian immigrant exclusion—after 1882 in the case of the Chinese and after 1907 in the case of the Japanese. Some were desperate to reunite with family members already living in the United States, while others were driven to escape deteriorating economic circumstances in their homeland. Many attempted to enter the United States with forged papers declaring them to be merchants (a permitted class of Chinese and Japanese immigrants) when they were not, or that they had been resident in the United States before the exclusion laws had gone into effect (and thus entitled to return). San Francisco was their principal port of entry, and Angel Island, in San Francisco harbor, became the counterpart of Ellis Island in New York harbor: the place where inspectors for the U.S. Bureau of Immigration interrogated them and scrutinized their documents and, more often than not, sent them back to Asia.

Other East Asian immigrants attempted to enter the United States through Canada or Mexico, hoping to find a non-patrolled part of the land border and to cross into the United States undetected. They became, in effect, America's first illegal aliens. That a certain percentage of East Asian immigrants had entered the country illegally, and were subject to deportation, generated considerable fear among the Asian immigrant populations resident in the United States, deepening tendencies within these communities to secrecy and to separation from mainstream American culture and society. Despite these considerable hardships, Asian immigrants would prove to be resourceful and would find ways to build homes and livelihoods in America.

Immigrant Labor

In the first decade of the 20th century, immigrant men and their male children constituted 70 percent of the workforce in 15 of the 19 leading U.S. industries. They concentrated in industries where work was the most backbreaking. Immigrants built the nation's railroads and tunnels; mined its coal, iron ore, and other minerals; stoked its hot and sometimes deadly steel furnaces; and slaughtered and packed its meat in Chicago's putrid packinghouses. In 1909, first- and second-generation immigrants—especially Greeks, Italians, Japanese, and Mexicans—constituted more than 96 percent of the labor force that built and maintained the nation's railroads. Of the 750,000 Slovaks who arrived in America before 1913, at least 600,000 headed for the coal mines and steel mills of western Pennsylvania. The steel mills of Pittsburgh, Buffalo, Cleveland, and Chicago also attracted disproportionately large numbers of Poles and other Slavs.

Immigrants also performed "lighter" but no less arduous work. Jews and Italians predominated in the garment manufacturing shops of New York City, Chicago, Philadelphia, Baltimore, and Boston. In 1900, French-Canadian immigrants and their children held one of every two jobs in New England's cotton textile industry. By 1920, the prosperity of California's rapidly growing agricultural industry depended primarily on Mexican and Filipino labor. In these industries, immigrant women and children, who worked for lower wages than men, formed a large part of the labor force. Few states restricted child labor. More than 25 percent of boys and 10 percent of girls aged 10 to 15 were "gainfully employed."

Immigrants were as essential as fossil fuels to the smooth operation of the American economic machine. Sometimes, however, the machine consumed workers as well as coal and oil. Those who worked in heavy industry, mining, or railroading were especially vulnerable to accident and injury. In 1901, for instance, 1 in every 400 railroad workers died on the job and 1 in every 26 suffered injury. Between the years 1906 and 1911, almost one-quarter of the recent immigrants employed at the U.S. Steel Corporation's South Works (Pittsburgh) were injured or killed on the job. Lax attention to safety rendered even light industry hazardous and sometimes fatal. In 1911, a fire broke out on an upper floor of the **Triangle Shirtwaist Company**, a New York City garment factory. The building had no fire escapes. The owners of the factory, moreover, had locked the entrances to each floor as a way of keeping their employees at work. A total of 146 workers, mostly young Jewish and Italian women, perished in the fire or from desperate nine-story leaps to the pavement below.

Chronic fatigue and inadequate nourishment increased the risk of accident and injury. Workweeks averaged 60 hours—10 hours every day except Sunday. Workers who were granted Saturday afternoons off, thus reducing their workweek to 55 hours, considered themselves fortunate. Steelworkers were not so lucky. They labored from 72 to 89 hours per week and were required to work one 24-hour shift every two weeks.

Most workers had to labor long hours simply to eke out a meager living. In 1900, the annual earnings of American

Triangle Shirtwaist Company Fire. In 1911, a fire at the Triangle Shirtwaist Company in New York City claimed the lives of 146 workers, most of them young Jewish and Italian women. Many died because they could not escape the flames. The building had no fire escapes, and the employer had locked the entrances to each floor to keep workers on the job. The tragedy spurred the growth of unions and the movement for factory reform in New York.

manufacturing workers averaged only $400 to $500 per year. Skilled jobs offered immigrants far more (as much as $1,500 to $2,000 per year), but most of these jobs were held by Yankees and by Germans, Irish, Welsh, and other "old immigrant" Europeans. Through their unions, workers of Northern European extraction also controlled access to new jobs that opened up and usually managed to fill them with a son, relative, or fellow countryman. Consequently, relatively few of the new immigrants rose into the prosperous ranks of skilled labor. In any case, employers were replacing many skilled workers with machines operated by cheaply paid operatives.

From the 1870s to 1910, real wages paid to factory workers and common laborers did rise, but not steadily. Wages fell sharply during depressions, and the hope for increases during periods of recovery often collapsed under the weight of renewed mass immigration, which brought hundreds of thousands of new job seekers into the labor market. One of every five industrial workers was unemployed, even during the boom years of the early 20th century.

Most working families required two or three wage earners to survive. If a mother could not go out to work because she had small children at home, she might rent rooms to some of the many single men who had recently immigrated. But economic security was difficult to attain. In his 1904 book, *Poverty*, social investigator Robert Hunter conservatively estimated that 20 percent of the industrial population of the North lived in poverty.

Living Conditions

Strained economic circumstances confined many working-class families to cramped and dilapidated living quarters. Many of them lived in two- or three-room apartments, with several people sleeping in each room. To make ends meet, one immigrant New York City family of eight living in a two-room apartment took in six boarders. Some boarders considered themselves lucky to have their own bed. That luxury was denied the 14 Slovaks who shared eight beds in a small Pittsburgh apartment and the New York City printer who slept on a door he unhinged every night and balanced across two chairs. The lack of windows in city tenements allowed little light or air into these apartments. Crowding was endemic. The population density of New York City's Lower East Side—where most of the city's Jewish immigrants settled—reached 700 per acre in 1900, a density matching or exceeding that of the world's poorest cities. Overcrowding and poor sanitation resulted in high rates of infectious diseases, especially diphtheria, typhoid fever, and pneumonia. In the early years of the twentieth century, improvements in the quality of housing and public health finally began to ease the dangers of urban life.

Building Ethnic Communities

Q **FOCUS QUESTION** In what ways did immigrants seek economic success and social mobility? How successful were they in their efforts?

The immigrants may have been poor, but they were not helpless. Migration had required a good deal of resourcefulness, self-help, and mutual aid—assets that survived in the new surroundings of American cities.

A Network of Institutions

Each ethnic group quickly established a network of institutions that supplied a sense of community and multiplied sources of communal assistance. Some immigrants simply reproduced those institutions that had been important to them in the Old Country. The devout established churches and synagogues. Lithuanian, Jewish, and Italian radicals reestablished Old World socialist and anarchist organizations. Irish nationalists set up clandestine chapters of the Clan Na Gael to keep alive the struggle to free Ireland from the English. Germans felt at home in their traditional *Turnevereins* (athletic clubs) and musical societies.

Immigrants developed new institutions as well. In the larger cities, foreign-language newspapers disseminated news, advice, and culture. Each ethnic group created fraternal societies to bring together immigrants who had known each other in the Old Country, or who shared the same craft, or who had come from the same town or region. Most of these societies provided members with a death benefit (ranging from a few hundred to a thousand dollars) that guaranteed the deceased a decent burial and the family a bit of cash. Some fraternal societies made small loans as well. Among those ethnic groups that prized home ownership, especially the Slavic groups, the fraternal societies also provided mortgage money. And all of them served as centers of sociability—places to have a drink, play cards, or simply relax with fellow countrymen. The joy, solace, and solidarity these groups generated helped countless immigrants adjust to American life.

The Emergence of an Ethnic Middle Class

Within each ethnic group, a sizable minority directed their talents and ambitions toward economic gain. Some of these entrepreneurs addressed their communities' needs for basic goods and services. Immigrants preferred to buy from fellow countrymen with whom they shared a language, a history, and presumably a bond of trust. Enterprising individuals responded by opening dry-goods stores, food shops, butcher shops, and saloons in their ethnic neighborhoods. Those who could not afford to rent a store hawked their fruit, clothing, or dry goods from portable stands, wagons, or sacks carried on their backs. The work was endless and the competition tough. Men often enlisted the entire family—wife, older children, younger children—in their undertakings. Few family members were ever paid for their labor, no matter how long or hard they worked. Although many of these small businesses failed, enough survived to give some immigrants and their children a toehold in the middle class.

Other immigrants turned to small industry, particularly garment manufacture, truck farming, and construction. A clothing manufacturer needed only a few sewing machines to become competitive. Many Jewish immigrants, having been tailors in Russia and Poland, opened such facilities. If a rented space proved beyond their means, they set up shop in their own apartments. Competition among these small manufacturers was fierce, and critics condemned the work environments as "sweatshops." Workers suffered from inadequate lighting, heat, and ventilation; 12-hour workdays and 70-hour workweeks during peak seasons, with every hour spent bent over a sewing machine; and poor pay and no employment security, especially for the women and children who made up a large part of this labor force. Even at this level of exploitation, many small manufacturers failed; but over time, significant numbers of them managed to firm up their position as manufacturers and to evolve into stable, responsible employers. Their success contributed to the emergence of a Jewish middle class.

The story was much the same in urban construction, where Italians who had established themselves as labor contractors, or *padroni*, went into business for themselves to take advantage of the rapid expansion of American cities. Although few became general contractors on major downtown projects, many of them did well building family residences or serving as subcontractors on larger buildings.

One who did make the leap from small to big business was Amadeo P. Giannini, the son of Italian immigrants, who used his savings from a San Francisco fruit and vegetable stand to launch a career in banking. Determined to make bank loans available and affordable to people of ordinary means, Giannini generated a huge business in small loans. Expanding on his ethnic base of small depositors, he eventually made his bank—the Bank of America—into the country's largest financial institution.

In southern California, Japanese immigrants chose agriculture as their route to the middle class. Working as agricultural laborers in the 1890s, they began to acquire their own land in the early years of the 20th century. Altogether, they owned only 1 percent of California's total farm acreage. Their specialization in fresh vegetables and fruits (particularly strawberries), combined with their family-labor-intensive agricultural methods, was yielding $67 million in annual revenues by 1919—one-tenth of the total California agriculture revenue that year. Japanese farmers sold their produce to Japanese fruit and vegetable wholesalers in Los Angeles, who had chosen a mercantile route to middle-class status. The success of Japanese farmers was all the more impressive given that the state of California had passed the Alien Land Law in 1913, prohibiting Japanese and other Asian aliens from owning property in the state. Japanese immigrant farmers thus depended on their native-born children or friendly whites to acquire land for them, arrangements that made them more vulnerable to losing the land—or control of it— than if they had been able to own it outright themselves.

Each ethnic group created its own history of economic success and social mobility. From the emerging middle classes came leaders who would provide their ethnic groups with identity, legitimacy, and power and would lead the way toward Americanization and assimilation. Their children tended to do better in school than the children of working-class ethnics, and academic success served as a ticket to upward social mobility in a society that increasingly depended on university-trained engineers, managers, lawyers, doctors, and other professionals.

Political Machines and Organized Crime

The underside of this success story was the rise of government corruption and organized crime. Many ethnic entrepreneurs operated on the margins of economic failure and bankruptcy, and some accepted the help of those who promised financial assistance. Sometimes the help came from honest unions and upright government officials, but other times it did not. Unions were generally weak, and some government officials, lacking experience and economic security, were susceptible to bribery. Economic necessity became a breeding ground for government corruption and greed. A contractor who was eager to win a city contract—to build a trolley system, a sewer line, or a new city hall, for example—would find it necessary to pay off government officials who could throw the contract his way. By 1900, such payments, referred to as "graft," had become essential to the day-to-day operation of government in most large cities. Graft, in turn, made local office holding a source of economic gain. Politicians began building political organizations called machines to guarantee their success in municipal elections. The machine "bosses" used a variety of legal and illegal means to bring victory on Election Day. They won the loyalty of urban voters—especially immigrants—by providing poor neighborhoods with paved roads and sewer systems. They helped newly arrived immigrants find jobs (often on city payrolls) and occasionally provided food, fuel, or clothing to families in need. Many of their clients were grateful for these services in an age when government provided little public assistance.

William Riordan, *Plunkitt of Tammany Hall*, excerpts (1905)

The bosses who ran the **political machines**—including "King Richard" Croker in New York, James Michael Curley in Boston, Tom Pendergast in Kansas City, Martin Behrman in New Orleans, and Abe Ruef in San Francisco—served their own needs first. They saw to it that construction contracts went to those who offered the most graft, not to those who were likely to do the best job. They protected gamblers, pimps, and other purveyors of urban vice who contributed large amounts to their machine coffers. They often required city employees to contribute to their campaign chests, to solicit political contributions, and to get out the vote on Election Day. And they engaged in widespread election fraud by rounding up truckloads of newly arrived immigrants and paying them to vote a certain way; having their supporters vote two or three times; and stuffing ballot boxes with the votes of phantom citizens who had died, moved away, or never been born.

"Keeping Tammany's Boots Shined." This 1880s cartoon by Joseph Keppler declares that the real boss of New York City was not its elected mayor, Hugh Graham, here depicted as a lowly shoe-shiner, but the Tammany Hall political machine. The loose strap underneath the boot, used to control both City Hall and Tammany, belongs to Richard Croker, Tammany's leader from 1886 to 1901.

Big-city machines, then, were both positive and negative forces in urban life. Reformers despised them for disregarding election laws and encouraging vice, but many immigrants valued them for providing social welfare services and for creating opportunities for upward mobility.

The history of President John F. Kennedy's family offers one example of the economic and political opportunities opened up by machine politics. Both of Kennedy's grandfathers, John Francis Fitzgerald ("Honey Fitz") and Patrick Joseph Kennedy, were the children of penniless Irish immigrants who arrived in Boston in the 1840s. Fitzgerald excelled at academics and won a coveted place in Harvard's Medical School but left Harvard that same year, choosing a career in politics instead. Between 1891 and 1905, Fitzgerald served as a Boston city councilor, Massachusetts state congressman and senator, U.S. congressman, and mayor of Boston. For much of this period, he derived considerable income and power from his position as the North End Ward boss, where he supervised the trading of jobs for votes and favors for cash in his section of Boston's Democratic and Irish-dominated political machine.

Patrick Kennedy, an East Boston tavern owner and liquor merchant, became an equally important figure in Boston city politics. In addition to running the Democratic Party's affairs in Ward Two, he served on the Strategy Board, a secret council of Boston's machine politicians that met regularly to devise policies, settle disputes, and divide up graft. Both

© Bettmann/CORBIS

Fitzgerald and Kennedy derived a substantial income from their political work and used it to lift their families into middle-class prosperity. Kennedy's son (and the future president's father), Joseph P. Kennedy, would go on to make a fortune as a Wall Street speculator and liquor distributor and to groom his sons for Harvard and the highest political offices in the land. His rapid economic and social ascent had been made possible by his father's and father-in-law's earlier success in Boston machine politics.

Underworld figures, too, influenced urban life. In the early years of the 20th century, gangsterism was a scourge of Italian neighborhoods, where Sicilian immigrants had established outposts of the notorious Mafia, and in Irish, Jewish, Chinese, and other ethnic communities as well. Favorite targets of these gangsters were small-scale manufacturers and contractors, who were threatened with violence and economic ruin if they did not pay a gang for "protection." Gangsters imposed their demands with physical force, beating up or killing those who failed to abide by the "rules." In Chinese communities, secret societies originating in China, or *tongs,* and initially set up in America to strengthen communal life among the immigrants, occasionally crossed the line into crime. Sometimes this transition resulted from good intentions—for example, tong members might smuggle into the United States the wife and children of an immigrant Chinese man who had no legal way of reuniting his family—but other times, tongs became enmeshed in far more damaging criminal activities, such as the opium trade, prostitution, and gambling.

Greedy for money, power, and fame, and willing to use any means necessary, many immigrant and ethnic criminals considered themselves authentic entrepreneurs cut from the American mold. By the 1920s, petty extortion had escalated in urban areas, and underworld crime had become big business. **Al Capone**, the ruthless Chicago mobster who made a fortune from gambling, prostitution, and bootleg liquor during Prohibition, once quipped: "Prohibition is a business. All I do is to supply a public demand. I do it in the best and least harmful way I can." New York City's Arnold Rothstein, whose financial sophistication won him a gambling empire and the power to fix the 1919 World Series, nurtured his reputation as "the J. P. Morgan of the underworld." Mobsters like Rothstein and Capone were charismatic figures, both in their ethnic communities and in the nation at large. Few immigrants, however, followed their criminal path to economic success.

African American Labor and Community

Q **FOCUS QUESTION** What were the similarities and differences between the African American and immigrant experiences in the early 20th century?

Unlike immigrants, African Americans remained a predominantly rural and southern people in the early 20th century. Most blacks were sharecroppers and tenant farmers. The markets for cotton and other southern crops had stabilized in the early 20th century, but black farmers remained vulnerable to exploitation. Landowners, most of them white, often forced sharecroppers to accept artificially low prices for their crops. At the same time, they charged high prices for seed, tools, and groceries at the local stores they controlled. Few rural areas generated enough business to support more than one store or to create a competitive climate that might force prices down. Those sharecroppers who traveled elsewhere to sell their crops or purchase their necessities risked retaliation—either physical assaults by white vigilantes or eviction from their land. Thus, most remained beholden to their landowners, mired in poverty and debt.

Some African Americans sought a better life by migrating to industrial areas of the South and the North. In the South, they worked in iron and coal mines, in furniture and cigarette manufacture, as railroad track layers and longshoremen, and as laborers in the steel mills of Birmingham, Alabama. By the early 20th century, their presence was growing in the urban North as well, where they worked on the fringes of industry as janitors, elevator operators, teamsters, and servants of various kinds. Altogether, about 200,000 blacks left the South for the North and West between 1890 and 1910.

In southern industries, blacks were subjected to hardships and indignities that even the newest immigrants were not expected to endure. Railroad contractors in the South, for example, treated their black track layers like prisoners. Armed guards marched them to work in the morning and back at night. Track layers were paid only once a month and forced to purchase food at the company commissary, where the high prices claimed most of what they earned. Their belongings were locked up to discourage them from running away. Although other southern employers of black workers did not engage in labor practices as harsh as those of the railroad contractors, they still confined blacks to the dirtiest and most grueling jobs. The Jim Crow laws passed by every southern state legislature in the 1890s legalized this rigid separation of the black and white races (see Chapter 18).

The nation's worsening racial climate adversely affected the southern blacks who moved north, even though these migrants had moved to states that generally did not have Jim Crow laws. Northern industrialists generally refused to hire black migrants for manufacturing jobs, preferring the labor of European immigrants. Only when those immigrants went on strike did employers turn to African Americans. Black workers first gained a foothold in the Chicago meat-packing industry in 1904, when 28,000 immigrant packinghouse workers walked off their jobs. Employers hoped that the use of black strike-breakers would inflame racial tensions between white and black workers and thus undermine labor unity and strength.

African Americans who had long resided in northern urban areas also experienced intensifying discrimination in the late 19th and early 20th centuries. In 1870, about one-third of the black men in many northern cities had been skilled tradesmen: blacksmiths, painters, shoemakers, and carpenters. Serving both black and white clients, these men enjoyed steady

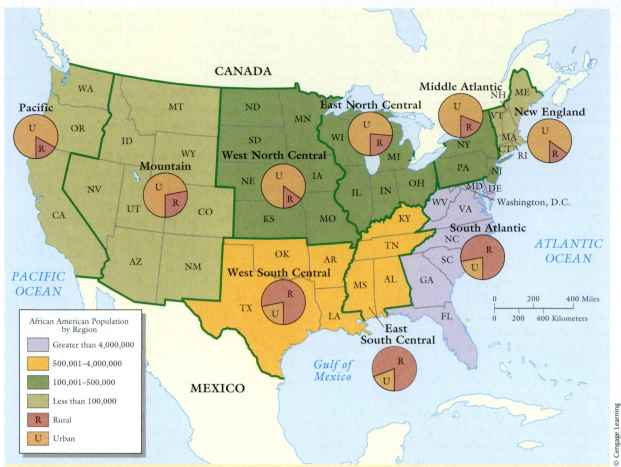

Map 20.1 African American Population, 1910. This 1910 map reveals that the African American population was mostly concentrated in rural areas of the South. Those relatively few African Americans living outside the South were predominantly in urban areas.

work and good pay, but by 1910 only 10 percent of black men made a living in this way. In many cities, the number of barber shops and food catering businesses owned by blacks also went into sharp decline, as did black representation in the ranks of restaurant and hotel waiters. These barbers, food caterers, and waiters had formed a black middle class whose livelihood depended on the patronage of white clients. By the early 20th century, this middle class was in decline, the victim of growing racism. Whites were no longer willing to engage the services of blacks, preferring to have their hair cut, beards shaved, and food prepared and served by European immigrants. The residential segregation of northern blacks also rose in these years, as whites excluded them from growing numbers of urban neighborhoods.

African Americans did not lack for resourcefulness. In urban areas of settlement, they laced their communities with the same array of institutions—churches, fraternal insurance societies, political organizations—that solidified ethnic neighborhoods. A new black middle class arose consisting of ministers, professionals, and businesspeople who serviced the needs of their racial group. Black-owned real estate agencies, funeral homes, doctors' offices, newspapers, groceries, restaurants, and bars opened for business on the commercial thoroughfares of African American neighborhoods. Many

businessmen had been inspired by the words of black educator Booker T. Washington, and specifically by his argument that blacks should devote themselves to self-help and self-sufficiency. **Madame C.J. Walker** offers one example of a black woman who built a lucrative business from the hair and skin lotions she devised and sold to black customers throughout the country. In many cities, African American real estate agents achieved significant wealth and power.

Booker T. Washington, Atlanta Exposition Address (1895)

Nevertheless, entrepreneurial success remained a tougher task among African Americans than among immigrants. Black communities were often smaller and poorer than their white ethnic ones; economic opportunities were fewer, and black businessmen found it more difficult than their white ethnic counterparts to cultivate customers outside of their core community. Racial prejudice stood as an obstacle to black business success. Meanwhile, blacks were so marginalized in politics that they had little opportunity to gain power or wealth through holding political office or controlling a political machine. Thus the African American middle class remained smaller and more precarious than did its counterpart in ethnic communities, less able to lead the way toward affluence and assimilation.

MUSICAL LINK TO THE PAST

Ragtime

Composer: Scott Joplin

Title: "Maple Leaf Rag" (probably written 1897; published 1899)

Upon writing the "Maple Leaf Rag," Scott Joplin proclaimed that the composition "will make me King of Ragtime Composers." With millions of worldwide sheet music sales stretching over two decades, and the continued popularity of this rag over a century later, Joplin was prescient in his prediction.

Ragtime represented a popular amalgam of African American and European American musical influences, combining a march-like bass foundation and syncopated melodic flourishes in the treble range. Its ecstatic, dance-inducing sound brought a welcome respite from sentimental Victorian "tear-jerker" ballads of the 19th century. Ragtime dominated the American music business between 1895 and 1910, providing a key source of inspiration for future songwriters Irving Berlin (see Chapter 23) and George Gershwin, among others.

Much like the waltz in the 1850s, and hip-hop in the 1980s, ragtime brought about heated controversy and numerous naysayers. Many viewed ragtime as a threat, sometimes for racist reasons. "Above all, as a black-originated music that was embraced by the youth of America, it was perceived as a negative influence that had to be confronted and eliminated," wrote Edward A. Berlin in his biography of Joplin.

John Stark, the white publisher who released "Maple Leaf Rag," promoted Joplin and other ragtime composers in a controversial way that flew in the face of ragtime's detractors. Stark proclaimed that rags, particularly Joplin's, were "the equal of classical music." One ad for the work proclaimed that it "has throttled and silenced those who oppose syncopations. It is played by the cultured of all nations, and is welcomed in the drawing rooms and boudoirs of good taste." Similar to marketing tactics used thirty years later for Duke Ellington (see Chapter 25), such advertising copy helped the process of overcoming bias against the artistic potential of blacks during a time of violent Jim Crow segregation, and widened the market for ragtime, bringing additional royalties to Stark and Joplin.

While rags were usually performed as solo piano pieces, there also existed a market for them as ensemble pieces. Expanded orchestration for "Maple Leaf Rag" and other compositions lent an even richer sound than usual to Joplin's music, proving irresistible to the crowds that gathered for ragtime performances on Sunday spring afternoons in municipal parks across the United States.

Q Can you think of new genres in American popular music that, like ragtime, were looked upon suspiciously for having originated among African Americans or other minority groups?

A'Lelia Bundles/Walker Family Collection/www.madamcjwalker.com

Madame C. J. Walker. This prominent African American entrepreneur, pictured here behind the wheel of her car, built a successful business selling hair and skin lotions to black customers throughout the country.

Working-class and Commercial Culture

 FOCUS QUESTION What kinds of commercial entertainment took root among urban workers in the late 19th and early 20th century? How did this commercial culture compare to the cultural initiatives undertaken by urban elites?

As much as the white elites and their middle-class allies attempted to impose a genteel order on city life, the city's vitality escaped such bounds. Most workers shared in a new culture of commercial entertainment that included dance halls, music halls, vaudeville theaters, nickelodeons (early storefront movie theaters), amusement parks, and ball parks. Storefront vaudeville theaters, for instance, began to advertise "cheap amusements" to a broad working public in the 1880s. With roots in such antebellum entertainments as minstrelsy, circuses, and dime museums, vaudeville shows offered a variety of miscellaneous short acts for only a dime: a typical show might include sentimental ballads, acrobats, soft-shoe dances, magicians, mind readers, one-act plays, blackface minstrelsy, sports stars from baseball or boxing, puppeteers, jugglers, and dancing bears. Not considered respectable middle-class fare at first, vaudeville became increasingly popular and eventually became a cross-class, national phenomenon.

Amusement parks such as Steeplechase Park at Coney Island, built in 1895, attracted a large working-class audience of men and women while soon also appealing to middle-class youth. Older middle-class commentators found the unchaperoned mingling of young men and women in an urban public space troubling, even shocking, but that loosening of restraint was what made Coney Island so pleasurable and exciting. A new kind of institution in American life, Coney Island was a structured world promoting gaiety and play, with dozens of rides and titillating attractions such as the "Blowhole Theater," whose jets of air blew women's skirts up. "Will she throw her

arms around your neck and yell?" asked a sign for the "Cannon Coaster," providing its own answer: "Well, I guess, yes!"

The rides at Coney Island offered young men and women a temporary escape from their industrial working lives, yet ironically enough many of the rides themselves imitated the industrial workplace. The 1884 Switchback Railroad, for instance, an early precursor to the roller coaster, was directly inspired by the operation of gravity-powered coal cars in the shafts of coal mines. New innovations in technology and transportation found a pleasurable mirror at Coney Island and at the other amusement parks around the country that quickly sprang up in imitation.

While vaudeville theaters and amusement parks at first attracted a primarily working-class crowd of pleasure-seekers, they appealed to growing middle-class audiences as well. These cross-class populations were the ones drawn in such large numbers to the sights and sounds of the Midway at the 1893 Columbia Exposition, their attraction to commercial entertainment on that strip subverting the work of those elites who were attempting to impose "White City" notions of order and demeanor on America's city dwellers.

Popular Literature

Just as in the antebellum period, urban workers read a wide variety of dime novels (paperbacks that sold for a dime; see Chapter 10) and newspapers. Beginning in the 1860s and 1870s, a flourishing cheap literature reflected the presence of working women in the new industrial order: the popular 1871 story "Bertha the Sewing Machine Girl; or, Death at the Wheel," inspired many imitators and was staged as a popular play in New York City. Its author, Laura Jane Libbey, published more than 60 novels in the 1880s appealing to a working-class audience. Working women read a variety of romances as well, purchasing dime novels from newsstands and pushcarts in large cities. Featuring wealthy heroines or working women who discovered that by birth they were actually aristocrats, these romantic tales offered fantasies that—in imagination, at least—closed

NICKELODEONS IN MAJOR AMERICAN CITIES, 1910

Cities	Population	Nickelodeons (estimate)	Seating Capacity	Population per Seat
New York	4,338,322	450	150,000	29
Chicago	2,000,000	310	93,000	22
Philadelphia	1,491,082	160	57,000	26
St. Louis	824,000	142	50,410	16
Cleveland	600,000	75	22,500	27
Baltimore	600,000	83	24,900	24
San Francisco	400,000	68	32,400	12
Cincinnati	350,000	75	22,500	16
New Orleans	325,000	28	5,600	58

Source: Garth Jowett, *Film: The Democratic Art* (Boston: Little, Brown, 1976), p. 46.

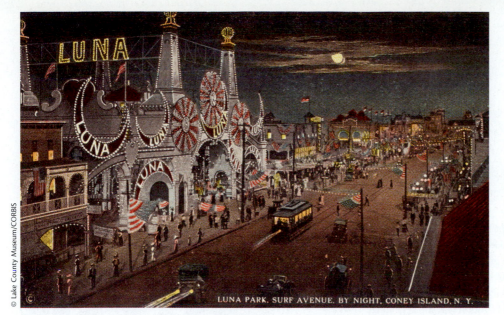

Surf Avenue and Luna Park, Coney Island, 1913. With its 1 million lights, Surf Avenue in Brooklyn, New York, advertised itself as the most brilliantly lit thoroughfare in the world. The avenue included the entrance to Luna Park, one of Coney Island's most popular attractions.

the gulf between the classes. Dime novels appealing to working-class men often told heroic stories of working-class manhood in which men overcame numerous obstacles to become the foremen or owners of factories. Such stories allowed a form of imagined compensation for the loss of independence men actually experienced as permanent wage earners.

If literature gestured toward the past, another form of commercial entertainment, the movies, pointed toward the future. Movies were well suited to poor city dwellers with little money, little free time, and little command of the English language. Initially, the movies cost only a nickel. The "nickelodeons" where they were shown were usually converted storefronts in working-class neighborhoods. Movies required little leisure time because at first they lasted only 15 minutes on average. Viewers with more time on their hands could stay for a cycle of two or three films (or for several cycles). And even non-English-speakers could understand what was happening on the "silent screen." By 1910, at least 20,000 nickelodeons dotted northern cities.

These early "moving pictures" were primitive by today's standards, but they were thrilling just the same. The figures appearing on the screen were "larger than life." Moviegoers could transport themselves to parts of the world they would otherwise never see, encounter people they would otherwise never meet, and watch boxing matches they could otherwise not afford to attend. The darkened theater provided a setting in which secret desires, especially sexual ones, could be explored. As one newspaper breathlessly commented in 1899: "For the first time in the history of the world it is possible to see what a kiss looks like."

No easy generalizations are possible about the content of these early films, more than half of which came from France, Germany, and Italy. American-made films tended toward slapstick comedies, adventure stories, and romances such as those generated by Buster Keaton and Fatty Arbuckle, two silent screen stars (see the *History Through Film* feature, p. 556). Producers did not yet shy away, as they soon would, from the lustier or seedier sides of American life. The Hollywood formula of happy endings had yet to be worked out. In fact, the industry,

centered in New York City and Fort Lee, New Jersey, had yet to locate itself in sunny southern California. In 1914, the movies' first sex symbol, Theda Bara, debuted in a movie that showed her tempting an upstanding American ambassador into infidelity and ruin. She would be the first of the big screen's vamps, so-called because the characters they portrayed, like vampires, thrived on the blood (and death) of men.

The New Sexuality and the Rise of Feminism

FOCUS QUESTION How did the early 20th-century movement toward sexual freedom contribute to the rise of feminism?

The appearance of the vamp was one sign that popular culture had become an arena in which Americans were beginning to experiment with more open expressions of sexuality. Another sign was the growing number of women who began insisting that they be accorded the same sexual freedom long enjoyed by men. This impulse was strongest among young, single, working-class women who were entering the workforce in large numbers and mixing at workplaces, in loosely supervised ways, with men their own age. The associations between young men and women that sprang up at work carried over into their leisure. Young people of both sexes flocked to the dance halls that were opening in every major city. They rejected the stiff formality of earlier ballroom dances such as the cotillion or the waltz for the freedom and intimacy of newer forms, such as the foxtrot, tango, and bunny-hug. They went to movies and to amusement parks together, and they engaged, far more than their parents had, in premarital sex. It is estimated that the proportion of women having sex before marriage rose from 10 to 25 percent in the generation that was coming of age between 1910 and 1920.

HISTORY THROUGH FILM

Coney Island (1917)

Directed by Roscoe "Fatty" Arbuckle (uncredited).
Starring Roscoe "Fatty" Arbuckle (Fatty), Buster Keaton (Rival), Alice Mann (Love Interest),
Agnes Neilson (Fatty's Wife), and Al St. John (Old Friend).

Coney Island was one of the first silent films to feature a classic comedy duo: Roscoe "Fatty" Arbuckle and Buster Keaton. The two met through a mutual friend in New York City in 1917 and quickly struck up a silver-screen partnership. Arbuckle, already a silent movie star, and Keaton, a veteran of the vaudeville circuit, crafted a crude, slapstick tour de force of pratfalls, gags, and fights. It was the beginning of a popular style of comedy on film, the fat/skinny buddy pic, which would be recast in famous teams like Abbot and Costello, Laurel and Hardy, and to an extent, the Three Stooges.

Coney Island opens to images of Luna Park at night, brightly lit towers, luminescent avenues, mechanized roller coasters. Highlighting these modern inventions, the film showcases the technological innovations of the late 19th and early 20th century. Coney Island itself—its state-of-the-art rides (The Witching Waves, Chutes), its street vendors hawking ice cream and candy, its carnival-like, consumer-driven atmosphere—is one of the most prominent "characters" in the film. It is cast as having irresistible allure. Like the Midway Plaisance and in contrast to the White City, Coney Island sought to fill urban dwellers' leisure time with adventure and fun rather than with moral improvement.

At the beginning of the film, Buster Keaton's character watches a parade with his girlfriend (Alice Mann) before the two decide to enter Luna Park. When Keaton comes up short on the entry fee, his lady friend drops him for a man who has the admission cash (Al St. John). Meanwhile, Fatty sits, bored, on the beach with his dowdy wife, but he eventually sneaks away from her after burying himself in the sand to hide. For the rest of the film, Keaton, Arbuckle, and St. John vie for Mann's attention, punching and pranking each other in the process. Keaton eventually wins back Mann's affection, and Fatty and St. John swear off women altogether, until they spy another young lady and run after her.

The raucous style of physical comedy that dominates this film offers us a glimpse of the values then coursing their way through working-class commercial culture. The cinematic displays of informal association between men and women, of adventure and sexuality, had been inspired by behaviors that many young urban dwellers, including sizable numbers of immigrants, had themselves embraced. The film is notable, too, for the breadth of its attack on social conventions and authority figures. In the movie, no relationship is sacred (the primary narrative follows Fatty's attempts to cheat on his wife), no authority figure powerful (the inadequate and often thickly mustachioed Keystone Kops all end up locked in jail, knocked out cold), and no gender line firm (Fatty cross-dresses to disguise himself from his wife). While the assault on authority in the movie is presented in a hilarious style, it carries a more serious message: namely that working-class individuals were going to make their own way in the world. It is precisely these declarations of cultural independence that made urban elites and their middle-class allies so

Fatty Arbuckle (center) getting clobbered by Buster Keaton (right) in a scene from *Coney Island*. Their love interest, played by Alice Mann, looks on.

Courtesy of Everett Collection

anxious about their ability to impose their own sense of order and morality on city life.

By the 1920s executives in the movie industry had taken steps to expunge Arbuckle-style antics from their films, and to make these art forms more suitable for refined middle-class audiences. Once decorum in the movies became the rule of the day, lords of cinematic anarchy, like Arbuckle, lost their footing. In fact, Arbuckle's career crashed in the twenties. In 1921, actress Virginia Rappe died four days after attending a bootleg liquor party at Fatty's San Francisco apartment. Arbuckle was accused of rape and was tried three times for manslaughter. Though eventually acquitted, his career as an actor never recovered. He died in 1933 of a heart attack at age 46. Buster Keaton, however, went on to become a successful actor, sharing the Hollywood limelight with the likes of Charlie Chaplin. ◼

Theda Bara as Cleopatra (1917). Bara was the first movie actress to gain fame for her roles as a "vamp"—a woman whose irresistible sexual charm led men to ruin. Because little effort was made to censor movies before the early 1920s, movie directors were able to explore sexual themes and to film their female stars in erotic, and partially nude, poses.

Working Women. A female army of department store employees surges into the streets of New York at the conclusion of the workday. Emboldened by the independence that working status conferred on them, these women began to challenge leisure patterns, dating conventions, and gender roles in early 20th-century America.

This movement toward sexual freedom was one expression of women's dissatisfaction with the restrictions that had been imposed on them by earlier generations. By the second decade of the 20th century, eloquent spokeswomen had emerged to make the case for full female freedom and equality. The author Charlotte Perkins Gilman called for the release of women from domestic chores through the collectivization of housekeeping. Social activist Margaret Sanger insisted in her lectures on birth control that women should be free to enjoy sexual relations without having to worry about unwanted motherhood. The anarchist Emma Goldman denounced marriage as a kind of prostitution and embraced the ideal of "free love"—love unburdened by contractual commitment. Alice Paul, founder of the National Women's Party, brought a new militancy to the campaign for woman suffrage (see Chapter 21).

These women were among the first to use the term **feminism** to describe their desire for complete equality with men. Some of them came together in Greenwich Village, a community of radical artists and writers in lower Manhattan, where they found a supportive environment in which to express and live by their feminist ideals. Crystal Eastman, a leader of the feminist **Greenwich Village** group called Heterodoxy, defined the feminist challenge as "how to arrange the world so that women can be human beings, with a chance to exercise their infinitely varied gifts in infinitely varied ways, instead of being destined by the accident of their sex to one field of activity."

The movement for sexual and gender equality aroused considerable anxiety. Parents worried about the promiscuity of their children. Conservatives were certain that sexual assertiveness among women would transform American cities into dens of iniquity. Vice commissions sprang up in every major city to clamp down on prostitution, drunkenness, and pornography. The campaign for prohibition—a ban on the sale of alcoholic beverages—gathered steam. Movie theater owners were pressured into excluding "indecent" films from their screens. Many believed lurid tales of international vice lords scouring foreign lands for innocent girls who could be delivered to American brothel owners. This "white slave trade" inspired passage of the 1910 Mann Act, which made the transportation of women across state lines for immoral purposes a federal crime (on the Mann Act, see Chapter 21).

Nor did it escape the attention of conservatives that Greenwich Village was home not only to the exponents of "free love" but also to advocates of class warfare. William "Big Bill" Haywood, leader of a newly-formed radical labor organization, the Industrial Workers of the World (IWW) (see Chapter 21) frequented Greenwich Village. So, too, did IWW organizer and Heterodoxy member, Elizabeth Gurley Flynn. Flynn's lover, Carlo Tresca, was an IWW theoretician.

© Bettmann/CORBIS

Margaret Sanger on Trial, 1916. Feminist Margaret Sanger, left, was put on trial for using the U.S. mail service to circulate her book, *The Woman Rebel*, which advocated birth control. A federal law barred the use of the mail system to spread birth control advice or techniques.

When Greenwich Village radicals began publishing an avant-garde artistic journal in 1914, they called it *The Masses;* its editor was Max Eastman, the brother of Crystal. This convergence of labor and feminist militancy intensified conservative feeling that the nation had strayed too far from its roots.

Re-Imagining American Nationality

Q **FOCUS QUESTION** How did Israel Zangwill, Horace Kallen, and Randolph Bourne re-imagine American nationality?

The large presence of immigrants in America also alarmed conservatives. Among the native-born middle and upper classes, the prevailing view was that immigrants should shed their ethnic backgrounds and become thoroughly American in speech, dress, and culture, and in their commitment to the principles of liberty and democracy. A refusal or inability to do so was increasingly interpreted by these conservative sectors of the population as marking the inferiority of the immigrant group in question or their unfitness for life in America. Such interpretations of immigrant behavior generated support for coercive Americanization campaigns and for legislation that would extend the ban on "undesirable" immigrants group from East Asians to Eastern and Southern Europeans, West Asians, and Africans. In 1907, Congress established the Dillingham Commission to collect information on every immigrant group in America with an eye toward making a factual case for closing America's immigrant gates.

As these pressures mounted, immigrants began to fight back, some insisting that all immigrants had the capacity to become fully American, others declaring that America would be a better place if it made room for at least some of the diversity that immigrants had brought to American culture. In 1908, Israel Zangwill, an Anglo-Jewish writer, debuted his play, *The Melting-Pot*, on Broadway. The play's theme was that all immigrants, even those originating from Eastern Europe, could become the most successful and best of Americans. The play's protagonist, David Quixano, belongs to a Russian Jewish family that has been killed in Russian anti-Jewish riots. David alone survives and flees to New York City, where he is taken in by his uncle and his uncle's mother, both older souls who will never successfully adapt their lives to the rhythms of America. But David himself has the youth, drive, and desire to succeed. A talented musician, he seizes the opportunity that America gives him, writes a successful American symphony, marries the Gentile girl of his dreams, and becomes a proud American.

It mattered greatly to Zangwill, the playwright, that David's success grew out of his willingness to abandon his ethnic and religious past and to embrace America. Zangwill imagined an America in which all immigrants, or at least all immigrants from Europe, would succeed in similar ways, leaving behind their Old World cultures (and grievances) and melting together to form a new and vigorous nationality. The climactic moment in the play comes when Zangwill puts these words in David's mouth: "America is God's Crucible, the great Melting-Pot where all the races of Europe are melting and reforming! . . . Germans and Frenchmen, Irishmen and Englishmen, Jews and Russians—into the Crucible with you all! God is making the American."

Zangwill was criticized at the time and by subsequent writers for believing that the shedding of one's Old World

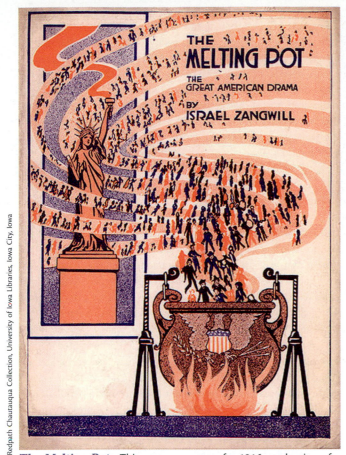

The Melting Pot. This program cover of a 1916 production of Zangwill's play visually recreates the process that unfolds in the drama itself: A swirl of diverse immigrants from many parts of the world are thrown into one great pot and fused into a strong freedom-loving people.

Randolph Bourne. An important early 20th-century intellectual who celebrated the "cosmopolitan" potential of American nationality. He died young, a victim of the influenza epidemic of 1918.

culture was both possible and desirable. But his celebration of the **melting pot** should not be understood as a simple-minded call for conformity of the sort that conservatives desired. Zangwill adhered to a dynamic conception of American nationality; the core of American culture, he believed, would change and become a different compound once varieties of immigrants had melted themselves and their cultures into it. Thus, even if the specific contributions of different immigrant cultures could not be precisely identified, they would nevertheless be present and influential. In such ways would the melting pot, as Zangwill imagined it, change and refresh American nationality.

Zangwill attracted prominent individuals to his point of view. President Theodore Roosevelt wrote Zangwill in 1908, after watching a performance of *The Melting-Pot,* that "I do not know when I have seen a play that stirred me as much." And President Woodrow Wilson declared in 1915 that America was "the only country in the world" that experiences a "constant and repeated rebirth." Wilson credited this rebirth to immigrants and to the contributions they had made to the "glory and majesty of a great country." In such ways did Zangwill's views resonate with prominent political figures who were beginning to identify themselves with reform.

Other immigrant thinkers were discomfited by the kind of melting that Zangwill had advocated. One of them was Horace Kallen, a German-Jewish immigrant, philosopher, and social critic. While an undergraduate at Harvard University in the first years of the 20th century, Kallen, along with fellow student Alain Locke (see Chapter 24), developed the doctrine of **cultural pluralism**. This doctrine called on America to become home to many cultures, not one; it argued against coercive assimilation and the melting pot and for the celebration of ethnic difference. Kallen believed that multiple cultures, if allowed to flourish in a democratic environment, would generate harmony not discord. In a famous 1915 article, "Democracy versus the Melting Pot," he imagined the American nation as an orchestra in which each ethnic group would have its own "theme and melody," contributing a distinctive part to the "symphony of [American] civilization."

The following year, another critic, the native-born Randolph Bourne, wrote an essay, "Trans-National America," in which he picked up on Kallen's insistence that immigrants be given a role in shaping culture in the United States. America, Bourne wrote in 1916, "shall be what the immigrant will have a hand in making it, and not what a ruling class, descendant of those British stocks which were the first permanent immigrants, decide[s] that America shall be." Bourne located America's uniqueness in the encounters that occurred between immigrant cultures on the one hand and the nation's atmosphere of freedom and democracy on the other. This atmosphere permitted individuals from all kinds of groups, both immigrant and native-born, both to preserve their own cultures and to partake of others. Bourne believed that immigrants delighted in the process of cultural exchange that America's environment of freedom encouraged. He celebrated such exchanges, and the variety of identities that arose from them, as essential to the American ideal. Through this process of exchange, Bourne argued, individuals would share more and more of their cultures with each other and would, as a result, become more cooperative with others. These exchanges, too, would make immigrants patriotic, able to believe that they "may have a hand in the destiny of America." Such integration, cooperation, and patriotism would create a nationality superior, Bourne wrote, to any emerging from a "narrow 'Americanism' or forced chauvinism."

Bourne's ideal of American nationality, one he labeled **cosmopolitanism**, allowed for more variation and choice than did Kallen's, which viewed cultural expressions in America as arising almost exclusively from the traditions that immigrants had brought with them to the New World. For Bourne, the New World was much more about creating new cultural forms out of the mélange of peoples and cultures that inhabited America than it was about preserving old forms; unlike Zangwill, Bourne did not look forward to an America in which everyone had been melted into one shape. Bourne celebrated variety, and he shared with Kallen a belief that America's atmosphere of freedom and commitment to democracy would allow such variety to flourish here as it had in few other places.

Zangwill, Kallen, and Bourne all failed to grapple sufficiently with race and with the discrimination that America imposed on groups marked as racially different, especially African Americans. Their writings did not address the perniciousness of Jim Crow, nor did they acknowledge the reality of Chinese and Japanese exclusion. Nevertheless, these thinkers' reckoning with diversity in America was innovative. They were among the first to articulate in public forums arguments for diversity that were percolating among the masses of immigrants living in America and struggling to find ways to make this new land their home. Today, Kallen and Bourne in particular are seen as early exponents of what late-20th-century Americans would call "multiculturalism."

Like feminism, pluralism and cosmopolitanism generated anxiety in large stretches of America, especially in farming communities and small towns, and in the South, where industrialization and urbanization were proceeding at a slower rate than elsewhere. To these Americans, it seemed as though the cultures that immigrants were creating in cities were taking the nation too far from its Anglo-Saxon roots.

The urban elites who exercised considerable cultural power in America were also troubled by the immigrant masses and the urban cultures they were creating. Many of their members, long frustrated by the apparent immigrant preference for movies, amusement parks, and saloons over the "civilizing forces" of museums, libraries, and lectures, were not predisposed to find virtue in immigrant cultures. Nevertheless, change was beginning to occur in these elite circles, as the positive reactions of Presidents Roosevelt and Wilson to Zangwill's ideas of the melting pot indicate. Both Roosevelt and Wilson had begun to understand that American nationality might be strengthened by the infusion into it of new peoples and new cultures, and that the resulting hybridity might be superior to an imagined Anglo-Saxon purity. Jane Addams, an important urban reformer who increasingly traveled in Roosevelt's and Wilson's political circles, ventured beyond where these two presidents were willing to go by acknowledging the importance of "immigrant gifts"—aspects of immigrant cultures that should be preserved even as immigrants assimilated into American nationality. Addams's concession to diversity was a small one, and she would continue to insist, across several decades of work with immigrants (see Chapter 21), on the importance of immigrant assimilation to American middle-class values and norms. Nevertheless, Addams's gesture was evidence that the peoples and cultures of the cities had begun to influence the ways in which broader circles of Americans thought about their nation.

Conclusion

By 1920, America's urban population outstripped its rural population for the first time in the country's history. Despite a political system that was chronically vulnerable to corruption, urban leaders found ways to build housing and infrastructure that enabled cities to address the demands placed on them by rapid growth. Through the invention of skyscrapers, elevators, electrified railroad and trolley lines, and sophisticated water systems, cities became centers of technological innovation. Urban elites wanted to make their cities centers of culture, too, and embarked on grand projects of architectural and landscape renovation to spread culture, civilization, and refinement through urban populations.

The gap between the elites and their cultural projects on the one hand and the lives of the urban masses on the other remained large, however. The numbers of new workers, many of them foreign born, arriving in cities was enormous. Their working and living conditions were often poor. Groups defined as racially different—African Americans, Chinese and Japanese immigrants, and even groups of southern and eastern European immigrants—suffered from prejudice as well. Every group could point to examples of economic success among their ranks, and, by the second decade of the 20th century, solid middle classes had emerged within them. Yet, majorities remained working-class, coming up short in their quest for equality and opportunity in America.

If economic success remained elusive, the new urban masses nevertheless demonstrated a spirit of creativity and independence that profoundly shaped urban culture. The culture emerging out of dance halls, amusement parks, and nickelodeons prized adventure rather than refinement, liberty rather than order, and diversity rather than conformity. Many urban dwellers thrived in this new environment. Working-class women discovered liberties in dress, employment, dating, and sex that they had not known and propelled feminism into being. Social critics began to imagine forms of American nationality that not only put immigrants on the same footing as the native born, but also that praised diversity as a central part of the American experience. Cities, meanwhile, acquired reputations for being innovative and as being places for forward-looking and independently minded Americans to settle.

This association of the cities with newness and difference only increased the cultural distance between them and the countryside. Within the cities, the popular culture of the immigrant masses also troubled urban elites and their middle-class allies. These cultural tensions had already begun to spill over into politics, shaping a new and important movement called *progressivism*.

CHAPTER REVIEW

REVIEW QUESTIONS

1. In what ways did urban elites seek to shape the physical and cultural character of their cities in the years between 1890 and 1910?
2. From which parts of the world did immigrants come in the years between 1880 and 1920? What caused them to migrate? What were their patterns of work and residence in the United States?
3. In what ways did immigrants seek economic success and social mobility? How successful were they in their efforts?
4. What were the similarities and differences between the African American and immigrant experiences in the early 20th century?
5. What kinds of commercial entertainment took root among urban workers in the late 19th and early 20th century? How did this commercial culture compare to the cultural initiatives undertaken by urban elites?
6. How did the early 20th-century movement toward sexual freedom contribute to the rise of feminism?
7. How did Israel Zangwill, Horace Kallen, and Randolph Bourne re-imagine American nationality?

CRITICAL THINKING QUESTIONS

1. Which group had a greater influence on urban life in the early 20th century: urban elites or immigrant masses?
2. Which philosophy, do you think, offered the best recipe for incorporating immigrants into American society in the early 20th century: melting-pot assimilation, cultural pluralism, or cosmopolitanism?

IDENTIFICATIONS

Review your understanding of the following key terms, people, and events for this chapter (terms in bold in text are included in the Glossary).

nickelodeons, p. 539
walking cities, p. 540
Frederick Law Olmsted, p. 541
White City, p. 542
City Beautiful movement, p. 543
Midway Plaisance, p. 543
Triangle Shirtwaist Company, p. 547
political machines, p. 550
Al Capone, p. 551
Madame C. J. Walker, p. 552

feminism, p. 557
Greenwich Village, p. 557
melting pot, p. 558
cultural pluralism, p. 559
cosmopolitanism, p. 560

SUGGESTED READINGS

On the changes in American cities in the late 19th century, see **Jon C. Teaford,** *The Unheralded Triumph: City Government in America, 1870–1900* (1984). On Chicago, see **William Cronon,** *Nature's Metropolis: Chicago and the Great West* (1991) and **Daniel Bluestone,** *Constructing Chicago* (1991). On New York, see **Roy Rosenzweig and Elizabeth Blackmar,** *The Park and the People: A History of Central Park* (1991). On the changing character of American elites during this time, see **Steve Fraser and Gary Gerstle, eds.,** *Ruling America: Wealth and Power in a Democracy* (2005). For an excellent overview of immigration, consult **Roger Daniels,** *Coming to America: A History of Immigration and Ethnicity in American Life* (2002). The best single-volume history of eastern and southern European immigrants during this period is **John Bodnar,** *The Transplanted: A History of Immigration* (1985).

The experience of Chinese immigrants during the period of American exclusion is discussed in **Erika Lee,** *At America's Gates: Chinese Immigration During the Exclusion Era, 1882–1943* (2003), while **Steven P. Erie,** *Rainbow's End: Irish Americans and the Dilemmas of Urban Machine Politics, 1840–1945* (1988), insightfully examines the benefits and costs of big-city machines. **John Hope Franklin and Alfred A. Moss Jr.,** *From Slavery to Freedom: A History of Negro Americans,* 8th ed. (2000), offers a comprehensive account of African-American life, while an important account of black female workers can be found in **Jacqueline Jones,** *Labor of Love, Labor of Sorrow: Black Women, Work and the Family from Slavery to the Present* (1985). On the rise of mass culture, see **David Nasaw,** *Going Out: The Rise and Fall of Public Amusements* (1993). On the new woman and feminism, consult **Nancy F. Cott,** *The Grounding of Modern Feminism* (1987) and **Christine Stansell,** *American Moderns: Bohemian New York and the Creation of a New Century* (2000). For an introduction to debates about American nationality in which Zangwill, Kallen, and Bourne took part, see **Jonathan M. Hansen,** *The Lost Promise of Patriotism: Debating American Identity, 1890–1920* (2003).

 Visit the CourseMate website at www.cengagebrain.com for additional study tools and review materials for this chapter.

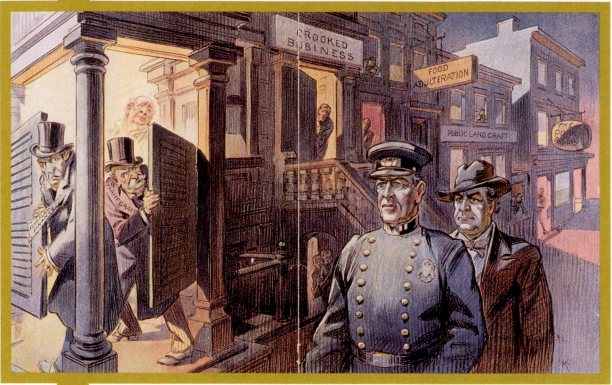

CHAPTER 21

Culver Pictures

"A New Captain in the District"

This cartoon depicts newly elected President Woodrow Wilson as a police captain who is determined to clean up Washington politics and regulate "crooked business." It illustrates a key belief shared by Wilson, Theodore Roosevelt, and most other progressives: An activist government was society's best hope for solving the nation's political and economic problems.

Progressivism

P ROGRESSIVISM was a reform movement that took its name from individuals who left the Republican Party in 1912 to join Theodore Roosevelt's new party, the Progressive Party. The term progressive, however, refers to a much larger and more varied group of reformers than those who gathered around Roosevelt in 1912.

As early as 1900, these reformers had set out to cleanse and reinvigorate an America whose politics and society they considered in decline. Progressives wanted to rid politics of corruption, tame the power of the "trusts," and in the process inject more liberty into American life. They fought against prostitution, gambling, drinking, and other forms of vice. They first appeared in municipal politics, organizing movements to oust crooked mayors and to break up local gas or streetcar monopolies. They carried their fights to the states and finally to the nation. Two presidents, Theodore Roosevelt and Woodrow Wilson, placed themselves at the head of this movement.

Progressivism was popular among a variety of groups who brought to the movement distinct, and often conflicting, aims. On one issue, however, most progressives agreed: the need for an activist government to right political, economic, and social wrongs. Some progressives wanted government to become active only long enough to clean up the political process, root out vice, upgrade the electorate, and break up trusts. These problems were so difficult to solve that many other progressives endorsed the notion of a permanently active government—with the power to tax income, regulate industry, protect consumers from fraud, empower workers, safeguard the environment, and provide social welfare. Many progressives, in other words, came to see the federal government as the institution best equipped to solve social problems.

Progressivism and the Protestant Spirit

Muckrakers and the Turn toward "Realism"

Settlement Houses and Women's Activism
Hull House
The Cultural Conservatism of Progressive Reformers
A Nation of Clubwomen

Socialism
The Several Faces of Socialism
Socialists and Progressives

Municipal Reform
The City Commission Plan
The City Manager Plan
The Costs of Reform

Reform in the States
Restoring Sovereignty to "the People"
Creating a Virtuous Electorate
The Australian Ballot
Personal Registration Laws
Disfranchisement
Disillusionment with the Electorate
Woman Suffrage
Robert La Follette and Wisconsin Progressivism
Progressive Reform in New York
Scientific Management on the Factory Floor

A Campaign for Civil Rights
The Failure of Accommodationism
From the Niagara Movement to the NAACP

The Roosevelt Presidency
Regulating the Trusts
Toward a "Square Deal"
Expanding Government Power: The Economy
Expanding Government Power: The Environment
Progressivism: A Movement for the People?
The Republicans: A Divided Party

(continued)

Such positive attitudes toward government power marked an important change in American politics. Americans had long been suspicious of centralized government, viewing it as the enemy of liberty. The Populists had broken with that view (see Chapter 19), but they had been defeated. The progressives had to build a new case for strong government as the protector of liberty and equality.

The Taft Presidency: Progressive Disappointment and Resurgence

Battling Congress
The Ballinger-Pinchot Controversy
Roosevelt's Return
The Bull Moose Campaign
The Rise of Woodrow Wilson
The Election of 1912

The Wilson Presidency

Tariff Reform and a Progressive Income Tax
The Federal Reserve Act
From the New Freedom to the New Nationalism

Progressivism and the Protestant Spirit

Q
FOCUS QUESTION

How did Protestantism influence reform?

Progressivism emerged first and most strongly among young, mainly Protestant, middle-class Americans who felt alienated from their society. Many had been raised in Protestant homes in which religious conviction had often been a spur to social action. They were expected to become ministers or missionaries or to serve their church in some other way. They had abandoned this path, but they never lost their zeal for righting moral wrongs and for uplifting the human spirit. They were distressed by the immorality and corruption in American politics and by the gap that separated rich from poor.

Other Protestant reformers retained their faith. This was true of William Jennings Bryan, the former Populist leader who became an ardent progressive and evangelical. Throughout his political career, Bryan insisted that Christian piety and American democracy were integrally related. Billy Sunday, a former major league baseball player who became the most theatrical evangelical preacher of his day, elevated opposition to saloons and the "liquor trust" into a righteous crusade. And Walter Rauschenbusch led a movement known as the Social Gospel, which emphasized the duty of Christians to work for the social good.

Protestants formed a large and diverse population, sizable sections of which showed little interest in reform. Thus it is important to identify smaller and more cohesive groups of reformers. Of the many that arose, three were of particular importance, especially in the early years: investigative journalists, who were called **"muckrakers"**; the founders and supporters of settlement houses; and socialists.

Muckrakers and the Turn toward "Realism"

Q
FOCUS QUESTION

What was "realism" and how did it spur investigative reporting and reform?

The term *muckraker* was coined by Theodore Roosevelt, who had intended it as a criticism of newspaper and magazine reporters who, for no purpose other than monetary reward, wrote stories about scandalous situations. But the label became a badge of honor among journalists who were committed to exposing repugnant aspects of American life. Ida Tarbell revealed the shady practices by which John D. Rockefeller had transformed his Standard Oil Company into a monopoly. Lincoln Steffens unraveled the webs of bribery and corruption that were strangling local governments in the nation's cities. George Kibbe Turner documented the extent of prostitution and family disintegration in the ethnic ghettos of those cities. These muckrakers wanted to shock the public into recognizing the shameful state of political, economic, and social affairs and to prompt "the people" to take action.

The tradition of investigative journalism reached back at least to the 1870s, when newspaper and magazine writers exposed the corrupt practices of New York City's Boss Tweed and his Tammany Hall machine. The 20th-century rise of the muckrakers reflected two factors, one economic—expanded newspaper and magazine circulation—and the other intellectual—increased interest in **"realism."** Together they transformed investigative reporting into something of national importance.

CHRONOLOGY

1889	Hull House established
1890–1904	All ex-Confederate states pass laws designed to disfranchise black voters ◆ Virtually all states adopt the Australian (secret) ballot
1900	La Follette elected governor of Wisconsin ◆ City commission plan introduced in Galveston, Texas
1901–1914	More than 1,000 African Americans lynched
1901	Johnson elected reform mayor of Cleveland ◆ McKinley assassinated; Roosevelt becomes president
1902	Direct primary introduced in Mississippi ◆ Initiative and referendum introduced in Oregon ◆ Roosevelt sides with workers in coal strike
1903	*McClure's Magazine* publishes Standard Oil exposé ◆ Federal court dissolves Northern Securities Company
1904	Roosevelt defeats Alton B. Parker for presidency
1905	National Forest Service established
1906	La Follette elected to U.S. Senate ◆ Congress passes Hepburn Act ◆ Upton Sinclair publishes *The Jungle* ◆ Congress passes Pure Food and Drug Act and Meat Inspection Act
1907	Reformer Hughes elected New York governor ◆ Financial panic shakes economy
1908	Taft defeats Bryan for presidency

1909	Congress passes Payne-Aldrich tariff bill
1910	Ballinger-Pinchot controversy ◆ NAACP founded ◆ Wilson elected governor of New Jersey
1911	National Urban League founded ◆ City manager plan introduced in Sumter, South Carolina ◆ Wisconsin Industrial Commission established ◆ Frederick Winslow Taylor publishes *The Principles of Scientific Management*
1912	Roosevelt forms Progressive Party ◆ Wilson defeats Roosevelt, Taft, and Debs for presidency
1913	16th (federal income tax) and 17th (direct election of U.S. Senators) Amendments ratified ◆ Congress passes Underwood-Simmons Tariff ◆ Congress establishes Federal Reserve
1914	Congress establishes Federal Trade Commission ◆ Congress passes Clayton Antitrust Act
1916	Louis Brandeis appointed to Supreme Court ◆ Kern-McGillicuddy Act, Keating-Owen Act, and Adamson Act passed ◆ National Park Service formed ◆ National Women's Party founded
1919	18th Amendment (Prohibition) ratified
1920	19th Amendment (Woman Suffrage) ratified

From 1870 to 1909, daily newspapers rose in number from 574 to 2,600, and their circulation increased from less than 3 million to more than 24 million. During the first decade of the 20th century, the magazine revolution of the 1880s and 1890s (see Chapter 19) accelerated. Cheap, 10-cent periodicals such as *McClure's Magazine* and *Ladies' Home Journal*, with circulations of 400,000 to 1 million, began to displace genteel and relatively expensive 35-cent publications such as *Harper's* and *The Atlantic Monthly*. The expanded readership brought journalists considerably more money and prestige and attracted many talented and ambitious men and women to the profession. Wider circulation also made magazine publishers more receptive to stories that might appeal to their expanded readership.

The American middle class's growing intellectual interest in "realism" (see Chapter 19) also favored the muckrakers. "Realism" was a way of thinking that prized detachment, objectivity, and skepticism. Those who embraced it pointed out that constitutional theory, with its emphasis on citizenship, elections, and democratic procedures, had little to do with the way government in the United States actually worked. What could one learn about bosses, machines, and graft from studying the Constitution? Others argued that the glorification of the "self-made man" and of "individualism" was preventing Americans from coping effectively with the centrality of large-scale organizations—corporations, banks, labor unions—to the economy. The realists, finally, criticized the tendency of American

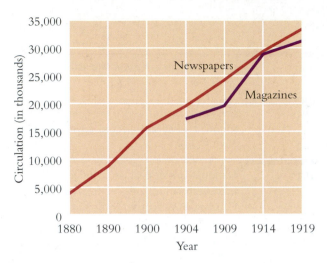

Circulation of Daily Newspapers and Magazines, 1880–1919.
Source: Data from *Historical Statistics of the United States, Colonial Times to 1970* (White Plains, NY: Kraus International, 1989).

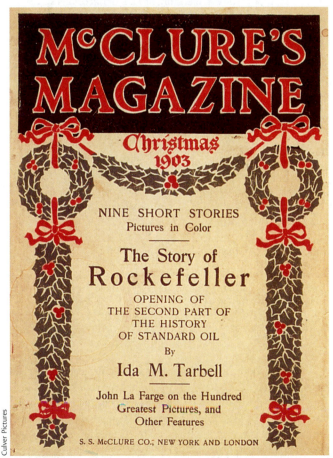

Pioneering Investigative Journalism. This Christmas 1903 issue of *McClure's Magazine* featured the second part of Ida Tarbell's exposé of John D. Rockefeller's business practices. Tarbell's revelations were regarded as sensational, and they convinced many middle-class Americans of the need for economic and political reform.

writers and artists to emulate European styles, calling instead for styles that would more accurately render American life and thought.

By the first decade of the 20th century, intellectuals and artists were attempting to create truer, more realistic ways of representing and analyzing American society. They brought shadowy figures vividly to life: the captain of industry who ruthlessly destroyed his competitors; the con artist who tricked young people new to city life; the innocent immigrant girl who fell prey to the white slave traders; the corrupt policeman under whose protection urban vice flourished.

A large middle class, uneasy about the state of American society, applauded the muckrakers for telling these stories and began trumpeting the virtues of reform. Members of this class pressured city and state governments to send crooked government officials to jail and to stamp out the sources of corruption and vice. Between 1902 and 1916, more than 100 cities launched investigations of the prostitution trade. The federal government, meanwhile, began to raise questions about "the trusts"—large corporations that had amassed overwhelming economic power. Progressivism began to crystallize into a political movement centered on the abuses the muckrakers had exposed.

Settlement Houses and Women's Activism

 Q

FOCUS QUESTION What contributions did associations of women's reformers make to progressivism?

Established by middle-class reformers, settlement houses were intended to help the largely immigrant urban poor cope with the harsh conditions of city life. Much of the inspiration for settlement houses came from young, college-educated, Protestant women from middle-class homes. Some had imbibed a commitment to social justice from parents and grandparents who had fought to abolish slavery. They rebelled against being relegated solely to the roles of wife and mother and sought to assert their independence in socially useful ways.

Hull House

Jane Addams and Ellen Gates Starr established the nation's first settlement house in Chicago in 1889. The two women had been inspired by a visit the year before to London's Toynbee Hall, where a small group of middle-class men had been living and working with that city's poor since 1884. Addams and Starr bought a decaying mansion that had once been the country home of a prominent Chicagoan, Charles J. Hull. By 1889, **"Hull House"** stood amidst factories, churches, saloons, and tenements inhabited by poor, largely foreign-born working-class families.

"The Poverty and Gloom of New York's Streets." Jacob Riis published this picture in his book, *How the Other Half Lives* (1890), a pioneering work in realist photography. The quoted words above are from Riis's text and reflect his efforts to rouse middle-class Americans from their complacency. This photograph depicts runaway boys who had no family and no home.

Addams quickly emerged as the guiding spirit of Hull House. She moved into the building and demanded that all who worked there do the same. She and Starr enlisted extraordinary women such as Florence Kelley, Alice Hamilton, and Julia Lathrop. They set up a nursery for the children of working mothers, a penny savings bank, and an employment bureau, soon followed by a baby clinic, a neighborhood playground, and social clubs. Determined to minister to cultural as well as economic needs, Hull House sponsored an orchestra, reading groups, and a lecture series. Members of Chicago's widening circle of reform-minded intellectuals, artists, and politicians contributed their energies to the enterprise. John Dewey taught philosophy, and Frank Lloyd Wright lectured on architecture. Clarence Darrow, the workingman's lawyer, and Henry Demarest Lloyd, Chicago's radical muckraker, spent considerable time at Hull House. In 1893, Illinois Governor John P. Altgeld named Hull House's Florence Kelley as the state's chief factory inspector. Her investigations led to Illinois's first factory law, which prohibited child labor, limited the employment of women to eight hours a day, and authorized the state to hire inspectors to enforce the law. (For the story of Kelley's time in Europe and how her education there contributed to her becoming one of America's leading advocates for working-class rights, see the Americans Abroad feature, "Florence Kelley: A European-Inspired Search for Social Justice.")

Julia Lathrop used her appointment to the State Board of Charities to agitate for improvements in the care of the poor, the handicapped, and the delinquent. With Edith Abbott and Sophonisba Breckinridge, she established the Department of Social Research at the University of Chicago (which would evolve into the nation's first school of social work). Alice

Jane Addams, Twenty Years at Hull House (1911)

AMERICANS ABROAD Florence Kelley

Hamilton, who had overcome gender discrimination to become a doctor, pioneered in the field of public health.

Hull House leaders did not command the instant fame accorded the muckrakers. Nevertheless, they were steadily drawn into the public arena. Thousands of women across the country were inspired to build their own settlement houses on the Hull House model (eventually more than 400 settlement houses would open nationwide). By 1910, Jane Addams had become one of the nation's most famous women. She and other settlement house workers played a critical role in fashioning the progressive agenda and in drafting pieces of progressive legislation.

The Cultural Conservatism of Progressive Reformers

In general, settlement house workers were more sympathetic toward the poor, the illiterate, and the downtrodden than the muckrakers were. Although she disapproved of machine politics, Jane Addams saw firsthand the benefits that machine politicians delivered to their constituents. She respected the cultural inheritance of the immigrants and admired their resourcefulness. Although she wanted them to become Americans, she encouraged them to integrate their "immigrant gifts" into their new identities. Those attitudes were more liberal than those of other reformers, who considered many immigrants to be culturally, even racially, inferior.

But there were limits even to Addams' sympathy for the immigrants. She disapproved of the new working-class entertainments that gave adolescents extensive and unregulated opportunities for intimate association. She was also troubled by the emerging sexual revolution (see Chapter 20). Addams tended to equate female sexuality with prostitution, and she joined many other women reformers in a campaign to suppress both. Addams and others had identified a serious problem in American cities, where significant numbers of

© Bettmann/ CORBIS

immigrant and rural women new to urban life were lured into prostitution or chose it as a job preferable to 65 poorly paid hours per week in a sweatshop.

Brown Brothers

Jane Addams. The founder of the settlement house movement, Addams was the most famous woman reformer of the progressive era. This photograph dates from the 1890s or 1900s, Hull House's formative period.

The reformers' zeal on this matter, however, exaggerated the dimensions of the problem and led to some questionable legislation, such as the Mann Act (1910), which made it illegal to transport a woman across state lines "for immoral purposes." If this law permitted the prosecution of true traffickers in women, it also allowed the government to interfere in the private sexual relations of consenting adults. This is what happened in the case of Jack Johnson, the African American heavyweight boxing champion, who was arrested and convicted for "transporting" his white secretary, Lucy Cameron, across state lines (see the History through Film feature on p. 581). That Johnson and Cameron's relationship was consensual and would culminate in marriage did not deter the authorities, who wanted to punish Johnson for his dominance of white boxers and his relationship with a white woman.

The cultural conservatism evident in the attitudes of Jane Addams and others on female sexuality also emerged in their attitudes toward alcohol. Drinking rivaled prostitution as a problem in poor, working-class areas. Many men wasted their hard-earned money on drinks at the local saloon, a drain on meager family resources that created tension between these men and their wives. Domestic fights and family violence sometimes ensued. Settlement house workers were well aware of the ill effects of alcoholism (250 saloons did business in Chicago's 19th Ward alone) and sought to combat it. They called on working people to refrain from drinking and pushed legislation that would shut down the saloons. The progressives joined forces with the Women's Christian Temperance Union (245,000 members strong by 1911) and the Anti-Saloon League. By 1916, through their collective efforts, these groups had won prohibition of the sale and manufacture of alcoholic beverages in 16 states. In 1919, their crowning achievement was the 18th Amendment to the U.S. Constitution, making prohibition the law of the land (see Chapter 23).

In depicting alcohol and saloons as unmitigated evils, however, the prohibition movement ignored the role saloons played in ethnic, working-class communities. On Chicago's South Side, for example, saloons provided thousands of workers

WOMEN ENROLLED IN INSTITUTIONS OF HIGHER EDUCATION, 1870–1930

Year	Women's Colleges (thousands of students)	Coed Institutions (thousands of students)	Total (thousands of students)	Percentage of All Students Enrolled
1870	6.5	4.6	11.1	21.0%
1880	15.7	23.9	39.6	33.4%
1890	16.8	39.5	56.3	35.9%
1900	24.4	61.0	85.4	36.8%
1910	34.1	106.5	140.6	39.6%
1920	52.9	230.0	282.9	47.3%
1930	82.1	398.7	480.8	43.7%

Source: From Mabel Newcomer, *A Century of Higher Education for American Women* (New York: Harper and Row, 1959), p. 46.

© CORBIS

Florence Kelley. A leading progressive reformer, member of Hull House, and Illinois's first chief factory inspector.

with the only decent place to eat lunch. The meatpacking plants where they labored had no cafeterias, and few workers could stomach eating their lunch where animals were slaughtered, dressed, and packed. Some saloons catered to particular ethnic groups: They served traditional foods and drinks, provided meeting space for fraternal organizations, and offered camaraderie to men longing to speak in their native tongue. Saloonkeepers sometimes functioned as informal bankers, cashing checks and making small loans. Not surprisingly, many immigrants shunned the prohibition movement.

A Nation of Clubwomen

Settlement house workers comprised only one part of a vast network of female reformers. Hundreds of thousands of women belonged to local women's clubs. Conceived in the 1860s and 1870s as self-help organizations in which women would be encouraged to sharpen their minds, refine their domestic skills, and strengthen their moral faculties (see Chapter 19), these clubs, by 1900, began taking on tasks of social reform. Clubwomen typically focused their energies on improving schools, building libraries and playgrounds, expanding educational and vocational opportunities for girls, and securing fire and sanitation codes for tenement houses. In so doing, they made traditional female concerns—the nurturing and education of children, the care of the home—questions of public policy.

Clubwomen rose to prominence in black communities, too, and addressed similar sorts of issues; on matters of sexuality and alcohol, they often shared the conservative sentiments of white clubwomen. Some groups of black clubwomen ventured into community affairs more boldly than their white counterparts, especially in southern states, where black men were being stripped of the right to vote, to serve on juries, and to hold political office. Whites were prepared to punish any African American, male or female, who showed too much initiative or was thought to be challenging the principles of white supremacy. Many black female activists persevered in the face of such threats, determined to provide leadership in their communities and voice their people's concerns.

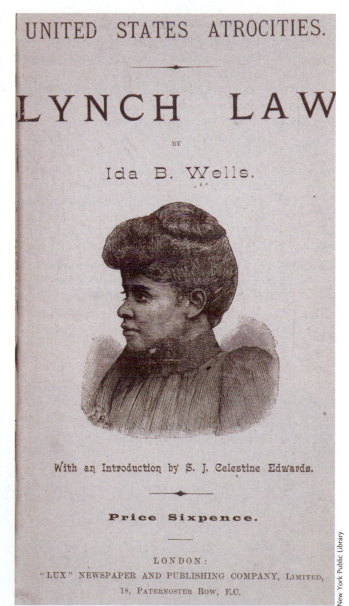

New York Public Library

Ida B. Wells. Wells is best known for her outspoken opposition to the lynching of African Americans—a campaign that she took to England in the 1890s, as the pamphlet pictured above indicates. Wells was also a proponent of female suffrage, a founder of the NAACP, and an active clubwoman. To honor her, black women named their activist organization the Ida B. Wells Club.

Socialism

Q **FOCUS QUESTION** What was the relationship of socialism to progressivism?

In the early 20th century, **socialism** stood for the transfer of control over big businesses from the capitalists who owned them to the laboring masses who worked in them. Socialists believed that such a transfer, usually defined in terms of government ownership and operation of corporations, would make it impossible for wealthy elites to control society.

The Socialist Party of America, founded in 1901, became a political force during the first 20 years of the century, and socialist ideas influenced progressivism. In 1912, at the peak of its influence, the Socialist Party enrolled more than 115,000 members. Its presidential candidate, the charismatic **Eugene Victor Debs** of Terre Haute, Indiana, attracted almost a million votes—6 percent of the total votes cast that year. In that same year, 1,200 Socialists held elective office in 340 different municipalities. Of these, 79 were mayors of cities as geographically

Eugene Debs, *How I Became a Socialist* (1902)

and demographically diverse as Schenectady, New York; Milwaukee, Wisconsin; Butte, Montana; and Berkeley, California. More than 300 newspapers and periodicals, with a combined circulation exceeding 2 million, spread the socialist gospel. The most important socialist publication was *Appeal to Reason*, published by Julius Wayland from Kansas and sent out each week to 750,000 subscribers. In 1905, Wayland published, in serial form, a novel by an obscure muckraker named Upton Sinclair, which depicted the scandalous working conditions in Chicago's meat-packing industry. When it was later published in book form in 1906, *The Jungle* created such an outcry that the federal government was forced to regulate the meat industry.

The Several Faces of Socialism

Socialists came in many varieties. In Milwaukee, they consisted of predominantly German working-class immigrants and their descendants; in New York City, their numbers were strongest among Jewish immigrants from Eastern Europe. In the Southwest, tens of thousands of disgruntled native-born farmers who had been Populists in the 1890s now flocked to the socialist banner. In the West, socialism was popular among miners, timber cutters, and others who labored in isolated areas where industrialists possessed extraordinary power over work, politics, and community life. These westerners gravitated to the militant labor union, the Industrial Workers of the World (IWW), which found a home in the Socialist Party from 1905 to 1913.

The IWW was the most radical socialist group. Unlike conventional labor unions such as the American Federation of Labor (see Chapter 19), the IWW refused to sign collective bargaining agreements with employers, arguing that such agreements only trapped workers in capitalist property relations. Capitalism had to be overthrown through struggles between workers and their employers. Although hundreds of thousands of workers passed through its ranks or participated in its strikes, the IWW's membership rarely exceeded 20,000. Nevertheless, the IWW acquired a national reputation by organizing the poorest and most isolated workers and leading them in strikes against employers who were unaccustomed to having their authority challenged. Violence lurked beneath the surface of these strikes and occasionally erupted in bloody skirmishes between strikers and police, National Guardsmen, or the private security forces hired by employers.

Mainstream socialists, led by Debs, shared the IWW's desire to end capitalism but wanted to work within rather than outside American political, cultural, and religious traditions. Debs and his followers saw themselves as the saviors of the American republic—as the true heirs of Thomas Jefferson. Their confidence that the nation could be redeemed through conventional politics—through the election of socialists to

Eugene V. Debs. This photograph captures the energy and charisma of Debs as he addresses a working-class audience in New York during his 1912 presidential campaign.

© Hulton Archive/Getty Images

office and ultimately to the presidency itself—is evidence of their belief in American democracy. And their faith in redemption reveals the degree to which Protestant religious beliefs underlay their quest for social justice and what they called a "cooperative commonwealth." Other socialists, led by Victor Berger of Milwaukee, abandoned talk of radicalism altogether and chose instead an aggressive brand of reform politics. They were dubbed "gas and water socialists" because of their interest in improving city services.

The differences among the socialists would, after 1912, fragment their movement. For a decade or so, however, these divergent groups managed to coexist in a single political party, thanks largely to the leadership of Debs. When he was released from a Chicago jail in 1895 after serving time for his role in the strike against the Pullman Company (see Chapter 19), Debs declared to a gathering of 100,000 admirers:

> Manifestly the spirit of '76 still survives. The fires of liberty and noble aspirations are not yet extinguished. . . . The vindication and glorification of American principles of government, as proclaimed to the world in the Declaration of Independence, is the high purpose of this convocation.

Socialists and Progressives

Debs' speeches both attracted and disturbed progressives. On the one hand, he spoke compellingly about the dangers of unregulated capitalism and excessively concentrated wealth, both progressive concerns. His confidence that a strong state could bring the economic system under control mirrored the progressives' own faith in the positive uses of government. Progressives often worked hand-in-hand with socialists to win economic and political reforms, especially at the municipal and state levels, and many intellectuals—including John Dewey, Richard Ely, and Thorstein Veblen—and reformers easily moved back and forth between socialism and progressivism. So did Helen Keller, the country's leading spokesperson for the disabled.

On the other hand, Debs's radicalism scared progressives, as did his efforts to organize a working-class political movement independent of middle-class involvement or control. Although progressives wanted to tame capitalism, they stopped short of wanting to eliminate it. They wanted to improve working and living conditions for the masses but not cede political control to them. The progressives hoped to offer a political program with

Map 21.1 Cities and Towns Electing Socialist Mayors or Other Major Municipal Officers, 1911–1920. This map reveals the strength of socialist electoral support in some unexpected areas: western Pennsylvania, Ohio, Illinois, Minnesota, a cluster of towns where Oklahoma, Missouri, and Kansas meet, Colorado, and Utah.

© Cengage Learning

Helen Keller, Labor Activist. Best known for her work in calling attention to the rights and needs of disabled Americans, Keller also agitated on behalf of America's workers. Here she stiffens the resolve of actors on strike against a New York City opera house. Her companion, Anne Sullivan Macy, stands to her right, serving as Keller's interpreter.

enough reform elements to counter the appeal of Debs's more radical movement. In this, they were successful.

Municipal Reform

Q **FOCUS QUESTION** What were the benefits and costs of municipal reform?

Progressive-era reform battles first erupted over control of municipal transportation networks and utilities. Private corporations typically owned and operated street railways and electrical and gas systems. Many of the corporations used their monopoly power to charge exorbitant fares and rates, and they often won that power by bribing city officials who belonged to one of the political machines. Corporations achieved generous reductions in real estate taxes in the same way.

The attack on private utilities and their protectors in city government gained momentum in the mid-1890s. In Detroit, reform-minded mayor Hazen S. Pingree led successful fights to control the city's gas, telephone, and trolley companies. In

Chicago in 1896 and 1897, a group of middle-class reformers ousted a corrupt city council and elected a mayor, Carter Harrison, Jr., who promised to protect Chicago's streetcar riders from exploitation. In Cleveland, the crusading reformer Tom Johnson won election as mayor in 1901, curbed the power of the streetcar interests, and brought honest and efficient government to the city.

Occasionally, a reform politician of Johnson's caliber would rise to power through one of the regular political parties. But this path to power was a difficult one, especially in cities where the political parties were controlled by machines. Consequently, progressives worked for reforms that would strip the parties of their power. Two of their favorite reforms were the city commission and the city manager forms of government.

The City Commission Plan

First introduced in Galveston, Texas, in 1900, in the wake of a devastating tidal wave, the city commission shifted municipal power from the mayor and his aldermen to five city commissioners, each responsible for a different department of city government. In Galveston and elsewhere, the impetus for this reform came from civic-minded businessmen who were determined to rebuild government on the principles of efficient and scientific management that had energized the private sector. The results were often impressive. The Galveston commissioners restored the city's credit after a brush with bankruptcy, improved the city's harbor, and built a massive seawall to protect the city from future floods. They accomplished all of this on budgets that had been cut by one-third. By 1913, more than 300 cities, most of them small to middling in size, had adopted the city commission plan.

The City Manager Plan

The city commission system did not always work to perfection, however. Sometimes the commissioners used their position to reward electoral supporters with jobs and contracts; other times, they pursued power and prestige for their respective departments. The city manager plan was meant to overcome such problems. Under this plan, the commissioners continued to set policy, but policy implementation now rested with a "chief executive." This official, who was not elected but appointed by the commissioners, would curtail rivalries among commissioners and ensure that no outside influences interfered with the impartial, businesslike management of the city. The job of city manager was explicitly modeled after that of a corporation executive. First introduced in Sumter, South Carolina, in 1911 and then in Dayton, Ohio, in 1913, by 1919 the city manager plan had spread to 130 cities.

The Costs of Reform

Although these reforms limited corruption and improved services, they were not universally popular. Poor and minority voters, in particular, saw their influence in local affairs weakened by the shift to city commissioners and city managers. Previously, candidates for municipal office (other than the mayor) competed in ward elections rather than in citywide elections. Voters in working-class wards commonly elected workingmen to represent them, and voters in immigrant wards made sure that fellow ethnics represented their interests on city councils. Citywide elections diluted the strength of these constituencies. Candidates from poor districts often lacked the money needed to mount a citywide campaign, and they were further hampered by the nonpartisan nature of such elections. Denied the support of a political party or platform, they had to make themselves personally known to voters throughout the city. That was a much easier task for the city's "leading citizens"—manufacturers, merchants, and lawyers—than it was for workingmen. In Dayton, the percentage of citizens voting Socialist rose from 25 to 44 percent in the years following the introduction of the commission manager system, but the number of Socialists elected to office declined from five to zero. Progressive political reforms thus frequently reduced the influence of radicals, minorities, and the poor in elections.

Reform in the States

FOCUS QUESTION What were the results of progressive efforts to create a "responsible" and "virtuous" electorate? What were the similarities and differences between John R. Commons's "Wisconsin Idea" and Frederick Winslow Taylor's program of scientific management?

As at the local level, political parties at the state level were often dominated by corrupt politicians who did the bidding of powerful private lobbies. In New Jersey in 1903, for example, industrial and financial interests, working through the Republican Party machine, controlled numerous appointments to state government, including the chief justice of the state supreme court, the attorney general, and the commissioner of banking and insurance. Such webs of influence ensured that New Jersey would provide large corporations such as the railroads with favorable political and economic legislation.

Restoring Sovereignty to "the People"

Progressives introduced reforms designed to undermine the power of party bosses, restore sovereignty to "the people," and encourage honest, talented individuals to enter politics. One such reform was the direct primary, a mechanism that enabled voters, rather than party bosses, to choose party candidates. Mississippi introduced this reform in 1902 and Wisconsin in 1903. By 1916, all but three states had adopted the direct primary. Closely related was a movement to strip state legislatures of their power to choose U.S. senators. State after state enacted legislation that permitted voters to choose Senate candidates in primary elections. In 1912, a reluctant U.S. Senate was obliged to approve the 17th Amendment to the Constitution, mandating the direct election of senators. The state legislatures ratified this amendment in 1913.

Populists had first proposed direct election of U.S. senators in the 1890s; they also proposed the **initiative** and the **referendum**, both of which were adopted first by Oregon in 1902 and then by 18 other states between 1902 and 1915. The initiative allowed reformers to put legislative proposals before voters in general elections without having to wait for state legislatures to act. The referendum gave voters the right in general elections to repeal an unpopular act that a state legislature had passed. Less widely adopted but important nevertheless was the **recall**, a device that allowed voters to remove from office public servants who had betrayed their trust. As a further control over the behavior of elected officials, numerous states enacted laws that regulated corporate campaign contributions and restricted lobbying activities in state legislatures. These laws neither eliminated corporate privilege nor destroyed the power of machine politicians. Nevertheless, they made politics more honest and strengthened the influence of ordinary voters.

Creating a Virtuous Electorate

Progressive reformers focused as well on creating a responsible electorate that understood the importance of the vote and that resisted efforts to manipulate elections. To create this ideal electorate, reformers had to see to it that all of those citizens who were deemed virtuous could cast their votes free of coercion and intimidation. At the same time, reformers sought to disfranchise citizens who were considered irresponsible and corruptible. In pursuing these goals, progressives substantially altered the composition of the electorate and strengthened government regulation of voting. As a result, progressives enlarged the electorate by extending the right to vote to women; but they also either initiated or tolerated laws that barred large numbers of minority and poor voters from the polls.

The Australian Ballot

Government regulation of voting had begun in the 1890s, when virtually every state adopted the **Australian ballot (secret ballot)**. This reform required voters to vote in private rather than in public. It also required the government, rather than political parties, to print the ballots and supervise the voting. Before this time, each political party had printed its own ballot with only its candidates listed. At election time, each party mobilized its loyal supporters. Party workers offered liquor, free meals, and other bribes to entice voters to the polls and to "persuade" them to cast the party ballot. Because the ballots were cast in public, few voters who had accepted gifts of liquor and food dared to cross watchful party officials. Critics argued that the system corrupted the electoral process. They also pointed out that it made "ticket splitting"—dividing one's vote between candidates of two or more parties—virtually impossible.

The Australian ballot solved these problems. Although it predated progressivism, it embodied the progressives' determination to use government power to encourage citizens to cast their votes responsibly and wisely.

The Australian Ballot in Action. This 1900 drawing of a New York City polling place shows the benefits of this election reform. A man on the left emerges from a booth where he voted in private and without intimidation. Moving right, he will deposit his "secret ballot" (held in his right hand) through a slit in a wooden box presided over by an impartial poll watcher.

Personal Registration Laws

That same determination was apparent in the progressives' support for the personal registration laws that virtually every state passed between 1890 and 1920. These laws allowed prospective voters to register to vote only if they appeared at a designated government office with proper identification. Frequently, these laws also mandated a certain period of residence in the state before registration and a certain interval between registration and actual voting.

Personal registration laws were meant to disfranchise citizens who showed no interest in voting until Election Day, when a party worker arrived with a few dollars and offered a free ride to the polls. However, they also excluded many hardworking, responsible, poor people who wanted to vote but had failed to register, either because their work schedules made it impossible or because they were intimidated by the complex regulations. The laws were particularly frustrating for immigrants with limited knowledge of English.

Disfranchisement

Progressives also promoted election laws expressly designed to keep noncitizen immigrants from voting. In the 1880s, 18 states had passed laws allowing immigrants to vote without first becoming citizens. Progressives reversed this trend. At the same time, the newly formed Bureau of Immigration and Naturalization (1906) made it more difficult to become a citizen. Applicants for citizenship now had to appear before a judge, who interrogated them, in the English language, on American history and civics. In addition, immigrants were required to provide two witnesses to vouch for their "moral character" and their "attachment to the principles of the Constitution." Finally, immigrants had to swear (and, if necessary, prove) that they were not anarchists or polygamists and that they had resided continuously in the United States for five years.

Most progressives defended the added rigor of the process. U.S. citizenship, they believed, carried responsibilities; it was not to be bestowed lightly. This position was understandable, given the electoral abuses progressives had exposed. Nevertheless, the reforms also denied the vote to a large proportion of the population. In cities and towns where immigrants dominated the workforce, the numbers of registered voters fell steeply. Nowhere was exclusion more startling than in the South, where between 1890 and 1904, every ex-Confederate state passed laws designed to strip blacks of their right to vote. Because laws explicitly barring blacks from voting would have violated the 15th Amendment, this exclusion had to be accomplished indirectly—through literacy tests, property qualifications, and poll taxes mandated by the legislatures of the ex-Confederate states. Any citizen who failed a reading test, or who could not sign his name, or who did not own a minimum amount of property, or who could not pay a poll tax, lost his right to vote. The citizens who failed these tests most frequently were blacks—who formed the poorest and least educated segment of the southern population—but a large segment of the region's poor whites also failed the tests. The effects of **disfranchisement** were stark. In 1900, only 1,300 blacks voted in Mississippi elections, down from 130,000 in the 1870s. Virginia's voter turnout dropped from 60 percent of adult men (white and black) in 1900 to 28 percent in 1904.

Many progressives in the North, such as Governor Robert La Follette of Wisconsin, criticized southern disfranchisement. Some, including Jane Addams and John Dewey, joined in 1910 with W. E. B. Du Bois and other black reformers to found the **National Association for the Advancement of Colored People (NAACP)**, an interracial political organization that made black equality its primary goal. In the South, however, white progressives rarely challenged disfranchisement, and most had little difficulty justifying it. Because progressives everywhere considered the right to vote a precious gift granted only to those who could handle its

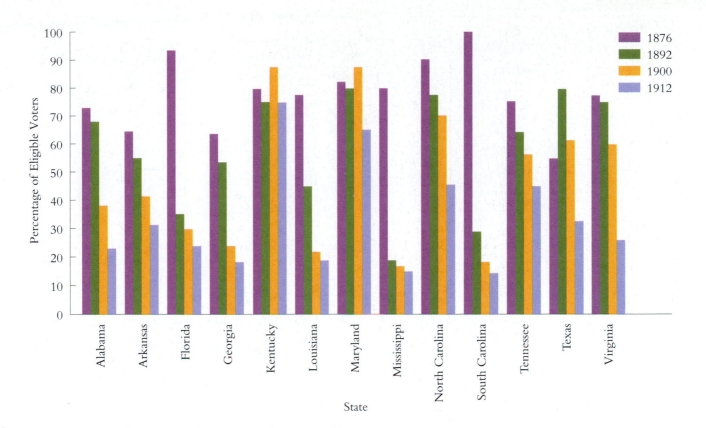

Voter Participation in 13 Southern States, 1876, 1892, 1900, 1912.
Source: Data from *Historical Statistics of the United States, Colonial Times to 1970* (White Plains, NY: Kraus International, 1989).

responsibilities, they equally believed that it must be withheld from people who were deemed racially or culturally unfit. Progressives in the North excluded many immigrants on just those grounds. Progressives in the South saw the disfranchisement of African Americans in the same light.

Disillusionment with the Electorate

In the process of identifying those groups as "unfit" to hold the franchise, some progressives soured on the electoral process altogether. The more they looked for rational and virtuous voters, the fewer they found. The growing disillusionment with the electorate, in combination with intensifying restrictions on the franchise, created an environment in which fewer and fewer Americans actually went to the polls. Voter participation rates fell from 79 percent in 1896 to only 49 percent in 1920.

Woman Suffrage

The major exception to this trend was the enfranchisement of women. This momentous reform was adopted by several states during the 1890s and the first two decades of the 20th century and became federal law with the ratification of the 19th Amendment to the Constitution in 1920.

Launched in 1848 at the famous Seneca Falls convention (see Chapter 12), the women's rights movement floundered in the 1870s and 1880s. In 1890, suffragists came together in a new organization, the **National American Woman Suffrage Association (NAWSA)**, led by Elizabeth Cady Stanton and Susan B. Anthony. Thousands of young, college-educated women campaigned door-to-door, held impromptu rallies, and pressured state legislators.

Wyoming, which attained statehood in 1890, became the first state to grant women the right to vote, followed in 1893 by Colorado and in 1896 by Idaho and Utah. The main reason for success in these sparsely populated western states was not egalitarianism but rather the conviction that women's supposedly gentler and more nurturing nature would tame and civilize the men who had populated the frontier.

Earlier generations had insisted that women were fundamentally equal to men, but the new suffragists argued that women were different from men. Women, they stressed, possessed a moral sense and a nurturing quality that men lacked. Consequently, they understood the civic obligations implied by the franchise and could be trusted to vote virtuously. Their votes would hasten to completion the progressive task of cleansing the political process of corruption. Their experience as mothers and household managers, moreover, would enable them to guide local and state governments in efforts to improve education, sanitation, family wholesomeness, and the condition of women and children in the workforce. In other words, the enfranchisement of women would enhance the quality of both public and private life without insisting that members of the female sex were the equals of men in all respects.

Suffragists were slow to ally themselves with blacks, Asians, and other disfranchised groups. In fact, many suffragists,

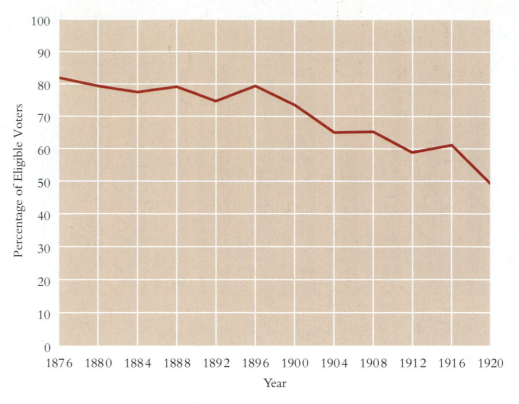

Voter Participation in Presidential Elections, 1876–1920.
Source: Data from *Historical Statistics of the United States, Colonial Times to 1970*
(White Plains, NY: Kraus International, 1989).

THE AWAKENING

© CORBIS

Woman Suffrage. The confident, torch-bearing suffragist striding across the continent in this 1915 cartoon conveys the conviction of woman suffragists everywhere that their most cherished goal, gaining the vote for women, was within reach. The cartoon also reveals the interesting split among the states: western states had already granted women the vote, whereas eastern states had not.

Humor and the Woman Suffrage Movement

The length and difficulty of the struggle for woman suffrage have left many Americans with an image of suffragists as a rather serious and humorless group. But the poem reproduced below, from a book by suffragist Alice Duer Miller, *Are Women People? A Book of Rhymes for Suffrage Times* (New York: George H. Doran Company, 1915), suggests that we need to rethink this image. The poems in this book make the case for woman suffrage and attack antisuffragists (known at the time simply as "antis") in a humorous, lighthearted way. The poem below ridicules a "consistent anti," meaning someone opposed to woman suffrage. The poem imagines this anti to be a mother anguished by the knowledge that her son, Willie, who has just turned 21 (then the voting age), must soon confront the "danger" of the polls, those "dark and dreadful places where many lose their souls." By making the fear of voting seem ludicrous, the poem attempts to discredit those who dreaded the consequences of extending the franchise to women.

A Consistent Anti to Her Son

You're twenty-one to-day, Willie,
And a danger lurks at the door,
I've known about it always,
But I never spoke before;
When you were only a baby
It seemed so very remote,
But you're twenty-one to-day, Willie,
And old enough to vote.
You must not go to the polls, Willie,
Never go to the polls,
They're dark and dreadful places
Where many lose their souls;
They smirch, degrade and coarsen,
Terrible things they do
To quiet, elderly women—
What would they do to you!
If you've a boyish fancy
For any measure or man,
Tell me, and I'll tell Father,
He'll vote for it, if he can.
He casts my vote, and Louisa's,
And Sarah, and dear Aunt Clo;
Wouldn't you let him vote for you?
Father, who loves you so?
I've guarded you always, Willie,
Body and soul from harm;
I'll guard your faith and honor,
Your innocence and charm
From the polls and their evil spirits,
Politics, rum and pelf;
Do you think I'd send my only son
Where I would not go myself?

Q What does this poem reveal about the arguments of the antis (those who opposed woman suffrage)?

Q Is the poem successful in its effort to poke fun at (and thus to undermine) these arguments?

Source: from Alice Duer Miller, *Are Women People? A Book of Rhymes for Suffrage Times*, New York (George H. Doran Company, 1915), pp. 11–12.

especially those in the South and West, opposed the franchise for Americans of color. They, like their male counterparts, believed that members of these groups lacked moral strength and thus did not deserve the right to vote. Unlike the suffrage pioneers of the 1840s and 1850s, many progressive-era suffragists were little troubled by racial discrimination and injustice.

Washington, California, Kansas, Oregon, and Arizona followed the lead of the other western states by enfranchising women between 1910 and 1912. After a series of setbacks in eastern and midwestern states, the movement regained momentum under the leadership of the strategically astute Carrie Chapman Catt, who became president of NAWSA in 1915 and successfully coordinated myriad grassroots campaigns. Equally important was Alice Paul, a radical who founded the Congressional Union in 1913 and later renamed it the National Woman's Party. Paul and her supporters focused their attention on the White House, picketing President Wilson's home 24 hours a day, brandishing large posters that chastised him for abandoning his democratic principles, and daring the police to arrest them. Several suffrage demonstrators were jailed, where they continued their protests by going on hunger strikes (refusing to eat). Aided by a heightened enthusiasm for democracy generated by America's participation in the First World War (see Chapter 23), which generated a more positive popular response to Paul's tactics than might otherwise have been the case, the suffragists achieved their goal of universal woman suffrage in 1920.

Predictions that suffrage for women would radically alter politics turned out to be false. The political system was neither cleansed of corruption, nor did the government rush headlong to address the private needs of women and their families. Although the numbers of voters increased after 1920, voter participation rates continued to decline. Still, the extension of the vote to women, 144 years after the founding of the nation, was a major political achievement.

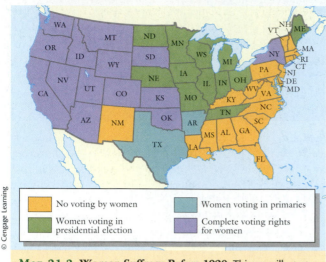

Map 21.2 **Woman Suffrage Before 1920.** This map illustrates how woman suffrage prior to 1920 had advanced furthest in the West.

Legend:
- No voting by women
- Women voting in presidential election
- Women voting in primaries
- Complete voting rights for women

© Cengage Learning

Robert La Follette and Wisconsin Progressivism

In some states, progressives extended reform efforts well beyond political parties and the electorate. Progressives also fought to limit corporate power, strengthen organized labor, and offer social welfare protection to the weak. Many state governments were pressured into passing such legislation by progressive alliances of middle-class and working-class reformers and by dynamic state governors.

Nowhere did the progressives' campaign for social reform flourish as it did in Wisconsin. The movement arose first in the 1890s, in hundreds of Wisconsin cities and towns, as citizens began to mobilize against the state's corrupt Republican Party and the special privileges the party had granted to private utilities and railroads. These reform-minded citizens came from varied backgrounds. They were middle class and working class, urban and rural, male and female, intellectual and evangelical, Scandinavian Protestant and German Catholic. Wisconsin progressivism had already gained considerable momentum by 1897, when Robert La Follette assumed its leadership.

La Follette was born into a prosperous farming family in 1855. He entered politics as a Republican in the 1880s and embraced reform in the late 1890s. Elected governor in 1900, he secured for Wisconsin both a direct primary and a tax law that stripped the railroad corporations of tax exemptions they had long enjoyed. In 1905, he pushed through a civil service law mandating that every state employee meet a certain level of competence.

A tireless campaigner and a spellbinding speaker, "Fighting Bob" won election to the U.S. Senate in 1906. Meanwhile, Wisconsin's advancing labor and socialist movements impelled progressive reformers to focus their legislative efforts on issues of corporate greed and social welfare. By 1910, reformers had passed state laws that regulated railroad and utility rates, instituted the nation's first state income tax, and provided workers with compensation for injuries, limitations on work hours, restrictions on child labor, and minimum wages for women.

Many of these laws were written by social scientists at the University of Wisconsin, with whom reformers had close ties. In the first decade of the 20th century, John R. Commons, University of Wisconsin economist, drafted Wisconsin's civil service and public utilities laws. In 1911, Commons designed and won legislative approval for the Wisconsin Industrial Commission, which brought together employers, trade unionists, and professionals and gave them broad powers to investigate and regulate relations between industry and labor throughout the state. Never before had a state government so plainly committed itself to the cause of industrial justice. For the first time, the rights of labor would be treated with the same respect as the rights of industry. Equally important was the responsibility the commission delegated to nonelected professionals: social scientists, lawyers, engineers, and others.

Wisconsin Historical Society, WHi-2390

Robert La Follette, Wisconsin Progressive. This photograph of La Follette campaigning in Wisconsin in 1897 captures the intensity and combativeness that "Fighting Bob" brought to progressivism.

These professionals, Wisconsin reformers believed, would succeed where political parties had failed—namely, in providing the public with expert and honest government.

The **"Wisconsin Idea"** found quick adoption in Ohio, Indiana, New York, and Colorado. In 1913, the federal government established its own Industrial Relations Commission and hired Commons to direct its investigative staff. In other areas, too, reformers began urging state and federal governments to shift the policy-making initiative away from political parties and toward administrative agencies staffed by professionals.

Progressive Reform in New York

New York was second only to Wisconsin in the vigor and breadth of its progressive movement. As in Wisconsin, New York progressives focused first on fighting political corruption. Revelations of close ties between leading Republican politicians and life insurance companies vaulted reform lawyer Charles Evans Hughes into the governor's mansion in 1907. Hughes immediately established several public service commissions to regulate railroads and utility companies. Also, as in Wisconsin, the labor movement exercised its influence. New York City garment workers struck and forced state legislators to regulate working conditions. With the establishment of the Factory Investigating Committee, New York, like Wisconsin, became a pioneer in labor and social welfare policy.

New York state legislators also faced pressure from middle-class reformers—settlement house workers such as Lillian Wald of the Henry Street Settlement and lawyers such as Louis Brandeis—who had become convinced of the need for new laws to protect the disadvantaged. This combined pressure from working-class and middle-class constituencies persuaded some state Democrats, including Assemblyman Alfred E. Smith and Senator Robert F. Wagner, to convert from machine to reform politics. Their appearance in the progressive ranks represented the arrival of a new reform sensibility. Wagner and Smith were both ethnic Catholics (Wagner was born in Germany, and Smith was the grandchild of Irish immigrants). They opposed prohibition, city commissions, voter registration laws, and other reforms whose intent seemed anti-immigrant or anti-Catholic. Meanwhile, they supported reforms meant to improve the working and living conditions of New York's urban poor. They agitated for a minimum wage, factory safety, workmen's compensation, the right of workers to join unions, and the regulation of excessively powerful corporations. Their participation in progressivism accelerated the movement's shift, first in New York and then elsewhere, away from a preoccupation with political parties and electorates and toward questions of economic justice and social welfare.

Scientific Management on the Factory Floor

Progressivism drew support, too, from businessmen who saw in this reform movement an opportunity to introduce more efficiency, science, and harmony into industrial relations. Just as business-oriented progressives in Galveston and elsewhere drew on the principles of scientific management to reform local government, so, too, some businessmen attempted to use those principles to create more productive and cohesive workplaces.

Scientific management had developed in the last two decades of the 19th century among managers and engineers who were looking to develop arrangements of machines and workers that would achieve the highest speed in production with the fewest human or mechanical interruptions. Their leader was **Frederick Winslow Taylor** who, as chief engineer at Philadelphia's Midvale Steel Company in the 1880s, had examined every human task and mechanical movement involved in his company's production process. Taylor pioneered the "time-and-motion study," the technique through which managers recorded every distinct movement a worker made in performing his or her job, how long it took, and how often it was performed. Taylor hoped thereby to identify and eliminate wasted human energy. Eliminating waste might mean reorganizing a floor of machinery so as to reduce "down time" between production steps; it might mean instructing workers to perform their tasks differently; or it might mean replacing uncooperative skilled workers with machines tended by unskilled, low-wage laborers. Regardless of the method chosen, the goal was the same: to make human labor emulate the smooth and apparently effortless operation of an automatic, perfectly calibrated piece of machinery.

Though Taylor's program of "scientific management" antedated progressivism, it fired the imagination of the business- and efficiency-oriented sectors of the reform movement. Taylor achieved his greatest popularity during the first two decades of the 20th century, and his 1911 book, *The Principles of Scientific Management*, drew the interest of countless corporate managers and engineers, many of whom sought to introduce "Taylorism" into their own production systems. By then, Taylor himself had been influenced by the spirit of progressive reform, and he offered his program as a way of achieving industrial peace. Scientific management, Taylor claimed, would allow each worker to be matched with a job well-suited to his abilities. Efficiency and wages would rise; so, too, would worker satisfaction. Most, if not all, workplace antagonism, would then dissolve.

Frederick W. Taylor, *Principles of Scientific Management* (1911)

Henry Ford, the pioneer in automobile manufacturing, was one of Taylor's disciples. By 1910, Ford's engineers had broken down the production of its main car, the "Model T," into a series of simple, sequential tasks. Each worker performed only one task: adding a carburetor to an engine, inserting a windshield, mounting tires onto wheels. Then in 1913, Ford's engineers introduced the first moving assembly line, a continuously moving conveyor belt that carried cars in production through each workstation. This innovation eliminated precious time previously wasted in transporting car parts (or partially built cars) by crane or truck from one work area to another. It also limited the time available to workers to perform their assigned tasks. Only the foreman, not the workers, could stop the line or change its speed.

By 1913, the continuous assembly line made Ford Motor Company's new Highland Park plant the most tightly integrated and continuously moving production system in American industry. It seemed to have leapt directly from the pages of

Frederick W. Taylor. Taylor's ideas for revolutionizing production techniques and worker management attracted many supporters in the early 20th century.

Taylor's *Principles of Scientific Management*. The pace of car production at Ford exceeded all expectations. Between 1910 and 1914, production time on Model Ts dropped by 90 percent, from an average of more than 12 hours per car to 1.5 hours. A thousand Model Ts began rolling off the assembly line each day. This striking increase in the rate of production enabled Ford to slash the price of a Model T from $950 in 1909 to only $295 in 1923, a reduction of 70 percent. The number of Model Ts purchased by Americans increased 16-fold between 1912 and 1921, from 79,000 to 1,250,000. The assembly line quickly became the most admired—and most feared—symbol of American mass production.

Problems immediately beset the system, however. Repeating a single motion all day long induced mental stupor, and managerial efforts to speed up the line produced physical exhaustion—both of which increased the incidence of error and injury. Some workers tried to organize a union to gain a voice in production matters, but most Ford workers expressed their dissatisfaction simply by quitting. By 1913, employee turnover at Highland Park had reached the astounding rate of 370 percent per year. At that rate, Ford had to hire 51,800 workers every year just to keep his factory fully staffed at 14,000.

A problem of that magnitude demanded a dramatic solution. Ford provided it in 1914 by raising the wage he paid his assembly-line workers to $5 per day, double the average manufacturing wage then prevalent in American industry. The result: Workers, especially young and single men, flocked to Detroit. Highland Park's high productivity rate permitted Ford to absorb the wage increase without cutting substantially into profits.

Taylor had believed that improved efficiency would lead to dramatic wage gains. Ford's ability to double his wage payout, in this respect, proved Taylor right. But Taylor's theory of human psychology remained primitive, inadequate to the task of comprehending the range of emotions that employees brought to the workplace and the multiple sources of employee–employer conflict. Ford recognized that workers were more complex than Taylor had allowed, which is why his innovations went well beyond what Taylor himself had contemplated. Thus, Ford set up a sociology department, forerunner of the personnel department, to collect job, family, and other information about his employees. He sent social workers into workers' homes to inquire into (and "improve") their personal lives. For the foreign-born, he instituted Americanization classes. He offered his employees housing subsidies, medical care, and other benefits. Ford's success was widely admired; nevertheless, it would take another generation or two for significant sectors of the corporate world to follow his lead. And thus throughout the first two decades of the 20th century, American industry remained more the target than the ally of progressive reform.

A Campaign for Civil Rights

 FOCUS QUESTION How did W. E. B. Du Bois's approach to African American reform differ from that of Booker T. Washington?

The reform energy unleashed by the progressives inspired a new generation of African American activists to insist that the nation grapple anew with issues of racial inequality. Indeed, the modern civil rights movement can be said to have started in the early years of the 20th century.

The Failure of Accommodationism

Booker T. Washington's message—that blacks should accept segregation and disfranchisement as unavoidable and focus their energies instead on self-help and self-improvement—faced increasing criticism from black activists such as **W. E. B. Du Bois**, Ida B. Wells, Monroe Trotter, and others. Washington's accommodationist leadership (see Chapter 18), in their eyes, brought southern blacks no reprieve from racism. More than 100 blacks had been lynched in 1900 alone; between 1901 and 1914, at least 1,000 others would be hanged.

Increasingly, unsubstantiated rumors of black assaults on whites became occasions for white mobs to rampage through black neighborhoods and destroy life and property. In 1908, a mob in Springfield, Illinois, attacked black businesses and

HISTORY THROUGH FILM

The Great White Hope (1970)

Directed by Martin Ritt.
Starring James Earl Jones (Jack Jefferson) and Jane Alexander (Eleanor Backman).

This movie is a fictional retelling of the life of Jack Johnson, the first black world heavyweight boxing champion, and of the furor that his dominance over white boxers, his outspokenness, and his relationships with white women generated in early 20th-century America. The movie opens with white boxing promoters persuading a former white champion (James Bradley) to come out of retirement to battle the black champion, here called Jack Jefferson (rather than Johnson). In a subsequent scene, Jefferson destroys Bradley in the ring and reacts with defiant cheeriness to the boos and racial epithets that rain down upon him from the predominantly white crowd.

Jefferson refuses to accept the limitations that white society placed on black men at the time. He is neither submissive nor deferential toward whites, and he openly dates white women. Whites fear and loathe him for defying the era's racial conventions. One evening, federal agents burst in on Jefferson and his white lover, Eleanor Backman (Jane Alexander), and accuse Jefferson of violating the Mann Act, a 1910 law that made it illegal to transport women across state lines for sexual purposes (see p. 568). At Jefferson's trial, prosecutors expected to convince a jury that Backman was coerced into sex, for no white woman, they intended to argue, would have freely chosen to consort with a black man in this way.

Jefferson manages to evade the authorities and flee to Europe, where Backman joins him. The early months abroad are invigorating for both, as Jefferson is celebrated for his fighting prowess and the couple's love for each other flourishes. Soon, however, the boxing opponents disappear, money stops coming in, and a sense of despair grows between the two lovers. Their exile ends disastrously in Mexico, where Backman kills herself after an argument with Jefferson. Jefferson, his spirit finally broken, agrees to throw a fight against the newest Great White Hope, Jess Willard, in return for an opportunity to end his fugitive status and return to the United States.

Made in 1970, *The Great White Hope* was inspired by the brash heavyweight champion of the 1960s, Muhammad Ali. The film is quite faithful to the story of the real Jack Johnson, who dated white women, was arrested for "violating" the Mann Act, fled the country rather than submit

James Earl Jones as Jack Jefferson.

20th Century Fox/THE KOBAL COLLECTION

to jail, and ultimately lost a heavyweight bout to Jess Willard. The film endows Backman, a fictional character, with more "class" and refinement than the real women who associated with Johnson usually possessed. The film also fictionalizes Johnson's fight against Willard by suggesting that Johnson could have won the fight had he not been required to throw it. Despite these changes, the film successfully re-creates the climate of the early years of the 20th century and the white hostility imperiling a black man who dared to assert his pride and independence. ◼

---

individuals; a force of 5,000 state militia was required to restore order. The troops were too late, however, to stop the lynching of two innocent black men, one a successful barber and the other an 84-year-old man who had been married to a white woman for more than 30 years.

Booker T. Washington had long believed that blacks who educated themselves or who succeeded in business would be accepted as equals by whites. As Du Bois and other black militants observed, however, white rioters made no distinction between rich blacks and poor, or between solid citizens and

Lynching. This grim photo records the death of five of the approximately 1,000 African Americans who were lynched between 1901 and 1914. The increase in lynching was one measure of the virulence of white racism in the early years of the 20th century.

petty criminals. All that had seemed to matter was the color of one's skin. Similarly, many black militants knew from personal experience that individual accomplishment was not enough to overcome racial prejudice. Du Bois was a brilliant scholar who became, in 1899, the first African American to receive a doctorate from Harvard University. Had he been white, Du Bois would have been asked to teach at Harvard or another elite academic institution, but no prestigious white university, in the South or North, made him an offer.

From the Niagara Movement to the NAACP

Seeing no future in accommodation, Du Bois and other young black activists came together at Niagara Falls in 1905 to fashion a new political agenda. They demanded that African Americans regain the right to vote in states that had taken it away, that segregation be abolished, and that the many discriminatory barriers to black advancement be removed. They declared their commitment to freedom of speech, the brotherhood of all men, and respect for the working man. Although their numbers were small, the members of the so-called Niagara movement were inspired by the example of the antebellum abolitionists. Meeting in Boston, Oberlin, and Harpers Ferry—all places of special significance to the abolitionist cause—they hoped to rekindle the militant, uncompromising spirit of that earlier crusade (see Chapters 12 and 14).

The 1908 Springfield riot had shaken many whites. Some, especially those already working for social and economic reform, now joined in common cause with the Niagara movement. Together, black and white activists planned a conference for Lincoln's birthday in 1909 to revive, in the words of author William English Walling, "the spirit of the

abolitionists" and to "treat the Negro on a plane of absolute political and social equality." Oswald Garrison Villard, the grandson of William Lloyd Garrison, called on "all believers in democracy to join in a National conference for the discussion of present evils, the voicing of protests, and the renewal of the struggle for civil and political liberty." The conference brought together distinguished progressives, white and black, including Mary White Ovington, Jane Addams, John Dewey, William Dean Howells, Ida B. Wells, and W. E. B. Du Bois. They drew up plans to establish an organization dedicated to fighting racial discrimination and prejudice. In May 1910, the National Association for the Advancement of Colored People (NAACP) was launched, with Moorfield Storey of Boston as president, Walling as chairman of the executive committee, and Du Bois as the director of publicity and research.

The formation of the NAACP marked the beginning of the modern civil rights movement. The organization launched a magazine, *The Crisis*, edited by Du Bois, to publicize and protest the lynchings, riots, and other abuses directed against black citizens. Equally important was the Legal Redress Committee, which initiated lawsuits against city and state governments for violating the constitutional rights of African Americans. The committee scored its first major success in 1915, when the U.S. Supreme Court ruled that the so-called grandfather clauses of the Oklahoma and Maryland constitutions violated the 15th Amendment. (These clauses extended the right to vote to whites who had failed to pay their state's poll tax or to pass its literacy test while denying the same right to blacks). NAACP lawyers won again in 1917 when the Supreme Court declared unconstitutional a Louisville, Kentucky, law that required all blacks to reside in predetermined parts of the city.

By 1914, the NAACP had enrolled thousands of members in scores of branches throughout the United States. The organization's success generated other civil rights groups. The National Urban League, founded in 1911, worked to improve the economic and social conditions of blacks in cities. It pressured employers to hire blacks, distributed lists of available jobs and housing in African American communities, and developed social programs to ease the adjustment of rural black migrants to city life.

Progress toward racial equality was sluggish. Attacking segregation and discrimination through lawsuits was, by its nature, a slow strategy that would take decades to complete. The growing membership of the NAACP, although impressive, was not large enough to qualify it as a mass movement, and its interracial character made the organization seem dangerously radical to millions of whites. White NAACP leaders responded to this hostility by limiting the number and power of African Americans who worked for the organization. This policy, in turn, angered black militants who argued that no civil rights organization should be in the business of appeasing white racists.

Despite its limitations, the NAACP made significant strides. It gave Du Bois the security and visibility he needed to carry on his fight against Booker T. Washington's accommodationist philosophy. Even before his death in 1915, Washington's influence in black and white communities had

Before Jazz: An Early African American Orchestra

Composer: Wilbur C. Sweatman
Title: "Down Home Rag"
Performer: James Reese Europe's Society Orchestra (December 29, 1913)

The dense, smeared, and exciting sound of "Down Home Rag," with its frenetic tempo that approximates the speed of today's punk rock, represented one of the first attempts to define black musical identity before jazz became a commercial force. The band on this disc, the first black orchestra to secure a major recording contract, was led by James Reese Europe, the son of an Alabama slave.

Jim Crow segregation laws and practices extended into the world of professional music, limiting the opportunities and respect accorded to black musicians and composers. The strict color line in musicians' unions meant that blacks earned lesser wages and were often asked to wash dishes or work more hours than white musicians to keep their nonunion jobs. African Americans were also kept from performing and composing in the more high-brow world of classical music. To combat these problems, Europe became the leading force behind the Clef Club, a New York City trade union and booking agency created in 1910 for and by African American musicians. The Club's signature event was their May 2, 1912, staging of a "Concert of Negro Music" at Carnegie Hall, America's premiere venue for classical music, a place where no African American performers or compositions had previously been featured. Blacks and whites sat in equal numbers in the capacity crowd, probably for the first time at an American concert. Following the show, more black composers and musicians received jobs, although the classical music market was still heavily skewed toward whites.

Europe believed that African American orchestras needed to demonstrate their own character apart from white orchestral music. In "Down Home Rag," we hear a scaled-down 18-piece version of the 125-piece orchestra that showcased Europe's musical vision at Carnegie. The orchestra boasted a full-bodied, percussive, and singular sound that included 14 upright pianos and unorthodox instruments, such as banjos, mandolins, and guitars, combined with more traditional string instruments and percussion. Europe's mixing of violin-led melodies that sounded like 19th-century Virginia reels with an aggressive and layered rhythmic foundation provided an early preview of the mixing of black and white genres that characterized American music in the 20th century.

Q How would you describe the music that James Reese Europe created with his orchestra?

Q Why do you think Europe argued that African American orchestral music had to be different in character from that usually performed in America's classical concert halls?

---

receded. The NAACP, more than any other organization, helped resurrect the issue of racial equality at a time when many white Americans had accepted as normal the practices of racial segregation and discrimination.

The Roosevelt Presidency

Q **FOCUS QUESTION** What would you identify as Roosevelt's three most important contributions to progressive reform?

Progressives sought to increase their influence in national politics. State regulations seemed inadequate to the task of curtailing the power of the trusts, protecting workers, or monitoring the quality of consumer goods. The courts repeatedly struck down as unconstitutional state laws regulating working hours or setting minimum wages, on the grounds that they impinged on the freedom of contract and trade. A national progressive movement could force passage of federal laws that were less vulnerable to judicial veto or elect a president who could overhaul the federal judiciary with progressive-minded judges.

National leadership would not emerge from Congress. The Populist challenge of the 1890s had left the Democratic Party badly divided between radical Bryanites and the conservative followers of Grover Cleveland. The Republican Party in Congress was in the hands of an "Old Guard." The impetus for innovation and reform thus shifted from the legislative to the executive branch, and to one chief executive in particular, Theodore Roosevelt.

When the Republican bosses chose Theodore Roosevelt as William McKinley's running mate in 1900, their purpose was more to remove this headstrong, unpredictable character from New York state politics than to groom him for national leadership. As governor of New York, Roosevelt had been a moderate reformer, but even his modest efforts to rid the state's Republican Party of corruption and to

Theodore Roosevelt. The youthful and animated president addresses a crowd in Evanston, Illinois, (a suburb of Chicago) in 1903.

institute civil service reform were too much for the state party machine, led by Thomas C. Platt. Consigning Roosevelt to the vice presidency seemed a safe solution. McKinley was a young, vigorous politician, fully in control of his party and his presidency. Less than a year into his second term, in September 1901, McKinley was shot by an anarchist assassin. The president clung to life for nine days, and then died. Upon succeeding McKinley, Theodore Roosevelt, age 42, became the youngest chief executive in the nation's history.

Although born to an aristocratic New York City family, Roosevelt developed an uncommon affection for "the people." Asthmatic, sickly, and nearsighted as a boy, he remade himself into a vigorous adult. With an insatiable appetite for high-risk adventure—everything from "dude ranching" in the Dakota Territory, to big-game hunting in Africa, to wartime combat—he was also a voracious reader and an accomplished writer. Aggressive and swaggering in his public rhetoric, he was in private a skilled, patient negotiator. A believer in the superiority of the English-speaking peoples, he nevertheless assembled an administration that was diverse by the standards of the time. Rarely has a president's personality so enthralled the American public. He is the only 20th-century president immortalized on Mount Rushmore.

Regulating the Trusts

Roosevelt quickly revealed his flair for the dramatic. In 1902, he ordered the Justice Department to prosecute the Northern Securities Company, a $400 million monopoly that controlled all railroad lines and traffic in the Northwest from Chicago to Washington state. Never before had an American president sought to use the Sherman Antitrust Act to break up a business monopoly. The news shocked the banker J. P. Morgan, who had brokered the deal that had created Northern Securities. Morgan rushed to the White House, where he is said to have told Roosevelt: "If we have done anything wrong, send your man to my man and they can fix it up." Roosevelt would have none of this "fixing." In 1903, a federal court ordered Northern Securities dissolved, and the U.S. Supreme Court upheld the decision the next year. Roosevelt was hailed as the nation's "trust-buster."

Roosevelt, however, did not believe in breaking up all, or even most, large corporations. Industrial concentration, he believed, brought the United States wealth, productivity, and a rising standard of living. Rather than bust them up, Roosevelt argued, government should regulate the industrial giants and punish those that used their power improperly. This new role would require the federal government to expand its powers. A newly fortified government—the centerpiece of a political program that Roosevelt would later call the **New Nationalism**—was to be led by a forceful president, who was willing to use his power to achieve prosperity and justice.

Toward a "Square Deal"

Roosevelt displayed his willingness to use government power to protect the economically weak in a 1902 coal miners' strike. Miners in the anthracite fields of eastern Pennsylvania wanted recognition for their union, the United Mine Workers (UMW). They also wanted a 10- to 20-percent increase in wages and an eight-hour day. When their employers, led by George F. Baer of the Reading Railroad, refused to negotiate, they went on strike. In October, the fifth month of the strike, Roosevelt summoned the mine owners and John Mitchell, the UMW president, to the White House. Baer expected Roosevelt to threaten the striking workers with arrest by federal troops if they failed to return to work. Instead, Roosevelt supported Mitchell's request for arbitration and warned the mine owners that if they refused to go along, 10,000 federal troops would seize their property. Stunned, the mine owners agreed to submit the dispute to arbitrators, who awarded the unionists a 10-percent wage increase and a nine-hour day.

The mere fact that the federal government had ordered employers to compromise with their workers carried great symbolic weight. Roosevelt enjoyed a surge of support from Americans convinced that he shared their dislike for ill-gotten wealth and privilege. He also raised the hopes of African Americans when, only a month into his presidency, he dined with Booker T. Washington at the White House and then shrugged off the protests of white southerners.

In his 1904 election campaign, Roosevelt promised that, if reelected, he would offer every American a "square deal." The slogan resonated with voters and helped carry Roosevelt to a victory (57 percent of the popular vote) over the conservative Democrat Alton B. Parker. To the surprise of many, Roosevelt had aligned the Republican Party with the cause of reform.

Expanding Government Power: The Economy

Emboldened by his victory, the president intensified his efforts to extend government regulation of economic affairs. His most important proposal was to give the government power to set railroad shipping rates and thereby to eliminate the industry's discriminatory marketing practices. The government, in theory, already possessed this power through the Interstate Commerce Commission (ICC), a regulatory body established by Congress in 1887, but the courts had so weakened the ICC's oversight and regulatory functions as to render it virtually powerless. Roosevelt achieved his goal in 1906, when Congress passed the Hepburn Act, which significantly increased the ICC's powers of rate review and enforcement. Roosevelt supported the Pure Food and Drug Act, passed by Congress that same year, which protected the public from fraudulently marketed and dangerous foods and medications. He also campaigned for the Meat Inspection Act (1906), which obligated the government to monitor the quality and safety of meat being sold to American consumers.

Expanding Government Power: The Environment

Roosevelt also did more than any previous president to extend federal control over the nation's physical environment. He was not a "preservationist" in the manner of John Muir, founder of the Sierra Club, who insisted that the beauty of the land and the well-being of its wildlife should be protected from all human interference. Instead, Roosevelt viewed the wilderness as a place to live strenuously, to test oneself against the rough outdoors, and to match wits against strong and clever game. He further believed that in the West—that land of ancient forests, lofty mountain peaks, and magnificent canyons—Americans could learn something important about their nation's roots and destiny. To preserve this West, Roosevelt oversaw the creation of 5 new national parks, 16 national monuments, and 53 wildlife reserves. The work of his administration led directly to the formation of the National Park Service in 1916.

Roosevelt also emerged a strong supporter of the **"conservationist"** movement. Conservationists cared little for national parks or grand canyons. They wanted to manage the environment scientifically so as to ensure that the nation's resources were put to the most efficient economic use. Roosevelt shared the conservationists' belief that the plundering of western timberlands, grazing areas, water resources, and minerals had reached crisis proportions.

Roosevelt therefore appointed a Public Lands Commission in 1903 to survey public lands, inventory them, and establish permit systems to regulate the kinds and numbers of users. Soon after, the Departments of the Interior and Agriculture placed certain western lands rich in natural resources and waterpower off-limits to agricultural users. Government officials also limited waterpower development by requiring companies to acquire permits and pay fees for the right to generate electricity on public land. When political favoritism and corruption within the Departments of the Interior and Agriculture threatened these efforts at regulation, Roosevelt authorized the hiring of university-trained experts to replace state and local politicians. Scientific expertise, rather than political connections, would now determine the distribution and use of western territory.

Gifford Pinchot, a specialist in forestry management, and Roosevelt's close friend, led the drive for scientific management of natural resources. In 1905, he persuaded Roosevelt to relocate jurisdiction for the national forests from the Department of the Interior to the Department of Agriculture, which, Pinchot argued, was the most appropriate department to oversee the efficient "harvest" of the nation's forest crop. The newly created National Forest Service, under Pinchot's control, quickly instituted a system of competitive bidding for the right to harvest timber on national forest lands. Pinchot and his expanding staff of college-educated foresters also exacted user fees from livestock ranchers who had previously used national forest grazing lands for free. Armed with new legislation and authority, Pinchot and fellow conservationists in the Roosevelt administration declared vast stretches of federal land in the West off-limits to mining and dam construction.

The Republican Old Guard disliked these initiatives. When Roosevelt recommended prosecution of cattlemen and lumbermen who were illegally using federal land for private gain, congressional conservatives struck back with legislation (in 1907) that curtailed the president's power to create new government land reserves. Roosevelt responded by seizing another 17 million acres for national forest reserves before the new law went into effect. To his conservative opponents, excluding commercial activity from public land was bad enough, but flouting the will of Congress with a 17-million-acre land grab violated constitutional principles governing the separation of powers. Yet, to millions of American voters, Roosevelt's willingness to defy western cattle barons, mining tycoons, and other "malefactors of great wealth" increased his popularity.

Progressivism: A Movement for the People?

Historians have long debated how much Roosevelt's economic and environmental reforms altered the balance of power between the "interests" and the people. Some have demonstrated that many corporations were eager for federal government regulation—that railroad corporations wanted relief from the rate wars that were driving them into bankruptcy, for example, and that the larger meatpackers believed that the costs of government food inspections would drive smaller meatpackers out of business. So, too, historians have shown that agribusinesses, timber companies, and mining corporations in the West believed that government regulation would aid them and hurt smaller competitors. According to this view, government regulation benefited the corporations more than it benefited workers, consumers, and small businessmen.

Indeed, these early reforms often curtailed corporate power only to a limited extent. But in 1907, the progressive program was still evolving. Popular anger over corporate power and political corruption remained a driving force of

Index Peak, Yellowstone National Park, 1914. An environmental movement emerged during the progressive era to protect beautiful areas of the American West such as those located in Yellowstone Park, the country's first national park. Thomas Moran painted this image of Index Peak.

progressivism. The presence in the Senate of La Follette, Albert Beveridge of Indiana, and other anticorporate Republicans gave that anger an influential national voice. Whether the corporations or the people would benefit most from progressive reforms had yet to be determined.

The Republicans: A Divided Party

The financial panic of 1907 further strained relations between Roosevelt reformers and Old Guard conservatives. A failed New York bank effort to corner the copper market triggered a run on banks, a short but severe dip in industrial production, and widespread layoffs. Everywhere, people worried that a major depression, like that of the 1890s, was in the offing. Only the timely decision of J. P. Morgan and a few other financiers to pour private cash into the collapsing banks saved the nation from an economic crisis.

The panic prompted Roosevelt to call for an overhaul of the banking system and for regulation of the stock market. The Republican Old Guard, meanwhile, was more determined than ever to run the "radical" Roosevelt out of the White House. Sensing that he might fail to win his party's nomination, and mindful of a rash promise he had made in 1904 not to run again in 1908, Roosevelt decided not to seek reelection. It was a decision he would soon regret. Barely 50 years old, he was too young and energetic to end his political career.

The Taft Presidency: Progressive Disappointment and Resurgence

 FOCUS QUESTION | What were the sources of tensions between Taft and the progressives?

Roosevelt thought he had found in William Howard Taft, his secretary of war, an ideal successor. Taft had worked closely with Roosevelt on foreign and domestic policies. Roosevelt believed Taft possessed both the ideas and the skills to complete the reform Republican program.

To reach that conclusion, however, Roosevelt had to ignore some obvious differences between Taft and himself. Taft neither liked nor was particularly adept at politics. With the exception of a judgeship in an Ohio superior court, he had never held elective office. He was by nature a cautious and conservative man. As Roosevelt's handpicked successor, Taft easily won the election of 1908, defeating Democrat William Jennings Bryan with 52 percent of the vote. His conservatism soon revealed itself in his choice of corporation lawyers, rather than reformers, for cabinet positions.

Battling Congress

Taft's troubles began when he appeared to side against progressives in an acrimonious congressional battle over tariff legislation. Progressives had long desired tariff reduction, believing that competition from foreign manufacturers would benefit American consumers and check the economic power of American manufacturers. Taft had raised expectations for tariff reduction when he called Congress into special session to consider a reform bill that called for a modest reduction of tariffs and an inheritance tax. The bill passed the House but was gutted in the Senate. The Payne-Aldrich Tariff Act that Taft signed into law in 1909 did little, as a result, to reduce tariffs. Progressive Republicans, bitterly disappointed, criticized Taft for not standing up to the Senate's Old Guard. A bruising fight over Taft's conservation policies brought relations between Taft and the insurgent Republicans to the breaking point.

The Ballinger-Pinchot Controversy

Richard A. Ballinger, Secretary of the Interior, had aroused progressives' suspicions by reopening for private commercial use 1 million acres of land that the Roosevelt administration had previously brought under federal protection. Gifford Pinchot, still head of the National Forest Service, obtained information implicating Ballinger in the sale of Alaskan

William Howard Taft. Roosevelt's handpicked successor, Taft, turned out to be much less of a progressive than his predecessor.

coal deposits to a private syndicate. Pinchot shared the information with Taft. When Taft defended Ballinger, Pinchot went public with his charges, and a contentious congressional investigation ensued. Whatever hope Taft may have had of escaping political damage disappeared when Roosevelt, returning from an African hunting trip by way of Europe in spring 1910, staged a publicized rendezvous with Pinchot in England. In so doing, Roosevelt signaled his continuing support for his old friend Pinchot and his displeasure with Taft.

Roosevelt's Return

Roosevelt had barely returned to the United States in summer 1910 when he dove back into politics. In September, Roosevelt embarked on a speaking tour, the high point of which was his elaboration at Osawatomie, Kansas, of his New Nationalism, an ambitious reform program that called for the federal government to stabilize the economy, protect the weak, and restore social harmony.

The 1910 congressional elections confirmed the popularity of Roosevelt's positions. Insurgent Republicans trounced conservative Republicans in primary after primary, and the Democrats' embrace of reform brought them a majority in the House of Representatives for the first time since 1894. When Robert La Follette, who was challenging Taft for the Republican presidential nomination, seemed to suffer a nervous breakdown in February 1912, Roosevelt announced his own candidacy. In the 13 states sponsoring preferential primaries, Roosevelt won nearly 75 percent of the delegates, but the party's national leadership remained in the hands of the Old Guard, and they were determined to deny Roosevelt the Republican nomination. At the Republican convention in Chicago, Taft won renomination on the first ballot.

The Bull Moose Campaign

Roosevelt had expected this outcome. The night before the convention opened, he had told an assembly of 5,000 supporters that the party leaders would not succeed in derailing their movement. "We stand at Armageddon," he declared, and "we battle for the Lord." The next day, Roosevelt and his supporters withdrew from the convention and from the Republican Party. In August, the reformers reassembled as the new **Progressive Party**, nominated Roosevelt for president and California governor Hiram W. Johnson for vice president, and hammered out the reform platform they had long envisioned: sweeping regulation of the corporations, extensive protections for workers, a sharply graduated income tax, and woman suffrage. "I am as strong as a bull moose," Roosevelt roared as he readied for combat; his proud followers took to calling themselves "Bull Moosers."

Some of them, however, probably including Roosevelt, knew that their mission was futile. They had failed to enroll enough Republican insurgents who had supported Roosevelt in the primaries but who now refused to abandon the GOP. Consequently, the Republican vote would be split between Roosevelt and Taft, making them both vulnerable to the Democrats' candidate, Woodrow Wilson.

The Rise of Woodrow Wilson

Few would have predicted in 1908 that the distinguished president of Princeton University, Woodrow Wilson, would be the 1912 Democratic nominee for president of the United States. Before 1910, Wilson had never run for elective office, nor had he ever held an appointed post in a local, state, or federal administration. The son of a Presbyterian minister from Virginia, Wilson had practiced law for a short time after graduating from Princeton (then still the College of New Jersey) in 1879 before settling on an academic career. Earning his doctorate in political science from Johns Hopkins in 1886, he taught history and political science at Bryn Mawr and Wesleyan (Connecticut) before returning to Princeton in 1890. He became president of Princeton in 1902, a post he held until he successfully ran for the governorship of New Jersey in 1910.

Identifying himself with the anti-Bryan wing of the Democratic Party, Wilson attracted the attention of wealthy conservatives, who saw him as a potential presidential candidate. They convinced the bosses of the New Jersey Democratic machine to nominate Wilson for governor in 1910. Wilson accepted the nomination and won the governorship handily. He then shocked his conservative backers by declaring his independence from the state's Democratic machine and moving New Jersey into the forefront of reform.

The Election of 1912

At the Democratic convention of 1912, Wilson was something of a dark horse, running a distant second to House Speaker Champ Clark of Missouri. When the New York delegation gave Clark a simple majority of delegates, virtually everyone assumed that Clark would soon command the two-thirds majority needed to win the nomination. But Wilson's managers held onto Wilson's delegates and began chipping away at Clark's lead. On the fourth day, on the 46th ballot, Wilson won the nomination.

Given the split in Republican ranks, Democrats had their best chance in 20 years of regaining the White House. A Wilson victory, moreover, would give the country its first southern-born president in almost 50 years. Finally, whatever its outcome, the election promised to deliver a vote for reform. Both Roosevelt and Wilson were running on reform platforms, and the Socialist Party candidate, Eugene V. Debs, was attracting larger crowds and generating greater enthusiasm than had been expected. Taft was so certain of defeat that he barely campaigned.

Debate among the candidates focused on the trusts. All three reform candidates—Roosevelt, Wilson, and Debs—agreed that corporations had acquired too much economic power. Debs argued that the only way to ensure popular control of that power was for the federal government to assume ownership of the trusts. Roosevelt called for the establishment of a powerful government that would regulate and, if necessary, curb the power of the trusts. This was the essence of his New Nationalism, the program he had been advocating since 1910.

Rather than regulate the trusts, Wilson declared his intention to break them up. He wanted to reverse the tendency toward economic concentration and thus restore opportunity to the people. This philosophy, which Wilson labeled the **New Freedom**, called for a temporary concentration of governmental power in order to dismantle the trusts. But once that was accomplished, Wilson promised, the government would relinquish its power.

Wilson won the November election with 42 percent of the popular vote to Roosevelt's 27 percent and Taft's 23 percent; Debs made a strong showing with 6 percent, the largest in his party's history.

© CORBIS

Woodrow Wilson. The Democratic presidential candidate campaigning from the back of a train in 1912, pledging to fulfill progressivism's promise.

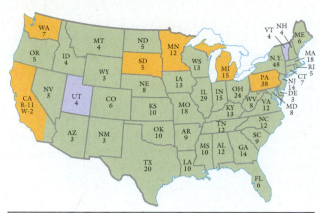

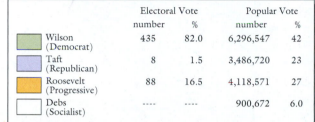

		Electoral Vote		Popular Vote	
		number	%	number	%
	Wilson (Democrat)	435	82.0	6,296,547	42
	Taft (Republican)	8	1.5	3,486,720	23
	Roosevelt (Progressive)	88	16.5	4,118,571	27
	Debs (Socialist)	----	----	900,672	6.0

Map 21.3 Presidential Election, 1912. Taft and Roosevelt split the Republican vote, allowing Wilson to win with a plurality of the popular vote (42 percent) and a big majority (82 percent) of the electoral vote.

The Wilson Presidency

Q FOCUS QUESTION What were the key similarities and differences in the progressive politics of Theodore Roosevelt and Woodrow Wilson?

Wilson quickly assembled a cabinet of talented men who could be counted on for wise counsel, loyalty, and influence over vital Democratic constituencies. He cultivated a public image of himself as a president firmly in charge of his party and as a faithful tribune of the people.

Tariff Reform and a Progressive Income Tax

Like Taft, Wilson first turned his attention to tariff reform. The House passed a tariff-reduction bill within a month, and Wilson used his leadership skills to push the bill through a reluctant Senate. The resulting Underwood-Simmons Tariff Act of 1913 reduced tariff barriers from approximately 40 to 25 percent. To make up for revenue lost to tariff reductions, Congress then passed an income tax law. The 16th Amendment to the Constitution, ratified by the states in 1913, had already given the government the right to impose an income tax. The law passed by Congress made good on the progressive pledge to reduce the power and privileges of wealthy Americans by requiring them to pay taxes on a greater percentage of their income than the poor.

The Federal Reserve Act

Wilson then asked Congress to overhaul the nation's financial system. The banking interests and their congressional supporters wanted the government to give the authority to regulate credit and currency flows either to a single bank or to several regional banks. Progressives opposed the vesting of so much financial power in private hands and insisted that any reformed financial system must be publicly controlled. Wilson worked out a compromise plan that included both private and public controls, and he marshaled the votes to push it through both the House and the Senate. By the end of 1913, Wilson had signed the **Federal Reserve Act**, the most important law passed in his first administration.

The Federal Reserve Act established 12 regional banks, each controlled by the private banks in its region. Every private bank in the country was required to deposit an average of 6 percent of its assets into its regional Federal Reserve bank. The reserve would be used to make loans to member banks and to issue paper currency (Federal Reserve notes) to facilitate financial transactions. The regional banks were also instructed to use their funds to shore up member banks in distress and to respond to sudden changes in credit demands by easing or tightening the flow of credit. A Federal Reserve Board appointed by the president and responsible to the public rather than to private bankers would set policy and oversee activities within the 12 reserve banks.

The Federal Reserve system strengthened the nation's financial structure and was in most respects an impressive political achievement for Wilson. In its final form, however, it revealed that Wilson was retreating from his New Freedom pledge. The Federal Reserve Board was a less powerful and less centralized federal authority than a national bank would have been, but it nevertheless represented a substantial increase in government control of banking. Moreover, the bill authorizing the system made no attempt to break up private financial institutions that had grown too powerful or to prohibit the interlocking directorates that large banks used to augment their power. Because it sought to work with large banks rather than to break them up, the Federal Reserve system seemed more consonant with the principles of Roosevelt's New Nationalism than with those of Wilson's New Freedom.

From the New Freedom to the New Nationalism

Wilson's failure to mount a vigorous antitrust campaign confirmed his drift toward the New Nationalism. For example, in 1914, Wilson supported the Federal Trade Commission Act, which created a government agency by that name to regulate business practices. The Federal Trade Commission (FTC) had wide powers to collect information on corporate pricing policies and on cooperation and competition among businesses. The FTC might have attacked trusts for "unfair trade practices," but the Senate stripped the FTC Act's companion legislation, the Clayton Antitrust Act, of virtually all provisions that would have allowed the government to prosecute the

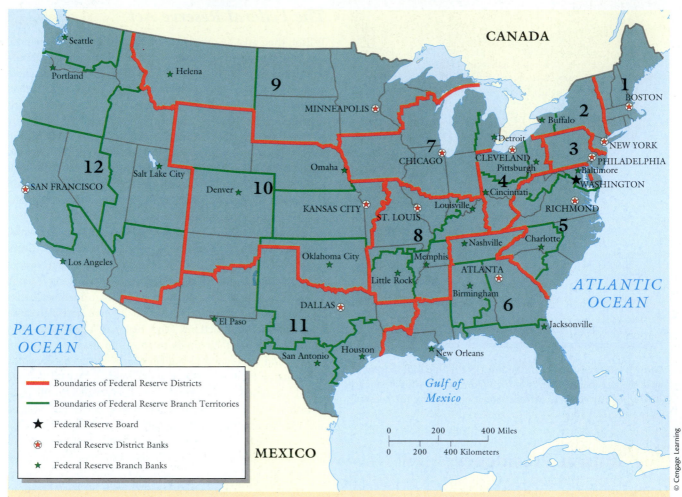

Map 21.4 Federal Reserve Districts. This map demonstrates in visual terms how the Federal Reserve (FR) attempted to impose order on the nation's financial system: 12 districts, each with an FR district bank. Most of the districts were subdivided into branches, in which the FR also established a banking presence.

Legend:
- **Boundaries of Federal Reserve Districts**
- **Boundaries of Federal Reserve Branch Territories**
- ★ **Federal Reserve Board**
- ★ **Federal Reserve District Banks**
- ★ **Federal Reserve Branch Banks**

© Cengage Learning

trusts. Wilson supported this weakening of the Clayton Act, having decided that the breakup of large-scale industry was no longer practical or preferable. The FTC, in Wilson's eyes, would help businesses, large and small, to regulate themselves in ways that contributed to national well-being. In accepting giant industry as an inescapable feature of modern life and in seeking to regulate industrial behavior by means of government agencies such as the FTC, Wilson had become, in effect, a New Nationalist.

At first, Wilson's shift to New Nationalist policies led him to support business interests. His nominations to the Federal Reserve Board, for example, were generally men who had worked for Wall Street firms and large industrial corporations. At the same time, he usually refused to use government powers to aid organized groups of workers and farmers. Court rulings had made worker and farmer organizations vulnerable to prosecution under the terms of the Sherman Antitrust Act of 1890. AFL president Samuel Gompers and other labor leaders tried but failed to convince Wilson to insert into the Clayton Antitrust Act a clause that would unambiguously grant labor and farmer organizations immunity from further antitrust prosecutions.

Nor did Wilson, at this time, view with any greater sympathy the campaign for African American political equality. He supported efforts by white southerners in his cabinet, such as Postmaster General Albert Burleson and Treasury Secretary William McAdoo, to segregate their government departments, and he largely ignored pleas from the NAACP to involve the federal government in a campaign against lynching.

In late 1915, however, Wilson moved to the left, in part because he feared losing his reelection in 1916. The Bull Moosers of 1912 were retreating back to the Republican Party. Wilson remembered how much his 1912 victory, based on only 42 percent of the popular vote, had depended on the Republican split. To halt the progressives' rapprochement with the GOP, he made a bid for their support. In January 1916, he nominated Louis Brandeis to the Supreme Court. Not only was Brandeis one of the country's most respected progressives, but he was also the first Jew nominated to serve on the country's highest court. Congressional conservatives did everything they could to block the confirmation of a man they regarded as dangerously radical, but Wilson, as usual, was better organized, and by June his forces in the Senate had emerged victorious.

Louis Brandeis, Associate Justice of the Supreme Court.
Appointed by President Woodrow Wilson in 1916, Brandeis became the first Jewish Supreme Court Justice. Closely identified with progressivism and the New Deal, he sat on the highest court until 1939.

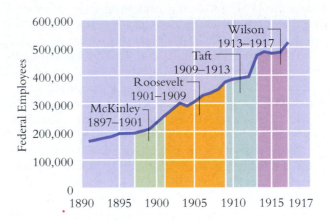

Growth in Federal Employment, 1891–1917.
Source: Reprinted with permission from *The Federal Government Service*, ed. W. S. Sayre (Upper Saddle River, NJ: Prentice-Hall, 1965), p. 41, The American Assembly.

Wilson followed up this victory by pushing through Congress the first federal workmen's compensation law (the Kern-McGillicuddy Act, which covered federal employees), the first federal law outlawing child labor (the Keating-Owen Act), and the first federal law guaranteeing workers an eight-hour day (the Adamson Act, which covered the nation's 400,000 railway workers). The number of Americans affected by these acts was relatively small. Nevertheless, Wilson had reoriented the Democratic Party to a New Nationalism that cared as much about the interests of the powerless as the interests of the powerful.

Trade unionists flocked to Wilson, as did most of the prominent progressives who had followed the Bull Moose in 1912. Meanwhile, Wilson had appealed to the supporters of William Jennings Bryan by supporting legislation that made federal credit available to farmers in need. He had put together a reform coalition capable of winning a majority at the polls. In the process, he had transformed the Democratic Party. From 1916 on, the Democrats, rather than the Republicans, became the chief guardians of the American reform tradition.

That Wilson did so is a sign of the strength of the reform and radical forces in American society. By 1916, the ranks of middle-class progressives had grown broad and deep. Working-class protest had also accelerated in scope and intensity. In Lawrence, Massachusetts, in 1912, and in Paterson, New Jersey, in 1913, for example, the IWW organized strikes of textile workers that drew national attention, as did a 1914 strike by Colorado mine workers. These protests reflected the mobilization of those working-class constituencies—immigrants, women, the unskilled—long considered inconsequential both by mainstream labor leaders and party politicians. Assisted by radicals, these groups had begun to fashion a more inclusive and politically ambitious labor movement. Wilson and other Democrats understood the potential strength of this new labor insurgency, and the president's pro-labor legislative agenda in 1916 can be understood, in part, as an effort to channel labor's new constituents into the Democratic Party. It was a successful strategy that contributed to Wilson's reelection in 1916.

Conclusion

By 1916, the progressives had accomplished a great deal. They demonstrated that traditional American concerns with democracy and liberty could be adapted to an industrial age. They exposed and curbed some of the worst abuses of the American political system. They enfranchised women and took steps to protect the environment. They broke the hold of laissez-faire economic policies on national politics and replaced it with the idea of a strong federal government committed to economic regulation and social justice. They transformed the presidency into a post of legislative and popular leadership. They enlarged the executive branch by establishing new commissions and agencies charged with administering government policies.

The progressives, in short, had begun to create a strong national government, one in which power increasingly flowed away from municipalities and states and toward Washington.

This reorientation followed a compelling logic: A national government stood a better chance of solving the problems of growing economic inequality, mismanagement of natural resources, and consumer fraud than did local and state governments. This emphasis on involving the federal government in economic and social affairs became progressivism's most enduring legacy. It made the movement a forerunner of the liberalism and "New Deal" that emerged under Franklin Roosevelt's leadership in the 1930s (see Chapter 25).

The promise of effective federal government intervention, however, also brought a new danger: the possibility that government administrators might use their power to fashion themselves into a new bureaucratic elite. Some progressives, such as Walter Lippmann, were already arguing that their knowledge, objectivity, and dedication equipped them to make critical decisions on behalf of the people without consulting them. Other progressives in government claimed to be responsive to the people while they cultivated close ties with corporations that they were expected to regulate on the people's behalf. In some instances, in other words, progressive reformers were doing as much to advance their own bureaucratic interests or those of their corporate allies as they were helping to improve the welfare of ordinary Americans.

These elitist tendencies did not go unchallenged. The democratic movements of the progressive era—those involving workers, women, minorities, consumers, and environmentalists—were determined to hold both elected and appointed government officials accountable to the popular will. Their success in moving Wilson to the left in 1916 demonstrated that the forces of democracy could win. But the struggle between the contrasting progressive impulses toward democracy and elitism would go on, manifesting itself not simply in domestic politics but also in foreign affairs, where the United States was seeking to balance its interest in spreading liberty with the protection of its international economic interests. ⚜

CHAPTER REVIEW

REVIEW QUESTIONS

1. How did Protestantism influence reform?
2. What was "realism" and how did it spur investigative reporting and reform?
3. What contributions did associations of women's reformers make to progressivism?
4. What was the relationship of socialism to progressivism?
5. What were the benefits and costs of municipal reform?
6. What were the results of progressive efforts to create a "responsible" and "virtuous" electorate? What were the similarities and differences between John R. Commons's "Wisconsin Idea" and Frederick Winslow Taylor's program of scientific management?
7. How did W. E. B. Du Bois's approach to African American reform differ from that of Booker T. Washington?
8. What would you identify as Roosevelt's three most important contributions to progressive reform?
9. What were the sources of tensions between Taft and the progressives?
10. What were the key similarities and differences in the progressive politics of Theodore Roosevelt and Woodrow Wilson?

CRITICAL THINKING QUESTIONS

1. Progressivism sought to reform all of American society—politics, economy, and culture. What were the most important reforms in each of these realms? Were these reforms successful in achieving their aims?

2. When the progressive reform movement peaked during the first Wilson Administration (1913–17), did it result in greater liberty and equality for ordinary Americans?

IDENTIFICATIONS

Review your understanding of the following key terms, people, and events for this chapter (terms in bold in text are included in the Glossary).

muckrakers, p. 564
realism, p. 564
Hull House, p. 566
socialism, p. 570
Eugene Victor Debs, p. 570
initiative, p. 573
referendum, p. 573
recall, p. 573
Australian ballot (secret ballot), p. 573
disfranchisement, p. 574
National Association for the Advancement of Colored People (NAACP), p. 574
National American Woman Suffrage Association (NAWSA), p. 575
"Wisconsin Idea", p. 579
Frederick Winslow Taylor, p. 579
W. E. B. Du Bois, p. 580
New Nationalism, p. 584
conservationist, p. 585

Progressive Party, p. 587
New Freedom, p. 588
Federal Reserve Act, p. 589

SUGGESTED READINGS

No topic in 20th-century American history has generated as large and rapidly changing a scholarship as has progressivism. Today, few scholars treat this political movement in the terms set forth by the progressives themselves: as a movement of "the people" against the "special interests." In *The Age of Reform: From Bryan to FDR* (1955), **Richard Hofstadter** argues that progressivism was the expression of a declining Protestant middle class at odds with the new industrial order. In *The Search for Order, 1877–1920* (1967), **Robert Wiebe** finds the movement's core in a rising middle class, closely allied to the corporations and bureaucratic imperatives that were defining this new order. **James Weinstein, *The Corporate Ideal in the Liberal State, 1900–1918*** (1969), argues that progressivism was the work of businessmen, who were eager to ensure corporate stability and profitability in a dangerously unstable capitalist economy.

Without denying the importance of this corporate search for order, **Alan Dawley, *Struggles for Justice: Social Responsibility and the Liberal State*** (1991), insists on the role of the working class, men and women, whites and blacks, in shaping the progressive agenda. **James T. Kloppenberg, *Uncertain Victory: Social Democracy and Progressivism in European and American Thought, 1870–1920*** (1986), emphasizes the influence of socialism on progressive thought, while **Martin J. Sklar, *The Corporate Reconstruction of American Capitalism, 1900–1916: The Market, the Law and Politics*** (1988), stresses the role of progressivism in "containing" or taming socialism.

Daniel T. Rodgers reconstructs the international networks of reform that nourished progressivism in **Atlantic Crossings: Social Politics in a Progressive Age** (1998). **Nick Salvatore** captures the charisma and enigma of Debs in his ***Eugene V. Debs: Citizen and Socialist*** (1982). **Paul Boyer, *Urban Masses and Moral Order in America, 1820–1920*** (1978), treats progressivism as a cultural movement to enforce middle-class norms on unruly urban and immigrant populations. **Theda Skocpol, *Protecting Soldiers and Mothers: The Political Origins of Social Policy in the United States*** (1992), and **Robyn Muncy, *Creating a Female Dominion in American Reform, 1890–1935*** (1991), reconstruct the central role of middle-class Protestant women in shaping progressive social policy, while **Robert M. Crunden, *Ministers of Reform: The Progressives' Achievement in American Civilization, 1889–1920*** (1982), stresses the religious roots of progressive reform. **Michael Kazin, *A Godly Hero: the Life of William Jennings Bryan*** (2006), is indispensable not just on Bryan but also on the religious dimensions of progressivism, while **Alexander Keyssar, *The Right to Vote: The Contested History of Democracy in the United States*** (2000), is an essential guide to political reform during this period. A recent attempt to synthesize the literature on progressivism is **Michael McGerr, *A Fierce Discontent: The Rise and Fall of the Progressive Movement in America, 1870–1920*** (2003).

CourseMate ►

Visit the CourseMate website at www.cengagebrain.com for additional study tools and review materials for this chapter.

CHAPTER 22

Culver Pictures

Uncle Sam Gets Cocky, 1901

From 1898 to 1917, the United States broadened its influence in world affairs and especially sought to establish its dominance in Latin America. This cartoon illustrates that dominance through the figure of a giant Uncle Sam rooster that dwarfs both the European chickens (gamely protesting, "you're not the only rooster in South America") and the diminutive Latin American republics.

Becoming a World Power, 1898–1917

The United States Looks Abroad
Protestant Missionaries
Businessmen
Imperialists

The Spanish-American War
"A Splendid Little War"

The United States Becomes a World Power
The Debate over the Treaty of Paris
The American-Filipino War
Controlling Cuba and Puerto Rico
China and the "Open Door"

Theodore Roosevelt, Geopolitician
The Roosevelt Corollary
The Panama Canal
Keeping the Peace in East Asia

William Howard Taft, Dollar Diplomat

Woodrow Wilson, Struggling Idealist

FOR MUCH OF THE 19TH CENTURY, most Americans were preoccupied by continental expansion. Elections rarely turned on international events, and presidents rarely made their reputations as statesmen in the world arena. The diplomatic corps, like most agencies of the federal government, was small and inexperienced. The government projected its limited military power westward and possessed virtually no capacity or desire for involvement overseas.

The nation's rapid industrial growth in the late 19th century forced a turn away from such continentalism. Technological advances, especially the laying of transoceanic cables and the introduction of steamship travel, diminished America's physical isolation. The babble of languages one could hear in American cities testified to how much the Old World had penetrated the New. Then, too, Americans watched anxiously as England, Germany, Russia, Japan, and other industrial powers intensified their competition for overseas markets and colonies. Some believed America also needed to enter this contest.

A war with Spain in 1898 gave the United States an opportunity to upgrade its military and acquire colonies and influence in the Western Hemisphere and Asia. Under Presidents William McKinley and Theodore Roosevelt, the United States pursued these initiatives and established a small but strategically important empire. Not all Americans supported this imperial project, and many protested the subjugation of the peoples of Cuba, Puerto Rico, and the Philippines that imperial expansion seemed to entail. In the eyes of anti-imperialists, the United States seemed to be becoming the kind of nation that many Americans had long despised—one that valued power more than liberty.

Roosevelt brushed aside these objections and set about creating an international system in which a handful of industrial nations pursued their global economic interests, dominated world trade, and kept the world at peace. Woodrow Wilson, however, was more troubled by America's imperial turn. His doubts became apparent in his efforts to devise a policy toward post revolutionary Mexico that restrained American might and respected Mexican desires for liberty. It was a worthy ambition but one that proved difficult to achieve.

The United States Looks Abroad

Q **FOCUS QUESTION** Which groups in American society were most interested in expanding U.S. influence abroad?

By the late 19th century, sizable numbers of Americans had become interested in extending their country's influence abroad. The most important groups were Protestant missionaries, businessmen, and imperialists.

Protestant Missionaries

Protestant missionaries were among the most active promoters of American interests abroad. Overseas missionary activity grew quickly between 1870 and 1900, most of it directed toward China. Between 1880 and 1900, the number of women's missionary societies doubled, from 20 to 40; by 1915, these societies enrolled 3 million women. Convinced of the superiority of the Anglo-Saxon race, Protestant missionaries considered it their Christian duty to teach the Gospel to the "ignorant" Asian masses and save their souls. Missionaries also believed that their conversion efforts would free those masses from their racial

CHRONOLOGY

1893	Frederick Jackson Turner publishes an essay announcing the end of the frontier
1898	Spanish-American War (April 14–August 12) ◆ Treaty of Paris signed (December 10), giving U.S. control of Philippines, Guam, and Puerto Rico ◆ U.S. annexes Hawaii
1899–1902	American-Filipino War
1899–1900	U.S. pursues Open Door policy toward China
1900	U.S. annexes Puerto Rico ◆ U.S. and other imperial powers put down Chinese Boxer Rebellion
1901	U.S. forces Cuba to adopt constitution favorable to U.S. interests
1903	Hay–Bunau-Varilla Treaty signed, giving U.S. control of Panama Canal Zone
1904	"Roosevelt corollary" to Monroe Doctrine proclaimed
1905	Roosevelt negotiates end to Russo-Japanese War

1906–1917	U.S. intervenes in Cuba, Nicaragua, Haiti, Dominican Republic, and Mexico
1907	Roosevelt and Japanese government reach a "gentlemen's agreement" restricting Japanese immigration to U.S. and ending the segregation of Japanese schoolchildren in California
1907–1909	Great White Fleet circles the world
1909–1913	William Howard Taft conducts "dollar diplomacy"
1910	Mexican Revolution
1914	Panama Canal opens
1914–1917	Wilson struggles to develop a policy toward Mexico
1917	U.S. purchases Virgin Islands from Denmark

destiny, enabling them to become "civilized." (For the story of how growing up in a missionary family in China inspired Henry Luce to build one of the great American media empires, see the Americans Abroad feature, "The Luce Family and China: Missionary Work, Education, and the Origins of an American Media Empire.")

Businessmen

Industrialists, traders, and investors also began to look overseas, sensing that they could make fortunes in foreign lands. Exports of American manufactured goods rose substantially after 1880. By 1914, American foreign investment equaled a sizable 7 percent of the nation's gross national product. Companies such as Eastman Kodak (film and cameras), Singer Sewing Machine, Standard Oil, American Tobacco, and International Harvester had become multinational corporations with overseas branch offices.

Some industrialists became entranced by the prospect of clothing, feeding, housing, and transporting the 400 million people of China. James B. Duke, who headed American Tobacco, was selling 1 billion cigarettes per year in East Asian markets. Looking for ways to fill empty boxcars heading west from Minnesota to Tacoma, Washington, the railroad tycoon James J. Hill imagined stuffing them with wheat and steel destined for China and Japan. He actually distributed wheat cookbooks throughout East Asia to convince Asians to shift from a rice-based to a bread-based diet (so that there would be a market there for U.S. flour exports). Although export trade with East Asia during this period never fulfilled the expectations of Hill and other industrialists, their talk

about the "wealth of the Orient" impressed on politicians its importance to American economic health.

Events of the 1890s only intensified the appeal of foreign markets. First, the 1890 U.S. census announced that the frontier had disappeared and that America had completed the task of westward expansion. Then, in 1893, a young historian named Frederick Jackson Turner published an essay, "The Significance of the Frontier in American History," that articulated what many Americans feared: that the frontier had been essential to the growth of the economy and to the cultivation of democracy.

Living in the wilderness, Turner argued, had transformed the Europeans who settled the New World into Americans. They shed their European clothing styles, social customs, and political beliefs, and acquired distinctively American characteristics—rugged individualism, egalitarianism, and a democratic faith. How, Turner wondered, could the nation continue to prosper now that the frontier had gone?

In recent years, historians of the American West have criticized **Turner's "frontier thesis."** They have argued that the very idea of the frontier as uninhabited wilderness overlooked the tens of thousands of Indians who occupied the region and that much else of what Americans believed about the West was based more on myth than on reality. They have also pointed out that it makes little sense to view the 1890s as a decade in which opportunities for economic gain disappeared in the West.

Even though these points are valid, they would have meant little to Americans living in Turner's time. For them, as for Turner, concern about the disappearing frontier expressed a

Singer Sewing Machine Advertisement. The Singer Sewing Machine Company was one of the first American multinational corporations. This advertisement, with its maps of the Western Hemisphere and its description of Singer as "the universal sewing machine," stresses Singer's global orientation.

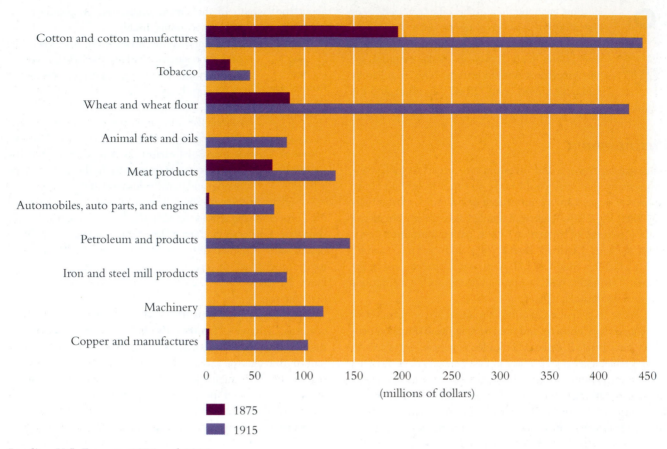

Leading U.S. Exports, 1875 and 1915.
Source: Data from *Historical Statistics of the United States, Colonial Times to 1970* (White Plains, NY: Kraus International, 1989).

fear that the increasingly urbanized and industrialized nation had lost its way. Turner's essay appeared just as the country was entering the deepest, longest, and most conflict-ridden depression in its history (see Chapter 19). What could the republic do to regain its economic prosperity and political stability? Where would it find its new frontiers? One answer to these questions focused on the pursuit of overseas expansion.

Imperialists

Eager to assist in the drive for overseas expansion was a group of politicians, intellectuals, and military strategists who viewed such expansion as essential to the pursuit of world power. They wanted the United States to join Britain, France, Germany, and Russia as a great imperial nation. They believed that the United States should build a strong navy, solidify a sphere of influence in the Caribbean, and extend markets into Asia. Their desire to control ports and territories beyond the continental borders of their own country made them **imperialists**.

One of the best-known imperialists of the period was Admiral **Alfred Thayer Mahan**. In an influential book, *The Influence of Sea Power upon History, 1660–1783* (1890), Mahan argued that past empires, beginning with Rome, had relied on their capacity to control the seas. Mahan called for the construction of a U.S. navy with enough ships and firepower to make its presence felt across the world. To be effective, that global fleet would require a canal across

Central America through which U.S. warships could pass swiftly from the Atlantic to the Pacific oceans. It would also require a string of far-flung service bases from the Caribbean to the southwestern Pacific. Mahan recommended that the U.S. government take possession of Hawaii and other strategically located Pacific islands with superior harbor facilities.

Presidents William McKinley and Theodore Roosevelt would eventually make almost the whole of Mahan's vision a reality, but in the early 1890s, Mahan doubted that Americans would accept the responsibility and costs of empire. Many Americans still insisted that the United States should not aspire to world power by acquiring overseas bases and colonizing foreign peoples.

Mahan underestimated, however, the government's alarm over the scramble of Europeans to extend their imperial control. Every U.S. administration from the 1880s on committed to a "big navy" policy. By 1898, the U.S. Navy ranked fifth in the world, and by 1900, it ranked third. Already in 1878, the United States had secured rights to Pago Pago, a superb deep-water harbor in Samoa (a collection of islands in the southwest Pacific inhabited by Polynesians), and in 1885, it had leased Pearl Harbor from the Hawaiians. Both harbors were expected to serve as fueling stations for the growing U.S. fleet.

These attempts to project U.S. power overseas had already deepened the government's involvement in the affairs of distant lands. In 1889, the United States established a protectorate over part of Samoa, a move meant to forestall

THE U.S. NAVY, 1890–1914: EXPENDITURES AND BATTLESHIP SIZE

Fiscal Year	Total Federal Expenditures	Naval Expenditures	Naval Expenditures as Percentage of Total Federal Expenditures	Size of Battleships (average tons displaced)
1890	$318,040,711	$22,006,206	6.9%	11,000
1900	520,860,847	55,953,078	10.7	12,000
1901	524,616,925	60,506,978	11.5	16,000
1905	657,278,914	117,550,308	20.7	16,000
1909	693,743,885	115,546,011	16.7	27,000 (1910)
1914	735,081,431	139,682,186	19.0	32,000

Source: (for expenditures) E. B. Potter, *Sea Power: A Naval History* (Annapolis: Naval Institute Press, 1982), p. 187; (for size of ships) Harold Sprout, *Toward a New Order of Sea Power* (New York: Greenwood Press, 1976), p. 52.

German and British efforts to weaken American influence on the islands. In the early 1890s, President Grover Cleveland's administration was increasingly drawn into Hawaiian affairs, as tensions between American sugar plantation owners and native Hawaiians upset the islands' economic and political stability. In 1891, U.S. plantation owners succeeded in deposing the Hawaiian king and putting into power Queen Liliuokalani. But when Liliuokalani strove to establish her independence from American interests, the planters, assisted by U.S. sailors, overthrew her regime, too. Cleveland declared Hawaii a protectorate in 1893, but he resisted the imperialists in Congress who wanted to annex the islands.

Still, imperialist sentiment in Congress and across the nation continued to grow, fueled by "jingoism." Jingoists were nationalists who thought that a swaggering foreign policy and a willingness to go to war would enhance their nation's glory. This predatory brand of nationalism emerged in each of the world's big powers in the late 19th century. In the United States, it manifested itself in terms of an eagerness for war. The anti-imperialist editor of the *Nation*, E. L. Godkin, exclaimed in 1894: "The number of men and officials of this country who are now mad to fight somebody is appalling." Recent feminist scholarship has emphasized the degree to which men of the 1890s saw war as an opportunity to revive frontier-like notions of masculinity—of men as warriors and conquerors—that were proving difficult to sustain in industrializing and bureaucratizing America. Spain's behavior in Cuba in the 1890s gave those men the war they sought.

The Spanish-American War

 Q FOCUS QUESTION In going to war against Spain in 1898, was the United States impelled more by imperialist or anti-imperialist motives?

Relations between the Cubans and their Spanish rulers had long been deteriorating. The Spanish had taken 10 years to subdue a revolt begun in 1868. In 1895, the Cubans staged another revolt, sparked by their continuing resentment of Spanish control and by a depressed economy caused in part by an 1894 U.S. tariff law that made Cuban sugar too expensive for the U.S. market. The fighting was brutal. Cuban forces destroyed large areas of the island to make it uninhabitable by the Spanish. The Spanish army, led by General Valeriano Weyler, responded in kind, forcing large numbers of Cubans into concentration camps. Denied adequate food, shelter, and sanitation, an estimated 200,000 Cubans—one-eighth of the island's population—died of starvation and disease.

Such tactics, especially those ascribed to "Butcher" Weyler (as he was known in much of the U.S. press), inflamed American opinion. Many Americans sympathized with the Cubans, who seemed to be fighting the kind of anti-colonial war Americans had waged more than 100 years earlier. Americans stayed informed about Cuban-Spanish struggles by reading the *New York Journal*, owned by William Randolph Hearst, and the *New York World*, owned by Joseph Pulitzer. Hearst and Pulitzer were transforming newspaper publishing in much the same way Sam McClure and others had revolutionized the magazine business (see Chapter 21). To boost circulation, they sought out sensational and shocking stories and described them in lurid detail. They were accused of engaging in **"yellow journalism"**—embellishing stories with titillating details when the true reports did not seem dramatic enough.

The sensationalism of the yellow press and its frequently jingoistic accounts failed to bring about American intervention in Cuba, however. In the final days of his administration, President Cleveland resisted mounting pressure to intervene. William McKinley, who succeeded him in 1897, denounced the Spanish even more harshly, with the aim of forcing Spain into concessions that would satisfy the Cuban rebels and end the conflict. Initially, this strategy seemed to work: Spain relieved "Butcher" Weyler of his command, began releasing incarcerated Cubans from concentration camps, and granted Cuba limited autonomy. Still, Spaniards living on the island refused the authority of a Cuban

Uncle Sam Gives Spain More Than It Can Handle. By going to war in 1898, this poster suggests, the United States had toppled "brutal Spain" and the remnants of its empire.

government, and Cuban rebels continued to demand full independence. Late in 1897, when riots broke out in Havana, McKinley ordered the battleship *Maine* into Havana harbor to protect U.S. citizens and their property. Then, two unexpected events set off a war.

The first was the February 9, 1898, publication in Hearst's *New York Journal* of a letter stolen from Enrique Dupuy de Lôme, the Spanish minister to Washington, in which he described McKinley as "a cheap politician" and a "bidder for the admiration of the crowd." The de Lôme letter also implied that the Spanish cared little about resolving the Cuban crisis through negotiation and reform. The news embarrassed Spanish officials and outraged many in the United States. Then, only six days later, the *Maine* exploded in Havana harbor, killing 260 American sailors. Although subsequent investigations revealed that the most probable cause of the explosion was a malfunctioning boiler, Americans were certain that it had been the work of Spanish agents. "Remember the *Maine!*" screamed the headlines in the yellow press. On March 8, Congress responded to the clamor for war by authorizing $50 million to mobilize U.S. forces. In the meantime, McKinley notified Spain of his conditions for avoiding war: Spain would pay an indemnity for the *Maine*, abandon its concentration camps, end the fighting with the rebels, and commit to Cuban

independence. On April 9, Spain accepted all the demands but the last. Nevertheless, on April 11, McKinley asked Congress for authority to go to war. Three days later, Congress approved a war resolution, which included a declaration (spelled out in the Teller Amendment) that the United States would not use the war as an opportunity to acquire territory in Cuba. On April 24, Spain responded with a formal declaration of war against the United States.

"A Splendid Little War"

Secretary of State John Hay called the fight with Spain "a splendid little war." Begun in April, it ended in August. More than 1 million men volunteered to fight, and fewer than 500 were killed or wounded in combat. The American victory over Spain was complete, not just in Cuba but in the neighboring island of Puerto Rico and in the Philippines, Spain's strategic possession in the Pacific.

Actually, the war was more complicated than it seemed. The main reason for the easy victory was U.S. naval superiority. In the war's first major battle, a naval engagement in Manila harbor in the Philippines on May 1, a U.S. fleet commanded by Commodore George Dewey destroyed an entire Spanish fleet and lost only one sailor (to heat stroke). On land, the story was different. On the eve of war, the U.S. Army consisted of only 26,000 troops. These soldiers were skilled at skirmishing with Indians but ill-prepared and ill-equipped for all-out war. A force of 80,000 Spanish regulars awaited them in Cuba, with another 50,000 in reserve in Spain. Congress immediately increased the army to 62,000 and called for an additional 125,000 volunteers. The response to this call was astounding, but outfitting, training, and transporting the new recruits overwhelmed the army's capacities. Its standard-issue, blue flannel uniforms proved too heavy for fighting in tropical Cuba. Rations were so poor that soldiers referred to one common item as "embalmed beef." Most of the volunteers had to make do with ancient Civil War rifles that still used black, rather than smokeless, powder. The initial invasion force of 16,000 men took more than five days to sail the short distance from Tampa, Florida, to Daiquiri, Cuba. Moreover, the army was unprepared for the effects of malaria and other tropical diseases.

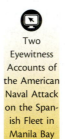

Two Eyewitness Accounts of the American Naval Attack on the Spanish Fleet in Manila Bay (1899)

That the Cuban revolutionaries were predominantly black also came as a shock to the U.S. forces. In their attempts to arouse support for the Cuban cause, U.S. newspapers had portrayed Cuban rebels as similar to white Americans. They were described as intelligent, civilized, and democratic, possessing an "Anglo-Saxon tenacity of purpose." And they were "fully nine-tenths" white, according to one report. The Spanish oppressors, by contrast, were depicted as dark-complexioned—"dark cruel eyes, dark swaggering men" wrote author Sherwood Anderson—and as possessing the characteristics of their "dark race": barbarism, cruelty, and indolence. The U.S. troops' first encounters with Cuban and Spanish forces challenged these stereotypes. Their Cuban allies appeared poorly outfitted, rough mannered, and largely black. The Spanish

"Remember the *Maine!*" The explosion of the battleship *Maine* in Havana harbor on February 15, 1898, killed 260 American sailors and helped drive the United States into war with Spain.

soldiers appeared well disciplined, tough in battle, and light complexioned.

The Cuban rebels were skilled guerrilla fighters, but racial prejudice prevented most U.S. soldiers and reporters from crediting their military expertise. Instead, they judged the Cubans harshly—as primitive, savage, and incapable of self-control or self-government. White U.S. troops preferred not to fight alongside the Cubans; increasingly, they refused to coordinate strategy with them.

At first, the U.S. Army's logistical unpreparedness and its racial misconceptions did little to diminish the soldiers' hunger for a good fight. No one was more eager for battle than Theodore Roosevelt, who, along with Colonel Leonard Wood, led a volunteer cavalry unit composed of Ivy League gentlemen, western cowboys, sheriffs, prospectors, Indians, and small numbers of Hispanics and ethnic European Americans. Roosevelt's **Rough Riders**, as the unit came to be known, landed with the invasion force and played an active role in the three battles fought in the hills surrounding Santiago. Their most famous action, the one on which Roosevelt would build his lifelong reputation as a military hero, was a furious charge up Kettle Hill into the teeth of Spanish defenses. Roosevelt's bravery was stunning, although his judgment was faulty. Nearly 100 men were killed or wounded. Reports of Roosevelt's bravery overshadowed the

equally brave performance of other troops, notably the **9th and 10th Negro Cavalries**, which played a pivotal role in clearing away Spanish fortifications on Kettle Hill and allowing Roosevelt's Rough Riders to make their charge. One Rough Rider commented: "If it had not been for the Negro cavalry, the Rough Riders would have been exterminated." The 24th and 25th Negro Infantry Regiments performed equally vital tasks in the U.S. Army's conquest of the adjacent San Juan Hill.

Theodore Roosevelt saw the Rough Rider regiment that he commanded in the Spanish-American War as a melting pot of different groups of white Americans. Combat, he further believed, would forge these many groups into one, as war had always done in the American past. African Americans were the group most conspicuously absent from the Rough Rider mix. Yet the fury of the fighting on Kettle Hill and San Juan Hill so scrambled the white and black regiments that by the time the troops reached the San Juan summit, they were racially intermixed. Combat had brought blacks into the great American melting pot. The black troops, Roosevelt declared, were "an excellent breed of Yankee," and no "Rough Rider will ever forget," he added, "the tie that binds us to the Ninth and Tenth Cavalry."

But Roosevelt did not truly believe that blacks were the equals of whites or that they could be absorbed into the

Leaders of the Cuban Struggle for Independence. By 1898, Cubans had been fighting to free their country from Spain for 30 years. This lithograph, a souvenir of the Grand Cuban-American Fair held in New York in 1896, depicts five leaders of the Cuban struggle: Máximo Gómez (upper left), Antonio Maceo (upper right), Calixto García (bottom right), and Salvador Cisneros (bottom left). At the center is José Martí, the "Father of the Revolution," killed in battle in 1895.

Rough Riders and 10th Cavalry. Roosevelt stands with his Rough Riders (top image) while members of the 10th Cavalry pose in the bottom image. Both groups played pivotal roles in the battles of San Juan and Kettle Hills, but America would celebrate only the Rough Riders, not the black cavalrymen.

American nation. So, a few months after returning home, he began downplaying the role of black troops and questioned their ability to fight. The attack on black fighting abilities would become so widespread that by the start of the First World War, the U.S. military had largely excluded black troops from combat roles. Thus, an episode that had demonstrated the possibility of interracial cooperation in America ended in the hardening of racial boundaries.

The taking of Kettle Hill, San Juan Hill, and other high ground surrounding Santiago gave the U.S. forces a substantial advantage over the Spanish defenders in Santiago. Nevertheless, the troops were short of food, ammunition, and medical facilities. Their ranks were devastated by malaria, typhoid, and dysentery, and more than 5,000 soldiers died from disease. Even the normally ebullient Roosevelt was close to despair: "We are within measurable distance of a terrible military disaster," he wrote his friend Henry Cabot Lodge on July 3.

Fortunately, the Spanish had lost the will to fight. On the very day Roosevelt wrote to Lodge, Spain's Atlantic fleet tried to retreat from Santiago harbor and was promptly destroyed

by a U.S. fleet. The Spanish army in Santiago surrendered on July 16; on July 18, the Spanish government asked for peace. While negotiations for an armistice proceeded, U.S. forces overran the neighboring island of Puerto Rico. On August 12, the U.S. and Spanish governments agreed to an armistice, but before the news could reach the Philippines, the United States had captured Manila and had taken prisoner 13,000 Spanish soldiers.

The armistice required Spain to relinquish its claim to Cuba, cede Puerto Rico and the Pacific island of Guam to the United States, and tolerate the American occupation of Manila until a peace conference could be convened in Paris on October 1, 1898. At that conference, American diplomats startled their Spanish counterparts by demanding that Spain also cede the Philippines to the United States. After two months of stalling, the Spanish government agreed to relinquish their coveted Pacific colony for $20 million. The transaction was sealed by the Treaty of Paris on December 10, 1898.

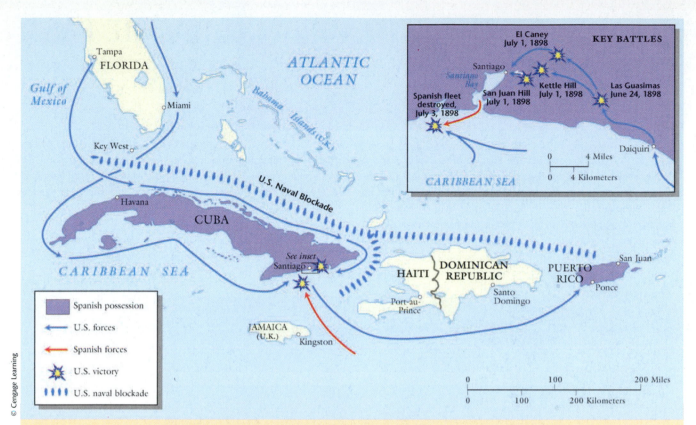

Map 22.1 Spanish-American War in Cuba, 1898. This map shows the following: the routes taken by U.S. ships transporting troops from Florida to Cuba; the concentration of troop landings and battles around Santiago, Cuba; and a U.S. naval blockade, stretching hundreds of miles from Puerto Rico to Cuba, that attempted to keep the Spanish troops in Cuba and Puerto Rico from being reinforced.

 View an animated version of this map or related maps on the CourseMate website.

The United States Becomes a World Power

Q FOCUS QUESTION What different mechanisms of control did the United States use to achieve its aims in Hawaii, Cuba, the Philippines, Puerto Rico, and China?

America's initial war aim had been to oust the Spanish from Cuba—an aim that both imperialists and anti-imperialists supported, but for different reasons. Imperialists hoped to incorporate Cuba into a new American empire; anti-imperialists hoped to see the Cubans gain their independence. But only the imperialists condoned the U.S. acquisition of Puerto Rico, Guam, and particularly the Philippines, which they viewed as integral to the extension of U.S. interests into Asia. Soon after the war began, President McKinley had cast his lot with the imperialists. First, he annexed Hawaii, giving the United States permanent control of Pearl Harbor. Next, he established a U.S. naval base at Manila. Never before had the United States sought such a large military presence outside the Western Hemisphere.

In a departure of equal importance, McKinley announced his intent to administer much of this newly acquired territory as U.S. colonies. Virtually all territory the United States had obtained

in the 19th century had been part of the North American continent. These lands had been settled by Americans, who had eventually petitioned for statehood. Of these new territories, however, only Hawaii would be allowed to follow this traditional path toward statehood. There, the powerful U.S. sugar plantation owners prevailed on Congress to pass an act in 1900 extending U.S. citizenship to all Hawaiian citizens and putting Hawaii on the road to statehood. No such influential group of Americans resided in the Philippines. The country was made a U.S. colony and placed under a U.S. administration that took its orders from Washington rather than from the Filipino people. Such colonization was necessary, in the eyes of American imperialists, to prevent other powers, such as Japan and Germany, from gaining a foothold somewhere in the 400-island archipelago and launching attacks on the U.S. naval base in Manila.

The United States might have negotiated an arrangement with **Emilio Aguinaldo**, the leader of an anti-colonial movement in the Philippines, that would have given the Philippines independence in exchange for a U.S. naval base at Manila. An American fleet stationed there would have been able to protect both American interests and the fledgling Philippine nation from predatory assaults by Japan, Germany, or Britain. Alternatively, the United States might have annexed the Philippines outright and offered Filipinos U.S. citizenship as the first step toward statehood. McKinley and his supporters, however, believed that the "inferior" Filipino people lacked the capacity for

Regular U.S. soldiers entered the Spanish-American War toting Norwegian-made Krag-Jorgensen rifles (top image), and the Spanish shouldered the German-made Mauser M93 (bottom image). Although the rifles look alike, the Mauser had a key advantage: it employed a stripper clip, a mechanism that allowed soldiers to load several bullets at once into the magazine. The Krag's magazine held five bullets, but they had to be loaded one at a time. Spanish soldiers with Mausers were able to fire off rounds quicker than the Americans. Criticized for its inferior weaponry, the U.S. government abandoned the Krag for the American-made Springfield M1903 soon after the war ended. This new Springfield rifle featured Mauser load-in technology.

Q What does America's reliance on foreign arms manufacturers reveal about the capacity and sophistication of its military industries in the years around 1900?

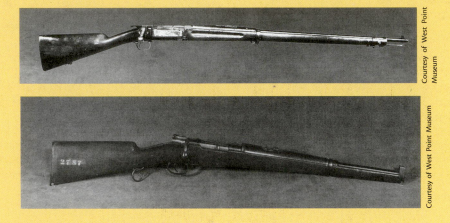

Courtesy of West Point Museum

Courtesy of West Point Museum

self-government. The United States would undertake a solemn mission to "civilize" the Filipinos and thereby prepare them for independence, but until that mission was complete, the Philippines would submit to rule by presidentially appointed U.S. governors.

The Debate over the Treaty of Paris

The proposed acquisition of the Philippines aroused opposition both in the United States and in the Philippines. The Anti-Imperialist League, strong in the Northeast, enlisted the support of several elder statesmen in McKinley's own party, as well as the former Democratic President Grover Cleveland, the industrialist Andrew Carnegie, and the labor leader Samuel Gompers. William Jennings Bryan, meanwhile, marshaled a vigorous anti-imperialist protest among Democrats in the South and West, while Mark Twain, William James, William Dean Howells, and other men of letters lent the cause their prestige. Some anti-imperialists believed that subjugating the Filipinos would violate the nation's most precious principle: the right of all people to independence and self-government. Moreover, they feared that the military and diplomatic establishment needed to administer the colony would threaten political liberties at home.

Other anti-imperialists were motivated more by self-interest than by democratic ideals. U.S. sugar producers, for example, feared competition from Filipino producers. Trade unionists worried that poor Filipino workers would flood the U.S. labor market and depress wage rates. Some businessmen warned that the costs of maintaining an imperial outpost would exceed any economic benefits that the colony might produce. Many Democrats, meanwhile, simply wanted to gain partisan advantage by opposing the Republican administration's foreign policy. Still other anti-imperialists feared the contaminating effects of contact with "inferior" Asian races.

Despite their contrasting motivations, the anti-imperialists almost dealt McKinley and his fellow imperialists a defeat in the U.S. Senate. On February 6, 1899, the Senate voted 57 to 27 in favor of the Treaty of Paris, only one vote beyond the minimum two-thirds majority required for ratification. Two last-minute developments may have brought victory. First, William Jennings Bryan, in the days before the vote, abandoned his opposition and announced his support for the treaty. Second, on the eve of the vote, Filipinos rose in revolt against the U.S. army of occupation. With another war looming and the lives of American soldiers imperiled, a few senators who had been reluctant to vote for the treaty may have felt obligated to support the president.

MUSICAL LINK TO THE PAST

Music for Patriots

Composer: John Philip Sousa
Title: "Stars and Stripes Forever" (c. 1895)

In the five years following the writing of "Stars and Stripes Forever," John Philip Sousa was probably the most famous musician in America. When he and his band arrived in town, a holiday atmosphere ensued: schools were closed, businesses released their workers for the day, and special flags were flown. Sousa furthered international respect for American music and helped dispel the pervasive stereotype that the United States could not produce musical works and performers worthy of the highest cultural respect. Sousa frowned upon symphonies, the musical form on which most famous composers had built their reputations. For him, symphonies were pretentious and full of padding, and they dawdled excessively before reaching their most crowd-pleasing sections. Instead, Sousa favored short, snappy, and often patriotic 3-minute pieces such as "Stars and Stripes Forever."

Sousa viewed music as entertainment and insisted on giving audiences what they wanted, and plenty of it. He did not mandate what audiences should hear as did most classical conductors; instead, he allowed listeners to render democratically their choices with applause. He mixed highbrow and lowbrow material, classical themes with march music, and frequently used humor in his arrangements, purposely avoiding what he regarded as the stuffiness of classical concerts. If audiences wished to hear "Stars and Stripes Forever" as an encore over and over (and they consistently did, until he died in 1932), then Sousa and his men would provide, with no withering of enthusiasm.

Besides his own works, Sousa championed the works of young American composers, but he demanded to know the stories behind their compositions. Musical inspiration, in Sousa's opinion, needed to be generated from "glorious events," and he avoided material from "atheistic composers" or those "crazily in love," because such works would not produce the appropriate nationalist feelings that he wished to cultivate in his audiences. "This was my mission. The point was to move all of America, while busied in its everyday pursuits, by the power of direct and simple music," he proclaimed in 1910. "I wanted to make a music for the people, a music to be grasped at once."

It was hardly an accident that Sousa's period of greatest popularity coincided with the wave of patriotic feeling that swept over America during the second half of the 1890s. The economy was recovering from the depression, and America was successfully flexing its muscles in a war with Spain. Many Americans wanted to wave the stars and stripes and found special inspiration in Sousa's music.

Q Does music, even instrumental music such as Sousa's, have the power to generate a patriotic mood?

Q Has any music produced in recent years in America—from 2001 to today—influenced Americans the way Sousa's music did in the 1890s?

Listen to an audio recording of this music on the Musical Links to the Past CD.

The American-Filipino War

The acquisition of the Philippines immediately embroiled the United States in a long, brutal war to subdue the Filipino rebels. In four years of fighting, more than 120,000 American soldiers served in the Philippines and more than 4,200 of them died. The war cost $160 million, or eight times what the United States had paid Spain to acquire the archipelago. The war brought Americans face-to-face with an unpleasant truth: American actions in the Philippines were virtually indistinguishable from Spain's actions in Cuba. Like Spain, the United States refused to acknowledge a people's aspiration for self-rule. Like "Butcher" Weyler, American generals permitted the use of savage tactics. Whole communities suspected of harboring guerrillas were driven into concentration camps, and their houses, farms, and livestock were destroyed. American soldiers killed so many Filipino rebels (whom they called "goo-goos") that the ratio of Filipino dead to wounded reached 15 to 1, a statistic that made

the American Civil War, in which one soldier had died for every five wounded, seem relatively humane. One New York infantryman wrote home that his unit had killed 1,000 Filipinos—men, women, and children—in retaliation for the murder of a single American soldier. A total of 15,000 Filipino soldiers died in the fighting. Estimates of total Filipino deaths from gunfire, starvation, and disease range from 50,000 to 200,000.

The United States finally gained the upper hand in the war after General Arthur MacArthur (father of Douglas) was appointed commander of the islands in 1900. MacArthur did not lessen the war's ferocity, but he understood that it could not be won by guns alone. He offered amnesty to Filipino guerrillas who agreed to surrender, and he cultivated close relations with the islands' economic elites. McKinley supported this effort to build a Filipino constituency sympathetic to the U.S. presence. He sent William Howard Taft to the islands in 1900 to establish a civilian government. In 1901, Taft became the colony's first "governor-general" and declared that he intended to prepare the

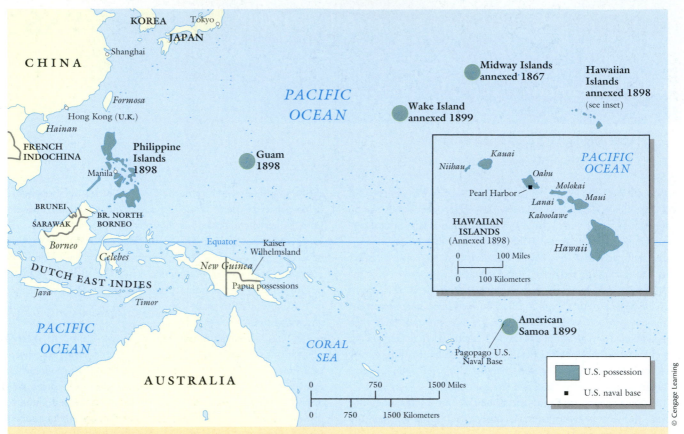

Map 22.2 American South Pacific Empire, 1900. By 1900, the American South Pacific empire consisted of a series of strategically located islands with superior harbor facilities, stretching from the Hawaiian Islands and Samoa in the middle of the Pacific to the Philippines on the ocean's western edge.

Filipinos for independence. He transferred many governmental functions to Filipino control and launched a program of public works (roads, bridges, schools) that would give the Philippines the infrastructure necessary for economic development and political independence. By 1902, this dual strategy of ruthless war against those who had taken up arms and concessions to those who were willing to live under benevolent American rule had crushed the revolt. Though sporadic fighting continued until 1913, Americans had secured control of the Philippines. The explicit commitment of the United States to Philippine

Emilio Aguinaldo and Filipino Anticolonial Insurgents, 1899–1901. Aguinaldo is in the first row, second from the right (he has his right hand on the shoulder of the man sitting in the center). Aguinaldo and his supporters initially welcomed the U.S. war against Spain in the Philippines but then fought U.S. efforts to turn the Philippines into an American colony.

The "Water Cure" in the Philippines. This photograph shows U.S. soldiers forcing water into the mouth of a Filipino guerrilla to the point where it would overflow his esophagus and pour into his breathing channels, creating the sensation of drowning. The image reveals U.S. forces using brutal tactics to break down the resistance of their Filipino opponents.

independence (a promise that was deferred until 1946), together with an extensive program of internal improvements, eased the nation's conscience.

Controlling Cuba and Puerto Rico

Helping the Cubans achieve independence had been a major rationalization for the war against Spain. Even so, in 1900 when General Leonard Wood, commander of U.S. forces in Cuba, authorized a constitutional convention to write the laws for a Cuban republic, the McKinley administration made clear it would not easily relinquish control of the island. At McKinley's urging, the U.S. Congress attached to a 1901 army appropriations bill the **Platt Amendment**, delineating three conditions for Cuban independence: (1) Cuba would not be permitted to make treaties with foreign powers; (2) the United States would have broad authority to intervene in Cuban political and economic affairs; and (3) Cuba would sell or lease land to the United States for naval stations. The delegates to Cuba's constitutional convention were outraged, but the dependence of Cuba's vital sugar industry on the U.S. market and the continuing presence of a U.S. army on Cuban soil rendered resistance futile. In 1901, by a vote of 15 to 11, the delegates reluctantly wrote the Platt conditions into their constitution. "There is, of course, little or no independence left Cuba under the Platt Amendment," Wood candidly admitted to his friend Theodore Roosevelt, who had recently succeeded the assassinated McKinley as president.

Cuba's status, in truth, differed little from that of the Philippines. Both were colonies of the United States. In the case of Cuba, economic dependence closely followed political subjugation. Between 1898 and 1914, U.S. trade with Cuba increased more than tenfold (from $27 million to $300 million), while investments more than quadrupled (from $50 million to

$220 million). In 1903, the United States compelled Cuba to lease it 45 square miles of land and water on the island nation's southeast coast. There the United States built the U.S. Naval Station at Guantanamo Bay, a facility that it maintains to this day. The United States also intervened in Cuban political affairs five times between 1906 and 1921 to protect its economic interests and those of the indigenous ruling class with whom it had become closely allied. The economic, political, and military control that the United States imposed on Cuba would fuel anti-American sentiment there for years to come.

Puerto Rico received somewhat different treatment. The United States annexed the island outright with the Foraker Act (1900). Unlike every previous annexation authorized by Congress since 1788, this act contained no provision for making the inhabitants of Puerto Rico citizens of the United States. Instead, Puerto Rico was designated an "unincorporated" territory, which meant that Congress would dictate the island's government and specify the rights of its inhabitants. Puerto Ricans were allowed no role in designing their government, nor was their consent to its establishment sought. With the Foraker Act, Congress had, in effect, invented a new, imperial mechanism for ensuring sovereignty over lands deemed vital to U.S. economic and military security. The U.S. Supreme Court upheld the constitutionality of this mechanism in a series of historic decisions, known as the Insular Cases, in the years from 1901 to 1904.

In some respects, Puerto Rico fared better than "independent" Cuba. Puerto Ricans were granted U.S. citizenship in 1917 and won the right to elect their own governor in 1947. Still, Puerto Ricans enjoyed fewer political rights than Americans in the 48 states. Moreover, throughout the 20th century, they endured a poverty rate far exceeding that of the mainland. As late as 1948, for example, three-fourths of Puerto Rican households subsisted on $1,000 or less annually, a figure below the U.S.

New Americans? The terms of Puerto Rico's 1900 annexation did not permit the island's inhabitants, such as those depicted in this 1900 photograph, to become citizens of the United States. Instead they became a colonized people.

poverty line. In its skewed distribution of wealth and its lack of industrial development, Puerto Rico resembled the poorly developed nations of Central and South America more than it did the affluent country that took over its government in 1900.

The subjugation of Cuba and the annexation of Puerto Rico troubled Americans far less than the U.S. takeover in the Philippines. Since the first articulation of the Monroe Doctrine in 1823, the United States had, in effect, claimed the Western Hemisphere as its sphere of influence. Within that sphere, many Americans believed, the United States possessed the right to act unilaterally to protect its interests. Before 1900, most of its actions (with the exception of the Mexican War) had been designed to limit the influence of European powers—Britain, France, Russia, and Spain—on the countries of the hemisphere. After 1900, however, the United States assumed a more aggressive role, seizing land, overturning governments it did not like, and forcing its economic and political policies on weaker neighbors in order to turn the Caribbean Sea into what policymakers called (with the example of ancient Rome in mind) an American Mediterranean.

China and the "Open Door"

Except for Hawaii, the Philippines, and Guam, the United States made no effort to take control of Asian lands. Such a policy might well have triggered war with other world powers that were already well established in the area. The United States opted for a diplomatic rather than a military strategy to achieve its foreign policy objectives. For China, in 1899 and 1900, it proposed the policy of the "open door."

The United States was concerned that the actions of the other world powers in China would block its own efforts to open up China's markets to American goods. Britain, Germany, Japan, Russia, and France each coveted a chunk of China, where they could monopolize trade, exploit cheap labor, and establish military bases. By the 1890s, each of these powers was building a sphere of influence, either by wringing economic and territorial concessions from the weak Chinese government or by seizing outright the land and trading privileges they desired.

To prevent China's breakup and to preserve U.S. economic access to the whole of China, McKinley's secretary of state, John Hay, sent **"open door" notes** to the major world powers. The notes asked each power to open its Chinese sphere of influence to the merchants of other nations and to grant them reasonable harbor fees and railroad rates. Hay also asked each power to respect China's sovereignty by enforcing Chinese tariff duties in the territory it controlled.

None of the world powers embraced either of Hay's requests, although Britain and Japan gave provisional assent. France, Germany, Russia, and Italy responded evasively, indicating their support for the Open Door policy in theory but insisting that they could not implement it until all of the other powers had done so. Hay put the best face on their responses by declaring that all of the powers had agreed to observe his Open Door principles and that he regarded their assent as "final and definitive." The rivals may have been impressed by Hay's diplomacy, but whether they intended to uphold the United States' Open Door policy was not at all clear.

The first challenge to Hay's policy came from the Chinese. In May 1900, a Chinese organization, colloquially known as the **"Boxers,"** sparked an uprising to rid China of all "foreign devils" and foreign influences. Hundreds of Europeans were killed, as were many Chinese men and women who had converted to Christianity. When the Boxers laid siege to the foreign legations in Beijing and cut off communication between that city and the outside world, the imperial powers raised an expeditionary force to rescue the diplomats and punish the Chinese rebels. The force, which included 5,000 U.S. soldiers, rushed over from the Philippines, broke the Beijing siege in August, and ended the Boxer Rebellion soon thereafter.

Hay feared that other major powers would use the rebellion as a reason to demand greater control over Chinese territory. He sent out a second round of Open Door notes, now asking each power to respect China's political independence and territorial integrity, in addition to guaranteeing unrestricted access to its markets. Impressed by America's show of military strength and worried that the Chinese rebels might strike again, the imperialist rivals responded more favorably to this second round of notes. Britain, France, and Germany endorsed Hay's policy outright. With that support, Hay was able to check Russian and Japanese designs on Chinese territory. Significantly, when the powers decided that the Chinese government should pay them reparations for their property and personnel losses during the Boxer Rebellion, Hay convinced them to accept payment in cash rather than in territory. By keeping China intact and open to free trade, the United States had achieved a major foreign policy victory.

Restoring Order in China.
This 1900 photograph depicts the international nature of the expeditionary force raised to defeat the Chinese rebels known as Boxers. The soldiers/marines depicted in this photo represented these nations (left to right): Great Britain, the United States, Russia, India, Germany, France, Austria-Hungary, Italy, and Japan.

Theodore Roosevelt, Geopolitician

FOCUS QUESTION What were the similarities and differences between Theodore Roosevelt's foreign policies in Latin America and East Asia? What explains the differences?

Roosevelt had been a driving force in the transformation of U.S. foreign policy during the McKinley Administration. As assistant secretary of the navy, as a military hero, as a speaker and writer, and then as vice president, Roosevelt worked tirelessly to remake the country into one of the world's great powers. He believed that Americans were a racially superior people destined for supremacy in economic and political affairs. He did not assume, however, that international supremacy would automatically accrue to the United States. A nation, like an individual, had to strive for greatness and cultivate physical and mental fitness; it had to build a military force that could convincingly project power overseas; and it had to be prepared to fight. All great nations, Roosevelt declared, ultimately depended on the skill and dedication of their warriors.

Roosevelt's appetite for a good fight caused many people to rue the ascension of this "cowboy" to the White House after McKinley's assassination in 1901. But behind his blustery exterior lay a shrewd analyst of international relations. As much as he craved power for himself and the nation, he understood that the United States could not rule every portion of the globe through military or economic means. Consequently, he sought a balance of power among the industrial nations through negotiation rather than war. Such a balance would enable each imperial power to safeguard its key interests and contribute to world peace and progress.

Absent from Roosevelt's geopolitical thinking was concern for the interests of less powerful nations. Roosevelt had little patience with the claims to sovereignty of small countries or the human rights of weak peoples. In his eyes, the peoples of Latin America, Asia (with the exception of Japan), and Africa were racially inferior and thus incapable of self-government or industrial progress.

The Roosevelt Corollary

Ensuring U.S. dominance in the Western Hemisphere ranked high on Roosevelt's list of foreign policy objectives. In 1904, he issued a "corollary" to the Monroe Doctrine, which had asserted the right of the United States to keep European powers from meddling in hemispheric affairs. In his corollary, Roosevelt declared that the United States possessed a further right: to intervene in the domestic affairs of nations in the Western Hemisphere to quell disorder and forestall European intervention. The **Roosevelt corollary** formalized a policy that the United States had already deployed against Cuba and Puerto Rico in 1900 and 1901. Subsequent events in Venezuela and the Dominican Republic had further convinced Roosevelt of the need to expand the scope of U.S. intervention in hemispheric affairs.

Both Venezuela and the Dominican Republic were controlled by dictators who had defaulted on debts owed to European banks. Their delinquency prompted a German-led European naval blockade and bombardment of Venezuela in 1902 and a threatened invasion of the Dominican Republic by Italy and France in 1903. The United States forced the German navy to retreat from the Venezuelan coast in 1903. In the Dominican Republic, after a revolution had chased the dictator from power, the United States assumed control of the nation's customs collections in 1905 and refinanced the Dominican national debt through U.S. bankers.

The willingness of European bankers to loan money to Latin America's corrupt regimes had created the possibility

Tarzan, The Ape Man (1932)

Directed by W. S. Van Dyke.
Starring Johnny Weismuller (Tarzan), Maureen O'Sullivan (Jane Parker), Neil Hamilton (Harry Holt), C. Aubrey Smith (James Parker), and Cheeta the Chimp.

This movie introduced Americans to Tarzan, one of the most popular screen figures of the 1930s, 1940s, and 1950s. Based on the best-selling novels of Edgar Rice Burroughs, this Tarzan movie, like the ones that followed, was meant to puncture the civilized complacency in which Americans and other Westernized, imperial peoples had enveloped themselves. The movie opens with an American woman, Jane Parker, arriving in Africa to join her father, James, and the crew he has assembled to search for the mythic elephant graveyard thought to contain untold riches in ivory tusks. Jane is depicted as bright, energetic, attractive, and defiant of female gender conventions. The rest of the white adventurers, however, are portrayed as greedy, haughty, contemptuous of the African environment, or just ignorant. The Africans who act as their servants and guides are presented as primitive and superstitious, more like animals than humans. This expedition in search of ivory is destined for disaster, and the movie provides thrills by showing expedition members succumbing to attacks by wild animals and "wild humans" who inhabit this "dark continent."

During one such attack by hippos and pygmies, Tarzan, played by handsome Olympic swimming champion Johnny Weismuller, comes to the rescue, scaring off the attackers by mobilizing a stampede of elephants with his piercing, high-pitched, and unforgettable jungle cry. He takes Jane,

Johnny Weismuller and Maureen O'Sullivan as Tarzan and Jane.

who has become separated from the group, to his tree house. Thus begins one of the more unusual and famous screen romances.

Tarzan's origins are not explained in the movie, although one intuits that he somehow lost his white family and was raised by apes. He has none of the refining features of civilization—decent clothes, language, manners—but he possesses strength, honesty, and virtue. As Jane falls in love with Tarzan and decides to share a jungle life with him, we, the viewers, are asked to contemplate, with Jane, the benefits of peeling off the layers of civilized life (which seem to drop away from Jane along with many of her clothes) and returning to a simpler, more wholesome, and more natural form of existence.

The movie critiques and lampoons the imperial pretensions and smugness of the West, but it never asks viewers to see the indigenous African peoples as anything other than savage. Tarzan may have been ignorant of civilized customs, but he was white and, as such, equipped with the "native" intelligence and character of his race. The Africans depicted in the movie show no such intelligence or character. They are presented as weak and superstitious or as brutally aggressive and indifferent to human life. Thus *Tarzan, the Ape Man* manages to critique the West without asking Western viewers to challenge the racism that justified the West's domination of non-Western peoples and territories.

---

that the countries ruled by these regimes would suffer bankruptcy, social turmoil, and foreign intervention. The United States, under Roosevelt, did not hesitate to intervene to make sure that loans were repaid and social stability restored. But rarely in Roosevelt's tenure did the United States show a willingness to help the people who had suffered under these regimes establish democratic institutions or achieve social justice. When Cubans seeking true national independence rebelled against their puppet government in 1906, the United States sent in the Marines to silence them.

The Panama Canal

Roosevelt had long believed, along with Admiral Mahan, that the nation needed a way of moving its ships swiftly between the Pacific and Atlantic oceans. Central America's narrow width, especially in its southern half, made it the logical place to build a canal. In fact, a French company had obtained land rights and had begun construction of a canal across the Colombian province of Panama in the 1880s. But even though a "mere" 40 miles of land separated the two oceans, the French

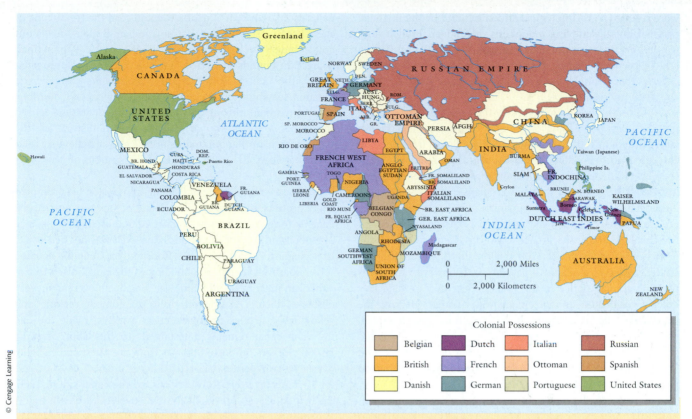

Map 22.3 Colonial Possessions, 1900. In 1900, the British Empire was the largest in the world, followed by the French and Russian Empires. The U.S. Empire, if measured by the square miles of land held as colonial possessions, was small by comparison.

Map 22.4 United States Presence in Latin America, 1895–1934. The United States possessed few colonies in Latin America but intervened (often repeatedly) in Mexico, Cuba, Nicaragua, Panama, Haiti, the Dominican Republic, and Venezuela to secure its economic and political interests.

were stymied by technological difficulties and by the financial costs of literally moving mountains. Moreover, French doctors found they were unable to check the spread of malaria and yellow fever among their workers. By the time Roosevelt entered the White House in 1901, the French Panama Company had gone bankrupt.

Roosevelt was not deterred by the French failure. He first presided over the signing of the Hay-Pauncefote Treaty with Great Britain in 1901, releasing the United States from an 1850 agreement that prohibited either country from building a Central American canal without the other's participation. He then instructed his advisers to develop plans for a canal across Nicaragua. Though the Panamanian route chosen by the French was shorter than the proposed Nicaraguan route, and the canal begun by the French was 40 percent complete, the French company wanted $109 million for it, more than the United States was willing to pay. In 1902, however, the company reduced the price to $40 million. Secretary of State Hay quickly negotiated an agreement with Tomas Herran, the Colombian chargé d'affaires in Washington. The agreement, formalized in the Hay-Herran Treaty, accorded the United States a six-mile-wide strip across **Panama** on which to build the **canal**. Colombia was to receive a one-time $10 million payment and annual rent of $250,000.

The Colombian legislature, however, rejected the proposed payment as insufficient and sent a new ambassador to the United States with instructions to ask for a one-time payment of $20 million and a share of the $40 million being paid to the French company. Actually, the Colombians were hoping to stall negotiations until 1904, when they would regain the rights to the Canal Zone and consequently to the $40 million sale price promised to the French company.

As negotiations failed to deliver the result he desired, Roosevelt encouraged the Panamanians to revolt against Colombian rule. Panamanians had staged several rebellions in the previous 25 years, all of which had failed. The 1903 rebellion succeeded, mainly because a U.S. naval force prevented the Colombian government from landing troops in its Panama province. Meanwhile, the U.S.S. Nashville put U.S. troops ashore to help the new nation secure its independence. The United States formally recognized Panama as a sovereign state only two days after the rebellion against Colombia began.

Philippe Bunau-Varilla, a director of the French company from which the United States had bought the rights to the canal, declared himself Panama's diplomatic representative, even though he was a French citizen operating out of a Wall Street law firm and hadn't set foot in Panama in 15 years. Before the true Panamanian delegation (appointed by the new Panamanian government) even reached the United States for negotiations over the canal, Bunau-Varilla and Secretary of State Hay signed the Hay–Bunau-Varilla Treaty (1903). The treaty granted the United States a 10-mile-wide canal zone in Panama in return for the package Colombia had rejected—$10 million down and $250,000 annually. Thus the United States secured its canal by dealing with Bunau-Varilla's French company rather than with the newly installed Panamanian government. When the Panamanian delegation arrived in Washington and read the treaty, one of them became so enraged that he knocked Bunau-Varilla out cold. Under the circumstances, however, the Panamanian delegation's hands were tied. If it objected to the counterfeit treaty, the United States might withdraw its troops from Panama, leaving the new country at the mercy of Colombia. The instrument through which the United States secured the Canal Zone is known in Panamanian history as "the treaty which no Panamanian signed," and it bedeviled relations between the two countries for much of the 20th century.

Roosevelt's severing of Panama from Colombia prompted angry protests in Congress. The Hearst newspapers decried the Panama foray as "nefarious" and "a quite unexampled instance of foul play in American politics." Roosevelt was not perturbed, later gloating, "I took the Canal Zone and let Congress debate!"

Roosevelt turned the building of the canal into a test of American ingenuity and willpower. Engineers overcame every obstacle; doctors developed drugs to combat malaria and yellow fever; armies of construction workers "made the dirt fly." The canal remains a testament to the labor of some 30,000 workers, imported mainly from the West Indies, who, over a 10-year period, labored 10 hours a day, 6 days a week, for 10 cents an hour. Roosevelt visited the canal site in 1906, the first American president to travel overseas while in office. When the canal was triumphantly opened to shipping in 1914, the British ambassador James Bryce described it as "the greatest liberty Man has ever taken with Nature." The canal shortened the voyage from San Francisco to New York by more than 8,000 miles and significantly enhanced the international prestige of the United States. The strategic importance of the canal, in turn, made the United States even more determined to preserve political order in Central America and the Caribbean.

In 1921, the United States paid the Colombian government $25 million as compensation for its loss of Panama. Panama waited more than 70 years, however, to regain control of the 10-mile-wide strip of land that Bunau-Varilla, in connivance with the U.S. government, had bargained away in 1903. President Jimmy Carter signed a treaty in 1977 providing for the reintegration of the Canal Zone into Panama, and the canal was transferred to Panama in 2000.

Keeping the Peace in East Asia

Roosevelt strove to preserve the Open Door policy in China and the balance of power throughout the region. The chief threats came from Russia and Japan, both of whom wanted to seize large chunks of China. At first, Russian expansion into Manchuria and Korea prompted Roosevelt to support Japan's 1904 attack on the Russian Pacific fleet anchored at Port Arthur, China. Once the ruinous effects of the war on Russia became clear, however, Roosevelt entered into secret negotiations to arrange a peace. He invited representatives of Japan and Russia to Portsmouth, New Hampshire, and prevailed on them to negotiate a compromise. The settlement favored Japan by perpetuating its control over most of the territories it had won during the brief **Russo-Japanese War**. Its chief prize was

© Cengage Learning

Map 22.5 Panama Canal Zone, 1914. This map shows the route of the completed canal through Panama and the 10-mile-wide zone surrounding it that the United States controlled. The inset map locates the Canal Zone in the context of Central and South America.

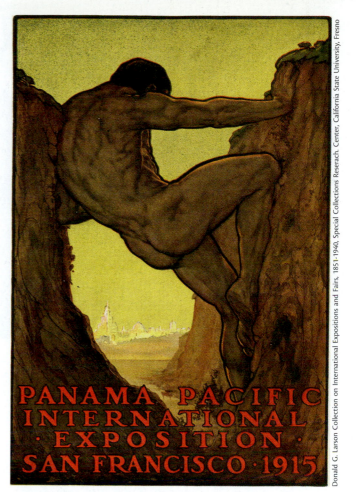

Donald G. Larson Collection on International Expositions and Fairs, 1851–1940, Special Collections Research. Center, California State University, Fresno

"The Thirteenth Labor of Hercules." In this poster designed by Perham W. Nahl for the 1915 Panama Pacific International Exposition in San Francisco, the building of the Panama Canal is celebrated as a work on the scale of Hercules, among the greatest—and the strongest—of Greek-Roman heroes.

© National Archives/CORBIS

Building the Canal with West Indian Labor. A ship delivers 1,500 Barbadian laborers to Panama in 1909 to work on the canal.

Korea, which became a protectorate of Japan, but Japan also acquired the southern part of Sakhalin Island, Port Arthur, and the South Manchurian Railroad. Russia avoided paying Japan a huge indemnity, and it retained Siberia, thus preserving its role as an East Asian power. Finally, Roosevelt protected China's territorial integrity by inducing the armies of both Russia and Japan to leave Manchuria. Roosevelt's success in ending the Russo-Japanese War won him the Nobel Prize for Peace in 1906; he was the first American to earn that award.

Although Roosevelt succeeded in negotiating a peace between these two world powers, he subsequently ignored, and sometimes encouraged, challenges to the sovereignty of weaker Asian nations. In a secret agreement with Japan (the Taft-Katsura Agreement of 1905), for example, the United States agreed that Japan could dominate Korea in return for a Japanese promise not to attack the Philippines. And in the Root-Takahira Agreement of 1908, the United States tacitly reversed its earlier stand on the inviolability of Chinese borders by recognizing Japanese expansion into southern Manchuria.

In Roosevelt's eyes, the overriding need to maintain peace with Japan justified ignoring the claims of Korea and,

Anti-Asian Hysteria in San Francisco. In 1906, in the midst of a wave of anti-Asian prejudice in California, the San Francisco school board ordered the segregation of all Asian schoolchildren. Here, a 9-year-old Japanese student submits an application for admission to a public primary school and is refused by the principal, Miss M. E. Dean.

increasingly, of China. The task of American diplomacy, he believed, was first to allow the Japanese to build a secure sphere of influence in East Asia (much as the United States had done in Central America and the Caribbean), and second to encourage them to join the United States in pursuing peace rather than war. This was a delicate diplomatic task that required both sensitivity and strength, especially when anti-Japanese agitation broke out in California in 1906.

White Californians had long feared the presence of East Asian immigrants (see Chapter 20). They had pressured Congress into passing the Chinese Exclusion Act of 1882, which ended most Chinese immigration to the United States. They next turned their racism on Japanese immigrants, whose numbers in California had reached 24,000. In 1906, the San Francisco school board ordered the segregation of Asian schoolchildren so that they would not "contaminate" white children. In 1907, the California legislature debated a law to end Japanese immigration to the state. Anti-Asian riots erupted in San Francisco and Los Angeles, encouraged in part by hysterical stories in the press about the "Yellow Peril."

Outraged militarists in Japan began talking of a possible war with the United States. Roosevelt assured the Japanese government that he, too, was appalled by the Californians' behavior. In 1907, he reached a **gentlemen's agreement** with the Japanese, by which the Tokyo government promised to halt the immigration of Japanese adult male laborers to the United States in return for Roosevelt's pledge to end anti-Japanese discrimination in California. Roosevelt did his part by persuading the San Francisco school board to rescind its segregation ordinance.

At the same time, Roosevelt worried that the Tokyo government would interpret his sensitivity to Japanese honor as weakness. So he ordered the main part of the U.S. fleet, consisting of 16 battleships, to embark on a 45,000-mile world tour, including a splashy stop in Tokyo Bay. Many Americans deplored the cost of the tour and feared that the appearance of the U.S. Navy in a Japanese port would provoke military retaliation. Roosevelt brushed his critics aside, and, true to his prediction, the Japanese were impressed by the show of strength by the **Great White Fleet**. Their response seemed to lend validity to the African proverb Roosevelt often invoked: "Speak softly and carry a big stick."

In fact, Roosevelt's handling of Japan was arguably the most impressive aspect of his foreign policy. Unlike many other Americans, he refused to let racist attitudes cloud his thinking. He knew when to make concessions and when to stand firm. His policies lessened the prospect of a war with Japan while preserving a strong U.S. presence in East Asia.

William Howard Taft, Dollar Diplomat

FOCUS QUESTION What was "dollar diplomacy," and how effective was it as a foreign policy tool for the United States under William Howard Taft?

William Howard Taft brought impressive foreign policy credentials to the job of president. He had gained valuable experience in colonial administration as the first governor-general of the Philippines. As Roosevelt's secretary of war and chief negotiator for the Taft-Katsura agreement of 1905, he had learned a great deal about conducting diplomacy with imperialist rivals. Yet Taft lacked Roosevelt's grasp of balance-of-power politics and capacity for leadership in foreign affairs. Furthermore, Taft's secretary of state, Philander C. Knox, a corporation lawyer from Pittsburgh, lacked diplomatic expertise. Knox's conduct of foreign policy seemed directed almost entirely toward expanding opportunities for corporate investment overseas, a disposition that prompted critics to deride his policies as **"dollar diplomacy."**

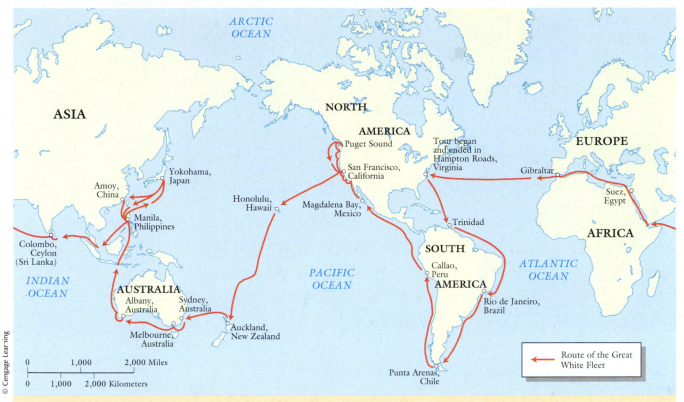

Map 22.6 Route of the Great White Fleet, 1907–1909. A 16-battleship-strong U.S. fleet left Virginia in 1907 for a 45,000-mile world tour, whose most important stop was Japan. The map reveals the enormous distance ships had to travel to cross from the Atlantic to the Pacific in the days before the Panama Canal.

Taft and Knox believed that U.S. investments would effectively substitute "dollars for bullets," and thus offer a more peaceful and less coercive way of maintaining stability and order. Taking a swipe at Roosevelt's "big stick" policy, Taft announced that "modern diplomacy is commercial."

The inability of Taft and Knox to grasp the complexities of power politics, however, led to a diplomatic reversal in East Asia. Prodded by banker associates, Knox sought to expand American economic activities in China—even in Manchuria, where they encroached on the Japanese sphere of influence. In 1911, Knox proposed that a syndicate of European and American bankers buy the Japanese-controlled South Manchurian Railroad to open up North China to international trade. Japan reacted by signing a friendship treaty with Russia, its former enemy, which signaled their joint determination to exclude American, British, and French goods from Manchurian markets. Knox's plan to purchase the railroad collapsed, and the United States' Open Door policy suffered a serious blow. Knox's further efforts to increase American trade with Central and South China triggered hostile responses from the Japanese and the Russians and contributed to the collapse of the Chinese government and the onset of the Chinese Revolution in 1911.

Dollar diplomacy worked better in the Caribbean, where no major power contested U.S. policy. Knox encouraged U.S. investment. Companies such as United Fruit of Boston, which established extensive banana plantations in Costa Rica and Honduras, grew powerful enough to influence both the economies and the governments of Central American

countries. When political turmoil threatened their investments, the United States simply sent in its troops. Thus, when Nicaraguan dictator José Santos Zelaya reportedly began negotiating with a European country to build a second trans-Isthmian canal in 1910, a force of U.S. Marines toppled his regime. Marines landed again in 1912 when Zelaya's successor, Adolfo Diaz, angered Nicaraguans with his pro-American policies. This time the Marines were instructed to keep the Diaz regime in power. Except for a brief period in 1925, U.S. troops would remain in Nicaragua continuously from 1912 until 1933. Under Taft, the United States continued to do whatever American policy makers deemed necessary to bolster friendly governments and maintain order in Latin America.

Woodrow Wilson, Struggling Idealist

FOCUS QUESTION

What does Woodrow Wilson's policy toward Mexico reveal about his underlying approach to foreign policy? How similar or different was his approach to the one favored by Theodore Roosevelt?

Woodrow Wilson's foreign policy in the Caribbean initially appeared no different from that of his Republican predecessors. In 1915, the United States sent troops to Haiti to put down a revolution; they remained as an army of occupation for 21

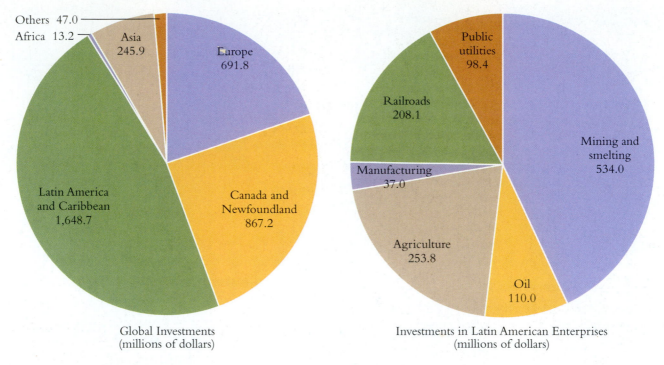

U.S. Global Investments and Investments in Latin America, 1914.
Source: From Cleona Lewis, *America's Stake in International Investments* (Washington, D.C.: The Brookings Institute, 1938), pp. 576–606.

years. In 1916, when the people of the Dominican Republic (who shared the island of Hispaniola with the Haitians) refused to accept a treaty making them more or less a protectorate of the United States, Wilson forced a U.S. military government upon them. When German influence in the Danish West Indies began to expand, Wilson purchased the islands from Denmark, renamed them the Virgin Islands, and added them to the U.S. Caribbean empire. By the time Wilson left office in 1921, he had intervened militarily in the Caribbean more often than any American president before him.

Wilson's relationship with Mexico in the wake of its revolution, however, reveals that he was troubled by a foreign policy that ignored a less powerful nation's right to determine its own future. He deemed the Mexicans capable of making democracy work and, in general, showed a concern for morality and justice in foreign affairs—matters to which Roosevelt and Taft had paid scant attention. Wilson wanted U.S. foreign policy to advance democratic ideals and institutions in Mexico.

Another motivation in Wilson's Mexican dealings was a fear that political unrest in Mexico could lead to violence, social disorder, and a revolutionary government hostile to U.S. economic interests. With a U.S.-style democratic government in Mexico, Wilson believed, property rights would be respected and U.S. investments would remain secure. Wilson's desire both to encourage democracy and to limit the extent of social change made it difficult to devise a consistent foreign policy toward Mexico.

The Mexican Revolution broke out in 1910 when dictator Porfirio Diaz, who had ruled for 34 years, was overthrown by democratic forces led by Francisco Madero. Madero's talk of democratic reform frightened many foreign investors, especially those in the United States and Great Britain, who owned more than half of all Mexican real estate, 90 percent of its oil reserves, and practically all of its railroads. Thus, when Madero was overthrown early in 1913 by Victoriano Huerta, a conservative general who promised to protect foreign investments, the dollar diplomatists in the Taft administration and in Great Britain breathed a sigh of relief. Henry Lane Wilson, the U.S. ambassador to Mexico, had helped engineer Huerta's coup. Before close relations between the United States and Huerta could be worked out, however, Huerta's men murdered Madero.

Woodrow Wilson, who became president shortly after Madero's assassination in 1913, refused to recognize Huerta's "government of butchers" and demanded that Mexico hold democratic elections. Wilson favored Venustiano Carranza and **Francisco ("Pancho") Villa**, two enemies of Huerta who commanded rebel armies and who claimed to be democrats. In April 1914, Wilson used the arrest of several U.S. sailors by Huerta's troops as a reason to send a fleet into Mexican waters. He ordered the U.S. Marines to occupy the Mexican port city of Veracruz and to prevent a German ship there from unloading munitions meant for Huerta's army. In the resulting battle between U.S. and Mexican forces, 19 Americans and 126 Mexicans were killed. The battle brought the two countries dangerously close to war. Eventually, however, American control over Veracruz weakened Huerta's regime to the point where Carranza was able to take power.

Carranza did not behave as Wilson had expected. Rejecting Wilson's efforts to shape his government, Carranza announced a bold land reform program. That program called for the distribution of some of Mexico's agricultural land to impoverished peasants and the transfer of developmental rights on oil lands from

Wilson's Mexico Policy. This 1916 cartoon illustrates the double character of Wilson's policy toward Mexico: On the one hand, he wanted Mexico to be successful in its efforts to become self-governing; On the other hand, he did not trust Mexico to find its way through its own revolution, so he felt compelled to put the country on his back and show it the way.

foreign corporations to the Mexican government. If the program went into effect, U.S. petroleum companies would lose control of their Mexican properties, a loss that Wilson deemed unacceptable. Wilson now threw his support to Pancho Villa, who seemed more willing than Carranza to protect U.S. oil interests. When Carranza's forces defeated Villa's forces in 1915, Wilson reluctantly withdrew his support of Villa and prepared to recognize the Carranza government.

Furious that Wilson had abandoned him, Villa and his soldiers pulled 18 U.S. citizens from a train in northern Mexico and murdered them, along with another 17 in an attack on Columbus, New Mexico. Determined to punish Villa, Wilson received permission from Carranza to send a U.S. expeditionary force under General John J. Pershing into Mexico to hunt down Villa's "bandits." Pershing's troops pursued Villa's forces 300 miles into Mexico but failed to catch them. The U.S. troops did, however, clash twice with Mexican troops under Carranza's command, once again bringing the countries to the brink of war. The United States, about to enter the First World War, could not afford a fight with Mexico; in 1917, Wilson quietly ordered Pershing's troops home and grudgingly recognized the Carranza government.

Wilson's policies toward Mexico in 1913–17 seemed to have produced few concrete results, except to reinforce an already deep antagonism among Mexicans toward the United States. His repeated changes in strategy, moreover, seemed to indicate a lack of skill and decisiveness in foreign affairs. Actually, however, Wilson recognized something that Roosevelt and

Taft had not: that more and more peoples of the world were determined to control their own destinies. The United States, under Wilson, was looking for a way to support these peoples' democratic aspirations while also safeguarding its own economic interests. The First World War would make this quest for a balance between democratic principles and national self-interest all the more urgent.

Conclusion

We can assess the dramatic turn in U.S. foreign policy after 1898 either in relation to the foreign policies of rival world powers or against America's own democratic ideals. By the first standard, U.S. foreign policy looks impressive. The United States achieved its major objectives in world affairs: It tightened its control over the Western Hemisphere and projected its military and economic power into Asia. It did so while sacrificing relatively few American lives and while constraining the jingoistic appetite for truly extensive military adventure and conquest. The United States added only 125,000 square miles to its empire in the years from 1870 to 1900, while Great Britain, France, and Germany enlarged their empires by 4.7, 3.5, and 1.0 million square miles, respectively. Relatively few foreigners were subjected to U.S. colonial rule. By contrast, in 1900, the British Empire extended more than 12 million square miles and embraced one-fourth of the world's population. At times, American rule could be brutal, as it was to Filipino soldiers and civilians alike, but on the whole it was no more severe than British or French rule and significantly less severe than that of German, Belgian, or Japanese imperialists. McKinley, Roosevelt, Taft, and Wilson all placed limits on American expansion and avoided, until 1917, extensive foreign entanglements and wars.

If measured against the standard of America's own democratic ideals, however, U.S. foreign policy after 1898 must be judged more harshly. It demeaned the peoples of the Philippines, Puerto Rico, Guam, Cuba, and Colombia as inferior and primitive and denied them the right to govern themselves. In choosing to behave like the imperialist powers of Europe, the United States abandoned its longstanding claim to being a different kind of nation—one that valued liberty more than power.

Many Americans of the time judged their nation by both standards and thus faced a dilemma that would extend throughout the 20th century. On the one hand, they believed with Roosevelt that the size, economic strength, and honor of the United States required it to accept the role of world power and policeman. On the other hand, they continued to believe with Wilson that they had a mission to spread the democratic values of 1776 to the farthest reaches of the earth. The Mexico example demonstrates how hard it was for the United States to reconcile these two very different approaches to world affairs.

CHAPTER REVIEW

REVIEW QUESTIONS

1. Which groups in American society were most interested in expanding U.S. influence abroad?
2. In going to war against Spain in 1898, was the United States impelled more by imperialist or anti-imperialist motives?
3. What different mechanisms of control did the United States use to achieve its aims in Hawaii, Cuba, the Philippines, Puerto Rico, and China?
4. What were the similarities and differences between Theodore Roosevelt's foreign policies in Latin America and East Asia? What explains the differences?
5. What was "dollar diplomacy," and how effective was it as a foreign policy tool for the United States under William Howard Taft?
6. What does Woodrow Wilson's policy toward Mexico reveal about his underlying approach to foreign policy? How similar or different was his approach to the one favored by Theodore Roosevelt?

CRITICAL THINKING QUESTIONS

1. What is the appropriate standard for judging the 1898 turn in U.S. foreign policy: the policies of rival world powers or America's own democratic ideals?
2. If you had been a president, secretary of state, or a leading senator in the period 1898–1917, with the power to alter U.S. foreign policy, what, if anything, would you have changed? What leads you to believe that your changes in policy would have been not only desirable but successful in achieving their aims?

IDENTIFICATIONS

Review your understanding of the following key terms, people, and events for this chapter (terms in bold in text are included in the Glossary).

Turner's "frontier thesis," p. 597
imperialists, p. 598
Alfred Thayer Mahan, p. 598
yellow journalism, p. 599
Rough Riders, p. 601
9th and 10th Negro Cavalries, p. 601
Emilio Aguinaldo, p. 603
Platt Amendment, p. 607
"open door" notes, p. 608
Boxers, p. 608
Roosevelt corollary, p. 610
The Panama Canal, p. 612
Russo-Japanese War, p. 614
gentlemen's agreement, p. 614
Great White Fleet, p. 614
dollar diplomacy, p. 615
Francisco ("Pancho") Villa, p. 617

SUGGESTED READINGS

General works on America's imperialist turn in the 1890s and early years of the 20th century include **Walter LaFeber, *The Cambridge History of Foreign Relations: The Search for Opportunity, 1865–1913*** (1993) and **Emily Rosenberg, *Spreading the American Dream: American Economic and Cultural Expansion, 1890–1945*** (1982). **David F. Trask, *The War with Spain in 1898*** (1981) is a comprehensive study of the

Spanish-American War. **Gerald F. Linderman, *The Mirror of War: American Society and the Spanish-American War*** (1974) brilliantly recaptures the shock that overtook Americans who discovered that their Cuban allies were black and the Spanish enemies were white. The role of gender in the Spanish-American War is explored in **Kristin L. Hoganson, *Fighting for American Manhood: How Gender Politics Provoked the Spanish-American and Philippine-American Wars*** (1998).

Paul A. Kramer, *The Blood of Government: Race, Empire, the United States, and the Philippines* (2006) analyzes the effects of U.S. colonialism on the Philippines and America. **Louis A. Perez, *Cuba Under the Platt Amendment, 1902–1934*** (1986), explores the extension of U.S. control over Cuba, while **Marilyn B. Young, *The Rhetoric of Empire: American China Policy, 1895–1901*** (1968) examines the unfolding Open Door policy. The history of Puerto Rico following its annexation by the United States is explored in **Raymond Carr, *Puerto Rico: A Colonial Experiment*** (1984).

Howard K. Beale, *Theodore Roosevelt and the Rise of America to World Power* (1956), is still a crucial work on Roosevelt's foreign policy. On the Panama Canal, see **Julie Greene, *The Canal Builders: Making America's Empire at the Panama Canal*** (2009). Consult **Emily Rosenberg, *Financial Missionaries to the World: The Politics and Culture of Dollar Diplomacy, 1900–1930*** (1999), on the "dollar diplomacy" that emerged during the Taft Administration. On Wilson's foreign policy, see **Thomas J. Knock, *To End All Wars: Woodrow Wilson and the Quest for a New World Order*** (1992); **Lloyd C. Gardner, *Safe for Democracy: The Anglo-American Response to Revolution, 1913–1923*** (1984); and **Mary A. Renda, *Taking Haiti: Military Occupation and the Culture of U.S. Imperialism, 1915–1940*** (2001).

 Visit the CourseMate website at www.cengagebrain.com for additional study tools and review materials for this chapter.

CHAPTER 23

© Mary Evans Picture Library/The Image Works

The Sinking of the *Lusitania*

On May 7, 1915, a German U-boat torpedoed and sank the British passenger liner *Lusitania*, killing 1,198 people, 128 of them Americans. The event turned U.S. opinion sharply against the Germans, especially because the civilians on board had been given no chance to escape or surrender.

War and Society, 1914–1920

THE FIRST WORLD WAR broke out in Europe in August 1914. The **Triple Alliance** of Germany, Austria-Hungary, and the Ottoman Empire squared off against the **Triple Entente** of Great Britain, France, and Russia. The United States entered the war on the side of the Entente (the Allies, or Allied Powers, as they came to be called) in 1917. Over the next year and a half, the United States converted its large, sprawling economy into a disciplined war production machine, raised a 5-million-man army, and provided both the war matériel and troops that helped propel the Allies to victory.

But the war also convulsed American society more deeply than any event since the Civil War. This was the first total war, meaning that combatants devoted virtually all of their resources to the fight. Thus the U.S. government had no choice but to pursue a degree of industrial control and social regimentation that was unprecedented in American history. This degree of government control was controversial in a society that had long distrusted state power. Moreover, significant numbers of Americans from a variety of constituencies opposed the war. To overcome this opposition, Wilson couched American war aims in disinterested and idealistic terms: The United States, he claimed, wanted a "peace without victory," a "war for democracy," and liberty for the world's oppressed peoples.

Although many people in the United States and abroad responded enthusiastically to Wilson's ideals, Wilson needed England and France's support to deliver peace without victory, and this support never came. At home, disadvantaged groups stirred up trouble by declaring that American society had failed to live up to its democratic and egalitarian ideals. Wilson supported repressive policies to silence these rebels and to enforce unity and conformity on the American people. In the process, he tarnished the ideals for which America had been fighting.

Europe's Descent into War

American Neutrality
Submarine Warfare
The Peace Movement
Wilson's Vision: "Peace without Victory"
German Escalation

American Intervention

Mobilizing for "Total" War
Organizing Industry
Securing Workers, Keeping Labor Peace
Raising an Army
Paying the Bills
Arousing Patriotic Ardor
Wartime Repression

The Failure of the International Peace
The Paris Peace Conference and the Treaty of Versailles
The League of Nations
Wilson versus Lodge: The Fight over Ratification
The Treaty's Final Defeat

The Postwar Period: A Society in Convulsion
Labor-Capital Conflict
Radicals and the Red Scare
Racial Conflict and the Rise of Black Nationalism

Europe's Descent into War

Q **FOCUS QUESTION** What caused Europe's descent into war?

Europe's descent into war began on June 28, 1914, in Sarajevo, Bosnia, when a Bosnian nationalist assassinated Archduke Franz Ferdinand, heir to the Austro-Hungarian throne. This act was meant to protest the Austro-Hungarian imperial presence in the Balkans and to encourage the Bosnians, Croatians, and other Balkan peoples to join the Serbs in establishing independent nations. Austria-Hungary responded to this provocation on July 28 by declaring war on Serbia, holding it responsible for the archduke's murder.

The conflict might have remained local if an intricate series of treaties had not divided Europe into two hostile camps. Germany, Austria-Hungary, and Italy, the so-called Triple Alliance, had promised to come to each other's aid if attacked. Italy would soon opt out of this alliance, to be replaced by the Ottoman Empire. Arrayed against the nations of the Triple Alliance were Britain, France, and Russia in the Triple Entente. Russia was obligated by another treaty to defend Serbia against Austria-Hungary, and consequently on July 30, it mobilized its armed forces to go to Serbia's aid. That brought Germany into the conflict to protect Austria-Hungary from Russian attack. On August 3, German troops struck not at Russia but at France, Russia's western ally. To reach France, German troops had marched through neutral Belgium. On August 4, Britain reacted by declaring war on Germany. Within the space of only a few weeks, Europe was engulfed in war.

Complicated alliances and defense treaties of the European nations undoubtedly hastened the rush toward war. But equally important was the competition among the European powers to build the strongest economies, the largest armies and navies, and the grandest colonial empires. Britain and Germany, in particular, were engaged in a bitter struggle for European and world supremacy. Few Europeans had any idea that these military buildups might lead to a terrible war that would kill millions and expose the barbarity lurking in their civilization. Historians now believe that several advisers close to the German emperor, Kaiser Wilhelm II, were actually eager to engage Russia and France in a fight for supremacy on the European continent. They expected that a European war would be swift and decisive—in Germany's favor.

Victory was not swift. The two camps were evenly matched. Moreover, the first wartime use of machine guns and barbed wire made defense against attack easier than staging an offensive. (Both tanks and airplanes had been invented, but military strategists were slow to put them to offensive use.) On the western front, after the initial German attack narrowly failed to take Paris in 1914, the two opposing armies confronted each other along a battle line stretching

CHRONOLOGY

1914	First World War breaks out (July–August)
1915	German submarine sinks the *Lusitania* (May 7)
1916	Woodrow Wilson unveils peace initiative ◆ Wilson reelected as "peace president"
1917	Germany resumes unrestricted submarine warfare (February) ◆ Tsar Nicholas II overthrown in Russia (March) ◆ U.S. enters the war (April 6) ◆ Committee on Public Information established ◆ Congress passes Selective Service Act and Espionage Act ◆ War Industries Board established ◆ Lenin's Bolsheviks come to power in Russia (November)
1918	Lenin signs treaty with Germany, pulls Russia out of war (March) ◆ Germany launches offensive on western front (March–April) ◆ Congress passes Sabotage Act and Sedition Act ◆ Allied Powers and U.S. advance toward Germany (April–October) ◆ Eugene V. Debs jailed for antiwar speech ◆ Germany signs armistice (November 11)
1919	Treaty of Versailles signed (June 28) ◆ Chicago race riot (July) ◆ Wilson suffers stroke (October 2) ◆ Police strike in Boston ◆ 18th Amendment (Prohibition) ratified
1919–1920	Steelworkers strike in Midwest ◆ Red Scare prompts "Palmer raids" ◆ Senate refuses to ratify Treaty of Versailles ◆ Universal Negro Improvement Association grows under Marcus Garvey's leadership
1920	Anarchists Sacco and Vanzetti convicted of murder

from Belgium in the north to the Swiss border in the south. Troops dug trenches to protect themselves from artillery bombardment and poison gas attacks. Commanders on both sides mounted suicidal ground assaults on the enemy by sending tens of thousands of infantry, armed only with rifles, bayonets, and grenades, out of the trenches and directly into enemy fire. Barbed wire further retarded forward progress, enabling enemy artillery and machine guns

THE ROAD TO WAR,
SUMMER 1914

1 June 28
   Assassination at Sarajevo

2 July 28
   Austria-Hungary declares
   war on Serbia

3 July 30
   Russia begins mobilization

4 August 1
   Germany declares war
   on Russia

5 August 3
   Germany declares war
   on France

6 August 4
   Great Britain declares war
   on Germany

7 August 6
   Russia and
   Austria-Hungary at war

8 August 12
   Great Britain declares war
   on Austria-Hungary

Legend:

- Allied powers and possessions, 1916
- Central powers and Ottoman Empire, 1916
- Neutral countries
- British naval blockade
- Trench line, Western front, 1915
- Eastern front, 1915

© Cengage Learning

Map 23.1 Europe Goes to War. In the First World War, Great Britain, France, and Russia squared off against Germany, Austria-Hungary, and the Ottoman Empire. Most of the fighting occurred in Europe along the western front in France (purple line) or the eastern front in Russia (red line). This map also shows Britain's blockade of German ports. British armies based in Egypt (then a British colony) clashed with Ottoman armies in Arabia and other parts of the Ottoman Empire.

View an animated version of this map or related maps on the CourseMate website.

to cut down appalling numbers of men. Many of those who were not killed in combat succumbed to disease that spread rapidly in the cold, wet, and rat-infested trenches. In Eastern Europe, the armies of Germany and Austria-Hungary squared off against those of Russia and Serbia. Although that front did not employ trench warfare, the combat was no less lethal. By the time the First World War ended, an estimated 8.5 million soldiers had died, and more than twice that number had been wounded. Total casualties, both military and civilian, had reached 37 million.

Gassed, by John Singer Sargent. An artist renders the horror of a poison gas attack in the First World War. The Germans were the first to use this new and brutal weapon, which contributed greatly to the terror of war.

American Neutrality

FOCUS QUESTION

Why did the U.S. policy of neutrality fail, and why did the United States get drawn into war?

Soon after the fighting began, Woodrow Wilson told Americans that this was a European war; neither side was threatening a vital American interest. The United States would therefore proclaim its neutrality and maintain normal relations with both sides while seeking to secure peace. Normal relations meant that the United States would continue trading with both camps. Wilson's neutrality policy met with opposition, especially from Theodore Roosevelt, who was convinced that the United States should join the Entente to check German power and expansionism. Most Americans, however, applauded Wilson's determination to keep the country out of war.

Neutrality was easier to proclaim than to achieve, however. Many Americans, especially those with economic and political power, identified culturally more with Britain than with Germany. They shared with the English a language, a common ancestry, and a commitment to liberty. Germany had no such attraction for U.S. policymakers. On the contrary, Germany's acceptance of monarchical rule, the prominence of militarists in German politics, and its lack of democratic traditions inclined U.S. officials to judge Germany harshly.

The United States had strong economic ties to Great Britain as well. In 1914, the United States exported more than $800 million in goods to Britain and its allies, compared with $170 million to Germany and Austria-Hungary (which came to be known as the Central Powers). As soon as the war began, the British and then the French turned to the United States for food, clothing, munitions, and other war supplies. The U.S. economy, which had been languishing in 1914, enjoyed a boom as a result. Bankers began to issue loans to the Allied Powers, further knitting together the American and British economies and giving American investors a direct stake in an Allied victory. Moreover, the British navy had blockaded German ports, which damaged the United States' already limited trade with Germany. By 1916, U.S. exports to the Central Powers had plummeted to barely $1 million, a fall of more than 99 percent in two years.

The Wilson administration protested the British navy's search and occasional seizure of American merchant ships, but it never retaliated by suspending loans or exports to Great Britain. To do so would have plunged the U.S. economy into a recession. In failing to protect its right to trade with Germany, however, the United States compromised its neutrality and allowed itself to be drawn into war.

Submarine Warfare

To combat British control of the seas and to check the flow of U.S. goods to the Allies, Germany unveiled a terrifying new weapon, the *Unterseeboot,* or U-boat, the first militarily effective submarine. Early in 1915, Germany announced its intent to use its U-boats to sink on sight enemy ships en route to the British Isles. On May 7, 1915, without warning, a German U-boat torpedoed the British passenger liner *Lusitania,* en route from New York to London. The ship sank in 22 minutes, killing 1,198 men, women, and children, 128 of them U.S. citizens. Shocked by the loss of life, the U.S. accused Germany of a barbaric and uncivilized act. The circumstances surrounding the sinking of the *Lusitania,* however, were more complicated than most Americans realized.

Before its sailing, the Germans had alleged that the *Lusitania* was secretly carrying a large store of munitions to Great Britain (a charge that later proved true), and that it therefore was subject to U-boat attack. Germany had warned American passengers not to travel on British passenger ships that carried munitions. Germany also claimed that the purpose of the U-boat attacks—the disruption of Allied supply lines—was no different from Britain's purpose in blockading German ports. Because German surface ships were outnumbered by British navy ships, Germany claimed that it had no alternative but to choose the underwater strategy. If a submarine attack seemed more reprehensible than a conventional sea battle, the Germans argued, it was no more so than the British attempt to starve the German people into submission with a blockade.

American political leaders might have used the *Lusitania* incident to denounce both Germany's U-boat strategy and Britain's blockade. Only Secretary of State Bryan had the courage to do so, however, and his stand proved so unpopular in Washington that he resigned from office; Wilson chose the pro-British Robert Lansing to take his place. Wilson denounced the sinking of the *Lusitania* and demanded that Germany pledge never to launch another attack on the citizens of neutral nations, even when they were traveling in British or French ships. Germany acquiesced to Wilson's demand.

In early 1916, the Allies began to arm their merchant vessels with guns and depth charges capable of destroying German U-boats. Considering this a provocation, Germany renewed its campaign of surprise submarine attacks. In March 1916, a German submarine torpedoed the French passenger liner *Sussex,* causing a heavy loss of life and injuring several Americans. Again Wilson demanded that Germany spare civilians from attack. In the so-called *Sussex* pledge, Germany once again relented but warned that it might resume unrestricted submarine warfare if the United States did not prevail upon Great Britain to permit neutral ships to pass through the naval blockade.

The German submarine attacks strengthened the hand of Theodore Roosevelt and others who had been arguing that war with Germany was inevitable and that the United States must prepare to fight. By 1916, Wilson could no longer ignore these critics. Between January and September of that year, he sought and won congressional approval for bills to increase the size of the army and navy, tighten federal control over National Guard forces, and authorize the building of a merchant fleet. Although Wilson had conceded ground to the pro-war agitators, he did not share their belief that war with Germany was either inevitable or desirable. To the contrary, he accelerated his diplomatic initiatives to secure peace, and he dispatched Colonel Edward M. House to London in January 1916 to draw up a peace plan with the British foreign secretary, Lord Grey. This initiative resulted in the House-Grey memorandum of February 22, 1916, in which Britain agreed to ask the United States to negotiate a settlement between the Allies and the Central Powers. The British believed that the terms of such a peace settlement would favor the Allies. They were furious when Wilson revealed that he wanted an impartial, honestly negotiated peace in which the claims of the Allies and Central Powers would be treated with equal respect. Britain now rejected U.S. peace overtures, and relations between the two countries grew unexpectedly tense.

The Peace Movement

Underlying Wilson's 1916 peace initiative was a vision of a new world order in which relations between nations would be governed by negotiation rather than war and in which justice would replace power as the fundamental principle of diplomacy. On May 27, 1916, Wilson formally declared his support for what he would later call the League of Nations, an international parliament dedicated to the pursuit of peace, security, and justice for all the world's peoples.

Many Americans supported Wilson's efforts to commit national prestige to the cause of international peace rather than conquest and to keep the United States out of war. Carrie Chapman Catt, president of the National American Woman Suffrage Association, and Jane Addams, founder of the Women's Peace Party, actively opposed the war. In 1915, an international women's peace conference at The Hague (in the Netherlands) had drawn many participants from the United States. A substantial pacifist group emerged among the nation's Protestant clergy. Midwestern progressives such as Robert La Follette, William Jennings Bryan, and George Norris urged that the United States steer clear of this European conflict, as did leading socialists such as Eugene V. Debs. In April 1916, many of the country's most prominent progressives and socialists joined hands in the American Union Against Militarism, pressuring Wilson to continue pursuing the path of peace. The country's sizable Irish and German ethnic populations, who wanted to block a formal military alliance with Great Britain, also supported Wilson's peace campaign.

AFTER TWO YEARS—WHO WANTS ME?

INDIANAPOLIS, IND., AUGUST 3, 1916

The Horror of War. This cover of the *United Mine Workers Journal* (1916) presents the Great War in the bleakest possible terms: as giving the Grim Reaper license to claim the bodies and souls of Europe's young men. Progressive labor unions were part of the broad coalition in the United States opposed to America's entry into war.

Wilson's Vision: "Peace without Victory"

The 1916 presidential election revealed the breadth of peace sentiment. At the Democratic convention, Governor Martin Glynn of New York, the Irish American speaker who renominated Wilson for a second term, praised the president for keeping the United States out of war. His portrayal of Wilson as the "peace president" electrified the convention and made "He kept us out of war" a campaign slogan. The slogan proved effective against Wilson's Republican opponent, Charles Evans Hughes, whose close ties to Theodore Roosevelt seemed to place him in the pro-war camp. Wilson's promise of peace along with a pledge to push ahead with progressive reform carried him to victory.

On December 16, 1916, Wilson sent a peace note to the belligerent governments, entreating them to consider ending the conflict and, to that end, to state their terms for peace. Although Germany refused to specify its terms and Britain and France announced a set of conditions too extreme for Germany ever to accept, Wilson pressed ahead, initiating secret peace negotiations with both sides. To prepare the American people for what he hoped would be a new era of international relations, Wilson appeared before the Senate on January 22, 1917, to outline his plans for peace. He reaffirmed his commitment to the League of Nations, but for such a league to succeed, Wilson argued, it would have to be handed a sturdy peace settlement. This entailed a **"peace without victory,"** one that refused to crown a victor or humiliate a loser. Only such a peace, Wilson argued, would last.

Wilson listed the crucial principles of a lasting peace: freedom of the seas; disarmament; and the right of every people to self-determination, democratic self-government, and security against aggression. He was proposing a revolutionary change in world order, one that would allow all of the world's peoples, regardless of their size or strength, to achieve political independence and to participate as equals in world affairs. These views, rarely expressed by the leader of a world power, stirred the masses of Europe and elsewhere caught in deadly conflict.

German Escalation

The German military responded to Wilson's entreaties for peace by throwing its full military might at France and Britain. On land it planned to launch a massive assault on the trenches, and at sea it prepared to unleash its submarines to attack all vessels heading for British ports. Germany knew that this last action would compel the United States to enter the war, but it was gambling on being able to strangle the British economy and leave France isolated before significant numbers of American troops could reach Europe.

Wilson continued to hope for a negotiated settlement until February 25, when the British intercepted and passed on to the president a telegram from Germany's foreign secretary, Arthur Zimmermann, to the German minister in Mexico. The infamous **Zimmermann telegram** instructed the minister to ask the Mexican government to attack the United States in the event of war between Germany and the United States. In return, Germany would pay the Mexicans a large fee and regain for them the "lost provinces" of Texas, New Mexico, and Arizona. Wilson, Congress, and the American public were outraged by this proposed deal.

In March, news arrived that Tsar Nicholas II's autocratic regime in Russia had collapsed and had been replaced by a liberal-democratic government under the leadership of Alexander Kerensky. As long as the tsar ruled Russia and stood to benefit from the Central Powers' defeat, Wilson could not honestly claim that America's going to war against Germany would bring democracy to Europe. The fall of the tsar and Russia's fledgling democratic government's need for assistance gave Wilson the rationale he needed to justify American intervention.

Appearing before a joint session of Congress on April 2, Wilson declared that the United States must enter the war because "the world must be made safe for democracy." He continued:

> We shall fight for the things which we have always carried nearest our hearts—for democracy, for the right of those who submit to authority to have a voice in their own Governments, for the rights and liberties of small nations, for a universal dominion of right by such a concert of free peoples as shall bring peace and safety to all nations and make the world itself at last free. To such a task we dedicate our lives and our fortunes.

Congress broke into thunderous applause. On April 6, it voted to declare war by a vote of 373 to 50 in the House and 82 to 6 in the Senate.

The United States thus embarked on a grand experiment to reshape the world. Wilson had given millions of people around the world reason to hope, both that the terrible war would end soon and that their strivings for freedom and social justice would be realized. Although he was taking America to war on the side of the Allies, he stressed that America would fight as an "associated power," a phrase meant to underscore America's determination to keep its war aims separate from and more idealistic than those of the Allies.

War Propaganda Pamphlet "10 Reasons Why We Are at War" (1917)

Still, Wilson understood all too well the risks of his undertaking. A few days before his speech to Congress, he had confided to a journalist his worry that the American people, once at war, will "forget there ever was such a thing as tolerance. To fight you must be brutal and ruthless, and the spirit of ruthless brutality will enter into the very fibre of our national life, infecting Congress, the courts, the policeman on the beat, the man in the street."

American Intervention

FOCUS QUESTION

What contribution did the United States make to the Allied Powers' victory?

The entry of the United States into the war gave the Allies the muscle they needed to defeat the Central Powers, but it almost came too late. Germany's resumption of unrestricted submarine warfare took a frightful toll on Allied shipping. From February through July 1917, German subs sank almost 4 million tons of shipping, more than one-third of Britain's entire merchant fleet. One of every four large freighters departing Britain in those months never returned; at one point, the British Isles were down to a mere four weeks of provisions. American intervention ended

Britain's vulnerability in dramatic fashion. U.S. and British naval commanders now grouped merchant ships into convoys and provided them with warship escorts through the most dangerous stretches of the North Atlantic. Destroyers armed with depth charges were particularly effective as escorts. Their shallow draft made them invulnerable to torpedoes, and their acceleration and speed allowed them to pursue slow-moving U-boats. The U.S. and British navies had begun to use sound waves (later called "sonar") to pinpoint the location of underwater craft, and this new technology increased the effectiveness of destroyer attacks. By the end of 1917, the tonnage of Allied shipping lost each month to U-boat attacks had declined by two-thirds, from almost 1 million tons in April to 350,000 tons in December.

The French and British armies had bled themselves white by taking the offensive in 1916 and 1917 and had scarcely budged the trench lines. The Germans had been content in those years simply to hold their trench position in the West because they were engaged in a huge offensive against the Russians in the East. The Germans intended first to defeat Russia and then to shift their eastern armies to the West for a final assault on the weakened British and French lines. Their opportunity came in the winter and spring of 1918.

A second Russian revolution in November 1917 had overthrown Kerensky's liberal-democratic government and had brought to power a revolutionary socialist government under Vladimir Lenin and his Bolshevik Party. Lenin pulled Russia out of the war on the grounds that the war did not serve the best interests of the working classes, that it was a conflict between rival capitalist elites interested only in wealth and power (and indifferent to the slaughter of soldiers in the trenches).

Russia's exit from the war hurt the Allies. Not only did it expose French and British troops to a much larger German force, but it also challenged the Allied claim that they were fighting a just war against German aggression. Lenin published the texts of secret Allied treaties showing that Britain and France, like Germany, had plotted to enlarge their nations and empires through war. The revelation that the Allies were fighting for land and riches rather than democratic principles outraged large numbers of people in France and Great Britain, demoralized Allied troops, and threw the French and British governments into disarray.

The treaties also embarrassed Wilson, who had brought America into the war to fight for democracy, not territory. Wilson quickly moved to restore the Allies' credibility by unveiling, in January 1918, a concrete program for peace. His **Fourteen Points** reaffirmed America's commitment to an international system governed by laws rather than by might and renounced territorial aggrandizement as a legitimate war aim. This document provided the ideological cement that held the Allies together at a critical moment. (The Fourteen Points are discussed more fully in this chapter in the section, "The Failure of the International Peace.")

Woodrow Wilson, Fourteen Points (1918)

In March and April 1918, Germany launched its huge offensive against British and French positions, sending Allied troops reeling. German troops advanced 10 miles a day—a faster pace than any on the western front since the earliest days of the war—until they reached the Marne River, within striking distance of Paris. The French government prepared to evacuate the city. At this perilous moment, a large American army—fresh, well-equipped, and oblivious to the horrors of trench warfare—arrived to reinforce what remained of the French lines.

In fact, these American troops, part of the American Expeditionary Force (AEF) commanded by General **John J. Pershing**, had begun landing in France almost a year earlier. During the intervening months, the United States had had to create a modern army from scratch, because its existing force was so small, ranking only 17th in the world. Men had to be drafted, trained, and supplied with food and equipment; ships for transporting them to Europe had to be found or built. In France, Pershing put his troops through additional training before committing them to battle. He was determined that the American soldiers—or "doughboys," as they were called—should acquit themselves well on the battlefield. The army

The Rock of the Marne. Mal Thompson's painting shows infantry units of the U.S. 30th and 38th regiments from the Third Division of the American Expeditionary Force engaging German troops in France in July 1918. Although he shows them under fire, Thompson depicts the soldiers as focused and calm, though operating in terrain desolated by war.

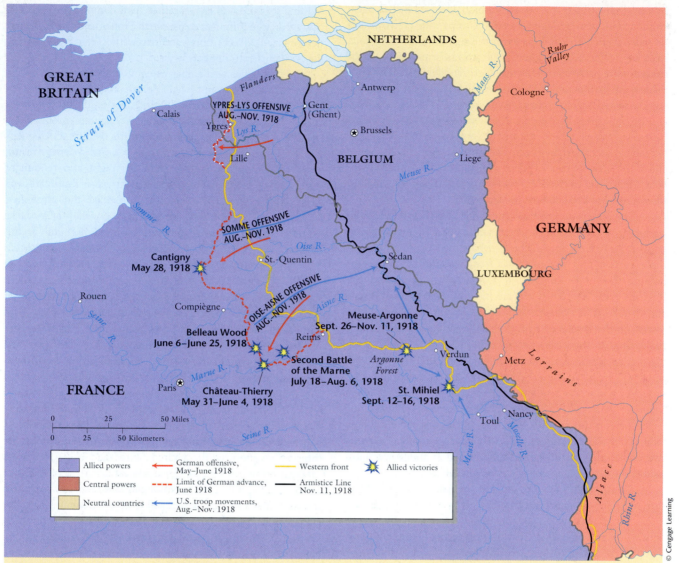

Map 23.2 America in the First World War: Western Front, 1918. In 1918, American forces joined the Allied forces in the climactic battles of the war. The red arrows show the major offensive by the Germans in the spring of 1918, and the blue arrows the decisive counteroffensive by the Allies in the fall of 1918. The fighting stopped along the black armistice line on November 11, 1918, after German capitulation.

he ordered into battle to counter the German spring offensive of 1918 fought well. Many American soldiers fell, but the German offensive ground to a halt. Paris was saved, and Germany's best chance for victory slipped from its grasp.

Buttressed by this show of AEF strength, the Allied troops staged a major offensive of their own in late September. Millions of Allied troops (including more than a million from the AEF) advanced across the 200-mile-wide Argonne Forest in France, cutting German supply lines. By late October, they had reached the German border. Faced with an invasion of their homeland and with rapidly mounting popular dissatisfaction with the war, German leaders asked for an armistice, to be followed by peace negotiations based on Wilson's Fourteen Points. Having forced the Germans to agree to numerous concessions, the Allies ended the war on November 11, 1918.

Mobilizing for "Total" War

Q FOCUS QUESTION — What problems did the United States encounter in mobilizing for total war, and how successfully were those problems overcome?

Compared to Europe, the United States suffered little from the war. The deaths of 112,000 American soldiers paled in comparison to European losses: 900,000 by Great Britain, 1.2 million by Austria-Hungary, 1.4 million by France, 1.7 million by Russia, and 2 million by Germany. The U.S. civilian population was spared most of the war's ravages—the destruction of homes and industries, the shortages of food and medicine, the spread of disease—that afflicted millions of Europeans.

Only with the flu epidemic that swept across the Atlantic from Europe in 1919 to claim approximately 500,000 lives did Americans briefly experience wholesale suffering and death.

Still, the war had a profound effect on American society. Every military engagement the United States had fought since the Civil War—the Indian wars, the Spanish-American War, the American-Filipino War, the Boxer Rebellion, the Latin American interventions—had been limited in scope. Even the troop mobilizations that seemed large at the time—the more than 100,000 needed to fight the Spanish and then the Filipinos—failed to tax American resources.

The First World War was different. It was a "total" war to which every combatant had committed virtually all of its resources. The scale of the effort in the United States became apparent early in 1917 when Wilson asked Congress for a conscription law that would permit the federal government to raise a multimillion-man army. The United States would also have to devote much of its agricultural, transportation, industrial, and population resources to the war effort if it wished to end the European stalemate. Who would organize this massive effort? Who would pay for it? Would Americans accept the sacrifice and regimentation it would demand? These were vexing questions for a nation long committed to individual liberty, small government, and a weak military.

Organizing Industry

At first, Wilson pursued a decentralized approach to mobilization, delegating tasks to local defense councils throughout the country. When that effort failed, however, Wilson created several centralized federal agencies, each charged with supervising nationwide activity in its assigned economic sector.

The success of these agencies varied. The Food Administration, headed by mining engineer and executive Herbert Hoover, substantially increased production of basic foodstuffs and put in place an efficient distribution system that delivered food to millions of troops and European civilians. (For more on Herbert Hoover's professional life and public service, see the Americans Abroad feature, "Herbert C. Hoover: International Mining Engineer, Businessman, and Public Servant.") Treasury

AMERICANS ABROAD
Herbert C. Hoover

Secretary William McAdoo, head of the U.S. Railroad Administration, also performed well in shifting the rail system from private to public control, coordinating dense train traffic, and making capital improvements that allowed goods to move rapidly to eastern ports, where they were loaded onto ships and sent to Europe. At the other extreme, the Aircraft Production Board and Emergency Fleet Corporation did a poor job of supplying the Allies with combat aircraft and merchant vessels. On balance, the U.S. economy performed wonders in supplying troops with uniforms, food, rifles, munitions, and other basic items; it did much less well in producing sophisticated weapons and machines such as artillery, aircraft, and ships.

Most of the new government agencies were more powerful on paper than in fact. Consider, for example, the **War Industries Board (WIB)**, an administrative body established by Wilson in July 1917 to harness manufacturing might to military needs. The WIB floundered for its first nine months, lacking the statutory authority to force manufacturers and the military to adopt its plans. Only the appointment of Wall Street investment banker Bernard Baruch as WIB chairman in March 1918 turned the agency around. Rather than force manufacturers to do the government's bidding, Baruch permitted industrialists to charge high prices for their products. He won exemptions from antitrust laws for corporations that complied with his requests. In general, he

Picture History

Herbert Hoover, Food Administration Chief. In this 1918 photograph, Hoover, seated in the middle, confers with French food administrators and private food industry officials about how best to distribute American foodstuffs to head off starvation and malnutrition in Europe.

"A Storm of Our People toward the North"

When jobs became available in the North during the First World War, African Americans from the South began journeying north in record numbers. Between 1916 and 1920, 500,000 made the journey, a population movement so large it became known as the Great Migration. That so many went north in such a brief period demonstrates how tough life was in the South for most African Americans and how ready they were to seize an opportunity to improve their situation. Many of the migrants were rural folk—tenant farmers, sharecroppers, and agricultural laborers—whose skills were not easily transferable to the urban and industrial economies of northern cities. They thus had to enter northern labor forces at the bottom—as unskilled industrial or service employees. But the Great Migration also counted educated African Americans in its ranks, as this excerpt from a letter sent to the *Chicago Defender*, a prominent black newspaper, demonstrates. The four letter-writers were educated women from Florida who had been teachers in black schools and were now looking for jobs as domestic servants with well-off Chicago families. We do not know whether the *Chicago Defender* responded to this particular letter, but we do know that in general the newspaper played a key role in facilitating migration by providing important information to southern migrants and northern employers.

We have several times read your noted newspaper and we are delighted with the same because it is a thorough Negro paper. There is a storm of our people toward the North and especially to your city. We have watched your want ad regularly and we are anxious for location with good families (white) where we can be cared for and do domestic work. We want to engage as cook, nurse, and maid. We have had some educational advantages, as we have taught in rural schools for few years but our pay so poor we could not continue. We can furnish testimonial of our honesty and integrity and moral standing. Will you please assist us in securing places as we are anxious to come but want jobs before we leave. Our chance here is so poor.

Q What, if anything, can we learn about these four potential migrants from this letter excerpt? In particular, how desperate were they to leave the South?

Q What steps had they taken to prepare for going north?

Q What risks were they willing to endure for the sake of gaining an opportunity for a better life?

Source: The Journal of Negro History, Vol. IV, ed. Carter G. Woodson, Lancaster, PA (The Association for the Study of Negro Life and History, Inc., 1919), pp. 318–319.

made war production too lucrative an activity to resist; however, he did not hesitate to unleash his wrath on corporations that resisted WIB enticements.

Baruch's forceful leadership worked reasonably well throughout his nine months in office. War production increased, and manufacturers discovered the financial benefits of cooperation between the public and private sectors. But Baruch's favoritism toward large corporations hurt smaller competitors. Moreover, the cozy relationship between government and corporation that he encouraged violated the progressive pledge to protect the people from the "interests." Achieving cooperation by boosting corporate profits, finally, was a costly way for the government to do business. The costs of the war soared to $33 billion, a figure more than three times expectations.

Securing Workers, Keeping Labor Peace

The government worried as much about labor's cooperation as about industry's compliance, for the best-laid production plans could be disrupted by a labor shortage or an extended strike. War increased the demand for industrial labor while cutting the supply. European immigrants had long been the most important source of new labor for American industry, and during the war they stopped coming. Meanwhile, millions of workers already in America were conscripted into the military and thus lost to industry.

Manufacturers responded to the labor shortage by recruiting new sources of labor from the rural South; 500,000 African Americans migrated to northern cities between 1916 and 1920. Another half-million white southerners followed the same path during that period. Hundreds of thousands of Mexicans fled their revolution-ridden homeland for the American Southwest and Midwest. Approximately 40,000 northern women found work as streetcar conductors, railroad workers, metalworkers, munitions makers, and in other jobs customarily reserved for men. The number of female clerical workers doubled between 1910 and 1920, with many of these women finding work in the government war bureaucracies. Altogether, a million women toiled in war-related industries.

These workers alleviated but did not eliminate the nation's labor shortage. Unemployment, which had hovered around 8.5 percent in 1915, plunged to 1.2 percent in 1918. Quick to recognize the benefits of the tight labor market, workers quit jobs they did not like and took part in strikes and other collective actions in large numbers. From 1916 to 1920, more than 1 million workers went on strike every year. Union membership almost doubled, from 2.6 million in 1915 to 5.1 million in 1920. Workers commonly sought higher wages and shorter hours through strikes and unionization. Wages rose an average of 137 percent from 1915 to 1920, although inflation largely negated these gains. The average

Mexicans Migrate to Chicago. Labor shortages caused by the war opened up new opportunities for Mexican immigrant laborers. In this 1917 photograph, a group of such laborers cuts grass alongside a road near Chicago.

workweek declined in that same period from 55 to 51 hours. Workers also struck in response to managerial attempts to speed up production and tighten discipline. As time passed, increasing numbers of workers began to wonder why the war for democracy in Europe had no counterpart in their factories at home. "Industrial democracy" became the battle cry of an awakened labor movement.

Wilson's willingness to include labor in his 1916 progressive coalition reflected his awareness of labor's potential power (see Chapter 21). In 1918, he bestowed prestige on the newly formed **National War Labor Board (NWLB)** by appointing former president William Howard Taft to be co-chair alongside Samuel Gompers, president of the American Federation of Labor. The NWLB brought together representatives of labor, industry, and the public to resolve labor disputes.

Raising an Army

To raise an army, the Wilson administration committed itself to conscription—the drafting of most men of a certain age, irrespective of their family's wealth, ethnic background, or social standing. The Selective Service Act of May 1917 empowered the administration to do just that. By war's end, local Selective Service boards had registered 24 million young men age 18 and older and had drafted nearly 3 million of them into the military; another 2 million volunteered for service.

Relatively few men resisted the draft, even among recently arrived immigrants. Foreign-born men constituted 18 percent of the armed forces—a percentage greater than their share of the total population. Almost 400,000 African Americans served, representing approximately 10 percent of armed forces, the same as the percentage of African Americans in the total population.

The U.S. Army, under the command of Chief of Staff Peyton March and General John J. Pershing, faced the difficult task of fashioning these ethnically and racially diverse millions

into a professional fighting force. Teaching raw recruits to fight was hard enough, Pershing and March observed; the generals refused the task of teaching them to put aside their racial prejudices. Rather than integrate the armed forces, they segregated black soldiers from white. Most African Americans were assigned to all-black units and barred from combat. Being stripped of a combat role was particularly galling to blacks, who, in previous wars, had proven to be among the best American fighters. Pershing was fully aware of the African American contribution. He had commanded African American troops in the 10th Cavalry, the all-black regiment that had distinguished itself in the Spanish-American War (see Chapter 22). Pershing's military reputation had depended so heavily on the black troops who fought for him that he had acquired the nickname Black Jack.

For a time, the military justified its intensified discrimination against blacks by referring to the results of rudimentary IQ (intelligence quotient) tests administered by psychologists to 2 million AEF soldiers. These tests allegedly "proved" that native-born Americans and immigrants from the British Isles, Germany, and Scandinavia were well endowed with intelligence, whereas African Americans and immigrants from Southern and Eastern Europe were poorly endowed. The tests were scientifically so ill-conceived, however, that their findings revealed nothing about the true distribution of intelligence in the soldier population. Their most sensational revelation was that more than half of the soldiers in the AEF—white and black—were "morons," men who had failed to reach the mental age of 13. After trying to absorb the apparent news that most U.S. soldiers were feeble-minded, the military sensibly rejected the pseudo-science on which these intelligence findings were based. In 1919, it discontinued the IQ testing program.

Given the racial and ethnic differences among American troops and the short time Pershing and his staff had to train recruits, the AEF's performance was impressive. The United

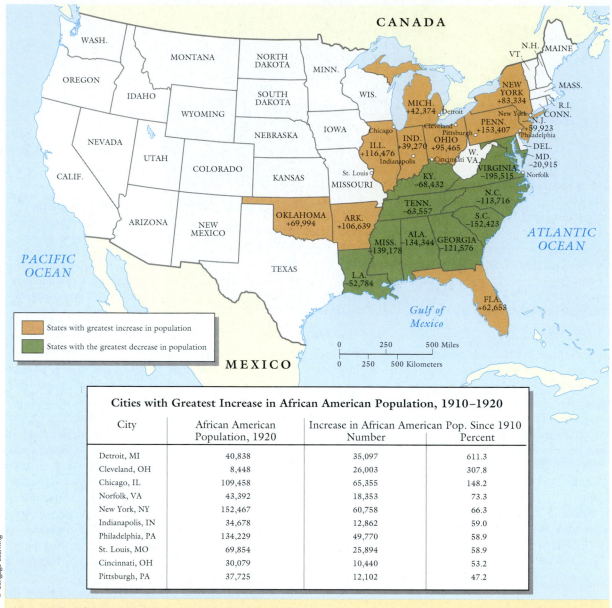

Cities with Greatest Increase in African American Population, 1910–1920

City	African American Population, 1920	Increase in African American Pop. Since 1910	
		Number	Percent
Detroit, MI	40,838	35,097	611.3
Cleveland, OH	8,448	26,003	307.8
Chicago, IL	109,458	65,355	148.2
Norfolk, VA	43,392	18,353	73.3
New York, NY	152,467	60,758	66.3
Indianapolis, IN	34,678	12,862	59.0
Philadelphia, PA	134,229	49,770	58.9
St. Louis, MO	69,854	25,894	58.9
Cincinnati, OH	30,079	10,440	53.2
Pittsburgh, PA	37,725	12,102	47.2

© Cengage Learning

Map 23.3 African American Migration, 1910–1920. Most southern states each lost 50,000 to 200,000 African Americans during the years of the Great Migration, while many northern states, in the industrial belt stretching from Illinois through New York, gained 40,000 to 150,000 apiece. The table inset on the map shows the cities posting the biggest gains.

States increased the army from a mere 100,000 to 5 million in little more than a year. The Germans sank no troop ships, nor were any soldiers killed during the dangerous Atlantic crossing. In combat, U.S. troops became known for their sharp-shooting skills. The most decorated soldier in the AEF was Sergeant Alvin C. York of Tennessee, who captured 35 machine guns, took 132 prisoners, and killed 17 German soldiers with 17 bullets. One of the most decorated AEF units was **New York's 369th Regiment,** a black unit recruited in Harlem. Bowing to pressure from civil rights groups to allow some black troops to fight, Pershing had offered the 369th to the French army. The 369th entered the French front line, served in the forward Allied trenches for 191 days (longer than any other U.S. regiment), and scored several major successes. In gratitude for its service, the French government decorated the entire unit with one of its highest honors—the *Croix de Guerre* (War Cross).

Paying the Bills

The government incurred huge debts buying food, uniforms, munitions, weapons, vehicles, and sundry other items for the U.S. military. To help pay its bills, it sharply increased tax rates. The richest were slapped with a 67-percent income tax and a 25-percent inheritance tax. Corporations were ordered to pay an "excess profits" tax. Progressives wanted to make sure that all Americans would sacrifice something for the war and that the "interests" would not be able to use the war to enrich themselves.

The 369th Returns to New York. Denied the opportunity to fight in the U.S. Army, this unit fought for the French. For the length and distinction of its service in the front lines, this entire unit was awarded the Croix de Guerre (War Cross) by the French government.

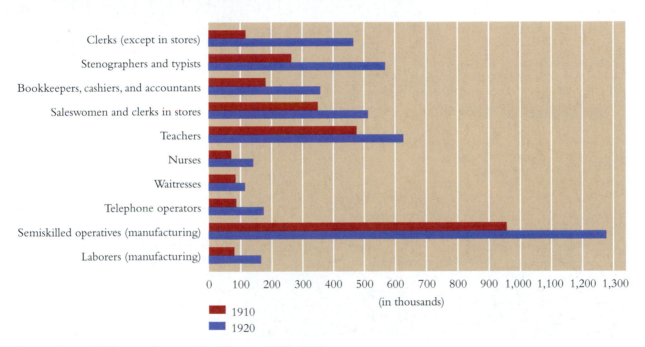

Occupations with Largest Increase in Women, 1910–1920.
Source: Joseph A. Hill, *Women in Gainful Occupations, 1870–1920*, U.S. Bureau of the Census, Monograph no. 9 (Washington, D. C. : Government Printing Office, 1929), p. 33.

Tax revenues, however, provided only about one-third of the $33 billion that the government ultimately spent on the war. The rest came from the sale of **Liberty Bonds**. These 30-year government bonds offered individual purchasers a return of 3.5 percent in annual interest. The government offered five bond issues between 1917 and 1920 and all quickly sold out, thanks, in no small measure, to a high-powered sales pitch, orchestrated by Treasury Secretary William G. McAdoo, that equated bond purchases with patriotic duty.

Arousing Patriotic Ardor

The Treasury's bond campaign was only one aspect of a wide-ranging government effort to arouse public support for the war. In 1917, Wilson set up a new agency, the **Committee on Public Information (CPI)**, to popularize the war. Under the chairmanship of George Creel, a midwestern progressive and a muckraker, the CPI distributed 75 million copies of pamphlets explaining U.S. war aims in several languages. It trained a force of 75,000 "Four-Minute Men" to deliver succinct, uplifting war speeches

Recruiting Poster, First World War, 1917. The government plastered public institutions with recruiting posters. This one represents navy work as glamorous, masculine, and brave, as a way of enticing more young men to join up.

Women Doing "Men's Work." Labor shortages during the war allowed thousands of women to take industrial jobs customarily reserved for men. Here women operate pneumatic hammers at the Midvale Steel and Ordnance Company, Nicetown, Pennsylvania, 1918.

to numerous groups in their home cities and towns. It papered the walls of virtually every public institution (and many private ones) with posters, placed advertisements in mass-circulation magazines, sponsored exhibitions, and peppered newspaper editors with thousands of press releases on the progress of the war.

Faithful to his muckraking past (see Chapter 21), Creel wanted to give the people the facts of the war, believing that well-informed citizens would see the wisdom of Wilson's policies. He also saw his work as an opportunity to achieve the progressive goal of uniting all Americans into a single moral community. Americans everywhere learned that the United States had entered the war "to make the world safe for democracy," to help the world's weaker peoples achieve

self-determination, and to bring a measure of justice into the conduct of international affairs. Americans were asked to affirm those ideals by doing everything they could to support the war.

This uplifting message affected the American people, although not necessarily in ways anticipated by CPI propagandists. It imparted to many a deep love of country and a sense of participation in a grand democratic experiment. Among others, particularly those experiencing poverty and discrimination, it sparked a new spirit of protest. Workers, women, European ethnics, and African Americans began demanding that America live up to its democratic ideals at home as well as abroad. Workers rallied to the cry of "industrial democracy." Women seized on the democratic fervor to bring their fight for suffrage to a successful conclusion (see Chapter 21). African Americans began to dream that the war might deliver them from second-class citizenship. European ethnics believed that Wilson's support of their countrymen's rights abroad would improve their own chances for success in the United States.

Although the CPI had helped to unleash it, this new democratic enthusiasm troubled Creel and others in the Wilson administration. The United States, after all, was still deeply divided along class, ethnic, and racial lines. Workers and industrialists regarded each other with suspicion. Cultural differences compounded this class division: the working class was heavily ethnic in composition, and the industrial and political elites consisted mainly of the native-born whose families had been Americans for generations. Progressives had fought hard to overcome these divisions. They had tamed the power of capitalists, improved the condition of workers, encouraged the Americanization of immigrants, and articulated a new, more inclusive idea of who could belong to the American nation.

But their work was far from complete when the war broke out. German immigrants still formed the largest foreign-born population group at 2.3 million. Another 2.3 million immigrants came from some part of the Austro-Hungarian Empire, and more than 1 million Americans—native-born and immigrants—supported the Socialist Party and the Industrial Workers of the World (IWW), both of which opposed the war. The decision to authorize the CPI's comprehensive unity campaign indicates that the progressives understood how widespread the discord was. Still, they had not anticipated that the promotion of democratic ideals at home would exacerbate, rather than lessen, the nation's social and cultural divisions.

Wartime Repression

By early 1918, the CPI's campaign had developed a darker, more coercive side. Inflammatory advertisements called on patriots to report on neighbors, coworkers, and ethnics who they suspected of subverting the war effort. Propagandists called on all immigrants, especially those from Central, Southern, and Eastern Europe, to pledge themselves to "100 percent Americanism" and to repudiate all ties to their homeland, native language, and ethnic customs. The CPI aroused hostility toward Germans by spreading lurid tales of German atrocities and encouraging the public to see movies such as The *Prussian Cur* and *The Beast of Berlin*. The Justice Department arrested thousands of German and Austrian immigrants suspected of subversive activities. Congress passed the Trading with the Enemy Act, which required foreign-language publications to submit all war-related stories to post office censors for approval.

German Americans became the objects of popular hatred. American patriots sought to expunge every trace of German influence from American culture. In Boston, performances of Beethoven's symphonies were banned, and the German-born conductor of the Boston Symphony Orchestra was forced to resign. Although Americans would not give up the German foods they had grown to love, they would no longer call them by their German names. Libraries removed works of German literature from their shelves, and Theodore Roosevelt and others urged school districts to prohibit the teaching of the German

RENAMED GERMAN AMERICAN WORDS

Original German Name	Renamed "Patriotic" Name
hamburger	salisbury steak, liberty steak, liberty sandwich
sauerkraut	liberty cabbage
Hamburg Avenue, Brooklyn, New York	Wilson Avenue, Brooklyn, New York
Germantown, Nebraska	Garland, Nebraska
East Germantown, Indiana	Pershing, Indiana
Berlin, Iowa	Lincoln, Iowa
pinochle	liberty
German shepherd	Alsatian shepherd
Deutsches Haus of Indianapolis	Athenaeum of Indiana
Germania Maennerchor of Chicago	Lincoln Club
Kaiser Street	Maine Way

Source: From La Vern J. Rippley, *The German Americans* (Boston: Twayne, 1976), p. 186; and Robert H. Ferrell, *Woodrow Wilson and World War* I, 1917–1921 (New York: Harper and Row, 1985), pp. 205–6.

language. Patriotic school boards in Lima, Ohio, and elsewhere burned the German books in their districts.

German Americans risked being fired from work, losing their businesses, and being assaulted on the street. A St. Louis mob lynched an innocent German immigrant they suspected of subversion. After only 25 minutes of deliberation, a St. Louis jury acquitted the mob leaders, who had brazenly defended their crime as an act of patriotism. German Americans began hiding their ethnic identity, changing their names, speaking German only in the privacy of their homes, and celebrating their holidays only with trusted friends.

The anti-German campaign escalated into a general anti-immigrant crusade. Congress passed the Immigration Restriction Act of 1917, over Wilson's veto, which declared that all adult immigrants who failed a reading test would be denied admission to the United States. The act also banned the immigration of laborers from India, Indochina, Afghanistan, Arabia, the East Indies, and several other countries within an "Asiatic Barred Zone."

Congress also passed the 18th Amendment to the Constitution, which prohibited the manufacture and distribution of alcoholic beverages (see Chapter 21). The campaign for prohibition was not new, but anti-immigrant feelings generated by the war gave it added impetus. Prohibitionists pictured the nation's urban ethnic ghettos as scenes of drunkenness, immorality, and disloyalty. They also accused German American brewers of operating a "liquor trust" to sap people's will to fight. The states quickly ratified the 18th Amendment, and in 1919, Prohibition became the law of the land.

A Light-Hearted Poke at Army Life

Composer: Irving Berlin

Title: "Oh, How I Hate to Get Up in the Morning" (written and originally performed in 1918)

The success of songwriter Irving Berlin, a Russian Jewish immigrant, was symbolic of the increasing influence of immigrants in America. By the 1910s, according to biographer Laurence Bergreen, Berlin became "a prominent exponent" of a movement that promoted the cultural worth of "homegrown" American music, dispelling notions that only European music was worthy of artistic consideration.

Berlin occasionally performed during his stage productions— usually a song that showcased his enthusiastic old-fashioned singing style, and did not put too harsh of a spotlight on his limited, somewhat whiny, vocal range, which we can hear in "Oh, How I Hate to Get Up in the Morning." The song emanated from a musical revue he wrote to boost the morale of American soldiers during the First World War. Berlin knew their trials; he was drafted in 1918. With the war winding down, the army decided to utilize Berlin to create an original production depicting military life, whose proceeds would be used to construct a community house at Camp Upton, located in Yaphank, New York, where Berlin was stationed.

Berlin's experiences showed in his songs for the revue, titled *Yip Yip Yaphank*. "I found out quickly I wasn't much of a soldier," he recalled. "There were a lot of things about army life I didn't like, and the thing I didn't like most of all was reveille." Such resentment inspired Berlin's hilarious lament, "Oh, I Hate to Get Up in the Morning," a huge hit, and a song any soldier could identify with, especially the desire to "murder the bugler" who woke the troops daily before dawn.

Yip Yip Yaphank premiered on Broadway in 1918. Though scheduled for only eight shows, the show's success inspired promoters to extend it a month, eventually netting $83,000 (almost $1.2 million in today's dollars).

But the community house was never built, and Berlin never discovered where the money went. Not that he minded: *Yip Yip Yaphank* and its songs expressed pride in his adopted country, and made Berlin even more of a national celebrity than before. Also, while composing the revue, he wrote a song called "God Bless America," which he had doubts about and shelved at the time. When finally released two decades later, it became one of the most patriotic, popular, and profitable songs of the American 20th century.

Q How do war-era songs such as this one, and the songs Stephen Foster wrote for the Civil War (in Chapter 15), compare to songs inspired by more recent American military conflicts in Iraq and Afghanistan?

Q How do immigrants contribute to today's American popular culture?

Source: From La Vern J. Rippley, *The German Americans* (Boston: Twayne, 1976), p. 186; and Robert H. Ferrell, *Woodrow Wilson and World War I, 1917–1921* (New York: Harper and Row, 1985), pp. 205–206.

In the **Espionage, Sabotage,** and **Sedition Acts** passed in 1917 and 1918, Congress gave the administration sweeping powers to silence and imprison dissenters. These acts went beyond outlawing behavior that no nation at war could be expected to tolerate, such as spying for the enemy, sabotaging war production, and calling for the enemy's victory. Now citizens could be prosecuted for writing or uttering any statement that could be construed as profaning the flag, the Constitution, or the military. These acts constituted the most drastic restrictions of free speech at the national level since the Alien and Sedition Acts of 1798 (see Chapter 8).

Government repression fell most heavily on the IWW and the Socialist Party. Both groups had opposed intervention. Although they subsequently muted their opposition, they continued to insist that the true enemies of American workers were to be found in the ranks of American employers, not in Germany or Austria-Hungary. The government responded by banning many socialist materials from the mails and by disrupting socialist and IWW meetings. By spring 1918, government agents had raided countless IWW offices and had arrested 2,000 IWW members, including its entire executive board. Many of those arrested would be sentenced to long jail terms. William Haywood, the IWW president, fled to Europe and then to the Soviet Union rather than go to jail. In summer 1918, Eugene V. Debs, the head of the Socialist Party, received a 10-year jail term for making an antiwar speech in Canton, Ohio.

This federal repression, carried out in an atmosphere of supercharged patriotism, encouraged local governments and private citizens to initiate their own antiradical crusades. In the mining town of Bisbee, Arizona, a sheriff with an eager force of 2,000 deputized citizens kidnapped 1,200 IWW members, herded them into cattle cars, and dumped them onto the New Mexico desert with little food or water. Vigilantes in Butte, Montana, chained an IWW organizer to a car and let his body scrape the pavement as they drove the vehicle through city streets. Next, they strung him up to a railroad trestle, castrated him, and left him to die. The 250,000 members of the American Protective League, most of them businessmen and professionals, routinely spied on fellow workers and neighbors. They opened mail and tapped phones and otherwise harassed those suspected of disloyalty. Attorney General Thomas Gregory publicly endorsed the group and sought federal funds to support its "police" work.

The spirit of coercion even infected institutions that had long prided themselves on tolerance. In July 1917, Columbia University fired two professors for speaking out against U.S. intervention in the war. The National Americanization Committee, which before 1917 had pioneered a humane approach to the problem of integrating immigrants into American life, now supported surveillance, internment, and deportation of aliens suspected of anti-American sentiments.

Wilson did attempt to block certain pieces of repressive legislation; for example, he vetoed both the Immigration Restriction Act and the Volstead Act (the act passed to enforce Prohibition), only to be overridden by Congress. But Wilson did little to halt Attorney General Gregory's prosecution of radicals or Postmaster General Burleson's campaign to exclude Socialist Party publications from the mail. He ignored pleas from progressives that he intervene in the Debs case to prevent the ailing 62-year-old from going to jail. His acquiescence in these matters cost him dearly among progressives and socialists. Wilson believed, however, that once the Allies, with U.S. support, won the war and arranged a just peace in accordance with the Fourteen Points, his administration's wartime actions would be forgiven and the progressive coalition would be restored.

The Failure of the International Peace

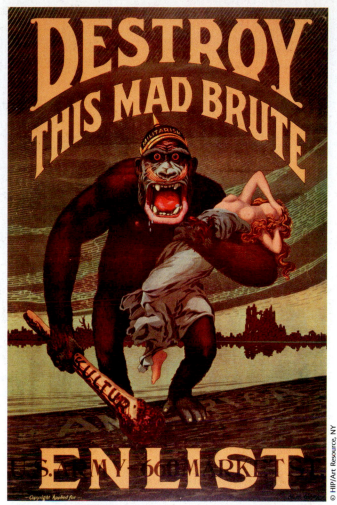

The Campaign of Fear. By 1918, the government's appeal to Americans' best aspirations—to spread liberty and democracy—had been replaced by a determination to arouse fear of subversion and conquest. Here the German enemy is depicted as a terrifying brute who violates Lady Liberty and uses his kultur club to destroy civilization.

Q FOCUS QUESTION

What were Woodrow Wilson's peace proposals, and how did they fare?

In the month following Germany's surrender on November 11, 1918, Wilson was confident about the prospects of achieving a just peace. Both Germany and the Allies had publicly accepted the Fourteen Points as the basis for negotiations. Wilson's international prestige was enormous. People throughout the world were inspired by his dream of a democratic, just, and harmonious world order free of poverty, ignorance, and war. Poles, Lithuanians, and other Eastern Europeans whose pursuit of nationhood had been frustrated for 100 years or more now believed that independence might be within their reach. Zionist Jews in Europe and the United States dared to dream of a Jewish homeland in Palestine within their lifetimes. Countless African and Asian peoples imagined achieving their freedom from colonial domination.

To capitalize on his fame and to maximize the chances for a peace settlement based on his Fourteen Points, Wilson broke with diplomatic precedent and decided to head the American delegation to the Paris Peace Conference in January 1919. Some 2 million French citizens—the largest throng ever assembled on French soil—lined the parade route in Paris to catch a glimpse of "Wilson, *le juste* [the just]." In Rome, Milan, and La Scala, Italians acclaimed him "The Savior of Humanity" and "The Moses from Across the Atlantic."

In the Fourteen Points, Wilson had translated his principles for a new world order into specific proposals for international peace and justice. The first group of points called for all nations to abide by a code of conduct that embraced free trade, freedom of the seas, open diplomacy, disarmament, and the resolution of disputes through mediation. A second group, based on the principle of self-determination, proposed redrawing the map of Europe to give the subjugated peoples of the Austro-Hungarian, Ottoman, and Russian empires national sovereignty. The last point called

"The Savior of Humanity." Wherever he went in Europe, Woodrow Wilson was greeted by huge crowds eager to thank him for ending Europe's terrible war and to endorse his vision of a peaceful, democratic world. Here millions of Italians greet Wilson's arrival in Milan.

New York Times, 1919

for establishing the League of Nations, an assembly in which all nations would be represented and in which international disputes would be given a fair hearing and an opportunity for peaceful solutions.

The Paris Peace Conference and the Treaty of Versailles

Although representatives of 27 nations began meeting in Paris on January 12, 1919, to discuss Wilson's Fourteen Points, negotiations were controlled by the "Big Four": Wilson, Prime Minister David Lloyd George of Great Britain, Premier Georges Clemenceau of France, and Prime Minister Vittorio Orlando of Italy. When Orlando quit the conference after a dispute with Wilson, the Big Four became the Big Three. Wilson quickly learned that his negotiating partners' support for the Fourteen Points was much weaker than he had believed. Clemenceau and Lloyd George refused to include most of Wilson's points in the peace treaty. The points having to do with freedom of the seas and free trade were omitted, as were the proposals for open diplomacy and Allied disarmament. Wilson won partial endorsement of the principle of self-determination: Belgian sovereignty was restored, Poland's status as a nation was affirmed, and the new nations of Czechoslovakia, Yugoslavia, Finland, Lithuania, Latvia, and Estonia were created. In addition, some lands of the former Ottoman Empire—Armenia, Palestine, Mesopotamia, and Syria—were to be placed under League of Nations' trusteeships with the understanding that they would someday gain their independence. Wilson failed in his efforts to block a British plan to transfer former German colonies in Asia to Japanese control, an Italian plan to annex territory inhabited by 200,000 Austrians, and a French plan to take from Germany its valuable Saar coal mines.

Nor could Wilson blunt the drive to punish Germany for its wartime aggression. In addition to awarding the Saar basin to France, the Allies gave portions of northern Germany to Denmark and portions of eastern Germany to Poland and Czechoslovakia. Germany was stripped of virtually its entire navy and air force, and forbidden to place soldiers or fortifications in western Germany along the Rhine. It was allowed to keep an army of only 100,000 men. In addition, Germany was forced to admit its responsibility for the war. In accepting this "war guilt," Germany was, in effect, agreeing to compensate the victors in cash (reparations) for the pain and suffering it had inflicted on them.

Lloyd George and Clemenceau brushed off the protests of those who viewed this desire to prostrate Germany as a cruel and vengeful act. That the German people, after their nation's 1918 defeat, had overthrown the monarch (Kaiser Wilhelm II) who had taken them to war, and had reconstituted their nation as a democratic republic—the first in their country's history—won them no leniency. On June 28, 1919, Great Britain, France, the United States, Germany, and other European nations signed the Treaty of Versailles. In 1921, an Allied commission notified the Germans that they were to pay the victors $33 billion, a sum well beyond the resources of a defeated and economically ruined Germany.

The League of Nations

The Allies' single-minded pursuit of self-interest disillusioned many liberals and socialists in the United States, but Wilson seemed undismayed. He had won approval of the most important of his Fourteen Points—that which called for the creation of the League of Nations. The League, whose structure and responsibilities were set forth in the Covenant attached to the peace treaty, would usher in Wilson's new world order. Drawing its membership from the signatories to the Treaty of Versailles (except, for the time being, Germany), the League would function as an international parliament and judiciary, establishing rules of international behavior and resolving disputes between nations through rational and peaceful means. A nine-member executive council—the United States, Britain, France, Italy, and Japan would have permanent seats on the council, while the other four seats would rotate among the smaller powers—was charged with administering decisions.

Wilson believed that the League would redeem the failures of the Paris Peace Conference. Under its auspices, free trade and freedom of the seas would be achieved, reparations against Germany would be reduced or eliminated, disarmament of the Allies would proceed, and the principle of self-determination would be extended to peoples outside Europe. Moreover, the **Covenant (Article X)** would endow the League with the power to punish aggressor nations through economic isolation and military retaliation.

Wilson versus Lodge: The Fight over Ratification

The League's success, however, depended on Wilson's ability to convince the U.S. Senate to ratify the Treaty of Versailles. Wilson knew that this would not be easy. The Republicans had gained a majority in the Senate in 1918, and two groups within their ranks were determined to frustrate Wilson's ambitions. One group was a caucus of 14 midwesterners and westerners known as the **"irreconcilables."** Most of them were conservative isolationists who wanted the United States to preserve its separation from Europe, but a few were prominent progressives—Robert La Follette, William Borah, and Hiram Johnson—who had voted against the declaration of war in 1917. The self-interest displayed by England and France at the peace conference convinced this group that the Europeans were incapable of decent behavior in international matters.

Senator **Henry Cabot Lodge** of Massachusetts led the second opposition group. Its members rejected Wilson's belief that every group of people on earth had a right to form their own nation; that every state, regardless of its size, its economic condition, and the vigor and intelligence of its people, should have a voice in world affairs; and that disputes between nations could be settled in open, democratic forums. They subscribed instead to Theodore Roosevelt's vision of a world controlled by a few great nations, each militarily strong, secure in its sphere of influence, and determined to avoid war through a carefully negotiated balance of power. These Republicans preferred to let Europe return to the power politics that had prevailed before the war rather than experiment

Wilson in Paris, 1919. This photograph shows President Wilson (on right), recently arrived in Paris to negotiate the Treaty of Versailles, striding confidently and comfortably alongside his two allies, British Prime Minister Lloyd George (on left) and French Premier Clemenceau (in center). In the negotiations themselves, Lloyd George and Clemenceau would prove to be as much adversaries as allies to Wilson.

© Bettmann/CORBIS

with a new world order that might constrain and compromise U.S. power and autonomy.

This Republican critique was a cogent one that merited extended discussion. Particularly important were questions that Republicans raised about Article X, which gave the League the right to undertake military actions against aggressor nations. Did Americans want to authorize an international organization to decide when the United States would go to war? Was this not a violation of the Constitution, which vested war-making power solely in Congress? Even if the constitutional problem could be solved, how could the United States ensure that it would not be forced into a military action that might damage its national interest?

It soon became clear, however, that several Republicans, including Lodge, were as interested in humiliating Wilson as they were in developing an alternative approach to foreign policy. They accused Wilson of promoting socialism through his wartime expansion of government power. They were angry that he had failed to include any distinguished Republicans, such as Lodge, Elihu Root, or William Howard Taft, in the Paris peace delegation. And they were still bitter about the 1918 congressional elections, when Wilson had argued that a Republican victory would embarrass the nation abroad.

As chairman of the Senate Foreign Relations Committee, charged with considering the treaty before reporting it to

Map 23.4 Europe and the Near East After the First World War. The First World War and the Treaty of Versailles changed the geography of Europe and the Near East. Nine nations in Europe, stretching from Yugoslavia in the south to Finland in the north, were created (or re-formed) out of the defeated Austro-Hungarian and Ottoman Empires. In the Near East, meanwhile, Syria, Lebanon, Palestine, Transjordan, and Iraq were carved out of the Ottoman Empire, placed under British or French control, and promised eventual independence.

the Senate floor, Lodge did everything possible to obstruct ratification. He packed the committee with senators who were likely to oppose the treaty. He delayed action by reading every one of the treaty's 300 pages aloud and by subjecting it to endless criticism in six long weeks of public hearings. When his committee finally reported the treaty to the full Senate, it came encumbered with nearly 50 amendments whose adoption Lodge made a precondition of his support. Some of the amendments expressed reasonable concerns—namely, that participation in the League not diminish the role of Congress in determining foreign policy, compromise American sovereignty, or involve the United States in an unjust or ill-advised war—but many were meant only to complicate the task of ratification.

Despite Lodge's obstructionism, the treaty's chances for ratification by the required two-thirds majority of the Senate remained good. Many Republicans were prepared to vote for ratification if Wilson indicated his willingness to accept some of the proposed amendments. Wilson could have salvaged the treaty and, along with it, U.S. participation in the League of Nations, but he refused to compromise with the Republicans and announced that he would carry his case directly to the American people instead. In September 1919, Wilson undertook a whirlwind cross-country tour that covered more than 8,000 miles with 37 stops. He addressed as many crowds as he could reach, sometimes speaking for an hour at a time, four times a day.

On September 25, after giving a speech at Pueblo, Colorado, Wilson suffered excruciating headaches throughout the

© CORBIS

Henry Cabot Lodge, Wilson's Adversary. Republican Senator Lodge led the fight in the Senate against ratifying the Treaty of Versailles.

night. His physician ordered him back to Washington, where on October 2 he suffered a near-fatal stroke. Wilson hovered near death for two weeks and remained seriously disabled for another six. His condition improved somewhat in November, but his left side remained paralyzed, his speech was slurred, his energy level low, and his emotions unstable. Wilson's wife, Edith Bolling Wilson, and his doctor isolated him from Congress and the press, withholding news they thought might upset him and preventing the public from learning how much his body and mind had deteriorated.

Many historians believe that the stroke impaired Wilson's political judgment. He refused to consider any of the Republican amendments to the treaty, even after it had become clear that compromise offered the only chance of winning U.S. participation in the League of Nations. When Lodge presented an amended treaty for a ratification vote on November 19, Wilson ordered Senate Democrats to vote against it; 42 of 47 Democratic senators complied, and with the aid of 13 Republican irreconcilables, the Lodge version was defeated. Only moments later, the unamended version of the treaty—Wilson's version—received only 38 votes.

The Treaty's Final Defeat

As the magnitude of the calamity became apparent, supporters of the League in Congress, the nation, and the world urged the Senate and the president to reconsider. Wilson would not

budge. A bipartisan group of senators desperately tried to work out a compromise without consulting him. When that effort failed, the Senate put to a vote, one more time, the Lodge version of the treaty. Because 23 Democrats, most of them southerners, still refused to break with Wilson, this last-ditch effort at ratification failed on March 8, 1920, by a margin of seven votes. Wilson's dream of a new world order died that day. The crumpled figure in the White House seemed to bear little resemblance to the hero who, barely 15 months before, had been greeted in Europe as the world's savior. Wilson filled out his remaining 12 months in office as an invalid, presiding over the interment of progressivism. He died in 1924.

The judgment of history lies heavily on these events, for many believe that the flawed treaty and the failure of the League contributed to Adolf Hitler's rise in Germany and the outbreak of a second world war more devastating than the first. It is necessary to ask, then, whether American participation in the League would have significantly altered the course of world history.

The mere fact of U.S. membership in the League would not have magically solved Europe's postwar problems. The U.S. government was inexperienced in diplomacy and prone to mistakes. Its freedom to negotiate solutions to international disputes would have been limited by the large number of American voters who remained strongly opposed to U.S. entanglement in European affairs. Even if such opposition could have been overcome, the United States would still have confronted European countries determined to go their own way.

Nevertheless, one thing is clear: No stable international order could have arisen after the First World War without the full involvement of the United States. The League of Nations required American authority and prestige in order to operate effectively as an international parliament. We cannot know whether the League, with American involvement, would have offered the Germans a less humiliating peace, allowing them to rehabilitate their economy and salvage their national pride; nor whether an American-led League would have stopped Hitler's expansionism before it escalated into full-scale war in 1939. Still, it seems fair to suggest that American participation would have strengthened the League and improved its ability to bring a lasting peace to Europe.

The Postwar Period: A Society in Convulsion

Q

FOCUS QUESTION

What issues convulsed American society in the immediate aftermath of war, and how were they resolved?

The end of the war brought no respite from the forces convulsing American society. Workers were determined to regain the purchasing power they had lost to inflation. Employers were determined to halt or reverse the wartime gains labor had made. Radicals saw in this conflict between capital and labor the possibility of a socialist revolution. Conservatives

WOODROW WILSON'S FOURTEEN POINTS, 1918: RECORD OF IMPLEMENTATION

1. Open covenants of peace openly arrived at	Not fulfilled
2. Absolute freedom of navigation upon the seas in peace and war	Not fulfilled
3. Removal of all economic barriers to the equality of trade among nations	Not fulfilled
4. Reduction of armaments to the level needed only for domestic safety	Not fulfilled
5. Impartial adjustments of colonial claims	Not fulfilled
6. Evacuation of all Russian territory; Russia to be welcomed into the society of free nations	Not fulfilled
7. Evacuation and restoration of Belgium	Fulfilled
8. Evacuation and restoration of all French lands; return of Alsace-Lorraine to France	Fulfilled
9. Readjustment of Italy's frontiers along lines of Italian nationality	Compromised
10. Self-determination for the former subjects of the Austro-Hungarian Empire	Compromised
11. Evacuation of Romania, Serbia, and Montenegro; free access to the sea for Serbia	Compromised
12. Self-determination for the former subjects of the Ottoman Empire; secure sovereignty for Turkish portion	Compromised
13. Establishment of an independent Poland with free and secure access to the sea	Fulfilled
14. Establishment of the League of Nations to secure mutual guarantees of independence and territorial integrity	Compromised

Source: From G. M. Gathorne-Hardy, *The Fourteen Points and the Treaty of Versailles*, Oxford Pamphlets on World Affairs, no. 6 (1939), pp. 8–34; and Thomas G. Paterson et al., *American Foreign Policy: A History*, 2nd ed. (Lexington, MA: Heath, 1983), vol. 2, pp. 282–93.

were certain that the revolution had already begun. Returning white servicemen were nervous about regaining their civilian jobs and looked with hostility on the black, Hispanic, and female workers who had been recruited to take their places. Black veterans were in no mood to return to segregation and subordination. The federal government, meanwhile, uneasy over the centralization of power during the war, quickly dismantled such agencies as the War Industries Board and the National War Labor Board.

Labor-Capital Conflict

Nowhere was the escalation of conflict more evident than in the workplace. In 1919, 4 million workers—one-fifth of the nation's manufacturing workforce—went on strike. In January 1919, a general strike paralyzed the city of Seattle when 60,000 workers walked off their jobs. By August, walkouts had been staged by 400,000 eastern and midwestern coal miners, 120,000 New England textile workers, and 50,000 New York City garment workers. Then came two strikes that turned public opinion sharply against labor. In September, Boston policemen walked off their jobs after the police commissioner refused to negotiate with their newly formed union. Rioting and looting soon broke out. Massachusetts Governor Calvin Coolidge, outraged by the policemen's betrayal of their sworn public duty, refused to negotiate with them, called out the National Guard to restore order, and fired the entire police force. His tough stand would bring him national fame and the Republican vice presidential nomination in 1920.

Hard on the heels of the policemen's strike came a strike by more than 300,000 steelworkers in the Midwest. No union had established a footing in the steel industry since the 1890s, when Andrew Carnegie had ousted the ironworkers' union from his mills in Homestead, Pennsylvania. Most steelworkers labored long hours (the 12-hour shift was still standard) for low wages in dangerous workplaces. The organizers of the **1919 Steel Strike** had somehow managed to persuade steelworkers with varied skill levels and ethnic backgrounds to put aside their differences and demand an eight-hour day and union recognition. When the employers rejected those demands, the workers walked off their jobs. Employers responded by procuring armed guards to beat up the strikers and by hiring nonunion labor to keep the plants running. In many areas, local and state police prohibited union meetings, ran strikers out of town, and opened fire on those who disobeyed orders. To arouse public support for their antiunion campaign, industry leaders portrayed the strike leaders as dangerous and violent radicals bent on the destruction of political liberty and economic freedom. They succeeded in turning public opinion against the steelworkers, and the strike collapsed in January 1920.

Radicals and the Red Scare

The steel companies succeeded in putting down the strike by fanning the public's fear that revolutionary sentiment was spreading among workers. Radical sentiment was indeed on the rise. Mine workers and railroad workers had begun calling for the permanent nationalization of coal mines and railroads.

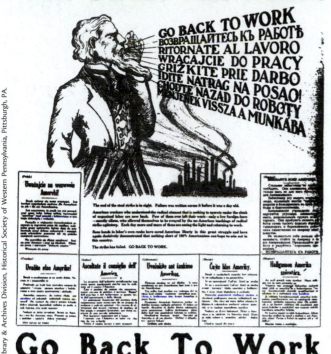

The Strike Has Failed

Go Back To Work

The 1919 Steel Strike Fails. The steel corporations were united in their opposition to the steelworkers' union and skillful in their use of media to demoralize the strikers. This poster reveals another reason for the strike's failure: a workforce so diverse that strike announcements had to be communicated in eight languages.

Longshoremen in San Francisco and Seattle refused to load ships carrying supplies to the White Russians who had taken up arms against Lenin's Bolshevik government. Socialist trade unionists mounted the most serious challenge to Gompers's control of the AFL in 25 years. In 1920, nearly a million Americans voted for the Socialist presidential candidate Debs, who ran his campaign from the Atlanta Federal Penitentiary.

This radical surge did not mean, however, that leftists had fashioned themselves into a single movement or political party. On the contrary, the Russian Revolution had split the American Socialist Party. One faction, which would keep the name Socialist and would continue under Debs's leadership, insisted that radicals follow a democratic path to socialism. The other group, which would take the name Communist, wanted to establish a Lenin-style "dictatorship of the proletariat." Small groups of anarchists, some of whom advocated campaigns of terror to speed the revolution, represented yet a third radical tendency.

Few Americans noticed the disarray in the radical camp. Most assumed that radicalism was a single, coordinated movement bent on establishing a communist government on American soil. They saw the nation's immigrant communities as breeding grounds for Bolshevism. Beginning in 1919, this perceived **Red Scare** prompted government officials and private citizens to embark on yet another campaign of repression.

The postwar repression of radicalism closely resembled the wartime repression of dissent. Thirty states passed sedition laws to punish those who advocated revolution. Numerous public and private groups intensified Americanization campaigns designed to strip foreigners of their subversive ways and remake them into loyal citizens. Universities fired radical professors, and vigilante groups wrecked the offices of socialists and assaulted IWW agitators. A newly formed veterans' organization, the American Legion, took on the American Protective League's role of identifying seditious individuals and organizations and ensuring the public's devotion to "100 percent Americanism."

The Red Scare reached its climax on New Year's Day 1920, when federal agents broke into the homes and meeting places of thousands of suspected revolutionaries in 33 cities. Directed by Attorney General A. Mitchell Palmer, these widely publicized "Palmer raids" were meant to expose the extent of revolutionary activity. Palmer's agents uncovered three pistols, no rifles, and no explosives. Nevertheless, they arrested more than 4,000 people and kept many of them in jail for weeks without formally charging them with a crime. Finally, those who were not citizens (approximately 600) were deported and the rest were released.

Palmer's failure to expose a revolutionary plot blunted support for him in official circles, but, undeterred, Palmer now alleged that revolutionaries were planning a series of assaults on government officials and government buildings for May 1, 1920. When nothing happened on that date, his credibility suffered another blow.

As Palmer's exaggerations of the radical threat became known, many Americans began to reconsider their fear of dissent and subversion. Even so, the political atmosphere remained hostile to radicals, as the **Sacco and Vanzetti Case** revealed. In May 1920, two Italian-born anarchists, Nicola Sacco and Bartolomeo Vanzetti, were arrested in Brockton, Massachusetts, and charged with armed robbery and murder. Both men proclaimed their innocence and insisted that they were being punished for their political beliefs. Their foreign accents and their defiant espousal of anarchist doctrines in the courtroom inclined many Americans, including the judge who presided at their trial, to view them harshly. Despite the weak case against them, they were convicted of first-degree murder and sentenced to death. Their lawyers attempted numerous appeals, all of which failed. Anger over the verdicts began to build among Italian Americans, radicals, and liberal intellectuals. Protests compelled the governor of Massachusetts to appoint a commission to review the case, but no new trial was ordered. On August 23, 1927, Sacco and Vanzetti were executed, still insisting they were innocent.

Racial Conflict and the Rise of Black Nationalism

The more than 400,000 blacks who served in the armed forces believed that a victory for democracy abroad would help them achieve democracy for their people at home. At first, despite the discrimination they encountered in the military, they maintained their conviction that they would be treated as full-fledged citizens upon their return. Many began to talk about the birth of a

HISTORY THROUGH FILM

Reds (1981)

Directed by Warren Beatty.
Starring Warren Beatty (John Reed), Diane Keaton (Louise Bryant), Edward Herrmann (Max Eastman), Jerzy Kosinski (Grigory Zinoviev), Jack Nicholson (Eugene O'Neill), and Maureen Stapleton (Emma Goldman).

In this epic film, Warren Beatty, producer, director, and screenplay co-writer, attempts to integrate the history of the American Left in the early 20th century with a love story about two radicals of that era, John "Jack" Reed and Louise Bryant. Reed was a well-known radical journalist whose dispatches from Russia during its 1917 revolution were published as a book, *Ten Days That Shook the World*, that brought him fame and notoriety. Bryant never developed the public reputation that Reed enjoyed, but she was an integral member of the radical circles that gathered in apartments and cafés in New York's Bohemian Greenwich Village before and during the First World War.

At times, the love principals in this movie seem to resemble Warren Beatty and Diane Keaton more than they do the historical figures they are meant to represent. In general, however, the movie keeps love and politics in balance and thus successfully conveys an important and historically accurate message about the American Left, especially before the First World War—namely, that its participants wanted to revolutionize the personal as well as the political. Thus equality between men and women, women's right to enjoy the same sexual freedom as men, and

marriage's impact on personal growth and adventure were issues debated with the same fervor as building a radical political party and accelerating the transition to socialism. (See Chapter 20, the section entitled: "The New Sexuality and the Rise of Feminism.")

Reds is also an exceptionally serious film about political parties and ideologies. The film follows the arc of John Reed's and Louise Bryant's lives from their prewar days as discontented members of the Portland, Oregon, social elite, through their flight to the freedom and radicalism of Greenwich Village, to the hardening of their radicalism as a result of repression during the First World War at home and the Bolshevik triumph in November 1917. In this movie, Beatty has recreated detailed and complex stories about internal fights within the Left both in the United States and Russia, through which he seeks to show how hopes for social transformation went awry. To give this film added historical weight, Beatty introduces "witnesses," individuals who actually knew the real Reed and Bryant and who appear on screen periodically to share their memories, both serious and whimsical, about the storied couple and the times in which they lived. ◼

Diane Keaton as Louise Bryant and Warren Beatty as John Reed, together in Russia in the midst of that country's socialist revolution.

Ben Shahn 1898-1969, The Passion of Sacco and Vanzetti, 1931-1932 Sacco-Vanzetti series. Tempera on canvas, Unframed: 84 1/2 x 48in. (214.6 x 121.9cm) Framed: 85 1/2 x 50x 4 in. (217.2 x 127cm). Whitney Museum of American Art, New York; Gift of Edith and Milton Lowenthal in memory of Juliana Force 49.22. Art © Estate of Ben Shahn/Licensed by VAGA, New York, NY.

The Passion of Sacco and Vanzetti, **by Ben Shahn.**
The 1920 trial and 1927 execution of Nicola Sacco and Bartolomeo Vanzetti became the passion of many immigrants, liberal intellectuals, and artists (such as Ben Shahn), who were convinced that the two anarchists had been unfairly tried and convicted.

New Negro—independent and proud. Thousands joined the National Association for the Advancement of Colored People (NAACP), an organization at the forefront of the fight for racial equality. By 1918, 100,000 African Americans subscribed to the NAACP's magazine, *The Crisis,* whose editor, W. E. B. Du Bois, had urged them to support the war.

This wartime optimism made the postwar discrimination and hatred African Americans encountered difficult to endure. Many black workers who had found jobs in the North were fired to make way for returning white veterans. Returning black servicemen, meanwhile, had to scrounge for poorly paid jobs as unskilled laborers. In the South, lynch mobs targeted black veterans who refused to tolerate the usual insults and indignities; 10 of the 70 blacks lynched in the South in 1919 were veterans.

The worst anti-black violence that year occurred in the North, however. Crowded city conditions during the war had forced black and white-ethnic city dwellers into uncomfortably close proximity. Many white ethnics regarded blacks with a mixture of fear and prejudice. They resented having to share neighborhoods, trolleys, parks, streets, and workplaces with blacks. Many also wanted African Americans barred from unions, seeing them as threats to their job security.

Racial tensions escalated into race riots. The deadliest explosion occurred in Chicago in July 1919, when a black teenager who had been swimming in Lake Michigan was killed by whites after coming too close to a whites-only beach. Rioting soon broke out, with white mobs invading black neighborhoods, torching homes and stores, and attacking innocent residents. Led by war veterans, some armed, blacks fought back, turning the border areas between white and black neighborhoods into battle zones. Fighting raged for five days, leaving 38 dead (23 black, 15 white) and more than 500 injured. Race rioting in other cities pushed the death toll to 120 before summer's end.

The riots made it clear to blacks that the North was not the Promised Land. Confined to unskilled jobs and to segregated neighborhoods with substandard housing and exorbitant rents, black migrants in Chicago, New York, and other northern cities suffered economic hardship throughout the 1920s. The NAACP carried on its campaign for civil rights and racial equality, but many blacks no longer shared its belief that they would one day be accepted as first-class citizens. They turned instead to a leader from Jamaica, **Marcus Garvey**, who gave voice to their bitterness: "The first dying that is to be done by the black man in the future," Garvey declared in 1918, "will be done to make himself free. And then when we are finished, if we have any charity to bestow, we may die for the white man. But as for me, I think I have stopped dying for him."

Garvey called on blacks to give up their hopes for integration and to set about forging a separate black nation. He reminded blacks that they possessed a rich culture stretching back over the centuries that would enable them to achieve greatness as a nation. Garvey's ambition was to build a black nation in Africa that would bring together all of the world's people of African descent. In the short term, he wanted to help American and Caribbean blacks to achieve economic and cultural independence.

Garvey's call for black separatism and self-sufficiency—or black nationalism, as it came to be known—elicited a favorable response among African Americans. In the early 1920s, the Universal Negro Improvement Association (UNIA), which Garvey had founded, enrolled millions of members in 700 branches in 38 states. His newspaper, the *Negro World,* reached a circulation of 200,000. The New York chapter of UNIA undertook an economic development program that included the establishment of grocery stores, restaurants, and factories. Garvey's most visible economic venture was the Black Star Line, a shipping company with three ships flying the UNIA flag from their masts.

This black nationalist movement did not endure for long. Garvey entered into bitter disputes with other black

Marcus Garvey, Black Nationalist. This portrait was taken in 1924, after Garvey's conviction on mail fraud charges.

deported to Jamaica, and the UNIA folded. Nevertheless, Garvey's philosophy of black nationalism endured.

Conclusion

The resurgence of racism in 1919 and the consequent turn to black nationalism among African Americans were signs that the high hopes of the war years had been dashed. Industrial workers, immigrants, and radicals also found their pursuit of liberty and equality interrupted by the fear, intolerance, and repression unleashed by the war. They came to understand as well that Wilson's commitment to these ideals counted for less than did his administration's and Congress's determination to discipline a people whom they regarded as dangerously heterogeneous and unstable. Of the reform groups, only woman suffragists made enduring gains—especially the right to vote—but for the feminists in their ranks, these steps forward failed to compensate for the collapse of the progressive movement and with it, their program of achieving equal rights for women across the board.

A similar disappointment engulfed those who had embraced and fought for Wilson's dream of creating a new and democratic world order. The world in 1919 appeared as volatile as it had been in 1914. More and more Americans—perhaps even a majority—were coming to believe that U.S. intervention had been a mistake.

In other ways, the United States benefited a great deal from the war. By 1919, the American economy was by far the world's strongest. Many of the nation's leading corporations had improved productivity and management during the war. U.S. banks were poised to supplant those of London as the most influential in international finance. The nation's economic strength triggered impressive growth in the 1920s, and millions of Americans rushed to take advantage of the prosperity that a "people's capitalism" had put within their grasp. But even affluence failed to dissolve the class, ethnic, and racial tensions that the war had exposed. And the failure of the peace process added to Europe's problems, delayed the emergence of the United States as a leader in world affairs, and created the preconditions for another world war. ⌇

leaders, including W. E. B. Du Bois, who regarded him as a flamboyant, self-serving demagogue. Garvey sometimes showed poor judgment, as when he expressed support for the Ku Klux Klan on the grounds that it shared his pessimism about the possibility of racial integration. Inexperienced in economic matters, Garvey squandered UNIA money on abortive business ventures. The U.S. government regarded his rhetoric as inflammatory and sought to silence him. In 1923, he was convicted of mail fraud involving the sale of Black Star stocks and was sentenced to five years in jail. In 1927, he was

CHAPTER REVIEW

REVIEW QUESTIONS

1. What caused Europe's descent into war?
2. Why did the U.S. policy of neutrality fail, and why did the United States get drawn into war?
3. What contribution did the United States make to the Allied Powers' victory?
4. What problems did the United States encounter in mobilizing for total war, and how successfully were those problems overcome?
5. What were Woodrow Wilson's peace proposals, and how did they fare?
6. What issues convulsed American society in the immediate aftermath of war, and how were they resolved?

CRITICAL THINKING QUESTIONS

1. Did the First World War do more to enhance or interrupt the pursuit of liberty and equality on the home front?
2. Do you think that the chances of a second world war breaking out in Europe in the late 1930s would have been substantially lessened had Woodrow Wilson prevailed on the U.S. Senate to ratify the Treaty of Versailles in 1919, thereby bringing the United States into the League of Nations?

IDENTIFICATIONS

Review your understanding of the following key terms, people, and events for this chapter (terms in bold in text are included in the Glossary).

Triple Alliance, p. 621
Triple Entente, p. 621
"peace without victory," p. 626
Zimmermann telegram, p. 626
Fourteen Points, p. 627
John J. Pershing, p. 627
War Industries Board (WIB), p. 628
National War Labor Board (NWLB), p. 631
New York's 369th Regiment, p. 632
Liberty Bonds, p. 633
Committee on Public Information (CPI), p. 633
Espionage, Sabotage, and Sedition Acts, p. 636
Covenant (Article X), p. 639
irreconcilables, p. 639
Henry Cabot Lodge, p. 639

1919 Steel Strike, p. 642
Red Scare, p. 643
Sacco and Vanzetti Case, p. 643
Marcus Garvey, p. 645

SUGGESTED READINGS

On America's neutrality and road to war, consult **John Milton Cooper, *Woodrow Wilson: A Biography*** (2009). On the effects of war on American society, consult **David Kennedy, *Over Here: The First World War and American Society*** (1980) and **Christopher Capozzola, *Uncle Sam Wants You: World War I and the Making of the Modern American Citizen*** (2008). For industrial mobilization and labor-management relations, see **Robert D. Cuff, *The War Industries Board: Business-Government Relations during World War I*** (1973) and **Joseph A. McCartin, *Labor's Great War: The Struggle for Industrial Democracy and the Origins of Modern Labor Relations, 1912–1921*** (1997).

For a pioneering effort to situate U.S. domestic politics during the war in an international context, see **Alan Dawley, *Changing the World: American Progressives in War and Revolution*** (2003). On the migration of African Americans to northern industrial centers and the movement of women into war production, see **Joe William Trotter Jr., ed., *The Great Migration in Historical Perspective: New Dimensions of Race, Class, and Gender*** (1991), and **Maurine W. Greenwald, *Women, War and Work*** (1980). **Stephen Vaughn, *Holding Fast the Inner Lines: Democracy, Nationalism, and the Committee on Public Information*** (1980), is an important account of the CPI. **Geoffrey R. Stone, *Perilous Times: Free Speech in War Time from the Sedition Act of 1798 to the War on Terrorism*** (2004), analyzes the repression of dissent.

On Wilson, Versailles, and the League of Nations, consult **Thomas J. Knock, *To End All Wars: Woodrow Wilson and the Quest for a New World Order*** (1992) and **Arno Mayer, *The Politics and Diplomacy of Peacemaking: Containment and Counterrevolution at Versailles, 1918–1919*** (1967). On Republican opposition to the League of Nations, see **William C. Widenor, *Henry Cabot Lodge and the Search for an American Foreign Policy*** (1980).

Beverly Gage, *The Day Wall Street Exploded: A Story of America in its First Age of Terror* (2009) offers a fresh analysis of the Red Scare. **Steven Hahn, *The Political Worlds of Slavery and Freedom*** (2009), does the same for Marcus Garvey and the United Negro Improvement Association.

Visit the CourseMate website at www.cengagebrain.com for additional study tools and review materials for this chapter.

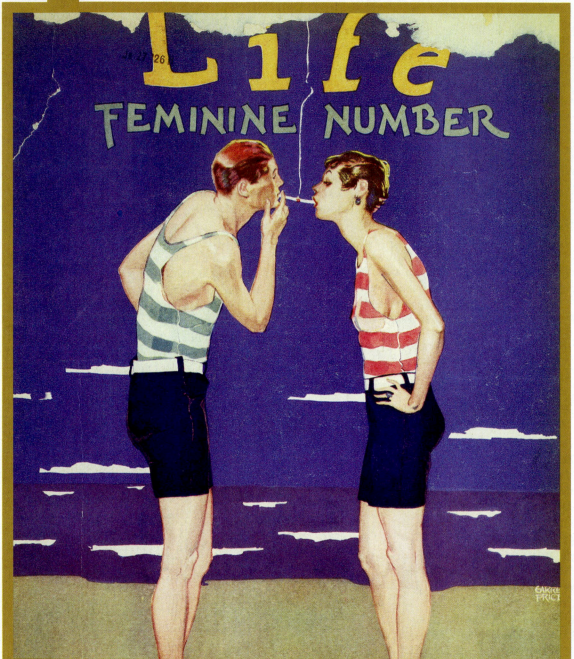

The Age of the Flapper

The 1920s witnessed the emergence of the "flapper," the name given to single women who deliberately flouted social rules governing female life. On this cover of *Life*, we see "Jill" sporting the same short hair and form-fitting bathing suit as her male friend, "Jack." Not only was she smoking in public, but she was also getting her light directly from a cigarette in Jack's mouth. Could a public kiss between Jack and Jill have been far behind?

The 1920s

N **1920,** AMERICANS ELECTED AS PRESIDENT, Warren G. Harding, a man who could not have been more different from his predecessor Woodrow Wilson. A Republican, Harding presented himself as a common man with common desires. In his 1920 campaign, he called for a "return to normalcy." Although he died in office in 1923, his carefree spirit is thought to characterize the 1920s.

To many Americans, the decade was one of fun rather than reform, of good times rather than high ideals. It was, in the words of novelist F. Scott Fitzgerald, the "Jazz Age," a time when the search for personal gratification seemed to replace the quest for public welfare.

Despite Harding's call for a return to a familiar past, America seemed to be rushing headlong into the future. The word *modern* began appearing everywhere: modern times, modern women, modern technology, the modern home, modern marriage. Although the word was rarely defined, it connoted certain beliefs: that science was a better guide to life than religion; that people should be free to choose their own lifestyles; that sex should be a source of pleasure for women as well as men; that women and minorities should be equal to white men and enjoy the same rights.

Many other Americans, however, reaffirmed their belief that God's word transcended science; that people should obey the moral code set forth in the Bible; that women were not equal to men; and that blacks, Mexicans, and Eastern European immigrants were inferior to Anglo-Saxon whites. They made their voices heard in a resurgent **Ku Klux Klan** and the fundamentalist movement, and on issues such as evolution and immigration. In seeking to restore an older America, some in their ranks were prepared to deny individual Americans the liberty to choose their own ways of living and to insist that all people were not fundamentally equal.

Modernists and traditionalists confronted each other in party politics, in legislatures, in courtrooms, and in the press. Their battles belie the vision of the 1920s merely as a time for the pursuit of leisure.

Prosperity
A Consumer Society
A People's Capitalism
The Rise of Advertising and Mass Marketing
Changing Attitudes toward Marriage and Sexuality
An Age of Celebrity
Celebrating Business Civilization
Industrial Workers
Women and Work
The Women's Movement Adrift

The Politics of Business
Harding and the Politics of Personal Gain
Coolidge and Laissez-Faire Politics
Hoover and the Politics of Associationalism
The Politics of Business Abroad

Farmers, Small-Town Protestants, and Moral Traditionalists
Agricultural Depression
Cultural Dislocation
Prohibition
The Ku Klux Klan
Immigration Restriction
Fundamentalism versus Liberal Protestantism
The Scopes Trial

Ethnic and Racial Communities
European American Ethnics
African Americans
The Harlem Renaissance
Mexican Americans

The "Lost Generation" and Disillusioned Intellectuals
Democracy on the Defensive

Prosperity

FOCUS QUESTION

What were the achievements and limitations of "people's capitalism" in the 1920s?

On balance, the First World War had been good for the American economy. American industries had emerged intact from, even strengthened by, the war. Manufacturers and bankers had exported so many goods and extended so many loans to the Allies that, by war's end, the United States was the world's leading creditor nation. New York City challenged London as the hub of world finance.

From 1919 to 1921, the country struggled to redirect industry from wartime to civilian production, a process slowed by the government's hasty withdrawal from its wartime role as economic regulator and stabilizer. Workers went on strike to protest wage reductions or increases in the workweek. Farmers were hit by a depression as the overseas demand for American foodstuffs fell from its 1918–19 peak. Disgruntled workers and farmers even joined forces to form statewide farmer-labor parties, which for a time threatened to disrupt the country's two-party system in the upper Midwest. In 1924, the two groups formed a national Farmer-Labor Party. Robert LaFollette, their presidential candidate, received an impressive 16 percent of the vote that year, but then the third-party movement fell apart.

Its collapse reflected a rising public awareness of how vigorous and productive the economy had become. Beginning in 1922, the nation embarked on a period of remarkable growth. From 1922 to 1929, the gross national product grew at an annual rate of 5.5 percent, rising from $149 billion to $227 billion. The unemployment rate never exceeded 5 percent, and real wages rose about 15 percent.

A Consumer Society

The variety of products being produced matched the rate of economic growth. In the 19th century, economic growth had rested primarily on the production of capital goods, such as factory machinery and railroad tracks. In the 1920s, however, growth rested more on consumer goods. Some products, such as cars and telephones, had been available since the early 1900s, but in the 1920s their sales reached new levels. In 1920, just 12 years after Ford introduced the Model T, 8 million cars were on the road. By 1929, there were 27 million—one for every five Americans. Other consumer goods became available for the first time: tractors, washing machines, refrigerators, electric irons, radios, and vacuum cleaners. The term "consumer durable" was coined to describe such goods, which, unlike food, clothing, and other perishables, were meant to last. Even perishables took on new allure. Scientists had discovered the importance of vitamins in the diet and began urging Americans to consume more fresh fruits and vegetables. The agricultural economy of southern California grew rapidly as urban demand for its products skyrocketed. Improvements in

CHRONOLOGY

1920	Prohibition goes into effect ◆ Warren G. Harding defeats James M. Cox for presidency ◆ Census reveals that a majority of Americans live in urban areas ◆ 8 million cars on roads
1921	Sheppard-Towner Act passed
1922	United States, Britain, Japan, France, and Italy sign Five-Power Treaty, agreeing to reduce size of their navies
1923	Teapot Dome scandal lands Secretary of the Interior Albert Fall in jail ◆ Harding dies in office ◆ Calvin Coolidge becomes president
1924	Dawes Plan to restructure Germany's war debt put into effect ◆ Coolidge defeats John W. Davis for presidency ◆ Ku Klux Klan membership approaches 4 million ◆ Johnson-Reed Act cuts immigration by 80 percent
1925	Scopes trial upholds right of Tennessee to bar teaching of evolution in public schools ◆ *Survey Graphic* publishes a special issue on the Harlem Renaissance ◆ F. Scott Fitzgerald publishes *The Great Gatsby* ◆ U.S. withdraws Marines from Nicaragua
1926	Revenue Act cuts income and estate taxes ◆ U.S. sends Marines back to Nicaragua to end civil war and protect U.S. property
1927	Coolidge vetoes high tariffs legislation (McNary-Haugen bill) ◆ Babe Ruth hits 60 home runs ◆ Charles Lindbergh flies across the Atlantic
1928	Fifteen nations sign Kellogg-Briand pact, pledging to avoid war ◆ Coolidge vetoes McNary-Haugen bill again ◆ Herbert Hoover defeats Alfred E. Smith for presidency
1929	Union membership drops to 3 million ◆ 27 million cars on roads ◆ William Faulkner publishes *The Sound and the Fury* ◆ Josh Gibson joins the National Negro League
1930	Los Angeles's Mexican population reaches 100,000

refrigeration and in packaging, meanwhile, allowed fresh produce to travel long distances and extended its shelf life in grocery stores. And more stores were being operated by large grocery chains that could afford the latest refrigeration and packaging technology.

The public responded to these innovations with excitement. American industry had made fresh food and stylish clothes available to the masses. Refrigerators, vacuum cleaners, and washing machines would spare women the drudgery of housework. Radios would expand the public's cultural horizons. Cars, asphalt roads, service stations, hot dog stands, "tourist cabins" (the forerunners of motels), and traffic lights seemed to herald a wholly new automobile civilization. By the middle of the decade, the country possessed a network of paved roads. City dwellers now had easy access to rural areas and made a ritual of daylong excursions. Camping trips and long-distance vacations became routine. Farmers and their families could now hop into their cars and head for the nearest town to take advantage of its stores, movie theater, amusement park, and sporting events. Suburbs proliferated, billed as the perfect mix of urban and rural life. Young men and women everywhere discovered that cars were a place where they could "make out," and even make love, without fear of reproach by prudish parents or prying neighbors.

In the 1920s, some Americans also discovered the benefits of owning stocks. The number of stockholders in AT&T, the nation's largest corporation, rose from 140,000 to 568,000. U.S. Steel stockholder numbers increased from 96,000 to 146,000. By 1929, as many as 7 million Americans owned stock, most of them people of middle- or upper-class means. The New York Stock Exchange, first organized in 1792, assisted in processing complicated transactions.

A People's Capitalism

Capitalists boasted that they had created a **"people's capitalism"** in which virtually all Americans could participate. Now everyone could own a piece of corporate America. Now everyone could have a share of luxuries and amenities. Poverty, capitalists claimed, was banished, but the gap between rich and poor all but closed.

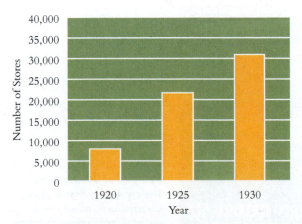

Growth of Six Leading Grocery Chains by Number of Stores, 1920–1930.
Source: From Godfrey M. Labhar, *Chain Stores in America, 1859–1962* (New York: Chain Store Publishing, 1963).

Actually, although wages were rising, millions of Americans still earned too little to partake fully of the marketplace. The percentage of Americans owning stocks remained small. Social scientists Robert and Helen Lynd discovered, in their celebrated 1929 study of Muncie, Indiana, that working-class families who bought a car often lacked money for other goods. One housewife admitted: "We don't have no fancy clothes when we have the car to pay for. . . . The car is the only pleasure we have." Many industrialists resisted pressure to increase wages, and workers lacked the organizational strength to force them to pay more.

One solution came with the introduction of consumer credit. Car dealers, home appliance salesmen, and other merchants began to offer installment plans that enabled consumers to purchase a product by making a down payment and promising to pay the rest in installments. By 1930, 15 percent of all purchases were made on the installment plan.

Even so, many poor Americans benefited little from the consumer revolution. Middle-class Americans acquired a disproportionate share of consumer durables. They also could afford to purchase more fresh fruits and vegetables and stocks than most working-class Americans.

The Rise of Advertising and Mass Marketing

But even middle-class consumers had to be wooed. How could they be persuaded to buy another car only a few years after they had bought their first one? General Motors (GM) had the answer: the annual model change. Beginning in 1926, GM cars took on a different look every year as GM engineers changed headlights and chassis colors, streamlined bodies, and added new features. The strategy worked. GM leaped past Ford and became the world's largest car manufacturer.

Henry Ford reluctantly introduced his Model A in 1927 to provide customers with a colorful alternative to the drab Model T. Having spent his lifetime selling a product renowned for its utility and reliability, Ford rejected the idea that sales could be increased by appealing to the intangible hopes and fears of consumers. He was wrong. The desire to be beautiful, handsome, or sexually attractive; to exercise power and control; to demonstrate competence and success; to escape anonymity, loneliness, and boredom; to experience pleasure—all such desires, once activated, could motivate a consumer to buy a new car even when the old one was still serviceable, or to spend money on goods that might have once seemed frivolous.

Arousing such desires required more than bright colors, sleek lines, and attractive packaging. It called for advertising campaigns intended to make a product seem to be the answer to the consumer's desires. To create those campaigns, corporations turned to a new kind of company: professional advertising firms. Advertising entrepreneurs, people such as Edward Bernays, Doris Fleischmann, and Bruce Barton, tended to be well educated, sensitive to public taste, and knowledgeable about human psychology. In their campaigns, advertisers played on the emotions and vulnerabilities of their target audiences. A perfume manufacturer's ad pronounced: "The first duty of woman is to attract. . . . It does not matter how clever or independent you may be, if you fail to influence the men you meet, consciously or unconsciously, you

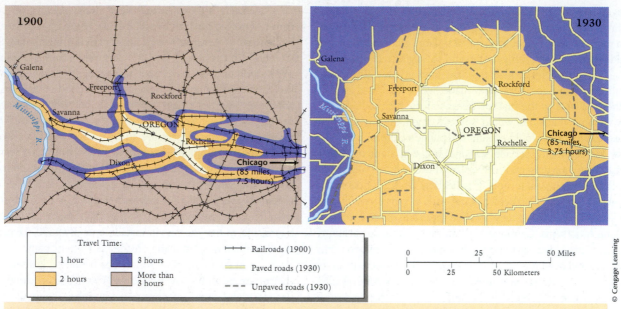

Map 24.1 **Automobile Civilization: Cars, Roads, and the Expansion of Travel Horizons in Oregon, Illinois.** In 1900, someone wanting to travel outside Oregon, Illinois, could not get very far in an hour or two, unless his or her destination lay exactly on the major train line running through town. By 1930, the distances a person could travel and the variety of destinations a person could reach in two hours—signified on the right-hand map by the white and tan circles surrounding Oregon—had expanded dramatically.

are not fulfilling your fundamental duty as a woman." A tobacco ad matter-of-factly declared: "Men at the top are apt to be pipe-smokers. . . . It's no coincidence—pipe-smoking is a calm and deliberate habit—restful, stimulating. His pipe helps a man think straight. A pipe is back of most big ideas."

Advertising professionals believed they were helping people to manage their lives in ways that would increase their satisfaction and pleasure. American consumers responded enthusiastically. The most enthusiastic of all were middle-class Americans, who could afford to buy what the advertisers were selling. Many of them were newcomers to middle-class ranks, searching for ways

to affirm—or even create—their new identity. The aforementioned ad for pipe tobacco, for example, was targeted at the new middle-class man, imagined by advertisers to be someone holding a salaried position in a corporate office or bank, or working as a commission salesman, or owning a small business.

As male wage earners moved into the new middle class, their wives were freed from the necessity of working outside the home. Advertisers appealed to the new middle-class woman, too, as she refocused her attention toward dressing in the latest fashion, managing the household, and raising children. Vacuum cleaners and other consumer durables would make her more

The Art of Selling Cars. The creators of this dazzling advertisement mixed female sexuality, bold colors, and the power and speed of lightning bolts to generate consumer interest in the "New Morris-Oxford Six" automobile.

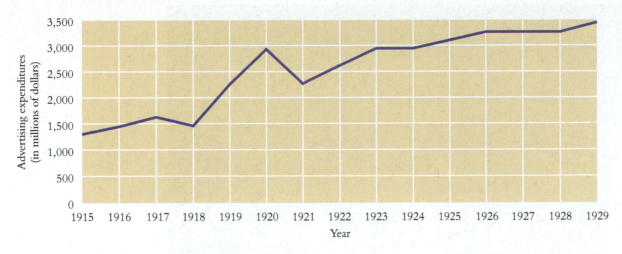

Expenditures on Advertising, 1915–1929.
Source: Data from *Historical Statistics of the United States, Colonial Times to 1970* (White Plains, NY: Kraus International, 1989), p. 856.

efficient, and books on childrearing, many imbued with a popularized Freudianism, would enable her to mold her children for future success in work and marriage. Cosmetics would aid women in their "first duty"—to be beautiful and sexual for their husbands and boyfriends.

Changing Attitudes toward Marriage and Sexuality

That husbands and wives were encouraged to pursue sexual satisfaction together was one sign of how prescriptions for married life had changed since the 19th century, when women were thought to lack sexual passion and men were tacitly expected to satisfy their drives through extramarital liaisons. Modern husbands and wives were expected to share other leisure activities as well—dining out, playing cards with friends, going to the movies, attending concerts, and discussing the latest selection from the newly formed Book-of-the-Month Club. Husbands and wives now aspired to a new ideal—to be best friends, full partners in the pursuit of happiness.

The public pursuit of pleasure was also noticeable among young and single middle-class women. The so-called **flappers** of the 1920s set out to break the informal rules governing young women's lives: they donned short dresses, rolled their stockings down, wore red lipstick, and smoked in public. Flappers were signaling their desire for independence and equality, but they had little thought of achieving those goals through politics as their middle-class predecessors had in the woman suffrage movement. Rather, they aimed to create a new female personality endowed with self-reliance, outspokenness, and a new appreciation for the pleasures of life.

An Age of Celebrity

The pursuit of pleasure became both an individual and a group endeavor. Mass marketers began to understand that they could make big sums of money by staging mega-events, mostly connected to sports, that tens of thousands would attend and that radio announcers would broadcast to a virtual audience of millions. Newspapers and word-of-mouth would ensure that enthusiasts would discuss these events for days, even weeks and months. Baseball and boxing became the two sports where mass marketing had advanced the farthest. When Yankee Stadium opened in 1923, it set a new standard for the scale and magnificence of sports amphitheaters. Boxing matches began drawing audiences that would have been unimaginable 20 years earlier. To succeed on this scale, these sports required not just stirring athletic competitions but also individual athletes who seemed larger than life and whose exploits and character could be endlessly promoted.

No sports figure achieved greater fame than George Herman "Babe" Ruth, who overcame the hardships of a poor and orphaned youth in Baltimore to become the slugging star—the "Sultan of Swat"—of the New York Yankees. In the 1920s, Ruth hit more home runs than baseball experts had thought humanly possible, culminating in 1927, when he hit a magical 60, a record that would last for 34 years and that would be surpassed only three times in the 20th century. A close second in popularity to Ruth was heavyweight prizefighter Jack Dempsey, whose combination of ruthlessness and efficiency in the ring with gentleness outside it enthralled millions.

Americans also drew their celebrities from the movies, where stars such as comedian Charlie Chaplin and the exotically handsome Rudolph Valentino stirred laughter and sexual longings, respectively, in audiences. These and other figures became so familiar on the silver screen that they created an insatiable appetite among movie fans for news about their private lives as well, an interest that the movie industry was only too eager to exploit.

The popular figures of the 1920s did not earn their status through their accomplishments in politics or war, but through their prowess at a game or their skill at acting in front of a camera. Historians have tended to criticize such celebrity worship, especially when the lionized individual seemed to

Babe Ruth at the Plate. The "Sultan of Swat" watches one of his towering shots soar toward the stadium fence.

possess no quality greater than the ability to hit a ball 400 feet or to smash an opponent's face. But such scholarly criticism perhaps has been too quick to overlook the human longing to experience the intensity of emotions associated with competition and triumph or to draw close to someone who demonstrates that the impossible—whether in the form of a physical feat, or a love relationship, or an escape from a confining life—could be accomplished.

Some of these sentiments can be discerned in the adulation bestowed on **Charles A. Lindbergh**, the young pilot who, in 1927, became the first individual to cross the Atlantic in a solo flight. Piloting his single-engine white monoplane, *The Spirit of St. Louis*, Lindbergh flew nonstop (and without sleep) for 34 hours from the time he took off from Long Island until he landed at Le Bourget Airport in Paris. Thousands of Parisians were waiting for him at the airfield and began charging his plane as soon as it landed. When he returned to New York, an estimated 4 million fans lined the parade route. None of this fame could have happened without the new machinery of celebrity culture—aggressive journalists and radio commentators, promoters, and others who understood how fame could yield a profit. It mattered, too, that Lindbergh performed his feat in an airplane, one of the era's newest and most exciting innovations. But Lindbergh's celebrity involved more than hype and technology: He accomplished what others said could not be done, and he did it on his own in a time when corporations and other private institutions of power seemed to be shrinking the realm for individual initiative. Some of Lindbergh's popularity no doubt rested on his ability to demonstrate that an individual of conviction and skill could still make a difference in an increasingly industrialized and bureaucratized world.

Celebrating Business Civilization

Industrialists, advertisers, and merchandisers in the 1920s began to claim that their accomplishments lay at the heart of American civilization. Business, they argued, made America great, and businessmen provided the nation with its wisest, most vigorous leadership. In 1924, President Calvin Coolidge declared, "the business of America is business." Even religion became a business. Bruce Barton, in his best-seller *The Man Nobody Knows* (1925), depicted Jesus as a business executive "who picked up twelve men from the bottom ranks of business and forged them into an organization that conquered the world." Elsewhere, Barton hailed Jesus as an early "national advertiser," and proclaimed that Peter and Paul were really not so different from Americans who sold vacuum cleaners.

Some corporate leaders adopted benevolent attitudes toward their employees. They set up workplace cafeterias, hired doctors and nurses to staff on-site medical clinics, and engaged psychologists to counsel troubled workers. They built ball fields and encouraged employees to join industry-sponsored leagues. They published employee newsletters and gave awards to employees who did their jobs well and with good spirit.

The real purpose of these measures—collectively known as welfare capitalism—was to encourage employees to be loyal to their firm and to convince them (contrary to what labor union critics had been arguing) that industry did have the best interests of its employees at heart. As the decade proceeded and as prosperity rolled on, welfare capitalism reflected the confidence that capitalism had become more responsive to employee concerns and thus more humane.

Charles A. Lindbergh and the *Spirit of St. Louis*. Lindbergh poses before the plane that will carry him from Long Island to Paris in the first solo flight across the Atlantic.

Industrial Workers

Many industrial workers benefited from the nation's prosperity. A majority enjoyed rising wages and a reasonably steady income. Skilled craftsmen in the older industries of construction, railroad transportation, and printing fared especially well. Their real wages rose by 30 to 50 percent over the decade. The several million workers employed in the large mass-production industries (such as automobile and electrical equipment manufacture) also did well. Their wages were relatively high, and some of them enjoyed good benefits—paid sick leave, paid vacations, life insurance, stock options, and retirement pensions. Although all workers in companies with these programs were eligible for such benefits, skilled workers were in the best position to claim them.

Semiskilled and unskilled industrial workers had to contend with a labor surplus throughout the decade. As employers replaced workers with machines, the aggregate demand for industrial labor increased at a lower rate than it had in the preceding 20 years. Despite a weakening demand for labor, rural whites, rural blacks, and Mexicans continued their migration to the cities, stiffening the competition for factory jobs. Employers could hire and fire as they saw fit and could therefore keep wage increases lagging behind increases in productivity.

This softening demand for labor helps explain why many working-class families benefited little from the decade's prosperity or from its consumer revolution. An estimated 40 percent of workers remained mired in poverty, unable to afford a healthy diet or adequate housing, much less any of the more costly consumer goods.

The million or more workers who labored in the nation's two largest industries, coal and textiles, suffered the most during the 1920s. Throughout the decade, both industries experienced severe overcapacity. By 1926, only half of the coal mined each year was being sold. Many New England textile cities experienced levels of unemployment that sometimes approached 50 percent. One reason was that many textile industrialists had shifted their operations to the South, where taxes and wages were lower. But the southern textile industry also suffered from excess capacity, exerting a downward pressure on prices and wages there as well. Plant managers pressured their workers to speed up production. Workers loathed the frequent "speed-ups" of machines and the "stretch-outs" in the number of spinning or weaving machines each worker was expected to tend. By the late 1920s, labor strife and calls for unionization were rising among disgruntled workers in both the South and the North.

Unionization of textiles and coal, and of more prosperous industries as well, would have brought workers a larger share of the decade's prosperity. Some labor leaders, such as Sidney Hillman of the Amalgamated Clothing Workers, argued that unionization would actually increase corporate profits by compelling employers to observe uniform wage and hour schedules that would restrain ruinous competition. Hillman pointed out—as Henry Ford had in the preceding decade (see Chapter 21)—that rising wages would enable workers to purchase more consumer goods and thus increase corporate sales and revenues. Hillman's views, however, were largely ignored outside the garment industry.

Elsewhere, unions lost ground, as business and government, backed by middle-class opinion, remained hostile to labor organization. Employers attacked unions as un-American. A conservative Supreme Court whittled away at labor's legal protections. In 1921, it ruled that lower courts could issue injunctions against union members, prohibiting them from striking or picketing an employer. State courts also enforced what union members called **"yellow dog" contracts**, written pledges by which employees promised not to join a union while they were employed. Any employee who violated that pledge was subject to immediate dismissal.

These measures crippled efforts to organize trade unions. Membership fell from a high of 5 million in 1920 to less than 3 million in 1929, a mere 10 percent of the nation's industrial workforce. Other forces contributed to the decline, too. Many workers, especially those benefiting from welfare capitalist programs, decided they no longer needed trade unions. And the labor movement hurt itself by moving too slowly to open its ranks to semiskilled and unskilled factory workers.

Women and Work

Women workers experienced the same hardships as men in the industrial workforce and fewer of the benefits. They were largely excluded from the ranks of the skilled craftsmen and thus missed out on the substantial wage increases that the men in those positions enjoyed. Women also had trouble finding work in the automobile industry, the highest paying of the mass-production industries. They had better access to the electrical equipment and meatpacking industries, although they were often segregated in departments given over to "women's work." Where women were allowed to compete for the same jobs as

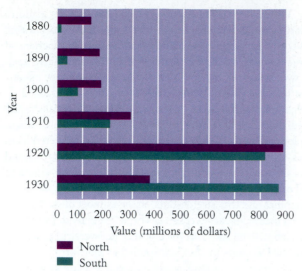

Value of Regional Cotton Textile Output, 1880–1930.
Source: Data from Nancy F. Kane, *Textiles in Transition: Technology,
Wages, and Industry Relocation in the U.S. Textile Industry, 1880–1939*
(New York: Greenwood Press, 1988), p. 29.

men, they usually earned less. Thus, a female trimmer in a meatpacking plant typically made 37 cents per hour, only two-thirds
of what a male trimmer earned. The textile industry had long
been a major source of employment for women, but in the
1920s, women and men alike in this ailing manufacturing sector
suffered high rates of unemployment and declining wages.

White-collar work established itself, in the 1920s, as a
magnet for women. Discrimination generally prevented women
from becoming managers, accountants, or supervisors, but they
did dominate the lower-level ranks of secretaries, typists, filing
clerks, bank tellers, and department store clerks. By the 1930s,
2 million women, or 20 percent of the female workforce, labored
in these and related occupations. Initially, these positions had a
glamour that factory work lacked. Work environments were
cleaner and brighter, and women had the opportunity—indeed
were expected—to dress well. But wages were low and managerial authority was absolute. Unions had virtually no presence in
white-collar places of employment, and workers had difficulty
finding alternative ways of protesting unfair managers or difficult
working conditions.

Women with ambitious work aspirations most often pursued the "female" professions, such as teaching, nursing, social
work, and librarianship. Opportunities in several of these fields,
especially teaching and social work, were growing, and women
responded by enrolling in college in large numbers. The number
of female college students increased by 50 percent during the
1920s. Some of these college graduates used their new skills in
new fields, such as writing for women's magazines. A few, drawing
strength from their feminist forebears during the progressive era,
managed to crack such male bastions of work as mainstream
journalism and university research and teaching. In every field of
endeavor, even such new and exotic ones as airplane flying, at least
one woman arose to demonstrate that her sex had the necessary
talent and drive to match or exceed what men had done.

Thus in 1932, Amelia Earhart became the first woman to
fly the Atlantic solo, matching Lindbergh's feat and inspiring
women everywhere. Even so, Earhart's feat failed to improve
substantially opportunities for women who wanted to work as
pilots in the airline industry. In this industry, as in most lines
of work, gender prejudices remained too entrenched, and the

**Amelia Earhart, Aviation
Pioneer.** Earhart strikes a flapper
pose in front of the biplane that
she was preparing to fly across the
Atlantic.

Subway—14th Street. In this vivid 1930 painting, Reginald Marsh endows a New York City subway scene with unexpected vitality. Marsh's women, in particular, draw our attention, as they stride confidently through the station in fashionable and colorful dresses. The men, by contrast, seem to have little color or purpose. Women were continuing to gain ground, Marsh seems to be suggesting, even as the organized women's movement faded away.

women who had broken the gender line remained, by and large, solitary figures.

The Women's Movement Adrift

Many supporters of the 19th Amendment to the Constitution, which, in 1920, gave women the right to vote, expected it to transform American politics. Women voters would reverse the decline in voter participation, cleanse politics of corruption, and launch a variety of reform initiatives that would improve the quality of life for women and men alike. This female-inspired transformation, however, failed to materialize. The women's movement, instead, seemed to succumb to the same exhaustion and frustration as had the more general progressive movement from which it had emerged 20 years earlier. Younger women searching for independence and equality (such as the flappers discussed earlier in this chapter) often turned away from reform altogether, preferring a lifestyle that emphasized private achievement and personal freedom to a political career devoted to improving the collective status of America's women. Those who continued to agitate for reform found progress more

difficult to achieve once the conservative Republican administrations of Harding and Coolidge took office.

Nevertheless, some female reformers made significant strides in the 1920s. In 1921, one group succeeded in getting Congress to pass the **Sheppard-Towner Act**, a major social welfare program that provided federal funds for prenatal and child healthcare centers throughout the United States. It remained in effect until 1929. In 1923, Alice Paul, still head of the National Woman's Party (NWP, see Chapter 20), and her allies prevailed on Congress to consider an Equal Rights Amendment (ERA) to the Constitution, phrased as follows: "Men and women shall have equal rights throughout the United States and every place subject to its jurisdiction." And in 1920, the National American Woman Suffrage Association, the major force behind the struggle for suffrage, transformed into the **League of Women Voters (LWV)**. During the next decade, the LWV launched numerous initiatives to encourage women to run for elective office, to educate voters about the issues before them, and to improve the condition of those Americans—the poor, female and child laborers, the mentally ill—who needed assistance.

Sometimes the women's movement was stymied not just by external opposition but also by internal division—as it was over the ERA. The NWP and other supporters of the ERA insisted that there could be no compromise with the proposition that women were the equals of men in every respect. But, the LWV countered, childrearing and mothering duties did render women different from men in key respects and thus, in some instances, in need of special treatment by Congress and other lawmaking bodies.

The question of female difference crystallized around the issue of protective labor legislation for women. Over the years, a series of state and federal laws had given women protections at the workplace—limitations on the hours of labor, prohibitions on overnight work, and other such measures—that men did not have. Many women reformers supported these measures, believing they were vital to protecting the masses of women workers from the worst forms of exploitation and thus enabling them to have enough time and energy to perform their vital roles as mothers and wives. Fearing that a successful ERA would render this protective legislation unconstitutional, the LWV and its allies opposed the ERA. Alice Paul and her allies countered by arguing that female protective laws did not really benefit women. Instead, employers used these laws as an excuse to segregate women in stereotyped jobs that were mostly low status and low paying and thus to deny women the opportunities for advancement and fulfillment open to men.

This issue of whether women should be treated like men in all respects or offered some protections that no men enjoyed was a genuinely complicated one, and women activists would continue to argue about it with each other for decades. In the 1920s, however, their inability to speak with a single voice on this matter weakened their cause in the eyes of their adversaries.

The Politics of Business

Q FOCUS QUESTION

What were the similarities and differences in the politics of Harding, Coolidge, and Hoover?

Republican presidents governed the country from 1921 to 1933. In the beginning, this transition engulfed national politics in scandal, as Warren Harding, the first of the decade's three Republican presidents, allowed high-ranking members of his administration to indulge in spectacular forms of corruption. But his successor, Calvin Coolidge, restored virtue and honor to the presidency while carrying out his 1924 campaign pledge to overturn the legacy of progressivism and reduce the role of the government in economic affairs. The most significant challenge to Coolidge's small government program came from his own secretary of commerce and then his successor as president, Herbert Hoover, who sought to sustain the spirit of activist government that Theodore Roosevelt had introduced to Republican politics, albeit in a somewhat altered form.

Harding and the Politics of Personal Gain

Warren Gamaliel Harding defeated Democrat James M. Cox for the presidency in 1920. From modest origins as a newspaper editor in the small town of Marion, Ohio, Harding had risen to the U.S. Senate chiefly because the powerful Ohio Republican machine knew it could count on him to do its bidding. He gained the presidency for the same reason. The Republican Party bosses believed that almost anyone they nominated in 1920 could defeat the Democratic opponent. They chose Harding because they could control him. Harding's good looks and geniality made him a favorite with voters, and he swept into office with 61 percent of the popular vote, the greatest landslide since 1820.

To his credit, Harding released the aging Socialist Party leader Eugene V. Debs from jail and took other measures to cool the passions unleashed by the Red Scare. He also included talented men in his cabinet. His choices of Herbert Hoover as secretary of commerce, Charles Evans Hughes as secretary of state, and Andrew Mellon as secretary of the treasury were particularly impressive appointments. Still, Harding lacked the will to alter his ingrained political habits. He had built his political career on a willingness to please the lobbyists who came to his Senate office asking for favors and deals. He had long followed Ohio boss Harry M. Daugherty's advice and would continue to do so with Daugherty as his attorney general. Harding apparently did not consider men such as Daugherty self-serving or corrupt. They were his friends; they had been with him since the beginning of his political career. He made sure the "boys" had jobs in his administration, and he continued to socialize with them. Many a night he could be found drinking (despite **Prohibition**), gambling, and womanizing with the "Ohio Gang" at its K Street hangout. Sometimes the gang even convened in the White House.

The K Street house was more than a place to carouse. It was a place of business where the Ohio Gang became rich selling government appointments, judicial pardons, and police protection to bootleggers. By 1923, the corruption could no longer be concealed. Journalists and senators began to focus public attention on the actions of Secretary of the Interior Albert Fall, who had persuaded Harding to transfer control of large government oil reserves at **Teapot Dome**, Wyoming, and Elk Hills, California, from the navy to the Department of the Interior. Fall had immediately leased the deposits to two oil tycoons, Harry F. Sinclair and Edward L. Doheny, who pumped oil from the wells in exchange for providing the navy with a system of fuel tank reserves. Fall had issued the leases secretly, without allowing other oil corporations to compete for them, and he had accepted almost $400,000 from Sinclair and Doheny.

Fall would pay for this shady deal with a year in jail. He was not the only Harding appointee to do so. Charles R. Forbes, head of the Veterans' Bureau, would go to Leavenworth Prison for swindling the government out of $200 million in hospital supplies. The exposure of Forbes's theft prompted his lawyer, Charles Cramer, to commit suicide; Jesse Smith, Attorney General Daugherty's close friend and housemate, also killed

Warren G. Harding with Friends and Attendants. This photograph was shot in St. Augustine, Florida. Harding is third from the right. Attorney General Harry M. Daugherty, boss of the Ohio Republican machine, stands to the left of the President, dressed in black and supporting himself with a cane.

himself, apparently to avoid being indicted and brought to trial. Daugherty managed to escape conviction and incarceration for bribery by burning incriminating documents held by his brother's Ohio bank. Still, Daugherty left government service in disgrace.

Harding initially kept himself blind to this widespread use of public office for private gain but grew depressed when he finally realized what had been going on. In summer 1923, in poor spirits, he left Washington for a West Coast tour. He fell ill in Seattle and died from a heart attack in San Francisco. The train returning his body to Washington attracted crowds of grief-stricken mourners who little suspected the web of corruption and bribery in which Harding had been caught. Even as the revelations poured forth in 1924 and 1925, few Americans seemed bothered. Some of this insouciance reflected the carefree atmosphere of the 1920s, but much of it had to do with the character of the man who succeeded Harding.

Coolidge and Laissez-Faire Politics

Calvin Coolidge rarely smiled. At the many dinners he attended as vice president, he said hardly a word. Silence was his public creed, much to the chagrin of Washington's socialites. He was never enticed into carousing with the "boys," nor did he ever stand by as liquor was being served. He believed that the best government was the government that governed least, and that the welfare of the country hinged not on politicians but on the people—their willingness to work hard, to be honest, and to live within their means.

Born in Vermont and raised in Massachusetts, Calvin Coolidge gained national visibility in September 1919, when as governor of Massachusetts he took a firm stand against

Boston's striking policemen (see Chapter 23). His reputation as a man who battled labor radicals earned him a place on the 1920 national Republican ticket. His image as an ordinary man helped convince voters in 1920 that the Republican Party would return the country to its commonsensical ways after a decade or more of progressive reform. Coolidge won his party's presidential nomination handily in 1924 and easily defeated his Democratic opponent, John W. Davis. Coolidge's popularity remained strong throughout his first full term, and he probably would have been renominated and reelected in 1928, but he chose not to run.

Coolidge took greatest pride in those measures that reduced the government's control over the economy. The Revenue Act of 1926 slashed the high income and estate taxes that progressives had pushed through Congress during the First World War. Coolidge curtailed the power of the Federal Trade Commission to regulate business affairs and endorsed Supreme Court decisions invalidating progressive-era laws that had strengthened organized labor and protected children and women from employer exploitation.

Hoover and the Politics of Associationalism

Republicans in the 1920s did more than simply remove government restraints and regulations from the economy. Some, led by Secretary of Commerce Herbert Hoover, conceived of government as a dynamic, even progressive, economic force. Hoover did not want government to control industry, but he did want government to persuade private corporations to abandon their wasteful, selfish ways and turn to cooperation and public service. Hoover envisioned an economy built on the principle of association. Industrialists, wholesalers, retailers,

A Stern Yankee. In contrast to Harding, President Calvin Coolidge did not enjoy informality, banter, or carousing. Here he seems to take little satisfaction in performing what most would have regarded as a pleasurable task: throwing out the first ball of the 1924 baseball season.

operators of railroad and shipping lines, small businessmen, farmers, workers, doctors—each of these groups would form a trade association whose members would share economic information, discuss problems of production and distribution, and seek ways of achieving greater efficiency and profit. Hoover believed that the very act of associating in this way—an approach that historian Ellis Hawley has called **"associationalism"**—would convince participants of the superiority of cooperation over competition, of negotiation over conflict, of public service over selfishness.

A graduate of Stanford University, Hoover had worked first as a mining engineer and then as an executive in multinational mining corporations. During the war, he had directed the government's Food Administration. From that experience, he had come to appreciate the role that government could play in coordinating the activities of thousands of producers and distributors scattered across the country.

Hoover's ambition as secretary of commerce was to make the department the grand orchestrator of economic cooperation, to which end he achieved some notable successes. He persuaded farmers to join together in marketing cooperatives, steel executives to abandon the 12-hour day for their employees, and some groups of bankers in the South to organize their institutions into regional associations with adequate resources and expertise. Hoover's dynamic

conception of government did not endear him to Coolidge, who declared in 1927: "That man has offered me unsolicited advice for six years, all of it bad."

The Politics of Business Abroad

Republican domestic policy disagreements over whether to pursue laissez-faire or associationalism spilled over into foreign policy as well. As secretary of commerce, Hoover intended to apply associationalism to international relations. He wanted the world's leading nations to meet regularly in conferences, to limit military buildups, and to foster an international environment in which capitalism could flourish. Aware that the United States must help to create such an environment, Hoover hoped to persuade American bankers to adopt investment and loan policies that would aid European recovery. If they refused to do so, he was prepared to urge the government to take an activist, supervisory role in foreign investment.

In 1921 and 1922, Hoover helped design the Washington Conference on the Limitation of Armaments. Although he did not serve as a negotiator at the conference—Secretary of State Charles Evans Hughes reserved that role for himself and his subordinates—Hoover did supply Hughes's team with a wealth of economic information that became the basis for bold, detailed proposals for disarmament. Those proposals gave U.S. negotiators a decided advantage over their European and Asian counterparts and helped them win a stunning accord, the Five-Power Treaty, by which the United States, Britain, Japan, France, and Italy agreed to scrap more than 2 million tons of warships. Hughes also obtained pledges from all of the signatories that they would respect the "Open Door" in China, long a U.S. foreign policy objective (see Chapter 22).

These triumphs redounded to Hughes's credit but not to Hoover's, and Hughes used it to consolidate his control over foreign policy. He rebuffed Hoover's efforts to put international economic affairs under the direction of the Commerce Department and rejected Hoover's suggestion to intervene in the international activities of U.S. banks.

Hughes's approach was not entirely laissez-faire, as he demonstrated in his 1923 reaction to a crisis in Franco-German relations. The victorious Allies had imposed on Germany an obligation to pay $33 billion in war reparations (see Chapter 23). When the impoverished German government suspended its payments in 1923, France sent troops to occupy the Ruhr valley, whose industry was vital to the German economy. German workers retaliated by going on strike. The crisis threatened to undermine Europe's precarious economic recovery. Hughes responded by intensifying American financial pressure on the French and by compelling them to attend a U.S.-sponsored conference in 1924 to restructure Germany's debt obligation.

The conference produced the **Dawes Plan** (after the Chicago banker and chief negotiator, Charles G. Dawes), which reduced German reparations from $542 million to $250 million annually and called on U.S. and foreign banks to stimulate the German economy with a quick infusion of $200 million in loans. Within a matter of days, banker J. P. Morgan, Jr., raised

Herbert Hoover, Secretary of Commerce. Hoover used his cabinet position to encourage innovation in American industry. In 1927, he participated in the nation's first television broadcast. Men in an ATT broadcast studio in New York speak and listen to Hoover and his associates in Washington.

© Bettmann/CORBIS

more than $1 billion from American investors. Money poured into German financial markets, and the German economy appeared to stabilize.

The Dawes Plan won applause on both sides of the Atlantic, but soon the U.S. money flooding into Germany created its own problems. American investors were so eager to lend to Germany that their investments became speculative and unsound. At this point, a stronger U.S. government effort to direct loans to sound investments, a strategy that Hoover supported, might have helped. But neither Hughes nor his successor as secretary of state, Frank Kellogg, was interested in such initiatives, and neither was Secretary of the Treasury Mellon. The laissez-faire approach had reasserted itself, and Hoover's plan to involve the U.S. government directly in international economic matters had been rebuffed.

Republican initiatives to ensure world peace continued, however. Secretary of State Kellogg drew up a treaty with Aristide Briand, the French foreign minister, outlawing war as a tool of national policy. In 1928, representatives of the United States, France, and 13 other nations met in Paris to sign the Kellogg-Briand pact, an agreement that soon attracted the support of 48 other nations. Coolidge viewed Kellogg-Briand as a way of reducing American military commitments abroad and thereby as a way of shrinking further the size of the U.S. government at home. With the threat of war removed, the United States could scale back its military forces and eliminate much of the bureaucracy needed to support a large standing army and navy. Unfortunately, the pact contained no enforcement mechanism, thus rendering itself ineffective as a foreign policy tool.

Republican administrations did attempt initially to curtail American military involvement in the Caribbean and Central America as well. Thus, the Coolidge administration pulled U.S. troops out of the Dominican Republic in 1924 and Nicaragua in 1925. But U.S. investments in the region, which more than doubled from 1917 to 1929, proved too important for the U.S. government to ignore. Coolidge sent the Marines back into Nicaragua in 1926 to end a war between liberals and conservatives there and to protect American property; this time they stayed until 1934. U.S. troops, meanwhile, occupied Haiti continuously between 1919 and 1934, keeping in power governments friendly to U.S. interests.

Farmers, Small-Town Protestants, and Moral Traditionalists

 FOCUS QUESTION What concerned farmers and conservative white Protestants in the 1920s, and what policies did they support?

Although many Americans benefited from the prosperity of the 1920s, others did not. Overproduction was impoverishing substantial numbers of farmers. Beyond these economic hardships, many white Protestants, especially those in rural areas and small towns, feared the new economy and new culture that was taking shape in the cities. Increasingly, these Americans made their voices heard in politics.

Agricultural Depression

The 1920s brought hard times to the nation's farmers. During the war, domestic demand for farm products had risen steadily and foreign demand had exploded as the war disrupted

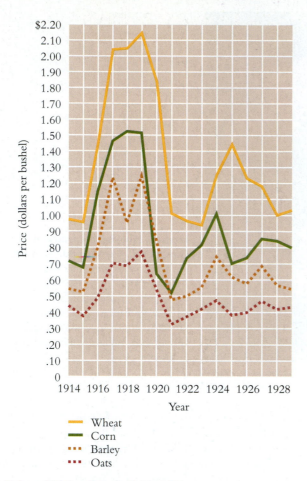

Price of Major Crops, 1914–1929.
Source: Data from *Historical Statistics of the United States, Colonial Times to 1970* (White Plains, NY: Kraus International, 1989), pp. 511–12.

agricultural production in France, Ukraine, and other European food-producing regions. Soon after the war, however, Europe's farmers quickly reestablished customary levels of production. Foreign demand for American foodstuffs fell precipitously, leaving U.S. farmers with an oversupply and depressed prices.

A rise in agricultural productivity made possible by the tractor also worsened the plight of many farmers. The number of tractors in use almost quadrupled in the 1920s, and 35 million new acres came under cultivation. Produce flooded the market. Prices fell even further, as did farm incomes. By 1929, the annual per capita income of rural Americans was only $223, one-quarter of that of the non-farm population. Hundreds of thousands had to sell their farms and scrape together a living as tenants or abandon farming altogether. Many chose to abandon farm life and headed for the city.

Those who stayed on the land grew increasingly assertive in their demands. Early in the decade, radical farmers led the movement, working through such organizations as the Nonpartisan League of North Dakota and farmer-labor parties in Minnesota, Wisconsin, and other midwestern states. By the second half of the decade, however, leadership had passed from farming radicals to farming moderates, and from small farmers in danger of dispossession to larger farmers and agribusinesses seeking to extend their holdings. By lobbying through such organizations as the Farm Bureau Federation, the more powerful agricultural interests pressured Congress to set up economic controls that would protect them from failure. Their proposals, embodied in the McNary-Haugen Bill, called on the government to erect high tariffs on foreign produce and to purchase surplus U.S. crops. The government would then sell the surplus crops on the world market for whatever prices they fetched. Any money lost in international sales would be absorbed by the government rather than by the farmers. The McNary-Haugen Bill passed Congress in 1927 and in 1928, only to be vetoed by President Coolidge both times.

Cultural Dislocation

Added to the economic plight of the farmers was a sense of cultural dislocation among the majority who were white, Protestant, and of northwest European descent. These farmers had long perceived themselves as the backbone of the nation—hardworking, honest, God-fearing yeomen, guardians of independence and liberty.

The 1920 census challenged the validity of that view. For the first time, a slight majority of Americans now lived in urban areas. That finding in itself signified little because the census classified as "urban" those towns with a population as small as 2,500. But the census figures did reinforce the widespread perception that both the economic and cultural vitality of the nation had shifted from the countryside to the metropolis. Industry, the chief engine of prosperity, was an urban phenomenon. Commercialized leisure—the world of amusement parks, department stores, professional sports, movies, cabarets, and theaters—was to be enjoyed in cities; so too were flashy fashions and open sexuality. Catholics, Jews, and African Americans, who together outnumbered white Protestants in many cities, seemed to be the principal creators of this new world. They were also thought to be the purveyors of Bolshevism and other kinds of radicalism. Cities, finally, were the home of secular intellectuals who had scrapped their belief in Scripture and in God and had embraced science as their new, unimpeachable authority.

Throughout the progressive era, rural white Americans believed that the cities could be redeemed, that city dwellers could be reformed, and that the Protestant values of rural America would triumph. War had crushed that confidence and had replaced it with the fear that urban culture and urban people would undermine all that "true" Americans held dear.

These fears grew more intense as urban-industrial America spread its consumer culture and its commodities to the countryside. Even small towns now sported movie theaters and automobile dealerships. Radio waves carried news of city life into isolated farmhouses. The growth in the circulation of national magazines also broke down the wall separating country from city. Mail-order catalogs invited farmers to fantasize that they too could fill their homes with refrigerators, RCA Victrola phonographs, and Hoover vacuum cleaners.

Women Singers and the Birth of Modern Country Music

Composer: A. P. Carter (credited as writer but probably was not)
Title: "Single Girl, Married Girl" (1927)
Performers: The Carter Family

Plaintive and never preachy, "Single Girl, Married Girl" explores women's roles and marriage in ways rarely seen in the country music of the 1920s. As she did throughout her career, Sara Carter, a country music pioneer, sang simply and passionately about the lives of common people, in this case women: "Single girl, single girl, she goes to the store and buys . . . Married girl, married girl, she rocks the cradle and cries . . . Single girl, single girl, she's going where she please . . . Married girl, married girl, baby on her knees." Is Sara sad or angry about the plight of this "married girl" tied down by her baby, or is she just plainly stating how women's lives change when children arrive? In either case, Sara Carter, in this song, offers us a glimpse of how country women of the 1920s, often thought to be conservative in outlook, were themselves struggling to balance traditional female responsibilities (in this case, motherhood) with the freedoms that modern society seemed to be offering young women.

The national commercialization of country and blues music in the 1920s opened up new, but still limited, roles for women in the mass media. The Carter Family was by far the most successful of the initial female country groups, producing hit recordings that sold well in the United States, England, and South Africa, among other places. The group consisted of Sara, who played autoharp and contributed lead vocals; her sister-in-law Maybelle on guitar; and her husband A. P., who occasionally sang with them, but whose most important job was traveling in search of material for the group, which he often took unwarranted credit for, a common practice at the time. Ralph Peer, talent scout for Victor Records, discovered the Carter Family at an open talent audition held in Bristol, Tennessee, on August 2, 1927. This recording, made at those sessions, provides us with a historic glimpse of the birth of modern country music.

The Carter women were relegated to the background in publicity concerning the group. Posters promised a "morally good" program in which a man (A. P.) appeared onstage, an important announcement because women who performed popular music independently were viewed as being morally suspect. Also, despite general agreement that Sara had a major hand in writing and arranging Carter Family material, her name rarely surfaced in the credits, where A.P.'s name typically dominated. Despite such caveats, the Carter Family represented an important example of women claiming new kinds of identities and expression in the modern mass media. Sara seemed to be an innovator in her personal life as well: Her relatives described her as "very liberated" for a Southern woman in the 1920s and 1930s, wearing slacks, shooting game, writing and arranging music, openly smoking, and divorcing A. P. in 1938.

© Michael Ochs Archives/CORBIS

Maybelle, A.P., and Sarah Carter posing for a photograph in Poor Valley, Virginia.

Q Why do you think women performing music independently were frowned on and viewed by many as morally suspect during this period?

Listen to an audio recording of this music on the Musical Links to the Past CD.

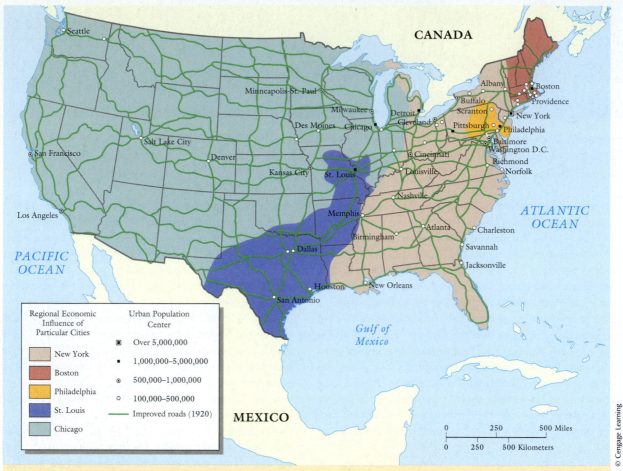

Map 24.2 Urbanization, 1920. By 1920, New York City had surpassed 5 million people, and Boston, Philadelphia, Pittsburgh, Detroit, Chicago, and St. Louis had surpassed 1 million. Another 10 cities, from Los Angeles, California, to Buffalo, New York, had surpassed 500,000. This map, through its color coding, also shows the regions in which the country's five largest cities exercised economic influence.

Rural white Americans showed ambivalence toward this cultural invasion. On the one hand, most country dwellers were eager to participate in the consumer marketplace. On the other hand, many worried that doing so would expose the countryside to atheism, immorality, and radicalism. They expressed their determination to protect their imperiled way of life in their support for Prohibition, the **Ku Klux Klan,** immigration restriction, and religious fundamentalism.

Prohibition

The 18th Amendment to the Constitution, which prohibited the manufacture and sale of alcohol, went into effect in January 1920. Initially it drew support from a large and varied constituency that included farmers, middle-class city dwellers, feminists, and progressive reformers who loathed the powerful "liquor trust" and who saw firsthand the deleterious effects of drink on the urban poor. It soon became apparent, however, that Prohibition was doing as much to encourage lawbreaking as abstinence. With only 1,500 federal agents to enforce the law, the government could not possibly police the drinking

habits of 110 million people. With little fear of punishment, those who wanted to drink did so, either brewing liquor at home or buying it from speakeasies and bootleggers.

Because the law prevented legitimate businesses from manufacturing liquor, organized crime added alcohol to its portfolio. Mobsters procured much of their liquor from Canadian manufacturers, smuggled it across the border, protected it in warehouses, and distributed it to speakeasies. Al Capone's Chicago-based mob alone employed 1,000 men to protect its liquor trafficking, which was so lucrative that Capone became the richest (and most feared) gangster in America. Blood flowed in the streets of Chicago and other northern cities as rival mobs fought one another to enlarge their share of the market.

These unexpected consequences caused many early advocates of Prohibition, especially in the cities, to withdraw their support. Not so for Prohibition's rural, white Protestant supporters, however. The violence spawned by liquor trafficking confirmed their view of alcohol as evil. The high-profile participation of Italian, Irish, and Jewish gangsters in the bootleg trade reinforced their belief that Catholics and Jews were threats to law and morality. Many rural white Protestants became more,

The Banjo

Carried to North America by African slaves, the banjo was adopted by Scots-Irish immigrants, who settled in the Appalachian Mountains. This versatile instrument crossed cultures and musical styles, prominently featuring in minstrel shows, ragtime bands, and later in jazz ensembles and bluegrass groups. The banjo's whimsical, bright tone appealed to many musicians during the Jazz Age. The instrument on the left is a mandolin-banjo, which was popular in 1920s jazz ensembles, such as "Jelly Roll" Morton (at piano) and the Red Hot Peppers, shown at the right.

Q Do you think that the banjo, with its appeal to both black and white musicians, might have played a role in promoting racial understanding and integration in the 1920s? If so, how? If not, why not?

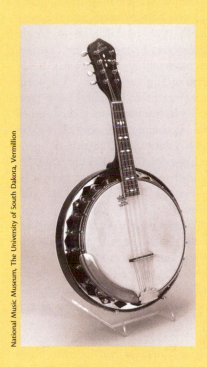

National Music Museum, The University of South Dakota, Vermillion

© The Granger Collection, New York

not less, determined to rid the country of liquor once and for all; some among them resolved to rid the country of Jews and Catholics as well.

The Ku Klux Klan

The original Ku Klux Klan, formed in the South in the late 1860s, had died out with the defeat of Reconstruction and the reestablishment of white supremacy (see Chapter 17). The new Klan was created in 1915 by William Simmons, a white southerner who had been inspired by D. W. Griffith's racist film, *Birth of a Nation*, in which the early Klan was depicted as having saved the nation from predatory blacks. (For a discussion of the film, see the History Through Film feature in Chapter 17, p. 479.) By the 1920s, control of the Klan had passed from Simmons to a Texas dentist, Hiram Evans, and its ideological focus had expanded from a loathing of blacks to a hatred of Jews and Catholics as well. Evans's Klan propagated a nativist message that the country should contain—or better yet, eliminate—the influence of Jews and Catholics and restore "Anglo-Saxon" racial purity, Protestant supremacy, and traditional morality to national life. This message swelled Klan ranks and expanded its visibility and influence in the North and South alike.

By 1924, as many as 4 million Americans are thought to have belonged to the Klan, including the half-million members

© Photos 12/Alamy

Al Capone, Chicago Mob Leader. Capone built a liquor distribution empire during Prohibition. In 1931, the government indicted him on tax evasion charges. In this photograph, Capone, third from the left, posts bail and is freed pending the outcome of his trial. He would be convicted and sent to prison in 1932.

of its female auxiliary, Women of the Ku Klux Klan. Not only was the Klan strong in states of the Old Confederacy, such as Louisiana and Texas, and in border states such as Oklahoma and Kansas, but it thrived, too, in such northern states as Indiana, Pennsylvania, Washington, and Oregon. It even drew significant membership from the cities of those states. Indiana, for example, was home to 500,000 Klansmen and women, many of them in the Indianapolis area. In 1924, Indiana voters elected a Klansman to the governorship and sent several other Klan members to the statehouse.

In some respects, the Klan resembled other fraternal organizations. It offered its members friendship networks, social services, and conviviality. Its rituals, regalia, and mock-medieval language (the Imperial Wizard, Exalted Cyclops, Grand Dragons, and such) gave initiates a sense of superiority, valor, and mystery similar to what other fraternal societies—from the Masons to the Knights of Columbus—imparted to their members.

But the Klan also thrived on hate. It spread lurid tales of financial extortion by Jewish bankers and sexual exploitation by Catholic priests. The accusations were sometimes general, as in the claim that an international conspiracy of Jewish bankers had caused the agricultural depression, or allegations that the pope had sent agents to the United States with instructions to destroy liberty and democracy. More common, and more incendiary, however, were the seemingly plausible, yet totally manufactured, tales of Jewish or Catholic depravity. Stories circulated of Jewish businessmen who had opened amusement parks and dance halls to which they lured innocent adolescents, tempting them with sexual transgression and profiting handsomely from their moral debasement. Likewise, Catholic priests and nuns were said to prey on Protestant girls and boys who had been forced into convents and Catholic orphanages. These stories sometimes provoked attacks on individual Jews and Catholics. More commonly, they prompted campaigns to boycott Jewish businesses and Catholic institutions, and to ruin reputations.

The emphasis on sexual exploitation in these stories reveals the anxiety Klan members felt about society's growing acceptance of sexual openness and sexual gratification. Many Klan supporters lived in towns suffused with these modern attitudes. That such attitudes might reflect the yearnings of Protestant children rather than the manipulation of deceitful Jews and Catholics was a truth some Protestant parents found difficult to accept.

Immigration Restriction

Although most white Protestants never joined the Klan, many of them did respond to the Klan's nativist argument that the country and its values would best be served by limiting the entry of outsiders. That was the purpose of the Johnson-Reed **Immigration Restriction Act of 1924**.

By the early 1920s, most Americans believed that the country could no longer accommodate the million immigrants who had been arriving each year before the war and the more than 800,000 who arrived in 1921. Industrialists no longer needed unskilled European laborers to operate their factories, their places having been taken either by machines or by African American, Mexican, or Filipino workers. Most labor movement leaders were convinced that the influx of workers unfamiliar with English and with trade unions had weakened labor solidarity. Progressive reformers no longer believed that immigrants could be easily Americanized or that harmony between the native-born and the foreign-born could be readily achieved. Congress responded to constituents' concerns by passing an immigration restriction act in 1921. In 1924, the more comprehensive Johnson-Reed Act imposed a yearly quota of 165,000 immigrants from countries outside the Western Hemisphere, effectively reducing total immigration to only 20 percent of the prewar annual average.

The sponsors of the 1924 act believed that certain groups—British, Germans, and Scandinavians, in particular—were racially superior and that, consequently, these groups should be allowed to enter the United States in greater numbers; however, because the Constitution prohibited the enactment of explicitly racist laws, Congress had to achieve this racist aim through subterfuge. Lawmakers established a formula to determine the annual immigrant quota for each foreign country, which was to be computed at 2 percent of the total number of immigrants from that country already resident in the United States in the year 1890. In 1890, immigrant ranks had been dominated by the British, Germans, and Scandinavians, so the new quotas would thus allow for a relatively larger cohort of immigrants from those countries. Immigrant groups that were poorly represented in the 1890 population—Italians, Greeks, Poles, Slavs, and Eastern European Jews—were effectively locked out.

The Johnson-Reed Act also reaffirmed the long-standing policy of excluding Chinese immigrants, and it added Japanese and other groups of East and South Asians to the list of groups that were altogether barred from entry. The act did not officially limit immigration from nations in the Western Hemisphere, chiefly because agribusiness interests in Texas and California had convinced Congress that cheap Mexican

ANNUAL IMMIGRANT QUOTAS UNDER THE JOHNSON-REED ACT, 1925–1927

Northwest Europe and Scandinavia		Eastern and Southern Europe		Other Countries	
Country	**Quota**	**Country**	**Quota**	**Country**	**Quota**
Germany	51,227	Poland	5,982	Africa (other than Egypt)	1,100
Great Britain and Northern Ireland	34,007	Italy	3,845	Armenia	124
Irish Free State (Ireland)	28,567	Czechoslovakia	3,073	Australia	121
Sweden	9,561	Russia	2,248	Palestine	100
Norway	6,453	Yugoslavia	671	Syria	100
France	3,954	Romania	603	Turkey	100
Denmark	2,789	Portugal	503	New Zealand and Pacific Islands	100
Switzerland	2,081	Hungary	473	All others	1,900
Netherlands	1,648	Lithuania	344		
Austria	785	Latvia	142		
Belgium	512	Spain	131		
Finland	471	Estonia	124		
Free City of Danzig	228	Albania	100		
Iceland	100	Bulgaria	100		
Luxembourg	100	Greece	100		
Total (number)	142,483	Total (number)	18,439	Total (number)	3,745
Total (%)	86.5%	Total (%)	11.2%	Total (%)	2.3%

Note: Total annual immigrant quota was 164,667.

Source: From *Statistical Abstract of the United States* (Washington, D.C.: Government Printing Office, 1929), p. 100.

labor was indispensable to their industry's prosperity. Still, the establishment of a Border Patrol along the U.S.–Mexican border and the imposition of a $10 head tax on all prospective Mexican immigrants made entry into the United States more difficult than it had been.

The Johnson-Reed Act accomplished Congress's underlying goal. Annual immigration from transoceanic nations fell by 80 percent. The large number of available slots for English and German immigrants regularly went unfilled, while the smaller number of available slots for Italians, Poles, Russian Jews, and others prevented hundreds of thousands of them from entering the country. A "national origins" system put in place in 1927 further reduced the total annual quota to 150,000 and reserved more than 120,000 of these slots for immigrants from northwestern Europe. Except for minor modifications in 1952, the Johnson-Reed Act would govern U.S. immigration policy until 1965.

Remarkably few Americans, outside of the ethnic groups being discriminated against, objected to these laws at the time they were passed—an indication of how broadly acceptable racism and nativism had become. In fact, racism and religious bigotry enjoyed a resurgence during the Jazz Age. The pseudoscience of eugenics, based on the idea that nations could improve the racial quality of their population by expanding its stronger racial strains and shrinking its weaker ones, found supporters not only in Congress but also among the ranks of prestigious scientists as well. Universities such as Harvard and Columbia set quotas similar to those of the Johnson-Reed Act to reduce the proportion of Jews among their undergraduates.

Fundamentalism versus Liberal Protestantism

Of all the movements protesting against the modern elements of urban life in the 1920s, Protestant fundamentalism was perhaps the most enduring. **Fundamentalists** regarded the Bible as God's word and thus the source of all "fundamental" truth. They believed that every event depicted in the Bible, from the creation of the world in six days to the resurrection of Christ, happened exactly as the Bible described it. For fundamentalists, God was a deity who intervened directly in the lives of individuals and communities and who made known both his pleasure and his wrath to those who acknowledged his divinity. Sin had to be actively purged, and salvation actively sought.

"Spoiling the Broth." This anti-immigrant cartoon, appearing in 1921, shows America's fabled melting pot being forced to take in far more immigrants from Europe and Asia than it could possibly handle. The result was hundreds of thousands, even millions, of immigrants being disgorged from the pot as "unassimilated aliens."

Aimee Semple McPherson. A famous 1920s evangelist, McPherson pioneered in the use of modern media to broadcast her religious message. In Los Angeles, McPherson built one of the country's first megachurches, the Angelus Temple. This photograph shows her in Washington, D.C., in 1927, where a crowd of 7,000 stormed the stage after her sermon to draw close to this charismatic woman.

The rise of the fundamentalist movement from the 1870s through the 1920s roughly paralleled the rise of urban-industrial society. Fundamentalists recoiled from the "evils" of the city—from what they perceived as its poverty, its moral degeneracy, its irreligion, and its crass materialism. Fundamentalism took shape in reaction against two additional aspects of urban society: the growth of liberal Protestantism and the revelations of science.

Liberal Protestants believed that religion had to be adapted to the skeptical and scientific temper of the modern age. The Bible was to be mined for its ethical values rather than for its literal truth. Liberal Protestants removed God from his active role in history and refashioned him into a distant and benign deity who watched over the world but did not intervene to punish or to redeem. They turned religion away from the quest for salvation and toward the pursuit of good deeds, social conscience, and love for one's neighbor. Although those with a liberal bent constituted only a minority of Protestants, they were articulate, visible, and influential in social reform movements. Fundamentalism arose in part to counter the "heretical" claims of the liberal Protestants.

Liberal Protestants and fundamentalists both understood that science was the source of most challenges to Christianity. Scientists believed that rational inquiry was a better guide to the past and to the future than prayer and revelation. Scientists even challenged the ideas that God had created the world and had fashioned humankind in his own image. These were assertions that many religious peoples, particularly fundamentalists, simply could not accept. Conflict was inevitable. It came in 1925, in Dayton, Tennessee.

The Scopes Trial

No aspect of science aroused more anger among fundamentalists than Charles Darwin's theory of evolution. There was no greater blasphemy than to suggest that man emerged from lower forms of life instead of being created by God. In Tennessee in 1925, fundamentalists succeeded in passing a law that forbade teaching "any theory that denies the story of the divine creation of man as taught in the Bible."

For Americans who accepted the authority of science, denying the truth of evolution was as ludicrous as insisting that the sun revolved around the earth. They ridiculed the fundamentalists, but they worried that the passage of the Tennessee law might signal the onset of a campaign to undermine First Amendment guarantees of free speech. The American Civil Liberties Union (ACLU), founded by liberals during the Red Scare of 1919 and 1920, began searching for a teacher who would be willing to challenge the constitutionality of the Tennessee law. They found their man in John T. Scopes, a 24-year-old biology teacher in Dayton, Tennessee. After confessing that he had taught evolution to his students, Scopes was arrested. The case quickly attracted national attention. William Jennings Bryan, the former Populist, progressive, and secretary of state, announced that he would help prosecute Scopes, and the famous liberal trial lawyer Clarence Darrow rushed to Dayton to lead Scopes's defense.

Scopes "Monkey" Trial transcripts (1925)

That Bryan and Darrow had once been allies in the progressive movement only heightened the drama. A small army of journalists descended on Dayton, led by H. L. Mencken, a Baltimore-based journalist famous for his savage critiques of the alleged stupidity and prudishness of small-town Americans.

The trial dragged on, and most of the observers expected Scopes to be convicted. He was, but the hearing took an unexpected turn when Darrow persuaded the judge to let Bryan testify as an "expert on the Bible." Darrow knew that Bryan's testimony would have no bearing on the question of Scopes's innocence or guilt. The jury was not even allowed to hear it. His aim was to expose Bryan as a fool for believing that the Bible was a source of literal truth and thus to embarrass the fundamentalists. In a riveting confrontation, Darrow made Bryan's defense of the Bible look problematic and led Bryan to admit that the "truth" of the Bible was not always easy to determine. But Darrow could not shake Bryan's belief that the Bible was God's word and thus the source of all truth.

In his account of the trial, Mencken portrayed Bryan as a pathetic figure devastated by his humiliating experience on the witness stand, a view popularized in the 1960 movie *Inherit the Wind*. When Bryan died only a week after the trial ended, Mencken claimed that the trial had broken Bryan's heart. Bryan deserved a better epitaph than the one Mencken had given him. Diabetes caused his death, not a broken heart. Nor was Bryan the innocent fool that Mencken made him out to be. He remembered when social conservatives had used Darwin's phrase "survival of the fittest" to prove that the wealthy and politically powerful were racially superior to the poor and powerless. His rejection of Darwinism evidenced his democratic faith that all human beings were creatures of God and thus capable of striving for perfection and equality.

The public ridicule attendant on the Scopes trial took its toll on fundamentalists. Many of them retreated from politics and refocused their attention on purging sin from their own hearts rather than from the hearts of others. In the end, the fundamentalists prevailed on three more states to prohibit the teaching of evolution, but the controversy had even more far-reaching effects. Worried about losing sales, publishers quietly removed references to Darwin from their science textbooks, a policy that would remain in force until the 1960s. In this respect, the fundamentalists had scored a significant victory.

Ethnic and Racial Communities

FOCUS QUESTION How were the experiences of ethnic and racial groups in 1920s America similar and how were they different?

The 1920s were a decade of change for ethnic and racial minorities. Some minorities benefited from the prosperity of the decade; others created and sustained vibrant subcultures. All, however, experienced a surge in religious and racial discrimination that made them uneasy in Jazz Age America.

European American Ethnics

European American ethnics—and especially the Southern and Eastern European majority among them—were concentrated in the cities of the Northeast and Midwest. Many were semiskilled and unskilled industrial laborers who suffered economic insecurity. In addition, they faced cultural discrimination. Catholics and Jews were targets of the Klan. Catholics generally opposed Prohibition, viewing it as a crude attempt by Protestants to control their behavior. Southern and Eastern Europeans, particularly Jews and Italians, resented immigration restriction and the implication that they were inferior to Anglo-Saxon whites. Many Italians were outraged by the execution of Nicola Sacco and Bartolomeo Vanzetti in 1927 (see Chapter 23). If the two men had been native-born white Protestants, many Italian Americans argued, their lives would have been spared.

Southern and Eastern Europeans everywhere endured intensive Americanization campaigns. State after state passed laws requiring public schools to instruct children in the essentials of citizenship. Several states, including Rhode Island, extended these laws to private schools as well, convinced that the children of immigrants who were attending Catholic parochial schools were spending too much time learning about their native religion, language, and country. An Oregon law tried to eliminate Catholic schools altogether by ordering all children aged 8 to 16 to enroll in public schools. But attending a public school was no guarantee of acceptance, either—a lesson learned by Jewish children who had excelled in their studies only to be barred from Harvard, Columbia, and other elite universities.

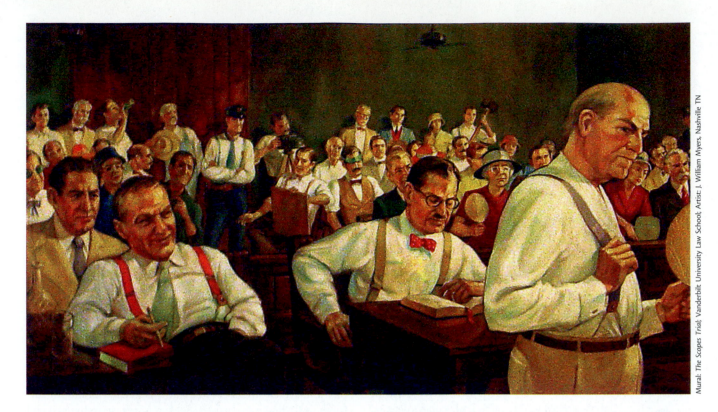

Mural: *The Scopes Trial:* Vanderbilt University Law School; Artist: J. William Myers, Nashville TN

Southern and Eastern Europeans responded to these insults and attacks by strengthening the very institutions and customs Americanizers sought to undermine. Ethnic associations flourished in the 1920s—Catholic churches and Jewish synagogues, fraternal and mutual benefit societies, banks and charitable organizations, athletic leagues and youth groups. Children learned their native languages and customs at home and at church if not at school, and they joined with their parents to celebrate their ethnic heritage. Among Italians and French Canadians, saints' days were occasions for parades, speeches, band concerts, games, and feasts, all serving to solidify ethnic bonds and affirm ethnic identity.

Many of these immigrants and their children, however, also embraced the new consumer culture. They flocked to movies and amusement parks, to baseball games and boxing matches. Children usually entered more enthusiastically into the world of American mass culture than did their immigrant parents, a behavior that often set off family conflicts. But many ethnics found it possible to reconcile their own culture with American culture.

European American ethnics also resolved to develop sufficient political muscle to defeat the forces of nativism and to turn government policy in a more favorable direction. One sign of this determination was a sharp rise in the number of immigrants who became U.S. citizens. The percentage of immigrant Poles, Slavs, Italians, Lithuanians, and Hungarians who became naturalized citizens nearly doubled during the decade; the percentage of naturalized Greeks almost tripled. Armed with the vote, ethnics turned out on election days to defeat unsympathetic city councilmen, mayors, state representatives, and even an occasional governor. Their growing national strength first became apparent at the Democratic national convention of 1924, when urban-ethnic delegates almost won

approval of planks calling for the repeal of Prohibition and condemnation of the Klan. After denying the presidential nomination to William G. McAdoo—Woodrow Wilson's treasury secretary, son-in-law, and heir apparent—they nearly secured it for their candidate, **Alfred E. Smith**, the Irish American governor of New York. McAdoo represented the rural and southern constituencies of the Democratic Party. His forces ended up battling Smith's urban-ethnic forces for 103 ballots, until both men gave up, and supporters from each camp switched their votes to a compromise candidate, the corporate lawyer John W. Davis.

The nomination fight damaged the Democratic Party in the short term, and popular Calvin Coolidge easily defeated the little-known Davis. The split between the party's rural Protestant and urban-ethnic constituencies would keep the Democrats from the White House for nearly a decade, but the convention upheaval of 1924 also marked an important milestone in the bid by European American ethnics for political power. They would achieve a second milestone at the Democratic national convention of 1928 when, after another bitter nomination struggle, they secured the presidential nomination for Al Smith. Never before had a major political party nominated a Catholic for president. Herbert Hoover crushed Smith in the general election, as nativists stirred up anti-Catholic prejudice yet again and as large numbers of southern Democrats either stayed home or voted Republican. Even so, the campaign offered encouraging signs, not the least of which was Smith beating Hoover in the nation's 12 largest cities.

African Americans

Despite the urban race riots of 1919 (see Chapter 23), African Americans continued to leave their rural homes for the industrial

The Scopes Trial. In this mural of the Scopes Trial painted by William Myers, William Jennings Bryan is shown interrogating John T. Scopes. Clarence Darrow is the bemused man in the red suspenders sitting on the left.

centers of the south and the north. In the 1920s alone, nearly a million blacks traveled north. In New York City and Chicago, their numbers grew so large—300,000 in New York and 234,000 in Chicago—that they formed cities unto themselves. When word of New York City's urban black enclave reached the Caribbean, thousands of West Indian blacks set off for Harlem. Within these black metropolises emerged complex societies consisting of workers, businessmen, professionals, intellectuals, artists, and entertainers. Social differentiation intensified as various groups—long-resident northerners and newly arrived

DEMOCRATIC PRESIDENTIAL VOTING IN CHICAGO BY ETHNIC GROUPS, 1924 AND 1928

	Percent Democratic	
	1924	**1928**
Czechoslovaks	40%	73%
Poles	35	71
Lithuanians	48	77
Yugoslavs	20	54
Italians	31	63
Germans	14	58
Jews	19	60

Source: From John M. Allswang, *A House for All Peoples: Ethnic Politics in Chicago, 1890–1936* (Lexington: University Press of Kentucky), p. 42.

southerners, religious conservatives and cultural radicals, African Americans and African Caribbeans—found reason to disapprove of one another's ways. Still, the diversity and complexity of urban black America were thrilling, nowhere more so than in Harlem, the "Negro capital." Black writer James Weldon Johnson described Harlem in the 1920s:

> Throughout colored America Harlem is the recognized Negro capital. Indeed, it is Mecca for the sightseer, the pleasure-seeker, the curious, the adventurous, the enterprising, the ambitious, and the talented of the entire Negro world. . . . Not merely a colony or a community or a settlement—not at all a "quarter" or a slum or a fringe—[Harlem is] . . . a black city, located in the heart of white Manhattan, and containing more Negroes to the square mile than any other spot on earth. It strikes the uninformed observer as a phenomenon, a miracle straight out of the skies.

Not even the glamour of Harlem could erase the reality of racial discrimination, however. Most African Americans could find work only in New York City's least-desired and lowest-paying jobs. Because they could rent apartments only in areas that real estate agents and banks had designated as "colored," African Americans suffered the highest rate of residential segregation of any minority group. Although Harlem had its fashionable districts where affluent blacks lived, much of the area's housing stock was poor and rents were high. Harlem became a black ghetto, an area set apart from the rest of the city by the skin color of its inhabitants, by its higher population density and poverty rate, by its higher incidence of infectious diseases, and by the lower life expectancy of its people.

Blacks did enjoy some important economic breakthroughs in the 1920s. Henry Ford, for example, hired large

HISTORY THROUGH FILM

The Jazz Singer (1927)

Directed by Alan Crosland.
Starring Al Jolson (Jake Rabinowitz/Jack Robin), May McAvoy (Mary Dale),
and Warner Oland (Cantor Rabinowitz).

The Jazz Singer was a sensation when it opened because it was the first movie to use sound (although relatively few words of dialogue were actually spoken). It also starred Al Jolson, the era's most popular Broadway entertainer, and bravely explored an issue that the film industry usually avoided—the religious culture and generational dynamics of a "new immigrant" family.

The movie focuses on Jake Rabinowitz and his immigrant parents, who are Jewish and devout. Jake's father is a fifth-generation cantor whose job it is to fill his New York City synagogue with ancient and uplifting melodies on the Sabbath and Jewish holidays. Cantor Rabinowitz looks upon his work as sacred, and he expects Jake to take his place one day. But Jake has other ideas. He loves music but is drawn to the new rhythmic ragtime and sensual jazz melodies emerging from his American surroundings. In an early scene, we encounter Jake at a dance hall, absorbed in playing and singing ragtime tunes and forgetting that he should be at home preparing for Yom Kippur, the holiest day in the Jewish calendar. His distraught father finds him and whips him, and Jake, in anger and pain, runs away. These early scenes allow us to glimpse an important theme in the immigrant experience of the early 20th century: the deep attraction among the children of immigrants to the energy and vitality of American popular culture and the strains that this attraction often caused between these children and parents desperate to maintain the traditions they had brought with them from Europe.

Jake's estrangement from his family and community gives him the space to reinvent himself as Jack Robin, the jazz singer. His love relationship with a prominent (and non-Jewish) stage actress, Mary Dale, brings him the big break he needs, a starring role in a Broadway show. Jack hopes to use his return to New York to reconcile with his father. This eventually happens when Jake, on the eve of Yom Kippur once again, agrees to skip his show's premiere in order to take his ailing father's place as cantor in the synagogue. Jake's melodies soar and reach his bedridden father who, thinking that his son has succeeded him as cantor and thus fulfilled his (the father's) deepest wish, peacefully dies.

His father is deceived, for Jake returns to his Broadway show as soon as Yom Kippur ends to deliver an outstanding performance as the "Jazz Singer." His future lies with Broadway, rather than with a synagogue, and with the gentile Mary. The movie, however, makes it seem as though everything will work out: Jake's mother is in the audience for the Broadway show, enjoying her son's success and in effect blessing him for the career and woman he has chosen. That this resolution requires misleading the father reminds us, however, that the strains between immigrant parents and their American-born children could be deep and sometimes not resolvable.

The movie also allows us to ask questions about the relationship between immigrants and African Americans. As part of his Broadway performance, Jake does a blackface routine, using burnt cork to turn his face and neck black and thus to appear to audiences as a "black" entertainer. From the early 19th to the early 20th centuries, "blacking up" was a performance style popular among white entertainers who wanted to appropriate and ridicule expressive aspects of black culture. What did it mean for a child of Jewish immigrants, himself vulnerable to being stigmatized as an outsider in America, to "black up"? Jake may have been expressing in part his desire to draw closer to rich elements in black musical culture. But Jake may also have been signaling his desire to distance himself from African Americans by participating in a tradition popular among white American entertainers. Ironically, "blacking up" may have been a way for an entertainer to embrace not black but white America, and for someone like Jake to be accepted by non-Jewish white Americans as one of them. ◄

A billboard in New York City advertising *The Jazz Singer*. Al Jolson is shown in blackface.

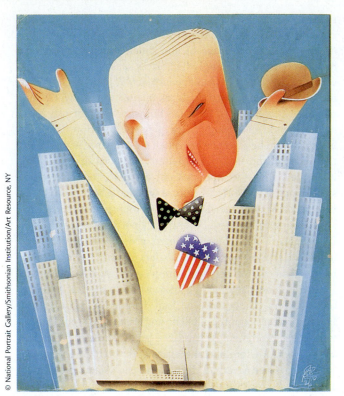

Alfred E. Smith, New York Democrat. This portrait of Al Smith, the New York–born Irish American politician who became the first Catholic to be nominated for the presidency by one of the two major parties, originally appeared in the *New Yorker* magazine in 1934. It suggests that his spirit was as buoyant and irrepressible as that of New York City, but there is a touch of sadness etched in his eyes and smile, a reflection perhaps of the defeats he had suffered, first in the 1928 presidential election and then in 1932, when the presidential nomination that he hoped would come his way again went instead to his successor as governor of New York, Franklin D. Roosevelt.

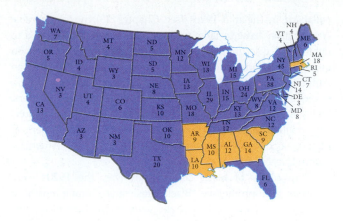

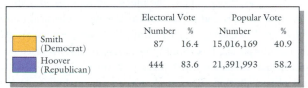

		Electoral Vote		Popular Vote	
		Number	%	Number	%
🟧	Smith (Democrat)	87	16.4	15,016,169	40.9
🟪	Hoover (Republican)	444	83.6	21,391,993	58.2

Map 24.3 Presidential Election, 1928. This map shows Hoover's landslide victory in 1928, as he carried all but eight states and won almost 84 percent of the electoral vote.

numbers of African Americans to work in his Detroit auto factories. Even here, however, a racist logic was operating, for Ford believed that automobile workers divided along racial lines would not challenge his authority. Until the 1940s, in fact, unions made less headway at Ford plants than at the plants of other major automobile manufacturers.

Racial divisions carried over from work to play. African Americans loved baseball as much as white Americans did, and Babe Ruth enjoyed a large black following, but black baseball players were barred from playing in the lily-white major leagues. In response, they formed their own Negro Leagues in the United States and also played professional ball in Mexico and the Caribbean, where they earned extra income and escaped some of the prejudice that met them everywhere in the United States. Cuba, Puerto Rico, Mexico, and other countries in which African Americans played did not organize baseball along racial lines.

The greatest black baseball player of the time was probably Josh Gibson, who joined the Homestead Grays of the National Negro League in 1929 at the age of 18. In his 17-year career, he compiled statistics that surpassed those of any professional ballplayer of his era, white or black, including those of the legendary Ruth. Gibson slugged 962 career home runs, hit 84 home runs in a single season, and compiled a .373 lifetime batting average. Because he died in 1947, at the age of 35, just months before the integration of major league baseball, Gibson never got the opportunity to test his skills against the best white ballplayers, and they never got a chance to play against him.

African Americans grew pessimistic about achieving racial equality. After Marcus Garvey's black-nationalist movement

DEATH RATES FROM SELECTED CAUSES FOR NEW YORK CITY RESIDENTS, 1925

Cause of Death	Total Population	African American Population
General death rate (per 1,000 population)	11.4	16.5
Pneumonia	132.8	282.4
Pulmonary tuberculosis	75.5	258.4
Infant mortality (per 1,000 live births)	64.6	118.4
Maternal mortality (per 1,000 total births)	5.3	10.2
Stillbirths (per 1,000 births)	47.6	82.7
Homicide	5.3	19.5
Suicide	14.8	9.7

Note: Population rate is per 100,000, unless noted otherwise.

Source: Cheryl Lynn Greenberg, *"Or Does It Explode?" Black Harlem in the Great Depression* (New York: Oxford University Press, 1991), p. 32.

collapsed in the mid-1920s (see Chapter 23), no comparable organization arose to take its place. The NAACP continued to fight racial discrimination, and the Urban League carried on quiet negotiations with industrial elites to secure jobs for African Americans. Black socialists led by A. Philip Randolph built a strong all-black union, the Brotherhood of Sleeping Car Porters, but the victories were small and white allies were scarce. The political initiatives emerging among European American ethnics had few counterparts in the African American community.

In terms of black culture, however, the 1920s were vigorous and productive. Black musicians coming north to Chicago and New York brought with them their distinctive musical styles, most notably the blues and ragtime. Influenced by the harmonies and techniques of European classical music, which black musicians learned from European American ethnic counterparts, these southern styles metamorphosed into jazz. Urban audiences, first black and then white, found this new music alluring. They responded to its melodies, its sensuality, its creativity, its savvy. In Chicago, Detroit, New York, New Orleans, and elsewhere, jazz musicians came together in cramped apartments, cabarets, and nightclubs to jam, compete, and entertain. Willie Smith, Charles P. Johnson, Count Basie, Fats Waller, Duke Ellington, and Louis Armstrong were among the most famous musicians of the day. By the late 1920s, they were being hailed in Europe as well.

Jazz seemed to express something quintessentially modern. Jazz musicians broke free of convention: they improvised and produced new sounds that created new sensations. Both blacks and whites found in jazz an escape from the routine, the predictability, and the conventions of their everyday lives.

The Harlem Renaissance

Paralleling the emergence of jazz was a black literary and artistic awakening known as the **Harlem Renaissance**. Black novelists, poets, painters, sculptors, and playwrights set about creating works rooted in their own culture instead of imitating the styles of white Europeans and Americans. The movement had begun during the war, when blacks sensed that they might at last be advancing to full equality. It was symbolized by the image of the "New Negro," a black man or woman who would no longer be deferential to whites but who would display his or her independence through talent and determination. The "New Negro" would be assertive in every field—at work, in politics, in the military, and in arts and letters. As racial discrimination intensified after the war, cultural activities took on special significance. The world of culture was one place where blacks could express their racial pride and demonstrate their talent.

Langston Hughes, a young black poet, said of the Harlem Renaissance: "We younger Negro artists who create now intend to express our individual dark-skinned selves without fear or shame. If white people are pleased, we are glad. If they are not, it doesn't matter. We know we are beautiful. And ugly, too." Writers Claude McKay, Jean Toomer, and Zora Neale Hurston; poet Countee Cullen; and painter Aaron Douglas were other prominent Renaissance participants. In 1925, *Survey Graphic*, a white liberal magazine, devoted an entire issue to "Harlem—the Mecca of the New Negro." Alain Locke, an art and literary critic and professor of philosophy at Howard University in Washington, D.C., edited both the issue and the book *The New Negro*, published later that year. Locke became the movement's leading visionary and philosopher.

But even these cultural advances failed to escape white prejudice. The most popular jazz nightclubs in Harlem, most of which were owned and operated by whites, often refused to admit black customers. The only African Americans permitted inside were the jazz musicians, singers and dancers, prostitutes, and kitchen help. Moreover, the musicians often had to perform what the white patrons wanted to hear. Duke Ellington, for example, was called on to play "jungle music," which for whites revealed the "true" African soul—sensual,

© Bettmann/CORBIS

Josh Gibson, Negro Leagues Star.
This photograph captures Gibson in 1944, near the end of his career, being tagged out at home plate by Ted Radcliffe in the 10th annual East-West All Star Game at Comiskey Park, Chicago.

innocent, primitive. Such pressures curtailed the artistic freedom of black musicians and reinforced racist stereotypes of African Americans as inferior people who were closer to nature than the "more civilized" white audiences who came to hear their music. Some black entertainers, such as Josephine Baker, the legendary dancer, left America for Europe in the 1920s, in the hope that they would find in Paris and elsewhere greater

AMERICANS
ABROAD
Josephine
Baker

artistic and personal freedom than what they could attain in the land of their birth. (For more on Josephine Baker's journey to achieve racial equality and artistic freedom, see the Americans Abroad feature, "Josephine Baker: An African American Entertainer in Paris.")

Black writers experienced similar pressures. Many of them depended for their sustenance on the support of wealthy white patrons. Those patrons were generous with their financial subsidies, but they wanted a return on their investment. Charlotte Mason, the New York City matron who supported Hughes and Hurston, for example, expected them to entertain her friends by demonstrating "authentic Negritude" in their work. Hurston accepted this role, but for Hughes it became intolerable. Both Hughes and Hurston paid a price for their patron's support, including the collapse of their once-close friendship with each other.

Mexican Americans

After the Johnson-Reed Act of 1924, Mexicans became the country's chief source of immigrant labor. A total of 500,000 Mexicans came to the United States in the 1920s. Some headed for the steel, auto, and meatpacking plants of the Midwest, but most settled in the Southwest, where they worked on the railroads and in construction, agriculture, and manufacturing. In Texas, three of four construction workers and eight of every ten migrant farm workers were Mexicans. In California, Mexican immigrants made up 75 percent of the state's agricultural workforce.

Mexican farm laborers in Texas worked long hours for little money. As a rule, they earned 50 cents to a dollar less per day than Anglo workers. They were usually barred from becoming machine operators or assuming other skilled positions. Forced to follow the crops, they had little opportunity to develop settled homes and communities. Mexican farm workers depended for shelter on whatever facilities farm owners offered. Because farm owners rarely required the services of Mexican workers for more than several days or weeks, few were willing to spend the money required to provide decent homes and schools. Houses typically lacked even wooden floors or indoor plumbing. Mexican laborers found it difficult to protest these conditions because their knowledge of English was limited. Few owned cars or trucks that would have allowed them to escape a bad employer and search for a good one. Many were in debt to employers who had advanced them money and who threatened them with jail if they failed to fulfill the terms of their contract. Others feared deportation; they lacked visas, having slipped into the United States illegally rather than pay the immigrant tax or endure harassment from the Border Patrol.

Increasing numbers of Mexican immigrants, however, found their way to California, where, on the whole, wages exceeded those in Texas. Some escaped agricultural labor altogether for construction and manufacturing jobs. Many Mexican men in Los Angeles, for example, worked in the city's large railroad yards, at the city's numerous construction sites, and as unskilled workers in local factories. Mexican women labored in the city's garment shops, fish canneries, and food processing plants. By 1930, Los Angeles had become the largest area of settlement for Mexicans in the United States.

The Los Angeles Mexican American community increased in complexity as it grew in size. By the mid-1920s, it included a sizable professional class, a proud group of *californios* (Spanish-speakers who had been resident in California for generations), many musicians and entertainers, a small but energetic band of entrepreneurs and businessmen, conservative clerics and intellectuals who had fled or been expelled from revolutionary Mexico, and Mexican government officials who had been sent to counter the influence of the conservative exiles and to strengthen the ties of the immigrants to their homeland. This diverse mix created much internal conflict, but it also generated considerable cultural vitality. Los Angeles became the same kind of magnet for Mexican Americans that Harlem had become for African Americans.

Mexican musicians flocked to Los Angeles, as did Mexican playwrights. The city supported a vigorous Spanish-language theater. Mexican musicians performed on street corners, at ethnic festivals and weddings, at cabarets, and on the radio. Especially popular were folk ballads, called *corridos*, that spoke to the experiences of Mexican immigrants. Although different in form and melody from the African American blues, *corridos* resembled the blues in their emphasis on the suffering, hope, and frustrations of ordinary people.

This flowering of Mexican American culture in Los Angeles could not erase the low wages, high rates of infant mortality, racial discrimination, and other hardships Mexicans faced; nor did it encourage Mexicans, in Los Angeles or elsewhere, to mobilize as a political force. Unlike European immigrants, Mexican immigrants showed little interest in becoming American citizens and acquiring the vote. Yet the cultural vibrancy of the Mexican immigrant community did sustain many individuals who were struggling to survive in a strange, often hostile, environment.

The "Lost Generation" and Disillusioned Intellectuals

Q

FOCUS
QUESTION

To whom did the phrase "Lost Generation" refer, and what caused these individuals to become disillusioned?

Many native-born white artists and intellectuals also felt uneasy in America in the 1920s. Their unease arose not from poverty or discrimination but from alienation. They despaired of American culture and regarded the average American as

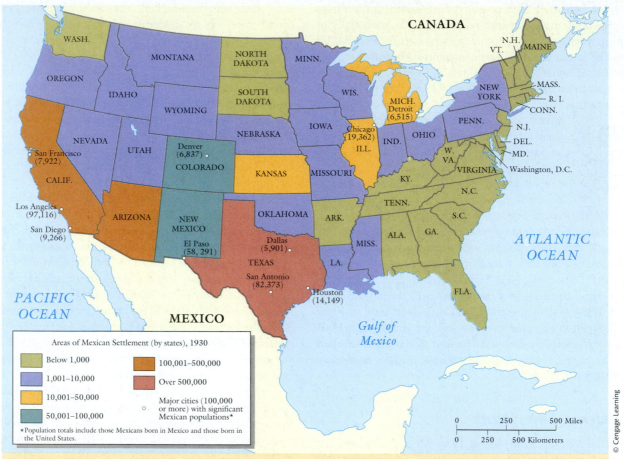

Map 24.4 Mexican Population in the United States, 1930. By 1930, Mexican immigrants had established their pattern of settling primarily in the U.S. Southwest. Texas had the largest concentration of Mexican immigrants, followed by California and Arizona, and then by New Mexico and Colorado. In the 1920s, Los Angeles surpassed San Antonio as the city with the largest Mexican community in the United States.

Legend:
Areas of Mexican Settlement (by states), 1930
- Below 1,000
- 1,001–10,000
- 10,001–50,000
- 50,001–100,000
- 100,001–500,000
- Over 500,000
- ○ Major cities (100,000 or more) with significant Mexican populations*

*Population totals include those Mexicans born in Mexico and those born in the United States.

anti-intellectual, small-minded, materialistic, and puritanical. The novelist Sinclair Lewis, for example, ridiculed small-town Americans in *Main Street* (1920), "sophisticated" city dwellers in *Babbitt* (1922), physicians in *Arrowsmith* (1925), and evangelicals in *Elmer Gantry* (1927).

Before the First World War, intellectuals and artists had been deeply engaged with "the people." Although they were critical of many aspects of American society, they believed they could help bring about a new politics and improve social conditions. The war, however, shook their confidence in Americans' capacity for reform. The wartime push for consensus created intolerance of radicals, immigrants, and blacks. Intellectuals had been further dismayed by Prohibition, the rebirth of the Ku Klux Klan, the rise of fundamentalism, and the execution of Sacco and Vanzetti. Not only had many Americans embraced conformity for themselves, but they also seemed determined to force conformity on others. The young critic Harold Stearns wrote in 1921, "the most moving and pathetic fact in the social life of America today is emotional and aesthetic starvation." Before these words were published, Stearns had sailed for France. So many alienated young men like Stearns showed up in Paris that Gertrude Stein, an American writer whose Paris

apartment became a gathering place for them, took to calling them the **"Lost Generation."**

Their indictment of America was often too harsh. Most of these writers possessed little knowledge of how most Americans lived. Still, they managed to convert their disillusionment into a rich literary sensibility. The finest works of the decade focused on the psychological toll of living in what the poet T. S. Eliot referred to as *The Waste Land* (1922). F. Scott Fitzgerald's novel *The Great Gatsby* (1925) told of a man destroyed by his desire to be accepted into a world of wealth, fancy cars, and fast women. In the novel *A Farewell to Arms* (1929), Ernest Hemingway wrote of an American soldier overwhelmed by the senselessness and brutality of war who deserts the army for the company of a woman he loves. Playwright Eugene O'Neill created characters haunted by despair, loneliness, and unfulfilled longing. Writers created innovations in style as well as in content. Sherwood Anderson, in his novel *Winesburg, Ohio* (1919), blended fiction and autobiography. John Dos Passos, in *Manhattan Transfer* (1925), mixed journalism with more traditional literary methods. Hemingway wrote in an understated, laconic prose that somehow drew attention to his characters' rage and vulnerability.

Security Pacific Collection/Los Angeles Public Library

Mexican American Women Workers, 1920s. These women were employed at a tortilla factory in Los Angeles.

White Southern writers found a tragic sensibility surviving from the South's defeat in the Civil War that spoke to their own loss of hope. One group of such writers, calling themselves the Agrarians, argued that the enduring agricultural character of their region offered a more hopeful path to the future than did the mass-production and mass- consumption regime that had overtaken the North. In 1929, William Faulkner published *The Sound and the Fury,* the first in a series of novels set in northern Mississippi's fictional Yoknapatawpha County. Faulkner explored the violence and terror that marked relationships among family members and townspeople, while maintaining compassion and understanding. Faulkner, Lewis, Hemingway, O'Neill, and Eliot would each receive the Nobel Prize for Literature.

Democracy on the Defensive

Disdain for the masses led many intellectuals to question democracy. Although few intellectuals were as frank as Mencken, who dismissed democracy as "the worship of jackals by jackasses," their distrust of democracy ran deep. Walter Lippmann, a former radical and progressive, declared that modern society had rendered democracy obsolete. In his view, average citizens, buffeted by propaganda emanating from powerful opinion makers, could no longer make the kind of informed, rational judgments needed to make democracy work. They were vulnerable to demagogues who played on their emotions and fears. Lippmann's solution, and that of many other political commentators, was to shift government power from the people to educated elites. Those elites, who would be appointed rather than elected, would conduct foreign and domestic policy in an informed, intelligent way. Only then, in Lippmann's view, could government be effective and just.

Mencken and Lippmann enjoyed especially strong influence and prestige among university students, whose ranks and political significance were growing. But their antidemocratic views did not go uncontested. The philosopher **John Dewey**, who taught at Columbia University but whose reputation and influence extended well beyond academia, was the most articulate spokesman for the "pro-democracy" position. He acknowledged that the concentration of power in giant organizations had eroded the authority of Congress, the presidency, and other democratic institutions, but democracy, he insisted, was not doomed. The people could reclaim their freedom by making big business subject to government control. Government could use its power to democratize corporations and to regulate the communications industry to ensure that every citizen had access to the facts needed to make reasonable, informed political decisions.

Dewey's views attracted the support of a wide range of liberal intellectuals and reformers, including Robert and Helen Lynd; Rexford Tugwell, professor of economics at Columbia; and Felix Frankfurter, a rising star at Harvard's law school. Some of these activists had ties to labor leaders and to New York Governor Franklin D. Roosevelt. They formed the

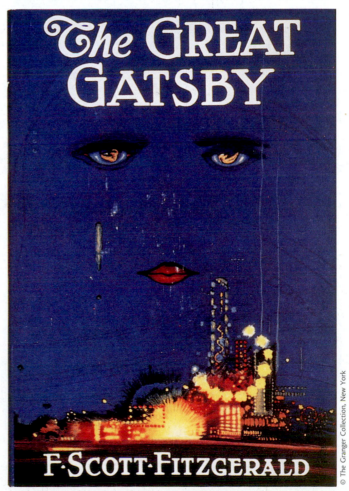

© The Granger Collection, New York

The Great Gatsby. F. Scott Fitzgerald emerged as a major American novelist with the publication of *The Great Gatsby.* Like so much of the best 1920s fiction, *Gatsby* tells the story of a man's disillusionment and ruin.

vanguard of a new liberal movement committed to taking up the work the progressives had left unfinished.

But these reformers were utterly without power, except in a few states, and they took little comfort in the presidential election of 1928. Hoover's smashing victory suggested that the trends of the 1920s—the dominance of the Republicans, the centrality of Prohibition to political debate, the paralysis of the Democrats, the growing economic might of capitalism, and the pervasive influence of consumer culture—would continue unabated.

Conclusion

Signs abounded in the 1920s that Americans were creating a new and bountiful society. The increased accessibility of cars, radios, vacuum cleaners, and other consumer durables; rising real wages, low unemployment, and installment buying; the widening circle of stock owners; the spread of welfare capitalism—all of these developments pointed to an economy that had become more prosperous, more consumer-oriented, even somewhat more egalitarian. Moves to greater equality within marriage and to enhanced liberty for single women suggested that economic change was propelling social change as well.

Even so, many working-class and rural Americans benefited little from the decade's prosperity. Moreover, the decade's social changes aroused resistance, especially from white farmers and small-town Americans, who feared that the rapid growth of cities and the large urban settlements of European and Mexican Catholics, Jews, and African Americans were rendering their white Protestant America unrecognizable.

In the Democratic Party, farmers, small-town Americans, and moral traditionalists fought bitterly against the growing power of urban, ethnic constituencies. Elsewhere, the traditionalists battled hard to protect religion's authority against the inroads of science and to purge the nation of "inferior" population streams. In the process they arrayed themselves against American traditions of liberty and equality, even as they posed as the defenders of the best that America had to offer.

Their resistance to change caused many of the nation's most talented artists and writers to turn away from their fellow Americans. Meanwhile, although ethnic and racial minorities experienced high levels of discrimination, they nevertheless found enough freedom to create vibrant ethnic and racial communities and to launch projects—as in the case of African Americans in Harlem and Mexican Americans in Los Angeles—of cultural renaissance.

The Republican Party, having largely shed its reputation for reform, took credit for engineering the new economy of consumer plenty. It looked forward to years of political dominance. A steep and unexpected economic depression, however, would soon dash that expectation, revive the Democratic Party, and destroy Republican political power for a generation.

CHAPTER REVIEW

REVIEW QUESTIONS

1. What were the achievements and limitations of "people's capitalism" in the 1920s?
2. What were the similarities and differences in the politics of Harding, Coolidge, and Hoover?
3. What concerned farmers and conservative white Protestants in the 1920s, and what policies did they support?
4. How were the experiences of ethnic and racial groups in 1920s America similar, and how were they different?
5. To whom did the phrase "Lost Generation" refer, and what caused these individuals to become disillusioned?

CRITICAL THINKING QUESTIONS

1. Can the deep cultural differences that divided Americans in the 1920s best be explained by where people lived (country versus city), where they were born (in the United States or abroad), their race (white or not), their class, or something else?

2. A Great Depression was the farthest thing from Americans' minds in the 1920s. Reviewing carefully what you have learned about the economy in these years, can you locate areas of economic trouble that contemporaries may have overlooked?

IDENTIFICATIONS

Review your understanding of the following key terms, people, and events for this chapter (terms in bold in text are included in the Glossary).

people's capitalism, p. 651
flappers, p. 653
Charles A. Lindbergh, p. 654
"yellow dog" contracts, p. 655
Sheppard-Towner Act, p. 657
League of Women Voters (LWV), p. 657
Prohibition, p. 658
Teapot Dome, p. 658

associationalism, p. 660

Dawes Plan, p. 660

Ku Klux Klan, p. 664

Immigration Restriction Act of 1924, p. 666

fundamentalists, p. 667

liberal Protestants, p. 668

Alfred E. Smith, p. 670

Harlem Renaissance, p. 674

californios, p. 675

Lost Generation, p. 676

John Dewey, p. 677

SUGGESTED READINGS

William Leuchtenberg, *The Perils of Prosperity, 1914–1932* (1958), and **Ellis Hawley,** *The Great War and the Search for a Modern Order: A History of the American People and Their Institutions, 1917–1933* (1979) offer useful overviews of the 1920s. Important works on consumer culture include **Roland Marchand,** *Advertising the American Dream: Making Way for Modernity, 1920–1940* (1985) and **Kathy Lee Peiss,** *Hope in a Jar: The Making of America's Beauty Culture* (1998). For a penetrating look at U.S. imperialism in the Caribbean in the 1920s, see **Mary A. Renda,** *Taking Haiti: Military Occupation and the Culture of U.S. Imperialism* (2001).

On agricultural distress and protest, see **Theodore Saloutos and John D. Hicks,** *Twentieth Century Populism: Agricultural Discontent in the Middle West, 1900–1939* (1951). For an examination of the economic and social effects of Prohibition, see **Norman Clark,** *Deliver Us From Evil: An Interpretation of American Prohibition* (1976). The best treatment of the Scopes trial can be found in **Michael Kazin,** *A Godly Hero: The Life of William Jennings Bryan* (2006). **John Higham,** *Strangers in the Land: Patterns of American Nativism, 1865–1925* (1955) and **Mae Ngai,** *Impossible Subjects: Illegal Aliens and the Making of Modern America* (2004) are excellent works on the spirit of intolerance that gripped America in the 1920s.

On ethnic communities, Americanization, and political mobilization in the 1920s, see **Gary Gerstle,** *Working-Class Americanism: The Politics of Labor in a Textile City, 1914–1960* (1989), and **George J. Sánchez,** *Becoming Mexican American: Ethnicity, Culture and Identity in Chicano Los Angeles, 1900–1945* (1993). On the Harlem Renaissance, see **Nathan Huggins,** *Harlem Renaissance* (1971). **Malcolm Cowley,** *Exiles Return* (1934), is a marvelous account of the writers and artists who comprised the "Lost Generation." For a provocative interpretation of the intertwined character of white and black literary cultures in 1920s New York, see **Ann Douglas,** *Terrible Honesty: Mongrel Manhattan in the 1920s* (1995).

Visit the CourseMate website at www.cengagebrain.com for additional study tools and review materials for this chapter.

Victims of the Depression

This image evokes the hardship of the 1930s in the form of a strong, able-bodied man in the prime of his life who is unable to find work and must depend on charity.

The Great Depression and the New Deal, 1929–1939

Causes of the Great Depression
  Stock Market Speculation
  Mistakes by the Federal Reserve
    Board
  An Ill-Advised Tariff
  A Maldistribution of Wealth

Hoover: The Fall of a Self-Made Man
  Hoover's Program
  The Bonus Army

A Culture in Crisis

The Democratic Roosevelt
  An Early Life of Privilege
  Roosevelt Liberalism

The First New Deal, 1933–1935
  Saving the Banks
  Economic Relief
  Agricultural Reform
  Industrial Reform
  Rebuilding the Nation's
    Infrastructure
  The TVA Alternative
  The New Deal and
    Western Development

Political Mobilization, Political Unrest, 1934–1935
  Populist Critics of the New Deal
  Labor Protests
  Anger at the Polls
  Radical Third Parties

The Second New Deal, 1935–1937
  Philosophical Underpinnings
  Legislation
  Victory in 1936: The New
    Democratic Coalition
  Rhetoric versus Reality
  Men, Women, and Reform
  Labor in Politics and Culture

America's Minorities and the New Deal
  Eastern and Southern
    European Ethnics
  African Americans
  Mexican Americans
  American Indians

The New Deal Abroad

Stalemate, 1937–1940
  The Court-Packing Fiasco
  The Recession of 1937–1938

T HE GREAT DEPRESSION began on October 29, 1929 (Black Tuesday), with a spectacular stock market crash. On that one day, stock values plummeted $14 billion. By the end of that year, stock prices had fallen 50 percent from their September highs. By 1932, the worst year of the depression, they had fallen another 30 percent. In three years, $74 billion of wealth had simply vanished. Meanwhile, the unemployment rate had soared to 25 percent.

Many Americans who lived through the Great Depression could never forget the scenes of misery they saw everywhere. In cities, the poor meekly awaited their turn for a piece of stale bread and thin gruel at ill-funded soup kitchens. Scavengers poked through garbage cans for food, scoured railroad tracks for coal that had fallen from trains, and sometimes ripped up railroad ties for fuel. Hundreds of thousands of Americans built makeshift shelters out of cardboard, scrap metal, and whatever else they could find in the city dump. They called their towns "Hoovervilles," after the president they despised for his apparent refusal to help them.

The Great Depression brought cultural crisis as well as economic crisis. In the 1920s, American business leaders had successfully redefined the national culture in business terms, as Americans' values became synonymous with the values of business: economic growth, freedom of enterprise, and acquisitiveness. But the swagger of American businessmen during the 1920s made them vulnerable to attack in the 1930s, as jobs, incomes, and growth all disappeared. With the prestige of business and business values in decline, how could Americans regain their hope and recover their confidence in the future? The first years of the 1930s held no convincing answers.

The gloom broke in early 1933 when Franklin Delano Roosevelt became president and unleashed the power of government to regulate capitalist enterprises, to restore the economy to health, and to guarantee the social welfare of Americans who were unable to help themselves. Roosevelt called his pro-government program a "new deal for the American people," and it would dominate national politics for the next 40 years. Hailed as a hero, Roosevelt became (and remains) the only president to serve more than two terms. In the short term, the New Deal failed to restore prosperity to America, but the **liberalism** it championed found acceptance among millions, who agreed with Roosevelt that only a large and powerful government could guarantee Americans their liberty.

Causes of the Great Depression

 Q What caused the crash of 1929, and why did the ensuing depression last so long?

FOCUS QUESTION

America had experienced other depressions, or "panics," and no one would have been surprised if the boom of the 1920s had been followed by a one- or two-year economic downturn. No one was prepared, however, for the economic catastrophe of the 1930s.

Stock Market Speculation

In 1928 and 1929, the New York Stock Exchange had undergone a remarkable run-up in prices. In less than two years, the Dow Jones Industrial Average had doubled. Money had poured into the market, but many investors were buying on 10 percent "margin," putting up only 10 percent of the price of a stock and borrowing the rest from brokers or banks. Few thought they would ever have to repay these loans with money out of their own pockets. Instead, investors expected to resell their shares within a few months at dramatically higher prices, pay back their loans from the proceeds, and still clear a handsome profit. And, for a while, that is exactly what they did.

The possibility of making a fortune by investing a few thousand dollars only intensified investors' greed. As speculation became rampant, money flowed indiscriminately into all kinds of risky enterprises. The stock market spiraled upward, out of control. When, in October 1929, confidence in future earnings faltered, creditors began demanding that investors who had bought stocks on margin repay their loans. The market crashed from its dizzying heights.

Still, the crash by itself fails to explain why the Great Depression lasted as long as it did. Poor decision making by the Federal Reserve Board, an ill-advised tariff that took effect soon after the depression hit, and a lopsided concentration of wealth in the hands of the rich deepened the economic collapse and made recovery more difficult.

Mistakes by the Federal Reserve Board

In 1930 and 1931, the Federal Reserve curtailed the amount of money in circulation and raised interest rates, thereby making credit more difficult for the public to secure. Although employing a tight money policy during the boom years of 1928 and 1929 might have restrained the stock market and strengthened the economy, it was disastrous once the market had crashed. What the economy needed in 1930 and 1931 was an expanded money supply, lower interest rates, and easier credit. Such a course would have made it easier for debtors to pay their creditors. Instead, by choosing the opposite course, the Federal Reserve plunged an economy starved for credit deeper into depression. Higher interest rates also triggered an international crisis, as the banks of Germany and Austria, heavily dependent on U.S. loans, went bankrupt. The German-Austrian collapse, in turn, spread financial panic through Europe and hurt U.S. manufacturers and banks specializing in European trade and investment.

An Ill-Advised Tariff

The Tariff Act of 1930, also known as the Hawley-Smoot Tariff Act, accelerated economic decline abroad and at home. Throughout the 1920s, agricultural interests had sought higher tariffs to protect American farmers against foreign competition. But Hawley-Smoot not only raised tariffs on 75

CHRONOLOGY

1929	Herbert Hoover assumes the presidency ◆ Stock market crashes on "Black Tuesday"
1930	Tariff Act (Hawley-Smoot) raises tariffs
1931	More than 2,000 U.S. banks fail
1932	Unemployment rate reaches 25 percent ◆ Reconstruction Finance Corporation established ◆ Bonus Army marches on Washington ◆ Roosevelt defeats Hoover for presidency
1933	Roosevelt assumes presidency ◆ Hundred Days legislation defines First New Deal (March–June) ◆ Roosevelt administration recognizes the Soviet Union ◆ Good Neighbor Policy toward Latin America launched
1934	Father Charles Coughlin and Huey Long challenge conservatism of First New Deal ◆ 2,000 strikes staged across country ◆ Democrats overwhelm Republicans in off-year election ◆ Radical political movements emerge in several states ◆ Indian Reorganization Act grants limited right of self-government to American Indians ◆ Reciprocal Trade Agreement lowers tariffs
1935	Committee for Industrial Organization (CIO) formed ◆ Supreme Court declares National Recovery Administration (NRA) unconstitutional

◆ Roosevelt unveils his Second New Deal ◆ Congress passes Social Security Act and National Labor Relations Act (Wagner Act) ◆ Holding Company Act breaks up utilities' near-monopoly ◆ Congress passes Wealth Tax Act ◆ Emergency Relief Administration Act passed; funds Works Progress Administration ◆ Rural Electrification Administration established ◆ Number of Mexican immigrants returning to Mexico reaches 500,000

1936	Roosevelt defeats Alf Landon for second term ◆ Supreme Court declares Agricultural Adjustment Act (AAA) unconstitutional ◆ Congress passes Soil Conservation and Domestic Allotment Act to replace AAA ◆ Farm Security Administration established
1937	United Auto Workers defeats General Motors in sit-down strike ◆ Roosevelt attempts to "pack" the Supreme Court ◆ Supreme Court upholds constitutionality of Social Security and National Labor Relations acts ◆ Severe recession hits
1938	Conservative opponents of New Deal do well in off-year election ◆ Superman comic debuts
1939	75,000 gather to hear Marian Anderson sing at Lincoln Memorial

© Bettmann/CORBIS

Unemployed Men in New York City, 1931. The thousands of men waiting to register at the Emergency Unemployment Relief office became so frustrated that they rioted. Police reserves arrived to restore order.

agricultural goods from 32 to 40 percent (the highest rate in American history), it also raised tariffs by a similar percentage on 925 manufactured products. Industrialists had convinced their supporters in the Republican-controlled Congress that such protection would give American industry much-needed assistance. The legislation was a disaster. Angry foreign governments retaliated by raising their own tariff rates to keep out American goods. International trade, already weakened by the tight credit policies of the Federal Reserve, declined even further.

A Maldistribution of Wealth

A maldistribution in the nation's wealth that had developed in the 1920s also stymied economic recovery. Although average income rose in the 1920s, the incomes of the wealthiest families rose higher than the rest. Between 1918 and 1929, the share of the national income that went to the wealthiest 20 percent of the population rose by more than 10 percent, while the share that went to the poorest 60 percent fell by almost 13 percent. The Coolidge administration contributed to this maldistribution by lowering taxes on the wealthy, thereby allowing a higher proportion of national wealth to remain in their hands. The deepening inequality of income distribution slowed consumption and held back the growth of consumer-oriented industries (cars, household appliances, processed and packaged foods, recreation), the most dynamic elements of the U.S. economy. Even when the rich spent their money lavishly—building huge mansions, buying expensive cars, vacationing on the French Riviera—they still spent a smaller proportion of their total incomes

on consumption than wage earners did. The average 1920s wage earner, for example, might spend one-quarter to one-half of his annual earnings to buy a car.

Putting more of the total increase in national income into the pockets of average Americans during the 1920s would have steadied the demand for consumer goods and strengthened the newer consumer industries. Such an economy might have recovered relatively quickly from the stock market crash of 1929. Instead, recovery from the Great Depression lagged until 1941, more than a decade later.

Hoover: The Fall of a Self-Made Man

FOCUS QUESTION Why did Hoover lose his popularity?

In 1928, Herbert Hoover seemed to embody the American dream. From modest beginnings, Hoover had parlayed his intelligence and drive into gaining admission to Stanford University, becoming a mining engineer, and then rising rapidly to top management positions in globe-spanning mining companies. A talented and tireless administrator, Hoover won an international reputation in the First World War for his success, as head of the U.S. Food Administration, in feeding millions of European soldiers and civilians. Then, in the 1920s, he became an active and influential secretary of commerce (see Chapters 23 and 24). As the decade wound down, no American seemed better qualified to become president of the United States, an office that Hoover assumed in March 1929. Hoover was certain he could make prosperity a permanent feature of American life. "We in America today are nearer to the final triumph over poverty than ever before in the history of any land," he declared in August 1928. A little more than a year later, the Great Depression struck.

Hoover's Program

To cope with the crisis, Hoover first turned to the associational principles he had followed as secretary of commerce (see Chapter 24). He encouraged organizations of farmers, industrialists, and bankers to share information, bolster one another's spirits, and devise policies to aid economic recovery. He urged farmers to restrict output, industrialists to hold wages at pre-depression levels, and bankers to help each other remain solvent. The federal government would provide them with information, strategies of mutual aid, occasional loans, and morale-boosting speeches.

Hoover also secured a one-year moratorium on loan payments that European governments owed American banks. He steered through Congress the Glass-Steagall Act of 1932, which was intended to help American banks meet the demands of European depositors who wished to convert their dollars to gold. And to ease the crisis at home, he began to expand the government's economic role. The Reconstruction Finance Corporation (RFC), created in 1932, made $2 billion

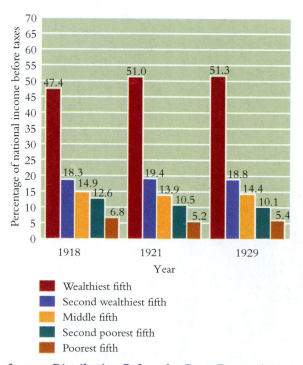

Income Distribution Before the Great Depression.
Source: From Gabriel Kolko, *Wealth and Power in America: An Analysis of Social Class and Income Distribution* (New York: Praeger, 1962), p. 14.

available in loans to ailing banks and to corporations willing to build low-cost housing, bridges, and other public works. The RFC was the biggest federal peacetime intervention in the economy up to that point in American history. The Home Loan Bank Board, set up that same year, offered funds to savings and loans, mortgage companies, and other financial institutions that lent money for home construction and mortgages.

Despite this new government activism, Hoover was uncomfortable with the idea that the government should be responsible for restoring the nation's economic welfare. When RFC expenditures, in 1932, created the largest peacetime deficit in U.S. history, Hoover tried to balance the federal budget. He also insisted that the RFC issue loans only to relatively healthy institutions that were capable of repaying them and that it favor public works, such as toll bridges, that were likely to become self-financing. As a result of these constraints, the RFC spent considerably less than Congress had authorized. Hoover was especially reluctant to engage the government in providing relief to unemployed and homeless Americans. To give money to the poor, he insisted, would destroy their desire to work and undermine their sense of self-worth.

Hoover saw no similar peril in extending government assistance to ailing banks and businesses. Critics pointed to the seeming hypocrisy of Hoover's policies. For example, in 1930, Hoover refused a request of $25 million to help feed Arkansas farmers and their families but approved $45 million to feed the same farmers' livestock. In 1932, shortly after rejecting an urgent request from the city of Chicago for aid to help pay its teachers and municipal workers, Hoover approved a $90 million loan to rescue that city's Central Republic Bank.

The Bonus Army

In spring 1932, a group of army veterans mounted a particularly emotional challenge to Hoover's policies. In 1924, Congress had authorized a $1,000 bonus for First World War veterans in the form of compensation certificates that would mature in 1945. Now the veterans were demanding that the government pay the bonus immediately. A group of Portland, Oregon, veterans, calling themselves the Bonus Expeditionary Force, hopped onto empty boxcars of freight trains heading east, determined to stage a march on Washington. As this "army" moved eastward, its ranks multiplied, so that by the time it reached Washington its numbers had swelled to 20,000, including wives and children. The so-called **Bonus Army** set up camp in the Anacostia Flats, southeast of the Capitol, and petitioned Congress for early payment of the promised bonus. The House of Representatives agreed, but the Senate turned them down. Hoover refused to meet with the veterans. In July, federal troops led by Army Chief of Staff Douglas MacArthur and 3rd Cavalry Commander George Patton entered the veterans' Anacostia encampment, set the tents and shacks ablaze, and dispersed the protestors. In the process, more than 100 veterans were wounded and one infant died.

© Bettmann/CORBIS

The Bonus Army's Encampment Set Ablaze. U.S. troops under the command of General Douglas MacArthur burned the tents and shacks that housed thousands of First World War veterans who had come to Washington to demand financial assistance from the government.

News that veterans and their families had been attacked in the nation's capital served only to harden anti-Hoover opinion. In the 1932 elections, the Republicans were voted out of office after having dominated national politics (excepting Woodrow Wilson's two terms) for 36 years. Hoover received only 39.6 percent of the popular vote and just 59 (of 531) electoral votes. He left the presidency in 1933 a bewildered man, reviled by Americans for his seeming indifference to suffering and his ineptitude in dealing with the economy's collapse.

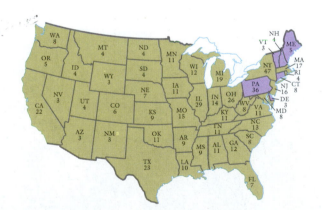

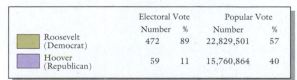

		Electoral Vote		Popular Vote	
		Number	%	Number	%
🟩	Roosevelt (Democrat)	472	89	22,829,501	57
🟪	Hoover (Republican)	59	11	15,760,864	40

© Cengage Learning

Map 25.1 Presidential Election, 1932. The trauma of the Great Depression can be gauged by the shifting fortunes of President Herbert Hoover. In 1928, he had won 444 electoral votes and carried all but eight states (see Map 24.3, p. 673). In 1932, by contrast, he won only 59 electoral votes and carried only seven states. His Democratic opponent, Franklin D. Roosevelt, was the big winner.

A Culture in Crisis

Q FOCUS QUESTION

In what ways did the political pessimism of the early 1930s influence American culture?

The economic crisis of the early 1930s expressed itself not just in politics but also in culture, especially in the literature and cinema of the time. Many writers who, in the 1920s, had castigated ordinary Americans for their small-mindedness and crass materialism now traveled among them, seeking signs of social renewal. But writers found mostly economic misery and spiritual depression. Edmund Wilson, a literary critic, traveled the country in 1930 and 1931 and wrote numerous essays about how Americans had lost their way and knew not where to turn. When he reached San Diego, he got hold of the city's coroner reports on the numerous individuals who, in desperation, had taken their own lives. Wilson had believed that this lovely outpost of the American frontier sitting astride the great and beckoning Pacific would be a place where the American dream still thrived. But here, too, failure suffused life and snuffed out hope.

A sense of aimlessness and hopelessness characterized one of the major literary works of the early 1930s, the Studs Lonigan trilogy (1932–35) written by the Chicago-born writer James T. Farrell. In another decade, one easily imagines that Farrell might have cast his scrappy Irish-American protagonist, Studs, as an American hero whose pluck and guile enable him to achieve wealth, success, and influence. But Studs lacks focus and is too easily overcome by the harshness of his environment. He dies poor and alone, not yet 30. Meanwhile, the popular writer Nathaniel West was publishing *Miss Lonelyhearts* (1933) and *A Cool Million* (1934), novels similarly built around central characters succumbing to failure, drift, even insanity.

One can detect parallel themes of despair in the period's cinema, especially in such movies as *I Am a Fugitive from a Chain Gang* (1932), in which an industrious and honorable man, James Allen, returns from Europe a war hero, only to sink into vagabondage. Caught by the police when he becomes an innocent accessory to a crime, Allen is sentenced to 10 years on a Georgia chain gang. Unable to tolerate the hardship and injustice of his punishment, Allen escapes from jail. But he is condemned to being a man on the run, unable to prove his innocence, earn a decent living, or build enduring relationships. This powerful, bleak film won an Academy Award for Best Picture.

Less grim but still sobering were the gangster movies of the early 1930s, especially *Little Caesar* (1930) and *The Public Enemy* (1931), which told stories of hard-nosed, crooked, violent men who became wealthy and influential by living outside the law and bending the people around them to their will. Moviegoers were gripped by the intensity, suspense, and violence of gangster–police confrontations in these films, but they were also drawn to the gangsters, modern-day outlaws who demonstrated how tough it was to succeed in America and how it might be necessary to break the rules.

Lawlessness also surfaced in the wild comedy of Groucho, Chico, Harpo, and Zeppo Marx, vaudevillians who, in the 1920s and 1930s, made the transition to the silver screen. The Marx Brothers ridiculed figures of authority, broke every rule of

Courtesy of The Everett Collection

Duck Soup. Zeppo, Chico, Groucho, and Harpo Marx strike a comic pose for the camera during the movie's final, and satirical, war scenes. Though filled with laughs, the movie delivered the dispiriting early 1930s message that politics lacked purpose.

etiquette, smacked around their antagonists (and each other), and deliberately and delightfully mangled the English language. Anarchy ruled their world. The Marx Brothers offered movie-goers a 90-minute escape from the harsh realities of their daily lives. Some Marx Brothers movies carried a more serious political message. *Duck Soup* (1933) is a withering political satire set in the fictional nation of Fredonia. Fredonia's leaders are pompous and small-minded, its legal system is a fraud, and its clueless citizens are easily misled. At the movie's end, Fredonians are called to arms through spectacularly ludicrous song and dance scenes, and then led off to fight a meaningless but deadly war. While hilarious to watch, *Duck Soup* also delivers the dispiriting message that people cannot hope to better themselves through politics, for politics has been emptied of all meaning and honesty. This cinematic sentiment paralleled the conviction held by many Americans in 1932 and early 1933 that their own politicians had failed them in a time of need. In such ways did the political pessimism of the early 1930s seep into the era's culture.

The Democratic Roosevelt

 Q **FOCUS QUESTION** What events transformed Franklin D. Roosevelt into a focused politician? What beliefs defined his liberalism?

Between 1933 and 1935, the mood of the country shifted sharply, and politics would, once again, generate hope rather than despair. This change was largely attributable to the personality and policies of Hoover's successor, **Franklin D. Roosevelt**, and to the social movements that emerged during his presidency.

An Early Life of Privilege

Roosevelt was born in 1882 into a patrician family descended, on his father's side, from Dutch gentry who in the 17th century had built large estates on the fertile land along the Hudson River. By the 1880s, the Hyde Park manor where Roosevelt grew up had been in the family for more than 200 years. His mother's family—the Delanos—traced its ancestry back to the *Mayflower*. Roosevelt's education at Groton, Harvard College, and Columbia Law School was typical of the path followed by the sons of America's elite.

The Roosevelt family was wealthy, although his parents' net worth of more than $1 million was relatively small in comparison to the wealth of industrialists and railroad tycoons, many of whom commanded fortunes of $50 million to $100 million or more. This widening gap in wealth concerned families like the Roosevelts, who worried that the new industrial elite would dislodge them from their social position. Moreover, they took offense at the newcomers' allegedly vulgar displays of wealth, lack of taste and etiquette, indifference to the natural environment, and hostility toward those less fortunate than themselves. Theodore Roosevelt, an older cousin of Franklin Roosevelt, had called on the men of his class to set a better example by devoting themselves to public service and the public good.

Though young Franklin wanted to follow in his famous cousin's footsteps, it took a long time for him to show Teddy's seriousness of purpose. Franklin distinguished himself neither at school nor at law. Prior to the 1920s, he could point to few significant political achievements, and he owed much of his political ascent in the Democratic Party to his famous name. He was charming, gregarious, and fun loving, always eager to sail, party, and enjoy the company of women other than his wife, Eleanor. Then in 1921, at the age of 39, Roosevelt was both stricken and transformed by a devastating illness, polio, which paralyzed him from the waist down for the rest of his life.

During the two years Roosevelt spent bedridden, he seemed to acquire a new determination and focus. He developed a compassion for those suffering misfortune that would later enable him to reach out to the millions caught in the Great Depression. Roosevelt's physical debilitation also transformed his relationship with Eleanor, with whom he had shared a testy and increasingly loveless marriage. Eleanor's dedication to nursing Franklin back to health forged a new bond between them. More conscious of his dependence on others, he now welcomed her as a partner in his career. Eleanor soon displayed a talent for political organization and public speaking that surprised those who knew her only as a shy, awkward woman. She was an indispensable player in the revival of Franklin's political fortunes, which began in 1928 with his election to the governorship of New York state. Eleanor would also become an active, eloquent First Lady, her husband's trusted ally, and an architect of American liberalism.

Roosevelt Liberalism

As governor of New York for four years (1929–33), Roosevelt had initiated various reform programs, and his success made him the front-runner for the 1932 Democratic presidential nomination. Even so, he had little assurance that he would be the party's choice. Since 1924, the Democrats had been divided between southern and midwestern agrarians on the one hand and northeastern ethnics on the other. The agrarians favored government regulation—both of the nation's economy and of the private affairs of its citizens. Their support of government intervention in the pursuit of social justice marked them as economic progressives, while their advocacy of Prohibition revealed a cultural conservatism as well as a nativistic strain. By contrast, urban ethnics opposed Prohibition and other forms of government interference in the private lives of its citizens. Urban ethnics were divided over whether the government should regulate the economy, with former New York governor Al Smith increasingly committed to a laissez-faire policy, and Senator Robert Wagner of New York and others supporting more federal control.

Roosevelt understood the need to carve out a middle ground. As governor of New York, and then as a presidential candidate in 1932, he surrounded himself with men and women who embraced a new reform movement called liberalism. Frances Perkins, Harry Hopkins, Raymond Moley, Rexford Tugwell, Adolph Berle, Samuel Rosenman—all were interventionist in economic matters and libertarian on questions of personal behavior.

Connecting with Ordinary Americans. In 1933, FDR began broadcasting "Fireside Chats," frank and accessible radio addresses about the problems confronting the nation and how Americans might solve them. Millions listened to these chats in their homes, gathered around the radio as though it were a hearth.

© Bettmann/ CORBIS

They shared with the agrarians and Wagner's supporters a desire to regulate capitalism, but they agreed with Al Smith that the government had no business telling people how to live their lives. Although it seemed unlikely at first, Roosevelt did manage to unite the party behind him at the 1932 Democratic Party convention. In his acceptance speech, he declared: "Ours must be the party of liberal thought, of planned action, of enlightened international outlook, and of the greatest good for the greatest number of citizens." He promised "a new deal for the American people."

The First New Deal, 1933–1935

Q **FOCUS QUESTION** What do you consider to be the three or four most important pieces of legislation in the First New Deal? Why?

By the time Roosevelt assumed office in March 1933, the economy lay in shambles. From 1929 to 1932, industrial production had fallen by 50 percent, while new investment had declined from $16 billion to less than $1 billion. In those same years, more than 100,000 businesses went bankrupt. In early 1933, with the nation's banking system on the verge of collapse, 34 states had ordered all the banks in their jurisdictions to close their doors. No one seemed to be able to bring the unemployment rate under control. Some Americans feared that the opportunity for reform had already passed.

Not Roosevelt. "This nation asks for action, and action now," Roosevelt declared in his inaugural address. Roosevelt was true to his word. In his first Hundred Days, from early March through early June 1933, Roosevelt persuaded Congress to pass 15 major

pieces of legislation to help bankers, farmers, industrialists, workers, homeowners, the unemployed, and the hungry. He also prevailed on Congress to repeal Prohibition. Not all of the new laws helped relieve distress and promote recovery, but in the short term that seemed to matter little. Roosevelt had brought excitement and hope to the nation. He was confident, decisive, and defiantly cheery. "The only thing we have to fear is fear itself," he declared.

Roosevelt used the radio to reach out to ordinary Americans. On the second Sunday after his inauguration, he launched a series of radio addresses known as "fireside chats," speaking in a plain, friendly, and direct voice to the forlorn and discouraged. In his first chat, he explained the banking crisis in simple terms but without condescension. "I want to take a few minutes to talk with the people of the United States about banking," he began. An estimated 20 million Americans listened.

Roosevelt's First Fireside Chat (March 12, 1933)

To hear the president speaking warmly and conversationally—as though he were actually there in the room—was riveting. An estimated 500,000 Americans wrote letters to Roosevelt within days of his inaugural address. Millions more would write to him and to **Eleanor Roosevelt** over the next few years. Many of the letters were simply addressed to "Mr. or Mrs. Roosevelt, Washington, D.C." Democrats began to hang portraits of Franklin Roosevelt in their homes, often next to a picture of Jesus or the Madonna.

Roosevelt skillfully crafted his public image. Compliant news photographers agreed not to show him in a wheelchair or struggling with the leg braces and cane he used to take even small steps. His political rhetoric sometimes promised more than he was prepared to deliver in actual legislation. Yet the bond that he developed with average Americans was strong, becoming a political force in its own right.

LEGISLATION ENACTED DURING THE "HUNDRED DAYS," MARCH 9–JUNE 16, 1933

Date	Legislation	Purpose
March 9	Emergency Banking Act	Provide federal loans to private bankers
March 20	Economy Act	Balance the federal budget
March 22	Beer-Wine Revenue Act	Repeal Prohibition
March 31	Unemployment Relief Act	Create the Civilian Conservation Corps
May 12	Agricultural Adjustment Act	Establish a national agricultural policy
May 12	Emergency Farm Mortgage Act	Provide refinancing of farm mortgages
May 12	Federal Emergency Relief Act	Establish a national relief system, including the Civil Works Administration
May 18	Tennessee Valley Authority Act	Promote economic development of the Tennessee Valley
May 27	Securities Act	Regulate the purchase and sale of new securities
June 5	Gold Repeal Joint Resolution	Cancel the gold clause in public and private contracts
June 13	Home Owners Loan Act	Provide refinancing of home mortgages
June 16	National Industrial Recovery Act	Set up a national system of industrial self-government and establish the Public Works Administration
June 16	Glass-Steagall Banking Act	Create Federal Deposit Insurance Corporation; separate commercial and investment banking
June 16	Farm Credit Act	Reorganize agricultural credit programs
June 16	Railroad Coordination Act	Appoint federal coordinator of transportation

Source: Arthur M. Schlesinger, Jr., *The Coming of the New Deal* (Boston: Houghton Mifflin, 1959), pp. 20–21.

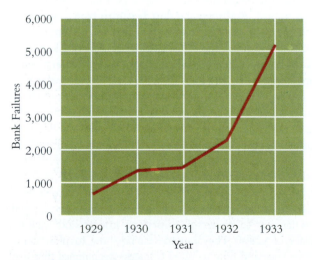

Bank Failures, 1929–1933.
Source: From C. D. Bremer, *American Bank Failures* (New York: Columbia University Press, 1935), p. 42.

Saving the Banks

Roosevelt's first order of business was to save the nation's financial system. By inauguration day, many of the nation's banks had shut their doors. Roosevelt immediately ordered all the nation's banks closed—a bold move he brazenly called a "bank holiday." At his request, Congress rushed through the Emergency Banking Act, which made federal loans available to private bankers, and the Economy Act, which committed the government to balancing the budget. Both were fiscally conservative programs that Hoover had proposed.

After the financial crisis eased, Roosevelt turned to the structural reform of banking. A second Glass-Steagall Act (1933) separated commercial banking from investment banking. It also created the Federal Deposit Insurance Corporation (FDIC), which assured depositors that the government would protect up to $5,000 of their savings. The Securities Act (1933) and the Securities Exchange Act (1934) imposed long-overdue regulation on the New York Stock Exchange, both by reining in buying on the margin and by establishing the Securities and Exchange Commission (SEC) to enforce federal law.

Economic Relief

Roosevelt understood the need to temper financial prudence with compassion. Congress responded swiftly in 1933 to Roosevelt's request to establish the Federal Emergency Relief Administration (FERA), granting it $500 million for relief to the poor. To head FERA, Roosevelt appointed a brash young reformer,

Harry Hopkins, who disbursed $2 million during his first two hours on the job. Roosevelt next won congressional approval for the Civilian Conservation Corps (CCC), which assembled more than 2 million single young men to plant trees, halt erosion, and otherwise improve the environment. The following winter, Roosevelt launched the Civil Works Administration (CWA), an ambitious work-relief program, also under Harry Hopkins's direction, which hired 4 million unemployed people at $15 per week and put them to work on 400,000 small-scale government projects. For middle-class Americans threatened with the loss of their homes, Roosevelt won Congressional approval for the Homeowners' Loan Corporation (1933) to refinance mortgages. These direct subsidies to millions of jobless and home-owning Americans lent credibility to Roosevelt's claim that the New Deal would set the country on a new course.

Agricultural Reform

In 1933, Roosevelt expected economic recovery to come not from relief, but through agricultural and industrial cooperation. He regarded the Agricultural Adjustment Act, passed in May, and the National Industrial Recovery Act (NIRA), passed in June, as the most important legislation of his Hundred Days. Both were based on the idea that curtailing production would trigger economic recovery. By shrinking the supply of agricultural and manufactured goods, Roosevelt's economists reasoned, they could restore the balance of normal market forces. As demand for scarce goods exceeded supply, prices would rise and revenues would climb. Farmers and industrialists, earning a profit once again, would increase their investment in new technology and hire more workers, and prosperity and full employment would be the final result.

To curtail farm production, the **Agricultural Adjustment Administration (AAA)**, which was set up by the Agricultural Adjustment Act, began paying farmers to keep a portion of their land out of cultivation and to reduce the size of their herds. The program was controversial. Many farmers were skeptical of a government offer to pay more money for working less land and husbanding fewer livestock, but few refused to accept payments. As one young Kansas farmer reported:

> There were mouthy individuals who seized every opportunity to run down the entire program . . . condemning it as useless, crooked, revolutionary, or dictatorial; but . . . when the first AAA payments were made available, shortly before Christmas, these same wordy critics made a beeline for the courthouse. They jostled and fell over each other in their mad scramble to be the first in line to receive allotment money.

The AAA had made no provision, however, for the tenant farmers and farm laborers who would be thrown out of work by the reduction in acreage. In the South, the victims were disproportionately black. A Georgia sharecropper wrote Harry Hopkins of his misery: "I have Bin farming all my life But the man I live with Has Turned me loose taking my mule [and] all my feed. . . . I can't get a Job so Some one said Rite you." New Dealers within the Department of Agriculture, such as Rexford Tugwell and Jerome Frank, were sympathetic to the plight of sharecroppers, but they failed during the First New Deal to extend to them the government's helping hand.

Searching for a Better Life. Scenes like this one were common in the 1930s as farm families in Oklahoma and Texas who had lost their land began heading to California. Here a family's entire belongings are packed onto a truck, and the mother tends to her baby on an isolated road. The woman's fur collar suggests that this family had once known better times.

The programs of the AAA also proved inadequate to Great Plains farmers, whose economic problems had been compounded by ecological crisis. Just as the depression rolled in, the rain stopped falling on the plains, and the land, stripped of its native grasses by decades of excessive plowing, dried up and turned to dust. And then the dust began to blow, sometimes traveling 1,000 miles across open prairie. Dust became a fixed feature of daily life on the plains (which soon became known as the Dust Bowl), covering furniture, floors, and stoves, and penetrating people's hair and lungs. The worst dust storm occurred on April 14, 1935, when a great mass of dust, moving at speeds of 45 to 70 miles per hour, roared through Colorado, Kansas, and Oklahoma, blackening the sky, suffocating cattle, and dumping thousands of tons of topsoil and red clay on homes and streets.

The government responded to this calamity by establishing the Soil Conservation Service (SCS) in 1935. Recognizing that the soil problems of the Great Plains could not be solved simply by taking land out of production, SCS experts urged plains farmers to plant soil-conserving grasses and legumes in place of wheat. They taught farmers how to plow along contour lines and how to build terraces—techniques that had been proven effective in slowing the runoff of rainwater and improving its absorption into the soil. Plains farmers were open to these suggestions, especially when the government offered to subsidize those willing to implement them. Bolstered by the new assistance, plains agriculture began to recover.

Still, the government offered little assistance to the rural poor—the tenant farmers and sharecroppers. Nearly 1 million had left their homes by 1935, and another 2.5 million would leave after 1935. Most headed west, piling their belongings onto

Helping Dust Bowl Victims. This poster by the artist and New Deal supporter Ben Shahn dramatizes the plight of the Dust Bowl's victims while expressing the belief that relief is forthcoming from a New Deal agency, the Resettlement Administration.

their jalopies, snaking along Route 66 until they reached California. They became known as Okies, because many, although not all, had come from Oklahoma. Their dispossession and forced migration disturbed many Americans, for whom the plight of these once-sturdy yeomen became a symbol of how much had gone wrong with the American dream.

In 1936, the Supreme Court ruled that AAA-mandated limits on farm production constituted an illegal restraint of trade. Congress responded by passing the Soil Conservation and Domestic Allotment Act, which justified the removal of land from cultivation for reasons of conservation rather than economics. This new act also called on landowners to share their government subsidies with sharecroppers and tenant farmers, although many landowners managed to evade this requirement.

The use of subsidies, begun by the AAA, did eventually bring stability and prosperity to agriculture, but at high cost. Agriculture became the most heavily subsidized sector of the U.S. economy, and the Department of Agriculture grew into one of the government's largest bureaucracies. The rural poor, black and white, never received a fair share of federal benefits. Beginning in the 1930s, and continuing in the 1940s and 1950s, they would be forced off the land and into the cities of the North and West.

Industrial Reform

American industry was so vast that Roosevelt's administration never contemplated paying individual manufacturers direct subsidies to reduce, or even halt, production. Instead, the government decided to limit production through persuasion and association—techniques that Hoover had also favored. The first task of the **National Recovery Administration (NRA)**, authorized under the National Industrial Recovery Act, was to persuade industrialists and businessmen to agree to raise employee wages to a minimum of 30 to 40 cents per hour and to limit employee hours to a maximum of 30 to 40 hours per week. The limitation on hours was meant to reduce the quantity of goods that any factory or business could produce.

The NRA undertook a high-powered publicity campaign, distributing pamphlets and pins throughout the country, promoting its goals on the radio, and urging employers to place a "blue eagle"—the logo of the NRA—on storefronts, at factory entrances, and on company stationery. Blue eagles began sprouting everywhere, usually accompanied by the slogan "We Do Our Part."

The NRA also brought together the largest producers in every sector of manufacturing and asked each group (or conference) to limit production and to develop a code of fair competition to govern prices, wages, and hours in their industry.

In summer and fall 1933, the NRA codes drawn up for steel, textiles, coal mining, rubber, garment manufacture, and other industries seemed to be working. The economy improved, and hard times seemed to be easing. But in winter and spring 1934, economic indicators plunged downward once again, and manufacturers began to evade the code provisions. By fall 1934, it was clear that the NRA had failed. When the Supreme Court declared the NRA codes unconstitutional in May 1935, the Roosevelt administration allowed the agency to die.

Rebuilding the Nation's Infrastructure

In addition to establishing the NRA, the National Industrial Recovery Act launched the Public Works Administration (PWA) to strengthen the nation's infrastructure of roads, bridges, sewage systems, hospitals, airports, and schools. The labor needed for these construction projects would shrink relief rolls and reduce unemployment, but the projects could be justified in terms that conservatives approved: economic investment rather than short-term relief.

The PWA authorized the building of three major dams in the West—Boulder, Grand Coulee, and Bonneville—that opened

Map Legend

- Area of severe wind erosion in 1935–1936
- Area of severe wind erosion in 1938
- Area of severe wind erosion in 1940
- Area of most severe wind erosion in 1935–1938

0   150   300 Miles
0   150   300 Kilometers

© Cengage Learning

Map 25.2 Dust Bowl, 1935–1940. This map shows the areas in six states—Texas, New Mexico, Oklahoma, Colorado, Kansas, and a bit of Nebraska—claimed by the Dust Bowl between 1935 and 1940. The pink color shows the area where the winds caused the worst damage.

© Bettmann/CORBIS

Selling the NRA Through Sex and Sunburn. Americans were asked to display their support for the NRA by pasting eagles onto their factory entrances, storefronts, and even clothes. The young women in this photo dispensed with pasting, choosing instead to allow the sun to burn their bare backs around a stenciled blue eagle and NRA lettering, which were being applied by the woman in the white gown.

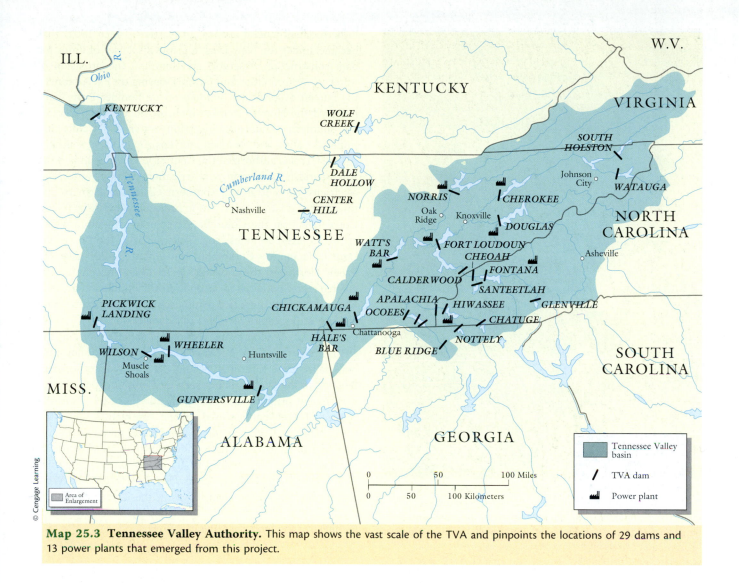

Map 25.3 **Tennessee Valley Authority.** This map shows the vast scale of the TVA and pinpoints the locations of 29 dams and 13 power plants that emerged from this project.

up large stretches of Arizona, California, and Washington to industrial and agricultural development. It funded the construction of the Triborough Bridge in New York City and the 100-mile causeway linking Florida to Key West. It also appropriated money for the construction of thousands of new schools.

The TVA Alternative

One piece of legislation passed during Roosevelt's First New Deal specified a strategy for economic recovery significantly different from the one promoted by the NIRA. The Tennessee Valley Authority Act (1933) called for the government—rather than private corporations—to promote economic development throughout the Tennessee Valley, a vast river basin winding through parts of Kentucky, Tennessee, Mississippi, Alabama, Georgia, and North Carolina. The act created the **Tennessee Valley Authority (TVA)** to control flooding on the Tennessee River, harness its water power to generate electricity, develop local industry (such as fertilizer production), improve river navigability, and ease the poverty and isolation of the area's inhabitants. In some respects, the TVA's mandate resembled that of the PWA, but the TVA enjoyed even greater authority.

The extent of its control over economic development reflected the influence of Rexford Tugwell and other New Dealers who were committed to a government-planned and government-operated economy. Although they rarely said so, these reformers were drawn to socialism.

The accomplishments of the TVA were many. It built, completed, or improved more than 20 dams, including the huge Wheeler Dam near Muscle Shoals in Alabama. At several of the dam sites, the TVA built hydroelectric generators and soon became the nation's largest producer of electricity. Its low electric rates compelled private utility companies to reduce their rates as well. The TVA also constructed waterways to bypass non-navigable stretches of the river, reduced the danger of flooding, and taught farmers how to prevent soil erosion and use fertilizers.

Although the TVA was one of the New Deal's most celebrated successes, it generated little support for more ambitious experiments in national planning. For the government to have assumed control of established industries and banks would have been quite a different matter from bringing prosperity to an impoverished region. Like Roosevelt, few members of Congress or the public favored the radical growth of governmental power that such programs would have

Improving the Nation's Infrastructure. The federal government built several major dams in the West to boost agricultural and industrial development. This is a photograph of the mammoth Boulder Dam (later renamed the Hoover Dam) on the Colorado River.

hitherto small federal agency (in existence since 1902) that became, under the New Deal, a prime dispenser of funds for dam construction, reservoir creation, and the provision of water to western cities and farms. Drawing on PWA monies, the bureau oversaw the building of the Boulder Dam (later renamed the Hoover Dam), which provided drinking water for southern California, irrigation water for California's Imperial Valley, and electricity for Los Angeles and southern Arizona. It also authorized the Central Valley Project and the All-American Canal to provide irrigation, drinking water, and electricity to central and southern California farmers and towns. The greatest construction project of all was the Grand Coulee Dam on the Columbia River in Washington, which created a lake 150 miles long. Together with the Bonneville Dam (also on the Columbia), the Grand Coulee gave the Pacific Northwest the cheapest electricity in the country and created a new potential for economic and population growth. Not surprisingly, these two dams also made Washington state the largest per capita recipient of New Deal aid.

These developments attracted less attention in the 1930s than the TVA because their benefits did not fully materialize until after the Second World War. Also, dam building in the West was not seen as a radical experiment in government planning and management. Unlike the TVA, the Bureau of Reclamation hired private contractors to do the work. Moreover, the benefits of these dams were intended to flow first to large agricultural and real estate interests, not to the poor; they were intended to aid private enterprise, rather than bypass it. In political terms, dam building in the West was more conservative than it was in the Tennessee Valley. Even so, this activity made the federal government a key architect of the modern American West.

entailed. Thus, the thought of replacing the NRA with a nationwide TVA, for instance, made little headway. The New Deal never embraced the idea of the federal government as a substitute for private enterprise.

The New Deal and Western Development

As the TVA showed, New Deal programs could make an enormous difference to a particular region's welfare. Other regional beneficiaries of the New Deal included the New York City area, which prospered from the close links of local politicians to the Roosevelt administration. The region that benefited most from the New Deal, however, was the West. Between 1933 and 1939, per-capita payments for public works projects, welfare, and federal loans in the Rocky Mountain and Pacific Coast states outstripped those of any other region.

Dam building was central to this western focus. Western real estate and agricultural interests wanted to dam the West's major rivers to provide water and electricity for urban and agricultural development, but the costs were prohibitive, even to the largest capitalists, until the New Deal offered to defray the expenses with federal dollars. Western interests found a government ally in the Bureau of Reclamation, a

Political Mobilization, Political Unrest, 1934–1935

FOCUS QUESTION

What forms did political unrest take in 1934 and 1935?

Although Roosevelt and the New Dealers dismantled the NRA in 1935, they could not stop the political forces it had set in motion. Ordinary Americans now believed they could make a difference. If the New Dealers could not achieve economic recovery, then the people would find others who could.

Populist Critics of the New Deal

Some critics were disturbed by what they perceived as the conservative character of New Deal programs. Banking reforms, the AAA, and the NRA, they alleged, all seemed to favor large economic interests. Ordinary people had been ignored.

In the South and Midwest, millions listened regularly to the radio addresses of Louisiana Senator **Huey Long**, a former

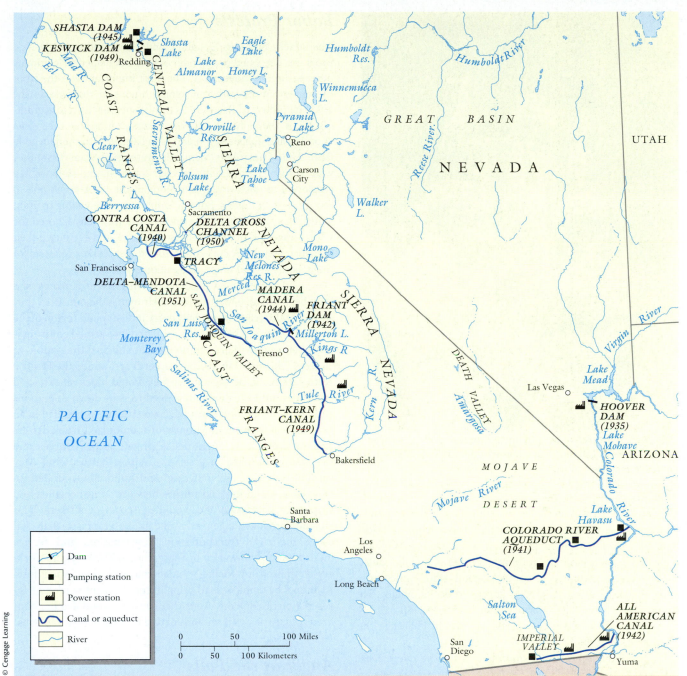

Map 25.4 Federal Water Projects in California Built or Funded by the New Deal. This map demonstrates how much California cities and agriculture benefited from water projects—dams, canals, aqueducts, pumping stations, and power plants—begun under the New Deal. The projects extended from the Shasta Dam in the northern part of the state to the All-American Canal that traversed the Imperial Valley south of San Diego, and included the Colorado River Aqueduct that carried vital drinking water to Los Angeles.

governor of that state and an accomplished orator. In attacks on New Deal programs, he alleged that "not a single thin dime of concentrated, bloated, pompous wealth, massed in the hands of a few people has been raked down to relieve the masses." Long offered a simple alternative: "Break up the swollen fortunes of America and . . . spread the wealth among all our people." He called for a redistribution of wealth that would guarantee each American family a $5,000 estate.

Long's rhetoric inspired hundreds of thousands of Americans to join the Share the Wealth clubs his supporters organized. Most came from middle-class ranks or from the ranks of skilled workers. By 1935, Roosevelt regarded Long as the man most likely to unseat him in the presidential election of 1936. Before that campaign began, however, Long was assassinated.

Meanwhile, in the Midwest, **Father Charles Coughlin**, the "radio priest," delivered a message similar to Long's. Like Long, Coughlin appealed to anxious middle-class Americans and to once-privileged groups of workers who believed that security and respectability were slipping from their grasp. A

Huey Long, Populist. A spellbinding speaker, Long influenced millions with his calls for redistributing America's wealth in a more equitable manner.

Labor Protests

The attacks by Long, Coughlin, and Townsend on New Deal programs deepened popular discontent and helped to legitimate other insurgent movements. The most important was the labor movement. Workers began joining unions in response to the National Industrial Recovery Act, and especially its clause granting them the right to join labor organizations of their own choosing and obligating employers to bargain with them in good faith. Union members' demands were modest at first: they wanted to be treated fairly by their foremen, and they wanted employers to observe the provisions of the NRA codes and to recognize their unions. But few employers were willing to grant workers any say in their working conditions. Many ignored the NRA's wage and hour guidelines altogether and even used their influence with NRA code authorities to get worker requests for wage increases and union recognition rejected.

Workers flooded Washington with letters of protest and then began to take matters into their own hands. In 1934 they staged 2,000 strikes in virtually every industry and region of the country. A few of these strikes escalated into armed confrontations between workers and police that shocked the nation. In Toledo, Ohio, in May, 10,000 workers surrounded the Electric Auto-Lite plant, declaring that they would block all exits and entrances until the company agreed to shut down operations and negotiate a union contract. Two strikers were killed in an exchange of gunfire. In Minneapolis, unionized truck drivers and warehousemen fought police, private security forces, and the National Guard in a series of street battles from May through July that left four dead and hundreds wounded. In San Francisco in July, skirmishes between longshoremen and employers killed two and wounded scores of strikers. This violence provoked a general strike in San Francisco that shut down the city's transportation, construction, and service industries for two weeks. In September, 400,000 textile workers at mills from Maine to Alabama walked off their jobs. Attempts by employers to bring in replacement workers triggered violent confrontations that caused several deaths, hundreds of injuries, and millions of dollars in property damages.

Anger at the Polls

In the fall of 1934, workers took their anger to the polls. In Rhode Island, they broke the Republican Party's 30-year domination of state politics. In the South Carolina gubernatorial race, working-class voters rejected a conservative Democrat, Coleman Blease, and chose instead Olin T. Johnston, a former mill worker and an ardent New Dealer. In the country as a whole, Democrats won 70 percent of the contested seats in the Senate and House. The Democrats increased their majority, from 310 to 319 (out of 432) in the House, and from 60 to 69 (out of 96) in the Senate. No sitting president's party had ever done so well in an off-year election.

The victory was not an unqualified one for Roosevelt and the First New Deal, however. The 74th Congress would include the largest contingent of radicals ever sent to Washington: Tom Amlie of Wisconsin, Ernest Lundeen of Minnesota, Maury Maverick of Texas, Vito Marcantonio of New York, and some 30 others. Their support for the New Deal depended on

former Roosevelt supporter, Coughlin had become a critic. The New Deal was run by bankers, he claimed. The NRA was a program to resuscitate corporate profits. Coughlin called for a strong government to compel capital, labor, agriculture, professionals, and other interest groups to do its bidding. He founded the National Union of Social Justice (NUSJ) in 1934 as a precursor to a political party that would challenge the Democrats in 1936.

As Coughlin's disillusionment with the New Deal deepened, a strain of anti-Semitism became apparent in his radio talks, as in his accusation that Jewish bankers were masterminding a world conspiracy to dispossess the toiling masses. Although Coughlin was a compelling speaker, he failed to build the NUSJ into an effective political force. Its successor, the Union Party, attracted only a small percentage of voters in 1936. Embittered, Coughlin moved further to the political right. By 1939, his denunciations of democracy and Jews had become so extreme that some radio stations refused to carry his addresses. Still, millions of Americans continued to put their faith in the "radio priest."

Another popular figure was Francis E. Townsend, a California doctor who claimed that the way to end the Depression was to give every senior citizen $200 a month. The Townsend Plan briefly garnered the support of an estimated 20 million Americans.

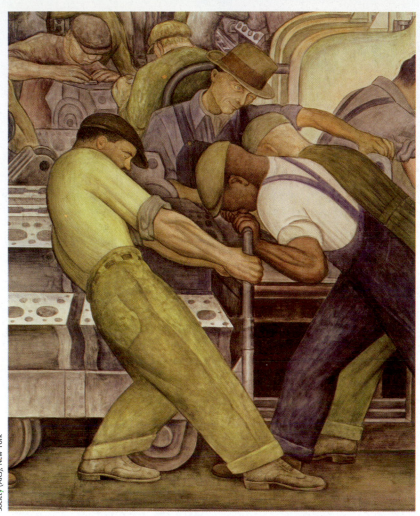

Men at Work. This is a detail from the huge mural that the Mexican artist Diego Rivera painted for the walls of the Detroit Art Museum in 1932–33. The strong, confident pose of Rivera's workers reveals his conviction (one he shared with other 1930s artists) that industrial workers stood at the heart of American civilization and that they would play a key role in rehabilitating a society devastated by depression.

whether Roosevelt delivered more relief, more income security, and more political power to farmers, workers, the unemployed, and the poor.

Radical Third Parties

Radical critics of the New Deal also made an impressive showing in state politics in 1934 and 1936. In Wisconsin Philip La Follette, the son of Robert La Follette (see Chapter 21), was elected governor in 1934 and 1936 as the candidate of the radical Wisconsin Progressive Party. In Minnesota, discontented agrarians and urban workers organized the Minnesota Farmer-Labor (MFL) Party and elected their candidate to the governorship in 1930, 1932, 1934, and 1936. In Washington, yet another radical third party, the Commonwealth Builders, elected both senators and almost half the state legislators in 1932 and 1934. And in California, the socialist and novelist Upton Sinclair and his organization, End Poverty in California (EPIC), came close to winning the governorship.

A widespread movement to form local labor parties offered further evidence of voter volatility, as did the growing appeal of the **Communist Party**. The American Communist Party (CP) had emerged in the early 1920s with the support of radicals who wanted to adopt the Soviet Union's path to socialism (see Chapter 23). In the early 1930s, CP organizers spread out among the poorest and most vulnerable populations in America—homeless urban blacks in the North, black and white sharecroppers in the South, Chicano and Filipino agricultural workers in the West—and mobilized them into unions and unemployment leagues. CP members also played significant roles in strikes described earlier, and they were influential in the Minnesota Farmer-Labor Party and in Washington's Commonwealth Builders. Once they stopped preaching world revolution in 1935 and began calling instead for a "popular front" of democratic forces against fascism (a term used to describe the new kinds of dictatorships appearing in Hitler's Germany and Mussolini's Italy), their ranks grew even more. By 1938, approximately 80,000 Americans were thought to have been members of the Communist Party.

Although the Communist Party proclaimed its allegiance to democratic principles beginning in 1935, it nevertheless remained a dictatorial organization that took its orders from the Soviet Union. Many Americans feared the growing strength of the CP and began to call for its suppression. The CP, however, was never strong enough to gain power for itself. Its chief role in 1930s politics was to channel popular discontent into unions and political parties that would, in turn, force New Dealers to respond to the demands of the nation's poor.

Monopoly

*M*onopoly's precursor was *The Landlord's Game*, a board game invented in 1903 by Lizzie Magie to promote reformer Henry George's economic ideas (see Chapter 19). By the 1930s, the appeal of the game's radical lessons had faded, and Philadelphia's Charles Darrow, an unemployed salesman, reworked the game and re-titled it *Monopoly*. He then licensed it to Parker Brothers, which distributed it nationwide in 1935. *Monopoly* immediately became the best-selling board game in the country.

Q *Monopoly* was fun to play, but did Americans also find meaning in a game of financial triumph and devastation that closely mirrored the economic highs and lows that the nation had itself experienced in the 1920s and 1930s?

© The Granger Collection, New York

The Second New Deal, 1935–1937

Q **FOCUS QUESTION** What was "underconsumptionism," and how did it inform the legislation of the Second New Deal? How was the Second New Deal different from the First New Deal?

The labor unrest of 1934 had taken Roosevelt by surprise. For a time, he kept his distance from the masses mobilizing in his name, but in spring 1935, with the 1936 presidential election looming, he decided to place himself at their head. He called for the "abolition of evil holding companies," attacked the wealthy for their profligate ways, and called for new programs to aid the poor and downtrodden. Rather than becoming a socialist, as his critics charged, Roosevelt sought to reinvigorate his appeal among poorer Americans and turn them away from radical solutions.

Philosophical Underpinnings

To point the New Deal in a more populist direction, Roosevelt turned increasingly to a relatively new economic theory,

underconsumptionism. Advocates of this theory held that a chronic weakness in consumer demand had caused the Great Depression. The path to recovery lay, therefore, not in restricting production, as the architects of the First New Deal had tried to do, but in boosting consumer expenditures through government support for strong labor unions (to force up wages), higher social welfare expenditures (to put more money in the hands of the poor), and ambitious public works projects (to create millions of new jobs).

Underconsumptionists did not worry that new welfare and public works programs might strain the federal budget. If the government found itself short of revenue, it could always borrow additional funds from private sources. These reformers, in fact, viewed government borrowing as a useful antidepression tool. Those who lent the government money would receive a return on their investment; those who received government assistance would have additional income to spend on consumer goods; and manufacturers would profit from increases in consumer spending. Government borrowing, in short, would stimulate the circulation of money through the economy, increase consumer demand, and end the depression. This fiscal policy, a reversal of the conventional wisdom that government should always balance its budget, would in the 1940s come to be known as Keynesianism, after John Maynard Keynes, the British economist who had been its advocate.

As the nation entered its sixth year of the depression, Roosevelt was willing to give these new ideas a try. Reform-minded members of the 1934 Congress were eager for a new round of legislation directed more to the needs of ordinary Americans than to the needs of big business.

Legislation

Congress passed much of that legislation in January to June 1935—a period that came to be known as the Second New Deal. Two of the acts were of historic importance: the **Social Security Act** and the National Labor Relations Act. The Social Security Act, passed in May, required the states to set up welfare funds from which money would be disbursed to the elderly poor, the unemployed, unmarried mothers with dependent children, and the disabled. It also enrolled a majority of working Americans in a pension program that guaranteed them a steady income upon retirement. A federal system of employer and employee taxation was set up to fund the pensions. Despite limitations on coverage and inadequate pension levels, the Social Security Act of 1935 provided a foundation on which future presidents and congresses would erect the American welfare state.

Equally historic was the passage, in June, of the National Labor Relations Act (NLRA). This act delivered what the NRA had only promised: the right of every worker to join a union of his or her own choosing and the obligation of employers to bargain with that union in good faith. The **NLRA**, also called the **Wagner Act** after its Senate sponsor, Robert Wagner of New York, set up a National Labor Relations Board (NLRB) to supervise union elections and to investigate claims of unfair labor practices. The NLRB was to be staffed by federal appointees with power to impose fines on employers who violated the law. Union leaders hailed the act as their Magna Carta.

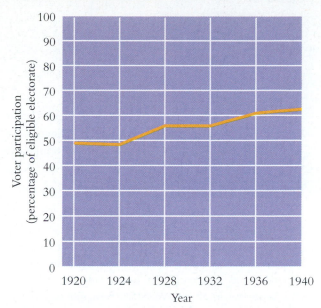

Voter Participation in Presidential Elections, 1920–1940.
Source: Data from *Historical Statistics of the United States, Colonial Times to 1970* (White Plains, NY: Kraus International, 1989), p. 1071.

Congress also passed the Holding Company Act to break up the 13 utility companies that controlled 75 percent of the nation's electric power. It passed the Wealth Tax Act, which increased tax rates on the wealthy from 59 to 75 percent, and on corporations from 13.75 to 15 percent; and it passed the Banking Act, which strengthened the power of the Federal Reserve Board over its member banks. It created the Rural Electrification Administration (REA) to bring electric power to rural households. Finally, it passed the huge $5 billion Emergency Relief Appropriation Act. Roosevelt funneled part of this sum to the PWA, the CCC, and the newly created National Youth Administration (NYA), which provided work and guidance to the nation's youth.

Roosevelt directed most of the new relief money, however, to the **Works Progress Administration (WPA)** under the direction of Harry Hopkins, now known as the New Deal's "minister of relief." The WPA built or improved thousands of schools, playgrounds, airports, and hospitals. WPA crews raked leaves, cleaned streets, and landscaped cities. In the process, the WPA provided jobs to approximately 30 percent of the nation's jobless.

By the time the decade ended, the WPA, in association with an expanded Reconstruction Finance Corporation, the PWA, and other agencies, had built 500,000 miles of roads, 100,000 bridges, 100,000 public buildings, and 600 airports. The New Deal had transformed America's urban and rural landscapes. The awe generated by these public works projects helped Roosevelt retain popular support at a time when the success of the New Deal's economic policies was uncertain. The WPA also funded a vast program of public art, supporting the work of thousands of painters, architects, writers, playwrights, actors, and intellectuals. Beyond extending relief to struggling artists, it fostered the creation of art that spoke to the concerns of ordinary Americans, adorned public buildings with colorful murals, and boosted public morale.

Mr. Deeds Goes To Town (1936)

Directed by Frank Capra.
Starring Gary Cooper (Longfellow Deeds), Jean Arthur (Babe Bennett), Lionel Stander (Cornelius Cobb), George Bancroft (McWade), and H. B. Warner (Judge Walker).

Mr. Deeds Goes to Town was one of several films made by Frank Capra, the most popular director of the 1930s, in which he charmed audiences with fables of simple, small-town heroes vanquishing the evil forces of wealth and decadence. The heroic ordinary American in *Mr. Deeds* is Longfellow Deeds from Mandrake Falls, Vermont, who goes to New York City to claim a fortune left to him by a deceased uncle. Deciding to give the fortune away, he becomes the laughingstock of slick, city lawyers, hardboiled newspapermen and women, cynical literati, and self-styled aristocrats. He also becomes a hero to the unemployed and downtrodden to whom he wishes to give the money. By making the conflict between the wealthy and ordinary Americans central to this story, Capra illuminated convictions that were popular in 1930s politics, as expressed by the New Deal.

The movie delivers its serious message, however, in an entertaining and often hilarious style. Capra was a master of what became known as "screwball" comedy. Longfellow Deeds slides down banisters, locks his bodyguards in a closet, uses the main hall of his inherited mansion as an echo chamber, punches a famous intellectual in the "kisser" (face), and turns his own trial for insanity into a delightful attack on the pretensions and peculiarities of corporate lawyers, judges, and psychiatrists. Central to the

story, too, is an alternately amusing and serious love story between Deeds and a newspaperwoman, Babe Bennett (Jean Arthur). Bennett insinuates herself into Deeds's life by pretending to be a destitute woman without work, shelter, family, or friends. Deeds has long dreamed about rescuing a "lady in distress," and he falls for the beautiful Bennett. Bennett, in turn, uses her privileged access to Deeds to learn about his foibles and to mock them (and him) in newspaper stories written for a ruthless and scandal-hungry public. But Deeds's idealism, honesty, and virtue overwhelm Bennett's cynicism and cause her to fall in love with him. By movie's end, she has proclaimed her love and seems ready to return with Deeds to Mandrake Falls, where she will become his devoted wife and the nurturing mother of his children.

In Babe Bennett's conversion from tough reporter to female romantic, we can detect the gender conservatism of 1930s culture. The movie suggests that Bennett's early cruelty toward Deeds arose as a consequence of her inappropriate involvement in the rough, male realm of newspaper work. Only by abandoning this realm and returning to the "natural" female realm of hearth and home can she recover her true and soft womanly soul. Thus this movie is as rich a document for exploring attitudes toward male and female behavior as for examining relations between the rich and poor. ◼

© The Granger Collection, New York

Gary Cooper as Longfellow Deeds (center of photo with hand on cheek) during his hilarious insanity trial. Cooper's bodyguard, Lionel Stander (Cobb), sits to the left of Cooper, and Cooper is looking at H. B. Warner (Judge Walker), who is presiding at the trial.

Victory in 1936: The New Democratic Coalition

Roosevelt described his Second New Deal as a program to limit the power and privilege of the wealthy few and to increase the security and welfare of ordinary citizens. In his 1936 reelection campaign, he excoriated the corporations as "economic royalists" who had "concentrated into their own hands an almost complete control over other people's property, other people's money, other people's labor—other people's lives." He called on voters to strip the corporations of their power and "save a great and precious form of government for ourselves and the world." American voters responded by handing Roosevelt the greatest victory in the history of American presidential politics. He received 61 percent of the popular vote; Alf Landon of Kansas, his Republican opponent, received only 37 percent. Only two

Construction and Renovation	Education, Health, and Art	Research and Records
East River Drive	Adult education: homemaking, trade and technical skills, and art and culture	Sewage treatment, community health, labor relations, and employment trends surveys
Henry Hudson Parkway	Children's education: remedial reading, lip reading, and field trips	Museum and library catalogs and exhibits
Bronx sewers	Prisoners' vocational training, recreation, and nutrition	Municipal office clerical support
Glendale and Queens public libraries	Dental clinics	Government forms standardization
King's County Hospital	Tuberculosis examination clinics	
Williamsburg housing project	Syphilis and gonorrhea treatment clinics	
School buildings, prisons, and firehouses	City hospital kitchen help, orderlies, laboratory technicians, nurses, doctors	
Coney Island and Brighton Beach boardwalks	Subsistence gardens	
Orchard Beach	Sewing rooms	
Swimming pools, playgrounds, parks, drinking fountains	Central Park sculpture shop	

Source: John David Millet, *The Works Progress Administration in New York City* (Chicago: Public Administration Service, 1938), pp. 95–126.

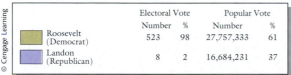

	Electoral Vote		Popular Vote	
	Number	%	Number	%
Roosevelt (Democrat)	523	98	27,757,333	61
Landon (Republican)	8	2	16,684,231	37

Map 25.5 Presidential Election, 1936. Franklin D. Roosevelt's reelection numbers were overwhelming: 98 percent of the electoral vote, and more than 60 percent of the popular vote. No previous election in American history had been so one-sided.

© Cengage Learning

for the first time, many of them European ethnics, 5 million voted for Roosevelt. Among the poorest Americans, Roosevelt received 80 percent of the vote. Black voters in the North left the Republican Party—the "Party of Lincoln"—calculating that their interests would be served better by the "Party of the Common Man." Roosevelt also did well among white middle-class voters, many of whom stood to benefit from the Social Security Act. These constituencies would constitute the "Roosevelt coalition" for most of the next 40 years, helping to solidify the Democratic Party as the new majority party in American politics.

Rhetoric versus Reality

Roosevelt's 1935–36 anti-corporate rhetoric was more radical than the laws he supported. The Wealth Tax Act took considerably less out of wealthy incomes and estates than was advertised, and the utility companies that the Holding Company Act was meant to break up remained largely intact. Moreover, Roosevelt promised more than he delivered to the nation's poor. Farm workers, for example, were not covered by the Social Security Act or by the National Labor Relations Act. Consequently, thousands of African American sharecroppers in the South, along with substantial numbers of Mexican American farm workers in the Southwest, missed out on protections and benefits brought by these laws. The sharecroppers were shut out because southern Democrats would not have voted for an act that was seen as improving the economic or social condition of southern blacks. For the same reason, the New Deal made little effort to restore voting rights to southern blacks or to protect their basic civil rights. White supremacy lived on in New Deal democracy.

states, Maine and Vermont, representing a mere eight electoral votes, went for Landon.

The 1936 election won the Democratic Party its reputation as the party of reform and the party of the "forgotten American." Of the 6 million Americans who went to the polls

Roosevelt's 1935–36 populist stance also obscured the support that some capitalists were giving the Second New Deal. In the West, Henry J. Kaiser headed a consortium of six companies that built the Hoover, Bonneville, and Grand Coulee dams; in Texas, building contractors Herman and George Brown were bankrolling a group of elected officials that included a young Democratic congressman named Lyndon Johnson. In the Midwest and the East, Roosevelt's corporate supporters included real estate developers, mass merchandisers (such as Bambergers and Sears, Roebuck), clothing manufacturers, and the like. These firms, in turn, had financial connections with recently established investment banks such as Lehman Brothers and Goldman Sachs, competitors of the House of Morgan and its allies in the Republican banking establishment, and with consumer-oriented banks such as the Bank of America and the Bowery Savings Bank. They tolerated strong labor unions, welfare programs, and high levels of government spending in the belief that these developments would strengthen consumer spending, but they had no intention of surrendering their own wealth or power. The Democratic Party had become, in effect, the party of the masses and one section of big business. The conflicting interests of these two constituencies would create tensions within the Democratic Party throughout the years of its political domination.

Men, Women, and Reform

The years 1936 and 1937 were exciting ones for academics, policymakers, and bureaucrats who designed and administered the rapidly growing roster of New Deal programs and agencies. Fueled by idealism and dedication, they were confident they could make the New Deal work. They planned and won congressional approval for the Farm Security Administration (FSA), an agency designed to improve the economic lot of tenant farmers, sharecroppers, and farm laborers. They drafted and passed legislation that outlawed child labor, set minimum wages and maximum hours for adult workers, and committed the federal government to building low-cost housing. They investigated and tried to regulate concentrations of corporate power.

Although they worked on behalf of "the people," the New Dealers constituted a new class of technocrats. The prospect of building a strong state committed to prosperity and justice fired their imaginations. They delighted in the intellectual challenge and the technical complexity of social policy.

Many of the male New Dealers had earned advanced degrees in law and economics at elite universities such as Harvard, Columbia, and Wisconsin. Not all had been raised among wealth and privilege, however. To his credit, Franklin Roosevelt was the first president since his cousin Theodore Roosevelt to welcome Jews and Catholics into his administration. Some became members of Roosevelt's inner circle of advisers—men such as Thomas "Tommy the Cork" Corcoran, Jim Farley, Ben Cohen, and Samuel Rosenman. These men had struggled to make their way, first on the streets and then in school and at work. They brought to the New Deal intellectual aggressiveness, quick minds, and mental toughness.

The profile of New Deal women was different. Although a few, notably Eleanor Roosevelt and Secretary of Labor

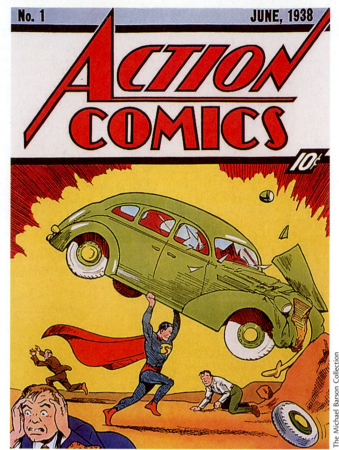

Man of Steel. The comic book *Superman* debuted in 1938, with the cover that appears in this reproduction. The character Superman partook of the New Deal's commitment to help ordinary Americans in need while offering men a fantasy about unconquerable male power.

Frances Perkins (the first woman to be appointed to the U.S. cabinet), were more visible than women in previous administrations had been, many of the female New Dealers worked in relative obscurity, in agencies such as the Women's Bureau or the Children's Bureau (both in the Department of Labor). Women who worked on major legislation, as did Mary Van Kleeck on the Social Security Act, or who directed major programs, as did Jane Hoey, chief of the Social Security's Bureau of Public Assistance, received less credit than men in comparable positions. Moreover, female New Dealers tended to be a generation older than their male colleagues and were more likely to be Protestant than Catholic or Jewish. Many of them had known each other since the days of progressive-era reform and woman suffrage (see Chapter 21).

The New Deal offered these female reformers little opportunity to advance the cause of women's equality. Demands for greater economic opportunity, sexual freedom, and full equality for women were put forward less often in the 1930s than they had been in the preceding two decades. One reason was that the women's movement had lost momentum after achieving the vote in 1920 (see Chapter 24). Another was that prominent New Deal women, rather than vigorously pursuing a campaign for equal rights, chose to

The Michael Barson Collection

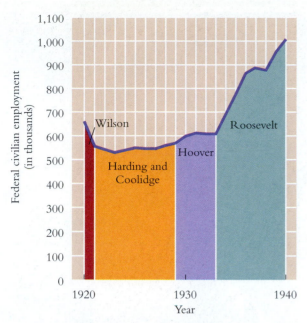

Growth in Federal Civilian Employment, 1920–1940.
Source: Data from *Historical Statistics of the United States, Colonial Times to 1970* (White Plains, NY: Kraus International, 1989), p. 1102.

concentrate instead on "protective legislation"—laws that safeguarded female workers. Those who insisted that women needed special protections could not easily argue that women were equal to men in all respects.

Feminism was also hemmed in on all sides by a male hostility that the depression had intensified. Many men had built their male identities on the value of hard work and the ability to provide economic security for their families. For them, the loss of work unleashed feelings of inadequacy. Male vulnerability increased as unemployment rates of men—most of whom labored in blue-collar industries—rose higher than those of women, many of whom worked in white-collar occupations less affected by job cutbacks. Many fathers and husbands resented wives and daughters who had taken over their breadwinning roles.

This male anxiety had political and social consequences. Several states passed laws outlawing the hiring of married women. New Deal relief agencies were reluctant to authorize aid for unemployed women. The labor movement made protection of the male wage earner one of its principal goals. The Social Security pension system left out waitresses, domestic servants, and other largely female occupations. Norman Cousins of the *Saturday Evening Post* suggested that the depression could be ended simply by firing 10 million working women and giving their jobs to men. "Presto!" he declared. "No unemployment, no relief rolls. No Depression."

Many artists introduced a strident masculinism into their painting and sculpture. Mighty *Superman*, the new comic-strip hero of 1938, reflected the spirit of the times. Superman was depicted as a working-class hero, who on several occasions saved workers from coal mine explosions and other disasters caused by the greed and negligence of villainous employers.

Superman's greatest vulnerability, however, other than kryptonite, was his attraction to the *working* woman, Lois Lane.

RATES OF UNEMPLOYMENT IN SELECTED MALE AND FEMALE OCCUPATIONS, 1930

Male Occupations	Percentage Male	Percentage Unemployed
Iron and steel	96%	13%
Forestry and fishing	99	10
Mining	99	18
Heavy manufacturing	86	13
Carpentry	100	19
Laborers (road and street)	100	13
Female Occupations	**Percentage Female**	**Percentage Unemployed**
Stenographers and typists	96%	5%
Laundresses	99	3
Trained nurses	98	4
Housekeepers	92	3
Telephone operators	95	3
Dressmakers	100	4

Source: U.S. Department of Commerce, Bureau of the Census, *Fifteenth Census of the United States, 1930, Population* (Washington, D.C.: Government Printing Office, 1931).

An Activist First Lady. No woman was more prominent in the 1930s than Eleanor Roosevelt. During the decade, she met with many different groups of Americans, including the miners depicted in this photo, seeking to learn more about their condition and the ways in which the New Deal could assist them.

He could never resolve his dilemma by marrying Lois and tucking her away in a safe domestic sphere, because the continuation of the comic strip demanded that Superman be repeatedly exposed to kryptonite and female danger. But the producers of male and female images in other mass media, such as the movies, faced no such technical obstacles. Anxious men could take comfort from the conclusion of the movie *Woman of the Year*, in which Spencer Tracy persuades the ambitious Katharine Hepburn to exchange her successful newspaper career for the bliss of motherhood and homemaking. From a thousand different points, 1930s politics and culture made it clear that a woman's proper place was in the home. Faced with such obstacles, it is not surprising that women activists failed to make feminism a major part of New Deal reform.

Labor in Politics and Culture

In 1935, John L. Lewis of the United Mine Workers, Sidney Hillman of the Amalgamated Clothing Workers, and the leaders of six other unions that had seceded from the American Federation of Labor (AFL) cobbled together a new labor organization. The Committee for Industrial Organization (**CIO**)—later renamed the Congress of Industrial Organizations—aspired to organize millions of unskilled and semiskilled workers whom the AFL had largely ignored. In 1936, Lewis and Hillman created a second organization, Labor's Non-Partisan League (LNPL), to channel labor's money, energy, and talent into Roosevelt's reelection campaign. Roosevelt welcomed the league's help, and labor would become a key constituency of the new Democratic coalition. The passage of the Wagner Act and the creation of the NLRB in 1935 enhanced the labor movement's status and credibility. Membership in labor unions climbed steadily, and in short order union members began flexing their muscles.

In late 1936, the United Auto Workers (UAW) took on General Motors, widely regarded as the most powerful corporation in the world. Workers occupied key GM factories in

Woody Guthrie. A bard from Okemah, Oklahoma, Guthrie was embraced by millions for his homespun melodies and lyrics and for his hopeful message that Americans could survive the depression with their dignity and sense of humor intact.

Flint, Michigan, declaring that their **sit-down strike** would continue until GM agreed to recognize the UAW and negotiate a collective bargaining agreement. Frank Murphy, the pro-labor governor of Michigan, refused to use National Guard troops to evict the strikers, and Roosevelt declined to send federal troops. A 50-year-old practice of using soldiers to break strikes ended, and General Motors capitulated after a month of resistance. Soon, the U.S. Steel Corporation, which had defeated unionists in the bloody strike of 1919 (see Chapter 23), announced that it was ready to negotiate a contract with the newly formed CIO steelworkers union.

The labor movement's public stature grew along with its size. Many writers and artists, funded through the WPA, depicted the labor movement as the voice of the people and the embodiment of the nation's values. Murals sprang up in post offices and other public buildings featuring portraits of blue-collar Americans at work. Broadway's most celebrated play in 1935 was Clifford Odets's *Waiting for Lefty*, a raw drama about taxi drivers who confront their bosses and organize an honest union. *Pins and Needles*, a 1937 musical about the hopes and dreams of garment workers, performed by actual members of the International Ladies Garment Workers Union, became the longest-running play in Broadway history (until *Oklahoma!* broke its record of 1,108 performances in 1943).

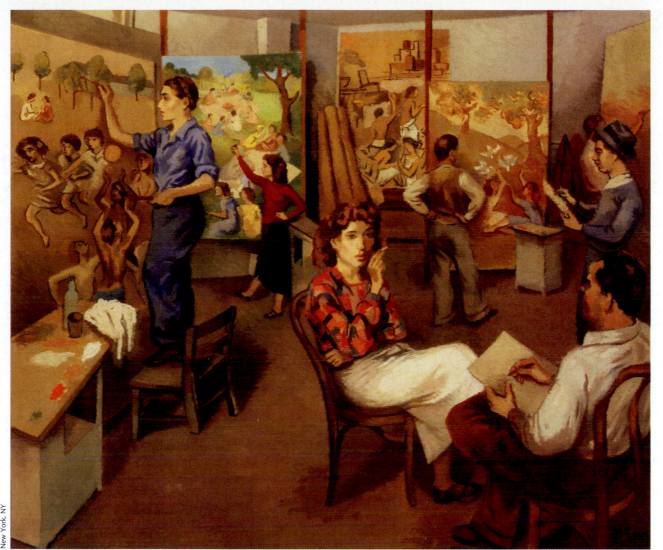

WPA Artists at Work. This 1935 painting by Moses Soyer shows painters hired by the WPA at work on their art, much of it commissioned by local and state governments to be hung in post offices, schools, city halls, train stations, and other public buildings.

Similarly, many of the most popular novels and movies of the 1930s celebrated the decency, honesty, and patriotism of ordinary Americans. In *Mr. Deeds Goes to Town* (1936) and *Mr. Smith Goes to Washington* (1939), Frank Capra delighted movie audiences with fables of simple, small-town heroes vanquishing the evil forces of wealth and decadence. Likewise, in *The Grapes of Wrath*, the best-selling novel of 1939, John Steinbeck told an epic tale of an Oklahoma family's fortitude in surviving eviction from their land, migrating westward, and suffering exploitation in the "promised land" of California. In 1940, John Ford turned Steinbeck's novel into one of that year's highest grossing and most acclaimed movies. Moviegoers found special meaning in the declaration of one of the story's main characters, Ma Joad: "We'll go on forever . . . cause we're the people."

The Okie migrants to California included a writer and musician named Woody Guthrie. Born in 1913 in Okemah, Oklahoma, Woody Guthrie grew up in nearby Pampa, Texas. He wasn't born poor—his father was a small businessman and a local politician—but by the time he reached his twenties, Guthrie had known a great deal of hardship: his father's business failed, three family homes burned down, one sister died from

burns, and then the drought and dust storms struck. In the 1930s, Guthrie joined the large migration of Okies to California. There, his musical gifts were discovered, chiefly because radio stations, in particular, were keen to put "singing cowboys" on the air. Guthrie had emerged from a country music tradition in Texas and Oklahoma and found an audience among the many people from those states who had gone to California.

Guthrie also developed a broader appeal as he cast himself as the bard of ordinary Americans everywhere. He loved America for the beauty of its landscape and its people, sentiments he expressed in one of his most popular songs, "This Land Is Your Land," which he wrote in 1940 in response to Irving Berlin's "God Bless America" (a song Guthrie did not like because of the false sense of complacency he thought it induced; for Berlin's own views about "God Bless America," see Chapter 23). Guthrie did not possess a refined singing voice, but his "hillbilly" lyrics, melodies, and humor were inventive and often inspiring. He would become a powerful influence on subsequent generations of musicians, including such major figures as Bob Dylan and Bruce Springsteen.

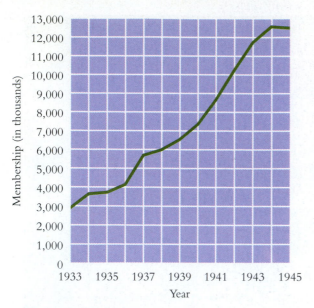

Labor Union Membership, 1933–1945.
Source: From Christopher Tomlins, "AFL Unions in the 1930s," in Melvyn Dubofsky and Stephen Burwood, eds., *Labor* (New York: Garland, 1990), p. 1023.

Guthrie traveled extensively in the 1930s, from Los Angeles to New York and from Texas to Washington state. The more he learned about the hardships of individual Americans, the angrier and more politically active he became. He drew close to the labor movement and to the Communist Party, and increasingly, in his writings and songs, he criticized the industrialists, financiers, and their political agents who, he believed, had brought the depression on America. But Guthrie always associated his criticism with the hope that the working people of America, if united, could take back their land—which is the message he meant to convey when he sang "This Land Is Your Land"—and restore its greatness. The optimism of his message underscored how much the cultural mood had changed since the early 1930s. In his focus on ordinary working Americans, in his hope for the future, and in his fusion of dissent and patriotism, Guthrie was emblematic of a major stream of culture and politics in the late 1930s.

America's Minorities and the New Deal

 FOCUS QUESTION Which minority groups in American society benefited the most from the New Deal, and which benefited the least?

Reformers in the 1930s generally believed that issues of capitalism's viability, economic recovery, and the inequality of wealth and power outweighed problems of racial and ethnic discrimination; only in the case of American Indians did New Dealers pass legislation specifically designed to improve a

minority's social and economic position. Because they were disproportionately poor, most minority groups did profit from the populist and pro-labor character of New Deal reforms, but the gains were distributed unevenly. Eastern and Southern European ethnics benefited the most, and African Americans and Mexican Americans advanced the least.

Eastern and Southern European Ethnics

Eastern and Southern European immigrants and their children had begun mobilizing politically in the 1920s in response to religious and racial discrimination (see Chapter 24). Roosevelt understood their political importance well, for he was a product of New York Democratic politics, where men such as Robert Wagner and Al Smith had begun to organize the ethnic vote even before 1920 (see Chapter 21). He made sure that a significant portion of New Deal monies for welfare, building and road construction, and unemployment relief reached the urban areas where most European ethnics lived. As a result, Jewish and Catholic Americans, especially those descended from Eastern and Southern European immigrants, voted for Roosevelt in overwhelming numbers. The New Deal did not eliminate anti-Semitism and anti-Catholicism from American society, but it did allow millions of European ethnics to believe, for the first time, that they would overcome the second-class status they had long endured.

Eastern and Southern European ethnics also benefited from their sizable presence in the mass-production industries of the Northeast, Midwest, and West Coast and in the new labor unions. Roosevelt understood and feared the power they wielded through their labor organizations.

African Americans

The New Deal did more to reproduce patterns of racial discrimination than to advance the cause of racial equality. African Americans who belonged to CIO unions or who lived in northern cities benefited from New Deal programs, but most blacks lived in the rural South, where they were barred from voting, largely excluded from AAA programs, and denied federal protection in their efforts to form agricultural unions. The CCC ran separate camps for black and white youth. The TVA hired few blacks. Those enrolled in the CWA and other work-relief programs frequently received less pay than whites for doing the same jobs. Roosevelt consistently refused to support legislation to make lynching a federal crime.

This failure to push a strong civil rights agenda did not mean that New Dealers were oblivious to concerns about race. Eleanor Roosevelt spoke out frequently against racial injustice. In 1939, she resigned from the Daughters of the American Revolution when the organization refused to allow black opera singer **Marian Anderson** to perform in its concert hall. She then pressured the federal government into granting Anderson permission to sing from the steps of the Lincoln Memorial. On Easter Sunday, 75,000 people gathered to hear Anderson and to demonstrate their support for racial equality. The president did not attend.

MUSICAL LINK TO THE PAST

An African American Rhapsody

Composer: Duke Ellington
Title: "Creole Rhapsody Parts One and Two" (1931—the second recording)
Performers: Duke Ellington and His Orchestra

By 1931, Duke Ellington had established himself as the premier African American bandleader, his hit songs airing nightly courtesy of a live national radio hook-up (the first for any black act) emanating from Harlem's Cotton Club. But Ellington was not satisfied with popularity and fame. "I have always been a firm believer in musical experimentation," he proclaimed during this period. "To stand still musically is equivalent to losing ground." Ellington wished to be viewed as a serious artist and composer, and "Creole Rhapsody" represented one of his first major bids to cultivate this image. Most pop records seldom broke the three-minute barrier, but "Creole" lasted nine minutes, spanning two sides of a 78-RPM record. While jazz and blues artists generally composed within 8-, 12-, and 16-bar forms, Ellington experimented with different phrase lengths. In an era when blacks were primarily associated with "torrid" dance records, the shifting tempos of "Creole" marked it as a record for concentrated listening. Ellington also composed the solos to ensure that they jelled with his elaborate arrangement, which did away with musical improvisation, a trademark of jazz and blues performances. Ellington was more involved with recording technique than most artists, sometimes placing microphones far away from his players to achieve a more evocative sound.

"Creole Rhapsody" reached only minor hit status, but Ellington and his manager Irving Mills nevertheless used this recording to bolster Ellington's image as a serious artist, a status that no other African American of his period had achieved in the white-dominated popular music marketplace. In contrast to the denigrating stereotypes that accompanied the appearance of most blacks in the mass media, Ellington was respectfully portrayed in the manner of a classical conductor, usually clad in a tuxedo and tails, baton in his hand.

Not all contemporary observers endorsed the idea of Ellington as a major composer. The English critic Constant Lambert wrote in 1934 that "Ellington is definitely a *petit maitre*," a "small master" not capable of extended composition. Many music lovers, however, embraced "Creole Rhapsody." The New York School of Music named it the best composition of the year because "it portrayed Negro life as no other piece had." Ellington attempted to continue the critics, both the laudatory and castigating ones, at a distance and to continue searching for musical innovation. He almost never took a formal political stand or made a speech demanding civil rights for blacks during the 1930s, choosing to let his music and his reputation as an innovative band leader speak for themselves.

Q From listening to "Creole Rhapsody," can you discern what the New York School of Music meant in celebrating this composition as a unique portrait of Negro life?

Listen to an audio recording of this music on the Musical Links to the Past CD.

Roosevelt did eliminate segregationist practices in the federal government that had been in place since Woodrow Wilson's presidency. He appointed Mary McLeod Bethune, Robert Weaver, William Hastie, and other African Americans to important second-level posts in his administration. Working closely with each other in what came to be known as the Black Cabinet, these officials fought hard to end discrimination in New Deal programs.

Roosevelt, however, refused to support the Black Cabinet if it meant alienating white southern senators who controlled key congressional committees. He believed that pushing for civil rights would cost him the support of the white South. Meanwhile, African Americans and their supporters were not yet strong enough as an electoral constituency or as a reform movement to compel Roosevelt to support a civil rights agenda.

Mexican Americans

The Mexican American experience in the Great Depression was particularly harsh. In 1931, Hoover's secretary of labor, William N. Doak, announced a plan for repatriating illegal aliens (returning them to their land of origin) and giving their jobs to American citizens. The federal campaign quickly focused on Mexican immigrants in California and the Southwest. The U.S. Immigration Service rounded up large numbers of Mexicans and Mexican Americans and demanded that each detainee prove his or her legal status. Those who failed to produce the necessary documentation were deported. Local and state governments pressured many more Mexicans into leaving. The combined efforts of federal, state, and local governments created a climate of fear in Mexican communities that prompted 500,000 to return to Mexico by 1935. This total equaled the number of Mexicans who had come to the United States in the 1920s. Los Angeles lost one-third of its Mexican population. Included in repatriate ranks were a significant number of legal immigrants who were unable to produce their immigration papers, the American-born children of illegals, and some Mexican Americans who had lived in the Southwest for generations.

The advent of the New Deal in 1933 eased but did not eliminate pressure on Chicano communities. New Deal agencies made money available for relief; Mexican Americans who worked in urban, blue-collar industries joined unions in large numbers. Most Chicanos, however, lived in rural areas and labored in agricultural jobs, and the New Deal offered them little help. The National Labor Relations Act did not protect their right to organize unions, and the Social Security Act excluded them from the new federal welfare system. Where Mexicans gained access to relief rolls, they often received payments lower than those given to "Anglos" (whites). New Dealers also did not do much to dissuade local officials from continuing their campaign to deport Mexican immigrants.

Life grew harder for immigrant Mexicans who stayed behind. The Mexican cultural renaissance that had emerged in 1920s Los Angeles (see Chapter 24) stalled. Mexicans in the city retreated into the separate community of East Los Angeles. To many, they became the "invisible minority."

American Indians

From the 1880s until the early 1930s, federal policy had contributed to the elimination of American Indians as a distinctive population. The Dawes Act of 1887 (see Chapter 18) had called for tribal lands to be broken up and allotted to individual owners in the hope that Indians would adopt the work habits and life styles of white farmers. But American Indians had proved stubbornly loyal to their languages, religions, and cultures. Few of them succeeded as farmers, and many lost land to white speculators. By 1933, nearly half the American Indians living on reservations whose land had been allotted were landless, and many who retained allotments held land that was largely desert or semidesert.

The shrinking land base in combination with a growing population deepened American Indian poverty. The assimilationist pressures on American Indians, meanwhile, reached a climax in the 1920s, when the Bureau of Indian Affairs (BIA) outlawed Indian religious ceremonies, forced children from tribal communities into federal boarding schools, banned polygamy, and imposed limits on the length of men's hair.

Government officials working in the Hoover administration began to question this assimilationist policy, but its reversal had to await the New Deal and Roosevelt's appointment of **John Collier** as the commissioner of the BIA. Collier pressured the CCC, AAA, and other New Deal agencies to employ Indians on

© Buyenlagre/Getty Images

Mexican Hardship. The Great Depression made it difficult for Mexican agricultural workers in California to find adequate work. Many suffered additional injury when state and local authorities pressured them into returning to Mexico.

Indian Children. An Arnold Rothstein photograph depicting three Indian children on the Mescalero Reservation in New Mexico in 1936.

projects that improved reservation land and trained Indians in land conservation methods. He prevailed on Congress to pass the Pueblo Relief Act of 1933, which compensated Pueblos for land taken from them in the 1920s, and the Johnson-O'Malley Act of 1934, which provided funds to the states for Indian health care, welfare, and education. As part of his campaign to make the BIA more responsive to American Indian needs, Collier increased the number of Indian BIA employees from a few hundred in 1933 to a 4,600 in 1940.

Collier also took steps to abolish federal boarding schools, encourage enrollment in local public schools, and establish community day schools. He insisted that American Indians be allowed to practice their traditional religions, and he created the Indian Arts and Crafts Board in 1935 to nurture traditional Indian artists and to help them market their work.

The centerpiece of Collier's reform strategy was the Indian Reorganization Act (IRA, also known as the Wheeler-Howard Act) of 1934, which revoked the allotment provisions of the Dawes Act. This landmark act recognized the rights of Native American tribes to chart their own political, cultural, and economic futures. It reflected Collier's commitment to "cultural pluralism," a doctrine that celebrated the diversity of peoples and cultures in American society and sought to protect that diversity against the pressures of assimilation (for the origins of cultural pluralism, see Chapter 20). Specifically, the IRA restored land to tribes, granted Indians the right to establish constitutions and bylaws for self-government, and provided support for new tribal corporations that would regulate the use of communal lands.

Collier encountered opposition everywhere: from Protestant missionaries and cultural conservatives who wanted to continue an assimilationist policy; to white farmers and businessmen who feared that the new legislation would restrict their access to Native American land; and even from a sizable number of Indian groups, some of which had embraced assimilation and others that viewed the IRA cynically, as one more attempt by the federal government to impose "the white man's will" on the Indian peoples. This opposition made the IRA a more modest bill than the one Collier had originally championed.

A vocal minority of Indians continued to oppose the act even after its passage. The Navajo, the nation's largest tribe, voted to reject its terms as did 76 other tribes. Still, 181 tribes, nearly 70 percent of the total, supported Collier's reform and began organizing new governments under the IRA. Although their quest for independence would suffer setbacks, these tribes gained significant measures of freedom and autonomy during the New Deal.

The New Deal Abroad

Q **FOCUS QUESTION** What were the achievements and limitations of the New Deal's turn toward internationalism?

When he first entered office, Roosevelt favored a nationalist approach to international relations. The United States, he believed, should pursue foreign policies to benefit its domestic affairs, without regard for the effects of those policies on world trade and international stability. Thus, in June 1933, Roosevelt pulled the United States out of the World Economic Conference in London, a meeting called by leading nations to strengthen the gold standard and thereby stabilize the value of their currencies. Roosevelt feared that the United States would be forced into an agreement designed to keep the gold content of the dollar high and U.S. commodity prices low, which would frustrate New Deal efforts to inflate the prices of agricultural and industrial goods.

Soon after his withdrawal from the London conference, however, Roosevelt put the United States on a more internationalist course. In November 1933, he became the first president to recognize the Soviet Union and to establish diplomatic ties with its Communist rulers. In December 1933, he inaugurated a **Good Neighbor Policy** toward Latin America by formally renouncing U.S. rights to intervene in the affairs of Latin American nations. To back up his pledge, Roosevelt ordered home the Marines stationed in Haiti and Nicaragua; scuttled the Platt Amendment that had given the United States control over the Cuban government since 1901; and granted Panama more political autonomy and a greater administrative role in operating the Panama Canal (see Chapter 22).

None of this, however, meant that the United States had given up its influence over Latin America. When a 1934 revolution brought a radical government to power in Cuba, the U.S. ambassador there worked with conservative Cubans to replace the government with a regime more favorable to U.S. interests. The United States did refrain from sending troops to Cuba. It also kept its troops at home in 1936 when Mexico nationalized several U.S.- and British-owned petroleum companies. Instead, the United States demanded that Mexico compensate the oil companies for their lost property,

Unemployment, 1920–1945

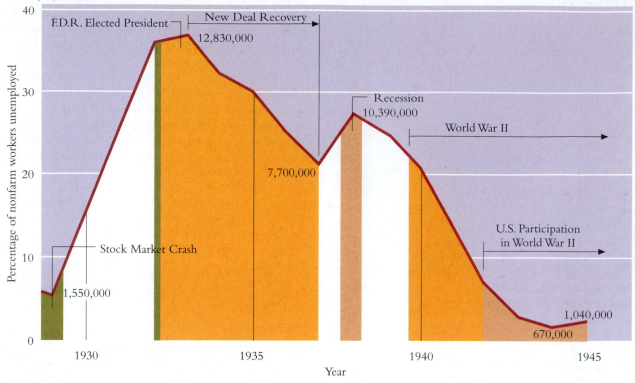

Unemployment in the Nonfarm Labor Force, 1929–1945.
Source: Data from *Historical Statistics of the United States, Colonial Times to 1970* (White Plains, NY: Kraus International, 1989), p. 126.

which Mexico eventually did. In such ways, the United States exercised restraint while remaining the dominant force in hemispheric affairs.

The Roosevelt administration's internationalism also reflected its interest in stimulating trade. American businessmen wanted access to the Soviet Union's domestic market. Latin America was already a major market for the United States, but one in need of greater stability. To win the support of American traders and investors, Roosevelt stressed how the Good Neighbor Policy would improve the region's business climate.

Roosevelt further expressed his commitment to international trade through his support for the Reciprocal Trade Agreement, passed by Congress in 1934. This act allowed the United States to lower its tariffs by as much as 50 percent in exchange for similar reductions by other nations. By the end of 1935, the United States had negotiated reciprocal trade agreements with 14 countries. Roosevelt's emphasis on international trade—a move consonant with the Second New Deal's program of increasing the circulation of goods and money through the economy—further solidified support for the New Deal in parts of the business community, especially among those firms, such as United Fruit and Coca-Cola, with large overseas investments.

Actually increasing the volume of international trade was more difficult than passing legislation to encourage it. In Germany and Italy, belligerent nationalists Adolf Hitler and Benito Mussolini told their people that the solution to their ills lay not in foreign trade but in military strength and conquest. Throughout the world, similar appeals to national pride proved more

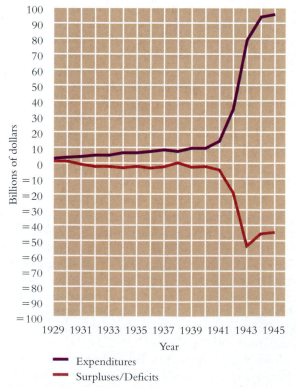

Federal Expenditures and Surpluses/Deficits, 1929–1945.
Source: Data from *Historical Statistics of the United States, Colonial Times to 1970* (White Plains, NY: Kraus International, 1989), p. 1105.

popular than calls for tariff reductions and increases in global trade. In the face of this historical current, the New Deal's internationalist economic policies made limited headway.

Stalemate, 1937–1940

 Q **FOCUS QUESTION** Why did the New Deal lose momentum in 1937 and 1938?

By 1937 and 1938, the New Deal had begun to lose momentum. One reason was an emerging split between working-class and middle-class Democrats. After the UAW's victory over General Motors in 1937, other workers began to imitate the successful tactics of the Flint, Michigan, militants. Sit-down strikes spread to many industries and regions, a development that worried many middle-class Americans.

The Court-Packing Fiasco

The president's proposal on February 5, 1937, to alter the makeup of the Supreme Court exacerbated middle-class fears. Roosevelt asked Congress to give him the power to appoint one new Supreme Court justice for every member of the court who was older than age 70 and who had served for at least 10 years. His stated reason was that the current justices were too old and feeble to handle the large volume of cases coming before them, but his real purpose was to prevent the conservative justices on the court—most had been appointed by Republican presidents—from dismantling his New Deal. His proposal, if accepted, would have given him the authority to appoint six additional justices, thereby securing a pro-New Deal majority.

The president seemed genuinely surprised by the indignation that greeted his **"court-packing"** proposal. Although working-class support for Roosevelt remained strong, many middle-class voters turned away from the New Deal. In 1937 and 1938, a conservative opposition took shape, uniting Republicans and conservative Democrats (many of them southerners) who believed that the changes unleashed by the New Deal had gone too far.

Ironically, Roosevelt's court-packing scheme may have been unnecessary. In March 1937, just one month after he proposed his plan, Supreme Court Justice Owen J. Roberts, a former opponent of New Deal programs, decided to support them. In April and May, the Court upheld the constitutionality of the Wagner Act and Social Security Act, both by a 5-to-4 margin. The principal reforms of the New Deal would endure. Roosevelt allowed his court-reform proposal to die in Congress that summer. Within three years, five of the aging justices had retired, giving Roosevelt the opportunity to fashion a court more to his liking. Nonetheless, Roosevelt's reputation had suffered.

The Recession of 1937–1938

Whatever hope Roosevelt may have had for a quick recovery from his attempt at court-packing was dashed by a sharp recession that struck the country in late 1937 and 1938. The New Deal programs of 1935 had stimulated the economy, prompting Roosevelt to scale back relief programs. Meanwhile, new payroll taxes took $2 billion from wage earners' salaries to finance the Social Security pension fund even though the government did not intend to begin paying benefits until 1941. Thus, the government substantially shrunk the volume of dollars it was putting into circulation. Starved for money, the economy and stock market crashed once again. Unemployment, which had fallen to 14 percent, shot back up to 20 percent. In the 1938 elections, voters vented their frustration by electing many conservative Democrats and Republicans who were opposed to the New Deal. These conservatives could not dismantle the New Deal reforms already in place, but they did block the passage of new programs.

Conclusion

Roosevelt first assumed the presidency in the same week that Adolf Hitler established a Nazi dictatorship in Germany. Some feared that Roosevelt, by accumulating more power into the hands of the federal government than had ever been held in peacetime, aspired to autocratic rule. Nothing of the sort happened. Roosevelt and the New Dealers not only strengthened democracy, they also inspired millions of Americans who had never before voted to go to the polls. Groups that had been marginalized—Eastern and Southern European ethnics, unskilled workers, American Indians—now believed that their political activism could make a difference.

Not everyone benefited to the same degree from the broadening of American democracy. Northern factory workers, farm owners, European American ethnics, and middle-class consumers (especially homeowners) were among the groups who benefited most. In contrast, the socialist and communist elements of the labor movement failed to achieve their radical aims. Unionization proceeded far more slowly among southern industrial workers, black and white. Sizable occupational groups, such as farm laborers and domestic servants, were denied Social Security benefits. Feminists made little headway. African Americans and Mexican Americans gained meager influence over public policy.

New Deal reforms might not have mattered to any group if the Second World War had not rescued the New Deal economic program. With government war orders flooding factories from 1941 on, the economy grew vigorously, unemployment vanished, and prosperity finally returned. The architects of the Second New Deal, who had argued that large government expenditures would stimulate consumer demand and trigger economic recovery, were vindicated.

The war also solidified the political reforms of the 1930s: an increased role for the government in regulating the economy and in ensuring the social welfare of those unable to help themselves; strong state support of unionization, agricultural subsidies, and progressive tax policies; and the use of government power and money to develop the West and Southwest. In contrast to progressivism, the reforms of the New Deal endured. Voters returned Roosevelt to office for unprecedented third and fourth terms, and these same voters remained wedded for the next 40 years to Roosevelt's central idea: that a powerful state would enhance the pursuit of liberty and equality. ⚡

CHAPTER REVIEW

REVIEW QUESTIONS

1. What caused the crash of 1929, and why did the ensuing depression last so long?
2. Why did Hoover lose his popularity?
3. In what ways did the political pessimism of the early 1930s influence American culture?
4. What events transformed Franklin D. Roosevelt into a focused politician? What beliefs defined his liberalism?
5. What do you consider to be the three or four most important pieces of legislation in the First New Deal? Why?
6. What forms did political unrest take in 1934 and 1935?
7. What was "underconsumptionism," and how did it inform the legislation of the Second New Deal? How was the Second New Deal different from the First New Deal?
8. Which minority groups in American society benefited the most from the New Deal, and which benefited least?
9. What were the achievements and limitations of the New Deal's turn toward internationalism?
10. Why did the New Deal lose momentum in 1937 and 1938?

CRITICAL THINKING QUESTIONS

1. How did the Great Depression and New Deal shape the literature and art of the 1930s?
2. Why did the New Deal prove so popular given that, in the 1930s, it failed to solve the problem of unemployment?

IDENTIFICATIONS

Review your understanding of the following key terms, people, and events for this chapter (terms in bold in text are included in the Glossary).

liberalism, p. 682
Bonus Army, p. 685
Franklin D. Roosevelt, p. 687
Eleanor Roosevelt, p. 688
Agricultural Adjustment Administration (AAA), p. 690
National Recovery Administration (NRA), p. 691
Tennessee Valley Authority (TVA), p. 693
Huey Long, p. 695

Father Charles Coughlin, p. 695
Communist Party, p. 697
underconsumptionism, p. 699
Social Security Act, p. 699
NLRA / Wagner Act, p. 699
Works Progress Administration (WPA), p. 699
CIO, p. 703
sit-down strike, p. 704
Marian Anderson, p. 706
John Collier, p. 708
Good Neighbor Policy, p. 709
court-packing, p. 711

SUGGESTED READINGS

T. H. Watkins, *The Great Depression: America in the 1930s* (1993), provides a broad overview of society and politics during the 1930s, and David M. Kennedy, *Freedom from Fear: The American People in Depression and War, 1929–1945* (1999) offers a more in-depth account.

The most complete biography of FDR, and one that is remarkably good at balancing Roosevelt's life and times, is Kenneth S. Davis, *FDR* (1972–1993), in four volumes. On Eleanor Roosevelt, see Blanche Wiesen Cook, *Eleanor Roosevelt, vol. 1* (1992). On the New Deal, see William E. Leuchtenberg, *Franklin D. Roosevelt and the New Deal, 1932–1940* (1963) and Steve Fraser and Gary Gerstle, eds., *The Rise and Fall of the New Deal Order, 1930–1980* (1989). For a sharply critical view of the New Deal, consult Amity Shlaes, *The Forgotten Man: A New History of the Great Depression* (2007).

Michael Denning, *The Cultural Front: The Laboring of American Culture in the Twentieth Century* (1996), is essential reading on the centrality of labor and the "common man" to literary and popular culture in the 1930s. For the economic and cultural ties between the New Deal and the rebirth of the labor movement, see Lizabeth Cohen, *Making a New Deal: Industrial Workers in Chicago, 1919–1939* (1990). On the gendered nature of New Deal reform, consult Alice Kessler-Harris, *In Pursuit of Equity: Women, Men, and the Quest for Economic Citizenship in Twentieth-Century America* (2001).

Harvard Sitkoff, *A New Deal for Blacks* (1978), is a wide-ranging examination of the place of African Americans in New Deal reform. **Abraham Hoffman, *Unwanted Mexican Americans in the Great Depression: Repatriation Pressures, 1929–1939*** (1974), analyzes the precarious situation of Mexican Americans in the 1930s. The importance of John Collier and the Indian Reorganization Act are treated well in **Lawrence C. Kelly, *The Assault on Assimilation: John Collier and the Origins of Indian Policy Reform*** (1983). **James T. Patterson, *Congressional Conservatism and the New Deal*** (1967), analyzes the growing opposition to the New Deal in the late 1930s, while **Alan Brinkley, *The End of Reform: New Deal Liberalism in Recession and War*** (1995), provocatively examines the efforts of New Dealers to adjust their beliefs and programs as they lost support, momentum, and confidence in the late 1930s.

Visit the CourseMate website at www.cengagebrain.com for additional study tools and review materials for this chapter.

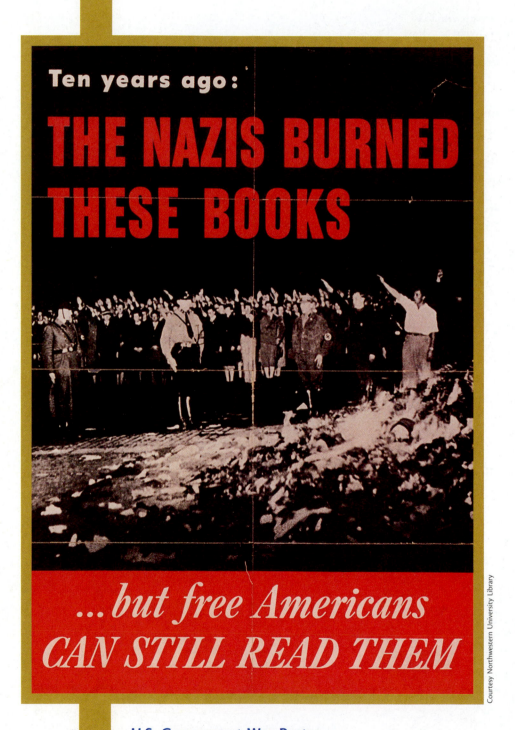

CHAPTER 26

Courtesy Northwestern University Library

U.S. Government War Poster

The governmental agencies charged with promoting support for U.S. participation in the Second World War often employed images from Nazi Germany as a way of dramatizing why we were fighting to preserve "the American way of life."

America During the Second World War

THE SECOND WORLD WAR vastly changed American life. The United States abandoned isolationism, moved toward military engagement on the side of the Allies, and emerged triumphant in a global war.

The mobilization for war finally lifted the United States out of the Great Depression. The nation's productive capacity—spurred by innovative technologies and by a new working relationship among government, business, labor, and scientific researchers—dwarfed that of all other nations and provided the economic basis for military victory.

At home, Americans reconsidered the meanings of liberty and equality. Although a massive publicity campaign initially stressed how wartime sacrifices would protect and preserve an "American way of life," the war raised questions. How would the nation, while striving for victory, reorder its economy, its politics, and the cultural and social patterns that had shaped racial, ethnic, and gender relationships during the 1930s? What processes of reconstruction, at home and abroad, might be required to build a prosperous and lasting peace?

The Road to War: Aggression and Response
The Rise of Aggressor States
U.S. Neutrality
The Mounting Crisis
The Outbreak of War in Europe
The U.S. Response to War in Europe
An "Arsenal of Democracy"
Pearl Harbor

Fighting the War in Europe and the Pacific
Campaigns in North Africa and Italy
Operation OVERLORD
Seizing the Offensive in the Pacific
China Policy
U.S. Strategy in the Pacific
A New President, the Atomic Bomb, and Japan's Surrender

The War at Home: The Economy
Government's Role in the Economy
Business and Finance
The Workforce
The Labor Front
Assessing Economic Change
A New Role for Government?

The War at Home: Social Issues
Selling the War
Gender Issues
Racial Issues
Internment of Japanese Americans
Challenging Racial Inequality

Shaping the Peace
International Organizations
Spheres of Interest and Postwar Settlements

The Road to War: Aggression and Response

FOCUS QUESTION

How did events in Asia and in Europe affect debate within the United States over whether or not to embrace more interventionist policies overseas?

The road to the Second World War began at least a decade before U.S. entry in 1941. In Japan, Italy, and Germany, economic stagnation created political conditions that nurtured ultranationalist movements bent on territorial expansion. Elsewhere in Europe and in the United States, economic problems made governments turn inward, concentrating on domestic recovery and avoiding foreign entanglements.

The Rise of Aggressor States

On September 18, 1931, Japanese military forces seized Manchuria and created Manchukuo, a puppet state of Japan. This action violated the League of Nations charter, the Washington Naval Treaties, and the Kellogg-Briand Pact (see Chapter 24). Focused on domestic matters, the international community hesitated to oppose Japan's move. The Hoover-Stimson Doctrine (1931) announced a U.S. policy of "nonrecognition" toward Manchukuo, and the League of Nations condemned Japan's action. Japan simply ignored these rebukes.

Meanwhile, ultranationalist states in Europe also sought to alleviate domestic ills through military aggression. **Adolf Hitler's** National Socialist (Nazi) Party came to power in Germany in 1933 and instituted a fascist regime, a one-party dictatorial state. Hitler denounced the Versailles peace settlement of 1919, blamed Germany's problems on a Jewish conspiracy, claimed a genetic superiority for the "Aryan race" of German-speaking peoples, and promised a new Germanic empire, the **Third Reich**. His regime withdrew from the League of Nations in 1933 and, in a blatant violation of the Versailles Treaty, dramatically boosted Germany's military budget. Another fascist government in Italy, headed by Benito Mussolini, also launched a military buildup and dreamed of empire. In October 1935 Mussolini's armies took over Ethiopia, an independent nation in Africa.

U.S. Neutrality

Many Americans wished to isolate their nation from these foreign troubles. Antiwar movies, such as *All Quiet on the Western Front* (1931), implicitly portrayed the First World War as a power game played by business and governmental elites, who

Nye Committee Hearings

used appeals to nationalism to dupe young soldiers into serving as cannon fodder. During the mid-1930s a Senate investigating committee headed by Republican Gerald P. Nye of North Dakota held well-publicized hearings and concluded that the United States had been maneuvered into the First World War to preserve the profits of bankers and munitions makers. By 1935, opinion polls suggested that Americans overwhelmingly opposed involvement in foreign conflicts.

CHRONOLOGY

1931	Japanese forces seize Manchuria
1933	Hitler takes power in Germany
1936	Spanish Civil War begins ◆ Germany and Italy agree to cooperate as the Axis Powers
1937	Neutrality Act broadens provisions of Neutrality Acts of 1935 and 1936 ◆ Roosevelt makes "Quarantine" speech ◆ Japan invades China
1938	France and Britain appease Hitler at Munich
1939	Hitler invades Poland; war breaks out in Europe ◆ Congress amends Neutrality Act to assist Allies
1940	Paris falls after German *blitzkreig* ◆ Roosevelt makes "destroyers-for-bases" deal with Britain ◆ Selective Service Act passed ◆ Roosevelt wins third term
1941	Lend-Lease established ◆ Roosevelt creates Fair Employment Practices Commission ◆ Roosevelt and Churchill proclaim the Atlantic Charter ◆ Congress narrowly repeals Neutrality Act ◆ Japanese forces attack Pearl Harbor (December 7)
1942	President signs Executive Order 9066 for internment of Japanese Americans ◆ General MacArthur driven from Philippines ◆ U.S. victorious in Battle of Midway ◆ German army defeated at Battle of Stalingrad ◆ Operation TORCH begins
1943	Axis armies in North Africa surrender ◆ Allies invade Sicily and Italy ◆ "Zoot suit" incidents in Los Angeles; racial violence in Detroit ◆ Allies begin drive toward Japan through South Pacific islands
1944	Allies land at Normandy (D-Day, June 6) ◆ Roosevelt reelected to fourth term ◆ Bretton Woods Conference creates IMF and World Bank ◆ Dumbarton Oaks Conference establishes plan for UN
1945	U.S. firebombs Japan ◆ Yalta Conference ◆ Roosevelt dies; Truman becomes president ◆ Germany surrenders ◆ Hiroshima and Nagasaki hit with atomic bombs ◆ Japan surrenders ◆ United Nations established

To prevent a repetition of the circumstances that had supposedly drawn the United States into the First World War, Congress enacted neutrality legislation. The **Neutrality Acts** of 1935 and 1936 mandated an arms embargo against belligerents, prohibited loans to them, and curtailed travel by Americans on ships belonging to nations at war. The Neutrality Act of 1937 extended the embargo to include all trade with any belligerent, unless the nation paid in cash and carried the purchases away in its own ships.

Critics charged that foreswearing U.S. intervention actively aided expansionist powers such as Nazi Germany. In March 1936 Nazi troops seized the Rhineland, a German area from which the 1919 peace settlement had barred military installations. A few months later, Hitler and Mussolini began assisting General Francisco Franco, a fellow fascist seeking to overthrow Spain's republican government. Republicans in Spain appealed to nonfascist nations for assistance, but only the Soviet Union responded. Britain, France, and the United States, fearing that the conflict would flare into world war if more nations took sides, remained uninvolved.

Although the United States remained officially aloof, the **Spanish Civil War** precipitated a major debate. Conservative groups generally hailed Franco as a staunch anticommunist who supported the Catholic Church and social traditionalism in Spain. In contrast, the political left championed republican Spain and denounced the fascism sweeping Europe. Cadres of Americans, including the famed "Abraham Lincoln Brigade," crossed the Atlantic to fight alongside republican forces in Spain. American peace groups splintered over the question of how to avoid a wider war. Some continued to advocate neutrality and isolation, but others argued for intervention against the spread of fascism.

FDR's Quarantine Speech

In October 1937 Roosevelt called for international cooperation to "quarantine" aggressor nations and suggested that Congress should modify its earlier Neutrality measures. Still suspicious of foreign entanglements, a majority of legislators refused to budge, even when this meant a victory by Franco in Spain's civil war.

The Mounting Crisis

As Americans debated how to deal with foreign aggression, Japan attacked China. In summer 1937, after an exchange of gunfire between Japanese and Chinese troops at the Marco Polo Bridge near Beijing, Japanese armies invaded and captured Shanghai, Nanjing, Shandong, and Beijing. Japan demanded that China become subservient to Tokyo. It also proposed an **East Asian Co-Prosperity Sphere** that would supposedly liberate Asian nations from Western colonialism and create a self-sufficient economic zone under Japanese leadership. In late 1937 Japanese planes sank the American gunboat *Panay* as it evacuated Americans from Nanjing. Japan's quick apology defused a potential crisis. Still, the *Panay* incident and Japan's brutality in occupying Nanjing—where perhaps 300,000 Chinese civilians were killed—alarmed Roosevelt.

Meanwhile, in Europe, Germany continued on the march. In March 1938 Hitler annexed Austria to the Third Reich and announced his intention to seize the Sudetenland, a portion of Czechoslovakia inhabited by 3.5 million people of German descent. In May FDR began a program of naval rearmament. French and British leaders, still hoping to avoid war, met with Hitler at the **Munich Conference** in September 1938. They acquiesced to Germany's seizure of the Sudetenland in return for Hitler's promise to seek no more territory. Hailed by Britain's prime minister as a guarantee of "peace in our time," the arrangement soon became a symbol of what interventionists called the "appeasement" of aggression.

In March 1939 Germans marched into Prague and, within a few months, annexed the rest of Czechoslovakia. In August 1939 Hitler signed a nonaggression pact with the Soviet Union, previously his bitter enemy. In a secret protocol, Hitler and Soviet leader Joseph Stalin agreed on a plan to divide up Poland and permit Soviet annexation of the Baltic States (Latvia, Lithuania, and Estonia).

The Outbreak of War in Europe

When Hitler's armies stormed into Poland on September 1, 1939, the Second World War officially began in Europe. Britain and France declared war against Germany, but these Allied powers could not mobilize in time to help Poland, which fell within weeks. Then an eerie calm settled over Europe during the winter.

In April 1940 a full-scale German *blitzkrieg*, or "lightning war," began moving swiftly, overrunning Denmark, Norway, the Netherlands, Belgium, Luxembourg, and France. The speed of the Nazi advance, employing massed tanks, motorized infantry, and air support, shocked Allied leaders in Paris and London. Britain barely managed to evacuate its troops, but not its equipment, from the French coastal town of Dunkirk, just before it fell to a German onslaught. Early in June, Italy joined Germany to form the Axis Powers, and they declared war on the Allies. Later in June, France fell, and Hitler installed a pro-Nazi government at Vichy in southern France. In only six weeks, Hitler's army had seized complete control of Europe's Atlantic coastline, from the North Sea south to Spain, where Franco remained officially neutral but decidedly pro-Axis. The Axis gained another member in September 1940, when Japan joined Germany and Italy in a Tripartite Pact.

The U.S. Response to War in Europe

Meanwhile, alarmed at the Nazi surge, Roosevelt pressured Congress to modify its neutrality legislation and called for other measures, "short of war," to help Britain and France. Late in 1939 Congress did lift the ban on selling military armaments to belligerents and substituted a cash-and-carry provision that permitted arms sales to belligerents who could pay cash and use their own ships for transport. This arrangement minimized risks to American exporters. Because its naval forces dominated the Atlantic sea lanes, Britain primarily benefited from this change in policy. Congress also boosted military funding and passed the Selective Training and Service Act of 1940, the first peacetime draft in U.S. history. Abandoning any pretense of neutrality, the United States also facilitated Britain's direct acquisition of U.S. "surplus" war materiel. In an attempt to broaden bipartisan support for these controversial measures, Roosevelt added pro-interventionist

Map 26.1 German Expansion at Its Height. This map shows the expansion of German power from 1938 through 1942. Which countries fell to German control? Why might Americans have differed over whether these moves by Germany represented a strategic threat to the United States?

Republicans to his cabinet—Henry Stimson as secretary of war and Frank Knox as secretary of Navy.

Meanwhile, from August through October 1940 Germany's *Luftwaffe* (air force) conducted daily raids on British air bases and nearly knocked out its Royal Air Force (RAF). On the verge of a knock-out, however, Hitler suddenly changed strategy and ordered, instead, the bombing of London and other cities. The use of airpower against civilians in the Battle of Britain, as it was called, steeled Britain's resolve and aroused sympathy among Americans who heard of events during dramatic radio broadcasts from London. CBS's Edward R. Murrow, observed the writer Archibald MacLeish, "skillfully burned the city of London in our homes, and we felt the flames."

In September 1940 Roosevelt agreed to transfer 50 First World War-era naval destroyers to the British navy. In return, the United States gained the right to build eight naval bases in British territories in the Western Hemisphere. This "destroyers-for-bases" deal infuriated isolationists. The America First Committee, organized by General Robert E. Wood, head of Sears, Roebuck, and Company, launched a campaign to shore up isolationist sentiment in Congress and among the public. The aviator hero Charles A. Lindbergh, America First's most famous member, flew around the country attending pro-isolationist rallies that denounced aid to Britain.

Although those who favored staying out of the war were generally lumped together as **"isolationists,"** this single term obscures their ideological diversity. Some pacifists opposed all wars as immoral, even those against fascist regimes. Some political progressives disliked fascism but feared even more the centralization of governmental power that conducting a war would require in the United States. Some conservatives sympathized with the anticommunism of fascist states, and some Americans shared Hitler's anti-Semitism.

A current of anti-Jewish sentiment existed in the United States. In 1939 congressional leaders had quashed the Wagner-Rogers bill, which would have boosted immigration quotas in order to allow for the entry of 20,000 Jewish children otherwise slated for Hitler's concentration camps. Bowing to anti-Semitic prejudices, the United States adopted a restrictive refugee policy. The consequences of these policies became especially grave after June 1941, when Hitler established the death camps that would systematically exterminate millions of Jews, gypsies, homosexuals, communists, and anyone else whom the Nazis deemed unfit for life in the Third Reich and its occupied territories. In September 1941 Burton K. Wheeler of Montana created a special Senate committee to investigate whether Hollywood movies were being used to promote pro-war views. Some isolationists, pointing out that many Hollywood producers were Jewish, expressed blatantly anti-Semitic views.

To counteract the isolationists, those who favored supporting the Allies also organized. The Military Training Camps Association lobbied on behalf of the Selective Service Act. The Committee to Defend America by Aiding the Allies, headed by William Allen White, a well-known Republican newspaper editor, organi-zed more than 300 local chapters in just a few weeks. Similar to the isola-tionists, interventionist organizations mobilized a diverse group of supporters. All, however, sounded alarms that fascist brutality, militar-ism, and racism might overrun Europe and threaten America as well.

Presidential electoral politics in 1940 forced Roosevelt, nominated for a third term, to tone down his pro-Allied rhetoric. The Republicans nominated Wendell Willkie, a lawyer and business executive with ties to the party's liberal, internationalist wing. To differentiate his policies from Willkie's, the president played to the popular opposition to war, promising not to send American troops to fight in "foreign wars." Once he had won an unprecedented third term, however, Roosevelt unveiled his most ambitious plan yet to support Britain's war effort.

The Fight Against Interventionism. The movement to keep the United States out of the Second World War mobilized powerful personalities, impassioned rhetoric, and colorful imagery. This emblem, for example, invokes nationalistic and patriotic imagery in the cause of avoiding, rather than engaging in, war.

© The Granger Collection, New York

An "Arsenal of Democracy"

Britain was nearly out of money, so the president proposed that the United States would now "lend-lease," or loan rather than sell, munitions to the Allies. Making the United States a "great arsenal of democracy," FDR claimed, would "keep war away from our country and our people." Congressional debate over the **Lend-Lease Act** was bitter, but it passed as House Resolution 1776 on March 11, 1941. When Germany turned its attention away from Britain and suddenly attacked in June its recent ally, the Soviet Union, Roosevelt extended Lend-Lease assistance to the communist regime of Joseph Stalin.

Roosevelt next began coordinating military strategy with Britain. He secretly pledged to follow a Europe-first approach if the United States were drawn into a two-front war against both Germany and Japan. Publicly, Roosevelt deployed U.S. Marines to Greenland and Iceland to free up the British forces that had protected these strategic Danish possessions after Germany's 1940 conquest of Denmark. In August 1941 Roosevelt and British Prime Minister Winston Churchill met on the high seas off the coast of Newfoundland to forge a formal wartime alliance.

They agreed to an eight-point Atlantic Charter that disavowed territorial expansion, endorsed protection of human rights and self-determination, and pledged the postwar creation of a new world organization that would ensure "general security." Roosevelt also agreed to Churchill's request that the U.S. Navy convoy American goods as far as Iceland. Soon, in an undeclared naval war, Germany's formidable submarine packs began attacking U.S. ships.

By this time Roosevelt and his advisors believed that defeating Hitler would require U.S. entry into the war, but public support still lagged. Privately, the president likely hoped that Germany would commit some provocative act in the North Atlantic that would jar public opinion. The October 1941 sinking of the U.S. destroyer *Reuben James* did just that. Congress repealed its earlier neutrality legislation, but the vote was so close and debate so bitter that Roosevelt knew he could not yet seek a formal declaration of war.

Pearl Harbor

As it turned out, Japan, rather than Germany, sparked America's involvement. In response to Japan's 1937 invasion of China, the

United States extended credit to China and curtailed sales of equipment to Japan. In 1939 the United States abrogated its Treaty of Commerce and Navigation with Japan, an action that further restricted U.S. exports to the island nation. A 1940 ban on the sale of aviation fuel and high-grade scrap iron to Japan was also intended to slow Japan's military advances.

These measures did not halt Japanese expansion but made it seem even more imperative to Japan's leaders. As the European war sapped the strength of France, the Netherlands, and Great Britain, Japanese militarists hoped to grab Europe's Asian colonies and incorporate them into Japan's own East Asian Co-Prosperity Sphere. Japan therefore pushed deep into French Indochina, seeking the raw materials it could no longer buy from the United States, and prepared to launch attacks on Singapore, the Netherlands East Indies (Indonesia), and the Philippines.

Roosevelt expanded the trade embargo against Japan, promised further assistance to China, and accelerated a U.S. military buildup in the Pacific. In mid-1941 he froze all Japanese assets in the United States, effectively bringing under presidential control all commerce between the two countries, including trade in petroleum, which was vital to the Japanese economy and war effort. Faced with impending economic strangulation, Japanese leaders did not reassess their plan to create an East Asian empire. Instead, they began planning a preemptive attack on the United States. With limited supplies of raw materials, especially oil, Japan had little hope of winning a prolonged war. Japanese military strategists gambled that a surprise, crippling blow would limit U.S. capabilities and force U.S. concessions. General Hideki Tojo, who became Japan's prime minister, knew the risks but remarked, "sometimes a man has to jump with his eyes closed."

On December 7, 1941, Japanese bombers swooped down on **Pearl Harbor**, Hawaii, and destroyed much of the U.S. Pacific Fleet. Altogether, 19 ships were sunk or severely damaged; nearly 200 aircraft were destroyed or disabled; and 2,200 Americans were killed. The attack could have been worse. U.S. aircraft carriers, out to sea at the time, were spared, as were the base's fuel storage tanks and repair facilities. In a dramatic message broadcast by radio on December 8, Roosevelt decried the attack and labeled December 7 as "a date which will live in infamy," a phrase that served as a battle cry throughout the war. Japan had rallied Americans, not brought them to terms.

A few Americans charged that Roosevelt had intentionally provoked Japan in order to open a "back door" to war. They asked why the fleet at Pearl Harbor lay vulnerable, not even in a state of full alert. The actions and inactions of leaders, however, were more confused than devious. Intelligence experts, who had broken Japanese diplomatic but not military code, expected Japan to move toward Singapore or other British or Dutch possessions in Asia. Intercepted messages, along with visual sightings of Japanese ships, seemed to confirm preparations for a strike in Southeast Asia (which did occur). American leaders doubted that Japan would risk a direct attack and doubted that Japan's military planners had the skill to plan an air attack of such distance.

FDR's "Infamy" Speech of December 8, 1941

On December 8, 1941, Congress declared war against Japan. Japan's allies, Germany and Italy, declared war on the United States three days later. Hitler mistakenly assumed that the fight against Japan would keep the United States preoccupied in the Pacific. The three Axis Powers drastically underestimated America's ability to mobilize swiftly and effectively.

Fighting the War in Europe and the Pacific

Q **FOCUS QUESTION** What military strategies did the United States and the Allies ultimately adopt when fighting in both the European and Asian theaters of the Second World War?

Initially, the war went badly for the Allies. German forces controlled most of Europe from Norway to Greece and had pushed eastward into the Soviet Union. Now they rolled

San Diego Historical Society

Is That a War Plant? This photo from 1945 shows an aircraft plant near San Diego bedecked with camouflage.

across North Africa, and German submarines endangered Allied supply lines in the Atlantic. Japan seemed unstoppable in the Pacific, overrunning Malaya, the Netherlands East Indies, and the Philippines and moving against the British in Burma and the Australians in New Guinea.

The United States had been unprepared for war, but new bureaucracies and technologies quickly guided a crash program for mobilization. The newly formed Joint Chiefs of Staff, consisting of representatives from each of the armed services, directed Roosevelt's strategy. The War Department's **Pentagon** complex, a giant, five-story, five-sided building, was completed in January 1943 after 16 months of around-the-clock work. In 1942 aircraft equipped with radar, a new technology developed in collaboration with Britain, proved effective against submarines, and during 1943 Germany's U-boat threat faded "from menace to problem," in the words of one U.S. naval commander. Perhaps most critical, a massive Allied code-breaking operation, based at Bletchley Park in England and employing 4000 people, perfected decryption techniques for use against Germany's supposedly inviolable encoding machine. Decrypted German messages, called "Ultra" for "ultrasecret," gave the Allies a crucial advantage. Throughout the war, Germans never discovered that many of their decoded radio communications were being forwarded to Allied commanders—sometimes even before they had reached their German recipients. In the postwar world, the code-breaking effort would contribute to the development of computer technology.

Campaigns in North Africa and Italy

Military strategy divided the Allied powers. All agreed that their primary focus would be on Europe, and Roosevelt and his military strategists established a unified command with the British. Stalin pleaded with Roosevelt and Churchill to open a second front in Western Europe, by way of an invasion across the English Channel into France, to relieve pressure on the Soviet Union. Many of Roosevelt's advisers agreed: If German troops succeeded in knocking the Soviet Union out of the war, Hitler could turn his full attention toward Britain. Churchill, however, urged instead the invasion of French North Africa, in order to nibble away at the edges of enemy power.

At a meeting in Casablanca, Morocco, in January 1943, Roosevelt sided with Churchill. He argued that a cross-Channel invasion of France carried too many risks at that time. To assuage Stalin's fear that his two allies might sign a separate peace with Hitler, however, Roosevelt and Churchill promised to remain in the fight until Germany agreed to an "unconditional surrender."

The North African operation, code-named TORCH, began with Anglo-American landings in Morocco and Algeria in November 1942. As TORCH progressed, the Soviets turned the tide of battle on the eastern front with a decisive victory at Stalingrad. The epic battle of Stalingrad, which lasted nearly six months between July 1942 and February 1943 and killed well over one million people, was perhaps the bloodiest in modern history.

Hitler poured reinforcements into North Africa but could stop neither TORCH nor the British drive westward from Egypt. In the summer of 1943 the Allies followed up their successful North African campaign by overrunning the island of Sicily and then fighting their way, slowly, northward through Italy's mountains.

Some U.S officials worried about the postwar implications of wartime strategy. Secretary of War Henry Stimson, for example, warned that the Allied campaigns through Africa and Italy might leave the Soviets dominant in most of Europe. Acting on this advice, Roosevelt finally agreed to set a date for the cross-Channel invasion that Stalin had long been promised.

Operation OVERLORD

Operation **OVERLORD**, directed by General Dwight D. Eisenhower began on June 6, 1944, D-Day. During the preceding months, probably the largest invasion force in history had assembled in England. Disinformation and diversionary tactics fooled the Germans into expecting a landing at the narrowest part of the English Channel rather than in the Normandy region. After several delays, because of the Channel's unpredictable weather, nervous commanders finally ordered the daring plan to begin. The night before, as naval guns pounded the Normandy shore, three divisions of paratroopers dropped behind enemy lines to disrupt German communications. Then at dawn, more than 4,000 Allied ships landed troops and supplies on Normandy's beaches. The first American forces to come ashore at Omaha Beach met especially heavy German fire and took enormous casualties, but the waves of invading troops continued. Only three weeks after D-Day, more than a million Allied personnel controlled the French coast and opened the long-awaited Second Front.

Just as the 1943 Battle of Stalingrad had reversed the course of the war in the East, so OVERLORD changed the momentum in the West. Within three months, U.S., British, and Free French troops entered Paris. After repulsing a desperate German counteroffensive in Belgium, at the Battle of the Bulge in December and January, Allied armies swept eastward, crossing the Rhine, and headed toward Berlin to meet up with westward-advancing Soviet troops.

As the war in Europe drew to a close, the horrors perpetrated by the Third Reich became fully visible to the world. Hitler's campaign of extermination, now called the Holocaust, killed more than 5 million Jews out of Europe's prewar population of 10 million. Hundreds of thousands more from various other groups were also murdered. Although only a military victory put an end to German death camps, the Allies might have saved thousands of Jews by helping them escape and emigrate. Allied leaders, however, worried about how to deal with large numbers of Jewish refugees, and they also claimed they could not spare scarce ships to transport them to sanctuary. The Allies would, in 1945 and 1946, bring 24 German high officials to trial at Nuremberg for "crimes against humanity." Large quantities of money, gold, and jewelry that Nazi leaders stole from victims of the Holocaust and deposited in Swiss banks, however, remained concealed for more than 50 years. Not until 1997 did Jewish groups and the U.S. government force an investigation of the Swiss banking industry's holdings of stolen "Nazi gold," an inquiry that finally prompted some monetary restitution for victims' families.

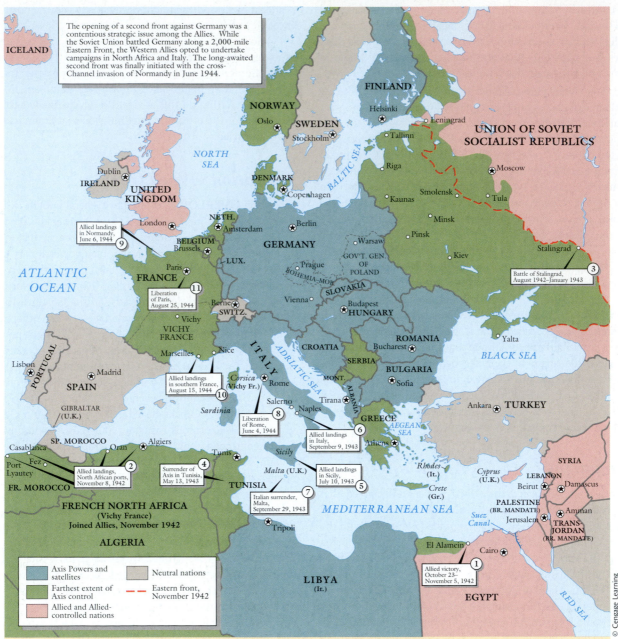

The opening of a second front against Germany was a contentious strategic issue among the Allies. While the Soviet Union battled Germany along a 2,000-mile Eastern Front, the Western Allies opted to undertake campaigns in North Africa and Italy. The long-awaited second front was finally initiated with the cross-Channel invasion of Normandy in June 1944.

Allied landings in Normandy, June 6, 1944 ⑨

Liberation of Paris, August 25, 1944 ⑪

Allied landings in southern France, August 15, 1944 ⑩

Liberation of Rome, June 4, 1944 ⑧

Allied landings in North African ports, November 8, 1942 ②

Surrender of Axis in Tunisia, May 13, 1943 ④

Allied landings in Italy, September 9, 1943 ⑥

Allied landings in Sicily, July 10, 1943 ⑤

Italian surrender, Malta, September 29, 1943 ⑦

Battle of Stalingrad, August 1942–January 1943 ③

Allied victory, October 23–November 5, 1942 ①

Legend:
- Axis Powers and satellites
- Farthest extent of Axis control
- Allied and Allied-controlled nations
- Neutral nations
- – – Eastern front, November 1942

© Cengage Learning

Map 26.2 Allied Military Strategy in North Africa, Italy, and France. This map shows the European theater of war from 1942 through 1944. Note how the crucial Battle of Stalingrad and the North African campaign began a rollback of German power. Why did June 1944 appear to be a critical month for the Allied effort?

With Hitler's suicide in April and Germany's surrender on May 8, 1945, the military foundations for peace in Europe were complete. Soviet armies controlled Eastern Europe; British and U.S. forces predominated in Italy and the rest of the Mediterranean; Germany and Austria fell under divided occupation. Governmental leaders now needed to work out a plan for transforming these military arrangements into a comprehensive political settlement for the postwar era. Meanwhile, the war in the Pacific was far from over.

Seizing the Offensive in the Pacific

For six months after Pearl Harbor, Japan's forces steadily advanced. Singapore fell easily. Japan overwhelmed U.S. naval garrisons in the Philippines and on Guam and Wake islands. Filipino and American troops surrendered at Bataan and Corregidor in the Philippines. Other Japanese forces headed southward to menace Australia and New Zealand.

When Japan finally suffered its first naval setback at the Battle of the Coral Sea in May 1942, Japanese naval commanders decided to hit back hard. They amassed 200 ships and 600 planes to destroy what remained of the U.S. Pacific fleet and to take Midway Island, from where they could assault Hawaii. U.S. Naval Intelligence, however, was monitoring Japanese codes and warned Admiral Chester W. Nimitz of the plan. Surprising the Japanese armada in the Battle of Midway, U.S. planes sank four Japanese carriers and destroyed a total of 322 planes.

HISTORY THROUGH FILM

Saving Private Ryan (1998)

Directed by Steven Spielberg.
Starring Tom Hanks (Captain John Miller), Matt Damon (Private James Ryan),
Harve Presnell (General George Marshall).

Hollywood marked the 50th anniversary of the Allied effort in the Second World War with a series of films about "the good war." Although *Saving Private Ryan* invited comparison with *The Longest Day* (1962) because of its depiction of the D-Day invasion of Normandy, Steven Spielberg's battlefield sequences represented a considerable advance in the art of waging war on film. His production team employed sophisticated computer graphics and nearly deafening Dolby sound to mount battle scenes so realistic that reviewers cautioned veterans susceptible to post-traumatic stress syndrome about watching the film.

The film also suggested the kind of family-centered melodrama that Spielberg had grafted onto the sci-fi genre in *E.T.: The Extra-Terrestrial* (1982). A heroic squad led by Captain John Miller is trying to locate a single U.S. soldier, Private James Ryan, whose mother has already lost her three other sons to the war. The film poses the question of whether such a family-related mission legitimates and sanctifies the sacrifices of the Second World War. *Private Ryan* answers "yes" to this question.

The major body of the film carefully justifies the rescue mission. Although Captain Miller wonders if his dangerous assignment is simply a public relations stunt, he quickly drops this idea and pursues his mission with the gallantry required of a Hollywood-commissioned

© RAC/Contributor/ Getty Images

Saving Private Ryan, which garnered four Academy Award nominations, celebrated the heroism of what popular historians called America's "greatest generation."

officer. Later, his platoon members debate the morality of risking eight lives to save one, but the cause of Ryan's mother always seems overriding. General George Marshall cuts off debate over the appropriateness of the Ryan mission by invoking an earlier war leader, Abraham Lincoln, who once faced a similar dilemma. When Miller's troops finally locate Private Ryan, the film's audience discovers that he is the kind of clean-cut Iowa farm boy who will stay with his would-be saviors rather than retreat to safety. Ryan survives, although most of his comrades perish. Captain Miller, dying, implores young Ryan to lead a "good" life to justify the sacrifice of so many others.

The film *Private Ryan*, in contrast to its characters, takes few risks. It secures its emotional investment in the rescue effort by bracketing the Second World War segments with two brief framing sequences in which an aging Ryan, along with his own family, returns to Normandy and visits the grave of Captain Miller. In the final segment, Ryan's wife provides the final reassurance that the trauma of the Second World War served a good cause, because Private Ryan's own family life has justified Miller's sacrifice. "Tell me I've led a good life. Tell me I'm a good man," he implores his wife. After nearly three hours of this Spielberg epic, the question is rhetorical.

Two months later, American forces splashed ashore at Guadalcanal in the Solomon Islands. The bloody engagements in the Solomons continued for months on both land and sea, but they accomplished one major objective: seizing the military initiative in the Pacific. According to prewar plans, the war in Europe was to have received highest priority, but by 1943 the two theaters were receiving roughly equal resources.

The bloody engagements in the Pacific reinforced racial prejudices and brutality on both sides. Japanese leaders hoped the war would confirm the superiority of their divine Yamato race. Prisoners taken by the Japanese, particularly on the Asian mainland, were brutalized in almost unimaginable ways. The Japanese Army's Unit 731 tested bacteriological weapons in China and conducted horrifying medical experiments on live

Map 26.3 Allied Advances and Collapse of German Power. This map depicts the final Allied advances and the end of the war in Germany. Through what countries did Soviet armies advance, and how might their advance have affected the postwar situation? How was Germany divided by occupying powers, and how might that division have affected postwar politics?

View an animated version of this map or related maps on the CourseMate website.

subjects. American propaganda images played on themes of racial superiority, portraying the Japanese people as animalistic subhumans. American troops often rivaled Japan's forces in their disrespect for the enemy dead and sometimes killed the enemy rather than take prisoners.

China Policy

U.S. policymakers hoped that China would fight effectively against Japan and emerge after the war as a strong, united nation. Neither hope seemed realized. China was beset by civil war.

Jiang Jieshi's Nationalist government was incompetent and unpopular. It avoided engaging the Japanese invaders and still made extravagant demands for U.S. assistance. A growing communist movement led by Mao Zedong fought more effectively against the Japanese invaders, but U.S. policy continued to support Jiang as China's future leader. Meanwhile, Japan's advance into China continued, and in 1944 its forces captured seven key U.S. air bases in China.

U.S. Strategy in the Pacific

In contrast to the European Theater, no unified command guided the war in the Pacific, and military actions often emerged from compromise. General Douglas MacArthur, commander of the army in the South Pacific, favored an offensive launched from his headquarters in Australia through New Guinea and the Philippines and on to Japan. After Japan had driven him out of the Philippines in May 1942, he promised to return. Admiral Nimitz disagreed. He favored an advance across the smaller islands of the central Pacific,

bypassing the Philippines. Unable to decide between the two strategies, the Joint Chiefs of Staff authorized both.

Both offensives moved forward, marked by fierce fighting and heavy casualties. MacArthur took New Guinea. Nimitz's forces liberated the Marshall Islands and the Marianas in 1943 and 1944. An effective radio communication system conducted by a Marine platoon of Navajo Indians, the Navajo Signal Corps, made a unique contribution to success. Navajo, a language unfamiliar to Japanese intelligence officers, provided a secure medium for sensitive communications.

In late 1944 the fall of Saipan brought American bombers within range of Japan. The capture of the islands of Iwo Jima and Okinawa during spring 1945 further shortened that distance. Okinawa illustrated the ferocity of the campaigns: 120,000 Japanese and 48,000 American soldiers died. Given these numbers, U.S. military planners dreaded the prospect of invading Japan's home islands.

Airpower looked more and more enticing. The results of the Allies' strategic bombing of Germany, including the

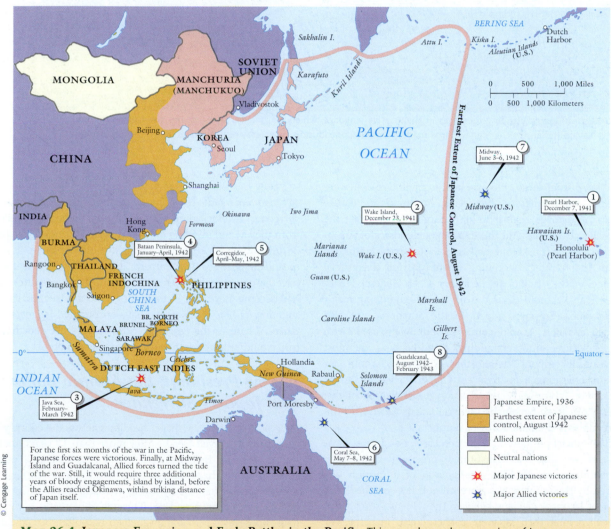

For the first six months of the war in the Pacific, Japanese forces were victorious. Finally, at Midway Island and Guadalcanal, Allied forces turned the tide of the war. Still, it would require three additional years of bloody engagements, island by island, before the Allies reached Okinawa, within striking distance of Japan itself.

© Cengage Learning

Map 26.4 Japanese Expansion and Early Battles in the Pacific. This map shows the expansion of Japanese power prior to the Battle of Midway. What countries were in the Japanese orbit? U.S. opinion polls from the late 1930s suggest that more Americans supported strong measures against this Japanese threat in Asia than against the German threat in Europe. What might be some explanations for this concern?

Navajo Signal Corps. Sending messages in their native language, which neither the Japanese nor the Germans could decipher, Navajo Indians in the Signal Corps made a unique contribution to preserving the secrecy of U.S. intelligence.

destruction of such large cities as Hamburg and Dresden, were ambiguous, and military historians continue to debate whether the damage against military targets really offset the huge civilian casualties and the unsustainable losses of American pilots and aircraft. Nonetheless, U.S. strategists continued to claim that strategic bombing might provide the crucial advantage in the Pacific. In February 1944 General Henry Harley ("Hap") Arnold devised a plan for firebombing major Japanese cities. Bombers added to the horror of war and terrorized civilians, Arnold conceded, but when used "with the proper degree of understanding" could become "the most humane of all weapons" by shortening the war. Arnold's air campaign, operating from bases in China, turned out to be cumbersome. It was replaced by a more effective and lethal operation run from Saipan by General Curtis LeMay, whom Arnold dubbed "the Babe Ruth of bombers."

The official position on the incendiary raids against Japanese cities was that they constituted "precision" rather than "area" bombing. In actuality, the success of a mission was measured by the number of square miles it left scorched. The number of Japanese civilians killed in the raids is estimated to have been greater than Japanese soldiers killed in battle. Air attacks on Tokyo during the night of March 9/10, 1945, inaugurated the new policy. They leveled nearly a quarter of the city and incinerated more than 100,000 people. LeMay summarized his strategy: "Bomb and burn them until they quit."

By the winter of 1944–45, a combined sea and air strategy had emerged: The United States sought "unconditional surrender" by blockading Japan's seaports, bombarding its cities from the air, and invading only if necessary. Critics of the policy of unconditional surrender, which most Japanese assumed meant the death of their emperor, later suggested that it might have hardened Japan's determination to fight even after defeat had become inevitable. Defenders of the policy suggest that any softening of U.S. terms would have encouraged Japanese resistance. Whatever the case, American leaders decided that victory would only come through massive destruction.

A New President, the Atomic Bomb, and Japan's Surrender

On April 13, 1945, newspaper headlines across the country read "President Roosevelt Dead." After more than 13 years in office, the increasingly frail president had succumbed to a massive cerebral hemorrhage. Sorrow and shock spread through the armed forces, where many young men and women had hardly known any other president. Through diplomatic conference halls, Roosevelt's personal magnetism had often brought unity, if not always clarity; and among his many supporters, he had symbolized optimism through economic depression and war. Roosevelt had also accumulated a host of critics and enemies. He had defeated Republican Thomas E. Dewey in the 1944

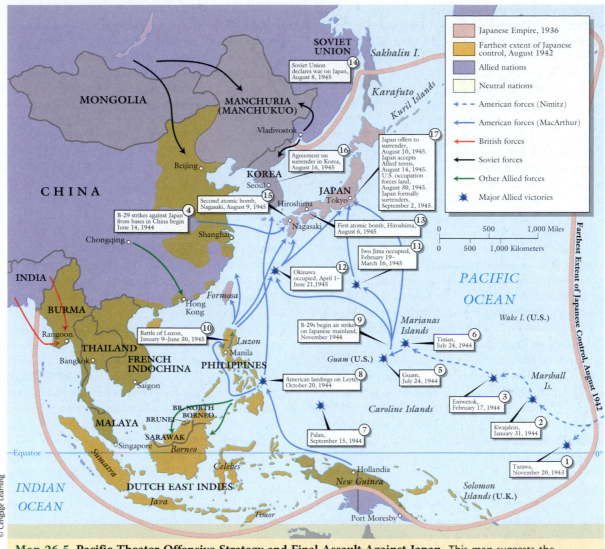

Map 26.5 Pacific Theater Offensive Strategy and Final Assault Against Japan. This map suggests the complicated nature of devising a war strategy in the vast Pacific region. What tactics did the United States use to advance upon and finally prevail over the island nation of Japan?

presidential election by the smallest popular-vote margin in nearly 30 years, and Republicans had further cut into the Democrat's once overwhelming majorities in the House and Senate. Unaware of Roosevelt's precarious health, however, both Republican and Democrats assumed FDR would lead the United States into the postwar world.

Emerging from Roosevelt's shadow, the new president, Harry S Truman, seemed an unimposing presence. Born on a farm near Independence, Missouri, Truman served in France during the First World War, became a U.S. Senator in 1934, and was tabbed as Roosevelt's running mate in 1944. Roosevelt offered an upper-class image of well-practiced and worldly charm. The blunt-spoken Truman proudly presented himself as a "little man from Missouri." He knew little about international affairs or about any informal understandings that Roosevelt may have made with foreign leaders.

Only after succeeding Roosevelt did Truman learn about events at Los Alamos, New Mexico. There, since the late 1930s, scientists from all across the world had been secretly working on a new weapon. Advances in theoretical physics had suggested that splitting the atom (fission) would release a tremendous amount of energy. Fearful that Germany was racing ahead of the United States in this research, Albert Einstein, a Jewish refugee from Germany, had urged Roosevelt to launch a secret program to build a bomb based on the latest atomic research. The government subsequently enlisted top scientists in the **Manhattan Project**, a huge, secret military operation. On July 16, 1945, the first atomic weapon was successfully tested at Trinity Site, near Alamogordo, New Mexico.

Truman and his top policymakers assumed that the weapon would be put to immediate use. They were eager to end the war, both because a possible land invasion of Japan might prove costly in American lives and because the Soviet Union was planning to enter the Pacific Theater, where Truman wished to limit Soviet power. Churchill called the bomb a "miracle of deliverance." Truman later publicly claimed that he had never lost a night's sleep over its use.

Privately, he and other U.S. officials admitted to more qualms. There was disagreement over where and how the bomb should be deployed. A commission of atomic scientists recommended a "demonstration" that would impress Japan with the bomb's power, yet cause no loss of life. General George C. Marshall suggested using it on purely military installations or only on manufacturing sites, after first warning away Japanese workers. Ultimately, the Truman administration discarded these options. The bomb, Secretary of War Henry Stimson said, had to make "a profound psychological impression on as many inhabitants as possible."

In the context of the earlier aerial bombardment of Japanese cities, dropping atomic bombs on the previously unbombed cities of **Hiroshima** and Nagasaki on August 6 and 9, 1945, seemed only a small departure from existing policy. "Fat Man" and "Little Boy," as the two bombs were nicknamed, could be regarded as merely bigger, more effective firebombs. Atomic weapons did, however, produce a new level of violence. Colonel Paul Tibbets, who piloted the U.S. plane that dropped the first bomb, reported, "the shimmering city became an ugly smudge . . . a pot of bubbling hot tar." Teams of U.S. observers who entered Hiroshima and Nagasaki in the aftermath were stunned at the instantaneous incineration of both human beings and manmade structures and shocked to contemplate the longer-lasting horror of radiation disease.

The mushroom clouds over Hiroshima and Nagasaki inaugurated a new "atomic age" in which dreams of peace mingled with nightmares of global destruction. Shortly after the bombing, Stimson wrote to Truman that atomic weapons represented "a new control by man over the forces of nature too revolutionary and dangerous to fit into old concepts." But in those late summer days of 1945 most Americans sighed with relief. News reports of August 15 proclaimed Japan's surrender, V-J Day. All across the nation people spontaneously flooded into the streets to celebrate the end of the Second World War.

The War at Home: The Economy

 Q **FOCUS QUESTION** How did mobilizing for war transform the American economy, its labor force, and the role of government?

The success of the U.S. military effort depended on economic mobilization at home. This effort ultimately brought the Great Depression of the 1930s to an end and transformed the nation's government, its business and financial institutions, and its labor force.

Government's Role in the Economy

The federal bureaucracy nearly quadrupled in size during the war. New economic agencies proliferated. The most powerful of these, the War Production Board, oversaw the conversion and expansion of factories, allocated resources, and enforced production priorities and schedules. The War Labor Board adjudicated labor-management disputes. The War Manpower Commission allocated workers to various industries. The Office of Price Administration regulated prices to control inflation and rationed such scarce commodities as gasoline, rubber, steel, shoes, coffee, sugar, and meat. Although most of the controls were abandoned after the war, the concept of greater governmental oversight of the economy survived, extending the New Deal's activist legacy that would begin to be called Keynesianism.

From 1940 to 1945 the U.S. economy expanded rapidly, and the gross national product (GNP) rose, year-by-year, by 15 percent or more. When Roosevelt called for the production of 60,000 planes shortly after Pearl Harbor, skeptics jeered. Yet within a few years the nation produced nearly 300,000 planes. The Maritime Commission oversaw the construction of millions of tons of new ships. The government's huge wartime spending provided a fiscal stimulus that eradicated the underconsumption of the Great Depression. The once stagnant economy sprang to life and spewed out prodigious quantities of all kinds of supplies, including 2.5 million trucks and 50 million pairs of shoes.

Striving to increase production, industry entered into a close relationship with government to promote scientific and technological research and development (R&D). Government money subsidized new industries, such as electronics, and transformed others, such as rubber and chemicals. Eventually, an Office of Scientific Research and Development contracted with universities and scientists for a variety of projects. Under this program, radar and penicillin (both British discoveries), rocket engines, and other new products were perfected for wartime use. The Manhattan Project, of course, provided the most dramatic example of the government's new involvement in military research. Refugees from Nazi tyranny contributed significantly to this scientific innovation.

Business and Finance

To finance the war effort, government spending rose from $9 billion in 1940 to $98 billion in 1944. In 1941 the national debt stood at $48 billion; by V-J Day it was $280 billion. With fewer goods to buy because of rationing, Americans invested in war bonds, turning their savings into tanks and planes. Although war bonds provided a relatively insignificant contribution to overall defense spending, they helped raise personal saving to record levels and gave those who purchased them a direct psychological and economic stake in the war effort.

As production shifted from autos to tanks, and from refrigerators to guns, consumer goods became scarce. Essentials such as food, fabrics, and gasoline were rationed and, consequently, were shared more equitably than before the war. Higher taxes on wealthier Americans redistributed income and narrowed the gap in wealth between the well-to-do and other citizens. War bonds, rationing, and progressive taxation encouraged a sense of shared sacrifice and helped ease the class tensions of the 1930s.

Even as the war fostered personal savings and lessened income inequality, however, it also facilitated the dismantling of some New Deal agencies most concerned with economic inequality. A Republican surge in the off-year elections of 1942—the GOP gained 44 seats in the House and 7 in the Senate—helped

© Bettmann/CORBIS

© Bettmann/CORBIS

Total War: Dresden and Hiroshima. The effects of "total war" are graphically illustrated in these photographs—of the devastation of Dresden, Germany (top), by the British Bomber Command and the U.S. 8th Air Force on February 13 and 14, 1945, and that of Hiroshima, Japan (bottom), by the U.S. 509th Composite Group on August 6, 1945. In the initial attack on Dresden, 786 aircraft dropped 5,824,000 pounds (2,600 long tons) of bombs on the city, killing an estimated 60,000 people and injuring another 30,000. An area of more than 2.5 square miles in the city center was demolished, and some 37,000 buildings were destroyed. To critics, the bombing of Dresden, a target that many argued was of little strategic value, exemplified the excessive use of airpower.

In sobering comparison, Hiroshima was devastated by one bomb weighing only 10,000 pounds (4.4 long tons)—an atomic bomb— dropped from one aircraft. The single U-235 bomb killed 68,000 people outright, injured another 30,000, and left 10,000 missing. (These figures do not include those who later developed diseases from deadly gamma rays.) The bomb obliterated almost five square miles of the city's center and destroyed 40,653 buildings. Truman reported the strike as "an overwhelming success." Many hailed the atomic bomb as a necessary step toward military victory; others worried about the dawn of the "nuclear age."

strengthen an anti-New Deal coalition in Congress. In 1943 legislators abolished the job-creation programs of the Works Progress Administration (WPA), the Civilian Conservation Corps (CCC), and the National Youth Administration (NYA) (see Chapter 25). They also shut down the Rural Electrification Administration (REA) and Farm Security Administration (FSA), agencies that had assisted rural areas. As business executives flocked to Washington, D.C., to run the new wartime agencies, the Roosevelt administration adopted a relatively cooperative stance toward big business.

Corporations considered essential to wartime victory flourished under governmental subsidies. What was essential, of course, became a matter of definition. Coca-Cola and Wrigley's chewing gum won precious sugar allotments by arguing that GIs overseas "needed" to enjoy these products. Both companies prospered. The California-based Kaiser Corporation, whose spectacular growth during the 1930s had been spurred by federal dam contracts, now turned its attention to building ships, aircraft, and military vehicles such as the famous "Jeep." By 1943 Kaiser controlled nearly a third of

Rita Hayworth Scraps Her Bumpers. Movie stars aided the war effort by promoting the sale of war bonds and urging sacrifice. Here Hayworth urges Americans to scrap their nonessential car parts.

the nation's military construction business and brought a boom to coastal California and Washington state. Federal subsidies and tax breaks enabled factories throughout the country to expand and retool. New manufacturing centers transformed the size and function of cities particularly in the South and West, areas previously dominated mostly by agricultural production.

The war concentrated power in the largest corporations. After Roosevelt ordered his justice department to postpone enforcement of antitrust laws, government lawyers tucked away long-planned legal cases, such as one against America's great oil cartel. Congressional efforts to investigate possible collusion in the awarding of large government contracts and to increase assistance to small businesses similarly made little headway. The top 100 companies, which had provided 30 percent of the nation's total manufacturing output in 1940, were providing 70 percent by 1943.

The Workforce

During the early years of the military buildup, people who had scrounged for jobs during the Great Depression found work. Employment in heavy industry invariably went to men, and most of the skilled jobs went to whites. But as military service depleted the ranks of white males, women and minorities became more attractive candidates for production jobs. Soon, both private

employers and public officials were encouraging women to go to work, southern African Americans to seek jobs in northern and western industrial cities, and Mexicans to enter the United States under the *bracero* guest farm worker program.

Hired for jobs never before open to them, women became welders, shipbuilders, lumberjacks, and miners. Women won places in prestigious symphony orchestras, and one Major League Baseball owner financed the creation of a women's league to give new life to the national pastime. Many employers hired married women, who before the war would have been lucky to obtain a position even in traditionally female occupations such as teaching. Minority women moved into clerical and sales jobs, where they had not previously been welcome. Most workplaces, however, continued to be segregated by sex.

The scope of unpaid labor, long provided primarily by women, also expanded. Volunteer activities such as Red Cross projects, civil defense work, and recycling drives claimed more and more of the time of women, children, and older people. As kids collected scrap and women rolled bandages, leisure time melted away and even seemed unpatriotic. Both in the home and in the workplace, women's responsibilities and workloads increased, but few complained. Government publications exhorted homemakers: "Wear it out, use it up, make it do, or do without." The Second World War became one in which people of all ages and occupations contributed either their fighting skills or their productive labor.

The new labor market improved the general economic position of African Americans. By executive order in June 1942, Roosevelt created the Fair Employment Practices Commission (FEPC), which aimed to ban discrimination in hiring. In 1943 his administration announced that it would not recognize as collective bargaining agents any unions that discriminated on the basis of race. The War Labor Board outlawed the practice of paying different wages to whites and nonwhites

Women Join the War Effort. Women employees at the Convair Company in California use a rivet gun and bucking bar, tools traditionally used only by men.

doing the same job. Before the war, the African American population had been mainly southern, rural, and agricultural; within a few years, a substantial percentage of African Americans had become northern, urban, and industrial. Although employment discrimination was hardly eliminated and many charged the FEPC with foot-dragging, twice as many African Americans held skilled jobs at the end of the war as at the beginning.

For both men and women, the war brought higher wages and longer work hours. Although the Roosevelt administration tried to limit wage increases during the war, overtime often raised paychecks. During the war, average weekly earnings for industrial workers rose nearly 70 percent. Farmers, who had suffered through many years of low prices and overproduction, doubled their income and then doubled it again.

The Labor Front

The scarcity of labor during the war substantially strengthened the union movement. Union membership rose by 50 percent. Although women and workers of color joined unions in unprecedented numbers, the main beneficiaries of labor's new clout were the white males who still comprised the bulk of union workers.

Especially on the national level, the commitment of organized labor to female workers was weak. Not a single woman served on the executive boards of either the American Federation of Labor (AFL) or the Congress of Industrial Organizations (CIO). The International Brotherhood of Teamsters even required women to sign a statement that their union membership could be revoked when the war was over. Unions did fight for contracts stipulating equal pay for men and women who worked in the same job, but these benefited women only as long as they held "male" jobs. The unions' primary purpose in advocating equal pay was to maintain wage levels for the men who would return to their jobs after the war. During the first year of peace, as employers trimmed their workforces, both businesses and unions gave special preference to returning veterans and worked to ease women and minority workers out of their wartime positions. Unions based their policies on seniority and their wage demands on the goal of securing male workers a "family wage," one sufficient to support an entire family.

Some union leaders feared that hiring traditionally lower-paid workers (women and minorities) would jeopardize the wage gains and recognition that unions had won during the labor struggles of the 1930s. Early in the war, some union locals in the well-paying aircraft and shipbuilding industries refused to enroll African Americans and opposed the FEPC. As growing numbers of African Americans were hired, racial tensions in the workplace increased. All across the country—at a defense plant in Lockland, Ohio; at a transit company in Philadelphia; at a shipbuilding company in Mobile—white

Children Enlist in the War Effort. These children, flashing the "V-for-Victory" sign, stand atop a pile of scrap metal. Collecting scrap of all kinds for war production helped engage millions of Americans young and old on the home front.

workers walked off the job to protest the hiring of African Americans, fearing that management might use the war as an excuse to erode union power.

The labor militancy of the 1930s, although muted by a wartime no-strike pledge, persisted into the 1940s. Wildcat strikes erupted among St. Louis bus drivers, Detroit assembly-line workers, and Philadelphia streetcar conductors. In Detroit, a group of aircraft workers, angry at the increasing regimentation of the production process, fanned out across a factory floor and cut off the neck ties worn by their supervisors. Despite the no-strike assurances, the United Mine Workers called a walkout in the bituminous coal fields in 1943. When the War Labor Board took a hard line against the union's demands, the strike was prolonged. The increasingly conservative Congress responded with the Smith-Connally Act of 1943, which empowered the president to seize plants or mines if strikes interrupted war production. Even so, the war helped to strengthen organized labor's place.

Assessing Economic Change

The economic impact of the war proved substantial. Most workplaces became more inclusive, in terms of gender and race, than ever before. So did labor unions. More people entered the paid labor force, and many earned more money than rationing restrictions on consumer goods allowed them to spend. Income inequality moderated. In a remarkable reversal of conditions during the Great Depression, jobs were plentiful and savings piled up.

More than anything else, the institutional scale of American life was transformed. Big government, big business, and big labor all grew even bigger during the war years. Science and technology forged new links of mutual interest among these three sectors and brought important new growth especially to still sparsely settled Western states. The old America of family farms, family-run businesses, and small towns did not disappear, but urban-based, bureaucratized institutions increasingly organized life.

A New Role for Government?

The growth of governmental power during the war years prompted debates over what the role of government should be in a postwar world. During the heyday of the New Deal, a broad view of governmentally guaranteed "security" had resulted in programs such as the Social Security System and federal agencies to secure home mortgages and personal savings accounts. At the same time, community-based groups and labor unions had begun to build a set of cooperative social welfare and health institutions they hoped would create a vast, nonprofit security-safety net.

As military victory began to seem likely, President Roosevelt and his advisers talked of harnessing the national government's power behind expanded efforts to enhance personal security in everyday life. Some dreamed of extending wartime health-care and day-care programs into a more comprehensive social welfare system.

In 1944 FDR introduced his ideas for the kind of expansive social agenda that some European governments were embracing.

Calling for a **"Second Bill of Rights,"** Roosevelt advocated measures to ensure that Americans could enjoy the "right" to

FDR's Second Bill of Rights Proposal

regular employment, adequate food and shelter, appropriate educational opportunities, and guaranteed health care. Translating this vision into reality, its proponents generally assumed, would require the government to continue the kind of economic and social planning it was doing in wartime.

Large insurance companies and some private businesses, recognizing the popularity of security-focused proposals, came forward with private alternatives to governmental programs. Insurers expanded their earlier efforts to market individual policies that would pay in cases of sickness, disability, and unexpected death. At the same time, insurance companies worked with large corporations to develop group insurance plans that would make expansion of government programs less attractive and provide supplements for existing New Deal-era programs such as Social Security. Questions about what should be the proper role for government in providing social safety nets would roil American life in the postwar era.

The War at Home: Social Issues

FOCUS QUESTION

How did the war propel movements for greater equality in American life?

Dramatic social changes accompanied the wartime mobilization. Many people, ordered by military service or attracted by employment, moved away from the communities where they had grown up. The war demanded sacrifice from all, and most Americans willingly obliged. The Roosevelt administration asked Americans to defend the "American way of life." Yet, for many, the war effort unsettled established patterns, and wartime ideals spotlighted the everyday inequalities that often clashed with rosy visions of the "American way."

Selling the War

Hollywood studios and directors answered the government's call to mobilize the country for war. The film factories produced both commercial movies with military themes, such as *Destination Tokyo* (1943), and documentaries, such as the *Why We Fight* series, directed by Frank Capra. Capra contrasted images of wholesome and diverse Americans with harrowing portrayals of the tightly regimented lifestyles in the military-dominated dictatorships of Germany, Italy, and Japan. Other famous directors enlisted their skills: Darryl F. Zanuck filmed Allied troops in North Africa; John Ford recreated the Pearl Harbor attack on film; Walt Disney's animation teams produced war-themed cartoons. Hollywood personalities sold war bonds, entertained the troops, and worked on documentaries for the Army's Pictorial Division.

Photojournalists helped bring the war into American living rooms. The U.S. Army, for example, accredited Margaret

Margaret Bourke-White. Famed photographer Margaret Bourke-White pursues her high-flying career covering the war.

FOOD IS A WEAPON

DON'T WASTE IT!
BUY WISELY – COOK CAREFULLY – EAT IT ALL

FOLLOW THE NATIONAL WARTIME NUTRITION PROGRAM

"Food Is a Weapon." This 1943 poster shows the Office of War Information skillfully extending its major theme: that people at home could assist the war by watching what they ate. The poster's final directive suggests how the war made better nutrition both a personal and patriotic goal.

Bourke-White as a war correspondent, the first woman so designated. She saw action in North Africa, Italy, and Germany, and documented the horrors of the Nazi death camps in *Life* magazine. The government, however, exercised close censorship over all journalists' war photos. Any images that censors felt might damage morale at home never made it into publication. (Read about one of the first photojournalists to document the horrors of Nazi death camps in the Americans Abroad feature, "Margaret Bourke-White: Adventure as a Photojournalist.")

AMERICANS ABROAD
Margaret Bourke-White

The advertising industry, lacking many consumer products to sell, turned its talents to promoting the war effort. Roosevelt encouraged advertisers to sell the benefits of freedom. Most obliged, and "freedom" often appeared in the form of new washing machines, improved kitchen appliances, streamlined automobiles, a wider range of lipstick hues, and other consumer products. As soon as the fighting ended, wartime ads promised, technological know-how would transform the United States into a consumer's paradise.

In the spring of 1942 Roosevelt created the **Office of War Information (OWI)** to coordinate propaganda and censorship. Many New Deal Democrats saw it catering to advertisers who preferred imagery extolling the future joys of consumerism to ones promoting broader visions of liberty and equality. Some Republicans, by contrast, blasted the agency for cranking out crass political appeals for causes favored by Roosevelt's New Dealers. Despite criticism from both left and right, the OWI established branch offices throughout the world, published a

magazine called *Victory*, and produced hundreds of films, posters, and radio broadcasts.

The work of illustrator Norman Rockwell exemplified wartime image making. Rockwell produced a set of paintings that visually represented the "Four Freedoms" for which President Roosevelt proclaimed Americans fought: Freedom of Speech, Freedom of Worship, Freedom from Want, and Freedom from Fear. Using his neighbors in Arlington, Vermont, as models, Rockwell depicted these values as rooted in small town America. Originally published in the *Saturday Evening Post* magazine in early 1943, the "Four Freedoms" came to adorn posters in millions of post offices and other buildings throughout the country.

Gender Issues

The changes sweeping American life became apparent in a range of social issues affecting women.

The wartime United States called on women to serve their country as more than wives and mothers. Some 350,000 women volunteered for military duty during the war, and more than a thousand became pilots for the Women's Airforce Service Pilots (WASPs). Not everyone approved. One member of Congress asked: "What has become of the manhood of America?" Most in Congress, however, supported the creation of a woman's corps in each branch of the military—an innovation proposed but never adopted during the First World War.

Even as the war narrowed gender differences in employment, widespread imagery frequently framed the changes as temporary. Women's expanded participation in the workplace was often portrayed as a short-term sacrifice intended, ultimately, to preserve and protect their "natural" sphere in the home. Stereotypes abounded. A typical ad suggesting that women take on farm work declared: "A woman can do anything if she knows she looks beautiful doing it."

An Equal Rights Amendment (ERA) to the Constitution continued to be debated both within Congress and around the country. Should the Constitution guarantee women "equal" status with men, or should the law continue to allow women some kind of "protected" status in view of their special vulnerability to exploitation? The war raised but did not settle this issue, over which even women's advocates were split.

In some ways, the war may have even widened the symbolic gap between notions of femininity and masculinity. Military culture fostered a "pin-up" mentality toward women.

Tanks and planes were decorated with images of female sexuality, and the home-front entertainment industry, led by Hollywood, promoted its glamorous female stars as anxious to "please" their "boys" in the military. Wartime popular culture often associated masculinity with misogyny. After the war, tough-guy fiction, on display in Mickey Spillane's "Mike Hammer" series of detective novels, portrayed female sexuality as both alluring and threatening to men.

Public policymaking sometimes worked to reinforce gender divisions. The military assigned most of the women who joined the armed services to stateside clerical and supply jobs. Day-care programs for mothers working outside their homes received reluctant and inadequate funding. The thousands of child-care centers set up during the conflict filled only a fraction of the need and were swiftly shut down after the war. Meanwhile, social scientists oftentimes blamed mothers for an apparent spike in rates of juvenile delinquency and divorce during the war years.

Racial Issues

Messages about race were as ambiguous as those related to gender. Before the war, America had been a sharply segregated

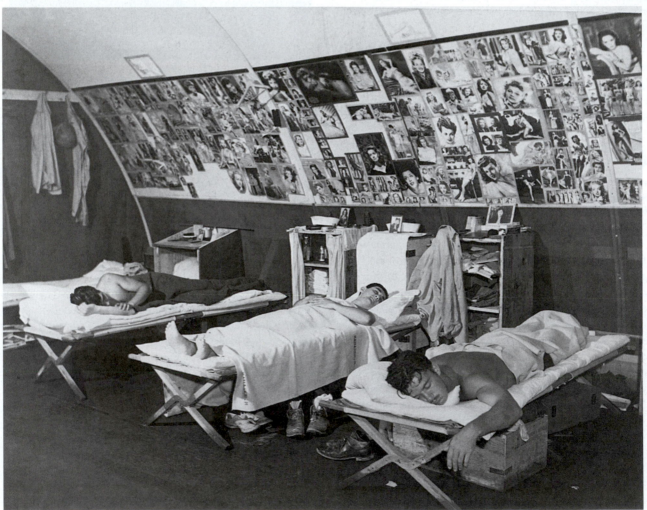

Pin-up Girls. Male GIs often surrounded themselves with pin-up girls, images very different from that of the home front "Rosie-the-Riveter."

© CORBIS

Songs of the Second World War

Songwriter: Cole Porter
Title: "Don't Fence Me In" (1944)
Artist: Bing Crosby (with the Andrews Sisters)

Harry Lillis ("Bing") Crosby (1903–77) was the dominant male vocalist during the Second World War. Although Crosby was not the first artist to embrace the style of singing known as "crooning," his careful attention to intonation, phrasing, and pacing provided a model for subsequent vocal stylists, including Frank Sinatra, Tony Bennett, and Peggy Lee. Crosby also melded a wide range of musical influences, including the "scat-singing" of African American vocalists, into his repertoire. The bandleader-musical critic Artie Shaw called Crosby "the first hip white person born in the United States."

During the war years, Crosby starred in motion pictures, headlined a network radio program, and toured the European Theater to entertain U.S. troops. This demanding schedule cost Crosby's voice some of its former suppleness but swelled his popularity. U.S. service personnel ranked him—ahead of President Franklin Roosevelt and General Dwight D. Eisenhower—as the person most responsible for boosting their morale.

Crosby's war-year recordings spanned the range of musical genres. Slow ballads such "White Christmas" (1942) and "I'll Be Home for Christmas" (1943) seemingly spoke to the hope that the war's end would allow Americans to re-embrace pre-war values and practices. His up-tempo version of "Don't Fence Me In" went in a different direction. Featuring the Andrews Sisters, a popular vocal trio during the 1940s, Crosby's recording acknowledged the new sound of western-swing bands and quickly shot to the top of the wartime music charts.

Q How did Bing Crosby's popularity suggest the importance of popular culture to the war effort?

Q How did a song entitled "Don't Fence Me In" express the readiness of Americans to tackle the challenges of wartime?

society. Disenfranchised in the South, African Americans in the rest of the country experimented with how best to use the political power they had gained during the 1930s. In California and throughout the Southwest, residents who traced their ancestry back to Mexico, including many who had long resided in the United States, also worked to address a wide range of discriminatory policies in employment, education, and housing.

President Roosevelt refused to abandon the policy of segregation in the armed forces. Although the Army integrated Latino and American Indian soldiers, along with those from various European ethnic groups, into its combat units, military leaders refused to do the same for people of African and Japanese ancestry. The National Association for the Advancement of Colored People (NAACP) and others pressed for integration, but Roosevelt's top advisers remained opposed to change. Desegregation of the armed forces found special opposition among politically powerful white Democrats in the South, who feared it might lead to broader demands for desegregation at home. The army even adopted the scientifically absurd practice of segregating donated blood into separate stores of "white" and "black" plasma. African Americans were relegated to inferior, often highly dangerous, jobs and excluded from combat duty. Toward the end of the war, when troop shortages forced the administration to put African American units into combat, they performed with distinction.

Meanwhile, on the home front, volatile social issues continued to simmer. As the wartime production system created more jobs, vast numbers of people from the rural South, including several hundred thousand African Americans, moved to cities such as Los Angles and Detroit. People already living in these areas often chafed at the influx of newcomers, who competed with them for jobs and housing and placed greater demands on public services such as transportation, education, and recreational facilities.

Social strains sometimes flared into violence. This escalation most often occurred in overcrowded urban spaces, where diverse populations and cultures already competed and clashed. In Detroit, in June 1943, conflict between white and black youth at an amusement park rapidly spiraled into a multiple-day riot. The violence left nearly 40 people, most of them African American, dead, injured hundreds, and inflicted millions of dollars worth of damage to property.

Racial disturbances were not restricted to confrontations between whites and blacks. In Los Angeles, complicated and long-standing ethnic tensions erupted in the "Zoot Suit Riots" of 1943. Soldiers and sailors from nearby military bases attacked young Mexican American and African American men wearing zoot suits: flamboyant outfits featuring oversized coats and trousers. Violence only escalated as the city's police force entered the fray, often beating and arresting Mexican Americans. A military order restricting servicemen to their bases finally helped quell the disorder.

A Segregated Military. This photo of an African American regiment eating in a mess hall during the Second World War illustrates racial segregation in the armed forces.

Even when wartime tensions did not produce the level of violence seen in Detroit and Los Angeles, the Second World War highlighted longstanding social divisions. For many Native Americans, for instance, the wartime years increased the pressures associated with longer-term patterns of migration and assimilation. Approximately 25,000 Indian men and several hundred Indian women served in the armed forces. Tens of thousands of other American Indians, many leaving their reservations for the first time, found wartime work in urban areas such as Rapid City, Minneapolis, Flagstaff, and Billings. Many Indians moved back and forth between city and reservation, seeking to live in two significantly different worlds.

Internment of Japanese Americans

People of Japanese descent faced a unique situation. Shortly after the attack on Pearl Harbor, fear of sabotage by pro-Japanese residents engulfed West Coast communities. One military report claimed that a "large, unassimilated, tightly knit racial group, bound to an enemy nation by strong ties of race, culture, custom, and religion . . . constituted a menace" that justified extraordinary action.

Although lacking evidence of disloyalty, the president in February 1942 issued Executive Order 9066, directing the relocation and **internment** of first- and second-generation Japanese Americans (called Issei and Nisei, respectively) at inland camps. Nearly 130,000 people were affected. Significantly, in Hawaii, where the presumed danger of subversion might have seemed

Executive Order 9066

much greater, military rule with intensive surveillance prevailed after the Pearl Harbor attack, and no internment took place. There, people of Japanese ancestry constituted nearly 40 percent of the population and were essential to the economy. Some Italian and German Americans were also closely watched and several thousand were interned in camps across America,

but these numbers paled beside the comprehensive internment of Japanese Americans.

Forced to abandon their possessions or sell them for a pittance, Japanese American evacuees were confined in flimsy barracks, enclosed by barbed wire and under armed guard. These camps, often located in remote locations such as Heart Mountain, Wyoming, offered only the barest accommodations: cots for beds, a low daily ration for food, overcrowded rooms. Two-thirds of the detainees were native-born U.S. citizens, and many gave up thriving agricultural enterprises that they had built in California over a generation. Some evacuated so quickly that they arrived in their camps with only the clothes they wore, hardly enough for cold-winter climates.

Internment was controversial. Civil libertarians charged that the measure was militarily unnecessary and unconstitutional. In December 1944, however, a divided U.S. Supreme Court upheld the constitutionality of Japanese relocation in *Korematsu* v. *U.S.* (1944). In 1988 Congress officially apologized for the internment, revealed that military investigators at the time had reported no cases of subversion, and authorized a cash indemnity for anyone who had been confined in the camps.

Korematsu v. U.S. arguments

Challenging Racial Inequality

The global fight against fascism proved helpful to movements that were working for greater racial equality in America. Nazism, based on the idea of racial inequality, exposed the racist underpinnings of older social-science research. The view that racial difference was not the result of biology but of culture gained wider acceptance during the war. "The Huns have wrecked the theory of the master race," stated an Alabama politician. The idea that a democracy could bridge racial differences provided a basis for the postwar struggle against discrimination.

Internment of Japanese Americans. Taken by the famous photographer Ansel Adams, this image shows internees walking in the snow at a remote relocation camp.

The *Amsterdam News*, a Harlem newspaper, called for a **"Double V" campaign**—victory at home as well as abroad. In January 1941 the labor leader A. Philip Randolph promised to lead tens of thousands of black workers in a march on Washington to demand more defense jobs and integration of the military forces. President Roosevelt feared the event would embarrass his administration and urged that it be canceled. Randolph's persistence ultimately forced Roosevelt to create the FEPC. Although this new agency gained little effective power, its very existence helped advance the ideal of nondiscrimination.

Double V Campaign announcement

Northward migration of African Americans accelerated demands for equality. Drawn by the promise of wartime jobs, nearly 750,000 African Americans relocated to northern cities, where many sensed the possibility of political power for the first time in their lives. They found an outspoken advocate of civil rights within the White House. First Lady Eleanor Roosevelt repeatedly antagonized southern Democrats and members of her husband's administration by her advocacy of civil rights and her participation in integrated social functions.

Particularly in urban areas, civil rights groups emerged from the wartime years with a strong base from which to fight for jobs and political power. Founded in 1942, the interracial Committee (later, Congress) on Racial Equality (CORE) devised new ways of opposing discrimination. CORE activists staged sit-ins to integrate restaurants, theaters, and other public facilities, especially in Washington, D.C.

In California and throughout the Southwest during the war years, Latino organizations also highlighted the irony of fighting overseas for a nation that denied equality at home. They challenged the United States to live up to its democratic rhetoric. Approximately 500,000 Mexican Americans served, often with great distinction, in the military. Not wishing to anger this constituency, the Roosevelt administration, also feared discrimination might harm the credibility of its Good Neighbor Policy in Latin America (see Chapter 25). The president's Coordinator of Inter-American Affairs allocated federal money to train Spanish-speaking workers for wartime employment, improve education in barrios, and provide high school graduates with new opportunities to enter college.

Although legal precedents in California and other Southwestern states classified Latinos as "white," actual practices, especially in public schools, usually discriminated against people of Mexican descent. Organizations such as the League of United Latin American Citizens (LULAC) mounted several drives against such discrimination during the war, and they prepared for greater challenges in the postwar period.

People of Japanese descent, despite their internment, also laid the basis for postwar campaigns for equality. The courage and sacrifice of Japanese American soldiers became legendary. The 100th Battalion and the 442nd Regimental

Civil Liberties in Wartime: *Korematsu v. United States*

Fred Korematsu, an American of Japanese background, was born in Oakland, California and had been a law-abiding citizen. In his early twenties, when the order to relocate Japanese Americans to internment camps was announced, he challenged the legality of the measure. Ultimately, the Supreme Court heard the case and in a controversial decision in December 1944, a divided court upheld the constitutionality of internment. The following selections suggest some of the arguments made in both the majority and minority opinions. Nearly 45 years later, after an examination of military records, Congress took a stand on the issue. Officially apologizing for internment, Congress stated that it was "not justified by military necessity, and . . . not driven by analysis of military conditions."

JUSTICE HUGO BLACK

from the majority opinion of the Supreme Court in *Korematsu v. U.S.* (1944), upholding the constitutionality of Executive Order 9066

Exclusion of those of Japanese origin was deemed necessary because of the presence of an unascertained number of disloyal members of the group, most of whom we have no doubt were loyal to this country. It was because we could not reject the finding of the military authorities that it was impossible to bring about an immediate segregation of the disloyal from the loyal. . . .

Compulsory exclusion of large groups of citizens from their homes, except under circumstances of direct emergency and peril, is inconsistent with our basic governmental institutions. But when under conditions of modern warfare our shores are threatened by hostile forces, the power to protect must be commensurate with the threatened danger. . . . To cast this case into outlines of racial prejudice, without reference to the real military dangers which were presented, merely confuses the issue.

JUSTICE FRANK MURPHY

from the dissenting opinion in *Korematsu v. U.S.*

We must accord great respect and consideration to the judgments of the military authorities who are on the scene and who have full knowledge of the military facts. . . . At the same time, however, it is essential that there be definite limits to military discretion, especially where martial law has not been declared. Individuals must not be left impoverished of their constitutional rights on a plea of military necessity that has neither substance nor support. . . .

In support of this blanket condemnation of all persons of Japanese descent, however, no reliable evidence is cited to show that such individuals were generally disloyal, or had . . . furnished reasonable ground for their exclusion as a group. . . . No adequate reason is given for the failure to treat these Japanese Americans on an individual basis by holding investigations and hearings to separate the loyal from the disloyal, as was done in the case of persons of German and Italian ancestry. . . . I dissent, therefore, from this legalization of racism.

Q Are there conditions that would constitutionally permit detention of citizens on the basis of their nationality or ethnic background?

Q What might explain Congress's later decision to issue an apology?

Combat Team, segregated units, suffered stunning casualities, often while undertaking extremely dangerous combat missions in Europe. Moreover, in the Pacific Theater, 6,000 Japanese-American members of the Military Intelligence Service provided invaluable service.

In the face of divisive issues and calls for greater equality in American life, wartime propaganda stressed national unity and contrasted America's "melting pot" ethos with German and Japanese obsessions about racial "purity." Wartime movies, plays, radio dramas, and music fostered a sense of national community by celebrating cultural diversity. As members of each of America's racial and ethnic groups distinguished themselves in the military, the claim of equality—"Americans All," in the words of a wartime slogan—took on greater moral force. Imagery extolling social solidarity and freedom provided a foundation for the antidiscrimination movements of the decades ahead.

Shaping the Peace

FOCUS QUESTION What major institutions and policies did the United States and the Allies adopt in their efforts to shape the reconstruction of the postwar world?

Even before the war ended, U.S. policymakers began considering postwar peace arrangements. The Truman administration built on Roosevelt's wartime conferences and agreements to shape the framework of international relations for the next half-century.

International Organizations

In the Atlantic Charter of 1941, and at a conference in Moscow in October 1943, the Allied powers had pledged to create a replacement for the defunct League of Nations. Internationalist-minded Americans hoped the new **United Nations (UN)** would offer a more realistic version of Woodrow Wilson's vision for a world body that could deter aggressor nations and promote peaceful political change. At the Dumbarton Oaks Conference in Washington in August 1944, and at a subsequent meeting in San Francisco in April 1945, the Allies worked out the UN's organizational structure. It included a General Assembly, in which each member nation would be represented and cast one vote. A smaller body, the Security Council, would include five permanent members from the Allied coalition—the United States, Great Britain, the Soviet Union, France, and Nationalist China—and six rotating members. The Security Council would have primary responsibility for maintaining peace, but permanent members could veto any council decision. A UN Secretariat, headed by a Secretary General, would handle day-to-day business, and an Economic and Social Council would sponsor measures to improve living conditions throughout the world.

The U.S. Senate, with only two dissenting votes, approved joining the UN in July 1945. This victory for internationalism contrasted sharply with the Senate's 1919 rejection of membership in the League of Nations. Opponents of Wilson's dream had worried that internationalist policies might limit the ability of the United States to pursue its own national interests. Following the Second World War, however, a newly powerful United States appeared able to dominate international organizations such as the UN. It seemed unlikely that decisions by it or other international bodies could hamstring U.S. foreign policy. In addition, most U.S. leaders recognized that the war had partly resulted from the lack of a coordinated, international response to aggression during the 1930s.

Eleanor Roosevelt, the former first lady and a committed social activist, played a prominent role in building the new postwar internationalist ethos. A delegate to the first meeting of the UN's General Assembly, she chaired its Commission on Human Rights and guided the drafting of a **Universal Declaration of Human Rights**, adopted by the UN in 1948. The document set forth "inalienable" human rights and freedoms as cornerstones of international law.

Universal Declaration of Human Rights, 1948

Economic agreements also illustrated a growing acceptance of international organizations. They sought to remedy some of the causes of international instability that had touched off the Great Depression and the war. At the Bretton Woods (New Hampshire) Conference of 1944, assembled nations created the International Monetary Fund (IMF), which was designed to maintain stable currency exchange rates by ensuring that each nation's currency could be converted into any other national currency at a fixed rate. The U.S. dollar, initially pegged at a value of $35 dollars for an ounce of gold, would provide the lynchpin. Exchange rates could be altered only with the agreement of the IMF.

The International Bank for Reconstruction and Development, later renamed the World Bank, was also created to provide loans to war-battered countries and promote the resumption of world trade. In 1948 the General Agreement on Tariffs and Trade (GATT) established the institutional groundwork for breaking up closed trading blocs and implementing free and fair trade agreements.

Spheres of Interest and Postwar Settlements

In wartime negotiations, Stalin, Churchill, and Roosevelt all had assumed that powerful nations—their own—would enjoy special "spheres of influence" in the postwar world. As early as January 1942 the Soviet ambassador to the United States reported to Stalin that Roosevelt had tacitly assented to Soviet postwar control over the Baltic states of Lithuania, Latvia, and Estonia. In 1944 Stalin and Churchill agreed, informally and secretly, that Britain would continue its sway over Greece and that the Soviets could control Romania and Bulgaria. U.S. leaders, meanwhile, assumed that Latin America would remain within their sphere of influence. Roosevelt sometimes seemed to imply that he accepted Stalin's goal of having states friendly to the USSR on his vulnerable western border, but at the Tehran Conference of November 1943 he also told Stalin that U.S. voters of Eastern European descent expected their homelands to be independent after the war.

Historians continue to differ on precisely how Roosevelt might have intended to reconcile his contradictory positions on a postwar Soviet sphere of influence. As long as the Soviet military remained essential to Germany's defeat—and Roosevelt also wanted the Soviet Union to join the war against Japan—the president struck a conciliatory tone with Stalin. After Roosevelt's death, however, the Soviets' powerful position in Eastern Europe became a focus of bipolar tensions.

Early in the war, both nations had urged the dismemberment and deindustrialization of a defeated Nazi Germany. At a conference held at Yalta, in Ukraine, in February 1945, the three Allied powers agreed to divide Germany into four zones of occupation (with France as the fourth occupying force). Later, as relations among the victors worsened, this temporary division of Germany hardened into a Soviet-dominated zone in the east and the other three zones to its west. Berlin, the German capital, also was divided, even though the city itself lay totally within the Soviet zone.

The future of Poland also posed difficult issues. At Yalta, the Soviets agreed to permit free elections in postwar Poland and to create a government "responsible to the will of the people," but Stalin believed that the other Allied leaders had tacitly accepted Soviet dominance over Poland. The agreement at Yalta was ambiguous at best. The war was still at a critical stage, and the western Allies chose to sacrifice clarity in order to encourage cooperation from the Soviets. After Yalta, the Soviets assumed that Poland would be in their sphere of influence, but many Americans charged the Soviets with bad faith for failing to hold free elections and for not relinquishing control.

In Asia, military realities likewise influenced postwar settlements. At Tehran and again at Yalta, Stalin pledged to send troops to fight Japan as soon as Germany surrendered. The first U.S. atomic bomb fell on Hiroshima, however, just one day before the Soviets were to enter the Pacific Theater of the war, and the United States assumed total charge of the occupation and postwar reorganization of Japan. The Soviet Union and the United States divided Korea, which had been controlled by Japan, into separate zones of occupation. Here, as in Germany, these zones would later emerge as two antagonistic states (see Chapter 27).

The fate of the European colonies seized by Japan in Southeast Asia was another contentious issue. Most U.S. officials preferred to see the former British and French colonies become independent nations, but they also worried about the left-leaning politics of many anticolonial nationalist movements. As the United States developed an anticommunist foreign policy after the end of the war, it moved to support British and French efforts to reassemble their colonial empires.

In the Philippines, the United States honored its long-standing pledge to grant independence. A friendly government that agreed to respect American economic interests and military bases took power in 1946 and enlisted American advisers to help suppress leftist rebels. In 1947 the United Nations designated the Mariana, Caroline, and Marshall Islands as the "Trust Territories of the Pacific" and authorized the United States to administer their affairs.

Although the nations of Latin America had been only indirectly involved in military conflict and peace negotiations, the war directly affected U.S. relations with them. During the 1930s the Roosevelt administration's Good Neighbor Policy had helped improve U.S.–Latin American relations. The Office of Inter-American Affairs (OIAA), created in 1937, further expanded cultural and economic ties. After the German invasion of Poland in 1939, Latin American leaders stood nearly united behind the Allies. After U.S. entry into the war, at a conference in Rio de Janeiro in January 1942, every Latin American country except Chile and Argentina broke diplomatic ties with the Axis governments. When naval warfare in the Atlantic severed commercial connections between Latin America and Europe, Latin American countries became critical suppliers of raw materials to the United States.

Wartime conferences avoided clear decisions about creating a Jewish homeland in the Middle East. The Second World War prompted survivors of the Holocaust and Jews from around the world to take direct action. Zionism, the movement to found a Jewish state in Palestine, attracted thousands of Jews to the Middle East. They began to carve out, against the wishes of Palestinians and other Arab people, the new nation of Israel.

Conclusion

The world changed dramatically during the Second World War. For the United States, wartime mobilization ended the Great Depression and focused attention on international concerns. The war brought victory over dictatorial, expansionist regimes, and the United States emerged as the world's preeminent power.

At home, a more powerful national government, concerned with preserving national security, assumed nearly complete power over the economy. New, cooperative ties were forged among government, business, and scientific researchers. These sectors worked together to provide the seemingly miraculous growth in productivity that ultimately won the war.

The early 1940s sharpened debates over liberty and equality. Many Americans saw the Second World War as a struggle to protect and preserve liberties they already enjoyed. Others, inspired by a struggle against racism and injustice abroad, insisted that a war for freedom overseas should extend to the redress of inequalities at home.

News of Japan's 1945 surrender prompted joyous celebrations throughout the United States. Still, Americans remained uncertain about postwar policies at home, where the dislocations of war would give way to the uncertainties of peace. They also worried about the recovery of Europe and relations with their wartime ally, the Soviet Union. And of course, the nation now faced the future without the charismatic leadership of Franklin D. Roosevelt. ⊁

CHAPTER REVIEW

REVIEW QUESTIONS

1. How did events in Asia and in Europe affect debate within the United States over whether or not to embrace more interventionist policies overseas?
2. What military strategies did the United States and the Allies ultimately adopt when fighting in both the European and Asian theaters of the Second World War?
3. How did mobilizing for war transform the American economy, its labor force, and the role of government?
4. How did the war propel movements for greater equality in American life?

5. What major institutions and policies did the United States and the Allies adopt in their efforts to shape the reconstruction of the postwar world?

CRITICAL THINKING QUESTIONS

1. In what ways had the United States already moved, even before the attack on Pearl Harbor, toward intervention in the Second World War?
2. How did Franklin Roosevelt's domestic policies during the Second World War both fulfill and retreat from the aspirations of his New Deal?

IDENTIFICATIONS

Review your understanding of the following key terms, people, and events for this chapter (terms in bold in text are included in the Glossary).

Adolf Hitler, p. 716
Third Reich, p. 716
Neutrality Acts, p. 717
Spanish Civil War, p. 717
East Asian Co-Prosperity Sphere, p. 717
Munich Conference, p. 717
isolationists, p. 719
Lend-Lease Act, p. 719
Pearl Harbor, p. 720
Pentagon, p. 721
OVERLORD, p. 721
Manhattan Project, p. 727
Hiroshima, p. 728
"Second Bill of Rights," p. 732
Office of War Information (OWI), p. 733
Internment, p. 736
"Double V" campaign, p. 737
United Nations (UN), p. 739
Universal Declaration of Human Rights, p. 739

 Visit the CourseMate website at www.cengagebrain.com for additional study tools and review materials for this chapter.

SUGGESTED READINGS

On the U.S. entry into the war see **Waldo H. Heinrichs,** *Threshold of War: Franklin D. Roosevelt and American Entry into World War II* (1988). For the war's military history consult **Gerald F. Linderman,** *The World Within War: America's Combat Experience in World War II* (1997). **J. Samuel Walker,** *Prompt and Utter Destruction: Truman and the Use of the Atomic Bombs against Japan* (2005) provides a judicious examination of the war's end, and **John Dower,** *War without Mercy: Race and Power in the Pacific War* (1987) is a powerful examination of the culture of violence.

On the home front, see **David Kennedy,** *The American People in World War II: Freedom from Fear* (2003), **William L. O'Neill,** *A Democracy at War: American's Fight at Home and Abroad in World War II* (1993), and **Gerald D. Nash,** *The American West Transformed: The Impact of the Second World War* (1990). **Thomas Patrick Doherty,** *Projections of War: Hollywood, American Culture, and World War II* (1993) examines wartime films. **Emily Yellin,** *Our Mothers' War: American Women at Home and at the Front During World War II* (2005) provides a readable overview of women's experiences. **Ronald Takaki,** *Double Victory: A Multicultural History of America in World War II* (2000) examines issues of race and ethnicity.

Hollywood in the Service of the Anticommunist Crusade

Fears about communist infiltration of the motion picture industry prompted Hollywood studios to display their anticommunist credentials by blacklisting left-leaning employees and by making films such as RKO's *I Married a Communist*. These anticommunist films, with their simplistic political messages, generally bombed at the box office. This particular film did better when re-released as *The Woman on Pier 13*.

The Age of Containment, 1946–1953

T HE SECOND WORLD WAR, popularly portrayed as a struggle to preserve the "American way of life," ended up transforming it. The fight against fascism propelled foreign-policy issues to the forefront of American politics, and postwar tensions kept them there. As combat operations gave way to friction between the United States and the Soviet Union, U.S. leaders overhauled military strategy. They claimed broad powers for the executive branch and called for a global stand against communism. The effort to shore up "national security" soon translated into an ever-larger military establishment and an economic system that could supply its needs.

At home, debate over increased governmental power generated immediate controversy. Wartime production, overseen by government bureaucracies in Washington, had finally ended the economic downturn of the 1930s. Should Washington help organize a postwar economy that satisfied household as well as military consumption? Should a more powerful and active government in Washington assist movements seeking greater equality? Could such a government limit security threats at home without endangering liberty? Questions such as these enlivened, and embittered, public debate in the aftermath the Second World War.

Creating a National Security State, 1945–1949
Onset of the Cold War
The Truman Doctrine and
    Containment Abroad
Truman's Loyalty Program and
    Containment at Home
The National Security Act, the
    Marshall Plan, and the Berlin
    Crisis
The Election of 1948

The Era of the Korean War, 1949–1952
NATO, China, and the Bomb
NSC-68 and the Korean War
Korea and Containment

Pursuing National Security at Home
Anticommunism and the U.S.
    Labor Movement
Containing Communism at Home
Targeting Difference
The "Great Fear"
Joseph McCarthy
The National Security
    Constitution and the Structure
    of Governance

Postwar Social-Economic Policymaking
The Employment Act of 1946
    and Economic Growth
Truman's Fair Deal
Civil Rights

Signs of a Changing Culture
The Baseball "Color Line"
The New Suburbia
Postwar Hollywood

The Election of 1952
Continuing Containment
A Soldier-Politician

Creating a National Security State, 1945–1949

FOCUS QUESTION What major conflicts between the United States and the Soviet Union shaped the Cold War and prompted a U.S. foreign policy focused on containment of communism?

The wartime alliance between the United States and the Soviet Union proved little more than a brief marriage of convenience. Defeating the Axis had forced the two nations to cooperate, but collaboration began unraveling even before war's end. A **Cold War** between the United States and the Soviet Union would feature mutual suspicion and massive military buildup but few direct confrontations between the two superpowers.

Onset of the Cold War

Historians have dissected the onset of the Cold War from different perspectives. A familiar view focuses on Soviet expansionism, stressing a historically rooted appetite for new territory, an ideological zeal to spread communism, or some interplay between the two. According to this interpretation, the United States needed to adopt firm, anti-Soviet policies. Other historians—generally called revisionists—see the Soviet Union's desire to secure its borders as an understandable response to the invasion of its territory during both world wars. The United States, in this view, should have tried to reassure the Soviet Union (USSR), pursing conciliatory measures instead of ones that intensified Soviet fears. Still other scholars maintain that assigning blame obscures how clashing interests and differing political cultures made postwar conflict between the two superpowers unavoidable.

Almost every view of the Cold War assigns the presidential administration of Harry Truman a central role. Truman initially hoped to bargain productively with the Soviet Union and its Premier, Joseph Stalin. As differences between the former allies sharpened, however, Truman came to distrust Stalin and listen to hardline, anti-Soviet advisers.

The atomic bomb became an important source of friction. At the Potsdam Conference of July 1945, Truman had casually told Stalin, without mentioning the bomb, about a new U.S. weapon of "unusual destructive force." Well informed by Soviet intelligence operations about the Manhattan Project, Stalin calmly advised Truman to make "good use" of this weapon. Stalin also ordered Soviet scientists, with far less calm, to intensify their nuclear weapons program. Truman likely hoped that the bomb would scare the Soviets—and it did. Historians debate whether it frightened Moscow into more cautious behavior or made it a more aggressive Cold War adversary.

As atomic warfare against Japan gave way to atomic diplomacy with the Soviet Union, U.S. leaders differed over how to proceed. One group, recognizing the Soviets would soon possess atomic weapons, urged Truman to share technology with the USSR in hopes of forestalling a future arms race. Hardliners, fearing Soviet intentions and underestimating their nuclear knowledge, rejected this approach.

CHRONOLOGY

1946	Employment Act passed ◆ Republicans gain control of Congress
1947	Truman Doctrine announced ◆ George Kennan's "Mr. X" article published ◆ National Security Act passed ◆ Marshall Plan proposed ◆ Taft-Hartley Act passed
1948	Marshall Plan adopted ◆ Berlin Airlift begins ◆ Truman wins reelection
1949	NATO established ◆ Soviet Union explodes atomic device ◆ Truman unveils his Fair Deal
1950	NSC-68 adopted ◆ Korean War begins
1951	Truman removes General MacArthur as commander in Korea ◆ *Dennis* decision in Supreme Court
1952	National Security Agency (NSA) created ◆ Republican Dwight Eisenhower elected president

In 1946 Truman authorized Bernard Baruch, his special representative at the United Nations, to explore ways of controlling atomic power. The Baruch Plan proposed that the United States abandon its atomic weapons if the USSR met certain conditions. These included the Soviets agreeing to outside monitoring of their weapons program and surrendering their veto power in the UN on atomic issues. Soviet leaders, after dismissing the Baruch Plan, counterproposed that the United States destroy its atomic weapons as the first step toward any bargain. The United States rejected this idea. Both nations used the deadlock to justify a stepped-up arms race.

Other sources of friction involved U.S. loan policy and Soviet domination of Eastern Europe. Truman ended Lend-Lease assistance to the Soviet Union at the end of the war and linked any new loans for postwar reconstruction to Soviet cooperation with the United States over the future of Europe. This linkage strategy failed. Lack of capital and suspicions about the intentions of the United States and its allies provided the Soviets with excuses for their own hard-line stance. A repressive Soviet sphere of influence, which Stalin called defensive and Truman labeled expansionist, spread over Eastern Europe. By 1946, the former allies seemed ready to become bitter adversaries. Early that year, Winston Churchill famously declared that an "Iron Curtain," with free nations on one side and communist ones on the other, had "descended across Europe." The communist countries to the East, under the control of the Soviet Union, threatened the security of Western Europe, the British leader proclaimed.

Testing the Atomic Bomb at Bikini Atoll.
This atomic test, one of 23 detonations at Bikini Atoll in the Marshall Islands during the late 1940s, raised a column of water 5,000 feet high. Although Bikini islanders were evacuated from the blast sites, the radiation still affected nearby people, including U.S. service personnel, and the area's ecology for years to come. As nuclear-related imagery spread through Cold War culture, new "bikini" swimsuits for "bombshell" women became a fashion rage.

Truman agreed and pledged to stop any communist aggression. His anticommunist initiatives, in both foreign and domestic affairs, extended the reach and power of the executive branch.

The Truman Doctrine and Containment Abroad

In March 1947, the president announced what soon became known as the **Truman Doctrine** when speaking to Congress about a civil war in Greece, where communist-led insurgents threatened to topple a pro-Western government. In private, London had informed Washington that it lacked the economic and military resources to act in Greece, long within Great Britain's sphere of influence. Truman's advisers feared a leftist victory in Greece would expose Turkey, a nation considered critical to the U.S. strategic position, to Soviet expansionism. In publically justifying U.S. aid to Greece and Turkey, Truman asserted that U.S. security interests now spanned the globe and that the fate of "free peoples" everywhere hung in the balance. Unless the United States aided people "resisting attempted subversion by armed minorities or by outside pressures," totalitarian communism would spread and ultimately threaten the United States.

The Truman Doctrine (1947)

The Truman Doctrine's global vision of national security encountered some skepticism. Henry Wallace, the most visible Democratic critic, chided Truman for exaggerating the Soviet threat and urged a more conciliatory approach toward Moscow. Conservative Republicans, though fervently anti-communist, looked with suspicion at the increase in presidential power and the vast expenditures that implementing the Truman Doctrine would seemingly entail. If Truman wanted broad support for his position, Republican Senator Arthur Vandenberg had already advised, he should "scare hell" out of people, something Truman proved quite willing to do when justifying his new doctrine. With votes from Republicans and Democrats, the president gained Congressional approval for $400 million in assistance to Greece and Turkey, most of it for military aid, in the spring of 1947. This vote signaled broad, bipartisan support for a national security policy that came to be called **containment**.

The term *containment* first appeared in a 1947 article in the journal *Foreign Affairs* by George Kennan, the State Department's premier Soviet expert. Writing under the pseudonym "X," Kennan argued that the "main element" in U.S. policy "must be that of a long-term, patient but firm and vigilant containment of Russian expansive tendencies." The measured and limited containment policy, which Kennan later claimed he had outlined in this article, soon became associated with the urgent tone and expansive approach of the Truman Doctrine.

Containment thus became a catchphrase for a global, anticommunist national security policy. As popularly articulated, containment linked all leftist insurgencies, wherever they occurred, to a totalitarian movement controlled from Moscow that directly threatened American security. Even a small gain for the Soviets in one part of the world could encourage communist aggression elsewhere. Although foreign policy debates included sharp disagreements over precisely how to pursue containment, most American leaders came to support an activist, anticommunist foreign policy that spanned the globe.

Truman's Loyalty Program and Containment at Home

Nine days after proclaiming the Truman Doctrine, the president issued Executive Order 9835. It authorized a system of government loyalty boards empowered to gather evidence in order to determine if there were "reasonable grounds" for concluding that a federal employee belonged to a subversive organization or espoused ideas that might endanger national security. Persons found to pose a "security risk" would lose their government jobs. The Truman administration also empowered the Justice Department to identify political organizations it deemed subversive and place them on a new Attorney General's List. The Loyalty Program, partly intended to show that Truman's administration considered communism a serious domestic threat, suggested that containing communist activities at home would require the type of aggressive measures being adopted overseas.

The Truman administration thus embarked on what became a controversial approach to containing communism, including Soviet espionage, at home. Although few people ever doubted that the Soviets were conducting spy operations inside the United States, there has long been sharp disagreement over their scope and effectiveness. Such debates now take place in light of recently declassified evidence from Soviet and U.S. surveillance files which reveal that both nations conducted a wide range of intelligence activity. By 1943, a U. S. Army unit had begun intercepting transmissions between Moscow and the United States. Collected as the VENONA files and finally released in 1995, these intercepted messages show that the Soviet Union had helped finance America's Communist Party, placed informants in governmental agencies, and obtained secret information about U.S. atomic work. Uncovering Soviet espionage, in short, was a legitimate objective. Historians remain divided, however, over the reliability and relevance of specific pieces of the evidence collected by the VENONA project—and also over how much of the intercepted information became immediately available to the Truman administration.

There is little doubt, though, that Truman's loyalty policy worried a diverse group of critics. The president defended the program by claiming that the harmful potential from a relatively few security risks demanded a response unprecedented in peacetime. Truman's position, however, angered more fervent anticommunists, particularly Republicans, who accused the president of doing too little to fight subversion at home. Civil libertarians, in contrast, charged Truman with whipping up fear about communist activity that far exceeded any actual threat. They called for a carefully targeted approach. Internal security policy, for example, needed to treat an atomic scientist with links to the Soviet Union differently from an outspoken clerical worker in a nonsensitive governmental position.

The National Security Act, the Marshall Plan, and the Berlin Crisis

Shaking off criticism, the Truman administration continued to extend its containment initiative. It secured congressional approval of The **National Security Act of 1947**, which created several new government bureaucracies. The old Navy and War Departments would become transformed, by 1949, into a new Department of Defense. An entirely new addition to the executive branch, the National Security Council, obtained broad authority over planning the new containment policy. The Air Force became a separate service equal to the Army and Navy. The National Security Act also created the Central Intelligence Agency (CIA) to gather information about communist threats and conduct covert activities outside the United States.

The CIA quickly became the most flexible arm of this new national security apparatus. A series of secret presidential directives expanded the CIA's role, while its activities and budget remained shrouded from public scrutiny. Soon, the CIA's covert operations crisscrossed the globe. CIA operatives cultivated ties with anti-Soviet groups in Eastern Europe and within the Soviet Union. The agency helped finance pro-U.S. labor unions in Western Europe to curtail the influence of leftist organizations. It orchestrated covert campaigns to prevent the Italian Communist Party from winning an electoral victory in 1948 and to bolster anticommunist political parties in France, Japan, and elsewhere.

The Truman administration also linked economic initiatives in Western Europe to its overall containment policy. Fearing that Europe's economic problems might create opportunities for local communist movements, Secretary of State General George C. Marshall sought to strengthen the region's economies. Under his 1947 proposal, known as the European Recovery Program or simply the Marshall Plan, U.S. funds would help postwar governments in Europe to coordinate programs of economic reconstruction. Although invited to participate, the Soviet Union quickly denounced the Marshall Plan as the economic component of a larger U.S. effort to dominate all of Europe.

The Marshall Plan, enacted by Congress in early 1948, ultimately achieved the hopes of its architects. It helped brighten the economic picture in Western Europe, where industrial production rebounded. Improved standards of living enhanced political stability and helped undercut the appeal of leftist movements. Between 1946 and 1951, the United States provided nearly $13 billion in assistance to 17 Western European nations. When critics in the United States condemned the Marshall Plan as an expensive "giveaway" scheme, supporters stressed how it would expand both overseas markets and investment opportunities for American businesses. They also hailed it for contributing to the larger containment strategy for safeguarding national security.

While lobbying for the Marshall Plan, the Truman administration also sought to expand U.S. military forces. The Soviet Union helped install a pro-Moscow government in Czechoslovakia in early 1948, and some U.S. officials warned of a Soviet military strike into Western Europe. Truman declared that "moral God-fearing peoples . . . must save the world from Atheism" and Soviet totalitarianism. As a brief war scare gripped Washington, national security planners successfully implored Congress to increase defense spending, largely for new aircraft, and reinstate a draft system for the military.

Policymakers in the United States viewed the future of Germany, initially divided into four zones of occupation, as crucial to the security of Western Europe. In June 1948, the United States, Great Britain, and France announced a program of currency reform as the first step toward integrating their separate sectors into a Federal Republic of Germany or West Germany.

The Marshall Plan. This poster, by an artist from the Netherlands, was the winning entry in a contest run in Marshall Plan countries. It suggests how the plan envisioned a united Europe transcending the divisions that had led to two world wars.

had been losing the support among those Democrats—led by his secretary of commerce, Henry A. Wallace—who considered Truman's containment policies overly confrontational. When Wallace continued to criticize these initiatives, the president had ousted him from the cabinet. Two months later, in the off-year national elections of November 1946, voters had given the Republicans control of Congress for the first time since 1928. Although Truman's political fortunes had improved somewhat by late 1947, few political handicappers liked his chances in 1948.

Truman faced three other presidential hopefuls. Challenged from the left by a new Progressive Party, which nominated Wallace, and from the right by Thomas E. Dewey, the Republican nominee, and J. Strom Thurmond, the pro-segregationist candidate of the new States' Rights Party, or Dixiecrats, the president waged a vigorous campaign. Only months before Election Day, Truman called the GOP-controlled Congress into special session and presented it with a list of domestic programs, including a plan for national health care, abhorrent to most Republicans. Then he denounced "that do-nothing, good-for-nothing, worst Congress" for failing to enact his agenda.

Truman's victory now seems less surprising to historians than it had to analysts in 1948. Despite the GOP's electoral successes in 1946, the Democratic Party was hardly enfeebled. Democratic congressional candidates identifying with the legacy of Franklin Roosevelt, rather than with the presidency of his successor, generally polled more votes in their districts than did Truman in 1948. Loyalty to the memory of Roosevelt and his New Deal programs helped bring the Democrats their victory.

After Truman endorsed his party's call for new civil rights measures, the president survived the revolt of the Dixiecrats. Their presidential candidate, South Carolina's

Having been invaded by German forces in both world wars, however, the Soviet Union worried about Germany again becoming an economic power. Hoping to sidetrack Western plans for strengthening Germany, the Soviets cut off all highways, railroads, and water routes into West Berlin, which was located within their zone of military occupation.

This **Berlin Blockade** failed. American and British aircraft, in what became known as the **Berlin Airlift**, delivered virtually all of the items West Berliners needed to continue their daily routines. Truman, hinting at a military response, dispatched to Great Britain two squadrons of B-29 bombers, reportedly able to bring atomic bombs within reach of Soviet territory. Unable to seal off West Berlin, Stalin abandoned his blockade in May 1949. The Soviets then created the German Democratic Republic, or East Germany, out of their military sector. West Berlin, which survived as an anticommunist enclave inside East Germany, would remain a focus of Cold War tensions for years to come.

The Election of 1948

Meanwhile, national security issues helped Harry Truman win the 1948 presidential election. For several years, the president

Dewey Defeats Truman? U.S. President Harry S Truman holds up an Election Day edition of the *Chicago Daily Tribune*, which mistakenly announced "Dewey Defeats Truman" in the 1948 presidential election. The president told well-wishers, "That is one for the books!"

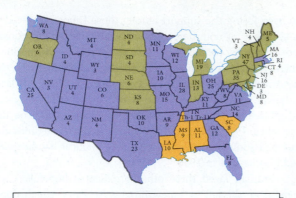

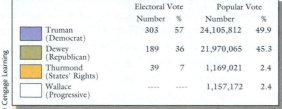

		Electoral Vote		Popular Vote	
		Number	%	Number	%
	Truman (Democrat)	303	57	24,105,812	49.9
	Dewey (Republican)	189	36	21,970,065	45.3
	Thurmond (States' Rights)	39	7	1,169,021	2.4
	Wallace (Progressive)	----	----	1,157,172	2.4

Map 27.1 Presidential Election, 1948. This electoral map helps show how, in this close election, Truman won the presidency with less than 50 percent of the popular vote.

Thurmond, denounced Truman for backing a "civil wrongs" program and assailed the national Democratic Party for having fallen under the control of "radicals, subversives, and reds." Although the Dixiecrat movement portended a political shift among Southern whites, who had voted overwhelmingly Democratic since the late 19th century, Truman carried all but four states of the old Confederacy in 1948.

Truman's staunch anticommunism helped bury Henry Wallace's challenge. Hampered by his Progressive Party's refusal to reject support from the U.S. Communist Party, Wallace received less than 3 percent of the popular tally and no electoral votes. The 1948 election suggested a blueprint for winning elections to come: Successful presidential candidates must never appear "soft" on national security issues.

The Era of the Korean War, 1949–1952

 How did the Korean War help reinforce and militarize the policy of containment?

FOCUS QUESTION

To implement his containment policy, Truman continued to mobilize the nation's economic and military resources. A series of Cold War crises in 1949 and the outbreak of war on the Korean peninsula in 1950, which heightened anticommunist fervor in the United States, boosted support for funding a vastly expanded national security state.

NATO, China, and the Bomb

In April 1949, the United States, Canada, and 10 European nations formed the **North Atlantic Treaty Organization (NATO)**. They pledged that an attack against one nation would automatically be treated as if a strike against all. Republican Senator Robert Taft called NATO a provocation to the Soviet Union, an "entangling alliance" in violation of settled foreign policy principles, and a threat to Congress's constitutional power to declare war. Still, the NATO concept prevailed, and the United States would continue to pursue its containment policy in Europe through this important "mutual defense" pact.

Meanwhile, events in China heightened Cold War tensions. Although the United States had extended Jiang Jieshi's struggling Nationalist government billions in military aid and economic assistance, Jiang's forces had steadily lost ground to those of Mao Zedong's communist movement. Mao pledged to transform China into a major world power. Experienced U.S. diplomats privately predicted that incompetence and corruption would speed Jiang's downfall, but the Truman administration publicly portrayed Jiang as the respected leader of an embattled but "free" China.

In 1949, when Mao's armies forced Jiang off the mainland to the nearby island of Formosa (Taiwan), many Americans wondered how communist forces could have triumphed. Financed by conservative business leaders, the powerful "China lobby" blamed Truman and his new secretary of state, Dean Acheson, for having "lost" China to communism. This domestic political pressure and new international tensions quickly convinced the Truman administration to embrace Jiang's fledgling government on Taiwan and to refuse diplomatic recognition for Mao's "Red China."

The communist threat grew more alarming when, in 1949, the Soviets exploded a crude atomic device, marking the end of the U.S. monopoly. Besieged by critics who saw recent history marked by Soviet gains and U.S. losses, Truman authorized U.S. scientists to develop a deadly new weapon, the hydrogen or "Super" bomb. "It is part of my responsibility as Commander-in-Chief to see to it that our country is able to defend itself against any possible aggressor," Truman declared.

NSC-68 and the Korean War

The Truman administration also reviewed its core assumptions about foreign policy. The task of coordinating this review fell to Paul Nitze, a hardliner who shaped a top-secret policy paper, **NSC-68** (National Security Council Document 68). It opened with a dramatic account of a global clash between "freedom," spread by U.S. power, and "slavery," promoted by the Soviet Union, the center of an international communist movement. Despairing of fruitful negotiations with the Soviets, NSC-68 urged a dramatic upgrade of U.S. national security capabilities. The United States should "find every weak spot in the enemy's armor" and "hit him with anything that comes to hand," one of NSC-68's architects insisted. NSC-68 thus endorsed covert

 Excerpts from NSC-68: U.S. Objectives and Programs for National Security (1950)

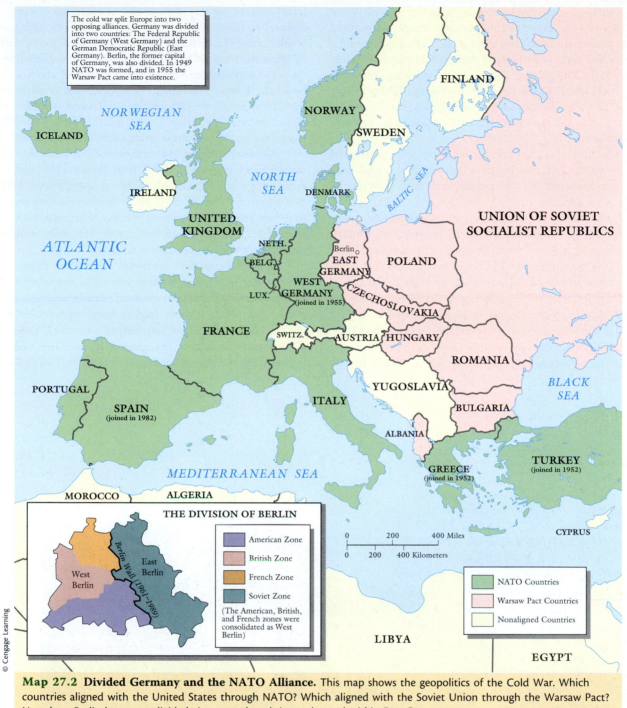

The cold war split Europe into two opposing alliances. Germany was divided into two countries: The Federal Republic of Germany (West Germany) and the German Democratic Republic (East Germany). Berlin, the former capital of Germany, was also divided. In 1949 NATO was formed, and in 1955 the Warsaw Pact came into existence.

THE DIVISION OF BERLIN

American Zone
British Zone
French Zone
Soviet Zone

(The American, British, and French zones were consolidated as West Berlin)

West Berlin
East Berlin
Berlin Wall (1961–1989)

© Cengage Learning

NATO Countries
Warsaw Pact Countries
Nonaligned Countries

Map 27.2 Divided Germany and the NATO Alliance. This map shows the geopolitics of the Cold War. Which countries aligned with the United States through NATO? Which aligned with the Soviet Union through the Warsaw Pact? Note how Berlin became a divided city, even though it was located within East Germany.

action, economic pressure, propaganda campaigns, and a massive military buildup. Because Americans might oppose larger military spending and budget deficits, the report cautioned, U.S. actions should be labeled as "defensive" and spending increases presented as a stimulus to the economy rather than as a drain on national resources. The details of NSC-68 remained classified until 1975, but the Truman administration immediately invoked its assumptions when framing specific policies and shaping public opinion.

The alarmist tone of NSC-68 seemed to be confirmed in June 1950 when communist North Korea invaded South

Korea. Truman characterized the invasion, which U.S. intelligence agencies had failed to anticipate, as a simple case of Soviet-inspired aggression and invoked the rhetoric of containment: "If aggression is successful in Korea, we can expect it to spread through Asia and Europe to this hemisphere," the president declared. The State Department characterized the relationship between the Soviet Union and North Korea as resembling "that between Walt Disney and Donald Duck."

The Korean situation, however, defied a one-dimensional analysis. Japanese military forces had occupied Korea between

1905 and 1945, and after Japan's defeat in the Second World War, Koreans had expected it to reemerge as one independent nation. Instead, the Soviet and U.S. zones of occupation resulting from the war became the basis for two separate states, artificially divided at the 38th parallel. The Soviet Union backed a communist government in North Korea, headed by the dictatorial Kim Il-sung. The United States supported Syngman Rhee, the leader of an unsteady and autocratic, but anticommunist, government in South Korea.

On June 25, 1950, after consulting with Soviet and Chinese leaders and receiving their tacit approval, Kim Il-sung moved troops across the 38th parallel in an attempt to reunify Korea. Rhee appealed to the United States for military assistance, and Truman responded without consulting Congress.

Korea quickly escalated into an international conflict, the **Korean War**. The Soviets, unaware of the details of Kim's plans, were boycotting the UN when North Korea's military action began and could not veto a U.S. proposal to send a UN peacekeeping force to Korea. Acting under UN auspices, the United States rushed assistance to Rhee, who moved to quell dissent in the South as well as to repel the armies of the North.

The United States confronted several options in Korea. It could simply contain communism by driving North Korea's forces back across the 38th parallel. It could risk a wider war and seek to reunify Korea under Rhee's leadership. This option seemed somewhat fanciful when North Korean forces pushed rapidly southward. Within three months, they captured Seoul, the capital of South Korea, and approached the southern tip of the Korean Peninsula. UN troops, most of them from the United States, seemed initially unprepared. American firepower, however, gradually took its toll on North Korea's elite troops and on the untrained recruits sent to replace them.

General Douglas MacArthur, the U.S. Army commander who led UN forces in Korea, then devised a plan that most other strategists considered crazy: an amphibious landing behind enemy lines. Those stunned by his audacious proposal were even more astounded by its results. On September 15, 1950, General MacArthur's troops landed at Inchon, suffered minimal casualties, and quickly recaptured Seoul.

The shifting tide of battle devastated Korea. The Korean War is called a "limited" war because it never spread off the Korean Peninsula or involved nuclear weapons, but its impact was hardly narrow. Intense bombing preceded every military move, and neither side seemed particularly concerned about civilian casualties. The number of estimated dead and wounded reached perhaps one tenth of North and South Korea's

Korean Refugees Move South. The Korean War disrupted life throughout the peninsula. Here, refugees flee their homes after receiving orders from the South Korean army to evacuate.

combined population. While rival armies battled for Seoul, the city became rubble, with only the capitol building and a train station left standing.

As MacArthur's troops drove northward, Truman faced a crucial decision. Emboldened by success, MacArthur urged moving beyond containment to an all-out war of "liberation" and reunification. Other U.S. military strategists warned that China would retaliate if MacArthur's forces approached its border. Truman did allow the General to carry the war into the North but cautioned against provoking intervention by China or the Soviet Union.

When MacArthur pushed near to the Chinese–Korean border, however, China sent at least 400,000 troops into North Korea and forced MacArthur back across the 38th parallel. China's Mao Zedong envisioned helping unite Korea under communist control. With China now in the war and

MacArthur seeking authority to use nuclear weapons, the Truman administration hastily reassessed U.S. priorities. "I could not bring myself to order the slaughter of 25,000,000 non-combatants" by using the atomic bomb, the president later claimed. Although Truman maintained a "limited" war, MacArthur's troops eventually regrouped and regained the initiative. As they moved back northward, Truman ordered the general to negotiate a truce at the 38th parallel. MacArthur, challenging the president, argued for a victory over North Korea—and over China, too. Truman thereupon relieved MacArthur of his command in April 1951. The Constitution made military officers subordinate to the president, the nation's commander in chief, Truman declared.

MacArthur returned to the United States a war hero. Initial polls reported strong opposition to Truman's dumping the popular general. Truman's approval ratings dipped under

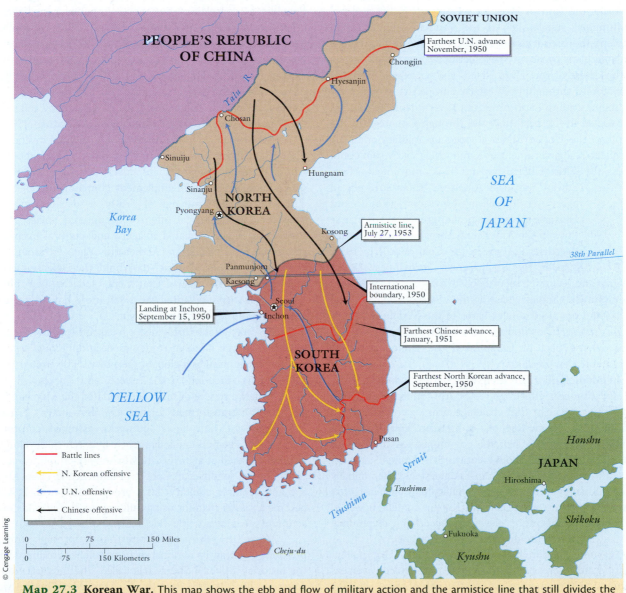

Map 27.3 Korean War. This map shows the ebb and flow of military action and the armistice line that still divides the two Koreas. Note the advances made first by North Korean and then by UN (United States–led) troops.

View an animated version of this map or related maps on the CourseMate website.

30 percent. Yet during Senate hearings on MacArthur's dismissal, other strategists dismissed his scenario for Korea as the "wrong war in the wrong place." Expanding and securing American power elsewhere around the world, particularly in Europe, should remain the central objective of U.S. policy. This broader goal dictated merely the containment, not a rollback, of communism in Korea, they successfully argued. MacArthur's once luminous image, along with his political ambitions, soon faded.

Truman still needed to secure a peace settlement for Korea. As negotiations stalled, another military hero, Dwight Eisenhower, the Republican candidate for president in 1952, promised to go to Korea if elected and accelerate the peace process. Harry Truman would leave office in 1953 without formally ending the Korean War.

Korea and Containment

Meanwhile, the Korean War, by seeming to justify a global anticommunist stance, helped the Truman administration implement the broad vision of NSC-68. The White House formulated plans to rearm West Germany, scarcely five years after the defeat of the Third Reich, and to expand NATO's military forces throughout Western Europe. Its proposal for direct military aid to Latin American governments, which had been rejected in the past, now slid through Congress. In the Philippines, the United States stepped up military and CIA assistance to the government of Ramon Magsaysay so it could suppress the leftist Hukbalahap (or Huk) movement. Here, Edward Lansdale, America's "super spy," played a key role in advising Magsaysay. (Read about Lansdale's psychological approach to spy operations in the Americans Abroad feature "Edward Lansdale: Psy-ops in the Cold War.") In 1951, Washington finally signed a formal peace treaty with Japan and secured a security pact that granted the United States a sprawling military base on the island of Okinawa. The United States acquired similar bases in the Middle East, bolstering its strategic position in that oil-rich area. The ANZUS mutual defense pact of 1952 linked the United States to Australia and New Zealand.

In addition, Truman greatly expanded economic assistance for France's effort to retain its colonial possession in Indochina against the challenge from communist Ho Chi Minh's Democratic Republic of Vietnam. Policymakers in Washington had hardly favored a communist-led government in Indochina but worries about identifying the United States too closely with French colonialism in Southeast Asia had initially limited U.S. support for France's military effort against Ho's forces. Following the outbreak of the Korean conflict, however, the Truman administration elevated preventing a communist victory in Indochina into an important policy goal.

Warning of potential communist gains, U.S. policymakers became increasingly insistent about opposing overseas movements that seemed to lean toward the political left. The U.S. occupation government in Japan, for example, restricted the activities of labor unions, suspended an antitrust program that American officials had earlier implemented, and barred communists from posts in Japan's government and universities. As in Germany, the United States tried to contain communism elsewhere by strengthening pro-U.S. elites and by promoting economic growth through marketplace rather than state-directed mechanisms.

Containment considerations also prompted the United States to ally with South Africa. In 1949 the all-white (and militantly anticommunist) Nationalist Party instituted a legal-social system called apartheid, based on elaborate rules of racial separation and subordination of blacks. Some State Department officials warned that a close relationship with South Africa, by implying support for apartheid, would damage America's international reputation, but the Truman administration nonetheless supported South Africa's white supremacist regime.

Most importantly, the elaboration of containment during the Korean War era featured the military buildup proposed in NSC-68. When the Truman administration asked for a dramatic increase in U.S. military capacities, congressional Republicans complained but most ultimately joined Democrats in voting the needed funding. By early 1953, U.S. military production totaled seven times what it had been before the North Korean attack. The United States also continued to expand its worldwide system of military bases. When later commenting on the importance of Korean War, Dean Acheson reportedly claimed that "Korea came along and saved" the Truman administration's plans for implementing NSC-68.

This expanded containment policy, shaped in line with NSC-68, included more than military moves. Throughout the world, economic pressure, CIA covert activities, and propaganda campaigns helped implement containment objectives. Truman's global "Campaign of Truth," a sustained informational and psychological offensive, countered Soviet propaganda with mass mediated imagery and cultural exchanges sponsored by Washington. A rhetoric organized around the concept of "national defense" took hold: the Defense Department replaced the War Department, and the new phrase *national security* supplanted the older, more limited language of gauging the best *national interest*.

NSC-68, in sum, provided a blueprint for how the United States, in the name of containment and national security, could reinvent itself as a global superpower. The United States extended its reach into Iran, Greece, and Turkey, all once inside Britain's sphere of influence; initiated the Marshall Plan and NATO; transformed former enemies—Italy, Germany, and Japan—into anti-Soviet bulwarks; assumed control of hundreds of Pacific islands; launched research to develop the H-bomb; winked at apartheid to win an anticommunist ally in South Africa; solidified its sphere of influence in Latin America; and acquired military bases around the world. NSC-68 became a master plan for using military, economic, and covert action to advance a worldwide national security policy.

While the Truman administration fortified strategic positions overseas, its national security policies produced what the historian Michael Sherry has called "the militarization of American life." By 1951, two-thirds of the federal budget went for military-related spending. With continued bipartisan support from Congress, the White House carried out a massive buildup that brought the increasing merger between military

AMERICANS ABROAD
Edward Lansdale

and economic policymaking. Congress granted a new Atomic Energy Commission broad authority to oversee development of a U.S. nuclear power industry. To develop ideas for advanced weaponry and the new policy initiatives that a global strategy of national security implied, Congress created a think tank called RAND, an acronym for Research and Development. Cost-conscious members of Congress complained about expensive defense contracts, but the prospect of these arrangements creating jobs in their home districts helped mute opposition.

Pursuing National Security at Home

Q FOCUS QUESTION
How did the foreign policy of containment affect domestic policymaking and American culture?

Although containment abroad generally gained bipartisan support, Harry Truman's programs for containing subversive influences at home encountered bitter, sustained opposition. Civil libertarians continued to complain about "witch hunts" against people who merely expressed dissent on prevailing policies. Militant anticommunists, taking their cue from Truman's own rhetoric, leveled increasingly alarming allegations about internal communist subversion being left unchecked. Even dedicated anticommunists began to worry that exaggerated charges and wild goose chases after unlikely subversives harmed the effort to identify authentic Soviet agents. The search for supposed subversives eventually touched many areas of postwar life.

Anticommunism and the U.S. Labor Movement

The politics of anticommunism helped unsettle the U.S. labor movement. After the end of the Second World War, many workers took part in strikes for increased wages and benefits and a greater voice in workplace routines and production decisions. Strikes brought both the auto and the electronics industries to a standstill. In Stamford, Connecticut, and Lancaster, Pennsylvania, general strikes led to massive work stoppages that spread to other cities. After Truman threatened to seize mines and railroads that had been shut down by work stoppages and to order strikers back to work, labor militancy began to subside.

In 1947 a Republican-controlled Congress effectively tapped anticommunist sentiment to help pass the Labor-Management Relations Act, popularly known as the **Taft-Hartley Act**. The law negated some gains made by organized labor during the 1930s. It limited a union's power to conduct boycotts, to compel employers to accept "closed shops" in which only union members could be hired, and to continue a strike that the president judged harmful to national security. In addition, the measure required union officials to sign affidavits stating that they did not belong to the Communist Party or any other "subversive" organization. A union that refused to comply was effectively denied protections under national labor laws. Truman vetoed Taft-Hartley, but Congress overrode him. By the end of the Truman era, some type of loyalty-security check had been conducted on about 20 percent of the U.S. workforce, more than 13 million people.

Anticommunism also affected internal union politics and labor–management relations. Some union members had long seen communist organizers as more loyal to the Communist Party than to their own unions or to the nation.

© Bettmann/CORBIS

Instructors on Strike, 1947. Employees of an Arthur Murray Dance Studio in New York City demonstrate the Conga, a popular Latin American dance—and their determination to form a union affiliated with the United Office and Professional Workers of America. In the immediate postwar period, in response to unionization campaigns, workers in a wide range of occupations used labor strikes to secure higher wages, better working conditions, and greater job security.

Differences over whether to support the Democratic Party or Henry Wallace's Progressive effort in 1948 had also splintered a number of unions. In the years following Truman's victory, the Congress of Industrial Organizations (CIO) expelled 13 unions—a full third of its membership. Meanwhile, many workers found that their political commitments could put their own jobs at risk.

Containing Communism at Home

Anticommunists scrutinized workers in the entertainment industry with special zeal. In 1947, the House Un-American Activities Committee (HUAC) opened hearings into communist influences in Hollywood. Basking in the glare of newsreel cameras, members of this committee seized on the refusal of ten screenwriters, producers, and directors—all current or former members of the American Communist Party—to testify about political allegiances within the film community. "The Hollywood Ten" claimed that the First Amendment barred HUAC from scrutinizing their political activities. The federal courts upheld HUAC's investigative powers, however, and the Hollywood Ten eventually went to prison for contempt of Congress.

Meanwhile, heads of the Hollywood studios drew up a "blacklist" of workers, allegedly subversives whom they agreed not to hire. Leaders in other sectors of the entertainment industry, particularly television, adopted a similar policy. The fate of prominent performers dominated media accounts of blacklisting activities, but many anonymous labor union members, who worked behind the scenes in technical and support positions, also lost their source of livelihood.

Soon, many workers in the entertainment field were unable to find jobs unless they agreed to appear as "friendly witnesses" before HUAC or other investigative committees. They were then asked to provide the names of people they had seen at some "communist meeting" in the increasingly distant past. Some of those called to testify, such as the screenwriter Lillian Hellman, refused to answer any questions. Others, such as the movie director Elia Kazan and the writer Budd Schulberg, cooperated. Decisions over whether or not to "name names" would divide people in the entertainment industry and the labor union movement for decades.

The search for subversives also created anticommunist celebrities. Ronald Reagan, who was president of the Screen Actors Guild and a secret informant for the FBI (identified as "T-10"), testified about communist influence in Hollywood. Richard Nixon, then an obscure member of Congress from California, began his remarkable political ascent in 1948 when Whittaker Chambers, a journalist formerly active in communist circles, came before HUAC. Chambers charged Alger Hiss, a prominent Democrat with a lengthy career in public service, with having been a party member and with passing classified information to Soviet agents during the late 1930s.

The Hiss-Chambers-Nixon affair continues to spark intense controversy. Hiss portrayed himself as the victim of a frame-up. Legal considerations barred an indictment of Hiss for espionage, but the government charged him with perjury for allegedly lying to Congress. Ultimately convicted on two counts,

Hiss spent nearly four years in prison. To Nixon and his supporters, the case of Alger Hiss, who had advised Franklin Roosevelt during the Yalta Conference (see Chapter 26), demonstrated how deeply rooted communist subversion had become and how only new political leadership in Washington could uncover it.

In the mid-1990s long-classified documents made newly available revived the Hiss controversy. A few scholars continued to see the Hiss case, like that of the Hollywood Ten, as more hype than substance. The vast majority, however, concluded that Hiss (along with several other high-ranking government officials) had likely passed information to the Soviets during the 1930s and 1940s. Historians continue to differ, however, over the precise nature of this material and its value to Moscow.

Meanwhile, the Truman administration pursued its own anticommunist course at home. It dismissed hundreds of federal employees under its loyalty program. Truman's attorney general, Tom Clark, secretly authorized J. Edgar Hoover, head of the FBI, to compile a list of alleged subversives the government could detain during any national emergency without any legal hearing.

Fear that subversives might immigrate to the United States helped shape several provisions of the **McCarran-Walter Act**. Also known as The Immigration and Nationality Act of 1952, this congressional statute authorized the denial of immigrant status to anyone who might compromise national security by bringing dangerous ideas into the country. The law also allowed the deportation of immigrants, even those who had become naturalized citizens, who belonged to organizations on the Attorney General's List. Calling these measures "un-American," Truman rejected McCarran-Walter, but Congress overrode his veto.

At the same time, Hoover's FBI undertook an extensive campaign of surveillance. It compiled confidential dossiers on a wide range of artists and intellectuals suspected of communist ties. Some of its targets, including the writers Ernest Hemingway and John Steinbeck, had no links to the Communist Party. The FBI often singled out prominent African Americans. Its agents kept close tabs, for instance, on civil rights activist Bayard Rustin. Richard Wright (author of the acclaimed novel *Native Son*), W. E. B. Du Bois (a celebrated African American historian), and Paul Robeson (a well-known entertainer-activist) encountered trouble from the State Department and immigration officials. Their association with the U.S. Communist Party and identification with anti-imperialist and antiracist organizations throughout the world threatened their ability to travel overseas. In addition, suspicions of homosexuality could make people, including the nominally closeted Rustin, targets for governmental surveillance and discrimination.

Targeting Difference

Public focus on homosexual behavior generally increased during the postwar era. During the Second World War, very visible gay and lesbian subcultures had emerged, particularly in larger cities such as New York and San Francisco. After the war, Dr. Alfred Kinsey's research on sexual behavior—his first volume, on male sexuality, appeared in 1948—claimed that homosexuality could

It's Okay—We're Hunting Communists

Herbert Block (1909–2001), who published editorial cartoons under the name of "Herblock," began his career in Chicago at the end of the 1920s. He published his last cartoon 72 years later, shortly before his death. It appeared in the paper for which he had worked since 1946, the *Washington Post*. His work garnered numerous awards, including three Pulitzer Prizes.

Developing his political perspective during the era of Franklin Roosevelt's New Deal, Block editorialized in favor of the national government playing an active role in both domestic and foreign policy. His cartoons thus supported anticommunist, Cold War policies such as the Marshall Plan. At the same time, however, Block's work satirized governmental measures that he saw threatening personal liberties, especially constitutionally protected expression.

During the era of the "Great Fear" Herblock cartoons portrayed the anticommunism of Richard Nixon, Joseph McCarthy, and the House Committee on Un-American Activities (HUAC) as threats to constitutionally protected liberties.

This 1947 cartoon for the *Washington Post* addresses HUAC's approach to investigating communist subversion.

Q Is the cartoon critical of the overall effort to contain communism at home? What, specifically, does "Herblock" find objectionable in HUAC's brand of anticommunism?

Q Would post-1989 evidence about the extent of Soviet espionage affect how viewers of the 21st century might evaluate such an editorial cartoon? Why or why not?

Library of Congress, Prints and Photographs Division

be found throughout American life and that many people pursued a wide range of sexual behaviors, from exclusively heterosexual to exclusively homosexual. In 1952, transsexuality hit the headlines when the press revealed that, after a series of "sex-change" operations in Europe, George W. Jorgensen, Jr. had become a "blonde beauty," Christine Jorgensen.

By this time, a small "homophile" movement had emerged to challenge the most egregious forms of discrimination. Gay men formed the Mattachine Society (in 1950), and lesbians later founded the Daughters of Bilitis, organizations that sought legal protection for the basic constitutional rights of people who were homosexual. They condemned police departments for singling out businesses catering to gays and lesbians when making raids for "disorderly conduct" and the Post Office for banning homosexual publications on the basis of "decency" requirements.

The homophile movement of the 1950s, however, confronted aggressive new efforts to restrict the visibility of homosexuality. The Kinsey Report's implicit claim that homosexuality was simply another form of sexuality, alongside the emergence of new gay and lesbian organizations, helped fuel this campaign. The fact that several founders of the Mattachine Society had also been members of the Communist Party, coupled with the claim that Soviet agents could blackmail homosexuals more easily than heterosexuals, helped link homosexuality with the communist threat to national security. "One homosexual can pollute a Government office," a U.S. Senate report claimed.

Today, historians of sexuality see a "Lavender Scare" about homosexuality accompanying the "Red Scare" about communism. Popular imagery portrayed both homosexuality and communism as subversive "diseases" that inwardly "sick" people, who seemed outwardly little different than other Americans, could spread throughout the body politic. Suspicion of "sexual deviance" became an acceptable basis for subjecting government employees to loyalty board hearings and, ultimately, denying them the legal and constitutional protections enjoyed by heterosexuals.

The "Great Fear"

The postwar search for subversion unfolded within an atmosphere of anxiety that some cultural historians call the "Great Fear." Genuine threats, such as the atomic program of the Soviets, helped heighten the impact of spurious claims about communist agents roaming military bases or gay subversives shaping foreign policy. A growing sense of insecurity, in turn, intensified efforts to safeguard national security.

As this sense of fear was settling over U.S. politics, the Justice Department announced the arrests, in 1950, of several members of a spy ring that had seemingly been channeling nuclear secrets to Moscow. Two of the arrested, Julius and Ethel Rosenberg, the parents of two young children and members of the Communist Party, became the central characters in a controversy over atomic espionage.

The Rosenberg spy case became a Cold War melodrama. The couple's trial, the guilty verdicts, the death sentences, the numerous legal appeals, the worldwide protests, and their 1953 executions for having committed espionage, captured media attention. To their supporters, the Rosenbergs (who died maintaining their innocence) had fallen victim to anticommunist hysteria. Federal officials, according to the couple's defenders, seemed primarily interested in sacrificing scapegoats at the altar of the Great Fear. To others, however, solid evidence pointed toward their involvement in an extensive operation, which included the confessed British spy Klaus Fuchs. Documents released after the fall of the Soviet Union in 1989 now clearly confirm Julius Rosenberg's spying activities. Ethel Rosenberg had apparently known about his work, but the evidence of her direct involvement in passing along information to the Soviets remains ambiguous.

The performance of the nation's criminal justice system in cases such as that of the Rosenbergs also helps to complicate the historical picture. Federal prosecutors never moved, for example, against some people who almost certainly were atomic spies. Theodore Hall, a physicist who worked on America's bomb and whose expertise about nuclear matters obviously exceeded that of Julius or Ethel Rosenberg, was among them. Officials may have feared revealing valuable counter-intelligence operations—or, perhaps, illegal surveillance activities. In any case, only the Rosenbergs, of all those who were prosecuted, faced a charge that carried the death penalty.

In addition, historians continue to differ over how well U.S. courts performed during the Great Fear. Did judges adequately balance the protection of national security concerns with those for civil liberties? During a 1949 prosecution of leaders of the American Communist Party for sedition, the trial judge accepted the Justice Department's argument that the 11 defendants be considered participants in an international conspiracy. Their Marxist ideas and publications, even without any proof of subversive acts, could justify convicting them of sedition against the U.S. government. In contrast, civil libertarians insisted that government prosecutors never showed how Communist Party publications and speeches, by themselves, posed any "clear and present danger" to national security. In this view, *political expression* should enjoy the protection of the First Amendment and only *illegal activity* should be put on trial.

When the convictions of the Communist Party leaders were appealed to the Supreme Court in *Dennis* v. *U.S.* (1951), a majority of the justices endorsed the view of national security advanced by the Truman administration: The Soviet threat was so serious that pro-communist expression, in the absence of any overt illegal activity, could constitute sedition. Several years later, with the passing of the Great Fear, the Supreme Court would back away from the *Dennis* decision (see Chapter 28).

Meanwhile, the Truman administration continued incurring the ire of more zealous red-hunters. In Congress, Republicans and conservative Democrats denounced Truman's anticommunist initiatives as too limited and passed the Subversive Activities Control Act of 1950. It created a Subversive Activities Control Board (SACB) to oversee the registration of groups allegedly controlled or infiltrated by communists. It barred communists from working in the defense industry, holding a labor-union office, and acquiring a passport. Unaware of J. Edgar Hoover's secret detention program, Congress also authorized the confinement of alleged subversives during any national emergency.

Truman responded ambiguously to the Subversive Activities Control Act. He vetoed the law, a futile gesture that Congress quickly overrode, but his administration continued to pursue its own loyalty program and to sanction the FBI's covert detention plan, which offered fewer legal safeguards than the one created by Congress. Still, Truman failed to erase doubts about his anticommunist credentials. **Joseph McCarthy**, a Republican senator from Wisconsin, eventually became the Truman administration's most tenacious critic.

Joseph McCarthy

An intelligence officer during the Second World War, McCarthy had entered politics as a battle-tested combat vet, "Tailgunner Joe." Elected to the U.S. Senate in 1946, McCarthy showed little interest in legislative matters, but he emerged as a two-fisted investigator of communist subversion during the height of the Great Fear.

McCarthy became a political celebrity when he claimed, during a 1950 speech in Wheeling, West Virginia, to have compiled a list of 205 communists then working in the State Department. Americans rightly feared the future, according to McCarthy, "not because our only powerful potential enemy has sent men to invade our shores, but rather because of the traitorous actions of those who have been treated so well by this Nation." Although McCarthy quickly shrank his number of subversives to 57, he also expanded his attacks. Secretary of State Dean Acheson and his predecessor, General George C. Marshall, soon came into range.

Adept at using political imagery and sexual innuendo, McCarthy linked the Lavender and Red Scares. He portrayed key members of Truman's administration as both overly privileged and insufficiently manly. People like Acheson who had been "born with silver spoons in their mouths," represented effete "enemies from within." McCarthy derided the smartly dressed Acheson as the "Red Dean of fashion" and as the leader of the "lace handkerchief crowd."

Initially, McCarthy seemed unstoppable. He substantiated none of his more sensational claims but lacked neither imagination nor targets. In the summer of 1950 a Senate subcommittee, after examining government files, concluded that McCarthy's charges against the State Department amounted to "the most nefarious campaign of half-truths and untruths in the history of this republic." McCarthy responded that the files had been "raped," and he went after Millard Tydings, the Democratic senator who had chaired the subcommittee. In the November 1950 elections, Tydings went down to defeat, in part because of a fabricated photograph that linked him to communist activities.

Despite McCarthy's erratic course, influential people initially tolerated, even encouraged, him. Conservative, anticommunist leaders of the Roman Catholic Church embraced McCarthy, himself a Catholic. Leading Republicans welcomed McCarthy's assaults on their Democratic rivals. Others insisted the senator's commitment to the cause of anticommunism outweighed complaints about his slapdash investigations and overzealous methods. In contrast, critics charged that the senator personified an old form of demagogic "attack politics," and they called his careless, flamboyant style "McCarthyism."

The National Security Constitution and the Structure of Governance

Focusing on the furor over the politics of McCarthyism, however, can obscure fundamental changes in constitutional governance that generated relatively little controversy. Except for the 22nd Amendment, adopted in 1951, which barred presidents from following Franklin Roosevelt's example and being elected to more than two terms, there were no formal modifications to the written Constitution during the era of the Great Fear. But congressional legislation, beginning with the National Security Act of 1947, and several executive orders by the office of the president significantly altered the nation's structure of governance. Scholars now see a new national security framework taking shape during the early postwar years.

The view that the office of the president possessed only limited powers, for example, gave way to the idea that protecting national security justified greatly extending the reach of the executive branch. Truman encountered no constitutional roadblocks when taking the United States into an undeclared war in Korea. Similarly, his desire to strengthen the executive branch's power to gather intelligence bore fruit. In 1952, Truman issued a secret executive order that created the super-secret National Security Agency (NSA). Using sophisticated technology, NSA began collecting any information, from communications networks around the globe, which might affect the nation's safety. Covert eavesdropping on a massive scale became part of the new, partially unwritten national security framework.

The specter of constitutional limitations on presidential power did arise in 1952, however, when Truman ordered his commerce secretary to seize control of the U.S. steel industry in order to prevent a threatened strike. Although Truman could have invoked a 60-day "cooling off" period under the Taft-Hartley Act, he sought to justify his action with a more fundamental, novel, and controversial constitutional claim: The president, as commander-in-chief, possessed extraordinary power whenever emergency action was required to safeguard national security. The steel companies quickly challenged this assertion in court.

When *Youngstown Sheet & Tube Company* v. *Sawyer* (1952) reached the Supreme Court, three justices who had been nominated by Truman supported his broad claim of executive power. Six others, for differing reasons, rejected Truman's position in this particular instance, but all supported a relatively expansive view of presidential authority whenever national security seemed more clearly at stake. Constitutional scholars would come to see this "Steel Seizure Case," then, as a short-term defeat for Truman but a long-term victory for those who claimed that national security considerations had reshaped the fundamental framework of American governance.

Postwar Social-Economic Policymaking

Q FOCUS QUESTION What assumptions dominated postwar policymaking, especially in Truman's Fair Deal? Which major initiatives seemed most likely to gain approval from Congress? Which proposals seemed likely to stall there?

Harry Truman embraced Franklin Roosevelt's domestic agenda, and many supporters of FDR's New Deal still championed his Second Bill of Rights of 1944 (see Chapter 26). This document envisioned all Americans someday having the "right" to a new set of substantive liberties, including employment, food and shelter, education, and health care. Whenever people could not obtain these "liberties," the national government should assume responsibility for providing access to them. Following the Second World War, most Western European nations were creating or expanding "welfare states" that provided people a broad range of substantive rights, including healthcare. Their governments also adopted ongoing economic and social planning and used state power aggressively.

In the United States, however, proposals for government planning and new social welfare measures met determined opposition. Many of their opponents had earlier assailed wartime Washington's role in economic decision making and FDR's Second Bill of Rights. Any postwar attempt to build on the New Deal and wartime arrangements, insisted most Republicans and some Democrats, would threaten unconstitutional governmental intrusions into people's liberties and undermine individual initiative and responsibility. Dixiecrat Democrats joined conservative Republicans to block any legislation that they feared might threaten local and state laws upholding white supremacy in the South. Business organizations, such as the National Association of Manufacturers (NAM), denounced the Truman administration as a menace to the nation's free-enterprise system. Fiscal conservatives worried about new commitments of tax money.

The Employment Act of 1946 and Economic Growth

The 1946 debate over the Full Employment Bill eventually provided a new template for domestic policymaking. This measure, initially, would have empowered Washington to ensure employment for all citizens seeking work. To the bill's opponents, the phrase "full employment" implied a step toward a European-style welfare state, even socialism.

As the effort to enact this bill stalled, a scaled-back approach emerged. The law that Congress finally passed, the **Employment Act of 1946**, called for "maximum" (rather than full) employment and specifically declared that private enterprise, not government, bore primary responsibility for economic decision making. This measure nonetheless created a new executive branch body, the Council of Economic Advisers, to formulate long-range policy recommendations, and it signaled that the national government would assume considerable responsibility for the performance of the economy. Constitutional observers thus judged the Employment Act of 1946, as with the National Security Act of 1947, as an informal amendment to the nation's fundamental framework of governance.

The Employment Act of 1946 also showed a growing faith that *advice* to public officials from economic experts, as an alternative to government *planning*, could guarantee a constantly expanding economy. Economic growth would, in turn, produce a growing number of jobs and, ultimately, an expanding array of consumer goods. An influential group of U.S. economists, disciples of Britain's John Maynard Keynes, were successfully arguing that their expertise could temper boom-and-bust cycles and rescue the nation's economy from uncoordinated decision making by private companies and poorly informed policymaking by government officials.

The promise of economic growth dazzled postwar leaders. Using the relatively new measure of gross national product (GNP), economists could calculate the nation's growing economic bounty. Developed in 1939, GNP—defined as the total dollar value of all goods and services produced in the nation during a given year—became the standard gauge of economic health. Corporate executives, who had feared that the end of the war would bring long-term labor unrest and trigger a deep recession, viewed a rising GNP as a guarantor of social stability. *U.S. News and World Report*, a generally conservative news magazine, suggested that economists had "found the magic formula for almost endless good times." The Truman administration welcomed the prospect of an expanding economy, which would increase federal tax revenues and, in turn, finance its foreign and domestic agendas. "With economic expansion, every problem is capable of solution," insisted one policy analyst.

Truman and his advisers spread the gospel of economic growth. This new faith nicely dovetailed with their national security plans. Spending for the Cold War could serve as an automatic "pump primer" for the entire U.S. economy. The sharp increase in military expenditures soon signaled a tilt in economic policy that some observers began calling "military Keynesianism," a policy of economic stimulation through governmental spending on the perceived needs of the Pentagon.

Moreover, Cold War assistance programs, such as the Marshall Plan, could create new markets, especially for agricultural products, and investment opportunities overseas. Economic growth at home during the postwar period thus became linked to development in the world at large—and to the all-pervasive concern with national security.

Truman's Fair Deal

In 1949, Harry Truman unveiled a series of legislative proposals he called the **"Fair Deal."** He called for extending popular New Deal programs such as Social Security and minimum wage laws; enacting legislation dealing with civil rights, national health care, and federal aid for education; and a measure repealing the Taft-Hartley Act of 1947. The Fair Deal also envisioned substantial spending on public housing projects and a complicated plan to support farm prices. The Fair Deal's core assumption—that sustained economic growth could finance new government programs—came to focus the Truman administration's policy planning.

Two prominent programs illustrate the emerging approach to domestic social policy. The **GI Bill** (officially titled the Serviceman's Readjustment Act of 1944), provided comprehensive benefits for those who had served in the armed forces. In theory, the measure applied to all veterans, but later studies showed that the 350,000 women who had served in the military tapped its provisions far less often than men, perhaps as a result of limited outreach by the Veterans Administration.

The GI Bill provided a wide array of assistance to those who used it. There was financial aid for college and job-training programs. By 1947, the year of peak enrollment, roughly half of the students enrolled in colleges and universities were receiving assistance under the GI Bill. Veterans also received preferential treatment when applying for government jobs; favorable financial terms when purchasing homes or businesses; and eventually, comprehensive medical care in veterans' hospitals. The Veterans Readjustment Assistance Act of 1952, popularly known as the "GI Bill of Rights," extended these programs to those who had served during the Korean War. Although the postwar Congress never enacted FDR's Second Bill of Rights, it did extend some of its key provisions to veterans.

The Social Security program also expanded. Conservatives continually challenged this New Deal measure as fiscally unsound and an unwarranted extension of federal power, but supporters of Social Security always prevailed. They defended its provisions for the disabled and the blind and successfully argued that older people had earned the "income security" through years of work and monetary contributions withheld from their paychecks. The combined magic of economic growth and compound interest rates promised to ensure Social Security's financial solvency. Under the Social Security Act of 1950, the level of benefits increased significantly; the retirement portions of the program expanded; and coverage was extended to more than 10 million people, including agricultural workers.

The more expansive (and expensive) proposals, however, either failed or were scaled back. One of the Fair Deal's

The Postwar College Scene. This picture by the famed photo journalist Margaret Bourke-White shows veterans of the Second World War dominating available space in a classroom at the University of Iowa. Tapping financial support offered under the GI Bill (1944), more than 600 vets enrolled in 1946 at Iowa. Returning servicemen, who at one point made up more than 60 percent of this university's total enrollment, often taxed existing facilities. Much the same pattern emerged at other colleges, universities, and technical schools throughout the country.

key goals, a national health insurance program, faced opposition from several different quarters. Consumer groups and labor unions, intent on creating nonprofit, community-run health plans, feared that a centralized system would unnecessarily bureaucratize medical care. The American Medical Association (AMA) and the American Hospital Association (AHA) opposed any governmental intervention in the traditional fee-for-service medical system, and they had already steered Congress toward a less intrusive alternative—greater federal funding for the new hospitals authorized under the Hill-Burton Act (1946). Large insurance companies, which were continuing to push their own private plans, also opposed the Truman initiative. Opinion polls suggested that many voters, many of whom were enrolling in private health insurance plans such as Blue Cross and Blue Shield, found Truman's proposals confusing. Truman, who had first proposed an expanded health care system in 1945, watched his Fair Deal version die in Congress.

The Fair Deal's housing proposals made some headway. Continued shortage of affordable housing in urban areas stirred support for home-building programs. Even some avowed conservatives such as Ohio's Senator Robert A. Taft supported the Housing Act of 1949. This law authorized construction of 810,000 public housing units and provided federal funds for "urban renewal" zones, areas to be cleared of rundown dwellings and replaced with new construction. The Housing Act proclaimed ambitious goals but provided relatively modest funding, especially for its public housing component. Private construction firms and real estate agents welcomed funding for federal home loan guarantee programs—such as those established under the GI Bill and through the Federal Housing Administration (FHA)—but they lobbied effectively against publicly financed housing projects.

An ambitious proposal for overhauling agricultural policy, which sought to address the continual problem of overproduction, produced more controversy than change. Supporters of New Deal era measures, which bolstered farm prices, credited them with balancing the interests of producers and consumers, but opponents complained they artificially inflated the cost of food. Truman's secretary of agriculture, Charles Brannan, unveiled a plan designed to guarantee farmers a minimum income but to allow commodity prices to fluctuate in line with marketplace conditions. Influential farming organizations saw the Brannan Plan as a bureaucratic nightmare, and congressional Republicans glimpsed a financial horror story. This Fair Deal idea joined national healthcare in the reject pile.

Postwar policymaking ultimately focused on specific groups, such as veterans and older Americans, rather than on more extensive programs such as national healthcare, a comprehensive housing program, or the Brannan Plan. With its opponents dismissing the Fair Deal as a move toward a European-style "welfare state," the White House found it easier to defend more narrowly targeted programs that it could present as economic security measures for specific recipients who deserved government assistance.

Civil Rights

The Truman administration also struggled to place the national government's power behind a growing civil rights movement. After returning to the home front, veterans of African, Latino, Asian, and American Indian descent increasingly refused to remain passive bystanders when laws and discriminatory practices reduced them to second-class citizens. Moreover, people of color who had moved to cities seeking to escape discrimination

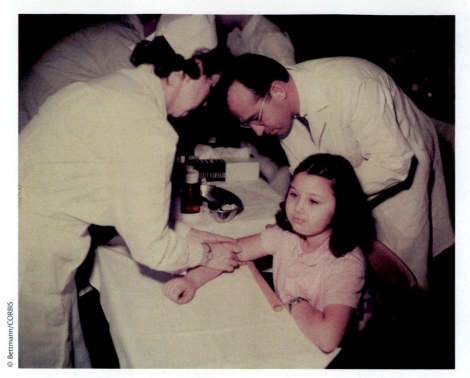

© Bettmann/CORBIS

An Anti-Polio Vaccine. Poliomyelitis became one of the most feared diseases of the postwar period. Because it tended to cripple and kill younger children, the disease became popularly known as "infantile paralysis." The response to polio in the United States and Canada highlighted key differences between the health-care systems of the two countries. The Canadian government placed public resources behind the research and testing of an anti-polio vaccine. In the United States, a private organization, the March of Dimes—famous for its solicitation of small donations—spearheaded the research effort. After working with Canadian scientists, Dr. Jonas Salk announced in early 1953 the successful testing of an effective anti-polio vaccine. Two years later, after further testing, a mass inoculation campaign began in the United States. Underscoring how the U.S. media liked to identify scientific breakthroughs with celebrity researchers, this 1955 photo shows a school nurse and Dr. Salk himself inoculating a stoic young student.

and find wartime employment wanted to build on the social and economic gains they had made during the earlier 1940s.

Drives to translate visions of liberty and equality into reality animated considerable grassroots pressure during the postwar period. African American organizations continued their earlier activism, including campaigns aimed at increasing job opportunities and access to affordable housing. On the West Coast, the Japanese American Citizens League (JACL) successfully campaigned against discriminatory laws affecting property ownership and immigration. The Community Service Organization (CSO) worked on issues that affected California's already sizeable Mexican American communities. These postwar activists hoped that the national government would assist their efforts.

During his 1948 presidential campaign, Truman did endorse the proposals of a civil rights commission he had established in 1946. Its report, entitled "To Secure These Rights," called for federal legislation against lynching; a special civil rights division within the Department of Justice; antidiscrimination initiatives in employment, housing, and public facilities; and desegregation of the military. These proposals helped prompt the Dixiecrat revolt of 1948, but they also gained Truman political support from civil rights groups that hoped for greater assistance in Washington.

Civil rights thus became an increasingly important political issue. After successive Congresses failed to enact any civil rights legislation—including a law against lynching and a ban on the poll taxes that prevented most Southern blacks from voting—leaders of the movement turned to the White House and to the federal courts. The Justice Department, under Truman, continued the Roosevelt-era practice of using its legal resources to intervene in civil rights cases, especially in the South. It showed particular concern for challenging work arrangements that burdened both female domestic workers

and rural agricultural laborers of African descent. These private employment contracts, the Justice Department argued, violated fundamental constitutional guarantees and justified greater use of government power to remedy their inequities.

The drive to end racial segregation in the U.S. military also gained the Truman administration's attention. A plan by labor leader A. Philip Randolph to organize a protest campaign helped prompt Executive Order 9981 (1948), which called for gradual desegregation of the armed forces. Truman later claimed that the United States "could not endorse a color line at home and still expect to influence the immense masses that make up the Asian and African peoples." His executive order began a lengthy, halting process in which the separate branches of the military proceeded at their own pace. In 1954, the secretary of defense finally announced the formal integration of the U.S. military, but informal discrimination continued. Mechanisms for using government power on behalf of advancing liberty and equality emerged much earlier in the armed services, however, than in almost any other area of American life.

Meanwhile, Harry Truman continued to note how segregation tarnished America's image in a Cold War world "which is 90 percent colored." Although Cold War politics could help justify government action against African American leaders allegedly linked to subversive causes, the crusade against communism on behalf of the "free world" also made racial discrimination into a foreign policy liability.

Truman's Justice Department thus appeared in court to support litigants who were contesting government-required segregation. Most notably, it weighed in against "restrictive covenants" (legal agreements that prevented racial or religious minorities from acquiring real estate) and against segregated education. In 1946 the Supreme Court declared restrictive covenants unconstitutional and began chipping away at the "separate-but-equal" principle used since *Plessey* v. *Ferguson* (1896) to justify segregated schools. A federal court in California, ruling on a case brought the previous year in Orange County by LULAC and the NAACP, held that segregating students of Mexican descent in separate, and unequal, schools violated their constitutional rights. In 1948, a second federal court—with the case now entitled *Westminster School District* v. *Mendez*—agreed with the first. In 1950 the Supreme Court ruled that, under the 14th Amendment, racial segregation in state-financed graduate and law schools was unconstitutional. The familiar arguments used to legitimize racial segregation in public education seemed ripe for a successful challenge.

The years immediately after the Second World War, in sum, marked a turning point in domestic policy-making. The New Deal's vision of comprehensive socioeconomic by government planning gave way to a less expansive view: The nation could expect uninterrupted economic growth, enabling Washington to finance, through rising tax revenues, programs designed to assist specific groups. As one supporter of this new approach argued, postwar policy-makers were sophisticated enough to embrace "partial remedies," such as the GI Bill, rather than to wait for fanciful "cure-alls," such as FDR's Second Bill of Rights.

Signs of a Changing Culture

 FOCUS QUESTION How did a resurgent civil rights movement and a new suburban culture help signal important cultural changes during the immediate postwar era?

The pace of cultural change accelerated during postwar years. Encouraged by the advertising industry, Americans seemed, in one sense, to view anything new as "progress." Yet, in another, the speed and scope of change appeared to accentuate feelings of uneasiness and anxiety. As a result, the impulse toward containment affected postwar culture as well as foreign and domestic policymaking.

The Baseball "Color Line"

The interplay between celebrating and containing change could be seen in the integration of organized baseball during the 1940s and early 1950s. In 1947, Jackie Robinson finally cracked Major League Baseball's policy of racial segregation. A graduate of UCLA who had battled segregation while serving in the U.S Army during the Second World War, Robinson had also played semi-professional football and in the Negro National Baseball League before joining the Brooklyn Dodgers. Some ballplayers opposed to integration, including several on Robinson's own club, considered a boycott. Baseball's leadership, seeking new sources of players and seeing a steady stream of African American fans coming through the turnstiles, threatened to suspend any player who would not play with or against Robinson.

Officially, Organized Baseball became desegregated. Shortly after Robinson's debut, the Cleveland Indians signed center fielder Larry Doby. Other top-flight players began abandoning the Negro leagues for clubs in the American and National circuits. Eventually, the skills of Robinson—named Rookie of the Year in 1947 and the National League's Most Valuable Player in 1949—and other players of African descent carried the day. Although light-skinned Latinos had long passed through the racial barrier, Orestes ("Minnie") Minoso, a Cuban-born veteran of the Negro circuits, became the first Afro-Latino to break into the big leagues in 1949. Major League teams began fielding greater numbers of African American and Latino players, and some accelerated recruitment efforts in Mexico and the Caribbean. During the 50th anniversary of Robinson's debut, Major League Baseball staged elaborate memorial ceremonies for Robinson, who had died in 1972, and congratulated the national pastime for having helped lead the fight for equal rights during the Cold War years.

These celebrations glossed over how postwar baseball's leadership had unofficially limited its own desegregation effort. Several teams waited years before integrating their rosters, claiming that they could find no talented African American or Latino prospects. More commonly, clubs restricted the number of nonwhite players they would take on and hired only whites as managers, coaches, and front-office personnel.

African American and Latino players who followed in Robinson's footsteps confronted continuing obstacles. They encountered overt, off-the-field discrimination during spring training in the South and Southwest and in many small towns elsewhere when playing in the minor leagues. Spanish-speaking players struggled to convince managers, sportswriters, and teammates that they could "understand" the subtleties of either baseball or North American culture.

The New Suburbia

In suburbia, too, change was simultaneously celebrated and feared—and thus subject to various strategies for limiting the impact of the new.

Suburban living had long been a feature of the "American Dream." The new Long Island town of Levittown, New York, which welcomed its first residents in October 1947, seemed to make that dream an affordable reality for middle-income families. Similar developments, such as Lakewood and Panorama City in California, soon began springing up in other parts of the country.

Nearly everything about Levittown and its counterparts seemed unprecedented. Levitt & Sons, a construction company that had mass-produced military barracks during the Second World War, claimed to be completing a five-room bungalow every 15 minutes. Architectural critics sneered at these "little boxes," but potential buyers stood in long lines for the chance to purchase one. By 1950, Levittown contained more than 10,000 homes and 40,000 residents. At the same time, bulldozers and construction crews were sweeping through other suburban developments across the country.

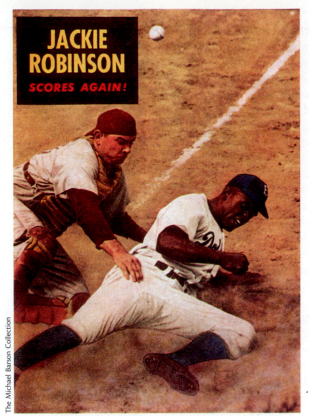

Jackie Robinson. In 1947 Jackie Robinson joined the Brooklyn Dodgers and became the first African American since the 19th century to play Major League baseball. As this photo of Robinson sliding into home illustrates, he and other veterans of the Negro Leagues brought a renewed emphasis on aggressive base running to Major League Baseball. Racial integration of the national pastime of baseball became a powerful symbol of progress in race relations.

occupying only about 15 percent of new suburban lots, large lawns served as private playgrounds. Suburban schools were as new as the homes, and their well-appointed facilities attracted both skilled, enthusiastic teachers and baby-boom children. In many respects, suburbia symbolized new possibilities, confidence in the future, and acceptance of change.

As contemporary observers noted, however, suburbia also appeared to offer a material and psychological refuge. Buying a suburban home seemed a way of containing the impact of the social and cultural changes of the Cold War era. As African American families continued to migrate to Northern and Western cities in search of jobs and greater opportunity, for example, whites began to see a move to the new suburbs as a way to avoid living in racially integrated neighborhoods. Governmental policies contributed to this trend through the financial incentives provided to homebuyers. Even after the Supreme Court declared restrictive covenants unconstitutional, local officials often successfully undercut the ruling's immediate impact. Various informal and extralegal arrangements prevented, until well into the 1960s, any African American from buying a home in Levittown.

Other policies and practices helped to limit diversity within the new postwar suburbs. Local governments could veto public housing projects in their communities. Although land and building costs would have been cheaper in the suburbs, public housing remained concentrated on relatively expensive, high-density urban sites. At the same time, the lending industry channeled government-guaranteed loans away from most urban neighborhoods, and private lenders

To assist potential buyers, the government offered an extensive set of programs. The FHA, established during the New Deal, helped underwrite an elaborate lending system. Typically, people who bought FHA-financed homes needed only 5 percent of the purchase price as a down payment; they could finance the rest with a long-term, government-insured mortgage. Veterans enjoyed even more favorable terms under the GI loan program. These government programs made it cheaper to purchase a suburban house than to rent an apartment in most cities. Moreover, the law provided suburban homeowners with an additional subsidy: They could deduct the interest payments on their mortgages from their federal income tax.

The new suburbs quickly gained a reputation for being ideal places for nurturing a **baby boom generation**. Sheer numbers helped identify "baby boomers," people born between 1946 and 1964, as a unique social and cultural force. The Great Depression and the Second World War had deflated the U.S. birth rate, but it began to soar even before the war's end. A number of factors, including earlier marriages and rising incomes, fueled a continuing boom in babies. More than 75 million babies were born in the United States during the baby boom era.

Although baby boomers lived everywhere, they became closely identified with the new suburbia. With houses

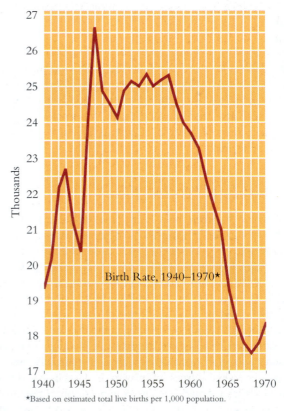

Birth Rate, 1940–1970*

*Based on estimated total live births per 1,000 population.

The Baby Boom.

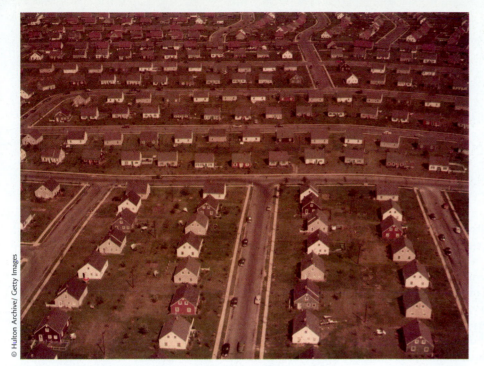

© Hulton Archive/ Getty Images

The New Suburbia: Levittown.
The success of Levittown, New York, in the late 1940s provided a pattern for mass-produced homes in new suburban developments elsewhere in the United States. Assistance from government financing programs, such as the GI Bill, and standardized production methods brought the cost of new suburban homes within the reach of millions of buyers.

routinely denied credit to African Americans and Latinos seeking to buy new suburban housing.

Leaders of the postwar housing industry denied any discriminatory intent. William Levitt could identify his private housing projects with the public crusade against communism. "No man who owns his house and lot can be a Communist," he remarked in 1948. "He has too much to do." Even as Levitt claimed he could help solve the problem of housing—and perhaps even that of communist subversion—he also resisted any suggestion that the private decisions of his construction business had anything to do with race.

Other architects of postwar suburbia saw nothing problematic about their operations. The private financial industry extended the vast majority of its loan guarantees to white men. Only rarely could single women, from any ethnic background, obtain loans. The FHA, a governmental agency, justified a similar policy on the grounds that men were the family breadwinners and that women seldom made enough money to qualify as good credit risks. Analogous justifications often kept men of non-European background from obtaining loans for housing in the new suburbs.

Postwar Hollywood

Hollywood turned out movies filled with powerful symbols of the Cold War era's fascination with—and containment of—change. The motion picture industry still commanded the nation's entertainment dollars at the start of the postwar period. As the overseas markets reopened and Hollywood's male stars returned from military service, the U.S. film industry expected to prosper and prepared to cheer the nation through the Cold War much as it had through the Depression and the Second World War. Attendance at movie theaters reached an all-time high in 1948.

The familiar musical genre, filled with lively stars, upbeat tunes, and flashy dance sequences, provided a ready formula for expressing postwar optimism. MGM's *On the Town* (1949) saturated movie screens with hopeful imagery. During 24 hours of shore leave, three U.S. sailors sing and dance their way through the streets of New York, sample the city's cultural life, and romance three equally vibrant young women. Ending with a title card proudly proclaiming it had been filmed in "Hollywood, USA," this musical seemed to herald the film industry's own bright future.

By the time *On the Town* arrived in movie theaters, however, Hollywood's fortunes were changing. Attendance figures—along with profits—began to plummet in 1949. A year before, the Supreme Court had ruled that antitrust laws required the major studios to give up their highly profitable ownership of local movie theaters. This decision rocked Hollywood just as it faced labor strife, internal conflict over blacklisting, and soaring production costs. The challenge of television delivered yet another blow to an industry already reeling backward.

Meanwhile, Hollywood continued to release a cycle of motion pictures that came to be called *film noir*, or "dark cinema." Almost always filmed in black and white and generally set in large cities, *film noir* purported to be peeking into the dark corner of postwar America. *Noir* characters still pursued their dreams and hopes but with little chance of attaining them. Failure and loss seemed to be the rule rather than the exception in these movies.

Film noir invariably featured alluring *femmes fatales*. These beautiful but dangerous female characters challenged the prevailing order, particularly its gender relationships. The *femmes fatale* disdained the confinement that came with being a faithful, nurturing wife and mother. Usually unmarried and childless, her continual scheming to escape her containment threatened both men and women.

HISTORY THROUGH FILM

High Noon (1952)

Directed by Fred Zinnemann.
Starring Gary Cooper (Will Kane), Grace Kelly (Amy Fowler Kane), Katy Jurado (Helen Ramirez).

During the early Cold War era, few Hollywood movies gained as much popular and critical acclaim—and created as much controversy—as *High Noon*.

Montana-born Gary Cooper, while starring in movies such *Mr. Deeds Goes to Town* (1936), had come to embody Hollywood's idealized version of "everyman." *High Noon* cast him as Will Kane, a veteran Old West lawman who retires as Hadleyville's marshal, marries a young woman (played by Grace Kelly), and prepares to become a storekeeper. Kane's plans are suddenly shattered when news arrives that Frank Miller, a vicious outlaw who had once controlled the town, has been released from prison. Slated to return on the noontime train, Miller has pledged to kill Kane and regain power. Will the marshal strap on his gun and defend Hadleyville against Miller and his henchmen? Or will he respect his new wife's Quaker pacifism, renounce violence, and flee from harm's way with her at his side?

Although the rules of the western genre require Kane to stand his ground, *High Noon*'s script greatly complicated his course. Although Kane had earlier saved the townspeople from Miller, they now refuse to help him defend their community. If Kane will simply leave, they hope to cut a deal with the returning outlaw. As images of clocks ticking toward high noon fill the screen, Kane prepares for a showdown with the Miller and his gang.

Reviewers invariably agreed that *High Noon* offered a parable about the Cold War era but disagreed about its meaning. While critics of extreme anticommunism viewed the movie as a commentary about how McCarthyism generated a fear that paralyzed American communities, including that of Hollywood, other commentators saw this view as too parochial. They considered *High Noon* a tale about the choices the United States faced in the postwar world. From this perspective, the movie's climactic gunfight—during which Kane, with unexpected assistance from his wife, dispatches the Miller gang—as a symbolic affirmation of the U.S. policy of containing, rather than negotiating with, communist aggressors.

High Noon's final sequence further complicated debates when a triumphant Will Kane throws down his marshal's badge and rides out of town on a buckboard with his wife. Was he expressing his disgust over the townspeople's refusal to help? Was he suggesting that he had dispatched Miller to uphold his personal code of honor rather than to defend Hadleyville or vindicate the rule of law?

Hollywood executives could hardly miss *High Noon*'s most obvious message. The movie, which won four Academy Awards, showed that the venerable western genre still resonated, for whatever reasons, with Cold War audiences. Hollywood and television stations began deluging audiences with westerns that generally ended, as had *High Noon*, with a showdown between two well-armed, well-defined adversaries. By the end of the 1950s, primetime TV featured more than 25 different series set in the Old West, and westerns remained reliable moneymakers for the motion picture industry. ◧

Gary Cooper as Marshal Will Kane.

© SUNSET BOULEVARD/CORBIS SYGMA

In *The File on Thelma Jordan* (1949), for instance, Barbara Stanwyck's title character destroys the marriage of a naïve district attorney. Neither love nor even lust drives her illicit affair with him. Instead, she seduces this public official as part of an ambitious, but ultimately unsuccessful, scheme to manipulate the criminal justice system. The postwar era's leading female stars—including Stanwyck, Joan Crawford, Rita Hayworth, and Lana Turner—achieved both popular and critical acclaim playing *femmes fatales*.

The Great Fear, at its height during the years from 1946 to 1953, accentuated pressure to contain supposed threats to

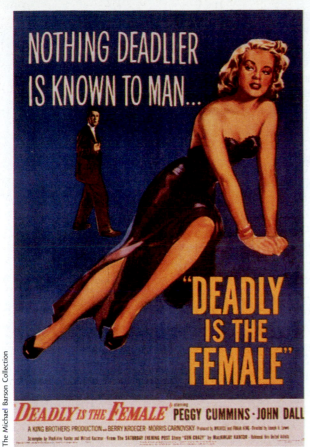

Deadly Is the Female. Also called *Gun Crazy* (1949), this example of a *film noir* played on fears of social breakdown and inspired the later movie *Bonnie and Clyde* (1967).

domestic security. Still, economic growth, new expectations stemming from the war, and demographic shifts worked to alter many social and cultural patterns. The everyday lives of Americans—racial hierarchies, living arrangements, and social-cultural expectations—were changing.

The Election of 1952

Q In what ways did the election of 1952 serve to confirm, rather than call into question, the major public policy decisions, especially in foreign affairs, of the earlier postwar era?

FOCUS QUESTION

Harry Truman, his popular approval rating ultimately falling to near 20 percent, declined to run for another term in 1952. His presidency had put his Democratic Party on the defensive, while denunciations of communism and of Truman's outgoing administration animated Republican campaign efforts.

Continuing Containment

Both major political parties embraced the policy of containment in 1952. Adlai Stevenson of Illinois, the Democratic presidential candidate, warned that "Soviet secret agents and their dupes"

had "burrowed like moles" into governments throughout the world. "We cannot let our guard drop for even a moment," he claimed. A solidly anticommunist stance, however, could not save Stevenson or his party. The Republicans linked Stevenson to the unpopular Truman presidency and highlighted several scandals that featured administration figures receiving kickbacks for granting government contracts. The GOP's vice presidential nominee, Senator Richard Nixon of California, called Stevenson "Adlai the appeaser." The Republican formula for electoral victory could be expressed in a simple equation, "K1C2": "Korea, corruption, and communism."

A Soldier-Politician

For a presidential candidate, Republicans ultimately turned to a hero of the Second World War, **General Dwight David Eisenhower**, popularly known as "Ike." Eisenhower grew up in Kansas; graduated from West Point; ascended through Army ranks; and, as Supreme Allied Commander, directed the Normandy invasion of 1944. He served as Army Chief of Staff from 1945 to 1948 and, after an interim period as president of Columbia University, became the commander of NATO, a post he held until resigning to seek the U.S. presidency. Eisenhower had never before sought elective office, but a half-century of military service had honed his political instincts and administrative skills. Still vigorous at 62 years of age, Eisenhower seemed much younger than the departing Truman, only six years his senior.

Eisenhower's personal appeal dazzled political insiders, media commentators, and ordinary voters. Although his partisan affiliations seemed hazy enough that Democrats (as well as Republicans) had courted him as their presidential choice in 1948, Eisenhower eventually emerged as the standard bearer of the GOP in 1952.

The crucial political battle of that year took place, before the general election, within Republican ranks. The more conservative party stalwarts rallied behind Senator Robert Taft of Ohio and his goals of reversing the New Deal and tempering Truman's global foreign policy. GOP leaders from the East and West Coasts saw Taft, his strength centered in the Midwest and South, leaning too far rightward on domestic issues and expressing insufficient enthusiasm for containment overseas. In contrast, Eisenhower had helped implement postwar national security policies as head of NATO and did not share Taft's animus toward the New Deal. After a fierce intra-party struggle, Eisenhower gained a narrow, first-ballot victory at the GOP national convention. Ike consoled Taft's supporters by endorsing a balanced federal budget and condemning "socialistic" domestic programs.

From the very outset, though, Eisenhower's major policy preferences, especially overseas, tilted more toward those of the Democrats than ones favored by Taft's wing of the GOP. Marketed as a middle-of-the-road candidate, Eisenhower appeared ready to direct the nation through a cold war as skillfully as he had led it through a hot one. The Republican effort of 1952, the first to feature televised appeals, downplayed Eisenhower's uncertain grasp of complicated

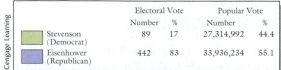

	Electoral Vote		Popular Vote	
	Number	%	Number	%
Stevenson (Democrat)	89	17	27,314,992	44.4
Eisenhower (Republican)	442	83	33,936,234	55.1

Map 27.4 Presidential Election, 1952. An overwhelming victory for Eisenhower, this election saw Stevenson carrying a handful of states. Note that the so-called "Solid South," though, remained largely Democratic. The nation's political configuration, especially for presidential elections, would change substantially over the next two decades.

a single-vote majority in the Senate and an eight-vote edge in the House of Representatives. The New Deal political coalition still survived but showed increasing signs of fraying in the South. There, some of the segregationist vote that had gone to the Dixiecrats in 1948 began moving toward the Republicans, and Eisenhower carried four states in the Democratic Party's once "Solid South" in 1952.

Conclusion

An emphasis on safeguarding national security helped reshape national life during the years that followed the Second World War. As worsening relations between the United States and the Soviet Union produced a Cold War, the Truman administration pursued foreign policy initiatives that expanded the power of the government, particularly the executive branch. The militarization of foreign policy intensified when the United States, after going to war in Korea in 1950, began implementing the assumptions laid out in NSC-68.

Americans also debated how best to safeguard security and calm cultural anxieties on the home front. Prospects for enacting any Second Bill of Rights faded, but postwar policymakers insisted that a careful application of Keynesian economic principles could guarantee economic growth and thereby provide tax revenues to underwrite a limited expansion of domestic programs. The Truman administration also expressed support, even when it alienated white Southerners, for a civil rights agenda.

The 1952 election of Dwight Eisenhower gave the Republicans the presidency for the first time in two decades. Eisenhower's personal appeal, however, did not signal the imminent demise of the New Deal coalition that had held sway since the 1930s or the postwar containment policies championed by his predecessor, Harry Truman. ⚜

policy issues in favoring of highlighting his winning personality. A GOP campaign button simply announced "I Like IKE!"

The first military leader to gain the presidency since Ulysses S. Grant (1869–77), Eisenhower could claim a great personal victory. The Eisenhower–Nixon ticket rolled up almost 7 million more popular votes than the Democrats and carried the Electoral College ballots by a nearly five-to-one margin. The Republican Party, however, made only modest gains. It managed

CHAPTER REVIEW

REVIEW QUESTIONS

1. What major conflicts between the United States and the Soviet Union shaped the Cold War and prompted a U.S. foreign policy focused on containment of communism?

2. How did the foreign policy of containment affect domestic policy and American life?

3. What assumptions dominated postwar policymaking, especially in Truman's Fair Deal? Which major initiatives seemed most likely to gain approval from Congress? Which proposals seemed likely to stall there?

4. How did a resurgent civil rights movement and a new suburban culture help signal important cultural changes during the immediate postwar era?

5. In what ways did the election of 1952 serve to confirm, rather than call into question, the major public policy decisions, especially in foreign affairs, of the earlier postwar era?

CRITICAL THINKING QUESTIONS

1. In what ways did U.S. foreign policy after the Second World War prompt important changes in the nation's system of constitutional governance? How did U.S. intervention in Korea help to underscore these changes?

2. How did postwar policymaking at home follow—and also depart from—the vision of Franklin Roosevelt's New Deal?

IDENTIFICATIONS

Review your understanding of the following key terms, people, and events for this chapter (terms in bold in text are included in the Glossary).

Cold War, p. 744
Containment, p. 745
Truman Doctrine, p. 745
National Security Act of 1947, p. 746
Berlin Blockade and Airlift, p. 747
North Atlantic Treaty Organization (NATO), p. 748
NSC-68, p. 748
General Douglas MacArthur, p. 750
Korean War, p. 750
Taft-Hartley Act, p. 753
McCarran-Walter Act, p. 754
Joseph McCarthy, p. 756
Employment Act of 1946, p. 758
Fair Deal, p. 758
GI Bill, p. 758
Baby Boom Generation, p. 762
General Dwight David Eisenhower, p. 765

SUGGESTED READINGS

David Reynolds, *One World Indivisible: A Global History since 1945* (2001) provides an international context for the origins of the Cold War. **Walter LeFeber,** *America, Russia, and the Cold War, 1945–2007* (rev. ed. 2006) and **Melvin P. Leffler,** *For the Soul of Mankind: The United States, the Soviet Union and the Cold War* (2008) offer more critical views of U.S. policy than **John Lewis Gaddis,** *The Cold War: A New History* (2005). **Bruce Cumings,** *Dominion from Sea to Sea Pacific Ascendancy and American Power* (2009) deals with both foreign and domestic issues, including the Korean War, from a westward-looking perspective.

The domestic consequences of national security policies are analyzed critically in **Garry Wills,** *Bomb Power: The Modern Presidency and the National Security State* (2010) and the relevant chapters of **Athan Theoharis,** *Chasing Spies* (2008). *Spies: The Rise and Fall of the KGB in America* (2010), **by John Earl Haynes, Harvey Klehr, and Alexander Vassiliev,** offers a different perspective. **David Oshinsky,** *A Conspiracy So Immense: The World of Joe McCarthy* (2005) offers the best account of the senator's still-controversial career.

On the major themes in Cold War culture, see **Stephen Whitfield,** *The Culture of the Cold War* (1996). This overview can be supplemented with **Thomas Doherty,** *Cold War, Cool Medium: Television, McCarthyism, and American Culture* (2005). **Jonathon Eig,** *Opening Day: The First Season of Jackie Robinson* (2008) is a recent study.

Important social-economic histories include **Elaine Tyler May,** *Homeward Bound: American Families in the Cold War Era* (rev. ed., 2008) and **Lisabeth Cohen,** *A Consumer's Republic: Mass Consumption in Cold War America* (2003).

On civil rights, see **Thomas J. Sugrue,** *Sweet Land of Liberty: The Forgotten Struggle for Civil Rights in the North* (2008) and **Risa L. Goluboff,** *The Lost Promise of Civil Rights* (2007).

CourseMate

Visit the CourseMate website at www.cengagebrain.com for additional study tools and review materials for this chapter.

The Queen of Abundance

The double-store, frost-free refrigerator offered consumers an elegant display case for the new prepackaged and frozen food products that became available during the 1950s. Advertisements such as this one proclaimed that Americans had become a "people of plenty."

Affluence and Its Discontents, 1953–1963

Reorienting Containment, 1953–1960
Eisenhower Takes Command
The New Look, Global Alliances, and Summitry
Covert Action and Economic Leverage
The Third World

Affluence—A "People of Plenty"
Economic Growth
Highways and Waterways
Labor–Management Accord
Political Pluralism
A Religious People

Discontents of Affluence
Conformity in an Affluent Society
Restive Youth
The Critique of Mass Culture

Debating the Role of Government
The New Conservatism
The Case for a More Active Government

New Frontiers, 1960–1963
The Election of 1960
Foreign Policy
Cuba and Berlin
Southeast Asia and Flexible Response
Domestic Policymaking

The Politics of Gender
The New Suburbs and Gender Politics
Signs of Women's Changing Roles
A New Women's Movement

The Expanding Civil Rights Movements, 1953–1963
The *Brown* Cases, 1954–1955
The Montgomery Bus Boycott
The Politics of Civil Rights: From the Local to the Global
The Politics of American Indian Policy
Spanish-Speaking Communities and Civil Rights
Urban-Suburban Issues
New Forms of Direct Action, 1960–1963

November, 1963
Policy Choices
The Assassination of John F. Kennedy

ONTAINMENT OF COMMUNISM continued to dominate American foreign policy between 1953 and 1963. President Dwight David Eisenhower modulated the pitch of the anticommunist rhetoric coming from a Republican White House, but both he and his Democratic successor, John F. Kennedy, supported the national bureaucracy's plans for new ways to fight the Cold War.

At home, Ike and JFK supported, with differing degrees of enthusiasm, social and economic programs that were initiated during the 1930s and 1940s. Eisenhower nudged the GOP away from the conservatism of the last Republican president, Herbert Hoover. Ike reminded fellow Republicans that many voters still blamed Hoover and their party for the Great Depression. Eisenhower's administration thus accepted the key elements of the New Deal: the economic regulatory structure, the safety net of Social Security, the ability of labor to bargain collectively, and the building of infrastructure projects. Calling Eisenhower's policies too cautious, Kennedy came to the presidency promising more vigorous governmental action at home and, especially, overseas.

The 1950s and early 1960s marked the midpoint of an economic expansion that had begun during the Second World War and would continue until the early 1970s. Sustained growth encouraged talk about "affluence." Economic data bolstered such optimistic claims. Between 1941 and 1950, the real income of the bottom 50 percent of the population grew by more than one third. The bottom 20 percent saw its income rise by a higher percentage than the top 20 percent. Economic growth also generated discontent, particularly over conformity, restive young people, and commercial mass culture. At the same time, continued economic disparities and racial discrimination sparked debate over greater use of governmental power—and the meanings of liberty and equality—in a time of affluence.

Reorienting Containment, 1953–1960

Q In what ways did the Eisenhower Administration retain but also reorient the foreign policy of containment that it inherited from the immediate postwar period?

FOCUS QUESTION

The U.S. strategy for containing communism shifted emphasis during the 1950s. Bipolar confrontation between the United States and the Soviet Union over European issues gave way to greater reliance on nuclear weaponry and on subtle power plays in the Third World: the Middle East, Asia, Latin America, and Africa.

Eisenhower Takes Command

Eisenhower honored a campaign pledge to travel to Korea and help end U.S. military involvement there. Negotiations temporarily broke down, however, over whether North Korean and Chinese prisoners of war (POWs) might refuse repatriation to their home nations and remain in South Korea. Anxious to conclude matters, Eisenhower began to hint about using nuclear weapons if diplomacy failed. Talks resumed, and on July 27, 1953, both sides signed a truce that established a commission of neutral nations to handle the issue of repatriating POWs. (Subsequently, the POWs were given the choice to be repatriated or not.) A conflict that claimed the lives of more than 2 million Asians, mostly noncombatants, and 53,000 Americans finally ended. A formal peace treaty remained unsigned, however, and the 38th parallel between the two Koreas became one of the most heavily fortified borders in the world.

At home, Ike patiently wrested control of the national security issue from more militant anticommunists. Anticommunist forces in Congress exceeded the wishes of the Eisenhower administration when enacting the Communist Control Act of 1954, which barred the American Communist Party from running candidates in elections and extended the Subversive Activities Control Act of 1950. With a GOP president in the White House, however, Republicans began turning away from the more confrontational styles of anticommunist politics associated with Joe McCarthy.

McCarthy finally careened out of control. He used his Senate subcommittee to rail against the Eisenhower administration and about supposed subversives in the U.S. Army. The senator also denounced, as "unfit to wear the uniform," a well-respected general who had denied McCarthy's charges. A special Senate committee began investigating the sensational allegations, and these "Army-McCarthy Hearings" turned into a television mini-series that began in April of 1954. Under the glare of TV lights, McCarthy could seem to be hurling slanders rather than offering evidence. And his habit of interrupting the proceedings with a "point of order" made for tiresome television. In late 1954 McCarthy's colleagues in the Senate, including half of his fellow Republicans, voted to "condemn" him for "unbecoming" conduct. Three years later, McCarthy died, still in office but

CHRONOLOGY

1953	Eisenhower becomes president ◆ Korean War ends
1954	New Look in foreign policy unveiled ◆ *Brown* Cases decided ◆ Geneva Peace Accords signed
1955	Montgomery bus boycott begins ◆ *National Review* founded
1956	Federal Highway Act passed ◆ Eisenhower reelected
1957	Eisenhower sends troops to Little Rock ◆ Congress passes Civil Rights Act ◆ Sputniks orbited
1958	National Defense Education Act passes
1959	Khrushchev visits U.S. ◆ Castro overthrows Batista in Cuba
1960	Kennedy elected President
1961	Bay of Pigs Invasion fails ◆ Berlin Wall goes up
1962	Cuban Missile Crisis endangers world
1963	Civil Rights groups hold March on Washington ◆ Kennedy assassinated

exiled from the national spotlight. Eisenhower's decision to allow McCarthy to self-destruct, rather than to confront him head-on, seemed vindicated.

Indeed, presidential historians now generally see Eisenhower as a skilled chief executive. By expanding the White House staff, he could employ the full power of the presidency while seeming to do relatively little. Eisenhower, in the words of one scholar, conducted a "hidden hand presidency." Ike encouraged the idea that George Humphrey, his first secretary of the treasury, and Sherman Adams, his first chief of staff, directed domestic matters. In foreign policy, he initially allowed John Foster Dulles, secretary of state from 1953 to 1959, to take center stage. Recognizing how regular TV coverage would increase presidential visibility, Ike honed his folksy image and became a capable television performer.

The New Look, Global Alliances, and Summitry

Working behind the scenes, Eisenhower collaborated with his national security advisers to reinforce executive branch leadership in foreign policy. He allowed Dulles to warn, repeatedly, that a new administration might seek to "roll back," rather than simply to contain, communism. The excesses of legislators like McCarthy helped the White House justify its claims for a constitutional privilege to withhold national security materials from Congress and against a constitutional amendment to limit presidential power in foreign affairs. Eisenhower also extended Harry Truman's earlier programs of domestic surveillance and continued a secret program to develop new aerial surveillance capabilities.

The Eisenhower administration also secretly reviewed overall military policy. It initially decided to rein in the military budget by introducing a **New Look**, which emphasized nuclear weaponry and air power as a way to halt the spiraling military expenditures, which had begun during Truman's presidency. Ike calculated that he could never find enough domestic spending cuts to achieve his dream of balancing the federal budget. The former general and his allies in the military, moreover, recognized that the Cold War would not end any time soon and that they needed a national security policy that would be affordable over the "long haul."

Eisenhower's New Look became associated with the doctrine of **massive retaliation**. In early 1954, John Foster Dulles announced that the United States reserved the right to respond to military aggression "vigorously at places and with means of our own choosing." This thinly veiled threat to unleash U.S. nuclear weaponry aimed at keeping Soviet expansion in check. To widen the U.S. nuclear umbrella, Eisenhower expanded NATO to include West Germany in 1955 and added other mutual defense pacts with noncommunist nations in Central and Southeast Asia.

The Eisenhower administration soon began modifying the New Look and massive retaliation by emphasizing more flexible approaches to national security policy. It embraced covert action and economic pressure as useful strategies. The administration also elevated psychological warfare and informational programs into additional weapons of the Cold War. The government run Voice of America extended its radio broadcasts globally. Washington secretly funded Radio Free Europe, Radio Liberty (beamed to the Soviet Union), and Radio Asia. In 1953 Eisenhower persuaded Congress to create the United States Information Agency (USIA) to coordinate anticommunist propaganda campaigns.

One piece of this cultural offensive fought the Cold War with jazz. Beginning in 1955, Willis Conover hosted a two-hour, six-night per week program that hailed jazz as "music of freedom." Opening with "Take the 'A' Train," Duke Ellington's signature tune, *Music USA: The Jazz Hour* reached more than 100 million listeners around the globe. After Conover's death in 1996, an admiring obituary quipped that his show would "bombard Budapest with Billy Taylor, strafe Poland with Oscar Peterson and drop John Coltrane on Moscow." (For more on Conover and his role in bringing American culture to the rest of the world, see the Americans Abroad feature, "Willis Conover: Fighting the Cold War with Music.")

AMERICANS ABROAD
Willis Conover

The United States and the USSR, in the hope of stabilizing their rocky relationship, began holding high-level "summit meetings" in 1955. In May, the same month the Warsaw Pact

Willis Conover: Fighting the Cold War with Music. From his Voice of America studio in Washington, D.C., Conover brought the sounds of jazz artists such as Miles Davis and Duke Ellington to the world.

AP Images

went into effect, U.S. and Soviet leaders finally agreed to end the occupation of Austria and to transform it into a neutral nation. Two months later, the United States, the Soviet Union, Britain, and France met in Geneva, Switzerland, and inaugurated cultural exchanges. Some optimistic observers began talking about the "Spirit of Geneva." During fall of 1959, hoping to heal a rift over the future of divided Berlin, Khrushchev toured the United States. He called on a farm family in Iowa, visited Hollywood, and toured Disneyland. Although a 1960 summit meeting in Paris fell apart after the Soviets shot down an American U-2 spy plane over their territory, the tone of Cold War rhetoric became somewhat less strident during Eisenhower's presidency.

The United States and the Soviet Union also began negotiations over their already vast stockpiles of nuclear weapons. Eisenhower's "Open Skies" initiative of 1955 proposed mutual reconnaissance flights over each other's territory to verify efforts at reduction. The Soviets balked, but some progress was made in limiting atomic testing. Responding to the health hazards of radioactive fallout, both nations slowed aboveground testing and discussed a broader test-ban agreement.

For some Americans, these efforts came too late. Documents finally declassified in the 1980s confirmed that people who had lived or worked "downwind" from nuclear test sites during the 1940s and 1950s suffered a number of atomic-related illnesses. More than one-third of the crew that worked on the Hollywood movie *The Conqueror* (1956), shot in a downwind area of Utah, contracted or died of cancer. Subsequent revelations also showed that the government had covertly experimented with radioactive materials on unsuspecting citizens.

Meanwhile, events in Eastern Europe tested the likelihood of the United States and the Soviet Union clashing militarily in this region. Dissidents within the Soviet-dominated "satellite" countries resented their badly managed communist economies and detested their police-state regimes. Seizing on hints that the Soviet Union might relax its heavy hand, insurgents in Poland staged a three-day rebellion in June 1956. They forced the Soviets to accept Wladyslaw Gomulka, an old foe of Moscow, as Poland's head of state.

Hungarians then rallied in support of Imre Nagy, a communist-nationalist who promised a multiparty political system for his country. After failed attempts at finding an accommodation, Soviet military forces moved against the new Hungarian government. Hungary's insurgents appealed to the United States for assistance. Apparently, they took seriously U.S. rhetoric from Secretary of State Dulles about "rolling back" Soviet power in Eastern Europe. Military strategists at the Pentagon, however, recognized the danger of mounting any military operation so close to Soviet territory. Soviet armies crushed the Hungarian uprising and killed thousands, including Nagy.

Covert Action and Economic Leverage

Meanwhile, the U.S. campaign to contain communism shifted toward the Third World, with covert action and economic pressure as primary tools. These approaches, less visible and less expensive than military deployments, also seemed less likely to provoke political controversy at home or a showdown with the Soviets abroad.

The CIA, headed by Allen Dulles, brother of the secretary of state, played a key role in advancing U.S. policy goals. In 1953 the CIA helped engineer the election of the anticommunist Ramón Magsaysay as president of the Philippines. That same year, the CIA facilitated a coup in Iran, overthrowing Mohammed Mossadegh's constitutional (and left-leaning) government and restoring Shah (emperor) Reza Pahlavi to power. The increasingly dictatorial Iranian leader ensured that his country would remain allied with Washington and supportive of American oil interests. In 1954 the CIA spearheaded a successful plot to topple President Jacobo Arbenz Guzmán's elected government in Guatemala. Officials in Washington and executives of the United Fruit Company desired the ouster of Arbenz, whose broad support included that of Guatemala's communist party. The CIA strategy included a full-scale propaganda offensive that helped undermine Arbenz's popular appeal among Guatemalans.

Impressed by these covert operations, the National Security Council widened the CIA's mandate. By 1961 the CIA deployed approximately 15,000 agents, as compared to about 6,000 only eight years earlier, around the world.

Eisenhower also employed economic strategies—trade and aid—to contain communism and win allies. Governmental initiatives sought to open new opportunities for American enterprises overseas, discourage other countries from adopting state-directed economic systems, and encourage expanded trade ties. Supporters of these efforts credited U.S. policy with encouraging greater stability in recipient countries. U.S. military aid to the

Third World nations also rose sharply between 1953 and 1963. This buildup of armaments provided the United States with stronger anticommunist allies but also contributed to the development of military dictatorships.

The Third World

When pursuing containment, the Eisenhower administration employed a broad definition of "communist." In many nations, groups advocating labor rights and land redistribution had allied with local communist movements. Opponents of these groups could hope to win U.S. support by mentioning the word "communist" to policymakers in Washington, D.C.

In Latin America, the White House gravitated toward dictatorial regimes that welcomed U.S. economic investment and opposed leftist movements. Eisenhower publicly honored dictators in Peru and Venezuela and privately praised the anticommunism of Paraguay's General Alfredo Stroessner, a tyrant who sheltered former Nazis and ran his country as if it were a private fiefdom. Eisenhower's administration cultivated close ties with Cuban dictator Fulgencio Batista, and the CIA secretly trained Batista's repressive security forces.

Events in Cuba dramatized growing hostility to U.S. policy. In late 1959, a revolutionary movement led by Fidel Castro toppled Batista's pro-U.S. regime and pledged to reduce Cuba's dependence on the United States. The Eisenhower administration responded with an economic boycott. Castro turned to the Soviet Union, openly embraced communism, squashed dissent at home, and promised to encourage Cuban-style insurgencies throughout Latin America.

This prompted the Eisenhower administration to revisit policies that seemed to be generating animosity and sparking anti-U.S. political movements throughout Latin America. Its review ultimately recommended greater emphasis on encouraging democratic political processes, human rights, and economic growth in Latin America. Meanwhile, the CIA pondered how best to hamstring, and then eliminate, Castro.

In the Middle East, distrust of nationalism and neutralism shaped U.S. policy. In 1954 when Colonel Gamal Abdel Nasser led a successful military coup in Egypt against a corrupt monarchy, he promised to rescue other Arab nations from European domination and guide them toward "positive neutralism" in the Cold War. Nasser denounced Israel, boosted Egypt's economic and military power, extended diplomatic recognition to the People's Republic of China, and purchased advanced weapons from communist Czechoslovakia.

The Eisenhower administration viewed Nassar's moves as neither positive nor neutral. It cancelled loans for the Aswan Dam, a project designed to improve agriculture along the Nile River and provide power for new Egyptian industries. Nasser responded, in July 1956, by seizing the British-controlled Suez Canal, which remained of economic and symbolic importance to Britain. Its forces, joined by those of France and Israel, attacked Egypt in October and seized back the canal.

Eisenhower distrusted Nasser but also opposed Britain's blatant attempt to retain its imperial position. Denouncing the Anglo-French-Israeli action, he threatened to destabilize Britain's currency unless the invasion ended. Eventually, a plan

Map 28.1 Israel, the Middle East, and the Suez Crisis, 1956. The creation of Israel and the Suez Crisis of 1956 shaped international politics in the Middle East in the postwar era. This map helps suggest some reasons why the establishment of Israel sharpened Arab nationalism and why the Suez Canal was considered to be such an important strategic location.

© Cengage Learning

supported by the United States and the UN gave Egypt control over the Suez Canal. Even so, U.S. influence in the area suffered as the Soviet Union underwrote construction of the Aswan Dam.

With Nasser-style nationalism now tilting toward Moscow, the Eisenhower administration feared "Nasserism" spreading throughout the energy-rich Middle East. In spring 1957 the **Eisenhower Doctrine** pledged that the United States would use military force to defend Middle Eastern countries "against overt armed aggression from any nation controlled by international communism." When governments in Lebanon and Jordan faced revolts by domestic forces friendly to Nasser, Eisenhower dispatched U.S. Marines to Lebanon, and Britain helped Jordan's King Hussein retain his throne. These actions dovetailed with Eisenhower's preference for supporting governments that embraced the status quo, but they also intensified Arab nationalism and anti-Americanism.

The Eisenhower administration tried to squelch left-leaning political movements in other parts of the Third World as well. In 1958 the CIA furnished planes and pilots to rebels trying to overthrow Achmed Sukarno, leader of Indonesia, who drew support from that nation's large communist party. The rebellion failed, and Sukarno tightened his grip on power. CIA operatives also became involved in a plot against Patrice Lumumba, a popular black nationalist in the Congo. Lumumba's opponents assassinated him in 1961, and scholars still debate the precise role the CIA played in his death.

Eisenhower's effort to thwart communism and neutralism in the Third World set the stage for the most substantial

U.S. commitment—in Indochina. During the Korean War, the Truman administration had dramatically increased economic aid for France's war to retain its colony in Indochina against a communist-nationalist movement led by Ho Chi Minh (Chapter 27). Eisenhower continued Truman's policy, but the French electorate increasingly soured on this colonial war. Then, during the early spring of 1954, French forces in the valley of Dien Bien Phu became surrounded by Ho's troops. France appealed to the Eisenhower administration for air support and, perhaps, for a nuclear strike. Opposition from both Great Britain and a bipartisan group in the U.S. Congress helped confirm Eisenhower's inclination to reject military invention. In May 1954, the trapped French troops surrendered, and previously scheduled peace negotiations opened in Geneva. The stunning defeat at Dien Bien Phu prompted France to abandon a colony it had created in 1887.

The **Geneva Peace Accords of 1954**, which the Eisenhower administration refused to sign, divided French Indochina into three new nations: Laos, Cambodia, and Vietnam. The accords temporarily split Vietnam at the 17th parallel into two jurisdictions—North Vietnam and South Vietnam—until a subsequent election could unify the country under a single government. Ho Chi Minh and his communist allies in China and the Soviet Union accepted this settlement, confident that Ho would win the political contest scheduled for 1956.

Eisenhower's advisers feared that a communist electoral victory in Vietnam might set off a geopolitical chain reaction that could "endanger the stability and security" of non-communist nations throughout Asia, a formulation known as the **"domino theory."** After Ho Chi Minh's communist government started consolidating its control over the Democratic Republic of Vietnam (North Vietnam), nearly 800,000 non-communist Vietnamese ultimately moved southward, Eisenhower ordered covert operations and economic programs to forestall Ho Chi Minh from assuming control of a unified Vietnam.

The United States sought to create a viable, anti-communist ally in the southern part of Vietnam. The CIA helped orchestrate a program for training an anticommunist combat force and stage a rigged 1955 election that installed Ngo Dinh Diem as the first president of the Republic of Vietnam (South Vietnam). Once again, "super spy" Edward Lansdale played a key role in the U.S. effort.

An anticommunist Catholic, Ngo Dinh Diem soon renounced the Geneva Peace Accords and the election intended to create a unified government for all of Vietnam. He consolidated his political power, augmented his military forces, and cracked down on his opponents. Diem's policies increasingly cost him support inside South Vietnam, especially among the sizeable Buddhist population, and encouraged the factions in North Vietnam that favored moving militarily against Diem rather than waiting for his regime to collapse from within. Diem became increasingly dependent on the United States and ever more disconnected from political conditions in his own country.

The Eisenhower administration sent billions of dollars and hundreds of military advisers to prop up Diem's government. Meanwhile, in early 1959, North Vietnam finally decided to send troops as well as supplies into the South. They traveled along a shifting route of highways and roads that became

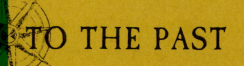

A Warning about the Future: President Dwight Eisenhower's Farewell Address, 1961

Eisenhower raised the stakes in the Cold War arms race with the Soviet Union: new missiles for the delivery of increasingly powerful nuclear bombs, new aerial surveillance techniques, and vast tracking centers to coordinate the nation's defenses. Yet he left office warning Americans about the growth in what he called the "military-industrial complex."

PRESIDENT DWIGHT D. EISENHOWER
farewell address, 1961

We annually spend on military security more than the net income of all United States corporations. This conjunction of an immense military establishment and a large arms industry is new in the American experience. The total influence—economic, political, even spiritual—is felt in every city, every State house, every office of the Federal government. We recognize the imperative need for this development. Yet we must not fail to comprehend its grave implications. . . .

In the councils of government, we must guard against the acquisition of unwarranted influence, whether sought or unsought, by the military-industrial complex. The potential for the disastrous rise of misplaced power exists and will persist.

We must never let the weight of this combination endanger our liberties or democratic processes. . . . I confess that I lay down my official responsibilities in this field with a definite sense of disappointment.

Q What did Eisenhower mean by the "military-industrial complex"?

Q Why did he think it threatened American democracy?

Q How might his warnings be evaluated today?

known as the "Ho Chi Minh Trail." Although Ike feared that any direct U.S. military involvement in South Vietnam would be a "tragedy," he supported increased aid and tied America's policy to Diem's shaky political and military fortunes. Any decision about whether Eisenhower's commitments would ever lead the United States to intervene with its own military forces would fall to his successors.

Affluence—A "People of Plenty"

Q How did economic growth change American life during the post-1953 decade?

FOCUS QUESTION

In his farewell address of 1961, Dwight Eisenhower warned that the greatest danger to the United States was not communism but the nation's own **military-industrial complex**. This term signified an informal relationship among military, political, and economic elites committed to expanding national security capabilities. This complex, the former general said, threatened to so accelerate the costs of Cold War containment that the burden of military expenditures would eventually harm the U.S. domestic economy.

Dwight Eisenhower, Farewell Address on the "Military-Industrial" Complex (1961)

Eisenhower's speech contained several ironies. Most obviously, his administration, while trying to contain costs, failed to prevent ever-larger sums of money from flowing to the military. Moreover, Ike's selection of corporate executives to head the Department of Defense seemingly dramatized the very same linkage his farewell address had decried. In addition, Eisenhower's warnings about possible impending danger came after eight years during which his White House had praised the nation's continued economic growth.

In 1940, the United States had still teetered on the brink of economic depression. Twenty years later, it could claim a GNP more than five times that of Great Britain and roughly 10 times that of Japan. National security policies facilitated U.S. access to raw materials and energy. Government spending for these same policies, what economists sometimes called "military Keynesianism," also pumped money into the economy. By 1955, military expenditures accounted for about 10 percent of the GNP.

Economic Growth

The post-1953 decade, despite three brief recessions, would mark the midpoint of a period of steady economic growth that would eventually stretch from the Second World War to the early 1970s. During the Fifties, the historian David Potter called Americans a "people of plenty." Corporations turned out vast quantities of consumer goods and enjoyed rising profits. The label "Made in America" announced both the quality of particular products and the economic power of the United States.

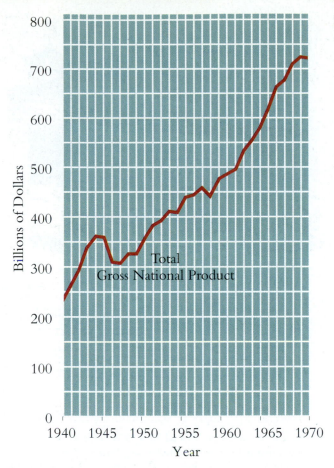

Steady Growth of Gross National Product, 1940–1970.

The "Mrs. America" Gas Kitchen. In 1959, the American National Exhibition in Moscow featured a "typical housewife" working in this RCA/Whirlpool "Mrs. America" gas kitchen, a symbol of the streamlined material progress of the postwar United States.

Newer American-based industries, such as those involving chemicals and electronics, dominated world markets. Corning Glass reported that most of its sales in the mid-1950s came from products that had been unknown in 1940. General Electric proclaimed, "progress is our most important product."

The new suburbs displayed the fruits of this booming economy. Because these outlying areas invariably lacked adequate mass transit, life revolved around the automobile. Car buying expanded during the 1950s as the two-car family and new suburban shopping malls, surrounded by acres of free parking, became tangible symbols of economic growth. Widespread ownership of kitchen appliances, television sets, and automobiles supported the claim that Americans were a people of plenty.

Complaints about the success of capitalism, a feature of political discourse during the 1930s, largely disappeared. Capitalism seemed to work—and spectacularly well. Only a new vocabulary could describe its wonders. *Fortune* magazine celebrated "The Rich Middle-Income Class" and the "Wonderful Ordinary Luxury Market." Harvard economist John Kenneth Galbraith reached the bestseller lists at the end of the 1950s with a book entitled *The Affluent Society* (1958).

The idea of affluence fit nicely with the dominant vision that celebrated constant economic growth and steady improvement of living standards as a uniquely American way of life. The gulf between rich and poor no longer seemed to be between people with cars and those without them, but

The Typical Housewife. This photograph depicts a different view of the "typical housewife" in her kitchen.

between people with Cadillacs and Lincolns and those with Fords and Chevrolets. "Luxury has reached the masses," proclaimed *Fortune* magazine.

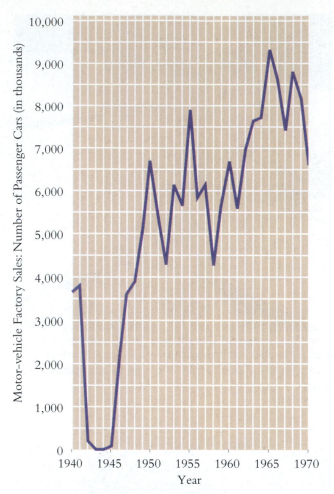

Auto Sales, 1940–1970.

We designed this car with mothers in mind

First big car that's light on its feet

the **AIR BORN B-58 BUICK**

Appealing to Mothers. This ad for a 1958 Buick seeks to appeal to affluent married women by emphasizing how modern consumer products bring comfort, convenience, and safety. Note how this ad, like so many others during the 1950s, extolled the central nurturing role of women in this Baby-Boom era.

Keynesian economists such as Galbraith argued that greater government expenditures would generate even faster growth, but the Eisenhower administration demurred. Fearing that increased spending would fuel inflation, it remained committed, at least rhetorically, to restraining even the Pentagon's budget. By the mid-1950s the federal government was running balanced budgets.

Highways and Waterways

Eisenhower did, however, endorse several costly new programs. He supported the **Highway Act of 1956**, citing national-security considerations. Financed largely by a national tax on gasoline, the act funded a nationwide system of limited-access expressways. It initially aimed at building, over a 10-year period, more than 40,000 miles of highway. Touted as the largest public works project in world history, this program delighted the oil, concrete, and tire industries; provided steady work for construction firms and labor unions; and boosted the interstate trucking business. It also confirmed the victory of the automobile over competing modes of surface transportation.

The White House also supported expensive water-diversion projects in the West. The Army Corps of Engineers and the Bureau of Reclamation, governmental agencies with powerful supporters in business and in Congress, spent billions

of dollars on dams, irrigation canals, and reservoirs. Irrigation turned desert into cropland, and elaborate pumping systems even forced rivers to flow uphill. By 1960 much of the West enjoyed access to trillions of gallons of water per year, and governmental expenditures laid the basis for substantial economic growth in the "sunbelt states" of Texas, California, and Arizona.

These water projects came at a price. Technologically complicated and costly to build, they spawned similarly complex bureaucracies to operate them. As a consequence, local communities lost power to government agencies and large-scale entrepreneurs, who pushed aside smaller farmers and ranchers. American Indian tribes, especially, found sections of their land being flooded for reservoirs or purchased by agribusinesses. Moreover, these vast projects—which diverted surface waters, tapped into groundwater tables, and dotted the West with dams and reservoirs—produced ecological problems. They degraded habitats and contributed to the buildup of salt byproducts in the water and the soil. Some scientists began to warn about the overuse of pesticides such as DDT.

Owner of a hobby farm in Pennsylvania, Eisenhower took a personal interest in agricultural policy. Although the number of farms in the United States plummeted during the 1950s, new machine technologies, corporate-style operations, and hybrid seeds spurred greater agricultural production. As

Turning Deserts into Crop Land.
California's 153-mile-long Friant-Kern Canal, one of many projects of the Army Corps of Engineers, allowed farmers to cultivate water-intensive fruit and other crops. Huge irrigation projects, financed by the federal government, turned dry western lands into farming areas but also carried long-term environmental implications for water tables and soil quality.

overproduction thus continued to drive down commodity prices, government support programs continued to prop up farm incomes. The idea that Washington should guarantee farmers "parity," or a fair price for their labor, remained the centerpiece of federal agricultural policy. Despite some efforts to tinker with existing arrangements, the parity system survived. The Eisenhower administration also tried to increase agricultural exports and began the "Soil Bank Program" that paid farmers for taking land out of production.

Labor–Management Accord

Most corporate leaders, supportive of the kind of government involvement required to build highways and water projects, were learning to live with labor unions as well. The auto industry showed the way.

Union leaders recognized that closer cooperation with corporate management could guarantee employment stability and political influence for their members. Roughly 35 per cent of the nonagricultural workers held a union card during the 1950s. Taking its cue from the United Auto Workers (UAW), one of the most militant unions back in the 1930s, organized labor agreed to bargain aggressively on issues that immediately affected worker paychecks and fringe benefits but to abide by their contracts with management and to disavow aggressive tactics such as wildcat strikes. To police this new labor-management détente, both sides looked to the federal government's National Labor Relations Board (NLRB). Meanwhile, in 1955, the American Federation of Labor (AFL) and the Congress of Industrial Organizations (CIO), long at odds, merged. The 1950s thus seemed to signal an end to the kind of labor-capital conflict that had marked the 1930s and late 1940s.

Labor activists expressed concern. Nearly two-thirds of all unionized workers lived in only 10 states. Worse, companies in some areas of union strength, such as the Northeast, were already beginning to move jobs to states in the South, where the union movement lacked strong roots. The 1947

Taft-Hartley Act, moreover, allowed for state laws that could frustrate new organizing drives, such as the unsuccessful effort in the South known as "Operation Dixie."

Business leaders, on the other hand, generally applauded the new direction in labor-management relations. *Fortune* magazine noted that General Motors had paid a price in terms of more costly employee benefits and higher wages, but that it "got a bargain" on the larger issue of labor peace. To safeguard their control over decision-making, corporations expanded their supervisory personnel, a practice that increased consumer prices. The labor-management accord also divided the industrial work force: Workers in the more profitable sectors could bargain far more effectively over wages and benefits than those in areas with smaller profit margins.

Some non-unionized businesses voluntarily expanded benefits for their workers. Companies such as Sears and Eastman Kodak encouraged a cooperative corporate culture, which included health and pension plans, profit-sharing arrangements, and social programs. Some firms created private recreational parks for exclusive use by their employees. Satisfying workers, corporate executives reasoned, would reduce the appeal of both unionization and governmental welfare measures.

During the 1950s and early 1960s real wages (what workers make after adjusting their paychecks for inflation) rose steadily, and jobs were plentiful. The frequency of industrial accidents dropped; fringe benefits (health insurance, paid vacation time, and retirement plans) improved; and job security was generally high.

Political Pluralism

Economic growth also gained credit for producing political stability. Observers of the political scene often framed the politics of the 1950s in terms of memories of the past and visions of the future. After the conflicts of the 1930s, the disruptions during the Second World War, and the Great Fear of the early Cold War period, the 1950s seemed an era of relative tranquility. An increasingly prosperous nation, most observers agreed, would effectively mute social conflict and eventually solve major problems. The future, according to one prominent sociologist, would see the end of clashing political ideologies.

According to this dominant viewpoint, which political scientists called "pluralism" (or "interest-group pluralism"), American politics already featured a roughly equal bargaining process among well-organized interest groups. John Kenneth Galbraith coined the term "countervailing power" when claiming that labor unions, consumer lobbies, farm organizations, and other groups could check the desires of giant corporations. No single group could dictate terms to the others, celebrants of political pluralism claimed, because so many interests felt so securely empowered. Pluralists shrugged off signs of decline in political participation, clearly evident in how few people cast ballots on election days, by arguing that voter behavior showed widespread satisfaction with how well the process of political pluralism worked.

In addition to praising the process, pluralists praised the results. Public leaders, it seemed, could find a solution to problems. Short-term conflicts over specific issues would never disappear, but supporters of the pluralist vision insisted that America's growing economy would continue to help moderate political passions and point warring interests toward agreement on fundamental arrangements. As a professor at Harvard Law School put it, constant economic growth meant that "in any conflict of interest," it was "always possible to work out a solution" because an expanding economy guaranteed that any settlement would leave all interests "better off than before."

A Religious People

Most observers professed an analogous faith in religious pluralism. Congress, as part of the crusade against "atheistic communism," constructed a nondenominational prayer room on Capitol Hill; added the phrase "under God" to the Pledge of Allegiance; and declared the phrase "In God We Trust," which had been emblazoned on U.S. currency for nearly a century, as the nation's official motto. In the view of pluralists, the intense religious allegiances no longer divided people as much as in the past. President Eisenhower declared that "our government makes no sense unless it is founded in a deeply felt religious faith—and I don't care what it is."

Religious leaders echoed the theme of pluralism. Will Herberg's *Protestant-Catholic-Jew* (1955) argued that these three faiths were really "saying the same thing" in affirming the "spiritual ideals" and "moral values" of the American way of life. The Rabbi who headed the Jewish Chaplain's Organization reassured Protestants and Catholics that they and their Jewish neighbors shared "the same rich heritage of the Old Testament . . . the sanctity of the Ten Commandments, the wisdom of the prophets, and the brotherhood of man." A 1954 survey claimed that more than 95 percent of the population identified with one of the three major faiths, and religious commentators praised how the "Judeo-Christian tradition" enriched American life.

This tradition could also produce religious celebrities. The Baptist evangelist Billy Graham achieved superstar status during the 1950s. Norman Vincent Peale, a minister in the Reformed Church of America, sold millions of books which declared that belief in a Higher Power could bring "health, happiness, and goodness" to daily life. His most famous volume, *The Power of Positive Thinking* (1952), remained a bestseller throughout the 1950s. The Catholic Bishop Fulton J. Sheen moved from radio to TV during the 1950s, and won an Emmy award for hosting a prime-time program entitled *Life Is Worth Living*.

Peale, Sheen, and Graham generally identified their religious ideals with conservative, anticommunist causes, but an emphasis on religious faith could be found all across the political spectrum. Dorothy Day, who had been involved in religiously based community activism since the early 1930s, continued to crusade for world peace and for domestic programs aimed at redistributing wealth. Church leaders and laypeople from all three major religions provided leadership in civil right efforts. Refusing to preach to segregated audiences, Billy Graham gradually aligned his ministry with major goals of the movement.

Discontents of Affluence

 FOCUS QUESTION What kinds of social criticism did the general economic prosperity of the post-1953 decade help to highlight?

A vibrant body of social criticism accompanied the celebrations of economic growth, political pluralism, and religious faith. By the late 1950s, a diverse body of critical commentary warned about the threat of conformity, the problems of young people, the disease of mass culture, the evils of discrimination, and the effects of economic inequality.

Conformity in an Affluent Society

The Organization Man (1956), written by the sociologist William H. Whyte, Jr., indicted corporate culture for contributing to an unwanted byproduct of affluence: conformity. This study saw corporate executives deferring to the dictates of their bosses, often at the expense of their own individual wishes and values. David Riesman, another sociologist, offered a broader critique of conformity in *The Lonely Crowd* (1950). This book envisioned a shift from an "inner-directed" culture, in which people looked to themselves and their immediate families for their sense of identity and self-worth, to an "other-directed" one, in which people looked to others for approval and increasingly measured their worth against images they saw in the mass media. An other-directed society, moreover, emphasized "adjustment" to the expectations of others rather than individual "autonomy."

The Lonely Crowd claimed that *Tootle the Engine*, a popular children's book, exemplified how mass culture taught

SPLIT-LEVEL LIVING

Split-Level Living. This 1960 cartoon, by the *Washington Post's* "Herblock" (Herbert Block), illustrates the growing critique of Eisenhower-era social policy. While suburbanites enjoy new affluence in a split-level home, public services and distressed people remain under-funded.

baby boomers conformist values. After "Tootle" shows a preference for jumping the rails and frolicking in the fields, intense pressure from his community gets him "back on the tracks." If he remains on the straight-and-narrow and follows lines laid down by others, Tootle learns, his future as a powerful and fast-moving locomotive seems assured.

The critique of conformity informed the bestselling books of journalist Vance Packard. *The Hidden Persuaders* (1957) criticized the advertising industry's calculated appeals to the insecurities of consumers for encouraging conformist behavior. His book, Packard claimed, could help its readers "to achieve a creative life in these conforming times" when so many people "are left only with the roles of being consumers or spectators."

Critics such as Whyte, Riesman, and Packard invariably highlighted signs of conformity and loss of selfhood supposedly evident among middle-class men, but Betty Friedan warned about an analogous malaise among women. Top business executives expected middle-class wives to help their husbands deal with the demands of corporate life, and many women found themselves trapped in a stultifying sphere of domestic obligations. A conformist "feminine mystique," Friedan wrote, stifled women's individuality and power.

The 1950s, then, hardly lacked for social and political criticism, some of it far more radical than complaints about conformity. The much-vaunted American way of life, according to the sociologist C. Wright Mills, suffered from increasingly regimented work routines and meaningless leisure-time activities that rarely produced genuine satisfaction. Mills also argued that a "power elite"—composed of corporate executives, military planners, political leaders, prominent academics, and media celebrities—set the agenda for crucial public policy discussions. As a result, this undemocratic group could dominate decisions about national security matters and domestic spending priorities.

Restive Youth

Another body of critical analysis targeted the culture of young people. Some critics linked an apparent rise in juvenile delinquency to the sale of comic books. The *Seduction of the Innocent* (1954), by the psychologist Frederick Wertham, blamed comics featuring images of sex and violent crime for "mass-conditioning" children and stimulating social unrest. Responding to regulatory legislation by some U.S. cities and to calls for federal measures, the comic book industry drafted its own self-censorship code. Publishers who followed the code's guidelines for portraying violence and deviant behavior could display a seal of approval. The "great comic book scare" soon faded away.

Other worrisome signs persisted, however. In 1954 Elvis Presley, a former truck driver from Memphis, rocked the pop music establishment and cultural purists with a string of "rock 'n' roll" hits on the tiny Sun record label. Presley's sensual, electric stage presence thrilled his young admirers and outraged critics. Presley and other youthful exponents of Fifties rock—including Buddy Holly from West Texas, Richard Valenzuela (Richie Valens) from East Los Angeles, Frankie Lymon from Spanish Harlem, and "Little Richard" (Penniman) from Georgia—leaped over cultural and ethnic barriers. They reshaped older musical forms, especially African American rhythm and blues and the "hillbilly" music of southern whites, into new sounds. Rock 'n' rollers claimed to sing about the hopes and fears of the millions of their young fans. They celebrated the joy of "having a ball tonight"; decried the pain of the "summertime blues"; complained about the torment of being "a teenager in love"; and preached the promise of deliverance, through the power of rock, from "the days of old." Songs such as "Roll over Beethoven" by Chuck Berry became powerful teen anthems.

Guardians of more genteel cultural forms recoiled at the sounds and sights of rock 'n' roll. They denounced its lyrics, pulsating guitars, and screeching saxophones as an assault on the very idea of music. Even its name, critics complained, brazenly appealed to raging teenage hormones. Religious groups denounced rock as the "Devil's music"; anticommunists detected a covert Red strategy to corrupt youth; and segregationists saw it as part of a plot to encourage "race-mixing." The FBI's J. Edgar Hoover called rock music "repulsive to right-thinking people" and a social force that would soon have "serious effects on our

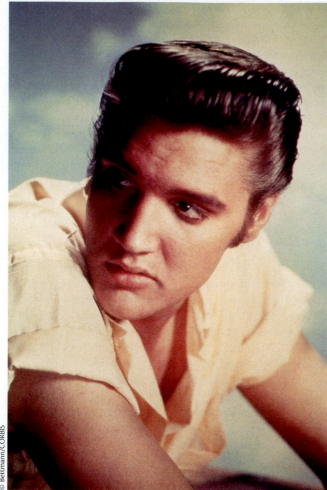

© Bettmann/CORBIS

Elvis Presley. "Elvis the Pelvis" drew upon blues, gospel, hillbilly, and pop music traditions to become the premier rock 'n' roll star of the 1950s.

young people." The danger of rock 'n' roll seemed on display in *The Blackboard Jungle* (1955), a movie about a racially mixed group of sexually active students who defy adult authority and terrorize high school classrooms.

Rock 'n' roll music spoke, however, to the concerns of its young fans. Chuck Berry's "School Days" challenged pieties about the benefits of schooling, as he sang of bored teenagers riding around "with no particular place to go." This kind of social criticism in songs anticipated the more overtly rebellious music of the 1960s.

At the same time, rock music and the larger youth culture of the 1950s could also merge into that era's general affluence. Sun Records, lacking sufficient capital to distribute Presley's hit songs and promote his image, sold his contract to RCA. Colonel Tom Parker, his personal promoter, soon had the "Elvis Brand" affixed to everything from 45 rpm records to Hollywood musicals. Record companies and Top-40 radio stations saw teenagers, with their part-time jobs and their own allowances, as a market segment worth targeting. In "Sweet Little Sixteen," Berry sang about an affluent teenager chasing after the latest fashions, the next rock 'n' roll show, and "about half-a million framed autographs." Record companies promoted

performers who exalted the pursuit of "fun, fun, fun," which apparently required the latest in "cool" clothes, late-model automobiles, and rock 'n' roll records.

The Critique of Mass Culture

Concern about social conformity and youth culture merged into the wider **mass culture critique** of the 1950s. Much of the anxiety about the decline of individualism and the rise of disruptive young people stemmed from fears that the "hidden persuaders" who promoted the entire commercial culture industry could reach millions of people with standardized imagery and messages. Cosmopolitan cultural critics worried that "bad" art—seemingly evident in comics and rock 'n' roll—would eventually purge anything "good" from the cultural marketplace. Moreover, they warned, the superficial imagery manufactured for a "mass" national audience threatened to wipe out vibrant local and regional cultural traditions.

Network television, dominated by three large corporations (NBC, CBS, and ABC) and sustained by advertising revenue, provided a prominent target for this mass-culture critique. Picturing millions of passive viewers gathered around "the boob tube," critics decried both the quality and the presumed impact of mass-produced TV programming. By the late 1950s the television networks were stocking their prime-time hours with western-themed series (about a mythical Old West) and staged quiz programs (whose contestants had been supplied the answers that they pretended to be puzzling over). Independent stations without network ties programmed the cultural leftovers: ancient B-pictures from Hollywood's movie vaults, cheaply produced adventure series, and amateurish local programming. The head of the Federal Communications Commission (FCC) would soon denounce TV as a "vast wasteland."

Critics also worried how TV was changing the fabric of everyday life. Architects rearranged living space so that the TV set could become the focal point of family gatherings. New products—such as the frozen TV dinner, the TV tray, the recliner chair, and *TV Guide* magazine—seemed banal.

The mass culture that critics decried, however, was embedded within the economic system and the pluralist political process that these same observers generally celebrated. Was it possible to eliminate the plague of mass culture without sacrificing economic growth and political pluralism? If, for example, Congress legislated against comic books, its effort at censorship might end up curtailing free expression. If local communities were to step in, as some had done with comics, the results might be even worse. The prospect of southern segregationists confiscating civil rights literature, or local censorship boards banning books by celebrated authors or "art films" from Europe, hardly appealed to the cosmopolitan, well-educated critics of mass culture. Their extensive critique seemed short on solutions. Criticism of mass culture thus did nothing to halt the flood of consumer products and forms of entertainment aimed at an ever-expanding popular audience.

Debating the Role of Government

Q FOCUS QUESTION How did the post-1953 decade help to focus competing views of the role of government? What did the new conservatism advocate? What did advocates of more active government hope to accomplish?

Although Eisenhower occasionally hinted at rolling back the New and Fair Deals, he actually presided over a modest expansion of the reach of the federal government. There was a broader Social Security system, a higher minimum wage, better unemployment benefits, and a new Department of Health, Education, and Welfare (HEW). Eisenhower liked to call his approach "modern Republicanism."

The New Conservatism

Eisenhower's brand of Republicanism angered members of a political movement eventually called the "new conservatism." This movement drew much of its energy from Republicans who conceded Eisenhower's popularity but questioned his commitment to conservative GOP principles. Moreover, Eisenhower appeared to be allowing too many congressional Republicans to cross the aisle and support Democratic-backed spending programs. And a leading modern Republican, New York's governor Nelson Rockefeller, seemed every bit as enamored of state-level welfare programs as his Democratic counterpart on the West Coast, California's Edmund (Pat) Brown.

Arizona Senator Barry Goldwater claimed to hear modern Republicans such as Rockefeller singing "the siren song of socialism." Goldwater emerged as the key political spokesperson for the new conservatism. After he won a second term in the U.S. Senate in 1958, a year when several other prominent GOP conservatives lost, a national magazine hailed him as "The Glittering Mr. Goldwater." Conservatives, Democrats as well as Republicans, saw a savior. Goldwater delighted them by assailing Eisenhower's policies as insufficiently conservative, overly enamored of elite constituencies on the East Coast, and too indebted to the Democratic Party's agenda. Modern Republicanism resembled a "Dime Store New Deal," a less expensive version of FDR's programs, according to Goldwater.

Goldwater's critique was summed up in a slim, ghost-written book, *The Conscience of a Conservative* (1960). By refusing to take stronger military measures against the Soviet Union and by not making "victory the goal" of U.S. policy, Eisenhower was likely endangering the nation's security. The senator from Arizona portrayed most domestic programs, including those supported by Eisenhower, as threats to individual liberty and as steps toward national bankruptcy. The GOP needed a clean break from the Democratic Party's "New Deal antics."

For economic ideas, the new conservatism looked not only to Europeans, such as Friedrich von Hayek and Ludwig von Mises, but to their American disciples, particularly Milton Friedman. Once a Keynesian, the quick-witted, fast-talking Friedman had later reoriented his economic ideas in a decidedly libertarian direction. Governmental action, he argued, generally interfered with self-correcting marketplace forces and thus generated additional problems rather than genuine solutions. When government absolutely needed to act, as it should have done more forcefully during the Great Depression, its touch must be as light as possible. Friedman wrote as clearly, and as quickly, as he spoke and could claim an impressive list of popular and scholarly publications. Headquartered at the University of Chicago, he helped symbolize a persistent pattern: Economists generally sympathetic to Keynesianism tended to migrate to institutions on either coast, while those embracing more classical, free market approaches generally gravitated toward the heartland.

Meanwhile, Friedman's eventual ally, the author-publisher William F. Buckley, Jr., was framing a broad, ideological platform for the new conservatism. In *God and Man at Yale* (1952), the devoutly Roman Catholic Buckley had attacked what he saw as a "collectivist" and antireligious tilt in higher education. He and his brother-in-law had later defended Senator Joe McCarthy in a book entitled *McCarthy and His Enemies* (1954). Then, in 1955, Buckley began his most ambitious enterprise: a new conservative magazine, the **National Review**. This publication avoided the anti-Semitism of some old-line conservatives and adopted an organizational strategy for the long run. To this end, conservatives established Young Americans for Freedom (YAF) in 1960, several years before similar college-based political organizations emerged on the political left.

Buckley's group adopted another long-term approach to building a conservative movement, "fusionism." Avoiding political litmus tests, the *National Review* featured a creative tension that fused three broad constituencies: "traditionalist" conservatives, who insisted that social stability depended on the educated, talented few, such as themselves, dominating the nation's institutions; "libertarians," who favored drastically limiting the power of any governmental system and enlarging the realm of personal and entrepreneurial freedom; and staunch anticommunists, who endorsed the aggressive use of military power against the Soviets.

The *National Review* assembled an eclectic group of writers. Some of its older contributors had come from the political left of the 1930s, and a few younger ones would eventually move to that of the 1960s. While at the *National Review* of the 1950s, however, they collaborated on developing ideas that could guide the new conservatism. Any program for coexistence with communism, according to the magazine's manifesto, was "neither desirable nor possible, nor honorable." Excessive "bipartisanship" was robbing politics of necessary conflict, while "Big Brother government" and "union monopolies" were threatening economic freedom. In addition to taking strong stands on foreign and domestic policy, the *National Review* promised to cover cultural affairs from a conservative perspective that made "excellence (rather than 'newness')" and "honest intellectual combat (rather than conformity)" its watchwords.

A zest for cultural combat animated other projects of the new conservatism. The writer Ayn Rand's fierce brand of secular libertarianism and commitment to sexual experimentation made her unwelcome at the staid *National Review*. The novel *Atlas*

Shrugged (1957), however, confirmed her iconic status among libertarians who endorsed her call for ignoring any "public good" and for advancing, instead, one's own self interest. To irritate conservatives such as Buckley, Rand called herself a "radical for capitalism." A number of conservative groups, however, did spread the religious ideals that Rand ridiculed. The Campus Crusade for Christ urged college students to live their lives according to traditional religious ideals and to preach this message among their peers. Seeking a wider audience, Clarence Manion, a prominent Catholic Democrat and former dean of Notre Dame Law School, staked out a forceful conservative presence on the radio dial of the 1950s. Off-air, Mansion helped spearhead an effort to draft Barry Goldwater to run as Eisenhower's successor in 1960.

The Manion Forum of Opinion, broadcast weekly, also helped Goldwater's western brand of conservatism to gain ground in the new suburbs of the Sunbelt states. Many of these conservatives derived their family incomes from high-tech jobs in the military-related sector, a consideration that likely reinforced their call for increased spending on national defense. On domestic issues, however, these "suburban warriors" championed a vision of much more limited government. Their ideal examples of legislation were measures to prevent "outside" authorities, both state and national, from infringing on the local liberties of suburban communities.

The Case for a More Active Government

While a new conservatism argued for scaling back the domestic role of government, an even more eclectic group urged expanding its reach, at home as well as overseas. These activists criticized Eisenhower's reluctance to use the power of his office more forcefully. When unemployment shot up during an economic downturn in 1958–59, economists indebted to Keynesianism ridiculed Eisenhower's commitment to a balanced budget. They called for greater government spending, even if this meant a temporary deficit, to stimulate economic activity. Even after economic conditions improved, Keynesian economists such as John Kenneth Galbraith and Paul Samuelson urged significant deficit spending as a spur to greater growth. During the 1950s, Samuelson's Keynesian-oriented textbook (or a less-demanding knockoff) became the standard choice for younger professors who taught introductory economics.

Other advocates for more active government, while avoiding the rhetoric of conservatives such as Goldwater and his suburban warriors, still criticized Eisenhower's national security policies for their timidity. *Deterrence and Survival in the Nuclear Age* (1957), better known as the **Gaither Report**, urged an immediate increase of about 25 percent in the Pentagon's budget. Prepared by analysts with ties to the defense industry and links to NSC-68 (see Chapter 27), the Gaither report also endorsed building fallout shelters, developing intercontinental ballistic missiles (ICBMs), and expanding conventional military forces. A report from the prestigious Rockefeller Foundation echoed the same themes and endorsed similar spending goals.

Eisenhower reacted cautiously. Keeping his defense budget well below the levels critics had proposed, he even reduced the size of several Army and Air Force units. As a consequence of super-secret U-2 surveillance flights over the Soviet Union, Eisenhower knew that the Soviets were lagging behind, rather than outpacing, the United States in military capability. Their missile program, he also learned, featured a few well-publicized successes but many unreported problems.

Concerns about national security and calls for greater government spending also affected U.S. educational policies. Throughout the 1950s critics complained about schools imparting "life-adjustment" skills instead of teaching traditional academic subjects. Rudolf Flesch's bestselling *Why Johnny Can't Read* (1956) anticipated books that asked why Johnny and his classmates couldn't add or subtract very well either, and why they lagged behind their counterparts in the Soviet Union in science. These critics urged more funding for public schools. Simultaneously, the nation's leading research universities sought greater federal aid for higher education, and prominent scientists urged expanded government funding for basic scientific research. The case for increased spending suddenly became more compelling when, in October 1957, the Soviets launched the world's first artificial satellite—a 22-inch sphere called *Sputnik* (Russian for "satellite") that circled the earth, initially accompanied by a "beep beep" soundtrack, for nearly three months.

A **Sputnik Crisis** soon gripped Washington when a second Soviet satellite, carrying a dog named Laika, went into orbit in early November. The USSR had seemingly soared beyond the United States in both space exploration and rocketry. The missile technology needed to lift up the *Sputniks*, argued Eisenhower's critics, could eventually rain down nuclear weapons on U.S cities. The United States needed, therefore, to expand its military arsenal, educational resources, and research capabilities.

After the *Sputniks*, phrases such as "national security" and "national defense" cleared the way for federal money to flow more freely to educational institutions. The National Defense Education Act of 1958 funneled financial aid to university programs in science, engineering, foreign languages, and the social sciences. This act marked a milestone in overcoming congressional opposition, especially from southerners who feared that economic aid could increase pressure for racial integration, to federal funding of education. The Soviets' apparent superiority in satellite technology also fueled an ambitious R&D effort overseen by a new National Aeronautics and Space Administration (NASA).

Many hoped that domestic social welfare programs would become similar beneficiaries of increased federal spending. Galbraith's *The Affluent Society* saw a dangerous tilt in the "social balance" away from "public goods." Affluent families could vacation in their new automobiles, but they needed to pass through shabby cities along litter-filled roadsides. The researcher who improved automobile performance was well rewarded. But anyone "who dreams up a new public service" is accused of wasting tax dollars, Galbraith's book sardonically noted.

Galbraith's critique seemed mild when compared to that of the socialist writer Michael Harrington. His

New Frontiers, 1960–1963

Q **FOCUS QUESTION** How did the foreign and domestic policies championed by the administration of John F. Kennedy both accept and reject those embraced by the Eisenhower administration during the 1950s? What policy changes did the early 1960s bring?

By 1960, it seemed that the time for translating some of the calls for a more active federal government into congressional legislation and executive orders was at hand. The off-year election of 1958 had not only deposed some conservative Republican stalwarts but helped embolden public officials sympathetic to more energetic government in both foreign and domestic policy. One of these people was John Fitzgerald Kennedy.

The Election of 1960

A wealthy, politically ambitious father claimed to have groomed John Fitzgerald Kennedy for the White House. The young Kennedy graduated from Harvard University, won military honors as a naval officer during the Second World War, became a representative from Massachusetts in 1946, and captured a Senate seat six years later. Kennedy was better known for his social life than his command of legislative details, but he parlayed charm and youthful good looks into political stardom. His 1953 marriage to Jacqueline Bouvier added another dash of glamour. A favorite of the media herself, Jackie won plaudits for her taste in the arts, stylish dress, and fluency in several languages. After John Kennedy narrowly missed winning the vice presidential nomination in 1956, he took aim at the top spot on the 1960 Democratic ticket.

Often accompanied by Jackie and by his brothers, Robert and Ted, John F. Kennedy (JFK), had begun barnstorming the country during the late 1950s. This early presidential campaigning, along with a talented staff and his family's vast wealth, helped Kennedy overwhelm two Democratic challengers, Senators Hubert Humphrey of Minnesota and Lyndon Johnson of Texas, who were also promising to support new governmental initiatives. By pledging to separate his Catholic religion from his politics and by confronting those who appealed to anti-Catholic prejudice, Kennedy defused the religious issue that had doomed the candidacy of Al Smith in 1928 (see Chapter 24).

Eisenhower's Vice President Richard Nixon, running for the Republicans, defied easy labeling. Champions of the new conservatism hardly needed to be reminded of Nixon's anti-communist credentials, but his record during the Eisenhower administration, particularly on civil rights, appeared that of a modern Republican. Nixon was never likely to be, conservatives lamented, Barry Goldwater. Indeed, some Democrats with suspicions about Kennedy's personal makeup could arguably insist that Nixon's stand on policy issues hardly differed from that of JFK. Arthur Schlesinger, Jr., who would become Kennedy's

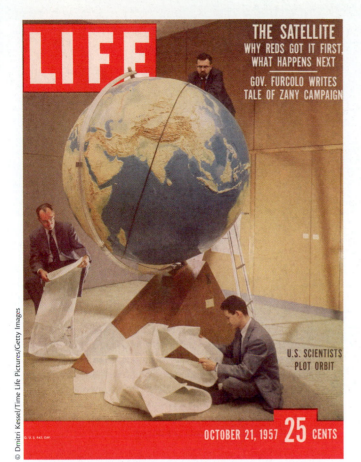

U.S. Scientists Plot Orbit. In the United States in October 1957 all eyes turned toward Sputnik, the first satellite to orbit the earth and a major achievement for the Soviet Union. American scientists took measure of the feat; magazines featured stories about the "Reds got it first"; and many people scanned the nighttime skies for a glimpse of the light refracted by the large rocket that had propelled Sputnik into space. A fear that the United States might lose the "space race" gripped national politics.

passionate essays about economic inequality recalled the radical literature of the 1930s and his own apprenticeship at Dorothy Day's *Catholic Worker* during the early 1950s. At least one-third of the nation's people—living in rural areas, small towns, and cities—barely subsisted in a land of supposed abundance. Avoiding detached economic analysis, Harrington crafted dramatic stories about how poverty ravaged the health and spirit of people whose lives had been largely untouched by the economic growth of the post-Depression era.

During the early 1960s, when addressing social and economic issues became a legislative priority, Galbraith and Harrington became political celebrities. They first entered the public arena, however, through the critical culture of the 1950s. The 1960 election, moreover, promised to feature presidential and congressional candidates who would generally draw on the calls for more active foreign and domestic policies that had emerged during modern Republican administration of Dwight Eisenhower.

"court historian," replied by dashing off an anti-Nixon manifesto that asked this rhetorical question: *Kennedy or Nixon: Does It Make Any Difference?*

Nixon spent much of the 1960 presidential campaign, however, on the defensive. Eisenhower would likely have run for a third term were it not for the 22nd Amendment, and he appeared unenthusiastic about Nixon's candidacy. Nixon himself seemed notably off-balance during the first of several televised debates in which a tanned, relaxed Kennedy emerged, according to surveys of TV viewers, with a clear victory over a pale, nervous Nixon. (Radio listeners, in contrast, awarded Nixon no worse than a draw.) Despite chronic and severe health problems, which his entourage concealed, Kennedy projected personal vigor and energy, if not much experience in directing affairs of state.

Kennedy's 1960 campaign highlighted issues from the 1950s that, taken together, became the agenda for his **New Frontier**. Although Senator Kennedy's civil rights record had been mixed, candidate Kennedy declared support for new legislation and, in an important symbolic act, dispatched aides to Georgia to assist the civil rights leader Martin Luther King, Jr., who was facing jail time for a minor traffic violation. Kennedy also endorsed new social programs to rebuild rural communities, increase educational opportunities, and improve urban conditions.

Two other key parts of Kennedy's New Frontier— promoting greater economic growth and conducting a more aggressive foreign policy—also emerged from the critical culture of the 1950s. Dismissing Eisenhower's policies as too moderate, Kennedy suggested using tax cuts and deficit spending to juice the economy. He also criticized Eisenhower for failing to rid the hemisphere of Castro in Cuba and for allowing a "missile gap" to develop in the arms race with the Soviet Union. By spending more on national security, Kennedy claimed, he could create a more "flexible response" against communism, especially in the Third World. Flexible response became the umbrella term to cover a wide range of military and non-military strategies that Kennedy promised to deploy against communism. The "American people are tired of the drift in our national course . . . and . . . they are ready to move again," Kennedy proclaimed.

The 1960 election brought Kennedy the narrowest of victories. He defeated Nixon by only about 100,000 popular votes, and his victory in the Electoral College rested on razor-thin margins in several states, including Illinois. Republicans urged their candidate to challenge Kennedy's suspicious vote total there, but Nixon chose to accept the disputed result. JFK's triumph owed a considerable debt to his vice presidential running mate, Lyndon Baines Johnson, whose regional appeal helped the Democratic ticket carry the Deep South and his home state of Texas. Even Johnson's political talents, though, could not help Kennedy when it came to the broader election results. The Democrats failed to duplicate their successes of 1958 and lost 20 seats in the House of Representatives and one in the Senate.

Supporters of the new president forgot about the closeness of his election, as JFK and Jackie, already first-name celebrities, riveted media attention on the White House. The

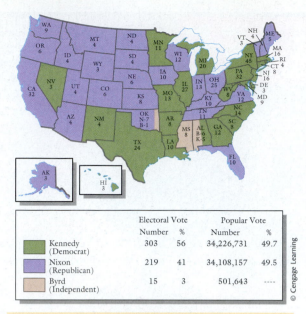

		Electoral Vote		Popular Vote	
		Number	%	Number	%
	Kennedy (Democrat)	303	56	34,226,731	49.7
	Nixon (Republican)	219	41	34,108,157	49.5
	Byrd (Independent)	15	3	501,643	----

© Cengage Learning

Map 28.2 Presidential Election, 1960. In one of the closest elections in American history in terms of the popular vote, Kennedy only narrowly outpolled Nixon. Kennedy's more commanding victory in the electoral vote produced some discussion about the consequences of the Electoral College one day producing a president who had failed to carry the popular vote, a situation that the election of 2000 actually produced.

couple hobnobbed with movie stars and hosted prominent intellectuals. Kennedy's inauguration featured designer clothing, a poignant appearance by the aged poet Robert Frost, and an oft-quoted speech in which JFK challenged people to "ask not what your country can do for you; ask what you can do for your country." The "best and the brightest," the name a journalist later bestowed on the hard-driving people who joined Kennedy's administration, promised to launch exciting and difficult crusades, even to the frontier of outer space.

Foreign Policy

Implementing flexible response gained Kennedy's immediate attention. Although Secretary of Defense Robert McNamara quickly found that the alleged missile gap never existed, the Kennedy administration boosted the defense budget anyway. It supported military assistance programs, propaganda agencies, and covert-action plans. In one of his most popular initiatives, the president created the Peace Corps, a volunteer program that sent Americans, especially young people, to nations around the world to work on development projects that might undercut communism's appeal. Peace Corps volunteers gained valuable experience, and many later staffed the growing number of non-governmental organizations that operated overseas.

Eisenhower's effort to reorient U.S.-Latin American policy away from dictators and toward socioeconomic programs was repackaged as Kennedy's "Alliance for Progress." Unveiled in spring 1961 in hopes of checking the spread of insurgencies that looked to Fidel Castro for inspiration and aid, the Alliance promised $20 billion in loans over a 10-year period to Latin American countries that would undertake land reform and economic development measures. Many Latin Americans judged Kennedy's Alliance, which underestimated obstacles to social and economic change, as more symbolic than substantive.

Cuba and Berlin

The worst fiasco of the Kennedy presidency, an ill-conceived 1961 CIA mission against Cuba, also had its roots in the Eisenhower administration. The CIA had been secretly planning an invasion to oust Fidel Castro. Overriding the doubts of key advisers, Kennedy approved this Eisenhower-era plan. On April 17, 1961, however, when U.S.-trained forces (mainly anticommunist Cuban exiles) landed at the Bahia de Cochinas (Bay of Pigs) on the southern coast of Cuba, the expected popular uprising against Castro failed to materialize. Instead, forces loyal to the Cuban revolution quickly surrounded and captured members of the mission. Kennedy rejected any additional steps, including the air strikes the Cuban exiles had expected, and initially denied any U.S. involvement in this **Bay of Pigs Invasion**. The CIA's role quickly became public knowledge, however, and anti-U.S. sentiment swept across Latin America. Castro tightened his grip over Cuban life and strengthened his ties to the Soviet Union.

Kennedy responded by calling the Bay of Pigs invasion a mistake—and by devising a new, covert program called "Operation Mongoose." It abandoned the idea of an invasion in favor of destabilizing Cuba's economy and, in concert with organized crime figures, trying to assassinate the Cuban leader.

Meanwhile, two other dramatic confrontations began unfolding, more slowly, in Berlin and in Cuba. In June 1961 Nikita Khrushchev and Kennedy met in Vienna, Austria, where the Soviets proposed ending the Western presence in Berlin and reuniting the city as part of East Germany. Kennedy refused to abandon West Berlin, but in August 1961 the communist regime began to erect a barbed-wire fence and then a concrete barrier to separate East from West Berlin. This Berlin Wall became a symbol of communist repression. Kennedy's assertion in 1963 speech, *"Ich bin ein Berliner,"* delivered in front of the wall to a cheering crowd of West Berliners, provided a memorable image of JFK's presidency.

Superpower confrontation, however, had already escalated to a potentially lethal level during the **Cuban Missile Crisis** of October 1962. The Soviet Union, responding to pleas from Castro, sent sophisticated armaments to Cuba. After U-2 spy planes revealed missile-launching sites in Cuba, the Kennedy administration declared it would never allow the Soviet Union to place nuclear warheads so close to U.S. soil. It demanded that the Soviets dismantle the missile silos and turn back supply ships heading for Cuba. After tense strategizing sessions with his top advisers, Kennedy rejected a military strike against Cuba, fearing it might lead to war with the Soviet Union. Instead, he ordered the Navy to "quarantine" Cuba. The Strategic Air Command went on full alert for a possible nuclear conflict. Both sides also began frantic, secret diplomatic maneuvers to forestall such a catastrophe.

Washington and Moscow, after 13 anxious days, did negotiate an end to this nuclear showdown. On October 28, 1962, Khrushchev ordered the Soviet missiles in Cuba dismantled and the supply ships brought home; Kennedy promised not to invade Cuba and secretly assured Khrushchev that he would complete a previously ordered withdrawal of U.S. missiles from Turkey. When Soviet archives were opened in the mid-1990s, Americans learned that the Missile Crisis had been even more dangerous than earlier imagined. Unknown to the Kennedy administration in 1962, the Soviets had already placed tactical nuclear weapons, which could have reached U.S. targets, inside Cuba. Some historical evidence suggests Castro favored atomic conflict over diplomatic concessions.

By underscoring the risk of nuclear conflict, however, the Cuban Missile Crisis made the two superpowers more cautious. To prevent a future confrontation or an accident, they established a direct telephone hot-line between Moscow and Washington, D.C.

Southeast Asia and Flexible Response

In Southeast Asia, Kennedy continued the U.S. effort to preserve a noncommunist state in South Vietnam. After the Bay of Pigs debacle, in which the overthrow of an already established communist government had failed, JFK became determined to prevent any communist-led "war of national liberation" from toppling a non-communist regime.

Even so, the odds against nurturing a pro-U.S. government in South Vietnam seemed to grow longer as Kennedy's own presidency lengthened. Opposition to the regime of Ngo Dinh Diem, in power since the mid-1950s, had now coalesced in the National Liberation Front (NLF). Formed in December 1960, the NLF included non-communist groups that resented Diem's dependence on the United States; communists who demanded more extensive land reform; an array of political leaders fed up with Diem's corruption and cronyism; and groups directly beholden to Ho Chi Minh's communist government in the North. North Vietnam continued sending supplies and troops to the South in support of the anti-Diem coalition.

The Kennedy administration saw Vietnam as the crucial test case for flexible response. It dispatched the Green Berets, elite U.S. troops who were trained in "counterinsurgency" tactics, to aid the South Vietnamese government. It also sent teams of social scientists, charged with "nation building," to consult on socioeconomic reforms and internal security. Finally, JFK dispatched U.S. combat troops. These forces, numbering nearly 24,000 by late 1963, would supposedly only advise, rather than actively fight alongside, South Vietnam's forces.

South Vietnam still lacked a credible government. Diem miscalculated badly when responding to protests from independent Buddhist groups, estranged from the president and his Catholic advisers. The decision, in May 1963, to fire on Buddhist demonstrators in the city of Hue prompted a series of confrontations between protestors and Diem's government. As part of the anti-government effort, several Buddhist monks committed suicide by setting fire to their robes. The Kennedy administration recognized these self-immolations as a sign of the deep-seated opposition to Diem—and as a public relations disaster. Diem dismissed the Buddhists as communist dupes, and his sister-in-law announced that she welcomed another "monk barbecue show." The Kennedy administration signaled to South Vietnam's powerful military that U.S. support for Diem was nearing its end.

Domestic Policymaking

Kennedy's campaign had promised an ambitious domestic agenda, but relatively little happened immediately. To begin, conservative Republicans and Southern Democrats retained enough clout in Congress to stall or vote down proposals with which they disagreed. Despite his own lengthy service in Congress, Kennedy seemed initially uncertain about how to deal with its old-line leadership. He eventually sided with confidants who advised that a slow approach would reap success toward the end of his first term.

This strategy meant that Kennedy did not press for the government-spending measures he had promised would speed economic growth. He feared any action that might unbalance the federal budget and thus alienate fiscal conservatives and business leaders. Relations with corporate leaders nevertheless turned ugly in 1962, when Kennedy clashed with the president of U.S. Steel over that company's decision to raise prices beyond the guidelines suggested by the White House. Kennedy's threat to retaliate against the steel company enraged his corporate critics, and his subsequent back peddling on price increases disappointed people desiring vigorous presidential leadership.

In 1962 the White House finally asked Congress to lower tax rates as a means of promoting economic growth. The economy continued its rebound from the downturn of 1957–58, but Kennedy now argued that lower tax rates for everyone, along with special deductions for businesses that invested in new plants and equipment, would produce more jobs and greater growth. Despite opposition from fiscal conservatives who feared an unbalanced federal budget and from those who thought Kennedy's proposal tilted toward corporations and the wealthy, the president's tax bill slowly moved through Congress. Kennedy publicly signaled support for Keynesian-style policies and denounced "myths" about an unbalanced budget, modest federal debt, and "big government."

On the social welfare issues, the Kennedy administration proposed a higher minimum wage and new urban rebuilding programs. It also supported the Area Redevelopment Bill of 1961, which called for directing federal grants and loans to impoverished areas such as Appalachia, the 13-state region running along the Appalachian Mountain chain from southern New York to northern Mississippi.

The Politics of Gender

Q What social, economic, and cultural forces worked to change gender roles during the 1950s and early 1960s?

FOCUS QUESTION

The 1950s and early 1960s saw significant changes in how and where people lived and worked. This era produced especially important changes in the everyday politics of gender.

The New Suburbs and Gender Politics

In middle-class homes, especially in the new suburbs, women discovered the ambiguous impact of technological innovation. If new appliances—automatic clothes washers, more powerful vacuum cleaners, home freezers—eased old burdens, they also created new ones. The time that women spent on domestic duties was not reduced so much as shifted to goals such as more frequently manicured floors and more carefully pressed clothes, which the latest household gadgets enabled.

Life in the new suburbs, moreover, was structured by a broad pattern of "separate spheres": a public sphere of paid work and politics dominated by men, and a private one of unpaid housework and childcare reserved for women. Because relatively few businesses initially located in the new suburbs, men commuted from home to work, while women found employment opportunities about as scarce as professional child-care facilities. Mothers thus spent considerable time tending to their baby-boomer children. In contrast to the urban neighborhoods or small-town communities where many suburban housewives had grown up, newly constructed suburbs contained few older relatives or younger single women who could help with household and child-care duties.

Without mothers or grandmothers living close by, young suburban mothers often turned to child-care manuals for advice. The various editions of *Baby and Child Care* (1946), written by Dr. Benjamin Spock, sold millions of copies. Like earlier advice books, Spock's assigned virtually all child-care duties to women and implied that the family and the nation itself depended on how well mothers looked after the Baby-Boom generation.

An alarmist tone in these books reflected—and helped generate—a widespread concern about juvenile delinquency. A problem teen, according to one 1950s study, sprang from a "family atmosphere not conducive to development of emotionally well-integrated, happy youngsters, conditioned to obey legitimate authority." The ideal mother devoted herself to rearing her children. Women who sought careers outside of the home and marriage risked being labeled as maladjusted and deviant—real-life versions of the *femme fatales* who populated *film noirs* (see Chapter 27).

Variations on this message appeared nearly everywhere. Even the nation's prestigious women's colleges assumed their graduates would pursue men and marriage. In a 1955 commencement address at Smith College, Adlai Stevenson, the Democratic Party's urbane presidential aspirant, reminded graduates of their "duty" to keep a husband "truly purposeful, to keep him whole." Popular magazines, psychological literature, and pop-culture imagery suggested that wives and mothers held the keys to social stability. This meant that women who desired alternative arrangements, either in their work or their sexual preferences, needed to be pressured, much as *Tootle the Engine*, to return to the straight and narrow.

Competing portraits, however, painted a somewhat more complicated picture of gender arrangements. Most men told researchers that they preferred an "active partner" to a "submissive, stay-at-home" wife. Popular TV shows, such as *Father Knows Best* and *Leave It to Beaver*, suggested that fathers should be more engaged in family life than they seemed to be. Advice manuals, while envisioning suburban husbands earning their family's entire income, increasingly urged them to be "real fathers" at home. Parenting literature increasingly emphasized family togetherness, and institutions such as the Young Men's Christian Association (YMCA) offered courses on how to achieve it.

This call for family togetherness was partly a response to what cultural historians now see as an incipient "male revolt" against the "male breadwinner role." Hugh Hefner's *Playboy* magazine, which debuted in 1953, epitomized this trend. It ridiculed men who neglected their own happiness in order to support a wife and children as suckers rather than saints. *Playboy*'s first issue proclaimed: "We aren't a 'family magazine.' " In Hefner's version of the good life, a man rented a "pad" rather than owned a home, drove a sports car rather than a station wagon, and admired the Playmate of the Month rather than the Mother of the Year.

Signs of Women's Changing Roles

Meanwhile, greater numbers of women were working outside the house. Female employment, even among married women, rose steadily as jobs expanded in the clerical and service sectors. In 1948 about 25 percent of married mothers worked outside the home; at the end of the 1950s nearly 40 percent did. With the 1960 introduction of a new method of oral contraception, the birth control pill, women could enjoy greater control over family planning and career decisions—and over decisions about their own sexual behavior. By 1964 one-quarter of the couples that used contraception relied on "The Pill." At the same time, activists began to press for an end to anti-abortion laws that restricted the ability of women to find legal and relatively safe ways to terminate pregnancies.

Employment opportunities still remained circumscribed. Virtually all of the nation's nurses, telephone operators, secretaries, and elementary school teachers were women. Historically, pay scales in these areas lagged behind those for men in occupations that required comparable training. Jobs for women in the unionized job sectors remained rare. And chances for advancement in the corporate field were similarly limited. As the number of low-paying jobs for women expanded during the 1950s, better-paying professional opportunities actually narrowed. Medical, law, and other professional schools admitted lower percentages of women than in the past. When Sandra Day (who would later become U.S. Supreme Court Justice Sandra Day O'Connor) graduated with honors from a prestigious law school during the 1950s, not a single private firm offered her a job. She worked, without pay, in the public sector. The number of women on college faculties shrank even from the low levels of earlier decades.

Although employers still invoked the "family wage" to justify higher pay for men, more women than ever before were trying to support a family on their own paychecks. This was especially true for women of color. Recognizing that images of domesticity hardly fit the lives of many African American women, *Ebony* magazine celebrated black women who combined success in parenting and at work.

Mass-circulation magazines aimed at women of European descent also carried increasingly mixed messages about gender roles. Although social commentators commonly labeled a woman's pursuit of activities outside the home as "unnatural," popular magazines increasingly featured stories about women in public life and in business. The 1950s, in short, saw growing diversity in both the social roles that women were assuming and the ways in which mass culture represented them.

A New Women's Movement

The seeds of a resurgent **women's movement** were also being sown, although more quietly, between 1953 and 1963. All across the political spectrum, women began speaking out on contemporary issues. The energy of women such as Phyllis Schlafly, whose book *A Choice, Not an Echo* (1964) became a leading manifesto from the political right, helped fuel the new conservatism. African American activists such as Bernice Johnson Reagon (whose work with the Freedom Singers combined music and social activism) and Fannie Lou Hamer (who spearheaded the organization of a racially integrated Freedom Democratic Party in Mississippi) fought discrimination based on both race and gender. Women union leaders pushed for greater employment opportunities and more equitable work environments. Chicana farm workers became key figures in union-organizing efforts in California. Women also played a central role in protests, through organizations such as the Committee for a Sane Nuclear Policy (SANE) and the Women's Strike for Peace, against the U.S.–Soviet arms race. During Kennedy's final year in office, Betty Friedan published *The Feminine Mystique*. Widely credited with helping to revive organized feminist activity in the United States, Friedan's book drew on her own social criticism from the late 1950s and articulated the dissatisfaction that many middle-class women felt about the narrow confines of domestic life and the lack of public roles available to them.

To address women's concerns, Kennedy appointed a Presidential Commission on the Status of Women, chaired by Eleanor Roosevelt. After negotiating differences between moderate and more militant members, the commission issued a report that documented discrimination against women in employment and wages. Kennedy responded with a presidential order to eliminate gender discrimination within the federal civil service. He also supported the Equal Pay Act of 1963, which made it a federal crime for employers to pay lower wages to women who did the same work as men.

Bernice Johnson Reagon. During the civil rights crusade, "freedom songs" fostered solidarity. The singers pictured here include Bernice Johnson Reagon, a member of the Freedom Singers. Later, she founded the all-woman a cappella singing group, Sweet Honey in the Rock.

© Danny Lyon/Magnum Photos, Inc.

The Expanding Civil Rights Movements, 1953–1963

Q **FOCUS QUESTION** How did expanding civil rights movements raise new political issues and visions during the 1950s and early 1960s? How did the nation's political and social institutions respond?

When Dwight Eisenhower took office, the U.S. Supreme Court was preparing to rehear a legal challenge to racially segregated educational systems. The NAACP and its chief legal strategist, Thurgood Marshall, spearheaded this cause. Before the rehearing took place, Eisenhower appointed Earl Warren, a former Republican governor of California, as chief justice. The Supreme Court, with Warren in its center chair, entered the widening civil rights struggle.

The *Brown* Cases, 1954–1955

The Supreme Court litigation popularly known as "the *Brown* decision" actually included a series of constitutional rulings, the **Brown** **Cases**. In 1954, Chief Justice Warren wrote a unanimous opinion (in *Brown* v. *Board of Education of Topeka*) declaring that states could not segregate their public schools on the basis of race without violating the constitutional right of

African American students to equal protection of the law. A companion case decided the same day (*Bolling* v. *Sharpe*) outlawed racially segregated schools in the District of Columbia.

Brown v. *Board of Education* (1955)

Although the *Brown* and *Bolling* decisions technically applied only to schools, they suggested that other segregated public facilities could no longer survive constitutional challenge. In 1955, though, a follow-up Supreme Court decision, known as "*Brown II*," decreed that the process of dismantling illegally segregated school systems should not go into effect immediately; desegregation could, instead, move forward "with all deliberate speed."

Implementing the *Brown* cases challenged the nation's political, social, and cultural institutions. The politics of civil rights sometimes seemed focused on the 16 states that the Census Bureau officially called "the South," but demographic changes helped make them more than a regional phenomenon.

During the 1950s the South was becoming more like the rest of the country. New cultural forces, such as network television, penetrated the region. Machines were displacing the region's predominantly black fieldworkers. The absence of strong labor unions and the presence of favorable tax laws attracted northern-based businesses. National chain stores extended throughout the South.

Meanwhile, the racial composition of cities in the West, Midwest, and Northeast became more like that of the South. In 1940, more than three-quarters of the nation's African

Segregation. Dressed in his Air Force uniform, a young man from New York City is faced with a "colored waiting room" in an Atlanta bus terminal in 1956. Before the civil rights revolution of the 1960s, southern states maintained legally enforced segregation in most public facilities, a practice popularly called Jim Crow (see Chapter 18).

Americans lived in the South, many on farms and in small towns. During and after the Second World War, much of this populaton left the rural South and became important to political life in northern urban areas, where Republicans joined Democrats in generally supporting efforts to end racial discrimination. As more African Americans voted Democratic, however, the GOP gained ground among white voters in the South and in the new suburban neighborhoods, especially in the Middle and Far West.

The most familiar stories about civil rights activities during the 1950s have long concentrated on the South, but recent histories emphasize how the struggle became nationwide in scope. Efforts to end segregation and racial discrimination emerged in virtually every Northern and Western city. These urban-based movements employed a variety of tactics, such as "shop where you can work" campaigns, which urged consumers to patronize only businesses that would employ them. They tried to bring more workers from non-European backgrounds into the union movement and the public-service sector, enlarging jobs in police and fire departments as well as in all of the agencies of state and local government. Increasingly, though, gaining legal-constitutional leverage seemed crucial to future successes.

As African Americans mounted new attacks on segregation and discrimination in the South, white segregationists pledged "massive resistance" to the *Brown* decisions and went

to court with delaying tactics. One hundred members of Congress signed a "Southern Manifesto" in 1956 that condemned the Supreme Court's desegregation rulings as a "clear abuse of judicial power" and pledged support for any state that intended "to resist forced integration by any lawful means."

Defiance went beyond the courtroom. White vigilantes unfurled the banners of the Ku Klux Klan and formed new racist organizations, such as the White Citizens Council. People who worked in the civil rights cause constantly risked injury and death. Racial tensions escalated. In August 1955, two white Mississippians murdered 14-year-old Emmett Till, a visitor from Chicago, because they thought he had acted "disrespectful" toward a white woman. Mamie Till Bradley insisted that her son's death not remain a private incident. She demanded that his maimed corpse be displayed for "the whole world to see" and that his killers be punished. When their case came to trial, an all-white Mississippi jury quickly found the two men—who would subsequently confess their crime to a magazine reporter—not guilty.

The Montgomery Bus Boycott

The southern civil rights movement increasingly supplemented legal maneuvering with direct action. Following an earlier, partially successful 1953 campaign to desegregate the transportation system in Baton Rouge, Louisiana, activists in Montgomery, Alabama, raised their sights. After police arrested Rosa Parks for defying a segregation ordinance that required segregated seating on municipal buses, Montgomery's black community demanded complete desegregation, boycotted public transportation, and organized carpools as alternative transit. Joining with Rosa Parks, a longtime bastion of the local NAACP chapter, many other black women in Montgomery helped coordinate the complicated, months-long boycott. Responding to events in Montgomery, the Supreme Court extended the premise of the *Brown* decisions on education and specifically declared segregation of public buses to be unconstitutional.

After a campaign lasting more than a year, the Montgomery bus boycott succeeded. City officials, saddled with financial losses and legal defeats, agreed to end Montgomery's separatist transit policy. Events in Montgomery suggested that black activists, even in the segregated South, could effectively mobilize—and then organize—community resources to fight racial discrimination.

The bus boycott also vaulted **Dr. Martin Luther King, Jr.,** one of its leaders, into the national spotlight. Born and educated in Atlanta, with a doctorate in theology from Boston University, King and other black ministers followed up the victory in Montgomery by forming the Southern Christian Leadership Conference (SCLC). In addition to demanding desegregated public facilities, the SCLC sought to organize an ongoing sociopolitical movement that would work for other changes.

The young, male ministers in the SCLC sought assistance across generational and gender divides. Tapping the strategic wisdom of Bayard Rustin, who had been involved in civil rights activism since the 1940s, and the tactical skills of Ella Baker, another veteran organizer, Dr. King led the SCLC's effort to register African American voters throughout the South.

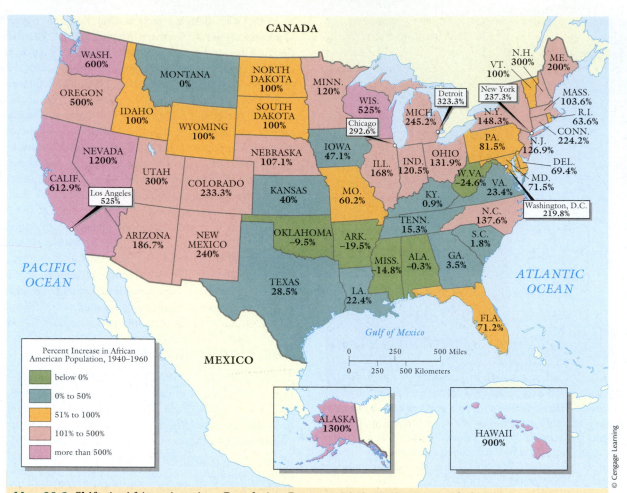

CANADA

WASH. 600%
OREGON 500%
MONTANA 0%
IDAHO 100%
NEVADA 1200%
UTAH 300%
CALIF. 612.9%
Los Angeles 525%
ARIZONA 186.7%
NEW MEXICO 240%
WYOMING 100%
COLORADO 233.3%
NORTH DAKOTA 100%
SOUTH DAKOTA 100%
NEBRASKA 107.1%
KANSAS 40%
OKLAHOMA −9.5%
TEXAS 28.5%
MINN. 120%
WIS. 525%
IOWA 47.1%
MO. 60.2%
ARK. −19.5%
LA. 22.4%
MISS. −14.8%
ALA. −0.3%
GA. 3.5%
FLA. 71.2%
Detroit 323.3%
Chicago 292.6%
MICH. 245.2%
ILL. 168%
IND. 120.5%
OHIO 131.9%
KY. 0.9%
TENN. 15.3%
W.VA. −24.6%
VA. 23.4%
N.C. 137.6%
S.C. 1.8%
N.H. 300%
VT. 100%
ME. 200%
New York 237.3%
N.Y. 148.3%
MASS. 103.6%
R.I. 63.6%
CONN. 224.2%
PA. 81.5%
N.J. 126.9%
DEL. 69.4%
MD. 71.5%
Washington, D.C. 219.8%

PACIFIC OCEAN

ATLANTIC OCEAN

Gulf of Mexico

MEXICO

0   250   500 Miles
0   250   500 Kilometers

Percent Increase in African American Population, 1940–1960

- below 0%
- 0% to 50%
- 51% to 100%
- 101% to 500%
- more than 500%

ALASKA 1300%

HAWAII 900%

© Cengage Learning

Map 28.3 Shifts in African American Population Patterns, 1940–1960. During and after the Second World War, large numbers of African Americans left the rural South and migrated to new locations. Which states had the largest percentage of outmigration? Which saw the greatest percentage of population increase? How might this migration have affected American life?

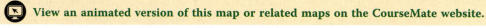 **View an animated version of this map or related maps on the CourseMate website.**

Montgomery Bus Boycott.
The drive to desegregate municipal buses in Montgomery, Alabama, required an elaborately organized and skillfully coordinated effort. It primarily relied on the talents and commitment of volunteers, particularly women. African American residents of Montgomery shared automobile transportation, coordinated by the boycott movement, while avoiding city buses like the one shown standing vacant across the street.

King and the SCLC relied on civil disobedience to obtain change. According to Dr. King, nonviolent direct action would dramatize, through both word and deed, the evil of racial discrimination. King's powerful presence and religiously rooted rhetoric carried the message of civil rights to most parts of the United States and the world.

The Politics of Civil Rights: From the Local to the Global

All across the country, civil rights activities went forward. Shortly after the conclusion of the Montgomery bus boycott, New York City passed the nation's first "open housing" ordinance, a model for other local and state measures aimed at ending racial discrimination in the sale and rental of homes and apartments. Efforts to change housing patterns faced tough going, however. Typically, white homeowners in those urban and older suburban neighborhoods where African Americans or Latinos might hope to buy or rent adopted the exclusionary strategies used so effectively by their counterparts in the new suburbs.

In cities and states outside the South, civil rights groups also sought legislation to outlaw discrimination in hiring. In 1958, for example, a labor union-civil rights coalition in California, joining under slogans such as "Fight Sharecropper Wages," defeated an anti-union right-to-work proposal they said threatened to drive down pay rates for all workers. Buoyed by this success, the same coalition began lobbying members of the legislature to enact a California-wide open housing measure.

Political institutions in Washington, D.C., felt similar pressure to act on civil rights. The Supreme Court lent its support at crucial times, such as during the Montgomery bus boycott, but Congress remained deeply divided on racial issues. With southern segregationists, all members of the Democratic majority, holding key posts on Capitol Hill, antidiscrimination measures faced formidable obstacles.

Even so, Congress did pass its first civil rights measure in more than 80 years. The **Civil Rights Act of 1957** expedited lawsuits by African Americans who claimed that southern states were systematically abridging their right to vote. The law also created a Commission on Civil Rights, an advisory body empowered to study alleged violations and recommend remedies. In 1960, with the crucial support of Lyndon Johnson of Texas, the Democratic leader in the Senate, a second civil rights act added more procedures to safeguard voting rights. These civil rights measures became law against fierce opposition from southern Democrats and conservative Republicans such as Barry Goldwater.

President Eisenhower initially hesitated to use his executive power to aid civil rights efforts. He did support the Civil Rights Act of 1957 but held back when some Republicans urged a dramatic presidential step—such as barring racial discrimination on all construction projects financed by federal funds. A confirmed gradualist, Eisenhower saw ending racial segregation as a slow, lengthy process. He also viewed desegregation as primarily a local matter and doubted that federal power could change the attitudes of people strongly opposed to integration.

In 1957, however, events in Little Rock, Arkansas, forced Eisenhower to invoke his executive power and enforce a federal court decree ordering the desegregation of the city's Central High School. Orval Faubus, the state's segregationist governor, had promised to prevent black students from entering the school building and deployed his state's National Guard to block them. Confronting this direct challenge to national authority, Eisenhower took command of the Arkansas National Guard and augmented its forces with members of the U.S. Army. Black students, escorted by armed troops, finally entered Central High. The primary issue at stake, Eisenhower insisted, was a state's defiance of a federal court order rather than school desegregation.

Dwight Eisenhower, Response to the Little Rock Crisis (September 24, 1957)

The confrontation in Little Rock also underscored the international dimension of civil rights politics in the United States. Washington often found itself on the defensive when foreign critics pointed to the U.S. record on civil rights. The Soviet Union delighted in telling people, particularly in the Third World, how racial discrimination showed "the façade of the so-called 'American democracy.'" When the U.S. Supreme Court, in *Cooper* v. *Aaron* (1958), unanimously invalidated an Arkansas law intended to block school integration, the Eisenhower administration's global informational campaign stressed America's support for liberty and equality, and it encouraged the world press to highlight this important constitutional decision.

Indeed the State Department during the 1950s sent Dizzy Gillespie, Louis Armstrong, Duke Ellington, and many other African American jazz musicians as "goodwill ambassadors" to build more cordial relationships with new states in Africa and Asia. These tours presented jazz as an authentic American art form symbolizing freedom. They tried to counter Soviet charges by highlighting the accomplishments of African Americans. America's cultural diplomacy, in fact, encouraged racially integrated musical acts to perform abroad—even though they might have been unwelcome in many venues at home. Racial discrimination and conflict, warned Secretary of State Dulles, was "not helpful to the influence of the United States abroad." The Cold War's battle for hearts and minds throughout the world provided yet one more pressure on behalf of civil rights efforts.

The Politics of American Indian Policy

The Eisenhower administration struggled with its policy toward American Indians. It attempted to implement two programs, **Termination and Relocation**, already underway before it took office. The first called for an end to the status of Indians as "wards of the United States" and a grant of all the "rights and privileges pertaining to American citizenship." The goals of Termination, to be pursued on a tribe-by-tribe basis, were to abolish reservations, liquidate tribal assets, and curtail the social services offered by the Bureau of Indian Affairs (BIA).

Under the Relocation program, which had begun in 1951, Indians were encouraged to leave rural reservations and seek jobs in urban areas. In 1954 the BIA intensified its relocation efforts, with Minneapolis, St. Louis, Dallas, and

Indian Women in Pacific Northwest, c. 1950. The programs of Termination and Relocation put traditional practices at risk. Here, women from the Muckleshoot Reservation in Washington state follow ancestral practices in preparing salmon to grill over an open fire of alderwood.

several other cities joining Denver, Salt Lake City, and Los Angeles as relocation sites. Proponents of Termination and Relocation insisted that American Indians could easily be assimilated into the mainstream of U.S. life.

These initiatives quickly failed. As several tribes were terminated during the 1950s, almost 12,000 people lost their status as tribal members, and the bonds of communal life for many Indians grew weaker. Land once held by tribes fell into the hands of commercial, non-Indian developers. Indians from terminated tribes also lost both their exemption from state taxation and social services from the BIA. They gained little in return. Relocation went no better. Most relocated Indians found only low paying, dead-end jobs and discrimination from both public and private institutions.

American Indian activists and their allies mobilized against Termination and Relocation. By 1957 their efforts forced the government to scale back the initial timetable, which had called for liquidating every tribe within five years. In 1960 the party platforms of both the Republicans and Democrats repudiated Termination, and in 1962 the policy was stopped. The Relocation program continued, however, and by 1967 almost half of the nation's Indians lived in relocation cities. This policy neither touched the deep-rooted problems that many Indians confronted, including a life expectancy only two-thirds that of whites, nor provided significantly better employment or educational opportunities.

Spanish-Speaking Communities and Civil Rights

Millions of Spanish-speaking people, many recently arrived in the United States, also began mobilizing in order to realize the nation's rhetorical commitment to liberty and equality. Puerto Ricans began moving in larger numbers from their island commonwealth to the mainland in the 1950s. By the early 1960s New York City's Puerto Rican population was nearly 100 times greater than it had been before the Second World War. Large numbers of Puerto Ricans also settled in Chicago, Boston, and Hartford, Connecticut. Officially U.S. citizens, most of the newcomers spoke only Spanish; social and cultural clubs helped them connect with the Puerto Rican communities they had left behind. At the same time, Puerto Ricans began to organize against the

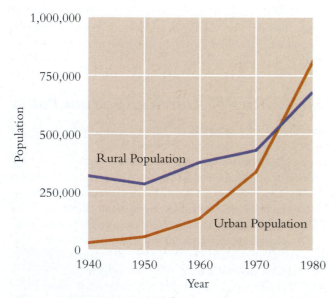

Total Urban and Rural Indian Population in the United States, 1940–1980.

discrimination they faced in housing and jobs. The Puerto Rican-Hispanic Leadership Forum, organized in 1957, presaged the emergence of groups that looked more to social and economic conditions—and, ultimately, greater political clout—in the United States than to cultural affinities with Puerto Rico.

Meanwhile, Spanish-speaking people from Mexico were continuing to move to California and the Southwest, where they joined long-established Mexican American communities. In 1940 Mexican Americans had been the most rural of all the major ethnic groups; by 1950, in contrast, more than 65 percent of Mexican Americans were living in urban areas, a figure that would climb to 85 percent during the 1960s. Mexican Americans were becoming a political force in many southwestern cities and an important constituency for the national Democratic Party.

Beginning in 1942 and continuing until 1967 the U.S. government sponsored the *bracero* (or farmhand) program, which brought nearly 5 million Mexicans northward to fill agricultural jobs. Many *braceros* and their families remained in the United States after their work contracts expired. Legal immigrants from Mexico joined them, as did undocumented immigrants, who became targets of a government dragnet called "Operation Wetback." ("Wetback" was a term of derision, implying a person of Mexican descent had illegally crossed the Rio Grande River to reach the United States.) During a five-year period the government claimed to have rounded up and deported to Mexico nearly 4 million undocumented immigrants. This operation, critics charged, helped stigmatize even U.S. citizens of Mexican heritage and justify further discriminatory treatment.

As a result, civil rights groups representing Mexican Americans intensified earlier mobilization efforts. Labor organizers sought higher wages and better working conditions in the factories and fields, even as the FBI labeled their efforts "communist inspired" and harassed unions with large Mexican American memberships, such as the United Cannery, Agricultural, Packing and Allied Workers of America (UCAPAWA). A lengthy mining strike in New Mexico became the subject of the independent motion picture *Salt of the Earth* (1954). Pressure from Washington, the film industry, and anticommunist labor unions throughout the 1950s prevented distribution of this collaboration among blacklisted filmmakers, striking miners, and their families.

Civil rights organizations such as the League of United Latin American Citizens (LULAC) and the Unity League sought to desegregate schools and other public facilities throughout California and the Southwest. Lawyers for these groups faced a strategic dilemma. Legal challenges brought on behalf of plaintiffs of African descent, as in the *Brown* cases, relied on the claim that state laws separating "whites" and "negroes" violated constitutional guarantees of equality. Most states, though, classified persons whose ancestors came from Mexico as legally "white." As earlier cases such as *Westminster* had shown (see Chapter 27), school officials in states such as California and Texas cited "language deficiencies," rather than "race," as justification for segregating students of Mexican descent. The "other white" legal status of Mexican Americans, in other words, complicated the ability of organizations such as LULAC to frame court challenges that could rely on legal precedents involving "white-against-black" discrimination.

Urban-Suburban Issues

The growth of suburbia during the 1950s helped to highlight urban issues, many of them related to changing racial patterns. Throughout this period, both public and private institutions began shifting financial resources away from cities, especially away from neighborhoods in which Latinos and African Americans lived. Adopting a policy called **redlining**, lending institutions generally denied loans for homebuyers and businesses in areas that were labeled "decaying" or "marginal" because they contained aging buildings, dense populations, and growing numbers of people of non-European descent. The Federal Housing Administration (FHA) and other governmental agencies channeled most lending toward the newer suburbs. In 1960, for example, the FHA failed to put up a single dollar for home loan guarantees in Camden or Paterson, New Jersey—cities in which minority populations were growing—while it poured millions of dollars into surrounding, largely all-white suburbs.

Urban renewal programs, authorized by the Housing Act of 1949 (see Chapter 27), often seemed aimed at "urban removal." Although this Fair Deal measure had called for "a feasible method for the temporary relocation" of persons displaced, developers generally ignored the requirement. For several decades, the person who directed New York City's vast construction projects, Robert Moses, consistently understated the number of people dislocated by his urban renewal and highway building programs. Defenders of Robert Moses insisted that he pursued a progressive vision that ultimately benefited all New Yorkers, but the costs of progress—and perhaps its benefits—hardly seemed equally shared.

Meanwhile, plans for federally built public housing faltered. Although suburban areas, where land was abundant and inexpensive, seemed the obvious place to locate affordable housing, middle-income homeowners used their political clout and zoning laws to freeze out government sponsored housing projects. At the same time, private housing interests lobbied to limit the number of public units actually constructed in urban areas and to ensure that they would offer tenants fewer amenities, including closets with doors, than could be found in private units. Originally conceived as short-term alternatives for families who would soon move to their own homes, publicly built facilities became stigmatized as "the projects," permanent housing of last resort for people with chronically low incomes.

The urban-suburban policies came under sustained criticism. In 1960 both the Democratic and Republican Parties pledged to create a new cabinet office for urban affairs and to reconsider Washington's role in addressing the cycle of continued suburban growth and onrushing urban decay.

New Forms of Direct Action, 1960–1963

Although John F. Kennedy had talked about new civil rights legislation, his administration initially tried to placate the segregationist wing of his Democratic Party. The president and his brother, Robert, who had become attorney general, listened sympathetically when J. Edgar Hoover, director of the FBI, falsely warned of continuing ties between Martin Luther King, Jr. and members of the Communist Party. To monitor King's activities, the FBI illegally recorded many of his private conversations and clamped a tight web of surveillance around his every move. King's movement also faced another challenge: that from activists who favored moving on to new forms of direct action.

In early 1960 African American students at North Carolina A & T College in Greensboro sat down at a drugstore lunch counter and politely asked to be served in the same manner as white customers. This was the beginning of the **sit-in movement**, a new phase of civil rights activism. In both the South and the North, young demonstrators staged nonviolent sit-ins at restaurants, bus and train stations, and other public facilities. Singing civil rights anthems such as "We Shall Overcome" to inspire solidarity, the sit-in movement encouraged further activism. In 1961 interracial activists from CORE and the Student Nonviolent Coordinating Committee (SNCC), a student group that emerged from the sit-in movement, risked racist retaliation by reviving a form of direct action that CORE had first tried in the 1940s: "freedom rides" across the South. The new **freedom riders** were challenging the Kennedy administration to enforce federal court decisions that had declared state laws requiring segregation on interstate buses (and in bus stations) to be unconstitutional.

The new grassroots activism forced the Kennedy administration into action of its own. It dispatched U.S. marshals and National Guard troops to protect the freedom riders. It also deployed federal power to help integrate educational institutions in the Deep South, including the Universities of Mississippi and Alabama. In November 1962 Kennedy issued the long promised executive order that banned racial discrimination in federally financed housing. The following February he sent Congress a civil rights bill that called for speedier trials in cases involving challenges to racial discrimination in voting.

Nearly 1500 civil rights demonstrations took place across the country the following spring. Protests in the urban Northeast and Midwest generally focused on improving educational opportunities. Most of these called for accelerating school integration plans, but a "Walk to Freedom March" in Detroit attracted more than 125,000 people on behalf of a broad agenda that included job creation and open housing legislation.

Events in the South, however, continued to attract the most attention. Beginning in the spring of 1963, violent conflict convulsed Birmingham. Direct action in this Alabama industrial center, according to Dr. King, was to create a situation "so crisis packed that it will inevitably open the door to negotiation" over desegregation of public facilities. Instead, white police officers unleashed dogs and turned high-pressure water hoses on demonstrators, including children. Four young girls were later murdered (and 20 people injured) when white supremacists bombed Birmingham's Sixteenth Street Baptist Church, a center of the local civil rights campaign. After thousands of African Americans rallied in protest—and two more children were killed, this time by police officers—the Kennedy administration again took action. It conceded that images from Birmingham played badly in the international scene and among African American communities outside of Alabama.

Birmingham's determined civil rights activists were starring in real-life dramas that were quickly reaching the entire world via television. Kennedy had already used the same medium when pleading for a national commitment to the battle against discrimination. Recent events had raised "a moral issue . . . as old as Scriptures and . . . as clear as the Constitution." Racial violence was "weakening the respect with which the rest of the world regards us," the president insisted in a June televised address.

The White House still hoped to influence the direction and pace of change. It crafted additional civil rights legislation designed to dampen enthusiasm for demonstrations and other forms of direct action. It now called for a ban against racial discrimination in public facilities and housing and for new measures to protect the voting rights of African Americans in the South. The administration soon recognized that its legislative proposals would

Racial Conflict in Birmingham. Images such as this 1963 photograph of a confrontation in Birmingham, Alabama, in which segregationists turned dogs on youthful demonstrators, helped rally public support for civil rights legislation. Events in Birmingham, however, also presaged the increasingly violent clashes that would punctuate the efforts to end racial discrimination.

not derail a **March on Washington for Jobs and Freedom**, modeled after the earlier march in Detroit and sponsored by a coalition of civil rights and labor organizations scheduled for the late summer of 1963. It belatedly endorsed the demonstration.

On August 28, 1963, an integrated group of more than 200,000 people marched through the nation's capital to the Lincoln Memorial. There, Dr. Martin Luther King, Jr., delivered his famous "I Have a Dream" speech. Speakers on that day generally applauded Kennedy's latest initiatives but urged a broader agenda, including a higher minimum wage and a federal program to guarantee new jobs. Well organized and smoothly run, the event received overwhelmingly favorable coverage from the national media and put additional pressure on the White House and Congress to lend a hand to civil rights efforts.

Martin Luther King, Jr., "I Have A Dream" Speech (1963)

November, 1963

FOCUS QUESTION What were the most important issues left unsettled at Kennedy's death?

As fall turned to winter in 1963, the United States confronted three major policy issues. All had historical roots, but they now carried special urgency.

Policy Choices

First, there was the issue of using government power to stimulate the rate of economic growth. Candidate Kennedy and his economic advisers had promised a vibrant economy. During the fall of 1963, as his tax-cut proposal still languished in Congress, Kennedy presented his case to a radio and TV audience. He claimed that his plan would benefit the entire nation. "Every taxpayer and his family," Kennedy promised, "will have more money left over after taxes for a new car, a new home, new conveniences, education and investment. Every businessman can keep a higher percentage of his profits in his cash register or put it to work expanding or improving his business." And greater economic growth would mean that "the federal government will ultimately end up with more revenues."

Then, there were many questions about U.S. policy in Vietnam. The Kennedy administration puzzled over how to recast Eisenhower's containment policy and execute its own flexible response approach to counterinsurgency and nation building. U.S. officials concluded that the effort in South Vietnam suffered from the Diem government's incompetence, and they gave disgruntled South Vietnamese military officers the green light to orchestrate its overthrow. On November 2, 1963, Diem was routed from his presidential palace and—despite assurances to the contrary from the coup's leaders—murdered. This coup, which brought a military regime to power in Saigon, bred even greater political instability throughout South Vietnam. The NLF and North Vietnam, in turn, ratcheted up their military pressure.

Photograph by Cecil Stoughton, White House, in the John F. Kennedy Presidential Library and Museum, Boston

JFK and Jackie Arrive at Love Field, November 22, 1963. President Kennedy and the First Lady, often treated in the manner of Hollywood movie stars, carefully orchestrated their public appearances. During Kennedy's final political trip to Texas, he and the First Lady traveled the short distance from Ft. Worth to Dallas by airplane, rather than automobile, as a way of making their arrival, marked by roses for the First Lady, appear more dramatic. Within hours, subsequent photographs of Jacqueline Kennedy would famously show her French-designed pink suit stained with the blood of the slain president, shot down while the presidential limousine passed through Dallas's Dealey Plaza.

HISTORY THROUGH FILM

JFK (1991)

Directed by Oliver Stone.
Starring Kevin Costner (Jim Garrison), Tommy Lee Jones
(Clay Shaw), Donald Sutherland ("Mr. X"), and Joe Pesci (David Ferrie).

JFK addressed two questions that have intrigued the history profession and the general public: Did John F. Kennedy fall victim to a lone assassin or a larger conspiracy? Might the course of U.S. history, including the nation's involvement in Vietnam, have been different if Kennedy's presidency had not ended in November 1963?

This movie restages the 1967 criminal prosecution by Jim Garrison, then the district attorney of New Orleans, against Clay Shaw, a local business leader. This real-life court case provides the vehicle for speculating that a shadowy conspiracy—involving government officials, military officers, and business executives—killed Kennedy because of fears he would end the U.S. commitment in South Vietnam.

To dramatize its claims, *JFK* employs numerous cinematic techniques. When showing the famous "Zapruder film," the home movie that provides the most important visual record of Kennedy's shooting, *JFK* inserts simulated, black-and-white images of sharpshooters catching the president in a deadly cross-fire. Later, the movie shows a mysterious figure planting the "magic bullet," a nearly pristine projectile the Warren Commission insisted came from the rifle of Lee Harvey Oswald and passed through Kennedy's body, on a hospital gurney.

JFK is vintage Oliver Stone. This controversial filmmaker-historian delights in disrupting dominant narratives about the past. His most successful historical movies—*JFK, Platoon* (1986), *Born on the Fourth of July* (1989), *The Doors* (1991), and *Nixon* (1995)—all feature disjuncture and uncertainty. When the Garrison character in *JFK* decides to challenge the official story of the Kennedy assassination, he warns his staff that "we're through the looking glass . . . white is black, and black is white."

Resembling Stone's equally controversial *Natural Born Killers* (1994), *JFK* focuses less on telling a coherent tale than using the film format to suggest tangled relationships between visual imagery and popular perception. The opening sequence of his Kennedy movie bombards the screen with quick-moving, seemingly disconnected images. Viewers, as if they themselves are passing "through the looking glass," immediately must struggle to connect the disjointed visual pieces contained in the cinematic puzzle that is *JFK*.

The movie, in this sense, seems more interested in posing, rather than settling, historical questions. Viewers might compare and contrast, for example, how *JFK* uses two very differently composed sequences, featuring performances by two very different character actors (Donald Sutherland and Joe Pesci), to speculate about Kennedy's death. Sutherland's "Mr. X," an entirely fictive employee in the national security bureaucracy, sees Kennedy's assassination as only one in a long line of machinations orchestrated by a military-industrial complex. During a scene shot against the iconography of the nation's capital, Sutherland calmly offers Garrison (and film viewers) a logically ordered, tightly packaged account of Kennedy's assassination. In contrast, the brief sequence featuring Joe Pesci's frenetic David Ferrie—a foot soldier in organized crime and Cuban-exile circles—lacks any coherent center. This real-life character, in contrast to Sutherland's fictional one, warns Garrison that he will never puzzle out Kennedy's death.

JFK, the movie, prompted a massive, congressionally ordered project to safeguard any evidence that might relate to Kennedy's assassination. Will the preservation of these sources ever bring historians any closer to solving, beyond reasonable doubts, Kennedy's assassination? Or, as Joe Pesci's character warns in *JFK*, will historians still confront "a mystery, inside a riddle, wrapped in an enigma"? ◾

Kevin Costner portrays New Orleans District Attorney Jim Garrison in *JFK*.

After nearly three years of constant fine-turning, Kennedy's Southeast Asian policy appeared no more coherent than Eisenhower's. The overall goal remained consistent: prevent communist forces from toppling an anticommunist government in Saigon. The United States could not afford to "lose" South Vietnam. By late November 1963, however, Kennedy's policy in Vietnam again appeared in a state of flux, perhaps even disarray.

Finally, there were political dilemmas associated with civil rights. Constantly pushed by spreading campaigns of direct action, the Kennedy administration renewed efforts to mobilize its political resources on behalf of long-promised congressional legislation. Recognizing that a measure to address discrimination in housing would never pass, White House strategists concentrated on using federal power to eliminate state-sanctioned segregation in the South and to advance a "fair employment" agenda everywhere. The latter goal, however, faced considerable opposition from business groups and from segments of the labor movement.

The Assassination of John F. Kennedy

The Kennedy White House, although still struggling to reframe both its foreign and domestic policies, expected JFK would win re-election in 1964. The apparent GOP candidate, Barry Goldwater, could count on his new conservative base, but it seemed too narrow, and likely too fragile, to provide a genuine threat to another Kennedy campaign.

On November 22, 1963, however, John F. Kennedy was assassinated as his presidential motorcade moved through Dallas. Vice President Lyndon Johnson, who had accompanied Kennedy to Texas, took the oath of office and rushed back to Washington. Equally quickly, the Dallas police arrested Lee Harvey Oswald and pegged him as JFK's assassin. FBI surveillance had already discovered what most everyone else would soon know: Oswald had vague ties to organized crime; had once lived in the Soviet Union; and had a bizarre set of political affiliations, including shadowy ones with groups interested in Cuba. Oswald declared his innocence but never faced trial. Jack Ruby, a Dallas nightclub owner, killed Oswald on national television, while the alleged gunman was in police custody. An investigation by a special commission headed by Chief Justice Earl Warren concluded that both Oswald and Ruby had acted alone.

The motivations for the president's assassination and the Warren Commission's account of a lone gunman came under intense scrutiny. Competing theories about the number of shots, the trajectory of the bullets, the nature of Kennedy's wounds, and the twisted affiliations of the assassin proliferated. The tragedy in Dallas still provokes myriad conspiracy theories and controversies.

Kennedy's life and presidency remain topics of historical debate and tabloid-style speculation. Researchers have provided new details about his poor health, reliance on exotic medications, and dalliances with women—all of which were kept from the public at the time. Historians speculate about how Kennedy's lifestyle might have affected his ability to make crucial decisions, and they debate what JFK might have done in Vietnam had he won the 1964 presidential election. The passage of time, in short, has diminished neither scholarly nor popular interest in John F. Kennedy and in his 1000-day presidency.

Conclusion

Tensions with the Soviet Union, which brought the superpowers to the brink of nuclear war during the Cuban Missile Crisis of 1962, dominated national security calculations between 1953 and 1963. The United States stockpiled nuclear weapons, employed new forms of economic pressure, and expanded covert activities. Left-leaning movements in the Third World, particularly in Cuba and Southeast Asia, became of growing concern to U.S. policymakers.

At home, the post-1953 decade brought economic growth. A cornucopia of new consumer products encouraged talk about an age of affluence but also generated apprehension about conformity, unruly youth, and mass culture. At the same time, the millions of people whom economic growth bypassed and those who faced racial and ethnic discrimination, saw their causes move toward the center of public debates over the meaning of liberty and equality. Critics charged the Eisenhower administration with failing to use government power to support civil rights efforts and to promote faster and more equitably distributed economic growth. Policy initiatives of the early 1960s, associated with Kennedy's New Frontier, grew out of the critical culture of the 1950s. More quietly, in both the political and cultural arenas, a new conservative movement was also taking shape. It saw government's social-economic role needing to be reduced, not expanded.

Although the Kennedy administration preferred to focus on foreign policy, the press coverage of domestic events, particularly those associated with direct action on behalf of civil rights, forced it to consider how government power might be used to address the issues of liberty and equality at home.

The years that immediately followed Kennedy's assassination would continue to highlight questions about liberty, equality, and power. Was the United States spreading freedom in Vietnam? Was government sufficiently active in pursuing egalitarian initiatives at home? The troubled era of "America's longest war," 1963–74, would turn on how different people and activist groups attempted to respond to these questions. ⟡

CHAPTER REVIEW

REVIEW QUESTIONS

1. In what ways did the Eisenhower Administration retain but also reorient the foreign policy of containment that it inherited from the immediate postwar period?
2. How did economic growth change American life during the post-1953 decade?
3. What kinds of social criticism did the general economic prosperity of the post-1953 decade help to highlight?
4. How did the post-1953 decade help to focus competing views of the role of government? What did the new conservatism advocate? What did advocates of more active government hope to accomplish?
5. How did the foreign and domestic policies championed by the administration of John F. Kennedy both accept and reject those embraced by the Eisenhower administration during the 1950s? What policy changes did the early 1960s bring?
6. What social, economic, and cultural forces worked to change gender roles during the 1950s and early 1960s?
7. How did expanding civil rights movements raise new political issues and visions during the 1950s and early 1960s? How did the nation's political and social institutions respond?
8. What were the most important issues left unsettled at Kennedy's death?

CRITICAL THINKING QUESTIONS

1. How did the policies of the Eisenhower and the Kennedy administrations toward the Cold War, economic growth, and civil rights show both differences and similarities?
2. Why does the relatively brief presidency of JFK loom so large in popular memory?

IDENTIFICATIONS

Review your understanding of the following key terms, people, and events for this chapter (terms in bold in text are included in the Glossary).

New Look, p. 771
massive retaliation, p. 771
Eisenhower Doctrine, p. 773
Geneva Peace Accords of 1954, p. 773

domino theory, p. 773
military-industrial complex, p. 774
Highway Act of 1956, p. 776
mass culture critique, p. 780
National Review, p. 781
Gaither Report, p. 782
Sputnik **Crisis**, p. 782
New Frontier, p. 784
Bay of Pigs Invasion, p. 785
Cuban Missile Crisis, p. 785
women's movement, p. 787
Brown **Cases**, p. 788
Dr. Martin Luther King, Jr., p. 789
Civil Rights Act of 1957, p. 791
Termination and Relocation, p. 791
redlining, p. 793
sit-in movement, p. 794
freedom riders, p. 794
March on Washington for Jobs and Freedom, p. 795

SUGGESTED READINGS

Peter G. Boyle, *Eisenhower* (2005) is a good, brief biography that can lead readers to the lengthier ones. **Robert R. Bowie, and Richard Immerman,** *Waging Peace: How Eisenhower Shaped an Enduring Cold War Strategy* (2000); **Kenneth Osgood**, *Total Cold War: Eisenhower's Secret Propaganda Battle at Home and Abroad* (2006); **Lawrence Friedman**, *Kennedy's Wars: Berlin, Cuba, Laos, and Vietnam* (2002); and **Mark Bradley**, *Vietnam at War* (2009) examine foreign policy. **Robert Dallek**, *An Unfinished Life: John F. Kennedy, 1917–1963* (2003) remains the best biography of JFK.

Major trends in economic and social policymaking can be found in the relevant chapters of **G. Calvin Mackenzie and Robert Weisbrot**, *The Liberal Hour: Washington and the Politics of Change in the 1960s* (2008).

On cultural themes, see **Karal Ann Marling**, *As Seen on TV: The Visual Culture of Everyday Life in the 1950s* (1994) and **Thomas Doherty**, *Cold War, Cool Medium: Television, McCarthyism, and American Culture* (2003). On the new conservatism, see **Rick Perlstein**, *Before the Storm: Barry Goldwater and the Unmaking of the American Consensus* (2001) and **Kim Phillips-Fein**, *Invisible Hands: The Making of the Conservative Movement from the New Deal to Reagan* (2009).

For major trends in gender politics, see **Elaine Tyler May,** *Homeward Bound: American Families in the Cold War Era* (rev. ed., 2008). On civil rights, begin with **Matt Garcia,** *A World of Its Own: Race, Labor, and Citrus in the Making of Greater Los Angeles* (2001); **Edward Charles** **Valandra,** *Not Without Our Consent: Lakota Resistance to Termination, 1953–59* (2006); and **Thomes J. Sugrue,** *Sweet Land of Liberty: The Forgotten Struggle for Civil Rights in the North* (2008).

 Visit the CourseMate website at www.cengagebrain.com for additional study tools and review materials for this chapter.

CHAPTER 29

© Joseph Sohm; ChromoSohm Inc./CORBIS

The Vietnam War Memorial

This memorial, a kind of "wailing wall" bearing the names of all Americans who died in the Vietnam War, was dedicated on the Mall in Washington, D.C., in 1982.

America During Its Longest War, 1963–1974

The Great Society
Closing the New Frontier
The Election of 1964
Lyndon Johnson's Great Society
Evaluating the Great Society

Escalation in Vietnam
The Gulf of Tonkin Resolution
The War Continues to Widen
The Media and the War

The War at Home
The Movement of Movements
A New Left
The Counterculture
Civil Rights and Black Power
The Antiwar Movement

1968
Turmoil in Vietnam, 1968
Turmoil at Home
The Election of 1968

Continued Polarization, 1969–1974
Lawbreaking, Violence, and a New President
Social Policy
Environmentalism
Controversies over Rights
The Economy

Foreign Policy in a Time of Turmoil, 1969–1974
Détente
Vietnamization and the Nixon Doctrine
The United States Leaves Vietnam
Expanding the Nixon Doctrine

A Crisis of Governance, 1972–1974
The Election of 1972
The Watergate Investigations
Nixon's Resignation

L YNDON BAINES JOHNSON (LBJ) promised to finish what John F. Kennedy (JFK) had begun. Ultimately, though, popular memories of LBJ's presidency would bear little resemblance to those of Kennedy's. At home, Johnson had already charted his course: He hoped to mobilize the power of government to promote liberty and advance equality. In Southeast Asia, however, Johnson saw no obvious route to follow. Should the United States pull back from earlier commitments to South Vietnam, roll out its vast military power, or follow some other course? Johnson's decisions about Vietnam generated political discord at home, and controversy also overtook his initially popular domestic moves. As America's longest war dragged on, public opinion turned against Johnson and his policies. By 1968, polarization over priorities at home and overseas embittered national politics.

The polarization so much in evidence during 1968 grew worse during the war years that followed. By the end of America's longest war and the Watergate crisis that brought President Richard Nixon's resignation, the nation's political culture and social fabric looked very different from how they had appeared in 1963.

The Great Society

FOCUS QUESTION How did the Johnson administration define its domestic goals, and how did it approach problem solving? Why did Johnson's "Great Society" produce so much controversy?

Lyndon Baines Johnson lacked Kennedy's charisma, but he possessed other political assets. As a member of the House of Representatives during the late 1930s and early 1940s and as majority leader of the U.S. Senate during the 1950s, Johnson mastered the art of interest group horse-trading. Few issues, it appeared, defied an LBJ-forged solution. Johnson flattered, cajoled, or threatened people until they lent him their support. During Johnson's time in Congress, his already wealthy Texas benefactors gained valuable oil and gas concessions and lucrative construction contracts. Johnson's skill in gaining congressional funding for building projects boosted Texas cities such as Dallas and Houston, along with much of the Southwest. LBJ himself acquired a personal fortune.

Kennedy's death gave Johnson the opportunity to deploy his political skills on the presidential stage. No previous president had ever taken office after having served so long in Congress. Although eager to enact a bold social-economic program, Johnson began cautiously. He asked Congress to honor JFK's memory by addressing three legislative issues proposed by Kennedy's administration: tax cutting, economic inequality, and civil rights.

Closing the New Frontier

Working behind the scenes, Johnson easily secured passage of the Kennedy tax cut, the measure that JFK had promised would stimulate economic growth. Although analysts still differ on the precise design of this legislation and its contribution to the economic boom of the mid-1960s, the tax measure appeared to work. GNP rose 7 percent in 1964 and 8 percent the following year, unemployment dropped, and inflation remained low.

In his January 1964 State of the Union address, Johnson upped the ante on Kennedy's cautious effort to address economic inequality by calling for "an unconditional war on poverty in America." Relentlessly prodded by the White House, Congress soon passed The Economic Opportunity Act of 1964. It created the Office of Economic Opportunity (OEO) to coordinate a multipart program. First headed by R. Sargent Shriver, a brother-in-law of John Kennedy, the OEO was charged with eliminating "the paradox of poverty in the midst of plenty." In addition to establishing the OEO, the act mandated loans for rural and small-business development; established a work-training program called the Jobs Corps; created Volunteers in Service to America (VISTA), a domestic version of the Peace Corps; provided low-wage, public service jobs for young people; began a "work-study program" to assist college students; and authorized the creation of federally funded social programs to be planned in concert with local community groups.

Johnson also helped push an expanded version of Kennedy's civil rights proposal through Congress. Although

CHRONOLOGY

1964 Civil Rights Act of 1964 passes ◆ Congress approves Gulf of Tonkin Resolution ◆ Johnson defeats Barry Goldwater

1965 Congress passes Voting Rights Act ◆ Violence hits Watts ◆ U.S role in Vietnam dramatically expands

1966 Supreme Court decides *Miranda* v. *Arizona* ◆ U.S. begins massive air strikes in North Vietnam

1967 Large antiwar demonstrations begin

1968 Tet offensive begins ◆ Martin Luther King, Jr. and Robert Kennedy assassinated ◆ Civil Rights Act passed ◆ Richard Nixon wins presidency

1969 Nixon announces "Vietnamization" policy ◆ My Lai massacre becomes public

1970 U.S. troops enter Cambodia ◆ Congress creates Environmental Protection Agency

1971 Stagflation upsets U.S. economy ◆ U.S. dollar begins to "float" on currency markets

1972 Watergate burglars caught inside Democratic headquarters ◆ Nixon crushes George McGovern in presidential election

1973 OPEC oil embargo begins ◆ Paris peace accords signed ◆ Supreme Court decides *Roe* v. *Wade* ◆ Special Senate committee begins hearings into "Watergate"

1974 House votes impeachment and Nixon resigns ◆ Gerald Ford assumes presidency

1975 Saigon falls to North Vietnamese forces

championing the measure as a memorial to JFK, LBJ knew that Southerners in their own Democratic Party would try to block it. Consequently, he successfully sought Republican support to curtail a southern-led filibuster. Johnson also helped hammer out compromises on several key provisions and reconcile the differing bills enacted by the House and Senate.

In July, Congress passed a landmark measure. The **Civil Rights Act of 1964** strengthened federal remedies, monitored by a new Equal Employment Opportunity Commission (EEOC), against racially inspired job discrimination. The act also prohibited racial discrimination in all public accommodations connected to interstate commerce, such as motels and restaurants.

The Presence of Lyndon B. Johnson. As both senator and president, Lyndon Johnson employed body language—the "Johnson treatment"—as one means of gaining support for his policies.

Moreover, Title VII, a provision added during congressional debate, barred discrimination based on sex and became important to the reviving women's movement. Although opponents of the 1964 act argued that its extension of federal power violated the Constitution, the Supreme Court, effectively a political ally of Lyndon Johnson during his presidency, curtly rejected such claims.

That same summer, a coalition of civil rights groups recruited nearly a thousand young volunteers for **Freedom Summer**. Sponsored by a coalition of activist groups and led by the Student Non-Violent Coordinating Committee (SNCC), this project targeted Mississippi with an effort to register African American voters and to begin other civil rights projects. During that tension-filled summer, at least six civil rights workers met violent deaths. In the most notorious incident, a conspiracy among KKK leaders and law-enforcement officers from Neshoba County, Mississippi, brutally murdered three volunteers—James Chaney, Michael Schwerner, and Andrew Goodman. This incident would roil Mississippi's legal and political life for years. Finally, in 2005, a Mississippi jury convicted a former KKK leader, by then in his eighties, of manslaughter for participating in the triple killing of 1964.

Meanwhile, supporters of Freedom Summer pressed forward, only to see the national Democratic Party reject their grassroots political work. Pressured by LBJ, the 1964 Democratic convention voted to seat Mississippi's "regular" all-white delegates rather than members of a new, racially diverse Mississippi Freedom Democratic Party (MFDP). The regulars had made clear their intention to support the GOP's presidential candidate, but Johnson declined to support the MFDP in hopes of keeping some other southern states in the Democratic camp in the fall election. LBJ's rebuff of the MFDP prompted its leaders, such as Fannie Lou Hamer, to question the president's commitment to their cause. What would Johnson—and Hubert Humphrey, his hand-picked vice presidential running mate—do for civil rights after the 1964 election?

The Election of 1964

After a bruising battle within GOP ranks, the Republicans nominated Senator **Barry Goldwater** of Arizona, hero of the new conservatism, to challenge Johnson. Goldwater's strategists claimed that a stoutly conservative GOP campaign would attract the vast number of voters who supposedly rejected both Democratic policies and Dwight Eisenhower's "modern Republican" ones. Goldwater denounced Johnson's foreign policy for tolerating communist expansion and attacked his domestic agenda, including civil rights, for destroying individual liberties. One of only eight Republican senators who had opposed the 1964 Civil Rights Act, Goldwater condemned the

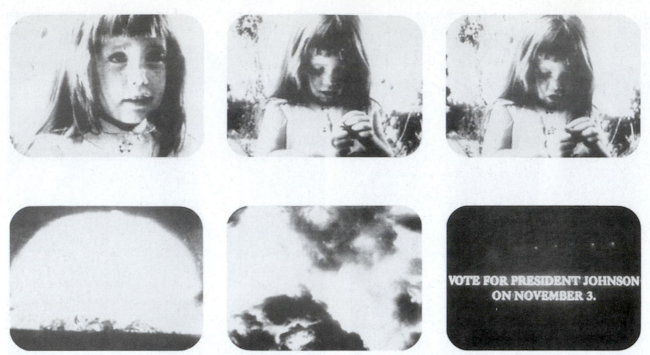

LBJ's 1964 Campaign against Barry Goldwater. In this television ad from the 1964 campaign, Lyndon Johnson's supporters exploited Republican Barry Goldwater's image as a far-right "extremist" who might take the nation into a nuclear war.

measure as an unconstitutional extension of national power on behalf of the laudable goal of combating discrimination. Issues of civil rights, Goldwater insisted, were matters for state and local governments.

The Goldwater campaign quickly fizzled. The Democratic campaign savaged the candidate's policies, his grasp of issues, and even his mental stability. A tendency to make ill-considered remarks already haunted Goldwater. He had suggested that people who feared nuclear war were "silly and sissified." He had wondered out loud if participation in the Social Security program should become voluntary. And during his acceptance speech at the 1964 Republican convention Goldwater proclaimed that "extremism in the pursuit of liberty is no vice" and "moderation in the pursuit of justice is no virtue." The phrase fed Democratic claims that "extremist" forces on the "radical right" would dominate a Goldwater presidency.

Many moderate Republicans deserted Goldwater, who led the GOP to a spectacular defeat in November. Johnson carried 44 states and won more than 60 percent of the popular vote; Democrats also gained 38 seats in Congress. In the short run, the 1964 election seemed a triumph for Lyndon Johnson's vision of government power.

The 1964 election, however, foreshadowed deep-rooted political changes that would undermine Johnson's agenda and, in time, the Democratic Party. Indeed, during the Democratic primaries of 1964, Alabama's segregationist governor, George Wallace, had run strongly against the president in several states. Already well positioned as an opponent of civil rights movements, Wallace denounced any "meddling" by Washington in local affairs. The 1964 election proved the last, until that of 2008, in which the Democratic Party would capture the White House by proposing an expansion in the power of the national government.

Goldwater's defeat invigorated rather than discouraged supporters of the new conservatism. His staff pioneered innovative campaign tactics, such as direct-mail fundraising. By refining these techniques during future campaigns, conservative strategists helped make 1964 the beginning, not the end, of their plan to push the Republican Party, and the country, to the right. Goldwater's continued criticism of the Civil Rights Act of 1964 helped him carry five Southern states. These victories—along with Wallace's earlier appeal to "white backlash" voters—suggested that opposition to additional civil rights measures could woo Southern whites away from the Democratic Party.

An important electoral issue in California also gave conservatives hope. The Democratic national ticket easily carried the state, but real-estate interests joined with suburban conservatives to sponsor a referendum measure that repealed the recently enacted "Rumford Act." This 1962 law had prohibited racial discrimination in the sale or rental of housing in California. Opponents of this open-housing measure adopted a political strategy that conservatives would increasingly embrace: downplay racial issues and, instead, denounce governmental regulations such as the Rumford Act for violating the principles of equal rights and individual liberties.

Finally, the Goldwater campaign introduced a new corps of conservative activists, many of them from the Sunbelt, to national politics. Ronald Reagan championed the new conservatism so effectively that Goldwater Republicans in California began grooming the former movie and TV actor for a political career. Younger conservatives, such as William Rehnquist and Newt Gingrich, entered the national arena as supporters of Goldwater's vision. Goldwater also enlisted Milton Friedman, the staunchly conservative economist and a critic of Keynesian policies, as an advisor. Historians now credit the Goldwater effort of 1964, for spearheading the overhaul of American conservatism—and the Republican Party.

Lyndon Johnson's Great Society

Lyndon Johnson rushed to capitalize on his electoral victory. Enjoying broad support in Congress, Johnson unveiled plans

Lyndon B. Johnson, "Great Society" Speech (1964)

for a **Great Society**, an array of federal programs designed to "enrich and elevate our national life." Some of the programs fulfilled the dreams of his Democratic predecessors. Nationally funded medical coverage for the elderly (Medicare) and for low-income citizens (Medicaid) grew out of healthcare proposals from the New- and Fair-Deal eras. Similarly, a new cabinet office, the Department of Housing and Urban Development (HUD), built on earlier plans for coordinating urban revitalization programs.

The **Voting Rights Act of 1965**, which created mechanisms for national oversight of state and local elections in the South, capped the long-term effort to eliminate racial and ethnic discrimination, especially sham "literacy tests," from political life. The measure gave the Justice Department broadly defined authority to monitor electoral procedures in jurisdictions with a history of discriminating against African American voters. Modified and extended over the years, most recently in 2008, the Voting Rights Act also came to require ballots printed in languages other than English.

Meanwhile, Congress enacted another milestone measure that addressed matters long discussed—and long avoided. The **Immigration and Nationality Act of 1965** finally abolished the discriminatory "national origins" quota system established in 1924 (see Chapter 24). Henceforth, roughly the same set of rules would apply to people wishing to immigrate to the United States from any part of the world. This change, in practice, would allow the entry of far more people from Asia and Africa than had previously been allowed.

Many of the Great Society's new proposals rested on the mid-century "affluence" that the Johnson administration expected to continue for years to come. Even a costly war in Southeast Asia could not dampen its optimism. Ongoing economic growth could provide the tax dollars to underwrite a bold expansion of national power without any overhaul of fundamental political and economic arrangements.

The array of Great Society initiatives that rolled through Congress during the mid-1960s heartened LBJ's supporters and appalled his critics. The Model Cities Program (1966) offered smaller-scale alternatives to urban renewal efforts. Rent supplements and an expanded food stamp program went to help low-income families. The Head Start Program (1965) provided help for children considered educationally unprepared for kindergarten. Other new federal educational programs aimed to upgrade classroom instruction, especially in low-income neighborhoods, and a legal services initiative provided lawyers to clients who could not afford to hire an attorney. These measures aimed at providing low-income people with the kind of professional expertise, routinely available to the more affluent, that could

help them fight their way out of social and economic distress. The Great Society's service-based approach, Johnson insisted, would give people a "hand up" rather than a "handout."

The Community Action Program (CAP) promised a different tack. It authorized grassroots activists, working through neighborhood organizations, to design community-based projects that could gain funding from Washington. By promoting "maximum feasible participation" by ordinary citizens rather than relying on planning experts, the architects of CAP proposed to nurture a grassroots democracy that could revitalize American politics from the bottom up.

Evaluating the Great Society

How did the Great Society become so controversial? Most obviously, the extension of Washington's reach rekindled old debates about the use, as both an issue of political principle and pragmatic policymaking, of the power of the national government. In addition, Johnson's rhetorical extravagance, such as promising an "unconditional" victory over poverty, announced long-term objectives that failed to survive the short-term rhythms of partisan politics. Republicans rebounded from the Democratic landslide of 1964 and picked up 47 seats in Congress in the midterm elections of 1966. The Great Society ideal would never again enjoy the overwhelming congressional support that had accompanied Johnson's initial proposals.

Finally, the expectation that continued economic growth would generate tax revenues sufficient to finance new social programs faded during the early 1970s. Worsening economic conditions, exacerbated by the escalating cost of the war in Vietnam, made social welfare measures more politically vulnerable than during the prosperous mid-1960s. Facing financial worries of their own, people who had been initially supportive of the Great Society became receptive to the claim, first championed by George Wallace and the Goldwater campaign in 1964, that bureaucrats in Washington would waste their hard-earned tax dollars on flawed social experiments.

Historians disagree about the impact of Johnson's programs. Charles Murray's *Losing Ground* (1984) charged the Great Society with encouraging antisocial behavior. This book argued that too many people, lured by welfare payments, abandoned the goals of marrying, settling down, and seeking jobs. Money spent on Johnson's programs, moreover, created government deficits that slowed economic growth. Had ill-advised social spending not undermined personal initiative and disrupted the nation's economy, its continued growth would have ultimately provided most Americans with a comfortable lifestyle, according to *Losing Ground*. A central text of the new conservatism, Murray's book saw Johnson's Great Society as a cause of, not a solution for, economic distress.

Other analysts more sympathetic to the Great Society rejected this view. First, where was the evidence for the claim that most people preferred welfare to meaningful work? Second, funds actually spent on Great Society programs neither matched Johnson's promises nor reached the lavish levels claimed by the new conservatism. Moreover, the charge that government expenditures choked off growth ignored the systemic economic problems that emerged in the early 1970s. In addition, Great Society advocates pointed to the significant decline in poverty rates, which fell from 19 percent in 1962 to 10 percent in 1969.

Antipoverty activists developed another critique that faulted the architects of the Great Society for not doing enough. They charged that the Johnson administration failed to challenge the prevailing distribution of political and economic power and favored large-scale bureaucratic solutions forged by people beholden to power-brokers in Washington. They noted that the administration jettisoned the CAP model of grassroots empowerment almost as soon as local politicians began complaining about having to compete for federal funding. In this view, the assumption that economic growth would fund the Great Society had precluded any serious attempt, such as a revised tax code, to redistribute income and wealth. The Johnson administration always lacked a viable plan to confront inequality, according to this critique.

Despite disagreements over how to interpret the Great Society, historians nevertheless concur over its impact on the federal budget. Washington's financial outlay for domestic programs increased more than 10 percent during every year of LBJ's presidency. In 1960, federal spending on social welfare constituted 28 percent of total governmental outlays; by 1970, this figure had risen to more than 40 percent. Moreover, Great Society programs such as Medicaid, legal assistance, and job training gave low-income families access to social services and slightly narrowed the disparity between rich and poor.

From the perspective of political viability, though, the Great Society proved a failure. Opposition to the assumptions and goals of Johnson's Great Society gave new energy to the conservative surge. As support for domestic spending programs waned, even some Democrats hesitated to defend Lyndon Johnson's vision. LBJ's domestic policies, based on extending national power, inflamed partisan passions; and calls for limiting the reach of Washington increasingly dominated political discussion and reshaped American political culture. For many years, the Democratic Party rarely recalled Lyndon Johnson's memory. Finally, in 2007, a Republican president signed a bill renaming the Department of Education Office Building in Johnson's honor.

Escalation in Vietnam

Q FOCUS QUESTION Through what incremental steps did the Johnson administration involve the United States ever more deeply in Vietnam? What was its major goal in Vietnam?

Lyndon Johnson's divisive crusade to build a Great Society at home found its counterpart abroad. His pledge to protect South Vietnam from communism demanded ever more of the nation's human and material resources. Johnson's foreign policy diminished the nation's international standing, further polarized its domestic politics, and strained its economy.

The Gulf of Tonkin Resolution

Immediately after John Kennedy's assassination, Johnson resisted additional support for South Vietnam. His fears of appearing soft on communism, however, soon led him to side with those advisers who saw air strikes against North Vietnam as the necessary first step toward preserving an anticommunist government in South Vietnam. Johnson prepared a congressional resolution authorizing this escalation of hostilities.

Events in the Gulf of Tonkin, off the coast of North Vietnam, provided the rationale for taking the resolution to Capitol Hill. On August 1, 1964, the U.S. destroyer *Maddox*, while on an intelligence-gathering mission, exchanged gunfire with North Vietnamese ships. Three days later, the *Maddox* returned with the *Turner Joy* and, during severe weather, reported what seemed to be signs of a failed torpedo attack. Although the *Maddox*'s commander advised that the episode needed further analysis, Johnson immediately denounced "unprovoked aggression" by North Vietnam against the United States. (A later study concluded that there had never been a North Vietnamese attack.) With only two dissenting votes in the Senate, Congress passed the **Gulf of Tonkin Resolution**, which authorized Johnson to take "all necessary measures to repel armed attack."

Lyndon B. Johnson, The Tonkin Gulf Incident Message to Congress (1964)

This resolution seemed to give Johnson what he needed. His strong stand against apparent aggression was politically popular, and the resolution gave the president numerous military options in Southeast Asia. He immediately began bombing strikes against North Vietnam and used the Gulf of Tonkin Resolution as tantamount to a congressional declaration of war.

The congressional resolution also helped Johnson position himself as a cautious moderate during the presidential campaign of 1964. When Barry Goldwater demanded stronger measures against North Vietnam and even hinted at possible use of tactical nuclear weapons, Johnson's campaign managers portrayed Goldwater as a threat to the survival of civilization. Johnson seemingly promised not to commit U.S. troops to any land war in Southeast Asia during the 1964 campaign.

Soon after the November election, however, Johnson faced a complicated decision. More than a year after the 1963 coup against Diem (see Chapter 28), South Vietnam still faced political disarray. The failure of successive military governments in Saigon was fueling popular discontent, and South Vietnamese troops were deserting at an alarming rate. North Vietnam continued expanding its military aid to the National Liberation Front (NLF) and then began sending a sizable number of its own troops into South Vietnam. By the beginning of 1965, the NLF controlled much of the countryside. Only in Saigon and other urban areas was national authority still relevant. In January, another Saigon regime collapsed, and factionalism stalled the emergence of any viable alternative.

Lacking an effective ally in Saigon, Johnson pondered conflicting advice. National Security Adviser McGeorge Bundy predicted Saigon's defeat unless the United States greatly increased its military role. Another key aide, Walt W. Rostow, assured Johnson that North Vietnam would give up its aggressive plans if the United States clearly showed its determination

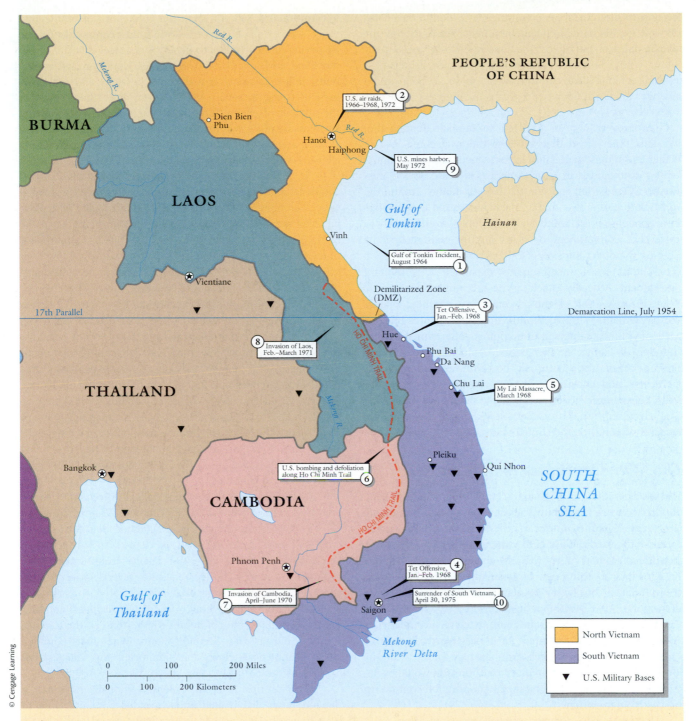

Map 29.1 Vietnam War. The war in Vietnam spread into neighboring countries as the United States sought to prevent North Vietnam from bringing supplies and troops southward along a network called the Ho Chi Minh Trail. Unlike the Korean War (see map on p. 752) the guerrilla-style war in Indochina had few conventional battle "fronts."

View an animated version of this map or related maps on the CourseMate website.

to oppose them. Undersecretary of State George Ball, by contrast, warned that U.S. troops could never prop up South Vietnam. He wrote, "no one has demonstrated that a white ground force of whatever size can win a guerrilla war—which is at the same time a civil war between Asians—in jungle terrain in the midst of a population that refuses cooperation to the white forces." Senate Majority Leader Mike Mansfield, an

expert in Asian history, urged finding some way of reuniting Vietnam as a neutral country. The Joint Chiefs of Staff, afflicted by inter-service rivalries, provided differing military assessments and, thus, no clear guidance.

Johnson was left wondering and worrying. He still privately doubted the chances for a successful U.S. intervention but seemed incapable of translating these doubts into a decision to alter the U.S. commitment to containing communism in Vietnam. Johnson became obsessed about the adverse political and diplomatic consequences of a U.S. pullout or compromise. He feared that domestic criticism of anything looking like a communist victory in Vietnam would endanger his Great Society programs and embolden the new conservatives.

Moreover, Johnson accepted the familiar domino theory. This theory held that a U.S. withdrawal could lead to further communist aggression in Asia, encourage communist-leaning insurgencies in Latin America, increase Soviet pressure on West Berlin, and damage U.S. credibility around the world. Both Eisenhower and Kennedy had staked U.S. prestige on a noncommunist South Vietnam. Johnson either had to revise that commitment or chart an uncertain course by ordering the direct infusion of U.S. combat troops.

Ultimately, Johnson greatly expanded U.S. military involvement. A deadly attack on the U.S. military outpost at Pleiku in early 1965 prompted retaliatory bombing against North Vietnam. Within a month, the United States inaugurated a sustained campaign of bombing, code-named Rolling Thunder. Washington also began deploying U.S. ground forces to regain lost territory in the South, expanding covert operations, and boosting economic aid to the beleaguered South Vietnamese government. Only six months after the 1964 election, with his advisers still divided, Johnson had decisively committed the United States to a wider war.

The War Continues to Widen

Combat operations in Vietnam grew steadily more intense. Hoping to break the enemy's spirit, U.S. military commanders sought to inflict more casualties. The Johnson administration authorized the use of napalm, an incendiary and toxic chemical that charred both foliage and people, and allowed the Air Force to bomb new targets. Additional U.S. combat troops arrived, but every escalation seemed to require a further one. After North Vietnam rejected a Johnson peace plan that Hanoi viewed as tantamount to its surrender, the United States again escalated its effort. North Vietnam's leadership, pursuing a long-term strategy of attrition in South Vietnam, became convinced that Johnson would eventually lose public and congressional support for continuing the costly intervention.

In April 1965 Johnson applied his Cold War, anticommunist principles closer to home. Responding to exaggerated reports about a communist threat in the Dominican Republic, Johnson sent U.S. troops to unseat a left-leaning, elected president and to install a government supportive of U.S. interests. This incursion violated a longstanding "good neighbor" pledge not to intervene militarily in the Western Hemisphere. Although the action angered critics throughout Latin America, the overthrow of a leftist government in the Dominican Republic seemed to steel Johnson's determination to hold the line against communism in Vietnam.

Later that spring, as another South Vietnamese government was forming in Saigon, U.S. strategists were still seeking a politically stable anticommunist ally. **General William**

Westmoreland, who directed the U.S. effort, recommended using "search and destroy" missions against communist forces. By relying on helicopters to deploy U.S. forces quickly, Westmoreland envisioned that U.S. troops would engage enemy units, inflict as many casualties as possible, and withdraw without trying to secure the battle-ground. "Body count"—the number of enemy forces killed or disabled—became the key measure of success for these missions. This strategy aimed at incapacitating NLF and North Vietnamese forces and at allowing a viable Saigon government the time to take shape.

In July 1965, Johnson publicly agreed to send 50,000 additional military personnel to Vietnam. Privately, he pledged to send another 50,000 and left open the possibility of deploying even more. LBJ also approved saturation bombing in the South Vietnamese countryside and intensified bombardment of the North.

Some advisers urged Johnson to inform the public candidly about the expanded U.S. military effort. They recommended seeking an outright declaration of war from Congress or at least legislation allowing the president to wield the economic and informational controls that previous administrations had used during wartime. But Johnson worried about provoking antiwar members of Congress and expanding a still-small antiwar movement. Rather than risk ramping up dissent, Johnson decided to stress the administration's willingness to negotiate and to act as if the war he was expanding was not really a war. The Johnson administration talked of seeing "light at the end of the tunnel" and apparently hoped that most people in the United States would remain largely in the dark about events in Vietnam.

Over the next three years, U.S. involvement steadily increased. The number of U.S. troops in Vietnam grew to 535,000. Operation Ranch Hand scorched South Vietnam's croplands and defoliated half its forests in an effort to eliminate the natural cover for enemy troop movements. Operation Rolling Thunder, despite several brief pauses, continued until the Pentagon finally declared it a strategic failure in late 1968. Overall, U.S. planes dropped approximately 1.5 million tons of bombs—more than all the tonnage dropped during the Second World War—that pounded North Vietnamese cities and pummeled the villages and hamlets of the South.

Despite this level of violence, Vietnam remained a "limited" war. The United States avoided bombing close to the Chinese border. China had stationed more than 300,000 troops in North Vietnam, and Johnson feared provoking their entry, or possibly even that of forces from the Soviet Union, into the conflict. The strategy remained one of containing the NLF and North Vietnam by steadily escalating the cost they would pay in lost lives and bombed-out infrastructure.

Body count continued to be the primary measure for gauging progress toward the goal of saving Saigon. Estimates that a kill ratio of 10 to 1 would force North Vietnam and the NLF to pull back encouraged the U.S. military command to unleash more firepower and further inflate enemy casualty figures. This same calculation provided an automatic justification for seeking additional U.S. troops. Whenever the number

Shocking Images

This 1968 photo, which won Eddie Adams a Pulitzer Prize, shows a South Vietnamese police official summarily executing a Viet Cong leader on the streets of Saigon. The photo was widely circulated in the U.S. media. The image seemed to reflect badly on South Vietnam's system of justice and shocked many Americans. It was one of many images that fueled doubts about whether the struggle in Vietnam advanced the democratic goals claimed by U.S. leaders. Much later, however, Adams apologized for how his still photo, which showed nothing of the background to this incident, had helped disgrace this once respected South Vietnamese military leader. "The general killed the Viet Cong; I killed the general with my camera," wrote Adams.

Q Why was this image so shocking to many Americans, and what might a careful viewer want to know about the overall context of this image?

AP Images/Eddie Adams

of enemy forces seemed to increase, the Pentagon required more U.S. troops to maintain the desired kill ratio.

Johnson, whose notorious temper flared at the first hint of bad news, used body count numbers to justify claims of victory being "just around the corner." Privately, though, a different picture began to emerge. Enjoying material assistance from the Soviet Union and China, North Vietnam could match every U.S. escalation. The North Vietnamese funneled troops and supplies into the South through the shifting network of roads and paths, primarily through Laos, called the Ho Chi Minh Trail. By the end of 1967, several of Johnson's key aides, most notably Secretary of Defense Robert McNamara, decided that the United States could not sustain its commitment to South Vietnam. The price for containing North Vietnam, McNamara now concluded, had become far too steep. He left office, he later recalled, in a daze. He had trouble remembering whether he had resigned or had been fired. The majority of Johnson's advisors, however, refused to accept McNamara's assessment.

Meanwhile, the destruction wreaked by U.S. forces was giving the NLF, North Vietnamese, Chinese, and Soviet leaders a decided propaganda advantage in what had become an international war of imagery. Pictures from Southeast Asia allowed critics from around the world to condemn the U.S. bombardments and its search-and-destroy strategy. In Western Europe, demonstrations against the United States became prominent features of political life. Antiwar protesters at home constantly hounded the president and members of his administration, and Johnson eventually complained of being a prisoner in his own White House.

He also continued to lack an effective ally in Saigon. The devastation of the countryside from the U.S. military strategy, the economic destabilization from the flood of U.S. dollars, and the political corruption of Saigon officials took their toll. The "pacification" and "strategic hamlet" programs, which gathered Vietnamese farmers into tightly guarded villages, sounded viable in Washington but created greater instability by uprooting many South Vietnamese from their villages and ancestral lands. Buddhist priests persistently demonstrated against foreign influence. In 1967, Generals Nguyen Van Thieu and Nguyen Cao Ky, having sustained a military regime in Saigon longer than any of their predecessors, tried to legitimate their rule by holding a new election. The effort failed. A voting process shot through with corruption only highlighted the precarious political position of Thieu and Ky and their dependence on aid from Washington.

The Media and the War

Johnson lectured the American public about upholding the nation's honor and diplomatic commitments, but dissent continually mounted. In previous wars, Washington had restricted media coverage. Hoping to avoid the controversy that overt censorship would surely cause, the Johnson administration employed informal ways of managing information. With television making Vietnam a "living room war"—one that people could watch in their own homes— Johnson kept three TV sets playing in his office in order to monitor what viewers were seeing. Most of what he saw, early on, he liked.

Antiwar activists initially assailed what they considered the media's uncritical reporting. American journalists, they claimed, generally accepted story frames constructed by the White House. Few reporters wrote stories that dissected either the limits of the U.S. military effort or the travails of its South Vietnamese ally. TV camera crews, trailing behind U.S. combat forces and reliant on them for protection, invariably framed their stories from perspectives supportive of "our guys." *Time* magazine initially praised General Westmoreland's leadership and named him its "Man of the Year" for 1965.

In time, however, media coverage changed. Images of unrelenting destruction coming across TV screens undercut the optimistic words coming from the White House and U.S. officials in Saigon. After gazing at his TV sets, LBJ started telephoning network executives, castigating them for broadcasts to which he objected. More and more journalists and reporters, finally following the lead of David Halberstam, began challenging the reassuring reports. Gloria Emerson's grim stories portrayed the war as one in which poor and disproportionately nonwhite troops fought and died so that wealthy families, with draft-exempt "fortunate sons," might reap war-related profits. Harrison Salisbury sent dispatches from North Vietnam that detailed the destructive impact of U.S. bombing missions. Younger journalists who traveled alongside U.S. troops, such as Michael Herr, came to represent the American mission as a drug-drenched trip into the surreal.

As the conflict dragged on, the media began to talk about a "war at home." Initially, commentators generally adopted a stark, bipolar story frame. It pitted the "hawks," people who wanted to fight in Vietnam until the United States "won," against those who desired to end U.S. involvement as quickly as possible, the "doves." Decrying media coverage, Johnson claimed to be following the time-tested policy of containment. Secretary of State Dean Rusk warned of the dangers of "appeasement." But influential U.S. politicians—led by J. William Fulbright of Arkansas, chair of the Senate Foreign Relations Committee—complained of misplaced priorities in Vietnam and of an "arrogance of power" by the Johnson administration.

In time, stories about a war at home expanded beyond those about hawks and doves. It came to seem as if the fundamental structures of domestic politics, society, and culture were up for grabs.

The War at Home

Q **FOCUS QUESTION** What domestic social movements emerged during America's longest war? How did they seek to change U.S. political culture and the direction of public policy? What role did commercial media play in the "movement of movements"?

Even as Lyndon Johnson's policy in Southeast Asia was coming under attack from antiwar activists, a broader culture of dissent emerged. Growing tensions produced a political landscape marked by bitterness, confrontation, polarization, and violence on a scale not seen in the United States for many years.

The Movement of Movements

The 1960s came to feature a variety of movements on the political and cultural left. These movements not only opposed the war in Vietnam but also demanded dramatic domestic changes that went beyond those envisioned in Lyndon Johnson's Great Society. A "New Left" sought to re-orient politics. Cultural activists urged people to expand their minds, often with a little help from drugs and rock music, and to seek alternative ways of living their lives. Iconic images from the 1960s provide a kaleidoscopic panorama of what can be called a "movement of movements."

This movement of movements rejected a dominant ideal of the 1950s and early 1960s: the faith that political pluralism would almost always unite the nation (see Chapter 28). As the war in Vietnam dragged on and conflict emerged at home, activists from different movements increasingly doubted that the existing political system could actually solve problems. At the same time, disparate movements based on deeply held values—involving issues such as war and peace, race relations, gender politics, the environment, and sexuality—appeared to head in different directions or to collide. Taken together, this complex

Antiwar Demonstration in Washington, D.C.
Mass rallies against U.S. involvement in the Vietnam War became an important part of antiwar politics during the late 1960s and early 1970s.

The Folk-Rock Movement and the Sixties

Songwriter: Bob Dylan
Title: "Subterranean Homesick Blues" (1965)

During the early 1960s, Bob Dylan emerged from the acoustic folk music revival with protest songs such as "Blowin' in the Wind." In 1965, however, Dylan adopted an amplified rock 'n' roll sound, with electric guitar and drums. For the next year, folk fans around the world booed when Dylan arrived onstage with his electric band.

The 1965 recording of "Subterranean Homesick Blues" displayed Dylan's revamped musical style. He dropped the relatively straightforward protest lyrics, which he dismissed as "finger-pointing songs," for a free-form approach that used "chains of flashing images" in a manner reminiscent of Beat writers of the 1950s such as Allen Ginsberg and Jack Kerouac. The words did not always immediately make sense, but many of the phrases entered national consciousness ("Don't follow leaders, watch the parking meters" and "You don't need a weatherman to know which way the wind blows"). Dylan's new compositions combined alienation with humor. According to one student of his music, some people "reacted by calling Dylan a 'sell-out,' not realizing, at least at first, that he was now making the most anti-establishment, revolutionary music of his or anyone's career." The new musical style of folk-rock, emblemized by Dylan, was about sweep across the world.

Q. Why do you think that stylistic turning points in musical history (such as Dylan's embrace of a rock sound or the arrival of the waltz in the 1850s) prompt popular resistance? Why do people view music as threatening, as something more than mere entertainment?

Q. How might Dylan's new style have influenced hip-hop songwriting, such as that displayed in "The Message" during the 1980s? (see Chapter 31)

Listen to an audio recording of this music on the Musical Links to the Past CD.

---

movement of movements soon became central to the historical era already being called "the Sixties."

Although media imagery alone could not create any particular movement, most activists sought the media spotlight to help demonstrate their disdain for policies they opposed and to attract support for their visions of change. Often beginning with posters and pamphlets, movement activists produced increasingly sophisticated imagery and eye-catching public demonstrations.

No single group can lay exclusive claim to the Sixties, the period from roughly 1963 to 1974 that coincided with America's longest war. Numerous movements sought to redirect national life down different paths, often with no clear maps. Still, those on the political and culture left, gaining recruits from the huge Baby Boom generation, initially dominated media accounts and the earliest histories of the Sixties. Four of the most prominent of the movements involved a New Left, a counterculture, a Black Power movement, and an antiwar coalition.

A New Left

While relatively few college students actually became active in left-leaning political movements, the activities of a **New Left** dominated politics on many campuses, attracted significant media attention, and in time generated popular controversy.

In 1962, two years after the new conservatism had given birth to Young Americans for Freedom (see Chapter 28), the left-leaning Students for a Democratic Society (SDS) emerged. Although SDS endorsed familiar causes, especially civil rights, it also attracted attention for the personalized style of its politics. SDS's *Port Huron Statement* (1962) pledged to fight the "loneliness, estrangement, isolation" that supposedly afflicted many people. Charging that the dominant political culture valued bureaucratic expertise over citizen engagement and economic growth over meaningful work, SDS spoke for alternative visions. In politics, it called for "participatory democracy"—grassroots activism and institutions responsive to local needs. Historians once framed SDS as *the* epicenter of the New Left, but recent accounts see it as only one of the left-leaning movements seeking a new politics.

Indeed, grassroots political efforts such as Freedom Summer in Mississippi provided tangible examples of participatory democracy. Organizing efforts in the Deep South attracted idealistic volunteers from the North. Risking racist violence, they joined local activists in registering African American voters and organizing for political action. Some volunteers remained in the South, working for civil rights; others returned to the North and joined neighborhood-based political projects. Small-scale movements of various kinds promised young people and their older allies the chance to reenergize political life and reorient its moral compass.

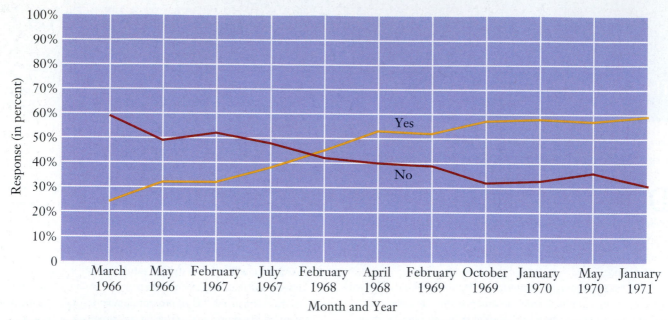

American Attitudes Toward the Vietnam War. Responses to the question: "Do you think that the United States made a mistake in sending troops to fight there?"

New Left activists constantly expanded their view of what counted as "politics." Although voter registration drives remained important in the South, for example, local movements came to place greater emphasis on alternative political forms, such as sit-ins and demonstrations. Young people claimed that their generation's numbers and educational attainments made them ideally suited to confront a political system dominated by powerful and entrenched interests.

On campus, discontent simmered. Even students generally indifferent to larger issues chafed at classes that seemed irrelevant to the issues of the day and at college bureaucracies that imposed restrictions on their living arrangements and lifestyle choices. Many students, for example, challenged whether deans of students should be able to establish dress codes and restrict visiting hours in dorms for students that, off campus, qualified as adults. Far worse, according to New Left activists, giant universities compromised their independence and integrity by welcoming funding from the military-industrial complex. Too many faculty members seemed oblivious to the social and moral implications of their war-related research.

The "Berkeley Revolt" of 1964 and 1965 saw dissident students and sympathetic faculty expand their activism. They first protested how the University of California restricted political activity on campus and then began speaking out against its complicity in the Vietnam War and in racial discrimination. The long-running drama of protest at Berkeley, which disrupted classes and polarized one of the world's most prestigious universities, came to symbolize the turmoil that the media began calling "the war on campus."

The Counterculture

Berkeley also hosted some of the earliest encounters between the political movements of the New Left and the vertiginous energies of a youth-dominated **counterculture**.

The counterculture of the mid-1960s remains a difficult "movement" to identify. One of its own slogans, after all, proclaimed "Do Your Own Thing." The counterculture elected no officers, held no formal meetings, and maintained no central office to issue manifestos. It first burst into view in low-income neighborhoods, such as San Francisco's Haight-Ashbury area, and along the streets bordering college campuses, such as Berkeley's Telegraph Avenue. Its self-appointed spokespeople embraced values, lifestyles, and institutions hailed as alternatives to those of the dominant culture.

Countercultural ventures drew on earlier models, especially those of the "Beat movement" of the 1950s. A loosely connected group of writers and poets, the Beats had denied that either the material abundance or conventional spiritual ideals of the 1950s provided fulfillment. Rejecting the benefits of "affluence" (see Chapter 28), the Beats claimed that an excess of consumer goods and oppressive technologies condemned most people to wander through alienated lives feeling oppressed, emotionally crippled, or just plain bored. Beat writers such as Jack Kerouac, author of *On the Road* (1957), praised the rebels and nonconformists for challenging settled routines and seeking more instinctual, sensual, and authentic ways of living. The Beat poet Allen Ginsberg, in works such as *Howl* (1956), decried soulless materialism and puritanical moral codes. He celebrated the kind of personal freedom that he found in drugs, Eastern mysticism, and same-sex love affairs. Ginsberg and other celebrities from the Beat era soon became iconic figures in the counterculture of the 1960s.

Countercultural energies eventually left their imprint on a wide range of social and cultural movements, including the cooperative movement, radical feminism, environmentalism, and the fight against legal restrictions on lifestyle choices. The counterculture also affected mainstream consumer culture. The mass media, for example, invariably highlighted the flamboyant clothing, hairstyles, and uninhibited sexuality among

San Francisco's Counterculture Gathers. Beat poet Allen Ginsberg addresses the 1967 Human Be-In with hippie singers backing him up in Golden Gate Park.

younger devotees of the counterculture. They liked to portray countercultural "hippies" as being on the cutting edge of a massive, fun-filled "youth rebellion" and focused on use of drugs, such as marijuana and LSD, communal living arrangements, and new forms of music, such as the folk-rock of the Byrds and the acid rock of the Grateful Dead.

As the counterculture developed its own soundtrack, it created its own media as well. Music-oriented publications such as *Rolling Stone* magazine (founded in 1967) celebrated singer-songwriters, such as Bob Dylan and Joni Mitchell, as the counterculture's prophet-laureates. Many radio stations featured folk-rock and other sounds associated with the counterculture. In a pre-Internet age, they also provided community billboards for promoting musical and political events. Some stations joined print publications, such as the *Berkeley Barb*, in dispatching youthful journalists to report on—and participate in—the countercultural scene.

Images and products from the counterculture soon found a ready market among otherwise conventional consumers. The ad agency for Chrysler Motors urged car buyers to break from older patterns, purchase a youthful-looking 1965 model, and thereby join the "Dodge Rebellion." Recognizing the appeal of bands such as San Francisco's Jefferson Airplane, the music industry, too, saw profits to be made. An early countercultural happening, the "Human Be-In," organized by community activists from San Francisco in early 1967, provided a model for subsequent, commercially dominated music festivals such as "Monterrey Pop" (later in 1967) and "Woodstock" (in 1969).

Back on college campuses, some of the students and faculty attracted to New Left political movements seemed initially baffled by the counterculture. The novelist Ken Kesey shocked a 1965 political demonstration at Berkeley with a style of politics indebted to the theatrics of the counterculture. Accompanied by veterans from the Beat movement and youthful members of his communal group, "the Merry Pranksters," Kesey alternated between singing choruses of "Home on the Range" and urging students to ignore politics and to refashion, especially through drugs such as LSD, how they lived their own lives.

Civil Rights and Black Power

The movement of movements of the mid-1960s also reshaped efforts to achieve liberty and equality for African Americans. Again, the media played an important and controversial role.

Civil rights leaders, of course, had long recognized the value of media coverage. TV images of the violence in Selma, Alabama, in 1965 had helped Dr. King's SCLC galvanize support for federal voting-rights legislation. At one point, ABC television interrupted a special showing of the anti-Nazi film *Judgment at Nuremberg* to show white Alabama state troopers beating peaceful, mostly African American, voting-rights marchers. Lyndon Johnson used television to promise, "we shall overcome" the nation's "crippling legacy of bigotry and injustice."

The turmoil associated with the civil rights campaigns prompted different views. Conservatives insisted that favorable media coverage of activism encouraged conflict and violence and that only a renewed commitment to law and order would ease social tensions. Movement activists who looked to Dr. King replied that racism, lack of opportunity, and inadequate government remedies produced the frustration that spawned violence. Other more militant voices within the broad movement of movements argued that governments could not be relied upon to address race-related issues effectively and that aggrieved groups needed to mobilize themselves.

In 1965, this debate intensified in the wake of racial conflict in Los Angeles. An altercation between a white highway patrol officer and a black motorist escalated into

Violence in Detroit, 1967. Outbreaks of violence swept through many U.S. cities between 1965 and 1969. The 1967 upheaval in Detroit, which federal troops had to quell, left many African American neighborhoods in ruin.

six days of violence, centered in the largely African American community of Watts in the South-Central area of Los Angeles. Thirty-four people died; hundreds of businesses and homes were burned; heavily armed National Guard troops patrolled the streets; and television camera crews carried images of the destruction across the nation and around the world.

What provoked this conflagration? Had TV cameras and radio reports helped to fan the flames? What should be the response to the violence in Watts? Stunned by what his trio of TV sets was showing, Lyndon Johnson responded according to his style of politics and ordered up new social welfare resources for Watts. "Let's move in—money, marbles, and chalk," LBJ reportedly ordered. The mayor and police chief of Los Angeles, conversely, blamed civil rights "agitators" and sought new resources for law enforcement. Local cultural leaders mobilized and created new organizations, such as the Watts Writers Workshop. When Dr. King rushed to the scene, preaching the politics of nonviolence, local activists generally ignored or even ridiculed him. They endorsed more militant action to gain political power. The previous year, they noted, white Californians from suburbia had voted overwhelmingly to junk the Rumford Act, the state's hard-won open housing law. Only a strategy of empowerment could produce access to more equitable policing practices, higher paying jobs, and better housing.

The basic structure of the post-Watts debate would change relatively little as violence continued to rock, usually during the summer, other urban neighborhoods. Commentators from different political camps applied their own value-soaked labels, including "riot," "rebellion," and "insurrection." The major outbreaks produced investigative commissions that debated these labels, parsed increasingly familiar arguments about causes, and pondered equally common recommendations for responding to the violence. According to one

estimate, there were more than 300 cases of serious urban violence between 1965 and 1969. Property damage reached into the billions, and hundreds of people lost their lives. Significant portions of major cities—but almost never the more affluent areas or nearby suburbs—became battlegrounds that would bear the scars of the Sixties for years to come.

How do these "long hot summers" fit into a history of the 1960s? The earliest narrative saw escalating violence producing movements that helped to splinter the earlier, more united, civil rights cause. The competing story about a "movement of movements," however, suggests that there was never one single civil rights *movement* that splintered. Long before Watts, a variety of black activist movements were advocating different ways to gain greater power for black communities.

Many efforts during the late 1950s and early 1960s looked to **Malcolm X**, who had initially gained attention as a minister in the Nation of Islam, a North American-based group popularly known as the "Black Muslims." In 1954, the same year as the *Brown* decisions (see Chapter 28), Malcolm X assumed leadership of the Nation of Islam's temple in Harlem. Using it as his base of operations, he forged ties with activist groups in other cities, particularly Detroit and Los Angeles. He oftentimes criticized Dr. King's gradual, nonviolent approach as largely irrelevant to the everyday problems of most African Americans and questioned the desirability or feasibility of racial integration. Malcolm X never advocated initiating confrontation, but he did endorse self-defense "by any means necessary."

Portrayed as a dangerous subversive by the FBI and most mainstream media, Malcolm X offered more than angry rhetoric. He also established a formidable presence among people and groups that would soon embrace what came to be called **Black Power**. Malcolm urged African Americans to "recapture our heritage and identity" and "launch a cultural

HISTORY THROUGH FILM

Malcolm X (1992)

Directed by Spike Lee.
Starring Denzel Washington (Malcolm X),
  Angela Bassett (Betty Shabbaz), Al Freeman, Jr. (Elijah Muhammad).

For more than 25 years, Hollywood tried to make a movie portraying the foremost advocate of Black Power, Malcolm X, whose *Autobiography* (1965) is a literary classic. Delays in obtaining financing, crafting a script, and finding a director always stymied production plans. Spike Lee, America's best-known African American film director, insisted that only he could do justice to the story of Malcolm X, who was assassinated by rivals at a speaking engagement in Harlem in 1965 at the age of 40. Finally, in 1992, with a budget of $34 million, Lee's independent production company (named Forty Acres and a Mule, after the land-distribution program for former slaves advocated after the Civil War) released a movie that argues for Malcolm X's continuing relevance.

The montage sequences that begin and end the movie underscore the film director's outlook. Against the backdrop of the Warner Brothers logo, the soundtrack introduces the actual voice of Malcolm X decrying the nature of racial politics over the course of U.S. history. Malcolm X's accusations continue as a giant American flag appears on screen and is cut into pieces by jagged images from an amateur video of Los Angeles police officers beating Rodney King, a notorious instance of police misconduct that took place in 1991. Next, the flag begins to burn until, revealed behind it, a giant "X," adorned with remnants of the flag, fills the frame. Some three hours later, the ending of the movie presents archival footage of Malcolm X, along with images of South African freedom fighter Nelson Mandela, while the voice of Ozzie Davis, the celebrated African American actor, gives a eulogy.

When first released, the film opened to packed movie houses. Despite a multimedia publicity blitz, box-office revenues steadily declined. Viewers reported that the lengthy, episodic movie taxed their patience and attention span.

Watching *Malcolm X* on video or DVD today, however, allows today's viewers to concentrate on its best sequences, speeding by ones that seem to drag, and returning to those that initially might seem

Denzel Washington stars as Malcolm X.

Everett Collection

muddled. *Malcolm X* offers a complex account of the early Black Power movement and the social ferment that gripped the nation during the 1960s. ◼

---

revolution to unbrainwash an entire people." Seeking a broad movement, Malcolm X eventually broke from the Black Muslims and established his own Organization of Afro-American Unity. Murdered in 1965 by enemies from the Nation of Islam, Malcolm X remained, especially after the posthumous publication of his *Autobiography* (1965), a powerful symbol for black-centered political and cultural visions of the future.

These visions increasingly diverged from those of LBJ's administration. Officially committed to additional civil rights legislation, the president privately struggled to understand movements with goals that differed from his. In fall 1965, the president hosted a "racial summit" at the White House. Among the several hundred black leaders who attended were two veteran activists: A. Philip Randolph and Bayard Rustin. They used this occasion to highlight their "Freedom Budget," an implicit criticism of their host's spending priorities. They called for spending $100 billion on infrastructure projects in low-income neighborhoods. Johnson privately denounced the sponsors of the Freedom Budget for "raising un-shirted hell and saying it's got to be a $100 billion" at *his* summit.

Meanwhile, events in the South highlighted other variations among the movements. SNCC and Dr. King's SCLC pressed forward, increasingly along separate paths. Both groups faced the constant threat of racist violence. State and local legal systems seemed unable to restrain or punish the segregationist vigilantes who attacked, or even killed, civil rights workers. White Southern legal officials appeared no better at overseeing electoral contests. Charging an SNCC-sponsored slate had been robbed of victory in a 1965 election in Lowndes County, Alabama, a young black activist named Stokely Carmichael organized a third-party movement. SNCC commissioned a special logo for it: a coiled black panther.

Carmichael himself achieved celebrity status the following summer. In June 1966, a KKK gunman shot James Meredith, who had integrated the University of Mississippi several years earlier and was conducting a one-person March against Fear from Tennessee to Jackson, Mississippi. Carmichael joined other activists in hastily organizing an enlarged March against Fear that would complete Meredith's walk. This was the first large-scale movement project—in contrast to the 1963 March on Washington and the 1965 voting-rights campaign in Alabama—that did not seek new civil rights legislation. It sought, instead, to demonstrate that movements for liberty and equality could focus on everyday struggles for safety, dignity, pride, and empowerment. The march also tried to capitalize on the national media coverage that Meredith's shooting had already attracted.

As Stokely Carmichael played to the omnipresent TV cameras, Dr. King, an old hand at this movement art form, admiringly acknowledged the younger activist's grasp of media routines. Shortly after having been jailed on a trumped-up charge, Carmichael delivered an emotional speech that secured his celebrity status. He questioned an unwavering commitment, no matter what the circumstances, to non-violence. The speech also explicitly urged that the civil rights struggle not remain just one for "Freedom," the byword of the SCLC, but for "Black Power." Black Power, Carmichael insisted, best described the objectives that direct-action movements must seek. As he later explained, Black Power was "a call for black people in this country to unite, to recognize their heritage, to build a sense of community." They should "define their own goals" and "lead their own organizations."

Black Power thus provided a sometimes inflammatory label for an often pragmatic set of claims that local civil rights groups had been making for some time. They sought greater on-the-ground power both in and for their own communities. Operating from this perspective, in 1966, several college students from Oakland announced a new Black Power organization that borrowed its name and logo from Carmichael's earlier movement in Lowndes County. The Black Panther Party's platform employed militant rhetoric on behalf of 10

objectives, including greater opportunities for housing, education, and employment; legal protections, especially against police misconduct; and improved health and nutrition initiatives in low-income black neighborhoods.

The Panther leadership quickly joined Carmichael as media-certified celebrities. A trio of its media-savvy young members—Huey Newton, Bobby Seale, and Eldridge Cleaver—adapted symbolism and rhetoric from Third World revolutionary movements. A 1967 rally in Sacramento, California, on behalf of the Second-Amendment right to use firearms for self-defense attracted the notice of J. Edgar Hoover. He made destroying the Black Panther Party a key goal of his FBI.

Less flamboyant groups and movements were also invoking the Black Power approach. Fully embracing the word *black* and a political-cultural agenda based on racial identity, they sought the power to pursue separate, African American–directed routes not just toward liberty and equality but also toward "liberation" from the prevailing political culture. "Black Is Beautiful" became a watchword. James Brown, the "Godfather of Soul," captured this new spirit with his song, "Say It Loud, I'm Black and I'm Proud" (1968).

Within this context, Congress passed the **Civil Rights Act of 1968**. One provision of this omnibus measure, popularly known as the "Fair Housing Act," followed in the wake of earlier state-level measures. It aimed at eliminating racial discrimination in the national real estate market but contained exemptions that enfeebled its own enforcement. Moreover, another section in the law declared it a crime to cross state lines in order to incite a "riot." Supporters hailed this provision as a law-and-order measure, while critics countered that it targeted political activists, especially those in the Black Power movement. Whenever tested in federal courts, though, this section passed constitutional scrutiny.

The Antiwar Movement

Meanwhile, another of these multifaceted movements was coming to overshadow all others: the one to end the war in Vietnam.

The antiwar movement, like its counterparts, never fell into neat categories. Some of the strongest "antiwar" sentiment, for example, blamed LBJ for not prosecuting the war *aggressively enough*. At the other end of the spectrum, several small movements called for a North Vietnam-NLF victory. The chant, "Ho, Ho, Ho Chi Minh/NLF is Gonna Win" enraged Johnson and distressed most others in the antiwar coalition.

The antiwar effort faced the same questions as the other movements of the Sixties. What kind of politics best expressed its ethical and spiritual values? How might it reach out to people not already in the movement? How could it mobilize enough support to change public policy?

The antiwar movement inexorably expanded the scope of its activism. On college campuses, for example, supporters and opponents of the war initially debated at "teach-ins." These academic-style events soon gave way to demonstrations and sit-ins. A draft-resistance effort emerged, often symbolized by the burning of draft cards, which urged young men to help alter Lyndon Johnson's policies by refusing to serve in the military. This movement gained its most cele-brated member when the heavyweight boxing champion Mohammed Ali refused induction into the military. (For more about Ali's life, international reputation, and his determina-

AMERICANS ABROAD
Cassius Clay

tion to gain conscientious-objector status, see the Americans Abroad feature "Cassius Clay/ Muhammad Ali: Champion of the Whole World.") Campus protests passed into a new phase when a pitched, bloody battle broke out between antiwar demonstrators and police at the University of Wisconsin in Madison in 1967.

That same year, Dr. Martin Luther King, Jr. crossed an important threshold in his personal politics. Antiwar clergy had been pressing him to proclaim publicly his opposition to the war, connect it to the civil rights cause, and elaborate his vision of the moral-spiritual issues at stake. Speaking at New York's Riverside Church in April 1967, Dr. King highlighted a black-and-white truth. African American troops, mostly from low-income communities, served and died in numbers far greater than their proportion of the U.S. population "for a nation that has been unable to seat them together in the same schools." The immoral "madness" in Vietnam "must cease," Dr. King concluded.

This speech provided a gauge of both the growing antiwar movement and the expanding polarization over the war. Many voices from the political-media mainstream, which had been supportive of Dr. King's civil rights activities, condemned his antiwar address. Although the *New York Times* did not follow some other newspapers in calling King a "traitor," it read his antiwar pronouncement through the narrow frame of interest-group politics. Dr. King risked damaging the civil rights cause by addressing a matter about which, according to the *Times*, he lacked any authority to speak. As Dr. King continued to broaden his political agenda, criticism from one-time supporters com-monly followed.

Dr. King's speech at Riverside Church raised the same issues—the nature of politics and the role of the media—that surrounded popular discussion of a massive 1967 antiwar demon-stration in Washington. This event underscored how the politics of the New Left and the spirit of the counterculture could march together, at least when opposing LBJ's policies in Vietnam. Noting the visual media's voracious appetite for pictures of colorful dis-senters, a small group of activists had invented a kind of "non-movement movement" that bypassed mobilization and organiza-tion in favor of making the media its primary constituency. Two members of this group, Abbie Hoffman and Jerry Rubin, pro-claimed themselves leaders of a (nonexistent) Youth International Party (or YIPPIE!) and waited for media coverage to surround their activities, as they knew it would.

Hoffman and Rubin raised the curtain on a new style of countercultural-political performance. In one incident, they mocked the symbolic value of stocks on the New York Exchange by tossing real dollar bills onto the trading floor. Invoking the sit-in movement, they joked about staging depart-ment store "loot-ins." Their contribution to the 1967 antiwar march in Washington would be to lead a separate trek to the Pentagon, where marchers would chant mystical incantations and try to levitate the building.

Although the Pentagon remained firmly planted, the march against it generated eye-catching media imagery. The event also gained the novelist and antiwar activist Norman Mailer a National Book Award for *Armies of the Night* (1968). Mailer's book, which wove together personal impressions and journalistic observation, helped to reinvent political reporting. Cultural observers identified accounts such as Mailer's as a "new journalism" and saw this form of reportage paralleling how political activists were creating a "new poli-tics" that expanded ideas about what counted as political involvement.

But the relationship between this new politics and the media seemed uncertain. Might not images of colorful quip-sters such as Hoffman and Rubin help fuel cultural polariza-tion rather than political action? Was the media's taste for spectacular demonstrations trivializing underlying issues? Such questions became even more pressing during the tumul-tuous 12 months of 1968.

1968

Q

FOCUS QUESTION

What helped to make the single year of 1968, even as it was still unfolding, seem such an important time in the history of America's longest war and of the Sixties?

This single year remains an important signpost in virtually every history of the period known as the Sixties. As world leaders rang in the New Year, many expressed hope that 1968 would bring better days. But the year ended on a very different note. Too many problems seemed to have grown worse; too many hopes appeared dashed.

Turmoil in Vietnam, 1968

At the end of January 1968, during a supposed truce in observance of Tet, the Vietnamese lunar New Year celebra-tion, NLF and North Vietnamese forces suddenly went on the attack throughout South Vietnam. U.S. military leaders had expected some kind of enemy offensive but badly under-estimated its potential breadth and ferocity. A small NLF force even temporarily seized the grounds of the U.S. embassy in Saigon. Very quickly, General Westmoreland's troops recovered and regained the areas that the other side had overrun, but the **Tet Offensive** nonetheless became a turning point.

Militarily, this offensive gained the NLF and the North relatively little territory at a very high cost. The NLF lost three-quarters of its military forces and much of its civilian support structure. Americans who backed the war blamed the antiwar movement and media imagery for exaggerating the early attacks, ignoring NLF and North Vietnamese losses, and thereby portraying a U.S. "victory" as a "defeat." Other obser-vers, however, countered that the offensive discredited Gen-eral Westmoreland's pre-Tet forecasts about seeing "light at the end of the tunnel." Even after rolling back the communist onslaught, the U.S. military command appeared ill prepared to pursue the badly mauled enemy forces.

Most importantly, the mere fact of a Tet Offensive undercut the optimistic story that the Johnson administration had been spinning. After CBS-TV anchor Walter Cronkite returned from a post-Tet trip to Vietnam, he told a national audience that the United States would never prevail militarily. Lyndon Johnson reportedly lamented that if he had lost "the most trusted person in America," as Cronkite was then known, he had lost the rest of the country on the issue of the Vietnam War.

Johnson received more bad news after summoning his most trusted advisers and a select group of senior outsiders, such as Dean Acheson, for advice on General Westmoreland's call for an additional 206,000 U.S. troops. Most criticized Westmoreland's request and insisted that South Vietnamese troops shoulder more of the military burden. The views of the senior members, the so-called "Wise Men," proved especially sobering since they had formulated America's anticommunist containment policy following the Second World War (see Chapter 27). Dean Acheson now advised the president that the United States "could no longer do the job we set out to do" in Vietnam "in the time we have left, and we must begin to take steps to disengage."

Other factors weighed on Johnson as well. As before, any plan for using U.S. military power to crush North Vietnam carried an unthinkable risk: a larger conflict with China and/or the Soviet Union. Now, public-opinion polls showed rapidly declining confidence in Johnson's more limited containment policy. And Westmoreland's call for another large increase in U.S troops, even if forces could be spared from other duties, would further fan antiwar opposition. Pressured by his new Secretary of Defense Clark Clifford, another early architect of Cold War containment, Johnson changed his guiding assumption about Vietnam. The cost of continuing the U.S. intervention vastly outweighed whatever benefit might accrue from continuing the effort against North Vietnam. He turned toward negotiations but found little success.

Turmoil at Home

The Tet offensive also destroyed Lyndon Johnson's political plans. The antiwar wing of the Democratic Party was trying to do what seasoned political pundits had declared impossible: deny Johnson renomination. The dissidents backed **Senator Eugene McCarthy** of Minnesota, the only prominent Democrat willing to challenge LBJ. An unorthodox candidate who avoided bombastic rhetoric in favor of calm warnings about how Johnson's course in Vietnam was dividing the nation, Gene McCarthy fronted an unusual campaign. The McCarthy movement's version of new politics relied on the wisdom of a few seasoned political strategists and the energy of thousands of college students. Young people packed away grubby campus attire, donned fresh clothing to "come clean for Gene," and stumped New Hampshire in the initial primary of 1968. Because Johnson refused to campaign personally, this "Dump Johnson" effort enjoyed unexpected media coverage. Johnson's forces actually won the New Hampshire's primary, but McCarthy came close enough to claim a symbolic victory.

Polls predicted he would easily beat Johnson, head-to-head, in the upcoming Wisconsin primary.

McCarthy's "children's crusade" thus rocked the Democratic Party—and U.S. policy in Vietnam. Even before McCarthy could claim the Wisconsin contest, Senator Robert Kennedy of New York, brother of the slain president, jumped into the race. He had refused earlier entreaties to challenge Johnson but now declared that the nation's "perilous course" impelled him to seek the presidency. Facing two Democratic challengers, President Johnson surprised all but his closest confidants when, during a live TV address in late March about Vietnam, he suddenly announced that he would not seek reelection. He also limited U.S. bombing of North Vietnam and signaled a readiness to begin peace negotiations in Paris.

Johnson's withdrawal created a three-way race for the Democratic nomination. McCarthy now faced Robert Kennedy and Johnson's ever-loyal vice president, Hubert H. Humphrey, who had entered the fray after LBJ's surprise announcement. Humphrey, however, steered clear of the remaining primaries, leaving the two senators to fight a series of brass-knuckled contests that pitted McCarthy's new politics against Kennedy's blend of the new and the old. Kennedy once quipped that the " 'A' students may have already flocked to McCarthy but that he was locking up those receiving 'Bs.' " The Democratic Party's A-level celebrities generally divided their support between the two, while Humphrey courted the Democratic powerbrokers who had been allied with LBJ.

Martin Luther King, Jr. welcomed LBJ's withdrawal and hoped that an antiwar candidate, ideally Kennedy, would head the Democratic ticket in November. On April 4, 1968, however, Dr. King took a break from planning an upcoming "Poor Peoples' March" on Washington and visited Memphis, Tennessee, in support of a strike by African American sanitation workers. There, he was assassinated while standing on the balcony of his motel. Law enforcement officials identified James Earl Ray, a career criminal, as the lone killer. Ray was eventually captured and charged with Kennedy's murder. He waived a jury trial, pleaded guilty, and received a 99-year prison sentence. Subsequently, Ray recanted and claimed to have been a pawn in a conspiracy directed by white supremacists. He died in prison still insisting on his innocence, but few people credit his claims.

News of Dr. King's murder immediately prompted another wave of violence. It swept through more than 100 cities and towns; 39 people died; 75,000 regular and National Guard troops were called to duty. When President Johnson proclaimed Sunday, April 7, as a day of national mourning for the slain civil rights leader, parts of the nation's capital city remained ablaze.

Following Dr. King's memorial service, Gene McCarthy and Robert Kennedy returned to campaigning. Their primary contests took on an increasingly surreal quality since the party insiders who controlled the selection of a majority of delegates to the Democratic national convention had unofficially anointed Hubert Humphrey as the party's presidential nominee. Campaigning at a breakneck pace, with only a minimal security detail, Robert Kennedy sought to demonstrate that popular opinion endorsed his candidacy. He also hoped to

The Funeral Procession of Dr. Martin Luther King, Jr., April 9, 1968. A vast crowd of mourners, including ordinary people and dignitaries, accompanied the body of Dr. King through the streets of Atlanta, Georgia. The simple, horse-drawn wagon had become the symbol of one of his final efforts, a Poor Peoples Campaign, that was to include a march on the nation's capital. After Dr. King's assassination in Memphis, a wagon would bear his body through the streets of the city in which he had grown up and gone to college.

convince the insiders now backing Humphrey that only a Democrat without ties to Lyndon Johnson, especially another Kennedy, could capture the White House in November.

On June 5, an ebullient Robert Kennedy defeated Gene McCarthy in California's Democratic Primary. He relished his dream of wresting the presidential nomination from Humphrey for only a few minutes, however. While preparing to leave the hotel that had hosted his victory celebration, Kennedy was slain by yet another political assassin. Bystanders grabbed Sirhan Sirhan, a Palestinian immigrant, who was later convicted of the killing. Television coverage of Kennedy's body being returned by train to Washington and his state funeral were reminders of Dr. King's recent murder and of the 1963 assassination of RFK's own brother. Bowing to the reality of Humphrey's delegate total, McCarthy effectively closed down his campaign.

Questions abounded. Was some "sickness" plaguing American political culture? Did "government by gunplay," rather than political pluralism, best describe the current system? Could the presidential election of 1968 possibly produce a legitimate victor?

The violence of 1968 continued. During the Republican national convention in Miami, as its presidential nominee **Richard Milhous Nixon** was promising to restore law and

order, racial conflict produced considerable property damage and took the lives of four people. Later that summer, thousands of antiwar demonstrators converged on Chicago, site of the Democratic Party's convention, to protest the nomination of Hubert Humphrey, still supporting Johnson's policy in Vietnam. Responding to provocative acts by some demonstrators, including Abbie Hoffman and Jerry Rubin of the Yippies, police officers attacked antiwar protestors and some nearby journalists. Tensions from this "Siege of Chicago" filtered into the convention hall, and antiwar delegates squared off, verbally, with supporters of the vice president. Humphrey easily captured the Democratic presidential nod, but disagreements over Johnson's Vietnam policy and the conduct of Chicago's police force left his party bitterly divided. Opinion polls showed that most people supported the use of force against the demonstrators, a judgment subsequently challenged by a special commission, whose report assessed the violence in Chicago as a "police riot."

The Election of 1968

Both Humphrey and Nixon worried about Alabama's George Wallace, who was running for president as a third-party

Robert F. Kennedy's Funeral. An elaborately staged funeral followed the 1968 assassination of Robert F. Kennedy. The shootings of the two leaders—Dr. King and Senator Kennedy—prompted widespread concern about the stability of America's social and political fabric.

candidate on the American Independent ticket. With his opposition to civil rights well established, Wallace concentrated his fire on the counterculture and the antiwar movement. If any "hippie" protestor ever blocked his motorcade, he once announced, it would "be the last car he'll ever lay down in front of." Although Wallace had generally supported the Democratic Party's domestic spending programs, he now courted voters who saw themselves the captives to "tax-and-spend" bureaucracies in Washington.

Wallace never expected to gain the presidency. If a candidate from the two major parties failed to win a majority of the electoral votes, however, the Constitution required that the president be selected by the House of Representatives. The Wallace strategy called for holding his core southern constituency, enticing conservatives elsewhere away from Nixon, and tipping several swing states to into the Humphrey camp. If everything fell into place, Wallace hoped to play the power-broker role when the House of Representatives selected the nation's next president.

As Wallace figured his odds and the new journalists wrote about a new politics, Humphrey and Nixon recalled the days of old. Humphrey promised fellow Democrats, still a majority of those likely to vote, the continuation of New Deal-Great Society programs. He struggled, though, with antiwar Democrats over his inability, until late in the campaign, to break from the Vietnam policies of Lyndon Johnson, his political patron. Conservative Republicans who favored Ronald Reagan as the GOP's 1968 nominee still suspected Richard Nixon to be an Eisenhower moderate. They also recognized, however, that the former vice president clearly stood to Humphrey's political right and that he appeared a safer guardian of conservative values than the mercurial Wallace. Nixon promised to restore order at home and hinted at a secret plan for ending U.S. involvement in Vietnam.

Nixon narrowly prevailed in November. Although he won 56 percent of the electoral vote, Nixon outpolled Humphrey in the popular vote by less than 1 percent. George Wallace's plan collapsed when he picked up only 46 electoral votes, all from the Deep South, and just 13.5 percent of the popular vote nationwide. Nixon won five crucial Southern states and attracted, all across the country, votes from people he called "the forgotten Americans, the non-shouters, the non-demonstrators."

The results in several states, however, were so close that relatively small shifts could have produced a victory for Humphrey or the scenario that Wallace had envisioned playing out in the House of Representatives. Humphrey's campaign suddenly gained momentum when normally Democratic voters decided they could not support Nixon or "waste a vote" on

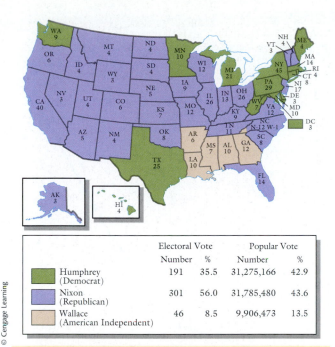

	Electoral Vote		Popular Vote	
	Number	%	Number	%
Humphrey (Democrat)	191	35.5	31,275,166	42.9
Nixon (Republican)	301	56.0	31,785,480	43.6
Wallace (American Independent)	46	8.5	9,906,473	13.5

Map 29.2 Presidential Election, 1968. George Wallace sought to throw the 1968 presidential election into the House of Representatives with his independent, third-party candidacy. What does this map suggest about the political changes already sweeping through the once solidly Democratic South?

Wallace. Humphrey also benefited when Lyndon Johnson temporarily halted all bombing of North Vietnam and sought to accelerate the peace talks in Paris. Nixon's forces responded with back-channel overtures to South Vietnamese leaders about getting a better deal if they stalled peace negotiations until a Nixon presidency. Although illegal wiretaps informed Johnson of this maneuver, he never intervened on Humphrey's behalf.

Continued Polarization, 1969–1974

 FOCUS QUESTION Why did the polarization that had developed over the 1960s continue into the 1970s? What foreign and domestic events contributed to the continued polarization?

Raised as Quaker, Richard Nixon had campaigned as someone able to restore the kind of tranquility he had known when growing up in Yorba Linda, California. His presidency, however, failed to calm the troubled waters.

Lawbreaking, Violence, and a New President

A handful of people on the leftist fringe embraced violence, generally through bomb attacks. There were nearly 200 actual and attempted bombings on college campuses during the 1969–70 academic year; an explosion at the University of Wisconsin claimed the life of a graduate student. Non-lethal attacks rocked other targets, including several large banks and the U.S. Capitol building. In 1970, three members of a small faction that had broken with SDS, "the Weather Underground," blew themselves apart when their bomb factory in New York City exploded.

At the same time, government officials stepped up their use of violent force. Fred Hampton of the Black Panthers and prison activist George Jackson died under circumstances their supporters called political assassination and public officials considered normal law enforcement. J. Edgar Hoover's FBI harassed activists, planted damaging rumors, and even dispatched *agent provocateurs* who incited protestors to undertake actions that officials could later prosecute as crimes.

State and local officials redoubled their efforts to bring order. During the fall of 1971, New York's Governor Nelson Rockefeller broke off negotiations with inmates at Attica State Prison, who had seized several cell-blocks and taken guards hostage in a protest over living conditions. He then ordered heavily armed state troopers and National Guard forces into the complex. When this "Attica Uprising" finally ended, 29 prisoners and 11 guards lay dead. On college campuses, too, local officials and administrators were increasingly ready to employ force against demonstrators.

Richard Nixon insisted that his vast public experience made him the ideal leader for such turbulent times. After graduating from Whittier College in California, Nixon studied law at Duke University and served in the Navy during the Second World War. He then began a political career that took him from a small-town law practice to the House of Representatives in 1946, the Senate in 1950, and the vice presidency in 1952.

Nixon claimed to thrive on confronting personal and political challenges. He entitled an early memoir *Six Crises*. After his narrow loss to Kennedy in 1960 and his failure, in 1962, to win the California governorship, Nixon denounced the media and announced his retirement from politics. He campaigned, however, loyally for Barry Goldwater in 1964 and tirelessly on behalf of Republican candidates in 1966. The GOP's comeback in that year's balloting boosted Nixon's stature within his party and even won him plaudits from media pundits. As he geared up for 1968, supporters talked about a "New Nixon" while detractors complained of "the same Old Nixon, now just a little older." Nixon narrowly captured the 1968 Republican nomination for president and emerged from his equally slim victory over Humphrey and Wallace with a new confidence.

Social Policy

Although Richard Nixon considered foreign policy to be his specialty, he initially crafted an ambitious domestic agenda. At the urging of Democrat Daniel Patrick Moynihan, a special presidential adviser on domestic issues, Nixon decided he could push through bolder programs than any Democratic president. Moynihan encouraged Nixon to think of himself as a conservative who could bring about progressive change. In 1969, Nixon thus proposed his **Family Assistance Plan (FAP)**, a dramatic

As a Percentage of Total Spending

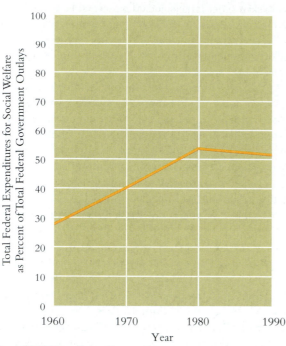

Total Expenditures

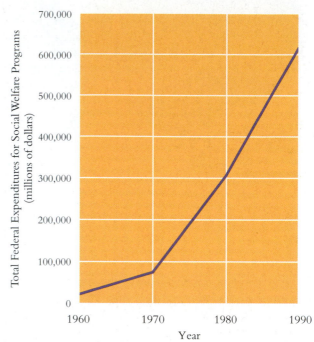

Social Welfare Spending, 1960–1990. These charts seem to present two very different views of social welfare spending in the 1970s and 1980s. What is the basis on which these different measurements rest, and which measure seems most useful?

overhaul of welfare policy. FAP proposed replacing most existing welfare measures, including the controversial Aid to Families with Dependent Children (AFDC). AFDC provided government payments to cover the basic costs of care for low-income children who had lost the support of a bread-winning parent.

Under the FAP proposal, *every* low-income family would be guaranteed an annual income of $1,600. Moynihan and Nixon touted FAP as advancing equality since it replaced existing arrangements that assisted only those with special circumstances, such as low-income mothers with small children. Nixon liked the measure because it promised to cut out the layers of bureaucracy needed to administer the requirements of a complicated program such as AFDC.

Nixon's FAP proposal debuted to tepid reviews. Conservatives claimed that income supplements for families with regularly employed, albeit low-paid, wage earners would be too costly. Proponents of more generous governmental assistance programs argued that FAP's income guarantee was too miserly. The House of Representatives approved a modified version of FAP in 1970, but a curious alliance of senators who opposed Nixon's proposal for very different reasons blocked its passage. Nixon eventually abandoned FAP, and the nation's welfare system would not be overhauled until the 1990s.

Although FAP failed to pass, other significant innovations in domestic policy were enacted. In an important move, Congress passed Nixon's revenue-sharing plan, part of his "new federalism," which returned a portion of federal tax dollars to state and local governments in the form of block grants. Instead of Washington specifying how these funds could be used, the block-grant concept allowed state and local officials, within general guidelines, to spend the funds as they saw fit.

A Democratic-controlled Congress and a Republican White House also cooperated to continue and even increase funding for many Great Society initiatives: Medicare, Medicaid, rent subsidies for low-income people, and Supplementary Security Insurance (SSI) payments to those who were elderly, blind, or disabled. In 1972, Social Security benefits were "indexed," which meant they would increase along with the inflation rate.

Nixon had adopted a complicated approach to civil rights during his campaign. He commonly criticized existing policies, such as the busing of children to advance school integration, but carefully distinguished his stance from that of George Wallace. The new Nixon administration, moreover, included Republicans anxious to aid civil rights causes. It thus allowed, and sometimes urged, federal bureaucracies to extend the reach civil rights measures when interpreting antidiscrimination legislation passed during the Great Society. In line with candidate Nixon's call for supporting "black capitalism" through small business loans, the new president helped extend the plan to other minority entrepreneurs, particularly Hispanics. His administration also helped implement the bilingual education programs that had been authorized in 1968 legislation. Indeed, the reach of many federal social welfare programs expanded during Nixon's first term, and the percentage of people living below the poverty line declined.

Environmentalism

Nixon also worked with the new environmental movement that became a significant political force during his presidency. Landmark legislation of the 1960s—such as the Wilderness Act of 1964, the National Wild and Scenic Rivers Act of 1968, and the National Trails Act of 1968—had already protected large areas of the country from commercial development. In the 1970s, a broader environmental movement focused on people's health and on ecological balances. Accounts such as *The Silent Spring* (1962) by Rachel Carson raised concerns that the pesticides used in agriculture, especially DDT, threatened bird populations. Air pollution (smog) in cities such as Los Angeles had become so toxic that simply breathing became equivalent to smoking several packs of cigarettes per day. Industrial processes, atomic weapons testing, and nuclear power plants prompted fear of cancer-causing materials. The Environmental Defense Fund, a private organization formed in 1967, went to court to try to limit DDT and other dangerous toxins. Earth Day, a festival first held in 1970, aimed to raise awareness about the many newly publicized hazards of environmental degradation.

The Nixon administration, although not a sponsor of Earth Day, took environmental issues seriously. The president supported creation of the Environmental Protection Agency (EPA) and signed major pieces of congressional legislation: the Resources Recovery Act of 1970 (dealing with waste management), the Clean Air Act of 1970, the Water Pollution Control Act of 1972, the Pesticides Control Act of 1972, and the Endangered Species Act of 1973. National parks and wilderness areas were expanded, and a new law required that "environmental impact statements" be prepared in advance of any major government project.

The new environmental standards brought both unanticipated problems and significant improvements. The Clean Air Act's requirement for taller factory smokestacks, for example, moved pollutants higher into the atmosphere, where they produced a dangerous byproduct, "acid rain." Still, the act's restrictions on auto and smokestack emissions cleared smog out of city skies and helped people with respiratory ailments. The law reduced six major airborne pollutants by one third in a single decade. Lead emissions into the atmosphere declined by 95 percent.

Controversies over Rights

Activism on social and environmental concerns accompanied fierce debate over the federal government's responsibility to protect the rights and liberties of citizens. The struggle to locate and define these rights soon embroiled the nation's constitutional culture in controversy.

A majority of the justices on the Supreme Court of the Sixties had supported the Great Society's political vision and sought to bring an expanding list of rights under constitutional protection. As this group charted the Court's path, two Eisenhower appointees, Chief Justice Earl Warren and Associate Justice William Brennan, often led the way. Although many of the Warren Court's decisions involving rights issues drew critical fire, the case that raised the most public controversy involved handling criminal suspects. *Miranda* v. *Arizona* (1966) held that the Constitution required police officers to advise persons suspected of having committed a felony offense of their constitutional right to remain silent and to consult an attorney, which would be provided to indigents by the

government. Defenders of this decision, which established the famous "Miranda Warning," saw it as the logical extension of settled precedents. The Court's critics, in contrast, accused its majority of "inventing" liberties not found in the Constitution. Amid rising public concern over crime, political conservatives made *Miranda* a symbol of the judicial "coddling" of criminals and the Warren Court's supposed disregard for constitutional law.

Richard Nixon had campaigned for president as an opponent of the Warren Court and promised to appoint federal judges who would "apply" rather than "make" the law on matters such as criminal rights and court-ordered school busing. As candidate Nixon continued to assail the Warren Court, the chief justice announced his retirement, and Lyndon Johnson's plan to anoint his close confidante, Associate Justice Abe Fortas as Warren's successor, stalled in Congress. Consequently, the victorious Nixon appointed a Republican loyalist, Warren Burger, as chief justice. Subsequent vacancies allowed Nixon to appoint three other Republicans to the High Court.

This new "Burger Court" immediately faced controversial rights-related cases of its own. Lawyers sympathetic to the Great Society vision of social welfare advanced the argument that access to adequate economic assistance from the federal government was a constitutionally protected right. The Burger Court, however, narrowly rejected this claim when deciding *Dandridge* v. *Williams* (1970). With the new chief justice casting the deciding vote, it held that a state could limit the amount it paid to welfare recipients. Payment schedules that varied from state to state did not violate the constitutional requirement of equal protection of the law.

Rights-related claims involving health-and-safety legislation generally fared better. A vigorous consumer movement, which had initially drawn inspiration from Ralph Nader's exposé about auto safety (*Unsafe at Any Speed*, 1965), joined with environmentalists to bolster rights claims in the context of workplace safety, consumer protection, and nontoxic environments. Their efforts, overcoming opposition from many business groups, found expression in such legislation as the Occupational Safety Act of 1973 and stronger consumer and environmental protection laws. The Burger Court invariably supported the constitutionality of these measures.

At the same time, the newly energized women's rights movement pressed another set of issues. The **Equal Rights Amendment (ERA)**, initially proposed during the 1920s, promised to explicitly guarantee women the same legal rights as men. Easily passed by Congress in 1972 and quickly ratified by more than half the states, the ERA suddenly stalled. Conservative women's groups, such as Phyllis Schlafly's "Stop ERA," charged that this constitutional amendment would undermine traditional "family values" and expose women to new dangers such as military service. The ERA failed to attain approval from the three quarters of states needed for ratification. Ultimately, women's groups abandoned the ERA effort in favor of using the courts to adjudicate equal rights claims on a case-by-case, issue-by-issue basis.

One of these issues, whether a woman possessed a constitutional right to terminate a pregnancy, became far more

Women's Rights Demonstrators, August 16, 1970. Activists, who gathered in Washington, D.C., to demonstrate on behalf of women's rights, take time to rest. Symbolically, they effectively "occupied" a statue erected in honor of a 19th-century military hero, Admiral David G. Farragut.

AP Images

controversial than the ERA. The abortion issue, in contrast to controversies over busing and criminal procedure, had never played a prominent role in Nixon's 1968 campaign, and his administration thus paid little attention to this rights-related question when nominating federal judges. In *Roe v. Wade* (1973), the Burger Supreme Court ruled, in a 7–2 decision, that a state law making abortion a criminal offense violated a woman's "right to privacy." Two of the three Justices appointed by Nixon voted with the majority. The *Roe* decision outraged antiabortion groups, who rallied under the "Right-to-Life" banner on behalf of the unborn fetus, providing new support for the already expanding conservative wing of the Republican Party. On the other side, feminist groups made the issue of individual choice in reproductive decisions a central rallying point.

Meanwhile, with little controversy, President Nixon supported other rights-related issues. He signed an extension of the Voting Rights Act of 1965, and in 1972 approved another civil rights measure popularly known as "Title IX." It banned sexual discrimination in higher education and became the legal basis for requiring colleges and universities to adopt "gender equity" in all areas, including intercollegiate athletics.

The Nixon administration also refined the "affirmative action" concept, which had surfaced during Lyndon Johnson's presidency, and required that all hiring and contracting that depended on federal funding take "affirmative" steps to enroll greater numbers of African Americans as union apprentices.

The Economy

Richard Nixon eventually confronted economic problems that had been unthinkable only a decade earlier. No single cause can account for them, but most analyses begin with the war in Vietnam. This expensive military commitment, along with increased domestic spending and a volatile international economy, began to curtail economic growth. Lyndon Johnson had been determined to contain communism in Indochina without cutting Great Society programs or raising taxes, and thus he had concealed the true costs of the war. Nixon inherited a deteriorating (although still favorable) balance of trade and rising rate of inflation. Between 1960 and 1965, consumer prices grew only about 1 percent per year; in 1968, this figure exceeded 4 percent.

By 1971, the unemployment rate topped 6 percent. According to conventional wisdom, expressed in an economic concept called "the Phillips curve," when unemployment rises, prices should remain constant or even decline. Yet *both* unemployment and inflation numbers were going up simultaneously. Economists coined the term **stagflation** to describe this puzzling convergence of economic stagnation and price inflation. Along with stagflation, U.S. exports were becoming less competitive in international markets and in 1971, for the first time in the 20th century, the United States ran a trade deficit, importing more products than it exported.

Nixon never expected to grapple with a faltering economy. One of his economic advisers conceded that the president had "an almost pathological block about economics." Although long critical of economic regulations, Nixon now needed a quick cure for the nation's economic ills. His narrow victory in 1968 and setbacks in the midterm election of 1970 left him fearful of the political fallout from stagflation and trade imbalances. In January 1971 he suddenly, and surprisingly, announced, "I am now a Keynesian in economics" and began proclaiming his faith in governmental remedies. In August, he unveiled a "New Economic Policy" that included a 90-day freeze on any increases in wages and prices, to be followed by government monitoring to detect "excessive" increases in either arena.

Nixon simultaneously took an even more daring step. Dating from the 1944 Bretton Woods agreement (see Chapter 26), the value of the U.S. dollar had been tied to the value of gold—at $35 for every ounce. This meant that the United States would exchange its dollars for gold at that rate whenever any other nation's central bank requested it to do so. Other countries had fixed their own currency exchange rate in relation to the values of the U.S. dollar. But U.S. trade deficits were undermining the dollar and allowing foreign banks to exchange U.S. dollars for gold at rates far more favorable than $35 per ounce. In response, the Nixon administration abandoned the fixed gold-to-dollar ratio. Henceforth, the U.S. dollar would "float" in value against the prevailing market price for gold and against all other currencies in the world. This change would devalue the dollar and hopefully make American exports more competitive in the global marketplace. The strategy fundamentally altered the international economic order by allowing the value of all currencies to float and fluctuate.

In October 1973, oil-producing nations in the Middle East further changed international economic arrangements. Citing the declining U.S dollar and falling oil revenues as justifications, petroleum producers began curtailing exports as a means of raising prices. About a week later, in response to U.S. military aid for Israel, then engaged in the Yom Kipper War with Egypt and Syria, Arab nations temporarily embargoed oil shipments to the United States. Nixon and Congress responded with a series of measures that included rationing, lowered speed limits, and the naming of a new "energy czar." As U.S. oil reserves declined, the days of "cheap oil" were coming to an end.

Foreign Policy in a Time of Turmoil, 1969–1974

FOCUS QUESTION What were the major aims of U.S. foreign policy during the presidency of Richard Nixon? How successful was the Nixon administration in carrying out these policies?

Even as it wrestled with divisive domestic concerns, the Nixon administration was far more interested in international affairs. Henry Kissinger, Nixon's national security adviser and then secretary of state, laid out a grand strategy: **détente** with the Soviet Union, normalization of relations with China, and disengagement from direct military involvement in South Vietnam.

Détente

Although Nixon had built his early political career on hard-line anticommunism, he and Kissinger worked to ease tensions with the two major communist nations: the Soviet Union and China. The Nixon–Kissinger team expected that improved relations might lead these nations to reduce their support for North Vietnam, increasing chances for a successful U.S. pullback of U.S. combat troops.

Arms control talks took top priority in U.S.–Soviet relations. In 1969, the two superpowers opened the Strategic Arms Limitation Talks (SALT); after several years of high-level diplomacy, they signed an agreement (SALT I) that limited further development of both antiballistic missiles (ABMs) and offensive intercontinental ballistic missiles (ICBMs). SALT I's impact on the arms race was limited because it said nothing about the number of nuclear warheads that a single missile might carry. Still, the ability to conclude any arms-control pact signaled improving relations.

Nixon's overtures toward the People's Republic of China eventually brought an even more dramatic break with the Cold War past. Secret negotiations, often conducted personally by Kissinger, led to a slight easing of U.S. trade restrictions and then to an invitation from China for Americans to compete in a table tennis match. This celebrated "ping-pong diplomacy" presaged more significant diplomatic exchanges. Most spectacularly, Nixon visited China in 1972, posing for photos with Mao Zedong and strolling along the Great Wall. A few months later, the UN admitted the People's Republic as the sole representative of China, and in 1973 the United States and China exchanged informal diplomatic missions.

Vietnamization and the Nixon Doctrine

In Vietnam, the Nixon administration decided to speed withdrawal of U.S. ground forces by embracing a policy called "Vietnamization," which had already informally begun during Lyndon Johnson's administration. Put simply, it meant that South Vietnamese, rather than U.S. troops, should bear the burden of ground combat operations. In July 1969, the **Nixon Doctrine** announced a broader version of this approach. It pledged that the United States would extend military assistance to anticommunist governments in Asia but would require them to supply their own combat forces. From the outset, the Nixon Doctrine for Vietnam envisioned the eventual removal of U.S. ground troops without accepting compromise or defeat. While officially adhering to Johnson's 1968 bombing halt over the North, Nixon and Kissinger accelerated both the ground and air wars by launching new offensives and by approving a military "incursion" into Cambodia, an ostensibly neutral country. The 1970 operation into Cambodia, which targeted a command center from which North Vietnam conducted the war in the South, aimed at shortening U.S. military engagement in Southeast Asia by temporarily expanding it.

The invasion of Cambodia set off a new wave of protests in the United States and around the world. U.S. campuses exploded in angry demonstrations against this apparent widening of the war, and a number of institutions began the summer vacation early. White police officers fatally shot two students at the all-black Jackson State College in Mississippi, and National Guard troops at Kent State University in Ohio fired on unarmed protestors, killing four students. As antiwar demonstrators descended on Washington, D.C., Nixon seemed personally unnerved by the furor, especially during an unscheduled, late-night meeting with protesting students.

A continuing controversy over the **My Lai Incident** further polarized sentiment over the war. Shortly after the 1968 Tet offensive, U.S. troops had entered the small South Vietnamese hamlet of My Lai and murdered more than 200 civilians, most of them women and children. This massacre only became public in 1969 and quickly refocused debate over U.S policy. Military courts convicted only one officer, Lieutenant William Calley, of any offense. Critics charged that the military was using Calley as a scapegoat for a failed strategy that emphasized body counts and lax rules of engagement. Injecting the White House into this controversy, Nixon ordered that the young lieutenant be confined to his officer's quarters pending the results of his appeal. Ultimately, Calley was ordered released based on procedural irregularities. The controversies over this case inflamed tensions between those Americans who backed and those who protested the war.

Meanwhile, the Nixon administration widened military operations to include Laos as well as Cambodia. Although it denied waging any such campaign, large areas of those agricultural countries were ravaged. As the number of refugees inside Cambodia swelled and food supplies dwindled, the communist guerrilla force there—the Khmer Rouge—became a well-disciplined army. The Khmer Rouge eventually came to power and in a murderous attempt to eliminate dissent turned Cambodia into a "killing field." It slaughtered more than 1 million Cambodians. While Nixon continued to plan U.S. troop withdrawals and conduct peace negotiations with North Vietnam in Paris, the Vietnam War broadened into a conflict that destabilized all of Indochina.

Even greater violence was yet to come. U.S. aid beefed up South Vietnam's army, but it never became a reliable fighting force. During the spring of 1972, North Vietnam's

Jackson State. The era of America's longest war was a time of violence overseas and at home. In May 1970, police gunfire killed two students and wounded 15 others at Jackson State University in Mississippi. This picture was taken through a bullet-riddled window in a women's dorm.

© Bettmann/CORBIS

"Easter Offensive" approached within 30 miles of Saigon before falling back. The surge showed the limits of Vietnamization and swelled South Vietnam's refugee population. Nixon responded with an escalation as great as that by Lyndon Johnson in 1965. He ordered the systematic bombing of North Vietnam, the mining of its harbors, and the institution of a naval blockade. Just weeks before the November 1972 elections in the United States, Henry Kissinger declared that "peace is at hand" and announced a cease-fire. After Nixon's reelection, however, the impending peace deal fell apart in Paris, and the United States unleashed even greater firepower over North Vietnam. During the "Christmas bombing" of December 1972, the heaviest bombardment in history, B-52 planes pounded military and civilian targets in North Vietnam around the clock. North Vietnam, which was also feeling diplomatic pressure from the Soviet Union and China, decided to conclude peace negotiations with Washington and Saigon.

The United States Leaves Vietnam

Much of the U.S. media, Congress, and public were also calling for an end to the war. Many were tired of the violence in Asia and of the administration's effort to stem dissent at home. In addition, sagging morale among U.S. troops hindered the missions that the U.S. command was still conducting. Soldiers questioned the purpose of their sacrifices; some refused to engage the enemy; and a few openly defied their superiors. At home, Vietnam Veterans Against the War (VVAW), a new organization, joined the antiwar coalition. Running out of non-bombing options, Nixon proceeded with full-scale Vietnamization.

In January 1973, the warring parties signed peace accords in Paris that provided for the withdrawal of U.S. troops. The actual terms closely resembled those in the pre-election deal that Kissinger had celebrated but which had later fallen apart. By allowing North Vietnamese troops to remain in the South, the Paris accords left Nguyen Van Thieu's government in an unenviable position, and Nixon may have anticipated preserving it by future bombing campaigns. As U.S. ground forces departed, the South Vietnamese army continued to fight, increasingly demoralized and ineffectual. In spring 1975, nearly two years after the Paris accords, South Vietnam's army and Thieu's government collapsed as North Vietnamese armies entered the capital of Saigon (see Chapter 30). America's longest war ended with its objective of maintaining a non-communist South Vietnam unfulfilled.

Between 1960 and 1973, approximately 3.5 million American men and women served in Vietnam: 58,000 died, 150,000 were wounded, and 2,000 were classified as missing. In the aftermath of this costly, divisive war, Americans struggled to understand why their country failed to defeat a small, barely industrialized nation. Those still supporting the war argued that it had been lost on the home front. They blamed an irresponsible media, a disloyal antiwar movement, and a Congress afflicted by a "failure of will." The war, they insisted, had been for a laudable cause. Politicians, setting unrealistic limits on the Pentagon, had prevented strategists from attaining victory. By contrast, those who had come to oppose the war stressed the overextension of U.S. power, the misguided belief in national omnipotence, the dangers of touching off a wider war with China, and the strategic miscalculations of decision makers. For them, the United States had waged a war in the wrong place for the wrong reasons. The human costs in both the United States and Indochina outweighed any possible gain.

Regardless of their position on the war, most Americans seemed to agree on a single proposition: There should be "no more Vietnams." The United States should not undertake another military operation unless it involved clear and compelling political objectives, sustained public support, and realistic means to accomplish its goals. Eventually, people who wanted to reassert U.S. power in the world came to worry that such caution, which they dismissed as "the Vietnam syndrome," might shape a timid foreign policy. The legacy of Vietnam era divisions would continue far beyond the era of America's longest war.

Expanding the Nixon Doctrine

Although the Nixon Doctrine initially applied to the Vietnamization of the war in Indochina, Nixon and Kissinger extended its premise to the entire world. The White House made clear that the United States would not dispatch its troops to quash insurgencies but would generously aid anticommunist regimes or factions willing to fight their own battles.

During the early 1970s, U.S. Cold War strategy came to rely on supporting staunchly anticommunist regional powers. These included nations such as Iran under Shah Reza Pahlavi, South Africa with its apartheid regime, and Brazil with its military dictatorship. All of these countries built large, U.S. trained military establishments. U.S. military assistance, together with covert CIA operations, also incubated and protected anticommunist dictatorships in South Korea, the Philippines, and much of Latin America. U.S. arms sales to the rest of the world skyrocketed. In one of its most controversial foreign policies, the Nixon administration employed covert action against the elected socialist government of Salvador Allende Gossens in Chile in 1970. After Allende took office, Kissinger pressed for the destabilization of his government. On September 11, 1973, the Chilean military overthrew Allende, immediately suspended democratic rule, and announced that Allende had committed suicide.

Critics charged that the United States, in the name of anticommunism, too often linked its diplomatic fortunes to questionable covert actions and unpopular military governments. In 1973, Democratic Senator Frank Church conducted Senate hearings into abuses of power by the executive branch, especially the CIA's actions in Chile. Supporters of Nixon and Kissinger, however, gave the pair high marks for a pragmatic foreign policy that combined détente toward the communist giants with containment directed against the spread of revolutionary regimes

A Crisis of Governance, 1972–1974

FOCUS QUESTION How did the constitutional controversies of the early 1970s lead the nation into a crisis of governance? How did this crisis ultimately undermine Richard Nixon's presidency and force his resignation?

Nixon's presidency came under constitutional scrutiny as a result of decisions made in the Oval Office. A political loner who ruminated about taking revenge against his enemies, Nixon often seemed his own greatest foe. He ordered the Internal Revenue Service (IRS) to harass prominent Democrats with expensive audits; placed antiwar and Black Power activists under surveillance; and conducted risky covert activities on the domestic front that even rattled the constitutional sensibilities of an old ally, J. Edgar Hoover. Isolated with a close-knit group of advisers, Nixon eventually created his own secret intelligence unit, "the Plumbers," which set up shop in the White House.

During the summer of 1971, Daniel Ellsberg, an antiwar activist who had once worked in the national security bureaucracy, leaked to the press a top-secret, highly critical history of U.S. involvement in the Vietnam War, subsequently known as the "Pentagon Papers." Nixon responded by seeking, unsuccessfully, a court injunction to stop publication and, more ominously, by unleashing his Plumbers unit to stop leaks to the media. Seeking something that might discredit Ellsberg, the Plumbers burglarized his psychiatrist's office. Thus began a series of secretive political "dirty tricks" and clear-cut crimes, sometimes financed by funds solicited for Nixon's 1972 reelection campaign.

The Election of 1972

Nixon's political strategists worried that domestic troubles and the war in Vietnam might deny the president another term. Creating a campaign organization separate from that of the Republican Party, with the ironic acronym of CREEP (Committee to Re-elect the President), they secretly raised millions of dollars, much of it from illegal contributions.

As the 1972 campaign took shape, Nixon's chances for reelection dramatically improved. An assassin's bullet crippled George Wallace and kept him from playing the spoiler's role in November. Senator Edmund Muskie of Maine, initially Nixon's leading Democratic challenger, made a series of blunders (some of them, perhaps, precipitated by Republican "dirty tricksters") that derailed his campaign. Eventually, Senator George McGovern of South Dakota, an outspoken opponent of the Vietnam War but a lackluster campaigner, won the Democratic nomination.

McGovern never seriously challenged Nixon. The Democratic candidate called for higher taxes on the wealthy, a guaranteed minimum income for all Americans, amnesty for Vietnam War draft resisters, and the decriminalization of marijuana. In foreign policy, he urged deep cuts in defense spending and peace in Vietnam—proposals that Nixon successfully portrayed as signs that McGovern would "weaken" national security. Nixon won an easy victory in November, receiving the Electoral College votes of all but one state and the District of Columbia. Although the 26th Amendment, ratified one year before the election, had lowered the voting age to 18, relatively few of the newly enfranchised voters cast ballots.

While helping achieve this victory, however, the president's supporters left a trail of crime and corruption that eventually led to a crisis of governance. The election of 1972 initially seemed a simple triumph for Richard Nixon, but the other branches of government soon began scrutinizing its legitimacy. In June 1972, a surveillance team with links to both CREEP and the White House had been arrested while fine tuning eavesdropping equipment in the Democratic Party's headquarters in Washington's Watergate office complex. In public, Nixon's spokespeople dismissed the Watergate break-in as a "third-rate burglary"; privately, the president and his inner circle launched a cover-up. They paid hush money to the Watergate burglars and ordered CIA officials to misinform the FBI that any investigation into the episode would jeopardize national security. Nixon succeeded in containing the political damage through the 1972 election, but events associated with **Watergate** soon overtook him.

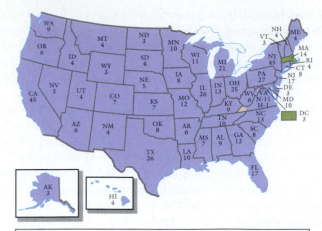

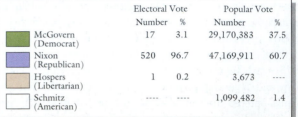

		Electoral Vote		Popular Vote	
		Number	%	Number	%
	McGovern (Democrat)	17	3.1	29,170,383	37.5
	Nixon (Republican)	520	96.7	47,169,911	60.7
	Hospers (Libertarian)	1	0.2	3,673	----
	Schmitz (American)	----	----	1,099,482	1.4

© Cengage Learning

Map 29.3 Presidential Election, 1972. In contrast to the closely contested election of 1968, the 1972 election produced a landslide victory for Richard Nixon. What helps explain the stark difference between these two elections? What events would force Richard Nixon, in 1974, to leave an office to which he had been overwhelmingly returned?

The Watergate Investigations

While reporters from the *Washington Post* pursued the taint of scandal coming from the election, Congress, the federal courts, and government prosecutors also sought evidence of illegal activities during the 1972 campaign. Federal District Judge John Sirica, a Republican appointee presiding over the trial of the Watergate burglars, suspected a cover-up and continually pressed the defendants before his court for additional information. In May 1973, U.S. Senate leaders convened a special, bipartisan Watergate Committee, headed by North Carolina's conservative Democratic Senator Sam Ervin, to investigate. Federal prosecutors uncovered evidence that seemed to link key administration figures, including John Mitchell, Nixon's former attorney general and later the head of CREEP, to illegal activities.

The Ervin hearings, carried live on TV, eventually attracted the most public attention. A succession of witnesses testified about illegal activities committed by CREEP and the White House. The Watergate Committee called Nixon's closest aides before the committee, and its sessions became a daily political drama that much of the country watched. Testimony from John Dean, who had been the president's chief legal counsel, linked Nixon himself to attempts to cover up Watergate and to other illegal activities. The president steadfastly denied Dean's charges.

Along the way, though, Senate investigators discovered that a voice-activated taping system had recorded every conversation in Nixon's Oval Office. These tapes made it possible to determine whether the president or Dean, Nixon's primary accuser, was lying. While contending he was not "a crook," Nixon also claimed an "executive privilege" to keep the tapes from being released, but Judge Sirica, Archibald Cox (a special, independent prosecutor in the Watergate case), and Congress all demanded access to them.

If Nixon's Watergate-related problems were not enough, his vice president Spiro Agnew suddenly resigned in October 1973 after pleading no contest to income-tax evasion. Agnew agreed to a plea-bargain arrangement to avoid prosecution for having accepted illegal kickbacks while in Maryland politics. Acting under the 25th Amendment (ratified in 1967), Nixon appointed—and both houses of Congress confirmed—Representative Gerald R. Ford of Michigan, a Republican Party stalwart, as the new vice president.

Nixon's Resignation

Nixon's clumsy efforts to protect himself backfired. During the fall of 1973, Nixon had abruptly fired Archibald Cox, hoping to prevent him from gaining access to the tapes. When this firing prompted an outcry, the president appointed an equally tenacious replacement, Leon Jaworski. Nixon's own release of edited transcripts of some Watergate-related conversations, including one key transcript reflecting an 18-minute gap in the tape, merely strengthened demand for the original recordings. Finally, by proclaiming that he would obey only a "definitive" Supreme Court decision, Nixon all but invited the justices to deliver a unanimous ruling on the question of the tapes. On July 24, 1974, the Burger Court did just that in the case of *U.S. v. Nixon*. No claim of executive privilege could justify the refusal to release evidence in a criminal investigation. With Nixon refusing to consider resignation, the House of Representatives began to consider his impeachment.

After televised deliberations, a bipartisan majority of the House Judiciary Committee voted three formal articles of impeachment against the president for obstruction of justice, violation of constitutional liberties, and refusal to produce evidence. Nixon promised to rebut these accusations before the Senate, the body authorized by the Constitution (Article I, Section 3) to render a verdict of guilty or not guilty after impeachment by the House.

Nixon's aides, however, were already orchestrating his departure. One of his own attorneys had discovered that a tape Nixon had been withholding contained the long-sought "smoking gun," clear evidence of a criminal offense. It confirmed that during a 1972 conversation, Nixon had helped hatch a plan by which the CIA would advance a fraudulent claim of national security in order to stop the FBI from investigating the Watergate break-in. At this point, Nixon's own secretary of defense ordered military commanders to ignore any order from the president, the constitutional commander-in-chief, unless the secretary had countersigned it. Abandoned by almost every prominent Republican and confronted by a Senate prepared to vote him guilty on the impeachment charges, Nixon went on television on August 8, 1974, to announce his resignation. On August 9, Gerald Ford became the nation's 38th chief executive. He assumed the post never having been elected president or vice president.

In 1974, most people told pollsters that the string of abuses collectively known as "Watergate" was one of the gravest crises in the history of the republic and that the Nixon administration had posed a serious threat to constitutional governance. As time passed, though, the details of Watergate-related events faded from memories. Opinion polls conducted on the 20th anniversary of Nixon's resignation suggested that Americans now only dimly recalled the crisis of governance that had once gripped the nation.

What might account for this change? First, although nearly a dozen members of Nixon's administration—including its chief law enforcement officer, John Mitchell—were convicted of criminal activities, the president avoided prosecution. Gerald Ford granted him an unconditional pardon. The nation was spared the spectacle of a former president undergoing trial, but it was also denied an authoritative accounting, in a court of law, of Nixon's misdeeds.

Another reason for fading memories may be the media's habit of attaching the Watergate label to nearly every political scandal of the post-Nixon era. The suffix-*gate* became affixed to grave constitutional episodes and to obviously trivial political events. Over time, then, "Watergate" became almost a synonym for "politics as usual." Finally, images of what the historian Stanley Kutler calls the "Wars of Watergate" have tended to blend into the broader picture of political, social, economic, and cultural turmoil that accompanied U.S. involvement in the nation's longest war.

Conclusion

The power of the national government expanded between 1963 and 1974. Lyndon Johnson's Great Society provided a blueprint for policymaking at home even as his administration dramatically escalated the war in Vietnam. This growth of government power prompted divisive debates that polarized the country. During Johnson's presidency, both the war effort and the economy faltered, top leaders became discredited, and Johnson abandoned the office he had so long sought. The use of presidential power by Johnson's Republican successor, Richard Nixon, prompted a crisis of governance that ultimately forced Nixon from office. The hopes of the early 1960s—that an active national government could promote liberty and equality both at home and throughout the rest of the world—ended in frustration.

The era of America's longest war was a time of political passion, cultural and racial conflict, and differing definitions of patriotism. It saw the slow convergence of an antiwar movement, along with the emergence of youthful dissent, Black Power, women's activism, and contests over what constituted Americans' basic rights. Different groups have invoked divergent explanations for the fates of both the Great Society and the war effort, and the divisions from this era shaped politics and culture for years to come. Many Americans became skeptical, many even cynical, about expanding the power of the federal government in the name of expanding liberty and equality.

CHAPTER REVIEW

REVIEW QUESTIONS

1. How did the Johnson administration define its domestic goals, and how did it approach problem solving? Why did Johnson's "Great Society" produce so much controversy?

2. Through what incremental steps did the Johnson administration involve the United States ever more deeply in Vietnam? What was its major goal in Vietnam?

3. What domestic social movements emerged during America's longest war? How did they seek to change U.S. political culture and the direction of public policy? What role did commercial media play in the "movement of movements"?

4. What helped to make the single year of 1968, even as it was still unfolding, seem such an important time in the history of America's Longest War and of the Sixties?

5. Why did the polarization that had developed over the 1960s continue into the 1970s? What foreign and domestic events contributed to the continued polarization?

6. What were the major aims of U.S. foreign policy during the presidency of Richard Nixon? How successful was the Nixon administration in carrying out these policies?

7. How did the constitutional controversies of the early 1970s lead the nation into a crisis of governance? How did this crisis ultimately undermine Richard Nixon's presidency and force his resignation?

CRITICAL THINKING QUESTIONS

1. What long-term repercussions did America's longest war exact on America's economy, social fabric, culture, and foreign policy?

2. Great Society proposals reinvigorated long-term debates over the extension of government power and over definitions of civil and personal liberties. What roles did issues of race, gender, and the distribution of wealth and income figure in these debates?

3. Why was the era of America's longest war marked by so much protest and unrest? How would the polarization of views during that era continue to affect how people saw the history and future of the United States?

IDENTIFICATIONS

Review your understanding of the following key terms, people, and events for this chapter (terms in bold in text are included in the Glossary).

Civil Rights Act of 1964, p. 802
Freedom Summer, p. 803
Barry Goldwater, p. 803
Great Society, p. 805
Immigration and Nationality Act of 1965, p. 805
Voting Rights Act of 1965, p. 805
Gulf of Tonkin Resolution, p. 806
General William Westmoreland, p. 808
New Left, p. 811
counterculture, p. 812
Black Power, p. 814
Malcolm X, p. 814
Civil Rights Act of 1968, p. 816
Tet Offensive, p. 817
Senator Eugene McCarthy, p. 818
Richard Milhous Nixon, p. 819
Family Assistance Plan (FAP), p. 821
Equal Rights Amendment (ERA), p. 823
Roe **v.** *Wade* **(1973)**, p. 824
stagflation, p. 825
Détente, p. 825
Nixon Doctrine, p. 826
My Lai Incident, p. 826
Watergate, p. 828

SUGGESTED READINGS

On policy making in the 1960s, see, again, **C. Calvin Mackenzie and Robert Weisbrot**, *The Liberal Hour: Washington and the Politics of Change in the 1960s* (2008). The best biographies of Lyndon Johnson include **Robert J. Dallek,** *Flawed Giant: Lyndon Johnson and His Times, 1961–1973* (1998) and **Randall B. Woods,** *LBJ: Architect of American Ambition* (2006).

The many outstanding histories of U.S. involvement in Vietnam include **Mark Philip Bradley,** *Vietnam at War* (2009); **Mark Atwood Lawrence,** *The Vietnam War: A Concise International History*, (2008), and **George Herring,** *America's Longest War: The United States and Vietnam, 1950–1975* (rev. ed., 2001).

The following books offer an introduction to the "movement of movements" during the 1960s: **Terry Anderson,** *The Movement and the Sixties: Protest in America From Greensboro to Wounded Knee* (1996); **Robert Self,** *American Babylon: Race and the Struggle for Postwar Oakland* (2003); **Thomas J. Sugrue,** *Sweet Land of Liberty: The Forgotten Struggle for Civil Rights in the North* (2008); and **Peniel E. Joseph, ed.,** *Neighborhood Rebels: Black Power at the Local Level* (2010). The year of 1968 is the subject of numerous volumes, including **Mark Kurlansky, *1968: The Year that Rocked the World*** (2003).

On the transition from the late 1960s to early 1970s, see **Andreas Hillen, *1973 Nervous Breakdown: Watergate, Warhol, and the Birth of Post-Sixties America*** (2006). On the riddle that was Richard Nixon, see **David Greenberg, *Nixon's Shadow: The History of an Image*** (2003). **Stanley**

I. Kutler, ed., *Abuse of Power: The New Nixon Tapes* (1997), provides evidence, in the president's own words, of Nixon's approach to politics and constitutional limitations. Other constitutional and legal issues can be followed in **John D. Skrentny, *The Minority Revolution*** (2002) and **Lucas A. Powe, Jr., *The Warren Court and American Politics*** (2000).

Visit the CourseMate website at www.cengagebrain.com for additional study tools and review materials for this chapter.

CHAPTER 30

© MCA/Universal Pictures-Courtesy: Everett Collection

Back to the Future

As president, Ronald Reagan seemed as fluent with the movie culture of the 1980s as with that from his own Hollywood past. His 1986 State of the Union Address invoked a line from *Back to the Future* (1985)—"Where we're going, we don't need roads"—to underscore his faith that reliance on the nation's history of technological innovation would ensure its future. Several quips from this same movie, which featured time travel between 1985 and 1955, also played on Reagan's own unorthodox path from the Silver Screen to the White House.

Uncertain Times, 1974–1992

T HE NATIONAL GOVERNMENT continually expanded its power following the onset of the Second World War. Most Americans supported increasing military and intelligence capabilities and using domestic programs to cushion against economic downturns and assist needy families.

Events of the 1960s and early 1970s, particularly Vietnam and Watergate, however, shook faith in government. Secrecy, corruption, and economic problems bred further disillusionment. During the 1970s and 1980s Americans debated how to respond to an aging industrial economy, a ballooning federal deficit, and a beleaguered social welfare system. Did the country need new governmental programs, or might conditions improve if Washington reduced its role?

Disagreement extended to foreign policy. Should the United States minimize anticommunism to pursue other goals, as Democratic president Jimmy Carter (1977–81) initially urged, or should it wage the Cold War even more vigorously, as his successor, Republican Ronald Reagan (1981–89), advocated? After 1989, when the Cold War ended unexpectedly, the United States needed to find a foreign policy for a post-Cold War world, a task that fell to the post-Reagan generation of national leaders.

Meanwhile, the "movement of movements," a legacy of the 1960s, refused to fade away. Social movements associated with women's rights, gay rights, and racial and ethnic identities affected how Americans saw themselves and their nation's future. Some of the goals of these movements, however, met strident opposition from the New Right that had helped build Reagan's popularity. During these years, the polarization of American politics that had become so evident during the Vietnam War and Watergate eras deepened and broadened, sparking new controversies over issues such as abortion, taxation, affirmative action, and environmental regulations.

Searching for Direction, 1974–1980
A Faltering Economy
Welfare and Energy Initiatives
Negotiation and Confrontation
    in Foreign Policy
The New Right

The Reagan Revolution, 1981–1992
The Election of 1980
Supply-Side Economics
Curtailing Unions, Regulations,
    and Welfare
Reagan to Bush

**Renewing and Ending
the Cold War**
The Defense Buildup
Deploying Military Power
The Iran-*Contra* Controversy
The Cold War Eases
Post-Cold War Policy and the
    Persian Gulf War
The Election of 1992

The Politics of Social Movements
Women's Issues
Sexual Politics
Activism Among African
    Americans
Activism Among American Indians
Activism in Spanish-Speaking
    Communities
Activism Among Asian Americans
Anti-Government Activism

Searching for Direction, 1974–1980

Q
How did the legacies of the Vietnam War and Watergate help shape U.S. politics in the decade that followed?

When Richard Nixon resigned in August 1974, **Gerald R. Ford**, his vice president, moved from one office to which voters had never elected him to another, the presidency. Emphasizing his long career in the House of Representatives, Ford promised to "heal the land," but he achieved limited success. A genial, unpretentious former college football star, Ford preferred that his public appearances be accompanied by the fight song of his alma mater, the University of Michigan, rather than "Hail to the Chief." He tried to present his administration as an updated version of the "modern Republicanism" of the 1950s, but this effort quickly foundered. His appointment of Nelson Rockefeller as vice president infuriated GOP conservatives, and his pardoning of former president Nixon, in September 1974, angered almost everyone. Ford's approval rating skidded downward, and his presidency proved to be short lived.

Ford nearly lost the GOP's 1976 presidential nomination. Conservative Republicans rallied behind Ronald Reagan, who ignited his effort by campaigning as a "true conservative" owing nothing to Washington insiders. Ford had already won just enough delegates in the early primaries, however, to eke out a narrow first-ballot victory at the Republican Party's national convention.

The Democrats did turn to an outsider, **James Earl (Jimmy) Carter**. A retired naval officer, engineer, peanut farmer, and former governor of Georgia, Carter campaigned by stressing personal character. He highlighted his small-town roots and his Southern Baptist faith. To balance the ticket, he picked Senator Walter Mondale of Minnesota as his running mate. In November of 1976 Carter won a narrow victory over Ford.

Carter's election rested on a transitory coalition. He carried every southern state except Virginia, running well among both whites who belonged to fundamentalist and evangelical churches and African Americans. Carter also courted former antiwar activists by promising to pardon most Vietnam-era draft resisters. Walter Mondale's appeal helped capture the Democratic strongholds of New York, Pennsylvania, and Ohio. The election was close, however, and voter turnout hit its lowest mark (54 percent) since the end of the Second World War.

Jimmy Carter's lack of a popular mandate and his outsider status proved serious handicaps. After leaving government, Carter reflected on his difficulties: "I had a different way of governing. . . . I was a southerner, a born-again Christian, a Baptist, a newcomer." Moreover, Carter was caught between advisers who, on the one hand, claimed that the national government exercised too much power and, on the other, argued that Washington did too little to address domestic and foreign problems. His policies often seemed hesitant and inconsistent.

The 865-day presidency of Ford and the one-term administration of Carter reflected the uncertainties of post-Vietnam

CHRONOLOGY

1974	Nixon resigns and Ford becomes president ◆ Ford soon pardons Nixon
1975	South Vietnam falls to North Vietnam ◆ Ford asserts U.S. power in *Mayaguez* incident
1976	Jimmy Carter elected president ◆ OPEC sharply raises oil prices
1978	Carter helps negotiate Camp David peace accords on Middle East
1979	Soviet Union invades Afghanistan ◆ *Sandinistas* come to power in Nicaragua ◆ U.S. hostages seized in Iran
1980	Reagan elected president ◆ U.S. hostages in Iran released
1981	Reagan tax cut passed
1983	U.S. troops removed from Lebanon ◆ Reagan announces SDI ("Star Wars") program
1984	Reagan defeats Walter Mondale
1986	Reagan administration rocked by revelation of Iran-*Contra* affair
1988	George H. W. Bush defeats Michael Dukakis in presidential election ◆ Congress enacts Indian Gaming Regulation Act
1989	Communist regimes in Eastern Europe collapse ◆ Berlin Wall falls ◆ Cold War, in effect, ends
1990	Bush angers conservative Republicans by agreeing to a tax increase
1991	Bush orchestrates Persian Gulf War against Iraq
1992	Bill Clinton defeats Bush

and post-Watergate America. The sense of national crisis seemed unrelenting, as politicians and citizens alike attempted to cope with a staggering economy, disruptive energy shortages, and sensationalized foreign challenges.

A Faltering Economy

Economic problems dominated the domestic side of Ford's caretaker presidency. Upon assuming the presidency after Nixon's resignation, Ford touted a program called "Whip

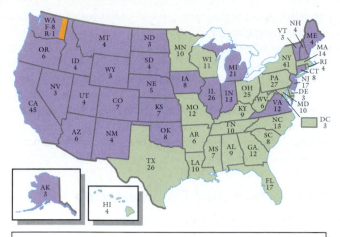

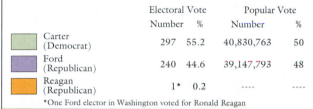

		Electoral Vote		Popular Vote	
		Number	%	Number	%
	Carter (Democrat)	297	55.2	40,830,763	50
	Ford (Republican)	240	44.6	39,147,793	48
	Reagan (Republican)	1*	0.2	----	----

*One Ford elector in Washington voted for Ronald Reagan

Map 30.1 Presidential Election, 1976. This map shows the low voter turnout and the very close election that made Jimmy Carter president. Notice how Carter, from Georgia, drew votes from Southern states.

Confronting Urban Decay in the 1970s. Some of financially strapped New York City's most pressing problems during the 1970s were in the South Bronx area. Here, President Jimmy Carter (in the center) poses with his Housing and Urban Development Secretary and New York's Mayor in front of several of the thousands of buildings that had fallen victim to decay, neglect, and arson. This widely circulated photo was intended to signal that national and local officials hoped to devise rebuilding programs for urban areas such as this.

Inflation Now" (WIN), which included a one-year surcharge on income taxes and cuts in federal spending as solutions. After both unemployment and prices still crept higher, Ford conceded WIN to be a loser. During 1975 unemployment reached 8.5 percent, and the inflation rate topped 9 percent.

Meanwhile, Ford clashed with the Democratic-controlled Congress over how to deal with the ever-rising price of oil and with stagflation, which combined economic stagnation with price inflation. Democrats tended to favor programs that might stimulate employment and economic growth; Republicans leaned toward policies that cut government spending. Ford, who vetoed nearly 40 spending bills while in office, finally agreed to a congressional economic package forged from an uneasy compromise of diverse goals. It included a tax cut, an increase in unemployment benefits, an unbalanced federal budget, and limited controls on oil prices. Democrats charged that Ford could not implement coherent programs of his own. Many Republicans complained that he could not stand up to congressional Democrats.

Once Carter took office, the problems of oil prices and stagflation only worsened. Carter pledged to lower both unemployment and inflation, rekindle economic growth, and balance the federal budget (which showed a deficit of about $70 billion in 1976). He pushed for tax cuts, increased public works spending, and pro-growth Federal Reserve Board policies. These measures, however, seemed to further aggravate matters. By 1980 the economy had virtually stopped expanding; unemployment (after temporarily dipping) continued to rise; and inflation topped an alarming 13 percent. Most voters told pollsters that their economic fortunes had deteriorated while Carter was in office.

Economic distress spread beyond individuals. New York City, beset by long-term economic problems and short-term fiscal mismanagement, faced bankruptcy. Private bankers and public officials had to secure congressional "bailout" legislation that granted special loan guarantees to America's largest city. Its troubles were hardly unique. According to one estimate, Chicago lost 200,000 manufacturing jobs during the 1970s. Bricks from demolished buildings in St. Louis became one of that city's leading products. Soaring unemployment, rising crime rates, deteriorating downtowns, and shrinking tax revenues afflicted most urban areas, even as inflation further eroded the buying power of city budgets.

Conservative economists and business interests charged that domestic programs favored by most congressional Democrats contributed to economic distress. Increasing the minimum wage and enforcing stringent safety and antipollution regulations, they argued, drove up the cost of doing business and forced companies to raise prices to consumers. During his last two years in office, Carter seemed to agree with some of this analysis. Defying many Democrats in Congress, he cut spending for social programs, sought to reduce capital gains taxes to encourage investment, and inaugurated the process of "deregulating" various industries, beginning with the financial and transportation sectors. This policy of deregulation would become a major emphasis that Republican administrations would pursue after 1980.

Welfare and Energy Initiatives

As the economic crisis spread during his presidency, Carter puzzled over how to respond to people's distress. His staff differed over whether to propose increasing monetary assistance to low-income families or to advocate federal spending to create several million public service jobs. A proposed compromise failed in Congress, although Carter did expand The Comprehensive Employment and Training Act (CETA) of 1973, an act that offered temporary public service jobs to people, especially students, with low incomes. Despite economic hardships, no agreement could be forged on behalf of a broad vision to overhaul the nation's social welfare system. Republicans tended to argue on behalf of less government spending on welfare programs; Democrats generally favored greater assistance to the under employed.

The president pushed harder on energy issues. The United States obtained 90 percent of its energy from fossil fuels, much of it from imported petroleum. In 1978, as in 1973, the Organization of Petroleum Exporting Countries (OPEC), a cartel dominated by oil-rich nations in the Middle East, dramatically raised the price of crude oil and precipitated acute worldwide shortages. As gasoline became expensive and scarce, drivers denounced high prices. Long lines at the gas pumps around the country sparked anger both at OPEC and at the administration. Carter, in response, promised to make the United States less dependent on imported fossil fuel.

The president had earlier charged James Schlesinger, head of a new Department of Energy, with developing a plan. Schlesinger outlined ambitious goals to decrease U.S. reliance on foreign sources: (1) expand domestic energy production through tax incentives and deregulation; (2) levy new taxes to discourage consumption; (3) foster conservation; and (4) promote non-petroleum energy sources, especially coal and nuclear power. Neither Carter nor Schlesinger consulted Congress or even some key members of the president's own administration. Instead, in early 1977, Carter announced that the **energy crisis** represented "the moral equivalent of war," and he abruptly advanced a complex plan that included more than 100 interrelated provisions.

Congress quickly rejected it. Gas and oil interests opposed higher taxes. Consumer activists blocked deregulation. Environmentalists charged that greater use of coal would increase air pollution. Carter, nonetheless, continued to press for energy conservation; for development of renewable sources, such as solar and wind-generated energy; and for greater use of nuclear power.

The nuclear option generated especially sharp controversy. In theory, nuclear reactors could provide inexpensive, almost limitless amounts of energy. The cost of building and maintaining them, however, far exceeded original estimates and posed safety risks. In 1979 a serious reactor malfunction at **Three Mile Island**, Pennsylvania, along with a popular movie about a similar event (*The China Syndrome*) heightened fears of a nuclear-reactor meltdown. Responding to growing concerns, power companies canceled orders for new reactors, and the nuclear power industry's expansion halted.

Meanwhile, OPEC oil prices continued to rise, from about $3.60 a barrel in 1971 to nearly $36 a decade later, at the end of Carter's presidency. Such dramatic price increases in a basic commodity that fueled the American economy helped drive the damaging stagflation of the 1970s. Although few Americans agreed on how to solve this oil crisis and America's broader energy problems, many lost confidence in Carter's leadership.

Negotiation and Confrontation in Foreign Policy

Foreign policy lurched along a similar uncertain course during the mid and late 1970s. Upon assuming office in late 1974, President Ford pledged a renewal of U.S. military support to the government in South Vietnam, if North Vietnam ever directly threatened its survival. The antiwar mood in the United States and battlefield conditions in Vietnam, however, made fulfilling this commitment impossible. North Vietnam's armies stormed across the South in March 1975, and Congress, relieved that U.S. troops had finally been withdrawn after the 1973 Paris peace accords, refused any new American involvement. Conducting their last mission in Vietnam, U.S. helicopters scrambled to airlift U.S. officials and top-ranking South Vietnamese officers off the American embassy's rooftop.

Spring 1975 brought new communist victories in Indochina. In early April, Khmer Rouge forces in Cambodia drove a U.S.-backed government from the capital of Phnom Penh, and on April 30, 1975, North Vietnamese troops finally overran the South Vietnamese capital of Saigon, renaming it Ho Chi Minh City. Debate over U.S. policy in Indochina became especially heated in the months that followed.

Within this charged atmosphere, Ford tried to demonstrate U.S military power. In May 1975 a contingent of Khmer Rouge boarded a U.S. ship, the *Mayaguez*, taking its crew hostage. Secretary of State Henry Kissinger declared that it was time to "look ferocious" and convinced Ford to order bombing strikes against Cambodia and a rescue operation for the crew. This military response, coupled with Chinese pressure on the Khmer Rouge, secured the release of the *Mayaguez* and its crew. Although the *Mayaguez* rescue cost more lives than it saved, Ford's approval ratings briefly shot up. His other foreign policy initiatives, which included extending Nixon's policy of détente with the Soviet Union and pursuing peace negotiations in the Middle East, achieved little.

Carter promised new directions away from the Nixon-Ford record on foreign policy. On his first day in office, he granted amnesty to most Vietnam-era draft resisters. He soon declared that he would not display an "inordinate fear of Communism" and would endorse human-rights initiatives. After four years, however, Carter's foreign policy initiatives seemed in as much disarray as were his economic and energy policies.

Carter had little background in foreign policy. Furthermore, his top aides—Secretary of State Cyrus Vance and national security adviser Zbigniew Brzezinski—pursued contradictory agendas. Vance preferred quiet diplomacy and avoidance of confrontations, while Brzezinski favored a hard line, anti-Soviet policy with an emphasis on military muscle. Pulled in divergent directions, Carter's foreign policy seemed to waffle. Carter himself favored settling disputes through negotiation, not military threats, and he elevated the promotion of human rights overseas into one of his most important priorities.

Carter's faith in negotiation and in his own skills as a facilitator yielded some successes. On the issue of the Panama Canal, the object of diplomatic negotiations for 13 years, Carter secured treaties that granted Panama increasing authority over the waterway and full control in 2000. Carter convinced skeptical senators, whose votes he needed in order to ratify any treaty, that the canal was no longer an economic or strategic necessity.

Carter's personal touch also emerged during the **Camp David Peace Talks of 1978**. Relations between Egypt and Israel had been strained since the Yom Kippur War of 1973, when Israel repelled an Egyptian attack and seized the Sinai Peninsula and territory along the West Bank (of the Jordan River). Reviving earlier Republican efforts to broker a peace settlement, Carter brought Menachem Begin and Anwar Sadat, leaders of Israel and Egypt, respectively, to the presidential retreat at Camp David. After 13 days of difficult bargaining, the three leaders announced a framework for further negotiations and a peace treaty. Middle East tensions hardly vanished, but the accords reached at Camp David kept alive high-level discussions, lowered the level of acrimony between Egypt and Israel, and bound both nations to the United States through Carter's promises of economic aid.

In Asia, the Carter administration built on Nixon's initiative, expanding economic and cultural relations with the communist government in China. The United States finally established formal diplomatic ties with the People's Republic on New Year's Day 1979.

Carter's foreign policy became best known for its emphasis on **human rights**. Carter argued that Cold War alliances with repressive dictatorships, even in the name of anticommunism, undermined U.S. influence in the world. The policy, however, proved difficult to orchestrate. His administration continued to support some harsh dictators, such as Ferdinand Marcos in the Philippines. Moreover, rhetoric about human rights helped justify uprisings against longstanding dictator-allies in Nicaragua and Iran. Revolutions in these countries, fueled by resentment against the United States, brought anti-American regimes to power and presented Carter with difficult choices.

In Nicaragua, the *Sandinista* movement toppled the dictatorship of Anastasio Somoza, which the United States had long supported. The *Sandinistas*, initially a coalition of moderate democrats and leftists, soon tilted toward a militant Marxism and began to expropriate private property. Republican critics charged that Carter's policies had given a green light to communism throughout Central America, and some pledged to oust the *Sandinistas*.

If events in Nicaragua brought dilemmas to Carter, those in Iran and Afghanistan all but shattered his uncertain presidency. The United States had steadfastly supported the dictatorial Shah Reza Pahlavi, who had reigned in oil-rich Iran since an American-supported coup in 1953. The shah's overthrow in the **Iranian revolution of January 1979**, by a movement dominated by Islamic fundamentalists, signaled a massive repudiation of U.S. influence. When the White House allowed the deposed shah to enter the United States for medical treatment in November 1979, Iranians seized the U.S. embassy in Tehran and 66 American hostages. Iran demanded the return of the shah in exchange for the hostages' release.

In response, Carter turned to tough talk, levied economic sanctions against Iran, and—over the objections of Cyrus Vance (who subsequently resigned)—sent a combat team to rescue the hostages. This military effort ended in an embarrassing failure. Carter's critics cited this "hostage crisis" as conclusive proof of his incompetence and used the issue relentlessly in the next presidential campaign. After Carter's defeat in the 1980 election, diplomatic efforts finally freed the hostages, but the United States and Iran remained at odds.

Criticism of Carter also focused on the Soviet Union's 1979 invasion of Afghanistan, a move primarily sparked by Soviet fear of the growing influence of Islamic fundamentalists along its borders. Carter responded in a nonmilitary manner.

© Bettmann/CORBIS

American Hostages in Iran.
The Iranian government presents American hostages to the press under a banner protesting Carter's decision to admit the shah into the United States to obtain medical treatment.

He halted grain exports to the Soviet Union (angering his farm constituency), organized a boycott of the 1980 Summer Olympic Games in Moscow, withdrew a new Strategic Arms Limitation Treaty (SALT) from the Senate, and revived registration for the military draft. Still, Republicans (along with some Democrats) charged Carter with allowing U.S. power and prestige to decline. They saw Soviet Union embarked on a new campaign of expanding communism, attempting to add new clients not only in Central America and in Afghanistan but also in other areas of the world.

For a time, after Senator Edward Kennedy of Massachusetts entered the 1980 presidential primaries, it seemed as if Carter's own Democratic Party might deny him a second term. Although Kennedy's challenge eventually fizzled, it popularized anti-Carter themes that Republicans would gleefully embrace in the election of 1980. "It's time to say no more hostages, no more high interest rates, no more high inflation, and no more Jimmy Carter," was Kennedy's standard stump speech.

The New Right

By 1976, the idea of preventing another Carter or another Kennedy presidency animated a diverse coalition of conservatives: a **New Right**. This broadly based movement succeeded in holding together several different constituencies. The already disparate group that had initially gathered around William F. Buckley's *National Review* during the 1950s provided one of these constituencies. Even as Buckley continued to use his magazine to push conservative ideas, he reached out to new converts through television. His long-running interview show, *Firing Line*, debuted on PBS in 1971 (and ran for another 28 years). The economist Milton Friedman—a frequent Buckley guest, 1976 Nobel laureate, and creator of a PBS series touting free-market economic principles—provided another important link between the conservatism of the 1950s and 1970s. In addition, many of the then-youthful conservatives who had energized Barry Goldwater's 1964 presidential campaign, such as Patrick Buchanan, came to the New Right after having worked in Richard Nixon's administration.

In contrast, the "neoconservative" (or "neocon") wing of the New Right of the 1970s had generally identified with Democrats, rather than Republicans, during the 1950s and much of the 1960s. Fiercely anticommunist, writers and academics such as Norman Podhoretz, Gertrude Himmelfarb, Jeane Kirkpatrick, and Irving Kristol saw too many Democrats criticizing Lyndon Johnson and then rallying behind George McGovern and his theme of "Come Home America." Fearful that the Democratic Party might abandon a strong anticommunist stance, neoconservatives also viewed most domestic movements of the 1960s, particularly those displaying countercultural values, as threatening the social stability and intellectual values they admired. This initial generation of neoconservatives, often the offspring of European-Jewish immigrants, also complained that U.S. foreign policy, even under Richard Nixon and Henry Kissinger, failed to support Israel strongly enough.

Conservative business leaders provided another important New Right constituency. Convinced that anti-corporate professors and students dominated most colleges and universities,

business magnates such as Joseph Coors, of the Colorado brewing family, placed at least portions of their fortunes at the service of their convictions. In their view, new regulatory legislation accepted by the Nixon administration, especially measures dealing with workplace safety issues and environmental concerns, threatened "economic freedom" and "entrepreneurial liberty." If colleges and universities could not provide intellectual support for conservative perspectives, then businesses should create counter-institutions in the form of right-leaning think tanks. Conservative business leaders and their philanthropic foundations generously funded existing research institutions, such as the American Enterprise Institute (founded in 1943), and created new ones, such as The Heritage Foundation (established in 1973).

Money from New Right businesspeople also financed lobbying efforts, such as those mounted by the Business Roundtable (created in 1973) and The Committee on the Present Danger (CPD). This bipartisan group, which took its name and much of its leadership from a similarly named group of the 1950s, argued that the foreign policy establishment of the 1970s, including "realists" such as Henry Kissinger, underestimated the threat that the Soviet Union still posed to the United States. The CPD's successes included persuading Gerald Ford's appointee as CIA director, George H. W. Bush, to order a review of the CIA's assessment of the communist menace by a group of outside analysts. Ultimately known as "Team B" and dominated by people close to the CPD, this panel warned of CIA complacency in the face of Soviet aggressiveness.

Groups such as the CPD also operated effectively outside of the Washington, D.C., beltway. In 1975, activists who had worked for Goldwater's 1964 campaign formed the National Conservative Political Action Committee (NCPAC), the first of many similar organizations aimed at organizing at the grassroots. Initiatives by the NCPAC backed conservative political candidates and advocated a wide range of policies. Forging a political strategy aimed at defending "family values," they opposed policies identified with feminism, such as legalized abortion, and with LGBT (lesbian, gay, bisexual, transgender) lifestyles.

The New Right of the 1970s also attracted grassroots support from Protestants in fundamentalist and evangelical churches. People from these religious groups had generally stayed clear of overtly partisan politics since the 1920s but continued to express concern, exemplified in the work of Billy Graham's organization, about public issues that involved spiritual and social matters. Already angered by Supreme Court decisions that seemed to eliminate religious prayers from public schools, many expressed greater outrage over *Roe* v. *Wade* (1973), the landmark abortion ruling. Reaching out to

Roe v. Wade (1973)

anti-abortion Catholics, people whom most members of southern Protestant congregations would have shunned a generation earlier, a "Religious Right" slowly took shape. The Reverend Jerry Falwell of the Thomas Road Baptist Church and The Old Time Gospel Hour television ministry declared that *Roe* showed the necessity of political action. Anti-religious elites in Washington "have been imposing morality on us for the last fifty years," Falwell proclaimed.

Leaders of the Religious Right insisted that sacred values should actively shape political policy making. A clear separation between church and state, a guiding principle of constitutionalism during the era of Earl Warren's Supreme Court, struck the Religious Right as a violation of a right specifically mentioned in the First Amendment: the "free exercise of religion." Particularly in the South, conservatives embarked on a lengthy legal struggle to prevent the Internal Revenue Service from denying tax-exempt status to the private Christian colleges and academies that opposed racial integration. Challenging older constitutional precedents against state aid to religious institutions, they also urged that government should use tax monies to help fund church-centered education and "faith-based" social programming. Most spokespeople for the Religious Right championed foreign policies that maximized the use of U.S. military power, especially on behalf of Israel. Protestants who embraced "dispensational premillennialism," the belief that the Second Coming of Christ would occur in their lifetimes, saw the survival of a Jewish state in the Middle East as crucial to the future they expected to unfold according to Biblical prophesy.

Especially in the South, the process of a political switch to the GOP could almost seem comparable to that of a religious conversion. In 1976 most evangelicals and fundamentalists from the South, including Jerry Falwell, supported Jimmy Carter. His religious values made him seem less committed to the *Roe* decision than Gerald Ford, whose spouse, Betty Ford, often identified herself with women's issues. Very soon, however, Falwell and others on the Religious Right began realigning their politics with those of the GOP's conservative bloc, placing their growing movement behind a refashioned Republican party under the leadership of Ronald Reagan.

The Reagan Revolution, 1981–1992

FOCUS QUESTION To what extent did Ronald Reagan's administration represent a victory for the New Right agenda in both domestic and foreign policy?

Ronald Reagan courted the New Right on national security, economic, and social issues. He used the hostage crisis with Iran as a symbol of Carter's failures, while his revitalized anticommunist rhetoric called for a stronger military posture and greater defense spending. At the same time, a taxpayer revolt that had swept through California politics during the late 1970s provided a model for Reagan's attack on "tax-and-spend" policymaking at the federal level. (The situation was ironic, however, because California's tax revolt had emerged in response to tax increases adopted while Reagan was the state's governor.) Across the country, people increasingly responded to the tax-reduction message. In addition to urging large tax cuts, Reagan opposed abortion rights, advocated prayer in school, and extolled conservative family values. Even Jimmy Carter's own Southern Baptists, who had rallied behind him in 1976, along with born-again Christians across the country, began flocking to Reagan.

The Election of 1980

Easily capturing the Republican nomination, and anointing one of his defeated rivals, George H. W. Bush, as a running mate, Ronald Reagan advanced an optimistic vision of a rejuvenated America. Punctuating his speeches with quips inspired by Hollywood movies, he stressed his opposition to domestic social spending and high taxes while promising support for a stronger national defense. To underscore the nation's economic problems under Carter, Reagan asked repeatedly, "Are you better off now than you were four years ago?" Quickly offering his own answer, Reagan cited what he called a "misery index," which added the rate of inflation to the rate of unemployment.

Reagan also seized issues that the Democratic Party had long regarded its own: economic growth and increased personal consumption. In 1979 one of Jimmy Carter's advisers had gloomily portrayed the nation's economic and energy problems as so severe that there was "no way we can avoid a decline in our standard of living. All we can do is adapt to it." In contrast, Reagan promised that sharp tax cuts and policies to increase the supply of oil would restore robust economic expansion.

The Reagan-Bush team swept to victory. Although it gained only slightly more than 50 percent of the popular vote (John Anderson, a middle-of-the-road Republican who ran as an independent, won about 7 percent), the GOP ticket captured the Electoral College tally by a 489 to 49 margin. Moreover, Republicans took away 12 Democratic Senate seats, gaining control of the Senate, though not the House of Representatives.

Although conservative think tanks deluged the Reagan administration with policy suggestions, the president focused

	Electoral Vote		Popular Vote	
	Number	%	Number	%
Carter (Democrat)	49	9.1	35,483,883	41
Reagan (Republican)	489	90.9	43,904,153	51
Anderson (Independent)	----	----	5,720,060	7

© Cengage Learning

Map 30.2 Presidential Election, 1980. Compare this map with the one showing the election of Jimmy Carter four years earlier. What factors might explain such a sudden downturn in Democratic fortunes?

on three major priorities: cutting federal taxes, reducing the governmental regulatory structure, and boosting national security capabilities.

Supply-Side Economics

To justify cutting taxes, Reagan touted **supply-side economics**. This economic theory held that tax reductions targeted toward investors and businesses would stimulate production, create jobs, and ameliorate the economic stagnation of the 1970s. Reagan pushed a tax-reduction plan through Congress in 1981. Many Democrats, who had supported more limited tax cuts during Carter's presidency, endorsed the plan. At the same time, the Federal Reserve Board under Paul Volker, a Carter appointee, kept interest rates high to drive down inflation.

In the short run, high interest rates continued to choke off growth, and economic conditions deteriorated. A severe economic downturn in 1981 and 1982 sent the Reagan's approval ratings diving below 40 percent, and the Republican Party experienced losses in the off-year election of 1982. Slowly, however, inflation moderated, and the economy rebounded to enter a period of non-inflationary growth. According to one study, the economy added nearly 17 million new jobs; figures on real income, after having declined throughout the 1970s, began to rise; and inflation dropped from double digits to around 2 percent. Although unemployment figures did not fall as sharply, Reagan's supporters hailed a "Reagan revolution" that had rescued the country from stagflation.

This revival and its causes, however, were controversial. Reagan had not matched tax cuts with sufficient spending reductions, and budget deficits soared. Reagan constantly inveighed against deficits and "big spenders," but his eight years in Washington, even after some of the early tax reductions were rolled back, saw annual deficits triple to nearly $300 billion. To finance such deficit spending, the United States borrowed abroad and piled up the largest foreign debt of any nation in the world at that time. Reagan's revolution, critical economists charged, stimulated recovery through unbalanced budgets but courted long-term problems with federal deficits and trade imbalances.

Moreover, the surge of the Reagan era prosperity brought upward mobility for some but growing uncertainty for others. Partisans of the Reagan revolution promised that its effects would ultimately "trickle down" and benefit everyone. Its detractors, however, countered that the country was developing a "Swiss-cheese" economy, in which many groups were falling through the holes. Farmers in the Midwest watched falling crop prices hamper their repayment of high-interest loans they had contracted during the inflation-ridden 1970s. Mortgage foreclosures, reminiscent of the 1930s, hit the farm states, and the ripple effect decimated the economies of small towns across the country. Urban areas fared even worse. Federal spending for urban areas declined, even as cities faced growing unemployment, population loss, and falling tax revenues. Federal funds for public transit and housing declined even as job-training programs such as CETA lost funding. One historian estimates that urban America bore two-thirds of the cost of Reagan-era budget cuts. The minimum wage, when adjusted for inflation, also declined in value during Reagan's presidency.

© Eve Arnold/Magnum Photos, Inc.

Selling off the Farm. Hard economic times during the early 1980s forced the liquidation of many small, family-run farms. Here, neighbors gather at a farm where everything, including a well-used pitchfork, headed to the auction block.

For African Americans, this mixed picture proved especially clear. The number of African American families earning a solid middle-class income, for example, more than doubled between 1970 and 1990. People with educational credentials and marketable skills made significant economic gains, and African American college graduates could expect incomes comparable to those of their white classmates. Partly as a result of affirmative action hiring plans put in place by the Nixon and Carter administrations, many could afford to leave problem-plagued inner-city neighborhoods. The situation looked different, however, for those who remained persistently unemployed, perhaps trapped in declining urban centers. At the end of the 1980s one-third of all African American families lived in poverty, and the number earning less than $15,000 per year had doubled since 1970. In inner cities, fewer than half of African American children were completing high school, and more than 60 percent were unemployed. The gap between the well off and the disadvantaged widened during the 1980s.

Curtailing Unions, Regulations, and Welfare

Meanwhile, Reagan pursued his second major goal: cutting back the role of the federal government in supporting labor unions and regulatory structures.

In 1981 Reagan fired the nation's air traffic controllers after their union refused to halt a nationwide strike. The action portended more aggressive anti-union strategies that both his administration and business interests would pursue during the 1980s. The percentage of unionized workers fell to just 16 percent by the end of Reagan's presidency. Recognizing the balance of power tilting against them, workers increasingly turned away from strikes as an economic weapon.

Reagan had entered office promising to tame OPEC by encouraging the development of new sources of supply. Rejecting environmentalists' calls to decrease U.S. dependence on fossil fuels by promotion of renewable sources, Reagan and his successor, George H. W. Bush, pursued a "cheap oil" policy. The tapping of new oil fields at home and abroad, together with rivalries among OPEC's members, weakened the cartel's hold on the world market and reduced energy prices worldwide. Lower energy costs, in turn, helped moderate the inflationary pressures.

To oversee environmental issues, Reagan appointed James Watt, an outspoken critic of governmental regulation, as secretary of the interior. Watt supported the so-called "sagebrush rebellion," in which western states demanded fewer federal restrictions on the use of public lands within their borders. Particularly in the timber states of the Pacific Northwest, people hotly debated protection of endangered species, such as rare bird populations, if it interfered with lumber-related opportunities. Reagan's first two appointees to the Department of Energy actually proposed eliminating the cabinet office they headed—an idea that Congress blocked. In both the Interior and Energy departments, the White House relaxed enforcement of federal safety and environmental regulations.

Reagan's agenda for **deregulation** focused especially on the financial system. His economic advisers insisted that financial markets were largely self-regulating and self-correcting. Minimal governmental interference in the marketplace, they argued, would bring greater economic efficiencies and therefore greater prosperity overall. The Carter administration had previously pursued programs of deregulation especially in the transportation sector, and many Democrats in Congress now joined Republicans in crafting a looser environment for banks. Before the 1980s, state usury laws limited the interest rates that lending institutions could charge their clients and "Savings and Loan" (S & L) institutions issued home mortgages under carefully controlled rules. Several pieces of legislation in the 1980s, however, wiped away these and other regulations, and the banking sector rapidly consolidated and transformed. More credit became available to more people, as a new "subprime loan" industry boomed. But there were hazards.

During Reagan's second term, corruption and mismanagement in the financial industry increasingly appeared as toxic byproducts of deregulation. S & L companies had ventured into risky loans, particularly in real estate. Regulators and politicians ignored forecasts of an impending meltdown until bankruptcies began to cascade through the S & L industry, eventually forcing the closure of 747 institutions. Finally, in 1989, Congress created a bailout plan designed to save some S & Ls and to transfer assets from already failed institutions to solvent ones. The plan proved astronomically expensive, and taxpayers footed costs that eventually reached around $125 billion. Meanwhile, the process by which large, well-connected commercial banks purchased the remaining assets of bankrupt S & Ls at bargain-basement prices reeked of corruption and scandal. As a result of the S & L debacle of the 1980s, the banking industry went through a sudden, unplanned consolidation. Many people lost savings.

The Reagan administration also sought a somewhat more limited role for government in social welfare spending. It decreased funding for various kinds of public-benefit programs, particularly Aid to Families with Dependent Children (AFDC). The Family Support Act of 1988 pressured states to inaugurate work-training programs and to begin moving people, including mothers receiving AFDC payments, off the welfare rolls. Reductions in food stamps and other programs increased poverty rates and fell disproportionately on female-headed households and on children. By the end of the 1980s, one of every five children was growing up in a household where the income fell below the official poverty line.

The president nevertheless steadfastly rejected suggestions of eliminating the basic set of New Deal programs that he called a "social safety net." Specifically, he rejected calls for curtailing the Social Security or Medicare systems. During the 1970s Social Security payments had been "indexed" to automatically increase along with the rate of inflation. Larger Social Security checks, along with Medicare benefits, enabled millions of Americans over 65 to do relatively well during the Reagan years.

The Reagan administration also placed its stamp on the federal legal system, nudging it in a more conservative direction. Almost immediately, Reagan nominated a Supreme Court justice, Sandra Day O'Connor (the first woman to sit on the Court), who appeared to be a conservative. With the Republican Party controlling the Senate until 1986, Reagan also named prominent conservative jurists, such as Robert Bork and Antonin Scalia, to lower federal courts. The New Right, which had decried the "rights revolution" of the Warren Supreme Court, welcomed the influx of conservative judges. Civil libertarians, by contrast, complained that the federal courts were becoming less hospitable to the legal-constitutional arguments of criminal defendants, labor unions, and political dissenters.

In 1986 the resignation of Warren Burger allowed Reagan to elevate **William Rehnquist** to the position of chief justice and appoint Antonin Scalia, a staunch conservative, to replace Rehnquist as an associate justice. In 1987 however, the Senate, now with a Democratic majority following the 1986 elections, rebuffed Reagan's attempt to place Robert Bork, a particular favorite of the New Right, on the High Court. Bork's rejection enraged conservatives, some blaming Reagan for not working hard enough on Bork's behalf. Still, by 1990, because of retirements, about half of all federal judges had reached the bench during Ronald Reagan's presidency. Reagan also sought out staunch conservatives for non-judicial appointments. He staffed the Justice Department with young attorneys, such as John Roberts and Samuel Alito, who expressed a desire to help conservative judges whittle back Warren-era judicial precedents.

Despite sometimes sharp criticism, especially over the soaring federal deficit, the widening gap between rich and

Riding the Presidential Range. Ronald Reagan, a master of both imagery and rhetoric, could casually and effectively adopt poses indebted to the Hollywood westerns in which he had once appeared. Here, the septuagenarian president, decked out in denim, stars in a western-themed parade.

poor, and the role that government should play in regulation and welfare, Reagan remained popular. His genial optimism seemed unshakable. His smile, jokes, and confident air disarmed and inspired many. He even appeared to rebound quickly—although close observers noted a clear decline in his energies—after being shot by a would-be assassin in March 1981. No matter what problems beset his administration, criticism rarely stuck to Reagan, whom one frustrated Democrat dubbed the "Teflon president."

Reagan to Bush

Democrats continually underestimated Reagan's appeal—a miscalculation that doomed their 1984 presidential effort. Walter Mondale, Jimmy Carter's vice president, ran on a platform calling for "the eradication of discrimination in all aspects of American life" and for an expansion of social welfare programs. Mondale proposed higher taxes to fund this agenda and chose as his running mate Representative Geraldine Ferraro of New York, the first woman to stand for president or vice president on a major party ticket.

Republican campaign ads—often framed by the slogan "It's Morning Again in America"—portrayed a glowing landscape of bustling small towns and lush farmlands. They attacked

Mondale's support from labor unions and civil rights groups as a vestige of the "old politics" of "special interests" and his tax proposal as a return to the policies popularly associated with the stagflation of the 1970s. The 1984 presidential election ended with Mondale, who projected the opposite of charisma, carrying only his home state of Minnesota and the District of Columbia.

Reagan never lacked for critics during his second term. Even some of his New Right supporters charged that he was insufficiently zealous in promoting Bork's appointment, antiabortion efforts, and other causes. Still conservatives would increasingly hail Ronald Reagan as a giant of their movement. Indeed, the Reagan revolution succeeded in advancing a new Republican agenda that helped change the nation's political vocabulary. Democrats had once invoked "liberalism" to stand for governmental initiatives to stimulate the economy, promote greater equality, and advance liberty for all. Republicans, however, deployed the term "liberal" as a code word for wasteful social programs devised by a bloated federal government that gouged hardworking people and squandered their tax dollars. By contrast, the new Republican Party that coalesced behind Reagan advanced the term "conservative" to stand for economic growth through the curtailment of governmental power and support for traditional sociocultural values. By the end of Reagan's presidency, the once-dominant Democratic Party of the New Deal, Fair Deal, and Great Society confronted a strong and refashioned Republican Party.

In the election of 1988, the Reagan legacy fell to the president's heir-apparent, Vice President **George H. W. Bush**. Born into a wealthy Republican family and educated at Yale, Bush had prospered in the oil business, served in the House of Representatives, and headed the CIA. To court the New Right, decidedly lukewarm to his candidacy, he pledged "no new taxes" and chose Senator J. Danforth (Dan) Quayle, a youthful conservative from Indiana, as a running mate. Quayle would soon delight political comedians who highlighted his verbal blunders.

Governor Michael Dukakis of Massachusetts emerged as the Democratic presidential candidate. Hoping to distance himself from the disastrous Mondale-Ferraro effort in 1984, Dukakis avoided talk of new domestic programs and higher taxes. Instead, he pledged to bring competence and honesty to the White House.

Although Bush emerged the winner, Democrats retained control of both houses of Congress. The turnout was the lowest for any national election since 1924, and polls suggested that many voters remained unimpressed with either Bush or Dukakis.

Once in the White House, Bush began to lose crucial support. He angered New Right Republicans by agreeing to an increase in the minimum wage and by failing to veto a law that allowed for some affirmative action in the hiring women and people of color into occupations where they were underrepresented. The Religious Right detected tepid support from the president in its campaigns against abortion and in favor of religious prayers in public schools. Most important, in 1990 Bush broke his "no new taxes" campaign pledge. Taxation had emerged as one of the New Right's central issues, even though Reagan himself had raised taxes during his second term. When Bush agreed to an upward revision in tax rates, trying to deal with the still-rising federal deficit, the New Right bitterly denounced his decision.

Meanwhile, the Democratic-controlled Congress and the Republican-occupied White House deadlocked over how

HISTORY THROUGH FILM

The First Movie-Star President

Ronald Reagan began his presidency in Hollywood. The political career of the "Great Communicator" built on, rather than broke away from, his days in the entertainment industry. His media advisers could count on directing a seasoned professional. Reagan always knew where to stand; how to deliver lines effectively; how to convey emotions through both body language and dialogue; and when to melt into the background so that other players in the cast of his presidency might carry a crucial scene.

Several of Reagan's movies provided rehearsals for roles he would play in the White House. Initially, Reagan's opponents thought that his old film parts, particularly in *Bedtime for Bonzo* (1947), where he co-starred with a chimpanzee, would be political liabilities. Instead of disavowing his days in Hollywood, Reagan accentuated his fluency with film-related imagery. His efforts to cheer on the nation during the 1980s consciously invoked his favorite film role, that of the 1920s Notre Dame football star, George Gipp, who Reagan played in *Knute Rockne, All American* (1940). Similarly, when tilting with a Democratic-controlled Congress over tax policy, Reagan invoked Clint Eastwood's famous screen character "Dirty Harry," promising to shoot down any tax increase. "Go ahead, make my day," he taunted. On another occasion, he cited *Rambo* (1982), an action thriller set in post-1975 Vietnam as a possible blueprint for dealing with countries that had seized U.S. hostages. As he freely drew from Hollywood motion pictures, Reagan occasionally seemed unable to separate "reel" from "real" life. During one session with reporters, he referred to his own dog as "Lassie," the canine performer who had been Reagan's Hollywood contemporary during the 1940s and 1950s.

Life in Hollywood also provided a prologue to President Reagan's conservative policies. Early in his film career,

Ronald Reagan as the "Gipper" in *Knute Rockne, All American.*

Reagan appeared in four films as the same character, a government agent named "Brass Bancroft." In these B-grade thrillers, Reagan developed an image that he later deployed in politics: the action-oriented character who could distinguish (good) friends from (evil) foes. *Murder in the Air* (1940), one of the Brass Bancroft movies, even featured a science fiction-style "death ray" that resembled the SDI ("Star Wars") armaments that President Reagan would champion more than 40 years later.

Subsequent film roles refined his Hollywood image. Poor eyesight kept Reagan out of combat during the Second World War, but he served long hours as an Army Air Corps officer, producing movies in support of the war effort. He appeared in several films, such as *For God and Country* (1943), and more often provided upbeat voiceovers, once even sharing a soundtrack with President Franklin Roosevelt. He also starred, on loan from the Air Corps, in *This Is the Army* (1943), one of the most successful of wartime Hollywood's military-oriented musicals. After the war, Reagan increasingly directed his energies toward Cold War politics in the film capital. His tenure as the anticommunist president of the Screen Actors Guild—and as a secret FBI informant—likely speeded his conversion from New Deal Democrat to right-leaning Republican. In his final onscreen roles Reagan usually portrayed the kind of independent, rugged individualist—often in westerns such as *Law and Order* (1953)—that he would later lionize in his political speeches.

Nancy Reagan, who costarred with her husband in *Hellcats of the Navy* (1957) and later as the nation's First Lady, offered her close-up view of the relationship between Reagan the actor and Reagan the politician: "There are not two Ronald Reagans." During the 1980s Hollywood and Washington, D.C., became embodied in the same character, Ronald Wilson Reagan. ◄

to address key domestic issues such as reorganization of the health care and social welfare systems. Worse for the president's political future, the economic growth of the Reagan years began slowing while the budget deficit continued to grow. George H. W. Bush's popularity and his chances for a second term dwindled. Meanwhile, both the Reagan and then Bush presidencies participated in one of the most momentous changes of the 20th century—the end of the Cold War.

Renewing and Ending the Cold War

Q *FOCUS QUESTION* What forces and events contributed first to heightened tensions in the Cold War and then to its end?

In foreign policy, Reagan promised to reverse what he derided as Carter's passivity. He declared that the Vietnam War had been a "noble cause" that politicians had refused to win. Renewing the rhetoric of strident anticommunism, Reagan denounced the Soviet Union as an "evil empire" and promised a military buildup to confront communism. This renewal of the Cold War, however, proved short lived. By the late 1980s, a variety of internal and external circumstances brought communist regimes under unsustainable pressure. Reagan had begun his presidency by renewing the Cold War; but he and his successor, George H. W. Bush, also presided over its end.

The Defense Buildup

In response to his campaign promises, Reagan's administration led off with dramatic increases in military spending, even as tax cuts reduced federal revenues. The Pentagon enlarged the Navy and expanded strategic nuclear forces, deploying new missiles throughout Western Europe. At the height of Reagan's military buildup, which produced gaping budget deficits, the Pentagon was purchasing about 20 percent of the nation's manufacturing output.

In 1983 Reagan proposed the most expensive defense system in history: a space-based shield against incoming missiles.

Ronald Reagan, "Star Wars" Speech (1983)

Beginning as a vague hope, this **Strategic Defense Initiative (SDI)** soon had its own Pentagon agency, which sought $26 billion, over five years, for research costs alone. Controversy swirled around SDI. Skeptics dubbed it "Star Wars" and shuddered at its astronomical costs. Although most scientists dismissed the plan as too speculative, Congress voted appropriations for SDI, and Reagan steadfastly insisted that a defensive missile shield could work. Reagan also suggested that, as Moscow increased the burden on its own fragile economy in order to compete in the accelerating arms race, the Soviet Union might collapse under the economic strain. SDI dominated both strategic debates at home and arms talks with the Soviets.

Reagan's foreign policy agenda included numerous non-military initiatives. A new "informational" offensive funded conservative media groups around the world and established Radio Martí, a Florida station beamed at Cuba and designed to discredit Fidel Castro's communist government. When the United Nations Educational, Scientific, and Cultural Organization (UNESCO) adopted an allegedly anti-American tone, Reagan cut off U.S. contributions to this agency. The White House also championed free markets, pressing other nations to minimize tariffs and restrictions on foreign investment. The Caribbean Basin Initiative, for example, rewarded with aid small nations in the Caribbean region that adhered to free-market principles.

The CIA, headed by William Casey, stepped up its covert activities. Some became so obvious they hardly qualified as covert. It was no secret, for instance, that the United States sent aid to anticommunist forces in Afghanistan, many of them radical Islamic fundamentalist groups. The CIA also helped train and support the *contras* in Nicaragua, a military force fighting to topple the *Sandinista* government. To contain the power of Iran, assistance went to its bitter enemy, Saddam Hussein in Iraq. Many of these moves would, in the future, have unintended and unwelcome consequences for U.S. policy.

Deploying Military Power

In renewing the global Cold War, Reagan promised military support to "democratic" revolutions anywhere, a move designed to contain the Soviet Union's sphere of influence. Reagan's UN ambassador, Jeane Kirkpatrick, wrote that "democratic" forces included almost any movement, no matter how autocratic, that was anticommunist. The United States thus funded opposition forces in countries aligned with the Soviet Union: Ethiopia, Angola, South Yemen, Cambodia, Guatemala, Grenada, Afghanistan, and Nicaragua. Reagan called the participants in such anticommunist insurgencies "freedom fighters," although few displayed any visible commitment to democratic values or institutions.

The Reagan administration also deployed U.S. military power, initially in southern Lebanon in 1982. Here, Israeli troops faced off against Islamic groups supported by Syria and Iran. Fearing loss of influence within Lebanon, the Reagan administration convinced Israel to withdraw and sent 1,600 U.S. Marines as part of an international "peacekeeping force." Islamic militias, however, turned against the U.S. forces. After a massive truck bomb attack against a military compound killed 241 U.S. troops, mostly Marines, in April 1983, Reagan decided to end this ill-defined undertaking. In February 1984 Reagan ordered the withdrawal of U.S. troops and disengaged from Lebanon.

Another military intervention seemed more successful. In October 1983 Reagan sent 2,000 U.S. troops to the tiny Caribbean island of Grenada, whose socialist leader was forging ties with Castro's Cuba. U.S. troops swept aside Grenada's government and installed one friendlier to U.S. policies.

Buoyed by Grenada, the Reagan administration fixed its sights on Nicaragua. Here, the Marxist-leaning *Sandinista* government was trying to break Nicaragua's dependence on the United States. The Reagan administration responded with economic pressure, a propaganda campaign, and greater assistance to the *contras*. These initiatives stirred considerable controversy, however, because of mounting evidence of the *contras'* corruption and brutality. Finally, Democrats in Congress broke with the president's policy and barred additional military aid to the *contras*, a group that Reagan had once compared to America's own Founding Fathers. Policymakers in the administration then encouraged wealthy American conservatives and foreign governments to help fund the *contra* cause.

Meanwhile, violence continued to escalate throughout the Middle East. Militant Islamic groups increased attacks against Israel and Western powers. Bombings and kidnappings of Westerners became more frequent. Apparently, Libya's Muammar al-Qaddafi and Iranian leaders encouraged such activities. In the spring of 1986 the United States launched an air strike into Qaddafi's personal compound. It killed his young daughter, but Qaddafi and his government survived. Despite what looked like a long-range assassination attempt against a foreign leader, an action outlawed by Congress. Americans generally approved of using strong measures against sponsors of terrorism and hostage taking.

The Iran-Contra Controversy

In November 1986 a magazine in Lebanon reported that the Reagan administration was selling arms to Iran in order to secure the release of Americans being held hostage by Islamic militants. These alleged deals violated the Reagan administration's own pledges against selling arms to Iran or rewarding hostage taking by negotiating for the release of captives. During the 1980 campaign, of course, Reagan had made hostages in Iran a symbol of U.S. weakness under Carter. When Iranian-backed groups continued to kidnap Americans during Reagan's own presidency, it seemed that Reagan had sought clandestine ways to recover hostages and avoid such charges being leveled at him.

As Congress began to investigate, the story became more bizarre. It appeared that the operatives in the Reagan administration had not only secretly sold arms to Iran but had funneled profits from these back-channel deals to the *contra* forces in Nicaragua, thereby circumventing the congressional ban on U.S. military aid. Oliver North, an aide to the national security adviser, had directed the effort, working with international arms dealers and private go-betweens. North's covert activities seemingly violated both the official policy of the White House and an act of Congress.

This **Iran-*contra* affair** never reached the proportions of the Watergate scandal. In contrast to Richard Nixon, Ronald Reagan stepped forward and testified, through a deposition, that he could not recall any details about either the release of hostages or the funding of the *contras.* His management skills might deserve criticism, Reagan admitted, but he had never intended to break any laws or violate any presidential promise. Vice President George H. W. Bush, whom investigators initially linked to Oliver North's machinations, also claimed ignorance. North and several others in the Reagan administration were convicted of felonies, including falsification of documents and lying to Congress, but appellate courts later overturned these verdicts. North destroyed so many documents and left so many false paper trails that congressional investigators struggled even to compile a simple narrative of his activities. Finally, in 1992, just a few days before the end of his presidency, George H. W. Bush pardoned six former Reagan-era officials connected to the Iran-*contra* controversy.

The Cold War Eases

After six years of renewed Cold War confrontation, Reagan's last two years saw a sudden thaw in U.S.–Soviet relations. The economic cost of superpower rivalry was burdening both nations.

Moreover, political change swept the Soviet Union and eliminated reasons for confrontation. **Mikhail Gorbachev**, who became general secretary of the Communist Party in 1985, promised a new style of Soviet leadership. He understood that his nation faced economic stagnation and environmental problems brought on by decades of poorly planned industrial development. To redirect the Soviet Union's course, he withdrew troops from Afghanistan, reduced commitments to Cuba and Nicaragua, proclaimed a policy of *glasnost* ("openness"), and began to implement *perestroika* ("economic liberalization") at home.

Gorbachev's policies gained him acclaim throughout the West, and summit meetings with the United States yielded breakthroughs in arms control. At Reykjavik, Iceland, in October 1986, Reagan shocked both Gorbachev and his own advisers by proposing a wholesale ban on nuclear weapons. Although negotiations at Reykjavik stumbled over Soviet insistence that the United States abandon SDI, Gorbachev later dropped that condition. In December 1987, Reagan and Gorbachev signed a major arms treaty that reduced each nation's supply of intermediate-range missiles and allowed for on-site verification, which the Soviets had never before permitted. The next year, Gorbachev scrapped the policy that forbade nations under Soviet influence from renouncing Communism. In effect, he declared an end to the Cold War.

Within the next few years, communist states began to topple like dominoes, falling out of the Soviet sphere of influence. In 1989, the first year of George H. W. Bush's presidency, Poland made the most significant move when its anticommunist labor movement, Solidarity, ousted a pro-Soviet regime. The pro-Moscow government in East Germany fell in November 1989. Both West and East Germans hacked down the Berlin Wall and then began the difficult process of reunifying Germany as a single nation. Popular movements similarly forced out communist governments throughout Eastern Europe. Yugoslavia quickly disintegrated, and warfare ensued as rival ethnic groups recreated separate states in Slovenia, Serbia, Bosnia, and Croatia. Latvia, Lithuania, and Estonia, which had been under Soviet control since the Second World War, declared their independence.

Most dramatically, the major provinces that had anchored the Soviet Union assumed self-government. The president of the new state of Russia, Boris Yeltsin, put down a coup by hard-line communists in August 1991, and he soon solidified his political position. In December 1991 Yeltsin brokered a plan to abolish the Soviet Union and replace it with 11 separate republics, loosely joined in a commonwealth arrangement.

Post-Cold War Policy and the Persian Gulf War

In response, the Bush administration set about redefining U.S. national security in a post-Cold War era. The collapse of the Soviet Union weakened support for the leftist insurgencies in Central America that had so preoccupied the Reagan administration. Nicaraguans voted out the *Sandinistas*, who became just another political party in a multiparty system. The Pentagon pondered new military missions, imagining rapid, sharply targeted strikes rather than lengthy, conventional campaigns. The armed forces assessed how they would serve in the "war

Berlin Wall, 1989. Berliners celebrated the end of the Cold War by chiseling away at the Berlin Wall, which the communist East German state had erected in 1962 to prevent the flow of refugees to West Berlin. Pieces of the Berlin Wall became coveted symbols of the fall of communism.

against drugs," an effort that Bush had suggested during his 1988 presidential campaign.

General Manuel Noriega, the president of Panama, was deeply involved in the drug trade, and the Reagan administration had secured an indictment against him for international narcotics trafficking. Confronting Noriega posed a potentially embarrassing problem for the Bush administration. The anti-communist general had been recruited as a CIA "asset" during the mid-1970s, when Bush had headed the Agency. Nevertheless, the United States needed a friendly and a stable government in Panama in order to complete the transfer of the Panama Canal to Panamanian sovereignty in 2000. Bush finally decided to topple the mercurial Noriega. During "Operation Just Cause," U.S. Marines landed in Panama in December 1989 and laid siege to the president's headquarters. Noriega soon surrendered, was extradited to Florida, and went to prison after a 1992 conviction for trafficking in cocaine.

The Panamanian operation carried major implications. Deposing the leader of a foreign government by unilateral military action raised questions of international law, but this operation, which involved 25,000 U.S. troops and few casualties, provided a model for the post-Cold War era. The Pentagon firmed up plans for creating highly mobile, rapid deployment forces. A test of its new strategy came during the Persian Gulf War of 1991.

On August 2, 1990, Iraq's Saddam Hussein ordered his troops to occupy the neighboring oil-rich emirate of Kuwait. U.S. intelligence analysts had been caught off guard, and they now warned that Iraq's next target might be Saudi Arabia, the largest oil exporter in the Middle East and a longtime U.S. ally.

Moving swiftly, Bush orchestrated a multilateral, international response. Four days after Iraq's invasion of Kuwait, he launched Operation Desert Shield by sending several hundred thousand U.S. troops to Saudi Arabia. Bush convinced the Saudi government, concerned about allowing Western troops on sacred Islamic soil, to accept a U.S. military presence in Saudi Arabia. After consulting with European leaders, Bush approached the UN, which denounced Iraqi aggression, ordered economic

sanctions against Iraq, and authorized the United States to lead an international force into the Gulf region if Saddam Hussein's troops did not withdraw from Kuwait.

Bush assembled a massive coalition force, ultimately nearly 500,000 troops from the United States and some 200,000 from other countries. He claimed a moral obligation to rescue Kuwait, and his policymakers also spoke frankly about the economic threat that Hussein's aggression posed for the oil-dependent economies of the United States and its allies. These arguments persuaded Congress to approve a resolution backing the use of force.

In mid-January 1991 the United States launched an air war against Iraq and, after a period of devastating aerial bombardment, began a ground offensive in late February. Coalition forces, enjoying air supremacy, decimated Saddam Hussein's armies in a matter of days. U.S. casualties were relatively light (148 combat deaths). Estimates of Iraqi casualties ranged from 25,000 to 100,000 deaths. Although this **Persian Gulf War** lasted scarcely six weeks, it took an enormous toll on highways, bridges, communications, and other infrastructure facilities in both Iraq and Kuwait.

In a controversial decision, Bush stopped short of ousting Saddam Hussein, a goal that the UN had never approved and that U.S. military planners considered too costly and risky. Instead, the United States, backed by the UN, maintained its economic pressure, ordered the dismantling of Iraq's capability to produce nuclear and bacteriological weapons, and enforced "no-fly" zones over northern and southern Iraq to help protect the Kurds and Shi'a Muslims from Hussein's continued persecution. The Persian Gulf War temporarily boosted George H. W. Bush's popularity. An increasingly vocal and influential group of critics, however, argued that Saddam Hussein should have been overthrown. Ten years later, with President Bush's son as president, they would get another chance.

Bush's economic foreign policy, although less visible than his leadership during the Persian Gulf War, comprised a key part of his post-Cold War vision. It pressed a program of international economic integration. During the mid-1980s huge debts that

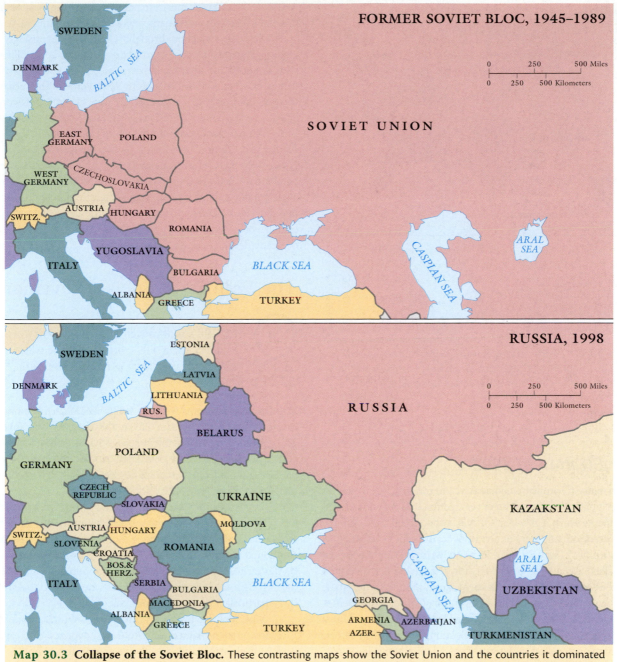

Map 30.3 Collapse of the Soviet Bloc. These contrasting maps show the Soviet Union and the countries it dominated before and after the fall of communist governments. What countries in Eastern Europe escaped Russian control after 1989? What new countries emerged out of the old Soviet Union?

Third World nations owed to U.S. institutions had threatened the international banking system, but most of these obligations had been renegotiated by the early 1990s. Market economies, which replaced centrally planned ones, began to emerge in former communist states. Western Europe moved toward economic integration. Most nations of the Pacific Rim experienced steady economic growth. The president supported (but was unable to pass) a North American Free Trade Agreement (NAFTA), which proposed to eliminate tariff barriers and join Canada, the United States, and Mexico together in the largest free-market zone in the world.

Ultimately, however, voters judged Bush's record on foreign affairs as something of a muddle. He had organized an international coalition against Iraq, assisted a peaceful post-Cold War transition in Russia and Eastern Europe, and embraced global economic integration. Despite these successes, the president publicly projected indecisiveness. The United States remained on the sidelines as full-scale warfare erupted among the states of the former Yugoslavia, with Serbs launching a brutal campaign of territorial aggrandizement and "ethnic cleansing" against Bosnian Muslims. In Africa, when severe famine wracked Somalia, Bush ordered U.S. troops to secure supply lines for humanitarian aid, but the American public remained wary of this military mission. As the old goal of containing the Soviet Union became irrelevant, George H. W. Bush failed to effectively articulate new ones that might inspire voters.

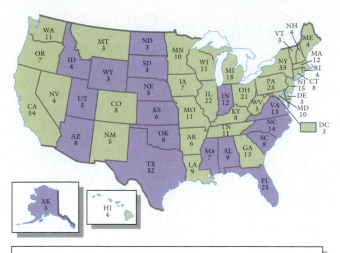

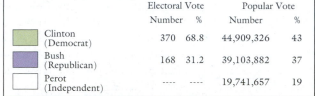

		Electoral Vote		Popular Vote	
		Number	%	Number	%
	Clinton (Democrat)	370	68.8	44,909,326	43
	Bush (Republican)	168	31.2	39,103,882	37
	Perot (Independent)	----	----	19,741,657	19

© Cengage Learning

Map 30.4 Presidential Election, 1992. Notice the substantial number of votes cast for an independent candidate, Ross Perot. How did Perot's vote totals affect Bill Clinton's mandate as president?

The Election of 1992

The inability to project a coherent vision for either domestic or foreign policy threatened Bush's reelection and forced concessions to the New Right. Dan Quayle, although clearly a liability with voters outside his conservative constituency, returned as Bush's running mate. The president allowed New Right activists, who talked about "a religious war" for "the soul of America" and pictured Democrats as the enemy of family values, to dominate the 1992 Republican National Convention. Conservative Democrats and independents that supported Ronald Reagan and Bush in the previous three presidential elections, found this rhetoric unsettling and looked back toward the Democratic side.

Bush's Democratic challenger, Governor William Jefferson Clinton of Arkansas, stressed economic issues. Campaigning as a "New Democrat," Bill Clinton promised job creation, deficit reduction, and an overhaul of the nation's healthcare system. Sounding almost like a Republican, Clinton pledged to shrink the size of government and to "end this [welfare] system as we know it." "People who can work ought to go to work, and no one should be able to stay on welfare forever," he insisted. This rhetoric made it difficult for Bush to label Clinton as a "big government liberal."

Clinton's focus on the economy helped deflect attention from the sociocultural issues on which he was vulnerable. As a college student, he had avoided service in Vietnam and, while in England as a Rhodes Scholar, had demonstrated against the Vietnam War. When Bush, a decorated veteran of the Second World War, challenged the patriotism of his Democratic challenger, Clinton countered by emphasizing, rather than repudiating, his roots in the 1960s. He appeared on MTV and touted his devotion

to (relatively soft) rock music. In addition, he chose Senator Albert Gore of Tennessee, a Vietnam veteran, as his running mate.

The 1992 election brought Clinton a surprisingly easy victory. The quixotic campaign of Ross Perot, a Texas billionaire who financed his own third-party run, took votes from both insider Bush and outsider Clinton. With Perot in the race, Clinton garnered only 43 percent of the popular vote but won 370 electoral votes by carrying 32 states and the District of Columbia. Bush won a majority only among white Protestants in the South. In contrast, Clinton carried the Jewish, African American, and Latino vote by large margins and even gained a plurality among people who had served in the Vietnam War. He also ran well among independents that had supported Reagan and Bush during the 1980s. Perhaps most surprising, about 55 percent of eligible voters went to the polls, a turnout that reversed 32 years of steady decline in voter participation.

The Politics of Social Movements

Q FOCUS QUESTION

How did social movements of the post-1960s era affect social life, culture, and the ways people saw their own personal identities?

The activism associated with the 1960s became firmly embedded in most areas of American life in the decades that followed. The proliferation of locally based activism, often focused on neighborhood-related projects, such as safer streets and cleaner parks, prompted one historian to see a "backyard revolution" taking place during the 1970s and 1980s. Even the U.S. Congress, hardly an institution inclined to fund domestic revolutions, recognized the value of locally based activism and created, in 1978, the National Consumer Cooperative Bank. Legislators envisioned it providing loans to support grass-roots enterprises. By the early 21st century, virtually every public forum featured the influence, and the clash, of activists who claimed to represent some particular constituency or goal.

Mass demonstrations reminiscent of those against the Vietnam War remained one tool of advocacy and protest. Both anti-abortion and pro-choice forces, for example, regularly demonstrated in Washington, D.C. During the 1980s, the Clamshell Alliance conducted a campaign of civil disobedience against a nuclear reactor being built in Seabrook, New Hampshire, and a coalition of West Coast activists waged a lengthy, unsuccessful struggle to close the University of California's Lawrence Livermore National Laboratory, which was developing nuclear weapons. In nearly every major city and many smaller towns, women's groups staged annual Take Back the Night rallies to call attention to the issue of sexual assault.

The media increasingly ignored most mass demonstrations, however, unless they sparked violent conflict. In 1991, for example, 30,000 Korean Americans staged a march for racial peace in Los Angeles. Although it was the largest demonstration ever conducted by any Asian American group, even the local media failed to cover it. Only C-Span, a niche network devoted to public affairs programming, provided minimal coverage of events of social and political protest. Social activism from all parts of the political spectrum and all sections of the country, in short, did not go away during the 1980s, but it did take forms less reliant than during the Sixties on media spectacles.

Women's Issues

In this political environment, women's groups adopted a range of methods to rally new supporters and re-energize their core constituencies. Struggles over gender-related issues had emerged within the labor movement and the civil rights and antiwar movements of the 1960s. Initially, many of the men involved in these causes complained that issues of gender equality interfered with broader fights to redirect labor, racial, or foreign policies. Women, however, insisted on calling attention to their second-class status in movements that claimed to be egalitarian. The spread of the birth control pill during the 1960s gave women greater control over reproductive choices but also complicated the meaning of "sexual freedom." Throughout the 1970s women promoted "consciousness-raising" sessions to discuss how *political* empowerment was inseparable from *personal* power relationships involving housework, child rearing, sexuality, and economic independence. "The personal is political" became a watchword for the new women's movement.

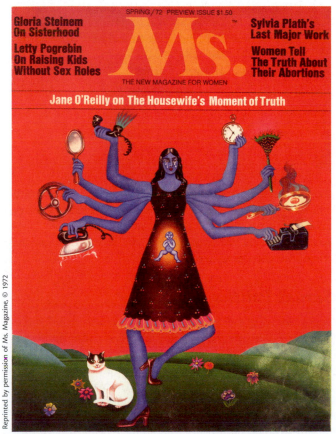

Ms. Debuts. Styling itself as "More than a Magazine—a Movement," *Ms.* has always featured eye-catching covers that help to chart the changing priorities of feminist activists. Initially an experimental offshoot of *New York* magazine, *Ms.* debuted in January 1972, under the editorship of Gloria Steinem, with this surrealistic, vividly symbolic cover.

The number of groups addressing issues of concern to women continually expanded. As part of the new activism, the National Organization for Women (NOW) became generally identified with the rights-based agenda of the mainstream of the Democratic Party. African American women often formed separate organizations that emphasized issues of cultural and ethnic identity. Chicana groups coalesced within the United Farm Workers' (UFW) movement and other Mexican American organizations. Lesbians also organized their own groups, often allying with an emerging gay rights movement. Many U.S. feminist organizations joined with groups in other nations on behalf of international women's rights. Although never embracing the word "feminism," conservative women also played important leadership roles in causes associated with the New Right.

With agendas often varying along lines of class, race, ethnicity, and religion, the women's movement remained highly diverse, but women from different backgrounds often cooperated to build new institutions and networks. Their efforts included battered-women's shelters; health and birthing clinics specializing in women's medicine; rape crisis centers; economic development counseling for women-owned businesses; union-organizing efforts led by women; organizations of women in specific businesses or professions; women and gender studies programs in colleges and universities; and academic journals and popular magazines devoted to women's issues. Pressure for gender equity also affected existing institutions. Country clubs and service organizations began admitting women members. Many Protestant denominations came to accept women into the ministry, and Reform Judaism placed women in its pulpits. Educational institutions adopted "gender-fair" hiring practices and curricula. American women by the beginning of the 21st century lived in an environment significantly different from that of their mothers.

Economic self-sufficiency became an especially pressing issue. Increases in AFDC payments and an expansion of the Food Stamp program had boosted social welfare payments for single mothers with children during the 1960s, but the economic dislocations of the following decades undercut the value, measured in constant dollars, of these benefits. Reagan-era budget cuts for social programs also took their toll, especially in urban locales. Homeless shelters, which once catered almost exclusively to single men, began serving growing numbers of women and children. As this feminization of poverty became of major concern, proposals proliferated on the state and federal levels for reshaping patterns of governmental support by limiting direct governmental payments and emphasizing strategies to move women, even those with young children, into the workforce.

The job market, however, remained laced with inequalities. Women constituted 30 percent of the labor force in 1950 and more than 45 percent in 2001. Although women increasingly entered the professions and gained unionized positions (by 2000 nearly 45 percent of union members were women, compared with 18 percent in 1960), the average female worker still earned around 75 cents for every dollar taken home by men. "Glass ceilings" limited women's chances for promotion, and childcare expenses often fell disproportionately on women who worked outside the home.

Cultural Disagreements: Equality for Women?

The changing role of women in America dramatically altered family and civic life during this era. Many of the cultural and political disputes of these years revolved around issues related to gender. Advocates of "full equality" for women, such as the National Organization for Women (NOW), clashed with New Right activists, who opposed gender equality as an affront to the "natural" order.

NATIONAL ORGANIZATION FOR WOMEN (NOW)

Statement of Purpose, 1966 ("Statement of Purpose," mimeographed, Washington D.C., p. 1)

[excerpt #1] *The purpose of NOW is to take action to bring women into full participation in the mainstream of American society now, exercising all the privileges and responsibilities thereof in truly equal partnership with men. . . . We reject the current assumptions that a man must carry the sole burden of supporting himself, his wife, and family, and that a woman is automatically entitled to lifelong support by a man upon her marriage, or that marriage, home and family are primarily woman's world and responsibility. . . . We believe that a true partnership between the sexes demands a different concept of marriage, an equitable sharing of the responsibilities of home and children and of the economic burdens of their support. . . .*

We will strive to ensure that no party, candidate, president, senator, governor, congressman, or any public official who betrays or ignores the principle of full equality between the sexes is elected or appointed to office.

JERRY FALWELL

calling for a "moral majority" in his 1980 book, *Listen America!* (New York, Doubleday 1980, pp. 150–151)

[excerpt #2] *I believe that at the foundation of the women's liberation movement there is a minority core of women who were once bored with life, whose real problems are spiritual problems. Many women have never accepted their God-given roles. . . . God Almighty created men and women biologically different and with differing needs and roles.*

He made men and women to complement each other and to love each other. Not all the women involved in the feminist movement are radicals. Some are misinformed, and some are lonely. . . . I believe that women deserve more than equal rights. . . . Men and women have differing strengths. . . . Because a woman is weaker does not mean that she is less important.

Q Different assumptions about gender roles led to public policy disputes, especially in areas related to military service, families and reproduction, and labor rights. What specific social and political issues seem to be grounded in the contest over women's rights?

Sexual harassment on the job became a controversial issue. Most women's groups pressed government and private employers to curtail sexually charged behaviors that they saw demeaning women and exploiting their lack of power vis-à-vis male supervisors and coworkers. In 1986, the U.S. Supreme Court ruled that sexual harassment constituted a form of discrimination covered by the Civil Rights Act of 1964.

In 1991, the issue gained national attention when Anita Hill, an African American law professor, accused Clarence Thomas, an African American nominee for the U.S. Supreme Court, of having sexually harassed her when both worked for the federal government. Feminists denounced the all-male Senate Judiciary Committee, which was responsible for considering Thomas's nomination, for failing even to understand, let alone investigate seriously, the issue of sexual harassment. Although the Senate narrowly approved Thomas for the High Court, women's groups mobilized female voters and elected four women as U.S. senators in 1992.

Sexual harassment also became of concern to the U.S. military, which began to recruit women more actively. The service academies accepted female cadets, and women found places within the military hierarchy. Soon, however, revelations

about harassment and even sexual assaults against female naval officers by male comrades revealed problems. Attempts by Navy officials to cover up sexual harassment during the 1991 "Tailhook" convention provoked outrage, and several high-ranking officers were forced to step down.

Sexual Politics

Issues involving gays and lesbians also became more public and political. In 1969 New York City police raided the Stonewall Inn, a bar in Greenwich Village with a largely homosexual clientele. Patrons resisted arrest, and the resultant confrontations pitted the neighborhood's gay and lesbian activists, who claimed to be the victims of police harassment, against law enforcement officials.

Historians of sexuality have come to criticize what they call "the Stonewall Narrative," in which events at a single Greenwich Village bar ignited what would become known as the Lesbian-Gay-Bisexual-Transgendered (LGBT) movement. Recent studies emphasize that LGBT activism did not suddenly emerge in 1969 but instead grew out of earlier

Aids "ACT-UP" Campaign. Healthcare issues increasingly galvanized grassroots activists. In 1989, members of ACT-UP, a group that embraced direct action, protested what they saw as the federal government's inattention to the issue of AIDS during the 1980s.

movements, such as the Mattachine Society, and cultural communities such as the Beats (see Chapter 29).

Still, the 1969 events at the Stonewall Inn, because of the prominence they received in mainstream and alternative media, marked an important benchmark in sexual politics. Gay and lesbian activism became an important part of the larger "movement of movements" that continued during the 1970s and 1980s. Thousands of advocacy and support groups, such as New York City's Gay Activist Alliance (GAA), sprang up. As many individuals "came out of the closet," newspapers, theaters, nightspots, and religious groups proudly identified themselves as activists. LGBT communities emerged particularly in larger cities and benefited from a general relaxation of legal and cultural controls over the portrayal and practice of sexuality. They demanded that law enforcement officials treat attacks against them no less seriously than attacks against all other communities. They also asserted constitutional claims to equal access to housing, jobs, and benefits for domestic partners.

One issue, with international implications, was especially urgent. A human immunodeficiency virus produced an immune deficiency syndrome, HIV-AIDS, a contagious disease for which medical science offered virtually nothing in the way of cure. The disease could be transmitted through the careless use of intravenous drugs, tainted blood supplies, and unprotected sexual intercourse. At first, the incidence of HIV-AIDS in the United States was primarily limited to gay men, and activists charged that, as a consequence, cultural and

religious conservatives placed a low priority on medical efforts to understand its causes, check its spread, or devise a cure. The resultant controversy over medical funding galvanized empowerment efforts among LGBT organizations, such as the Aids Coalition to Unleash Power, or ACT UP. With the development of prevention programs and drugs that could combat HIV-AIDS, however, most public figures came to support new efforts both at home and overseas, particularly in Africa, to address HIV-AIDS. It has remained a modern scourge threatening advancement in many parts of the world, but its specific identification with LGBT rights has faded.

Activism Among African Americans

The emphasis on group identity as the fulcrum for social activism became especially strong among racial and ethnic communities. Extending the movement of movements of the 1960s, groups emphasized pride in their distinctive cultural traditions and insisted that differences should be affirmed rather than feared.

Having accomplished many of the legislative goals of the 1960s, African American activists, one observed, were "heading into a completely new era, and we don't know what to make of it." Mobilizing to promote political and economic advancement, however, continued in many directions.

African American leaders became increasingly prominent in national and local politics. One media spotlight fell on the Reverend Jesse Jackson. Jackson had spent the late 1960s in

Chicago directing a local effort sponsored by Dr. Martin Luther King, Jr.'s Southern Christian Leadership Conference (SCLC). After Dr. King's 1968 assassination, Jackson soon clashed with the SCLC's new leadership, and in 1971 he created his own Chicago-based organization, Operation PUSH. One of many local efforts, Operation PUSH pressured public officials and corporations to create jobs and promote community development projects. Abundant media coverage, however, made Reverend Jackson best known for addressing a wide range of national and international issues, including the status of the Palestinians and apartheid in South Africa. During the 1980s, he formed the National Rainbow Coalition to provide a broad geographic and ethnic umbrella for his movement and to facilitate his campaigns for the Democratic Party's presidential nomination in 1984 and 1988. Jackson's efforts garnered some primary victories but made only a minimal impact on national or even Democratic Party politics.

Other types of political activism, however, left a significant imprint on electoral politics during the 1970s and 1980s. The civil rights movement of the 1960s (see Chapter 29) provided the legal-constitutional basis for greater political participation by African Americans, and change came rapidly. In 1970, 13 African American members of Congress established the Congressional Black Caucus (CBC) to form a common front on a wide range of foreign and domestic issues. Picking up the mantle of A. Philip Randolph and Bayard Rustin's "Freedom Budget" of the 1960s, the CBC regularly issued a hypothetical "Alternative Budget," which targeted more money toward social initiatives. The caucus also campaigned on behalf of better relations between the United States and African nations and took stands on issues, such as inequities in drug sentencing, that particularly affected African Americans.

Hoping to create a more broadly based movement, a diverse group convened in 1972 at a National Black Political Convention in Gary, Indiana. They pieced together a National Black Political Agenda, a lengthy list of far-reaching social and economic initiatives. The document's divergent goals and conflicting principles ultimately divided more than it unified, but the Gary gathering did anticipate African American political movements that gained momentum during the two decades that followed. By the end of the 1980s, more than 7,000 African Americans (including nearly 1500 women) held political office. The year the Voting Rights Act passed, 1965, there had been fewer than 200. Urban centers with significant African American populations, such as Gary and Detroit, elected black mayors, but so did cities such as Denver, where African American candidates successfully formed cross-ethnic alliances. The new direction pursued by the Republican Party during the 1970s and 1980s meant that virtually all of this political activity occurred within Democratic ranks.

In addition to experiencing ballot-box victories, African Americans also moved into government-related employment. By the end of the 1980s, nearly half of all black professionals worked at some level of government or in some public sector position. These jobs provided the economic basis for an expanding African American middle class.

This form of black political activism confronted clear limits. Few mayors, whatever their ethnic identity, could mobilize the economic resources that large cities required to deal with rising crime rates, decaying infrastructures, and galloping inflation. African American voters had been crucial to Jimmy Carter's 1976 victory, and his administration did use CETA job-training money and public works spending to try to stabilize employment opportunities. Still, the stagnant economy under Carter and the urban budget cutting, which characterized the Reagan years, hit African Americans in inner cities with severity.

In addition to political activism, a diverse set of cultural movements sought to build on the identity politics that had emerged during the 1960s. The hyper-violent cycle of "Blaxploitation movies," such as *Shaft* (1971) and *Coffy* (1973), of the 1970s prompted heated debate over whether representing urban black life "like it [supposedly] was," rather than "like it [supposedly] should be," advanced African American interests. The 1980s movies of Spike Lee also created controversy by tackling issues such as politics of gender and "light skin" in African American life. *Do the Right Thing* (1989), arguably an even more ambitious movie—though smaller budgeted—than the epic *Malcolm X* (1991), provided a complex meditation about African American heroes, multiculturalism, law enforcement patterns, and personal activism amidst the uncertainties of urban life in the 1980s.

Prominent academics such as **Henry Lewis Gates, Jr.** worked in another venue to complicate the study of the African American experience and to challenge the movement that advocated creating an "Afrocentric" school curriculum. African American culture, in the view of Gates, was not "a thing apart, separate from the whole, having no influence on the shape and shaping of American culture." Gates insisted on viewing African American authors, such as Toni Morrison and Alice Walker, as writers who take "the blackness of the culture for granted" and use this as "a springboard to write about those human emotions that we share with everyone else." The cultural works of African Americans, in short, could simultaneously be seen as unique and different, *and also* be viewed in relationship to broader cultural traditions.

Activism Among American Indians

Native Americans mounted activist movements along two broad fronts. Indians had, of course, longstanding identities based on their tribal affiliation, and many issues, particularly those involving land and treaty disputes, turned on specific, tribal-based claims. Other questions, which seemed to require strategies that extended beyond a single tribe or band, became identified as "pan-Indian" in nature.

In 1969, people from several tribes began a two-year sit-in designed to dramatize a history of broken treaty promises, at the former federal prison on Alcatraz Island in San Francisco harbor. Expanding on this tactic, the American Indian Movement (AIM), created in 1968 by young activists from several Northern Plains tribes, adopted even more confrontational approaches. Violent clashes with both federal officials and older American Indian leaders erupted in 1973 on the Pine Ridge Reservation in South Dakota. In response, federal officials targeted members of AIM with illegal surveillance and a series of controversial criminal prosecutions.

Meanwhile, important social and legal changes were taking place. In the Civil Rights Act of 1968, which contained several

Gaming at Potawatomi Casino. During the 1980s, casino style gaming began to emerge as one of the nation's leading entertainment enterprises. Native Americans embraced casinos, such as this one located near Milwaukee, Wisconsin, as important ways to generate jobs and capital on Indian reservations. The Potawatomi complex, which opened in 1991, juxtaposes traditional style sculptures, an Indian heritage center and gift shop, an imaginatively designed building, more than 1000 slot machines, and a cabaret-style dinner theater patterned after ones in Las Vegas.

sections that became known as the "Indian Bill of Rights," Congress extended most of the provisions of the constitutional Bill of Rights to Native Americans living on reservations, while reconfirming the legitimacy of tribal laws. Federal legislation and several Supreme Court decisions in the 1970s subsequently reinforced the principle of "tribal self-determination." Tribal identification itself required legal action. By the early 21st century, the federal government officially recognized nearly 600 separate tribes and bands. After 1978 Congress also provided funds for educational institutions that would teach job skills and preserve tribal cultures.

Tapping the expertise of the Native American Rights Fund (NARF), tribes pressed demands that derived from old treaties with the U.S. government. Some campaigns sought recognition of fishing and agricultural rights and often provoked resentment among non-Indians who argued that these claims, based on federal authority, should not take precedence over state and local laws. American Indians also sued to protect tribal water rights and traditional religious ceremonies, some of which included the ritualistic use of drugs such as peyote. In 1990, Congress passed the Native American Graves Protection and Repatriation Act, which required universities and museums to return human remains and sacred objects to tribes that requested them.

Claiming exemption from state gaming laws, Native Americans began to open bingo halls and then full-blown casinos. In 1988 the U.S. Supreme Court ruled that states could not prohibit gambling operations on tribal land, and Congress responded with the Indian Gaming Regulatory Act. Gambling emerged as one of the most lucrative sectors of the nation's entertainment business, and Indian-owned casinos thrived. Ironically, the glitzy, tribal-owned casinos often financed tribal powwows and other efforts to nurture traditional cultural practices. Sometimes the competition to establish casinos in prime locations prompted intertribal political and legal conflicts.

To forestall the disappearance of native languages, American Indian activists urged bilingualism and renewed attention to tribal rituals. Indian groups also denounced the use of stereotypical nicknames, such as "Chiefs" and "Redskins," and Indian-related logos in amateur and professional sports. The federal government assisted this cultural-pride movement by funding two National Museums of the American Indian, one in New York and the other in Washington, D.C. The National Park Service changed the name of "Custer Battlefield" in Montana to "Little Bighorn Battlefield," redesigning its exhibits to honor American Indian culture.

Activism in Spanish-Speaking Communities

Spanish-speaking Americans, who constituted the fastest-growing ethnic group in the United States, highlighted the diversity and complexity of identity. Many Spanish-speaking people, especially in the Southwest, preferred the umbrella term "Latino," whereas others, particularly in Florida, used the term "Hispanic." At the same time, people the U.S. Census began (in 1980) labeling "Hispanic" most frequently identified themselves according to the specific Spanish-speaking country or commonwealth from which they or their ancestors had immigrated.

Mexican Americans, members of the oldest and most numerous Spanish-speaking group, could tap a long tradition of social activism. The late 1960s saw an emerging spirit of **Chicanismo**, a populist-style pride in a heritage that could be traced back to the ancient civilizations of Middle America. Young activists made "Chicano/a," terms of derision that most Mexican Americans had generally avoided in the past, into a rallying cry.

In cities in the Southwest during the 1970s, advocates of *Chicanismo* gained considerable cultural influence. Members of La Raza Unida, a political party founded in 1967, began to win local elections. At the same time, Mexican American communities experienced a cultural flowering. New Spanish-language newspapers and journals reinforced a growing sense of pride, and many churches sponsored festivals with ethnic dancing, mural painting, poetry, and literature. Mexican Americans successfully pushed for programs in Chicano/a Studies at colleges and universities.

Developments in San Antonio, Texas, a city with a large Mexican American population, suggested the potential fruits of grassroots political organizing. In the 1970s, Ernesto Cortes, Jr., took the lead in founding Communities Organized for Public Service (COPS), a group that brought the energy and talents of Mexican Americans, particularly women, into the city's public arena for the first time. Mexican American activists worked with Anglo business leaders and Democratic politicians such as Henry Cisneros, who became the city's mayor in 1981. Other locally based organizations formed on the model of COPS, such as United Neighborhood Organization (UNO) in Los Angeles, also worked on community concerns.

On the national level, the Mexican American Legal Defense and Education Fund (MALDEF), established in 1968, emerged as a highly visible advocacy group ready to lobby or litigate. Professional groups, such as the National Network of Hispanic Women, also proliferated. Mexican American activists, however, became especially well known for their labor-organizing efforts, particularly among farm workers and in the rapidly expanding service sector.

Efforts to organize agricultural workers, who were largely of Mexican and Filipino descent, dramatized both the successes and the difficulties of expanding the union movement to largely immigrant workers. **Dolores Huerta and Cesar Chavez**, charismatic leaders who emulated the nonviolent tactics of Martin Luther King, Jr., vaulted the United Farm Workers (UFW) into public attention during the 1970s. Chavez undertook personal hunger strikes, and Huerta helped organize well-publicized consumer boycotts of lettuce and grapes to pressure growers into collective bargaining agreements with the UFW. Despite some successes, the UFW steadily lost ground during the later 1970s and the 1980s. Strong anti-union stands by growers and the continued influx of new immigrants eager for work undercut the UFW's efforts. When Chavez died in April 1993, the UFW was struggling.

Social activism among Puerto Ricans in the United States emerged more slowly. Some stateside Puerto Ricans focused their political energy on the persistent "status" question—that is, whether Puerto Rico should seek independence, strive for statehood, or retain a commonwealth connection to the mainland. New York City's Puerto Rican Day Parade became the city's largest ethnic celebration and an important focus of cultural pride. A 1976 report by the U.S. Commission on Civil Rights, however, concluded that Puerto Ricans remained "the last in line" for government-funded benefits and opportunity programs. Over time, the Puerto Rican Legal Defense and Education Fund and allied groups helped Puerto Ricans surmount obstacles to the ballot box and political office.

©Ralf-Finn Hestoft/CORBIS

Mural Art in Chicago. Themes in Mexican history and culture, inspired by the great Mexican muralists, appeared in Mexican American communities throughout the country.

Cuban Americans, who had begun immigrating in large numbers to south Florida after Fidel Castro came to power, generally enjoyed greater access to education and higher incomes. These Cuban immigrants also tended to be politically conservative, generally voted Republican, and lobbied for a hard line toward Castro's communist government. Cuban Americans quickly developed a dense network of institutions that leveraged them into positions of power in Florida politics and civic affairs.

Beneath a common Spanish language, then, lay great diversity in terms of economic status, national and cultural identification, political affiliation, and activist goals and organizations. Established communities that identified with Mexico, Puerto Rico, and Cuba developed a wide range of mobilizing and organizing styles. More recent immigrants from the Dominican Republic and Central America, who were the most economically deprived and the least organized, also began to add their voices and concerns.

Activism Among Asian Americans

Americans of Chinese, Japanese, Korean, Filipino, and other backgrounds began to create an Asian American movement in the 1970s. Organizations such as the Asian Pacific Planning Council (APPCON), founded in 1976, lobbied to obtain government funding for projects that benefited Asian American communities. The Asian Law Caucus, founded during the early 1970s by opponents of U.S. intervention in Vietnam, and the Committee against Anti-Asian Violence, created a decade later in response to a wave of racially motivated attacks, mobilized for a wide range of legal battles. During the 1970s Asian American studies programs also took shape at colleges and universities, particularly on the West Coast. By the early 1980s, Asian American political activists enjoyed growing influence, especially within the Democratic Party, and began gaining public office.

Emphasizing a broad, Asian American identity, however, raised questions of inclusion, exclusion, and rivalry. Filipino American activists, members of the second largest Asian American group in the United States in 1990, often resisted the Asian American label because they believed that Chinese Americans or Japanese Americans dominated groups such as APPCON. Many people of Filipino descent focused on specific goals, particularly an effort to obtain citizenship and veteran's benefits for former soldiers of the Second World War who had fought against Japan in the Philippines. Japanese American groups also lobbied on behalf of specific issues, and in 1988 Congress formally apologized and voted to approve a reparations payment of $20,000 to every living Japanese American who had been confined in internment camps during the Second World War. Similarly, Hmong and Vietnamese groups pursued their own concerns related to the aftermath of the struggles in Indochina.

Socioeconomic differences often made it difficult to frame a single Asian American agenda. Although many groups showed remarkable upward educational and economic mobility during the late 1980s and early 1990s, immigrants who were especially recent or impoverished often struggled to find jobs that paid more than the minimum wage.

As a result of combined pressure from different ethnic groups, the federal government finally decided to designate "Asian or Pacific Islanders" (API) as a single pan-ethnic category in the censuses of 1990 and 2000. It also provided, however, nine specifically enumerated subcategories (such as Hawaiian or Filipino) and allowed other API groups (such as Hmong or Samoan) to write in their respective ethnic identifications. Thus, the term Asian American—which by the beginning of the 21st century applied to more than 10 million people and dozens of different ethnicities—both reflected, and was challenged by, the new emphasis on ethnic identity.

© Nik Wheeler/Corbis

Vietnamese American Businesses in Los Angeles. New Asian immigrants, especially from Southeast Asia, established a growing economic presence in many U.S. cities and helped revitalize older urban neighborhoods.

Anti-Government Activism

Ronald Reagan's first Inaugural Address declared that "government is not the solution to our problem; government is the problem." As president, Reagan exempted national security institutions from this principle and rarely applied it literally to basic safety-net programs such as Social Security and Medicare. In the face of budget deficits, Reagan proved willing to raise taxes to support government's expenditures. His claim that government action was almost always harmful, however, did appeal to the all-important New Right segment of the larger Reagan coalition, reason enough for its titular leader to lace his speeches with condemnations of the same government over which he presided. During the 1980s, denunciations of federal power spread throughout the culture, propelled especially by controversies over affirmative action and various regulatory rules.

Affirmative action programs had grown from bi-partisan roots in the administrations of Lyndon Johnson and Richard Nixon. Public officials, proponents argued, should act affirmatively to help people who belonged to groups with a shared history of discrimination—especially African Americans, Latinos, and women—obtain an equitable share of the nation's jobs, public spending, and educational programs. Affirmative action would help compensate for past discrimination and for continued, sometimes hidden, prejudice that laws merely guaranteeing formal equality failed to reach. Advocates of affirmative action emphasized that *any* process of selection inevitably "affirmed" some qualities, such as family or old school lineages, at the expense of others. Efforts at undoing years of discrimination against entire groups of people, in this view, required a complicated, seemingly paradoxical view of what counted as "equal" treatment by government.

Critics of affirmative action, however, began to identify it as one of the most dangerous examples of increased governmental power. They delighted in noting that until the mid-1960s even supporters of civil rights had opposed government officials categorizing individuals according to group identities based on race or ethnicity. They often quoted Dr. King's words about judging people by the "content of their character" rather than the "color of their skin" and argued that government should remain "blind" to color and gender by treating everyone equally. They rejected the claim that policymakers needed to craft special rules or programs in order to eliminate discriminatory barriers to individual opportunity. Even some beneficiaries of these programs, such as the Supreme Court Justice Clarence Thomas, charged that the derogatory label of "affirmative action applicant" threw into question the talents and capabilities of individuals. More broadly, critics of affirmative action programs denounced "set aside" job programs and special educational admission procedures for previously disadvantaged groups as examples of illegal quotas, violations of constitutional guarantees, and even harbingers of totalitarianism. Did not affirmative action *on behalf of* people in some groups always constitute "reverse discrimination" *against* those in others? The claim of reverse discrimination became particularly emotional when members of one affirmative action group, despite apparently inferior scores on aptitude or admissions exams, received preferences for employment or for entry into educational institutions.

In the midst of this controversy, federal courts managed to square affirmative action programs with older antidiscrimination precedents. They struck down affirmative action plans that contained inflexible quotas but upheld ones that made group identity only one of several criteria for making hiring or educational decisions. In the celebrated Supreme Court decision popularly known as the *Bakke* case (1978), a majority of justices endorsed affirmative action. Affirmative action programs in educational settings could pass constitutional muster because they aimed at redressing past discrimination *and* because they contributed to "diversity," an intangible social and psychological quality important in any social, educational, or business environment. Many leaders of corporations, educational establishments, and the military came to endorse this *Bakke* principle: Diversity benefited not just applicants from historically discriminated groups but *all* people who worked within those environments as well as *all* those who relied on their services and expertise.

This apparent acceptance of affirmative action programs, which government power would ultimately enforce, mobilized anti-government activists who opposed such programs. They mounted new informational, as well as political offensives, and found a close ally in New Right radio. During the 1970s the FM dial had become dominated by musical programming, and many AM radio stations switched to an all-talk format. One of the personalities who made the switch was Rush Hudson Limbaugh, III. Raised in a staunchly conservative Republican family, Limbaugh broke into AM as a radio host in several different markets under (as was the custom) several different names. Then in 1984 Limbaugh took over an already-prominent New Right talk show in California. Four years later, Limbaugh's ability to galvanize anti-government listeners earned him a spot in New York City and propelled him to the top ranks of a rapidly expanding, informal network for anti-government activism.

New Right radio also thrived by attacking federal environmental regulations in the name of defending property rights. During the 1970s, western entrepreneurs associated with the sagebrush rebellion advocated transferring to state and private hands some of the vast amount of land held by the federal government for recreational parks and environmental purposes. Freed of restrictions from Washington, the rebels argued, the land could be developed. As part of a broader effort sometimes called the "wise use movement," they insisted that westerners knew better than faraway government bureaucrats how to make productive use of lands that lay within their states. A parallel effort, the "property rights movement" emerged across much of the country, particularly in areas of scenic beauty and where plans of suburban developers encountered environmental restrictions. Private builders denounced government for insisting on environmental impact assessments, thus limiting the ability of property owners to do what they thought best with their land. In this movement, anti-government activists fought not only regulations from Washington but from any governmental body that claimed the power to regulate the use of private property in the name of some larger public purpose.

The New Right radio programs that denounced government rules flourished within a freshly deregulated communications

Anti-Abortion Protest, 1989. Legalized abortions became a major political issue after the 1973 Supreme Court decision in *Roe* v. *Wade.* Here, on the 16th anniversary of *Roe,* protesters assemble in front of the Supreme Court building.

industry. Beginning in 1949, the Federal Communications Commission (FCC), the government agency that regulated broadcasting, had required stations to represent a diversity of viewpoints. This "Fairness Doctrine" survived constitutional challenge in the courts. Anti-government activists in the legal community, however, persevered in their effort to overturn the doctrine. In 1986, two conservative jurists, Atonin Scalia and Robert Bork, authored a federal court decision ruling that Congress had never given the FCC any authority to mandate fairness. One year later, this decision prompted an FCC dominated by members appointed by Ronald Reagan to eliminate the Fairness Doctrine. New Right radio now enjoyed freedom to ramp up its rhetoric against governmental power.

The overturning of the Fairness Doctrine dovetailed with perhaps the central tenet of the new anti-government activism: "Free markets," not government, provided the best structure for enhancing individual freedom and ensuring social-economic progress. The faith that markets served people better than governments, an idea older than the U.S. Constitution, had taken a considerable hit during the economic disarray of the 1930s. As a consequence, New Dealers had built on a very different conviction popularized under the label of Keynesianism: that government regulation must tame market excesses and prevent them from unleashing irrational and self-destructive forces into the larger political economy (see Chapters 25, 27, and 28). In the 1950s and 1960s, conservative academics such as Milton Friedman had fired away at the Keynesian underpinnings of the New Deal-Great Society governmental structure, but during the 1970s and 1980s, conservatives rolled out much heavier weaponry.

A talented group of activist-academics in the fields of law and economics at the University of Chicago took the lead. The economists crafted highly technical, mathematically complex arguments for ideas that soon became the new economic orthodoxy. Government regulators could never understand the risks from economic activities such as trading stocks or lending money as well as the people who actually worked in the marketplace. Markets almost always got things right, at least in the long run, while government regulators invariably got them wrong. Moreover, governmental bureaucracies such as the

Securities and Exchange Commission (SEC) and the Federal Reserve Board were not really regulating markets in the public interest. Government bureaucrats were just another "special interest" looking out for themselves or for some other interest groups. They seldom acted as honest brokers between contending interests, as the interest-group pluralist model of the 1950s had claimed.

Most importantly, the argument went, bureaucrats armed with the power of government invariably interfered with the most magical quality of free markets—their ability to provide self-correcting mechanisms that allowed a complex economy to run efficiently with little intervention. On those rare occasions when economic markets seemingly failed, such as during the 1930s, the failure would be temporary. From this perspective, the flood of government regulations unleashed during the New Deal era had prolonged, rather than ended, the economic downturn by preventing the free market from correcting itself. Moreover, the continued reliance on government regulation explained the economic malaise of the early 1970s. The market's ability to rebound during the deregulation of the 1980s seemed proof of the new economic assumptions.

A widening circle of academic and legal proponents of these anti-government ideas actively pressed this case. New economic textbooks challenged the Keynesian-oriented ones that had once dominated college and university classrooms. A new legal field, called "law and economics," attracted lawyers and judges (including Bork and Scalia) who began to craft doctrines that accorded with free-market assumptions rather than the pro-regulatory ones that had guided New Deal-Great Society jurisprudence. Economist-activists carried the case against government regulation into the conservative think tanks, such as the Heritage Foundation, which were helping to shape public policy during the late 1970s and 1980s. Taking advantage of the loosened regulations, the business and financial world began to test the theories of self-regulating markets on Wall Street by devising new modes of investment and creative financial instruments.

By the end of the 1980s, opposition to government had become a prominent feature of American political culture. Although the left-leaning movements of the 1960s still argued for an activist government to promote social equality and economic fairness, they found a significant challenge in those who claimed that reducing the power of government would be the best way to solve social-economic problems and preserve liberty. Within this debate, anti-government activists, like other activists, hardly moved in lockstep. Some cared deeply about opposing new rules for affirmative action; others placed greater priority on economic or environmental deregulation. While remaining a coalition of disparate parts, however, anti-government activism (always linked to anti-tax sentiment) became a powerful force. It drew populist strength from the expertly crafted speeches of Ronald Reagan and the bombast of New Right radio. It found justification within the mathematically informed papers of Nobel Prize winners and top-rung law professors. Successfully challenging the once-dominant political agendas of the Democratic Party, it propelled the mainstream of the Republican Party decidedly rightward, established a strong foothold in public policy and media discussions, and succeeded in remapping the nation's cultural and informational landscape.

Conclusion

The Reagan revolution of the 1980s rested on a conservative movement that had been taking shape for several decades. New Right Republicans distrusted extending federal government power, advocated sharp tax cuts with deregulation, and stressed a socio-cultural agenda emphasizing "traditional" values. The dozen years of Republican dominance of the White House, from 1980 to 1992, helped shift the terms of political debate in the United States. The "liberal" label became one that most Democrats sought to avoid. In the international realm, the Reagan and Bush presidencies facilitated the end of the Cold War, a struggle that had defined U.S. foreign policy since the end of the Second World War.

Meanwhile, American society seemed to fragment into specialized identifications. Social activism increasingly organized around sexual, racial, ethnic, and ideological identities. The New Right's stress on limiting the power of government and promoting conservative values increasingly reconfigured discussions about how government power could best promote liberty and equality. ⚜

CHAPTER REVIEW

REVIEW QUESTIONS

1. How did the legacies of the Vietnam War and Watergate help shape U.S. politics in the decade that followed?
2. To what extent did Ronald Reagan's administration represent a victory for the New Right agenda in both domestic and foreign policy?
3. What forces and events contributed first to heightened tensions in the Cold War and then to its end?
4. How did social movements of the post-1960s era affect social life, culture, and the ways people saw their own personal identities?

CRITICAL THINKING QUESTIONS

1. In domestic policy, the Reagan presidency represented a decisive swing away from the liberal Democratic agenda that had dated from the New Deal. Discuss this proposition.
2. Discuss the many ways in which social activism continued to play an important role in politics and culture during the 1970s and 1980s?

IDENTIFICATIONS

Review your understanding of the following key terms, people, and events for this chapter (terms in bold in text are included in the Glossary).

Gerald R. Ford, p. 834
James Earl (Jimmy) Carter, p. 834
Three Mile Island, p. 836
energy crisis, p. 836
Camp David Peace Talks of 1978, p. 837
human rights policy, p. 837
Iranian revolution of January 1979, p. 837
New Right, p. 838
Ronald Reagan, p. 839
supply-side economics, p. 840
deregulation, p. 841
William Rehnquist, p. 841
George H. W. Bush, p. 842
Strategic Defense Initiative (SDI), p. 844
Iran-*contra* affair, p. 845
Mikhail Gorbachev, p. 845
Persian Gulf War, p. 846
Chicanismo, p. 854
Dolores Huerta and Cesar Chavez, p. 854

SUGGESTED READINGS

For differing perspectives on political trends that came together during the 1980s and early 1990s, see **Douglas Brinkley, *The Unfinished Presidency: Jimmy Carter's Journey to the Nobel Peace Prize* (1998); Gil Troy, *Morning in America: How**

Ronald Reagan Invented the 1980s (2005); **Jacob Hacker, *The Great Risk Shift: The Great Economic Insecurity and the End of the American Dream*** (2008); **Steven F. Hayward, *The Age of Reagan: Conservative Counterrevolution, 1980–1989*** (2009); and **Betty Glad, *An Outsider in the White House: Jimmy Carter, His Advisors, and the Making of American Foreign Policy*** (2010).

See also, **Bruce J. Schulman, *The Seventies: The Great Shift in American Culture, Society, and Politics*** (2001); **Sean Wilentz, *The Age of Reagan: A History, 1974–2008*** (2008).

Suggestive studies about social and cultural activism include **Juan P. Garcia, ed., *Mexican Americans in the***

1990s (1997); **Lisa McGirr, *Suburban Warriors: The Origins of the New American Right*** (2001); **Frank Wu, *Yellow: Race in America Beyond Black and White*** (2002); **Larry Nesper, *The Walleye War: The Struggle for Ojibwe Spearfishing and Treaty Rights*** (2002); **Sara Evans, *Tidal Wave: How Women Changed America at Century's End*** (2003); **David Carter, *Stonewall: The Riots that Sparked the Gay Revolution*** (2004); **Ruth Rosen, *The World Split Open: How the Modern Women's Movement Changed America*** (rev. ed., 2006); and **Alan J. Lichtman, *White Protestant Nation; The Rise of the American Conservative Movement*** (2008).

Visit the CourseMate website at www.cengagebrain.com for additional study tools and review materials for this chapter.

21st-Century Los Angeles

Billboards such as these, one in English and the other in Chinese, showed how the advertising industry, like other American institutions, adjusted to America's growing linguistic diversity.

Economic, Social, and Cultural Change in the Late 20th Century

T HE FINAL DECADES of the 20th century brought sweeping change to American life. A dramatic increase in immigration, along with movements of people throughout metropolitan areas and into states in the West and South, altered the demographic landscape. The continuing decline of employment in the manufacturing sector changed the workplace for many Americans. A digital revolution transfigured how people communicated in both the public and private spheres. A vast entertainment-informational complex, with an emphasis on professional sports, also emerged. At the same time, religious life in America became more diverse and more closely intertwined with the nation's politics.

A Changing People
    An Aging, Shifting Population
    The New Immigration
    The Metropolitan Nation

Economic Transformations
    New Technologies
    Changes in the Structure
      and Operations of Business
    The Financial Sector
    The Sports-Entertainment
      Industry

Culture and Media
    The Video Revolution
    Hollywood
    The Changing Media Environment
      for Pop Music
    The New Mass Culture Debate
    The Religious Landscape

A Changing People

Q **FOCUS QUESTION** What major demographic trends characterized the post-1970 United States? How did they help change daily life?

America's population changed significantly during the final three decades of the 20th century, becoming older, more metropolitan, and more ethnically and racially diverse. Moreover, the nation's centers of power continued shifting away from the Northeast and toward the South and West.

An Aging, Shifting Population

During the 1950s, the height of the Baby Boom, the population had grown by 1.8 percent per year; after 1970, even with new waves of immigration and longer life expectancies, the growth rate slowed to about 1 percent per year. Younger people were delaying marriage until well into their 20s; most raised smaller families than had their parents; and many adults remained unmarried for much of their lives. The number of households with at least one child under 18 continually shrank. In 1960, nearly half fell into this category; by 1999, only about a third of U.S. households contained even one person under the age of 18. Consequently, by the mid-1980s, people in the 25–44 age category constituted a larger slice of the U.S. population than any other, and the number of teens to early twenties was relatively small.

The steady rise of the median age of the population brought public policy, as well as personal, dilemmas. As aging baby boomers pondered retirement, policymakers began exploring various ways of covering projected Social Security and Medicare payouts to the Baby Boom generation of retirees. Trend watchers of the 1960s had talked of a "youth revolt." By the end of the 20th century, their counterparts pondered the "graying of America."

The changing geographical distribution of population restructured political and economic power. After 1970, most of the population growth occurred in the South and the West. Nevada, California, Florida, and Arizona became the fastest

CHRONOLOGY

1971	Starbucks Coffee opens first store
1972	Congress passes Title IX (Patsy Mink Equal Opportunity in Education Act)
1973	Federal Express opens for business
1977	Congress passes Community Reinvestment Act
1978	Supreme Court decision frees banks to relocate credit-card operations
1979	ESPN joins the cable TV lineup
1981	MTV and CNN debut on cable TV
1982	Congress relaxes regulations on S&Ls
1986	Congress passes Immigration Reform and Control Act
1987	Prices crash on NY Stock Exchange and then rebound
1988	Fox television network begins
1989	Congress enacts bailout plan for S&L industry
1990	Congress passes another Immigration Act
1991	First McDonalds opens in Moscow
1995	Amazon.com begins selling books online
1996	Fox News Network debuts
2000	Human Genome Project issues preliminary draft

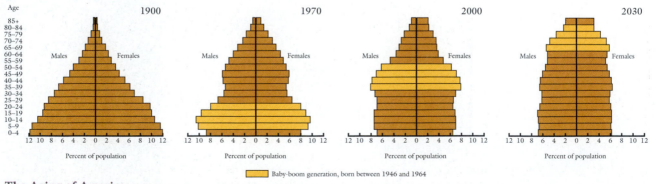

The Aging of America.

Source: U.S. Census Bureau. Adapted from C. L. Himes, "Elderly Americans," *Population Bulletin*, 2002, 56(4), p. 4.

growing states, and by 2000 more than one in ten Americans lived in California. Between 1990 and 2001, California gained eight seats in the House of Representatives, Florida added six, New York lost five, and several Northeastern states shed two or three. Presidential politics increasingly focused on Florida, Texas, and California. Many reasons helped account for this demographic shift: affordable air-conditioning; the expansion of tourism and new retirement communities; and for businesses, the attraction of lower labor costs and the absence of strong unions.

The development of high-tech industries connected to military related spending and the computer revolution also played an important role. California's Santa Clara County, a once rural area near San Francisco, exemplified the trend. Eventually propelled by spectacular growth in its semiconductor industry and its network of computer related enterprises, this locale became known as "Silicon Valley" during the early 1970s. It spawned companies such as Google and Yahoo!

The government financed space program, directed from the National Aeronautics and Space Administration (NASA) installations in Texas and Florida, signified the shift of research and technology to the Sun Belt. In 1961, President Kennedy had announced plans for the manned Apollo program, and in July 1969, astronaut Neil Armstrong had walked on the lunar surface. Apollo flights continued until 1972, when NASA began to develop a space station. In the 1980s, NASA started operating space shuttles, manned craft that served as scientific laboratories in outer space and could be flown back to earth for reuse. In early 1986, the program suffered a tragic setback when a *Challenger* shuttle exploded shortly after liftoff. After a hiatus of more than two years, the program resumed its operations, with new safety procedures in place.

Individual entrepreneurs and giant corporations also migrated to the Sunbelt and crafted multiple versions of a single product: *entertainment*. The Sunbelt featured a host of

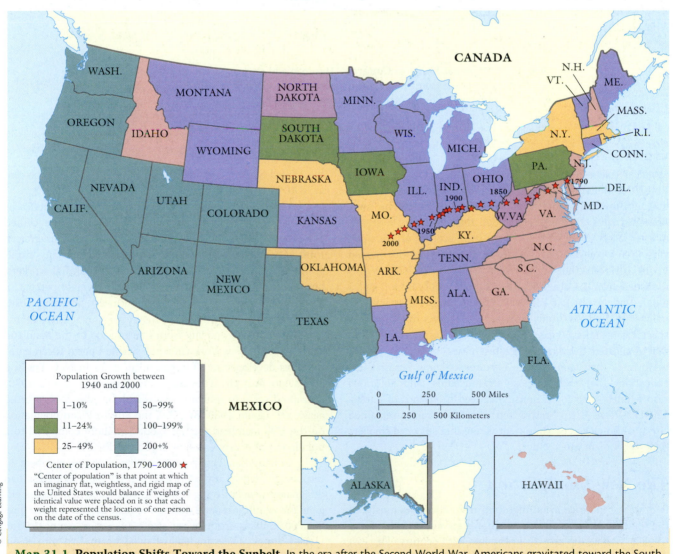

Map 31.1 Population Shifts Toward the Sunbelt. In the era after the Second World War, Americans gravitated toward the South and West. Which states grew the fastest? What might be some of the causes and consequences of such population shifts?

▶ **View an animated version of this map or related maps on the CourseMate website.**

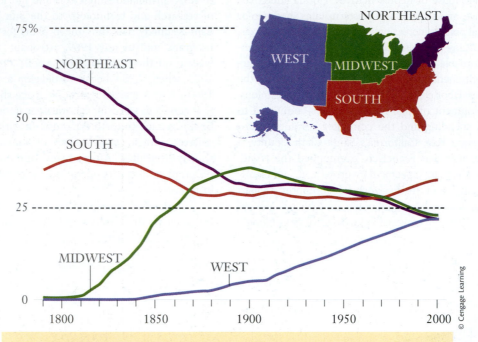

Regional Shifts in Congress
Percent of House seats representing each region

Map 31.2 Regional Shifts in Congress. This map and chart show the changing regional balance in the House of Representatives. Which regions have gained and lost the most political power? Which region is now strongest in the House?
Source: Clerk of the House.

"magical" places such as Disneyland and Las Vegas. These tourist destinations predated the 1970s, but they boomed during the final decades of the 20th century. The sun-drenched sites constantly expanded their offerings in search of ever-larger crowds and ever-greater profits. An enlarged version of Disneyland in Florida, Walt Disney World, opened in 1971. From the 1970s through the 1900s Las Vegas morphed from an underworld controlled outpost for sin, a jungle with green felt gaming tables, into an entertainment magnet that added family-oriented attractions to the mix. A spectacle itself, Las Vegas hosted other spectacles: architecture that replicated the world's greatest cities, past and present; performers that came from every area of show business; art collections that rivaled those in museums; and luxurious resort-hotels that could house and feed thousands of guests. The Las Vegas "strip," retrofitted with mass transit, remained a round-the-clock entertainment venue that spawned smaller-scale versions in other cities.

The New Immigration

A dramatic increase in immigration from countries mostly to the south and west of the United States accounted for much of the U.S. population growth in the late 20th century. The vast bulk of post-1970 immigration came from Asia, Oceania, Latin America, and Africa rather than from Europe, which had previously been the primary source of immigrants. In 2000, roughly 12 percent of the U.S. population had been born outside the United States, compared to the all-time high of 15 percent in 1890.

The largest number of non-European immigrants came from Mexico. Responding to labor shortages in the United States and poor economic prospects at home, immigration from Mexico rose substantially in every decade. Many immigrants from Mexico arrived as seasonal agricultural workers, but most formed permanent communities. Ninety percent of all Mexican Americans lived in the Southwest, primarily Texas and California.

Most people moving from Puerto Rico to the mainland settled around New York City, but sizable Puerto Rican communities developed in Chicago and in cities in New England and Ohio as well. The economic problems of the 1970s prompted some to return to the island, but the flow reversed again after about 1980. By 2000, the Puerto Rican population on the U.S. mainland totaled about 3 million, compared to a population of nearly 4 million in Puerto Rico.

Cubans had begun immigrating in large numbers in response to Fidel Castro's revolution. In 1962, Congress had designated people fleeing from Castro's Cuba as refugees eligible for admittance, and during the next 20 years, more than 800,000 Cubans from every strata of society came to the United States. They gradually moved northward into many major American cities, but the greatest impact was in south Florida. An agreement with Castro in 1995 brought the first U.S. restrictions on the flow of immigrants from Cuba. By 2000, however, about half of all Miamians were of Cuban descent.

The number of Spanish-speaking people in the United States at the end of the 20th century exceeded that of all but four countries of Latin America. Los Angeles became the second largest "Mexican city" in the world, trailing only Mexico City, and its Salvadoran population just about equaled that of San Salvador. More Puerto Ricans lived in New York City than in San Juan, and the Big Apple's Dominican population rivaled that of Santo Domingo.

The broad changes in immigration patterns began with the landmark **Immigration and Nationality Act of 1965**, which spurred not only population growth but diversity as well. Since the 1920s, rates of immigration were determined by quotas based on national origin (see Chapter 24). The 1965 act abolished these. Instead, it placed a ceiling of 20,000 immigrants for every country, gave preference to people with close family ties in the United States, and accorded priority to those with special skills and those classified as "refugees." Although largely unforeseen at the time, this legislation laid the basis for not only a resumption of high-volume immigration but also for a substantial shift in region of origin.

International events also affected U.S. immigration policy. Following the American withdrawal from Vietnam, for example, U.S. officials facilitated the admittance of many Vietnamese, Cambodians, Laotians, and Hmong (an ethnically distinct people who inhabited lands extending across the borders of these three Asian countries). The goal was to resettle some of the people who had allied with the United States during the Vietnam War and whose families were consequently in peril.

In response to the growing number of people seeking admission to the United States, Congress passed the Refugee Act of 1980. It favored political refugees, "those fleeing overt persecution," over people seeking simply to improve their economic circumstances. In practice, U.S. officials interpreted the terms "political" and "economic" so that people leaving communist regimes were admitted but those fleeing right-wing dictatorships were turned away or deported. For example, Cubans and Soviet Jews were admitted, but Haitians often were not. Many Guatemalans and Salvadorans, hoping to escape repressive military governments backed by the United States during the 1980s, stood little chance of being admitted.

Immigration became an ongoing political issue. **The Immigration Reform and Control Act of 1986** (or the **Simpson-Mazzoli Act**) imposed stricter penalties on businesses employing undocumented workers and granted permanent residency to people who could prove that they had been living in the United States since 1982. Immigration continued to soar as the economic upturn of the 1990s acted as a magnet for newcomers. Another Immigration Act in 1990 raised the number of people who could be admitted on the basis of special job skills or the investment capital they could bring into the United States. The prosperity of the 1990s encouraged a continuing flow of immigrants. Those favoring continued high levels of immigration saw potential benefits for the entire nation, but proponents of more rigorous restrictions decried the economic, social, and cultural burdens that newcomers supposedly posed. Starkly

Somalis in Minneapolis. Minnesota hosted the largest concentration in the United States of immigrants from Somalia. Many settled in high-rise apartments near downtown Minneapolis, Minnesota. Several decades earlier, the Riverside Plaza high rises were used in the opening to the popular *Mary Tyler Moore Show.*

conflicting perspectives stalemated any further change in immigration policy.

The new immigration likely affected California more than any other state. In the Golden State, Los Angeles and Orange counties seemed microcosms of world culture. By 2000, more than half of schoolchildren in LA lacked proficiency in English, and no single ethnic group represented a majority of the city's population. Like the wave of immigration that had peaked shortly after 1900, the immigration of the late 20th century produced ethnic rivalries and tensions but also cooperation and hope.

The Metropolitan Nation

Urban–suburban demographics, too, were in a state of flux. At the end of the 20th century, more than 80 percent of Americans lived in vast metropolitan areas. With the overall population growing, the relationship between central cities and adjacent suburbs changed. The suburbs melded into "urban corridors," metropolitan strips running between older cities such as Seattle and Tacoma or Washington and Baltimore. Outlying areas sprouted "edge cities" such as Irvine in California or Boca Raton

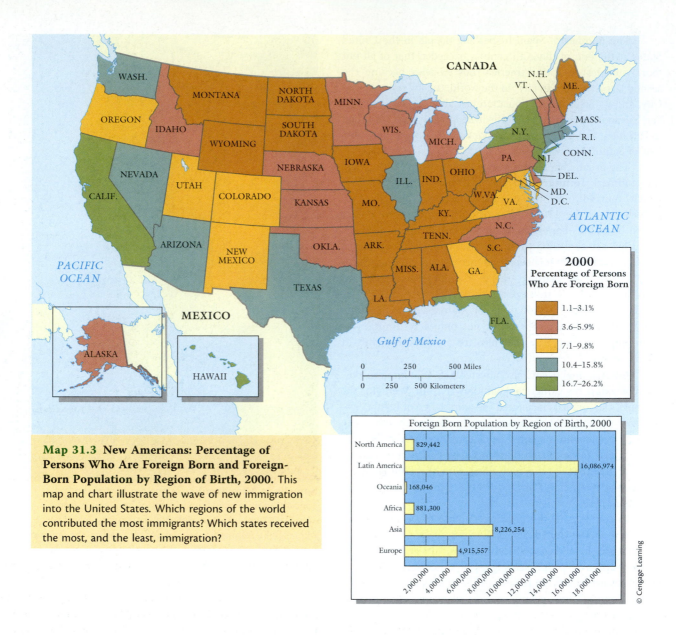

Map 31.3 New Americans: Percentage of Persons Who Are Foreign Born and Foreign-Born Population by Region of Birth, 2000. This map and chart illustrate the wave of new immigration into the United States. Which regions of the world contributed the most immigrants? Which states received the most, and the least, immigration?

2000
Percentage of Persons Who Are Foreign Born

- 1.1–3.1%
- 3.6–5.9%
- 7.1–9.8%
- 10.4–15.8%
- 16.7–26.2%

Foreign Born Population by Region of Birth, 2000

Region	Population
North America	829,442
Latin America	16,086,974
Oceania	168,046
Africa	881,300
Asia	8,226,254
Europe	4,915,557

© Cengage Learning

in Florida. These areas competed with older urban centers for businesses, job opportunities, retail shopping outlets, and residents. People living in edge cities, according to surveys, rarely found the need to visit the nearby center cities such as Los Angeles or Miami.

Demographic patterns within suburban areas also changed. Especially in the last decade of the century, more people from non-European backgrounds began moving to suburbs, just as more Americans of European descent were relocating in cities. As a result, the percentage of African Americans residing in urban centers steadily declined, and the percentage living in suburbia increased. With immigrants settling outside central cites, some suburbs—even in urban areas such as Chicago and Minneapolis—came to contain more foreign-born residents than the central cities they surrounded.

Moreover, new suburbs sprouted up further and further away from either core or edge cities. A frenzy of new construction, financed by innovative lending arrangements, transformed farmland and small towns into a series of sprawling housing developments, which demographers called **"exurbs"**. Built on relatively inexpensive land, exurbs offered homebuyers more space for less money. When commuting to work, however, these exurbanites could easily spend several hours every day trapped inside a car, inching in and out of these areas where transportation seldom kept pace with home construction.

Meanwhile, central cities were transformed. During the 1970s and 1980s, as manufacturing jobs left urban areas and as retail shopping shifted to suburban malls, cities became primarily financial, administrative, and entertainment centers. Most large cities faced rising rates of homelessness and crime and deterioration in schools and infrastructure, especially sewage and water systems. Big-city mayors complained that the government in Washington did little to address urban problems. Federal funding decreased from $64 per urban resident in 1980 to less than $30 by the early 1990s.

At the same time, however, certain areas within many central cities underwent stunning revivals. A building boom brought new office towers, residential buildings, arts complexes

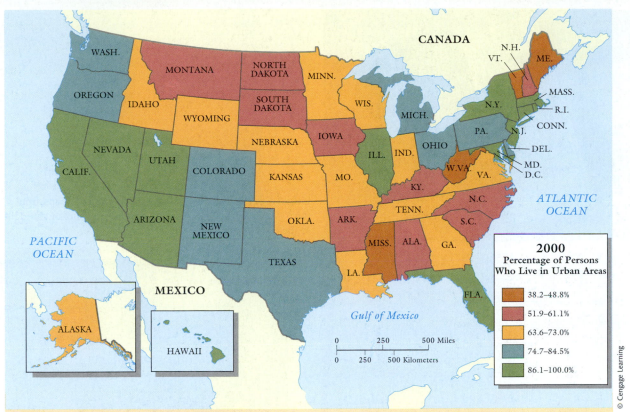

Map 31.4 Urbanization: Percentage of Persons Who Live in Urban Areas in 2000. More and more Americans moved from rural areas in the postwar period. Which states had the most rural dwellers? Which states were the least rural? What might be some economic and political consequences of this demographic change?

and sports facilities to many downtowns across the country. People with cash or credit to spend on housing, restaurants, and entertainment began returning to select areas, which became labeled as "gentrified."

This urban renaissance, which especially gained momentum during the 1990s, sprang from many sources. A vibrant national economy and improved air and water quality helped. Innovations in urban design skillfully integrated diverse architectural styles with new green spaces and revitalized riverbanks and lakefronts. Community development corporations (CDCs), grassroots efforts indebted to movement cultures of the 1960s, supported initiatives for affordable housing, better childcare facilities, and expanded employment opportunities. The **Community Reinvestment Act of 1977**, which obliged banks to finance some home buying in low-income neighborhoods, stimulated economic activity. Subsequently, both major political parties pressed lenders to adopt policies and practices that favored expanded opportunities for home ownership. Community policing, a trend toward harsher sentencing, and an aging population lowered urban crime rates during the 1990s. Moreover, commuters, frustrated by increasingly clogged freeways, discovered that they could save both time and money by moving from distant suburbs to the revitalizing downtowns. In addition, new immigrants repopulated once-declining neighborhoods, refurbishing the housing stock and

reviving the commercial zones. Many U.S. cities featured vibrant, transnational spaces.

Urban life often attracted college-educated professionals who had benefited from the dramatic expansion of higher education. In the 1960s, colleges and universities had doubled their enrollment. The boom continued as the federal government's Pell Grant program softened the impact of uncertain economic times. (Created in 1973, the Pell program financially assists students from low-income families.) More students of non-European ancestry and increasing numbers of women enrolled. By 1980, more than 50 percent of students were women. Gaining a college degree increased a person's income and occupational mobility. By the end of the 20th century, a college graduate's median income was nearly double that of someone with a high school diploma.

The ability to live and play in the new metropolitan spaces, of course, largely depended on household income. During the two decades after 1980, households in the top 10 percent of the income pyramid saw a substantial increase. The incomes of those at *very* top, the super wealthy, fared even better. The vast majority of individuals and families, by contrast, saw far more modest if any gains. An important part of this story involved the transformations that were occurring throughout the U.S. and international economies.

A Changing People ❧ **867**

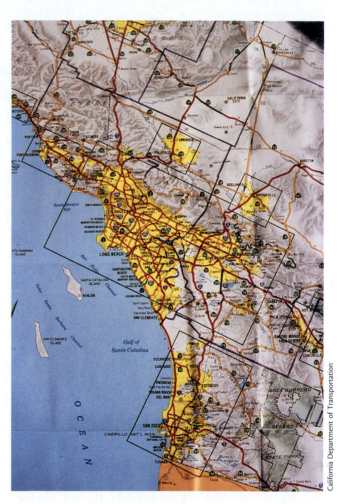

Urban Corridors. These official California road maps, from the 1940s and the 1990s, show development of urban corridors in the Los Angeles area.

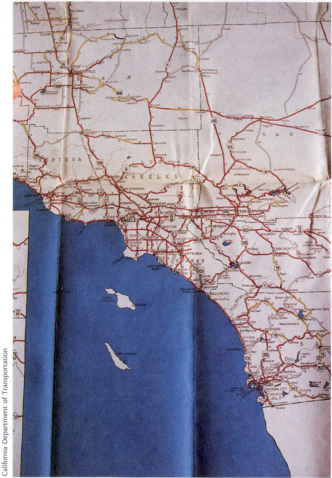

Economic Transformations

FOCUS QUESTION What were the most important post-1970 economic changes? How did economic change create both new problems and new possibilities?

A latter day "Rip van Winkle," awakening from a 30-year sleep in 1999, would have marveled at the consumer products in daily use. People could awaken to sounds from a digital device; glance at the morning news on a personal computer; use the same PC or Mac to work from home; and later watch a daytime soap opera they had recorded earlier. They could also enter a fantasy world through a video game or catch up with the world and friends via the Internet or mobile phone. If one could look past large pockets of persistent poverty, it would seem as if Americans lived in a consumption paradise provided by new technologies and innovative businesses.

New Technologies

The computer revolution, which had begun during the 1940s, entered a new phase after 1970. Microchips increased hardware capacity and reduced the size and cost of computers. Microsoft and Apple, two companies founded during the 1970s, challenged mighty IBM for supremacy in the personal computer market and introduced competing operating systems and Web browsers. Their celebrity CEOs, Bill Gates and Steve Jobs, became two of the wealthiest and most influential people in the world—and came to symbolize key differences between these cyber-era giants. Although Microsoft quickly beat out Apple for domination in the war over lucrative operating systems, the companies continued to battle over virtually everything else, from their complex technologies to the design details of their products. They also fought over that all-important intangible: the loyalty of customers who saw their computers, especially if they owned a Mac, as part of their personal identity.

Changes in the speed and accessibility of informational systems rearranged how people interacted with the larger economy and lived their daily lives. Enhanced memory capacity and parallel processors, which allow many computer operations to run simultaneously, rapidly transformed the handling of words and images. Enhanced by new communications technologies, such as fiber optic networks and then satellite transmission, successive generations of computers fueled an **"information revolution."** Libraries replaced card catalogs with networked computer databases; screens replaced paper. Voicemail, fax transmissions, e-mail, and text messaging came to supplement or substitute for posted mail and telephone conversations. The use of cellular phones spread rapidly during the 1990s and, along with improved computer access, made telecommuting from home to work an attractive option.

Technological innovations in other fields such as biotechnology promised to produce the same kind of dramatic effects. Beginning in 1990, for example, the **Human Genome Project** sought to map the genetic code. This international effort, which unveiled a preliminary draft of the human genome in 2000, sought to introduce new techniques for gene transfer, embryo manipulation, tissue regeneration, and even cloning. Other biotechnological research portended new approaches to the treatment of cancer and other diseases.

Some of the more immediate, and controversial, results of work in biotechnology occurred in the genetic manipulation that began to revolutionize farming, waste conversion, and toxic cleanup. Large food producers, for example, heralded the use of genetically modified crops as an extension of the earlier "green revolution," which had boosted agricultural yields. (Read about how Norman Borlaug's agricultural innovations fueled the "green revolution" and saved lives by preventing famine in the Americans Abroad feature "Norman Borlaug: The 'Green Revolution.'") Foods that had been modified, beginning with those derived from soybeans and corn, first reached consumers during the early 1990s. A genetically modified tomato, which would ripen without softening, debuted in 1994.

AMERICANS ABROAD
Norman Borlaug

Norman Borlaug at His Field Station. In Sonora, Mexico, Borlaug established a major research center for advancing the "green revolution."

These new technologies raised legal and ethical questions. How would the computer revolution, for example, affect traditional ideas and laws about privacy? Biotechnological research generated even more controversial questions. Almost immediately after the Supreme Court decided the abortion case of *Roe* v. *Wade*, for instance, Congress banned federal funding for research involving fetal tissue. Fears that experimentation with embryonic stem cells would increase abortions blocked federal support for research, except when an executive order from Bill Clinton was briefly in effect. Proponents of stem cell research, sustained by other sources of funding, however, argued for its benefits in regenerating human tissue. Controversy, more gradually, came to swirl around genetically modified foods (or GM for short). By the end of the 20th century, critics asked how GM foods might affect individuals with allergies. More ominously, they wondered, could GM crops harm biodiversity across the entire planet and drive out small producers?

Changes in the Structure and Operations of Business

Computerization encouraged businesses to change their modes of operation. Computer networks helped lower costs and boost productivity (the output of goods per labor hour). Companies increasingly abandoned paperwork in favor of computerized tracking systems. The resulting improvement in information processing helped businesses more accurately calculate the relationship between what they produced (or ordered from suppliers) and sales projections. Computers thus enabled "just in time production" or JIT. This streamlined process eliminated waste throughout the production–consumption loop and permitted the downscaling of warehousing operations for unsold products and unused supplies.

The computer revolution also speeded the continued expansion of chain and franchise businesses. McDonald's and

Holiday Inn had pioneered nationwide standardization in the fast food and travel industries during the late 1950s. Similarly organized operations adapted their models after 1970. Starbucks Coffee Company began as a local operation in 1971, rapidly expanded beyond Seattle during the 1980s, and opened a new store somewhere in the world every day during the 1990s. Starbucks helped to add a new term to the labor lexicon, *barista*, and to elevate a once-simple beverage into a pricey designer commodity.

Sam Walton's Wal-Mart chain prospered by moving in the opposite direction: the company promised customers it was constantly rolling back prices. Wal-Mart initially avoided the upscale metropolitan areas where Starbucks was thriving. During the 1970s and 1980s, as Wal-Mart slowly moved beyond its base of operations in Bentonville, Arkansas, it focused on small towns and exurban areas, places where someone other than a *barista* was likely to be preparing coffee. Here, the company could find workers, called "associates," willing to work part-time at relatively low pay. Wal-Mart's labor force thus contained many people, such as married women and retirees, who could not find or did not desire full-time employment. After undertaking an aggressive outreach effort, Wal-Mart became the largest private employer in the United States. By the end of the century, one of about every 120 workers, and nearly one of every 20 in the retail sector, worked for Wal-Mart. Communities were often divided over the arrival of a Wal-Mart. While the retail giant did offer consumers a wide array of merchandise at lower prices, it also crushed local, independent retailers in thousands of midsized and small towns.

U.S.-owned chain and franchise businesses also expanded overseas, especially after the end of the Cold War. In 1991, McDonald's opened to great fanfare in Moscow, and its Pushkin Square restaurant immediately claimed the title of the world's busiest "Mickey D's." U.S.-based hotel chains such as Hilton and Sheraton opened competing, luxury facilities in the former Soviet Union and throughout Eastern Europe. The demise of the Soviet Union also allowed Pepsi and Coke to carry their ongoing "cola wars" into new territory. During the 1970s, Pepsi had struck a special deal with the Kremlin that allowed its cola to be the first American product sold in the Soviet Union. During the 1990s, however, Coca Cola debuted and quickly challenged its rival for cola supremacy in Russia's newly competitive soft-drink market.

A byproduct of the spread of personal computers, Amazon.com led a different kind of retailing revolution during the 1990s—e-commerce, or the practice of selling over the Internet. Launched in 1995, Amazon.com began with books but soon added other products. Toward the very end of the 1990s, a wave of new "dot-com" businesses flooded the Internet and set off a short-term bubble in dot-com stocks that Amazon.com managed to survive. Buying and selling over the Internet quickly became a settled feature of consumer culture. Amazon and the online auction site, eBay, became models for doing business in cyberspace.

Important changes in the transportation of products, when joined to the computer revolution, transformed the global economic marketplace—and the place of the United States within it. Air cargo service improved dramatically after 1970. The fledgling Federal Express Corporation (or FedEx), for example, could claim annual revenues of $1 billion dollars only a decade after its debut in 1973. The greatly expanded use of **steel cargo containers** similarly facilitated national and international commerce. Containers could be easily stacked, insulated, and refrigerated. Even when stretched to 40 feet in length, they could be unloaded from a boat or plane and trucked to their final destination. Containers dramatically lowered the cost of transporting finished goods and raw materials over long distances.

© Keren Su/CORBIS

Lattes in Shanghai. American chain businesses spread throughout the world, part of the process known as globalization.

As suppliers and markets increasingly gave businesses worldwide scope, commercial publications began to refer to the process as **"globalization."** U.S. automakers, for example, increasingly looked outside the United States to procure parts and even to assemble its automobiles and trucks. The trend toward the privatization (the sale of government-owned industries to private business) in many overseas economies provided firms based in the United States with new opportunities for acquisitions. Conversely, foreign buyers purchased U.S. companies and real estate holdings. RCA, Doubleday, Mack Truck, and Goodyear were just some of the traditionally American brands owned by foreign-based corporations during the 1990s. So many industrial giants had become globalized by the end of the 20th century that it became difficult to define what constituted a U.S. company or a foreign one.

New technologies and globalization interacted to change the basic structure of American businesses and their workforces. Citing pressure from declining profits and international competitors, which usually paid workers a fraction of the U.S. wage rate, many industrial companies cut back their labor pools and trimmed their management staffs. This process became known as **"downsizing."** The U.S. auto industry began to lay off thousands of workers, and many older steel plants closed entirely. During the 1990s, the auto and steel industries temporarily regained profitability, but other sectors took their turn at downsizing.

Business restructuring, encouraged by globalization and generous interpretations of anti-trust laws by both Republican and Democratic administrations, touched off a merger boom. During the late 1990s, huge mergers, with acquisitions totaling more than $1.6 trillion per year, brought a concentration in production unseen since the 1890s.

As employment in traditional manufacturing and extractive sectors (such as mining) declined, jobs in service, high-tech, and information and entertainment sectors increased. In 1960, the production of goods, as opposed to services, engaged roughly a quarter of the U.S. workforce. By the end of the 20th century, the comparable figure stood at about 15 percent. Positions in financial services, computing, and other high-tech industries offered high salaries—astronomical ones for top management—but most jobs in the rapidly expanding service sector, such as clerks and cleaners, remained low paying, part-time, and non-unionized. Wal-Mart's enormous non-union workforce, for example, earned an average of $7 to $8 per hour, and had limited, or no, health benefits. Moreover, U.S. manufacturers, wanting to lower costs to compete for the huge Wal-Mart purchasing contracts, moved plants to countries with cheap labor environments. Such moves further contributed to the decline of relatively better-paid manufacturing jobs in the United States.

Some economists worried that this shift toward a "post-industrial" service economy would effectively change the domestic wage-structure, "de-skill" the American labor force, and eventually erode the standard of living in the United States. They warned that the widening gulf between highly paid, skilled positions and minimum-wage jobs with low wages

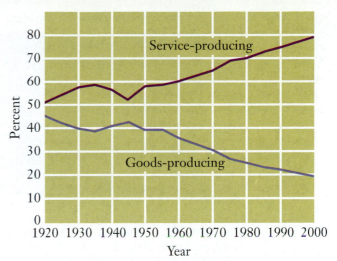

Growth of Service Sector Jobs, 1920–2000.
Source: U.S. Census Bureau.

and few benefits would undermine the middle-class nature of American society.

Other economists were more sanguine. Globalization and corporate downsizing would temporarily mean lost jobs, but gains in productivity would soon translate into lower consumer prices and a rise in living standards for everyone. Celebrants of change also pointed to many success stories, especially in high-tech industries, where constant technological innovation paved a broad avenue of upward economic mobility for people with skills in post-industrial areas such as computing. Real wages did rise a little in the late 1990s, especially for women.

The structure of the labor market changed in other ways. Skilled workers during the middle of the 20th century, for example, tended to stick to one profession and even the same place of employment throughout their working life. By the end of the century, however, both blue- and white-collar workers were likely to switch employers several times before retiring. The need for training and retraining programs that served people of all ages transformed ideas about the relationship between education and work.

Economic restructuring also contributed to a dramatic drop in labor union membership. During the 1950s, more than 30 percent of American workers belonged to a union. By the end of the 20th century, the figure stood at only 13 percent. Although the labor movement mounted organizing drives among clerical, restaurant, and hotel workers, it struggled to make significant inroads into these sectors of the economy. The major growth for organized labor came among government employees and healthcare workers. Most businesses adamantly fought unionization. The health and retirement benefits that American companies had once proudly offered, inexorably began to disappear.

The system of benefits found in the United States, which many companies had greatly expanded after the Second World War, came under increasing pressure. During the 1940s and 1950s, a generous benefit package helped employers attract workers without having to pay dramatically high wages

Average Hourly Earnings, 1964–2008 (*in 2008 dollars*)

1972: $20.06
1979: $18.76
2008: $18.52
1964: $17.54
1993: $16.82

Hourly Wages. Between 1972 and 1993, the average hourly wage dropped from $20.06 to $16.82 in 2008 dollars. Since 1993, the average hourly wage has regained only a part of the ground lost, rising to $18.52 in 2008.

and salaries. Moreover, the amount of money a company paid toward its share of a health plan did not count, under federal law, as part of an employee's taxable compensation. Labor and management both stood to gain, it had seemed, from generous benefit programs.

Things began to change, however, during the 1970s as U.S. companies faced increasing foreign competition and rising costs for healthcare. In 1960, only about 7 percent of the entire U.S. gross domestic product (GDP) went for healthcare; some 40 years later, the comparable figure neared 15 percent, a greater percentage than people paid for food. (In Canada, by contrast, healthcare totaled less than 10 percent of GDP.) The annual cost of providing healthcare for a family, according to most estimates, came to about what a full-time, minimum-wage worker would earn over a year and twice the pay of the average Wal-Mart employee. U.S. companies facing foreign competition, such as the large auto manufacturers, complained about maintaining extensive benefit packages that included healthcare for their aging work forces.

Individuals and families increasingly maintained their lifestyles by incurring rising levels of debt. Economists began to analyze the **"household deficit"**—the difference between what U.S. households earned and what they spent. As late as 1980, the rate of indebtedness for households, though higher than that during the 1950s, still remained lower than it had been during the 1920s. The 1980s, however, inaugurated a trend that would accelerate into the next century. As more people shouldered greater debt, the number of personal bankruptcies increased, and the rate of personal savings in the United States fell to the lowest in the industrialized world.

The Financial Sector

The household deficit became intertwined with one of the most dramatic post-1970 economic changes: The expansion of a vast, highly innovative financial industry. A wide range of financial institutions—from international "super banks" such as Citigroup and Bank of America, to payday loan

institutions like Check 'n Go and Moneytree, to pawnshop chains such as Pawn America, right on down to illegal loan-sharking operations—profited from people who seemed increasingly unable to balance their personal books. By the end of the century, loans to homebuyers who lacked the resources to repay them were helping to sustain the financial industry. The industry also thrived, however, on wealthy investors who appeared awash in assets to invest. By the end of the 20th century, according to one estimate, more than 40 percent of U.S. corporate profits came from the financial services sector while only about 10 percent derived from manufacturing.

The computer revolution helped the financial industry expand and changed its everyday relationship to customers. American consumers had long used a variety of credit arrangements, for example, but bank-issued credit cards, monitored through computerized systems, vastly expanded their reach after 1970. Issuing credit via "plastic" became a highly lucrative enterprise, especially after a 1978 U.S. Supreme Court decision declared that national banks headquartered in one state could move their card operations to any other. This decision effectively eliminated anti-usury laws, which had traditionally limited interest rates, as states competed to attract the credit-card operations of giant banks. These institutions deluged potential cardholders, particularly college students, with competing enticements. "Free" credit cards, once interest and service charges began piling up, proved anything but free to those who used them. Other innovations of the 1980s and 1990s—automated teller machines (ATMs), automatic deposits, debit cards, and electronic bill payment—moved Americans ever closer to a cashless economy.

The financial system increasingly shed the regulatory restrictions crafted earlier in the century, particularly during the New Deal (see Chapter 25). As free-market economists criticized government bureaucrats for ignoring the magical qualities of markets, deregulating the financial industry seemed an obvious way to free up the flow of investment capital. Congress thus lifted many of the restrictions on Savings and Loan institutions (S&Ls) in 1982. Long limited in the services they could provide and the interest rate they could pay depositors, S&Ls boomed. Too many, however, enjoyed deregulation far too much. They made risky loans, speculated in real estate, or simply cooked their books. By the end of the 1980s, the S&L industry was in turmoil and required a massively expensive governmental bailout. (See Chapter 30)

The problems elsewhere in the financial sector, however, seemed limited to individual firms and to specific times, such as the meltdown on the New York Stock Market in October 1987. A rapid rebound seemingly confirmed claims that all markets, including the larger financial ones, were self-correcting, even self-regulating. The S&L debacle, from this perspective, signaled no structural problem in the larger financial industry.

During the last two decades of the 20th century, then, most observers applauded the financial sector's remarkable growth and dynamism. Wall Street investment firms, such as Lehman Brothers, and large banks, such as Chase Manhattan, did well. Newer types of financial ventures, such as the "hedge fund" operations, which managed complicated investment portfolios for a limited number of affluent clients, performed *very* well. Taking in vast pools of money and paying out sizeable profits to their investors, these funds came to make up a "shadow banking system"—one whose financial dealings were not covered by the regulatory system that oversaw more traditional banking institutions. Financial investments—whether in real estate, individual stocks, corporate bonds, or hedge funds—still risked losing money, but a new generation of managers claimed the ability to forecast and thus *manage* risk.

The financial sector could also create, and then trade, new forms of investment that carried the generic name of "derivatives," because they had been "derived" from other financial transactions. During the late 1980s, for example, entrepreneurs in the financial sector began purchasing individual home-loan contracts. Combining those of dubious value with sounder ones, they would market the resultant package of loan contracts as a new form of investment called a "collateralized debt obligation" (CDO). Complex mathematical calculations, which relatively few people in the financial industry fully understood, supposedly ensured that a CDO carried little risk to the financial firm that had created it or to investors who purchased it. Financial analysts argued that the chance of so many different loan contracts defaulting at the same time were so slim that a CDO carried virtually no risk to investors.

CDOs based on home loans were only one of many different types of new securities derived from other kinds of financial transactions. This part of the larger financial system produced huge profits. It also provided similarly outsized payouts, in bonuses and stock options, to the people who worked in this largely unregulated, little understood enterprise. Economists and public officials, including those at the Treasury Department and the Federal Reserve System, cheered the creation of new types of securities. Governmental regulation of them, according to Alan Greenspan, Chairman of the Federal Reserve Board from 1987 to 2006, would discourage innovation and prevent the financial system from performing the task it seemed to be doing so well: delivering an ever-increasing array of secure investments to clients all over the world. The deregulation and globalization of the financial industry, then, echoed other late economic transformations of the last three decades of the 20th century transformations. The hazards would become apparent in 2008.

The Sports-Entertainment Industry

The sports-entertainment industry also grew exponentially during this era. Metropolitan areas competed to obtain—or retain—professional teams. TV contracts and tax write-offs tempted tycoons such as George Steinbrenner of the New York Yankees to run a sporting empire. An older generation of owners such as the Halas family in football and the Griffiths in baseball, who had supported themselves only through a sports franchise, passed from the scene.

Baseball led off this expansionist era. Seeking a better fit with emerging economic, demographic, and social forces, the leadership of Major League Baseball (MLB) realigned the "national pastime." During a single decade, the 1970s, MLB shuffled teams in and out of Milwaukee, Seattle, and Washington, D.C. By relocating franchises from struggling to thriving metropolitan areas, MLB acquired new ticket buyers, advantageous TV deals, and stadiums financed by public money. If moving existing franchises made sense, creating new ones seemed an even shrewder option. During the mid-1950s, there had been only 16 Big League teams, none located west of Chicago; at the end of the 20th century, 30 MLB franchises stretched across the United States and into Canada.

The National Football League (NFL) and the National Basketball Association (NBA) challenged MLB for the professional sports spotlight. Surveys showed fans shifting their allegiances from baseball to faster-paced sports. Having operated in the shadow of MLB until the 1960s, the NFL and the NBA expanded into new metropolitan areas and created lengthy schedules that overlapped with the once sacrosanct baseball season.

Just in time for the 1970 season, the NFL merged with the American Football League (AFL), with which it had been playing a "Super Bowl" since 1967. In contrast to the economic philosophy of MLB, that of the revamped NFL helped small-market teams such as the Green Bay Packers remain competitive with larger market franchises over the long run. During the 1970s, ABC began televising an NFL game during primetime hours, and the success of *Monday Night Football* signaled the growing importance of football to TV and to the nation's popular culture.

Basketball's small court made NBA games more TV-friendly than those of football and baseball, and entrepreneurs easily gained television contracts to underwrite new professional franchises. As a result, the NBA faced a lengthy off-the-court rivalry with the upstart American Basketball Association (ABA). When the two leagues finally merged in 1976, the NBA jettisoned the ABA's garish, multicolored basketball but retained its 3-point shot and emphasis on marketing African American stars like Julius ("Dr. J") Irving. After joining the league in 1984, Michael Jordan soon became the preeminent symbol for marketing the NBA and anchored the "Dream Team" of professionals that captured basketball's Gold Medal at the 1992 Olympic Games. The NBA also elevated African Americans into coaching and management positions far more quickly than did the NFL and MLB.

Several efforts to make soccer a major attraction in the United States faltered, but most other sports-entertainment operations flourished. The venerable National Hockey League (NHL) outlasted the rival league World Hockey Association (WHA) and entered the 1980s with a 21-team operation that stretched across both Canada and the United States. By the end of the 20th century, the NHL supported 28 franchises, three fewer than the NFL and only one fewer than the NBA. Professional play in tennis, aided by TV coverage, featured rapidly expanding tours for both men and women.

Professional golf for men—tightly controlled by the Professional Golfing Association (PGA)—continually grew in popularity, especially after it found its own version of Michael Jordan, Eldrick (Tiger) Woods, during the early 1990s. Woods soon became *the* brand name for a sports-business that attracted corporate sponsors, sold a vast array of high-end products, and sustained a media presence that included a separate Golf Channel (1995–) on cable TV. Although the economic and cultural impact of the Ladies Professional Golf Association (LPGA) lagged behind that of the men's, the women's tour prospered. It also emulated the post-Woods PGA and the NBA by attracting a growing number of players from outside the United States to its ranks.

The national romance with automobiles helped to speed the growth of auto racing. The Indianapolis 500 initially vied with the Super Bowl for recognition as the most spectacular one-day event in sports, but events sponsored by the National Association for Stock Car Racing (NASCAR) eventually overtook those of Indy-style racing. As new technologies brought TV viewers onto the track and even into the race cars, NASCAR moved beyond its traditional base in the South. Its signature event, the Daytona 500, replaced the Indy 500 as the nation's premier automobile race.

College sports grew in similar fashion. Television coverage mushroomed, especially after TV entrepreneurs created **ESPN** (1979–), a cable network devoted entirely to sports. ESPN initially helped so-called minor collegiate sports, such as gymnastics and lacrosse, gain TV time, but college football and basketball ultimately benefited the most. Television allowed football's longstanding post-season bowl system to create more games and reap greater revenues. The playoff arrangement in college basketball, which had begun in 1939, evolved into an extended extravaganza that became known during the 1980s as "March Madness." University administrators often claimed that success on their playing fields and arenas, which became ever larger and more luxurious, translated into greater visibility and prestige, and garnered more donations for the educational mission of their institutions.

The glamour and excitement generated by the sports-entertainment industry increasingly merged with political culture. Candidates competed to sign up prominent athletes for their campaign squads, and some retired players, including football's Jack Kemp and Hall of Fame hurler Jim Bunning, made the transition from the sports to the political field. In addition to tapping his family connections, George W. Bush used his partial ownership of the Texas Rangers baseball team as an entrée into electoral politics. The position that Bush reportedly desired more than any other, however, was that of MLB's commissioner.

With the business of sports booming, its legal foundations inevitably shifted. MLB's star players, armed with union advisers and attorneys, successfully spearheaded new legal challenges to old doctrines that contractually bound players to a single franchise year after year. Court rulings eventually brought differing versions of "free agency" to the major team sports. These systems soon produced powerful new players in the sporting world: sports agents who could help professional athletes auction their services and marketing potential to the highest bidder. Although some fans and sportswriters grumbled when highly paid players seemed to under perform, owners discovered that steadily rising TV revenues, tax breaks, and favorable stadium deals allowed them to adjust to the new salary structures and strong union movements. Knowledgeable fans became as conversant in contract law and labor-management relations as with more traditional matters such as batting averages and yards-per-carry.

Sports and legal disputes also became intertwined with social issues. Women's rights advocates condemned big-time sports for promoting sexism—pointing, for example, to NFL cheerleading squads that resembled Las Vegas chorus lines—and urged equality for women athletes. One result of this pressure was **"Title IX"** of a 1972 congressional measure, which was later re-titled the **Patsy Mink Equal Opportunity in Education Act**. By mandating gender equity in intercollegiate sports activities, Title IX required colleges and universities to upgrade the financing and promotion of women's sports. A 1973 exhibition tennis match between Billy Jean King, the leading women's player of the day, and a former male star from the 1940s, Bobby Riggs, helped dramatize the gender-equity issues that Title IX addressed. (Billy Jean King won the match.) Over time, professional tennis surpassed every other sport in narrowing the gender gap in prize money, endorsement contracts, and media coverage.

The sports-entertainment industry continued to provide a cultural mirror on racial issues. The effort to measure how much opportunity sports really offered to African American athletes, especially at the collegiate level, remained a persistent concern. By the end of the 20th century, for example, the number of African Americans playing professional baseball was in decline while the number of Latino ballplayers was soaring. And as NBA scouts began identifying talented international players, especially from Eastern Europe, some observers predicted that the strong African American presence in the NBA might suffer as well.

While the sports-entertainment complex was growing in visibility and profitability, traditionalists detected signs of decline. The familiar complaint about intercollegiate athletics corrupting educational standards gained new force. Critics also found many sporting enterprises awash in hyper-commercialism, financial double-dealing, and on-field cheating. The success of MLB, for example, seemingly owed much to the prodigious feats of homerun hitters led by Mark McGwire of the St. Louis Cardinals, who hit a record 70 home runs in 1998. It soon became apparent, however, that performance enhancing drugs—and perhaps souped-up baseballs—were aiding sluggers like McGwire. Sports historians now argue that the late 1980s ushered in baseball's "Steroid

Era." The super-knowledgeable sports fan might wish for a background not only in legal but in pharmaceutical matters as well.

Culture and Media

Q **FOCUS QUESTION** How did new forms of media change the ways in which people received entertainment, information and even religious instruction? How did the debate over popular culture in the 1980s and 1990s differ from the earlier debate of the 1950s?

A broader range of knowledge could also prove handy for fans of all forms of popular culture. New technologies significantly altered how people received and used books, movies, TV, music, and other sources of information and entertainment. By the end of the 20th century, virtually every home or apartment had at least one television and an accompanying recording device. About 80 percent had a personal computer. People began using the Internet to access newspapers, books, music, and movies. E-mail became, before the popularity of text messaging, the first choice for contacting friends. The omnipresent video screen, more portable than ever before, seemed the preeminent symbol of American culture by the end of the 20th century.

The Video Revolution

At the beginning of the 1970s, TV broadcasters still expected a hit program to attract more viewers in a single evening than did a successful motion picture over an entire year. The three networks could also promise advertisers that a rough cross-section of the American public would be watching their night-time sales pitches.

During the 1970s, however, viewing trends increasingly forced the networks to embrace the strategy called **"narrow-casting"** in which programmers fragmented the TV audience into carefully targeted segments. CBS replaced several highly watched programs, such as *The Beverly Hillbillies*, with "edgier" shows aimed at viewers under the age of 40, who were coveted by advertisers because they were most likely to purchase products and services. *All in the Family*, a sitcom about intergenerational conflict within a blue-collar family, made its proudly bigoted protagonist, "Archie Bunker," a lightning rod for issues involving race and gender. Although *The Mary Tyler Moore Show* rarely took overtly feminist positions, it did address the personal politics of working women. Other CBS shows, such as *M*A*S*H*, also merged comedy with social commentary.

With CBS leading the way, the new programming strategy helped the entire TV industry prosper between the mid-1970s and mid-1980s. ABC found its niche among high school- and college-age viewers, emphasizing sex-and-action programs (*Charlie's Angels*), mildly risqué sitcoms (*Three's Company*), and shows about teen life (*Happy Days*). NBC belatedly brought the barbed humor of the 1960s counterculture to network television by nurturing *Saturday Night Live*. At the end of the 1970s, 9 of every 10 television sets were tuned to a network program during primetime viewing hours.

A decade later, however, people were beginning to desert network TV, and programmers were struggling to attract viewers. NBC could claim two now-classic hits, *The Cosby Show* (featuring an affluent African American family), and *Cheers* (which was set in a Boston tavern where "everybody knows your name"). Its other primetime programs, however, garnered disappointing ratings. Facing a similar situation, the other two networks joined NBC in slashing budgets and staff, especially in their news divisions. Local stations, which had been limping along without a network affiliation, began picking up viewers who were deserting network offerings. These independents programmed older Hollywood films, sporting events, and reruns of canceled primetime shows now being syndicated to individual stations. Several hundred independent television stations debuted during the 1980s.

Capitalizing on the rise of these independents, the media mogul Rupert Murdoch introduced his Fox TV network in 1988. Using a pattern later imitated by far less-successful challengers, Fox offered a limited schedule to previously nonaffiliated stations. Fox's first big hit, *The Simpsons* (1989–), an animated send-up of the standard family sitcom, became a pop culture phenomenon and mass-marketing bonanza. In 1993 Fox outbid CBS for the TV rights to carry NFL games. Throughout the 1990s, Fox and the other fledgling networks introduced programs—such as *In Living Color* and *Buffy the Vampire Slayer*—for audiences that contained more minority, young, and urban viewers than those of the three older networks.

New technologies, which promised viewers greater choice, challenged all four networks. The remote control, an innovation introduced during the 1960s that finally clicked during the 1980s, created a television aesthetic called "channel surfing," in which viewers flip rapidly from program to program. Videocassette recorders (VCRs), introduced during the 1970s, became the first of the record-and-view-later technologies allowing viewers to create their own TV schedules.

The primary challenge to the networks came from cable television, which had wired nearly three-quarters of the nation's homes by 2000. The expansion of cable during the 1980s accelerated audience fragmentation and narrowcasting. Atlanta's Ted Turner led the way by introducing the Cable News Network (CNN), several movie channels, and an all-cartoon network before his communication empire merged with that of Time-Warner in 1996. Challenging the networks and cable, companies selling direct satellite transmission began gaining an important share of the viewing audience. By the end of the 20th century, the percentage of viewers watching primetime network programs had fallen to less than 60 percent, and cable shows were beginning to compete with those carried on the networks for the industry's annual Emmy awards.

Hollywood

Hollywood also adapted to changing business arrangements and new technologies. With movie attendance in 1970 about the same as it had been in 1960, the film industry began raising ticket prices, betting on a few blockbuster films such as the highly profitable *Star Wars* series (1977–2005), and hoping for

Family Guy. As the U.S. TV audience began to fragment, animated shows increasingly found exceedingly loyal niche markets. The Fox network introduced *Family Guy* in 1999 but canceled the series in 2000. Noting the popularity of *Family Guy* in reruns and the strong DVD sales, Fox soon began producing new episodes. Although the inept antihero of the series, Peter Griffin, recalls Fred Flintstone and Homer Simpson, aficionados of this series consider his antics and *Family Guy*'s references to popular culture several cuts above those found on *The Flintstones* and *The Simpsons.*

a surprise hit such as *The Blair Witch Project* (1999). Although Hollywood endured super-expensive flops such as *Heaven's Gate* (1980) or *Eyes Wide Shut* (1999), motion pictures survived and even thrived through adaptation.

Volatility in the movie market encouraged most filmmakers to play it safe. Many of them recycled titles and special effects that had made money in the past. They transferred popular stories, such as *How the Grinch Stole Christmas* (2000), and TV shows, such as *The Brady Bunch* (1995), to the big screen and produced sequels for any movie, such as *Speed* (1992), that had even approached blockbuster status. In addition, Hollywood expanded the older practice of targeting younger viewers with movies such as *Ferris Bueller's Day Off* (1986). Meanwhile, celebratory stories that tapped themes in popular history, such as *Braveheart* (1995) and *Titanic* (1997), impressed both ticket buyers and industry insiders.

At the same time, however, a cultural complex that nurtured "independent" films emerged. Woody Allen became one of the first U.S. filmmakers to specialize in movies, such as *Annie Hall* (1977), which borrowed techniques and themes from European cinema. In 1981, Robert Redford launched the Sundance Film Institute in hopes of encouraging innovative screenwriting and direction. Its annual Sundance Festival, held in Park City, Utah, began attracting Hollywood moguls. They sought the next small movie, such as *The Brothers McMullan* (1995), that might find a large audience. Sundance supported the work of African American, Latino, and Asian American directors by showcasing movies like *Hoop Dreams* (1994), *El Mariachi* (1993), and *Picture Bride* (1995). It also celebrated women directors such as Lizzie Borden (*Working Girls*, 1986)

and Barbara Kopple (*American Dream*, 1990). The Landmark movie chain led the way in screening independent films unlikely to find space in any of the growing number of suburban multiplexes. Major studios even created special divisions, such as Fox Searchlight Pictures, which specialized in so-called independent films.

Hollywood became increasingly intertwined with the changing television establishment, once its feared rival, and with the emerging home-viewing industries. Hollywood gained badly needed revenue by licensing its offerings to TV and for VCR and DVD distribution. For a brief time, during the early 1990s, the United States could claim more video rental outlets than movie theaters. Advances in DVD technology gave viewers improved visual imagery, bonus attractions (such as footage that had been cut from a theatrical release), wide-screen prints, and the kind of expert commentary hitherto available only at film schools. As the Hollywood movie industry discovered that DVD sales could match theatrical receipts, it came to favor action films with elaborate special effects that promised to sell well in the home viewing and international markets. Filmmakers also confronted new "pirating" technologies that meant their movies might appear in bootlegged editions at virtually the same time they debuted in theaters.

The Changing Media Environment for Pop Music

New business ventures and technologies also transformed the relationship between the media and the lucrative pop music industry. A Music Television channel (MTV) debuted in 1981 and subsequently adjusted to changes in the cable TV and

HISTORY THROUGH FILM

Star Wars (1977)

Directed by George Lucas.
Starring Mark Hamill (Luke Skywalker), Alec Guinness (Obi-Wan Kenobi), Harrison Ford (Han Solo), Carrie Fisher (Princess Leia), and James Earl Jones (voice of Darth Vader).

The series of *Star Wars* movies, which began in 1977, eventually gained a vast following. The initial *Star Wars* broke all previous box-office records and launched thousands of merchandising tie-ins. Marketing campaigns for *Star Wars* began in the era of low-tech products, such as Luke Skywalker lunch boxes, and extended into the age of interactive computer video games. The movie's creator, George Lucas, earned more money from licensing images from *Star Wars* than he made from the movie's unprecedented box-office receipts.

Star Wars, which took three years and the then-astronomical sum of $30 million to produce, generated a similarly outsized popular response. Within three years, it returned nearly 2,000 percent profit. It gained 10 Academy Award nominations, seven Oscars, and three Grammies. The movie also financed Lucas's own private media empire, Lucasfilm Ltd.; introduced six-track Dolby stereo sound to movie theaters; helped to make viewers in their teens and early 20s Hollywood's primary target audience; and

Star Wars' C-3PO and R2-D2, a 'droid and a robot with personalities, generated considerable non-film revenue from product tie-ins.

pioneered computerized breakthroughs in the use of graphic imagery and camera movement. The bottom line for Hollywood increasingly depended less on producing a steady supply of successful films than on releasing a few "blockbusters" modeled on *Star Wars*. Blockbusters were designed to attract a huge initial audience, create an expectation of sequels, sustain a variety of ancillary products, do well overseas, and sell briskly in formats aimed at the home viewing market.

The initial *Star Wars* entry, eventually the third installment of a six-part series, arguably tells an allegorical story that works against the cynicism and divisions of the Vietnam era. Young Luke Skywalker, aided by the wizened Obi-Wan Kenobi and Han Solo, joins the fight to defeat the "Empire" and to rescue Princess Leia from the villainous Darth Vader. The movie embellishes this sparse tale with imagery borrowed from various Hollywood genres, including science fiction, combat films, westerns, and the Saturday-morning serials of the 1930s and 1940s.

The film's major event, Luke Skywalker's destruction of the "Death Star," can appear to soothe the traumatic history of U.S. involvement in Southeast Asia with a heroic folktale about triumph over evil. Similarly, the alliance between the youthful Skywalker and the aging Obi-Wan Kenobi might seem a parable about the need to move beyond the "generation gap" of the 1960s.

Seen another way, though, a film product such as *Star Wars* seemed to rest less on crafting the kind of political-historical allegory found in a Cold War-era movie such as *High Noon* (1952) than on simple market logic. A successful blockbuster primarily became a venue for eye-popping special effects (often portraying considerable violence and mayhem) and for images (such as those of cute robots and cuddly creatures) for marketing in off-screen forms. In this sense, spectacles such as *Star Wars* merit attention primarily as contributions to the economic health of the Hollywood film industry. 🎬

music industries. Initially offering a 24-hour supply of rock videos, MTV came under fire for portraying women as sex objects and excluding artists of color. Eventually, however, MTV defused complaints, especially after featuring Michael Jackson's 29-minute video based on his hit single "Thriller" (1983). By the end of the 20th century, MTV and other cable channels programmed videos that represented the increasingly multiethnic nature of the music industry.

MTV also seemed on the cutting edge of changes in media programming. MTV's stars of the 1980s such as Jackson and Madonna used MTV to forge a new relationship between music and visual imagery: the **"MTV aesthetic."** This fast-paced visual style played with traditional ideas about time and space, recycled images from earlier movies and TV programs, and often carried a sharply satirical edge. During the 1990s, MTV introduced a wide range of youth-oriented programming such as *The Real World* (1992–). MTV's longest running program, *The Real World* inaugurated the "reality TV" genre that spread to other cable channels and the broadcast networks.

Entertainment conglomerates began marketing music in ever-newer formats. The 45-rpm record and the long-play album (LP), associated with the musical revolutions of the 1950s and 1960s, all but disappeared. Analog cassette tapes, which could be played through a variety of portable stereo devices including Sony's Walkman, arrived during the 1970s. The compact discs (CDs) of the early 1980s changed not only the technology for delivering pop music but also, eventually, the nature of the product and the listening experience. The now-classic rock LPs of the 1960s and early 1970s, such as the Beatles' *Magical Mystery Tour* (1967), had featured 10 to 12 songs, split between the two sides and often organized around a core concept. By the late 1990s, however, CD offerings were coming to mirror those that MP3 technology was just beginning to provide by offering unusual musical mixes that generally lacked any unifying theme.

New formats enabled listeners to obtain, preserve, and exchange music in entirely new ways. FM radio stations began to stream their programs over the Internet during the early 1990s, and one of rock's most venerable bands, The Rolling Stones, was the first to simulcast a live concert in 1994. After several years in which Internet users experimented with the sharing of musical files, in 1999 a college student introduced Napster. This short-lived venture provided a technology by which users could freely share music gleaned from commercially produced CDs. Artists as well as corporate executives confronted a serious threat to CD sales—and the future of their industry. They charged Internet technologies with facilitating the "pirating" of copyrighted material. Their legal actions prompted a prolonged battle—which extended into the new century—over how music was made, stored, and distributed.

The New Mass Culture Debate

New trends in mass commercial culture generated other controversies, many of them also legalistic ones. In 1975, the Federal Communications Commission (FCC) ordered the television networks to dedicate the first 60 minutes of primetime each evening to "family" programming free of violence and "mature" themes. Eventually, federal courts struck down this family-hour requirement as a violation of the First Amendment. Demands that Congress regulate rock lyrics and album covers also ran afoul of complaints that legislation of this kind would be unconstitutional. TV programmers, record producers, and new Internet gaming ventures, following the example of the Hollywood film industry, began to adopt "warning labels" that supposedly informed parents about products with violent and sexually explicit imagery.

Commercial pop culture also produced new aesthetic disputes. Unlike the cultural critics of the 1950s, who had dismissed mass fare as trivial and degenerate (see Chapter 28), analysts from the new academic field of "cultural studies" often seemed unabashed fans of the commercial products they studied. They jettisoned any bright-line distinction between lowbrow and highbrow as untenable. The music of the Beatles could be studied along with that of Beethoven, Bob Dylan's lyrics alongside classic poetry. Rejecting the elitist-themed criticism of the 1950s, which had seen consumers as cultural dupes who passively soaked up junk, cultural studies stressed people's creative interaction with commercial culture. Scholarly accounts of *Star Trek*, for example, examined how, through self-produced magazines (called "fanzines"), conventions, and the Internet, Trekkies created a grassroots subculture that used the original TV series and its spinoffs to launch serious discussions about social and political issues. The cultural studies approach also tended to embrace multiculturalism, highlighting works produced by women, political outsiders, and non-Western writers and artists. It encouraged students to see traditional texts within their political and historical contexts rather than as timeless works. Traditionalists condemned this "cultural turn" as a legacy of the counterculture of the 1960s and blamed it for eroding settled ideas about the quality and value of artistic expression.

Some of the fiercest debates over popular culture involved the impact of "infotainment." An imprecise cultural category, infotainment signaled that the always-delicate balance between actually informing and merely amusing audiences had tilted decisively toward the latter.

Cable TV's news operations, for example, emphasized infotainment in ways that the major networks had long avoided. While maintaining a 24/7 schedule, CNN initially followed the networks in pursuing a "hard-news" agenda from camera crews and correspondents stationed around the globe. CNN's motto was "news is the star." CNN also introduced, however, programs such as *Crossfire*, which featured the in-studio pyrotechnics of verbally dueling pundits. The cacophony of claims and counter-claims, indebted to the legal-drama format popularized throughout the 1990s (see Chapter 32), increasingly bore slight resemblance to the kind of news analysis that network radio and TV had traditionally offered. CNN's eventual rival, the Fox News Channel (FNC), which debuted in 1996, retrofitted the *Crossfire* approach to much of its programming. FNC featured verbally nimble personalities who covered the news from studio sets and emphasized, despite labels such as "fair and balanced," political opinions that tilted toward those of the New Right.

Public affairs broadcasting on cable TV increasingly adopted a narrowcasting strategy. This represented a significant break with the traditional broadcast format, going back to network radio, which had always sought a "big tent" audience. FNC made clear, for example, that its idea of "balance" would attract viewers who saw the major networks and CNN as "biased." CNN and MSNBC, in response, began positioning their coverage toward people uncomfortable with FNC. This new approach, critics charged, featured news programming that reinforced rather than broadened the perspectives of core constituencies. A "fake" news program, *The Daily Show*, satirized the narrowness of its cable TV counterparts. It also arguably produced—or simply attracted—viewers more broadly informed about issues than were the aficionados of

MUSICAL LINK TO THE PAST

Hip-Hop Leaps In

Songwriters: E. Fletcher, M. Glover, C. Chase, S. Robinson
Title: "The Message" (1982)
Performers: Grandmaster Flash and the Furious Five

Black radio formats in the early 1980s were generally staid and conservative, favoring such easy listening, corporate-associated artists as Lionel Richie. According to critic Nelson George, New York-based black music professionals "were so office-bound, taking meetings with managers and listening to tapes from song publishers [in midtown Manhattan], that they failed to venture up the road to Harlem and the South Bronx, where, in the middle of the nation's most depressing urban rot, something wonderful was happening." That "wonderful" innovation was hip-hop music, which began in the mid-1970s with DJs using other artists' records (Chic's "Good Times" was a perennial favorite) as instrumental backing tracks for live rappers. Hip-hop assembled elaborate rhyming stories, messages, and boasts—often improvised on the spot.

Although early hits such as the Sugar Hill Gang's 1979 "Rapper's Delight" promoted a genial party mood, "The Message" presented a sobering litany of inner-city ghetto life: police brutality, junkies, pimps, homeless people "pissing on the stairs," and random violence, punctuated with the mantra of "sometimes it makes me wonder, how I keep from going under." It presaged the even harder-edged, more politically minded, and economically successful rap artists, such as Public Enemy, NWA, and KRS-One. Despite commercial success

("The Message" achieved top-five R&B hit status), major label executives veered away from the angry black, mostly male, performers of rap music until the mid-1980s. Like earlier controversial American music innovations such as bebop and rock 'n' roll, rap was initially confined to independent label distribution.

Hip-hop also introduced revolutionary musical approaches. DJ Grandmaster Flash, who was unable to afford studio-recording time in the mid-1970s, created his own backing tracks by manipulating turntables and vinyl records in new ways. He, along with DJ Kool Herc, pioneered the effects of "scratching" (turning records manually to make the needle repeat brief lengths of groove) and "phasing" (altering turntable speeds to change the sound of recordings). These and other new technologies enabled "The Message" to offer a complex soundscape that represented the urban atmosphere of the early 1980s.

Q How did hip-hop artists convert a turntable into a musical instrument?

Q What might this use of a century-old technology say about the role of technology in musical change and the specific cultural climate that gave birth to hip-hop?

"real" newscasts. After Jon Stewart assumed the "anchor desk" in January 1999, the *Daily Show* quickly became a favorite news source for college students.

The Religious Landscape

A pervasive religiosity differentiated the United States from most European nations during the last decades of the 20th century. Attention commonly focused on Americans drawn to the Religious Right, but a propensity to see daily life and world events through religious teachings spanned the political and cultural spectrum. Polls taken at the end of the 20th century suggested that more than three-quarters of Americans believed in a divine being that performed miracles on earth.

The nation's religious landscape showed greater diversity than ever before. During the 1950s, for example, Will Herberg could see his book entitled *Protestant-Catholic-Jew* (1955) as characterizing the religious dimensions of the "American way of

life." A half-century later, however, these three faiths represented only some of the religious denominations in the United States.

After about 1970, cultural and social change helped produce this religious diversity. Movements such as the Jesus People were loosely associated with the counterculture. A few other countercultural groups withdrew to communal retreats organized around religious teachings. Many people drawn to alternative cultures also embraced spiritual and religious impulses outside of the Protestant-Catholic-Jewish triad. Asian-inspired traditions, such as Transcendental Meditation and Buddhism, proved particularly appealing. A variety of New Age spiritual movements, which stressed individual insights over group doctrines, also traced their most immediate origins back to the early 1970s.

The same era also saw the beginnings of a significant movement toward Islam among Americans of African descent, especially those who had been affected by the Black Power movement. Following the 1975 death of Elijah Muhammad,

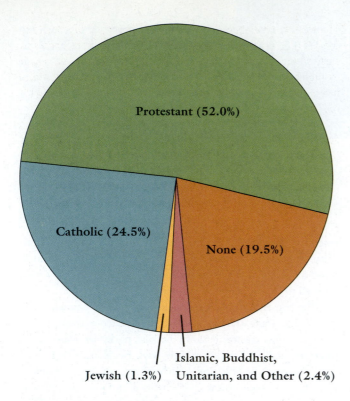

Religion in America, 2001. This chart shows the self-described religious affiliations of the American people compiled through sampling techniques.

Source: Data adapted from *The American Religious Identification Survey*, Graduate Center, City University of New York.

Meanwhile, the Immigration and Nationality Act of 1965 enabled larger numbers of immigrants from many religious backgrounds, including Islam, to settle in the United States. As the array of different faiths expanded, for instance, the weekly directory of religious services in the Los Angeles *Times* noted times and places for nearly 600 different denominations. Immigration from countries with large Islamic populations brought several million Muslims to the United States during the 1990s. According to some estimates (the official U.S. Census does not track religious affiliations) the number of residents who were practicing Muslims by the year 2000 surpassed those practicing Judaism, and even those identifying with several mainline Protestant denominations, including Presbyterian and Episcopalian. Adapting to American cultural practices, mosques began making Sunday, rather than the traditional Friday, the week's major Islamic holy day. The faith's leading institutions, such as the Islamic Center of Southern California, provided a variety of religious and non-religious services for their congregations. They also sought to inform non-Muslims about Islam, which claimed more followers worldwide than any other religion.

Other religions experienced similar growth. The number of Protestant evangelicals grew faster than the U.S. population. Between 1970 and the late 1990s, the Southern Baptist Convention expanded beyond its traditional regional base and added 6 million new members. The Church of Jesus Christ of the Latter-day Saints (the Mormon faith) gained more than half that many. Along with augmenting their membership rolls at home, many of these groups greatly expanded their international missionary activities.

Religious faith did not determine political belief. Most fundamentalists and evangelicals favored the politics of the New Right, but there were evangelical groups that espoused diametrically opposed political-social positions. As Jim Wallis of the Sojourner movement wrote in 1995, an "illness of spirit has spread across the land, and our greatest need" was a "new kind of politics—a politics with spiritual values" that pursued many of the "social justice" issues identified with the political left. Moreover, some evangelicals joined mainline religious

the longtime leader of the Nation of Islam (NOI) or "Black Muslims," his successors moved closer to Sunni Islam. The dynamic and outspoken Louis Farrakhan, once a rival to Malcolm X, revived the NOI during the 1980s, but it attracted far fewer members than other versions of Islam. By 1990, American-born converts, the majority of them of African descent, comprised more than 40 percent of those who practiced Islam in the United States.

The Islamic Center of America, Dearborn, Michigan. This 70,000-square-foot facility dramatizes the growing presence of Islam in the United States. It features building materials imported from all over the world, a gold dome, twin minarets, and a prayer hall that accommodates a thousand worshippers.

movements in espousing environmental causes that were generally anathema to the New Right. "Justice-seeking work without concern for the earth is naïve and narrow minded," another leader of the Sojourners insisted in a 1990 article. The following year, the United States Conference of Catholic Bishops issued a lengthy document focused on the relationship between Church teachings and environmental movements for the "planetary common good."

Most organized religious groups also struggled with the relationship between their spiritual faith and other social and cultural causes. Religious communities offered very different responses, for example, to the emergence of Lesbian-Gay-Bisexual-Transgendered (LGBT) movements. Most leaders of the Religious Right, such as Jerry Falwell and Pat Robertson, mobilized against what they saw as the "moral decay" posed by LGBT activism. Orthodox Judaism, Islam, and Catholicism, without mobilizing on the scale of the Religious Right, still labeled same-sex relationships as sinful. In stark contrast, a minority of churches, synagogues, and temples—especially in larger cities—welcomed LGBT members. A few denominations accepted gays and lesbians as ministers and rabbis, and recognizable bodies of "gay theology," grounded in specific Biblical passages and on more general principles of tolerance, began to emerge. Churches also confronted, along with the nation at large, growing pressure to address the legality of gay marriages (see Chapter 32).

Religious divisions emerged over foreign policy questions. The movement to contain the spread of nuclear weaponry attracted a number of religious groups. After prolonged internal debate, for example, the Conference of Catholic Bishops issued a pastoral letter entitled "The Challenge of Peace" (1983). It joined statements by several Protestant groups and, in effect, declared U.S. nuclear policy in conflict with religious teachings. At about the same time, some Catholic priests joined dissident Protestant congregations in offering sanctuary to undocumented refugees from Latin America, particularly El Salvador and Guatemala, who were fleeing U.S.-supported military regimes and, once they reached the United States, American immigration authorities. On the other hand, many spiritual leaders and laypeople, particularly those associated with evangelical churches, gravitated toward the fervent anticommunist initiatives supported by the New Right and the Reagan administration.

Three prominent religious figures, who entered the partisan arena, exemplified the diversity of religion's relationship to political action. Father Robert F. Drinan, a member of the U.S. House of Representatives from 1971 to 1981, often embraced positions on issues, such as abortion, contrary to the pronouncements of his own Roman Catholic Church. Eventually, the Church hierarchy decreed that no priest should hold a political office, and Father Drinan resigned. The presidential bids, in 1984 and 1988, of the Reverend Jesse Jackson, a Baptist, recalled movement-style politics that looked back to the religious fervor of the civil rights crusade but also moved in step with the largely secular multiculturalism of the 1980s. Pat Robertson, in contrast, hoped he could use his firm identification with the Religious Right to successfully challenge Vice President George H. W. Bush for the 1988 GOP presidential nomination. After some success in early Republican primaries, which prompted a reticent Bush to highlight his religious faith, Robertson's presidential effort ultimately attracted few Republicans not already aligned with the Religious Right.

Pat Robertson did, however, shore up his religious empire at a time when several other media-enabled religious movements were being swamped by controversy. Jim and Tammy Faye Bakker of the "Praise the Lord" (PTL) movement and Jimmy Lee Swaggart saw their multimillion-dollar, multimedia operations collapse as a result of violating the financial and moral values their ministries preached. After being convicted on multiple counts of fraud, Jim Bakker landed in jail. Swaggart's dalliances with prostitutes left his ministry, which had once claimed a worldwide media audience of more than 500 million people, with a drastically scaled back outreach that included appearances on cable TV's public access channels.

Others religious ministries, however, prospered in the manner of Pat Robertson's. The Billy Graham Evangelistic Association crusade (created in 1950) avoided even the hint of financial or moral malfeasance, and Reverend Graham himself remained one of the nation's most admired—and officially nonpartisan—citizens. Another charismatic Baptist minister, Rick Warren, painstakingly established one of the important evangelical "mega-churches" in Southern California in 1980. Within 20 years, Warren's Saddleback Church ranked among the 10 largest congregations in the country.

Successful movements on the Religious Right, such as Falwell's and Warren's, became cultural conglomerates. They established publishing enterprises, bookstores, radio and TV outlets, Christian academies and other "charter" schools, religiously affiliated colleges and seminaries, and even schools of law and of public policy. Apocalyptic novels from this religious milieu featured page-turning tales about Earth's "final days" before the Rapture that would carry true believers to heaven. The *Left Behind Series*, authored by Tim LaHaye and Jerry Jenkins, became a publishing phenomenon that sold tens of millions of books. *A Thief in the Night* (1972), by the evangelist-director Donald W. Thompson, demonstrated that Christian-themed movies could find a sizeable audience, and a Christian music industry, also a product of the early 1970s, easily surpassed the classical and jazz genres in sales by the end of the 20th century.

The Religious Right framed several influential cultural narratives about the nation's past and the role that people of faith must play in shaping its future. The influential historian-theologian Francis Schaeffer, a committed evangelical, offered a powerful story that pictured the Enlightenment as giving birth to a "secular humanism" that opposed religious faith. The secularist ideas on which the United States had been founded, argued Schaeffer, bequeathed an insufficiently solid religious base. According to an alternative history that slowly gained ascendancy over that of Schaeffer, the original intent of the Founding Fathers was to create a "Christian Nation." The subsequent movement toward secularism, grounded in mistaken claims about a "separation between church and state," lacked historical and, more importantly, legal-constitutional grounding. Both of these historical narratives, of course, pointed toward forging a politics devoted to joining the sacred with the secular.

The Republican Party remained the primary political vehicle for this project. The Religious Right, in addition to gravitating to the post-Reagan GOP at the national level, became a vital force in state and local politics, steadily pressing Republican organizations toward its perspective on issues such as school curricula and textbook selection. It also placed supporters on officially non-partisan bodies such as local school boards. From the grassroots to the White House, then, the Religious Right began to play an increasingly active role in American political culture.

Conclusion

Sweeping changes occurred in demographics, economics, culture, and society during the last quarter of the 20th century. The nation aged, and more of its people gravitated to the Sun Belt. Sprawling urban corridors challenged older central cities as sites for development. Rapid technological change fueled the growth of globalized industries and the restructuring of the labor force to fit a postindustrial economy.

The most prominent development in American popular culture was the proliferation of the video screen. Television, motion pictures, the Internet, and even services for phones increasingly targeted specific audiences, and the fragmented nature of cultural reception was exemplified by the rise of new, particularistic media ventures. ⊱

CHAPTER REVIEW

REVIEW QUESTIONS

1. What major demographic trends characterized the post-1970 United States? How did they contribute to changing daily life?
2. What were the most important post-1970 technological and economic changes? How did technological change create both new problems and new possibilities?
3. How did new forms of media change the ways in which people received entertainment, information and even religious instruction? How did the debate over popular culture in the 1980s and 1990s differ from the earlier debate of the 1950s?

CRITICAL THINKING QUESTIONS

1. In what ways might the major demographic changes of the late 20th century have accelerated economic restructuring?
2. How did the spread of video screens help to change so many areas of cultural life?

IDENTIFICATIONS

Review your understanding of the following key terms, people, and events for this chapter (terms in bold in text are included in the Glossary).

Immigration and Nationality Act of 1965, p. 865
Immigration Reform and Control Act of 1986 (Simpson-Mazzoli Act), p. 865
exurbs, p. 866

Community Reinvestment Act of 1977, p. 867
information revolution, p. 869
Human Genome Project, p. 869
steel cargo containers, p. 870
globalization, p. 871
downsizing, p. 871
household deficit, p. 872
ESPN, p. 874
Title IX or Patsy Mink Equal Opportunity in Education Act, p. 874
narrowcasting, p. 875
MTV aesthetic, p. 877

SUGGESTED READINGS

An overview of the demographic landscape at the end of the 20th century can be found in **Robert E. Lang and Bruce Katz, eds., Redefining Urban and Suburban America: Evidence from Census 2000** (2006). See also, the splendid study by **Jon Teaford, The Metropolitan Revolution: The Rise of Post-Urban America** (2006).

The economic ferment can be surveyed in **Justin Fox, The Myth of the Rational Market: A History of Risk, Reward, and Delusion on Wall Street** (2009); **Joseph Stiglitz, Free Fall: America, Free Markets, and the Sinking of the World Economy** (2009); and **Michael Lewis, Liar's Poker** (rev. ed., 2010).

On the sports-entertainment complex, see **Walter LaFeber, Michael Jordan and the New Global Capitalism** (2002); **Karen Blumenthal, Let Me Play: Title IX—The Law that Changed the Future of Girls in America** (2005); **Michael Oriard, Brand NFL: Making and Selling America's Favorite**

Sport (2007); **Benjamin G. Rader,** *American Sports: From the Age of Folk Games to the Age of Televised Sports* (6th ed., 2008)

The cultural scene comes into view in **Robert G. Kolker,** *The Cinema of Loneliness: Penn, Kubrick, Scorsese, Spielberg, Altman* (rev ed., 2000); **Alan Wolfe,** *The Transformation of American Religion: How We Actually Live Our Faith* (2005); **David Bordwell,** *The Way Hollywood Tells It: Story and Style in Modern*

Movies (2006); **Thomas Hine,** *The Great Funk: Falling Apart and Coming Together (On a Shag Rug) in the Seventies* (2007); **Tricia Rose,** *The Hip-Hop Wars: What We Talk About When We Talk About Hip-Hop—And Why It Matters* (2008); **Alexander B. Maquon,** *Television: The Life Story of a Technology* (2009); and **Steve Knopper,** *Appetite for Self-Destruction: The Spectacular Crash of the Record Industry in the Digital Age* (2009).

 Visit the CourseMate website at www.cengagebrain.com for additional study tools and review materials for this chapter.

CHAPTER 32

© Lee Snider/Photo Images/CORBIS

Ground Zero, September 11, 2001
The South Tower of the World Trade Center collapses as the North Tower burns, after terrorists commandeered two airliners and used them as deadly missiles.

A Time of Hope and Fear, 1993–2011

T HE DECADES that directly proceeded and followed the turn of the 21st century featured a tension between hope and fear. With the collapse of the Soviet Union, it seemed that America's military, economic, and cultural institutions had not only survived the challenge of communism but had become the envy of the world. American consumers enjoyed an expanding array of products and services, and stock markets reached record highs in early 2000 and again in late 2007.

Hopes for the future, however, found their match in new fears. Were the nation's economic and cultural institutions strong enough to withstand domestic changes such as the restructuring of the economy and increased immigration? Was its political structure flexible enough to meet the challenges of 21st century governance? Could the nation's economic and military power overcome new threats from terrorist networks? The attacks of September 11, 2001 brought a new urgency to fears about the future. How could Americans best protect national security? Might new powers for fighting terrorism endanger liberty and equality at home?

The two-term presidencies of Bill Clinton and George W. Bush inspired both adoration and contempt. These leaders tried, in different ways, to redesign the political landscape, yet the nation remained polarized. The sudden economic meltdown in 2008 helped bring a new Democratic face to the White House, Barack Obama. The first African American president and the second youngest in U.S. history, Obama offered what he called "the audacity of hope" in a time of war and economic uncertainty.

The Politics of Polarization, 1993–2008
   A New Democrat
   A Decade of Legal Investigations and Trials
   The Investigation and Trial of a President
   The Long Election and Trials of 2000
   A Conservative Washington, 2001–2008
   Politics and Social-Cultural Issues

Foreign Policies of Hope and Terror: 1993–2008
   Clinton's Internationalist Agenda
   Globalization
   Protecting the Planet
   September 11, 2001 and the Bush Doctrine
   Unilateralism and the Iraq War
   National Security and Presidential Power
   Divisions over Foreign Policy Direction

An Economy of Bubble and Bust, 1993–2008
   Deregulation of the Financial Sector During the 1990s
   Economics for a New Century, 2000–2006
   The Bubble Bursts, 2006–2008
   The Election of 2008

Changing Times, 2009–
   Political Polarization
   The Culture of Social Networking and Liberty, Equality, Power

The Politics of Polarization, 1993–2008

Q
FOCUS QUESTION
What political and cultural forces helped to polarize national politics during the years between 1993 and 2008? What impact did this polarization have on public policymaking in Washington?

William Jefferson Clinton, the first Democratic president since Jimmy Carter, brought images of youth, vitality, and cultural diversity to Washington. Events at his inauguration

AMERICANS ABROAD
Madeleine Albright

included separate parties for different musical tastes, including one broadcast on MTV. His initial cabinet included three African Americans and two Latinos; three cabinet posts went to women. Ruth Bader Ginsburg, his first nominee to the Supreme Court, became only the second woman to sit on the High Court. As ambassador to the United Nations, Clinton named Madeleine Albright, who, during his second term, would become the country's first female Secretary

of State. (Read about Albright's life and international journey to become the first woman to hold America's top foreign policy job in the Americans Abroad feature "Madeleine Albright: A Woman on the World Stage.")

A New Democrat

The Clinton administration moved quickly on the domestic front. It steered a family leave plan for working parents through Congress; helped establish AmeriCorps, a program that allowed students to repay college loans through community service; and secured passage of the Brady Bill, which instituted restrictions on handgun purchases that the Supreme Court subsequently declared unconstitutional. A presidential order ended the Reagan era's ban on federal funding for abortion counseling.

Vice President Al Gore's tiebreaking vote in the Senate allowed passage of Clinton's 1993 economic package. It featured a modest tax increase and a spending-cut package aimed at reducing the federal deficit and lowering interest rates to stimulate economic growth. The plan also expanded an existing governmental program, the **Earned Income Tax Credit (EITC)**, which assisted low and moderate income households

CHRONOLOGY

1993	Congress approves North American Free Trade Agreement (NAFTA)
1994	Republicans gain control of Congress ◆ O. J. Simpson saga begins
1996	Congress overhauls national welfare system ◆ Clinton reelected president ◆ *FOX Cable News* debuts
1997	Congress and White House agree on deficit reduction plan
1998	House of Representatives impeaches Clinton
1999	Senate Trial ends with Clinton's acquittal
2000	*Bush* v. *Gore* decision clears way for George W. Bush to become president
2001	Congress passes Bush tax cut ◆ Terrorists from al-Qaeda destroy World Trade Center and attack Pentagon ◆ Congress passes Patriot Act ◆ U.S. forces invade Afghanistan
2002	*National Security Strategy of 2002* reasserts the Bush Doctrine
2003	Congress enacts Medicare Drug Plan ◆ Bush secures another tax cut
2004	Bush defeats Kerry in the presidential race ◆ Facebook debuts at Harvard
2005	Hurricane Katrina hits Gulf Coast ◆ YouTube goes online ◆ Insurgency in Iraq continues as permanent Iraqi government debuts
2006	Democrats gain control of Congress ◆ Housing "bubble" reaches its peak
2007	"Surge" begins in Iraq ◆ Housing "bubble" bursts
2008	Bush administration and Federal Reserve Board respond to financial meltdown ◆ Great Recession, worst since 1930s, begins ◆ Barack Obama wins presidential race
2009	Obama administration passes economic stimulus plan ◆ U.S. devotes more resources to war in Afghanistan
2010	Congress passes Affordable Health Care for America Act ◆ BP's massive oil spill endangers the Gulf Coast

with children. This provided an important safety net for millions of people.

Identifying himself as a **"New Democrat"** (see also Chapter 30), Clinton broke with his party's recent orthodoxy on criminal justice issues. He backed a 1994 law that provided funding for more police officers and more prisons. Its controversial "three strikes" provision required a life sentence for a third felony conviction. Clinton later supported limiting appeals by prisoners on death row and an anti-terrorist bill opposed by civil libertarian groups.

The administration's ambitious effort to revamp the nation's healthcare system, though, ended in failure. A task force chaired by Hillary Rodham Clinton began with two basic goals: extend coverage to the tens of millions who lacked insurance and contain the rising cost of care, which was burdening the larger U.S. economy. The plan that emerged, however, contained exceedingly complex mechanisms for financing and delivering health care. Republicans denounced it, extolled the existing health care system, and assailed the president as a proponent of "big government." Sick on arrival, the healthcare proposal died in Congress during early 1994.

Clinton's hope for another try at overhauling healthcare ended when the November 1994 elections brought dramatic victories for the GOP. An aggressive campaign spearheaded by Representative Newt Gingrich of Georgia produced Republican majorities in both houses of Congress for the first time in 40 years. Republicans also won several new governorships, gained ground in most state legislatures, and made significant headway in many city and county elections, particularly across the South. Gingrich claimed a mandate for what he called a **"Contract with America."** It drew from Ronald Reagan's 1985 State of the Union Address and included calls for dramatically overhauling the welfare system, enacting anti-crime legislation, streamlining federal legal procedures, requiring a three fifths majority for any increase in taxation, and revising the nation's relationship to the UN.

Gingrich downplayed polls that showed few voters knew much about the Contract and overplayed his new role as Speaker of the House. A deadlock between a Democratic president and a GOP Congress over spending issues produced two brief shutdowns of federal agencies in late 1995 and early 1996. Most people blamed Gingrich and the Republicans rather than Clinton and the Democrats for interrupting the delivery of government services.

A continually improving economy sustained Clinton's approval ratings. The annual rise in GDP averaged nearly 4 percent. Clinton's economic team shared credit with Alan Greenspan, head of the Federal Reserve Board since 1987. Admirers hailed Greenspan as "the Maestro" for keeping down inflation, adroitly managing interest rates, and encouraging rising productivity. Clinton and Congress agreed that Greenspan should begin a third term at Fed in 1996 and a fourth in 2000. Economic growth spurred millions of new jobs, decreased the federal deficit, boosted corporate profits, propelled stock and bond markets to new heights, and enabled the astronomical boom in the financial sector.

The fruits of economic expansion, however, were distributed unequally. An increasingly corporatized agricultural economy continued to push smaller farmers off the land. The gap between earnings of corporate executives, especially in the financial sector, and the earnings of their employees grew steadily wider. And the income gulf between the wealthiest 1 percent of households and the other 99 percent deepened. Still, most people did see their economic fortunes improve, however slightly. Unemployment fell, averaging less than 2 percent a year during the 1990s, and real income headed upward for the first time in nearly 15 years.

Surveying the political and economic landscapes, Clinton focused on an agenda that built on his self-identification as a New Democrat. He hired Dick Morris, a conservative political consultant who was shunned by most other Democrats. In his 1996 State of the Union address, the president declared the end of the era of "big government" and suggested a willingness to work with congressional Republicans in reducing social welfare costs.

The Personal Responsibility and Work Opportunity Reconciliation Act of 1996 incorporated a series of accommodations between the Republican dominated Congress and Clinton, who had vetoed two earlier welfare measures. Although critical of some provisions of this law, Clinton embraced its central feature: eliminating the controversial AFDC program. AFDC provided funds and services to poor families headed by single, unemployed women. The new law supplanted AFDC with a program called **Temporary Assistance to Needy Families (TANF)** that allowed the 50 states to design, under general federal guidelines, their own welfare-to-work programs.

TANF angered many traditional Democrats who did not share Clinton's vision. Provisions limiting governmental assistance over a person's lifetime to five years and authorizing states to suspend benefits if recipients failed to find employment within two years seemed blind to the difficulties faced by people without job skills. TANF's opponents also feared its impact on children, particularly in states with already minimal child care, nutrition, and medical care programs. Senator Daniel Patrick Moynihan, who had earlier devised Richard Nixon's FAP program (see Chapter 28), denounced TANF as "the most brutal act of social policy" since the 19th century. Edward Kennedy condemned it as "legislative child abuse."

New Democrats such as Clinton and Al Gore, however, claimed that it merged political principle with electoral reality. It expressed the conservative Republican faith in a smaller federal government; the widespread criticism of the existing system; and the ideal of work, rather than welfare, being the primary source of personal income. TANF's New Democratic supporters predicted it would encourage states to experiment with programs to reduce welfare costs, devise job-training programs, and even create jobs. It immediately benefited the Clinton-Gore team by eliminating the welfare issue from partisan debate and re-emphasizing the president's claim that he was reducing the size and cost of government.

In the 1996 election, Clinton and Gore defeated Republicans Robert Dole and Jack Kemp by about the same margin they had beaten George H. W. Bush and Dan Quayle four years earlier. Although Ross Perot, as a third-party candidate, again denied the Democratic ticket a popular majority, his low-key campaign effort gained less than 10 percent of the vote. Clinton became the first Democratic president since Franklin D. Roosevelt to win back-to-back terms. Republicans retained control of Congress, however, and gained several new governorships.

Clinton and congressional Republicans soon agreed on a timetable for eradicating the federal deficit, which the president accurately predicted would begin to disappear. He also secured Republican support for the State Children's Health Insurance Program (SCHIP), a 1997 measure extending medical care coverage to several million children from moderate-income families that made too much money to qualify for the Medicaid program. The White House even seemed poised, in early 1998, to work with congressional Republicans on reshaping the Social Security and Medicare programs. The nation's political culture, however, was about to start revolving around a legal-constitutional debate over the future of Bill Clinton's presidency rather than policy initiatives.

A Decade of Legal Investigations and Trials

Intensive inquiries into Clinton's public and private life capped a decade of popular fascination with investigations and trials. Americans, of course, had long been drawn to legal spectacles—such as the Scopes Trial of the 1920s (see Chapter 24) and the trials of communists during the early Cold War era (see Chapter 27). During the 1990s, however, investigative and courtroom dramas, both fictional and real, came to dominate popular culture.

Fictive accounts that featured legal pyrotechnics did big business. The legal thrillers of John Grisham catapulted this former attorney into the best-selling fiction writer of the 1990s. Six of his ten novels became feature motion pictures. Tom Cruise, perhaps Hollywood's most famous male star of the decade, played a lawyer in two Oscar-nominated legal movies, *A Few Good Men* (1992) and *The Firm* (1993), adapted from Grisham novels. 1990 marked the debut of what would become one of TV's longest running drama series, *Law & Order* (1990-2010). It divided every episode between investigative and courtroom segments. And the much anticipated final episode of the comedy series *Seinfeld* (1989–98) revolved around a satirical trial sequence that featured all the fictional crimes the leading characters had allegedly committed during the 1990s.

Coverage of real trials, long a feature of mass culture, began a new phase when Court TV (renamed truTV in 2008) arrived in 1991. This cable channel helped drive the media feeding frenzy that surrounded the trials of O. J. Simpson, which began in mid-1994. The Simpson saga—which involved race, sex, money, and a celebrity defendant—ran for nearly three years. TV cameras closely followed an investigation into the double homicide of Simpson's former wife and one of her acquaintances that led to the indictment of Simpson, a football star turned actor. Simpson's high-profile attorneys, known as

the "dream team," argued to a jury with an African American majority that racist police officers had conspired to frame an innocent black person.

As cable TV news stations fixated on Simpson's case, pundits christened the result "All OJ, All-the-Time." Television coverage featured legal commentators able to subject the smallest bits of evidence to the maximum amount of analysis. These adversarial analysts became surrogate attorneys, arguing on behalf of Simpson or his prosecutors. The trial itself finally ended in October 1995 with the jury quickly returning a "not guilty" verdict. Debates over whether their decision represented a reasonable view of the evidence or an emotional rebuke to the police system sustained innumerable media retrospectives. A sequel to this criminal trial featured relatives of the victims bringing a civil suit against Simpson for monetary damages. TV cameras were barred from the courtroom, but legal commentators continued to dissect the case, which ended with Simpson being held liable for damages. Eventually, however, a new round of investigations and legal actions, these involving the President of the United States, commandeered the media spotlight.

The Investigation and Trial of a President

Long before the Simpson saga ended, groups on the New Right were bankrolling private inquiries into Bill Clinton's past. Hardcore critics attacked not simply the propriety of Clinton's activities but the legitimacy of his presidency. New Right stalwarts such as the Reverend Jerry Falwell insisted that "Sixties radicalism" had shaped Clinton's allegedly flawed character and morally disqualified him for the White House. Falwell even endorsed a scurrilous video alleging that Clinton had silenced a former aide from Arkansas by arranging his murder.

Two less extreme charges against Clinton also concerned his pre-presidential activities. One concerned a scandal-plagued real-estate venture called "Whitewater," to which Hillary and Bill Clinton had been financially connected. Confident of rebutting the Whitewater allegations, the Clinton administration asked for the appointment of a special independent prosecutor to investigate them. The president also faced a seemingly frivolous civil suit for monetary damages by Paula Corbin Jones, who alleged that Clinton, while governor of Arkansas, had sexually harassed her. After the U.S. Supreme Court ruled that this private legal action could proceed while Clinton still held public office, the Jones case became entangled with the Whitewater inquiry when Kenneth Starr replaced the initial head prosecutor. A conservative attorney with Supreme Court ambitions, Starr had little background in criminal work. Starr's ultra-conservative staff pressed him to extend the Whitewater investigation into allegations that Clinton was concealing sexual encounters with other women.

Clinton's denial of sexual liaisons crumbled in early 1998 after conservative activists helped Starr obtain irrefutable evidence of White House trysts between Clinton and a young

HISTORY THROUGH FILM

The Big Lebowski (1998)

Director: Joel Coen.
Starring: Jeff Bridges ("The Dude"), John Goodman (Walter), Steve Buscemi (Donny), and Sam Elliott ("The Stranger").

There are many possible ways of recalling the 1990s and almost as many reasons to begin with *The Big Lebowski*. This loosely structured, irony-soaked comedy is set at the decade's beginning, "just about the time of your conflict with Saddam and the Iraqis," according to its narrator, "The Stranger" (Sam Elliot).

The Big Lebowski meanders through historical events such as military interventions in Korea and Vietnam, the New Left and counterculture of the Sixties, the sexual revolution, and the new immigration. The film also wanders through the history of the Hollywood film industry, drawing snippets from the western, the musical, and the *film noir* of the 1940s, particularly *The Big Sleep* (1945, 1946). It also reworks the Hollywood "bio-pic," a traditional genre that offers highly sanitized biographies of invariably male heroes.

The heroic figure for the nineties is "Jeffrey Lebowski" (Jeff Bridges). Portrayed as a burnout from the Sixties, he claims that he wrote the initial draft of the *Port Huron Statement* (the 1962 manifesto of the Students for a Democratic Society). Known as "the Dude," he embraces the "slacker life" and concentrates on, in no particular order, White Russian cocktails, pot, and bowling. One of his bowling buddies, "Walter Sobchak" (John Goodman), is a satirical portrayal of a gun-toting whacko, mocking Hollywood's representation of veterans of the Vietnam War.

The storyline, such as it is, begins with a gang of thugs mistaking "the Dude"

"The Dude" abides.

for "the Big Lebowski," a paraplegic veteran of the Korean conflict and celebrated philanthropist, whose young wife, "Bunny," owes a gambling debt. Loosely paralleling *The Big Sleep*, the "Big Lebowski" improbably hires "the Dude" to broker a ransom deal for "Bunny," who has allegedly been kidnapped. Falling into the role of private investigator, "the Dude" must survive a series of trial-like encounters in order to save, as did noble knights of old, a "damsel in distress."

In this film, however, the surreal misadventures of a private investigator of the 1990s, provide another opportunity for the reworking of various Hollywood movie clichés. It all ends with "the Dude" drinking beer at his favorite bowling alley, talking to "the Stranger" and telling him (and all of us) that all the "strikes and gutters, ups and downs" of life will never bother or change him. We are thus assured that "the Dude abides."

Initially a box-office disappointment, the movie subsequently spawned the inevitable 10th Anniversary DVD, a series of Facebook sites, and the annual "Lebowski Fests" where the movie's devoted fans bowl, dress in costume, sip White Russians, and shout out its signature line: "I'm a Lebowski. You're a Lebowski."

In *The Big Lebowski*, the 1990s randomly unfolds as a time that lacks a coherent theme. Coming after the end of the Cold War, and with 9/11 still unimaginable, the movie portrays an era that, much like "the Dude," simply "abides."

intern, Monica Lewinsky. The president's problems further escalated when Republican leaders in the House of Representatives claimed that Clinton's conduct justified his removal from office. Democrats condemned Clinton's behavior but supported his legal-constitutional claim: Congress could not impeach, let alone convict, a president for private failings that did not qualify as "high crimes or misdemeanors."

GOP leaders, however, pressed on. At Newt Gingrich's insistence, Republicans made Clinton's character their major issue during the off-year elections of 1998, but Clinton won this informal political trial. Republicans surprisingly lost five seats in the House of Representatives. Even worse for Gingrich, public revelation of his long-term extramarital affair forced his own resignation from the House. Although Kenneth Starr conceded that all the original charges against Clinton lacked merit, the official report of his lengthy investigation detailed the dalliances

The Starr Report, excerpts (1998)

with Monica Lewinsky and highlighted Clinton's efforts to conceal them when testifying under oath in the Jones lawsuit and the Whitewater investigation. Using evidence gathered by Starr's investigators, the Republican majority in the lame-duck House of Representatives mobilized enough votes, in mid-December 1998, for two articles of impeachment (one for perjury and another for obstruction of justice) against Clinton.

Thirteen Republican members of the House, called "Managers," served as Clinton's prosecutors during the televised trial in which members of the U.S. Senate served as jurors. This legal-constitutional showdown lacked first-rate dramatic quality, however, as the Managers' courtroom skills proved no match for those of Clinton's own "dream team" of defense lawyers. The Senate trial concluded on February 12, 1999, with both articles of impeachment gaining nowhere near the 67 votes that the Constitution required for conviction on an impeachment charge.

Although Clinton could justifiably complain about a well-funded public-private campaign to unseat him, more than a partisan vendetta produced his legal-constitutional trials. First, of course, the president was hardly an innocent. He would ultimately be ordered to pay $850,000 to settle the Jones lawsuit, be cited for contempt of court for "misleading" testimony, and be forced to surrender his license to practice law.

In addition, the transition from "All OJ, All the Time" to "All Clinton, All the Time" meant that an adversarial, legalistic model would shape media coverage of the president's problems. Indeed, commentators who had made their TV debut during the OJ era, such as Greta van Sestern, reappeared during the Clinton impeachment saga. TV news, in short, began featuring dueling opinions—for or against—about every rumor or potential legal charge, however far-fetched, involving Clinton and other public figures.

The Fox News Channel's 1996 launch added a spicy new ingredient to the cable TV mix. Fox's rightward political slant was less important initially than its role in refining the adversarial OJ format for TV news. The channel perfected a cost-cutting technique by which its camera crews gathered eye-catching imagery and brief interviews for re-editing and recycling. On-air commentators became ever more skillful in using fleeting imagery and brief sound bites as the basis for trading opinions and speculation without leaving the studio or doing any actual reporting. New digital technologies, moreover, facilitated the retrieval of archived footage. After the Clinton-Lewinsky story became a media obsession, a fleeting glimpse of the two passing one another during a public reception began accompanying virtually every mention of the president's legal troubles.

Finally, a medium newer and more adversarial than cable TV—political sites on the Internet—came online at a critical point in the Clinton investigation. Although other outlets eventually might have reported rumors about the president's involvement with Monica Lewinsky, there was a long

history (most evident during John Kennedy's presidency) of burying such stories as purely private matters. In any event, the first news of the Clinton-Lewinsky relationship came from a fledgling Internet enterprise, *The Drudge Report*, a conservative opinion-gossip site that other media had previously disdained. Very quickly, *The Drudge Report* became a much-visited stop on the Internet and a model for subsequent sites that featured an adversarial approach to political coverage. Over the course of the 1990s, in short, discussions of public affairs increasingly took on the investigative format that came to envelop—indeed, almost paralyze—the work of the Clinton administration.

The Long Election and Trials of 2000

The lengthy presidential election of 2000 also ended in a legal drama that attracted this same style of coverage, especially on cable TV news programs.

A retro aura initially surrounded the presidential campaign of 2000. Al Gore, Clinton's vice president for eight years, reappeared as the Democratic presidential nominee and selected Senator Joseph Lieberman of Connecticut as his running mate. The Republican ballot, for the fifth time in the last six elections, bore the name of Bush. **George W. Bush** chose **Richard (Dick) Cheney**—a conservative Republican stalwart who had served in Bush senior's administration—to be his vice-presidential running mate. The veteran lawyer-activist Ralph Nader ran on the Green Party ticket but attracted less than 3 percent of the popular vote, a far less impressive showing than Ross Perot had made in 1992 or even in 1996.

The campaign of 2000 energized the Republican Party's base but stirred less passion elsewhere. Bush claimed his record as governor of Texas showed he could work with Democrats, appeal to African Americans and Hispanics, and pursue a "compassionate conservatism." While the Bush camp stayed on message, Gore's disorganized campaign struggled to articulate coherent themes. By distancing himself from Clinton, the vice president likely squandered his primary asset—eight years of economic prosperity—and kept some Democratic voters at home. In contrast, New Right voters who reviled Clinton did turn out—and overwhelmingly favored Bush over Gore.

Still, barely 50 percent of eligible voters went to the polls in 2000. Following a pattern evident since the presidency of Ronald Reagan, the vote highlighted the gender, racial, and ethnic differences between the two parties. According to exit polls, Bush attracted 54 percent of the ballots cast by men but only 43 percent of those from women. He received 38 percent of the votes from Latinos, 37 percent from Asian Americans, and 9 percent from African Americans.

The election of 2000 ended in a near dead heat. Republicans narrowly maintained control of the House of Representatives, and the Senate ended up evenly split between the two parties. Al Gore carried the popular vote by about 500,000 ballots, but the only tally that mattered, the one in the Electoral College, turned on the 25 votes from Florida. Only about 1,000 popular votes initially separated the two candidates. As

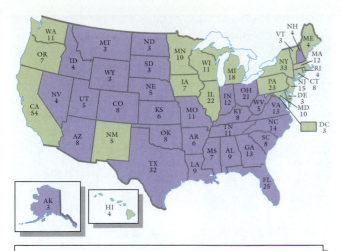

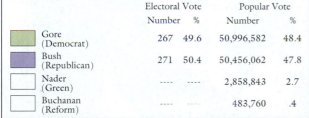

		Electoral Vote		Popular Vote	
		Number	%	Number	%
	Gore (Democrat)	267	49.6	50,996,582	48.4
	Bush (Republican)	271	50.4	50,456,062	47.8
	Nader (Green)	----	----	2,858,843	2.7
	Buchanan (Reform)	----	----	483,760	.4

© Cengage Learning

Map 32.1 Presidential Election, 2000. Although Gore won the popular vote, Bush won the electoral vote after a bitter fight over disputed ballots in Florida.

When it became evident that no clear winner had emerged in Florida, the partisan fervor that had remained muted during the campaign suddenly flared. Cable TV news shifted to an "All Election, All the Time" focus on Florida, where Bush's brother Jeb was governor and the GOP dominated the state legislature. After a count of absentee ballots, Republican officials declared Bush the victor in Florida by a margin of 930 votes. Democrats charged that numerous irregularities—including antiquated voting machines, deliberately confusing ballots, and apparent efforts to discourage voting by African Americans—had distorted the count. A torrent of lawsuits, by Democrats and Republicans alike, quickly ensued. Both parties, especially the GOP, flooded Florida with cadres of lawyers and party activists who performed for the benefit of TV cameras. Florida's highest court finally ordered hand recounts in several counties where Gore's totals seemed suspiciously low. When early results seemed to be reducing Bush's already slim margin, Republicans charged Democrats with stealing his victory and appealed to the U.S. Supreme Court.

As the nation's highest court heard the case of **Bush v. Gore** (2000), legal reporting and TV commentary approached a near-frenzied state. On the evening of December 12, 2000, the Court handed down its final decision. Five conservative Republicans (over the dissents of two other Republicans and two Democrats) ruled that no more ballots could be recounted. Moreover, they announced that their legal holding only applied to this particular case and should not be cited as precedent for any future lawsuit. Outflanked in court, Gore conceded political defeat, and George W. Bush became the 43rd President of the United States. Statisticians later advised that no procedure for hand counting so many disputed Florida ballots could have yielded a universally agreed-upon result in such a close election.

other media outlets held back, *Fox News,* at the urging of an employee who was also Bush's cousin, declared that the Republican ticket had carried Florida—and gained the presidency. Most other media, and even Al Gore for a time, accepted this verdict.

AP Images/Gary I. Rothstein

The 2000 Presidential Campaign, Phase 2. The inconclusive popular vote in Florida extended the 2000 presidential election process. Partisan activists, especially on the Republican side, rushed to Florida and on TV. GOP demonstrators insisted that George W. Bush had carried the Sunshine State and that the hand counting of ballots was meant to steal his victory.

A Conservative Washington, 2001–2008

The Bush presidency's program for tax cuts, educational reform, and expanding oil drilling got off to a fast start, using the Reagan administration's high-octane entry into Washington, D.C., as its model. Conservative think tanks had already assembled thousands of policy proposals and a similar number of resumes from reliably conservative job seekers. Bush chose a cabinet and White House staff as diverse in gender and ethnicity as Clinton's first one. It included General Colin Powell in the key post of Secretary of State, three women, two Asian Americans, and even a Democrat who had briefly served in Clinton's administration.

Several divisive issues immediately dominated Bush's presidency. An economic downturn accompanied by an early 2001 plunge in U.S stock markets—a consequence of a bubble in high-tech stocks and fraudulent activities by several large corporations—signaled the end of the boom of the 1990s. Revenue surpluses at the national and state levels began dwindling and then turning to deficits. Consumer confidence slumped. The Bush administration responded by urging a tax cut to provide an economic stimulus.

The White House pressed two other proposals. First, Vice President Cheney put together an ambitious energy plan, focused on easing restrictions on oil drilling and regulations on pricing. Critics complained that it primarily benefited large oil and gas firms—many headquartered in Texas—and did little to develop alternative sources of energy. Second, the president himself championed an educational program called "No Child Left Behind" that would require nationwide testing to determine which schools were teaching students effectively.

Bush's initiatives were bolder than either his campaign rhetoric or his loss of the popular vote might have suggested. A revised tax plan, which phased in the substantial cuts that tilted toward the wealthiest 1 per cent of Americans, became law in June 2001. "No Child Left Behind," supported by Democratic icon Ted Kennedy, also passed. Opponents of the pro-oil and gas energy bill blocked its passage but only until 2005. In 2003 the administration narrowly passed a costly addition (the first in 35 years) to the Medicare system. **The Medicare Prescription Drug Improvement and Modernization Act** created complex rules by which federal funds would pay for some, but not all, of the drug costs of Medicare recipients. Benefiting drug companies as well as patients, this measure helped further increase the federal deficit.

In contrast to Clinton, who preferred lengthy, loosely structured intellectual give-and-take sessions, Bush favored brief, tightly controlled meetings that moved toward clearly delineated decisions. According to some members of his administration, Bush rarely seemed interested in exploring, or sometimes even hearing or reading, ideas in conflict with his instincts. He initially allowed Vice President Cheney and Donald Rumsfeld, the secretary of defense, wide latitude to set policy directions. Bush also proclaimed that religious faith *directly* shaped his political outlook.

AP Images/Pablo Martinez Monsivais

George W. Bush Shows Texas Style. The 43rd president, in contrast to his father, George H. W. Bush, always emphasized his Texas roots. Here, he steps out at an Inaugural Ball.

The president's approval ratings, which had hovered under 50 percent, soared after the attacks on the World Trade Center and the Pentagon on September 11, 2001. (For the foreign policy implications of 9/11, especially in the Middle East, see below, pp. 896–897.) The mid-term elections of 2002 left the GOP with secure control of the U.S. Senate and an even larger margin in the House of Representatives.

Downplaying the rapidly growing federal deficit, largely the result of Bush's earlier tax reductions, the White House secured yet another tax cut in 2003. It again insisted that this measure would spur economic growth. Democrats condemned these cuts for tilting toward the already wealthy in an economy that had shed nearly 3 million jobs and had shown a widening gap between rich and poor.

The White House's political strategy for the 2004 elections, fine tuned by consultant Karl Rove, stressed Bush's role in combating terrorism. The Democratic nominee, Senator John Kerry of Massachusetts, had served in Vietnam during the 1960s before becoming an antiwar activist. Kerry endorsed the Bush administration's national security initiatives but criticized its strategy and tactics and kept his distance from the small antiwar movement.

A fiercely partisan campaign ensued. Some Bush supporters disparaged Kerry's Vietnam War record, and his campaign portrayed a Kerry presidency as a danger to national security. Democrats charged Bush with bumbling leadership, saddling future generations with a horrendous burden of debt, and enabling a small percentage of the wealthy to enjoy tax cuts. The GOP's mobilization effort produced an unusually large turnout and charges of voter fraud, especially in Ohio. Bush defeated Kerry by about 3 percent of the popular vote and 15 electoral ballots. As in 2000, Bush did best in suburbia and small towns, among men, and with people who attended church regularly. Kerry failed to do as well as had Al Gore in 2000 among white voters—still more than three-quarters of the electorate—or to win enough middle-income voters, who Democrats had claimed were suffering from Bush's economic policies.

Bush claimed an electoral mandate and announced an ambitious second-term agenda that featured substantial overhauls of the Social Security system and the tax code. He barnstormed the country on behalf of these initiatives, but most people appeared wary. A shaky economy and a yawning federal deficit seemed reason enough to defer action on significant policy changes with uncertain economic consequences. Moreover, a Republican controlled Congress became less of an asset to the White House. Revelations of illegal contributions from lobbyists and personal misconduct forced the resignation of several GOP legislators, including the powerful Tom DeLay, and sent Congress's approval skidding below that of Bush.

Politics and Social-Cultural Issues

On most domestic issues, differences between the national Republican and Democratic parties widened and deepened. It became increasingly difficult to find common ground on a wide range of political and social questions. With the major political parties locked in partisan stalemate, a variety of movement groups tried to seize the initiative on specific issues.

Immigration policy emerged as one of the most contentious problems. Entering the United States in near-record numbers, immigrants were now seeking jobs throughout the country, particularly in the South. This encouraged organizations that opposed immigration to mobilize on a national scale. A few formed militia-like patrols and threatened to turn back people trying to enter the United States along the southwestern border. Others lobbied Congress, demanding new immigration restrictions, tighter border security, and stronger penalties for employers of undocumented immigrants.

Pro-immigrant organizations responded, particularly in California and other states with large Mexican American populations. Tapping the power of Spanish-language radio and TV, they staged temporary work stoppages and street demonstrations intended to demonstrate the economic importance of immigrant workers and the political clout of their movement. They cited economic studies that challenged

claims that immigrants "took away" jobs and depressed wage levels.

Political leaders moved cautiously. House Republicans from districts with strong anti-immigration movements favored new restrictions, but enough Republicans in the Senate joined Democrats to block any such measure. The Bush administration promised a more vigorous effort to secure the U.S.-Mexican border but angered congressional Republicans by endorsing a "guest worker" arrangement, an option favored by most business interests. Uncertain about how immigration legislation might affect electoral results in 2008, Republicans backed off taking action at the national level.

Differences over the role of government in dealing with possible public health risks also sharpened. Business interests joined prominent Republicans in supporting continued deregulation and opposing new governmental restrictions. The free market, they contended, would self-correct to protect the public, and regulators would stifle business growth.

In response to this position, environmentalist groups increasingly merged social-justice concerns with quality of life issues. They argued that hazardous wastes, though a potential threat to everyone, most directly affected people with low incomes who lacked the political power to keep toxic byproducts out of their neighborhoods and off their lands. Activists also highlighted how the relatively few corporations that dominated the global production and sale of beef, poultry, grains, and other foodstuffs did business. They charged that large feed lot complexes and poultry factories brutalized animals, overused antibiotics, and polluted the environment with waste products. Grain corporations used their financial leverage to press farmers in the United States and overseas to produce single crops, often soybeans or corn (which were found in more and more non-food products), and to use agricultural methods that threatened soil quality and vital rain forests. Governmental regulations, they argued, were needed to protect the quality of soil and water as well as to insure the health and safety of consumers.

Critics of the food industry especially examined the patterns of distribution and consumption. By buying from the largest producers at the lowest possible prices, the giant fast-food and grocery chains contributed to environmental problems. "Good food" advocates who were also environmentalists, such as Alice Waters and Michael Pollan, spearheaded a "local food" movement that sparked a growing consumer demand for organic products, local farmers' markets, and well-prepared "slow food."

The issue of "gay marriage" also emerged as a major political-cultural flashpoint, as LGBT movements sought legal recognition of long-term partnerships that they viewed to be as legitimate as heterosexual marriages. When the U.S. Supreme Court struck down state anti-sodomy laws (in *Lawrence v. Texas*, 2003), it signaled that the same constitutional logic might apply to bans on same-sex marriage. Opinion polls suggested sharply divided views about gay marriage but fairly broad support for civil unions or other legal arrangements that would recognize LGBT partnerships. In several states, though, courts held that the bedrock principle of legal constitutional equality guaranteed gays and lesbians a "right to marry," a liberty that a controversial 2008 referendum in California rejected but one that several state legislatures subsequently affirmed.

Conservative organizations, which usually gained support from the GOP, responded by reiterating their case against gay marriage. They claimed that gay couples were unsuited for raising children and joined the Bush administration in seeking an amendment to the U.S. Constitution which specifically declared marriage as a "union between a man and a woman." Opponents of the amendment narrowly turned back a congressional effort to send such a measure to the states for ratification in 2006. In response, conservatives mobilized to overturn, by constitutional amendment or referendum, legislative and court actions that legalized gay marriage in a number of states.

Mobilization on the political right also highlighted conflict between religious belief and scientific-medical research. Moving beyond opposition to abortion, "right-to-life" activists condemned other practices, such as assisted suicide and removal of feeding tubes; anti-pregnancy drugs; and medical research that used stem cells from human embryos. In July 2006, after Congress passed a measure in support of stem cell research, President Bush responded by issuing, on live television, the first veto of his presidency, on "culture-of-life" grounds.

Many of these political-cultural issues involved court decisions, and a conservative legal movement enjoyed considerable success in elevating lawyers who had worked for previous Republican administrations to federal judgeships. During Bill Clinton's presidency, conservative Republican lawyers had worried that an influx of Clinton appointees might cancel out the impact of Reagan-era appointees. Following the GOP electoral surge of 1994, they had managed to block confirmation of the Clinton nominees they labeled "liberal activists." With Bush doing the nominating during the early 2000s, the GOP's Senate leadership, however, threatened to change long-standing rules that enabled filibusters if Democrats sought to block Bush's judicial choices.

Despite an embarrassing misfire, when a Bush nominee for the Supreme Court, Harriet Myers, met determined opposition from within Republican ranks, the conservative legal movement succeeded in placing many jurists on lower federal courts. In addition, the White House easily obtained Senate confirmations for two staunchly conservative Supreme Court nominees who had done legal work in the Reagan administration. In 2005, John Roberts replaced William Rehnquist as Chief Justice of the United States, and the following year Samuel Alito (rather than Harriet Myers) succeeded the retiring Sandra Day O'Connor as an associate justice.

The **"Roberts Court"** seemed even more attuned to the conservative legal movement than its predecessor, headed by the conservative William Rehnquist. In one of several key decisions breaking 5–4—with Justice Anthony Kennedy replacing Justice O'Connor as the swing vote—the Roberts Court limited women's access to abortion without accepting

Justice Clarence Thomas' invitation to overrule *Roe* v. *Wade*. It rebuffed traditional civil rights groups with a similarly restrictive view of the ability of local school districts to use racial identification when assigning students to particular schools in pursuit of a desegregation strategy. In a 5–4 decision that thrilled Second Amendment activists, the Roberts Court ruled that the right to bear arms included that of individual citizens to possess firearms and struck down an ordinance regulating gun ownership in the nation's capital. The logic of this decision, *District of Columbia* v. *Heller* (2008), suggested that the ruling would extend to similar regulations at the state and local levels, a step taken in *McDonald* v. *City of Chicago* (2010). And the Court invariably sided with claims made by corporations fighting government regulations.

Foreign Policies of Hope and Terror: 1993–2008

 FOCUS QUESTION How did the Clinton administration attempt to redesign foreign policy for a post-Cold War world? How did the administration of George W. Bush, especially after September 11, 2001, seek to re-orient Clinton's approach?

For nearly half a century, the goal of containing Soviet communism had shaped U.S. foreign policy. After the collapse of the Soviet Union, George H. W. Bush's measured attempt to fashion new goals for a post-Cold War world had failed to impress either his Democratic or Republican critics (see Chapter 30). Thus, Bill Clinton came to the White House with a more ambitious foreign policy agenda. A committed internationalist, he assigned top priority to devising guidelines for military intervention, improving relations with the UN, promoting free-market policies that supported globalization, addressing environmental concerns that were both global and local in nature, and reducing threats from nuclear materials.

Clinton's Internationalist Agenda

One of the most perplexing foreign policy issues involved decisions about when to employ U.S. military power in localized conflicts that no longer could automatically be connected to the now-defunct Soviet Union. No consistent guidelines for intervention ever emerged. In Somalia, U.S. troops, under the umbrella of a UN mission since May 1992, had been assisting a humanitarian effort to provide food and relief supplies. After a battle in Mogadishu (subsequently portrayed in the book and movie *Black Hawk Down*) took the lives of 18 U.S. service personnel in the fall of 1993, however, domestic criticism mounted. Clinton ordered a pullout the following spring. Recalling the criticism of involvement in Somalia, Clinton withheld support from a UN peacekeeping effort in Rwanda, where 500,000 Tutsis died during a genocidal civil war. In Haiti, though, Clinton dispatched U.S. troops, in cooperation with the UN, to reinstall the elected president, Jean-Bertrand Aristide, who had been ousted in a coup. The White House, in cooperation with NATO, also sent 20,000 U.S. troops to Yugoslavia to prevent Bosnian Serbs from massacring Bosnian Muslims. U.S. forces remained in Bosnia to oversee a ceasefire and peace-building process that resulted from the U.S.-brokered Dayton (Ohio) Peace Accords of 1995.

In March 1999 Clinton supported a NATO bombing campaign to protect Albanian Muslims from an "ethnic cleansing" program in the Serbian province of Kosovo carried out by Serbia's president, Slobodan Milosevic. The Albanian Muslims constituted nearly 90 percent of the population in Kosovo. After 78 days of bombardment had decimated Serbia's infrastructure, Milosevic withdrew his forces from Kosovo. Serbs soon elected a new president supportive of multi-ethnic democracy and the West, and Milosevic faced trial before an international human rights court. As in Bosnia, U.S. and allied troops remained in Kosovo as peacekeepers.

Clinton's military moves in Haiti, Bosnia, and Kosovo provoked controversy. Republican critics accused the president of lacking clear guidelines about when, where, and how to employ U.S. force. Suspicious of cooperating with the UN, they denounced peacekeeping and "nation-building" programs, and demanded clear-cut exit strategies to prevent the United States from getting bogged down in lengthy occupations. Defenders of intervention insisted that Clinton's flexibility and willingness to work with NATO and the UN were strengths, not weaknesses, in a post-Cold War world.

Globalization

In addition, the Clinton administration placed great emphasis on lowering barriers to trade and expanding global markets to advance the international economic process called "globalization." Building on Reagan-Bush policies, Clinton argued that globalization would boost prosperity and foster democracy around the world, to the ultimate benefit of the U.S. economy. His stance angered many labor leaders, who warned that globalization was contributing to the loss of industrial jobs in the United States. It also sparked a highly visible anti-globalization movement that emerged in most nations during the 1990s.

In pursuit of his support for globalization, Clinton first promoted the stalled North American Free Trade Agreement (NAFTA) among the United States, Canada, and Mexico. In late 1993 he pushed NAFTA through Congress in a close vote that depended on Republican support and faced fierce opposition from normally pro-Democratic labor unions. Then in early 1995, Mexico's severe debt crisis and a drastic devaluation of its currency prompted Clinton to extend a $20 billion loan. Unprecedented and controversial, this loan stabilized the Mexican economy and, within a few years, had been repaid with $1 billion in interest. When Asian economies later faltered, Clinton lobbied the International Monetary Fund (IMF) to provide emergency credits to shore up financial systems from Korea to Indonesia.

Clinton's administration signed more than 300 trade agreements. Its trade negotiators, promising that expanded trade ties would benefit all nations, completed the so-called Uruguay Round of the General Agreement on Tariffs and Trade (GATT) in late 1993. In early 1995 GATT was replaced by a more powerful **World Trade Organization (WTO).** Anxious to move China toward a market economy, Clinton reversed his earlier position and backed China's entry into the WTO, in exchange for its promise to relax trade restrictions. Similarly, in February 1994, the United States ended its 19-year-old trade embargo against Vietnam. Everywhere he went, Clinton extolled the coming of a "New Century" in which freer trade would expand prosperity, and "liberty will spread by cell phone and cable modem."

Protecting the Planet

International environmental issues were a third area of major concern for the Clinton administration. At home, it negotiated plans to manage and protect old-growth forests in the Pacific Northwest, implement a conservation framework in nine national forests in the Sierra Nevada, and handle the crowds of tourists in Yosemite National Park. In controversial moves, Clinton's secretary of the interior set aside 16 new national monuments and blocked road construction and logging in nearly 60 million acres of wild areas in national forests. Building on the work of its Republican predecessors, Clinton's administration placed almost 6 million new surface and underwater acres under federal protection. It preferred to promote change through incentives rather than penalties. The Conservation Reserve Program, a farm subsidy program that earlier paid farmers to remove land from tillage, for instance, began payments to those who would restore their wetlands to decrease polluted runoff into streams and preserve wildlife habitat.

The U.S. government, however, often seemed to be one of the country's most flagrant polluters. Throughout the Cold War, governmental nuclear facilities had spewed toxic wastes, and workers had been inadequately warned about the dangers of radiation. In 1993 Clinton's energy secretary released long-secret medical records relating to radiation and promised programs to inform and compensate victims. The legacy of other military-related pollutants also became evident after many of the nation's military bases were shut down during the post-Cold War 1990s.

Most importantly, Clinton supported the environmental movement's increasing focus on international ecological dangers. Environmentalists warned of holes in the ozone layer caused by chlorofluorocarbons (CFCs), potentially catastrophic climate change associated with deforestation and desertification, pollution of the world's oceans, and the decline of biodiversity in plant and animal species. Solutions to global environmental problems seemingly required worldwide cooperation toward "sustainable development," and international meetings on environmental issues became more frequent. An "Earth Summit" was held in Brazil in 1992. International conventions signed in Kyoto in 1997 and at The Hague in 2000 pointed toward establishing international standards on emissions of CFCs and gases that contributed to global climate changes. The climate-change issue, however, was becoming increasingly polarized as some Republicans began insisting that the issue was a scientific hoax that would cripple the American economy.

Clinton's post–Cold War agenda included several other priorities. Clinton supported nonproliferation of nuclear weapons. He dismantled some of the U.S. nuclear arsenal and increased economic aid to Ukraine, then the third greatest nuclear power in the world, in exchange for a pledge to disarm its 1,600 Soviet-era warheads. After promises of U.S. help, North Korea also agreed to begin halting its fledgling nuclear program and permitting international inspections—agreements it later repudiated. The White House successfully pressed for a new Nuclear Nonproliferation Treaty in the spring of 1995, and three years later neared the brink of war with Iraq to maintain international inspections of Saddam Hussein's weapons programs. After enduring punishing air strikes, however, Iraq still expelled the investigators and left analysts wondering if Hussein had resumed building weapons of mass destruction (WMD).

September 11, 2001 and the Bush Doctrine

During the 1990s, intelligence experts highlighted a growing concern about attacks by a foreign terrorist network called al-Qaeda. Its operatives bombed the World Trade Center in New York City in 1993; U.S. embassies in Kenya and Tanzania in 1998; and a U.S. battleship, the *Cole*, docked in Yemen in 2000. These bombings prompted heightened security efforts and special efforts that began to track al-Qaeda's leaders. As the Clinton administration left office, however, national security officers worried about what al-Qaeda's leader Osama bin Laden, an Islamic fundamentalist from Saudi Arabia, might be plotting next.

On September 11, 2001, 19 suicide terrorists, organized in separate squads, seized four jetliners, already airborne and loaded with highly flammable jet fuel, for use as high-octane, human-guided missiles. Two planes toppled the Twin Towers of New York's World Trade Center; another ripped into the Pentagon in Washington; and only the courageous action of passengers on a fourth plane, which crashed in Pennsylvania, prevented a second attack against the nation's capital. Nearly 3,000 people, including several hundred passengers and an even larger number of police and fire officers in New York City, perished.

President Bush, donning the mantle of a wartime president, declared a war on terrorism. Tracing the attacks to Osama bin Laden and al-Qaeda operating out of Afghanistan, the Bush administration organized a multinational invasion force. In December 2001, U.S.-led troops toppled the Taliban regime that had been dominating Afghanistan with bin Laden's help and installed a pro-U.S. government in Afghanistan's capital city of Kabul. The effort failed, however, to secure that nation's countryside or to capture bin Laden and his top aides.

Meanwhile, the president proclaimed what became known as the **Bush Doctrine**. As fully expressed in **The National Security Strategy of 2002**, it denounced not only terrorist networks but any nation sponsoring terrorism or accumulating WMD that terrorists might use. The Bush Doctrine additionally proclaimed that the United States possessed the unilateral authority to wage preemptive war against any force, including any foreign nation, that endangered American security.

Congressional legislation bolstered the Bush doctrine. Many Democrats joined Republicans in passing the USA Patriot Act, which gave the executive branch broad latitude to watch over and detain people it considered threats to national security. A newly created agency, the Department of Homeland Security, launched an array of new measures including screenings for all passengers at airports. Fear of more terrorist attacks, heightened by mysterious mailings of deadly anthrax bacteria to several public officials, reverberated through American culture and strengthened the case for extending the power of the executive branch.

Unilateralism and the Iraq War

As Osama bin Laden dropped from sight, the White House invoked the Bush Doctrine against Iraq and Saddam Hussein, the old nemesis of the president's father, who controlled some of the richest oil reserves in the world. The Bush administration contended that Iraq posed a clear and immediate danger to the United States. Claiming that intelligence reports showed that Saddam possessed WMDs and had ties to al-Qaeda, the Bush administration called for "regime change." The White House asked the UN and other nations to support a military strike to remove Hussein on the claim that Iraq had frustrated the weapons inspections mandated by the Gulf War settlement of 1991. Led by France, Germany, and Russia, however, the UN favored giving weapons inspectors another try.

Bush's presidential campaign had emphasized conservative Republicans' distrust of working with international bodies and a preference for unilateralism. Moreover, the president had appointed to his administration a group of **neoconservatives** who had called throughout the 1990s for "regime change" in Iraq. According to neoconservative advisers to Vice President Dick Cheney and Secretary of Defense Donald Rumsfeld, the United States should use its enormous military power to go on the offensive and clear away threatening, repressive regimes, beginning with that in Iraq. In this effort to spread liberty around the globe and enhance U.S. influence especially in the Middle East, they argued, the United States could not be hampered by international organizations and agreements. Unlike his father, an internationalist who had carefully courted UN backing for the Persian Gulf War, Bush proved determined to overthrow Hussein regardless of the UN's position.

Acting without UN authorization, in early 2003 the Bush administration assembled its own "coalition of the willing"—troops from the United States and Great Britain, plus smaller contingents from Poland, Italy, Spain, and several other countries. On March 20, the coalition launched an air and ground

Baghdad, Iraq, 2006. Bombings aimed at both Iraqis and U.S. personnel followed the fall of Saddam Hussein. In May 2006, a bomb attack hit a news crew from CBS, underscoring the danger that journalists, as well as troops, confronted whenever they left the relative safety of the U.S.-controlled "Green Zone" in central Baghdad.

assault against Iraq. Overriding military planners who desired at least 300,000 U.S. troops, Operation Iraqi Freedom deployed only one-third that many forces. Saddam Hussein's regime did fall in less than two months, and on May 1 President Bush proclaimed, from the deck of the aircraft carrier *Abraham Lincoln*, that "significant combat" had ended in Iraq. This carefully crafted media event quickly rebounded against the president, however, as resistance flared against the American-dominated occupation, which aimed at creating a pro-U.S. government and a new economic order closely tied to U.S. companies. Iraqi insurgents also attacked aid workers from the United Nations, the Red Cross, and other international relief agencies.

As U.S. officials and cooperating Iraqis tried to create a system of governance, they faced an evolving insurgency that brought rising American and Iraqi casualties. In part, violence stemmed from Iraq's ethnic, religious, and regional divisions. Under Hussein, Sunni Arabs who lived in areas around Baghdad had dominated political power. The Shi'a Arabs, a majority of the nation's population who were concentrated in the South, and the northern Kurds, mostly Sunni but non-Arabs, had been persecuted outsiders. They now wanted a share of governmental power. Divisions also emerged between Iraqis who insisted that any new government remain secular (as it

had been under Hussein) and those who desired one based on Islamic law. Moreover, terrorist groups from outside Iraq, particularly ones claiming connections to al-Qaeda, joined the insurgency.

Factional struggles, complicated by the presence of Western troops with little knowledge of Iraq's socio-religious dynamics, embroiled the country in civil war. The Joint Chiefs of Staff warned that the Iraq war was stretching the military so thin that it might not be able to respond in other areas of the globe. As U.S. casualties in Iraq mounted, so did the costs. The lack of international support for U.S. action meant that, unlike the 1991 Persian Gulf War, U.S. taxpayers directly bore the costs of this operation. The Bush administration had suggested that the sale of Iraqi oil could pay for the "liberation" effort, but revenues remained low as financial mismanagement of the occupation left billions of U.S. dollars in aid unaccounted for. The administration repeatedly needed to ask Congress for additional billions of dollars to fund ongoing operations in Iraq. Meanwhile, the war in Afghanistan stalled, the Taliban regrouped, and the al-Qaeda leaders who had attacked on September 11, 2001, retreated into mountainous safe havens.

As the Iraqi operation became more and more difficult, the Bush administration's public rationale for having undertaken it fell apart. The White House never documented any connection between al-Qaeda and Saddam Hussein, and an exhaustive official report concluded that Iraq had possessed no biological or nuclear WMD at the time of the invasion. Later evidence suggested that intelligence had been distorted to bolster the justification for war. In response to the clear failures in intelligence gathering and assessment, Congress in December 2004 placed existing efforts under a new umbrella agency and created a new director of national intelligence as the key coordinating official.

As the initial case for war came under fire, so did its conduct. Photographs showing abuse of detained Iraqis, especially at Baghdad's Abu Ghraib prison, and stories of a few U.S. troops deliberately killing civilians called into question the wisdom of having U.S. forces occupy a country about which they knew relatively little. Controversy developed over whether methods of what the Bush administration called "enhanced interrogation" had been a euphemism for what others called "torture."

During 2005, conditions in Iraq continued to deteriorate. Iraqis elected a national assembly, chose an interim prime minister, and produced a constitution that gained popular approval. The civil war, however, only intensified. Ever-growing Iranian influence within Iraq was especially irksome to those neoconservatives who had claimed that deposing Saddam Hussein would increase U.S. power in the Middle East. Furthermore, the Iraqi government included factions that opposed the U.S. presence and expressed scant sympathy for Western-style democracy. In addition, widespread hatred for U.S. intervention in Muslim lands inflamed many people across the Middle East. The conflict between Israelis and Palestinians consequently became more complicated than ever. Contrary to the Bush Doctrine, it seemed that regime change in Iraq was producing neither a stable nor a pro-American region.

National Security and Presidential Power

Hurricane Katrina, slamming into the U.S. Gulf Coast region in late August 2005, prompted an intense, if temporary, debate over national security on the home front. Local and state officials bumbled through the first post–9/11 emergency. The Department of Homeland Security, presumably created to deal more efficiently with threats, seemed unprepared to assist people battered by the storm or caught in its aftermath. Although the White House would claim no one had "anticipated the breach of levees" intended to protect New Orleans from flood waters, videotapes later showed the president receiving precisely such a warning. Katrina exacted an especially heavy toll on the Gulf Coast's oldest, poorest, and African American residents. After failing to provide effective aid to hundreds of thousands, neither state nor national authorities could supply a precise figure, presumably in the several thousands, of those who perished as a result of Katrina.

The Bush administration's limited response to Katrina departed from its usual preference for expanding the reach of the executive branch. On issues that involved national security

and the president's role as commander-in-chief, Vice President Cheney and Secretary of Defense Rumsfeld, who had served in the executive branch during the immediate post-Watergate era of the 1970s, were especially insistent that Bush challenge the congressional and judicial restrictions that had been put in place in response to Richard Nixon's actions. The Bush administration convinced Congress to renew the Patriot Act, which otherwise would have automatically expired in 2006. Bush's nomination of John Bolton to become ambassador to the UN faced bipartisan opposition. Bolton had long been an arch-critic of the UN, and critics doubted his ability to work effectively with ambassadors from other nations. Bush, however, used an interim process that did not require Senate confirmation to send Bolton to the UN.

Several issues raised special controversy over presidential power. Initially, when dealing with alleged terrorists captured overseas, especially in Afghanistan, the Bush administration chose to operate outside both domestic and international agreements and detain captives at a new facility in the U.S. enclave at Guantanamo Bay, Cuba. Later, it devised special legal proceedings for trying detainees, which the U.S. Supreme Court, on three separate occasions, declared unconstitutional. The Bush administration also bypassed the Foreign Intelligence Surveillance Act of 1978 (FISA), which mandated special procedures before undertaking domestic wiretaps. The White House insisted that the post-September 11 congressional resolution on fighting terrorism and the president's inherent powers as commander-in-chief allowed him to forgo FISA's provisions in order to save lives. Congress and the White House agreed on revisions to FISA, in 2007 and 2008, that granted surveillance agencies, in the name of national security, broader power to monitor communication networks.

Changes in Washington drained some urgency and partisan discord from the issues of the war and presidential powers during the final years of the Bush presidency. An apparent antiwar backlash helped the Democratic Party capture control of Congress in the mid-term elections of November 2006. The following month, Bush named Robert Gates, a skillful bureaucratic manager, to replace the mercurial Donald Rumsfeld as head of the Department of Defense. Gates helped the Bush administration adopt a new strategy for Iraq: **"the surge."** It temporarily increased U.S. troop levels and placed in command **General David Petraeus**, an expert on counterinsurgency warfare. Deploying U.S. troops more selectively, General Petraeus also stepped up training for Iraqi forces and ramped up payments to Sunni factions in Iraq to rebuff foreign insurgents in favor of political participation. The "surge" strategy soon reduced the level of civil violence and decreased political tension within Iraq as Bush prepared to leave office.

Divisions over Foreign Policy Direction

By the end of Bush's presidency, the wars in Afghanistan and Iraq had claimed the lives of nearly 5000 U.S. troops. Iraqi civilian casualties numbered, by the most conservative

Hurricane Katrina Hits New Orleans, 2005. These photos provide birds-eye and ground-level views of New Orleans after Hurricane Katrina made landfall. They suggest the devastation that befell the Crescent City and the challenges faced by those charged with devising an effective response. Katrina temporarily highlighted the domestic dimensions of "Homeland Security."

estimates, in the tens of thousands. The ongoing occupation of Iraq was costing the United States $6 billion per month. George W. Bush, who had run for office as a critic of "nation-building" projects, had embarked on just such an effort in Iraq, the largest in the history of the United States. With Americans deeply divided over the justification for the invasion and the conduct of the occupation, popular support for Bush dropped below 30 percent.

Democratic critics, looking toward the election of 2008, developed a foreign policy agenda that would repudiate the Bush administration's policies and offer new approaches. They advocated a timetable for removing U.S. combat troops from Iraq, a renewed military and diplomatic effort to stabilize Afghanistan, and a clearer focus on al-Qaeda, which seemed increasingly entrenched in remote areas of Pakistan and Yemen. Critics also urged moving away from the military emphasis of the Bush years. In their view, Bush had neglected threats to national security that required international cooperation. One involved securing loose stockpiles of nuclear material before they fell into the hands of terrorists.

Another threat involved climate change. Republican neoconservatives had opposed the Clinton-era Kyoto Protocol, under which nations would agree to curb emissions that contributed to global warming. The Bush administration claimed that the science behind climate change remained uncertain. It also objected to the fact that targets would not be applied equally to developed nations and to certain developing nations, especially China. The Republican-dominated Senate failed to approve the Kyoto Protocol, but some prominent Democrats such as the former vice-president Al Gore continued to publicize the dangers of climate change and advocate rejoining the international forums working on the issue. They also pressed for development of "green energy" sources that would both lessen U.S. reliance on supplies of oil from the Middle East and help reduce carbon output.

An Economy of Bubble and Bust, 1993–2008

Q FOCUS QUESTION

What forces fueled the various economic bubbles from the late 1990s to 2008? How did governmental officials respond to the financial meltdown of 2008 and the subsequent recession?

In 2003, the Nobel Prize-winning economist Robert Lucas credited his generation with effectively mastering the "central problem of depression-prevention." He spoke for those who believed that the U.S. and world economies were enjoying "The Great Moderation," a term that signified a faith that the economy, increasingly free from the burdens of government regulations, would no longer face the extremes of boom and bust. At times, the economy might not perform to its optimum level, but downturns would be temporary—and moderate. This conviction dominated economic thought and policy-making during the 1990s and the first years of the 21st century. Then, beginning in 2006, the American economy reached the highpoint of what, in retrospect, was an economic-financial bubble that helped conceal other, dismal economic trends. During the 96 months of the Bush presidency, for example, the economy gained only about 3 million new jobs, a fraction of the total added during the 1990s. Economic trouble loomed on the horizon.

Deregulation of the Financial Sector During the 1990s

The financial sector had become, of course, the most dynamic and exciting part of the economy during the 1990s (see Chapter 31). Its leaders could take credit for generating roughly 30 percent of all domestic profits by the mid-nineties. The financial industry produced more than profits and wealth. It gained an aura of excitement and innovation. Talented college graduates, primarily but not exclusively men, began abandoning plans to become physicians or engineers in favor of careers in the financial sector.

Robert Rubin, the Clinton administration's leading economic celebrity, accepted a huge pay cut when leaving Goldman Sachs to head up the National Economic Agency (NEC). Created by Clinton with Rubin in mind, the NEC assumed responsibility for coordinating economic policymaking. To execute this demanding and delicate task, which centered on promoting globalization and reducing the federal government's deficit, Rubin recruited talented theorists and technicians from academia and the financial industry. In 1995, he left the NEC to become Secretary of the Treasury, a post that he passed along in 1999 to Larry Summers, a Rubin protégé whose resume included stints at Harvard University and the World Bank.

Clinton's economic brain trust concluded that the late 20th century economy had outgrown the New Deal regulatory structure, but it still saw a limited economic role for government. If the economy were to continue growing, these New Democrats argued, Washington occasionally needed to mount activist rescue efforts both at home and abroad to ensure that problems remained moderate in nature. They viewed the effort that helped restore Mexico's financial, economic, and political stability in 1995 and another that bailed out a shoddily run financial venture known as Long-Term Capital Management in 1998 as textbook examples of their preference for government rescuing rather than regulating. When the economy appeared to be running smoothly, though, government needed to stay out of the way, except to remove outmoded regulations that might frustrate innovative financiers.

The Clinton administration and the Federal Reserve Board under Alan Greenspan thus showed scant reverence for financial regulations from the New Deal era. In 1999, Rubin and Summers supported Republican Senator Phil Gramm's effort to repeal the Glass-Steagall Act (see Chapter 25). "We have learned government is not the answer," according to Gramm.

"We have learned that freedom and competition are the answers" in the financial world.

The Clinton administration also resisted regulating new financial products because it feared hampering financial innovation. Applying regulatory ideas of the 1930s to securities trading in the 1990s, Larry Summers once quipped, would be akin to forcing modern tennis pros play with outmoded wooden rackets. Advocates of "Rubinomics" sided with forces outside the administration that wanted to translate the dominant faith in minimal regulation into congressional legislation. The Commodities Futures Modernization Act of 2000 prohibited Washington from regulating the new financial inventions called "derivatives."

Economics for a New Century, 2000–2006

The administration of Republican George W. Bush surpassed that of New Democrat Bill Clinton in its enthusiasm for supporting deregulation and promoting financial innovation. Bush's first two heads of the Treasury Department had come from the manufacturing and transportation sectors, but Henry (Hank) Paulson, who became secretary of the treasury in 2006, was another alumnus of Goldman Sachs. Just before joining the Bush administration, Paulson had successfully pressed the Securities and Exchange Commission (SEC) to exempt the five largest investment houses, which included Goldman Sachs, from a general regulation that required investment firms to reserve a specific amount of capital to cover their debt obligations. This SEC ruling dramatically increased these five firms' capacity to borrow and, consequently, their ability to speculate in risky investments.

Observers skeptical of deregulation noted early signs of trouble. During 2002, several fraud-plagued firms fell into bankruptcy. The most spectacular case involved Enron, a Texas-based energy firm with close ties to members of the Bush administration. Enron had gained an ill-deserved reputation for innovation among market analysts of the 1990s, and the value of its stock had soared. The absence of effective regulation, however, allowed the company to engage in legally suspect speculation in the trading of energy-related contracts and in illegal bookkeeping that lifted its profits to fictional heights. Seeking to restore popular confidence, Congress passed regulatory legislation (the Sarbanes-Oxley Act of 2002) that mandated new rules designed to prevent publically traded companies from fraudulently reporting their financial condition as Enron and others had done.

The political and financial impact of the scandals of the early 2000s soon paled in comparison to the systemic problems posed by the real estate and financial industries. The Bush administration quickly abandoned its predecessor's commitment to balanced budgets and a small federal deficit, but it retained its goal of promoting home ownership. Owning a home, according to conventional wisdom, increased peoples' commitment to their communities and provided a rock-solid financial investment. Bush touted the importance of an "ownership society," and his administration emulated Clinton's in pressing government connected financial institutions to help low-income buyers find the house of their dreams. These policies helped to create a residential real estate market that boosted the financial sector and, in turn, the larger economy. By 2006, nearly 70 percent of households lived in their own homes, an all-time high.

Why had the nation become caught up in an unsustainable **housing "bubble"** rather than a genuine "boom"? First, as more buyers entered the housing market, prices for new and existing homes moved upward and then skyrocketed toward the stratosphere. This meant that many people who desired—and were being urged—to become home owners lacked household incomes that could handle a conventional mortgage.

Second, the home lending industry responded by devising an array of "non-conventional" mortgages for people whose incomes or credit histories disqualified them from obtaining a fixed rate loan. By 2006, far too many new loans involved **"sub-prime mortgages,"** meaning that they, unlike those of higher quality, carried a "high risk" of defaulting. In 2001, less than 10 percent of home mortgages qualified as less than "prime" quality. In contrast, 40 percent of the new loans processed between 2001 and 2006 fell into this category.

Worse, problems extended beyond sub-prime mortgages. People with houses whose market value had dramatically increased could refinance their existing mortgage at a lower interest rate. As if by magic, refinancing on the basis of the higher valuation gave them more money to spend on consumer purchases or on investments even riskier than their new mortgages. Mortgage refinancing, then, helped stimulate overall economic activity but at the risk of creating mortgage holders who would, if the economy seriously faltered, be unable to meet their payments.

Third, people at the commanding heights of the financial system worked overtime to boost the residential housing market. They recognized that the home-buying and home-building industries were the primary engines driving the U.S., and even much of the world, economy. The Federal Reserve Board, under Alan Greenspan (who began a fifth term in 2002) and his successor Ben Bernanke (who took over in 2006), kept interest rates at historic lows. This allowed relatively "cheap money" to continue flowing through the financial sector—and kept the residential housing market bubbling. Greenspan and Bernanke insisted, however, that "the fundamentals" remained sound.

Finally, the giant firms at the top of the financial structure kept their optimistic risk assessments in place. Compliant investing services such as Moody's provided "low risk" ratings for the mortgage-backed CDOs that investment firms such as Goldman Sachs and Lehman Brothers were marketing as top-grade securities (see, also, Chapter 31).

By 2006, some people detected a bubble about to burst. Perceptive lenders at the grass roots privately joked about offering "pick-a-payment loans" and dealing with "zombie buyers," whose newly minted mortgages were virtually certain to go into default. Further up the analytical ladder, several prominent economists such as Joseph Stiglitz and Robert Shiller came to similar, and better articulated, judgments. The famed investor Warren Buffett called mortgage-backed CDOs "financial weapons of mass destruction" and forecast trouble for the home loan industry: "Dumb lending always has its consequences."

The Bubble Bursts, 2006–2008

Buffett, hailed as "the Oracle of Omaha," proved prophetic. Beginning in late 2006, the rise in housing prices first slowed and, then, home prices headed rapidly downward. The financial industry—riddled by its unrealistic assessments of risk, unsound lending practices, and fraudulent activities—soon fell victim to the housing bubble it had helped inflate. Self-correcting mechanisms, contrary to what free-market economists promised, had never appeared.

As loans went into default, the ripple effect cascaded into financial institutions overloaded with mortgage-derived securities. Credit stopped flowing, and economies throughout the world began to contract. Stock and bond values reversed course, leaving individual and institutional investors to watch the worth of their portfolios shrink. As economic growth halted in most places in the world, future factory orders declined, and unemployment figures rose.

The Bush administration and the Fed's Bernanke sought to respond. First, the Fed extended massive financial assistance to the banking industry. Then, during spring 2008, Bernanke's Fed and the Treasury Department's Hank Paulson helped J. P. Morgan Chase acquire Bear Stearns, a rival Wall Street firm headed for bankruptcy, but later allowed Lehman Brothers, another Wall Street stalwart, to collapse. The Bush administration and the Fed appeared to be signaling that a short-lived era of governmental rescue was over.

Almost instantaneously, a complete global financial meltdown loomed. In a massive sell-off, the Dow Jones stock average plummeted nearly 20 percent during a single week in early October. People began draining their savings and money market accounts. The world's financial system seized up, as it had done at the start of the Great Depression of the 1930s.

Bush's Treasury Department, the Fed, and governments around the world recognized the need for a coordinated, dramatic response. Paulson hastily designed a rescue plan and Congress passed a revised version as the Emergency Economic Stabilization Act of 2008, enacted with greater support from Democrats than from Republicans. It included the **Troubled Assets Relief Program (TARP)**. Implicitly based on the principle that giant financial institutions were "too big to fail" or go through normal bankruptcy procedure, TARP empowered the Treasury Department, guided only by loosely defined rules, to spread $700 billion throughout the financial system.

The Election of 2008

Differences over how to respond to this Great Recession dominated the 2008 political season. The presidential contest featured septuagenarian Republican Senator John McCain of Arizona and his much-younger senatorial colleague, Democrat **Barack Obama**. The first major-party presidential candidate of African descent, Obama capitalized on a media-savvy campaign staff, an innovative fundraising operation, his skills at oratory, and the unpopularity of the outgoing Bush Administration. The Obama campaign also energized many of the movements, such as those opposing immigration restriction and favoring gay rights, which had become so active during the early years of the 21st century. Many voters blamed Bush for the economic morass and viewed McCain, who admitted to knowing little about the economy, as lagging behind Obama in economic sagacity. Obama's campaign featured two words: "HOPE" and "CHANGE."

McCain's zigzag effort undercut his always slim chances. He admirably rejected conducting a smear campaign that falsely

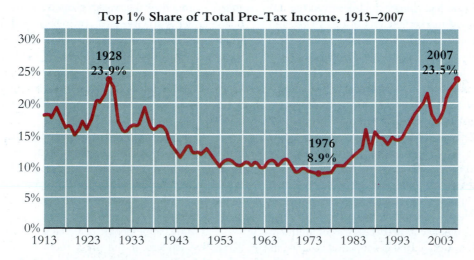

Top 1% Share of Total Pre-Tax Income, 1913–2007

Rising Income Inequality. Even before the financial crisis and Great Recession that began in 2008, income equality had been on the rise. In 2007 the top 1 percent took in 23.5 percent of total pre-tax income, the highest level since 1928.

Source: Thomas Piketty and Emmanuel Saez, "Income Inequality in the United States, 1913-1998," *Quarterly Journal of Economics*, 118(1), 2003. Updated to 2007 at http://emlab.berkeley.edu/users/saez.

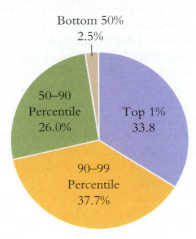

Distribution of Wealth in America, 2007. Half of the U.S. population holds only 2.5 percent of the total wealth in America. The top 10 percent holds 71.5 percent.

Source: Arthur B. Kennickell, "Ponds and Streams: Wealth and Income in the U.S., 1989 to 2007," *Federal Reserve Board Working Paper*, January 7, 2009, Figure A3a, p. 63.

Barack, Michelle, Malia, and Sasha Obama. When the Obama family moved into the White House in 2009, Sasha became the first resident to have been born in the 21st century.

claimed Obama had not been born in United States (and therefore was ineligible for the presidency) or secretly practiced Islam. McCain's biggest gamble, selecting Alaska's half-term Governor Sarah Palin as a running mate, produced scant returns at the polls. By inching away from the political center, McCain mollified some of the most conservative Republicans but also lost independents and crossover Democrats.

Although veteran prognosticators who personally admired McCain expected a closer presidential finish, younger Internet-based forecasters anticipated an Obama victory. FiveThirtyEight.com, a blog site which employed rigorous statistical analysis, almost precisely predicted Obama's margin of victory. Young black voters, especially women, turned out in record numbers. The turnout among Latinos and Asian Americans also reached all-time highs. In contrast, the percentage of Americans of European descent casting ballots fell slightly from that of 2004. Forty-three percent of this vote, a slight increase from what Kerry had gained four years prior, went to Obama. In addition to the presidency, the Democratic Party picked up seats in both branches of Congress and in many state and local races, especially outside the South.

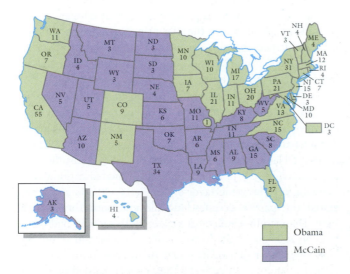

Map 32.2 Presidential Election, 2008. The victory of Barack Obama over John McCain is illustrated in this state-by-state tally of votes in the Electoral College. How did the 2008 presidential election break from the regional pattern that had boosted George W. Bush to the White House (see Map 32.1)? What states did Obama carry that Al Gore failed to win in 2000?

Changing Times, 2009–

Q FOCUS QUESTION What hopes did the Obama administration bring to Washington and what fears did its arrival produce among Republicans? What hopes and fears did the emerging culture of social networking generate?

Barack Obama's administrative team brought even greater diversity—and more star power—than those of Clinton and Bush. The key position of Secretary of State went to Hillary

Clinton. Steven Chu, a Nobel Prize winner, became Secretary of Energy. General Eric Shenseki, forced into retirement by the Bush administration, became head of Veterans Affairs. The actor Kal Penn left the TV series *House* for a brief stint in the White House's office of Public Engagement. Perhaps most crucially, Robert Gates, a Republican who had been a calming presence toward the end of Bush's presidency, agreed to remain as Secretary of Defense. The president's inaugural address urged the nation to tackle the current crises with "hope and virtue."

Political Polarization

The appointment of Gates signaled Obama's inclination for continuing some Bush-era policies and thus disappointed supporters hoping for fundamental changes. The new administration's stance on counter-terrorism, for instance, initially resembled that employed during the final years of the Bush presidency. It set aside, in response to fierce criticism from Republicans, Obama's earlier pledge to close the detention facility at Guantanamo and try terrorist suspects in U.S. courts. Similarly, civil libertarians found only minor differences between the broad legal-constitutional claims for executive power made by the Bush and Obama administrations. On the crucial economic front, Timothy Geithner, a Federal Reserve official who had helped devise the Bush administration's financial bailout of 2008, became Obama's treasury secretary, and the new president re-appointed Ben Bernanke to lead the Fed.

In the Middle East the Obama administration brought modest changes of emphasis. In Afghanistan and along that nation's border with Pakistan, Obama upped troop levels, placed increased reliance on air attacks by drones operated by computer technicians, and budgeted additional financial resources. It authorized Generals David Petraeus and Stanley McChrystal to devise an ambitious counterinsurgency effort, modeled on the "surge" in Iraq, against the Taliban. The United States tried to increase pressure on Afghanistan's Hamid Karzai, to rein in corruption and pressed Pakistan's government to move more determinedly against Taliban forces. These moves won more support from Republican than Democratic ranks.

Most domestic initiatives produced steadily escalating Republican opposition. The Obama administration could claim some victories—Senate confirmation of two Supreme Court nominees (Sonia Sotomayor and Elena Kagan), a law regulating tobacco products, another extending land conservation policies, and yet another creating a "bill of rights" for credit card holders. It encountered fierce GOP opposition on almost everything else. Only three Republican senators (and no representatives in the House) supported its plan to stimulate the economy through greater government spending, The American Recovery and Reinvestment Act of 2009 provided $212 billion in tax cuts and $575 billion in federal spending to halt the spreading recession. A congressional measure to re-regulate parts of the financial industry passed in the face of Republican criticism.

Months of negotiation among the White House, House Speaker Nancy Pelosi, and Senator Majority Leader Harry Reid also yielded the **Affordable Health Care for America Act** of 2010. Republicans revived the strategy used to derail the Clinton healthcare plan sixteen years earlier and unanimously opposed the measure. Its proponents, however, rounded up just enough Democratic votes to pass a law designed to extend, over time, coverage to some 30 million people. The act also expanded the Medicaid system, created mechanisms (called "exchanges") for increasing competition among insurance companies, and prohibited the use of pre-existing health conditions to deny coverage. Its most controversial provision required every American to carry health insurance. Critics warned that this complex legislation might cost much more than official estimates, endanger the Medicare program, and create uncertainty throughout the healthcare system.

Republican resistance to healthcare legislation signaled even broader opposition to Obama and his presidency. The GOP's most conservative factions rebranded themselves as part of a "Tea Party" movement and threatened primary challenges to any Republican incumbent tempted to support White House initiatives. Pressed by its Tea Party wing, the GOP increasingly portrayed Obama as a danger to fundamental liberties. It assailed his economic suggestions, including hints about the need for additional spending to stimulate a still-sputtering economy, as misguided. To the horror of economists supportive of Keynesian policies, Republicans insisted that cutting governmental programs and lowering the federal deficit should take precedence over increased spending for job creation and aid to unemployed workers. Familiar questions resurfaced: Was domestic action the core of economic problems or could it be part of their solutions?

The explosion on April 30, 2010 of a BP (formerly British Petroleum) pumping rig in the Gulf of Mexico—which took 11 lives and sent 62,000 barrels of oil a day spilling into the water and fragile coastal habitats—focused further debate over these contentious questions. The White House immediately joined BP in devising a response effort, but environmental groups criticized Obama for having failed to change the regulatory approach of his predecessor quickly enough and for permitting BP to direct the clean-up. Republicans simultaneously blamed the president for over-managing the federal government's response and for pressuring BP and the oil industry to change their drilling practices.

The GOP ran squarely against Obama and his domestic policies in the mid-term elections of 2010. The party's most conservative activists, rebranded as the Tea Party movement, denounced Democrats as well as Republican Rhinos ("Republicans in Name only"), whom they considered insufficiently oppositional. GOP primary contests eliminated a number of Republican stalwarts in favor of Tea Party activists and accelerated the party's decades-long move toward the political right. Democratic candidates, especially those who had benefitted in 2006 and 2008 from economic turmoil and an unpopular Republican president, found themselves burdened by a jobless economic recovery and their own embattled president. In contrast to 2008, many younger voters stayed home in 2010 while older ones, who tended to favor Republican candidates, turned out in higher numbers. Republicans linked Obama to continued high unemployment and federal budget deficits, legacies of the Great Recession that began before his presidency. As a result, the 2010 mid-term elections followed a

The Future of Print Media?

This final edition of Denver's *Rocky Mountain News*—which appeared on February 27, 2009—offered a poignant and perceptive look at the past and present of newspaper publishing. This tabloid source of news and opinion, which had garnered four coveted Pulitzer Prizes during its final decade of publishing, accompanied many other newspapers around the country into oblivion.

As the arrival of the Internet transformed how people communicated with one another, the familiar medium of the newspaper lost its economic viability. People who wanted to obtain the day's news, sample political opinion, or survey evening entertainment options began firing up their computers rather than glancing at the printed page. Sports fans, especially, found that the morning sports page, long a major incentive for opening up a newspaper, seemed a pale imitation of what they could find on ESPN and its constantly expanding web site.

Sources of revenue for newspapers steadily shrank. As print papers began developing their own sites in cyberspace, they found that they were "giving away" material that they were still asking print readers to purchase. Moreover, with fewer readers, newspaper publishers saw advertising revenues, the life blood of their business, dry up. The economics of publishing meant that most cities, even ones as large as Denver, could no longer support several newspapers.

Q Look carefully at this page from the final day in the life of the *Rocky Mountain News*. How do the paper's publishers seek to tell, in *prose*, the story of a nearly 150-year relationship with Denver?

Q How does the visual composition of this same page, which harkens back to a time

when Denver was not yet a city and Colorado not a state, show that the *Rocky Mountain News* and the citizens of Denver were now living in different era? What, for example, do you see running down the left-hand side of this re-creation of a mid-19th century newspaper that you might see sprinkled through an early 21st century website?

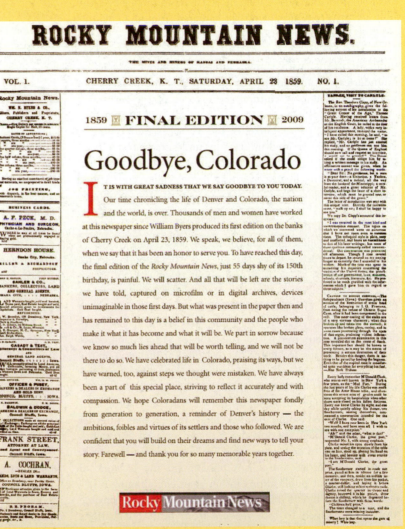

Newspapers Became a Casualty of the Internet Era.

AFP PHOTO/ROCKY MOUNTAIN NEWS/Newscom

long-familiar pattern: The party controlling the White House and Congress almost always lost legislative seats.

The results of the GOP's well-funded electoral effort, however, exceeded the historical averages and the early projections of most analysts. Republicans took control of the House of Representatives, cut into the Democrats' majority in the Senate, and gained more than 600 legislative seats and 20 gubernatorial offices in states throughout the country. A national political culture marked by extreme partisanship, dramatically shifting electoral outcomes, and

The Culture of Social Networking and Liberty, Equality, Power

The Obama administration and its critics increasingly drew on the culture of **social networking sites**. The Obama electoral movement had successfully employed the Internet to gain the Democratic nomination and the presidency. One of the creators of the networking service Facebook joined the Obama team and helped elaborate its Internet operations. In contrast, the McCain effort attracted few tech-savvy people, and its main site earned low marks for both style and performance. The Obama effort ultimately raised more far more money over the Internet than McCain's campaign gathered from all of its outreach to individual contributors.

Use of various Internet-based sites to create communities of people with similar interests, while transcending boundaries of time and space, quickly became perhaps the most important new cultural-social force of the early 21st century. It transformed not only political mobilization but nearly everything else. LinkedIn and MySpace went online in 2003. Facebook, created in 2004 by undergraduates at Harvard University to facilitate links with other students, quickly attracted wealthy investors from Silicon Valley and tapped enough advertising revenues to make its operations profitable in 2009.

YouTube, developed by Silicon Valley entrepreneurs in 2005, offered a different kind of social networking model. It allowed people to post footage derived from motion picture and TV sources; music from just about anywhere; and, most importantly, original material created by individual users. Its rate of growth, a measure of the popular desire to produce as well as consume visual imagery, surpassed even that of Facebook. Google soon purchased YouTube for $1.65 billion. *Time* magazine, perhaps seeing the handwriting (or imagery) on the wall, selected "You," all of the millions of people using networking sites, as its "Person of the Year" for 2008.

The changes brought by the Internet and social networking worried some people. They feared that Internet news and commentary only made the adversarial framework that had come to dominate cable TV news more ubiquitous. They saw Internet journalism preying on the legwork of writers for print publications rather than encouraging original reporting by its bloggers. At the same time, on-line journalism helped to lure readers from print publications and to diminish their value to potential advertisers. Losing readers and revenue, magazines and newspapers began to cease publication. Frequent Internet postings, moreover, seemed to be making the 24/7 news cycle move even faster. American politics "has become an almost minute-by-minute spectacle," growled an editor at the embattled *New York Times*. While voicing analogous concerns about the cultural impact of social networking sites, critics also feared that the process of "linking up" was destroying traditional notions of privacy was well as threatening the safety of the young and the innocent.

The most enthusiastic champions of social networking, however, praised it—and the larger Internet environment—for creating patterns that could not only transcend old barriers of time and space but help people re-imagine liberty, power, and equality. Freely shared and communally developed software might liberate communication from corporate control. Interactive Internet sites might empower ordinary people and challenge hierarchical arrangements. Political figures used websites and Facebook to issue policy pronouncements that bypassed the traditional process media gatekeepers. Bloggers took on, and sometimes took down, media commentators and special interests. Networking sites such as Yelp helped reconfigure restaurant, TV, and motion picture reviews by drawing upon audience and user responses. Wikipedia supplanted hard-copy encyclopedias with a collaboratively written, ever-changing, and controversial source on virtually everything. And even history textbooks began to devise more participatory formats.

Conclusion

Two presidents, one Democrat and one Republican, dominated political life at the end of the 20th and the beginning of the 21st centuries. Bill Clinton's administration pressed a modest domestic agenda that moved the Democratic Party away from its "big government" image. Although failing to achieve its major goal of healthcare overhaul, it cut back the welfare system and eliminated the federal deficit. As political polarization escalated during the 1990s, however, Clinton's personal behavior ensnared him in legal investigations that stalled his presidency. When the presidential election of 2000 ended in a near dead heat, a 5–4 Supreme Court decision declared Republican George W. Bush the 43rd president. The Bush administration's conservative agenda featured tax cuts, deregulation, and reform of education. It also converted the budget surplus left by Clinton into a rising federal deficit. Numerically closely matched, the political parties of these years launched partisan attacks that exaggerated the buoyant hopes and the deepest fears of the age.

Both Clinton and Bush tried to chart foreign policies for a post-Cold War world. Clinton's internationalist policy deployed military power selectively and concentrated on measures fostering the "globalization" of economic relationships. After the terrorist attacks of 9/11, the Bush administration focused its unilateralist foreign policy on fighting a global "war on terror." The U.S. first invaded Afghanistan and then attacked Iraq. When the rapid success that the White House had expected never materialized, the administration shifted its energies and U.S. resources toward the kind of expensive "nation-building" project in Iraq that Republicans had once opposed.

The U.S. economy enjoyed its longest period of sustained growth during the 1990s. The financial sector did especially well. The early years of the 21st century, however, produced a mixed picture. The financial industry continued to reap phenomenal profits, aided by a spectacular bubble in the residential housing market. In 2007, however, declining home prices and a wave of mortgage foreclosures rocked the financial sector, and the impact rippled quickly through the entire global economy. The Bush administration and the Federal Reserve Board, with more Democratic than Republican support, devised a 2008 effort that rescued the financial sector. The larger economy, however, slid into the Great Recession, the worst since the 1930s.

President Bush's unpopularity and the country's economic distress helped the Democratic Party regain control of Congress in 2006 and lifted its standard bearer, Barack Obama, to the presidency in 2008. Backing a flurry of new initiatives, Obama sought to shift the military focus from Iraq to Afghanistan, revamp the healthcare system, and reverse the trend toward deregulation, especially in the financial sector and for health and environmental matters. Discussions of social policy, international relations, and economic recovery, however, continued against the backdrops of hope and fear that circulated within rapidly changing forms of media. ⚸

CHAPTER REVIEW

REVIEW QUESTIONS

1. What political and cultural forces helped to polarize national politics during the years between 1993 and 2008? What impact did this polarization have on the policymaking process in Washington?
2. How did the Clinton administration attempt to redesign foreign policy for a post-Cold War world? How did the administration of George W. Bush, especially after September 11, 2001, seek to re-orient Clinton's approach?
3. What forces fueled the various economic bubbles from the late 1990s to 2008? How did governmental officials respond to the financial meltdown of 2008 and the subsequent recession?
4. What hopes did the Obama administration bring to Washington and what fears did its arrival produce among its critics? What hopes and fears did the emerging culture of social networking generate?

CRITICAL THINKING QUESTIONS

1. Before the 1980s, Republicans had generally opposed expensive domestic programs and large deficits, which they identified with Democratic administrations. What factors help explain how, between 1980 and 2000, Republican administrations created large government deficits, while New Democrats offered their party as the guarantor of fiscal prudence? How did the financial meltdown of 2008 and the subsequent recession alter the situation?
2. How did Bill Clinton and George W. Bush, who espoused differing visions of government power and social policy, generate different popular followings? How could Bush, who generally lacked the strong approval ratings of Clinton, become such a "strong" chief executive, especially during the early years of his two-term presidency?

IDENTIFICATIONS

Review your understanding of the following key terms, people, and events for this chapter (terms in bold in text are included in the Glossary).

William Jefferson (Bill) Clinton, p. 886
Earned Income Tax Credit (EITC), p. 886
New Democrat, p. 887
Contract with America, p. 887
Temporary Assistance to Needy Families (TANF), p. 887
George W. Bush, p. 890
Richard (Dick) Cheney, p. 890
Bush **v.** *Gore*, p. 891
The Medicare Prescription Drug Improvement and Modernization Act, p. 892
Roberts Court, p. 894
World Trade Organization (WTO), p. 895.
Bush Doctrine, p. 896
National Security Strategy of 2002, p. 896
neoconservatives, p. 896
the surge, p. 898
General David Petraeus, p. 898
housing bubble, p. 901
sub-prime mortgages, p. 901
Troubled Assets Relief Program (TARP), p. 902
Barack Obama, p. 902
Affordable Health Care for America Act, p. 904
social networking, p. 906

SUGGESTED READINGS

William L. O'Neill, *A Bubble in Time: America During the Interwar Years, 1989–2001* (2009) is a superb, popular study by an academic historian. **Taylor Branch**, *The Clinton Tapes: Wrestling with the President* (2009) is a unique collaboration between a president and a designated historian-chronicler. **Ken Gormley, *The Death of American Virtue: Clinton v. Starr*** (2010) is an exhaustive analysis of the investigation and trial of a president by an indefatigable lawyer-historian. On the "long election," see **Jeffrey Toobin, *Too Close to Call: The Thirty-Six Day Battle to Decide the 2000 Election*** (2002). His earlier book, ***The Run of His Life: The People vs. O. J. Simpson*** (1997) remains one of the better accounts of the Simpson saga.

On the political stalemate of this era, see **Earl and Merle Black, *Divided: The Ferocious Power Struggle in American Politics*** (2008). On Bush's foreign policy, especially in Iraq, consult two books by **Thomas Ricks, *Fiasco: The American Military Adventure in Iraq, 2003–2005*** (2006) and ***The Gamble: General David Petraeus and the American Military Adventure in Iraq, 2006–2008*** (2009). See also, **Philip Bobbit, *Terror and Consent: The Wars for the 21st Century*** (2008).

The story of the fiscal-economic crack-up can be followed in these outstanding books: **John Cassidy, *How Markets Fail: The Logic of Economic Calamities*** (2009); **Simon Johnson and James Kwak, *13 Bankers: The Wall Street Takeover and the Next Financial Meltdown*** (2010); and **Andrew Ross Sorkin, *Too Big To Fail: The Inside Story of How Washington and Wall Street Sought to Save the Financial System—And Themselves*** (2010).

David Plouffe, *The Audacity to Win: The Inside Story and Lessons of Barack Obama's Historic Victory* (2009) and **David Remnick, *The Bridge: The Life and Rise of Barack Obama*** (2010) are early efforts at understanding the 44th president and his 2008 victory.

For introductions to some of this era's major cultural forces, see **Yochei Benkler, *The Wealth of Networks*** (2007); and **James Livingston, *The World Turned Inside Out: American Thought and Culture at the end of the 20th Century*** (2009).

Visit the CourseMate website at www.cengagebrain.com for additional study tools and review materials for this chapter.

APPENDIX

The Declaration of Independence — A-3

The Constitution of the United States of America — A-5

Admission of States — A-13

Population of the United States — A-14

Presidential Elections — A-17

Justices of the U.S. Supreme Court — A-23

A-1

The Declaration of Independence
The Unanimous Declaration of the Thirteen United States of America

When in the Course of human events it becomes necessary for one people to dissolve the political bands which have connected them with another, and to assume among the Powers of the earth, the separate and equal station to which the Laws of Nature and of Nature's God entitle them, a decent respect to the opinions of mankind requires that they should declare the causes which impel them to the separation.

We hold these truths to be self-evident, that all men are created equal, that they are endowed by their Creator with certain unalienable Rights, that among these are Life, Liberty and the pursuit of Happiness. That to secure these rights, Governments are instituted among Men, deriving their just Powers from the consent of the governed. That whenever any Form of Government becomes destructive of these ends, it is the Right of the People to alter or to abolish it, and to institute new Government, laying its foundation on such principles and organizing its Powers in such form, as to them shall seem most likely to effect their Safety and Happiness. Prudence, indeed, will dictate that Governments long established should not be changed for light and transient causes; and accordingly all experience hath shewn, that mankind are more disposed to suffer, while evils are sufferable, than to right themselves by abolishing the forms to which they are accustomed. But when a long train of abuses and usurpations, pursuing invariably the same Object evinces a design to reduce them under absolute Despotism, it is their right, it is their duty, to throw off such Government, and to provide new Guards for their future security. Such has been the patient sufferance of these Colonies; and such is now the necessity which constrains them to alter their former Systems of Government. The history of the present King of Great Britain is a history of repeated injuries and usurpations, all having in direct object the establishment of an absolute Tyranny over these States. To prove this, let Facts be submitted to a candid world.

He has refused his Assent to Laws, the most wholesome and necessary for the public good.

He has forbidden his Governors to pass Laws of immediate and pressing importance, unless suspended in their operation till his Assent should be obtained; and when so suspended, he has utterly neglected to attend to them.

He has refused to pass other Laws for the accommodation of large districts of people, unless those people would relinquish the right of Representation in the Legislature, a right inestimable to them and formidable to tyrants only.

He has called together legislative bodies at places unusual, uncomfortable, and distant from the depository of their Public Records, for the sole Purpose of fatiguing them into compliance with his measures.

He has dissolved Representative Houses repeatedly, for opposing with manly firmness his invasions on the rights of the People.

He has refused for a long time, after such dissolutions, to cause others to be elected; whereby the Legislative Powers, incapable of Annihilation, have returned to the People at large for their exercise; the State remaining in the mean time exposed to all the dangers of invasion from without, and convulsions within.

He has endeavoured to prevent the Population of these States; for that purpose obstructing the Laws for Naturalization of Foreigners; refusing to pass others to encourage their migrations hither, and raising the conditions of new Appropriations of Lands.

He has obstructed the Administration of Justice, by refusing his Assent to Laws for establishing Judiciary Powers.

He has made Judges dependent on his Will alone, for the tenure of their offices, and the amount and payment of their salaries.

He has erected a multitude of New Offices, and sent hither swarms of Officers to harass our People, and eat out their substance.

He has kept among us, in times of peace, Standing Armies without the Consent of our legislatures.

He has affected to render the Military independent of and superior to the Civil Power.

He has combined with others to subject us to a jurisdiction foreign to our constitution, and unacknowledged by our laws; giving his Assent to their Acts of pretended Legislation: For Quartering large bodies of armed troops among us: For protecting them, by a mock Trial, from Punishment for any Murders which they should commit on the Inhabitants of these States: For cutting off our Trade with all parts of the world: For imposing Taxes on us without our Consent: For depriving us in many cases, of the benefits of Trial by Jury: For transporting us beyond Seas to be tried for pretended offences: For abolishing the free System of English Laws in a neighbouring Province, establishing therein an Arbitrary government,

---

Text is reprinted from the facsimile of the engrossed copy in the National Archives. The original spelling, capitalization, and punctuation have been retained. Paragraphing has been added.

and enlarging its Boundaries so as to render it at once an example and fit instrument for introducing the same absolute rule into these Colonies: For taking away our Charters, abolishing our most valuable Laws, and altering fundamentally the Forms of our Governments: For suspending our own Legislatures, and declaring themselves invested with Power to legislate for us in all cases whatsoever.

He has abdicated Government here, by declaring us out of his Protection, and waging War against us.

He has plundered our seas, ravaged our Coasts, burnt our towns, and destroyed the lives of our people.

He is at this time transporting large Armies of foreign Mercenaries to compleat the works of death, desolation and tyranny, already begun with circumstances of Cruelty and perfidy scarcely paralleled in the most barbarous ages, and totally unworthy the Head of a civilized nation.

He has constrained our fellow Citizens taken Captive on the high Seas to bear Arms against their Country, to become the executioners of their friends and Brethren, or to fall themselves by their Hands.

He has excited domestic insurrections amongst us, and has endeavoured to bring on the inhabitants of our frontiers, the merciless Indian Savages, whose known rule of warfare, is an undistinguished destruction of all ages, sexes and conditions.

In every stage of these Oppressions We have Petitioned for Redress in the most humble terms: Our repeated Petitions have been answered only by repeated injury. A Prince, whose character is thus marked by every act which may define a Tyrant, is unfit to be the ruler of a free People.

Nor have We been wanting in attentions to our British brethren. We have warned them from time to time of attempts by their legislature to extend an unwarrantable jurisdiction over us. We have reminded them of the circumstances of our emigration and settlement here. We have appealed to their native justice and magnanimity, and we have conjured them by the ties of our common kindred to disavow these usurpations, which, would inevitably interrupt our connections and correspondence. They too have been deaf to the voice of justice and of consanguinity. We must, therefore, acquiesce in the necessity, which denounces our Separation, and hold them, as we hold the rest of mankind, Enemies in War, in Peace Friends.

We, therefore, the Representatives of the United States of America, in General Congress, Assembled, appealing to the Supreme Judge of the world for the rectitude of our intentions, do, in the Name, and by Authority of the good People of these Colonies, solemnly publish and declare, That these United Colonies are, and of Right ought to be Free and Independent States; that they are Absolved from all Allegiance to the British Crown, and that all political connection between them and the State of Great Britain, is and ought to be totally dissolved; and that, as Free and Independent States, they have full Power to levy War, conclude Peace, contract Alliances, establish Commerce, and to do all other Acts and Things which Independent States may of right do. And for the support of this Declaration, with a firm reliance on the protection of divine Providence, we mutually pledge to each other our Lives, our Fortunes and our sacred Honor.

The Constitution of the United States of America

We the People of the United States, in Order to form a more perfect Union, establish Justice, insure domestic Tranquility, provide for the common defence, promote the general Welfare, and secure the Blessings of Liberty to ourselves and our Posterity, do ordain and establish this Constitution for the United States of America.

ARTICLE I.

SECTION 1. All legislative Powers herein granted shall be vested in a Congress of the United States, which shall consist of a Senate and House of Representatives.

SECTION 2. The House of Representatives shall be composed of Members chosen every second Year by the People of the several States, and the Electors in each State shall have the Qualifications requisite for Electors of the most numerous Branch of the State Legislature.

No Person shall be a Representative who shall not have attained to the Age of twenty five Years, and been seven Years a Citizen of the United States, and who shall not, when elected, be an Inhabitant of that State in which he shall be chosen.

Representatives and direct Taxes[1] shall be apportioned among the several States which may be included within this Union, according to their respective Numbers, which shall be determined by adding to the whole Number of free Persons, including those bound to Service for a Term of Years, and excluding Indians not taxed, three fifths of all other Persons.[2]

The actual Enumeration shall be made within three Years after the first Meeting of the Congress of the United States, and within every subsequent Term of ten Years, in such Manner as they shall by Law direct. The Number of Representatives shall not exceed one for every thirty Thousand, but each State shall have at Least one Representative; and until such enumeration shall be made, the State of New Hampshire shall be entitled to chuse three; Massachusetts eight; Rhode Island and Providence Plantations one; Connecticut five; New York six; New Jersey four; Pennsylvania eight; Delaware one; Maryland six; Virginia ten; North Carolina five; South Carolina five; and Georgia three.

When vacancies happen in the Representation from any State, the Executive Authority thereof shall issue Writs of Election to fill such Vacancies.

The House of Representatives shall chuse their Speaker and other Officers; and shall have the sole Power of Impeachment.

SECTION 3. The Senate of the United States shall be composed of two Senators from each State, chosen by the Legislature thereof, for six Years; and each Senator shall have one Vote.[3]

Immediately after they shall be assembled in Consequence of the first Election, they shall be divided as equally as may be into three Classes. The Seats of the Senators of the first Class shall be vacated at the Expiration of the second Year, of the second Class at the Expiration of the fourth Year, and of the third Class at the Expiration of the sixth Year, so that one third may be chosen every second Year; and if Vacancies happen by Resignation, or otherwise, during the Recess of the Legislature of any State, the Executive thereof may make temporary Appointments until the next Meeting of the Legislature, which shall then fill such Vacancies.[4]

No Person shall be a Senator who shall not have attained to the Age of thirty Years, and been nine Years a Citizen of the United States, and who shall not, when elected, be an Inhabitant of that State for which he shall be chosen.

The Vice President of the United States shall be President of the Senate, but shall have no Vote, unless they be equally divided.

The Senate shall chuse their other Officers, and also a President pro tempore, in the Absence of the Vice President, or when he shall exercise the Office of President of the United States.

The Senate shall have the sole Power to try all Impeachments. When sitting for that Purpose, they shall be on Oath or Affirmation. When the President of the United States is tried, the Chief Justice shall preside: And no Person shall be convicted without the Concurrence of two thirds of the Members present.

Judgment in Cases of Impeachment shall not extend further than to removal from Office, and disqualification to hold and enjoy any Office of honor, Trust or Profit under the United States: but the Party convicted shall nevertheless be liable and subject to Indictment, Trial, Judgment and Punishment, according to Law.

SECTION 4. The Times, Places and Manner of holding Elections for Senators and Representatives, shall be prescribed in each State by the Legislature thereof, but the Congress may at any time by Law make or alter such Regulation, except as to the Places of chusing Senators.

The Congress shall assemble at least once in every Year, and such Meeting shall be on the first Monday in December, unless they shall by Law appoint a different Day.[5]

SECTION 5. Each House shall be the Judge of the Elections, Returns and Qualifications of its own Members, and a Majority

---

Text is from the engrossed copy in the National Archives. Original spelling, capitalization, and punctuation have been retained.

1 Modified by the Sixteenth Amendment.
2 Replaced by the Fourteenth Amendment.
3 Superseded by the Seventeenth Amendment.
4 Modified by the Seventeenth Amendment.
5 Superseded by the Twentieth Amendment.

of each shall constitute a Quorum to do Business; but a smaller Number may adjourn from day to day, and may be authorized to compel the Attendance of absent Members, in such Manner, and under such Penalties as each House may provide.

Each House may determine the Rules of its Proceedings, punish its Members for disorderly Behaviour, and, with the Concurrence of two thirds, expel a Member.

Each House shall keep a Journal of its Proceedings, and from time to time publish the same, excepting such Parts as may in their Judgment require Secrecy; and the Yeas and Nays of the Members of either House on any question shall, at the Desire of one fifth of those Present, be entered on the Journal.

Neither House, during the Session of Congress, shall, without the Consent of the other, adjourn for more than three days, nor to any other Place than that in which the two Houses shall be sitting.

SECTION 6. The Senators and Representatives shall receive a Compensation for their Services, to be ascertained by Law, and paid out of the Treasury of the United States. They shall in all Cases, except Treason, Felony and Breach of the Peace, be privileged from Arrest during their Attendance at the Session of their respective Houses, and in going to and returning from the same; and for any Speech or Debate in either House, they shall not be questioned in any other Place.

No Senator or Representative shall, during the Time for which he was elected, be appointed to any civil Office under the Authority of the United States, which shall have been created, or the Emoluments whereof shall have been encreased during such time; and no Person holding any Office under the United States, shall be a Member of either House during his Continuance in Office.

SECTION 7. All Bills for raising Revenue shall originate in the House of Representatives; but the Senate may propose or concur with Amendments as on other Bills.

Every Bill which shall have passed the House of Representatives and the Senate shall, before it become a Law, be presented to the President of the United States; If he approve he shall sign it, but if not he shall return it, with his Objections to that House in which it shall have originated, who shall enter the Objections at large on their Journal, and proceed to reconsider it. If after such Reconsideration two thirds of that House shall agree to pass the Bill, it shall be sent, together with the Objections, to the other House, by which it shall likewise be reconsidered, and if approved by two thirds of that House, it shall become a Law. But in all such Cases the Votes of both Houses shall be determined by yeas and Nays, and the Names of the Persons voting for and against the Bill shall be entered on the Journal of each House respectively. If any Bill shall not be returned by the President within ten Days (Sundays excepted) after it shall have been presented to him, the Same shall be a Law, in like Manner as if he had signed it, unless the Congress by their Adjournment prevent its Return, in which Case it shall not be a Law.

Every Order, Resolution, or Vote to which the Concurrence of the Senate and House of Representatives may be necessary (except on a question of Adjournment) shall be presented to the President of the United States; and before the Same shall take Effect, shall be approved by him, or being disapproved by him shall be repassed by two thirds of the Senate and House of Representatives, according to the Rules and Limitations prescribed in the Case of a Bill.

SECTION 8. The Congress shall have power To lay and collect Taxes, Duties, Imposts and Excises, to pay the Debts and provide for the common Defence and general Welfare of the United States; but all Duties, Imposts and Excises shall be uniform throughout the United States; To borrow Money on the credit of the United States; To regulate Commerce with foreign Nations, and among the several States, and with the Indian Tribes; To establish an uniform Rule of Naturalization, and uniform Laws on the subject of Bankruptcies throughout the United States; To coin Money, regulate the Value thereof, and of foreign Coin, and fix the Standard of Weights and Measures; To provide for the Punishment of counterfeiting the Securities and current Coin of the United States; To establish Post Offices and post Roads; To promote the Progress of Science and useful Arts, by securing for limited Times to Authors and Inventors the exclusive Right to their respective Writings and Discoveries; To constitute Tribunals inferior to the supreme Court; To define and punish Piracies and Felonies committed on the high Seas, and Offences against the Law of Nations;

To declare War, grant Letters of Marque and Reprisal, and make Rules concerning Captures on Land and Water; To raise and support Armies, but no Appropriation of Money to that Use shall be for a longer Term than two Years; To provide and maintain a Navy; To make Rules for the Government and Regulation of the land and naval Forces; To provide for calling forth the Militia to execute the Laws of the Union, suppress Insurrections and repel Invasions; To provide for organizing, arming, and disciplining, the Militia, and for governing such Part of them as may be employed in the Service of the United States, reserving to the States respectively, the Appointment of the Officers, and the Authority of training the Militia according to the discipline prescribed by Congress; To exercise exclusive Legislation in all Cases whatsoever, over such District (not exceeding ten Miles square) as may, by Cession of particular States, and the Acceptance of Congress, become the Seat of the Government of the United States, and to exercise like Authority over all Places purchased by the Consent of the Legislature of the State in which the Same shall be, for the Erection of Forts, Magazines, Arsenals, dock-Yards, and other needful Buildings;— And To make all Laws which shall be necessary and proper for carrying into Execution the foregoing Powers, and all other Powers vested by this Constitution in the Government of the United States, or in any Department or Officer thereof.

SECTION 9. The Migration or Importation of such Persons as any of the States now existing shall think proper to admit, shall not be prohibited by the Congress prior to the Year one thousand eight hundred and eight, but a Tax or duty may be imposed on such Importation, not exceeding ten dollars for each Person.

The Privilege of the Writ of Habeas Corpus shall not be suspended, unless when in Cases of Rebellion or Invasion the public Safety may require it.

No Bill of Attainder or ex post facto Law shall be passed. No Capitation, or other direct, Tax shall be laid, unless in Proportion to the Census or Enumeration herein before directed to be taken.

No Tax or Duty shall be laid on Articles exported from any State.

No Preference shall be given by any Regulation of Commerce or Revenue to the Ports of one State over those of another: nor shall Vessels bound to, or from, one State, be obliged to enter, clear, or pay Duties in another.

No Money shall be drawn from the Treasury, but in Consequence of Appropriations made by Law, and a regular Statement and Account of the Receipts and Expenditures of all public Money shall be published from time to time.

No Title of Nobility shall be granted by the United States: And no Person holding any Office of Profit or Trust under them, shall, without the Consent of the Congress, accept of any present, Emolument, Office, or Title, of any kind whatever, from any King, Prince, or foreign State.

SECTION 10. No State shall enter into any Treaty, Alliance, or Confederation; grant Letters of Marque and Reprisal; coin Money; emit Bills of Credit; make any Thing but gold and silver Coin a Tender in Payment of Debts; pass any Bill of Attainder, ex post facto Law, or Law impairing the Obligation of Contracts, or grant any Title of Nobility.

No State shall, without the Consent of the Congress, lay any Imposts or Duties on Imports or Exports, except what may be absolutely necessary for executing its inspection Laws: and the net Produce of all Duties and Imposts, laid by any State on Imports or Exports, shall be for the Use of the Treasury of the United States; and all such Laws shall be subject to the Revision and Controul of the Congress.

No State shall, without the Consent of Congress, lay any Duty of Tonnage, keep Troops, or Ships of War in time of Peace, enter into any Agreement or Compact with another State, or with a foreign Power, or engage in War, unless actually invaded, or in such imminent Danger as will not admit of delay.

ARTICLE II.

SECTION 1. The executive Power shall be vested in a President of the United States of America. He shall hold his Office during the Term of four Years, and, together with the Vice President, chosen for the same Term, be elected, as follows: Each State shall appoint, in such Manner as the Legislature thereof may direct, a Number of Electors, equal to the whole Number of Senators and Representatives to which the State may be entitled in the Congress: but no Senator or Representative, or Person holding an Office of Trust or Profit under the United States, shall be appointed an Elector.

The Electors shall meet in their respective States, and vote by Ballot for two Persons, of whom one at least shall not be an Inhabitant of the same State with themselves. And they shall make a List of all the Persons voted for, and of the Number of Votes for each; which List they shall sign and certify, and transmit sealed to the Seat of the Government of the United States, directed to the President of the Senate. The President of the Senate shall, in the Presence of the Senate and House of Representatives, open all the Certificates, and the Votes shall then be counted. The Person having the greatest Number of Votes shall be the President, if such Number be a Majority of the whole Number of Electors appointed; and if there be more

than one who have such Majority, and have an equal Number of Votes, then the House of Representatives shall immediately chuse by Ballot one of them for President; and if no Person have a Majority, then from the five highest on the List the said House shall in like Manner chuse the President. But in chusing the President, the Votes shall be taken by States, the Representation from each State having one Vote; A quorum for this Purpose shall consist of a Member or Members from two thirds of the States, and a Majority of all the States shall be necessary to a Choice. In every Case, after the Choice of the President, the Person having the greatest Number of Votes of the Electors shall be the Vice President. But if there should remain two or more who have equal Votes, the Senate shall chuse from them by Ballot the Vice President.[6]

The Congress may determine the Time of chusing the Electors, and the Day on which they shall give their Votes; which Day shall be the same throughout the United States.

No Person except a natural born Citizen, or a Citizen of the United States, at the time of the Adoption of this Constitution, shall be eligible to the Office of President, neither shall any Person be eligible to that Office who shall not have attained to the Age of thirty five Years, and been fourteen Years a Resident within the United States.

In Case of the Removal of the President from Office, or of his Death, Resignation, or Inability to discharge the Powers and Duties of the said Office, the Same shall devolve on the Vice President, and the Congress may by Law provide for the Case of Removal, Death, Resignation or Inability, both of the President and Vice President, declaring what Officer shall then act as President, and such Officer shall act accordingly, until the Disability be removed, or a President shall be elected.[7]

The President shall, at stated Times, receive for his Services, a Compensation, which shall neither be encreased nor diminished during the Period for which he shall have been elected, and he shall not receive within that Period any other Emolument from the United States, or any of them.

Before he enter on the Execution of his Office, he shall take the following Oath or Affirmation:—"I do solemnly swear (or affirm) that I will faithfully execute the Office of President of the United States, and will to the best of my Ability, preserve, protect and defend the Constitution of the United States."

SECTION 2. The President shall be Commander in Chief of the Army and Navy of the United States, and of the Militia of the several States, when called into the actual Service of the United States; he may require the Opinion, in writing, of the principal Officer in each of the executive Departments, upon any Subject relating to the Duties of their respective Offices, and he shall have Power to grant Reprieves and Pardons for Offences against the United States, except in Cases of Impeachment.

He shall have Power, by and with the Advice and Consent of the Senate, to make Treaties, provided two thirds of the Senators present concur; and he shall nominate, and by and with the Advice and Consent of the Senate, shall appoint Ambassadors, other public Ministers and Consuls, Judges of the supreme Court, and all other Officers of the United States,

---

6 Superseded by the Twelfth Amendment.
7 Modified by the Twenty-fifth Amendment.

whose Appointments are not herein otherwise provided for, and which shall be established by Law; but the Congress may by Law vest the Appointment of such inferior Officers, as they think proper, in the President alone, in the Courts of Law, or in the Heads of Departments.

The President shall have Power to fill up all Vacancies that may happen during the Recess of the Senate, by granting Commissions which shall expire at the End of their next Session.

SECTION 3. He shall from time to time give the Congress Information of the State of the Union, and recommend to their Consideration such Measures as he shall judge necessary and expedient; he may, on extraordinary Occasions, convene both Houses, or either of them, and in Case of Disagreement between them, with Respect to the Time of Adjournment, he may adjourn them to such Time as he shall think proper; he shall receive Ambassadors and other public Ministers; he shall take Care that the Laws be faithfully executed, and shall Commission all the Officers of the United States.

SECTION 4. The President, Vice President and all civil Officers of the United States, shall be removed from Office on Impeachment for, and Conviction of, Treason, Bribery, or other high Crimes and Misdemeanors.

ARTICLE III.

SECTION 1. The judicial Power of the United States, shall be vested in one supreme Court, and in such inferior Courts as the Congress may from time to time ordain and establish.

The Judges, both of the supreme and inferior Courts, shall hold their Offices during good Behaviour, and shall, at stated Times, receive for their Services, a Compensation, which shall not be diminished during their Continuance in Office.

SECTION 2. The judicial Power shall extend to all Cases, in Law and Equity, arising under this Constitution, the Laws of the United States, and Treaties made, or which shall be made, under their Authority;—to all Cases affecting Ambassadors, other public Ministers and Consuls;—to all Cases of admiralty and maritime Jurisdiction;—to Controversies to which the United States shall be a Party;—to Controversies between two or more States;—between a State and Citizens of another State;[8]—between Citizens of different States,—between Citizens of the same State claiming Lands under Grants of different States, and between a State, or the Citizens thereof, and foreign States, Citizens or Subjects.

In all Cases affecting Ambassadors, other public Ministers and Consuls, and those in which a State shall be Party, the supreme Court shall have original Jurisdiction. In all the other Cases before mentioned, the supreme Court shall have appellate Jurisdiction, both as to Law and Fact, with such Exceptions, and under such Regulations as the Congress shall make.

The Trial of all Crimes, except in Cases of Impeachment, shall be by Jury; and such Trial shall be held in the State where the said Crimes shall have been committed; but when not committed within any State, the Trial shall be at such Place or Places as the Congress may by Law have directed.

SECTION 3. Treason against the United States, shall consist only in levying War against them, or in adhering to their

---

8 Modified by the Eleventh Amendment.

Enemies, giving them Aid and Comfort. No Person shall be convicted of Treason unless on the Testimony of two Witnesses to the same overt Act, or on Confession in open Court.

The Congress shall have Power to declare the Punishment of Treason, but no Attainder of Treason shall work Corruption of Blood, or Forfeiture except during the Life of the Person attainted.

ARTICLE IV.

SECTION 1. Full Faith and Credit shall be given in each State to the public Acts, Records, and judicial Proceedings of every other State. And the Congress may by general Laws prescribe the Manner in which such Acts, Records and Proceedings shall be proved, and the Effect thereof.

SECTION 2. The Citizens of each State shall be entitled to all Privileges and Immunities of Citizens in the several States.

A Person charged in any State with Treason, Felony, or other Crime, who shall flee from Justice, and be found in another State, shall on Demand of the executive Authority of the State from which he fled, be delivered up, to be removed to the State having Jurisdiction of the Crime.

No Person held to Service or Labour in one State, under the Laws thereof, escaping into another, shall, in Consequence of any Law or Regulation therein, be discharged from such Service or Labour, but shall be delivered up on Claim of the Party to whom such Service or Labour may be due.

SECTION 3. New States may be admitted by the Congress into this Union; but no new State shall be formed or erected within the Jurisdiction of any other State, nor any State be formed by the Junction of two or more States, or Parts of States, without the Consent of the Legislatures of the States concerned as well as of the Congress.

The Congress shall have Power to dispose of and make all needful Rules and Regulations respecting the Territory or other Property belonging to the United States; and nothing in this Constitution shall be so construed as to Prejudice any Claims of the United States, or of any particular State.

SECTION 4. The United States shall guarantee to every State in this Union a Republican Form of Government, and shall protect each of them against Invasion; and on Application of the Legislature, or of the Executive (when the Legislature cannot be convened) against domestic Violence.

ARTICLE V.

The Congress, whenever two thirds of both Houses shall deem it necessary, shall propose Amendments to this Constitution, or, on the Application of the Legislatures of two thirds of the several States, shall call a Convention for proposing Amendments, which, in either Case, shall be valid to all Intents and Purposes, as Part of this Constitution, when ratified by the Legislatures of three fourths of the several States, or by Conventions in three fourths thereof, as the one or the other Mode of Ratification may be proposed by the Congress; Provided that no Amendment which may be made prior to the Year One thousand eight hundred and eight shall in any

Manner affect the first and fourth Clauses in the Ninth Section of the first Article; and that no State, without its Consent, shall be deprived of its equal Suffrage in the Senate.

ARTICLE VI.

All Debts contracted and Engagements entered into, before the Adoption of this Constitution, shall be as valid against the United States under this Constitution, as under the Confederation.

This Constitution, and the Laws of the United States which shall be made in Pursuance thereof; and all Treaties made, or which shall be made, under the Authority of the United States, shall be the supreme Law of the Land; and the Judges in every State shall be bound thereby, any Thing in the Constitution or Laws of any State to the Contrary notwithstanding.

The Senators and Representatives before mentioned, and the Members of the several State Legislatures, and all executive and judicial Officers, both of the United States and of the several States, shall be bound by Oath or Affirmation, to support this Constitution; but no religious Test shall ever be required as a Qualification to any Office or public Trust under the United States.

ARTICLE VII.

The Ratification of the Conventions of nine States, shall be sufficient for the Establishment of this Constitution between the States so ratifying the Same.

Done in Convention by the Unanimous Consent of the States present the Seventeenth Day of September in the Year of our Lord one thousand seven hundred and Eighty seven and of the Independence of the United States of America the Twelfth. In witness whereof We have hereunto subscribed our Names,

Articles in Addition to, and Amendment of, the Constitution of the United States of America, Proposed by Congress, and Ratified by the Legislatures of the Several States, Pursuant to the Fifth Article of the Original Constitution.

AMENDMENT I[9]

Congress shall make no law respecting an establishment of religion, or prohibiting the free exercise thereof; or abridging the freedom of speech, or of the press; or the right of the people peaceably to assemble, and to petition the Government for a redress of grievances.

AMENDMENT II

A well regulated Militia, being necessary to the security of a free State, the right of the people to keep and bear Arms shall not be infringed.

AMENDMENT III

No Soldier shall, in time of peace, be quartered in any house, without the consent of the Owner, nor in time of war, but in a manner to be prescribed by law.

AMENDMENT IV

The right of the people to be secure in their persons, houses, papers, and effects, against unreasonable searches and seizures, shall not be violated, and no Warrants shall issue, but upon probable cause, supported by Oath or affirmation, and particularly describing the place to be searched, and the persons or things to be seized.

AMENDMENT V

No person shall be held to answer for a capital or otherwise infamous crime, unless on a presentment or indictment of a Grand Jury, except in cases arising in the land or naval forces, or in the Militia, when in actual service in time of War or public danger; nor shall any person be subject for the same offence to be twice put in jeopardy of life or limb; nor shall be compelled in any criminal case to be a witness against himself, nor be deprived of life, liberty, or property, without due process of law; nor shall private property be taken for public use, without just compensation.

AMENDMENT VI

In all criminal prosecutions, the accused shall enjoy the right to a speedy and public trial, by an impartial jury of the State and district wherein the crime shall have been committed, which district shall have been previously ascertained by law, and to be informed of the nature and cause of the accusation; to be confronted with the witnesses against him; to have compulsory process for obtaining witnesses in his favor, and to have the Assistance of Counsel for his defence.

AMENDMENT VII

In suits at common law, where the value in controversy shall exceed twenty dollars, the right of trial by jury shall be preserved, and no fact tried by a jury, shall be otherwise reexamined in any Court of the United States, than according to the rules of the common law.

AMENDMENT VIII

Excessive bail shall not be required, nor excessive fines imposed, nor cruel and unusual punishments inflicted.

AMENDMENT IX

The enumeration in the Constitution, of certain rights, shall not be construed to deny or disparage others retained by the people.

---

9 The first ten amendments were passed by Congress September 25, 1789. They were ratified by three-fourths of the states December 15, 1791.

AMENDMENT X

The powers not delegated to the United States by the Constitution; nor prohibited by it to the States, are reserved to the States respectively, or to the people.

AMENDMENT XI[10]

The Judicial power of the United States shall not be construed to extend to any suit in law or equity, commenced or prosecuted against one of the United States by Citizens of another State, or by Citizens or Subjects of any Foreign State.

AMENDMENT XII[11]

The Electors shall meet in their respective States and vote by ballot for President and Vice-President, one of whom, at least, shall not be an inhabitant of the same State with themselves; they shall name in their ballots the person voted for as President, and in distinct ballots the person voted for as Vice-President, and they shall make distinct lists of all persons voted for as President, and of all persons voted for as Vice-President, and of the number of votes for each, which lists they shall sign and certify, and transmit sealed to the seat of the government of the United States, directed to the President of the Senate;—The President of the Senate shall, in the presence of the Senate and House of Representatives, open all the certificates and the votes shall then be counted;—The person having the greatest number of votes for President, shall be the President, if such number be a majority of the whole number of Electors appointed; and if no person have such majority, then from the persons having the highest numbers not exceeding three on the list of those voted for as President, the House of Representatives shall choose immediately, by ballot, the President.

But in choosing the President, the votes shall be taken by states, the representation from each state having one vote; a quorum for this purpose shall consist of a member or members from two-thirds of the states, and a majority of all the states shall be necessary to a choice. And if the House of Representatives shall not choose a President whenever the right of choice shall devolve upon them, before the fourth day of March next following, then the Vice-President shall act as President, as in the case of the death or other constitutional disability of the President.—The person having the greatest number of votes as Vice-President, shall be the Vice-President, if such number be a majority of the whole number of Electors appointed, and if no person have a majority, then from the two highest numbers on the list, the Senate shall choose the Vice-President; a quorum for the purpose shall consist of two-thirds of the whole number of Senators, and a majority of the whole number shall be necessary to a choice. But no person constitutionally ineligible to the office of President shall be eligible to that of Vice-President of the United States.

AMENDMENT XIII[12]

SECTION 1. Neither slavery nor involuntary servitude, except as a punishment for crime whereof the party shall have been duly convicted, shall exist within the United States, or any place subject to their jurisdiction.

SECTION 2. Congress shall have power to enforce this article by appropriate legislation.

AMENDMENT XIV[13]

SECTION 1. All persons born or naturalized in the United States, and subject to the jurisdiction thereof, are citizens of the United States and of the State wherein they reside. No State shall make or enforce any law which shall abridge the privileges or immunities of citizens of the United States; nor shall any State deprive any person of life, liberty, or property, without due process of law; nor deny to any person within its jurisdiction the equal protection of the laws.

SECTION 2. Representatives shall be apportioned among the several States according to their respective numbers, counting the whole number of persons in each State, excluding Indians not taxed. But when the right to vote at any election for the choice of electors for President and Vice-President of the United States, Representatives in Congress, the Executive and Judicial officers of a State, or the members of the Legislature thereof, is denied to any of the male inhabitants of such State, being twenty-one years of age, and citizens of the United States, or in any way abridged, except for participation in rebellion, or other crime, the basis of representation therein shall be reduced in the proportion which the number of such male citizens shall bear to the whole number of male citizens twenty-one years of age in such State.

SECTION 3. No person shall be a Senator or Representative in Congress, or elector of President and Vice-President, or hold any office, civil or military, under the United States, or under any State, who, having previously taken an oath, as a member of Congress, or as an officer of the United States, or as a member of any State legislature, or as an executive or judicial officer of any State, to support the Constitution of the United States, shall have engaged in insurrection or rebellion against the same, or given aid or comfort to the enemies thereof. But Congress may by a vote of two-thirds of each House, remove such disability.

SECTION 4. The validity of the public debt of the United States, authorized by law, including debts incurred for payment of pensions and bounties for services in suppressing insurrection or rebellion, shall not be questioned. But neither the United States nor any State shall assume or pay any debt or obligation incurred in aid of insurrection or rebellion against the United States, or any claim for the loss or emancipation of any slave; but all such debts, obligations, and claims shall be held illegal and void.

SECTION 5. The Congress shall have the power to enforce, by appropriate legislation, the provisions of this article.

---

10 Passed March 4, 1794. Ratified January 23, 1795.
11 Passed December 9, 1803. Ratified June 15, 1804.

12 Passed January 31, 1865. Ratified December 6, 1865.
13 Passed June 13, 1866. Ratified July 9, 1868.

AMENDMENT XV[14]

SECTION 1. The right of citizens of the United States to vote shall not be denied or abridged by the United States or by any State on account of race, color, or previous conditions of servitude—

SECTION 2. The Congress shall have power to enforce this article by appropriate legislation.

AMENDMENT XVI[15]

The Congress shall have power to lay and collect taxes on incomes, from whatever source derived, without apportionment among the several States, and without regard to any census or enumeration.

AMENDMENT XVII[16]

The Senate of the United States shall be composed of two Senators from each State, elected by the people thereof, for six years; and each Senator shall have one vote. The electors in each State shall have the qualifications requisite for electors of the most numerous branch of the State legislatures.

When vacancies happen in the representation of any State in the Senate, the executive authority of such State shall issue writs of election to fill such vacancies: Provided, That the legislature of any State may empower the executive thereof to make temporary appointments until the people fill the vacancies by election as the legislature may direct.

This amendment shall not be so construed as to affect the election or term of any Senator chosen before it becomes valid as part of the Constitution.

AMENDMENT XVIII[17]

SECTION 1. After one year from the ratification of this article the manufacture, sale, or transportation of intoxicating liquors within, the importation thereof into, or the exportation thereof from the United States and all territory subject to the jurisdiction thereof for beverage purposes is hereby prohibited.

SECTION 2. The Congress and the several States shall have concurrent power to enforce this article by appropriate legislation.

SECTION 3. This article shall be inoperative unless it shall have been ratified as an amendment to the Constitution by the legislatures of the several States, as provided in the Constitution, within seven years from the date of the submission hereof to the States by the Congress.

AMENDMENT XIX[18]

The right of citizens of the United States to vote shall not be denied or abridged by the United States or by any State on account of sex.

Congress shall have power to enforce this article by appropriate legislation.

AMENDMENT XX[19]

SECTION 1. The terms of the President and Vice-President shall end at noon on the 20th day of January, and the terms of Senators and Representatives at noon on the 3d day of January, of the years in which such terms would have ended if this article had not been ratified; and the terms of their successors shall then begin.

SECTION 2. The Congress shall assemble at least once in every year, and such meeting shall begin at noon on the 3d day of January, unless they shall by law appoint a different day.

SECTION 3. If, at the time fixed for the beginning of the term of the President, the President elect shall have died, the Vice-President elect shall become President. If a President shall not have been chosen before the time fixed for the beginning of his term, or if the President elect shall have failed to qualify, then the Vice-President elect shall act as President until a President shall have qualified; and the Congress may by law provide for the case wherein neither a President elect nor a Vice-President elect shall have qualified, declaring who shall then act as President, or the manner in which one who is to act shall be selected, and such person shall act accordingly until a President or Vice-President shall have qualified.

SECTION 4. The Congress may by law provide for the case of the death of any of the persons from whom the House of Representatives may choose a President whenever the right of choice shall have devolved upon them, and for the case of the death of any of the persons from whom the Senate may choose a Vice-President whenever the right of choice shall have devolved upon them.

SECTION 5. Sections 1 and 2 shall take effect on the 15th day of October following the ratification of this article.

SECTION 6. This article shall be inoperative unless it shall have been ratified as an amendment to the Constitution by the legislatures of three-fourths of the several States within seven years from the date of its submission.

AMENDMENT XXI[20]

SECTION 1. The eighteenth article of amendment to the Constitution of the United States is hereby repealed.

SECTION 2. The transportation or importation into any State, Territory, or possession of the United States for delivery or use therein of intoxicating liquors, in violation of the laws thereof, is hereby prohibited.

SECTION 3. This article shall be inoperative unless it shall have been ratified as an amendment to the Constitution by conventions in the several States, as provided in the Constitution, within seven years from the date of the submission hereof to the States by the Congress.

---

14 Passed February 26, 1869. Ratified February 2, 1870.
15 Passed July 12, 1909. Ratified February 3, 1913.
16 Passed May 13, 1912. Ratified April 8, 1913.
17 Passed December 18, 1917. Ratified January 16, 1919.
18 Passed June 4, 1919. Ratified August 18, 1920.

---

19 Passed March 2, 1932. Ratified January 23, 1933.
20 Passed February 20, 1933. Ratified December 5, 1933.

AMENDMENT XXII[21]

No person shall be elected to the office of the President more than twice, and no person who has held the office of President, or acted as President, for more than two years of a term to which some other person was elected President shall be elected to the office of the President more than once.

But this Article shall not apply to any person holding the office of President when this Article was proposed by the Congress, and shall not prevent any person who may be holding the office of President, or acting as President, during the term within which this Article becomes operative from holding the office of President or acting as President during the remainder of such term.

AMENDMENT XXIII[22]

SECTION 1. The District constituting the seat of Government of the United States shall appoint in such manner as the Congress may direct: A number of electors of President and Vice President equal to the whole number of Senators and Representatives in Congress to which the District would be entitled if it were a State, but in no event more than the least populous State; they shall be in addition to those appointed by the States, but they shall be considered, for the purposes of the election of President and Vice President, to be electors appointed by the State; and they shall meet in the District and perform such duties as provided by the twelfth article of amendment.

SECTION 2. The Congress shall have power to enforce this article by appropriate legislation.

AMENDMENT XXIV[23]

SECTION 1. The right of citizens of the United States to vote in any primary or other election for President or Vice President, or for Senator or Representative in Congress, shall not be denied or abridged by the United States or any State by reason of failure to pay any poll tax or other tax.

SECTION 2. The Congress shall have power to enforce this article by appropriate legislation.

AMENDMENT XXV[24]

SECTION 1. In case of the removal of the President from office or of his death or resignation, the Vice President shall become President.

SECTION 2. Whenever there is a vacancy in the office of the Vice President, the President shall nominate a Vice President who shall take office upon confirmation by a majority vote of both Houses of Congress.

SECTION 3. Whenever the President transmits to the President pro tempore of the Senate and the Speaker of the House of Representatives his written declaration that he is unable to discharge the powers and duties of his office, and until he transmits them a written declaration to the contrary, such powers and duties shall be discharged by the Vice President as Acting President.

SECTION 4. Whenever the Vice President and a majority of either the principal officers of the executive department or of such other body as Congress may by law provide, transmit to the President pro tempore of the Senate and the Speaker of the House of Representatives their written declaration that the President is unable to discharge the powers and duties of his office, the Vice President shall immediately assume the powers and duties of the office of Acting President

Thereafter, when the President transmits to the President pro tempore of the Senate and the Speaker of the House of Representatives his written declaration that no inability exists, he shall resume the powers and duties of his office unless the Vice President and a majority of either the principal officers of the executive department or of such other body as Congress may by law provide, transmit within four days to the President pro tempore of the Senate and the Speaker of the House of Representatives their written declaration that the President is unable to discharge the powers and duties of his office. Thereupon Congress shall decide the issue, assembling within forty-eight hours for that purpose if not in session. If the Congress, within twenty-one days after receipt of the latter written declaration, or, if Congress is not in session, within twenty-one days after Congress is required to assemble, determines by two-thirds vote of both Houses that the President is unable to discharge the powers and duties of his office, the Vice President shall continue to discharge the same as Acting President; otherwise, the President shall resume the powers and duties of his office.

AMENDMENT XXVI[25]

SECTION 1. The right of citizens of the United States, who are eighteen years of age or older, to vote shall not be denied or abridged by the United States or by any State on account of age.

SECTION 2. The Congress shall have power to enforce this article by appropriate legislation.

AMENDMENT XXVII[26]

No law, varying the compensation for the service of the Senators and Representatives, shall take effect, until an election of Representatives shall have intervened.

---

21 Passed March 12, 1947. Ratified March 1, 1951.
22 Passed June 16, 1960. Ratified April 3, 1961.
23 Passed August 27, 1962. Ratified January 23, 1964.
24 Passed July 6, 1965. Ratified February 11, 1967.

25 Passed March 23, 1971. Ratified July 5, 1971.
26 Passed September 25, 1789. Ratified May 7, 1992.

Order of admission	State	Date of admission	Order of admission	State	Date of admission
1	Delaware	December 7, 1787	26	Michigan	January 26, 1837
2	Pennsylvania	December 12, 1787	27	Florida	March 3, 1845
3	New Jersey	December 18, 1787	28	Texas	December 29, 1845
4	Georgia	January 2, 1788	29	Iowa	December 28, 1846
5	Connecticut	January 9, 1788	30	Wisconsin	May 29, 1848
6	Massachusetts	February 6, 1788	31	California	September 9, 1850
7	Maryland	April 28, 1788	32	Minnesota	May 11, 1858
8	South Carolina	May 23, 1788	33	Oregon	February 14, 1859
9	New Hampshire	June 21, 1788	34	Kansas	January 29, 1861
10	Virginia	June 25, 1788	35	West Virginia	June 20, 1863
11	New York	July 26, 1788	36	Nevada	October 31, 1864
12	North Carolina	November 21, 1789	37	Nebraska	March 1, 1867
13	Rhode Island	May 29, 1790	38	Colorado	August 1, 1876
14	Vermont	March 4, 1791	39	North Dakota	November 2, 1889
15	Kentucky	June 1, 1792	40	South Dakota	November 2, 1889
16	Tennessee	June 1, 1796	41	Montana	November 8, 1889
17	Ohio	March 1, 1803	42	Washington	November 11, 1889
18	Louisiana	April 30, 1812	43	Idaho	July 3, 1890
19	Indiana	December 11, 1816	44	Wyoming	July 10, 1890
20	Mississippi	December 10, 1817	45	Utah	January 4, 1896
21	Illinois	December 3, 1818	46	Oklahoma	November 16, 1907
22	Alabama	December 14, 1819	47	New Mexico	January 6, 1912
23	Maine	March 15, 1820	48	Arizona	February 14, 1912
24	Missouri	August 10, 1821	49	Alaska	January 3, 1959
25	Arkansas	June 15, 1836	50	Hawaii	August 21, 1959

Year	Total population	Number per square mile	Year	Total population	Number per square mile	Year	Total population	Number per square mile
1790	3,929	4.5	1822	10,268		1854	26,561	
1791	4,056		1823	10,596		1855	27,386	
1792	4,194		1824	10,924		1856	28,212	
1793	4,332		1825	11,252		1857	29,037	
1794	4,469		1826	11,580		1858	29,862	
1795	4,607		1827	11,909		1859	30,687	
1796	4,745		1828	12,237		1860	31,513	10.6
1797	4,883		1829	12,565		1861	32,351	
1798	5,021		1830	12,901	7.4	1862	33,188	
1799	5,159		1831	13,321		1863	34,026	
1800	5,297	6.1	1832	13,742		1864	34,863	
1801	5,486		1833	14,162		1865	35,701	
1802	5,679		1834	14,582		1866	36,538	
1803	5,872		1835	15,003		1867	37,376	
1804	5,065		1836	15,423		1868	38,213	
1805	6,258		1837	15,843		1869	39,051	
1806	6,451		1838	16,264		1870	39,905	13.4
1807	6,644		1839	16,684		1871	40,938	
1808	6,838		1840	17,120	9.8	1872	41,972	
1809	7,031		1841	17,733		1873	43,006	
1810	7,224	4.3	1842	18,345		1874	44,040	
1811	7,460		1843	18,957		1875	45,073	
1812	7,700		1844	19,569		1876	46,107	
1813	7,939		1845	20,182		1877	47,141	
1814	8,179		1846	20,794		1878	48,174	
1815	8,419		1847	21,406		1879	49,208	
1816	8,659		1848	22,018		1880	50,262	16.9
1817	8,899		1849	22,631		1881	51,542	
1818	9,139		1850	23,261	7.9	1882	52,821	
1819	9,379		1851	24,086		1883	54,100	
1820	9,618	5.6	1852	24,911		1884	55,379	
1821	9,939		1853	25,736		1885	56,658	

Figures are from *Historical Statistics of the United States, Colonial Times to 1957* (1961), pp. 7, 8; *Statistical Abstract of the United States: 1974*, p. 5, Census Bureau for 1974 and 1975; and *Statistical Abstract of the United States: 1988*, p. 7.
Note: Population figures are in thousands. Density figures are for land area of continental United States.

Year	Total population	Number per square mile	Year	Total population[1]	Number per square mile	Year	Total population[1]	Number per square mile
1886	57,938		1919	105,063		1952	157,553	
1887	59,217		1920	106,466	35.6	1953	160,184	
1888	60,496		1921	108,541		1954	163,026	
1889	61,775		1922	110,055		1955	165,931	
1890	63,056	21.2	1923	111,950		1956	168,903	
1891	64,361		1924	114,113		1957	171,984	
1892	65,666		1925	115,832		1958	174,882	
1893	66,970		1926	117,399		1959	177,830	
1894	68,275		1927	119,038		1960	178,464	60.1
1895	69,580		1928	120,501		1961	183,642	
1896	70,885		1929	121,700		1962	186,504	
1897	72,189		1930	122,775	41.2	1963	189,197	
1898	73,494		1931	124,040		1964	191,833	
1899	74,799		1932	124,840		1965	194,237	
1900	76,094	25.6	1933	125,579		1966	196,485	
1901	77,585		1934	126,374		1967	198,629	
1902	79,160		1935	127,250		1968	200,619	
1903	80,632		1936	128,053		1969	202,599	
1904	82,165		1937	128,825		1970	203,875	57.5[2]
1905	83,820		1938	129,825		1971	207,045	
1906	85,437		1939	130,880		1972	208,842	
1907	87,000		1940	131,669	44.2	1973	210,396	
1908	88,709		1941	133,894		1974	211,894	
1909	90,492		1942	135,361		1975	213,631	
1910	92,407	31.0	1943	137,250		1976	215,152	
1911	93,868		1944	138,916		1977	216,880	
1912	95,331		1945	140,468		1978	218,717	
1913	97,227		1946	141,936		1979	220,584	
1914	99,118		1947	144,698		1980	226,546	64.0
1915	100,549		1948	147,208		1981	230,138	
1916	101,966		1949	149,767		1982	232,520	
1917	103,414		1950	150,697	50.7	1983	234,799	
1918	104,550		1951	154,878		1984	237,001	

[1] Figures after 1940 represent total population including armed forces abroad, except in official census years.

[2] Figure includes Alaska and Hawaii.

(Continued)

POPULATION OF THE UNITED STATES, CONTINUED

Year	Total population[1]	Number per square mile	Year	Total population[1]	Number per square mile	Year	Total population[1]	Number per square mile
1985	239,283		1994	261,875		2003	290,326	
1986	241,596		1995	263,434		2004	293,046	
1987	234,773		1996	266,096		2005	295,753	
1988	245,051		1997	267,901		2006	298,593	
1989	247,350		1998	269,501		2007	301,580	
1990	250,122	70.3	1999	272,700		2008	304,375	
1991	254,521		2000	282,172	80.0	2009	307,007	
1992	245,908		2001	285,082				
1993	257,908		2002	287,804				

[1] Figures after 1940 represent total population including armed forces abroad, except in official census years.

PRESIDENTIAL ELECTIONS

Year	Number of states	Candidates[1]	Parties	Popular vote	Electoral vote	Percentage of popular vote[2]
1789	11	**George Washington**	No party designations		69	
		John Adams			34	
		Minor Candidates			35	
1792	15	**George Washington**	No party designations		132	
		John Adams			77	
		George Clinton			50	
		Minor Candidates			5	
1796	16	**John Adams**	Federalist		71	
		Thomas Jefferson	Democratic-Republican		68	
		Thomas Pinckney	Federalist		59	
		Aaron Burr	Democratic-Republican		30	
		Minor Candidates			48	
1800	16	**Thomas Jefferson**	Democratic-Republican		73	
		Aaron Burr	Democratic-Republican		73	
		John Adams	Federalist		65	
		Charles C. Pinckney	Federalist		64	
		John Jay	Federalist		1	

[1] Before the passage of the Twelfth Amendment in 1804, the Electoral College voted for two presidential candidates; the runner-up became vice president. Figures are from Historical Statistics of the United States, Colonial Times to 1957 (1961), pp. 682–83; and the U.S. Department of Justice.

[2] Candidates receiving less than 1 percent of the popular vote have been omitted. For that reason the percentage of popular vote given for any election year may not total 100 percent.

Year	Number of states	Candidates	Parties	Popular vote	Electoral vote	Percentage of popular vote[1]
1804	17	**Thomas Jefferson**	Democratic-Republican		162	
		Charles C. Pinckney	Federalist		14	
1808	17	**James Madison**	Democratic-Republican		122	
		Charles C. Pinckney	Federalist		47	
		George Clinton	Democratic-Republican		6	
1812	18	**James Madison**	Democratic-Republican		128	
		DeWitt Clinton	Federalist		89	
1816	19	**James Monroe**	Democratic-Republican		183	
		Rufus King	Federalist		34	
1820	24	**James Monroe**	Democratic-Republican		231	
		John Quincy Adams	Independent Republican		1	
1824	24	**John Quincy Adams**	Democratic-Republican	108,740	84	30.5
		Andrew Jackson	Democratic-Republican	153,544	99	43.1
		William H. Crawford	Democratic-Republican	46,618	41	13.1
		Henry Clay	Democratic-Republican	47,136	37	13.2
1828	24	**Andrew Jackson**	Democratic	647,286	178	56.0
		John Quincy Adams	National Republican	508,064	83	44.0
1832	24	**Andrew Jackson**	Democratic	687,502	219	55.0
		Henry Clay	National Republican	530,189	49	42.4
		William Wirt	Anti-Masonic		7	
		John Floyd	National Republican	33,108	11	2.6
1836	26	**Martin Van Buren**	Democratic	765,483	170	50.9
		William H. Harrison	Whig		73	
		Hugh L. White	Whig	739,795	26	
		Daniel Webster	Whig		14	
		W. P. Mangum	Whig		11	
1840	26	**William H. Harrison**	Whig	1,274,624	234	53.1
		Martin Van Buren	Democratic	1,127,781	60	46.9
1844	26	**James K. Polk**	Democratic	1,338,464	170	49.6
		Henry Clay	Whig	1,300,097	105	48.1
		James G. Birney	Liberty	62,300		2.3

[1] Candidates receiving less than 1 percent of the popular vote have been omitted. For that reason the percentage of popular vote given for any election year may not total 100 percent.

(Continued)

Year	Number of states	Candidates	Parties	Popular vote	Electoral vote	Percentage of popular vote[1]
1848	30	**Zachary Taylor**	Whig	1,360,967	163	47.4
		Lewis Cass	Democratic	1,222,342	127	42.5
		Martin Van Buren	Free Soil	291,263		10.1
1852	31	**Franklin Pierce**	Democratic	1,601,117	254	50.9
		Winfield Scott	Whig	1,385,453	42	44.1
		John P. Hale	Free Soil	155,825		5.0
1856	31	**James Buchanan**	Democratic	1,832,955	174	45.3
		John C. Frémont	Republican	1,339,932	114	33.1
		Millard Fillmore	American	871,731	8	21.6
1860	33	**Abraham Lincoln**	Republican	1,865,593	180	39.8
		Stephen A. Douglas	Democratic	1,382,713	12	29.5
		John C. Breckinridge	Democratic	848,356	72	18.1
		John Bell	Constitutional Union	592,906	39	12.6
1864	36	**Abraham Lincoln**	Republican	2,206,938	212	55.0
		George B. McClellan	Democratic	1,803,787	21	45.0
1868	37	**Ulysses S. Grant**	Republican	3,013,421	214	52.7
		Horatio Seymour	Democratic	2,706,829	80	47.3
1872	37	**Ulysses S. Grant**	Republican	3,596,745	286	55.6
		Horace Greeley	Democratic	2,843,446	[2]	43.9
1876	38	**Rutherford B. Hayes**	Republican	4,036,572	185	48.0
		Samuel J. Tilden	Democratic	4,284,020	184	51.0
1880	38	**James A. Garfield**	Republican	4,453,295	214	48.5
		Winfield S. Hancock	Democratic	4,414,082	155	48.1
		James B. Weaver	Greenback-Labor	308,578		3.4
1884	38	**Grover Cleveland**	Democratic	4,879,507	219	48.5
		James G. Blaine	Republican	4,850,293	182	48.2
		Benjamin F. Butler	Greenback-Labor	175,370		1.8
		John P. St. John	Prohibition	150,369		1.5
1888	38	**Benjamin Harrison**	Republican	5,477,129	233	47.9
		Grover Cleveland	Democratic	5,537,857	168	48.6
		Clinton B. Fisk	Prohibition	249,506		2.2
		Anson J. Streeter	Union Labor	146,935		1.3

[1] Candidates receiving less than 1 percent of the popular vote have been omitted. For that reason the percentage of popular vote given for any election year may not total 100 percent.

[2] Greeley died shortly after the election; the electors supporting him then divided their votes among minor candidates.

Year	Number of states	Candidates	Parties	Popular vote	Electoral vote	Percentage of popular vote[1]
1892	44	**Grover Cleveland**	Democratic	5,555,426	277	46.1
		Benjamin Harrison	Republican	5,182,690	145	43.0
		James B. Weaver	People's	1,029,846	22	8.5
		John Bidwell	Prohibition	264,133		2.2
1896	45	**William McKinley**	Republican	7,102,246	271	51.1
		William J. Bryan	Democratic	6,492,559	176	47.7
1900	45	**William McKinley**	Republican	7,218,491	292	51.7
		William J. Bryan	Democratic; Populist	6,356,734	155	45.5
		John C. Wooley	Prohibition	208,914		1.5
1904	45	**Theodore Roosevelt**	Republican	7,628,461	336	57.4
		Alton B. Parker	Democratic	5,084,223	140	37.6
		Eugene V. Debs	Socialist	402,283		3.0
		Silas C. Swallow	Prohibition	258,536		1.9
1908	46	**William H. Taft**	Republican	7,675,320	321	51.6
		William J. Bryan	Democratic	6,412,294	162	43.1
		Eugene V. Debs	Socialist	420,793		2.8
		Eugene W. Chafin	Prohibition	253,840		1.7
1912	48	**Woodrow Wilson**	Democratic	6,296,547	435	41.9
		Theodore Roosevelt	Progressive	4,118,571	88	27.4
		William H. Taft	Republican	3,486,720	8	23.2
		Eugene V. Debs	Socialist	900,672		6.0
		Eugene W. Chafin	Prohibition	206,275		1.4
1916	48	**Woodrow Wilson**	Democratic	9,127,695	277	49.4
		Charles E. Hughes	Republican	8,533,507	254	46.2
		A. L. Benson	Socialist	585,113		3.2
		J. Frank Hanly	Prohibition	220,506		1.2
1920	48	**Warren G. Harding**	Republican	16,143,407	404	60.4
		James N. Cox	Democratic	9,130,328	127	34.2
		Eugene V. Debs	Socialist	919,799		3.4
		P. P. Christensen	Farmer-Labor	265,411		1.0

[1] Candidates receiving less than 1 percent of the popular vote have been omitted. For that reason the percentage of popular vote given for any election year may not total 100 percent.

(Continued)

Year	Number of states	Candidates	Parties	Popular vote	Electoral vote	Percentage of popular vote[1]
1924	48	**Calvin Coolidge**	Republican	15,718,211	382	54.0
		John W. Davis	Democratic	8,385,283	136	28.8
		Robert M. La Follette	Progressive	4,831,289	13	16.6
1928	48	**Herbert C. Hoover**	Republican	21,391,993	444	58.2
		Alfred E. Smith	Democratic	15,016,169	87	40.9
1932	48	**Franklin D. Roosevelt**	Democratic	22,809,638	472	57.4
		Herbert C. Hoover	Republican	15,758,901	59	39.7
		Norman Thomas	Socialist	881,951		2.2
1936	48	**Franklin D. Roosevelt**	Democratic	27,752,869	523	60.8
		Alfred M. Landon	Republican	16,674,665	8	36.5
		William Lemke	Union	882,479		1.9
1940	48	**Franklin D. Roosevelt**	Democratic	27,307,819	449	54.8
		Wendell L. Willkie	Republican	22,321,018	82	44.8
1944	48	**Franklin D. Roosevelt**	Democratic	25,606,585	432	53.5
		Thomas E. Dewey	Republican	22,014,745	99	46.0
1948	48	**Harry S. Truman**	Democratic	24,105,812	303	49.5
		Thomas E. Dewey	Republican	21,970,065	189	45.1
		J. Strom Thurmond	States' Rights	1,169,063	39	2.4
		Henry A. Wallace	Progressive	1,157,172		2.4
1952	48	**Dwight D. Eisenhower**	Republican	33,936,234	442	55.1
		Adlai E. Stevenson	Democratic	27,314,992	89	44.4
1956	48	**Dwight D. Eisenhower**	Republican	35,590,472	457	57.6
		Adlai E. Stevenson	Democratic	26,022,752	73	42.1
1960	50	**John F. Kennedy**	Democratic	34,227,096	303	49.9
		Richard M. Nixon	Republican	34,108,546	219	49.6
1964	50	**Lyndon B. Johnson**	Democratic	43,126,506	486	61.1
		Barry M. Goldwater	Republican	27,176,799	52	38.5
1968	50	**Richard M. Nixon**	Republican	31,785,480	301	43.4
		Hubert H. Humphrey	Democratic	31,275,165	191	42.7
		George C. Wallace	American Independent	9,906,473	46	13.5
1972	50	**Richard M. Nixon**	Republican	47,169,911	520	60.7
		George S. McGovern	Democratic	29,170,383	17	37.5

[1] Candidates receiving less than 1 percent of the popular vote have been omitted. For that reason the percentage of popular vote given for any election year may not total 100 percent.

Year	Number of states	Candidates	Parties	Popular vote	Electoral vote	Percentage of popular vote[1]
1976	50	**Jimmy Carter**	Democratic	40,827,394	297	50.0
		Gerald R. Ford	Republican	39,145,977	240	47.9
1980	50	**Ronald W. Reagan**	Republican	43,899,248	489	50.8
		Jimmy Carter	Democratic	35,481,435	49	41.0
		John B. Anderson	Independent	5,719,437		6.6
		Ed Clark	Libertarian	920,859		1.0
1984	50	**Ronald W. Reagan**	Republican	54,281,858	525	59.2
		Walter F. Mondale	Democratic	37,457,215	13	40.8
1988	50	**George H. Bush**	Republican	47,917,341	426	54
		Michael Dukakis	Democratic	41,013,030	112	46
1992	50	**William Clinton**	Democratic	44,908,254	370	43.0
		George H. Bush	Republican	39,102,343	168	37.4
		Ross Perot	Independent	19,741,065		18.9
1996	50	**William Clinton**	Democratic	45,628,667	379	49.2
		Robert Dole	Republican	37,869,435	159	40.8
		Ross Perot	Reform	7,874,283		8.5
2000	50	**George W. Bush**	Republican	50,456,062	271	47.9
		Albert Gore	Democratic	50,996,582	266	48.4
		Ralph Nader	Green	2,858,843		2.7
2004	50	**George W. Bush**	Republican	62,040,606	286	51
		John F. Kerry	Democratic	59,028,109	252	48
		Ralph Nader	Green/Independent	411,304		1
2008	50	**Barack Obama**	Democratic	66,882,230	365	53
		John McCain	Republican	58,343,671	173	46

[1] Candidates receiving less than 1 percent of the popular vote have been omitted. For that reason the percentage of popular vote given for any election year may not total 100 percent.

Term	President	Vice President	Term	President	Vice President
1789–1793	George Washington	John Adams	1901–1905	William McKinley (d. 1901)	Theodore Roosevelt
1793–1797	George Washington	John Adams		Theodore Roosevelt	
1797–1801	John Adams	Thomas Jefferson	1905–1909	Theodore Roosevelt	Charles W. Fairbanks
1801–1805	Thomas Jefferson	Aaron Burr	1909–1913	William H. Taft	James S. Sherman (d. 1912)
1805–1809	Thomas Jefferson	George Clinton			
1809–1813	James Madison	George Clinton (d. 1812)	1913–1917	Woodrow Wilson	Thomas R. Marshall
1813–1817	James Madison	Elbridge Gerry (d. 1814)	1917–1921	Woodrow Wilson	Thomas R. Marshall
			1921–1925	Warren G. Harding (d. 1923)	Calvin Coolidge
1817–1821	James Monroe	Daniel D. Tompkins		Calvin Coolidge	
1821–1825	James Monroe	Daniel D. Tompkins	1925–1929	Calvin Coolidge	Charles G. Dawes
1825–1829	John Quincy Adams	John C. Calhoun	1929–1933	Herbert Hoover	Charles Curtis
1829–1833	Andrew Jackson	John C. Calhoun (resigned 1832)	1933–1937	Franklin D. Roosevelt	John N. Garner
1833–1837	Andrew Jackson	Martin Van Buren	1937–1941	Franklin D. Roosevelt	John N. Garner
1837–1841	Martin Van Buren	Richard M. Johnson	1941–1945	Franklin D. Roosevelt	Henry A. Wallace
1841–1845	William H. Harrison (d. 1841)	John Tyler	1945–1949	Franklin D. Roosevelt (d. 1945)	Harry S Truman
	John Tyler			Harry S Truman	
1845–1849	James K. Polk	George M. Dallas	1949–1953	Harry S Truman	Alben W. Barkley
1849–1853	Zachary Taylor (d. 1850)	Millard Fillmore	1953–1957	Dwight D. Eisenhower	Richard M. Nixon
	Millard Fillmore		1957–1961	Dwight D. Eisenhower	Richard M. Nixon
1853–1857	Franklin Pierce	William R. D. King (d. 1853)	1961–1965	John F. Kennedy (d. 1963)	Lyndon B. Johnson
				Lyndon B. Johnson	
1857–1861	James Buchanan	John C. Breckinridge	1965–1969	Lyndon B. Johnson	Hubert H. Humphrey, Jr.
1861–1865	Abraham Lincoln	Hannibal Hamlin			
1865–1869	Abraham Lincoln (d. 1865)	Andrew Johnson	1969–1974	Richard M. Nixon	Spiro T. Agnew (resigned 1973);
	Andrew Johnson				Gerald R. Ford
1869–1873	Ulysses S. Grant	Schuyler Colfax	1974–1977	Gerald R. Ford	Nelson A. Rockefeller
1873–1877	Ulysses S. Grant	Henry Wilson (d. 1875)	1977–1981	Jimmy Carter	Walter F. Mondale
1877–1881	Rutherford B. Hayes	William A. Wheeler	1981–1985	Ronald Reagan	George Bush
1881–1885	James A. Garfield (d. 1881)	Chester A. Arthur	1985–1989	Ronald Reagan	George Bush
	Chester A. Arthur		1989–1993	George Bush	J. Danforth Quayle III
1885–1889	Grover Cleveland	Thomas A. Hendricks (d. 1885)	1993–2001	William Clinton	Albert Gore, Jr.
1889–1893	Benjamin Harrison	Levi P. Morton	2001–2005	George W. Bush	Richard Cheney
1893–1897	Grover Cleveland	Adlai E. Stevenson	2005–2009	George W. Bush	Richard Cheney
1897–1901	William McKinley	Garret A. Hobart (d. 1899)	2009–	Barack Obama	Joseph Biden

Name	Term of service	Years of service	Appointed by	Name	Term of service	Years of service	Appointed by
John Jay	1789–1795	5	Washington	Robert C. Grier	1846–1870	23	Polk
John Rutledge	1789–1791	1	Washington	Benjamin R. Curtis	1851–1857	6	Fillmore
William Cushing	1789–1810	20	Washington	John A. Campbell	1853–1861	8	Pierce
James Wilson	1789–1798	8	Washington	Nathan Clifford	1858–1881	23	Buchanan
John Blair	1789–1796	6	Washington	Noah H. Swayne	1862–1881	18	Lincoln
Robert H. Harrison	1789–1790	—	Washington	Samuel F. Miller	1862–1890	28	Lincoln
James Iredell	1790–1799	9	Washington	David Davis	1862–1877	14	Lincoln
Thomas Johnson	1791–1793	1	Washington	Stephen J. Field	1863–1897	34	Lincoln
William Paterson	1793–1806	13	Washington	**Salmon P. Chase**	1864–1873	8	Lincoln
John Rutledge[1]	1795	—	Washington	William Strong	1870–1880	10	Grant
Samuel Chase	1796–1811	15	Washington	Joseph P. Bradley	1870–1892	22	Grant
Oliver Ellsworth	1796–1800	4	Washington	Ward Hunt	1873–1882	9	Grant
Bushrod Washington	1798–1829	31	J. Adams	**Morrison R. Waite**	1874–1888	14	Grant
Alfred Moore	1799–1804	4	J. Adams	John M. Harlan	1877–1911	34	Hayes
John Marshall	1801–1835	34	J. Adams	William B. Woods	1880–1887	7	Hayes
William Johnson	1804–1834	30	Jefferson	Stanley Matthews	1881–1889	7	Garfield
H. Brockholst Livingston	1806–1823	16	Jefferson	Horace Gray	1882–1902	20	Arthur
Thomas Todd	1807–1826	18	Jefferson	Samuel Blatchford	1882–1893	11	Arthur
Joseph Story	1811–1845	33	Madison	Lucius Q. C. Lamar	1888–1893	5	Cleveland
Gabriel Duval	1811–1835	24	Madison	**Melville W. Fuller**	1888–1910	21	Cleveland
Smith Thompson	1823–1843	20	Monroe	David J. Brewer	1890–1910	20	B. Harrison
Robert Trimble	1826–1828	2	J. Q. Adams	Henry B. Brown	1890–1906	16	B. Harrison
John McLean	1829–1861	32	Jackson	George Shiras, Jr.	1892–1903	10	B. Harrison
Henry Baldwin	1830–1844	14	Jackson	Howell E. Jackson	1893–1895	2	B. Harrison
James M. Wayne	1835–1867	32	Jackson	Edward D. White	1894–1910	16	Cleveland
Roger B. Taney	1836–1864	28	Jackson	Rufus W. Peckham	1895–1909	14	Cleveland
Philip P. Barbour	1836–1841	4	Jackson	Joseph McKenna	1898–1925	26	McKinley
John Catron	1837–1865	28	Van Buren	Oliver W. Holmes, Jr.	1902–1932	30	T. Roosevelt
John McKinley	1837–1852	15	Van Buren	William R. Day	1903–1922	19	T. Roosevelt
Peter V. Daniel	1841–1860	19	Van Buren	William H. Moody	1906–1910	3	T. Roosevelt
Samuel Nelson	1845–1872	27	Tyler	Horace H. Lurton	1910–1914	4	Taft
Levi Woodbury	1845–1851	5	Polk	Charles E. Hughes	1910–1916	5	Taft

Note: Chief justices appear in bold type.

[1] Acting chief justice; Senate refused to confirm appointment.

(Continued)

Name	Term of service	Years of service	Appointed by	Name	Term of service	Years of service	Appointed by
Willis Van Devanter	1911–1937	26	Taft	Tom C. Clark	1949–1967	18	Truman
Joseph R. Lamar	1911–1916	5	Taft	Sherman Minton	1949–1956	7	Truman
Edward D. White	1910–1921	11	Taft	Earl Warren	1953–1969	16	Eisenhower
Mahlon Pitney	1912–1922	10	Taft	John Marshall Harlan	1955–1971	16	Eisenhower
James C. McReynolds	1914–1941	26	Wilson	William J. Brennan, Jr.	1956–1990	34	Eisenhower
Louis D. Brandeis	1916–1939	22	Wilson	Charles E. Whittaker	1957–1962	5	Eisenhower
John H. Clarke	1916–1922	6	Wilson	Potter Stewart	1958–1981	23	Eisenhower
William H. Taft	1921–1930	8	Harding	Byron R. White	1962–1993	31	Kennedy
George Sutherland	1922–1938	15	Harding	Arthur J. Goldberg	1962–1965	3	Kennedy
Pierce Butler	1922–1939	16	Harding	Abe Fortas	1965–1969	4	Johnson
Edward T. Sanford	1923–1930	7	Harding	Thurgood Marshall	1967–1994	24	Johnson
Harlan F. Stone	1925–1941	16	Coolidge	Warren E. Burger	1969–1986	18	Nixon
Charles E. Hughes	1930–1941	11	Hoover	Harry A. Blackmun	1970–1994	24	Nixon
Owen J. Roberts	1930–1945	15	Hoover	Lewis F. Powell, Jr.	1971–1987	15	Nixon
Benjamin N. Cardozo	1932–1938	6	Hoover	William H. Rehnquist[1]	1971–2005	34	Nixon
Hugo L. Black	1937–1971	34	F. Roosevelt	John P. Stevens III	1975–	—	Ford
Stanley F. Reed	1938–1957	19	F. Roosevelt	Sandra Day O'Connor	1981–2006	25	Reagan
Felix Frankfurter	1939–1962	23	F. Roosevelt	Antonin Scalia	1986–	—	Reagan
William O. Douglas	1939–1975	36	F. Roosevelt	Anthony M. Kennedy	1988–	—	Reagan
Frank Murphy	1940–1949	9	F. Roosevelt	David Souter	1990–2009	—	Bush
Harlan F. Stone	1941–1946	5	F. Roosevelt	Clarence Thomas	1991–	—	Bush
James F. Byrnes	1941–1942	1	F. Roosevelt	Ruth Bader Ginsburg	1993–	—	Clinton
Robert H. Jackson	1941–1954	13	F. Roosevelt	Stephen G. Breyer	1994–	—	Clinton
Wiley B. Rutledge	1943–1949	6	F. Roosevelt	John G. Roberts, Jr.	2005–	—	G. W. Bush
Harold H. Burton	1945–1958	13	Truman	Samuel Anthony Alito, Jr.	2006–	—	G. W. Bush
Fred M. Vinson	1946–1953	7	Truman	Sonia Sotomayor	2009–	—	Obama

[1] Chief justice from 1986 on (Reagan administration).

1919 steel strike Walkout by 300,000 steelworkers in the Midwest demanding union recognition and an eight-hour day. It was defeated by employers and local and state police forces, who sometimes resorted to violence.

40 acres and a mule Largely unfulfilled hope of many former slaves that they would receive free land from the confiscated property of ex-Confederates.

9th and 10th U.S. Cavalry African-American army units that played pivotal roles in the Spanish-American war.

abolitionism Movement begun in the North about 1830 to abolish slavery immediately and without compensation to owners.

abolitionist A person who wanted to abolish slavery.

abrogating a treaty Process of abolishing a treaty so that it is no longer in effect.

affirmative action Program or policy that attempted to compensate for past injustice or discrimination to ensure more employment and educational opportunities.

affluence Abundance of material goods or wealth.

Affordable Health Care for America Act Designed to extend healthcare to some 30 million people, expand the Medicaid system, create mechanisms for increasing competition among insurance companies, prohibit the use of pre-existing health conditions do deny coverage, and provide every American health insurance.

Agricultural Adjustment Administration (AAA) 1933 attempt to promote economic recovery by reducing supply of crops, dairy, and meat produced by American farmers.

Aguinaldo, Emilio Anti-colonial leader who fought for independence of the Philippines first from Spain and then from the United States.

Alamo Battle between Texas revolutionaries and the Mexican army at the San Antonio mission called the *Alamo* on March 6, 1836, in which all 187 Texans were killed.

Albany Congress An inter-colonial congress that met in Albany, New York, in June 1754. The delegates urged the Crown to assume direct control of Indian relations beyond the settled boundaries of the colonies, and they drafted a plan of confederation for the continental colonies. No colony ratified it, nor did the Crown or Parliament accept it.

Algonquians Indian peoples who spoke some dialect of the Algonquian language family.

alien Person from another country who is living in the United States.

American Anti-Slavery Society Organization created by northern abolitionists in 1833 that called for immediate, uncompensated emancipation of the slaves.

American Colonization Society Established by elite gentlemen of the middle and upper-south states in 1816, this organization encouraged voluntary emancipation of slaves, to be followed by their emigration to the West African colony of Liberia.

American System Program proposed by Henry Clay and others to foster national economic growth and interdependence among the geographical sections. It included a protective tariff, a national bank, and internal improvements.

American Temperance Society Society established in 1826 by northeastern evangelicals that headed the crusade for alcohol temperance.

Amerind The forerunner of the vast majority of Indian languages in the Americas.

amnesty General pardon granted to a large group of people.

anarchist Activist who called for the violent destruction of the capitalist system so that a new socialist order could be built.

Anasazi An advanced pre-Columbian cliff-dwelling culture that flourished for two centuries in what are now the states of Arizona, New Mexico, Utah, and Colorado before abandoning these sites in the late 13th century A.D.

Anderson, Marian Black opera singer who broke a color barrier in 1939 when she sang to an interracial audience of 75,000 from the steps of the Lincoln Memorial.

Anglican A member of the legally established Church of England, or that church itself.

Anglos English-speaking people.

anxious bench Bench at or near the front of a religious revival meeting where the most likely converts were seated.

apartheid Legal system practiced in South Africa and based on elaborate rules of racial separation and subordination of blacks.

armistice A temporary stop in fighting. Often in effect before a final peace treaty is signed.

Article X of the Covenant Addendum to the Treaty of Versailles that empowered the League of Nations to undertake military actions against aggressor nations.

artisan A skilled laborer who works with his hands. In early America, artisans often owned their own shops and produced goods either for general sale or for special order.

Association Groups created by the First Continental Congress in local committees to enforce its trade sanctions against Britain. The creation of these groups was an important sign that Congress was beginning to act as a central government.

associationalism Herbert Hoover's approach to managing the economy. Firms and organizations in each economic sector would be asked to cooperate with each other in the pursuit of efficiency, profit, and the public good.

astrolabe A device that permitted accurate calculation of latitude or distances north and south.

Atlantic slave trade A European commerce that led to the enslavement of millions of people who were shipped from their African homelands to European colonies in the Americas.

attrition A type of warfare in which an effort is made to exhaust the manpower, supplies, and morale of the other side.

Auburn system Prison system designed to reform criminals and reduce expenses through the sale of items produced in workshops. Prisoners slept in solitary cells, marched in military formation to meals and workshops, and were forbidden to speak to one another at any time.

Australian ballot (secret ballot) Practice that required citizens to vote in private rather than in public and required the government (rather than political parties) to supervise the voting process.

Aztec The last pre-Columbian high culture in the Valley of Mexico. It was conquered by the Spaniards in 1519–1521.

Baby Boom Sudden increase in births in the years after World War II.

Baby Boom Generation People born between 1946 and 1964; more than 75 million babies were born in the U.S. during this time.

backcountry Term used in the 18th and early 19th centuries to refer to the western settlements and the supposed misfits who lived in them.

Bacon's Rebellion The most serious challenge to royal authority in the English mainland colonies prior to 1775. It erupted in Virginia in 1676 after the governor and Nathaniel Bacon, the principal rebel, could not agree on how best to wage war against frontier Indians.

balance of trade The relationship between imports and exports. The difference between exports and imports is the balance between the two. A healthy nation should export more than it imports. This is known as a favorable balance of trade.

bandeirantes Brazilian frontiersmen who traveled deep into South America to enslave Indians. The slaves then were worked to death on the sugar plantations.

banknotes Paper money, issued by banks, that circulated as currency.

barrios Spanish-speaking urban areas, usually separate districts in southwestern towns and cities.

bateau A light, flat-bottomed boat with narrow ends that was used in Canada and the northeastern part of the colonies.

Battle of Lexington The first military engagement of the Revolutionary War. It occurred on April 19, 1775, when British soldiers fired into a much smaller body of minutemen on Lexington green.

Battle of Little Big Horn A battle in eastern Montana Territory on the bluffs above Little Big Horn River on June 25, 1876.

Bay of Pigs Site of an ill-fated 1961 invasion of Cuba by a U.S.-trained force that attempted to overthrow the government of Fidel Castro.

Beatles Preeminent musical group associated with the "British invasion" in the 1960s.

belligerent Country actively engaged in a war.

Beringia A land bridge during the last ice age across the Bering Strait between Siberia and Alaska. It was once an area where plants, animals, and humans could live.

Berlin Airlift American and British aircraft that provided all of the items needed in West Berlin during the Berlin Blockade.

Berlin Blockade Soviet Union cut off all highways, railroads, and water routes into West Berlin, Germany in attempt to weaken the nation.

bicameral legislature A legislature with two houses or chambers.

Bill of Rights First ten amendments to the Constitution, which protect the rights of individuals from abuses by the federal government.

Black Codes Laws passed by southern states that restricted the rights and liberties of former slaves.

Black Power Mid-1960s movement that called for modifying integrationist goals in favor of gaining political and economic power for separate black-directed institutions and emphasized pride in African-American heritage.

Black Republicans Label coined by the Democratic Party to attack the Republican Party as believers in racial equality. The Democrats used this fear to convince many whites to remain loyal to them.

blacklist In the postwar years, a list of people who could no longer work in the entertainment industry because of alleged contacts with communists.

blitzkrieg A "lightning war"; a coordinated and massive military strike by German army and air forces.

block grants Part of Nixon's new economic plan in which a percentage of federal tax dollars would be returned to state and local governments to spend as they deemed fit.

blockade runner A ship designed to run through a blockade.

blockade The closing of a country's harbors by enemy ships to prevent trade and commerce, especially to prevent traffic in military supplies.

blockhouse A wooden fort with an overhanging second floor. The white settlers of Kentucky used blockhouses to defend themselves against Indians.

blood sports Sporting activities emphasizing bloodiness that were favored by working-class men of the cities. The most popular in the early 19th century were cockfighting, ratting, dogfights, and various types of violence between animals.

bonanza farms Huge wheat farms financed by eastern capital and cultivated with heavy machinery and hired labor.

Bonus Army Army veterans who marched on Washington, D.C., in 1932 to lobby for economic relief but who were rebuffed by Hoover.

Boone, Daniel A pioneer settler of Kentucky, Boone became the most famous American frontiersman of his generation.

border ruffians Term used to describe proslavery Missourians who streamed into Kansas in 1854, determined to vote as many times as necessary to install a proslavery government there.

Boston Massacre The colonial term for the confrontation between colonial protestors and British soldiers in front of the customs house on March 5, 1770. Five colonists were killed and six wounded.

Boston Tea Party In December 1773, Boston's Sons of Liberty threw 342 chests of East India Company tea into Boston harbor rather than allow them to be landed and pay the hated tea duty.

bounty jumpers Men who enlisted in the Union army to collect the bounties offered by some districts to fill military quotas; these men would enlist and then desert as soon as they got their money.

Boxers Chinese nationalist organization that instigated an uprising in 1900 to rid China of all foreign influence.

braceros Guest workers from Mexico allowed into the United States because of labor shortages from 1942 to 1964.

Brown v. Board of Education 1954 case in which the U.S. Supreme Court unanimously overruled the "separate but equal" doctrine and held that segregation in the public schools violated the principle of equal protection under the law.

"broad" wives Wives of slave men who lived on other plantations and were visited by their husbands during off hours.

Brown **Cases** Refers to several Supreme Court cases that challenged the nation's political, social and cultural institutions by outlawing racial segregation in public schools and public facilities.

Brown, John Prominent abolitionist who fought for the antislavery cause in Kansas (1856) and led a raid to seize the Harpers Ferry arsenal in 1859.

Bryan, William Jennings A two-term Democratic congressman from Nebraska who won the party's presidential nomination in 1896 after electrifying delegates with his "Cross of Gold" speech. Bryan was twice more nominated for president (1900 and 1908); he lost all three times.

Bull Moosers Followers of Theodore Roosevelt in the 1912 election.

bulldozing Using force to keep African Americans from voting.

Burr, Aaron Vice President under Thomas Jefferson who killed Alexander Hamilton in a duel and eventually hatched schemes to detach parts of the west from the United States.

Bush Doctrine Denounced terrorist networks and proclaimed that the U.S. had the right to wage war against any force that endangered American as expressed in the National Security Strategy of 2002.

Bush v. Gore Court case over the 2000 election between George W. Bush and Al Gore; the courts ceased the recounting of ballots in Florida and ruled George W. Bush the 43rd President of the United States.

Bush, George H. W. Republican President (1989–1993) who directed an international coalition against Iraq in the Persian Gulf War.

Bush, George W. Republican president (2001–2009) elected in the highly disputed 2000 contest decided by the Supreme Court.

bushwhackers Confederate guerrilla raiders especially active in Missouri. Jayhawkers were the Union version of the same type of people. Both groups did a tremendous amount of damage with raids, arson, ambush, and murder.

Butternuts Democrats from the southern river-oriented counties of the Northwest region whose name came from the yellow vegetable dye with which they colored their homespun clothing.

Cahokia The largest city created by Mississippian mound builders. Located in Illinois near modern St. Louis, it thrived from A.D. 900 to 1250 and then declined.

californios Spanish-speaking people whose families had resided in California for generations.

Camp David Peace Talks of 1978 President Carter negotiated a peace treaty with Menachem Begin and Anwar Sadat, leaders of Israel and Egypt.

camp meeting Outdoor revival often lasting for days; a principal means of spreading evangelical Christianity in the United States.

Capone, Al Chicago mobster who made a fortune from gambling, prostitution, and bootleg liquor during Prohibition.

Capra, Frank Popular 1930s filmmaker who celebrated the decency, honesty, and patriotism of ordinary Americans in such films as *Mr. Deeds Goes to Town* and *Mr. Smith Goes to Washington.*

caravel A new type of oceangoing vessel that could sail closer to a head wind than any other sailing ship and make speeds of from three to twelve knots per hour.

Carnegie, Andrew A Scottish immigrant who became the most efficient entrepreneur in the U.S. steel industry and earned a great fortune.

carpetbaggers Northerners who settled in the South during Reconstruction.

Carson, Rachel American marine biologist and author best known for *Silent Spring* (1962), a widely read book that questioned the use of chemical pesticides and helped stimulate the modern environmental movement.

Carter, Jimmy Democratic president (1977–1981) whose single term in office was marked by inflation, fuel shortages, and a hostage crisis.

cash and carry U.S. foreign policy prior to American entry into World War II that required belligerents to pay cash and carry products away in their own ships. This arrangement minimized risks to American exports, loans, and shipping.

Cavaliers Supporters of the Stuart family of Charles I during the civil wars.

changing system Elaborate system of neighborhood debts and bartering used primarily in the South and West where little cash money was available.

Chavez, Cesar Political activist, leader of the United Farm Workers of America, and the most influential Mexican American leader during the 1970s.

Cheney, Richard (Dick) Conservative republican who served as vice president to George W. Bush.

Cherokee War Between December 1759 and December 1761, the Cherokee Indians devastated the South Carolina backcountry. The British army intervened and in turn inflicted immense damage on the Cherokee.

Chicanismo Populistic pride in the Mexican American heritage that emerged in the late 1960s. Chicano, once a term of derision, became a rallying cry among activists.

chinampas The highly productive gardens built on Lake Taxcoco by the Aztecs.

Chinese Exclusion Act Suspended Chinese immigration for 10 years with the exception of a few job categories.

Chisholm Trail Trail used to get longhorn cattle from Texas to Abilene, Kansas where they were loaded into railcars and shipped to Kansas City or Chicago.

CIO The Committee (and then Congress) for Industrial Organization, founded in 1935 to organize the unskilled and semiskilled workers ignored by the AFL. The CIO reinvigorated the labor movement.

circuit court Court that meets at different places within a district.

circuit-riding preachers Methodist ministers who traveled from church to church, usually in rural areas.

City Beautiful movement A movement of urban architectural renovation.

Civil Rights Act of 1957 First civil-rights act since Reconstruction, aimed at securing voting rights for African Americans in the South.

Civil Rights Act of 1964 Bipartisan measure that denied federal funding to segregated schools and barred discrimination by race and sex in employment, public accommodations, and labor unions.

Civil Rights Act of 1968 Measure that banned racial discrimination in housing and made interference with a person's civil rights a federal crime. It also stipulated that crossing state lines to incite a riot was a federal crime.

Civilized Tribes 60,000 Cherokees, Creeks, Choctaws, Chickasaws, and Seminoles who remained on their ancestral lands in the Old Southwest and were considered sovereign peoples.

Clay, Henry Speaker of the House, senator from Kentucky, and National Republican presidential candidate who was the principal spokesman for the American System.

Clinton, Bill Democratic president (1993–2001) whose two-term presidency witnessed rapid economic growth but also a sexual scandal that fueled an impeachment effort, which he survived.

close-order assault Military tactic of attacking with little space between men. In the face of modern weapons used during the Civil War, such fighting produced a high casualty rate.

Clovis tip A superior spear point developed before 9000 B.C. It was in use nearly everywhere in North and South America and produced such an improvement in hunting ability that it contributed to the extinction of most large mammals.

Coercive (Intolerable) Acts Four statutes passed by Parliament in response to the Boston Tea Party, including one that closed the port of Boston until the tea was paid for, and another that overturned the Massachusetts Charter of 1691. The colonists called them the Intolerable Acts and included the Quebec Act under that label.

Cold War The political, military, cultural, and economic rivalry between the United States and the Soviet Union that developed after the Second World War and lasted until the disintegration of the Soviet State after 1989.

collective bargaining Negotiations between representatives of workers and employers on issues such as wages, hours, and working conditions.

Collier, John Activist head of the Bureau of Indian Affairs who improved U.S. policy toward Native Americans and guided the landmark Indian Reorganization Act through Congress.

colonial economy Economy based on the export of agricultural products and the import of manufactured goods; sometimes used to describe the dependence of the South on the North.

Columbian Exchange A term coined by Alfred W. Crosby to describe the exchange of plants, animals, diseases, culture, and people between the American and European continents following the Spanish discovery of the New World.

Columbus, Christopher The Genoese mariner who persuaded Queen Isabella of Spain to support his voyage of discovery across the Atlantic in 1492. Until his death in 1506, he believed he had reached East Asia. Instead he had discovered America.

Committee on Public Information U.S. Government agency established in 1917 to arouse support for the war and, later, to generate suspicion of war dissenters.

committees of correspondence Bodies formed on both the local and colonial levels that played an important role in exchanging ideas and information. They spread primarily anti-British material and were an important step in the first tentative unity of people in different colonies.

common law The heart of the English legal system was based on precedents and judicial decisions. Common-law courts offered due process through such devices as trial by jury, which usually consisted of local men.

common schools Tax-supported public schools built by state and local governments.

Communist Party Radical group that wanted America to follow the Soviet Union's path to socialism. The CP organized some of the country's poorest workers into unions and pushed the New Deal leftward, but was never popular enough to bid for power itself.

Community Reinvestment Act of 1977 Forced banks to finance home buying in low-income neighborhoods to stimulate economic activity.

commutation fee $300 fee that could be paid by a man drafted into the Union army to exempt him from the current draft call.

compensated emancipation Idea that the federal government would offer compensation or money to states that voluntarily abolished slavery.

competence Understood in the early republic as the ability to live up to neighborhood economic standards while protecting the long-term independence of the household.

Compromise of 1850 Series of laws enacted in 1850 intended to settle all outstanding slavery issues.

Congressional Black Caucus (CBC) Congressional group formed in 1969 that focused on eliminating disparities between African Americans and white Americans.

congressional caucus In the early republic, the group of congressmen who traditionally chose the party's presidential candidates. By the 1820s, the American public distrusted the caucus as undemocratic because only one party contested for power. The caucus was replaced by the national nominating convention.

conquistadores The Spanish word for conquerors.

Conscience Whigs A group of antislavery members of the Whig Party.

Conservation Movement that called for managing the environment to ensure the careful and efficient use of the nation's natural resources.

conservationist Scientific environmentalists who were concerned with making sure the nation's resources were not being wasted.

consumer durable Consumer goods that were meant to last, such as washing machines and radios.

containment Label used to describe the global anticommunist national-security policies adopted by the United States to stop the expansion of communism during the late 1940s.

contraband of war Term used to describe slaves who came within the Union lines.

"Contract with America" Headed by Newt Gingrich, called for an overhaul of the welfare system, endorsement of an anti-crime legislation, reform for federal legal procedures, a three fifths majority for any increase in taxation, and a revised relationship with the UN.

contras Military force in Nicaragua, trained and financed by the United States, that opposed the Nicaraguan socialist government led by the Sandinista Party.

convention In England, a meeting, usually of the houses of Parliament, to address an emergency, such as the flight of James II to France in 1688. The convention welcomed William and Mary, who then restored the traditional parliamentary system. In the United States by the 1780s, conventions had become the purest expression of the popular will, superior to the legislature, as in the convention that drafted the Massachusetts Constitution of 1780.

cooperatives Marketing groups established by such groups as the Farmers Alliance that eliminated "middlemen" and reduced prices to farmers. The idea also was tried by some labor groups and included other types of businesses, such as factories.

Copperheads Term used by some Republicans to describe Peace Democrats to imply that they were traitors to the Union.

corrupt bargain Following the election of 1824, Andrew Jackson and his supporters alleged that, in a "corrupt bargain," Henry Clay sold his support during the House vote in the disputed election of 1824 of John Quincy Adams in exchange for appointment as Secretary of State.

Cortés, Hernán The Spanish conquistador who vanquished the Aztecs.

cosmopolitanism Ideal of American nationality developed by Randolph Bourne that encouraged creating new cultural forms from the combinations of peoples and cultures.

cotton Semitropical plant that produced white, fluffy fibers that could be made into textiles.

Coughlin, Father Charles The "radio priest" from the Midwest who alleged that the New Deal was being run by bankers. His growing anti-Semitism discredited him by 1939.

counterculture Antiestablishment movement that symbolized the youthful social upheaval of the 1960s. Ridiculing traditional attitudes toward such matters as clothing, hair styles, and sexuality, the counterculture urged a more open and less regimented approach to daily life.

coureur de bois A French phrase interpreted as "a roamer of the woods," referring to French colonists who participated in the fur trade with the Indians and lived part of the year with them.

court-packing plan 1937 attempt by Roosevelt to appoint one new Supreme Court justice for every sitting justice over the age of 70 and who had sat for at least 10 years. Roosevelt's purpose was to prevent conservative justices from dismantling the New Deal, but the plan died in Congress and inflamed opponents of the New Deal.

Covenant Chain of Peace An agreement negotiated by Governor Edmund Andros in 1677 that linked the colony of New York to the Iroquois Five Nations and was later expanded to include other colonies and Indian peoples.

covenant theology The belief that God made two personal covenants with humans: the covenant of works and the covenant of grace.

coverture A common-law doctrine under which the legal personality of the husband covered the wife, and he made all legally binding decisions.

Crazy Horse War chief of the Oglala Lakota (Sioux) Indians, who forged an alliance with Cheyenne chiefs to resist white expansion into the Black Hills in 1874–1875; led the attack on Custer's 7th Cavalry at Little Big Horn.

Credit Mobilier Construction company for the Union Pacific Railroad that gave shares of stock to some congressmen in return for favors.

crisis conversion Understood in evangelical churches as a personal transformation that resulted from directly experiencing the Holy Spirit.

crop lien system System of credit used in the poor rural South, whereby merchants in small country stores provided necessary goods on credit in return for a lien on the crop. As the price of crops fell, small farmers, black and white, drifted deeper into debt.

Cuban Missile Crisis (1962) Serious Cold War confrontation between the United States and the Soviet Union over the installation of Soviet missiles in Cuba.

cultural pluralism Doctrine that encouraged Americans to celebrate their ethnic differences.

Custer, George A. Civil War hero and postwar Indian fighter who was killed at Little Big Horn in 1876.

Dartmouth College v. Woodward 1816 Supreme Court case that showcased one of many important decisions made by John Marshall to protect the sanctity of contracts and corporate charters against state legislatures.

Davis, Jefferson Mississippi planter and prominent leader of the Southern Democrats in the 1850s, who later served as president of the Confederacy.

Dawes Plan 1924 U.S.-backed agreement to reduce German reparation payments by more than half. The plan also called on banks to invest $200 million in the German economy.

Dawes Severalty Act 1887 legislation that called for the dissolution of Indian tribes as legal entities, offered Indians citizenship, and allotted each head of family 160 acres of farmland or 320 acres of grazing land.

Debs, Eugene V. Leader of the Socialist Party who received almost a million votes in the election of 1912.

Declaration of Independence A document drafted primarily by Thomas Jefferson of Virginia; this document justified American independence to the world by affirming "that all men are created equal" and have a natural right to "life, liberty, and the pursuit of happiness." The longest section of the Declaration condemned George III as a tyrant.

deflation Decline in consumer prices or a rise in the purchasing power of money.

Deism Belief that God created the universe but did not intervene in its affairs.

deists People who believed that God made the universe but did not intervene in its affairs.

Denmark Vesey Leader of a slave conspiracy in and around Charleston, South Carolina, in 1822.

deregulation To reduce or remove government rules or policies; Reagan's deregulation agenda focused on the financial system.

deskilling Process in which the employment market produces jobs requiring

fewer skills (and offering less income) than in the past.

détente An easing of tensions, particularly between the United States and the Soviet Union.

Dewey, John Philosopher who believed that American technological and industrial power could be made to serve the people and democracy.

direct election of senators Constitutional amendment that mandated the election of senators by the people rather than by selection by state legislatures.

dirty tricks Actions designed to destroy the reputation and effectiveness of political opponents of the Nixon administration.

disfranchisement Process of barring groups of adult citizens from voting.

dissenter Person who disagrees openly with the majority opinion.

Dix, Dorothea Boston reformer who traveled throughout the country campaigning for humane, state-supported asylums for the insane.

dollar diplomacy Diplomatic strategy formulated under President Taft that focused on expanding American investments abroad, especially in Latin America and East Asia.

Dolores Huerta and Cesar Chavez Political activists, leaders of the United Farm Workers of America, and the most influential Mexican American leaders during the 1970s.

domestic fiction Sentimental literature that centered on household and domestic themes that emphasized the toil and travails of women and children who overcame adversity through religious faith and strength of character.

"domino theory" Refers to the threat of communism spreading throughout Asia as the result of a communist electoral victory in Vietnam.

"Double V" campaign Urged for a victory against racial discrimination abroad as well as at home during World War II.

Douglas, Stephen A. Senator from Illinois who emerged as a leading Democrat in 1850 and led efforts to enact the Compromise of 1850.

downsizing Process of cutting back in labor pools and management staffs by businesses usually due to declining profits.

doves Opponents of military action, especially those who wanted to end quickly U.S. involvement in the Vietnam War.

dower rights The right of a widow to a portion of her deceased husband's estate (usually one-third of the value of the estate). It was passed to their children upon her death.

dowry The cash or goods a woman received from her father when she married.

drawbacks Form of rebate offered to special customers by the railroads.

Dred Scott Missouri slave who sued for freedom on grounds of prolonged residence in a free state and free territory; in 1857, the Supreme Court found against his case, declaring the Missouri Compromise unconstitutional.

Du Bois, W. E. B. Leader of the NAACP, the editor of its newspaper, *The Crisis,* and an outspoken critic of Booker T. Washington and his accomodationist approach to race relations.

Earned Income Tax Credit (EITC) Assisted lower and moderate income households with children.

East Asian Co-Prosperity Sphere Proposition from Japan to China that would liberate Asian nations from Western colonialism and create a self-sufficient economic zone under Japanese leadership.

economy of scale Term used in both industry and agriculture to describe the economic advantages of concentrating capital, units of production, and output.

Edison, Thomas Alva Inventor of the 1800s who developed an array of devices including the phonograph, incandescent light bulb, and movie camera.

Eisenhower Doctrine Policy that stated that the United States would use armed force to respond to imminent or actual communist aggression in the Middle East.

Eisenhower, Dwight D. Supreme Commander of the Allied Forces in Europe, orchestrator of the Normandy Invasion, and President of the United States (1953–1961).

elect Those selected by God for salvation.

Electoral College The group that elects the president. Each state receives as many electors as it has congressmen and senators combined and can decide how to choose its electors. Every elector votes for two candidates, one of whom has to be from another state.

emancipation Refers to release from slavery or bondage. Gradual emancipation was introduced in Pennsylvania and provided for the eventual freeing of slaves born after a certain date when they reached age 28.

embargo Government order prohibiting the movement of merchant ships or goods in or out of its ports.

Employment Act of 1946 Called for maximum employment and declared private enterprises responsible for economic decision making.

encomienda A system of labor introduced into the Western Hemisphere by the Spanish. It permitted the holder, or *encomendero,* to claim labor from Indians in a district for a stated period of time.

energy crisis OPEC raised the price of crude oil and precipitated acute worldwide shortages in 1978; gasoline became expensive and scarce.

enfranchise To grant the right to vote.

Enlightenment The new learning in science and philosophy that took hold, at least in England, between 1660 and the American Revolution. Nearly all of its spokesmen were religious moderates who were more interested in science than religious doctrine and who favored broad religious toleration.

entail A legal device that required a landowner to keep his estate intact and pass it on to his heir.

enumerated commodities A group of colonial products that had to be shipped from the colony of origin to England or another English colony. The most important commodities were sugar and tobacco.

Environmental Protection Agency (EPA) Organization established in 1970 that brought under a single institutional umbrella the enforcement of laws intended to protect environmental quality.

environmentalism Movement with roots in earlier conservation, preservation, and public health movements that grew in power after 1970, when concern mounted over the disruption of ecological balances and critical habitats.

Equal Rights Amendment (ERA) Proposed amendment to the Constitution providing that equal rights could not be abridged on account of sex. It won congressional approval in 1972 but failed to gain ratification by the states.

Erie Canal Canal linking the Hudson River at Albany with the Great Lakes at Buffalo that helped commercialize the farms of the Great Lakes watershed and channel that commerce into New York City.

Espionage, Sabotage, and Sedition Acts Laws passed in 1917 and 1918 that gave the federal government sweeping powers to silence and even imprison dissenters.

ESPN Cable network devoted entirely to sports.

established church The church in a European state or colony that was sustained by the government and supported by public taxes.

evangelical A style of Christian ministry that includes much zeal and enthusiasm. Evangelical ministers emphasized personal conversion and faith rather than religious ritual.

evangelicals Religious groups that generally placed an emphasis on conversion of non-Christians.

excise tax Internal tax on goods or services.

Exodusters Name given to the 20,000 African Americans who moved to Kansas believing rumors of free land for settlers and supplies from the government in 1879.

external taxes Taxes based on oceanic trade, such as port duties. Some colonists thought of them more as a means of regulating trade than as taxes for revenue.

exurbs Housing developments that expanded further away from larger cities into farmlands and small towns.

factories A term used to describe small posts established for the early slave trade along the coast of Africa or on small offshore islands.

Fair Deal Proposed in 1949 by President Truman to extend New Deal programs, enact legislation dealing with civil rights, national health care, and federal aid for education, provide funds for public housing, and support farm prices.

fall line A geographical landmark defined by the first waterfalls encountered when going upriver from the sea.

These waterfalls prevented oceangoing ships from sailing further inland and thus made the fall line a significant early barrier. Land between the falls and the ocean was called the tidewater. Land above the falls but below the mountains was called the piedmont.

Family Assistance Plan (FAP) Proposed by Nixon in 1969 to replace the existing welfare policy; it called to provide every low-income family an annual income of $1,600.

fascism Type of highly centralized government that used terror and violence to suppress opposition. Its rigid social and economic controls often incorporated strong nationalism and racism. Fascist governments were dominated by strong authority figures or dictators.

favorite son Candidate for president supported by delegates from his home state.

Federal Reserve Act Act that brought private banks and public authority together to regulate and strengthen the nation's financial system.

Federalists Supporters of the Constitution during the ratification process. Anti-Federalists resisted ratification.

feminism Desire for complete equality between men and women.

feudal revival The reliance on old feudal charters for all of the profits that could be extracted from them. It took hold in several colonies in the mid-18th century and caused serious problems between many landowners and tenants.

fiat money Paper money backed only by the promise of the government to accept it in payment of taxes. It originated in Massachusetts after a military emergency in 1690.

filibuster Congressional delaying tactic involving lengthy speeches that prevent legislation from being enacted.

filibustering A term used to describe several groups that invaded or attempted to invade various Latin American areas to attempt to add them to the slaveholding regions of the United States. The word originated from *filibustero*, meaning a freebooter or pirate.

fire-eaters Southerners who were eager, enthusiastic supporters of southern rights and later of secession.

First Continental Congress This intercolonial body met in Philadelphia in

September and October 1774 to organize resistance against the Coercive Acts by defining American rights, petitioning the king, and appealing to the British and American people. It created the Association, local committees in each community to enforce nonimportation.

Five-Power Treaty 1922 treaty in which the United States, Britain, Japan, France, and Italy agreed to scrap more than 2 million tons of their warships.

flappers Rebellious middle-class young women who signaled their desire for independence and equality through style and personality rather than through politics.

flexible response Kennedy's approach to the Cold War that aimed to provide a wide variety of military and nonmilitary methods to confront communist movements.

Ford, Gerald A GOP member of the House of Representatives, Gerald Ford became the first person to be appointed Vice President of the United States. When Richard Nixon resigned in 1974, Ford became President.

Fort Sumter Fort in Charleston's harbor occupied by United States troops after the secession of South Carolina.

Fourteen Points Plan laid out by Woodrow Wilson in January 1918 to give concrete form to his dream of a "peace without victory" and a new world order.

Freemasons A religion of manliness, complete with mysterious rituals that extolled sobriety, industry, brotherhood, benevolence, and citizenship.

free silver Idea that the government would purchase all silver offered for sale and coin it into silver dollars at the preferred ratio between silver and gold of 16 to 1.

Freedmen's Bureau Federal agency created in 1865 to supervise newly freed people. It oversaw relations between whites and blacks in the South, issued food rations, and supervised labor contracts.

freedom riders Members of interracial groups who traveled the South on buses to test a series of federal court decisions declaring segregation on buses and in waiting rooms to be unconstitutional.

Freedom Summer Summer of 1964 when nearly a thousand white volunteers went to Mississippi to aid in voter registration and other civil-rights projects.

free-labor ideology Belief that all work in a free society is honorable and that manual labor is degraded when it is equated with slavery or bondage.

Free-Soilers A term used to describe people who opposed the expansion of slavery into the territories. It came from the name of a small political party in the election of 1848.

French and Indian War Popular name for the struggle between Britain and France for the control of North America, 1754 to 1763, in which the British conquered New France. It merged into Europe's Seven Years' War (1756–1763) that pitted Britain and Prussia against France, Austria, and Russia.

Friedan, Betty Author of *The Feminine Mystique* (1963) and founder of the National Organization for Women (1966).

frontier An area on the advancing edge of American civilization.

fugitive slaves Runaway slaves who escaped to a free state.

Fulton, Robert Builder of the *Clermont*, the first practical steam-driven boat.

fundamentalists Religious groups that preached the necessity of fidelity to a strict moral code, individual commitment to Christ, and faith in the literal truth of the Bible.

funded national debt The state agreed to pay the interest due to its creditors before all other obligations.

Gabriel's rebellion Carefully planned but unsuccessful rebellion of slaves in Richmond, Virginia, and the surrounding area in 1800.

gag rule Procedure in which Congress voted at each session from 1836 to 1844 to table antislavery petitions without reading them in order avoid any debate.

Gaither Report Report that encouraged President Eisenhower to increase national security and government spending in 1957.

gang labor A system where planters organized their field slaves into gangs, supervised them closely, and kept them working in the fields all day. This type of labor was used on tobacco plantations.

Garrison, William Lloyd Abolitionist and publisher of the first issue of the *Liberator*.

Garvey, Marcus Jamaican-born black nationalist who attracted millions of African Americans in the early 1920s to a movement calling for black separatism and self-sufficiency.

gas and water socialists Term used to describe evolutionary socialists who focused their reform efforts on regulating municipal utilities in the public interest.

Gates, Henry Lewis, Jr. Activist for the academics of African American's in the 1990s.

General William Westmoreland Recommended the "search and destroy" method in North Vietnam to incapacitate NLF and North Vietnamese forces and to allow Saigon government time to develop.

Geneva Peace Accords of 1954 Divided French Indochina into three new nations: Laos, Cambodia, and Vietnam; Vietnam was also split into two jurisdiction at the 17th parallel until an election could unify the country.

gentleman Term used to describe a person of means who performed no manual labor.

gentlemen's agreement (1907) Agreement by which the Japanese government promised to halt the immigration of its adult male laborers to the United States in return for President Theodore Roosevelt's pledge to end the discriminatory treatment of Japanese immigrant children in California's public schools.

Ghost Dance Indian ritual involving days of worship expressed in part through dance.

GI Bill Officially called the Serviceman's Readjustment Act of 1944. It provided veterans with college and job-training assistance, preferential treatment in hiring, and subsidized home loans, and was later extended to Korean War veterans in 1952.

girdled trees Trees with a line cut around them so sap would not rise in the spring.

glasnost Russian term describing increased openness in Russian society under Mikhail Gorbachev.

globalization Spread of businesses throughout world.

Glorious Revolution The overthrow of King James II by Whigs and Tories, who invited William of Orange to England. William landed in November 1688, the army defected to him, James fled to France, and in early 1689, Parliament offered the throne to William and his wife Mary, a daughter of James. Contemporaries called the event "glorious" because almost no blood was shed in England.

gold bugs "Sound money" advocates who wanted to keep the United States on the international gold standard and believed the expanded coinage of silver was foolhardy.

Goldwater, Barry Republican candidate defeated by Lyndon B. Johnson in the 1964 presidential election.

Gompers, Samuel F. America's most famous trade unionist while serving as president of the AFL (1896–1924). He achieved his greatest success in organizing skilled workers.

Good Neighbor Policy Roosevelt's foreign policy initiative that formally renounced the right of the United States to intervene in Latin American affairs, leading to improved relations between the United States and Latin American countries.

Gorbachev, Mikhail Became general secretary of the Communist Party in 1985; he agreed to Reagan's proposal to ban nuclear weapons and eliminated the policy that prohibited nations under Soviet influence from rejecting Communism, which brought an end to the Cold War.

governor-general The French official responsible for military and diplomatic affairs and for appointment of all militia officers in a colony.

graduated income tax Tax based on income with rates that gradually rise as the level of income rises.

Grangers Members of the Patrons of Husbandry (a farmers' organization) and a contemptuous name for farmers used by ranchers in the West.

Grant, Ulysses S. General-in-chief of Union armies who led those armies to victory in the Civil War.

Great American Desert The treeless area in the plains that most Americans considered unsuitable for settlement. It generally was passed over by settlers going to the Pacific Coast areas.

Great Awakening An immense religious revival that swept across the Protestant world in the 1730s and 1740s.

Great Depression Economic downturn triggered by the stock market crash in October 1929 and lasting until 1941.

Great Railroad Strike of 1877 Strike that occurred during a time of depression that caused employers to cut wages and lay off workers.

Great Society Series of domestic initiatives announced in 1964 by President Lyndon Johnson to "end poverty and racial injustice." They included the Voting Rights Act of 1965; the establishment of the Department of Housing and Urban Development, Head Start, and job-training programs; Medicare and Medicaid expansion; and various community action programs.

Great White Fleet Naval ships sent on a 45,000-mile world tour by President Roosevelt (1907–1909) to showcase American military power.

Greeley, Horace Editor of the *New York Tribune*, one of the most influential newspapers in the country.

greenbacks Paper money issued by the federal government during the Civil War to help pay war expenses. They were called greenbacks because of their color.

Greene, Nathanael A general from Rhode Island whose superb strategy of irregular war reclaimed the Lower South for the American cause in 1780–1781.

Greenwich Village Community of radical artists and writers in lower Manhattan that provided a supportive environment for various kinds of radical ideals.

Grenville, George As head of the British government from 1763 to 1765, Grenville passed the Sugar Act, Quartering Act, Currency Act, and the Stamp Act, provoking the imperial crisis of 1765–1766.

Grimke, Sarah Along with her sister Angelina, this elite South Carolina woman moved north and campaigned against slavery and for temperance and women's rights.

gross national product (GNP) Total value of all goods and services produced during a specific period.

Gulf of Tonkin Resolution Measure passed by Congress in August 1964 that provided authorization for an air war against North Vietnam after U.S. destroyers were allegedly attacked by North Vietnamese torpedoes. Johnson invoked it as authority for expanding the Vietnam War.

Gullah A language spoken by newly imported African slaves. Originally, it was a simple second language for everyone who spoke it, but it gradually evolved into modern black English.

habeas corpus Right of an individual to obtain a legal document as protection against illegal imprisonment.

haciendas Large, landed estates established by the Spanish.

Hale, Sarah Josepha Editor of *Godey's Ladies Book* and an important arbiter of domesticity and taste for middle-class housewives.

Half-Way Covenant The Puritan practice whereby parents who had been baptized but had not yet experienced conversion could bring their children before the church and have them baptized.

Hamilton, Alexander Secretary of the Treasury under Washington who organized the finances of the new government and led the partisan fight against the Democratic Republicans.

Hard Money Democrats Democrats who, in the 1830s and 1840s, wanted to eliminate paper money and regarded banks as centers of trickery and privilege.

Harlem Renaissance 1920s African-American literary and artistic awakening that sought to create works rooted in black culture instead of imitating white styles.

Harpers Ferry Site of John Brown's 1859 raid on a U.S. armory and arsenal for the manufacture and storage of military rifles.

hawks Supporters of intensified military efforts in the Vietnam War.

Haymarket Bombing at an Anarchist protest meeting at Haymarket Square in Chicago on May 4 resulting in 10 deaths, 6 of them policemen.

Haywood, William Labor organizer known as "Big Bill," who led the radical union Industrial Workers of the World.

headright A colonist received 50 acres of land for every person whose passage to America he financed, including himself. This system was introduced in Virginia.

heathen A term used sometimes by Christians to refer to anyone who was not a Christian or a Jew.

herrenvolk democracy Concept that emphasized the equality of all who belonged to the master race—not all mankind.

Hessians A term used by Americans to describe the 17,000 mercenary troops hired by Britain from various German states, especially Hesse.

hidalgos The minor nobility of Spain. Many possessed little wealth and were interested in improving their position through the overseas empire.

High Federalists A term used to describe Alexander Hamilton and some of his less-moderate supporters. They wanted the naval war with France to continue and also wanted to severely limit the rights of an opposition party.

Highway Act of 1956 Act that appropriated $25 billion for the construction of more than 40,000 miles of interstate highways over a 10-year period.

hippies People who identified with the 1960s counterculture. They were often depicted as embracing mind-altering drugs, communal living arrangements, and new forms of music.

Hiroshima Japanese city destroyed by an atomic bomb on August 6, 1945.

Hiss, Alger High-level State Department employee who was accused, in a controversial case, of being a communist and Soviet spy.

Hitler, Adolph German fascist dictator whose aggressive policies touched off the Second World War.

HIV-AIDS Acquired immune deficiency syndrome (AIDS) resulting from infection with the human immunodeficiency virus (HIV). It progressively impedes the body's ability to protect itself from disease.

Hmong Ethnically distinct people who inhabited lands extending across the borders of the Indochinese countries of Vietnam, Cambodia, and Laos.

Homestead (Strike) Carnegie Steel Company closed its Homestead plant planning to reopen with nonunion workers; the union went on strike refusing to leave the building, which led to a gun battle and several deaths.

Homestead Act Legislation that took effect on January 1, 1863 to provide free land for western settlers.

House of Burgesses The assembly of early Virginia that settlers were allowed to elect. Members met with the governor and his council and enacted local laws. It first met in 1619.

House Un-American Activities Committee (HUAC) Congressional committee (1938–1975) that zealously investigated suspected Nazi and Communist sympathizers.

household deficit Difference between what U.S. households earned and what they spent.

household industry Work such as converting raw materials into finished products done by women and children to provide additional household income.

housing "bubble" Refers to people who became home owners but lacked the incomes to handle a conventional mortgage.

Howe, William (General) Howe commanded the British army in North America from 1776 to 1778. He won major victories in New York and northern New Jersey in 1776, but Washington regained control of New Jersey after his Trenton-Princeton campaign. Howe took Philadelphia in September 1777 but was recalled in disgrace after Britain's northern army surrendered at Saratoga.

Huguenots French Protestants who followed the beliefs of John Calvin.

Hull House First American settlement house established in Chicago in 1889 by Jane Addams and Ellen Gates Starr.

Human Genome Project Program launched in 1985 to map all genetic material in the 24 human chromosomes. It sparked ongoing debate over the potential consequences of genetic research and manipulation.

human rights Rights and freedoms that all people deserve; this was a major emphasis of Carter's foreign policy.

Hutchinson, Anne A religious radical who attracted a large following in Massachusetts, especially in Boston. She warned that nearly all of the ministers were preaching a covenant of works instead of the covenant of grace. Convicted of the Antinomian heresy after claiming that she received direct messages from God, she and her most loyal followers were banished to Rhode Island in 1638.

hydraulic mining Use of high-pressure streams of water to wash gold or other minerals from soil.

Immigration Act of 1924 (Johnson-Reed Act) Limited immigration to the United States to 165,000 per year, shrank immigration from southern and eastern Europe to insignificance, and banned immigration from East and South Asia.

Immigration and Nationality Act of 1965 Law eliminating the national-origins quota system for immigration and substituting preferences for people with certain skills or with relatives in the United States.

Immigration Reform and Control Act of 1986 (Simpson-Mazzoli Act) Created stricter penalties for employing undocumented workers and provided residency for people that had lived in the U.S. since 1982.

Immigration Restriction Act of 1917 Measure that denied any adult immigrant who failed a reading test entry into the United States, and banned immigration from the "Asiatic Barred Zone."

impeach To charge government office-holders with misconduct in office.

impeachment Act of charging a public official with misconduct in office.

imperialists Those who wanted to expand their nation's world power through military prowess, economic strength, and control of foreign territory (often organized into colonies).

impressment Removal of sailors from American ships by British naval officers.

Inca The last and most extensive pre-Columbian empire in the Andes and along the Pacific coast of South America.

indentured servants People who had their passage to America paid by a master or ship captain. They agreed to work for their master for a term of years in exchange for cost of passage, bed and board, and small freedom dues when their terms were up. The number of years served depended on the terms of the contract. Most early settlers in the English colonies outside of New England arrived as indentured servants.

Independent Treasury Bill 1840 bill that permitted the federal government to hold and dispense money without depositing it in banks and required that customs and land purchases be paid in gold and silver coins or notes from specie-paying banks.

Indian Removal Act (1830) Legislation that offered the native peoples of the lower South the option of removal to federal lands west of the Mississippi. Those who did not take the offer were removed by force in 1838.

indigo A blue dye obtained from plants that was used by the textile industry. The British government subsidized the commercial production of it in South Carolina.

information revolution Acceleration of the speed and availability of information resulting from use of computer and satellite systems.

initiative Reform that gave voters the right to propose and pass a law independently of their state legislature.

Inns of Court England's law schools.

intendant The officer who administered the system of justice in New France.

interchangeable parts Industrial technique using machine tools to cut and shape a large number of similar parts that can be fitted together with other parts to make an entire item such as a gun.

internal improvements 19th-century term for transportation facilities such as roads, canals, and railroads.

internal taxes Taxes that were imposed on land, people, retail items (such as excises), or legal documents and newspapers (such as the Stamp Act). Most colonists thought that only their elective assemblies had the constitutional power to impose internal taxes.

Iran-*contra* affair Reagan administration scandal in which the U.S. secretly sold arms to Iran, a country implicated in holding American hostages, and diverted the money to finance the attempt by the *contras* to overthrow the Sandinista government of Nicaragua. Both transactions violated acts of Congress, which had prohibited funding the *contra* and selling weapons to Iran.

Iranian revolution of January 1979 Islamic fundamentalists overthrew Iranian dictator Shah Reza Pahlavi; the rebellion led to 66 Americans taken hostage when Carter allowed the shah into the U.S. for medical assistance.

Iroquois League A confederation of five Indian nations centered around the Mohawk Valley who were very active in the fur trade. They first worked with the Dutch and then the English. They were especially successful in using adoption as a means of remaining strong.

irreconcilables Group of 14 midwestern and western senators who opposed the Treaty of Versailles.

irregular war A type of war using men who were not part of a permanent or professional regular military force. It also can apply to guerilla-type warfare, usually against the civilian population.

isolationists Name given to people who were not in favor of war during World War II.

itinerant preachers Ministers who lacked their own parishes and who traveled from place to place.

Jackson State (incident) Killing of two students on May 13, 1970, after an escalation in tensions between students at Jackson State University, a historically black institution, and National Guard troops in Mississippi.

Jackson, Andrew President of the United States (1829–1837) who founded the Democratic Party, signed the Indian Removal Act, vetoed the Second Bank, and signed the Force Bill.

Jackson, Thomas J. ("Stonewall") A native of Virginia, he emerged as one of the Confederacy's best generals in 1861–1862.

Jamestown Founded in 1607, Jamestown became England's first permanent settlement in North America. It served as the capital of Virginia for most of the 17th century.

Japanese internment Removal of first- and second-generation Japanese Americans into secured camps, a 1942 action then justified as a security measure but since deemed unjustified by evidence.

Jim Crow laws Laws passed by southern states mandating racial segregation in public facilities.

Jim Crow laws Laws passed by southern states mandating racial segregation in public facilities of all kinds.

Johnson, Lyndon B. President (1963–1969) who undertook an ambitious Great Society program and a major military effort in Vietnam.

joint resolution An act passed by both houses of Congress with a simple majority rather than the two-thirds majority in the Senate.

joint-stock company A form of business organization that resembled a modern corporation. Individuals invested in the company through the purchase of shares. One major difference between then and today was that each stockholder had one vote regardless of how many shares he owned. The first permanent English colonies in North America were established by joint-stock companies.

journeyman Wage-earning craftsman.

judicial review Supreme Court's power to rule on the constitutionality of congressional acts.

Kansas-Nebraska Act Law enacted in 1854 to organize the new territories of Kansas and Nebraska that effectively repealed the provision of the 1820 Missouri Compromise by leaving the question of slavery to the territories' settlers.

Kennan, George (Mr. X) American diplomat and historian who recommended the policy of containment toward Soviet aggression in a famous article published under the pseudonym "X."

Kennedy, John F. President from 1961 to 1963, noted for his youthful charm and vigor and his "New Frontier" vision for America.

Kent State (incident) Killing of four students on May 4, 1970, by the National Guard at a Kent State University protest against the U.S. incursion into neutral Cambodia.

King George's War Popular term in North America for the third of the four Anglo-French wars before the American Revolution (1744–1748). It is sometimes also applied to the War of Jenkins's Ear between Spain and Britain (1739–1748).

King, Martin Luther, Jr. African American clergyman who advocated nonviolent social change and shaped the civil-rights movement of the 1950s and 1960s.

Knights of Labor Secret fraternal organization founded in 1869 in Philadelphia.

Know-Nothings Adherents of nativist organizations and of the American party who wanted to restrict the political rights of immigrants.

Korean War Conflict lasting from 1950 to 1953 between communist North Korea, aided by China, and South Korea, aided by United Nations forces consisting primarily of U.S. troops.

Ku Klux Klan White terrorist organization in the South originally founded as a fraternal society in 1866. Reborn in 1915, it achieved popularity in the 1920s through its calls for Anglo-Saxon purity, Protestant supremacy, and the subordination of blacks, Catholics, and Jews.

La Raza Unida Mexican American–based movement that scored some political successes in the Southwest in the late 1960s and early 1970s.

lame duck Elected official who is about to reach the end of service and/or whose successor is already elected

lame-duck administration Period of time between an incumbent party's or officeholder's loss of an election and the succession to office of the winning party or candidate.

League of Women Voters Successor to the National American Woman Suffrage Association, it promoted women's role in politics and dedicated itself to educating voters.

Lee, Robert E. U.S. army officer until his resignation to join the Confederacy as general-in-chief.

legal tender Any type of money that the government requires everyone to accept at face value.

Lend-Lease Act A 1941 act by which the United States "loaned" munitions to the Allies, hoping to avoid war by becoming an "arsenal" for the Allied cause.

levee Earthen dike or mound, usually along the banks of rivers, used to prevent flooding.

Lewis and Clark Explorers commissioned in 1804 by President Jefferson to survey the Louisiana Purchase.

liberal Protestants Those who believed that religion had to be adapted to science and that the Bible was to be mined for its ethical values rather than for its literal meaning.

Liberty bonds Thirty-year government bonds with an annual interest rate of 3.5 percent sold to fund the war effort.

liberty tree A term for the gallows on which enemies of the people deserved to be hanged. The best known was in Boston.

limited liability Liability that protected directors and stockholders of corporations from corporate debts by separating those debts from personal liabilities.

Lincoln, Abraham Illinois Whig who became the Republican Party's first successful presidential candidate in 1860 and who led the Union during the Civil War.

Lincoln-Douglas debates Series of seven debates between Abraham Lincoln and Stephen Douglas in their contest for election to the U.S. Senate in 1858.

Lindbergh, Charles A. First individual to fly solo across the Atlantic (1927) and the greatest celebrity of the 1920s.

lintheads Term used by wealthier whites to describe poor whites who labored in southern cotton mills.

living room war Phrase suggesting that television coverage had brought the Vietnam War into the living rooms of Americans and may have led many to question the war.

lockout Act of closing down a business by the owners during a labor dispute.

Lodge, Henry Cabot Republican Senator from Massachusetts who led the campaign to reject the Treaty of Versailles.

logistics Military activity relating to such things as the transporting, supplying, and quartering of troops and their equipment.

long knives The term Indians used to describe Virginians.

Long, Huey Democratic senator and former governor of Louisiana who used the radio to attack the New Deal as too conservative. FDR regarded him as a major rival.

longhorn Breed of cattle introduced into the Southwest by the Spanish that became the main breed of livestock on the cattle frontier.

Lost Generation Term used by Gertrude Stein to describe U.S. writers and artists who fled to Paris in the 1920s after becoming disillusioned with America.

Louisiana Purchase Land purchased from France in 1803 that doubled the size of the United States.

Lowell, Francis Cabot Wealthy Bostonian who, with the help of the Boston Associates, built and operated integrated textile mills in eastern Massachusetts.

loyalists People in the 13 colonies who remained loyal to Britain during the Revolution.

Ludlow massacre Murder of 66 men, women, and children in April 1914 when company police of the Colorado Fuel and Iron Company fired randomly on striking United Mine Workers.

Luftwaffe German air force.

Lusitania British passenger ship sunk by a German U-boat on May 7, 1915, killing more than 1,000 men, women, and children.

MacArthur, Douglas Supreme commander of Allied forces in the southwest Pacific during the Second World War; leader of the occupation forces in the reconstruction of Japan; and head of United Nations forces during the Korean War.

magistrate An official who enforced the law. In colonial America, this person was usually a justice of the peace or a judge in a higher court.

Mahan, Alfred Thayer Influential imperialist who advocated construction of a large navy as crucial to the successful pursuit of world power.

Malcolm X Charismatic African American leader who criticized integration and urged the creation of separate black economic and cultural institutions. He became a hero to members of the Black Power movement.

mandamus A legal writ ordering a person, usually a public official, to carry out a specific act. In Massachusetts in 1774, the new royal councilors were appointed by a writ of mandamus.

Manhattan Project Major secret military operation that involved the development of the first atomic weapon.

manifest destiny The belief that the United States was destined to grow from the Atlantic to the Pacific and from the Arctic to the tropics. Providence supposedly intended for Americans to have this area for a great experiment in liberty.

manumission of slaves The act of freeing a slave, done at the will of the owner.

Marbury v. Madison 1803 case involving the disputed appointment of a federal justice of the peace in which Chief Justice John Marshall expanded the Supreme Court's authority to review legislation.

March on Washington for Jobs and Freedom On August 28, 1960, 200,000 people marched through Washington D.C. to the Lincoln Memorial for the rights of African Americans; Dr. Martin Luther King Jr. delivered his famous "I Have a Dream" speech on this day.

maritime Of, or relating to, the sea.

Marshall Plan Plan of U.S. aid to Europe that aimed to contain communism by fostering postwar economic recovery. Proposed by Secretary of State George C. Marshall in 1947, it was known formally as the European Recovery Program.

Marshall, John Chief Justice of the United States Supreme Court from 1801 to 1835. Appointed by Federalist President John Adams, Marshall's decisions tended to favor the federal government over the states and to clear legal blocks to private business.

martial law Government by military force rather than by citizens.

mass culture critique Fear that the cultural traditions of the 1950s would be drastically altered due to the influences of art, music, and TV.

mass production High-speed and high-volume production.

Massachusetts Bay Company A joint-stock company chartered by Charles I in 1629. It was controlled by Non-Separatists, who took the charter with them to New England and, in effect, converted it into a written constitution for the colony.

massive retaliation Assertion by the Eisenhower administration that the threat of U.S. atomic weaponry would hold Communist powers in check.

matrilineal A society that determines inheritance and roles in life based on the female or maternal line.

Maya A literate, highly urbanized Mesoamerican civilization that flourished for more than a thousand years before its sudden collapse in the ninth century A.D.

McCarran-Walter Act Authorized the denial of immigrant status to anyone who might compromise national security by bringing dangerous ideas into the country; it also allowed the deportation of immigrants who belonged to organizations on the Attorney General's List.

McCarthy, Joseph 1946 U.S. Senator who unfairly accused numerous people of being Communists.

McCarthy, Senator Eugene Senator of Minnesota who challenged Lyndon B. Johnson for the presidency in 1968; McCarthy shut down his campaign upon realizing Johnson's vice president, Hubert Humphrey, was the favored democrat candidate.

McCarthyism Public accusations of disloyalty made with little or no regard to actual evidence. Named after Senator Joseph McCarthy, these accusations and the scandal and harm they caused came to symbolize the most virulent form of anticommunism.

McClellan, George B. One of the most promising young officers in the U.S. army, he became the principal commander of Union armies in 1861–1862.

McCulloch v. Maryland Supreme Court case in which the Bank of the United States Baltimore branch challenged the Maryland legislature's attempt to tax the bank; lead by John Marshall, the Court decided in favor of the Bank and denied Maryland's right to tax the Bank or any other federal agency.

McKinley, William A seven-term Republican congressman from Ohio whose signature issue was the protective tariff. He was the last Civil War veteran to be elected president.

melting pot Term first used in the early 1900s that referred to the fusing of immigrants' culture with American culture as a continuous rebirth of the nation.

Menéndez, Francisco An escaped South Carolina slave who fought with the Yamasee Indians against the colony, fled to Florida, was reenslaved by the Spanish, became a militia captain, was freed again, and was put in charge of the free-black town of Mose near St. Augustine in the late 1730s, the first community of its kind in what is now the United States.

Pedro Menendez de Aviles The Spanish Admiral charged with Havana's protection after it was sacked by the Huguenots. Forces under Aviles' command expanded Spanish influence in the region, attacking and conquering settlements on Florida's Atlantic coast in 1565.

Mercantilism An economic theory that stresses a direct relationship between a nation's wealth and its power. Mercantilist nations in the 17th century sought to increase their wealth and power through aggressive trade expansion within their colonies.

merger movement Late-19th and early 20th-century effort to integrate different enterprises into single, giant corporations able to eliminate competition, achieve economic order, and boost profits.

Mesoamerica An area embracing Central America and southern and central Mexico.

Metacom's War (King Philip's War) A war that devastated much of southern New England in 1675–1676. It began as a conflict between Metacom's Wampanoags and Plymouth Colony but soon engulfed all of the New England colonies and most of the region's Indian nations.

Mexican repatriation Secretary of Labor William Doak's plan to deport illegal Mexican aliens to Mexico. By 1935, more than 500,000 Mexicans had left the United States.

microchips Technological improvement that boosted the capability and reduced the size and cost of computer hardware.

middle class Social group that developed in the early 19th century comprised of urban and country merchants, master craftsmen who had turned themselves into manufacturers, and market-oriented farmers—small-scale entrepreneurs who rose within market society.

Middle Ground The area of French and Indian cooperation west of Niagara and south of the Great Lakes. No one exercised sovereign power over this area, but the French used Indian rituals to negotiate treaties with their Algonquian trading partners, first against the Iroquois and later against the British.

midnight judges Federal judicial officials appointed under the Judiciary Act of 1801, in the last days of John Adams's presidency.

Midway Plaisance A section of the Columbia Exposition of 1893 that included concessions, games, the Ferris Wheel, traveling museums, and freak shows.

military-industrial complex Refers to the relationship between military, political, and economic elites committed to expanding national security capabilities.

militia A community's armed force, made up primarily of ordinary male citizens rather than professional soldiers.

Millennium The period at the end of history when Christ is expected to return and rule with his saints for a thousand years.

minstrel show Popular form of theater among working men of the northern cities in which white men in blackface portrayed African Americans in song and dance.

missions Outposts established by the Spanish along the northern frontier to aid in Christianizing the native peoples. They also were used to exploit these peoples' labor.

Missouri Compromise Compromise that maintained sectional balance in Congress by admitting Missouri as a slave state and Maine as a free state and by drawing a line west from the 368 309 parallel separating future slave and free states.

modernists Those who believed in science rather than religion and in moving toward equality for men and women and for whites and nonwhites.

Monroe Doctrine Foreign policy doctrine proposed by Secretary of State John Quincy Adams in 1823 that denied the right of European powers to establish new colonies in the Americas while maintaining the United States' right to annex new territory.

Montgomery bus boycott Political protest campaign mounted in 1955 to oppose the city's policy of racial segregation on its public transit system. The Supreme Court soon declared segregation on public transit unconstitutional.

morale The general feeling of the people toward such events as a war. Good morale greatly enhances an ability to fight or sacrifice for a cause.

Morgan, J. P. Most celebrated and powerful banker of the late 19th century.

Mormons Members of the Church of Jesus Christ of Latter-Day Saints, founded by Joseph Smith in 1830; the *Book of Mormon* is their Bible.

Mourning War An Indian war often initiated by a widow or bereaved relative who insisted that her male relatives provide captives to repair the loss.

MTV aesthetic Created a relationship between music and visual imagery.

muckrakers Investigative journalists who propelled Progressivism by exposing corruption, economic monopolies, and moral decay in American society.

Munich Conference French and British leaders met with Adolf Hitler in 1938 to avoid war.

My Lai Incident U.S. troops murdered more than 200 civilians, most of them women and children, in the small South Vietnamese village of My Lai in 1968.

napalm Incendiary and toxic chemical contained in bombs used by the United States in Vietnam.

narrowcasting Tactic used by TV programmers to target specific audiences with corresponding shows.

National American Woman Suffrage Association (NAWSA)

National American Women Suffrage Association Organization established in 1890 to promote woman suffrage; stressed that women's special virtue made them indispensable to politics.

National Association for the Advancement of Colored People (NAACP) Organization launched in 1910 to fight racial discrimination and prejudice and to promote civil rights for blacks.

National Recovery Administration (NRA) 1933 attempt to promote economic recovery by persuading private groups of industrialists to decrease production, limit hours of work per employee, and standardize minimum wages.

National Review Magazine started in 1955 by William F. Buckley Jr. that represents conservative opinions and commentary about current events and politics.

National Road A road that attempted to link west and east through the Chesapeake by connecting the Potomac River with the Ohio River at Wheeling, Virginia in 1818.

National Security Act (1947) Reorganized the U.S. military forces within a new Department of Defense, and established the National Security Council and the Central Intelligence Agency.

National Security Strategy of 2002 Denounced terrorist networks and proclaimed that the U.S. had the right to wage war against any force that endangered Americans.

National War Labor Board U.S. government agency that brought together representatives of labor, industry, and the public to resolve labor disputes.

nativism Hostility of native-born Americans toward immigrants.

naturalization Process by which people born in a foreign country are granted full citizenship with all of its rights.

Navajo Signal Corp Navajo Indians who conveyed military intelligence in their native language to preserve its secrecy.

naval stores Items such as pitch, resin, and turpentine that were used to manufacture ships. Most of them were obtained from pine trees.

neoconservatives Group of intellectuals, many of whom had been anticommunist Democrats during the 1950s and 1960s, who came to emphasize hard-line foreign policies and conservative social stances.

neo-Federalists Nationalist Republicans who favored many Federalist economic programs, such as protective tariffs and a national bank.

Neolithic The period known also as the late Stone Age. Agriculture developed, and stone, rather than metal, tools were used.

Neutrality Acts of 1935 and 1936 Legislation that restricted loans, trade, and travel with belligerent nations in an attempt to avoid the entanglements that had brought the United States into the First World War.

neutrality U.S. policy toward World War I from 1914 to 1917 that called for staying out of war but maintaining normal economic relations with both sides.

"New Democrat" Refers to Clinton and his series of political decisions that clashed with the classic democratic viewpoint.

New Freedom Wilson's reform program of 1912 that called for temporarily concentrating government power so as to dismantle the trusts and return America to 19th-century conditions of competitive capitalism.

New Frontier Term used by John F. Kennedy in his 1960 campaign as a reference to what lied ahead for the country. Kennedy spoke of new social programs to rebuild rural communities, increase educational opportunities and improve urban conditions; he also promoted economic growth and more aggressive foreign policy.

New Left 1960s movement that sought to re-orient politics; people were urged to expand their minds and seek alternative ways of living.

New Lights Term used to describe pro-revival Congregationalists.

New Look President Eisenhower's attempt to minimize the military budget by focusing on nuclear weaponry and air power.

New Nationalism Roosevelt's reform program between 1910 and 1912, which called for establishing a strong federal government to regulate corporations, stabilize the economy, protect the weak, and restore social harmony.

New Right A diverse coalition of conservatives that focused on social issues and national sovereignty; they supported the Republican party under the leadership of Ronald Reagan.

New Sides Term used to describe evangelical Presbyterians.

"New Woman" 1890s depiction of women in cartoons, paintings, and short stories as a public figure who was athletic, self-confident, young, and independent.

New York's 369th Regiment Black army unit recruited in Harlem that served under French command and was decorated with the *Croix de Guerre* for its valor.

New-York Magdalen Society Female established society whose mission was to separate prostitutes from male power, pray with them, and convert them to middle-class morality.

nickelodeons Converted storefronts in working-class neighborhoods that showed early short silent films usually lasting 15 minutes, requiring little comprehension of English, and costing only a nickel to view.

Nixon Doctrine Pledged that the U.S. would extend military assistance to anticommunist governments in Asia but would require them to supply their own combat forces.

Nixon, Richard President of the United States (1969–1974) during the final years of the Vietnam War. He resigned the presidency when he faced impeachment for the Watergate scandals.

nonimportation agreements Agreements not to import goods from Great Britain. They were designed to put pressure on the British economy and force the repeal of unpopular parliamentary acts.

Non-Separatists English Puritans who insisted that they were faithful members of the Church of England while demanding that it purge itself of its surviving Catholic rituals and vestments.

normal schools State colleges established to train teachers.

North American Free Trade Agreement (NAFTA) 1994 agreement that aimed to lower or eliminate barriers restricting the trade of goods and services among the United States, Canada, and Mexico.

North Atlantic Treaty Organization (NATO) Established by treaty in 1949 to provide for the collective defense of noncommunist European and North American nations against possible aggression from the Soviet Union and to encourage political, economic, and social cooperation.

Northwest Ordinance Established the Northwest Territory between the Ohio River and the Great Lakes. Adopted by the Confederation Congress in 1787, it abolished slavery in the territory and provided that it be divided into three to five states that would eventually be admitted to the Union as full equals of the original thirteen.

NSC-68 National Security Council Document number 68 (1950) that provided the rationale and comprehensive strategic vision for U.S. policy during the Cold War.

nullification Beginning in the late 1820s, John C. Calhoun and others argued that the Union was a voluntary compact between sovereign states, that states were the ultimate judges of the constitutionality of federal law, that states could nullify federal laws within their borders, and that they had the right to secede from the Union.

Obama, Barack 44th President of the United States and the first president of African descent; voted into office in 2008 with a campaign for "hope" and "change."

Office of War Information (OWI) Created in 1942 by President Roosevelt to coordinate propaganda and censorship.

Old Lights Antirevival Congregationalists.

Old Northwest The region west of Pennsylvania, north of the Ohio River, and east of the Mississippi River.

Old Sides Antirevival Presbyterians.

oligarchy A society dominated by a few persons or families.

Olmec The oldest pre-Columbian high culture to appear in what is now Mexico.

Olmsted, Frederick Law Principal designer of Central Park in New York City.

Onontio An Algonquian word that means "great mountain" and that was used by Indians of the Middle Ground to designate the governor of New France.

Open Door notes (1899–1900) Foreign policy tactic in which the United States asked European powers to respect China's independence and to open their spheres of influence to merchants from other nations.

Open Skies Eisenhower's proposal that U.S. and Soviet disarmament be verified by reconnaissance flights over each other's territory.

open-field agriculture A medieval system of land distribution used only in the New England colonies. Farmers owned scattered strips of land within a common field, and the town as a whole decided what crops to plant.

OVERLORD Massive invasion of Germany that began on June 6, 1944, known as D-Day; this event was the beginning of the end to the war in Europe.

pacifist A person opposed to war or violence. The religious group most committed to pacifism is the Quakers.

Panama Canal An engineering marvel completed in 1914 across the new Central American nation of Panama. Connecting the Atlantic and Pacific oceans, it shortened ship travel between New York and San Francisco by 8,000 miles.

parish A term used to describe an area served by one tax-supported church. The term was used primarily in regions settled by members of the Church of England.

Parks, Rosa African American seamstress in Montgomery, Alabama, who, after refusing to give up her bus seat to a white man, was arrested and fined. Her protest sparked a subsequent bus boycott that attracted national sympathy for the civil-rights cause and put Martin Luther King, Jr., in the national spotlight.

parochial schools Schools associated with a church, usually Roman Catholic. The funding of these schools became a major political issue in the 1850s.

passive civil disobedience Nonviolent refusal to obey a law in an attempt to call attention to government policies considered unfair.

patronage The act of appointing people to government jobs or awarding them government contracts, often based on political favoritism rather than on abilities.

patronships Vast estates along the Hudson River that were established by the Dutch. They had difficulty attracting peasant labor, and most were not successful.

Peace of Paris The 1763 treaty that ended the war between Britain on the one side and France and Spain on the other side. France surrendered New France to Britain. Spain ceded Florida to Britain, and France compensated its ally by ceding all of Louisiana to Spain.

peace without victory Woodrow Wilson's 1917 pledge to work for a peace settlement that did not favor one side over the other but ensured an equality among combatants.

Pearl Harbor Japan's December 7, 1941 attack on a U.S. base in Hawaii that brought the United States into the Second World War.

Penn, William A convert to the Society of Friends in the 1660s, Penn used his friendship with Charles II and James, Duke of York, to acquire a charter for Pennsylvania in 1681, and he then launched a major migration of Friends to the Delaware Valley.

Pentagon Completed in January of 1943, this five-story, five-sided building houses the United States' War Department.

people's capitalism An egalitarian capitalism in which all Americans could participate and enjoy the consumer goods that U.S. industry had made available.

per capita Term used to measure the wealth of a nation by dividing total income by population.

perestroika Russian term describing the economic liberalization that began in the late 1980s.

Perkins, Frances Secretary of Labor under Roosevelt and the first female Cabinet member.

Pershing, John J. Commander of the American Expeditionary Force that began landing in Europe in 1917 and that entered battle in the spring and summer of 1918.

Persian Gulf War Conflict that lasted six weeks in 1991 between the U.S. and Iraq; Bush ordered aid to Kuwait when Saddam Hussein and his armies invaded their land.

personal liberty laws Laws enacted by nine northern states to prohibit the use of state law facilities such as jails or law officers in the recapture of fugitive slaves.

Petraeus, General David Expert on counterinsurgency warfare, recommended into command by Robert Gates.

piedmont A term referring to the land above the fall line but below the Appalachian Mountains.

Pilgrims A pious, sentimental term used by later generations to describe the settlers who sailed on the Mayflower in 1620 and founded Plymouth Colony.

Pitt, William One of the most popular public officials in 18th-century Britain, he was best known as the minister who organized Britain's successful war effort against France in the French and Indian War.

Placemen Appointed office holders who sat in the British Parliament. The Country party in 18th century England lobbied to ban placemen, whom they saw as a threat to the natural balance of the British system of government.

placer mining Mining where minerals, especially gold, were found in glacial or alluvial deposits.

Platt Amendment Clause that the U.S. forced Cuba to insert into its constitution giving the U.S. broad control over Cuba's foreign and domestic policies.

Plessy v. Ferguson 1896 Supreme Court case that sanctioned Jim Crow laws as long as the separate facilities for black and whites were equal.

plumbers Nixon's secret intelligence unit designed to stop information leaks to the media.

Plymouth Founded by Separatists in 1620, Plymouth was England's first permanent colony in New England.

political machines Organizations that controlled local political parties and municipal governments through bribery, election fraud, and support of urban vice while providing some municipal services to the urban poor.

politics of harmony A system in which the governor and the colonial assembly worked together through persuasion rather than through patronage or bullying.

politique A man who believed that the survival of the state took precedence over religious differences.

poll tax A tax based on people or population rather than property. It was usually a fixed amount per adult.

polygamy The act of having more than one wife.

Pontiac An Ottawa chief whose name has been attached to the great Indian uprising against the British in 1763–1764.

Pontiac's War A large group of Indians, including Seneca, Mingo, Delaware, Shawnee, Wyandot, Miami, Ottawa, and other warriors, joined forces in 1763, attacking 13 British posts in the West in hopes to drive British settlers back to the Eastern seaboard.

pools Technique used by railroads to divide up traffic and fix rates, thereby avoiding ruinous competition.

popular sovereignty The concept that settlers of each territory would decide for themselves whether to allow slavery.

postal campaign Abolitionist tactic to force the nation to confront the slavery question by flooding the mails, both North and South, with antislavery literature. Their hope was to raise controversy within an area that was the province of the federal government.

postmillennialism Belief (held mostly by middle-class evangelists) that Christ's Second Coming would occur when missionary conversion of the world brought about a thousand years of social perfection.

postmillennialists Middle-class evangelicals that believed that Christ's Second Coming would occur at the end of 1,000 years of social perfection brought about by the missionary conversion of the world.

powwow Originally, a word used to identify tribal prophets or medicine men. Later it was used also to describe the ceremonies held by them.

praying Indians The Christian Indians of New England.

predestination A theory that states that God has decreed, even before he created the world, who will be saved and who will be damned.

premillennialism A view assumed by Baptists, Methodists, and Disciples of Christ that the millennium would arrive with world-destroying violence, followed by 1,000 years of Christ's rule on Earth.

Presbytery An intermediate level of organization in the Presbyterian church, above individual congregations but below the synod. One of its primary responsibilities was the ordination and placement of ministers.

presidios Military posts constructed by the Spanish to protect the settlers from hostile Indians. They also were used to keep non-Spanish settlers from the area.

Presley, Elvis Known as "the King" of Rock and Roll, he was the biggest pop star of the 1950s.

Primogeniture The right, by law or custom, of the first-born to inherit the entire estate, to the exclusion of younger siblings.

private fields Farms of up to five acres on which slaves working under the task system were permitted to produce items for their own use and sale in a nearby market.

privateers A privately owned ship that was authorized by a government to attack enemy ships during times of war. The owner of the ship got to claim a portion of whatever was captured. This practice damaged any enemy country that could not dramatically increase naval protection for its merchant ships.

Proclamation of 1763 Issued by the Privy Council, it tried to prevent the colonists from encroaching upon Indian lands by prohibiting settlement west of the Appalachian watershed unless the government first purchased those lands by treaty.

Progressive Party Political party formed by Theodore Roosevelt in 1912 when the Republicans refused to nominate him for president. The party adopted a sweeping reform program.

Prohibition Constitutional ban on the manufacture and sale of alcohol in the United States (1920–1933).

proprietary colony A colony owned by an individual(s) who had vast discretionary powers over the colony. Maryland was the first proprietary colony, but others were founded later.

protective tariff Tariff that increases the price of imported goods that compete with American products and thus protects American manufacturers from foreign competition.

Protestant Reformation A religious movement begun by Martin Luther in 1517 that led to the repudiation of the Roman Catholic Church in large parts of northern and central Europe.

provincial congress A type of convention elected by the colonists to organize resistance. They tended to be larger than the legal assemblies they displaced, and they played a major role in politicizing the countryside.

public Friends The men and women who spoke most frequently and effectively for the Society of Friends. They were as close as the Quakers came to having a clergy. They occupied special elevated seats in some meetinghouses.

public virtue Meant, to the revolutionary generation, patriotism and the willingness of a free and independent people to subordinate their interests to the common good and even to die for their country.

Pueblo Revolt In the most successful Indian uprising in American history, the Pueblo people rose against the Spanish in 1680, killed most Spanish missionaries, devastated Spanish buildings, and forced the surviving Spaniards to retreat down the Rio Grande. The Pueblos maintained their autonomy for about a decade, but Spain reasserted control in the early 1690s.

Pullman Strike 1894 Labor strike that became the first nationwide workers' strike against the railroad.

Puritans An English religious group that followed the teachings of John Calvin. They wanted a fuller reformation of the Church of England and hoped to replace The Book of Common Prayer with sermons. They wanted to purify the Church of England of its surviving Catholic ceremonies and vestments.

Quakers A term of abuse used by opponents to describe members of the Society of Friends, who believed that God, in the form of the Inner Light, was present in all humans. Friends were pacifists who rejected oaths, sacraments, and all set forms of religious worship.

quasi-slavery Position that resembled slavery, such as that created by the Black Codes.

quitrent A relic of feudalism, a quitrent was a small required annual fee attached to a piece of land. It differed from other rents in that nonpayment did not lead to ejection from the land but to a suit for debt.

R&D Research and development.

racial profiling Law enforcement practice of using racial appearance to screen for potential wrongdoing.

railhead End of a railroad line, or the farthest point on the track.

railroad gauge Distance between the rails on which wheels of railroad cars fit.

"rainfall follows the plow" Erroneous belief that settlement and cultivation somehow changed the weather. It evolved due to heavier-than-normal precipitation during the 1870s and 1880s.

RAND Think tank developed by the U.S. military to conduct scientific research and development.

Reagan, Ronald Republican president (1981–1989) who steered domestic politics in a conservative direction and sponsored a huge military buildup.

real wages Relationship between wages and the consumer price index.

realism Form of thinking, writing, and art that prized detachment, objectivity, and skepticism.

rebates Practice by the railroads of giving certain big businesses reductions in freight rates or refunds.

recall Reform that gave voters the right to remove from office a public servant who had betrayed their trust.

Red Scare Widespread fear in 1919–1920 that radicals had coalesced to establish a communist government on American soil. In response, U.S. government and private citizens undertook a campaign to identify, silence, and, in some cases, imprison radicals.

redemptioners Servants with an indentured contract that allowed them to find masters after they arrived in the colonies. Many German immigrant families were redemptioners and thus were able to stay together while they served their terms.

redlining Refusal by banks and loan associations to grant loans for home buying and business expansion in neighborhoods that contained aging buildings, dense populations, and growing numbers of nonwhites.

referendum Procedure that allows the electorate to decide an issue through a direct vote.

Refugee Act of 1980 Law allowing refugees fleeing political persecution entry into the United States.

Rehnquist, William Appointed to Chief Justice of the Supreme Court by Reagan in 1986.

religious bigotry Intolerance based on religious beliefs or practices.

religious right Christians who wedded their religious beliefs to a conservative political agenda and gained growing influence in Republican party politics after the late 1960s.

Republic of Texas Independent nation founded in 1836 when a revolution by residents in the Mexican province of Texas won their independence.

republics Independent Indian villages that were willing to trade with the British and remained outside the French system of Indian alliances.

Restoration era The period that began in 1660 when the Stuart dynasty under Charles II was restored to the throne of England. It ended with the overthrow of James II in 1688–1689.

restorationism Belief that all theological and institutional changes since the end of biblical times were manmade mistakes and that religious organizations must restore themselves to the purity and simplicity of the apostolic church.

restraint of trade Activity that prevented competition in the marketplace or free trade.

revival A series of emotional religious meetings that led to numerous public conversions.

revolving gun turret A low structure, often round, on a ship that moved horizontally and contained mounted guns.

rifling Process of cutting spiral grooves in a gun's barrel to impart a spin to the bullet. Perfected in the 1850s, it produced greater accuracy and longer range.

"robber barons" Industrial leaders who began to restrain their displays of wealth and make significant philanthropic contributions to the public.

"Roberts Court" Refers to the Supreme Court after John Roberts became Chief Justice in 2005.

Robinson, Jackie African American whose addition to the Brooklyn Dodgers in 1947 began the lengthy process of integrating Major League Baseball.

rock 'n' roll Form of popular music that arose in the 1950s from a variety of musical styles, including rhythm and blues, country, and gospel. Its heavily accented beat attracted a large following among devotees of the emerging youth culture.

Rockefeller, John D. Founder of the Standard Oil Company, whose aggressive practices drove many competitors out of business and made him one of the richest men in America.

Roe v. Wade Supreme Court decision in 1973 that ruled that a blanket prohibition against abortion violated a woman's right to privacy and prompted decades of political controversy.

rolling stock Locomotives, freight cars, and other types of wheeled equipment owned by railroads.

Roosevelt corollary 1904 corollary to the Monroe Doctrine, stating that the United States had the right to intervene in domestic affairs of hemispheric nations to quell disorder and forestall European intervention.

Roosevelt liberalism New reform movement that sought to regulate capitalism but not the morals or behavior of private citizens. This reform liberalism overcame divisions between southern agrarians and northeastern ethnics.

Roosevelt, Eleanor A politically engaged and effective First Lady, and an architect of American liberalism.

Roosevelt, Franklin D. President from 1933 to 1945 and the creator of the New Deal.

Rough Riders Much-decorated volunteer cavalry unit organized by Theodore Roosevelt and Leonard Wood to fight in Cuba in 1898.

royal colony A colony controlled directly by the English monarch. The governor and council were appointed by the Crown.

Russo-Japanese War Territorial conflict between imperial Japan and Russia mediated by Theodore Roosevelt at Portsmouth, New Hampshire. The peace agreement gave Korea and other territories to Japan, ensured Russia's continuing control over Siberia, and protected China's territorial integrity.

Sacco and Vanzetti Case (1920) Controversial conviction of two Italian-born anarchists accused of armed robbery and murder.

sachem An Algonquian word that means "chief."

Safety-Fund Law New York state law that required banks to pool a fraction of their resources to protect both bankers and small stockholders in case of bank failures.

Salem witch trials About 150 people were accused of witchcraft in Massachusetts between March and September 1692. During the summer trials, 19 people were hanged and one was pressed to death after he refused to stand trial. All of those executed insisted they were innocent. Of the 50 who confessed, none was executed.

Sand Creek massacre Attack led by Colonel John Chivington that killed 200 Cheyenne Indians that returned in peace to their Colorado reservation.

Saratoga A major turning point in the Revolutionary War. American forces prevented John Burgoyne's army from reaching Albany, cut off its retreat, and forced it to surrender in October 1777. This victory helped bring France into the war.

saturation bombing Intensive bombing designed to destroy everything in a target area.

scabs Strikebreakers who were willing to act as replacements for striking workers, thus undermining the effect of strikes as leverage against company owners.

scalawags Term used by southern Democrats to describe southern whites who worked with the Republicans.

scientific management Attempt to break down each factory job into its smallest components to increase efficiency, eliminate waste, and promote worker satisfaction.

secession The act of a state withdrawing from the Union. South Carolina was the first state to attempt to do this in 1860.

"Second Bill of Rights" President Roosevelt's ambition to ensure that Americans could enjoy regular employment, adequate food and shelter, educational opportunities, and health care.

Second Continental Congress The intercolonial body that met in Philadelphia in May 1775 a few weeks after the Battles of Lexington and Concord. It organized the Continental Army, appointed George Washington commander-in-chief, and simultaneously pursued policies of military resistance and conciliation. When conciliation failed, it chose independence in July 1776 and in 1777 drafted the Articles of Confederation, which finally went into force in March 1781.

sedentary Societies that are rooted locally or are nonmigratory. Semisedentary societies are migratory for part of the year.

seditious libel The common-law crime of openly criticizing a public official.

seigneurs The landed gentry who claimed most of the land between Quebec and Montreal. They were

never as powerful as aristocrats in France.

Seneca Falls Convention (1848) First national convention of women's rights activists.

separation of powers The theory that a free government, especially in a republic, should have three independent branches capable of checking or balancing one another: the executive, the legislative (usually bicameral), and the judicial.

Separatists One of the most extreme English Protestant groups that were followers of John Calvin. They began to separate from the Church of England and form their own congregations.

September 11, 2001 Day on which U.S. airliners, hijacked by Al Qaeda operatives, were crashed into the World Trade Center and the Pentagon, killing around 3,000 people.

serfdom Early medieval Europe's predominant labor system, which tied peasants to their lords and the land. They were not slaves because they could not be sold from the land.

Seward, William H. Secretary of State under Abraham Lincoln and Andrew Jackson. He was best known for his purchase of Alaska from Russia.

share wages Payment of workers' wages with a share of the crop rather than with cash.

sharecropping Working land in return for a share of the crops produced instead of paying cash rent.

Shays's Rebellion An uprising of farmers in western Massachusetts in the winter of 1786–1787. They objected to high taxes and foreclosures for unpaid debts. Militia from eastern Massachusetts suppressed the rebels.

Sheppard-Towner Act Major social welfare program providing federal funds for prenatal and child health care, 1921–1929.

Sherman Antitrust Act of 1890 Intended to declare any form of trade restraint illegal, but proved to be useless in prosecution of corporations.

sickle cell A crescent- or sickle-shaped red blood cell sometimes found in African Americans. It helped protect them from malaria but exposed some children to the dangerous and painful condition of sickle cell anemia.

Sir Walter Raleigh An Elizabethan courtier who, in the 1580s, tried but failed to establish an English colony on Roanoke Island in what is now North Carolina.

sit-down strike Labor strike strategy in which workers occupied their factory but refused to do any work until the employer agreed to recognize the workers' union. This strategy succeeded against General Motors in 1937.

sit-in movement Activity that challenged legal segregation by demanding that blacks have the same access to public facilities as whites. These nonviolent demonstrations were staged at restaurants, bus and train stations, and other public places.

Sitting Bull Hunkapapa Lakota (Sioux) chief and holy man who led warriors against the U.S. Army in Montana Territory in 1876, culminating in the Battle of Little Big Horn.

slash and burn A system of agriculture in which trees were cut down, girdled, or in some way destroyed. The underbrush then was burned, and a crop was planted. Men created the farms, and women did the farming. The system eventually depleted the fertility of the soil, and the entire tribe would move to a new area after 10 or 20 years.

Smith, Alfred E. Irish American, Democratic governor of New York who became in 1928 the first Catholic ever nominated for the presidency by a major party.

Smith, John (Captain) A member of the Virginia Council; his strong leadership from 1607 to 1609 probably saved the colony from collapse.

Smith, Joseph Poor New York farm boy whose visions led him to translate the *Book of Mormon* in late 1820s. He became the founder and the prophet of the Church of Jesus Christ of Latter-day Saints (Mormons).

Social Darwinism Set of beliefs explaining human history as an ongoing evolutionary struggle between different groups of people for survival and supremacy that was used to justify inequalities between races, classes, and nations.

social networking sites Internet-based sites that unite communities of people based on similar interests.

Social Security Act Centerpiece of the welfare state (1935) that instituted the first federal pension system and set up funds to take care of groups (such as the disabled and unmarried mothers with children) that were unable to support themselves.

socialism Political movement that called for the transfer of industry from private to public control, and the transfer of political power from elites to the laboring masses.

sodbuster Small farmer in parts of the West who adapted to the treeless plains and prairies, such as the construction of homes out of sod.

soddies Houses built by Great Plains settlers made from prairie sod that was cut into blocks and stacked to form walls.

southern yeoman Farmer who owned relatively little land and few or no slaves.

sovereign power A term used to describe supreme or final power.

space shuttle Manned rocket that served as a space laboratory and could be flown back to the earth for reuse.

Spanish Civil War Conflict between Spain's republican government and nationalist rebels led by General Francisco Franco.

specie Also called "hard money" as against paper money. In colonial times, it usually meant silver, but it could also include gold coins.

Specie Circular Provision added to the Deposit Act in 1836 that required speculators to pay in silver and gold coins when buying large parcels of public land.

spirituals Term later devised to describe the religious songs of slaves.

Spock, Dr. Benjamin Pediatrician who wrote *Baby and Child Care* (1946), the most widely used child-rearing book during the baby-boom generation.

spoils system System by which the victorious political party rewarded its supporters with government jobs.

Sputnik First Soviet satellite sent into orbit around the earth in 1957.

Sputnik Crisis Following Russia's second successful satellite launch, the possibility of nuclear weapons development forced President Eisenhower to expand military arsenal, educational resources, and research capabilities.

stagflation Condition of simultaneous economic stagnation and price inflation.

Stalin, Joseph Soviet communist dictator who worked with Allied leaders during Second World War.

Stamp Act Passed by the administration of George Grenville in 1765, the Stamp Act imposed duties on most legal documents in the colonies and on newspapers and other publications. Massive colonial resistance to the act created a major imperial crisis.

Stanton, Elizabeth Cady Feminist abolitionist who organized the Seneca Falls Convention.

staple crop A crop grown for commercial sale. It usually was produced in a colonial area and was sold in Europe. The first staple crops were sugar and tobacco.

Starr, Kenneth Republican lawyer appointed as independent counsel to investigate possible wrongdoing by President Clinton.

States General The legislative assembly of the Netherlands.

stay laws A law that delays or postpones something. During the 1780s, many states passed stay laws to delay the due date on debts because of the serious economic problems of the times.

steel cargo containers Made shipping goods and raw materials long distances easier and less expensive.

Strategic Defense Initiative (SDI) Popularly termed "Star Wars," a proposal to develop technology for creation of a space-based defensive missile shield around the United States.

Student Nonviolent Coordinating Committee (SNCC) Interracial civil-rights organization formed by young people involved in the sit-in movement that later adopted a direct-action approach to fighting segregation.

"sub-prime mortgages" Mortgages that carried a high risk of defaulting.

subtreasuries Plan to help farmers escape the ruinous interest rates of the crop lien system by storing their crops in federal warehouses until market prices were more favorable. Farmers could draw low-interest loans against the value of these crops.

subversive Systematic, deliberate attempt to overthrow or undermine a government or society by people working secretly within the country.

Sun Belt Southern rim of the United States running from Florida to California.

Sunday schools Schools that first appeared in the 1790s to teach working-class children to read and write but that by the 1820s and 1830s were becoming moral training grounds.

supply-side economics Economic theory that tax reductions targeted toward investors and businesses would stimulate production and eventually create jobs.

sweated Describes a type of worker, mostly women, who worked in her home producing items for subcontractors, usually in the clothing industry.

synod The governing body of the Presbyterian church. A synod was a meeting of Presbyterian ministers and prominent laymen to set policies for the whole church.

table a petition or bill Act of removing a petition or bill from consideration without debate by placing it at the end of the legislative agenda.

Taft-Hartley Act Limited a union's power to conduct boycotts, force employers to hire only union members, and to continue a strike harmful to national security; it also required union officials to sign affidavits stating that they did not belong to the Communist Party.

Taft, William Howard Roosevelt's successor as president (1909–1913), who tried but failed to mediate between reformers and conservatives in the Republican Party.

Tallmadge Amendments Two amendments proposed by James Tallmadge Jr. to be added to the Missouri statehood bill before Missouri's admission to the union; the first barred slaved from being brought into Missouri and the second emancipated Missouri slaves born after admission once they reached their 25th birthday.

tariff A tax on imports.

"Tariff of Abominations" Refers to the protective tariffs passed by the Democratic Congress in 1828 that hurt the South by diminishing exports of cotton and raised prices of manufactured goods.

task system A system of slave labor under which slaves had to complete specific assignments each day. After these assignments were finished, their time was their own. It was used primarily on rice plantations. Slaves often preferred this system over gang labor because it gave them more autonomy and free time.

Taylor, Frederick Winslow Chief engineer at Philadelphia's Midvale Steel Company whose goal was to make human labor mimic the efficiency of a piece of machinery.

Teapot Dome scandal Political scandal by which Secretary of Interior Albert Fall allowed oil tycoons access to government oil reserves in exchange for $400,000 in bribes.

Tecumseh Shawnee leader who assumed political and military leadership of the pan-Indian religious movement began by his brother Tenskwatawa.

tejanos Spanish-speaking settlers of Texas. The term comes from the Spanish word *Tejas* for Texas.

temperance Movement that supported abstaining from alcoholic beverages.

Temporary Assistance to Needy Families (TANF) Program that allowed each state to design its own welfare-to-work programs under general federal guidelines.

tenancy System under which farmers worked land that they did not own.

Tennessee Valley Authority (TVA) Ambitious and successful use of government resources and power to promote economic development throughout the Tennessee Valley.

Tenochtitlán The huge Aztec capital city destroyed by Cortés.

Tenskwatawa Brother of Tecumseh, whose religious vision of 1805 called for the unification of Indians west of the Appalachians and foretold the defeat and disappearance of the whites.

termination and relocation Policies designed to assimilate American Indians by terminating tribal status and relocating individuals off reservations.

Tet offensive Surprise National Liberation Front (NLF) attack during the lunar new year holiday in early 1968 that brought high casualties to the NLF but fueled pessimism about the war's outcome in the United States.

The Medicare Prescription Drug Improvement and Modernization Act 2003 act that created Medicare Part D, a new program that would provide prescription drug benefits for Medicare recipients. The law was controversial because of its enormous cost and because the Federal government was prohibited from negotiating discounts with drug companies.

The Man That Nobody Knows Bruce Barton's best-selling, 1925 book depicting Jesus as a business executive.

"the strenuous life" A time in the 1890s when middle-class and wealthy Americans took great interest in competitive sports, physical fitness, and outdoor recreation.

"the surge" Strategy developed by Robert Gates, temporarily increased U.S. troops in Iraq and placed General David Petraeus in command; reduced the level of civil violence and decreased political tension.

think tank Group or agency organized to conduct intensive research or engage in problem solving, especially in developing new technology, military strategy, or social planning.

Third Reich New empire that Adolf Hitler promised the German people would bring glory and unity to the nation.

Third World Less economically developed areas of the world, primarily the Middle East, Asia, Latin America, and Africa.

Three Mile Island Housed a nuclear power plant in Pennsylvania that experienced a major reactor malfunction in 1979; the industry stopped development following this event.

Tierra del Fuego The region at the southern tip of South America.

tithe A portion of one's income that is owed to the church. In most places, it was one-tenth.

Title IX or Patsy Mink Equal Opportunity in Education Act Required colleges and universities to improve the financing and promotion of women's sports in 1972.

toll roads Roads for which travelers were charged a fee for each use.

tories A term for Irish Catholic peasants who murdered Protestant landlords. It was used to describe the followers of Charles II and became one of the names of the two major political parties in England.

total war New kind of war requiring every combatant to devote virtually all his or her economic and political resources to the fight.

totalitarian movement Movement in which the individual is subordinated to the state and all areas of life are subjected to centralized, total control—usually by force.

Townshend Revenue Act Passed by Parliament in 1767, this act imposed import duties on tea, paper, glass, red and white lead, and painter's colors. It provoked the imperial crisis of 1767–1770. In 1770, Parliament repealed all of the duties except the one on tea.

traditionalists Those who believed that God's word transcended science and that America should continue to be guided by older hierarchies (men over women, whites over nonwhites, native-born over immigrants).

transcontinental railroad Railroad line that connected with other lines to provide continuous rail transportation from coast to coast.

treasury notes Paper money used by the Union to help finance the Civil War. One type of treasury note was known as a greenback because of its color.

Treaty of Guadalupe Hidalgo Treaty that authorized the purchase of California, New Mexico, and a Texas border on the Rio Grande from Mexico for 15 million dollars.

Triangle Shirtwaist Company New York City site of a tragic 1911 industrial fire that killed 146 workers who were unable to find their way to safety.

Triple Alliance One set of combatants in World War I, consisting of Germany, Austria-Hungary, and Italy. When Italy left the alliance, this side became known as the Central Powers.

Triple Entente One set of combatants in World War I, consisting of Britain, France, and Russia. As the war went on, this side came to be known as the Allies or Allied Powers.

Troubled Assets Relief Program (TARP) Section of the Emergency Economic Stabilization act of 2008 that authorized the Treasury Department to spread $700 billing throughout the financial system.

Truman Doctrine Policy established by President Truman in 1947 to aid Greece and Turkey in order to prevent Soviet expansionism and the spread of communism.

Truman, Harry S. Franklin Roosevelt's Vice President who became president when Roosevelt died on April 13, 1945.

trust Large corporations that controlled a substantial share of any given market.

Turner, Nat Baptist lay preacher whose religious visions encouraged him to lead a slave revolt in southern Virginia in 1831 in which 55 whites were killed —more than any other American slave revolt.

Turner's frontier thesis Theory developed by historian Frederick Jackson Turner, who argued that the frontier had been central to the shaping of American character and the success of the U.S. economy and democracy.

Twenty Negro Law Confederate conscription law that exempted from the draft one white man on every plantation owning 20 or more slaves. The law's purpose was to exempt overseers or owners who would ensure discipline over the slaves and keep up production but was regarded as discrimination by nonslaveholding families.

U-2 spy plane Aircraft specializing in high-altitude reconnaissance.

Ulster The northern province of Ireland that provided 70 percent of the Irish immigrants in the colonial period. Nearly all of them were Presbyterians whose forebears had moved to Ireland from Scotland in the previous century. They sometimes are called Scots-Irish today.

Uncle Tom's Cabin Published by Harriet Beecher Stowe in 1852, this sentimental novel told the story of the Christian slave Uncle Tom and became a best seller and the most powerful antislavery tract of the antebellum years.

underconsumptionism Theory that underconsumption, or a chronic weakness in consumer demand, had caused the depression. This theory guided the Second New Deal, leading to the passage of laws designed to stimulate consumer demand.

underground railroad A small group who helped slaves escape bondage in the South. It took on legendary status, and its role was much exaggerated.

UNESCO (United Nations Educational, Scientific, and Cultural Organization) UN organization intended to create peace and security through collaboration among member nations.

unicameral legislature A legislature with only one chamber or house.

Union Leagues Organizations that informed African American voters of, and mobilized them to, support the Republican Party.

Unionists Southerners who remained loyal to the Union during the Civil War.

United Nations (UN) An international organization of Allied powers formed in 1945 to promote peaceful political change and to deter aggressive nations.

Universal Declaration of Human Rights Document adopted by the United Nations in 1948 that established human rights and freedoms as cornerstones of international law.

universal male suffrage System that allowed all adult males to vote without regard to property, religious, or race qualifications or limitations.

urban corridors Metropolitan strips of population running between older cities.

vaqueros Mexican cowboys who rounded up cattle, branded them, and drove them to San Francisco.

vestry A group of prominent men who managed the lay affairs of the local Anglican church, often including the choice of the minister, especially in Virginia.

vice-admiralty courts These royal courts handled the disposition of enemy ships captured in time of war, adjudicated routine maritime disputes between, for example, a ship's crew and its owner, and occasionally tried to decide cases involving parliamentary regulation of colonial commerce. This last category was the most controversial. These courts did not use juries.

Victorianism Moral code of conduct that advocated modesty, sexual restraint, and separate spheres of activity and influence for men and women.

Vietnam War Conflict lasting from 1946 to 1975, with direct U.S. military involvement from 1964 to 1973. Highly controversial, the war devastated the Vietnam countryside, spilled into all of Indochina, and ended in a victory for communist North Vietnam, which then united the country under its rule.

Vietnamization Policy whereby the South Vietnamese were to assume more of the military burdens of the war and allow the United States to withdraw combat troops.

Villa, Francisco ("Pancho") Favored by Woodrow Wilson to be elected Mexico's leader in 1913.

virtual representation The English concept that Members of Parliament represented the entire empire, not just a local constituency and its voters. According to this theory, settlers were represented in Parliament in the same way that nonvoting subjects in Britain were represented. The colonists accepted virtual representation for nonvoting settlers within their colonies but denied that the term could describe their relationship with Parliament.

VJ Day August 15, 1945, day on which the war in the Pacific was won by the Allies.

Voting Rights Act of 1965 Law that provided new federal mechanisms to help guarantee African Americans the right to vote.

Wagner Act (NLRA) Named after its sponsor Senator Robert Wagner (D-NY), this 1935 act gave every worker the right to join a union and compelled employers to bargain with unions in good faith.

Walker, Madame C. J. Black entrepreneur who built a lucrative business from the hair and skin lotions she devised and sold to black customers throughout the country.

walking cities Compact residential areas near working districts with different income and ethnic groups living in close proximity.

Waltham A town in Massachusetts that was the site of the first mill built by the Boston Manufacturing Company in 1813.

War Hawks Members of the 12th Congress, most of them young nationalists from southern and western areas, who promoted war with Britain.

War Industries Board U.S. government agency responsible for mobilizing American industry for war production.

war on terrorism Global effort, adopted after the attacks of September 11, 2001, by the United States and its allies to neutralize international groups deemed "terrorists," primarily radical Islamic groups such as Al Qaeda.

Washington, George A veteran of the French and Indian War, Washington was named commander-in-chief of the Continental Army by the Second Continental Congress in 1775 and won notable victories at Boston, Trenton, Princeton, and Yorktown, where Lord Cornwallis's army surrendered to him in 1781. His fellow delegates chose him to preside over the deliberations of the Philadelphia Convention in 1787, and after the federal Constitution was ratified, he was unanimously chosen the first president of the United States for two terms.

Washington Temperance Society Society established in 1840 by reformed drinkers of the laboring classes who operated separate from the church and converted drinkers through compassion and persuasion.

Washington, Booker T. Founder of Tuskegee Institute and most famous for his controversial speech at the 1895 Atlanta Exposition.

Watergate Business and residential complex in Washington, D.C., that came to stand for the political espionage and cover-ups directed by the Nixon administration. The complicated web of Watergate scandals brought about Nixon's resignation in 1974.

Wells, Ida B. Anti-lynching activist who wrote and spoke in protest, gaining the attention of the North only after taking her campaign to England.

Western development Disproportionate amount of New Deal funds sent to Rocky Mountain and Pacific Coast areas to provide water and electricity for urban and agricultural development.

Western Federation of Miners (WFM) Association of union mine workers established in 1893 to protect their rights.

wheat blast A plant disease that affected wheat and first appeared in New England in the 1660s. There were no known remedies for the disease, and it gradually spread until wheat production in New England nearly ceased.

Wheatley, Phillis Eight-year-old Phillis Wheatley arrived in Boston from Africa in 1761 and was sold as a slave to wealthy John and Susannah Wheatley. Susannah taught her to read and write, and in 1767 she published her first poem in Boston. In 1773, she visited London to celebrate the publication there of a volume of her poetry, an event that made her a transatlantic sensation. On her return to Boston, the Wheatleys emancipated her.

Whigs The name of an obscure sect of Scottish religious extremists who favored the assassination of Charles and James of England. The term was used to denote one of the two leading political parties of late 17th-century England.

Whiskey Rebellion Revolt in Western Pennsylvania against the federal excise tax on whiskey.

whiskey ring Network of distillers and revenue agents that cheated the government out of millions of tax dollars.

White City Monument created for the Columbia Exposition of 1893 in Chicago.

Whitney, Eli The Connecticut-born tutor who invented the cotton gin.

Wilmot Proviso Famous proviso made by Congressman David Wilmot regarding an amendment to an army appropriations bill that framed the national debate over slavery for the next 15 years.

"Wisconsin Idea" Refers to Wisconsin's decision to bring together employers, trade unionists, and professionals and give them power to control relations between industry and labor; many states followed this model.

wolfpacks German submarine groups that attacked enemy merchant ships or convoys.

women's movement Took place between 1953 and 1963; women began speaking out about their political rights, race and gender discrimination, employment opportunities and equitable working environments, and the lack of public roles available to them.

Works Progress Administration Federal relief agency established in 1935 that disbursed billions to pay for infrastructural improvements and funded a vast program of public art.

World Trade Organization Established in 1995 to head international trade between nations.

Wounded Knee Site of a shootout between Indians and Army troops at the Pine Ridge Indian reservation in southwestern South Dakota.

XYZ Affair Incident that precipitated an undeclared war with France when three French officials (identified as X, Y, and Z) demanded that American emissaries pay a bribe before negotiating disputes between the two countries.

Yankee A Dutch word for New Englanders that originally meant something like "land pirate."

yankeephobia Popular term describing strong dislike of the United States, whose citizens were referred to as "yankees," in Latin America.

yellow dog contracts Written pledges by employees promising not to join a union while they were employed.

yellow journalism Newspaper stories embellished with sensational or titillating details when the true reports did not seem dramatic enough.

yeoman A farmer who owned his own farm.

"Young America" movement A group of young members of the Democratic Party who were interested in territorial expansion in the 1840s.

Yorktown The last major engagement of the Revolutionary War. Washington's army, two French armies, and a French fleet trapped Lord Cornwallis at Yorktown and forced his army to surrender in October 1781.

Zenger, John Peter Printer of the *New York Weekly Journal* who was acquitted in 1735 by a jury of the crime of seditious libel after his paper sharply criticized Governor William Cosby.

Zimmerman telegram Telegram from Germany's foreign secretary instructing the German minister in Mexico to ask that country's government to attack the United States in return for German assistance in regaining Mexico's "lost provinces" (Texas, New Mexico, and Arizona).

Zion A term used by the Mormons to describe their "promised land" where they could prosper and live without persecution.

INDEX

AAA. *See* Agricultural Adjustment Administration
Abbott, Edith, 567
ABC television, 780, 875. *See also* Television
Abell, Mary, 487, 489, 497
Abilene, Kansas, 492
Abolition and abolitionism
   education for freedpeople and, 467
   Niagara movement and, 582
   women's rights and, 473
Abortion, 787, 894
   rights to, 869
   right wing and, 838
Abraham Lincoln (ship), 897
Abraham Lincoln Brigade, 717
Accidents. *See also* Safety
   industrial, 525, 547, 777
   in mining, 492
Accommodationism
   failure of, 580–582
   Washington, Booker T., and, 506
Acheson, Dean, 748, 752, 756, 818
Acid rain, 823
Acid-rock music, 813
Acquired immune deficiency syndrome. *See* AIDS
Activism. *See also* Civil-rights movement; Grassroots activism
   African American, 580, 760, 851–852
   American Indian, 792, 852–853
   anti-government, 856–858
   antiwar movement and, 816–817
   Asian American, 855
   civil-rights, 737
   conservative, 838
   environmental, 822–823
   government, 658, 858
   labor, 492, 777
   Lesbian-Gay-Bisexual-Transgendered (LGBT) movement and, 850–851
   mass demonstrations and, 848–849
   Mexican American, 793
   of New Left, 810–811
   Puerto Rican, 792–793
   after Second World War, 759–761
   in Spanish-speaking communities, 792–793, 853–855
   by women, 575–577, 787, 849–850
ACT-UP. *See* "Aids Coalition to Unleash Power"
Adams, Ansel, 737
Adams, Eddie, 809
Adams, Sherman, 770
Addams, Jane, 566–567
   female sexuality and, 567
   immigrant culture and, 560, 567–568

as NAACP founder, 574, 582
   peace movement and, 625
Addiction. *See* Alcohol and alcoholism; Drugs
Adolescents. *See* Youth
Advertising, 779
   of appliances, 769
   of cigarettes, 518
   counterculture and, 813
   expenditures on, 520, 653
   in 1920s, 651–653
   of ragtime music, 553
   in Second World War, 733
   visual imagery in, 520
AFDC. *See* Aid to Families with Dependent Children
Affirmative action, 840, 843, 856
   Johnson and, 824
   Nixon and, 824
Affluence. *See also* Prosperity; Wealth and wealthy
   Beats and, 812
   discontents of, 778–780
   Great Society and, 805
   in post-1953 decade, 774–778
Affluent Society, The (Galbraith), 775, 782
Affordable Health Care for America Act (2010), 904
Afghanistan, 900, 904
   bin Laden and, 896
   Carter and, 837–838
   Soviet withdrawal from, 845
   U.S. aid to, 844
AFL. *See* American Federation of Labor
Africa. *See also* African Americans; North Africa
   famine in, 847
   immigration from, 864
   Tarzan movies and, 610
African Americans. *See also* Civil-rights movement; Slaves and slavery
   activism by, 580, 760, 851–852
   affirmative action and, 840, 856
   alliance movement and, 532
   banjo and, 665
   baseball and, 761
   Black Codes and, 467
   Brown Cases and, 788
   citizenship and, 470
   civil rights for, 788–791
   clubwomen and, 569
   Columbian Exposition and, 543–544
   communities of, 552
   as cowboys, 492, 494
   discrimination against, 671
   election of 1936 and, 701

as Exodusters, 504–505
   FBI and, 754
   after First World War, 643–646
   in First World War, 631
   as "goodwill ambassadors," 791
   Great Railroad Strike and, 526
   Harlem Renaissance and, 674–675
   hip-hop music and, 879
   Homestead Act and, 489
   immigrants and, 672
   Jim Crow laws and, 506, 551
   Ku Klux Klan and, 472, 477–478
   labor of, 551–552
   labor unions and, 527, 528, 731–732
   lynchings of, 505, 569, 582, 590
   Malcolm X and, 814–815
   Malcolm X (movie) and, 815
   in middle class, 506, 840
   migrations by, 487, 504–505, 551, 630, 632 (map), 670–671, 735, 737, 762
   Mississippi Plan and, 480, 481
   movies and, 852, 876
   in New Deal, 706–707
   in New Orleans, 897
   in New South, 504–506
   in 1920s, 670–675
   as officeholders, 475–477
   orchestra of, 583
   in Paris, 675
   in politics, 851–852
   population of (1910), 552 (map)
   in professional sports, 761, 762
   racism toward, 580–581, 582
   rock 'n' roll and, 779
   Second World War and, 730–731, 731–732, 734–736
   segregation of, 472, 734–735, 736
   shifts in population patterns of (1940-1960), 790 (map)
   in Spanish-American War, 601–602
   in sports, 873, 874
   in state constitutional conventions, 473 (map)
   as teachers, 468
   voting and, 464, 465, 469, 471, 482, 507, 789, 791
   westward movement by, 487
   Wilson and, 590
   in women's club movement, 523
   women's organizations of, 849
   working women, 787
   Zoot Suit Riots and, 735
Africanization myth, of southern governments, 477
African Methodist Episcopal (AME) Church, 506

Afrocentric curriculum, 852
Afro-Latinos, in baseball, 761
Age, of American population, 862–864
Agent provocateurs Hoover and, 821
Age of containment, 743–766
Agnew, Spiro, 829
Agrarianism. *See* Agriculture; Farms and
    farming
Agribusiness, 662, 776
Agricultural Adjustment Act (1933), 689
Agricultural Adjustment Administration
    (AAA), 690
Agriculture. *See also* Farms and farming
    big businesses in, 893
    crop lien system in, 504
    depression in (1920s), 661–662
    Eisenhower and, 776–777
    in Great Depression, 690
    immigrant labor in, 547
    Indian rights and, 853
    Japanese Americans in, 549
    labor decline in, 521
    Mexican Americans in, 708
    overproduction and, 759
    pesticides and, 823
    in South, 504
    tariffs on, 684
    union movement and, 854
Agriculture Department, 489, 585, 690
Aguinaldo, Emilio, 606
AIDS, HIV and, 851
"Aids Coalition to Unleash Power"
    (ACT-UP), 851
Aid to Families with Dependent Children
    (AFDC), 822, 841, 849
AIM. *See* American Indian Movement
Air cargo, 870
Aircraft Production Board, 629
Air Force, 746
    in Second World War, 718, 725–726,
        729, 733
Air pollution, 823. *See also* Environment;
    Pollution
Air power
    Earhart and, 656–657
    Lindbergh and, 654
    Second World War and, 718, 725–726,
        728, 729, 733
    women pilots and, 733–734
Air traffic controllers, firing of, 841
Alabama (commerce raider), 475
Alabama, racial violence in, 503, 813
Alabama Claims, 475
Alamogordo, New Mexico, atomic testing at,
    727
Alaska, 534
Albania, 895
Albany & Susquehanna Railroad, 516
Albright, Madeleine, 886
Alcatraz Island, Indian occupation
    of, 852
Alcohol and alcoholism. *See also* Prohibition
    Indians and, 499
    organized crime in 1920s and, 664–665
    progressive reformers and, 568
Alcott, Louisa May, 522

Algeria, 721
Ali, Muhammad, 581, 817
Alien Land Law (California, 1913), 549
Alito, Samuel, 841, 894
All-American Canal, 694, 695 (map)
Allen, Woody, 876
Allende Gossens, Salvador, 827
Alliance for Progress, 785
Alliances. *See also* specific alliances
    ANZUS, 752
    Atlantic Charter and, 719
    in First World War, 621
    NATO, 748, 749 (map)
Allies (First World War), 621. *See also* First
    World War
    U.S. intervention and, 626–628,
        628 (map)
Allies (Second World War). *See also* Second
    World War
    advances and collapse of German power,
        724 (map)
    bombings by, 725–726
    European war and, 717
    Latin America and, 740
    North Africa campaign of, 721
    at Potsdam Conference (1945), 744
    United Nations and, 739
    wartime conferences of, 739–740
All Quiet on the Western Front (Remarque),
    716
al-Qaeda, 896, 900
    Iraq and, 897
Alternating current (AC), 515
"Alternative Budget" (CBC), 852
Altgeld, John P., 530, 567
Amalgamated Association of Iron, Steel, and
    Tin Workers, 529
Amalgamated Clothing Workers, 703
Amazon.com, 870
AME Church. *See* African Methodist
    Episcopal (AME) Church
America First Committee, 718
American Bar Association, 523
American Basketball Association (ABA), 873
American Civil Liberties Union (ACLU),
    Scopes Trial and, 669
American Communist Party (CP), 643, 697
    election restrictions on, 770
    homosexuals and, 755
    labor unions and, 753–754
    movie industry and, 754
    sedition trial and (1949), 756
    Soviet financing of, 746
"American dream," 761
American Economic Association, 523
American Empire, 617
American Enterprise Institute, 838
American Equal Rights Association
    (AERA), 473
American Expeditionary Force (AEF), in
    First World War, 627–628, 631–632
American Federation of Labor (AFL), 528,
    570, 590
    CIO and, 703, 777
    First World War and, 631
    women in, 731

American-Filipino War, 605–607
    casualties in, 605
American Football League (AFL), 873
American Historical Association, 523
American Hospital Association (AHA), 759
American Impressionism, 521
American Independent Party, 820,
    821 (map)
American Indian Movement (AIM), 852
American Indians. *See also* Indian policy;
    specific groups
    activism of, 852–853
    "Bill of Rights" for, 853
    buffalo extermination and, 496, 500
    citizenship for, 791
    Dawes Severalty Act and, 500
    flooding of lands for agriculture and
        ranching, 776
    gambling casinos of, 853
    Ghost Dance and, 501
    Homestead Act and, 489
    land and, 500
    New Deal and, 705–706,
        708–709
    peace policy for, 500
    Relocation program and, 791–792
    reservations for (1875 and 1900),
        499 (map)
    resistance by, 499–500, 501
    Sand Creek massacre and, 500
    schools for, 501, 502
    in Second World War, 735, 736
    Sioux uprising and, 499
    Termination program and, 791, 792
    in trans-Mississippi West, 487, 498–503
    urban and rural population of
        (1940-1960), 792
    as wards of nation, 500
    western water projects and, 776
    westward expansion and, 487
    Wounded Knee massacre and, 500
Americanization
    ethnic groups and, 550, 558
    after First World War, 644
    of immigrant workers at Ford, 580
American Legion, 643
American Medical Association (AMA),
    523, 759
American Museum of Natural History,
    541, 542
American National Exhibition (Moscow),
    775
American nationality
    Bourne and, 559–560
    Kallen and, 559
    Zangwill and, 558–559
American Protective League, 637, 643
American Railway Union (ARU), 530
American Recovery and Reinvestment Act
    (2009), 904
American Smelting and Refining Company,
    536
American Tobacco Company, 517, 597
American Union Against Militarism, 625
"American way of life," Roosevelt, Franklin
    D., and, 732

American Woman Suffrage Association, 473
AmeriCorps, 886
Ames, Adelbert, 480, 481
Amlie, Tom, 696
Amnesty
    for ex-Confederates, 465
    for Vietnam-era draft resisters, 836
Amnesty Proclamation (1865), land for
        freedpeople and, 468
Amsterdam News (newspaper), 737
Amusement parks, 539, 554, 555
Amusements, at Columbian Exposition,
        543, 544
Anacostia Flats, Bonus Army at, 685
Anarchists, 529, 534, 549, 643
    Haymarket bombing and, 528
Ancient Order of Hibernians, 526
Anderson, John, 839
Anderson, Marian, 706–707
Anderson, Sherwood, 600, 676
Andrews Sisters, 735
Angel Island, Asian immigrants on, 546, 547
Anglo-Americans
    Mexican American lands and, 491, 496
    in Texas, 496
Anglo-Saxons
    attitudes of superiority, 522
    Protestant missionaries and, 596–597
    racism and, 665–666
Angola, 844
Animals, production and sale of meats, 893
Annexation, of Puerto Rico, 607
Anshutz, Thomas, 512, 521
Antebellum era. *See also* South
    slave education in, 469
Anthony, Susan B., woman suffrage and,
        473, 575
Antiabortion groups, demonstrations by,
        824, 848
Antiballistic missiles (ABMs), limitations
        on, 825
Anti-Catholicism, 706
Anticommunism
    Carter and, 833, 836
    Eisenhower and, 770
    in entertainment industry, 754
    in film, 742
    homosexuality and, 755
    Johnson, Lyndon B., and, 808
    Kennedy, John F., and, 784, 785
    labor movement and, 753–754
    McCarthy, Joseph, and, 756–757
    of neoconservatives, 838
    Nixon and, 826, 827
    Reagan and, 839, 844
    after Second World War, 740
    Truman and, 745, 754
Antidiscrimination efforts, 760. *See also*
        Discrimination
Antidraft riots, 478
Anti-government activism, 856–858
Anti-immigration sentiment, 490, 579
Anti-Imperialist League, 604
Anti-lynching campaign, 505
Antimonopoly parties, 531
Anti-New Deal coalition, 729

Anti-Saloon League, 568
Anti-Semitism. *See also* Jews and Judaism
    of Coughlin, 696
    immigration and, 545
    in New Deal, 706
    before Second World War, 719
Anti-trust laws, mergers and, 871
Antitrust legislation (1880s and 1890s),
        517–518
Anti-usury laws, 872
Antiwar movements, in Vietnam War, 809,
        810, 816–817, 818, 826, 827–828, 849
Antiwar movies, 716
ANZUS, 752
Apartheid, in South Africa, 752
Appalachia, loans to, 786
APPCON. *See* Asian Pacific Planning
        Council
Appeal to Reason (socialist publication), 570
Appeasement
    of Hitler, 717
    Vietnam War and, 810
Apple computers, 869
Appliances, 775
    advertising of, 769
    consumer, 652–653
Arab-Israeli conflicts, 825
Arab world. *See also* Middle East
    Nasser and, 773
Arapaho Indians, 500
Arbenz Guzmán, Jacobo, covert actions
        against, 772
Arbitration, in UMW strike, 584
Arbuckle, Fatty, 555, 556
Architecture
    Beaux-Arts, 541, 543
    Chicago School of, 542
    City Beautiful, 543
    economic elite and, 539
    skyscrapers and, 539, 540, 542
    of White City, 542–543
Area Redevelopment Bill (1961), 786
*Are Women People? A Book of Rhymes for
        Suffrage Times* (Miller), 577
Argentina, Second World War and, 740
Aristide, Jean-Bertrand, 895
Arizona, 492, 577
Arkansas, 464
    integration in, 791
Armed forces. *See also* Military; Militia;
        specific branches
    blood segregated by, 735
    after Cold War, 845–846
    desegregation of, 760
    Japanese Americans in, 737–738
    Mexican Americans in, 737
    music about, 636
    Native Americans in, 736
    segregation in, 735, 736
    in South Vietnam, 785
Armenia, 638
    immigrants from, 545
Armies of the Night (Mailer), 817
Armistice
    in First World War, 628, 628 (map), 638
    in Spanish-American War, 602

Armistice line, dividing Korea, 751 (map)
Armories, as urban fortresses, 527
Armour (meatpacking), 517
Arms and armaments. *See also* Arms race;
        Weapons
    embargo before Second World War, 717
    limitation on, 660
Arms-control talks, with Soviets, 825
Arms race, 784
    Cold War and, 744, 774
    protests against, 787
    Reagan and, 844
    SALT I and, 825
Arms reduction treaty (1987), 845
Armstrong, Louis, 674, 791
Army Chief of Staff, Eisenhower
        as, 765
Army Corps of Engineers, 776, 777
Army-McCarthy Hearings, 770
Arnold, Henry Harley ("Hap"), 726
Arrowsmith (Lewis), 676
"Arsenal of democracy," U.S. as, 719
Art(s). *See also* Intellectual thought; specific
        arts
    economic elites in cities and, 539
    in Harlem Renaissance, 674–675
    masculinism in, 702
    "New Woman" in, 523, 524
    WPA and, 699, 705
Arthur, Chester A., 507–508
Arthur Murray Dance Studio, strike
        at, 753
Article X (Covenant), of League of Nations,
        639
Artisans, as wage earners, 525
"Aryan race," in Nazi Germany, 716
Asia. *See also* Vietnam War; specific
        locations
    Carter and, 837
    domino effect in, 773
    economic crisis in, 895
    after First World War, 638
    immigration from, 546–547, 555, 864
    post-Second World War settlements in,
        739–740
Asian Americans
    activism of, 848, 855
    movies by, 876
    prejudice against, 614
Asian American studies programs, 855
Asian Law Caucus, 855
"Asian or Pacific Islanders" (API), on
        census, 855
Asian Pacific Planning Council (APPCON),
        855
Asiatic Barred Zone, 635
Assassinations
    of Franz Ferdinand (Austria), 622
    of Garfield, 507
    of Kennedy, John F., 795, 796, 797
    of Kennedy, Robert F., 819
    of King, Martin Luther, Jr., 818
    of Madero, 616
    of McKinley, 584, 609
Assemblies, of Knights of Labor, 527
Assembly line, at Ford, 579–580

Assimilation
    ethnic groups and, 550
    immigrants and, 560
    of Indians, 500, 501, 708–709, 792
Assisted suicide, 894
Associationalism, of Hoover, 659–660
Aswan Dam, 772, 773
AT&T, 651
Atchison, Topeka, and Santa Fe Railroad, 489
Athletics, 522. *See also* Sports
    Title IX and, 824
Atlanta, Georgia, race riots in, 506
Atlanta *Constitution*, 503
Atlanta Exposition, Washington,
    Booker T., at, 506
Atlantic Charter (1941), 719, 739
Atlantic Monthly, The, 565
Atlas Shrugged (Rand), 781–782
Atmosphere, pollution in, 823
ATMs (automated teller machines), 872
Atomic age, 728
Atomic bomb
    Baruch Plan and, 744
    Cold War and, 744
    development of, 727
    Hiroshima, Nagasaki, and, 728
    Soviets and, 748
    testing of, 745, 771
Atomic Energy Commission, 753
Atomic spies, 756
Attica State Prison, protests at, 821
Attorney General's List, of subversives, 746,
    754
Australia
    ANZUS and, 752
    in Second World War, 722, 725
Australian ballot (secret ballot), 573
Austria
    German annexation of, 717
    occupation ended in, 771
Austria-Hungary, 622 640 (map). *See also*
    First World War
    immigrants from, 497, 635
Autobiography (Malcolm X), 815
Automated teller machines. *See* ATMs
Automobiles and automobile industry, 515,
    782
    emissions and, 823
    globalization and, 871
    highways and, 776
    marketing of, 651, 652
    mass production of, 518
    in 1920s, 650
    racing and, 874
    safety issues and, 823
    sales of (1940-1970), 776
    scientific management in, 579–580
    in suburbs, 775
Aviation. *See* Air power
Axis Powers, 717, 740

Babbitt (Lewis), 676
Baby and Child Care (Spock), 786
Baby Boom, 762
    population growth during, 862
    women and, 786

Bachelor girls, 522
Back to the Future (movie), 832
Backyard revolution, 848
Baer, George F., 584
Baghdad, Iraq, 898
Bailout
    of New York City, 835
    of S & Ls, 841
Baker, Ella, 789
Baker, Josephine, 675
Bakke case, 856
Bakker, Jim and Tammy Faye, 881
Balanced budget. *See also* Budget
    Eisenhower and, 776
    as goal, 771
    Kennedy, John F., and, 786
    Keynes and, 782
Balance of trade, 824
Balkan region, in First World War, 622
Ball, George, 807
Ballinger, Richard A., Pinchot controversy and,
    587
Ball parks, 554
Baltic region
    after Second World War, 739
    Soviets and, 717
Baltimore and Ohio Railroad, 525
Banjo, 665
Bank holiday, 689
Banking. *See also* Financial institutions
    changes in, 872–873
    deregulation of, 841
    failures of, 529, 689
    Federal Reserve system and, 589
    Giannini and, 549
    in Great Depression, 694
    Roosevelt, F. D., and, 689
    S & L debacle and, 841
Banking Act (1935), 699
Bank of America, 549, 872
Bankruptcies
    in later 19th century, 514, 529
    of New York City, 835
    personal, 872
    in 2002, 901
Baptists, 778
Bara, Theda, 555, 557
Barrios, 737
Barton, Bruce, 651, 654
Baruch, Bernard, 629–630, 744
Baruch Plan, 744
Baseball, 653, 654, 873
    color line in, 673
    desegregation of, 761
    steroid use in, 874–875
    women's league in, 730
Basie, Count, 674
Bataan, 722
Batista, Fulgencio, 772
Battle of Britain, 718
Battles. *See* specific battles and wars
Bay of Pigs Invasion, 785
Bayonet rule, in South, 478, 480, 483
Bear Stearns, 902
Beatles, 878
Beat movement (1950s), 811, 812

Beaux-Arts architecture, 541, 543
Beef, cattle, in United States
    (1867-1897), 494
Beer-Wine Revenue Act (1933), 689
Begin, Menachem, 837
Behrman, Martin, 550
Beijing, Japan and, 717
Belgium, 622
    Second World War in, 717, 721
Bell, Alexander Graham, 515
Bellamy, Edward, 522
Benefits, for workers, 580, 655, 777, 871–872
Berger, Victor, 571
Berkeley Revolt. *See* University of California
Berkman, Alexander, 534
Berle, Adolph, 687
Berlin
    occupation zones in, 739, 749 (map)
    U.S.-Soviet crisis over, 785
Berlin, Edward A., 553
Berlin, Irving, 553, 636, 705
Berlin Airlift, 747
Berlin Blockade, 747
Berlin Wall, 785, 845, 846
Bernanke, Ben, 901, 902, 904
Bernays, Edward, 651
Berry, Chuck, 779, 780
"Bertha the Sewing Machine Girl; or, Death
    at the Wheel" (Libbey), 554
Beveridge, Albert J., 586
Bible
    gays and, 881
    Protestant fundamentalists on, 667
    Scopes Trial and, 669
Bicycles, 522, 523
Big business. *See also* Business
    Democratic Party and, 702
    Duke and, 597
    mining and, 491–492
    railroads as, 516
    ranching as, 494
    Second World War and, 729–730
Big Four, after First World War, 638
"Big Four" of the Central Pacific, 489, 491
Big government, Clinton on, 887
Big Lebowski, The (movie), 889
Big stick policy, of Roosevelt, T., 614, 615
Big Three, after First World War, 638
Bikini Atoll, atomic testing at, 745
Bilingual education, 822
Bilingualism, Indians and, 853
Bill of Rights, 484
    Second, 732, 757
Billy Graham Evangelistic Association
    crusade, 881
Bin Laden, Osama, 896
Biodiversity, in West, 509
Biotechnology, 869
Bipartisanship, new conservatism and, 781
Birmingham, Alabama
    iron industry in, 503
    racial conflict in, 794
Birth control
    Comstock Law and, 523
    pill for, 787, 849
    Sanger and, 557, 558

Birth of a Nation, The (movie), 479, 665
Bison. *See* Buffalo
Black, Hugo, 738
Blackboard Jungle, The (movie), 779
Black capitalism, Nixon and, 822
Black Codes, 467
Black Hawk Down (movie), 894
Black Hills, Sioux and gold discovery in, 499
"Black Is Beautiful," 816
Black Kettle (Cheyenne chief), 500
Blacklisting
    Mexican American strikers and, 793
    in movie industry, 742, 754
Black Muslims, 814, 815, 879–880
Black nationalist movement (Garvey), 645
Black Panthers, 816, 821
Black Power movement, 814, 816, 827,
    879–880
    Malcolm X and, 814–815
Blacks. *See also* African Americans; Slaves
    and slavery
    Cubans as, 600–601
Black Star Line, 645
Blackwell, Elizabeth, 523
Blaine, James G., 507, 508
Blair, Frank, 474
Bland-Allison Act (1878), 532
Blanket amnesty, for ex-Confederates, 465
"Blaxploitation movies," 852
Blease, Coleman, 696
Bletchley Park, code-breaking at, 721
Blitzkrieg ("lightning war"), 717
Block, Herbert. *See* Herblock (Herbert
    Block)
Blockade(s)
    of Berlin, 747
    in First World War, 624–625
    in Second World War, 726
Block grants, 822
Blues music, 674
Boarding schools, for Indian children, 501,
    502
Board of Indian Commissioners, 500
Body count (Vietnam War), 808–809
Bohemians, as immigrants, 545
Bolling v. *Sharpe*, 788
Bolsheviks and Bolshevism, 627, 643
Bolton, John, 897–898
Bombs and bombings. *See also* Atomic
    bomb; Nuclear weapons
    in Birmingham, 794
    on colleges campuses (1969-1970), 821
    in Haymarket Square, 522, 523, 527–528
    of Iraq, 846
    in Korean War, 750
    of Marine barracks (Lebanon), 844
    in Second World War, 718, 725–726,
        728, 729
    of Vietnam, 806, 808, 821, 826
Bonds, Liberty, 633
Bonneville Dam, 693, 694
Bonnie and Clyde (movie), 765
Bonsack, James Albert, 518
Bonus Army, 685
Book(s). *See also* Literature; Novels
    Nazi burning of, 714

Book-of-the-Month Club, 653
Boom-and-bust cycles, 758
"Boomers," in Indian Territory, 500
Borah, William, Versailles Treaty ratification
    and, 639
Borden, Lizzie, 876
Border(s), immigration and, 547, 893
Borderlands communities, railroads and, 491
Border Patrol, 667, 675
Bork, Robert, 841, 857
Borlaug, Norman, 869
Born-again Christians, Reagan and, 839
Bosnia, 622, 845
Bosnian Muslims, 895
Bosses (political), 550, 573
Boston
    Kennedy family in, 550–551
    strike in, 643
Boston Public Library, 541
Boulder Dam, 693, 694
Bourke-White, Margaret, 732–733, 759
Bourne, Randolph, on cultural exchange,
    559–560
Boxers (China), rebellion by, 608
Boxing, 581, 653
Boycotts
    bus, 789, 790
    against Cuba, 772
    of 1980 Moscow Olympics, 838
    of Pullman cars, 530
BP (British Petroleum), Gulf of Mexico rig
    explosion and, 904
Bracero program, 730, 793
Bradley, Mamie Till, 789
Brady Bill, 886
Brandeis, Louis, 579, 590, 591
Brands, national, 520
Brannan, Charles, 759
Brannan Plan, 759
Brazil, funding of, 827
Breckinridge, John C., 470
Breckinridge, Sophonisba, 567
Brennan, William, 823
Bretton Woods Conference (1944), 739, 825
Briand, Aristide, 661
Bribery, 489, 564
Bridges, steel suspension, 539
Britain, Battle of, 718
British Empire, 617. *See also* Colonies and
    colonization; England (Britain)
    in 1900, 611 (map)
British North America Act (1867), 475
Brookline, Massachusetts, 540
Brooklyn Dodgers, integration of, 761, 762
Brotherhood of Locomotive Firemen, 530
Brotherhood of Sleeping Car Porters, 674
Brown II, 788
Brown, Edmund (Pat), 781
Brown, Herman and George, 702
Brown, James, 816
Brown Cases, 788, 789
Brown v. *Board of Education of Topeka*, 788
Bruce, Blanche K., 476
Bryan, Louise, 644
Bryan, William Jennings, 564, 583, 586, 591
    as anti-imperialist, 604

"Cross of Gold" speech of, 533, 534
    election of 1896 and, 534,
        535 (map)
    election of 1900 and, 534
    election of 1908 and, 586
    First World War and, 625
    Scopes Trial and, 669, 670–671
Bryce, James, 612
Brzezinski, Zbigniew, 836–837
Bubbles (economic), in 1990s and 2000s,
    900, 901–902
Buchanan, Patrick, 838
Buckley, William F., Jr., 781, 782,
    838
Buddhism, 879
    in South Vietnam, 773, 786, 809
Budget. *See also* Balanced budget
    deficits under Reagan, 840
    Eisenhower and, 771
    in First World War, 635
    Great Society programs and, 806
    Kennedy, John F., and, 786
Buffalo
    destruction of, 496, 500, 509
    Plains Indians and, 498
Buffalo Bill Cody's Wild West Show,
    501–503
Buffet, Warren, 902
Bulgaria, 739
Bulgarian immigrants, 545
Bulge, Battle of the, 721
Bulldozing (Democratic intimidation
    techniques), 482, 507
Bull Moose campaign, 587, 590, 591
Bunau-Varilla, Philippe, 612
Bundy, McGeorge, 806
Bunning, Jim, 874
Burchard, Samuel, 508
Bureaucracy
    civil service reform and, 474–475
    in Cold War, 746
    during Second World War, 728
    for western water projects, 776
Bureau of Immigration and Naturalization,
    574
Bureau of Indian Affairs (BIA), 501,
    708–709, 791, 792
Bureau of Reclamation, 694, 776
Bureau of Refugees, Freedmen, and
    Abandoned Lands. *See* Freedmen's
    Bureau
Burger, Warren, 823, 841
Burger Court, 823, 824, 829
Burleson, Albert, 590, 638
Burnham, Daniel, 543
Burroughs, Edgar Rice, 610
Bush, George H. W., 841, 881
    as CIA director, 838, 842
    Cold War end and, 845
    economy and, 843
    election of 1980 and, 839
    election of 1992 and, 842, 848, 887
    foreign policy of, 845–847, 894
    Iran-*contra* and, 845
    Persian Gulf War and, 846
    presidency of, 842–843

Bush, George W., 846, 874, 906
    conservatism of, 892–893
    economy and, 901–902
    election of 2000 and, 890–891
    election of 2004 and, 892–893
    immigration policy and, 893
Bush Doctrine, 896, 897
Bush v. *Gore*, 891
Business. *See also* Big business
    African American, 551–552
    changes in, 869–872
    conservative leaders in, 838
    in First World War, 629–630
    foreign markets for, 597–598
    FTC and, 590
    in 1920s, 654
    Nixon and, 822
    organization of, 516–517
    overseas, 660
    politics of, 658–661
    progressivism and, 579–580
    in Second World War, 729–730
    vertical integration and, 516
    women in, 849
Business cycle
    corporations and, 516
    immigration and, 546
Business Roundtable, 838
Busing, for school integration, 822
Butte, Montana, mining in, 492
Byrds, The, 813

Cabinet (presidential)
    of Clinton, 886
    of Grant, 475
    of Obama, 903–904
    of Roosevelt, F. D., 718
    of Truman, 747
    of Wilson, 590
    women in, 702
Cable television, 874, 875. *See also*
      Television
    MTV and, 876–877
    public affairs broadcasting on, 878–879
California, 577
    anti-Asian sentiment in, 614
    Chinese immigrants in, 490–491
    election of 1964 and, 804
    gay marriage in, 894
    high-tech industries in, 863
    immigration in, 544, 547, 865
    irrigation projects in, 777
    Japanese Americans in, 549
    Latinos in, 737
    Mexican-American lands in, 494–495
    Mexicans in, 488, 675, 793
    open housing in, 804, 814
    population growth in, 863
    radical third party in, 697
    Reagan as governor of, 839
    water projects in, 695 (map)
California Gold Rush, 490, 491, 497
Californios, 494–495, 496, 675
Calley, William, 826
Cambodia, 773, 826, 836, 844
    immigrants from, 865

Cameron, Lucy, 568
"Campaign of Truth" (Truman), 752
Campaigns (political). *See* Political
      campaigns
Camp David Peace Talks (1978), 837
Campus Crusade for Christ, 782
Canada. *See also* French Canada
    in NAFTA, 847
    in NATO, 748
    Treaty of Washington and, 475
Canals. *See also* Panama Canal
    irrigation, 776, 777
    trans-Isthmian, 615
Canal Zone. *See* Panama Canal Zone
Cancer
    environmental agents and, 823
    nuclear testing and, 771
Capital (financial)
    labor and, 513, 527, 643
    for New South industrialization, 503
    for railroads, 516
    southern investment of, 477
Capitalism, 775. *See also* Market economy
    black, 822
    IWW and, 570
    in 1920s, 651
    Roosevelt, F. D., and, 701
    welfare, 654
Capone, Al, 551, 664, 665
Capra, Frank, 700, 704, 732
CAPs. *See* Community Action Programs
Cardozo, Francis L., 476
Caribbean Basin Initiative, 844
Caribbean region
    as American sea, 608
    blacks from, 671
    dollar diplomacy in, 615
    U.S. military in, 661
    Wilson's foreign policy in, 616
Carlisle School, 501
Carmichael, Stokely, 816
Carnegie, Andrew, 521
    as anti-imperialist, 604
    "Gospel of Wealth" of, 517, 534
    philanthropy of, 517, 535
    steel industry and, 516, 517, 643
Carnegie foundations, 535
Carnegie Hall, 535, 583
Carnegie Institute (Carnegie-Mellon
      Univertity), 535
Carnegie Steel Company, 514, 516
    Homestead strike and, 514, 529
Caroline Islands, 740
Carpetbaggers, 471, 477, 480
Carranza, Venustiano, 616–617
Cars. *See* Automobiles and automobile
    industry
Carson, Rachel, 823
Cartels (business), 516
Carter, James Earl ("Jimmy"), 833
    African Americans and, 852
    Camp David Accords and, 837
    economy and, 835–836
    election of 1976 and, 834, 835 (map), 852
    election of 1980 and, 837, 838, 839,
      839 (map), 845

evangelicals, fundamentalists, and, 839
    foreign policy of, 836–838
    human rights and, 836, 837
    presidency of, 834
Carter family, country music and, 663
Cartoons. *See also* Political cartoons
    in Second World War, 732
Casablanca meeting (1943), 721
Casey, William, CIA under, 844
"Cash-and-carry" provision, in Neutrality
    Act (1937), 717
Cash crops, cotton as, 504
Cash indemnity, to Japanese Americans, 736
Castro, Fidel, 784, 785, 844
    Bay of Pigs and, 785
    Cuban Americans and, 864
    Cuban Revolution by, 772
Casualties. *See* specific battles and wars
Catalogues, mail-order, 520, 532
Catholicism
    abortion and, 838
    environmental movements and, 881
    ethnicity and, 669–670
    of immigrants, 545
    of Kennedy, John F., 783
    Klan and, 666
    McCarthy, Joseph, and, 757
    presidency and, 670, 673
    Roosevelt, F. D., administration and, 702
    of Spanish-speaking peoples, 496
Catholic Worker magazine, 783
Catt, Carrie Chapman, 577, 625
Cattle, 492, 493, 494
Cattle drives, 492–493, 493 (map)
CBC. *See* Congressional Black Caucus
CBS television, 780, 875. *See also* Television
CCC. *See* Civilian Conservation Corps
CDO. *See* Collateralized debt obligation
CDs, 878
Celebrities, in 1920s, 653–654
Censorship, in Second World War, 733
Census
    frontier line and, 509
    Hispanic label in, 854
    subcategories on, 855
Central America
    immigrants from, 855
    leftist insurgencies in, 845
    navy and, 598
    Panama Canal in, 610–612
    United Fruit in, 615
    U.S. military in, 661
Central High School, Little Rock, integration
    of, 791
Central Intelligence Agency (CIA), 746, 752.
    See also Covert operations
    Bay of Pigs Invasion and, 785
    Bush, George H. W., and, 838, 842
    Noriega and, 846
    Third World communism and, 772, 773
Central Pacific Railroad, 486, 489, 490
Central Park (New York City), 541, 542
Central Powers, 624, 625. *See also* Triple
    Alliance
Central Valley Project, 694
Century (magazine), 521

Century of Dishonor, A (Jackson), 500
CETA. *See* Comprehensive Employment and
    Training Act
Chain businesses, 869–870
"Challenge of Peace, The" (Conference of
    Catholic Bishops), 881
Challenger shuttle, 863
Chambers, Whitaker, 754
Chaney, James, 803
Channel surfing, 875
Chaplin, Charles, 653
Chase, C. (songwriter), 879
Chase, William Merrit, 521
Chase Manhattan, 873
Chavez, Cesar, 854
"Cheap oil" policy, 841
Chemical warfare, in Vietnam, 808
Cheney, Richard ("Dick"), 890, 892, 897
Cherokee Indians, 498
Cheyenne Indians, 499, 500
Chiang Kai-shek. *See* Jiang Jieshi
Chicago, 835
    African Americans in, 551, 671
    Columbian Exposition in, 542–544
    Democratic presidential voting by ethnic
        groups in, 671
    Harrison, Carter, in, 572
    Haymarket bombing in, 522, 523,
        527–528
    Hull House in, 566–567
    innovation and conflict in, 542
    meatpacking industry in, 492, 547, 551,
        570
    Mexican American mural art in, 854
    Operation PUSH in, 852
    organized crime in, 551, 664, 665
    population growth in, 540
    Pullman strike in, 529–530
    race riot in (1919), 645
    saloons in, 568–569
    typhoid epidemic in, 541, 542
    water and sewage systems in, 540–541
Chicago Daily Tribune, 1948 election and,
    747
Chicago Defender, 630
Chicago Fire (1871), 541
Chicago School, 542
Chicanismo, 854
Chicano/a, 708, 787, 849, 854. *See also*
    Mexican Americans
Chickasaw Indians, 498
Chief Joseph (Nez Percé), 500
Chief Justice. *See* Supreme Court (U.S.);
    specific justices
Child, Lydia Maria, 521
Child care, 734, 786
Child labor
    federal outlawing of, 591, 702
    immigrant, 547
    Kelley, Florence, and, 567
    in southern textile industry, 504
    in sweatshops, 549
Children. *See also* Families; Schools
    African American, 840
    immigrant, 544, 546, 549, 550
    Indian, 501, 502

mothers and, 786
in poverty, 841
in Second World War war effort, 730,
    731
Spock and, 786
Children's Bureau, 702
"Children's crusade," of McCarthy, Eugene,
    818
Chile
    covert actions in, 827
    Second World War and, 740
China
    business investment in, 597
    Carter and, 837
    civil war in, 724–725, 748
    communism in, 748
    diplomatic relations with, 837
    immigrants excluded from, 491, 546,
        666–667
    immigrants from, 487, 488, 490, 491, 544,
        546–547
    Japan and, 613–614, 717, 719, 725
    Korean War and, 751
    markets in, 895
    Nixon and, 825
    Open Door policy toward, 608, 660
    sexual slavery of women from, 497
    U.S. trade with, 615
    Vietnam and, 773, 808, 809
"China lobby," 748
China Syndrome, The (movie), 836
Chinatown, San Francisco, 490, 491
Chinese Americans, 855
    tongs and, 551
Chinese Exclusion Act (1882), 491, 546
Chinese laborers
    Homestead Act and, 489
    prejudice and discrimination against,
        490–491
    railroads and, 486, 490
Chinese Revolution (1911), 615
Chisholm Trail, 493
Chivington, John, 500
Chlorofluorocarbons (CFCs), 895
Choctaw Indians, 498
Choice, Not an Echo, A (Schlafly), 787
Christian entertainment, 881
Christianity. *See also* Evangelicals and
    evangelicalism; Missions and
    missionaries; Religion
    fundamentalism in, 667–668
    vs. science, 668
Christmas bombing, of Vietnam (1972), 826
Chu, Steven, 904
Church(es). *See also* Church and state;
    Religion
    immigrant, 549
Church, Frank, 827
Church and state, separation of, 839, 882
Churchill, Winston, 721, 727
    Atlantic Charter and, 719
    at Casablanca, 721
    "Iron Curtain" and, 744
    postwar spheres of influence and, 739
Church of Jesus Christ of Latter-Day Saints.
    See Mormons

CIA. *See* Central Intelligence Agency
Cigarettes, 503. *See also* Tobacco and
    tobacco industry
    Duke and, 517, 518
CIO. *See* Committee for Industrial
    Organization; Congress of Industrial
    Organizations
Cisneros, Henry, 854
Cisneros, Salvador, 602
Cities, 865–867. *See also* Metropolitan areas;
    Town(s); Urban areas; specific
    locations
    African Americans in, 788–789
    air pollution in, 823
    American Indians in, 791–792
    commercial culture in, 539
    corruption in, 541, 550–551
    cultural institutions in, 541
    elites in, 539, 540–544
    farm culture vs., 662
    growth of, 539
    immigrants in, 538
    municipal reform and, 572–573
    in 1920, 664
    race riots in, 813–814
    racism in, 645
    residential areas and, 540
    restoration in, 866–867
    Second World War bombing of,
        725–726, 729
    segregation of blacks in, 789
    socialist mayors and other officers in,
        570, 571 (map)
    strikes in, 753
    transportation in, 540
    urban cores in, 540
    urban renewal and, 793, 805
    walking, 540
    water and sewage systems in, 540–541
    working class in, 539
Citigroup, 872
Citizens and citizenship
    Asian immigrants and, 546
    Chinese laborers and, 489
    education for, 669
    Filipino Americans and, 855
    Fourteenth Amendment and, 470
    freedpeople and, 470
    immigrants and, 574, 575
    Indians and, 500, 791
    in Puerto Rico, 607
    requirements for, 574
    slaves of five civilized tribes and, 498
City Beautiful movement, 543
City commission plan, 572, 573
City manager plan, 572, 573
Civic organizations, of black middle class,
    506, 523
Civil disobedience
    King and, 791
    against Lawrence Livermore National
        Laboratory, 848
Civilian(s), in Second World
    War, 718, 726
Civilian Conservation Corps (CCC),
    690, 729

Civil libertarians
    on Japanese-American internment, 736
    Reagan and, 841
    Truman and, 746, 753
Civil liberties. *See also* Civil rights;
    Liberty(ies)
    in Second World War, 738
Civil rights. *See also* Civil-rights movement;
    Liberty(ies); Rights
    for American Indians, 791–792
    Eisenhower and, 791
    failure of accommodationism and, 580–582
    Fourteenth Amendment and, 470
    Goldwater and, 803–804
    Johnson, Lyndon B., and, 801–802,
        815–816
    Kennedy, John F., and, 784, 793–795, 797
    law protecting, 478
    NAACP and, 582–583
    in New Deal, 706–707
    Nixon and, 822
    politics of, 791
    religion and, 778
    Roberts Court on, 894
    Roosevelt, Eleanor, and, 737
    in Second World War, 736–738
    for Spanish-speaking people, 792–793
    Truman and, 747, 758, 759–761
Civil Rights Act
    of 1875, 481, 482
    of 1957, 791
    of 1964, 482, 802–803, 804, 850
    of 1968, 816, 852–853
Civil rights bills
    in congressional Reconstruction, 469, 470
    of Kennedy, John F., 794
Civil Rights Cases (1883), 481
Civil rights commission (1946), 760
Civil-rights laws, in states, 482
Civil-rights movement(s)
    American Indian, 791–792
    of Spanish-speaking people, 792–793
Civil-rights movement (African American),
    789, 815–816. *See also* Civil rights
    beginning of, 582
    Brown Cases and, 788
    demonstrations in, 794
    electoral politics and, 852
    Freedom Summer and, 803
    gender equality and, 849
    Malcolm X and, 814–815
    media and, 813–814
    Montgomery bus boycott and, 789
    in 1960s, 793–795, 852
    Till murder and, 789
    Truman and, 759–761
Civil-rights workers, deaths of (1964), 803
Civil service
    reform of, 474–475, 507–508
    in Wisconsin, 578
    women in, 787
Civil service commission, of Grant, 475
Civil war(s)
    in China, 724–725, 748
    in Greece, 745
    in Spain, 717

Civil War (U.S.). *See also* Confederacy;
    Reconstruction
    Indians in, 498
Civil Works Administration (CWA), 690
Clamshell Alliance, 848
Clan Na Gael, 549
Clark, Champ, 588
Clark, Tom, 754
Clarke, Edward H., 523
Class conflict, advocates of, 557
Classes. *See also* Elites; Planters and
    plantations; specific groups
    demarcation of, 521
    distinctions in late 19th century,
        521–522
Clay, Cassius Marcellus, Jr. *See* Ali,
    Muhammad
Clayton Antitrust Act, 589–590
Clean Air Act (1970), 823
"Clear and present danger," national security
    and, 756
Cleaver, Eldridge, 816
Clef Club, 583
Clemenceau, Georges, in Big Four, 638
Cleveland (city), Johnson, Tom, in, 572
Cleveland, Grover, 533, 583
    as anti-imperialist, 604
    Cuba and, 599
    election of 1884 and, 507, 508
    election of 1888 and, 507
    election of 1892 and, 507, 508
    Hawaii and, 599
    Panic of 1893 and, 532
    Pullman strike and, 530
    tariff issue and, 508
Cleveland Indians, 761
Clifford, Clark, 818
Climate
    of Great Plains, 497
    warming of, 900
Clinton, Hillary Rodham
    healthcare and, 887
    as Secretary of State, 903–904
    Whitewater and, 887
Clinton, William Jefferson ("Bill"),
    886–890, 906
    economic policy and, 900–901
    election of 1992 and, 848, 886
    election of 1996 and, 887–888
    foreign policy of, 894–895
    globalization and, 895
    Gore, election of 2000 and, 890–891
    impeachment of, 888–890
    international environmental issues and,
        895–896
    Republican confirmation of appointees,
        894
    stem cell research and, 869
    trade agreements and, 895
"Closed shops," 753
Clothing and clothing industry
    of flappers, 653
    Jews in, 549
    "New Woman" and, 523
Clubwomen, 569
CNN, 875, 878

Coal and coal industry, 514, 836
    film about, 526
    industrial accidents in, 492, 525, 547
    in 1920s, 655
    strike in, 584
Coalition force, in Gulf War, 846
Coca-Cola, 729, 870
Code-breaking, in Second World War, 721
Cody, Buffalo Bill, 501–503
Coeur d'Alene, Idaho, mining strike at, 492
Coffy (movie), 852
Cohen, Ben, 702
Cold War. *See also* Communism;
    Containment; National Security;
    Soviet Union
    Berlin Blockade and, 747
    business expansion during, 870
    deportation of immigrants in, 754
    economic growth and, 758
    Eisenhower and, 769, 771, 774
    election of 1952 and, 765–766
    end of, 833, 845
    funding of anticommunist regimes in,
        816, 827, 837
    Korean War and, 748–753, 751 (map)
    military expenditures in, 752–753
    movies in, 763–765
    national security after, 845–847
    Nixon and, 825
    NSC-68 and, 748–749, 752
    onset of, 744–748
    Reagan and, 833, 843, 844–845
    segregation in, 760–761
    space race and, 783
    spying in, 746, 756
    Truman Doctrine and, 745
    U.S. racial discrimination and, 791
Cole (ship), 896
Colfax Massacre, 478
Collateralized debt obligation (CDO), 873
Collective bargaining, 527
    IWW and, 570
Collier, John, 709
Colombia, Panama Canal and, 610, 612
Colonial economy, of South, 504
Colonies and colonization. *See also*
    American Indians
    after First World War, 637–638
    in 1900s, 611 (map)
    Philippines as, 603–604
    after Second World War, 740
    U.S. Latin American, 611 (map)
Colorado, 491, 500
    woman suffrage in, 575
Colored Farmers' Alliance, 532
Color line, in baseball, 761
Columbian Exposition (Chicago, 1893),
    542–544, 554
Columbia River, 694
Comedy, in films, 555, 556
Comics, juvenile delinquency and, 779
Commerce. *See* Business; Corporations;
    Trade
Commerce and Navigation, Treaty of
    (U.S.-Japan), 720
Commerce raiders, 475

Commercial banks, S & L debacle and, 841
Commercial culture, 539, 554–555, 780
Commission on Civil Rights, 791
Commission on Human Rights (UN), 739
Committee against Anti-Asian Violence, 855
Committee for a Sane Nuclear Policy (SANE), 787
Committee for Industrial Organization (CIO), 703. *See also* Congress of Industrial Organizations
Committee on Public Information (CPI), in First World War, 633–635
Committee on Racial Equality (CORE), 737. *See also* Congress on Racial Equality
Committee on the Present Danger, The (CPD), 838
Committee to Defend America by Aiding the Allies, 719
Commodities Futures Modernization Act (2000), 901
Commodity Credit Corporation (1930s), 532
Common people. *See also* Popular culture
Democratic Party and, 702
Commons, John R., 578, 579
Commonwealth Builders (Washington), 697
Communes, in 1960s, 813
Communications
deregulation of industry, 856–857
digital technology for, 861
government control of, 532
in Second World War, 725
Communism. *See also* Anticommunism; Cold War; Containment; Soviet Union
Castro and, 772
in China, 725, 748
domino theory and, 773, 808
Eisenhower Doctrine and, 773
Great Fear and, 755, 756
in Greece, 745
in Indochina, 752
Korean War and, 750
labor unions and, 753–754
McCarthyism and, 756–757
movie industry and, 754
Nazis and, 719
in Nicaragua, 837
overseas movements and, 752
in Third World, 772–774
in Vietnam, 773
Communist Control Act (1954), 770
Communist Party (CP). *See* American Communist Party; Communism
Communities
African American, 552
borderlands, 491
ethnic, 549–551
Spanish-speaking, 853–855
Communities Organized for Public Service (COPS), 854
Community Action Programs (CAPs), 805, 806
Community Reinvestment Act (1977), 867
Community Service Organization (CSO), 760

Competition
athletic, 522
corporate restraints on, 516–518
from foreign business, 872
railroads and, 531
Comprehensive Employment and Training Act (CETA, 1973), 836, 852
Compromise of 1877, 483–484
Computers. *See also* Digital technology; High-tech industries; Internet
business operations and, 869–870
personal computer and, 868
Second World War and, 721
Comstock Law (1872), 523
Comstock Lode, 491, 492
Concentration camps, Nazi, 719
"Concert of Negro Music," 583
Coney Island, 554, 555
Coney Island (film), 556
Confederacy (Civil War). *See also* Civil War (U.S.)
Indians and, 498
wartime reconstruction and, 464
Confederate States of America. *See* Confederacy (Civil War)
Conference of Catholic Bishops, 881
Conformity, 778–779
Congo, Lumumba in, 773
Congress (U.S.). *See also* Elections; specific branches
African Americans in, 476, 507, 852
corruption in, 474
ex-Confederates in, 466
Iran-*contra* affair and, 845
Johnson, Andrew, and, 469, 472
locally-based activism and, 848
Nixon impeachment and, 829
political stalemate and, 507
racial issues and, 791
Southern Manifesto in, 789
Taft, William Howard, and, 587
Truman and, 756
Congressional Black Caucus (CBC), 852
Congressional Reconstruction, 469–472
Congressional Union, 577
Congress of Industrial Organizations (CIO), 703, 731, 754, 777
Congress on Racial Equality (CORE), 737, 793
Conover, Willis, 771
Conqueror, The (movie), 771
Conscience of a Conservative, The (Goldwater), 781
Conscience Whigs, 508
Consciousness-raising sessions, for women, 849
Conscription. *See* Draft (military)
Conservation, 895
of energy, 836
of land, 904
movement, 509, 585
Conservation Reserve Program, 895
Conservatives and conservatism. *See also* New Right; Religious Right
abortion rights and, 824
Bush, George W., and, 892–893

civil-rights movement and, 813
Cuban Americans and, 855
cultural, 567–569
economy and, 835
election of 1964 and, 802–804
environment and, 585
ERA and, 823
feminism and, 849
gay marriage and, 894
Goldwater and, 804–805
immigrants and, 558
new conservatism, 781–782, 787, 803
new sexuality and, 557
of progressives, 567–569
Reagan and, 842
Second World War and, 719
support for Franco, 717
on Supreme Court, 841
Consolidation
in banking industry, 841
of corporations, 516–518
Conspicuous consumption, 520
Constitution(s)
disfranchising southern blacks, 506
in states during Reconstruction, 466, 471, 472
Constitution (U.S.). *See* specific Amendments
Constitutional conventions
black and white participation in (1867-1868), 473 (map)
in South, 471, 472
Constitutional governance, Watergate and, 829
Construction industry
Italians in, 549
technological advances in, 540
Consumer credit, 651, 872
Consumer culture, 520, 812
Internet shopping and, 870
in 1920s, 650–651
urban vs. rural, 662–664
Consumer goods, 520, 728, 774
Consumer movement, 823
Consumption
conspicuous, 520
culture of, 520, 523–525
Container shipping, 870
Containment, 769, 818
election of 1952 and, 765
Johnson, Lyndon B., and, 810, 818
Kennan and, 745
Kennedy, John F., and, 795
in Korea War era, 752
Third World and, 772–774
Truman's Loyalty Program and, 746
Contraception. *See* Birth control
Contracts
bracero program and, 793
with craft unions, 528
defense, 753
free-labor, 467
government, in Second World War, 730
Justice Department and, 760
yellow dog, 655

Contract with America, 887
Contras (Nicaragua), 844
   Iran-*contra* controversy and, 845
Conventions. *See* Political conventions
Cooke, Jay, 480, 516
Coolidge, Calvin, 660
   on business, 654, 658
   election of 1924 and, 659, 670
   maldistribution of wealth and, 684
   postwar riots and, 643
Cool Million, A (West), 686
Cooperative movement, 812
Cooperatives
   farm, 531, 532
   worker, 527
Cooper v. *Aaron*, 791
Coordinator of Inter-American affairs, 737
Coors, Joseph, 838
Copper, mining of, 492
Copperheads, 507
COPS. *See* Communities Organized for
    Public Service
Coral Sea, Battle of the, 722
Corcoran, Thomas ("Tommy the
    Cork"), 702
CORE. *See* Congress on Racial Equality
Corning Glass Company, 775
Corporate culture, 778
Corporate order
   in later 19th century, 513
   of post-Civil War era, 512
   social costs of, 522
Corporations. *See also* Business; Trusts
   businesses organized as, 516
   consolidation of, 516–518
   "countervailing power" and, 778
   cultural impact of, 520–522
   in First World War, 632
   government regulation and, 585
   government support for, 516
   group insurance plans for, 732
   growth of, 514
   Homestead Act and, 489
   management revolution and, 518–520
   mass production and, 518
   merger movement and, 517
   mining, 491
   multinational, 597
   municipal transportation and, 572
   in 1920s, 651
   in 1950s, 774
   power of, 509, 585–586, 588
   Roosevelt, T., and, 584
   in Second World War, 729–730
   support for Roosevelt, F. D., 702
   technological innovation and, 515
   workers in, 521, 523–530, 654
Corregidor, 722
Corridos, 675
Corruption, 566
   in Chicago, 542
   in cities, 541, 564
   financial, 841
   in Grant Administration, 474
   Harding and, 658
   Homestead Act and, 489

in New York (state), 579
   organized crime and, 551
   political machines and, 474, 550–551
   progressives and, 562, 563, 579
   in railroad boom, 489–491
   in South, 477, 480, 482
Cortes, Ernesto, Jr., 854
Cosmopolitanism, of Bourne, 560
Cost(s). *See also* Price(s)
   of municipal reform, 572–573
Cost-accounting methods, 519
Costa Rica, United Fruit in, 615
Cotton and cotton industry, 530. *See also*
    Textiles and textile industry
   in New South, 503, 504
   overproduction in, 504
   value of output, 656
Coughlin, Charles (Father), 695–696
Council of Economic Advisers, 757
Counterculture, 817
   media and, 812–813, 817
"Countervailing power," 778
Country music, women singers and, 663
Coups
   in Egypt, 772
   in Iran, 772, 837
   in Russia, 845
   in South Vietnam, 795
Court(s). *See also* Supreme Court (U.S.)
   affirmative action and, 856
   during Great Fear, 756
   HUAC and, 754
   labor unions and, 528
Court-packing proposal, by
    Roosevelt, F. D., 711
Court TV (truTV), 888
Cousins, Norman, 702
Covenant (Article X), of League of Nations,
   639
Covert operations, 746
   against Cuba, 785
   eavesdropping and, 757
   Eisenhower and, 771
   in Latin America, 772
   Nixon and, 827
   Reagan and, 844
   in Vietnam, 773
Cowboys
   African American, 492, 494
   cattle drives and, 492
   strikes by, 492
   vaqueros as, 494
Cox, Archibald, 829
Cox, James M., 658
Coxey, Jacob, 529
Coxey's army, 529
CPD. *See* Committee on the Present
    Danger, The
Craft unions, 528, 530
   labor unrest and, 525
Cramer, Charles, 658
Crazy Horse (Sioux leader), 499
Credit
   consumer, 651
   crop lien system and, 504
   economic decline of 2000s and, 902

for farmers, 504, 531–532, 591
   Federal Reserve and, 589
   Great Depression and, 682
   Hispanic farmers and, 491
Credit cards, 872
   "bill of rights" for holders
    of, 904
Credit Mobilier affair, 474, 489
Creek Indians, 498
Creel, George, 633–634
CREEP (Committee to Re-Elect the
   President), 828
"Creole Rhapsody Parts One and Two"
   (Ellington), 707
Crime and criminals. *See also* Prison(s)
   in cities, 866, 867
   organized, 551
   in Reconstruction South, 467
   rights of criminals and, 823
   "three strikes" provision, 887
   urban, 835
Crimes against humanity, Nuremberg trials
   and, 721
Cripple Creek, Colorado, mining strike at,
   492
Crisis, The (magazine), 582, 645
Croatia, 622, 845
Croatian immigrants, 545
Crocker, Charles, 489
Croix de Guerre, to black soldiers, 632, 633
Croker, Richard ("King Richard"), 550
Croly, Jane ("Jenny June"), 522, 523
Cronkite, Walter, 818
Crop lien system, 504
Crops
   genetically modified, 869
   price of (1914-1929), 662
   in South, 504
Crosby, Harry Lillis ("Bing"), 735
"Cross of Gold" speech (Bryan), 533, 534
Crow Indians, 500
Cuba
   Batista in, 772
   Castro in, 772
   CIA and, 785
   independence for, 602, 603, 607
   intervention in, 610, 611 (map), 709
   Radio Martí and, 844
   Soviet Union and, 845
   Spanish-American War in, 599–602,
    600–602, 603 (map)
   U.S. control of, 607
   U.S. prison at, 898
Cuban Americans, 855, 864, 865
Cuban Missile Crisis, 785
Cuen, Rafael, 494, 496
Cullen, Countee, 674
Cultural conservatism, of progressives,
   567–569
Cultural diplomacy, 791
Cultural exchange, 559–560
Cultural movements, identity politics and,
   852
Cultural pluralism, 709
   Kallen and Locke on, 559
Cultural studies, 878

Culture. *See also* Counterculture; Gays and
   lesbians; Mass culture; Society
   African American, 674–675, 852
   Chicanismo and, 854
   class distinctions in, 521
   commercial, 539, 554–555
   consumer, 520, 523–525
   corporations and, 520–522, 778
   critique of mass, 780
   diversity and, 559
   in farm communities, 662–664
   of immigrants, 497
   Indians and, 500, 853
   labor and, 703–705
   media and, 875–882
   Mexican, 708
   middle class, 521
   military, 734
   in 1930s, 686–687
   political issues and, 857–858, 893–894
   popular, 555
   of social networking, 904–906
   Spanish-language, 496
   suburban, 761–763
   urban elites and, 541–542
   urban vs. rural, 662–664
   working-class, 539, 554–555
   youth (1950s), 779–780
Curley, James Michael, 550
Currency
   deflation and, 532
   dual (greenbacks and gold), 532
   Federal Reserve and, 589
   "In God We Trust" on, 778
Curriculum, Afrocentric, 852
Curtis, George William, 475
Custer, George A., 499
Cyberspace. *See also* Internet
   business in, 870
Czechoslovakia
   creation of, 638
   Nazi annexation of, 717
   Soviets and, 746
Czech region, immigrants from, 497

Daily Show, The (television program),
   878–879
Dakota Territory, Sioux reservation in, 499
Dallas, Kennedy, John F., assassination
   in, 795, 797
Dams
   from New Deal, 693, 694
   in West, 694, 702, 776
Dance halls, 539, 554
Dandridge v. *Williams*, 823
Danish West Indies, 616
DAR. *See* Daughters of the American
   Revolution
"Dark horse" candidate, 588
Darrow, Charles, 698
Darrow, Clarence, 567
   Scopes Trial and, 669, 670–671
Darwin, Charles, 669
   Social Darwinism and, 521
Daugherty, Harry M., 658–659
Daughters. *See* Families; Women

Daughters of Bilitis, 755
Daughters of the American Revolution
   (DAR), 505
   Anderson, Marian, and, 706–707
Davis, Henry Winter, 465
Davis, Jefferson, 470
Davis, John W., 670
Dawes, Charles G., 660
Dawes Plan (1924), 660–661
Dawes Severalty Act (1887), 500, 708, 709
Day, Dorothy, 778, 783
Day, Sandra. *See* O'Connor, Sandra Day
Day-care, in Second World War, 734
Dayton, Ohio
   city manager plan in, 572
   city reform in, 573
Daytona, 500, 874
Dayton (Ohio) Peace Accords (1995), 895
D-Day, 721
DDT, 776, 823
Dean, John, 828, 829
Death. *See* Mortality rates
Death camps, Nazi, 719, 721
Death rates, in New York City
   (1925), 673
Debates, Kennedy-Nixon, 784
Debs, Eugene Victor, 658
   American Railway Union (ARU) and, 530
   election of 1912 and, 570, 588, 589 (map)
   election of 1920 and, 643
   First World War and, 625, 636
   jailing of, 571, 636
   Pullman strike and, 530, 571
   socialism and, 570–571
Debt. *See also* National debt
   of farmers, 504
   after First World War, 660
   household, 872
   of investment firms, 901
   Reagan and foreign, 840
   Third World, 846–847
Debt crisis, in Mexico, 895
Decryption techniques, in Second World
   War, 721
Deep South. *See also* South
   organizing in, 811
Defense Department, 746, 752
   business links to, 774
Defense spending, 717, 782, 784. *See also*
   Military spending
   in Second World War, 728
Deficit, 710
   budget, 840
   federal, 888
   household, 872
   Reagan and, 840
   trade, 825
Deflation
   currency expansion and, 525
   in 1897, 534
   in late 19th century, 532
   price, from 1865 to 1897, 531
DeLay, Tom, 893
Delinquents, Lathrop and, 567
De Lôme, Enrique Dupuy. *See* Dupuy de
   Lôme, Enrique

Demagogues, in 1920s, 677
Democracy
   ideals vs. reality, 618
   in 1920s, 677–678
   support of foreign, 617
"Democracy versus the Melting Pot"
   (Kallen), 559
Democratic Party
   African Americans in, 852
   anti-Vietnam War wing of, 818
   Cleveland, Grover, and, 533
   ethnic group voting for, 671
   Freedom Democratic Party at
      convention (1964), 803
   Jackson, Jesse, and, 852
   Johnson, Andrew, and, 465,
      466–467, 473
   Mississippi Plan and, 480, 481
   New Deal coalition of, 700–701
   New Democrats and, 887
   political stalemate and, 507
   in Reconstruction, 470–471
   in South, 474, 477, 480–481, 482
   voter intimidation techniques of, 480,
      482
   white-only primaries of, 506
   Wilson and, 590, 591
Democratic Republicans. *See also* Elections;
   Republican Party
Democratic Republic of Vietnam. *See* North
   Vietnam
Demographics. *See also* Population; Religion
   in suburbs, 866
Demonstrations. *See also* Protest(s)
   in civil-rights movement, 794
   after 1960s, 848–849
   by suffragists, 577
   against Vietnam War, 826
Dempsey, Jack, 653
Denmark
   German territory given to, 638
   Second World War in, 717, 719
Dennis v. *U.S.*, 756
Department stores, 520
Deportation, of immigrants on Attorney
   General's List, 754
Depressions (financial). *See also* Great
   Depression; Panics (financial)
   of 1873-78, 480, 514, 516, 525
   of 1882-1885, 514
   of 1893-1897, 514, 517, 522, 529
   in agriculture, 661–662
   preventing, 900
Deregulation
   Carter and, 836, 841
   of economic sector, 900–901
   of financial industry, 841, 872–873
   Reagan and, 841
Derivatives, 873, 901
Desegregation. *See also* Integration;
   Segregation
   in armed forces, 735, 760
   of baseball, 761
   Brown Cases and, 788
   Eisenhower and, 791
   of military, 760

Desegregation (*continued*)
 Montgomery bus boycott
   and, 789, 790
 Roberts Court on, 894
 Spanish-speaking peoples and, 793
Deserts, irrigation of, 776, 777
Destination Tokyo (movie), 732
"Destroyers-for-bases" deal, 718
Détente policy, 825, 836
Detention, of subversives, 756
Deterrence and Survival in the Nuclear Age.
   See Gaither Report
Detroit
 Pingree in, 572
 racial violence in, 735
 strike in, 732
 "Walk to Freedom March" in, 794
Devaluation, of dollar, 825
Dewey, George, 600
Dewey, John, 567, 677
 as NAACP founder, 574, 582
 progressivism, socialism, and, 571
 on role of government, 677
Dewey, Thomas E.
 election of 1944 and, 726–727
 election of 1948 and, 747, 748
Diaz, Adolfo, 615
Diaz, Porfirio, 616
Dickens, Charles, 523
Dictators and dictatorships. *See also* specific
   individuals
 Carter and, 837
 in Latin America, 772
 U.S. support for, 827
Diem, Ngo Dinh, 773, 774, 785–786,
   795
Dien Bien Phu, battle of, 773
Digital compact discs. *See* CDs
Digital technology, media revolution
   through, 861
Dillingham Commission (1907), 558
Dime novels, 503, 521, 554–555
Diphtheria epidemic, 548
Diplomacy. *See also* Foreign policy
 atomic, 744
 cultural, 791
 Hay, Open Door notes, and, 608
 Hoover-Stimson Doctrine and, 716
 ping-pong, 825
 Roosevelt, T., on, 612–614
 of Taft, 614–615
 Wilson and, 625
Direct election of senators, 532,
   533, 573
Direct-mail fundraising, for
   campaigns, 804
Direct primary, 573, 578
Dirty tricks, under Nixon, 828
Disabled people
 Keller, Helen, and, 572
 Lathrop and, 567
Disarmament
 Clinton and, 896
 after First World War, 639
 in 1920s, 660
 Open Skies initiative and, 771

Discrimination. *See also* Antidiscrimination
   efforts; Race and racism
 against African Americans, 551–552,
   582, 631, 671
 against Chinese immigrants, 490–491
 as foreign policy liability, 760
 against gays and lesbians, 755
 by gender, 567, 787
 in housing, 762–763, 816
 against Mexicans, 737
 in public transportation and
   accommodations, 481
 reverse, 856
 sexual, 824
 sexual harassment as, 850
 struggle against, 789
 Title VII and, 803
 against working women, 656
 in workplace, 730–731
Diseases. *See also* Epidemics; specific
   conditions
 in cities, 540
 among Indians, 499
 from nuclear testing, 771, 823
 in tenements, 548
Disfranchisement
 of blacks, 506, 574, 575
 of ex-Confederates, 471, 472
 of noncitizen immigrants, 574, 575
 in Reconstruction state constitutions,
   506
Disney, Walt, 732
Disneyland, 864
Dispensational premillennialism, 839
Dissent and dissenters. *See also* Protest(s)
 during Cold War, 753, 772
 after First World War, 637, 643
 student, 812
Distribution
 of industries (1900-1920), 519 (map)
 mass production and, 518
District of Columbia, segregated schools
   outlawed in, 788
District of Columbia v. *Heller*, 894
Diversity
 affirmative action and, 856
 in cities, 539
 immigrants and, 558
 intellectual thought on, 558–560
 linguistic, 860
 in Obama administration, 903–904
 in suburbs, 762–763
Dixiecrat Democrats. *See* States' Rights Party
Dixiecrat revolt (1948), 760
Doak, William N., 707
Doby, Larry, 761
Doctors. *See* Medicine
Dodge City, Kansas, 493
Doheny, Edward L., 658
Dole, Robert, election of 1996 and, 887
Dollar (U.S.)
 floating, 825
 in New Deal, 709
Dollar diplomacy, of Taft, 614–615
Domesticity, politics and, 787
Domestic slave trade. *See also* Slave trade

Domestic surveillance programs, 754, 771
Dominican Republic, 475
 immigrants from, 855
 intervention in, 609, 611 (map), 616, 661
 Johnson, Lyndon B., and, 808
Dominion of Canada, 475
Domino theory, 773, 808
"Don't Fence Me In" (Porter), 735
Dos Passos, John, 676
Dot-com businesses, 870
Do the Right Thing (movie), 852
"Double V" campaign, 737
Doughboys, U.S. soldiers as, 627–628
Douglas, Aaron, 674
Douglass, Frederick, 544
 Johnson, Andrew, and, 466
 on Supreme Court and civil rights, 482
Doves, in Vietnam War, 810
Dow Jones Industrial Average, 682, 902
"Down Home Rag" (song), 583
Downsizing, 871
Downtowns, revitalizing, 867
Draft (military)
 Carter and, 838
 in First World War, 631
 resistance to, 816–817
 in Second World War, 717
Draft riot (1863), 478
Dresden, bombing of, 726, 729
Drinan, Robert F., 881
Drinking, 563, 568. *See also* Alcohol and
   alcoholism; Prohibition
Drought, in Great Plains, 497, 498
Drudge Report, The, 890
Drugs
 counterculture and, 813
 in Indian religious ceremonies, 853
 Noriega and trade in, 846
 war against, 845–846
Du Bois, W. E. B., 580, 581
 anticommunism and, 754
 criticism of Washington, Booker T., by,
   506
 on education crusade, 468
 after First World War, 645
 NAACP and, 574, 582
Duck Soup (movie), 686, 687
Due process, Fourteenth Amendment
   and, 470
Dukakis, Michael, 842
Duke, James Buchanan, 503, 517,
   518, 597
Dulles, Allen, 772
Dulles, John Foster, 770–771, 772, 791
Dumbarton Oaks Conference (1944), 739
Dunkirk, British evacuation of, 717
DuPont Corporation, 514
Dupuy de Lôme, Enrique, 600
Durables, consumer, 650, 651
Durant, Thomas C., 489
Dust bowls, 509, 690, 691, 692 (map)
Dutch. *See* Netherlands
Dutch East Indies, 720
DVDs, 876
Dwellings. *See* Housing
Dylan, Bob, 705, 811, 813

Eakins, Thomas, 521
Earhart, Amelia, 656–657
Earned Income Tax Credit (EITC), 886–887
Earnings. *See* Income; Wages
Earth Day (1970), 823
Earth Summit (Brazil, 1992), 895
East Asia. *See also* Asia
    immigrants from, 546–547, 614
    peacekeeping in, 612–614
East Asia Co-Prosperity Sphere, 717, 720
Eastern Europe, 530, 739. *See also* Europe and Europeans
    ethnics from, 669–670, 706
    immigration from, 545
    revolts by satellite countries in, 773, 845
    Soviets and, 722, 744
Eastern front
    in First World War, 623 (map)
    in Second World War, 721
Easter Offensive (North Vietnam), 826
East Germany (German Democratic Republic), 747, 845
Eastman, Crystal, 557
Eastman, Max, 558
Eastman Kodak, 597, 777. *See also* Kodak camera
eBay, 870
Ebony magazine, on black women, 787
Ecology. *See* Environment
E-commerce, 870
Economic and Social Council (UN), 739
Economic bubbles, in 1990s and 2006, 900, 901–902
Economic inequality, socialist essays on, 783
Economic Opportunity Act (EOA, 1964), 802
Economic relief, in Great Depression, 689–690
Economics, supply-side, 840
Economic sanctions, against Iraq, 846
Economy. *See also* Depressions (financial); Great Depression; Panics (financial); Recessions
    African Americans in, 671–673
    anti-government activists and, 857
    boom-and-bust cycles and, 758
    Bush, George H. W., and, 843
    Carter and, 835–836
    Clinton and, 886–887, 900–901
    depression of 1890s and, 534
    deregulation of, 900–901
    European, 746
    after First World War, 650
    First World War and, 624, 629–631, 632–633, 635
    of five civilized tribes, 498
    Ford, Gerald, and, 834–835
    global, 869–872
    government power over, 585, 795
    growth of, 514–520, 758, 769, 774–776, 777
    industrial, 833
    Johnson, Lyndon B., and, 802
    Kennedy, John F., and, 784, 786
    in later 19th century, 514–520
    1993-2008, 900–902

Nixon and, 824–825
post-Second World War agreements and, 739
progressivism and, 592
Reagan and, 840
restraints on money supply and, 532
Roosevelt, T., and, 585
Second World War and, 728–732, 743
in South, 504
transformation after 1970, 868–875
Truman and, 758
from 2000-2006, 901–902
underconsumption theory and, 699
Vietnam War and, 824
Economy Act (1933), 689
Edison, Thomas Alva, 515, 516
Edison Electric Light Company, 515
Editors, women as, 522
Education. *See also* Higher education; Public schools; Schools; Universities and colleges
    for American Indians, 853
    bilingual, 822
    church-centered, 839
    federal aid to, 758
    for freedpeople, 462, 468, 469
    Great Society programs for, 805
    Indian schools, 501, 502
    national security and, 782
    for women, 523
EEOC. *See* Equal Employment Opportunity Commission
Egalitarianism, in Homestead Act, 489
Egypt
    Camp David Accords (1978) and, 837
    Israel and, 825
    Nasser in, 772–773
Eighteenth Amendment, 568, 635
Eight-hour day, 525, 527, 528, 567
Einstein, Albert, 727
Eisenhower, Dwight David ("Ike")
    civil rights issues and, 791
    Cold War and, 769, 771
    covert action under, 772
    defense spending and, 782
    election of 1952 and, 752, 765–766
    farewell address of, 774
    foreign policy of, 770–774
    Highway Act and, 776
    Indian policy and, 791–792
    New Look of, 771
    "new Republicanism" of, 781, 803
    as president, 769, 770
    on religion, 778
    in Second World War, 721
    Third World politics and, 772
    Vietnam and, 773–774
Eisenhower Doctrine (1957), 773
Elections. *See also* Voting
    of 1864, 465
    of 1866, 469, 470–471
    of 1867, 472
    of 1868, 472, 473–474
    of 1870, 525
    of 1872, 478–480
    of 1875 (Mississippi), 480–481

of 1876, 482–483, 483–484, 483 (map), 507, 508
between 1876 and 1892, 507
of 1878, 525, 527–528
of 1880, 507, 525
of 1884, 507, 508
of 1888, 507, 508
of 1890, 533
of 1892, 507, 508, 533
of 1894, 533
of 1896, 533–534, 535 (map)
of 1900, 534, 583
of 1904, 584
of 1908, 586
of 1910, 587
of 1912, 570, 587–588, 589 (map)
of 1916, 590, 591, 626
of 1920, 643, 658
of 1924, 659, 670, 671
of 1928, 670, 671, 673 (map), 678
of 1932, 685 (map)
of 1936, 700–701, 701 (map)
of 1940, 719
of 1942, 728
of 1944, 726–727
of 1946, 747
of 1948, 747–748, 748 (map), 754
of 1952, 752, 765–766, 766 (map)
of 1960, 783–784, 784 (map), 821
of 1964, 797, 803–805, 806, 821
of 1966, 805
of 1968, 818, 819–821, 821 (map)
of 1972, 826, 828, 828 (map)
of 1976, 834, 835 (map), 852
of 1980, 837, 838, 839–840, 839 (map), 845
of 1984, 842, 852
of 1988, 842, 852
of 1992, 848, 848 (map), 886
of 1996, 887–888
of 1998, 889
of 2000, 890–891, 891 (map)
of 2004, 892–893
of 2006, 898
of 2008, 902–903, 903 (map)
in cities, 573
direct, of senators, 532, 533, 573
disfranchisement and, 574–575
participation in (1920-1940), 699
political stalemate and, 507
reforms in, 573
voter participation in presidential (1920-1940), 576
Electoral College. *See also* Elections
    election of 2000 and, 890–891
Electoral commission, for 1876 election, 483
Electorate. *See also* Voting
    progressive disillusionment with, 575
    virtuous, 573
Electric Auto-Lite plant, strike at, 696
Electricity
    in cities, 539
    late 19th century innovations in, 515
    rural, 699
    in transportation, 540
    TVA and, 693–694, 693 (map)

Electric lights, 515
Electric power plant, financing of, 516
Electric railways, 540
Electronic banking, 872
Electronics, 728
Elevators, 515, 539, 540
Eliot, T. S., 676
Elites
    bureaucratic, 592
    Californios, 494–495
    in Gilded Age, 520–521
    immigrant cultures and, 560
    in New Mexico, 496
    power, 779
    urban, 539, 540–544
Ellington, Duke, 553, 674–675, 707, 771, 791
Elliott, Rober B., 476
Ellis Island, 547
Ellsberg, Daniel, 827
Elmer Gantry (Lewis), 676
El Salvador
    immigrants from, 865
    refugees from, 881
Ely, Richard, progressivism, socialism, and, 571
E-mail, 869
Embargo
    of arms before Second World War, 717
    against Japan, 720
    of oil, 825
Embassies, terrorist bombings of, 896
Emergency Banking Act (EBA, 1933), 689
Emergency Economic Stabilization
    Act (2008), 902
Emergency Farm Mortgage Act (1933), 689
Emergency Fleet Corporation, 629
Emergency Relief Appropriation
    Act (1935), 699
Emergency Unemployment Relief
    office, 683
Emerson, Gloria, 810
Emigration. *See also* Immigrants and
    immigration
    of blacks from New South, 504–505
    of blacks to Liberia, 504
    policy for freedpeople, 464
Empires. *See also* British Empire
    American Pacific, 606 (map)
    in 1900, 611 (map)
Employment. *See also* Unemployment
    for African Americans, 852
    discrimination and, 760
    by federal government, 703
    Second World War and, 730
    by sector, 871
    of women, 787
Employment Act (1946), 758
Endangered species, Reagan and, 841
Endangered Species Act (1973), 823
End Poverty in California (EPIC), 697
Energy
    Bush, George W., and, 892
    green, 900
    Reagan and, 841
    renewable sources of, 836
Energy Department, 836, 841

Enforcement acts (1870-1871), 478, 481
Enfranchise, 465
Enfranchisement. *See* Voting
Engineering
    profession, 521
    of urban water systems, 541
Engines, gasoline, 515
England (Britain). *See also* British Empire;
        First World War; Royal Navy
    Alabama Claims and, 475
    colonies and, 740
    in First World War, 622, 626–627
    Hay-Pauncefote Treaty with, 612
    imperialism of, 599
    lend-lease assistance to, 719
    Mexico and, 616
    Open Door policy and, 608
    Second World War in, 717, 721
    southern cotton industry and, 504
    Suez crisis and, 772–773, 773 (map)
    Wells' anti-lynching campaign and, 505
English language, proficiency in Los
        Angeles, 865
Enron, 901
Entertainment. *See also* Commercial culture
    Christian, 881
    for immigrants, 567
    industry, anticommunism and, 754
    information and, 861
    mass, 503
    sports and, 873–875
    in Sunbelt, 863–864
Entrepreneurs
    black, 552, 822
    ethnic, 549, 550
    in Sunbelt, 863–864
Environment
    BP rig explosion and, 904
    government control over, 585
    of Great Plains, 497
    international issues in, 895–896
    laws protecting, 823
    mining and, 492
    New Right and, 856, 881
    progressivism and, 592
    Reagan and, 841
    Roosevelt, T., and, 585
    western irrigation projects and, 776
    westward movement and, 509
Environmental Defense Fund, 823
Environmental impact statements, 823, 856
Environmentalism, 812
    Nixon and, 822–823
Environmental Protection Agency (EPA),
        823
EPA. *See* Environmental Protection Agency
Epidemics. *See also* Diseases
    in cities, 541, 542
    diphtheria, 548
    flu (1919), 629
Equal Employment Opportunity
        Commission (EEOC), 802
Equality. *See also* Equal rights; Race and
        racism
    political stalemate and, 507
    as product of frontier, 509

racial, 506, 582–583
    in Second World War, 736–738
    sexual and gender, 557, 824, 850
    social networking and, 904–906
    of women, 734, 849
Equal Pay Act (1963), 787
Equal rights. *See also* Equality
    for freedpeople, 467, 469
Equal Rights Amendment (ERA)
    in 1920s, 657–658
    of 1972, 823
    in Second World War, 734
Ervin, Sam, 828
Escalation, of Vietnam War, 808
Espionage, Sabotage, and Sedition Acts
        (1917 and 1918), 636
ESPN, 874
Estate taxes, 658
Estonia, 638, 717, 739, 845
Ethics, of technology, 869
Ethiopia, 716, 844
Ethnic cleansing
    in Kosovo, 895
    by Serbs, 847
Ethnic groups and ethnicity, 669–675. *See
        also* Immigrants and immigration;
        Race and racism; specific groups
    African Americans and, 670–674
    associations of, 670
    Columbian Exposition and, 543
    Democratic presidential voting in
        Chicago by, 671
    Eastern European, 669–670, 706–707
    European American, 669–670
    in First World War, 634–635
    immigration discrimination against,
        666–667
    institutions and, 549
    Mexican Americans and, 793
    middle class groups and, 549–550
    in Midwest and northern plains, 497
    saloons and, 568–569
    schools and, 669
    in Second World War, 735
    from Southern Europe, 669–670,
        706–707
    Spanish-speaking Americans,
        853–854
    in Yugoslavia, 845
Eugenics, 667
Europe, James Reese, 583
European Americans, ethnic groups among,
        669–670
Europe and Europeans. *See also* First
        World War
    after First World War, 640 (map)
    in First World War, 623 (map)
    immigrants from, 544, 545–546, 666
    imperialism of, 598
    Second World War in, 717–719,
        718 (map), 720, 721–722, 722 (map)
European Recovery Program. *See* Marshall
        Plan
Evangelicals and evangelicalism, 777, 880
    McPherson and, 668
    New Right support by, 838

politics and, 880–881
progressivism and, 564
in South, 839
Evans, Hiram, 665
Evanston, Illinois, 540
Evolution, Scopes Trial and, 669
Excess profits tax, in First World War, 632
"Exchanges," insurance, 904
Executive branch. *See also* Presidency
enlargement of, 591, 896
powers of, 743, 757
Executive clemency, for Santee Sioux, 499
Executive Orders
9066, 736, 738
9835, 745–746
9981 (1948), 760
banning discrimination in federally
financed housing, 794
government structure and, 757
Executive privilege, Nixon and, 829
Exodus movement, 504–505
Exodusters, 505
Expansion and expansionism. *See also*
Westward movement
in cities, 540
Indians and, 498–499
Japanese, 612–614, 717, 719–720,
725 (map)
Nazi, 717, 718 (map)
Russian, 612–613
Soviet, 744
by United States, 595, 598–599
Expenditures. *See* Spending
Exploration. *See* Space exploration
Exports, 777
to Asia, 597
in 1875 and 1915, 598
in international markets, 825
to Japan, 720
Expressways. *See* Roads and
highways
Exurbs, 866

Facebook, 904, 905, 906
Factories
growth of, 514
scientific managment in, 579–580
worker autonomy in, 525
Factory Investigating Committee
(New York), 579
Factory law, in Illinois, 567
Fair Deal, 758–759, 793
Fair Employment Practices Commission
(FEPC, 1942), 730, 731, 737
Fair Housing Act, 816. *See also* Civil Rights
Act, of 1968
Fairness Doctrine, of FCC, 857
"Faith-based" social programs, 839
Fall, Albert, 658
Fallout shelters, 782
Falwell, Jerry, 838, 839, 850, 881, 888
Families. *See also* Marriage
AFDC and, 822
farm, 532
Great Society and, 805
homesteading on Great Plains, 497, 498

immigrant, 545–546, 547, 549
poverty of, 548, 840
sharecropping and, 467, 468
TV images of, 787
of workers, 525, 548
Family Assistance Plan (FAP), 821–822, 887
Family leave plan, 886
Family planning, 787
Family Support Act (1988), 841
Family values
neoconservatives on, 838
1992 election and, 847
Reagan and, 839
Famine, in Somalia, 847
FAP. *See* Family Assistance Plan
Farewell address, of Eisenhower, 774
Farewell to Arms, A (Hemingway), 676
Farley, Jim, 702
Farm Credit Act (1933), 689
Farmer-labor parties, in 1920s, 662
Farmer-Labor Party (Minnesota), 650
Farmers' Alliance, 532–533. *See also* People's
Party (Populists)
Farmers' movements, 530–533
alliance movement, 532–533
free silver movement, 531–532
Grange, 531, 532
Greenback Party, 531–532
resistance to railroads, 531
Farms and farming. *See also* Agriculture;
Rural areas
by African Americans, 551
bracero program and, 730, 793
credit and, 504, 531–532, 591
crop lien system and, 504
cultural dislocation in, 662–664
after First World War, 650
free silver movement and, 532
grangers, range wars, and cattle ranchers,
493
in Great Depression, 690
Greenback Party and, 532
by immigrants, 497, 549
Mexican labor in, 675
in New South, 504
in 1920s, 661–664
parity system and, 777
prices for cotton and grain,
530–531
price supports for, 758
railroads and, 491
Reagan and, 840
resistance to railroads and, 531
in Second World War, 731
sharecropping and, 467, 468, 504
Soil Bank Program and, 777
subsidies to, 895
tenancy and, 504
UFW and, 854
in West, 497
Farm Security Administration (FSA), 702,
729
Farm workers, Mexican, 675
Farragut, David G., 824
Farrakhan, Louis, 879
Farrell, James T., 686

Far West. *See* West
Fascism
in Italy, 716
in Nazi Germany, 716
in Spain, 717
Fathers. *See also* Families
family roles of, 787
"Fat Man" (bomb), 728
Faulkner, William, 677
FBI. *See* Federal Bureau of Investigation
FCC. *See* Federal Communications
Commission
FDIC. *See* Federal Deposit Insurance
Corporation
Fears. *See* Red Scare; Subversion
Federal Bureau of Investigation (FBI), 754
harassment of activists by, 821
King monitored by, 793–794
Mexican American activism and, 793
Reagan as informer for, 843
surveillance of artists and intellectuals
by, 754
Federal Communications
Commission (FCC), 780
Fairness Doctrine of, 857
television family programming and, 878
Federal Deposit Insurance
Corporation (FDIC), 689
Federal elections law (1890), 507
Federal Emergency Relief Act (1933), 689
Federal Emergency Relief Administration
(FERA), 689
Federal government. *See* Government
(U.S.)
Federal Housing Administration (FHA), 759,
762, 793
Federal Republic of Germany (West
Germany). *See* West Germany
Federal Reserve Act (1913), 589
Federal Reserve Board (FRB), 589, 590, 835,
900–901
in Great Depression, 682
Greenspan and, 873, 887
market regulation by, 857
Volcker and, 840
Federal Reserve System
districts of, 590 (map)
financial sector and, 873, 902
Federal Trade Commission (FTC), 589, 590
Coolidge and, 659
Federal Trade Commission Act (1914), 589
FedEx, 870
Feed lots, 893
Felons. *See* Crime and criminals
"Feminine mystique," Friedan on, 779
Feminine Mystique, The (Friedan), 787
Femininity, in Second World War, 734
Feminism. *See also* Women; Women's rights
movements and, 849
New Right and, 838
radical, 812
Religious Right and, 838
on Spanish-American War, 599
use of term, 557
Feminization, of poverty, 841, 849
Femmes fatales, 763–764, 786

FEPC. *See* Fair Employment Practices
Commission
FERA. *See* Federal Emergency Relief
Administration
Ferraro, Geraldine, 842
Ferris Wheel, 543, 544
FHA. *See* Federal Housing Administration
Fiction. *See also* Literature; Novels
tough-guy, 734
Field, James G., 533
Fifteenth Amendment, 472–473, 475, 484,
574
File on Thelma Jordan, The (movie), 764
Filibuster
against Civil Rights Act (1964), 802
in House, Compromise of 1877 and, 483
Filipinos, 544, 855. *See also* Philippines
as agricultural labor, 547, 854
Fillmore, Millard, 507
Film noirs, 763, 765, 786
Films. *See* Movies and movie industry
Finance(s). *See also* Banking; Panics;
Taxation
in Second World War, 728
Financial institutions
deregulation of, 836, 841
Federal Reserve and, 589
lending practices of, 762–763
"subprime loan" industry and, 841
Financial system
decline in 2000s, 902
derivatives and, 901
in early 2000s, 901
expansion of, 872–873
regulation of, 904
Financing
of hospitals, 759
of housing, 762
of railroads, 489–490, 516
Finland, 638, 640 (map)
Firebombings, in Second World War, 726
Fireside chats, 688
Firing Line (television program), 838
First Amendment
HUAC and, 754
political expression vs. illegal activity
and, 756
Religious Right on, 839
Scopes Trial and, 669
First New Deal (1933-1935), 688–694, 696.
See also New Deal
First World War
armed forces in, 631–632
armistice in, 628, 628 (map), 637
casualties in, 623, 628
Europe after, 640 (map)
failure of peace after, 637–641
federal budget and, 635
immigrants during, 635
Mexico and, 626
mobilization for, 628–637
movie about, 716
neutrality of U.S. in, 624–625
peace movement in, 625
postwar period and, 643–646
repression during, 635–637

Russian exit from, 626, 627
societal impact of, 629–637, 643–646
trusteeships after, 638
U-boats in, 620, 624–625, 626–627
United States in, 626–628, 628 (map)
western front in, 622, 628
workers during, 630–631, 634
FISA. *See* Foreign Intelligence
Surveillance Act
Fish, Hamilton, 475
Fishing and fishing industry
Indian rights and, 853
Washington Treaty and, 475
Fission, atomic, 727
Fitzgerald, F. Scott, 649, 676, 677
Fitzgerald, John Francis ("Honey Fitz"),
550–551
Five "civilized tribes," alliance with
Confederacy, 498
Five-dollar-per-day wage, by Ford, Henry,
580
Five-Power Treaty (1922), 660
FiveThirtyEight.com, 903
Flappers, 648, 653
Fleischmann, Doris, 651
Flesch, Rudolf, 782
Fletcher, E., 879
Flexible response policy, 784, 785–786, 795
Floating dollar, 825
Florida, 480
Cuban Americans in, 855
election of 2000 and, 890–891, 891 (map)
Hispanics in, 853
Flour. *See* Wheat
Flu epidemic, in 1919, 629
Flush toilets, 540
Flynn, Elizabeth Gurley, 557
Folk-rock movement, Sixties and, 811, 813
Food(s)
green revolution and, 869
healthy, 522
in 1920s, 650–651
rations from Freedmen's Bureau, 467
regulation of, 585
Food Administration, 629
Hoover and, 629, 660, 684
Food industry, 894
"Food Is a Weapon" poster, 733
Food stamps, 805, 841, 849
Football, 522, 873
Foraker Act (1900), 607
Forbes, Charles R., 658
Ford, Betty, 839
Ford, Gerald R., 838, 839
economy and, 834–835
election of 1976 and, 834, 835 (map)
foreign policy of, 836
as president, 829, 834
as vice president, 829
Ford, Henry, 518
African Americans and, 671–673
Taylorism and, 579–580
Ford, John, 704, 732
Ford Motor Company
automobiles of, 518, 579, 580, 650, 651
workers at, 579, 580

Foreign Affairs (journal), 745
Foreign-born Americans. *See* Immigrants
and immigration
Foreign Intelligence Surveillance Act (FISA,
1978), 898
Foreign investment, 597
Foreign Miners' Tax (California, 1850), 490,
495–496
Foreign policy. *See also* Containment;
Imperialism
anticommunist, 740
of Bush, George H. W., 845–847
of Carter, 836–838
after Cold War, 833
containment in, 745, 769
Democratic agenda for, 900
vs. democratic ideals, 618
divisions over, 898–900
Eisenhower and, 770–774
of Ford, 836
Grant and, 475
Great Fear and, 756
of Kennedy, John F., 784–785
neoconservatives on, 838
neutrality as, 716–717
1993-2008, 894–900
of Nixon, 825–827
of Obama, 904
Open Door in, 660
of Reagan, 844–845
religious divisions over, 881
Roosevelt, T., and, 612–614
after September 11, 2001, 896
of Taft, 614–615
of Truman, 745, 746, 748–749
unilateralism as, 896–897
Vietnam syndrome and, 827
of Wilson, 615–617, 624
before World War I, 595–618
Foreign relations, in New Deal, 709–711
Foreign trade. *See* Trade
Forests
destruction of, 509
protection of, 895
regulation of, 585
Formosa (Taiwan), 748
Forrest, Nathan Bedford, 474
Fortas, Abe, 823
Fort Lee, New Jersey, movie industry in, 555
Fortune magazine
on American affluence, 775
on labor at General Motors, 777
"40 acres and a mule," 468
Fossil fuels. *See also* Energy
energy from, 836
Reagan and, 841
U.S. reliance on, 836
"Four Freedoms" (Rockwell), 733
442nd Regimental Combat Team, 737–738
"Four-Minute Men," 634
Fourteen Points, 627, 628, 637–638
Fourteenth Amendment, 470, 471, 472,
482, 484
school segregation and, 761
Fox News Channel (FNS), 878, 890, 891
Fox TV, 875

France. *See also* West Indies
   African Americans soldiers in, 632, 633
   colonies of, 740
   Dominican Republic and, 609
   in First World War, 622, 626
   Indochina and, 752, 773
   occupation of Ruhr by, 660
   Open Door policy and, 608
   Panama Canal and, 610–612
   in Second World War, 717, 721,
      722 (map)
   Suez Crisis and, 772–773, 773 (map)
   Vichy regime in, 717
Franchise businesses, 869–870
Franco, Francisco (Spain), 717
Frank, Jerome, 690
Frankfurter, Felix, 677
Franz Ferdinand (Austria), 622
Fraternal societies
   immigrant, ethnic, 549
   Klan as, 666
Freedmen's Bureau, 467, 468, 469,
      470, 474
   education for freedpeople and, 468
Freedmen's school, burning of, 471
Freedom(s). *See* Liberty(ies); Rights
Freedom Budget, 816, 852
Freedom Democratic Party (FDP), 787
Freedom riders, 793
Freedom Singers, 787, 788
Freedom Summer, 803, 811
Freedpeople, 464
   education for, 468, 469
   free-labor contracts and, 467
   land for, 467–468
   Lincoln and, 464
   in Reconstruction South, 467
   sharecropping and, 467, 468
   symbolism of, 462
Free France, in Second World War, 721
Free-labor contracts, 467
Free-labor ideology, 513
Free love, in Greenwich Village, 557
Free market(s)
   anti-government activists on, 857
   Friedman on, 781, 838, 857
   Reagan and, 844
Free silver movement, 532, 533, 534
Free Speech, 505
Free trade. *See also* North American Free
      Trade Agreement
   Clinton and, 895
   after First World War, 638
Freight, railroads and, 491
French Canada, immigrants from, 544, 545,
      547
French Empire. *See* Canada; Colonies and
      colonization; France
French Indochina, Japan and, 720
Freud, Sigmund, child-raising books and,
      653
Friant-Kern Canal, 777
Frick, Henry Clay, 529, 534
Friedan, Betty, 779, 787
Friedman, Milton, 781, 804–805, 838, 857
Frontier, disappearance of, 597

Frontier thesis, of Turner, 509, 597–598
Front-porch campaign, of McKinley, 534
Frost, Robert, 784
FTC. *See* Federal Trade Commission
Fuchs, Klaus, 756
Fuel. *See* Fossil fuels
Fulbright, J. William, 810
Full Employment Bill, 758
Fundamentalism
   Islamic, 837, 844
   vs. liberal Protestantism, 667–668
   Protestant, 838–839
   Scopes Trial and, 669
Funding, military, 717. *See also* Defense
      spending; Military spending
Fusionism, 781

Gaither Report, 782
Galbraith, John Kenneth, 775, 776, 778, 782,
      783
Galveston
   city commission plan in, 572
   scientific management and, 579
Gambling, 563
   Indian casinos and, 853
Gang labor, 467, 468
Gangsterism, 551, 664–665
García, Calixto, 602
Garfield, James A., 507
Garment industry. *See also* Clothing and
      clothing industry
   immigrant labor in, 547, 549
   strike in, 643
Garrison, Jim, 796
Garrison, William Lloyd, 582
Garvey, Marcus, 645
"Gas and water socialists," 571
Gas attacks, in First World War, 624
Gasoline. *See* Oil and oil industry
Gassed (Sargent), 624
Gates, Bill, 869
Gates, Henry Lewis, Jr., 852
Gates, Robert, 898, 904
GATT. *See* General Agreement on Tariffs
      and Trade
Gay Activist Alliance (GAA), 851
Gay marriage, 893–894
Gay rights, 833
Gays and lesbians. *See also* Homosexuality
   activism of, 850–851
   LGBT movement and, 881
   subcultures of, 754–755
Gay theology, 881
GDP. *See* Gross domestic product
Geithner, Timothy, 904
Gender and gender issues. *See also* Men;
      Women
   discrimination by, 567, 787, 803
   equality and, 824, 849, 850
   in New Deal, 702–703
   "New Woman" and, 523, 524
   politics of, 786–788, 850–851
   in Second World War, 730, 733–734
   in sports, 874
   western settlement and, 497–498
   woman suffrage and, 473

General Agreement on Tariffs and Trade
      (GATT), 739, 895
General Assembly (UN), 739
General Electric, 775
General Motors (GM), 651, 777
   sit-down strike against, 704
General strikes, after Second World War,
      753
Genetically modified foods, 869
Genetic code, 869
Geneva Medical College, women in, 523
Geneva meeting (1955), on cultural
      exchanges, 771
Geneva Peace Accords (1954), 773
Genocide. *See* Ethnic cleansing; Holocaust
Gentlemen's agreement, with Japan, 546,
      614
Geopolitics
   of Cold War, 749 (map)
   of Roosevelt, T., 609–614
George, Henry, 496, 698
German Americans
   First World War and, 625, 635–636
   Haymarket bombing and, 528
   Turnevereins of, 549
German Democratic Republic. *See* East
      Germany
Germany. *See also* East Germany; First
      World War; Nazi Germany; West
      Germany
   Danish West Indies and, 616
   immigrants from, 497, 549
   imperialism of, 599
   Lusitania and, 620, 624
   occupation zones in, 739, 749 (map)
   Open Door policy and, 608
   reparations after First World War,
      660–661
   reunification of, 845
   Ruhr and, 660
   submarine warfare by, 620, 624–625,
      626–627
   as U.S. ally, 752
   Venezuela and, 609
   war guilt after First World War, 638
Gershwin, George, 553
Ghettos, 564
Ghost Dance, 501, 503
Giannini, Amadeo, 549
Gibbs, Jonathan, 475–476
GI Bill (1944), 758, 759
GI Bill of Rights (1952), 758
Gibson, Josh, 673, 674
Gilded Age
   literary indictment of, 522
   Twain and, 520
Gilded Age, The (Twain and Warner), 474
Gillespie, Dizzy, 791
Gilman, Charlotte Perkins, 522, 557
Gingrich, Newt
   Contract with America and, 887
   election of 1964 and, 804
   election of 1998 and, 889
   extramarital affair by, 889–890
Ginsberg, Allen, 811, 812, 813
Ginsburg, Ruth Bader, 886

Gipp, George, 843
Glasnost, 845
"Glass ceiling," 849
Glass-Steagall Act (1932), 684, 900
Glass-Steagall Banking Act (1933), 689
Globalization, 871. *See also* International
   interactions
      Clinton and, 895
      economic, 846–847, 869–872
      western industrialization and, 489
Global warming, 900
Glover, M., 879
Glynn, Martin, 626
GNP. *See* Gross national product
God and Man at Yale (Buckley), 781
"God Bless America" (song), 705
Godkin, E. L., 599
Gold
      Black Hills discovery, 499
      discoveries of, 532, 534
      dual currency with greenbacks, 532
      gold-to-dollar ratio, 825
      mining of, 491–492
      vs. silver, 532
Gold bugs, 532
Golden spike, 486, 491
Goldman, Emma, 557
Goldman Sachs, 901
Gold Repeal Joint Resolution (1933), 689
Gold Rush, in California, 490, 491
Gold standard, 532
Goldwater, Barry, 781, 783, 791, 797
      election of 1964 and, 803–805, 838
Golf, 874
Gómez, Máximo, 602
Gompers, Samuel F., 528, 590, 604, 631, 643
Gomulka, Wladyslaw, 772
Goodman, Andrew, 803
Good Neighbor Policy
      Mexican Americans and, 737
      in 1930s, 709, 710, 740
Goods and services, consumer goods and,
   650
Google, 906
Gorbachev, Mikhail, 845
Gordon, John B., 474
Gore, Albert, 848, 886, 887–888
      climate change and, 900
      election of 2000 and, 890–891, 891 (map)
"Gospel of Wealth," of Carnegie, 517
Gould, Jay, 516
Government. *See also* Municipal
      government
      of Puerto Rico, 607–608
Government (U.S.). *See also* Progressives
      and progressivism
      activist, 562, 563, 658, 782–783
      centralized, 564
      civil service reform and, 474–475
      corporate support by, 516
      economy and, 585, 728, 795
      employment by, 703
      environment and, 585
      Hoover and, 684–685
      housing built by, 702
      New Right and, 856–858

pollution by, 895
power of, 732, 833
Reconstruction and, 484
Grady, Henry, 503
Graft (payments), 489, 550
Graham, Billy, 777, 838, 881
Graham, Hugh, 550
Grain. *See also* Wheat
      exports of, 530
      production of, 893
Gramm, Phil, 900–901
Grand Coulee Dam, 693, 694
Grandfather clauses, 506
      NAACP challenge to, 582
Grange, 531, 532
Granger laws, 531
Grangers, range wars and, 493
Grant, Ulysses S., 473, 491, 766
      administration of, 474
      civil service reform and, 474–475
      election of 1868 and, 473–474
      election of 1872 and, 478–480
      foreign policy and, 475
      Hamburg Massacre and, 482
      Ku Klux Klan and, 478
      Mississippi election of 1875 and, 480
      peace policy toward Indians of, 500
Grapes of Wrath, The (Steinbeck), 704
Grassroots activism
      in civil rights movement, 794
      Great Society and, 805
      in 1960s, 811–812
Grateful Dead, The, 813
Great American Desert, 497
Great Britain. *See* England (Britain)
Great Depression, 681. *See also* New Deal;
   Roosevelt, Franklin D.
      agricultural reforms in, 690
      causes of, 682–684
      First New Deal in, 688–694
      Mexicans in, 707–708
      Second World War and, 728, 740
      stock market crash and, 681
      victims of, 681
Great Fear, communism and, 755, 756
Great Gatsby, The (Fitzgerald), 676, 677
Great Migration, 630
"Great Moderation, The," 900
Great Northern Railroad, 530
Great Plains region, 497, 531
      Dust Bowl in, 690
Great Railroad Strike (1877), 490, 513, 514,
   515, 525–527
Great Society, of Johnson, Lyndon B., 802,
   805–806, 822
Great War. *See* First World War
Great White Fleet, 614, 615 (map)
Great White Hope, The (movie), 581
Greece, 720, 739, 752
      immigrants from, 545
      U.S. aid to, 745
Greeley, Horace
      election of 1872 and, 478–480
      homestead law and, 489
Greenbackers, 525
Greenback-Labor Party, 525

Greenback Party, 532
Greenbacks, gold and, 532
Green Berets, 785
Green energy, 900
Greenland, 719
Green revolution, 869
Greenspan, Alan, 873, 887, 900, 901
Greenwich Village
      feminists and labor leaders in, 557–558
      Stonewall Narrative and, 850–851
Gregory, Thomas, 637
Grenada, 844
Grey (Lord), 625
Griffith, D. W., 479, 665
Grisham, John, 888
Grocery chains, in 1920-1930, 651
Gross domestic product (GDP), 872
Gross national product (GNP)
      from 1869 to 1873, 514
      from 1897 to 1901, 514
      in 1920s, 650
      by 1960, 774
      in 1960s, 802
      growth of (1940-1970), 775
      in Second World War, 728
      Truman and, 758
Ground Zero. *See* September 11 2001
      terrorist attacks
Guadalcanal, 723
Guam, 602, 722
Guantanamo Bay
      detention center at, 898, 904
      U.S. Naval Station at, 607
Guatemala, 844
      CIA in, 772
      refugees from, 865, 881
Guerrilla warfare. *See also* Kansas Territory
      by Molly Maguires, 525, 526
Guggenheim, Daniel and Simon, 536
Guiteau, Charles, 507
Gulf of Mexico region
      BP rig explosion in, 904
      Hurricane Katrina and, 897, 899
Gulf of Tonkin Resolution, 806–808
Gulf War. *See* Persian Gulf War
Gun control, 886, 894
Gun Crazy (movie), 765
Guthrie, Woody, 704–705, 706
Gypsies, Nazi death camps and, 719

Habeas corpus, writ of, presidential power to
      suspend, 478
Hague, The
      environmental convention in, 896
      international women's peace
         conference at, 625
Haight-Ashbury district (San Francisco), 812
Haiti, 464, 616, 895
      immigrants from, 865
      intervention in, 611 (map), 615, 661
      troops in, 709
Halas family (football), 873
Halberstam, David, 810
Half-Breeds, 507
Hall, Theodore, 756
Hamburg, bombing of, 726

Hamburg Massacre, 482
Hamer, Fannie Lou, 787, 803
Hamilton, Alice, 567
Hampton, Fred, 821
Hampton Institute, 502
Hancock, Winfield Scott, 507
Handguns. *See also* Gun control
    restrictions on, 886
Handicapped people. *See* Disabled people
Hanna, Mark, 534
Hanoi, 808
Harding, Warren G., 649, 658–659
Harlem, New York, 671
Harlem Renaissance, 674–675
Harper's New Monthly, 515, 521, 565
Harrington, Michael, 782–783
Harrison, Carter, Jr., 508, 572
Hassam, Childe, 521
Havana, Cuba, riots in, 600
Hawaii
    Japanese immigrants to, 546
    Pearl Harbor attack in, 719–720
    as protectorate, 599
    statehood for, 603
    U.S. involvement in, 598, 599
Hawks, in Vietnam War, 810
Hawley, Ellis, 660
Hawley-Smoot Tariff Act (1930), 682–684
Hay, John, 612
    Open Door policy and, 608
Hay-Bunau-Varilla Treaty, 612
Hayek, Friedrich von, 781
Hayes, Rutherford B.
    election of 1876 and, 482–483, 483–484,
      483 (map)
    end of Reconstruction and, 484, 513
    Great Railroad Strike and, 526
Hay-Herran Treaty, 612
Haymarket bombing, 522, 523, 527–528
Hay-Pauncefote Treaty, 612
Haywood, William ("Big Bill"), 492, 557, 636
Hayworth, Rita, 730
Hazardous waste disposal, 893
H-bomb. *See* Hydrogen bomb
Head Start Program (1965), 805
Health
    environmental focus on, 823
    public, 548, 567
Health, Education, and Welfare, Department
    of (HEW), 781
Healthcare
    ACT UP and, 851
    Clinton and, 887
    in GDP, 872
    Johnson, Lyndon B., and, 805
    Truman and, 747, 758, 759
    in 2010, 904
Health insurance
    national, 759
    private, 759
Hearst, George, 491
Hearst, William Randolph, 599
Hedge funds, 873
Hefner, Hugh, 787
Heirs. *See* Inheritance
Hellman, Lillian, 754

Hemingway, Ernest, 676
    FBI and, 754
Henry Street Settlement, 579
Hepburn Act (1906), 585
Herberg, Will, 778, 879
Herblock (Herbert Block)
    on Eisenhower-era social policy, 779
    on HUAC, 755
Heritage Foundation, The, 838, 857
Herran, Tomas, 612
Hester Street (Luks), 538
Heterodoxy, 557
HEW. *See* Health, Education, and Welfare,
    Department of
Hidden Persuaders, The (Packard), 779
Higher education. *See also* Universities and
    colleges
    for African Americans, 468
    sexual discrimination banned in, 824
    urban life and, 867
    for women, 523, 568
Highland Park Ford plant, 579–580
High Noon (movie), 764
High-tech industries, 863, 871
Highway Act (1956), 776
Highways. *See* Roads and highways
Hill, Anita, 850
Hill, James J., 597
Hill-Burton Act (1946), 759
Hillman, Sidney, 703
Himmelfarb, Gertrude, 838
Hip-hop music, 879
Hippies, 812
Hiring, discrimination in, 791
Hiroshima, atomic bombing of, 728, 729
Hispanics. *See also* Latinos; Spanish-
    speaking people
    Homestead Act and, 489
    use of term, 854
    western railroad expansion and, 491
Hispaniola, 616
Hiss, Alger, 754
Hiss-Chambers-Nixon affair, 754
History and historians
    on economic and environmental reforms
      of Theodore Roosevelt, 585
    frontier thesis and, 509
    on Great Society, 805–806
    on onset of Cold War, 744
    revisionists, 744
Hitler, Adolf, 710–711, 716. *See also* Nazi
    Germany
    appeasement of, 717
    League and, 641, 716
    in Rhineland, 717
    Spain and, 717
    suicide of, 722
HIV-AIDS, 851
Hmong people, 855, 865
Ho Chi Minh, 752, 773, 785
Ho Chi Minh City, 836
Ho Chi Minh Trail, 774, 809
Hoffman, Abbie, 817
Holding Company Act (1935), 699, 701
Holiday Inn, 870
Holland. *See* Netherlands

Holly, Buddy, 779
Hollywood. *See* Movies and movie industry
"Hollywood Ten, The," 754
Holocaust, 721. *See also* Hitler, Adolf; Nazi
    Germany
Home front
    in First World War, 628–637
    in Second World War, 728–738
    in Vietnam War, 810–817
Homeland Security, Department of, 896,
    897, 899
Homelessness, 866
    of women and children, 849
Home Loan Bank Board, 685
Home loans, 872, 873
Home Owners Loan Act (1933), 689
Homeowners' Loan Corporation (1933), 690
Homer, Winslow, 462
Homestake Mine (Black Hills), 491
Homestead Act (1862), 489, 497
Homesteading, in West, 489, 497
Homestead Strike (1892), 514, 529
Homophile movement, 755
Homosexuality. *See also* Gays and lesbians
    anticommunism and, 754, 755
    LGBT movement and, 881
    Nazi death camps and, 719
    in postwar era, 754–755
Honduras, United Fruit in, 615
Hoover, Herbert, 769
    associationalism of, 659–660
    election of 1928 and, 670, 673 (map), 678
    election of 1932 and, 685 (map)
    in First World War, 629
    presidency of, 684–685
    as secretary of commerce, 658, 660, 661
Hoover, J. Edgar
    agent provocateurs and, 821
    Black Panthers and, 816
    detention of subversives and, 756
    illegal surveillance by, 754, 827
    King and, 793–794
    on rock music, 779–780
    secret subversives file of, 754
Hoover Dam. *See* Boulder Dam
Hoover-Stimson Doctrine (1931), 716
Hopkins, Harry, 687, 690
Hopkins, Mark, 489
Horseless carriages, 515
Hospitals, federal financing of, 759
Hostage crisis, in Iran, 837, 839, 845
Hot-line, between Soviet Union and U.S.,
    785
House, Edward M., 625
Households, deficit in, 872
House of Representatives. *See also*
    Congress (U.S.)
    African Americans in, 476
    impeachment by, 472
House Un-American Activities Committee
    (HUAC), 754, 755
Housing
    "bubble" in 2000s, 901, 902
    discrimination and, 671, 760, 794,
      816
    of elites, 539

Housing (*continued*)
federal building of, 702
federal funds for, 840
financing for, 762, 793
for GIs, 758, 759
in low-income neighborhoods, 867
middle class, 540
public, 758, 759, 762, 793
redlining in, 793
residential segregation in, 791
restrictive covenants in, 760–761, 762
Rumford Act and, 804, 814
soddies (sod houses) as, 497, 498
suburbs and, 521, 761–762
urban renewal and, 793
for working class, 540, 548
Housing Act (1949), 759, 793
Housing and Urban Development,
Department of (HUD), 805, 835
Housing projects, 793
Howard, Oliver O., 467
Howells, William Dean, 521–522, 582
Howl (Ginsberg), 812
How the Other Half Lives (Riis), 567
HUAC. *See* House Un-; American Activities
Committee
HUD. *See* Housing and Urban Development,
Department of
Huerta, Dolores, 854
Huerta, Victoriano, 616
Hughes, Charles Evans, 579, 626, 658, 660,
661
Hughes, Langston, 674
Hukbalahaps (Huks), in Philippines, 752
Hull, Charles J., 566
Hull House, 566–567
"Human Be-In," 813
Human Genome Project, 869
Human immunodeficiency virus (HIV). *See*
HIV-AIDS
Humanitarian aid, to Somalia, 847
Human rights
Carter and, 836, 837
Milosevic trial and, 895
UN and, 739
Humor, and woman suffrage
movement, 577
Humphrey, George, 770
Humphrey, Hubert, 783
election of 1964 and, 803
election of 1968 and, 818–819, 819–821,
821 (map)
Hundred Days (1933), legislation in,
688–694
Hungary
in First World War, 622
immigrants from, 497, 545
revolution in (1956), 772
Hunger strikes, by suffragists, 577
Hunter, Robert, 548
Hunting, of buffalo, 509
Huntington, Collis P., 489
Hurricane Katrina, 897, 899
Hurston, Zora Neale, 674
Husbands. *See* Families; Men
Hussein (Jordan), 773

Hussein, Saddam
al-Qaeda and, 897
Iraq after, 898
Iraq War and, 896–897
Persian Gulf War and, 846
U.S. assistance to, 844
weapons programs of, 896
Hydraulic mining, 492
Hydrogen bomb, 748

I Am a Fugitive from a Chain Gang
(movie), 686
ICBMs. *See* Intercontinental ballistic
missiles
ICC. *See* Interstate Commerce Commission
Iceland, Second World War and, 719
Idaho, 533
woman suffrage in, 575
Identity politics, cultural movements and, 852
Igler, David, 494
"I Have a Dream" speech (King), 795
ILGWU. *See* International Ladies Garment
Workers Union
Illegal immigrants. *See also* Undocumented
immigrants
from Asia, 547
from Mexico, 793
in New Deal, 707–708
Illinois, election of 1960 and, 784
Illiteracy
of freedpeople, 468, 469
of southern blacks, 475, 476–477
I Married a Communist (movie), 742
IMF. *See* International Monetary Fund
Immigrants and immigration. *See also*
Migration
African Americans and, 672
American nationality and, 558–560
Asian, 491, 546–547, 614, 855
cartoons against, 668
Chinese Exclusion Act and, 491
to cities, 544
corporations and, 536
culture of, 497
Dillingham Commission and, 558
disfranchisement of, 574, 575
between 1880 and 1920, 544–545
ethnicity, religion, schools, and, 669–670
European, 544, 545–546
in First World War, 631, 635–636
foreign-born Americans and, 866 (map)
Homestead Act and, 489
illegal, 547
from Islamic countries, 880
Jewish, 538, 545, 546
labor, 547–548
McCarran-Walter Act and, 754
Mexican, 496, 675, 676 (map), 707–708
in Midwest, 497
national origins system of, 667
"new" (19th century), 545, 548
new immigration (20th century),
864–865
in northern plains region, 497
"old," 545, 548
political disagreement over, 893

prohibition movement and, 569
rate of return for, 546
reasons for, 545–547
refugee policy and, 719
restrictions in 1920s, 666–667
social institutions of, 549
from Somalia, 865
sources of, 545
in 20th century, 861
undocumented, 793
urban living conditions for, 548
voting by, 574
in West, 487
Immigration Act (1990), 865
Immigration and Nationality Act (1952). *See*
McCarran-Walter Act
Immigration and Nationality Act (1965),
805, 865, 880
Immigration Reform and Control Act
(1986), 865
Immigration Restriction Act
of 1917, 635, 637
of 1924, 666
Impeachment
of Clinton, 888–890
of Johnson, Andrew, 472
of Nixon, 829
Imperialism, 598–599
after Spanish-American War, 603–608
Imperial Valley, water for, 694, 695 (map)
Imports. *See* Tariff(s)
Impressionism, 521
Inauguration
of Kennedy, John F., 784
of Obama, 904
of Reagan, 856
Incandescent bulb, 515
Inchon, 750
Income. *See also* Wages
of college graduates, 867
FAP and, 822
farm, 662
rising inequality in, 902
in South, 504
Income tax, 527, 532, 659
progressive, 589
Independence
for Cuba, 602, 603, 607
in Eastern Europe, 845
of Panama, 612
for Philippines, 607
Independent films, 876
Indexing, of Social Security, 822, 841
Index Peak, Yellowstone National Park, 1914
(Moran), 586
Indiana, electoral balance and, 507
Indianapolis, 500, 874
Indian Arts and Crafts Board, 709
Indian Bill of Rights, 853
Indian boarding schools, 501, 502
Indian policy. *See also* American Indians
of concentration, 498
peace policy, 500
reservations for, 499, 500
Termination and Relocation, 791–792
Indian Reorganization Act (IRA, 1934), 709

Indian Territory
 cattle drives in, 492
 five civilized tribes in, 498
 land opened to white settlement in, 500
 reconstruction of, 498–499
Indigenous peoples. *See* American Indians
Indochina, 836. *See also* Cambodia; Laos;
  Vietnam
 destabilization of, 826
 France and, 752, 773
 Truman and, 752
Indonesia. *See also* Dutch East Indies
 CIA and, 773
Industrial accidents, 525, 547, 777
Industrial democracy, 631, 634
Industrial economy, 833
Industrialist philanthropic foundations
  (1905-1925), 535
Industrialization. *See* Industry and
  industrialization
Industrial Relations Commission, 579
Industrial unions, 528. *See also* Labor
  unions
Industrial workers, 655
Industrial Workers of the World (IWW),
  492, 557, 570, 635, 636
 textile strikes and, 591
Industry and industrialization, 512. *See also*
  Labor
 accidents and, 525, 547
 African American migration and, 551
 electric-powered, 515
 financing for, 516
 after First World War, 650
 in First World War, 629–630
 in Germany, 660
 in Great Depression, 690–693
 high-tech, 863
 immigrant labor and, 547–548, 549
 New South and, 503–506
 in 1900-1920, 519 (map)
 in 1950s, 775
 race and, 504
 railroad expansion and, 491
 of ranching, 494
 in Second World War, 728
 in South, 551
 of West, 486, 488–498
 Wisconsin idea and, 578–579
Inflation
 economic growth and, 776
 in First World War, 630
 Ford and, 834–835
 in 1970s, 835
 in 1980s, 840, 841
 Nixon and, 824
 Social Security and, 822
Influence of Sea Power upon History, The
  (Mahan), 598
Information. *See also* Digital technology
 business operations and, 869
 conservative, 844
 entertainment and, 861
 programs in Cold War, 771, 844
Information revolution, 869
Infotainment, debate over, 878

Infrastructure
 of cities, 541
 deterioration of, 866
 in Iraq, 846
 in New Deal, 692–693, 694
Ingersoll, Robert, 508
Inherit the Wind (movie), 669
Inheritance tax, in First World War, 632
Initiative, 573
Injunctions, strikes and, 528, 530
Inner cities, African Americans in, 840
Inspection, of nuclear facilities, 896
Institutions
 African American, 552
 ethnic, 549
Insurance, health, 759, 904
Insurance companies, security-focused
  plans of, 732
Integration. *See also* Segregation
 of baseball, 761
 Brown Cases and, 788
 of military, 631
 Roosevelt, Eleanor, and, 737
 in Second World War, 737
Intellectual thought. *See also* Art(s);
  Literature
 on American nationality, 558–560
 conservatives and, 838
 Hull House and, 567
 Lost Generation and, 675–678
 realism and, 564–566
 Social Darwinism and, 520–521
Intelligence (military), 746, 897
Intelligence tests, in First World
  War, 631
Intercollegiate athletics, 874
Intercontinental ballistic missiles (ICBMs),
  782, 825
Interest-group pluralism, 778
Interest rates
 credit cards and, 872
 Great Depression and, 682
 in 2000s, 901
Interior Department, 585, 841
Intermediate-range missiles, 845
Internal combustion engine, 515
Internal Revenue Service (IRS), 839
 harassment by, 827
International Bank for Reconstruction and
  Development, 739
International Brotherhood of Teamsters,
  women in, 731
International Harvester, 514, 597
International interactions. *See also* specific
  issues
International interactions. *See also* Foreign
  policy; Globalization; Immigrants and
  immigration
 Alabama Claims, 475
 associationalism in, 660
 cotton overproduction and, 504
 devaluation of dollar, 825
 drug trafficking, 846
 economic integration, 846–847
 imperialism and, 598–618
 League of Nations and, 638–641

Open Door policy and, 608
 Persian Gulf War, 846
International Ladies Garment Workers
  Union (ILGWU), 528, 704
International Monetary Fund (IMF), 739,
  895
International relations
 immigrant sources and, 865
 nationalism and, 709
International system, Roosevelt, T., and, 595
Internet, 869
 Clinton investigation and, 890
 culture and, 875
 e-commerce on, 870
 music file sharing via, 878
 social networking and, 904–906
Internment, of Japanese Americans, 736, 737
Interstate Commerce Act (1887), 507, 531
Interstate Commerce Commission (ICC),
  531, 585
Intervention
 in Cuba, 785
 in Dominican Republic, 808
 in Grenada, 844
 in Lebanon, 844
 in Nicaragua, 844, 845
Interventionist organizations, in Second
  World War, 719
Inventions and inventors, economic growth
  and, 515
Investment, 873, 901
 in Caribbean region, 615
 foreign, 597
 in Germany, 660–661
 Great Depression and, 682
 in mining, 491
 northern, in southern industry, 503–504
 in railroads, 516
 in South, 477
 U.S. global and Latin American, 616
Investment banking, 516, 517, 873
IQ tests, in First World War, 631
Iran, 844
 American hostages in, 837, 839, 845
 CIA-facilitated coup in, 772, 837
 Cold War strategy toward, 752
 Iraq and, 844
 Shah in, 772, 827
Iran-*contra* affair, 845
Iranian revolution (January, 1979), 837
Iraq
 in Persian Gulf War, 846
 weapons inspection in, 896
Iraq War (2003-), 896–897
Ireland, immigrants from, 545, 546, 549
Irish Americans, 508, 525, 526, 550–551. *See
  also* Ireland
 Clan Na Gael and, 549
 First World War and, 625
 as railroad labor, 490
Iron and iron industry, 514
 industrial accidents in, 525
 in New South, 503
Iron Curtain. *See also* Cold War; Soviet
  Union
 Churchill on, 744

Ironworkers' Noontime, The (Anshutz), 512
Irreconcilables, 641
Irrigation, in West, 694, 776, 777
IRS. *See* Internal Revenue Service
Irving, Julius ("Dr. J"), 873
Islam. *See also* Muslims
    Black Muslims and, 879–880
Islamic Center of America (Dearborn,
    Michigan), 880
Islamic Center of Southern California, 880
Islamic fundamentalism, 837, 844
Isolationists and isolationism
    in Second World War, 715, 717, 718
    before World War I, 595
Israel. *See also* Jews and Judaism; Palestine
    Camp David Accords (1978) and, 837
    founding of, 740
    Lebanon and, 844
    Religious Right and, 839
    Suez Crisis in (1956), 772–773,
      773 (map)
    Yom Kipper War and, 825, 837
Issei, 736
Italian Americans, 551, 643, 669
Italy. *See also* First World War; Mussolini,
    Benito
    Communist Party in, 746
    Dominican Republic and, 609
    Ethiopia invaded by, 716
    fascism in, 716
    after First World War, 638
    immigrants from, 545, 546, 547
    in Second World War, 717, 721
    as U.S. ally, 752
Itinerant laborers, in West, 496–497
Ivy League schools, football at, 522
Iwo Jima, in Second World War, 725
IWW. *See* Industrial Workers of the World

Jackson, George, 821
Jackson, Helen Hunt, 500
Jackson, Jesse, 851–852
    political actions by, 881
Jackson, Michael, 877
Jackson State College, killings at, 826
James, William, 604
James Reese Europe's Society Orchestra, 583
Japan
    atomic bombing of, 728
    as Axis Power, 717
    China and, 717, 719, 725
    expansionism of, 612–614
    firebombings of, 726
    after First World War, 638
    gentlemen's agreement with, 614
    immigrants from, 544, 546–547
    Korea and, 613, 749–750
    Manchuria and, 613, 716
    Open Door policy and, 608
    peace treaty with, 752
    Pearl Harbor attack by, 719–720
    Russia and, 615
    after Second World War, 740, 752
    in Second World War, 717, 722–724,
      725–726, 725 (map), 727 (map)
    sphere of influence of, 615

surrender of, 728
    as U.S. ally, 752
Japanese American Citizens
    League (JACL), 760
Japanese Americans, 855
    cash indemnity for internment, 736, 855
    internment of, 736, 737
    prejudice against, 614
    in Second World War, 737–738
Jaworski, Leon, 829
Jazz
    fighting Cold War with, 771, 791
    in 1920s, 674–675
Jazz Age, 649
    racism and religious bigotry during, 667
Jazz Singer, The (movie), 672
Jeep, 729
Jefferson, Thomas, 570
Jefferson Airplane, 813
Jenkins, Jerry, 881
Jesus People, 879
Jews and Judaism. *See also* Anti-Semitism
    as European American ethnics, 669–670
    after First World War, 637
    in garment industry, 549
    German death camps and, 719
    Holocaust and, 721, 740
    as immigrants, 538, 545, 546, 547
    immigration quotas on, 719
    Jazz Singer and, 672
    Klan and, 666
    Nazi Germany and, 716, 719
    in New York City, 538
    quotas on, 667, 669
    Roosevelt, F. D., administration and, 702
    socialism and, 570
    Soviet immigrants and, 865
    on Supreme Court, 590
    Zionism and, 740
JFK (movie), 796
Jiang Jieshi, 725, 748
Jim Crow, 560
    laws, 506, 551
    in music, 583
Jim Crow (character), in minstrel show, 506
Jingoism, 599
Job Corps, 802
Jobs. *See also* Employment
    and unemployment in 1930 by gender,
      703
Jobs, Steve, 869
Johnson, Andrew, 465, 507
    Amnesty Proclamation of, 465, 468
    Congress and, 469
    election of 1868 and, 473
    elections of 1866 and, 470–471
    Fourteenth Amendment and, 470
    impeachment of, 472
    presidential pardons by, 466, 468
    Reconstruction and, 465–467, 471–472
Johnson, Charles P., 674
Johnson, Hiram W., 587, 639
Johnson, Jack, 568, 581
Johnson, James Weldon, 671
Johnson, Lyndon B., 797, 813, 838
    affirmative action and, 824

antiwar movement and, 816
    civil rights and, 791
    Dominican Republic and, 808
    election of 1960 and, 783, 784
    election of 1964 and, 803–805, 806
    election of 1968 and, 818
    Great Society of, 802, 805–806
    after Kennedy assassination, 801
    New Frontier and, 802–803
    in Second New Deal, 702
    Tet Offensive and, 818
    Vietnam War and, 806–810
    Watts riot and, 814
Johnson, Tom, 572
Johnson County War (Wyoming), 493
Johnson-Reed Immigration Restriction Act
    (1924), 666–667, 675
Johnston, Joseph E., 470
Johnston, Olin T., 696
Joint Chiefs of Staff
    in Second World War, 721, 725
    Vietnam and, 807
Jones, Paula Corbin, 888, 890
Joplin, Scott, 553
Jordan, Eisenhower and, 773
Jordan, Michael, 873
Jorgensen, George W., Jr.
    (Christine Jorgensen), 755
Joseph (Chief, Nez Percé), 500
Journalism. *See also* Media; Newspapers;
    Yellow journalism
    Internet, 906
    investigative, 564–566
    new, 817
    in Vietnam War, 810
    women in, 522
    "yellow," 599
J. P. Morgan Chase, 902
Judeo-Christian tradition, 778
Jungle, The (Sinclair), 570
Justice Department
    civil rights division in, 760
    conservatives in, 841
Juvenile delinquency
    comic books and, 779
    mothers and, 734, 786

Kabul, Afghanistan, 896
Kagan, Elena, 904
Kaiser, Henry J., 702
Kaiser Corporation, 729–730
Kallen, Horace, cultural pluralism of, 559
Kansas, 577
    black emigration to, 504–505
Kansas City, 492
Kansas Pacific Railroad, 492
Kansas Territory, Indians in, 498
Karzai, Hamid, 904
Katrina (Hurricane), 897, 899
Kazan, Elia, 754
Kearney, Dennis, 490
Keaton, Buster, 555, 556
"Keeping Tammany's Boots Shined"
    (Keppler), 550
Keller, Helen, 571, 572
Kelley, Florence, 567, 569

Kellogg, Frank, 661
Kellogg-Briand Pact, 661, 716
Kemp, Jack, 874, 887
Kennan, George, 745
Kennedy, Anthony, 894
Kennedy, Edward (Ted), 783, 838
Kennedy, Jacqueline, 783, 795
Kennedy, John F.
  anticommunism of, 784, 785
  assassination of, 795, 796, 797
  civil rights and, 784, 793–795, 797
  Cold War and, 769
  commission on women's status and, 787
  Cuban Missile Crisis and, 785
  domestic policy of, 786
  election of 1960 and, 783–784, 784 (map)
  family history of, 550–551
  foreign policy of, 784–785
  New Frontier of, 784
  space program and, 863
  Vietnam and, 785–786, 795–797
Kennedy, Joseph P., 551
Kennedy, Patrick Joseph, 550–551
Kennedy, Robert F., 783, 793
  assassination of, 819
  election of 1968 and, 818–819
  funeral of, 820
Kennedy or Nixon:...(Schlesinger), 784
Kent State University, killings at, 826
Kenya, embassy bombing in, 896
Keppler, Joseph, 550
Kerensky, Alexander, 627
Kern-McGillicuddy Act, 591
Kerouac, Jack, 811, 812
Kerr, Orpheus C., 474
Kerry, John, election of 2004 and,
  892–893
Kesey, Ken, 813
Kettle Hill, battle at, 601
Key, David, 484
Keynes, John Maynard, 699, 758
Keynesianism, 699, 728, 758, 774, 776, 782,
  786, 804. *See also* Underconsumption
  theory
  New Deal and, 857
  Nixon and, 825
Khmer Rouge, 826, 836
Khrushchev, Nikita, 771, 785
Kim Il-sung, 750
Kinetoscope (movie camera), 515
King, Billy Jean, 874
King, Martin Luther, Jr., 856
  antiwar stance of, 817
  assassination of, 818
  Birmingham and, 794
  civil disobedience and, 791
  FBI monitoring of, 793–794
  funeral of, 819
  "I Have a Dream" speech by, 795
  Kennedy, John F., and, 784
  Montgomery bus boycott and, 789
  SCLC and, 789, 791, 852
  in Watts, 814
King, Rodney, 815
Kinsey, Alfred, 754–755
Kinsey Report, The (Kinsey), 755

Kirkpatrick, Jeane, 838
Kissinger, Henry, 826, 827
  Cambodia and, 836
  foreign policy and, 825
  New Right on, 838
Knights of Labor, 527, 528, 532
Knights of the White Camelia, 477
Knox, Frank, 718
Knox, Philander C., 614, 615
Kodak camera, 515. *See also* Eastman Kodak
Kopple, Barbara, 876
Korea. *See also* Korean War
  division of, 740, 749
  Japan and, 613, 749–750
  Russia and, 612
  Soviets and, 749, 750
Korean Americans, 848
Korean War, 750–752, 751 (map), 773
  casualties in, 750–751, 770
  containment policy and, 752
  Eisenhower and, 752, 770
  refugees from, 750
  truce in, 770
Korematsu, Fred, 738
Korematsu v. *U.S.*, 736, 738
Kosovo, 895
Kristol, Irving, 838
Ku Klux Klan, 649, 803
  in film, 479
  Garvey and, 645
  integration and, 789
  in 1920s, 649, 665–666
  in South, 474, 666
  terrorism by, 472, 477–478
Ku Klux Klan Act (1871), 478
Kurds, 897
  in Iraq, 846
Kuwait, Saddam Hussein's occupation of, 846
Ky, Nguyen Cao, 809
Kyoto Protocol (1997), 896, 897

Labor. *See also* Child labor; Free-labor
  ideology; Labor unions; Management;
  Strikes; Workers
  African American, 551–552
  in agriculture, 521, 549
  capital and, 643
  changes in, 871
  Chinese immigrants as, 666–667
  Clinton and, 895
  for cotton industry, 504
  discontent of, 525
  female wage earners and, 702
  in First World War, 625, 630–631, 635
  of freedpeople, 467, 468
  immigrant, 539, 547–548, 549
  industrial, 655
  itinerant, 496–497
  local parties and, 697
  Mexican Americans as, 675
  for Panama Canal, 613
  in politics and culture, 703–705
  protests in 1930s, 696
  for railroads, 486, 490
  scientific management and, 579–580
  in Second World War, 728, 730–732

  in South, 467
  unemployment in (1929-1945), 710
  for wages, 513
  at Wal-Mart, 870
  white collar, 521
  Wilson and, 591
  of women, 849
Labor-capital conflict, in late-19th century,
  539
Labor-management relations
  anticommunism and, 753
  in 1950s and early 1960s, 777
Labor-Management Relations Act (1947).
  See Taft-Hartley Act (1947)
Labor movement. *See also* Labor unions
  anticommunism and, 753–754
  gender equality and, 849
  in Great Depression, 703–704
  in New York City, 541, 579
  in Wisconsin, 578
Labor Reform Party, 525
Labor's Non-Partisan League (LNPL), 703
Labor strikes. *See* Strikes
Labor unions, 655. *See also* Craft unions;
  Labor movement; Trade unions
  African Americans and, 527, 528, 731
  American Federation of Labor, 528
  anticommunism and, 753–754
  black, 674
  CIO and, 703
  election of 1948 and, 754
  First World War and, 630
  government and, 528
  in Great Depression, 703
  highway system and, 776
  Knights of Labor, 527
  legal system and, 528
  limitations on, 753
  management accords with, 777
  membership in, 528, 706
  Mexican Americans and, 854
  in mining, 492
  new immigrants and, 548
  in 1920s, 655
  Reagan and, 841
  in Second World War, 731–732
  white-collar employment and, 656
  women and, 527, 528, 731, 787, 849
Labor violence. *See also* Strikes
  Haymarket bombing and, 522, 523,
  527–528
Ladies' Home Journal, 520, 565
Ladies' Professional Golf Association (LPGA),
  874
La Follette, Philip, 697
La Follette, Robert ("Fighting Bob"), 587
  corporations and, 586
  Farmer-Labor Party and, 650
  First World War and, 625
  on southern disfranchisement, 574
  Versailles Treaty ratification and, 639
  Wisconsin progressivism and, 578–579
LaHaye, Tim, 881
Laissez-faire approach
  economic, 591
  Hughes and, 660

Land. *See also* Public lands
 for blacks in New South, 504
 conservation of, 904
 for cotton vs. land for food crops, 504
 for freedpeople, 464, 467–468
 Homestead Act and, 489
 Indians and, 498, 500, 708, 709, 791
 of Japanese Americans, 549
 Mexican Americans' loss of, 494–496
 preservation of, 585
 for railroads, 516
 wise use movement and, 856
Land-grant colleges, 523
Landon, Alf, 700–701, 701 (map)
Languages
 American Indian, 853
 on ballots, 805
 diversity of, 860
 English, 865
 First World War and, 635
 Navajo, 725
Lansdale, Edward G., 752, 773
Lansing, Robert, 625
Laos, 773, 809, 826
 immigrants from, 865
Las Gorras Blancas (White caps), 491
Las Vegas, 864
Lathrop, Julia, 567
Latin America. *See also* specific locations
 Alliance for Progress and, 785
 Good Neighbor Policy toward, 709,
  710, 737
 immigration from, 544–545, 864
 intervention in, 772–774, 827
 military aid to, 752
 refugees from, 881
 Roosevelt corollary and, 609–610
 in Second World War, 740
 U.S. and, 594, 611 (map), 616,
  739, 752
Latinos. *See also* Spanish-speaking people
 affirmative action and, 856
 in baseball, 761
 movies by, 876
 in Second World War, 735
 in sports, 874
 use of term, 854
Latvia, 638, 717, 739, 845
"Lavender Scare," 755, 756
Law(s). *See also* specific laws
 Granger, 531
 women and, 522
"Law and economics" (legal field), 857
Lawrence Livermore National
  Laboratory, 848
Lawrence v. *Texas*, 893
Lead emissions, 823
League of Nations, 638–640, 739
 Covenant (Article X) of, 639
 Japanese violation of, 716
 U.S. ratification and, 639–641
 Wilson on, 625, 626
League of United Latin American Citizens
  (LULAC), 737, 761, 793
League of Women Voters (LWV), 657
Lease, Mary, 533

Lebanon
 Eisenhower and, 773
 immigrants from, 545
 intervention in, 844
Lee, Robert E., 470
Lee, Spike, 815, 852
Left (political). *See* Communism; New Left;
  Radicals and radicalism; Socialism
Left Behind Series (LaHaye and Jenkins), 881
Legal Redress Committee (NAACP), 582
Legal system. *See also* Court(s); Law(s);
  Supreme Court (U.S.)
 adversarial, 890
 Reagan and, 841
Legislation. *See also* Law(s); specific laws
 environmental, 585, 823
 health-and-safety, 823
 in Hundred Days (1933), 688–694
 political stalemate and, 507
 in Second New Deal, 699
Lehman Brothers, 873, 902
Leisure
 in cities, 539, 555
 in 1920s, 651
LeMay, Curtis, 726
Lending. *See* Loans
Lending industry
 discrimination by, 762–763
 redlining by, 793
Lend-Lease Act (1941), 719
Lend-Lease assistance, to Soviet Union,
  719, 744
Lenin, Vladimir, 627, 643
Lesbian-Gay-Bisexual-Transgendered
  (LGBT) movement, 850–851, 881
 activism for gay marriage and,
  893–894
 New Right and, 838
Lesbians. *See* Gays and lesbians;
  Homosexuality
Levees, in Mississippi, 483
Levitt, William, 763
Levittown, New York, 761, 762, 763
Lewinsky, Monica, 889, 890
Lewis, John L., 703
Lewis, Sinclair, 676
LGBT. *See* Lesbian-Gay-Bisexual-
  Transgendered movement
Libbey, Laura Jane, 554
Liberalism. *See also* New Left
 progressivism and, 592
 of Roosevelt, F. D., 682, 687–688
 use of term, 842
Liberal Protestants, 668
Liberal Republicans, 478, 480
Liberia, black emigration to, 504
Libertarians, 781
Liberty(ies). *See also* Rights
 as product of frontier, 509
 social networking and, 904-906?
Liberty Bonds, in First World War, 633
Libraries
 Carnegie-funded, 535
 public, 541
Libya, 845
Life expectancy, population growth and, 862

Life Is Worth Living (television program), 778
Lifestyle
 affluence and, 774–778
 counterculture and, 812–813
 in Great Depression, 692
 LGBT, 838
 of Mexican Americans, 675
 militarization of, 752–753
 television and, 780
 of urban working class, 548
Liliuokalani (Hawaii), 599
Limbaugh, Rush Hudson, III, 856
Limited war
 Korean War as, 750, 751
 Vietnam War as, 808
Lincoln, Abraham
 executive clemency for Santee Sioux, 499
 Wartime Reconstruction and, 463, 464,
  465
Lindbergh, Charles A., 654, 655
 in America First Committee, 718
LinkedIn, 905
Lippmann, Walter, 592, 677
Liquor. *See* Alcohol and alcoholism
Literacy
 of freedpeople, 468, 469
 for voting, 506, 574, 805
Literature. *See also* Fiction; Novels; specific
  works and authors
 African American, 852
 of Beat writers, 812
 conformity critiqued in, 778–779
 feminist, 787
 genteel standards in, 521
 in Harlem Renaissance, 674, 675
 of new conservatism, 781–782
 from New South, 505
 of nostalgia for slavery, 521
 popular, 554–555
 realism in, 521–522
 romanticizing slavery, 505
 utopian, 522
 women and, 522, 554–555
Lithography, technological improvements
  for, 520
Lithuania, 638, 717, 739, 845
Lithuanian immigrants, 545
Little, Malcolm. *See* Malcolm X
Little Bighorn
 Battlefield, 853
 Battle of, 499
"Little Boy" (bomb), 728
Little Caesar (movie), 686
Little Crow (chief), 499
"Little Richard" Penniman, 779
Little Rock, Arkansas, Central High
  integration in, 791
Lloyd, Henry Demarest, 567
Lloyd George, David, in Big Four, 638
Loans
 financial bubble of 2000s and, 901–902
 after First World War, 684
 to homeowners, 872, 873
 risky, 873
 by S & Ls, 841
 small business, 822

Loan sharks, 872
Lobbying, by New Right, 838
Lochner v. *New York*, 528
Locke, Alain, 559, 674
Lockouts, 529
Lodge, Henry Cabot, Versailles Treaty ratification and, 639
London, England, Nazi bombing of, 718
Lonely Crowd, The (Riesman), 778–779
Long, Huey, 695, 696
Longest Day, The (movie), 723
Longhorn cattle, 492, 493
Longshoremen, after First World War, 643
Long-Term Capital Management, 900
Looking Backward (Bellamy), 522
Los Alamos, New Mexico, atomic bomb and, 727
Los Angeles
    English language proficiency in, 865
    Korean Americans in, 848
    Mexican Americans in, 675, 676 (map), 865
    in 21st century, 860
    water for, 695 (map)
    Watts riot (1965) in, 813–814
    Zoot Suit Riots in, 735
Losing Ground (Murray), 805
Lost Cause, in New South, 505
Lost Generation, 676
Louisiana, 478, 480
    reconstruction of, 464, 465
Lower East Side (New York), 548
Loyalty Program, of Truman, 745–746
Loyalty-security checks, on workforce, 753, 755
LPs, 878
LSD, 813
Lucas, George, 877
Lucas, Robert, 900
Luce, Henry, 597
Luftwaffe, 718
Luks, George, 538
LULAC. *See* League of United Latin American Citizens
Lumber industry, 503, 585
    endangered species and, 841
Lumumba, Patrice, 773
Lundeen, Ernest, 696
Lusitania (ship), sinking of, 620, 624–625
Luxembourg, Second World War in, 717
Lymon, Frankie, 779
Lynchings
    of African Americans, 505, 569, 582, 645, 760
    after First World War, 645
    of German Americans, 636–637
    Wilson and, 590
Lynd, Robert and Helen, 651, 677

MacArthur, Arthur, 605
MacArthur, Douglas
    Bonus Army and, 685
    in Korea, 750, 751
    removal of, 751–752
    in Second World War, 725

Macedonian immigrants, 545
Maceo, Antonio, 602
Machine politics. *See* Political machines
Machines, skilled workers and, 518, 525
Machine tools, 515, 518
MacLeish, Archibald, 718
Macy, Anne Sullivan, 572
Macy's, R. H., 520
Maddox (ship), 806
Madero, Francisco, 616
Mafia, 551
Magazines
    circulation of (1880-1919), 566
    of counterculture, 813
    feminist, 849
    gender roles in, 787
    muckrakers and, 564, 565
    revolution in, 565
    visual imagery in, 520
Magie, Lizzie, 698
Magsaysay, Ramón, 752, 772
Mahan, Alfred Thayer, 598
Mail, birth control literature in, 558
Mailer, Norman, 817
Mail-order catalogues, 520, 532
Maine (battleship), 600
Main Street (Lewis), 676
Major League Baseball (MLB), 873, 874. *See also* Baseball
    integration of, 761
Malaria, Panama Canal and, 612
Malcolm X, 814–815, 879
Malcolm X (movie), 815, 852
MALDEF. *See* Mexican American Legal Defense and Education Fund
Male revolt, 787
Management, 525
    labor accords with, 777
    revolution in, 518–520
Manchukuo, 716
Manchuria
    Japan and, 613, 615, 622, 716
    Russia and, 612
Mandela, Nelson, 815
Manhattan Project, 727, 728, 744
Manhattan Transfer (Dos Passos), 676
Manila
    in Spanish-American War, 600
    U.S. occupation of, 602
Manion, Clarence, 782
Manion Forum of Opinion, The (radio program), 782
Mann Act (1910), 557, 568, 581
Man Nobody Knows, The (Barton), 654
Mansfield, Mike, 807
Manufacturing
    in cities, 866
    ethnic, 549
    federal government control and, 518
    in First World War, 629–630
    in Great Depression, 690–691
    growth of, 514
    railroad expansion and, 514
    tariffs on, 684
    technological innovation and, 515
Mao Zedong, 725, 748, 751, 825

"Maple Leaf Rag" (Joplin), 553
March, Peyton, 631
March Against Fear, 816
March Madness, 874
March of Dimes, 760
March on Washington
    for Jobs and Freedom (1963), 795
    in Second World War, 737
Marco Polo Bridge, 717
Marcos, Ferdinand, 837
Margin buying, 682
Mariana Islands, 725, 740
Marijuana, 813
Marines (U.S.). *See also* Intervention
    to Greenland and Iceland, 719
    in Latin America, 661
    in Lebanon, 773, 844
    in Nicaragua, 661
    in Panama, 846
    in Second World War, 725
Maritime Commission, in Second World War, 728
Market(s). *See also* Free market(s); Overseas markets
    for American agricultural products, 530–531
    anti-government activists and, 857
    foreign, 597–598, 660–661, 870
    global, 870
    in 1930s, 710–711
    for tobacco, 518
Market economy
    in China, 895
    in former communist states, 847
Marketing
    mass, 651–653
    of ragtime music, 553
Marne River, battle at, 627
Marriage
    feminists on, 557
    gay, 893–894
    in 1920s, 653
Marsh, Reginald, 657
Marshall, George C., 723
    atomic bomb and, 728
    European economy and, 746
    McCarthy, Joseph, and, 756
Marshall, Thurgood, 788
Marshall Field & Co., 520
Marshall Islands, 725, 740
Marshall Plan, 746, 747, 752, 758
Martí, José, 602
Martin, Bradley (Mrs.), 534
Marx Brothers, 686–687
Marxism. *See* American Communist Party; Communism
Masculinity, in Second World War, 734
Mason, Charlotte, 675
Mass culture, debate over, 778–779
Mass culture critique, 780
Mass demonstrations, 848–849
Mass entertainment, 503
Masses, The (journal), 558
Mass immigration, 545
Massive retaliation doctrine, 771
Mass marketing, in 1920s, 651–653

Mass media. *See* Media
Mass production, Ford, Henry, and, 518
Mattachine Society, 755, 851
Matthews, Joseph Warren, 496–497
Maverick, Maury, 696
Mayaguez (ship), 836
Mayors
  black, 852
  socialist, 570, 571 (map)
McAdoo, William G., 590, 629, 633, 670
McCain, John, 902–903, 903 (map)
McCarran-Walter Act (1952), 754
McCarthy, Eugene, 818, 819
McCarthy, Joseph, and McCarthyism, 755,
    756–757, 770
McCarthy and His Enemies (Buckley), 781
McChrystal, Stanley, 904
McClure, Sam, 599
McClure's Magazine, 565, 566
McCormick farm machinery plant, 528
McDonald's, 869–870
McGovern, George, 828, 838
McGwire, Mark, 874
McKay, Claude, 674
McKinley, William
  election of 1896 and, 533–534, 535 (map)
  election of 1900 and, 534, 583
  expansion under, 595
  as imperialist, 598, 599, 603
  open door policy and, 608
  on Philippines, 603–604
  Roosevelt, T., and, 584, 609
McKinley Tariff (1890), 508
McNamara, Robert, 784, 809
McNary-Haugen Bill, 662
McPherson, Aimee Semple, 668
Meat Inspection Act (1906), 585
Meatpacking industry, 494, 517, 570
  black workers in, 551
Media. *See also* specific forms
  civil-rights movement and,
    813–814, 816
  counterculture and, 812–813
  culture and, 875–882
  demonstrations and, 811, 848–849
  popular culture and, 875–882
  print, 905
  religious movements and, 881
  Vietnam War and, 809–810
  Watergate and, 829
  Watts riot and, 814
  YIPPIES and, 817
Mediation, international, 637
Medicaid, 805, 806, 822, 888, 904
Medicare, 805, 822
  Clinton and, 888
  Reagan and, 841
Medicare Prescription Drug Improvement
    and Modernization Act, 892
Medication, regulation of, 585
Medicine. *See also* Diseases
  women and, 522, 523, 567
Mega-churches, 881
Mellon, Andrew, 658, 661
Melting pot, 559, 668
Melting-Pot, The (Zangwill), 558–559

Memphis
  anti-lynching campaign in, 505
  King's assassination in, 818
  race riot in, 470, 471
Men
  as immigrants, 546, 547
  as New Dealers, 702
  revolt by, 787
  unemployment of, 703
  in West, 497
Mencken, H. L., 669, 677
Menlo Park, New Jersey, Edison
  and, 515
Mercantonio, Vito, 696
Merchants. *See also* Business; Commerce
  crop lien system and, 504
Meredith, James, 816
Mergers, 517, 871
Mescalero Reservation, New Mexico, 709
Mesopotamia, 638
Metalworking industry, 515
Metropolitan areas, 865–867. *See also* Cities;
    Urban areas
Metropolitan Museum of Art (New York
    City), 541, 542
Mexican American Legal Defense and
    Education Fund (MALDEF), 854
Mexican Americans, 675, 849
  activism by, 793, 854
  as agricultural labor, 793, 854
  Chicanismo and, 854
  as cowboys, 494
  cultural renaissance of, 708
  in First World War, 630, 631
  immigration issues and, 893
  loss of property and political influence in
    West, 494–496
  in New Deal, 707–708
  population of (1930), 676 (map)
  in Second World War, 730, 737
  segregation of, 761, 793
  in Southwest, 793
  in West, 488
  women workers and, 677
  Zoot Suit Riots and, 735
Mexican Revolution (1910), 616
  immigration after, 545
Mexico
  debt crisis in, 895
  illegal immigrants from, 793
  immigrants from, 487, 496, 544, 547,
    666–667, 864
  intervention in, 611 (map), 616, 709–710
  NAFTA and, 847
  reforms in, 616–617
  revolution in (1910), 616
  unrest in, 616
  Zimmermann telegram and, 626
Miami, Cuban Americans in, 864
Microchips, 869
Microsoft, 869
Middle class
  African American, 506, 552
  in cities, 541
  commercial amusements and, 554
  conformity and, 779

  culture of, 521–522
  ethnic groups in, 549–550
  in late 19th century, 521
  movies and, 556
  progressivism and, 564, 591
  realism and, 565–566
  reform and, 566–567
  suburbanization movement and, 521
  "white-collar," 521
  women in, 522–523, 787
  women's club movement in, 523
  working class and, 527, 556
Middle East. *See also* Arab world; specific
    locations
  Camp David Accords and, 837
  Eisenhower policy toward, 773
  Jewish state in, 740
  military bases in, 752
  oil-producing nations in, 825, 836
  peace negotiations in, 836
  Reagan and, 844–845
  Suez Crisis in (1956), 772–773,
    773 (map)
Middle managers, in corporations, 519
Midvale Steel Company, 579
Midway Island, Battle of, 722, 725 (map)
Midway Plaisance, of Columbian Exposition,
    543, 544, 554, 556
Midwest
  civil rights protests in, 794
  immigrants in, 497, 545
  racial composition in, 788–789
Migrant workers, 704
Migration
  African American, 487, 504–505, 551,
    630, 632 (map), 670–671, 735, 737,
    762
  Mexican American, 675
Militancy
  black, 581, 582, 814–816
  labor, 732, 753
Militarization, of American life, 752–753
Military. *See also* Armed forces; Soldiers
  blacks in, 601–602
  during Cold War, 752
  desegregation of, 760
  Eisenhower and, 782
  First World War and, 622, 625, 627,
    631–632, 638
  funding of, 717
  high-tech industries and, 863
  integration of, 631
  in Iraq, 898
  Japanese Americans in, 737–738
  Kellogg-Briand pact and, 661
  Kennedy, John F., and, 785
  Mexican Americans in, 737
  My Lai massacre and, 826
  in Nazi Germany, 716
  pollution related to, 895
  Pullman strike and, 530
  Second World War and, 733–734
  segregation of, 735, 736, 760
  sexual harassment in, 850
  strikes broken by, 528
  U.S. base in Cuba, 607

U.S. intervention and, 661
in Vietnam, 785
women in, 733–734
Military bases. *See also* Naval bases
in Cold War, 752
Military districts, in South, 471, 472
Military draft. *See* Draft (military)
Military-industrial complex, Eisenhower's
warning against, 774
"Military Keynesianism," 758, 774
Military occupation. *See* Occupation
(military)
Military spending, 717, 752–753, 758. *See
also* Defense spending
Eisenhower and, 771, 774
by Reagan, 844
Military Training Camps Association, 719
Militia
Great Railroad Strike and, 526
Indian warfare and, 499
Islamic, 844
race riots and, 581
in South, 466, 478, 481, 482
strikes and, 529
Miller, Alice Duer, poem by, 577
Miller & Lux (ranching company), 494,
496, 497
Millionaires, in 1890s, 520
Mills, C. Wright, on power elite, 779
Mills, in New South, 504
Milosevic, Slobodan, 895
Mines and mining. *See also* Coal and coal
industry; Gold
accidents in, 547
in California gold rush, 491
camps, 497
Chinese immigrants in, 490
Hispanics in, 491
hydraulic mining, 492
immigrant labor for, 547
mechanized violence in, 525
Mexican Americans in, 495–496
strikes in, 492, 584, 591, 732, 793
strip-mining, 492
in West, 490, 491–492, 493 (map)
Minimum wage, 579, 702, 758, 781, 835
Bush, George H. W., and, 842
decline in value of, 840
Minneapolis, labor protests in, 696
Minnesota, 497, 499
Somalis in, 865
Minnesota Farmer-Labor (MFL)
Party, 697
Minorities. *See also* Ethnic groups and
ethnicity; Race and racism
discrimination against, 523
in New Deal, 705–709
in Second World War, 730
Minoso, Orestes ("Minnie"), 761
Minstrels and minstrelsy, 554
Miranda v. *Arizona*, 823
Miranda Warning, 823
"Misery index," 839
Mises, Ludwig von, 781
Misogyny, masculinity and, 734
"Missile gap," 784

Missiles
in Cuba, 785
in Turkey, 785
Missions and missionaries
freedmen's schools of, 468, 469
Protestant, 596–597
Mississippi, 480, 574
civil-rights workers murdered in, 803
direct primary in, 573
election of 1875 and, 480–481
Till, Emmett, murder in, 789
Mississippi Freedom Democratic Party
(MFDP), 803
Mississippi Plan, 480, 481
Miss Lonelyhearts (West), 686
Missouri Pacific Railroad, 527
Mitchell, John (attorney general), 829
Mitchell, John (UMW), 584
Mitchell, Joni, 813
MLB. *See* Major League Baseball
Mobility. *See* Social mobility
Mobilization
for First World War, 622
for Second World War, 715, 721,
728–732
Model A Ford, 651
Model Cities Program, 805
Model T Ford, 518, 579, 580, 650
"Modern," use of term in 1920s, 649
Modern Republicanism, of Ford, 834
Mogadishu, 894
Moley, Raymond, 687
Molly Maguires, 525
Molly Maguires, The (movie), 526
Mondale, Walter
election of 1976 and, 834
election of 1984 and, 842
Monday Night Football, 873
Monetary system, dual currency (greenbacks
and gold), 532
Money. *See* Currency
Money Power, 532
Monopolies, 518
Standard Oil as, 516–517
Monopoly (game), 698
Monroe Doctrine, 608
Roosevelt corollary to, 609–610
Montana, 533
Battle of Little Bighorn in, 499
"Monterrey Pop" music festival, 813
Montgomery bus boycott, 789, 790
Morale, during Vietnam War, 827
Moral Majority, 850
Moran, Thomas, 586
Morgan, J. P., 517. *See also* J. P. Morgan
Chase
industrial investment by, 516
Northern Securities and, 584
panic of 1907 and, 586
Morgan, J. P., Jr., foreign investment and,
660
Mormons, 880
Morocco, 721
Morris, Dick, 887
Morrison, Toni, 852
Mortality rates, urban, 541

Mortgages, 841, 872
foreclosures on, 840
in Great Depression, 690
interest payments on, 762
sub-prime, 901
Morton, "Jelly Roll," 665
Moscow, McDonald's in, 870
Moses, Robert, 793
Mossadegh, Mohammed, CIA-facilitated
overthrow of, 772
Mothers
advertising appeals to, 776
juvenile delinquency and, 734, 786
working, 787
Motion pictures. *See* Movies and movie
industry
Mount Rushmore, 584
Movement of movements, in 1960s,
810–811, 813, 814, 833, 851
Movement of peoples. *See* Immigrants and
immigration; Migration; Westward
movement
Movies and movie industry
African Americans in, 815, 852
anticommunism and, 742, 754
"Blaxploitation movies," 852
celebrities and, 653
Christian-themed, 881
in cities, 555
comedy in, 555, 556
communism and, 754
entertainment technology and, 875–876
Hollywood Ten and, 754
musicals in, 763
nickelodeons and, 539, 554, 555
in 1930s, 704
pirated, 876
Reagan in, 754, 843
after Second World War, 763–765
in Second World War, 719, 730, 732
sexuality in, 555, 557
silent, 555
technology changes and, 875–876
Moynihan, Daniel Patrick, 821
on PRWORA, 887
Mr. Deeds Goes to Town (movie), 700, 704,
764
Mr. Smith Goes to Washington (movie), 704
MS. magazine, 849
MSNBC, 878
MTV, 876–877
Muckleshoot Reservation, 792
Muckrakers, 564–566, 567
Mugwumps, 507, 508
Muhammad, Elijah, 879
Muir, John, 585
Multiculturalism, 560
Multinational corporations, 597
Muncie, Indiana, study of, 651
Munich Conference (1938), 717
Municipal government
reform of, 572–573
socialist mayors and other officers in,
570, 571 (map)
Munn v. *Illinois*, 531
Mural art, Mexican American, 854

Murdoch, Rupert, 875
Murphy, Frank, 704
Murray, Charles, 805
Murrow, Edward R., 718
Muscle Shoals, Alabama, 693
Museums, 541
Music
    army life and, 636
    banjo in, 665
    black, 674, 707
    blues, 674
    Christian, 881
    of counterculture, 813
    country and blues, 663
    early African American orchestra, 583
    folk-rock, 811, 813
    in Harlem Renaissance, 674–675
    hip-hop, 879
    jazz, 674, 771, 791
    of Joplin, Scott, 553
    in 1930s, 704–705
    patriotic, 605
    pop, 876–878
    ragtime, 553
    rock 'n' roll, 779–780
    in Second World War, 735
Music Entertainment Channel. See MTV
Music halls, 554
Music industry, 876–878
Music USA: The Jazz Hour (radio
        program), 771
Muskie, Edmund, election of 1972 and, 828
Muslims, 880. See also Islam
    attitudes toward U.S., 897
    Bosnian, 895
    Shi'a, 846
Mussolini, Benito, 710–711, 716, 717
Myers, Harriet, 894
Myers, William, 671
My Lai Incident, 826
MySpace, 905
Myths, of West, 503

NAACP (National Association for the
        Advancement of Colored People),
        569, 574, 582–583, 590, 735, 761
    after First World War, 645
Nader, Ralph, 823, 891 (map)
NAFTA. See North American Free Trade
        Agreement
Nagasaki, atomic bombing of, 728
Nagy, Imre, 772
Nahl, Perham W., 613
Nanjing, 717
Napalm, 808
Napster, 878
Narcotics. See Drugs
Narrowcasting, 875, 878
NASA. See National Aeronautics and Space
        Administration
Nasser, Gamal Abdel, 772
Nasserism, 773
Nast, Thomas, cartoons of, 470, 478
Nation (magazine), 599
National Aeronautics and Space
        Administration (NASA), 782, 863

National Americanization Committee, 637
National American Woman Suffrage
        Association (NAWSA), 575, 577,
        625, 657
National Association for Stock Car Racing
        (NASCAR), 874
National Association for the Advancement
        of Colored People (NAACP). See
        NAACP
National Association of Colored Women,
        506
National Association of Manufacturers
        (NAM), 757
National Basketball Association (NBA), 873
National Black Political Convention (1972),
        852
National brands, 520
National Conservative Political Action
        Committee (NCPAC), 838
National Consumer Cooperative Bank, 848
National Cordage Company, 529
National debt, Second World War and, 728
National defense
    Cold War and, 752
    Reagan and, 844–845
National Defense Education Act (1958), 782
National Economic Agency (NEC), 900
National Farmers' Alliance and Industrial
        Union, 532
National Football League (NFL), 873
National forests, conservation of, 585, 895
National Forest Service, 585
    Ballinger-Pinchot controversy and, 587
National government. See Government (U.
        S.)
National Guard
    Attica Uprising and, 821
    at Central High School, 791
    freedom riders and, 794
    labor strikes and, 492, 570
    Watts riot and, 814
National health insurance, 759
National Hockey League (NHL), 874
National Industrial Recovery Act (NIRA,
        1933), 689, 690, 696
National Industrial Recovery Administration
        (NRA), 689, 690
Nationalism. See also Imperialism
    black, 645
Nationalism (of Bellamy), 522
Nationalist China
    Second World War and, 725
    U.S. aid to, 748
Nationalist Party (South Africa), 752
Nationalization
    after First World War, 643, 645
    in Mexico, 709–710
National Labor Relations Act (NLRA, 1935),
        699, 701, 703, 708, 711
National Labor Relations Board (NLRB),
        699, 703, 777
National Labor Union, 525
National Liberation Front (NLF), 785, 806
National Museums of the American Indian,
        853
National Negro League, 673

National Network of Hispanic Women, 854
National Organization for Women (NOW),
        849, 850
National origins system
    of immigration, 667, 865
    quotas and, 805
National parks, 585, 823
National Park Service, 585, 853
National Rainbow Coalition, 852
National Recovery Administration (NRA),
        691, 692, 696
National Review (magazine), 781, 838
National security
    anticommunism and, 743
    Bush Doctrine and, 896
    after Cold War, 845–847
    in Cold War, 744–747, 752–753
    education and, 782
    Eisenhower and, 771, 782
    at home, 753–757
    Kennedy, John F., and, 784
    presidential power and, 897–898
    spying and, 746
    Truman Doctrine and, 745
National Security Act (1947), 746, 757, 758
National Security Agency (NSA), 757
National Security Council (NSC), 746
    CIA mandate and, 772
    NSC-68 and, 748–749, 752
National Security Strategy (2002), 896
National Socialist (Nazi) Party, 716. See also
        Nazi Germany
National Trails Act (1968), 823
National Union of Social Justice
        (NUSJ), 696
National Union Party, 470–471
National Urban League, 582, 674
National War Labor Board (NWLB), 631,
        642
National Wild and Scenic Rivers Act (1968),
        822
National Woman's Party (NWP), 577, 657
National Woman Suffrage Association, 473
National Women's Party (NWP), 557
National Youth Administration (NYA),
        699, 729
Nation building
    as policy, 895
    in South Vietnam, 785
Nation of Islam (NOI). See Black Muslims
Native American Graves Protection and
        Repatriation Act (1990), 853
Native American Rights Fund (NARF), 853
Native Americans. See American Indians
Native Son (Wright), 754
NATO. See North Atlantic Treaty
        Organization
Naturalization. See Citizens and citizenship
Natural resources, preservation of, 585
Natural science, 521
Navajo Indians, 709
    language of, 725
Navajo Signal Corps, 725, 726
Naval bases
    at Guantanamo Bay, 607
    in Manila, 603

Navy. *See also* Navy (U.S.); Royal Navy
(Britain)
limits on warships, 660
Navy (U.S.)
expenditures and battleship size in
(1890-1914), 599
Great White Fleet and, 614, 615 (map)
Guantanamo base for, 607
imperialism and, 598–599
rearmament and, 717
in Second World War, 720, 722
sexual harassment in, 850
in Spanish-American War, 600
NAWSA. *See* National American Woman
Suffrage Association
Nazi Germany. *See also* Death camps;
Germany; Hitler, Adolf; Second
World War
Austria and, 717
blitzkrieg by, 717
bombing of, 725–726
dismemberment of, 739
expansion by, 717, 718 (map)
Holocaust of, 721, 740
images of, 714
Japanese attack on Pearl Harbor and, 720
Soviet pact with, 717
surrender by, 722
war crimes by, 721
"Nazi gold," 721
Nazism, 736
NBA. *See* National Basketball Association
NBC television, 780, 875. *See also* Television
NCPAC. *See* National Conservative Political
Action Committee
Near East. *See also* Middle East
after First World War, 640 (map)
immigrants from, 545
Nebraska Territory, Indians in, 498
Negroes. *See* African Americans; Blacks;
Slaves and slavery
Negro Leagues, in baseball, 673, 674, 761,
762
Negro rule, 477, 507
Negro World, 645
Neo-Confederate violence, 466, 474
Neoconservatives, 896, 897, 900
Neoconservatives (neocons), in New Right,
838
Netherlands, Second World War in, 717
Netherlands East Indies. *See* Dutch East
Indies
Network TV, 875
Neutralism, in Cold War, 772, 773
Neutrality Acts (1935, 1936, 1937), 717
Neutrality policy
in First World War, 624–625
before Second World War, 716–717
Nevada, 491
New Age spiritual movements, 879
"New Captain in the District, A," 562
New conservatism, 781–782, 787, 803, 804,
805, 811
New Deal, 592. *See also* Great Depression
African Americans in, 706–707
American Indians in, 705–706, 708–709

banking in, 689
court-packing fiasco and, 711
First, 688–694
foreign relations in, 709–711
Keynesianism and, 857
labor protests in, 696
Mexican Americans in, 707–708
minorities in, 705–709
populist critics of, 694–696
recession of 1937-1938 and, 711
Second, 698–705
Second World War and, 728–729
Truman and, 758
TVA in, 693–694
western development and, 694,
695 (map)
New Democrats, 848, 887
New Economic Policy, of Nixon, 825
New England, immigrants in, 544, 545, 547
New federalism, of Nixon, 822
New Freedom (Wilson), 588
New Nationalism and, 589–591
New Frontier (Kennedy), 784
Johnson, Lyndon B., and, 802–803
New Guinea, 725
New immigration, 545, 548, 864–865. *See
also* Immigrants and immigration
New Jersey, corporations in, 573
"New journalism," 817
New Left, 817
on college campuses, 811–812
political and cultural movements of,
810–811
New Look, in U.S. military, 771
New Mexico
Anglo-Americans and Mexican
Americans in, 491, 496
mining strike in, 793
New Nationalism
New Freedom and, 589–591
Roosevelt, T., and, 584, 587, 588
New Negro
after First World War, 643, 646
Harlem Renaissance and, 674
New Negro, The (Locke), 674
New Orleans
Hurricane Katrina and, 897, 899
race riot in, 470
"New politics," 817
New Right
affirmative action and, 856
anti-government activism of, 856–858
Bush, George H. W., and, 842
business leaders in, 838
election of 1992 and, 848
on environmental regulation, 856,
880–881
on gender equality, 850
in 1970s, 838–839
Reagan and, 833, 841, 842
women in, 849
News
"fake" programs as, 878–879
on television, 878
New South. *See also* South
agriculture in, 504

industrialization in, 503–504
Jim Crow laws in, 506
labor force in, 504
race relations in, 505
Newspapers
celebrities in, 653
circulation of, 565, 566
expansion of, 520
foreign-language, 549
future of, 905
socialist, 570
Newton, Huey, 816
"New Woman," 523, 524
New York (city)
African Americans in, 671
aqueducts in, 541
bankruptcy and, 835
death rates in (1925), 673
draft riot in, 478
garment workers strike in, 642
Greenwich Village in, 557–558
immigrants in, 538
movie industry in, 555
museums and parks in, 541, 542
"open housing" in, 791
political machine in, 474, 550, 564
population of, 540, 548
poverty in, 567
Puerto Ricans in, 792, 854
terrorist attack in, 896
unemployment in Great Depression, 683
urban decay in, 835
WPA projects in, 701
New York (state)
electoral balance and, 507, 508
progressive reforms in, 579
New York Journal, 599, 600
New York Press Club, 523
New York Stock Exchange
crash of 1873 and, 516
in 1920s, 651, 682
in 1987, 873
railroads listed on, 516
New York World, 599
New Zealand
ANZUS and, 752
in Second World War, 722
Nez Percé Indians, 500
NFL. *See* National Football League
NHL. *See* National Hockey League
Niagara movement, NAACP and, 582
Nicaragua
canal through, 612
Carter and, 837
intervention in, 611 (map), 615, 661, 844
Iran-*contra* affair and, 845
Sandinistas in, 837, 845
Soviet Union and, 845
U.S. intervention in, 709
Nicholas II (Russia), 626
Nickelodeons, 539, 554, 555
Nimitz, Chester W., 722, 725
Nineteenth Amendment, 575, 657
9th and 10th Negro Cavalries, 601
Nisei, 736
Nitze, Paul, 748

Nixon, Richard Milhous, 838, 845
    anticommunism of, 755
    China and, 825
    economy and, 824–825
    election of 1952 and, 765, 766
    election of 1960 and, 783–784,
        784 (map), 821
    election of 1968 and, 819–821, 821 (map)
    election of 1972 and, 826, 828, 828 (map)
    environmental legislation and, 822–823
    FAP program of, 887
    foreign policy of, 825–827
    Hiss affair and, 754
    impeachment and, 829
    pardon of, 829, 834
    presidency of, 827–828
    resignation of, 801, 829
    rights-related issues and, 823–824
    social policy of, 821–822
    Vietnam and, 821, 825–827
    Watergate scandal and, 801, 828–829
Nixon Doctrine, 826, 827
NLF. See National Liberation Front
NLRA. See National Labor Relations Act
    (NLRA, 1935)
NLRB. See National Labor Relations Board
Nobel Prize
    for literature, 677
    Peace Prize to Roosevelt, T., 613
No Child Left Behind program, 892
"No-fly" zones, in Iraq, 846
Nonaggression pact, Soviet-Nazi, 717
Nonpartisan League of North Dakota, 662
Nonproliferation, of nuclear weapons, 896
Nonrecognition, toward Manchukuo, 716
Nonviolence. See also Protest(s)
    King on, 791, 814
    as UFW tactic, 854
Noriega, Manuel, 846
"Normalcy," Harding on, 649
Normandy landing, in Second World War,
    721, 722 (map)
Norris, George, 625
North (region)
    African American migration to, 551, 630,
        632 (map), 671, 735, 737
    anti-lynching campaign and, 505
    investment in southern industry, 503–504
    Reconstruction and, 480
North, Oliver, 845
North Africa, in Second World War, 721,
    722 (map)
North American Free Trade Agreement
    (NAFTA), 847, 895
North Atlantic Treaty Organization
    (NATO), 748, 749 (map), 752, 765,
    895
    expansion of, 771
North Carolina, 465, 794. See also South
    Carolina
North Carolina A&T University, sit-ins and,
    794
North Dakota, 533
Northeast
    civil rights protests in, 794
    racial composition in, 788

Northern Pacific Railroad, 489, 491
    Panic of 1873 and, 480, 516
Northern Plains tribes, activism of, 852
Northern Securities Company, prosecution
    of, 584
North Korea, 749, 750. See also Korea;
    Korean War
    nuclear weapons program in, 896
North Vietnam, 752, 773, 795, 836. See also
    Vietnam; Vietnam War
    bombing of, 806, 826
    Easter Offensive of, 826
Norway
    immigrants from, 497
    Second World War in, 717, 720
Novels. See also Literature
    dime, 503, 521, 554–555
    in 1930s, 704
    about trials, 888
November 11, 1918 First World War
    armistice on, 628, 628 (map)
NOW. See National Organization for
    Women
NRA. See National Recovery Administration
NSC. See National Security Council
NSC-68, 748–749, 752, 782
Nuclear Nonproliferation Treaty (1995), 896
Nuclear power
    cancer and, 823
    development of, 753
    energy from, 836
    pollution by, 895
Nuclear weapons. See also Atomic bomb
    ban on, 845
    Clinton and, 896
    Cold War arms race and, 744, 774
    in Cuba, 785
    demonstrations against, 848
    health effects of testing, 823
    Korean War and, 750, 751
    limitations on, 825, 900
    massive retaliation and, 771
    religious groups and, 881
    testing of, 771
Nuremberg trials, 721
Nursing, women in, 522, 787
NWLB. See National War Labor Board
Nye, Gerald P., 716

Oath of allegiance, for ex-Confederates,
    464–465
Obama, Barack, 885, 902–903, 903 (map),
    906
    cabinet of, 903–904
    family of, 903
    inaugural address of, 904
Ocala, Florida, Farmers' Alliance at, 532
Occupation (military). See also Zones of
    occupation
    of Austria, 771
    of Japan, 740, 752
    of South, 467
Occupational Safety Act (1973), 823
Occupations (jobs). See Jobs; Professions
Oceania, immigration from, 864
O'Connor, Sandra Day, 787, 841, 894

Odets, Clifford, 704
OEO. See Office of Economic Opportunity
Officeholders
    Asian Americans as, 855
    blacks as, 475–477, 507, 852
    ex-Confederates and, 466
    socialists as, 570, 571 (map)
Office of Economic Opportunity (OEO), 802
Office of Inter-American Affairs (OIAA),
    740
Office of Price Administration, 728
Office of Scientific Research and
    Development, 728
Office of War Information (OWI), 733
Office work, women in, 522
Ohio, electoral balance and, 507
Oil and oil industry, 835. See also Energy;
    Organization of Petroleum Exporting
    Countries
    Carter and, 836
    Persian Gulf War and, 846
    Reagan and, 841
    Rockefeller in, 516–517
Oil embargo, 825
Okies, 690
    Steinbeck on, 704
Okinawa, 725, 752
Oklahoma! (movie), 495
Oklahoma! (musical play), 704
Old Guard. See Republican Party
Old immigrants, 545, 548
Olmsted, Frederick Law, 541
Olympic Games, boycott of (1980), 838
100th Battalion, 737–738
O'Neill, Eugene, 676
On the Road (Kerouac), 812
On the Town (movie), 763
OPEC. See Organization of Petroleum
    Exporting Countries
"Open door" notes, 608
Open Door policy, toward China, 608, 660
Open housing
    in California, 804
    in New York, 791
Open-range grazing, 493
Open Skies initiative (1955), 771
Opera companies, 541
Operation Desert Shield, 846
"Operation Dixie," 777
Operation Iraqi Freedom, 897
Operation Just Cause, 846
Operation Mongoose, 785
Operation OVERLORD, 721, 722 (map)
Operation PUSH, 852
Operation Ranch Hand, 808
Operation Rolling Thunder, 808
Operation Wetback, 793
Opium Wars (China), 490
Orchestras, African American, 583
Oregon, 577
Oregon, Illinois, automobiles and travel in,
    652 (map)
Organization Man, The (Whyte), 778
Organization of Afro-American Unity, 815
Organization of Petroleum Exporting
    Countries (OPEC), 836, 841

Organized Baseball, desegregation of, 761
Organized crime, 551, 664–665
Orlando, Vittorio, in Big Four, 638
Oswald, Lee Harvey, 796, 797
Otis elevators, 515
Ottoman Empire, First World War and, 622, 638, 640 (map)
Overland trails, 498. *See also* Trail(s)
OVERLORD, Operation, in Second World War, 721, 722 (map)
Overseas markets
    business in, 660–661, 870
    Cold War assistance programs and, 758
Ovington, Mary White, 582
OWI. *See* Office of War Information
Ozone layer, 895

Pacification program, in Vietnam, 809
Pacific Fleet, U.S., Japanese attack on, 720, 722
Pacific Northwest
    American Indians in, 792
    Grand Coulee Dam in, 694
    timber industry in, 841
Pacific Ocean region
    Pearl Harbor attack in, 719–720
    in Second World War, 720, 721, 722–724, 725–726, 725 (map), 727 (map)
    U.S. sphere of influence in, 752
Pacific Railroad Bill (1862), 489
Pacific Rim, economic growth in, 846
Pacifism
    in First World War, 625
    in Second World War, 719
Packard, Vance, 779
Padroni (labor contractors), 549
Page, Thomas Nelson, 505
Pago Pago, 598
Pahlavi, Reza (Shah), 772, 827, 837
Painting. *See also* Art(s)
    in Harlem Renaissance, 674
    Impressionism in, 521
    realism in, 521
    in Second World War, 733
Paiute Indians, 501
Pakistan, al-Qaeda in, 900
Palestine. *See also* Israel
    after First World War, 638
    Jewish state in, 740
Palin, Sarah, 903
Palmer, A. Mitchell, 643
Palmer raids, 643
Panama
    independence of, 612
    intervention in, 611 (map)
    Noriega and, 846
Panama Canal, 610–612, 613 (map)
    building of, 613
    Carter treaties for, 837
    transfer to Panama, 612, 846
Panama Canal Zone, 612, 613 (map)
Panay (gunboat), 717
Panics (financial)
    of 1873, 480, 506, 514, 516, 525
    of 1893, 506, 529, 530, 532, 533
    of 1907-08, 546, 586

Paraguay, dictator in, 772
Paramilitary organizations, in South, 480
Pardons
    for ex-Confederates, 466, 468
    of Iran-*contra* officials, 845
    of Nixon, 829, 834
Paris, 721
    African American expatriates in, 675
    in First World War, 628
    peace accords in (1973), 827
    summit planned for, 771
Paris, Treaty of, of 1898, 602, 604
Paris Peace Conference
    in 1898, 602
    in 1919, 637–639
Park, Tom (Colonel), 780
Parker, Alton B., 584
Parks
    national, 585
    urban, 541
Parks, Rosa, 789
Participatory democracy, SDS on, 811
Passion of Sacco and Vanzetti, The (Shahn), 643
Patriot Act. *See* USA Patriot Act
Patriotism
    in First World War, 633–635
    music for, 605
Patronage, political machines and, 475
Patrons of Husbandry. *See* Grange
Patsy Mink Equal Opportunity in Education Act, 874
Patton, George, Bonus Army and, 685
Paul, Alice, 557, 577, 657, 658
Paulson, Henry (Hank), 901, 902
Pawn America, 872
Payne-Aldrich Tariff Act (1909), 587
Peace
    after First World War, 637–641, 660–661
    after Second World War, 738–740
Peace accords (Paris), ending Vietnam War, 827, 836
Peace Corps, 784, 802
Peace groups. *See also* Antiwar movements
    Spanish Civil War and, 717
Peacekeeping
    Clinton and, 895
    by Roosevelt, T., in East Asia, 612
    UN force in Korean War, 750
    U.S., in Lebanon, 844
Peace movements. *See also* Antiwar movements; Copperheads
    in First World War, 625
Peace negotiations
    in Middle East, 836
    in Vietnam War, 821, 826
"Peace Policy," for Indians, 500
"Peace without victory," Wilson on, 626
Peale, Norman Vincent, 777
Pearl Harbor
    Japanese attack on, 719–720
    U.S. leasing of, 598
Pell Grants, 867
Pelosi, Nancy, 904
Pendergast, Tom, 550

Pendleton Civil Service Act (1883), 474, 507
Penicillin, 728
Penn, Kal, 904
Pennsylvania
    coal industry in, 525, 526
    Homestead strike in, 529
    September 11, 2001, terrorist attack and, 896
Pensions, 508, 699, 711, 777
Pentagon
    budget increase for, 782
    after Cold War, 845, 846
    Reagan and, 844
    in Second World War, 721
    September 11, 2001, attack on, 892
    YIPPIEs and, 817
"Pentagon Papers," 828
People of color. *See also* specific groups
    Columbian Exposition and, 543
    after Second World War, 759–760
People's capitalism, 651
People's Party (Populists)
    launch of, 532–533
    rise and fall of, 533–534
People's Republic of China. *See* China
Pepsi Cola, 870
Per capita production and income, and real wages (1870-1900), 525
Perestroika, 845
Periodicals. *See also* Magazines; Newspapers
    socialist, 570
Perkins, Frances, 687, 702
Perot, Ross, 848, 887–888
Pershing, John J.
    in First World War, 627, 631
    in Mexico, 617
Persia. *See* Iran
Persian Gulf War, 846
Personal computers, 868
Personal registration laws, 574
Personal Responsibility and Work Opportunity Reconciliation Act (PRWORA, 1996), 887
Personal savings, decline of, 872
Peru, dictator in, 772
Pesticides, 776, 823
Pesticides Control Act (1972), 823
Petit jury, Senate as, 472
Petraeus, David, 898, 904
Petroleum industry. *See* Energy; Oil and oil industry
Peyote, 853
Phelps, Elizabeth Stuart, 522
Philadelphia, 732
    population of, 540
Philanthropy, 517, 535–536
Philippines, 827. *See also* Filipino Americans
    independence for, 607, 740
    Japan and, 613
    Magsaysay and CIA in, 752, 772
    Marcos in, 837
    in Second World War, 720, 722, 725
    Spanish-American War and, 602
    Spanish cession to U.S., 602
    Taft, William Howard, as governor-general, 605–606

Philippines (*continued*)
    as U.S. colony, 603–604
    U.S. war with, 605–606
Phillips curve, 825
Philosophy, Social Darwinism as, 521
Phonograph, 515
Photography
    of Bourke-White, Margaret, 732–733,
        759
    of Japanese American internment, 737
    Kodak camera and, 515
    in magazines, 520
    in Second World War, 732–733
    of Vietnam War, 809
Physical fitness, 522
Physics, fission and, 727
Pill, the, 787, 849
Pinchot, Gifford, 585, 587
Pine Ridge Reservation, 501, 852
"Ping-pong diplomacy," 825
Pingree, Hazen S., 572
Pinkerton agency, 529
Pins and Needles (musical play), 704
"Pin-ups," in Second World War, 734
Pirating
    of copyrighted materials, 878
    of movies, 876
Plains Indians
    Ghost Dance and, 501
    "peace policy" and, 500
    Sioux uprising and, 499
    suppression of, 500
    westward expansion by whites and,
        498–499
Planter (dispatch steamer), 476
Planters and plantations, romanticization of,
    505
Platform (political). *See also* specific parties
    of Black Panther Party, 816
    of People's Party, 533
Platt, Thomas C., 584
Platt Amendment, 607, 709
Playboy magazine, 787
Pledge of Allegiance, "under God" in, 778
Pleiku, attack on, 808
Plessy v. *Ferguson*, 506, 761
Plumbers unit, 828
Pluralism
    cultural, 559
    political, 777–778, 810
Podhoretz, Norman, 838
Poets and poetry
    Beat, 812, 813
    in Harlem Renaissance, 674
Poison gas, in First World War, 624
Poland
    after First World War, 638
    immigrants from, 497, 545
    rebellion in (1956), 772
    Second World War in, 717
    Solidarity movement in, 845
    Soviets and, 739
Polarization, of politics, 833, 886–894
Police
    Haymarket bombing and, 528
    strikes and, 570

Polio
    of Roosevelt, F. D., 687, 688
    vaccine against, 760
Political bosses. *See* Bosses (political)
Political campaigns. *See also* Whistle-stop
    campaign
    Goldwater's tactics in (1964), 804
Political cartoons
    anti-Bryan, 534
    anti-immigrant, 668
    for freedom, 470
    Herblock on anticommunism, 755
    Herblock on Eisenhower-era social policy,
        779
    "Keeping Tammany's Boots Shined"
        (Keppler), 550
    on Mississippi Plan, 481
    Nast's anti-Greeley cartoons, 478
    "New Captain in the District,
        A," 562
    on Wilson's Mexico policy, 617
    on woman suffrage, 576
Political conventions, Democratic Party
    (1964), 803
Political machines, 550–551, 572, 584
    Addams, Jane, and, 567
    patronage and, 475
Political parties. *See also* Elections; specific
    parties
    labor, 525
    reform and, 572
    spoils system and, 474
Political refugees, 545
Politics
    African Americans in, 851–852
    of American Indian policy, 791–792
    of anticommunism, 753–754
    Asian Americans in, 855
    attitudes toward in 1930s, 686–687
    of business, 658–661
    of civil rights, 791
    ethnics in, 670
    Farmers' Alliance and, 532–533
    gender, 786–788
    in Great Depression, 694–697
    identity, 852
    labor and, 703–705
    Mexican Americans in, 854
    in New Deal, 694–697
    New Left and, 810, 812
    pluralism in, 777–778
    polarization of, 833, 886–894
    progressivism and, 563, 583–584
    of race, 504
    religion and, 880–881
    sexual, 850–851
    social-cultural issues and, 893–894
    of socialists, 570–571
    of social movements, 848–858
    South and West in, 863
    sports figures in, 874
    of stalemate (late 1800s), 506–508
    women's club movement and, 523
Polk, Leonidas L., 533
Pollan, Michael, 894
Poll taxes, 574, 760

Pollution. *See also* Environment
    air, 823
    by government, 895
    legislation and, 823
    water, 541, 893
Pools (business), railroads and, 516, 531
Poor people. *See also* Poverty
    Homestead Act and, 489
    urban, 541, 567, 579
Poor Peoples Campaign, 818, 819
Pop music, 876–878
Popular culture
    in Second World War, 734
    sexuality in, 555
Popular literature, 554–555
Population
    African American, 552 (map), 790 (map)
    aging of, 862–864
    of American Indians, 792
    of Chinese immigrants, 490, 491
    in cities (late 19th century), 540, 548
    European, 544, 545–546
    foreign-born, 866 (map)
    immigrants in, 544, 546, 864
    millionaires in, 520
    of Puerto Ricans on U.S. mainland, 864
    shifts in, 862–864, 863 (map)
    in trans-Mississippi West, 487
    urban vs. rural, 560
Populism, of Roosevelt, F. D., 702
Populists. *See also* People's Party (Populists)
    New Deal criticized by, 694–696
    reforms by, 573
Port Arthur, China, 612
Porter, Cole, 735
Port Huron Statement (1962), 811
Post-industrial service economy, 871
Postwar period, after First World War,
    641–646
Potawatomi Casino, gaming at, 853
Potsdam Conference (1945), atomic bomb and,
    744
Potter, David, 774
Poverty
    among African Americans, 840
    in cities, 567
    feminization of, 841, 849
    Great Society and, 806
    Harrington on, 783
    Indian, 499, 708
    Johnson, Lyndon B., and, 802
    of northern laborers, 548
    in Puerto Rico, 607–608
    Reagan and, 841
    in South, 504
Poverty (Hunter), 548
Powderly, Terence, 527, 528
Powell, Colin, as secretary of state, 892
Power (energy). *See* Electricity; Energy;
    Nuclear power
Power (political). *See also* Imperialism;
    Superpowers; World powers
    governmental, 564, 732, 833
    of president, 745, 757, 897–898
    social networking and, 904–906
"Power elite" (Mills), 779

Power of Positive Thinking, The (Peale), 778
Power politics, Taft and, 615
Prague, Nazis in, 717
"Praise the Lord" (PTL) movement, 881
Prayer
   in 1950s, 778
   in public schools, 838
Predatory pricing, 516
Pregnancy, abortion and, 787, 823–824
Prejudice. *See also* Discrimination; Race and
     racism
   against Asian Americans, 614
   against Chinese laborers, 486,
     490–491
Preservation, of environment, 585
Presidency
   geographical availability of candidates
     for, 507
   progressives and, 591
President. *See also* Elections; specific
     individuals
   power of, 745, 757, 770, 897–898
   Reconstruction and (Andrew Johnson),
     465–467
   after September 11, 2001, 896
   two-term limit for, 757
Presidential Commission on the Status of
     Women, 787
Presidential elections. *See* Elections
Presidential pardons, for ex-Confederates,
     466, 468
Presley, Elvis, 779, 780
Press. *See* Media; Newspapers
Price(s)
   agricultural, 504, 530–531
   of crops (1914-1929), 662
Price indexes, wholesale and consumer
     (1865-1897), 530
Priests. *See also* Missions and missionaries
   in political office, 881
Primary elections
   direct primary and, 573, 578
   white only, 506
Princeton University, 588
Principles of Scientific Management, The
     (Taylor), 579, 580
Printing, 520
Print media, future of, 905
Prisoners of war (POWs)
   in Civil War, 754–755
   in Korean War, 770
   in Second World War, 723–724
Privacy, women's rights to, 824
Private property. *See* Property
Private schools. *See* Public schools; Schools
Privatization, in overseas economies, 871
Prizefights. *See* Boxing
Pro-choice demonstrations, 848
Proclamation of Amnesty and
     Reconstruction (1863), 464
Production
   agricultural, 662
   from 1865 to 1900, 514
   at Ford's Highland Park plant, 579–580
   mass, 518
   in Second World War, 715, 728

Products, transportation of, 870
Professional Golfing Association (PGA), 874
Professionalization, women, minorities, and,
     523
Professional organizations
   barriers to women and, 523
   Mexican American, 854
Professions
   "female," 656
   white-collar, 521
   women in, 523, 787
Profit sharing, 777
Progress and Poverty (George), 496
Progressive income tax, 589
Progressive Party
   of 1912, 563, 587
   of 1948, 747, 748
   in Wisconsin (1934 and 1936), 697
Progressives and progressivism, 560. *See also*
     La Follette, Robert
   accomplishments of, 591–592
   activist government and, 562
   business and, 579–580
   business interests vs. people and,
     585–586
   citizenship requirements and, 574
   cultural conservatism of, 567–569
   disfranchisement and, 574–575
   First World War and, 625, 635
   municipal reform and, 572–573
   in New York (state), 579
   opposition to Second World War, 719
   Protestant reformers and, 564
   Roosevelt, T., and, 562, 563, 587
   socialists and, 571–572
   state reforms and, 573–580
   in states, 578
   Taft and, 587
   use of term, 563
   virtuous electorate and, 573
   Wilson and, 589, 590
Prohibition
   campaign for, 568
   18th amendment and, 568, 635
   Harding and, 658
   in 1920s, 664–665
   organized crime and, 551
   repeal of, 698
Promontory, Utah, transcontinental railroad
     and, 480, 486, 491
Propaganda
   in Cold War, 752, 771
   in First World War, 633–635
   racist, 505
   in Second World War, 724, 732–733,
     738
   in Vietnam War, 809
Property, for voting, 574
Property rights
   environmental regulations and, 856
   for women, 489
Property rights movement, 856
Prospectors, in California Gold Rush, 492
Prosperity. *See also* Affluence; Wealth and
     wealthy
   in late 1890s, 534

of middle class African Americans, 506
   in 1920s, 650–658
   in Reagan era, 840
   workers and, 655
Prostitution, 563
   investigations of, 564, 566
   Mann Act and, 557, 568
   in mining towns, 497
   reformers and, 567–568
Protectorate
   Hawaii as, 599
   Samoa as, 598–599
Protest(s). *See also* Dissent and dissenters;
     Resistance
   in civil rights movement, 794
   by labor, 696
   in prisons (1971), 821
   songs of, 811
   women and, 787
Protestant-Catholic-Jew (Herberg), 778, 879
Protestants and Protestantism. *See also*
     Fundamentalism
   evangelicalism and, 838, 880
   fundamentalist, 838
   liberal, 668
   missionaries and, 596–597
   pacifism in First World War, 625
   progressivism and, 564
Provisional governors, in Reconstruction,
     465
Psychological warfare, under Eisenhower,
     771
Public affairs broadcasting, 878–879
Public education. *See* Education; Schools
Public Enemy, The (movie), 686
Public facilities
   discrimination and, 760
   Jim Crow laws and segregation in, 506
Public health. *See* Healthcare
Public housing, 758, 759, 762, 793
Public lands
   Ballinger-Pinchot controversy and, 587
   Reagan and, 841
   regulation of, 585
Public Lands Commission, 585
Public libraries. *See* Libraries
Public opinion, Republican policies in South
     and, 480
Public policy, Heritage Foundation and, 857
Public schools
   citizenship education in, 669
   Mexicans in, 737
   prayer in, 838
   during Reconstruction, 468
   segregation in, 788
   in South, 472
Public service jobs, CETA and, 836
Public utilities. *See* Utilities
Public works
   Coxey and, 529
   under New Deal, 699
   in Philippines, 606
   in West, 694
Public Works Administration (PWA),
     692–693
Pueblo Relief Act (1934), 709

Puerto Rican-Hispanic Leadership Forum, 793
Puerto Rican Legal Defense and Education Fund, 854
Puerto Ricans
    communities of, 792, 864
    social activism among, 792–793, 854
Puerto Rico
    annexation of, 607–608
    Spanish-American War and, 602
    status question of, 854
Pulaski, Tennessee, Klan in, 477
Pulitzer, Joseph, 599
Pullman, George M., 529, 530
Pullman strike, 529–530
Pure Food and Drug Act (1906), 585
PWA. *See* Public Works Administration

al-Qadaffi, Muammar, 845
al Qaeda. *See* Al-Qaeda
Quasi-slavery, in Reconstruction, 467
Quayle, J. Danforth ("Dan"), 842, 848, 887
Quebec, 545
Queue ordinances, 491
Quotas
    on immigration, 666, 667, 805, 865
    on Jews, 667, 669

Race and racism. *See also* Activism; Anti-Semitism; Civil rights; Civil-rights movement; Ethnic groups and ethnicity; Ku Klux Klan; Minorities; Race riots; Slaves and slavery
    African Americans and, 551–552, 560, 580–581, 582
    Anglo-Saxon superiority and, 665
    against Asian immigrants, 546, 547
    Columbian Exposition and racial hierarchy, 543–544
    after First World War, 643–646
    industrialization in New South and, 504
    Ku Klux Klan and, 665–666
    Mann Act and, 568
    movements against, 736–738
    "new immigrants" and, 545
    in New South, 505, 506
    in 1920s, 667
    in North, 505
    Protestant missionaries and, 596–597
    racial fitness and, 522
    Roosevelt, T., and, 609
    in Second World War, 723–724, 731–732, 734–738
    Social Darwinism and, 521
    in Spanish-American War, 600–601
    in sports, 673
    stereotypes in, 674–675
    suffragists and, 577
    Tarzan movies and, 610
Race riots
    antiblack, 506
    after First World War, 645
    in Reconstruction, 470, 471
    in Second World War, 735
    in Springfield, Illinois, 580–581, 582
    in Watts, 813–814

Racial discrimination. *See* Discrimination; Race and racism
Racial equality. *See* Equality; Race and racism
Racial identity, Black Power approach and, 821
Racial segregation. *See* Military; Segregation
"Racial summit," 815–816
Racing, auto, 874
Radar, 721, 728
Radcliffe, Ted, 673
Radiation
    from atomic bombings, 728
    covert experiments with, 771
    victims of, 771, 895
Radical Republicans
    Johnson, Andrew, and, 465–466
    Reconstruction and, 464–465
Radicals and radicalism. *See also* Radical Republicans
    Debs and, 571
    in election of 1934, 696–697
    after First World War, 642–645
    Haymarket bombing and, 527–528
    labor and feminist, 557–558
    organizations of, 549
    suffragists and, 473
    third parties in Great Depression, 697
Radio, 651
    conservatives on, 782
    Coughlin on, 695–696
    counterculture music on, 813
    New Right programs on, 856–857
    psychological warfare and, 771
    in Second World War, 718, 725
Radioactivity. *See* Radiation
Radio Asia, 771
Radio Free Europe, 771
Radio Liberty, 771
Radio Martí, 844
RAF. *See* Royal Air Force
Ragtime, 553, 674
Railroad(s), 532
    as big business, 516
    black labor for, 551
    borderlands communities and, 491
    cattle and, 492, 493, 494
    Chinese labor for, 490–491
    cooperative arrangements among, 516
    economic growth and, 514
    expansion of (1870-1890), 490 (map)
    farmers' resistance to, 531
    financing of, 489–490
    Great Railroad Strike and, 490, 513, 514, 515, 525–527
    Homestead Act and, 489
    immigrant labor for, 547
    industrial accidents on, 525, 547
    land grants for, 516
    mining and, 492
    monopolies and, 584
    Panic of 1873 and, 480
    pools and, 516, 531
    refrigerated rail cars and, 492
    regulation of, 531, 578, 579, 585
    in South, 503

standardization of time by, 520
    strikes against, 490, 513, 514, 527, 529–530
    tax exemptions for, 578
    technological advances for, 515
    transcontinental, 480, 486, 491
    West and, 489–490
Railroad Coordination Act (1933), 689
"Railroad time," 520
Ranching
    beef cattle in U.S. (1867-1897), 494
    Californio ranchers, 494–495
    cattle drives and, 492–493
    Hispanic methods of, 494
    industrialization of, 494
    itinerant laborers in, 496–497
    longhorn cattle and, 492, 493
    open-range grazing and, 493
    in West, 492–494, 493 (map)
RAND (government think tank), 753
Rand, Ayn, 781–782
R&D. *See* Research and development
Randolph, A. Philip, 674, 737, 760, 815, 852
Range wars, 493
Rappe, Virginia, 556
Rate-cutting wars, among railroads, 531
Ratification, of Versailles Treaty, 639–641
Rationing, 728, 825
Rauschenbusch, Walter, 564
Ray, James Earl, 818
Raza Unida, La, 854
REA. *See* Rural Electrification Administration
Reading. *See* Literacy
Reading Railroad, 529, 584
Reagan, Nancy, 843
Reagan, Ronald, 832
    anticommunism of, 754
    assassination attempt on, 842
    as California governor, 839
    Cold War and, 833, 843, 844–845
    economy and, 840
    election of 1964 and, 804
    election of 1968 and, 820
    election of 1976 and, 835 (map)
    election of 1980 and, 839–840, 839 (map)
    election of 1984 and, 842
    as FBI informant, 843
    FCC and, 857
    on government action, 856
    Grenada intervention and, 844
    Iran-*contra* controversy and, 845
    in movies, 754, 843
    presidency of, 840–842
    second term of, 842
Reagan revolution, 840, 842
Reagon, Bernice Johnson, 787, 788
Real estate, in early 2000s, 901
Real estate market
    African American agents in, 552
    racial discrimination eliminated from, 816
    restrictive covenants in, 760–761
    risky loans in, 841
Real income, growth in, 769
Realism, 521, 564–566

Real wages, 525, 777
Rearmament, in Second World War, 717
"Reason Why the Colored American Is Not in the World's Columbian Exposition, The" (Wells), 543
Rebates, by railroads, 516, 531
Rebellions. *See* Revolts and rebellions
Recall, 573
Recessions. *See also* Depressions (financial); Economy
    in 1937-1938, 711
    in 2009, 904
Reciprocal Trade Agreement (1934), 710
Reconnaissance flights, for disarmament efforts, 771
Reconstruction, 462–484
    Black Codes in, 467
    carpetbaggers in, 471, 477
    completion of formal, 472
    Compromise of 1877 and, 483–484
    congressional, 469–472
    election of 1868 and, 473–474
    end of, 484, 513
    film on, 479
    Freedmen's Bureau and, 467, 468, 469, 470
    freedpeople in, 467–468, 469, 471
    goals of, 484
    Indians and, 498–499
    Johnson, Andrew, and, 465–467, 471–472
    Ku Klux Klan in, 472, 477–478
    Radical Republicans and, 464–465
    retreat from, 480–484
    scalawags and, 471, 477
    second, 484
    in South, 466–467, 471, 475, 475 (map)
    Supreme Court and, 481–482
    Wade-Davis bill and, 465
    Wartime, 464–465
Reconstruction acts (1867), 471–472, 474
Reconstruction Finance Corporation (RFC), 684–685, 699
Recordings. *See also* Music
    45-rpm and LP, 878
Recreation, outdoor, 522
Recruitment, for First World War, 635
Recycling, in Second World War, 730
Red China. *See* China
Red Cross, 730
Redford, Robert, 876
Redistribution of income, in Second World War, 728
Redlining, 793
Reds (movie), 644
Red Scare
    after First World War, 642–643, 658, 669
    after Second World War, 755, 756
Red Shirts, 480, 482
Reed, John ("Jack"), 644
Referendum, 573
Reform and reformers. *See also* Abolition and abolitionism; New Deal; Progressives and progressivism
    civil service reform, 474–475, 507–508
    by clubwomen, 569

farmers' movements, 530–533
Indian policy and, 500
industrial, 690–691
in Mexico, 616–617
muckrakers and, 564–566
municipal, 572–573
in New York (state), 579
Roosevelt, F. D., and, 687–688
Roosevelt, T., and, 584
in states, 573–580
tariff, 589
urban water systems and, 541
in Wisconsin, 578–579
women as, 702
women's club movement and, 523
Reformed Church of America, 777
Refrigeration, in rail cars, 492, 651
Refugee Act (1980), 865
Refugees
    Cuban, 864
    immigrants classified as, 865
    Jewish, 721
    from Korean War, 750
    political, 545
    restrictions on, 719
    in Second World War, 728
Registration, of voters, 803
Regulation
    anti-government activists and, 857
    economic, 585, 900
    of environment, 585, 893
    of financial system, 872–873
    of industrial safety, 525
    of meat industry, 570
    Nixon and, 838
    of railroads, 531, 578, 579
    Reagan and, 841
    of trusts, 584
Rehnquist, William, 804, 841, 894
Reid, Harry, 904
Relief. *See also* Social welfare
    in Great Depression, 689–690
    in New Deal, 699
Religion. *See also* Evangelicals and evangelicalism; Fundamentalism; Missions and missionaries; specific groups
    in administration of George W. Bush, 892
    of American Indians, 853
    city vs. town, 662
    gays and, 881
    Ghost Dance and, 501
    Indian, 500
    of new immigrants, 545
    New Right and, 838
    in 1950s, 778
    after 1970s, 879–882
    politics and, 880–881
    in 2001, 880
Religious Right, 838–839, 881
    Bush, George H. W., and, 842
    cultural conglomerates in, 881
Relocation
    Indian, 791–792
    of Japanese Americans, 736–737

"Remember the Maine!", 600
Renaissance
    in Harlem, 674–675
    Mexican, 708
Renewable energy sources, 836
Rent subsidies, 805, 822
Reparations
    German, after First World War, 660–661
    for Japanese American internment, 855
Repatriation
    of Korean War POWs, 770
    of Mexicans, 707–708
Repression, in First World War, 635–637
Republicanism, artisan, 527
Republican Party. *See also* Elections; Radical Republicans
    anti-government activism and, 858
    conservationist movement and, 585
    Contract with America and, 887
    Goldwater and, 805
    Harding and, 658
    Ku Klux Klan and, 478
    Mississippi Plan and, 480, 481
    in 1920s, 678
    political stalemate and, 507
    progressivism and, 563, 587
    Reconstruction and, 469–472, 480
    Religious Right and, 839, 882
    Roosevelt, T., and, 583–584
    in South, 471, 472, 474, 475–476, 477, 480–481, 482, 483, 484
    split in, 507, 583, 586
    Versailles Treaty ratification and, 639–641
    Wartime Reconstruction and, 464–465
Republicans (Spain), 717
Republics, in former Soviet Union, 845
Research and development (R&D)
    in Cold War, 752
    NASA and, 782
    scientific, 894
    in Second World War, 728
Research departments, corporate, 519–520
Reservations (Indian), 498, 500
    in 1875 and 1900, 499 (map)
    relocation from, 791–792
    in Second World War, 736
Reservoirs, 776
Resettlement Administration, 691
Resistance. *See also* Protest(s); Revolts and rebellions
    to draft, 816–817
    by Hispanics, 491
    by Indians, 499–500, 501
    to railroads, 531
    of whites to *Brown* Cases, 789
    of workers, 523–530
Resource extraction. *See also* Mines and mining
    western processes of, 488–489, 492
Resources Recovery Act (1970), 823
"Restraint of trade," Sherman Antitrust Act and, 518
Restrictive covenants, 760–761, 762
Retirement, communities for, 863
Reuben James (ship), 719

Reunification, of Germany, 845
Revenue Acts, of 1926, 659
Revenue-sharing plans, of Nixon, 822
Reverse discrimination, 856
Revolts and rebellions. *See also* Resistance
    Berkeley Revolt, 812
    in Cuba, 599–600
    in Eastern Europe, 773, 845
    male, 787
    against Philippine occupation, 604
    youth rebellion, 813
Revolution(s)
    in China (1911), 615
    in Cuba (1959), 772
    in Iran, 837
    management, 518–520
    in Mexico, 616
    Reagan and democratic, 844
    Russian, 627
Reykjavik, summit meeting at, 845
RFC. *See* Reconstruction Finance
        Corporation
Rhee, Syngman, 750
Rhineland region, 638
    Nazis in, 717
Riesman, David, 778, 779
Rifle, in Spanish-American War, 604
Rifle Clubs, 480
Riggs, Bobby, 874
Right (political). *See also* Conservatives and
        conservatism; New Right
    Fox News and, 890
    Religious Right and, 838–839
Rights. *See also* Civil rights; Liberty(ies);
        Women's rights
    for freedpeople, 467, 469
    Nixon and, 823–824
    of women, 657–658
Right-to-Life movement, 824, 894
Riis, Jacob, 567
Rio Arriba County, New Mexico, 491
Rio de Janeiro, conference in (1942), 740
Riots. *See also* Race riots
    anti-Asian, 614
    antidraft, 478
    against Chinese workers, 490
    after First World War, 642, 646
Risk management, 873
Rivera, Diego, 697
Rivers. *See* Waterways; specific river regions
Riverside Church, King at, 817
Roads and highways
    Highway Act and, 776
    in 1920s, 652 (map)
"Robber barons," 517, 525, 534–536
Roberts, John, 841, 894
Roberts, Owen J., 711
Roberts Court, 894
Robertson, Pat, 881
Robeson, Paul, anticommunism and, 754
Robinson, Jackie, 761, 762
Robinson, S., 879
Rockefeller, John D., 521
    oil industry and, 516–517, 564, 566
    philanthropy of, 535–536
Rockefeller, Nelson, 781, 821, 834

Rockefeller Foundation, 535, 782
Rockefeller University, 536
Rock 'n' roll, 779–780
Rock of the Marne, The (Thompson), 627
Rock Springs, Colorado, massacre of
        Chinese workers in, 490
Rockwell, Norman, 733
Roe v. *Wade*, 824, 838, 839, 869, 894
Rolling Stone magazine, 813
Rolling Thunder (Vietnam bombing
        campaign), 808
Roman Catholicism. *See* Catholicism
Romances (literature), 554–555
Romania, 739
Roosevelt, Eleanor, 687, 688, 702, 704, 787
    African Americans and, 737
    United Nations and, 739
Roosevelt, Franklin D., 673, 677, 687, 740.
        See also Great Depression; New Deal
    Atlantic Charter and, 719
    at Casablanca, 721
    corporations and, 730
    court-packing scheme of, 711
    death of, 726–727
    Democratic coalition and, 701
    election of 1932 and, 685 (map)
    election of 1936 and, 700–701, 701 (map)
    election of 1940 and, 719
    election of 1944 and, 726–727
    Fair Employment Practices Commission
        and, 730, 737
    Good Neighbor Policy of, 709, 710, 737,
        740
    government power and, 732
    Japanese American internment by, 736
    liberalism of, 682, 687–688
    New Deal and, 592
    Pearl Harbor attack and, 720
    quarantine of aggressor nations and, 717
    Second Bill of Rights of, 732, 757
    Second World War and, 717–718, 719,
        721, 733
    segregation and, 735
    spheres of influence and, 739
    at Tehran Conference, 739
    workplace discrimination and, 730–731
Roosevelt, Theodore, 562
    American nationality and, 560
    big stick policy of, 614, 615
    diplomacy and, 612–614
    election of 1900 and, 583–584
    election of 1904 and, 584
    election of 1908 and, 586
    election of 1912 and, 587, 588, 589 (map)
    environment and, 585
    expansion under, 595
    First World War and, 625, 635
    geopolitics of, 609–614
    government activism and, 658
    as imperialist, 598
    on *Melting-Pot, The*, 559
    muckrakers and, 564
    New Nationalism of, 584, 587, 588
    Panama Canal and, 612
    Progressive Party and, 563
    Roosevelt, F. D., and, 687

    in Spanish-American War, 601–602
    Square Deal of, 584
    on strenuous life, 522
    trusts and, 584
Roosevelt corollary, 609–610
Root, Elihu, 639
Root, John Wellborn, 542
Root-Takahira Agreement (1908), 613
Rosenberg, Julius and Ethel, 756
Rosenman, Samuel, 687, 702
Rosenwald, Julius, philanthropy of, 536
Rostow, Walt W., 806
Rothstein, Arnold, 551, 709
Rough Riders, 601
Route 66, 690
Rove, Karl, 892–893
Royal Air Force (RAF), 718
Royal Navy (Britain), in Second World War,
        717
Rubin, Jerry, 817
Rubin, Robert, 900, 901
Ruby, Jack, 797
Ruef, Abe, 550
Ruhr region, French occupation of, 660
Rumford Act (California), 804, 814
Rumsfeld, Donald, 892, 897
Rural areas. *See also* Farms and farming
    in Great Depression, 690
Rural Electrification Administration (REA),
        699, 729
Rusk, Dean, 810
Russia. *See also* First World War; Soviet
        Union
    Bolsheviks in, 627
    exit from First World War, 626, 627
    expansionism of, 612–613
    after fall of Soviet Union, 845
    in First World War, 622
    immigrants from, 545
    Japanese treaty with, 615
    Open Door policy and, 608
Russian Revolutions, 627
Russo-Japanese War, 612–613
Rustin, Bayard, 754, 789, 815, 852
Rustling, 493
Ruth, George Herman ("Babe"), 653, 654, 673
Rwanda, U.N. peacekeeping in, 895

Saar region, after First World War, 638
Sabotage Act, in First World War, 636
Sacco, Nicola, 643, 669
Sacco and Vanzetti case, 643
Sacrilegious Candidate, The (political
        cartoon), 534
Sadat, Anwar, 837
Saddam Hussein. *See* Hussein, Saddam
Saddleback Church, 881
Safety
    industrial, 525, 547, 579
    regulations, Reagan and, 841
    on urban construction projects, 541
Sagebrush rebellion, 841, 856
Saigon. *See also* South Vietnam;
        Vietnam War
    Diem government in, 795
    North Vietnamese capture of, 827, 836

St. Louis, 732, 835
Saipan, in Second World War, 725, 726
Salisbury, Harrison, 810
Salk, Jonas, 760
Saloons, 568–569
SALT I, 825
Salt of the Earth (movie), 793
SALT talks. *See* Strategic Arms Limitation
    Talks
Salvadoran immigrants, 865
Salvation. *See also* Missions and missionaries
    Protestant fundamentalists on, 667
Same-sex relationships. *See* Gays and
    lesbians; Homosexuality
Samoa, U.S. rights to, 598–599
Samuelson, Paul, 782
San Antonio, 676 (map)
    Mexican Americans in, 854
Sand Creek massacre, 500
Sandinistas in Nicaragua, 837,
    844, 845
S & Ls
    bailout of, 841
    crisis in, 872–873
    deregulation and debacle in, 841
SANE. *See* Committee for a Sane Nuclear
    Policy
San Francisco
    Asian immigrants in, 547
    Chinatown in, 490, 491
    counterculture in, 812, 813
    segregation of Asian children in, 614
    strikes in, 696
Sanger, Margaret, 557, 558
Sanitation, in cities, 548
San Juan Hill, battle at, 601
Santa Fe Railroad, 491. *See also* Atchison,
    Topeka, and Santa Fe Railroad
Santa Fe Trail, 489, 496
Santee Sioux Indians, conflict with, 499
Santiago, Cuba, 602
Santo Domingo (Dominican Republic). *See
    also* Dominican Republic
    attempts to annex, 475
Sarajevo, Bosnia, Franz Ferdinand
    assassination in, 622
Sarbanes-Oxley Act (2002), 901
Sargent, John Singer, 523, 524, 624
Satellite countries, in Eastern Europe, 772
Satellites, for space exploration, 782, 783
Saturation bombing, in Vietnam, 808
Saturday Evening Post, 733
Saudi Arabia, Persian Gulf War and, 846
Saving Private Ryan (movie), 723
Savings and loan (S & L) institutions. *See* S &
    Ls
Savings rate, decline of, 872
"Say It Loud, I'm Black and I'm Proud"
    (Brown), 816
Scabs (strikebreakers), 527
Scalawags, 471, 477
Scalia, Antonin, 841, 857
Scandinavia, immigrants from, 497
Schaeffer, Francis, 881–882
Schlafly, Phyllis, 787, 823
Schlesinger, Arthur, Jr., 783–784

Schlesinger, James, 836
Schofield, John M., 472
"School Days" (rock song), 780
Schools. *See also* Education; Higher
    education; Universities and colleges
    for blacks, 469, 472, 478
    Brown Cases and, 788
    busing and integration of, 822
    freedmen's, 471
    Indians in, 501, 502, 709
    public, 468, 472, 838
    segregation in, 472, 761, 793
Schulberg, Budd, 754
Schurz, Carl, 480
Schwerner, Michael, 803
Science. *See also* Natural science; Scientific
    method; Technology
    vs. Christianity, 668
Scientific management, 579–580
Scientific method, applied to society, 521
Scientific research, 728
Scientific Research and Development, Office
    of, 728
SCLC. *See* Southern Christian Leadership
    Conference
Scopes, John T., 669
Scopes Trial, 669, 670–671
    Inherit the Wind (movie) and, 669
Scopes Trial, The (Myers), 670–671
Screen Actors Guild, 843
Scribner's magazine, 521
SDI. *See* Strategic Defense Initiative
SDS. *See* Students for a Democratic Society
Seale, Bobby, 816
"Search and destroy" missions (Vietnam
    War), 808, 809
Sears, Roebuck, 536, 718, 777
Seattle, strike in (1919), 642
SEC. *See* Securities and Exchange
    Commission
Second Amendment, 816, 894
Second Bill of Rights, 732, 757, 758
Second Front, in Second World War, 721
Second New Deal (1935-1937), 698–705. *See
    also* New Deal
Second World War, 714–740
    aftermath of, 743
    atomic bombs in, 728
    casualties in, 721, 725, 729
    corporations in, 729–730
    economy and, 728–732
    in Europe, 717–719, 718 (map), 720,
      721–722, 722 (map), 724 (map)
    events leading to, 716–717
    Holocaust in, 721, 740
    home front in, 728–738
    Japanese surrender in, 728
    mobilization for, 715, 721, 728–732
    movies on, 723, 732
    Nazi surrender in, 722
    New Deal and, 711–712
    in North Africa, 721, 722 (map),
      724 (map)
    in Pacific, 720, 722–724, 725–726,
      725 (map), 727 (map)
    peace after, 738–740

    Pearl Harbor attack in, 719–720
    social issues during, 732–738
    spheres of influence after, 739–740
    support for, 719
    U.S. neutrality before, 716–717
    U.S. entry into, 720
    U.S. response to war in Europe, 717–719
    war posters in, 714, 733
    wartime conferences in, 739–740, 744,
      754
Secretariat (UN), 739
Secret ballot, 573
Sectionalism, East vs. West, 532
Secular humanism, 881
Securities, 873
Securities Act (1933), 689
Securities and Exchange Commission (SEC),
    857, 901
Securities Exchange Act (1934), 689
Security. *See* National security
Security Council (UN), 739
Sedalia, Missouri, 492
Sedition Act, in First World War, 636
Seduction of the Innocent, The (Wertham),
    779
Segregation. *See also* Desegregation
    of African Americans, 582, 706, 707, 735
    in armed forces, 735
    colored waiting room and, 789
    Eisenhower and, 791
    fight against, 789
    by gender, 730
    of government departments, 590
    of Mexican American children, 761, 793
    of military, 631, 735, 736, 760
    Montgomery bus boycott and, 789, 790
    in New South, 506
    in public facilities, Jim Crow laws and,
      506
    in schools, 472, 761
    of transportation, 789
Selective Service Act (1917), 631
Selective Training and Service Act (1940),
    717, 719
Self-determination, after First World War,
    639
Self-government
    by Filipinos, 603–604
    for Indians, 709
Self-interest, of anti-imperialists, 604
Selma, Alabama, racial violence in, 813
Seminole Indians, 498
Semiskilled labor, 655
    AFL and, 528
    wages for, 525
Senate (U.S.)
    African Americans in, 476
    impeachment and, 472
    Versailles Treaty ratification fight, 639–
      641
    Watergate Committee in, 828–829
Senators
    direct election of, 532, 533, 573
    election by legislatures, 573
    women as, 850
Seneca Falls Convention, 473, 575

Sensationalism, of yellow journalism, 599
Seoul, 750, 751
Separate-but equal-principle, 506, 761
Separation of church and state, 839, 882
September 11, 2001, terrorist attacks, 884, 885, 892, 896
Serbia, 845
    First World War and, 622
    Kosovo and, 895
Serbian immigrants, 545
Serbs, ethnic cleansing by, 847
Service economy, 871
Serviceman's Readjustment Act (1944). See GI Bill (1944)
Settlement
    Indians and, 498
    in West, 489, 497–498
Settlement houses, 566–567, 579
Seventeenth Amendment, 573
74th Congress, 696–697
Sewage systems, in cities, 540–541
Sewing machine, 549, 597
Sex and sexuality. See also Gender; Homosexuality
    counterculture and, 812–813
    feminism and, 557
    Kinsey on, 754–755
    in movies, 555, 557
    new sexuality and, 555–558
    in 1920s, 649, 653
    politics of, 786–787
    premarital sex, 555
    in Second World War, 734
    transsexuality and, 755
"Sex-change" operations, 755
Sexual assaults
    in military, 850
    Take Back the Night rallies against, 848
Sexual freedom, 849
Sexual harassment, 850
    Clinton and, 888
    Thomas, Clarence, and, 850
Sexual politics, 850–851
Sexual revolution
    Addams and, 567–568
    working-class women and, 539
Seymour, Horatio, 473–474
Shadow banking system, 873
Shaft (movie), 852
Shahn, Ben, 645, 691
Shah of Iran. See Pahlavi, Reza (Shah)
Shandong, 717
Shanghai, 717
    Starbucks in, 870
Sharecropping, 467, 468, 551
    in Great Depression, 690
    in New South, 504
Share the Wealth program, of Long, 695
Share wages, in southern free-labor contracts, 467
Shasta Dam, 695 (map)
Shaw, Clay, 796
Sheen, Fulton J., 777
Sheep, grazing, Hispanics and, 491
Shenseki, Eric, 904
Sheppard-Towner Act (1921), 657

Sheridan, Philip, 499, 500
Sherman, William T., 500
    land for freedpeople and, 468
Sherman Antitrust Act (1890), 507, 518, 590
    labor unions and, 528
    Roosevelt, T., and, 584
    strikes and, 530
Sherman Silver Purchase Act (1890), 532, 533
Shi'a Muslims, 846, 897
Shiller, Robert, 901
Ships and shipping. See also Railroad(s); Roads and highways; Transportation
    container shipping and, 870
    in First World War, 624–625, 626–627
    limits on warships, 660
    before Panama Canal, 615 (map)
    Second World War and, 717, 719, 728
Shopping malls, 775
Shriver, R. Sargent, 802
Siberia, Russia and, 613
Sicilian immigrants, 551
Sicily, in Second World War, 721
Sierra Club, 585
Sierra Nevada Mountains, national forests in, 895
Silent Spring, The (Carson), 823
Silicon Valley, 863
Silver
    coinage of, 532, 533
    free silver movement and, 532, 533, 534
    mining of, 491, 492
Simmons, William, 665
Simpson, O. J., trial of, 888
Simpson-Mazzoli Act (1986), 865
Sin, Protestant fundamentalists on, 667
Sinai Peninsula, 837
Sinclair, Harry F., 658
Sinclair, Upton, 570, 697
Singapore, 720, 722
Singer Sewing Machine Company, 597
Singleton, Benjamin, 504
Sioux Indians, 499
    Ghost Dance religion and, 501
    Wounded Knee massacre of, 501
Sirhan, Sirhan, 819
Sirica, John, 828, 829
Sitcoms, 875
Sit-down strikes, 704, 711
Sit-ins, 737, 793
Sitting Bull (Sioux leader), 499, 501, 503
Six Crises (Nixon), 821
Sixteenth Amendment, 589
Sixteenth Street Baptist Church (Birmingham), bombing of, 794
Skilled labor, 655, 871
    AFL and, 528
    immigrants and, 548
    mass production and, 518
Skyscrapers, 539, 540, 542
Slaveholders, Indians as, 498
Slaves and slavery. See also Abolition and abolitionism; Slave trade
    sexual slavery of women, 497
    tribal citizenship for slaves of civilized tribes, 498

Slave trade, white, 557
Slavs, as immigrants, 545, 546
Slovak immigrants, 545
Slovenia, 845
Slovenian immigrants, 545
Small businesses, loans to, 822
Smith, Alfred E., 579, 670, 673, 687, 706
Smith, Jesse, 658–659
Smith, Willie, 674
Smith College, 787
Smith-Connally Act (1943), 732
Smog, 823
Smokestacks, emissions of, 823
Smoking. See Tobacco and tobacco industry
SNCC. See Student Nonviolent Coordinating Committee
Soccer, 874
Social activism. See Activism
Social classes. See Classes
Social Darwinism, 520–521
    "racial superiority" and, 522, 669
Socialism
    in Dayton, 573
    economic inequality and, 783
    in First World War, 625
    Nationalism form of, 522
    organizations for, 549
    progressivism and, 571–572
    use of term, 570
    varieties of, 570–571
    in Wisconsin, 578?
Socialist Labor Party, 527–528
Socialist Party of America, 570, 588, 635, 636, 637, 643
Social mobility, 509, 840
Social movements
    African Americans and, 580, 760
    politics of, 848–858
    social activism after 1960s, 833
Social networking, culture of, 904–906
Social orders. See Classes
Social policy, of Nixon, 821–822
Social programs, faith-based, 839
Social reform. See Reform and reformers
Social sciences, 521
Social Security
    Bush, George W., and, 893
    Clinton and, 888
    expansion of, 758, 781
    indexing of, 822, 841
    Reagan and, 841
Social Security Act
    of 1935, 699, 701, 711
    of 1950, 758
Social welfare
    Carter and, 835, 836
    costs of, 805
    Gingrich and, 887
    Nixon and, 821–822
    political machines and, 550
    Reagan and, 841
    reducing costs of, 887
    in southern states, 472
    spending on, 782, 822
    women and, 849

Social work and social workers
  at Ford, 580
  at University of Chicago, 567
Society. *See also* Families; Gender and
    gender issues; Men; Women
  affluence in, 774–780
  conformity in, 778–779
  consumer, 650–651
  corporate, 516
  cultural crisis in, 686–687
  after First World War, 642–646
  First World War and, 621, 629–637
  militarization of American life and,
    752–753
  Social Darwinism and, 521
Soddies (sod houses), 497, 498
Sodomy, laws on, 894
Soil, quality of, 893
Soil Bank Program, 777
Soil Conservation and Domestic Allotment
    Act (1936), 690
Soil Conservation Service (SCS), 690
Soil erosion, 509
Sojourner movement, 880
Soldiers. *See also* Armed forces; specific
    battles and wars
  in First World War, 622–623, 627–628,
    631–632
  Japanese American, 737–738
  as strike-breakers, 704
  in Vietnam, 810, 827
Solidarity movement (Poland), 845
Solid South, 482, 766
Solomon Islands, 723
Somalia, 865, 894
  U.S. troops in, 847
Somoza, Anastasio, 837
Sony, Walkman and, 878
Sorosis (women's club), 523
Sotomayor, Sonia, 904
Souls of Black Folk, The (Du Bois), 506
Sound and the Fury, The (Faulkner),
    677
Sousa, John Philip, "Stars and Stripes
    Forever," 605
South. *See also* Confederacy (Civil War);
    Deep South; New South;
    Reconstruction
  African American migration and, 551,
    630, 632 (map)
  African American migration from, 487,
    504–505, 551, 735, 790 (map)
  bayonet rule in, 478, 480, 483
  Black Codes in, 467
  black officeholders in, 475–477
  carpetbaggers in, 471, 477, 480
  civil-rights movement and, 789–791, 794
  after Civil War, 467
  disfranchisement of blacks in, 574, 575
  illiteracy in, 468, 469, 475, 476–477
  Jim Crow laws in, 506, 551
  Klan in, 472, 474, 477–478, 666
  lynchings of blacks in, 505
  military districts in, 471, 472
  movement of jobs to, 777
  in 1950s, 788

population growth in, 862–863
  public schools in, 472
  Reconstruction in, 466–467, 471, 475,
    475 (map), 483–484
  Religious Right in, 838, 839
  Republican Party in, 475–476, 507, 839
  segregation in, 472, 789
  sharecropping in, 467, 468, 504
  voter participation in (1876, 1892, 1900,
    1912), 575
South Africa, 534, 827
  apartheid in, 752
South Carolina, 480. *See also* North Carolina
  New Deal voting in, 696
South Dakota, 533
Southeast Asia. *See also* Vietnam War
  immigrants from, 855
  Johnson, Lyndon B., and, 801
  Kennedy, John F., and, 785–786,
    795–797
  after Second World War, 740, 752
Southern Baptists, 839, 880
Southern Christian Leadership Conference
    (SCLC), 789, 816, 852
Southern Europe
  ethnics from, 669–670, 706
  immigrants from, 545
Southern Farmers' Alliance, 532
Southern Manifesto, 789
Southern Pacific Railroad, 489
Southern Republican Party, 477
South Korea, 749, 750, 827. *See also* Korea;
    Korean War
South Manchurian Railroad, 615
South Pacific region
  American empire in (1900),
    606 (map)
  Second World War in, 725
South Vietnam, 809, 825–826. *See also*
    Vietnam; Vietnam War
  Diem in, 773, 774, 785–786
  Johnson, Lyndon B., and, 806–807
  Kennedy, John F., and, 785–786,
    795–797
  after peace accords, 773–774, 836
Southwest
  Hispanic population in, 496
  immigrants in, 544
  Latinos in, 737, 854
  Mexican Americans in, 793, 864
South Yemen, 844
Sovereignty
  after First World War, 638
  for "the people," 573
Soviet Union. *See also* Cold War;
    Communism; Russia; Second World
    War
  Afghanistan invasion by, 837–838
  American Communist Party and, 746
  atomic bomb and, 748
  Berlin and, 747, 785
  collapse of, 847 (map)
  Cuba and, 772, 785
  détente with, 825, 836
  Eastern Europe and, 722, 744
  Egypt and, 773

end of, 845
  expansionism of, 744
  Gorbachev in, 845
  Jewish immigrants from, 865
  Korea and, 749, 750
  lend-lease assistance to, 719, 744
  as market, 710
  massive retaliation doctrine and, 771
  Nazis and, 717, 719, 720
  New Right on, 838
  Olympic Games in (1980), 838
  postwar spheres of influence and, 739–740
  Reagan and, 844
  recognition of, 709
  Second World War and, 721, 724 (map),
    727
  Spanish Civil War and, 717
  Sputnik and, 782
  spying and, 746, 756, 782
  U.S. business chains in, 870
  on U.S. racial discrimination, 791
  Vietnam and, 774, 809
Soyer, Moses, 705
Space exploration
  NASA installations and, 863
  Sputnik and, 782
Space race, 783
Space shuttles, 863
Spain. *See also* Spanish-American War
  Cuba and, 601–602
Spanish-American War, 599–602, 631
  in Cuba, 599–602, 603 (map)
  rifles from, 604
Spanish Civil War, 717
Spanish-speaking people, 864–865. *See also*
    Hispanics
  activism of, 853–855
  civil rights and, 792–793
  in West, 476
Special electoral commission, for 1876
    election, 483
Speculation
  in corporate society, 516
  in Germany, 661
  Homestead Act and, 489
  Panic of 1873 and, 480
  railroad financing and, 516
  in stock market, 682
"Speed-ups," of machines, 655
Spencer, Herbert, 521
Spending (governmental), 710, 835, 904. *See
    also* Budget; Finance(s); Military
  on defense, 782, 784, 844
  Ford and, 835
  Keynesian economists and, 782
  military, 752–753, 758, 771, 774
  on navy (1890-1914), 599
  Reagan and, 840, 841
  in Second World War, 728
  on social welfare, 782, 822
Spheres of influence
  of Great Britain, 745
  Japanese, 615
  after Second World War, 739–740, 752
  of Soviet Union, 744, 844, 845
  in Western Hemisphere, 608

Spies and spying
    atomic spies, 756
    in Cold War, 746
    Rosenbergs and, 756
    U-2 spy planes and, 771, 782
Spillane, Mickey, 734
Spirit of St. Louis, The (airplane), 654, 655
Spock, Benjamin, 786
Spoils system, reform of, 474, 507–508
Sports
    college, 874
    in late 19th century, 522
    in 1920s, 653, 654
    racism in, 673
    women in, 874
Sports-entertainment industry, 873–875
Springfield, Illinois, race riot in, 580–581, 582
Springsteen, Bruce, 705
Sputnik Crisis, 782, 783
Square Deal, of Roosevelt, T., 584
Squatters, on Mexican-American lands, 496
SSI. *See* Supplementary Security Insurance
Stagflation, 825, 835, 840
Stalin, Joseph, 717
    at Casablanca, 721
    Cold War and, 744
    lend-lease assistance to, 719
    postwar spheres of influence and, 739
    at Potsdam Conference (1945), 744
    at Tehran Conference, 739
    at Yalta, 739
Stalingrad, Battle of, 721, 722 (map)
Stalwarts, 507
Standardization
    in fast-food and travel industries, 870
    of railroad tracks, 503
    of time, 520
Standard of living. *See* Lifestyle
Standard Oil Company, 474, 564, 597
    Rockefeller and, 516–517, 535
Stand Watie (Cherokee leader), 498
Stanford, Leland, 489
Stanton, Edwin M., 472
Stanton, Elizabeth Cady, woman suffrage
    and, 473, 575
Stanwyck, Barbara, 764
Starbucks, 870
Stark, John, 553
Starr, Ellen Gates, 566, 567
Starr, Kenneth, 888, 890
"Stars and Stripes Forever" (Sousa), 605
Star Trek scholarly studies of, 878
Star Wars. *See* Strategic Defense Initiative
Star Wars (movie), 877
State (nation), separation of church from,
    882
State(s). *See also* specific locations
    aid to religious institutions, 839
    block grants to, 822
    financial regulation by, 841
    public education in, 788
    railroad regulation by, 531
    readmission of, 464, 465, 470, 471
    reform in, 573–580
State Children's Health Insurance Program
    (SCHIP, 1997), 888

State Department, McCarthy, Joseph, and,
    756, 757
Statehood, for Hawaii, 603
State legislatures, U.S. senators elected by,
    573
State militia. *See* Militia
State of the Union address
    of Johnson, Lyndon B., 802
    of Reagan (1986), 832
States' Rights (Dixiecrat) Party, 747–748,
    757
Status. *See* Classes
Steam power, electricity and, 515
Stearns, Harold, 676
Steel and steel industry
    cargo containers and, 870
    Carnegie in, 516, 642
    immigrant labor for, 547
    industrial accidents in, 525, 547
    labor in, 704
    mass production in, 518
    merger movement in, 517
    railroad expansion and, 514
    skyscrapers and, 540
    strikes in, 642, 704
    Truman and, 757
Steeplechase Park (Coney Island), 554
Steffens, Lincoln, 564
Stein, Gertrude, 676
Steinbeck, John, 704, 754
Steinbrenner, George, 873
Stem cell research, 869, 894
Stephens, Alexander H., 466, 470
Stereotypes
    of African Americans, 674–675
    in film, 479
    gender, 734
    Indian, 853
Steroid use, in sports, 874–875
Stevens, Thaddeus, 464
Stevenson, Adlai, 765, 766 (map), 786–787
Stiglitz, Joseph, 901
Stimson, Henry, 718, 721
    atomic bomb and, 728
Stock Growers' Association, 493
Stock market
    crash of 1929 and, 681
    in 1920s, 651
    speculation in, 682
Stocks, 516. *See also* Stock market
    railroad, 489–490
Stokes, I. N. and Edith Minturn, Sargent
    portrait of, 524
Stone, Oliver, 796
Stonewall Narrative, 850
Storey, Moorfield, 582
Story of Avis, The (Phelps), 522
Strategic Air Command (SAC), Cuban
    Missile Crisis and, 785
Strategic Arms Limitation Talks (SALT),
    825
    SALT I, 825
Strategic Arms Limitation Treaty (SALT),
    Carter and, 838
Strategic Defense Initiative (SDI), 844, 845
Strategic hamlet program, in Vietnam, 809

"Strenuous life, the," 522
"Stretch-outs," of machines, 655
Strikebreakers, 527, 529, 551
Strikes. *See also* Wildcat strikes
    African Americans as strikebreakers, 551
    at Arthur Murray Dance Studio, 753
    by cowboys, 492
    after First World War, 642
    in First World War, 630–631
    government and, 528
    in Great Depression, 696, 711
    Great Railroad Strike of 1877, 490, 513,
        514, 515, 525–527
    Homestead (1892), 514, 529
    injunctions against, 528, 530
    by IWW, 570, 591
    Knights of Labor and, 527
    at McCormick farm machinery plant, 528
    in mining industry, 492, 591, 732, 793
    Pullman, 529–530
    against railroads, 490, 513, 514, 515, 527,
        530
    Reagan and, 841
    after Second World War, 753
    in Second World War, 732
    steel, 529, 642
    by textile workers, 591
    by UMW, 584
Strip-mining, 492
Stroessner, Alfredo, 772
Student Nonviolent Coordinating
    Committee (SNCC), 793, 803, 816
Students for a Democratic Society (SDS), 811,
    821
Studs Lonigan trilogy (Farrell), 686
Subcultures. *See* Gays and lesbians
Submarines
    in First World War, 620, 624–625, 626
    in Second World War, 719, 720
"Subprime loan" industry, 841
Sub-prime mortgages, 901
Subsidies
    farm, 895
    to home owners, 690
    for railroads, 489, 516
    rent, 805, 822
    in Second World War, 728, 729, 730
"Subterranean Homesick Blues" (Dylan), 811
Subtreasuries (federal warehouses), in
    Farmers' Alliance agenda, 532, 533
Suburbs, 539, 540
    affluence in, 775
    conservatism in, 782
    demographics in, 866
    gender politics and, 786–787
    middle class and, 521
    new, 786, 793
    postwar development of, 761–763
    public housing and, 793
Subversion. *See also* Cold War;
    Communism; Movies and movie
    industry
    communism, homosexuality, and, 755
    FBI and, 756
    HUAC and, 754
    postwar fears of, 753

Subversive Activities Control Act (1950), 756, 770
Subversive Activities Control Board, 756
Subway, 540
Subway—14th Street (Marsh), 657
Sudetenland, Hitler and, 717
Suez Crisis (1956), 772–773, 773 (map)
Suffrage. *See also* Woman suffrage
    universal, 472
    women's club movement and, 523
Suffragists, 473, 575–577
Sugar and sugar industry, 503, 518
    in Cuba, 607
    imperialism and, 603
    in Second World War, 729
Sugar colonies. *See* West Indies
Suicide, assisted, 894
Sukarno, Achmed, 773
Sullivan, Louis, 542, 543
Summers, Larry, 900, 901
Summit meetings
    Eisenhower and, 771
    Reagan-Gorbachev, 845
Sumner, Charles, 478
    Reconstruction and, 464, 465
Sumter, South Carolina, city manager
    plan in, 572
Sunbelt
    conservatism in, 782, 804
    economic growth in, 776
    population shift to, 862–864, 863 (map)
Sundance Film Institute, 876
Sunday, Billy, 564
Sunday Morning in Virginia (Homer), 462
Sunni Muslims, 897
Sun Records, 780
Super banks, 872
Super Bowl, 873
Superman (comic-strip hero), 702–703, 704
Superpowers. *See also* Soviet Union
    conflict between, 744
    confrontations of, 785
    United States as, 752
Supplementary Security Insurance (SSI), 822
Supply-side economics, 840
Supreme Court (U.S.)
    on antitrust laws and movie industry, 763
    Bakke case and, 856
    Brandeis on, 590
    Brown Cases and, 788
    on civil rights, 482, 791, 803
    constitutional protection of rights
        and, 823
    disfranchisement clauses in southern
        constitutions and, 506
    on executive power, 757
    on federal authority over
        manufacturing, 518
    on gambling on tribal land, 853
    on grandfather clauses, 582
    injunctions against strikes and, 530
    integration and, 791
    on Japanese-American internment, 736,
        738
    labor unions and, 528
    Nixon and, 823

nominees to, 894, 904
Northern Securities and, 584
on pro-communist expression, 756
on public bus segregation, 789
Reagan and, 841
Reconstruction and, 481–482
Religious Right and, 838, 839
on residency segregation, 582
on restrictive covenants, 760–761,
    762
Roberts and, 894
Roosevelt, F. D., and, 711
on school segregation, 761
on separate but equal facilities for
    blacks, 506
on sexual harassment, 850
on state regulation of railroads, 531
Thomas on, 850
on tribal self-determination, 853
U.S. v. *Nixon* and, 829
Warren on, 788
women on, 841, 886
Surge, the, in Iraq, 898
Surgeons. *See* Medicine
Surplus
    budget, 710
    of war materiel, 717–718
Survival of the fittest, 521, 669
Sussex (ship), 625
Sussex pledge, 625
Sustainable development, 895
Swaggart, Jimmy Lee, 881
Sweatman, Wilbur C., 583
Sweatshops, 549
Sweden, immigrants from, 497
Sweet Honey in the Rock, 788
"Sweet Little Sixteen" (rock song), 780
Swift (meatpacking), 517
Switzerland, Nazi deposits in, 721
Symphonies, 541
Synagogues, immigrant, 549
Syria
    after First World War, 638
    immigrants from, 545
    Israel and, 825, 844

Taft, Robert, 748, 759, 765
Taft, William Howard
    dollar diplomacy of, 614–615
    election of 1908 and, 586
    election of 1912 and, 587, 588,
        589 (map)
    NWLB and, 631
    as Philippine governor-general, 605–606
    presidency of, 587
    Versailles Treaty and, 639
Taft-Hartley Act (1947), 753, 757, 777
Taft-Katsura Agreement (1905), 613, 614
"Tailhook" convention, 850
Taiwan. *See* Formosa (Taiwan)
Take Back the Night rallies, 848
Taliban, 896, 897, 904
Tammany Hall, 474, 550, 564
TANF. *See* Temporary Assistance to Needy
    Families
Tanzania, embassy bombing in, 896

Tarbell, Ida, Standard Oil exposé by, 535,
    564, 566
Tariff(s), 507
    of 1930 (Hawley-Smoot), 682–684
    Cleveland and, 508
    McKinley Tariff (1890), 508
    Taft and, 587
    Wilson and, 589
TARP. *See* Troubled Assets Relief Program
Tarzanthe Ape Man (movie), 610
Tax-and-spend policy, Reagan and, 839
Taxation. *See also* Finance(s); Income tax;
    Tariff(s)
    Bush, George H. W., and, 842
    Bush, George W., and, 892, 893
    Carter and, 835–836
    cuts in, 904
    estate, 658
    in First World War, 632–633
    income, 527, 532, 589, 658
    Johnson, Lyndon B., and, 802
    Kennedy, John F., and, 786, 795
    railroads and, 578
    Reagan and, 839, 840, 842
    Religious Right on, 839
    in Second New Deal, 699
    in Second World War, 728
Tax revolt, in California, 839
Taylor, Frederick Winslow, and "Taylorism,"
    579–580
Teaching profession
    in freedpeople's schools, 468, 469
    women in, 520, 656, 787
Teach-ins, 816
"Team B," 838
Tea Party movement, 904
Teapot Dome scandal, 658
Technocrats, New Dealers as, 702
Technology, 595. *See also* Weapons
    for advertising, 520
    in cities, 539, 540
    for information collection, 757
    innovations in, 869
    manufacturing growth and, 515
    mining, 492
    network TV and, 875
    for pirating movies, 876
    in printing, 520
    in Second World War, 721, 728
Teflon president, Reagan as, 842
Teheran, hostage crisis in, 837
Teheran Conference (1943), 739
Tejanos (Mexican Texans), 496
Telegraph, 532
Telephones, 515, 532
    U.S.-Soviet hot-line, 785
Television. *See also* Cable television
    animated shows on, 876
    Army-McCarthy Hearings on, 770
    blacklist in, 754
    conservatives on, 838
    Eisenhower and, 770
    in 1950s, 780
    in 1964 campaign, 804
    presidential debates on, 784
    programs on, 875

Television (*continued*)
  religious programs on, 777, 838
  role of women on, 787
  sports coverage on, 873
  video revolution and, 875
  Vietnam War on, 809, 810
  Watergate hearings on, 828
  Watts riot on, 814
Temperance. *See* Prohibition
Temporary Assistance to Needy Families
    (TANF), 887
Tenant farmers, 551
  in Great Depression, 690
  in New South, 504
Ten Days That Shook the World (Reed), 644
Tenements, 548
Tennessee
  reconstruction of, 464, 470
  Scopes Trial in, 669
Tennessee Valley Authority (TVA, 1933),
    693–694, 693 (map)
Tennessee Valley Authority Act (1933), 689,
    693
10th Negro Cavalry, 631
Tenure of Office Act (1867), 472
Termination and Relocation programs, for
    Indians, 791–792
Terms of office
  limits on, 757
  of Roosevelt, F. D., 757
Terrell, Mary Church, 506
Terrorism
  by Islamic militants, 844–845, 897
  of Ku Klux Klan, 472, 474, 477–478
  presidential power and, 897–898
  on September 11, 2001, 884, 885, 892, 896
Tesla, Nikola, 515
Tet Offensive, 817–818, 826
Texas
  Anglo-Americans and Mexican
      Americans in, 496
  cattle industry in, 492
  Johnson, Lyndon B., and, 802
  Mexican Americans in, 675
Texas Rangers, as Anglo vigilante force, 496
Textiles and textile industry
  immigrant labor in, 547
  industrial accidents in, 525
  in New South, 503, 504
  in 1920s, 655
  strikes in, 591, 696
  value of cotton output, 656
Theory of the Leisure Class, The (Veblen),
    520
Thief in the Night, A (movie), 881
Thieu, Nguyen Van, 809, 827
Think tanks, 892
  conservative, 839
  RAND as, 753
Third parties. *See also* specific parties
  Farmer-Labor, 650
  Perot and, 848
  radical, 697
  of Wallace, George, 819–820
Third Reich, 716, 717, 721. *See also* Nazi
    Germany

Third World
  CIA and, 772
  debt to U.S. by, 846–847
  economic aid to, 772
Thirteenth Amendment, 466, 484
38th parallel, 750, 751, 770
"This Land Is Your Land" (Guthrie), 705
Thomas, Clarence, 850, 856, 894
Thompson, Donald W., 881
Thompson, Mal, 627
369th Regiment (New York), 632, 633
Three Mile Island, reactor malfunction at,
    836
"Thriller" (Michael Jackson), 877
Thurmond, J. Strom, election of 1948 and,
    747–748
Tibbets, Paul, 728
Tilden, Samuel J., 482–483, 483 (map), 507
Till, Emmett, murder of, 789
Tillman, Benjamin, 533
Timber. *See* Lumber industry
Time, transportation and, 520
Time-and-motion studies, 579
Time magazine, 810
  person of the year 2008 in, 906
Title VII, of Civil Rights Act (1964), 803
Title IX, 824, 874
Tobacco and tobacco industry
  advertising of, 652
  Duke and, 517, 597
  in New South, 503, 504
  regulation of, 904
Toilets, flush, 540
Tojo, Hideki, 720
Tokyo, air attacks on, 726
Tomatoes, 869
Tongs (Chinese secret societies), 551
"Too big to fail" institutions, 902
Toombs, Robert, 470
Toomer, Jean, 674
Tootle the Engine, 778–779, 787
TORCH campaign, in Second World
    War, 721
Torture, by U.S. of Filipino guerrillas, 607
"To Secure These Rights," 760
Totalitarianism, Soviet, 746
Total war
  in First World War, 628–637
  in Second World War, 729
Tourism, in Sunbelt, 864
Town(s). *See also* Cities
  cow towns, 493
  mining, 497
Townsend, Francis E., 696
Toxic waste, 895
Toynbee Hall, 566
Tractors, 662
Trade. *See also* Commerce; Slave trade;
      Transportation
  with China, 615
  Clinton and, 895
  with England, 624
  GATT and, 739
  imbalances in, 840
  in 1930s, 710–711
  in prostitution, 497

restraint of, trusts and, 518
  with Third World, 772
  trails for, 496
Trade deficit, 825
Trade unions. *See also* Labor unions
  anarchists in, 528
  in 1920s, 655
  Wilson and, 591
Trail(s)
  for cattle drives, 492, 493, 493 (map)
  Chisholm, 493
Transcendental Meditation, 879
Transcontinental railroad
  Chinese laborers for, 490
  completion of, 480, 486, 491
  western settlement and, 489
Transit systems, electric-powered, 540
Trans-Mississippi West. *See also* West
  American Indians in, 487, 498–503
  black land ownership in, 504
  white population in, 487
Transportation. *See also* Automobiles and
      automobile industry; Railroad(s)
  automobiles and road expansion,
      652 (map)
  deregulation in, 835, 841
  electricity and, 540
  government control of, 532
  Highway Act (1956) and, 776
  of products, 870–871
  racial discrimination in, 481, 506
  reform of municipal, 572
  segregation of, 789
  suburbanization and, 540
Transsexuality, 755
Traverse des Sioux, Treaty of, 499
Treasury Department, 902
Treaties. *See also* specific treaties
  to annex Santo Domingo, 475
  on arms limitations, 660
  between Confederacy and five "civilized
      tribes," 498
  Indians and, 500, 852, 853
  peace treaty with Japan, 752
Trees. *See* Forests; Lumber
Trench warfare, in First World War, 622, 623
Tresca, Carlo, 557
Trials, novels about, 888
Triangle Shirtwaist Company, fire at, 547, 548
Tribes (Indian). *See also* American Indians;
      specific groups
  self-determination for, 853
  termination of, 792
Tripartite Pact, 717
Triple Alliance, 621, 622. *See also* Central
      Powers
Triple Entente, 621. *See also* Allies (First
      World War)
Trolleys, electrical, 540
Troops. *See* Military
Trotter, Monroe, 580
Troubled Assets Relief Program (TARP),
    902
Truman, Harry S
  anticommunism of, 745, 754, 756
  assumption of presidency by, 727

atomic bomb and, 727–728
civil rights and, 747, 758, 759–761
Cold War and, 744–745
containment and, 752
election of 1948 and, 747–748, 748 (map)
election of 1952 and, 765
executive power and, 757
Fair Deal of, 758–759
Korean War and, 750, 751
Loyalty Program of, 745–746
MacArthur and, 751–752
McCarthy, Joseph, and, 756
peace after Second World War and, 738
at Potsdam Conference (1945), 744
strikes and, 753
Truman Doctrine, 745
Trusteeships, after First World War, 638
Trusts, 516, 566
FTC and, 589–590
regulation and, 588
Rockefeller and, 516
Roosevelt, T., and, 584
Trust Territories of the Pacific, 740
Tugwell, Rexford, 677, 687, 690
Turkey, 752
immigrants from, 545
U.S. aid to, 745
U.S. missiles withdrawn from, 785
Turner, Frederick Jackson, frontier thesis of, 509, 597–598
Turner, George Kibbe, 564
Turner, Ted, 875
Turner Joy (ship), 806
Turnevereins, 549
Tuskegee Institute, 506
Tutsis, 895
TVA. *See* Tennessee Valley Authority
Twain, Mark, 474, 520
as anti-imperialist, 604
Tweed, William Marcy ("Boss"), 474, 564
Twenties, 648, 649
Twenty-fifth Amendment, Ford as vice president and, 829
24th and 25th Negro Infantry Regiments, 601
Twenty-second Amendment, 757, 784
Twenty-sixth Amendment, 828
Tydings, Millard, 757
Tyler, John, 507
Typhoid, in cities, 541, 542, 548

UAW. *See* United Auto Workers
U-boats. *See also* Submarines
in First World War, 620, 624–625, 626
in Second World War, 721
UFW. *See* United Farm Workers
Ukraine, economic aid to, 896
Ukrainian immigrants, 545
Ultranationalism, before Second World War, 716
UMW. *See* United Mine Workers
UN. *See* United Nations
Uncle Sam, Spanish-American War and, 600
Unconditional surrender policy (Second World War), 721, 726

Underconsumption theory, 699
Understanding clauses, black voting rights and, 506
Underwood-Simmons Tariff (1913), 589
Undocumented immigrants, 865. *See also* Illegal immigrants
refugees as, 881
Unemployment. *See also* Employment
in 1920s, 681
in 1950s, 782
in 1960s, 802
in 1970s, 835
in 1980s, 840
Clinton and, 887
in depression of 1893-1897, 529
in First World War, 630
in Great Depression, 711
of men and women, 703
Nixon and, 825
in nonfarm labor force (1929-1945), 710
Panic of 1873 and, 480
Reagan revolution and, 840
Unemployment Relief Act (1933), 689
UNESCO, Reagan funding and, 844
Unilateralism, Iraq War and, 896–897
Unionists
in border states, 465
election of 1866 and, 470
in South, 466
Union Leagues, in Reconstruction South, 471, 477
Union Pacific Railroad, 474, 486, 489, 490
Irish laborers of, 490
strikes against, 527
Union Party, 465
Unions (labor). *See* Labor unions
Union Station, Washington, D.C., 543
United Auto Workers (UAW), 704, 777
United Cannery, Agricultural, Packing and Allied Workers of America (UCAPAWA), 793
United Daughters of the Confederacy (UDC), 505
United Farm Workers (UFW), 849, 854
United Fruit Company, Arbenz ouster and, 772
United Fruit of Boston, 615
United Mine Workers (UMW), 528, 703, 732
United Mine Workers Journal on First World War, 625
United Nations (UN), 739, 895
China in, 825
Iraq War (2003–) and, 896–897
Korean War and, 750
Persian Gulf War and, 846
Rwanda peacekeeping effort by, 895
"Trust Territories of the Pacific" and, 740
United Neighborhood Organization (UNO), 854
United Office and Professional Workers of America, 753
United States, as Christian nation, 881–882
U.S. Bureau of Immigration, 547
U.S. Bureau of Indian Affairs. *See* Bureau of Indian Affairs (BIA)

U.S. Commission on Civil Rights, on Puerto Ricans, 854
United States Conference of Catholic Bishops, 881
United States Information Agency (USIA), 771
U.S. marshals, freedom riders and, 794
U.S. News and World Report, 758
U.S. Steel Corporation, 517
CIO contract with, 704
injuries at South Works plant, 547
Kennedy, John F., and, 786
strike against, 529
U.S. v. Cruikshank, 481
U.S. v. E.C. Knight Company, 518
U.S. v. Nixon, 829
U.S. v. Reese, 481
Unit 731 (Japanese army), 723
Unity League, 793
Universal Declaration of Human Rights, 739
Universal male suffrage, 472
Universal Negro Improvement Association (UNIA), 645
Universities and colleges. *See also* Higher education
antiwar movement in, 816–817, 826
Asian American studies programs at, 855
athletics in, 522
black, 468, 506
bombings at, 821
Chicano/a studies in, 854
corporate training in, 519
federal aid for, 782
gender politics and, 786–787
land-grant, 523
New Left and, 811–812, 813
New Right and, 838
public, 523
quotas on Jews in, 667, 669
Religious Right and, 839
after Second World War, 758, 759
in Second World War, 728
sports in, 874
urban life and, 867
women and, 523, 568, 849
work-study programs at, 802
University of Alabama, 794
University of California
Berkeley Revolt at, 812
Lawrence Livermore National Laboratory of, 848
University of Chicago, 535
law and economics activist-academics at, 857
school of social work at, 567
University of Iowa, 759
University of Mississippi, 794, 816
University of Wisconsin
antiwar protests at, 817
bombing at, 821
reform laws and, 578
Unsafe at Any Speed (Nader), 823
Unskilled labor, 655
AFL and, 529
wages for, 525

Upper South. *See also* South
  black land ownership in, 504
Urban areas. *See also* Cities
  African Americans in, 840, 852
  decay in, 835
  Indians in, 791–792
  lifestyle in, 867
  Mexican Americans in, 793
  population growth in, 662
  race riots in, 813–814
  Reagan and, 840
Urbanization, 545
  in 1920, 664 (map)
  in 2000, 867 (map)
Urban League. *See* National Urban
  League
Urban renewal, 759, 793, 805
Uruguay Round, of GATT, 895
USA Patriot Act, 896, 897
USIA. *See* United States Information
  Agency
USSR. *See* Soviet Union
Usury, regulating, 872
Utah, woman suffrage in, 575
Utilities, private, 572
U-2 spy planes, 771, 782

VA. *See* Veterans Administration
Vacations, in 1920s, 651
Vaccine, against polio, 760
Valens, Richie (Richard Valenzuela), 779
Valentino, Rudolph, 653
"Vamps," in movies, 555, 557
Vance, Cyrus, 836–837
Vandenberg, Arthur, 745
Van Kleeck, Mary, 702
Vanzetti, Bartolomeo, 643, 669
Vaqueros, 494, 496
Vassar college, 523
Vast wasteland, TV as, 780
Vaudeville, 554, 686
VCRs, 875, 876
Veblen, Thorstein, 520, 571
Venezuela
  dictator in, 772
  intervention in, 609, 611 (map)
VENONA files, 746
Veracruz, intervention in, 616
Versailles, Treaty of, 638–641, 640,
  map, 716
Vertical integration, 516
Veterans
  Bonus Army and, 685
  Confederate, 467
  after First World War, 645
  after Second World War, 731, 758,
    759, 855
Veterans Administration (VA), 758
Veterans' Readjustment Assistance Act
  (1952). *See* GI Bill of Rights
Veto
  by Ford, 835
  by Hayes, 532
  by Johnson, Andrew, 469, 471
  by Lincoln, 465
  by Truman, 753, 756

Vice, 566
Vice commissions, 557
Vice president, Roosevelt, T., as, 584
Vichy regime (France), 717
Victory (magazine), 733
Video revolution, 875
Viet Cong, 809
Vietnam
  Eisenhower and, 773–774
  Ford and, 836
  immigrants from, 865
  Johnson, Lyndon B., and, 801
  Kennedy, John F., and, 785–786,
    795–797
  trade with, 895
Vietnamese Americans, 855
Vietnamization policy, 825–826, 827
Vietnam Veterans against the War
  (VVAW), 827
Vietnam War, 801, 806–810, 807 (map)
  antiwar movement in, 809, 810, 816–817,
    818
  body count measure in, 808–809
  casualties in, 827
  escalation of, 808–809, 825–826
  Gulf of Tonkin Resolution and, 806–808
  at home, 810–817, 818–819
  King on, 817
  media coverage of, 809–810
  Nixon and, 825–827
  peace accords ending, 827
  saturation bombing in, 808
  Tet offensive in, 817–818
Vietnam War Memorial, 800
Vigilantes
  Texas Rangers as, 496
  white, 467
Villa, Francisco ("Pancho"), 616, 617
Villard, Oswald Garrison, 582
Violence. *See also* Civil-rights movement;
    Race riots
  against Chinese workers, 490
  after King's death, 818
  by Ku Klux Klan, 472, 474, 478
  labor, 525
  neo-Confederate, 466
  in 1968, 818, 819
  in 1969-1974, 821
  racial, 813
  against war protesters, 826
  in Watts, 813–814
Virtuous electorate, 573
VISTA. *See* Volunteers in Service to
  America
Visual imagery, in advertising, 520
V-J Day, 729
Voice of America, 771
Volcker, Paul, 840
Volstead Act, 637. *See also* Prohibition
Volunteers, women as, 730, 733
Volunteers in Service to America (VISTA),
  802
Voting. *See also* Elections; Suffrage; Woman
    suffrage
  by African Americans, 464, 465, 469, 471,
    482, 507, 789

Australian (secret) ballot and, 573
  bulldozing and, 482, 507
  in cities, 573
  disfranchisement and, 574–575
  in election of 1868, 474
  in election of 1896, 534, 535 (map)
  in election of 1934, 696–697
  in election of 1936, 701
  in election of 1964, 804
  in election of 2008, 903
  Fifteenth Amendment and, 472–473
  Fourteenth Amendment and, 470
  government regulation of, 573–574
  laws protecting, 478
  Mississippi Plan and, 480
  in New South, 506
  participation and, 575, 576, 577, 777, 848
  personal registration laws and, 574
  political machines and, 550
  progressives and, 573, 574–575
  in Reconstruction, 465, 466, 469, 472
  requirements for, 574
  in South, 470, 474, 482, 789
  virtuous electorate and, 573
  voter registration drive and, 803
  by women, 473, 575–577, 578 (map), 657
Voting age, lowered to 18, 828
Voting Rights Act (1965), 805, 824, 852

Wade, Benjamin, 465
Wade-Davis reconstruction bill (1864), 465
Wage labor, 489
  Hispanic, 491
  in mining, 491
  Powderly on, 527, 528
Wages. *See also* Income
  family, 731, 787
  in First World War, 630
  at Ford, 580
  hourly, 872
  in late 19th century, 523–525
  in mining, 492
  in 1900, 547–548
  real, 525, 777
  rises and declines in, 548
  in Second World War, 730–731
  share, 467
  of skilled workers, 655, 871
  of southern labor, 504
  strikes and cuts in, 525
  for women, 655–656, 731, 787, 849
"Wages of whiteness," southern mill workers
  and, 504
Wagner, Robert F., 579, 687, 706
Wagner-Rogers bill, 719
Waiting for Lefty (Odets), 704
Wake Island, 722
Wald, Lillian, 579
Walker, Alice, 852
Walker, Madame C. J., 552, 553
Walking cities, 540
"Walk to Freedom March" (Detroit), 794
Wallace, George, 822
  assassination attempt on, 828
  election of 1964 and, 804
  election of 1968 and, 819–821, 821 (map)

Wallace, Henry A., 745
    election of 1948 and, 747, 748, 754
Waller, Fats, 674
Walling, William English, 582
Wallis, Jim, 880
Wall Street. *See* Financial institutions;
    Investment
Wal-Mart, 870
Walt Disney World, 864
Walton, Sam, 870
War against drugs, 845–846
War bonds, in Second World War, 728
Ward, A. Montgomery, mail-order
    catalogue of, 520
War Democrats, 465
War Department, 472, 721
War guilt, of Germany, 638
War Industries Board (WIB), 629–630,
    642
War Labor Board, 728, 730–731, 732
War Manpower Commission, 728
Warner, Charles Dudley, 474
War on Poverty, Johnson, Lyndon B., and,
    802
War Production Board (Second World
    War), 728
Warren, Earl, 788
Warren, Rick, 881
Warren Commission, 796, 797
Warren Court, 841
    decisions of, 823
    Religious Right and, 839
Wars and warfare. *See also* specific battles
    and wars
    Indians and, 499–500
    limited, 750, 751, 808
Warsaw Pact, 749 (map), 771
Wartime conferences (Second World War),
    739–740, 744, 754
Wartime Reconstruction, 464–465
Washington (state), 577
Washington, Booker T., 505, 552, 580, 581,
    582–583
    Atlanta Exposition speech by, 506
    Roosevelt, T., and, 584
Washington, Treaty of, 475
Washington Conference on the Limitation
    of Armaments, 660
Washington Naval Treaties, 716
Washington Post Watergate and, 828
WASPs. *See* Women's Air Force Service
    Pilots
Waste Land, The (Eliot), 676
Waste management, 823, 893
Water
    California projects and, 695 (map)
    in cities, 539, 540–541
    development of resources, 585
    diseases from, 541
    tribal rights to, 853
    in West, 694, 776
Water filtration systems, 541
Watergate Crisis, 801, 828–829
Water pollution, 541, 893
Water Pollution Control Act (1972), 823
Waters, Alice, 894

Waterways. *See also* Canals; specific
    waterways
    in West, 776
Watt, James, 840
Watts riot, of 1965, 813–814
Watts Writers Workshop, 814
"Waving the bloody shirt" rhetoric, 507, 508
Wayland, Julius, 570
WCTU. *See* Woman's Christian
    Temperance Union
Wealth and wealthy. *See also* Affluence
    income tax on, 589
    of labor, 527
    maldistribution in Great Depression, 684
    redistribution of, 695, 696
    robber barons and, 534–536
    Second World War and, 728
    Social Darwinism and, 520–521
    from southern industry, 503
Wealth gap
    in Chicago, 542
    Reagan and, 840
    Second World War and, 728
Wealth Tax Act (1935), 699, 701
Weapons. *See also* Bombs and bombings;
    Nuclear power
    atomic, 727–728
    limitations on, 660
Weapons of mass destruction (WMDs), 896,
    897
Weather Underground, 821
Weaver, James B., 533
Web. *See* Internet
Web browsers, 869
Weeks, Philip, on Indian "policy of
    concentration," 498
Welfare capitalism, 654
Welfare programs. *See* Social welfare
Welfare recipients, payments to, 823
Welfare state, in Europe, 757
Wells, Ida B., 580
    anti-lynching campaign of, 505, 569
    on Columbian Exposition's exclusion of
    blacks, 543–544
    NAACP and, 569, 582
Wertham, Frederick, 779
"We Shall Overcome" (song), 794
West
    African American migration to, 504–505
    Chinese in, 490–491, 546, 547
    cowboys in, 492, 494
    ecological balance in, 509
    in film, 495, 764
    frontier theory and, 597–598
    Homestead Act (1862) and, 489
    homesteading and farming in, 489, 497
    immigrants in, 546, 547
    industrialization of, 488–498
    itinerant laborers in, 496–497
    Mexican Americans in, 494–496
    migration to, 487
    mining in, 490, 491–492
    population growth in, 862–863
    preservation of, 585
    public works projects in, 694
    racial composition in, 788–789

    railroad expansion in, 489–490, 491
    ranching in, 492–494
    sagebrush rebellion and, 841
    Second New Deal in, 702
    settlement of, 487
    socialism in, 570
    water projects in, 694, 695 (map)
    wise use movement in, 856
    woman suffrage in, 498, 575, 578 (map)
West, Nathaniel, 686
West Bank, 837
West Berlin. *See* Berlin
Western Europe. *See also* Europe and
    Europeans
    economic integration and, 846
    after Second World War, 744, 746
Western Federation of Miners (WFM), 492
Western front, in First World War, 622, 628
Western Hemisphere
    Monroe Doctrine and, 608
    Roosevelt Corollary and, 609–610
Westerns, on television, 780
West Germany (Federal Republic of
    Germany), 746
    German reunification and, 845
    rearmament of, 752
West Indies, Danish, 616
Westinghouse, George, 515
Westminster School District v. *Mendez*, 761,
    793
Westmoreland, William, 808, 810, 817, 818
Westward movement
    environmental impact of, 509
    in post-Civil War era, 487
Weyler, Valeriano ("Butcher"), 599
Wheat, 530
Wheeler, Burton K., 719
Wheeler Dam, 693
Whip Inflation Now (WIN) program,
    834–835
Whistle-stop campaign, of Bryan, 534
White, William Allen, 719
White Citizens Council, 789
White City, of Columbian Exposition,
    542–543, 554
White-collar workers, 521
    women as, 656
White Leagues, 480, 482
White Russians, Bolsheviks and, 643
Whites. *See also* White supremacy
    anti-Asian attitudes of, 547
    Homestead Act and, 489
    movement to suburbs, 762
    segregationists, 789
    in South, 464, 467
White slave trade, 557
White supremacy, 533
    Dixiecrats and, 757
    of Johnson, Andrew, 466
    Ku Klux Klan and, 478, 665–666
    in New Deal, 701
    in New South, 504, 505, 506
Whitewater scandal, 888
Wholesale and consumer price indexes
    (1865-1897), 530
Why Johnny Can't Read (Flesch), 782

Whyte, William H., Jr., 778, 779
Why We Fight (documentary), 732
Wikipedia, 906
Wildcat strikes, in Second World War, 732
Wilderness, preservation of, 585
Wilderness Act (1964), 822
Wild West Show, of Buffalo Bill Cody, 501–503
Wilhelm II (Germany), 638
Willard, Frances, 523
Willard, Jess, 581
Williams v. *Mississippi*, 506
Willkie, Wendell, 719
Wilmington, North Carolina, race riot in, 506
Wilson, Edith Bolling, 641
Wilson, Henry Lane, 616
Wilson, Woodrow
    American nationality and, 560
    in Big Four, 638
    Brandeis appointment by, 590
    election of 1912 and, 587–588, 589 (map)
    election of 1916 and, 590, 591, 626
    First World War and, 624, 637
    foreign policy of, 615–617
    Fourteen Points of, 627, 628
    on immigrants, 559
    New Freedom of, 588, 589–591
    Paris Peace Conference and, 637–638
    "peace without victory" and, 626
    presidency of, 589–591
    progressivism and, 562, 563, 589, 590
    stroke of, 641
    Versailles Treaty ratification and, 639–641
WIN. *See* Whip Inflation Now (WIN) program
Winesburg, Ohio (Anderson), 676
Wiretaps, 898
Wisconsin
    direct primary in, 573
    progressivism and La Follette in, 578–579
"Wisconsin idea," 579
Wisconsin Progressive Party, 697
"Wise Men," Vietnam War and, 818
Wise use movement, 856
"Witch hunts," 753
Wives. *See* Families; Women
WMDs. *See* Weapons of mass destruction
Woman of the Year (movie), 703
Woman Rebel, The (Sanger), 558
Woman's Christian Temperance Union (WCTU), 523, 568
Woman suffrage, 557, 575–577, 578 (map)
    Fifteenth Amendment and, 473, 569
    humor and, 577
    before 1920, 578 (map)
    in western states, 498, 575
Women. *See also* Gender and gender issues; Woman suffrage
    affirmative action and, 856
    African American, 506, 552, 553
    agriculture and, 547
    changing roles of, 787
    as country music singers, 663

domesticity vs. work and, 786
    in First World War, 630, 634
    gender politics and, 786–787
    glass ceiling and, 849
    Grange and, 532
    Great Railroad Strike and, 526
    higher education and, 523
    Homestead Act provisions for, 489, 497
    in Ku Klux Klan, 666
    labor unions and, 527, 528, 731
    libertarians and, 781–782
    Mexican American, 677, 854
    in middle class, 522–523
    missionary societies of, 596
    movies and, 763–764, 876
    as New Dealers, 702
    new sexuality and, 555–557
    "New Woman" and, 523, 524
    in 1920s, 649, 652–653
    in 1950s, 775
    physical activities by, 522
    Populists and, 533
    professional organizations and, 523
    reform by, 567–569
    in Second World War, 730, 731, 732–733, 733–734
    in Senate, 850
    settlement house movement and, 566–567
    as settlers, 497, 498
    sexual harassment of, 850
    sexual slavery of Chinese, 497
    in sports, 874
    strikes and, 526
    on Supreme Court, 841, 886
    in sweatshops, 549
    unemployment of, 703
    as vice presidential nominee, 842
    voting rights for, 657
    wages for, 871
    western settlement and, 497–498
    as workers, 504, 520, 549, 655–657, 702, 849
    in working class, 539, 548
Women's Airforce Service Pilots (WASPs), 733
Women's Bureau, 702
Women's club movement, 506, 523
Women's colleges, gender politics in, 786–787
Women's movement, 575, 823–824, 833, 849–850. *See also* Feminism; Women; Women's rights
    in 1920s, 657–658
    after 1960s, 849–850
    resurgence of (1953-1963), 787
Women's Peace Party, 625
Women's rights. *See also* Feminism; Women's movement
    abortion and, 823–824
    demonstrators for, 824
    ERA and, 823
Women's Strike for Peace, 787
Wood, Leonard, 601, 607
Wood, Robert E., 718
Woods, Eldrick (Tiger), 874

"Woodstock" music festival, 813
Work (Alcott), 522
Workday, 547
    eight-hour, 525, 527, 528
    limits on, 702
    Supreme Court and, 528
    for women, 567
Workers. *See also* Labor; Strikes; Working class
    African American, 645
    agricultural, 854
    on assembly line, 580
    benefits for, 580, 777, 871–872
    ethnic, 549
    after First World War, 642, 650
    in First World War, 630–631
    industrial, 655
    Mexican, 708
    migrant, 704
    protective legislation for, 702
    rights of, 528
    Rivera mural of, 697
    in Second World War, 730–731
    in sweatshops, 549
    undocumented, 865
    unions and, 841
    voting by, 696–697
Workers' cooperatives, 527
Workforce
    distribution of (1870-1920), 517
    immigrants in, 547
    in Second World War, 730–731
    women in, 504, 522, 557, 655–657, 730, 787, 849
Working class
    commercial culture of, 539, 554–555
    families in, 525, 548
    in film, 556
    immigrants in, 544
    living conditions of, 548
    middle class and, 539
    strikes by, 591
    urban, 540
Working conditions
    dangerous, 525
    garment workers and, 579
    in mines, 492
Workingman's Party of California, 490
Workingmen's Benevolent Association, 526
Workmen's compensation, 525, 591
Workplace. *See also* Safety
    scientific management in, 579–580
    segregation by sex in, 730
    women in, 734
Works Progress Administration (WPA), 699, 729
    arts under, 705
    projects in New York City, 701
Work-study programs, 802
Workweek
    in First World War, 630
    industrial, 547
World Bank. *See* International Bank for Reconstruction and Development
World Economic Conference, 709

World Hockey Association (WHA), 874
World market(s), for American agricultural
    products, 530–531
World powers
    Open Door policy and, 608
    United States as, 595, 603–608
World Series, of 1919, 551
World's Fair, in Chicago, 542–543
World Trade Center
    attack on, 892
    Ground Zero and, 884
    September 11, 2001, destruction
        of, 896
World Trade Organization
    (WTO), 895
World War I. *See* First World War
World War II. *See* Second World War
World Wide Web. *See* Internet
Worship. *See* Religion
Wounded Knee massacre, of Sioux
    Indians, 501
Wovoka (Paiute shaman), 501
WPA. *See* Works Progress Administration
WPA Artists at Work (Soyer), 705
Wright, Frank Lloyd, 542, 567
Wright, Richard, 754
Wrigley's chewing gum, 729

Writers. *See* Literature; Novels
Writing (literary). *See* Literature
WTO. *See* World Trade Organization
Wyoming, 533
    woman suffrage in, 575

Yalta Conference (1945), 739, 754
Yankee Stadium, sports and, 653
Yellow dog contracts, 655
Yellow journalism, 599
"Yellow Peril," 614
Yellowstone Park, 586
Yellow Wallpaper, The (Gilman), 522
Yelp, 906
Yeltsin, Boris, 845
Yemen
    al-Qaeda in, 900
    Cole attacked in, 896
YIPPIEs, 817
YMCA. *See* Young Men's Christian
    Association
Yom Kippur War (1973), 825, 837
York, Alvin C., 632
Young Americans for Freedom
    (YAF), 811
Young Men's Christian Association
    (YMCA), 787

Youngstown Steel & Tube Company v.
    Sawyer, 757
Youth
    counterculture and, 812–813
    culture in 1950s, 779–780
    new sexuality and, 555
    population and, 862
Youth International Party (YIPPIEs). *See*
    YIPPIEs
YouTube, 905–906
Yugoslavia
    creation of, 638, 640 (map)
    disintegration of, 845
    war in former, 847

Zangwill, Israel, 560
    American nationality and, 558–559
Zanuck, Darryl F., 732
"Zapruder film," 796
Zelaya, José Santos, 715
Zimmermann telegram, 626
Zionism, 637, 740
Zitkala-Sa (Yankton Sioux writer), 501
Zones of occupation
    in Germany, 739, 746
    in Korea, 740
Zoot Suit Riots (1943), 735